The Cambridge Handbent in Human Development

Families, communities, and societies influence children's learning and development in many ways. This is the first handbook devoted to the understanding of the nature of environments in child development. Utilizing Urie Bronfenbrenner's idea of embedded environments, this volume looks at environments from the immediate environment of the family (including fathers, siblings, grandparents, and day-care personnel) to the larger environment (including schools, neighborhoods, geographic regions, countries, and cultures). Understanding these embedded environments and the ways in which they interact is necessary to understand development.

Dr. Linda C. Mayes is the Arnold Gesell Professor of Child Psychiatry, Pediatrics, and Psychology in the Yale Child Study Center, a department in the Yale School of Medicine. She is also a member of the directorial team of the Anna Freud Centre, London. As a clinical investigator she works at the interface of three fields – pediatrics, developmental psychology, and child psychiatry. Formally trained as a pediatrician and neonatologist, in her work Dr. Mayes integrates perspectives from child development, behavioral neuroscience, psychophysiology, neurobiology, developmental psychopathology, and neurobehavioral teratology. She is the author of nearly 200 peer-reviewed papers and more than 100 chapters and reviews. Dr. Mayes is the author of a book for parents, *The Yale Child Study Center Guide to Understanding Your Child*. She is also special adviser to the dean in the Yale University School of Medicine and a member of the National Scientific Council on the Developing Child.

Michael Lewis is University Distinguished Professor of Pediatrics and Psychiatry and Director of the Institute for the Study of Child Development at Robert Wood Johnson Medical School, University of Medicine and Dentistry of New Jersey. He also is Professor of Psychology, Education, Cognitive Science, and Biomedical Engineering at Rutgers University. Dr. Lewis has published more than 300 articles in scientific journals and has written or edited more than 35 books, including *Social Cognition and the Acquisition of Self* (1979), *Children's Emotions and Moods: Developmental Theory and Measurement* (1983), *Shame: The Exposed Self* (1992), and *Altering Fate: Why the Past Does Not Predict the Future* (1997). He edited the *Handbook of Developmental Psychopathology*, second edition (2001) and the *Handbook of Emotions*, third edition (2009). He recently won the Urie Bronfenbrenner Award from the American Psychological Association for Lifetime Contribution to Developmental Psychology in the Service of Science and Society.

The Cambridge Handbook of Environment in Human Development

Edited by

LINDA C. MAYES
Yale University School of Medicine

MICHAEL LEWIS
Robert Wood Johnson Medical School

CAMBRIDGE
UNIVERSITY PRESS

CAMBRIDGE
UNIVERSITY PRESS

University Printing House, Cambridge CB2 8BS, United Kingdom

Cambridge University Press is part of the University of Cambridge.

It furthers the University's mission by disseminating knowledge in the pursuit of education, learning and research at the highest international levels of excellence.

www.cambridge.org
Information on this title: www.cambridge.org/9781107531680

© Cambridge University Press 2012

First published 2012
First paperback edition 2015

A catalogue record for this publication is available from the British Library

Library of Congress Cataloguing in Publication data
    The Cambridge handbook of environment in human development / [edited by] Linda Mayes, Michael Lewis.
        p.   cm.
    Includes bibliographical references and index.
    ISBN 978-0-521-86882-2 (hbk.)
    1. Child development.   2. Child psychology.   3. Environmental psychology.   I. Mayes, Linda C.   II. Lewis, Michael, 1937 Jan. 10–
    HQ767.9.H348   2012
    305.231–dc23   2012000796

ISBN 978-0-521-86882-2 Hardback
ISBN 978-1-107-53168-0 Paperback

Contents

Notes on Contributors

THOMAS M. ACHENBACH
Thomas M. Achenbach, Ph.D., is Professor of Psychiatry and Psychology and President of the nonprofit Research Center for Children, Youth, and Families at the University of Vermont. His research currently focuses on multicultural assessment and epidemiology of psychopathology and adaptive functioning from age one to ninety-plus years.

MARC H. BORNSTEIN
Marc H. Bornstein, Ph.D., is Senior Investigator and Head of Child and Family Research at the Eunice Kennedy Shriver National Institute of Child Health and Human Development. Bornstein has published in experimental, methodological, comparative, developmental, and cultural science as well as neuroscience, pediatrics, and aesthetics. Visit www.cfr.nichd.nih.gov and www.tandfonline.com/HPAR.

W. THOMAS BOYCE
W. Thomas Boyce, M.D., is the Sunny Hill Health Centre/BC Leadership Chair in Child Development at the University of British Columbia. He is also Co-Director of the Experience-Based Brain and Biological Development Program of the Canadian Institute for Advanced Research, a member of the Institute of Medicine, and a member of Harvard University's National Scientific Council on the Developing Child.

ROBERT H. BRADLEY
Robert H. Bradley, Ph.D., is Professor and Director of the Family and Human Dynamics Research Institute at Arizona State University. Former Associate Editor for *Child Development and Early Childhood Research Quarterly*, in his research he focuses on parenting, the impact of home environment on child well-being, child care, early education, and the measurement of children's environments. He was an investigator in the NICHD Study of Early Child Care and Youth Development and the Early Head Start Research and Evaluation Study.

KELLY BRIDGES
Kelly Bridges is an adjunct faculty member and Ph.D. student in the Department

of Communicative Sciences and Disorders at New York University, where she is studying the speech and language of adults who have neurological disease and psychiatric disorders. She received her master's degree in experimental psychology with a focus on child language acquisition from Florida Atlantic University in 2008, and her bachelor's degree in psychology from Loyola University Maryland in 2006.

JEANNE BROOKS-GUNN
Jeanne Brooks-Gunn, Ph.D., is the Virginia and Leonard Marx Professor of Child Development at Columbia University's Teachers College and the College of Physicians and Surgeons. Brooks-Gunn is a Developmental Psychologist and a member of the National Academy's Institute of Medicine. She directs the National Center for Children and Families at Columbia University. Her work focuses on the development and health of children and youth, with special foci on how families, schools, and neighborhoods influence development; on how children from poor, single-parent, or low-education families fare; and on how policies and programs can enhance well-being.

BRENDA K. BRYANT
Brenda K. Bryant, Ph.D., is Professor Emeritus of Human Development at the University of California, Davis. Her research focuses on children's sources of support in the family, school, and community and their relationship to social-emotional functioning in middle childhood. In addition, she is finalizing a longitudinal study that addresses these issues in middle childhood in relation to vocational and social-emotional development in adulthood.

SANDRA L. CALVERT
Sandra L. Calvert, Ph.D., is a Professor of Psychology at Georgetown University. She is also the Co-Founder and Director of the Children's Digital Media Center, which hosts an interdisciplinary group of scholars who are funded primarily by the National Science Foundation. Professor Calvert's current research focuses on the role of digital media, particularly the characters who populate onscreen stories, in the lives of children and youth.

SCOTT COLTRANE
Scott Coltrane, Ph.D., is Dean of the College of Arts and Sciences and Professor of Sociology at the University of Oregon. His research focuses on fathers, families, social inequalities, and gender equity.

E. MARK CUMMINGS
E. Mark Cummings, Ph.D., is professor and Notre Dame Endowed Chair in Psychology at the University of Notre Dame, in his research interests focuses on family factors, especially socioemotional processes, associated with normal development and the development of psychopathology in children.

STACEY B. DAUGHTERS
Stacey B. Daughters, Ph.D., is an assistant professor in the Department of Behavioral and Community Health and Director of the Stress, Health, and Addiction Research Program (SHARP) at the University of Maryland, College Park. Her research interests include understanding the interaction of neurobiological and behavioral determinants of stress and addiction and the translation of this knowledge into effective prevention and intervention programs.

CINDY DECOSTE
Cindy DeCoste is a Research Associate in the Department of Psychiatry at Yale University School of Medicine and Project Director for a research program focused on developing and evaluating attachment- and mentalization-based interventions for mothers who have substance abuse disorders.

MARC DE ROSNAY
Marc de Rosnay, Ph.D., Department of Psychology, University of Sydney, Australia, specializes in the development of emotional competence during infancy and early childhood.

JACQUELYNNE S. ECCLES

Jacquelynne S. Eccles, Ph.D., is the McKeachie/Printrich Distinguished University Professor at the University of Michigan, Ann Arbor. She is past President of Division 35 (Psychology of Women) of the APA and of the Society for Research on Adolescence, past Editor of the *Journal of Research on Adolescence*, and current Editor of *Developmental Psychology*. Her research focuses on development in the second two decades of life with particular focus on the Eccles Expectancy Value Model of Achievement-Related Choices and on the contextual influences on social and achievement-related developmental trajectories.

HADAS EIDELMAN

Hadas Eidelman is a doctoral student at the Harvard Graduate School of Education. Hadas has a long background of work in early childhood education, including teaching, administrating, and facilitating infant and early childhood art programming. Currently, Hadas' research involves longitudinal statistical modeling of family mental health and social emotional outcomes in children.

RUTH FELDMAN

Ruth Feldman, Ph.D., is a Professor of Psychology and Neuroscience at Bar-Ilan University, Israel and director of a community clinic for parents and young children. Her research focuses on the neurobiology of affiliation; biobehavioral aspects in disorders associated with maternal-infant bond formation including prematurity, postpartum depression, and childhood PTSD; children's social-emotional development; and methods for the observation of social interactions between attachment partners.

PETER FONAGY

Peter Fonagy, Ph.D., F.B.A., is Freud Memorial Professor of Psychoanalysis and Head of Department, Research Department of Clinical, Educational and Health Psychology at University College London and is Chief Executive of the Anna Freud Centre, London. Professor Fonagy is a clinical psychologist and a training and supervising analyst in the British Psycho-Analytical Society (http://www.psychoanalysis.org.uk/) in child and adult analysis. His clinical interests center around issues of borderline psychopathology, violence, and early attachment relationships. His work attempts to integrate empirical research with psychoanalytic theory.

WALTER S. GILLIAM

Walter S. Gilliam, Ph.D., is an associate professor of child psychiatry and psychology at the Yale Child Study Center and Director of the Edward Zigler Center in Child Development and Social Policy. His research involves policies regarding early childhood education and child care, methods to improve the quality of early childhood services, the impact of early childhood education programs on children's school readiness, and early childhood mental health consultation.

ANDREA L. GOLD

Andrea L. Gold, M.S., M.Phil., is a doctoral student in the Department of Psychology at Yale University. Her research interests focus on neurobiological mechanisms of emotion-cognition interactions underlying risk for psychopathology following exposure to traumatic life events, including childhood maltreatment.

ELENA L. GRIGORENKO

Elena L. Grigorenko, Ph.D., is Emily Fraser Beede Associate Professor of Developmental Disabilities, Child Studies, Psychology, and Epidemiology and Public Health at Yale University.

SARA HARKNESS

Sara Harkness, Ph.D., M.P.H., is Professor of Human Development, Pediatrics, and Public Health at the University of Connecticut, where she also is Director of the Center for the Study of Culture, Health, and Human Development. Her research focuses on the cultural organization of children's environments and its implications for policies and programs in health and education.

SYBIL L. HART

Sybil L. Hart, Ph.D., is Professor of Human Development and Family Studies at Texas Tech University. She received her Ph.D. in Psychology from Tufts University and recently edited *Handbook of Jealousy: Theory, Research and Multidisciplinary Approaches* (Wiley-Blackwell, 2010).

JESSICA S. HENRY

Jessica S. Henry, M.A., is currently a doctoral student in the Clinical Psychology program in the Department of Psychology at the George Washington University. She received her bachelor's degree in psychology from Howard University and her master's degree in clinical psychology with a Specialization in Psychology of Education from Teachers College, Columbia University. Her research interests are identifying race and culturally relevant sources of protection for youth exposed to stressful experiences and traumatic life events.

ERIKA HOFF

Erika Hoff, Ph.D., is Professor of Psychology at Florida Atlantic University. Her research examines the effects of socioeconomic status and dual-language input on early language development. Her books include *The Blackwell Handbook of Language Development* (with Marilyn Shatz, Blackwell, 2007), *Childhood Bilingualism: Research on Infancy through School Age* (with Peggy McCardle, Multilingual Matters, 2006), *Research Methods in Child Language*, and *Language Development* (Wiley-Blackwell, 2012). She is currently Associate Editor of *Child Development* (Cengage, 2013).

TOM HOLLENSTEIN

Tom Hollenstein received his Ph.D. at the University of Toronto in 2005 and is currently an Associate Professor in the Developmental Psychology program at Queen's University in Kingston, Ontario, Canada. His research foci are adolescent emotional development and dynamic systems approaches.

STEPHANIE M. JONES

Stephanie M. Jones' basic developmental research focuses on the longitudinal effects of poverty and exposure to violence on social and emotional development in early childhood and adolescence. In addition, she conducts evaluation research focusing on the developmental impact of school-based interventions targeting children's social-emotional skills and aggressive behavior, as well as their basic academic skills.

JULIA KIM-COHEN

Julia Kim-Cohen, Ph.D., is Assistant Professor of Psychology in the Department of Psychology at Yale University. Dr. Kim-Cohen received her Ph.D. in Clinical Psychology from the University of Rochester and was a postdoctoral trainee at the Social, Genetic, and Developmental Psychiatry Centre at the Institute of Psychiatry, King's College London. Her research focuses on genetic and environmental influences on risk for disruptive behavior problems and resilience in children exposed to maternal depression and maltreatment.

PAMELA K. KLEBANOV

Pamela K. Klebanov, Ph.D., is a Senior Research Scientist at the National Center for Children and Families at Columbia University's Teachers College and a Visiting Research Collaborator at Princeton University's Center for Research on Child Wellbeing. Klebanov's research focuses on the effects of poverty and risk factors on child health and development.

BRETT LAURSEN

Brett Laursen, Ph.D., is Professor of Psychology and Director of Graduate Training at Florida Atlantic University and Docent Professor of Social Developmental Psychology at the University of Jyvaskyla, Finland. He has authored numerous papers on parent-child and peer relationships and edited several volumes on adolescent development and developmental methodology, the most recent of which are *Relationship Pathways: From Adolescence to Young Adulthood* (with Andy Collins, Sage, 2012) and *The Handbook of Developmental Research Methods* (with Todd Little and Noel Card, Guilford, 2012). He is a recipient of an Honorary Doctorate from the Orebro University, Sweden, and he is currently Editor of the Methods and Measures section of the *International Journal of Behavioral Development*.

MARY J. LEVITT
Mary J. Levitt, Ph.D., is a Professor in the Developmental Science program, Department of Psychology at Florida International University, with a focus on the development of social relationships across the life span. Her current research addresses social network change and postmigration adaptation of newly immigrant children and adolescents. She received her Ph.D. from the Life Span Developmental Psychology program at Syracuse University.

ALICIA F. LIEBERMAN
Alicia F. Lieberman, Ph.D., is Professor and Vice-Chair for Academic Affairs at the University of California San Francisco Department of Psychiatry. She holds the Irving B. Harris Endowed Chair in Infant Mental Health and is Director of the Child Trauma Research Program at San Francisco General Hospital.

SHOON LIO
Shoon Lio, Ph.D., is an assistant professor of sociology/anthropology at the University of Illinois, Springfield. His interests include neighborhood context for sociopsychological development and civic engagement, political sociology, collective memory, and social psychology.

JESSICA F. MAGIDSON
Jessica F. Magidson, M.S., is a doctoral student in the Clinical Psychology program at University of Maryland, College Park. Her research and clinical interests focus on treatment development for substance use and depression comorbidity as well as improving HIV medication adherence.

ANN S. MASTEN
Ann S. Masten, Ph.D., LP, is a Distinguished McKnight University Professor in the Institute of Child Development at the University

of Minnesota. She directs the Project Competence studies of risk and resilience; is President of the Society for Research in Child Development (2011–2013); and is a member of the Board on Children, Youth and Families of the Institute of Medicine/National Academies.

DAVID L. MOLFESE
David L. Molfese, Ph.D., completed graduate training in both molecular and cognitive neuroscience. He is currently a postdoctoral Fellow at the University of Houston.

PETER J. MOLFESE
Peter J. Molfese, Ph.D., completed his graduate work at the University of Houston in Developmental Cognitive Neuroscience and is now a postdoctoral associate at Yale School of Medicine and Haskins Laboratories, New Haven. He specializes in learning and language development as well as neuroimaging theory, methods, and statistics.

LYNNE MURRAY
Lynne Murray, Ph.D., is affiliated with the School of Psychology and Clinical Language Sciences at the University of Reading in the United Kingdom. Professor Murray's research focuses on the impact of parental psychiatric disorders on child development. She has published widely on the influence of postnatal depression on child development and the intergenerational transmission of psychopathology.

JELENA OBRADOVIĆ
Jelena Obradović, Ph.D., is an assistant professor at Stanford University in the Developmental and Psychological Sciences program in the School of Education. Dr. Obradovic's research focuses on how contextual risk and adversity influence children's adaptation across multiple domains of functioning over time. She studies how individual differences in children's physiological reactivity and self-regulatory abilities enable some disadvantaged children to demonstrate remarkable resilience, while placing others at risk for maladaptive outcomes.

LAUREN M. PAPP

Lauren M. Papp, Ph.D., is the assistant Professor in the Department of Human Development and Family Studies at the University of Wisconsin. He has research interests that include intimate relationship quality and psychological distress, interparental conflict and child development, and quantitative methods and modeling of family and relationship processes.

ROSS D. PARKE

Ross D. Parke, Ph.D., is a distinguished professor of psychology, Emeritus, and past director of the Center for Family Studies at the University of California, Riverside. His interests include fatherhood, the relation between families and peers, ethnic variation in families, and the impact of the new reproductive technologies on families. His current project is a book entitled *Future Families: Diverse Forms, Rich Possibilities*.

YAACOV PETSCHER

Yaacov Petscher, Ph.D., is the Director of Research at the Florida Center for Reading Research. He is interested in the assessment, measurement theory, and the study of individual differences in literacy research assessment.

AELESIA PISCIELLA

Aelesia Pisciella received her Ph.D. in Applied Developmental Psychology from Fordham University. At Fordham, her research focused on mothers' participation in family leave on children's and mothers' well-being, as well as an examination of the links between maternal employment and the quality of parent-child relationships. She has also conducted research on the economic and housing instability of young children and families to determine how these early experiences impacted children's social-emotional development.

ALIZA W. PRESSMAN

Aliza W. Pressman, Ph.D., is a clinical instructor in the Department of Pediatrics in the Division of Behavioral and Developmental Health at the Mount Sinai School of Medicine, where she teaches behavior and child development and investigates and designs parent education programs for at-risk mothers. She was previously a Fellow at the National Center for Children and Families at Teachers College, Columbia University.

SARAH RABBITT

Sarah Rabbitt, M.S., M.Phil, is a doctoral student in the Clinical Psychology program in the Department of Psychology at Yale University. Her research interests include developing ways to improve access to evidence-based treatment for children and adolescents who have behavior disorders.

CRAIG T. RAMEY

Craig T. Ramey, Ph.D., is the Distinguished Research Scholar of Human Development at the Virginia Tech Carilion Research Institute, Professor of Psychology at Virginia Tech, and Professor of Pediatrics at the Virginia Tech Carilion School of Medicine. He specializes in the study of factors affecting children's health and the development of intelligence, social competence, and academic achievement. Over the past forty years he and his wife, Sharon Landesman Ramey, have conducted multidisciplinary longitudinal research with more than 100,000 children in more than forty states. He is the Founding Director of several frequently cited early intervention programs, including the Abecedarian Project, Project CARE, and the Infant Health and Development Program, and currently serves as the Chief Science Officer for the statewide preschool educational program for preK children in Louisiana.

SHARON LANDESMAN RAMEY

Sharon Landesman Ramey, Ph.D., is Distinguished Research Scholar of Human Development at the Virginia Tech Carilion Research Institute, Professor of Psychology at Virginia Tech, and Professor of Psychiatry at the Virginia Tech Carilion School of Medicine. She is a developmental scientist who studies the multiple biosocial and environmental influences on prenatal and early child development, the transition to school and academic achievement, family dynamics, and intergenerational vitality and competence. She is engaged in multiple large-scale and multisite trials to improve the health and education outcomes of vulnerable children, including children from challenging life circumstances and children who have disabilities.

JESSICA M. RICHARDS

Jessica M. Richards, M.S., University of Maryland College Park, Department of Psychology, is a graduate student in the doctoral program in Clinical Psychology.

ROBERT W. ROESER

Robert W. Roeser is Professor of Psychology and Human Development in the Department of Psychology at Portland State University in Portland, Oregon. Dr. Roeser's expertise is in teachers' professional development and school as a primary cultural context of adolescents' motivation to learn, achievement, and identity development. His current research is focused on how contemplative practices like mindfulness and yoga can improve teaching and learning in schools through the effects of these practices on stress reduction, the enhancement of well-being, the sharpening of attention and awareness, and the cultivation of empathy and compassion among educators and students alike.

THOMAS J. SCHOFIELD

Thomas J. Schofield, Ph.D., is a postdoctoral scholar at the University of California, Davis. His interests include the antecedents and consequences of parenting practices, the contexts in which parents attempt to shape child and adolescent development, and ethnic variation in families.

RONALD SEIFER

Ronald Seifer, Ph.D., is Professor of Psychiatry and Human Behavior at Alpert Medical School of Brown University and Director of Research at E. P. Bradley Hospital. Research interests are in the area of developmental psychopathology and public health, with ongoing studies on resilience in maltreated children, early development in the context of preventive interventions for postpartum depression, program evaluation of integration

of mental health in primary care and child care settings, and program evaluation of implementation of nurse home visiting programs. Dr. Seifer received his Ph.D. in developmental psychology from the University of Rochester in 1981. He spent eight years at the Institute for the Study of Developmental Disabilities at the University of Illinois Chicago, before moving to Brown University and E. P. Bradley Hospital in 1986.

ANNE SHAFFER

Anne Shaffer, Ph.D., is an assistant professor of psychology at the University of Georgia. Dr. Shaffer's research focuses on identifying contextual factors at multiple levels of analysis that may mediate or moderate the effects of adversity on outcomes in childhood and adulthood. A current area of research is the sequelae of maltreatment and family stress, with a specific focus on emotional maltreatment.

MICHELLE SLEED

Michelle Sleed is a Senior Research Psychologist at the Anna Freud Centre in London and University College London. Her research focuses on parent-infant relationships and interaction, parental representations, parental mental health, and outcomes of psychotherapeutic interventions for parents and infants. She teaches and supervises in the area of parent-infant research and service evaluation.

LAURA STOUT SOSINSKY

Laura Stout Sosinsky, Ph.D., is an assistant professor of applied developmental psychology in the Fordham University Department of Psychology. Her research involves early childhood development in the contexts of parenting and early care and education; family, industry, and policy contributors to the quality, availability, affordability, and accessibility of child care and early education services; and parental child care decision making.

NANCY E. SUCHMAN

Nancy E. Suchman, Ph.D., is Associate Professor in the Department of Psychiatry and in the Child Study Center at Yale University School of Medicine. Her clinical research focuses on developing and evaluating attachment- and mentalization-based interventions for mothers who have substance use disorders and psychiatric illnesses.

CHARLES M. SUPER
Charles M. Super, Ph.D., is Professor of Human Development and Pediatrics at the University of Connecticut, where he is Co-Director of the Center for the Study of Culture, Health, and Human Development. His primary research concerns how culture interacts with emerging biological systems to shape early development.

LOUIS TUTHILL
Louis Tuthill, Ph.D., formerly a Social Science Analyst at the National Institute of Justice, is an assistant professor in the Department of Sociology, Anthropology, and Criminal Justice at Rutgers-Camden. He has worked closely with law enforcement agencies in crime mapping, performance measures, and evaluation research. His interests include neighborhood violence, gang activity, illicit firearms and drug trafficking, and juvenile delinquency.

PATRICIA VAN HORN
Patricia Van Horn, Ph.D., is a Clinical Professor at the University of California San Francisco Department of Psychiatry. She is Director of the Division of Infant, Child, and Adolescent Psychiatry at San Francisco General Hospital and Associate Director of the Child Trauma Research Program.

ERIC VEGA
Eric Vega, Ph.D., is a Resident Scholar in the Center for Family Studies at the University of California, Riverside. His interests include schooling, immigrant families, and the formation of educational capital in ethnic family networks. His current research is on educational policy reform and academic achievement of immigrant children.

SARAH WARD
Sarah Ward is a graduate student in the Clinical Science and Psychopathology Research Program at the University of Minnesota.

MONICA YUDRON
Monica Yudron is a doctoral student at the Harvard Graduate School of Education with more than 15 years of experience in education-related fields including teaching, publishing, and policy making. Her research interests are centered on understanding formal programs of early childhood education and care as primary settings for intervening in the lives of young children facing a variety of poverty-related risks.

The Role of Environments in Development: An Introduction

Michael Lewis and Linda C. Mayes

In this volume, we explicate the role of environment in children's development. On the surface, the volume's focus may seem accepted if not mundane. All scholars agree that children's environment, defined in multiple ways but basically as all those events, persons, and circumstances outside the physical body and biological endowment of the child, impacts children's developmental trajectories and outcome through a host of mechanisms. However, for the most part environment is thought of as the "other variable or variables" that either confound longitudinal predictions or contribute difficult-to-measure noise and/or variance in models focusing on individual child outcome. Indeed, the features of the environment and their various effects are poorly understood. Although we have focused on the taxonomy of organism behaviors, little attention has been paid to measures of the environment. Given the diverse features of environments and the important roles attributed to them, it is surprising that so little systematic work has gone into their study. For the most part, mothers and families have received the most attention as

environmental factors. However, other people as well as other features of environments have not. This handbook is intended to make us more aware of the many ways to consider environments.

Because other people make up one important aspect of our environment, the work on the structure of the *social* environment is particularly relevant. From a developmental perspective, some work exists on this topic, and an attempt has been made to expand the numbers of potentially important people in the child's environment through the study of social networks (Lewis &Takahashi, 2005), as well as to create an analysis of the structure of the social environment itself. Although considerable effort has been focused on the importance of the mother to the child, other persons also play a significant role, even from birth, including fathers, siblings, grandparents, and peers. This social network also may extend to the relationships in schools and communities as well as the broader culture.

The role of environments in the developmental processes has been underplayed because most investigators seek to find

1

structure and change within the organism itself. Likewise in the study of psychopathology, even though we recognize that environments can cause disturbance and abnormal behavior, we prefer to treat the person – to increase his or her coping skills or alter specific behaviors – rather than change the environment. Our belief that the thrust of development resides in the organism rather than in the environment, in large part, raises many problems. For example, at cultural levels, we assume that violence (and its cure) must be met in the individual – a trait model – rather than in the structure of the environment. The murder rate using handguns in the United States is many times higher than in any other Western society. We seek responsibility in the nature of the individual (e.g., XYY males or the genetics of antisocial behavior), when the alternative of environmental structure is available. In this case, murders may be due more to the culture's nonrestriction of handguns. Thus, we conclude either that Americans are by their nature more violent than Europeans or that other Western societies do not allow handguns and therefore have lower murder rates. Other examples include models for understanding various health conditions such as heart disease, obesity, and addictions. The incidence of all three is on the rise in American culture, but more often than not, we look to genetic risks, weaknesses in self-control, or poor understanding in the individual as singular or primary explanatory variables rather than more complex interactions of individual, society, and culture.

While scholars understand the necessity of grappling with individual differences in children's environment, we intend this volume to explicate the variety of environments, how environments are also dynamic and often change as children develop, and how the science of assessing and understanding developmental environments is increasingly complex and sophisticated and introduces new methods for understanding how complex systems change over time. In this Introduction, we hope to accomplish three tasks that will be echoed in the structure of this volume. First, in order to

understand the role of environment in the development of the child we need to articulate the various models used in understanding the child by environment interaction. Such models vary from trait views in which the child may impact the response of his or her caring environment to epigenetic models where environments interact at the genome level, producing differences in replication of the genetic code.

The second section will review the various dimensions of environments that have been articulated and that are considered in the chapters to follow. Bronfenbrenner's analysis of embeddedness speaks to the need for our analysis to consider, besides the child's mother, other members of the family, school/peers, the larger community, and the culture as well. The social domain contains various people, and our analysis should address such concepts as the social networks and the functions of this complex structure. By going past the mother and child relationship, we broaden our perspective of the social environment.

Following this we need to consider that events "out there" need to be considered from the perspective of the child. Thus, an event that may be stressful for one child may not be stressful for another. Similarly, events may be more meaningful for one child than for another. Moments of mentoring, caring acts, even moments of harsh, albeit caring advice have their impact in different ways on individuals depending on the child's cognitive and emotional state and needs at the time. Environments can be defined by the experimenter or by the parent or even by an observer; however, ultimately, environments must be seen from the point of view of the child as well. Children's construction and memories of reality, here taken to mean environments, may be quite different from the ways we might characterize them. While few of the chapters take this up in any detail, the need to consider environments from the child's constructionist position highlights how our analyses of important environmental events may be missing important information. This point underscores too the ever-present tension of an epistemology of individual experience and perspective versus one of interrater agreement, shared themes, and group commonality.

Finally, the last section will consider the structure and frame of the chapters to follow. Our conceptualization and types of integration of the various analyses of environments will also touch on areas missing from the typical ways of considering environmental vectors and forces.

Models of Development

Models of development represent worldviews about human nature and the environments that create an individual human life course. Models of abnormal development also reflect these views, and the data from normal and abnormal lives inform our theories of development. So, for example, the trait notion of personality and the invulnerable or "resilient" child both share the view that some fixed pattern of behavior once formed may be unaffected by environmental factors.

More than 30 years ago, Riegel (1978) developed a scheme for considering models that involve the child and the environment. All of these elements can be active or passive agents. The passive child–passive environment model is of relatively less interest because it arose from the views of John Locke and David Hume and now receives little attention. Such models as these originally had some use, for example, in our belief about short-term memory, where memories were stored in a small box that was sequentially filled; when a new memory was entered and there was no more room, the first (or oldest) memory dropped out.

The second model of development, passive child with an active environment, is an environmental control view, because here the environment actively controls, by reward and punishment, the child's behavior. The characteristics of this environment may differ, as may the nature of the different reinforcers, but the child's behavior is in response to and is determined by its environment. We are most familiar with

this model in operant conditioning (Skinner, 1953). It is a model used in diverse areas, such as behavior modification treatment to alter maladaptive behavior, as well as in theories that explain normal sex role learning by parental or peer reinforcement. It is also implicit in many parent education or parent guidance programs focused on empowering parents with the skills and approaches that will shape their child's behavior into socially accepted norms.

In the third model, we are confronted with the view of an active person and a passive environment. These models have in common an active child extracting and constructing its world from the material of the environment. Piaget's theory fits well within this framework (Piaget, 1952). It is easy to see that although the child needs the environment to construct knowledge, the environment itself play little role. In psychopathology and therapy, we often employ such a model when we attempt to help patients alter their behavior (active person) but discount the role of the environment except for the therapist. Such models are also at play in training programs that teach children mastery skills so that they can "meet all challenges" that come their way. In this perspective, the control and active stance rest within the child.

The last model is most familiar to contemporary developmentalists because of its interactive nature. An active person and an active environment are postulated as creating, modifying, and changing behavior. These interactive models take many forms, varying from the interactional approach to transactional models to newer epigenetic models. They also include Chess and Thomas (1984) and Lerner's (1984) goodness-of-fit models, and from a developmental psychopathology point of view, the notion of vulnerability and risk status (Garmezy, Masten, & Tellegen, 1984).

Even though Riegel's (1978) approach is useful, other systems of classification are available. We offer three additional models of development: a *trait model*, an *environmental model*, and an *interactional model*. Although each of these models has variations, the interactional model is the most variable. These three models, which are prototypes of the various views of development, make clear how such models diverge in the role of environments and how they can be used to understand development. Unfortunately, by describing sharp distinctions, we may draw too tight an image and, as such, may make them appear as caricatures. Nevertheless, it is important to consider them in this fashion in order to reach our goal of more clearly explicating the complex role of environments in children's development.

Trait or Status Model

The trait or status model is often called the *medical model*, that is, predicting a later outcome based on earlier features. It is characterized by its simplicity and holds to the view that a trait, or the status of the child at one point in time, is likely to predict a trait or status at a later point in time. A trait model is not a traditionally interactive one and does not provide for the effects of the environment or usually for the effects of the trait on the response of the environment. In fact, in the most extreme form, the environment is thought to play no role either in affecting its display or in transforming its characteristic. A particular trait may interact with the environment, but in this model, the trait is not changed by that interaction.

Traits can be processes, coping skills, attributes, or tendencies to respond in certain ways and are not usually seen as readily open to transformation. Traits can be "innate" features, such as temperament or particular genetic codes, and can also be habitual patterns of behavior acquired though learning or through more interactive processes. However, once a trait, however defined, is acquired, it may be relatively impervious to subsequent interactions with a host of environmental factors. The trait model is most useful in many instances; for example, when considering potential genetic or biological causes of subsequent psychopathology. A child who is born with a certain gene or set of genes is likely to display illness or psychopathology at some later time. This model

characterizes some of the research in the genetics of mental illness. Here the environment, or its interaction with genes, plays little role in the potential outcome. Although a trait model is appealing in its simplicity, there are any number of problems with it; for example, not all people who possess a trait or have a particular status at one point in time are likely to show subsequent psychopathology. The examples of this point are myriad and include the relationship between early abuse and later depression (Cicchetti, Rogosch, Gunnar, & Toth, 2010), the long-term relationship of various "risk" polymorphisms such as the serotonin transporter gene to later outcome (Kaufman et al., 2006), the relationship between impulsivity as a trait in childhood and later addictive disorders (Chambers, Taylor, & Potenza, 2003), and the relationship of the *ApoE* gene and the onset of Alzheimer's disease later in life (Borroni, Costanzi, & Padovani, 2010).

In some trait models, attachment, for example, there is initially an interaction with the environment that produces the trait. However, once that trait is established through the interaction with the environment, the environment is unlikely to play a further role. This trait model has much in common with what we have seen in most of the attachment literature, where the early environment, the mother and child interaction, leads to a certain type of attachment, and it is this type of attachment that predicts subsequent behavior. However, we have now learned that traits can be affected by later environmental interaction (Lewis, 1997). The same trait model is apparent in the concept of invulnerability; that is, there are attributes of children that appear to protect them from environment stressors. This invulnerability trait serves to make the child stress-resistant. Such a mechanism is used to explain why not all at-risk children develop psychopathology (Garmezy et al., 1984).

Trait models in personality theory are not new (Allport & Allport, 1921) and the problems identified in personality research apply here as well. The major problem related to trait models is the recognition that individual traits are likely to be situation specific

(Mischel, 1965). As such they can only partially characterize the organism. Problematic with the trait notion is the fact that such models do not consider the impact of environment on subsequent developmental growth or dysfunction.

The Environmental Model

The prototypic environmental model holds that it is the exogenous factors that influence development. In the simplest model, behavior, normal or maladaptive, is primarily a function of the environmental forces acting on the organism at any point in time. In such a model, for example, a child does behavior X but not behavior Y, because behavior X is positively rewarded by his parents and Y is punished. Notice that, in this model, the environmental forces act continuously on the organism, and the behavior emitted is a direct function of this action. Although this model may apply for some behavior, it is more likely the case that environmental forces act on the child, directly at that point in time and indirectly at later points in time. Our hypothetical child may do behavior X, not because it has immediate reward value, but because the child remembers that X is a rewarded behavior. Clearly, much of our behavior is controlled by this indirect effect of environmental pressure. Many other forms of indirect reward and punishment have been observed. For example, consider the situation in which a child is present when the mother scolds the older sibling for writing on the walls of the house. The younger child, although not directly punished, does learn that writing on the walls is not an action to be performed.

A general environmental model suggests that children's behavior is a function of the environment in which the behavior occurs. As long as the environment appears consistent, the child's behavior will be consistent; if the environment changes, so too will the child's behavior. If a more active organism model is used, it is still the case that maladaptive environments produce abnormal behavior; however, the abnormal behavior is produced by the child's perception and construction of its reality. From a developmental psychopathology point of view, maladaptive behavior is caused by maladaptive environments; if we change those environments, we alter the behavior. Consistency and change in the child's behavior are supported by exogenous rather than endogenous factors. Such a model of change as a function of the environment can be readily tested but rarely is. This failure reflects the bias of the trait model. Consider the case of attachment. Although it is recognized that the environment at Time 1 affects the child at Time 1, it is the attachment type that is hypothesized to determine the child's later development. Rarely is the environment, and the consistency of the environment, factored into the model as a possible cause of subsequent child behavior: Consider that it is poor parenting that produces an insecure child at Time 1, and this parenting remains poor at Time 2. Moreover, a nonresponsive mother at Time 1 also may not be responsive at Time 2 so that her child's behavior at Time 2 may also be a function of the consistency of her behavior at Time 2 as much as of the child's attachment type at Time 1. That most research in this area fails in this regard constitutes evidence for the relative lack of interest in the environmental mode. (See Lewis, 1997, for a full description of this problem.)

Although the environmental model can be more complex, this model suggests in all cases that the child's concurrent status is determined by the environment. If the environment changes, then the child's status will change. The degree to which the environment remains consistent is the degree to which the psychopathology or adaptive development will be consistently found within the subject. Therefore, the environmental model is characterized by the view that holds that the constraints, changes, and consistencies in children's development and/or risk for psychopathology rest not so much within intrinsic structures located in the child as in the nature, structure, and environment of the child.

The environmental model also raises the issue of the nature and degree of prior experience: that is, the notion of the critical period. Certain environmental influences may have a greater effect at some points in time than at others. For example, a responsive environment in the first year and a less responsive environment in the second year should lead to better consequences than a nonresponsive environment in the first year. Although critical period suggests some organism characteristic, the effects of the environment as a function of past experience remain relevant here. In its simplest form, it is important to know whether a series of positive environmental events that are followed by a negative event affect the negative event, so the number or the timing of the positive events is important to consider. In similar fashion, the same question applies for a series of negative events. This suggests that the embeddedness of environmental events is important as is the event itself.

The Interactional Model

Interactional models vary; some researchers prefer to call them "interactional" and others "transactional" (Lewis, 1972; Sameroff & Chandler, 1975). As we shall see, all these models have in common the role of both child and environment in determining the course of development. In these models, the nature of the environment and the characteristics or traits of the child are needed to explain concurrent as well as subsequent behavior and adjustment. The stability and change in the child need to be viewed as a function of both factors, and, as such, the task of any interactive model is to study both features. In our earlier attachment example, the infant who is securely attached, as a function of the responsive environment in the first year, will show competence at a later age as a function of the earlier events as well as the nature of the environment at that later age.

One of the central issues of the developmental theories that are interactive in nature is the question of transformation. Two models of concurrent behavior as a function of traits and environments can

be drawn. In the first, both trait and environment interact and produce a new set of behaviors. However, neither the trait nor the environment is altered by the interaction. From a developmental perspective, this is an additive model because new behaviors are derived from old behaviors/traits and their interaction with the environment, but these new behaviors are added to the repertoire of the set of old behaviors (Lewis, 1997). For example, an impulsive, anxious adolescent encountering substance using peers may experience relief from anxiety with drug use. A new repertoire of behaviors, an addicted process, develops, though the traits of impulsivity and anxiety remain and the adolescent's peers remain substance using. Or consider the case of the temperamentally active child. If such a child is raised in a household where activity and noise are valued – where there is a match between the active child and the environment – no maladaptive behavior results. However, if this same child is raised in a household where quiet behavior and inhibition are valued, we would expect to see more adjustment problems. Similarly, for the quiet lethargic child, again depending on the match between the behavior and environment, different degrees of maladjustment can occur.

In terms of transformation, such a model is relatively silent. Even so, it would seem reasonable to imagine that new behaviors arise as a result of either match or mismatch, but these new behaviors do not require the old behaviors to be transformed. The active child may learn to move more slowly, but the trait of activity is not lost or transformed. The environment, too, may change, because less is required of the child, but the values or goals underlying the requirement remain and are not changed.

In the second model, both trait and environment interact, producing both a new set of and a transformation of both old traits and environment. From a developmental perspective, this is a transformational model because the interaction of old behaviors and environment gives rise to new behaviors, and the old behaviors and environment are themselves altered by the interaction.

The goodness-of-fit model was proposed by Thomas and Chess (1977) with regard to individual differences in children's temperament. The major feature of this model is that discord arises when the child's characteristics do not match the environmental demand, or, stated in another way, the environmental demand does not match the child's characteristic. Notice that maladjustment is the consequence of the *mismatch*. It is not located in the nature of the child's characteristic nor in the environmental demand. The goodness-of-fit model suggests that psychopathology is the consequence of the mismatch between trait and environment, and, as such, it is an interactive model. In this instance, the poor fit results in both a new repertoire of behaviors in response to the mismatch and an intensification in those aspects of both the child's temperament and the environment that are poorly matched.

These types of models, which require that all features that make up interaction are transformed by their interaction, are called *transactional* (Sameroff, 1975). For example, if we believe that the child's characteristics at Time 1 interact with the environment at Time 1 to produce a transformed child characteristic and environment at Time 2, then it is likely that both the child and environment at Time 1 also were transformed from some earlier Time, Time n − 1, and that therefore each feature is never independent of the other. Such models reject the idea that child or environment characteristics are ever independent or exist as "pure" forms; there is an ultimate regression of effects. Moreover, from a future perspective of development, these features interact and transform themselves at each point in development. The linear functions that characterize the other models are inadequate for the transformation view. The parent's behavior affects the child's behavior; however, the parent's behavior was affected by the child's earlier behavior and will be subsequently changed by changes in the child's behavior.

Consider the irritable child who interacts with a positive environment and produces a negative environment that subsequently produces a negative irritable child. The causal chain does not simply pass in a continuous fashion either through the environment or though the irritable child as the trait or environmental model would have it. In fact, it is a circular pattern of child causes affecting the environment and environmental causes affecting the child. Such models have intrinsic appeal but by their nature are difficult to test. Nonlinearity requires a mathematics that is still being developed. Moreover, it is difficult not to treat a child or environmental characteristic as a "pure" quantity even though we might know better. As such, we tend to test interactive models that require less transformation. Clearly the new work in epigenetics also renders the trait and environment model relatively obsolete. The interaction of environments can have a direct effect on gene expression, which can subsequently affect behavior and the child's interaction with its environment. These new models need to articulate which aspects of environments can affect gene expression and how this happens.

Types of Environments

As we have discussed, when environment has been assessed and considered as a variable or condition that not only changes with the child but also impacts the child's developmental trajectory, it is most often defined as the most proximal environment, that of maternal (and less often, paternal) care, especially in the first months and years of life. In this volume, we expand the definition of environment along the dimension of proximal versus distal experience (that is, day-to-day caregiving compared to the standards of caregiving in a community or culture or the less regular caregiving of an occasional caregiver such as a grandparent or aunt) and along the idea of a broader social network of experiences offered to children across development. With more and more children entering child care programs at earlier ages (Halle et al., 2009), children's early social-caregiving experiences are far more diverse in terms of practices and in terms of persons. Indeed, while multiple caregiving is difficult to manage empirically, most children seen in studies of early social development are not cared for just by their mothers or their parents – and to assume that an interaction session between a parent and child captures the child's average day-to-day experience is likely erroneous. Their interactions with their parents are only a portion of their day-to-day social caregiving experiences.

Similarly, all too often overlooked is that many children are looked after for significant periods by their older siblings. It is not just that sibling relationships are an important component of a child's social environment but that those siblings often care for their younger brothers and sisters while the adults in the family are working a second job or a late shift. Indeed, among poorer families, children are more often cared for by other children (e.g., siblings) as well as neighbors and other family members (e.g., aunts, uncles, stepparents, grandparents, and great-grandparents). In this way, socioeconomic status or economic status impacts a child's caring environment as well as the amount of stimulation and resources available to the child. Poverty is also likely a surrogate variable for the amount of chronic stress experienced by parents and hence by their children. Thus, poverty is both an index of the social-caring environment as well as an indirect measure of family stress and family emotional health. Similarly, there is the difference between rural and urban environments that offer differences in community cohesion and networks, community resources, and cultural mores. For example, rural poverty may be experienced by children quite differently from urban poverty even at the same ratio of income to need in part because in smaller communities there may be less apparent disparity between the economically advantaged and disadvantaged.

Extending beyond the family or the caregiving network especially for younger children is the environment of education and schools. At younger and younger ages, children are spending significant amounts of time outside the home whether in child care, school, or after-school programs. Schools – and their teachers, coaches,

administrators – are significant members of a child's social and caring environment, and often mentoring relationships formed through schools have significant and memorable impacts long into adulthood. Characterizing those relationships at the individual, classroom, and programmatic levels is critical to better understanding these significant environmental contexts in children's lives. And schools are embedded in communities and neighborhoods – sometimes they are the hub of their community; sometimes they are only one of a number of threads that hold a neighborhood, town, or community together. But children are a part of their neighborhoods and their communities, and those environments become a part of their identity. When adults say, "I grew up in South Boston" or "I'm from a farm in Iowa," they are implicitly saying these are the communities that will tell any listener more about them and about their experiences. These communities have their cultures, their beliefs, their pride and shame that are passed along to children and influence again the broader social-environmental network and the caring environment.

But in the twenty-first century, these neighborhoods and communities are also virtual, and increasingly the media in the form of television, film, the Internet, social networking sites, gaming communities, and so on, form another influential environment for children. Simultaneously opening up the broader world to children and at the same time often diminishing direct peer to peer time, the influence of these different forms of media is just beginning to be studied (and harnessed). Even at the basic level of understanding how much familiarity children do or do not have with computers, assessments of children's developing cognitive and social skills are influenced by experience with the media environment. It may also be that the media environment defines another disparity line much like economic advantage or disadvantage and hence becomes a significant environmental variable even in its relative absence in some children's lives.

Finally, though not exhaustively, we need to consider explicitly those examples of environments that are problematic and disruptive, from the effects of community violence and natural disasters to the impact of parental psychopathology on children's proximal caring environments. While the literature on parental depression is extensive, there is far less literature on parental psychopathology in general and on how children understand their parents' mental illness at different developmental ages. Parental psychopathology, like every other "environment" we discuss, is not a fixed construct – it ebbs and flows, improves and worsens, and often those fluctuations are tied to children's differing developmental needs. Similar is the impact of neglect and trauma in childhood. While neglect and trauma are topics for which there is an extensive literature in terms of long-term sequelae, what is less well incorporated into developmental models is an understanding of neglect and trauma in terms of an environmental failure that is experienced over and over in terms of memories, repeated foster care placements, continued or resumed contact with biological parents. And especially for examples of environmental failure, it is as much the child's experience and construction of these circumstances as the veridical events that carry the impact, an observation leading us to the next section.

"Material" or Constructed Environments

Here we call attention to an issue that is not explicitly considered in every chapter in this volume but is nonetheless a significant consideration as we investigate the dynamic, changing qualities of different environments. As outlined in the previous section, in this volume, we present various perspectives on environments. The idea that we respond to literal environmental events, persons, or circumstances is at the core of the interaction model and is the core justification for this handbook. Yet there is also the idea that our constructive perceptions, thoughts, and memories of events are what really constitute our psychic reality, and it is

that constructed environmental reality, not the veridical environment, to which we are responding. Often hard to reconcile with general theories of development is the possibility that our constructed memories of our past may be little related to what "really happened" or to veridical accounts and moreover that our constructed past may have a more powerful effect on us in the present than what really happened in the past. Thus while, for example, Bowlby (1969) suggested that the young child constructs a model of its relationship to its mother, that model is based as much, if not more, on the child's constructed experience of interactions with the mother or on the child's expectations of those interactions as it is on what really happened.

This issue has been around in various theories of psychological development for a long time but is perhaps best captured in the psychoanalytic perspective on experience: That is, what matters in that perspective is the individual's construction of past and present experiences, not what really happened, for it is those constructions that influence current and future behavior and ways of seeing and experiencing the world. Freud's treatment of this issue, is what he called deferred action, in German *nachtraglichkeit*. Although Freud was a determinist who believed in a temporal direction where what happened in the past determines the future, he also had the view that reinvestment with meaning could occur later after the original event. In a word, Freud (1896) wrote to Fliess, "I am working on the assumption that our psychical mechanism has come into being by a process of stratification; the material present in the form of memory – traces being subjected from time to time to a re-arrangement in accordance with fresh circumstances." It was also an idea of Jung when he talked about retrospective phantasies, *Zuruckphantasieren*. Thus, we need to consider that humans even from early childhood can perceive the same event differentially and can reconstruct memories not in keeping to what "really happened." The examples of this are well considered in psychology, from projective tests like the thematic apperception test (TAT) or Rorschach test, to the memory research of Rovee-Collier with infants. Recall that, in her research she has amply shown that associations can be made through connecting events that give rise to action patterns learned with one event becoming associated to another event (Giles & Rovee-Collier, 2011).

Since the mother is an important environment factor in the development of the child we can ask whether the model or memory of the mother is a real event or construction. Perhaps most relevant to our focus on development is a study done by Marian Radke Yarrow, John D. Campbell, and Roger V. Burton (1970) of both mothers' and their children's recollections of their relationship in the past. In this study they gathered what they called the "baseline data," which were derived when the children were young. Through observations, tests, ratings, and reports gathered years before, information on their earlier mother-child relationships was evaluated and the participants in that research recontacted and reinterviewed. Yarrow and her colleagues found that there was little overall relation between children's recollection of their relationships with their mothers and their actual relationships with them. Mothers' recall of the earlier relationships was no better. As Yarrow and her colleagues (1970) stated, "Mothers who have had pleasant and rewarding experiences in rearing their children, mothers who feel hostile to their children, and mothers who have had especially stressful life situations may not be equally able to report on their own rearing behavior or on the behavior of their children." Even more important to this discussion, however, was that Yarrow and her colleagues found that mothers' and children's recall of their earlier relationships depended on their current relationships. The degree of warmth or coolness in the *current* relationship shifted the *recollection* of the past in the direction of the current status. "For groups in which the [current] relationships were rated as 'cold', shifts in recall tended to be in an unfavorable direction, and for groups in which the relationships were rated as 'warm', shifts in recall tended to increase the felicity of earlier times."

Mothers' recollections of the preschool personalities of their children were structured so as to conform to their perceptions of their children's present personalities. For example, if the children were not seen as shy, mothers tended to recall them as having been less shy in early childhood relative to the actual data collected. If, on the other hand, the children were described as outgoing in the present, they were rated as having been more outgoing when they were younger than the data suggested. This occurred not only for the dimensions of children's response to authority and of their independence. The shift in ratings was also true for the children themselves. If they rated themselves shy now, they also rated themselves as having been shy when they were younger.

Another example is from the work of one of our laboratories. Lewis et al. (2000), in a study of attachment over time, examined data from a longitudinal study of one hundred children followed from infancy to eighteen years of age. We wished to determine whether the young adults' perception of their own degree of attachment at 18 bore any resemblance to observations made of their early childhood attachment and whether the current environment affected their current perception of their past. We had collected attachment data taken during infancy, data about their current lives, and, because we were interested in the models of attachment, the standard adult attachment interview assessing their current model of attachment to their parents. In other words, we wanted to determine whether the teenagers' models of their own attachment bore a resemblance to what their attachment had been when they were infants or whether their current environment affected their current working model of attachment relationships. In addition, we wanted to determine whether what occurred in their early childhood affected their current environment. To get some picture of the nature of the participants' current lives, we asked them and their teachers to fill out a commonly used scale that measures teenagers' emotional adjustment.

The findings were quite clear. First, young adults' current attachment bore no relation to what they actually were like at one year of age, neither for the entire group of children nor even for those children who were insecurely attached earlier. Second, the young adults' current mental health status, as measured either by the teachers' report or by the teens themselves, bore no relation to their early attachment relationship. Their early attachment patterns did not influence subsequent mental health status, although 20 percent of these young adults did show some mild form of psychopathology. Thus, as in many studies on eighteen-year-olds, there was evidence of poor adjustment, but this adjustment was unrelated to their early attachment relationships with their mothers. In other words, there was no predictive usefulness of the attachment relationship at one year of age to young adults' attachment models or their mental health.

What we found was a relation between current life adjustment and current attachment models. Young adults who now had positive and healthy adjustment patterns had current secure attachment models, while young adults who had negative and maladjusted current lives had current insecure attachment models. Moreover, there were no complex interactions, such as the past affecting current life adjustment and current life adjustment in turn affecting the current working models. Should we think that this issue of what is the material or "real" environment and what is the individual's construction is restricted to social relations? Probably not, for the same can be seen in many studies on pain and distress. In a recently reported study we obtained measures of the child's experience of pain in relation to a suture for a cut on the head or body and an observer's ratings. There was no agreement between someone observing the child from the outside and the child's experience of the pain during the suturing.

Such findings suggest that in order to understand the nature of the environment in which the child develops truly, we need not only measures of that environment but measures of the child's perception of that environment. This is so whether we are describing environments in terms of relationships or in terms of its physical characteristics, and is a perspective only rarely incorporated into studies examining the impact of environments and experiences on child outcome.

Structure of the Chapters

There are four sections in this volume. In the first section, four chapters explore the concept of environment including concepts of risk, proximal and distal environmental constructs, parenting, and new approaches to characterizing environments. The second section presents the perspectives of five chapters including a detailed review of notions of environment beyond the usual conceptualization of parental care, gene-environment interaction (or the interaction model), and how we must necessarily consider environments as changing developmentally as much as the individual and the utility of dynamic systems perspectives in this regard. The third section takes up the range of perspectives on environments as discussed previously, from parenting to couples' relationships, families, siblings, peers, schools, rural and urban communities, neighborhoods, the media, and psychopathology. The fourth and final section offers perspectives on measurement including assessments of the home environment, psychopathology, social networks, and economic advantage and disadvantage. In this section, we also undertake a review of the notion of stress, a key environmental construct that cuts through so many definitions of environment as events, circumstance, and/or relationships. Finally, this section concludes with a review of statistical approaches to assessing change over time and especially interactional models in which both child and environment change.

In each chapter authors were asked not only to review the state of the art in their area of expertise, but also to comment on approaches to assessment and what areas still need considerable attention in order to capture the complexity of environmental perspectives more adequately. We fully appreciate that as comprehensive as we have attempted to be, we cannot fully encompass as broad and complex a topic as the environment, which impacts each of us through every moment of our day and throughout our lives. Our intent is to raise awareness and discussion of considering the complexity and richness of broader and deeper models of environment. We hope this volume will be the beginning of new models and new understandings.

References

Allport, F. H. & Allport, G. W. (1921). Personality traits: Their classification and measurement. *Journal of Abnormal and Social Psychology*, 16, 1–40.

Borroni, B., Costanzi, C., & Padovani, A. (2010). Genetic susceptibility to behavioural and psychological symptoms in Alzheimer's disease. *Current Alzheimer Research*, 7(2), 158–164.

Bowlby, J. (1969). *Attachment and loss*: Vol. 1. *Attachment*. New York: Basic Books.

Chambers, R. A., Taylor, J. R., & Potenza, M. N. (2003). Developmental neurocircuitry of motivation in adolescence: A critical period of addiction vulnerability. *American Journal of Psychiatry*, 160(6), 1041–1052.

Chess, S. & Thomas, A. (1984). *Origins and evolution of behavior disorders*. New York: Brunner/Mazel.

Cicchetti, D., Rogosch, F. A., Gunnar, M. R., & Toth, S. L. (2010). The differential impacts of early physical and sexual abuse and internalizing problems on daytime cortisol rhythm in school-aged children. *Child Development*, 81(1), 252–269.

Freud, S. (1896). Letter from Freud to Fliess, December 6, 1896. In J. M. Masson (1985, Trans. & Ed.), *The complete letters of Sigmud Freud to Wilhelm Fliess*, 1887–1904, pp. 207. Cambridge, MA: The Belknap Press of Harvard University Press.

Garmezy, N., Masten, A. S., & Tellegen, A. (1984). The study of stress and competence in children: A building block for developmental psychopathology. *Child Development*, 55, 987–1111.

Giles, A. & Rovee-Collier, C. (2011). Infant long-term memory for associations formed during mere exposure. *Infant Behavior and Development*, 34, 327–338.

Halle, T., Hair, E., Nuenning, M., Weinstein, D., Vick, J., Forry, N., & Kinukawa, A. (2009). *Primary child care arrangements of U.S. infants: Patterns of utilization by poverty status, family structure, maternal work status, maternal work schedule, and child care assistance.* Washington, D.C.: Child Trends.

Kaufman, J., Yang, B., Douglas-Palumberi, H., Grasso, D., Lipschitz, D., Houshyar, S., Krystal, J. H., & Gelernter, J. (2006). Brain-derived neurotrophic factor-5-*HHTLPR* gene interactions and environmental modifiers of depression in children. *Biological Psychiatry*, 59(8), 673–680.

Lerner, R. H. (1984). *On the nature of human plasticity*. New York: Cambridge University Press.

Lewis, M. (1972). State as an infant-environment interaction: An analysis of mother-infant interaction as a function of sex. *Merrill-Palmer Quarterly*, 18, 95–121.

Lewis, M. (1997). *Altering fate: Why the past does not predict the future*. New York: Guilford Press.

Lewis, M., Feiring, C., & Rosenthal, S. (2000). Attachment over time. *Child Development*, 71(3), 707–720.

Lewis, M., & Takahashi, K. (Eds.) (2005). *Human development: Special issue: Beyond the dyad: Conceptualization of social networks.* Switzerland: Karger.

Mischel, W. (1965). *Personality assessment.* New York: Wiley.

Piaget, J. (1952). *The origins of intelligence in children.* New York: International Universities Press.

Riegel, K. F. (1978). *Psychology, mon amour: A countertext.* Boston: Houghton Mifflin.

Sameroff, A. (1975). Transactional models in early social relations. *Human Development*, 18, 65–79.

Sameroff, A. & Chandler, M. J. (1975). Reproductive risk and the continuum of caretaking causality. In F. D. Horowitz (Ed.), *Review of child development research*, Vol. 4, pp. 187–244. Chicago: University of Chicago Press.

Skinner, B. F. (1953). *Science and human behavior.* New York: Macmillan.

Thomas, A. & Chess, S. (1977). *Temperament and development.* New York: Brunner/Mazel.

Yarrow, M. R., Campbell, J. D., & Burton, R. V. (1970). Recollections of childhood: A study of the retrospective method. *Monographs of the Society for Research in Child Development*, 35(5), 1–83.

Part I

THE "ENVIRONMENTAL" VARIABLE

CHAPTER 1

Proximal to Distal Environments in Child Development

Theoretical, Structural, Methodological, and Empirical Considerations

Marc H. Bornstein

Introduction

Children do not grow up in isolation. Rather, human beings are reared in and are exquisitely sensitive to their natural and designed environments, and they are intensely social creatures. Thus, theoreticians and researchers who ignore the multiple environments of child development risk failing to understand childhood fully (Bronfenbrenner & Morris, 2006). Different environments, ecologies, or contexts provide children with different physical, cognitive, and social experiences. In this chapter, I explore several significant environments in which children develop.

In Western industrialized cultures, parents typically play the major role in structuring young children's environments and experiences, and consequently child-parent relationships constitute the first ecological focus of this chapter. However, highlighting relationships involving children and their parents can overshadow the extent child-parent relationships themselves are embedded in broader contexts. Families provide children with a richly textured array of developmental environments. The family

shapes and is shaped by component relationships within it (for example, the relationship between the parents) as well as by its several surrounding communities. In this chapter, therefore, I also discuss the family system, focusing on the ways in which mothers, fathers, siblings, and children interrelate and influence one another. The patterns of influence of different individuals in the family on children are complex because changing family dynamics shape the style and significance of each relationship (Bornstein & Sawyer, 2006). Families also take different forms, but whichever form it takes the family – social and physical – constitutes the child's proximal environment.

Families represent only one of a variety of distinct developmental ecologies of childhood. In addition to frequent opportunities to interact with peers, children in many places are tended by a variety of nonparental care providers, whether in family day care, day care centers, fields, or schools. I discuss these nonfamilial ecologies of childhood in the third section of the chapter. These situations represent one of the ways in which people outside the family meaningfully affect children. Even broader circumstances are also influential. Social classes and cultures vary with respect to the patterns of development they expect and encourage. For example, cultural prescriptions determine, to a great extent, the more immediate environments experienced by children; the short- and long-term goals parents have for their children; and the practices parents use in attempting to meet those goals. These several extrafamilial contexts constitute distal environments of childhood, and I conclude with a consideration of their influences.

The chapter begins, however, with a brief discussion of tools we need to approach the multiple environments of childhood, including the roles of environmental experiences, measurement issues in child-environment interactions, and the overarching theoretical orientation of the chapter. These perspectives are intended to bring a deeper understanding and a greater coherence to an exposition of the environments of child development. The chapter then moves to an equally brief review of the important issue of what the child brings to his or her interactions with the several environments of development. Children not only evoke specific responses from their environments, they seek out environments that fit them best, and they experience and interpret their environments idiosyncratically.

Child-Environment Interactions

Roles of Experience

Sensitivity to the environment is the destiny of the developing organism from the very beginning of ontogenesis. Stem cells are found in all multicellular organisms. One broad class of mammalian stem cells are embryonic stem cells that are found in blastocysts. In a developing embryo, stem cells retain the ability to renew themselves through mitotic cell division but, importantly, can differentiate into a diverse range of specialized cell types because stem cells are highly plastic to their environment and can be grown and transformed through cell culture into specialized cells with characteristics consistent with cells of various tissues such as muscles or nerves. Stem cells, which are either totipotent or pluripotent, can give rise to any mature cell type and can become any tissue in the body (excluding a placenta) because of environmental cues of their particular niche. So, from the earliest stages of ontogenesis, sensitivity to the environment engendered by experience is a key characteristic of organism development.

This plasticity to the environment continues as cells in the brain and body respond to specific features of their internal and external environments. For example, selectivity characterizes cells in cortical areas of primate brains at birth (Wiesel & Hubel, 1974), and in cats and ferrets at eye opening, but selectivity sharpens with visual experience (Chapman, Godecke, & Bonhoeffer, 1999; Chapman & Stryker, 1993). The modifiability of cellular sensitivity by experience is illustrated in the way individual cells in the cat visual cortex respond to stimuli of different orientations. In the absence of specific orientation experiences, the "naive" cortex contains cells sensitive to all orientations. However, exposure to vertical stripes for 1 hour at a sensitive period early in life is sufficient to bias the sensitivity of cells in the visual cortex. More units are devoted to vertical and near-vertical orientations, whereas fewer units are devoted to other orientations. Indeed, 3 to 33 hours of selective exposure does not sharpen cortical sensitivity to vertical much more than does 1 hour of exposure, illustrating a threshold rather than linear dose-effect experience-sensitivity relation. Rearing kittens under conditions in which they view one particular orientation causes an overrepresentation of that orientation in the cortex (Sengpiel, Stawinski, & Bonhoeffer, 1999). In general terms, it may be that organisms are born with a brain and body ready to respond to critical features of its environment, and brain and body readily adapt to the environment in which the organism finds itself.

In addition to the functional differentiation of cells based on experience, two kinds of plasticity commonly characterize the nervous system: modifiability and compensation. Modifiability means that, although cells are predestined for specific functions, those functions may be transmuted or attuned. Presumptive visual system cells, for example, can function competently in new roles with new partners when transplanted to other organ systems. (To be successful, however, transplantation must occur within a temporal window; after a certain sensitive period, transplanted cells will die.) If a section of cortex is moved to a different part of the brain, the transplanted part adapts structurally and functionally to its new location (e.g., if moved to the visual cortex, cells from the auditory cortex become responsive to visual stimuli). Compensation is the second kind of neuronal plasticity. Compensation involves the ability of some cells to substitute for others, permitting recovery of function after neuronal loss or damage, such as the functional "reassignment" of motor neurons following amputations. Young neurons and young brains are less specialized with regard to function and so are able to compensate more flexibly (see Chugani, 1994; Kolb, 1989).

For its part, the type of environment experienced makes a difference to development, as does how the environment is experienced. Rats raised in "visually enriched" environments develop visual cortexes that are heavier and thicker than those of litter mates raised in barren, standard laboratory cages (e.g., Black & Greenough, 1986; Greenough, 1975, Rosenzweig, 1971); they also show improved performance on problem-solving tasks (Greenough, Black, & Wallace, 1987). Likewise, human children who are reared in an enriched ecology tend to have more developed skills (Sameroff, 1983). Self-produced experiences alter development differently to passive ones. Held and Hein (1963) showed that kittens that were allowed to explore their visual environment actively later mastered visual tasks in more sophisticated ways than did their yoked-control litter mates that experienced the same visual environment under conditions of motor restraint.

All theories of human development are experiential, environmental, and necessarily contextualist. They may differ with respect to the degree to which they assert that environmental variation is fundamental and to whether physical or social aspects of the environment are more central (Hunt, 1961). Greenough et al. (1987) distinguished experience-expectant from experience-dependent processes. Experience-expectant processes are common to all members of the species and presumably evolved as neural preparation for incorporating general information from the environment efficiently and satisfactorily. For example, binocular vision, and the experience of a single three-dimensional image rather than the two-dimensional images created by light in each eye, depend on expected experience. Experience-expectant plasticity fine-tunes aspects of development that cannot proceed to optimum outcomes as a result of solely genetic factors (Greenough, Black, & Wallace, 1993). By contrast, experience-dependent processes, in which development is altered as a result of learning in and from the environment, reflect brain changes unique to the organism's experience in its environments.

Shared environmental influences are those aspects of the environment that act to make children similar, and nonshared environmental influences are those aspects of the environment that act to make children different (Plomin & Daniels, 1987). Nonshared environmental influences acting on individuals in the same situation or setting may be nonsystematic, or they may be systematic. Nonsystematic influences include accidents, illnesses, or other chance circumstances that contribute to individual differences and that influence individual development. By contrast, systematic nonshared influences include gender differences and birth order but also differential treatment by the family or other family or social factors. Significant sibling similarity across a number of diverse outcome domains, such as antisocial behavior (Goodman, 1991; Pike, McGuire, Hetherington, Reiss, & Plomin, 1996), development of attitudes (Hoffman, 1991), and reading achievement (Thompson, 1996), points to the operation of shared environmental influences. Nonshared environmental influences appear to be the major means through which the environment influences development (Rowe, 1994). Note that the same dimensions of the environment can be shared or nonshared depending on whether the dimension is common to one or all of the siblings in the family (Goodman, 1991; Wachs, 1995).

Finally, environments give rise to different possible developmental trajectories given different levels of maturation before the onset of the environmental experience and the nature of different experiences afterward. If a construct, structure, function, or process is undeveloped at the time of the onset of environmental experience, experience may induce it or prevent its emergence; without experience, the construct, structure, function, or process will not develop. If a construct, structure, function, or process is partially developed, experience may maintain it at its immature level or attune or facilitate its further development or suppress it. If the construct, structure, function, or process is fully developed, experience could serve to maintain or suppress it. In the case of partially or fully developed constructs, structures, functions, or processes at what would be the onset of experience, the lack of effective experience could eventuate in its loss.

Measurement of the Environment, Phenomenology, and Development

There is no one way to partition the environment. There are an infinite number of environmental events, and we have no taxonomy of them. A subjective in-the-eye-of-the-beholder determinism prevails. We see the world – literally and figuratively – through adult eyes. Children do not. They see the world through child eyes. What looks like one thing to an adult may look quite differently to a baby, a child, or even an adolescent. It is a serious error to misattribute adult perspectives on environment and experience to the child. As a consequence, developmental environmental research needs to be especially sensitive to the child's point of view. For example, the "complexity"

of a visual stimulus may appear one way to an adult, but quite another to a child. An adult might see a 2 × 2 checkerboard as "simpler" than, say, a 24 × 24 checkerboard. However, when confronted with a 24 × 24 board, a child may look at only one square or along one border. Consequently, the 2 × 2 and the 24 × 24 boards might be equally "simple" structures for the child. The "scale error" is another example (DeLoache, 2004). Young children will sometimes treat a miniature car or slide or chair as they would a normal sized car or slide or chair and try to enter the miniature car, slip down the miniature slide, or sit in the miniature chair.

Thus, parsing environment, while usually done through the perceptions of adults, must necessarily be done through the senses of children; that means that the nature of the effective environment remains a central (and surprising) question across development. DeLoache (1987, 1989) showed toddlers a scale model of a room and told them that a miniature toy was hidden in the scale model in the same place as in a real room. Three-year-olds know where in the real room to search for the hidden toy, but 2-year-olds do not. The younger child seems not to understand how or that the model maps to the actual room. A moment's reflection summons the revelation that other common environmental experiences that project themselves as this task does – books and television – might be interpreted uniquely by young children. Even teens' brains function differently from those of adults when processing emotional information from external stimuli. In a study mapping differences between the brains of adults and teens, Yurgelun-Todd (2002) subjected teenage and adult volunteers to magnetic resonance imaging (MRI) and monitored how their brains responded to a series of pictures of facial emotions. All the adults identified one emotion as fear, but many of the teenagers reported that they saw a different emotion, such as shock or anger. When their brains were scanned, teenagers were found to be using the amygdala when reading the images, where adults were using the prefrontal cortex. Thus, even the teen brain appears to respond differently to some aspects of the outside world compared to the adult brain. Adults look at fearful faces and perceive them as fearful faces, and they label them as such, whereas teenagers do not see the same faces in the same way. Teens read some external visual cues differently, or they look at affect differently. Infants, children, and adolescents do not necessarily take the information that is in the outside world, organize it, and understand it the same way adults do. These examples, and many others, imply that children do not perceive or experience their environments, however defined, in the ways that adults do, even those adults close to them.

Bioecological Theory

The child's home, school, and community contexts all help shape the child's development. Factors in the child's immediate environment influence development by providing and constraining the child's opportunities both to practice and develop specific skills and to gain familiarity with and develop expertise in specific domains.

Bronfenbrenner's (1999; Bronfenbrenner & Morris, 2006) bioecological theory asserts that process, person, context, and time are basic to understanding human development. Process is viewed as mediating between the individual and an environment. Proximal processes are the "engines of development" and provide the links, the interrelations, and the mutual influences between individual and environment. Proximal processes also constitute the typically occurring practices to which the child is exposed. According to Bronfenbrenner (Bronfenbrenner & Crouter, 1983; Bronfenbrenner & Morris, 2006) human development takes place in progressively more complex reciprocal interactions between the active, evolving biopsychological human organism and the persons, objects, and symbols that inhabit the proximal-to-distal external environments. Proximal processes are defined as enduring forms of interaction in the immediate environment. Their form, power, content, and direction vary with characteristics of the developing person, of the immediate and remote environments in which they take place; the nature of the developmental outcomes and continuities and changes that occur throughout the life course and the historical period. Proximal processes thus link between children's everyday activities with more competent members of the community and more distal environments. This idea of process requires us to study the typically occurring activities and interactions in which children engage, while assessing how those proximal processes are themselves influenced both by characteristics of the individuals involved and by aspects of the broader environment.

The person in bioecological theory is active, capable of discovering, maintaining, or transforming opportunities afforded by his or her environment. This dynamic implies focusing on individual characteristics, both psychological and biological; personal response styles to the environment; the intensity of involvement of the individual; and the extent to which the individual plays an active role in initiating activities and recruiting others to engage with him or her. As Bronfenbrenner (1999, p. 5) asserted, "in the bioecological model, the characteristics of the person are both the product and producers of development."

Context in development is characterized by a series of systems, defined hierarchically, from the most proximal to the most distal. Bronfenbrenner defined these "systems" in the following ways: A microsystem includes patterns of activities, social roles, and interpersonal relationships experienced by the developing person in a given face-to-face setting with particular physical, social, and symbolic features that invite, permit, or inhibit engaging in sustained, progressively more complex interactions with, and activity in, the immediate environment. The mesosystem comprises the linkages and processes that take place between two or more settings containing the developing person and include extended family, peers, schools, and neighborhoods. The exosystem comprises the linkages and processes that take place between two or more settings, at least one of which does not contain the developing person, but in which events occur that indirectly influence processes within the immediate setting in which the developing person lives, such as workplaces and mass media. The macrosystem consists of the overarching pattern of micro-, meso-, and exosystems characteristic of a given culture or subculture, with particular reference to the belief systems, bodies of knowledge, material resources, customs, lifestyles, opportunity structures, hazards, and life course options that are embedded in each of these broader systems (see Bronfenbrenner, 1994, pp. 1645–1646). Bioecological theory reminds us that interactions with the environment occur at multiple levels, and all constitute effective environmental stimulants to development.

The Person

Since Piaget, developmental scientists have recognized the importance of the child and the child's action to the child's learning about, and attaining mastery over, the environment. In Piaget's view, the environment does not act on a passive, receptive child. Rather, the child actively engages and changes to understand the environment. Newborns seek visual stimulation and input, scanning the environment in a controlled and alert fashion, to find things to inspect. When egocentrism declines, children become increasingly aware of the relation between their own behavior and the environment. For example, when children accidentally produce environmental events, they may repeat them, suggesting that they want to review their effects on the environment. Several attributes that children carry with them across different situations shape development and their experience of their environment. Two central (relatively) stable characteristics of children that do so are gender and personality.

In this connection, developmentalists have distinguished several genotype-environment interactions (see Buss & Plomin, 1984; Plomin, deFries, & Loehlin, 1977; Scarr & McCartney, 1983). "Active" interactions

occur when children seek out and create environments (presumably ones compatible with their genotypes), and "evocative" interactions occur when children draw out particular characteristics from the environment. Thus, children help to construct or evoke certain responses from their environments based on their attributes, and these responses, in turn, affect children's development. More generally, the principle of "transaction" states that children shape their experiences with the environment just as they are shaped by those experiences (Bornstein, 2009; Sameroff, 2009). Students of child temperament (Putnam, Sanson, & Rothbart, 2002), for example, report that the extent to which children are perceived as "easy" or "difficult" influences how parents respond to them. A highly sociable child may elicit interest and play from adults, and this social stimulation may have many kinds of beneficial results for the child. Parents' responses, in turn, further shape children's development. As children grow older, their individual temperaments lead them to prefer certain environments to others, especially those that best suit their behavioral style. A highly active child may choose to become involved in sports, whereas a reserved child may select settings that foster sedentary activities, like reading. This kind of "niche-picking" (Scarr & McCartney, 1983) expresses itself in the child's selective interest in certain environments and activities over others.

Individuals not only shape their environments but experience them differently on the basis of their idiosyncratic attributes (Ellis, Boyce, Belsky, Bakermans-Kranenburg, & van IJzendoorn, 2011; Wachs & Gandour, 1983). An unexpected encounter with a friendly but unfamiliar adult will be experienced much differently by a child who is temperamentally sociable and positive in mood, compared to a child who is low in adaptability and fearful. Here, Escalona's (1968) concept of "effective experience" is important. An active child may seek out toys, whereas an inactive child may wait for an adult to offer them. Thus, the same environmental structure – the presence of toys in the surround – affords different experiences to different children. Crowded noisy environments may pose greater problems for some children than for others; fearful withdrawn children may need more measured introductions to new stimulation than assertive and outgoing children. Children with different characteristics are differentially susceptible to experience and environment: Those with moderate and flexible temperaments are in general more affected by their environments than those with extreme and stable temperaments (Pluess & Belsky, 2010).

In brief, people are prompted by their unique genetic endowments to selectively experience and shape whatever environments they encounter. Environments are not only shaped by individual differences, they are experienced differently. The environment is often regarded as working uniform effects on individuals, but in actuality individual reactivity determines how comparable environments are experienced, and so individual differences mediate experience. Children evoke specific responses from the environment in which they find themselves; they seek out those environments that best fit their predilections and talents; and they experience and interpret their environments uniquely.

It follows from this line of thought that children also vary in terms of their (or their brain's) plasticity to experience. That is, some people "possess brains that are better able to adapt their neurocircuitry to environmental stimulation" (Garlicky, 2002, p. 121). In this view, child development is partly a function of the brain's relative ability to adapt to its environments. Normally, people are exposed to the same general environmental experiences – from physical properties of the world to cause-effect relations to social associations – and so individuals with more plastic brains would be more highly adaptive. A neural network that is better able to adapt to its environment can learn faster and accommodate information from that environment better. It could be, then, that babies who process information efficiently also expose themselves to more optimal amounts, kinds, or patterns of environmental stimulation. Other individual differences may be effective

as well. Children's motivation to master the environment often results in longer periods of object exploration (i.e., attention) and thereby increased competence (Yarrow et al., 1983; Yarrow et al., 1982). Children oriented to master the environment are likely to learn more quickly about objects they see or hear, because they are able to attend to or to concentrate on them for long periods. Effectance may be an especially important type of motivation (White, 1958) – a motivation to try to act on and alter the environment. In short, the same environment has different meanings and implications for children who differ in terms of their perceptions, temperament, developmental status, or other individual-difference factors.

The Proximal Environment of Child Development

Microsystem

The microsystem refers to the most proximate level of environmental influences, in which variables in the immediate situation impact the child. It has been said that parents largely "create" persons (Sroufe, Egeland, Carlson, & Collins, 2005) because mothers and fathers influence the development of their children in many ways. Direct effects are most obvious. Parents not only contribute directly to the genetic makeup of their children, but they also directly shape their children's experiences. Parents also serve as their children's most immediate social partners. In the natural course of things, these two main sorts of direct effects are confounded: Parents who endow their child with their genetics also structure their child's environment and experiences. Can we disentangle heritable from experiential influences on children? Can we tell how the two are influential in development? To try to study heritable and experiential direct effects, developmental scientists have sometimes appealed to so-called natural experiments involving twins and adoptees where the effects of heredity and experience on the individual can be distinguished, at least to a degree.

DIRECT FAMILY EFFECTS – HERITABILITY
Parents contribute directly to the nature
and development of their children by passing on biological characteristics. Modern
behavior genetics asserts that characteristics
of offspring in a host of different realms –
height and weight, temperament and intelligence – reflect inheritance in some degree
(e.g., Bouchard, Lykken, McGue, Segal, &
Tellegen, 1990; Plomin, 1989). Typical twin
studies involve assessing the extent to
which certain characteristics are shared by
(1) monozygotic twins reared together versus apart or (2) monozygotic versus dizygotic twins. To the degree a characteristic is
inherited or shaped by experience, monozygotic (identical) twins reared together
should be more alike, just as monozygotic
twins should be more alike than dizygotic
(fraternal) twins. Behavior geneticists also
use adoption designs to examine the degree
to which adopted children share traits
with their adoptive and biological parents,
respectively. The degree to which a characteristic is inherited or shaped by experience
may be evidenced by however biological
parents and their children are more or less
alike than adoptive parents and their children. On average, siblings share about 50
percent of their genes; hence genetic differences account for some of the variation
among siblings. Genetic differences do not
account for all the variation, however. Even
if heredity accounts for a proportion of variance in human development (an assertion
itself often challenged; Lerner, 2002), heredity rarely accounts for as much as 50 percent
(see McCartney, Harris, & Bernieri, 1990).
Thus, even within the same family, parents
(and others) create different effective environments for different children. Indeed, gene
action always involves the environment.

DIRECT FAMILY EFFECTS – EXPERIENCES
Evidence for heritability does not negate or
even diminish equally compelling evidence
for direct (and indirect) effects of experience on children's growth and development
(Collins, Maccoby, Steinberg, Hetherington,
& Bornstein, 2000). Although parental genes
may contribute to children's proclivities and

abilities in different domains, all prominent
theories of development put experience
in the world as either the principal source
of individual growth or a major contributing component (Lerner, Lewin-Bizan, &
Warren, 2011). It is parents (and other caregivers) who furnish and shape their young
children's experiences. Parents directly
influence child development by the beliefs
they hold and by the behaviors they exhibit.
For example, warm, attentive, stimulating,
responsive, and nonrestrictive parenting
promotes intellectual and social competencies in children. Maternal attentiveness and
mood during feeding in the first months predict children's language abilities at 3 years
(Bee et al., 1982). Mothers' affectionately
touching, rocking, holding, and smiling at
their 6-month-olds predict cognitive competencies at 2 years (Olson, Bates, & Bayles,
1984). Mothers who speak more, prompt
more, and respond more during the first
year have 6-month-olds to 4-year-olds who
score higher in standardized cognitive evaluations (Bornstein, 1985; Bornstein & Tamis-
LeMonda, 1989, 1995; Tamis-LeMonda &
Bornstein, 1989, 1990; Vibbert & Bornstein,
1989). Bornstein (2002, 2006) distinguished
among major experience-based domains of
parenting: nurturant caregiving, aimed at
promoting children's survival (protection,
supervision, and sustenance); social caregiving, involving children in interpersonal
exchanges (soothing, touching, smiling, and
vocalizing); and didactic caregiving, facilitating children's understanding of the world
around them (directing attention to and
interpreting external events and providing
opportunities to learn). These domains are
not mutually exclusive, and two or more parenting domains may occur simultaneously
as, for example, when a parent attempts to
read with a child (didactic caregiving) while
seating the child in her lap and stroking her
(social caregiving).
   Vygotsky (1962) proposed that growth in
children proceeds by children's exercising
partially mastered skills and adults' providing
the necessary supports or scaffolds to enable
children to execute those skills successfully at more advanced levels. Along these

lines, Rogoff and Gardner (1984) described behaviors mothers used to help their children attempt new problems and, thereby, advance their skills. Mothers use a variety of supportive strategies, such as showing how a new problem relates to a more familiar context, providing task-relevant information, explaining why particular strategies are helpful, directing children's attention to specific details in the problem context, and giving children opportunities to execute steps in the process before attempting entire tasks by themselves. Mothers who are knowledgeable about development generally are more likely to create environments that are appropriate to their children's developing abilities (e.g., Hunt & Paraskevopoulos, 1980). Miller (1988) showed how awareness of developmental milestones helps mothers create stimulating and challenging environments for their young children. Mothers formulate relatively accurate schemas about specific areas of their children's accomplishments, and their schemas are a stable part of mothers' knowledge base (at least over brief periods). Mothers match their children's play during free-play interactions (e.g., Damast et al., 1996; Tamis-LeMonda & Bornstein, 1991), and they adjust the level of their own play over time in close synchrony with changes to their children's play (Tamis-LeMonda & Bornstein, 1991). Similarly, mothers modulate the complexity of their speech to meet their children's current language abilities (Ferguson, 1978; Snow, 1977).

INDIRECT FAMILY EFFECTS: EXPERIENCE
Indirect effects of parent-provided experience on child development are effective as well. The mere presence of attachment figures provides children with security to explore the environment extensively and adaptively on their own (Bowlby, 1969).

FAMILY EFFECTS: SIBLINGS
Experiences interacting with other children also foster the development of a sophisticated and flexible repertoire of skills by providing exposure to different individuals who have different behavioral styles and contrasting patterns of interaction. In some cultures, children spend relatively little time playing with younger or older siblings; when they do, most of their interactions, like those of Western parents, involve protection or caregiving. Siblings in many non-Western nonindustrialized countries assume much more responsibility for child care (Zukow-Goldring, 2002). Sibling relationships appear to incorporate features of both the child-adult and child-peer systems. On the one hand, child-sibling dyads share common interests and have more similar behavioral repertoires than do child-adult dyads. On the other hand, sibling pairs resemble child-adult pairs to the extent that they differ in experience and levels of both cognitive and social ability. Zukow-Goldring (2002) described the ways in which Mexican siblings not only care for those younger than they are but, through play, teach skills (like how to make tortillas) their younger siblings need to succeed in the society. Older siblings tend to "lead" interactions: They engage in more dominant, assertive, and directing behaviors than their younger siblings. Children appear inordinately interested in what their siblings are doing; they follow them around, attempting to imitate or explore the toys just abandoned by the older children. This strategy maximizes the amount the sibling can learn about the environment from an older child.

In summary, siblings play a salient role in children's development from early in life. In addition, older siblings may be important socializing agents in their own right, shaping both prosocial and aggressive behavior in younger siblings. Older siblings influence the cognitive and social development of younger children through combinations of teaching and modeling.

Effects of the Natural and Designed Environments

It is also central for an environmental psychology of childhood to identify unique as well as interactive effects related to the child's natural and designed environments. Proximal environmental influences are specific social, physical, or symbolic contextual characteristics that directly impinge on the child (Bronfenbrenner & Ceci, 1994). Child rearing practices, like structuring of the environment, are often credited with providing experiences that influence the course and the eventual outcome of child development. Natural physical hazards have a direct impact on child rearing practices, and thereby on child development, by influencing the degree to which caregivers restrict children's attempts at locomotion and independent exploration of the environment (Kaplan & Dove, 1987; McSwain, 1981). Material caregiving involves the manner in which parents structure children's physical environments (provision of toys and books, restrictions on physical freedom, and the like). Specific aspects of the child's designed environment influence specific aspects of the child's development. For example, Wachs and Chan (1986) assessed different aspects of the environment in conjunction with different dimensions of children's communicative development. Parents who provided their children with new toys and changed their children's room decorations were also likely to name objects, but physical parameters of the environment that parents manipulated exerted influences on child language acquisition separate and apart from parental language interactions, and not only as a function of parental naming.

Many aspects of the proximal physical environment – from toxins and noise to books and museums – exert unique effects on child development (Evans, 2006). The Home Observation for Measurement of the Environment (HOME Inventory; Bradley, 2010) captures both direct and indirect experiences in subscales that include responsivity, acceptance of the child, organization of the environment, provision of appropriate play materials, involvement with the child, variety of stimulation in the home, language stimulation, and encouragement of social maturity. Elardo, Bradley, and Caldwell (1977) reported that emotional and verbal responsivity of the mother; the provision of appropriate play materials; and maternal involvement with the child all promoted child language development. Bradley and Caldwell (1984b)

reported that several HOME subscales at 12 months predicted first-grade achievement-test scores. For example, the type of play materials that mothers gave their 12-month-olds predicted children's first-grade reading, language, and math achievement. Even when the children's early intellectual development was taken into consideration (using the Bayley Mental Development Index score at 12 months and the Stanford-Binet score at 3 years), the HOME subscale assessing provision of appropriate toys still predicted first-grade reading scores. Later, Bradley, Caldwell, and Rock (1988) examined children as infants and at age 10, finding significant correlations between home environments measured at both 2 and 10 years and children's later achievement test scores and classroom behavior. Luster and Dubow (1992) hypothesized that, when multiple aspects of the home environment are evaluated (as is done in the HOME Inventories), and when children are assessed at younger rather than older ages, the home environment accounts for significant amounts of variance in children's intelligence, even when maternal intelligence is also considered. In analyses of the National Longitudinal Survey of Youth, these investigators unearthed a relation between the HOME Inventory and verbal intelligence scores of children from 3 to 8 years.

Distal Environments of Child Development

Mesosystem, Exosystem, and Macrosystem

So far, we have seen how a greater understanding of children must acknowledge the richness, diversity, and complexity of their early environmental experiences, especially those involving the full complement of close family members and children's local environments. The meso-, exo-, and macrosystems refer to more distal nonfamilial social structures, settings, or other related circumstances that help shape the course of children's development. Two prominent meso- and exosystem environments that involve the child directly are peers and day care.

Peers

Social interaction between nonrelated children is less frequent in infancy, and it is not sustained very long when it does occur (Rubin, Coplan, Chen, Bowker, & McDonald, 2011). Soon, however, even young children show interest in peers, and although early child-peer interactions may be simple and fleeting, they deepen and broaden rather quickly. Still in the first year, children begin to interact in more complex ways – initiating exchanges and responding to one another's social overtures with combinations of looks, smiles, and vocalizations. Children's sensitivity to social cues from peers leads them to continue interacting when their partners are responsive, whereas children tend to cease social bids when their partners are nonresponsive. Child-peer interaction increases developmentally with responsiveness to peer overtures and imitation becomes increasingly common. Some have proposed that peer group socialization eventually supplants parents and family as children's main influences (Harris, 1995).

Day Care

The majority of children in the United States are now cared for at some time by someone other than a parent (Lamb & Ahnert, 2006), and child care situations have a variety of effects on children's development. Because so many children are placed in out-of-home care, extensive efforts have been made to conceptualize and measure child care. The National Center for Children, Toddlers, and Families identified eight criteria that ensure high-quality care (Fenichel, Lurie-Hurvitz, & Griffin, 1999). These include (1) health and safety, (2) small groups (no more than three to four children per caregiver), (3) assigning each child to a primary caregiver, (4) continuity in care, (5) responsive caregiving, (6) meeting individual needs in the context of the larger group, (7) cultural and linguistic continuity, and (8) a stimulating physical environment. Measures of quality of care typically fall into two types: Structure (group size, teacher-child ratio,

and teacher training) assesses broad markers of the social and physical environments that bear a straightforward relation to a child's interactions in the setting; and process (language and reasoning experiences, caregivers' interactional competence with children, and the breadth and diversity of the learning curriculum) assesses the actual quality of care experienced by children (Lamb & Ahnert, 2006). Structural measures appear to be associated with process measures: Higher staff-to-child ratios and better training correlate positively with caregiver-child interaction and the frequency of parent-caregiver communication (Helburn, 1995; National Institute of Child Health and Human Development (NICHD) Early Child Care Research Network, 1996).

Children in child care facilities are not only exposed regularly to additional sets of experiences at child care, but also have experiences at home that differ from those experienced by peers who do not receive regular nonparental care. For example, parents interact more intensely with children who attend child care centers as if attempting to make up for the time they are apart (Booth, Clarke-Stewart, Vandell, McCartney, & Owen, 2002). Relationships with care providers also affect children's development. The security of both child-mother and child–care provider attachments are correlated with the level of children's social competence evident when playing with adults as well as the degree of engagement in play with peers (Howes & Hamilton, 1993; Howes, Matheson, & Hamilton, 1994).

Major macrosystem determinants in child development include ethnic group membership, education, socioeconomic status, and culture. These determinants represent the most general influences on the child. I briefly consider how socioeconomic status and culture as they relate to children's environmental experiences.

Socioeconomic Status

Socioeconomic status (SES) traditionally is defined by a complex grouping of financial, educational, and occupational characteristics of parents (Bornstein & Bradley, 2003; Hernandez, 1997; Hoff, Laursen, & Tardif, 2002). SES often has a substantial impact on the quality of relationships between parents and on the quality of their parenting. The stress of poverty and economic hardship can directly impact parents' ability to care for children optimally, and poverty and economic failure are associated with punitive parenting and increased child abuse and neglect (Gottfried, Gottfried, & Bathurst, 2002; McLoyd, Aikens, & Burton, 2006). Stress not only affects each parent's behavior directly, it also reduces mutual supportiveness and adversely affects the quality of the partner's behavior.

Hoff et al. (2002) noted that middle-SES parents expect their children to show an early mastery of academic-related skills. By contrast, lower-SES parents expect their children to have as little opportunity for self-actualization and leadership as they themselves had and, hence, tend to emphasize obedience and conformity, values thought to maximize their children's chances of success in the roles they are expected to fill in society. Studies of SES differences in the treatment of children reveal differences consistent with these predictions. Middle-SES American mothers talk to their babies more than lower-SES mothers, even though children are not yet talking themselves (Hart & Risley, 1995). Similar social-status differences in maternal speech to children are observed elsewhere, as in Israel, where lower-SES mothers talk, label, and ask "what" questions of their children less often than do upper-middle-SES mothers (Ninio, 1980).

Extreme economic disadvantage affects child development in ways that go beyond parental values and expectations (McLoyd et al., 2006). Compared to children in middle-SES environments, children living in poverty experience lower levels of emotional and verbal responsivity, fewer opportunities for variety in daily stimulation, fewer appropriate play materials, and more chaotic, disorganized, and unstructured environments (Bradley et al., 1994; Garrett, Ng'andu, & Ferron, 1994; Hart & Risley, 1995). Poverty is also associated with reduced intellectual

functioning, and with oppositional, antisocial behavior that increases in frequency from the preschool years onward (Magnuson & Duncan, 2002).

In summary, family socioeconomic status exerts direct and indirect influences on child development. Social status affects parents' conceptions of development and enhances or diminishes parents' ability to respond effectively to their children, structure and organize their children's environments, and provide children with levels of stimulation needed to support optimal child development.

Culture

Consider two children: One is born into a group of nomadic hunter-gatherers, living in temporary homes and spending much of each day in large multiage groups obtaining food (Hewlett & Lamb, 2005). The other is born in a modern Western setting, isolated at home with a single adult, where food is purchased prepared. Culture is the system of beliefs, conventions, behaviors, and symbolic representations that are shared by a people, persist over time, and are transmitted to new members of the group; it reflects the social, economic, and psychological adaptation of a people (Goodnow, 2010). Culture influences values and beliefs as well as norms and expectations for acceptable behavior, and it prescribes general rules of conduct. Cultural variation is manifest in the frequency with which the child is cared for by a parent, other children, or unrelated adults; the extent to which the child is allowed to explore; and whether the child's experiences are expansive or restrictive. Culture thus helps to construct children in myriad ways, for example, by influencing parental beliefs about child rearing and attributions about the developmental capacities of children, which in turn influence parents' practices (Bornstein, 1991, 2010; Cole & Packer, 2011). After studying developmental timetables in two groups of Australian mothers (Australian born and Lebanese born), Goodnow, Cashmore, Cotton, and Knight (1984) determined that cultural differences shaped parents' developmental expectations of children more than SES, gender, or birth order.

Cross-cultural research shows systematic culture differences in all sorts of experiences that affect children. In their study of the nomadic hunter-gatherer Aka and Ngandu farming communities in central Africa, Hewlett et al. (1998) observed that 3- to 4-month-old Aka children experienced more "proximal" relationships with their caregivers (they were more likely to be held and fed) than were same-age Ngandu children, who were more likely than Aka children to be left alone. The neighboring Aka and Ngandu have similarly high levels of child mortality, equivalently hazardous living conditions, equally healthy children, and comparable maternal workloads, and thus these sociodemographic factors do not explain differences in the child caregiving practices of the two cultural groups.

Variations in culture can make for subtle, but still meaningful, differences in patterns of parent-child interaction. Harwood, Schölmerich, Schulze, and Gonzalez (1999) observed that European American mothers of 12- to 15-month-olds emphasize the development of individual autonomy, whereas Puerto Rican mothers focus on maternal-child interdependence and connectedness. These differences in cognitions relate to the mothers' actual practices, with European American mothers using suggestions (rather than commands) and other indirect means to structure their children's behavior, and Puerto Rican mothers using more direct means of structuring, such as commands, physical positioning and restraints, and blunt attempts to get their children's attention. U.S. American mothers respond more to their children's orienting to the environment relative to their children's social orienting, whereas Japanese mothers respond more to their children's social than environmental orienting (Bornstein, Cote, Haynes, & Bakeman, 2012). When responding to their children, Japanese mothers tend to direct their children's attention to themselves, whereas U.S. American mothers tend to direct their children's attention away from themselves and toward the environment.

Of course, culture-specific patterns of childrearing can be expected to be adapted to each specific society's setting and needs. It is likely that cultural variation in childrearing cognitions mediates differences in childrearing practices vis-à-vis the environment. So, parents in different cultures may structure their children's environments differently, make different stimuli of one sort or another (e.g., books) available, and interpret the meaning, usefulness, and so forth, of different aspects of the environment differently on the basis of their culture. Thus, Hewlett et al. (1998) speculated that Aka parents stayed closer to their children because of their frequent moves from one location to the next in search of food. Aka parents are consequently always less familiar with their home surroundings than are Ngandu parents, who live a comparatively sedentary existence, and thus Aka parents may stay in closer proximity to their children to protect them better in unfamiliar environments. It is important to keep cultural relativity about child development in mind because it explains variation and sets limits on generalizability. The cultural environment defines how people live, what they value, and what they do, and it exerts effects on how children develop. Even if their school learning may suffer, Brazilian street children do the math required for survival in their street businesses quite well (Carraher, Carraher, & Schliemann, 1985), Zambian children excel in wire media (Serpell, 1979), and children in Botswana are accustomed to storytelling and have excellent memories for stories (Dube, 1982).

Thematicity – the repetition of the same cultural idea across mechanisms and contexts – has special importance to culture qua an organizer of behavior (Schank & Abelson, 1977). Every culture is characterized and distinguished from other cultures by thoroughgoing and consistent themes that inculcate what the child needs to know in order to think and behave as a functioning member of the culture (Quinn & Holland, 1987). So, for example, in the United States personal choice is closely bound up with how individuals think of themselves and make sense of their lives. Personal choice is firmly rooted in principles of liberty and freedom and is an outstanding psychological construct and persistent force in the lives of United States–born children (Tamis-LeMonda & McFaden, 2010). U.S. children are permitted much personal freedom and say in their lives – from the foods they eat to clothes they wear to the academic courses they take.

In summary, macrosystem characteristics of social class and cultural ideology (along with physical ecology, economy, and political orientation) shape children's development in profound ways. Although distal, macrosystem influences on child development are embedded in all of the more proximal nested levels of the ecological systems model. It has been observed that perhaps the single most influential factor in deciding the course of a person's development is the culture where the person is born (Weisner, 2002).

Conclusions

We do well not to overlook key roles of multiple environments in child development. Children grow in worlds that (hopefully) meet their needs and provide them with influential adaptive experiences; these external possibilities help to direct their development. But shared and nonshared environments can be expected to interact with individual proclivities to affect different ends in different children. Intelligence and sociability alike are defined by the ability to adapt, understand, and successfully negotiate the environment. Bronfenbrenner organized environments into a multilevel hierarchically integrated structure, with bidirectional patterns of influence both within and across levels: The macrosystem (culture, subcultures, societal institutions), the exosystem (environments that affect the child's development but that the child does not directly encounter), the mesosystem (links between proximal settings that are directly encountered by the child), and the microsystem (proximal settings of children's

development). The boundaries of the child's home, school, and community contexts determine to some degree the child's opportunities to practice specific skills and to develop familiarity with particular content domains. Consequently, child development is shaped directly, as adults teach children specific strategies or rules to follow in certain situations, and indirectly, by children being exposed to or not being exposed to different skills and domains. These systems are further characterized by their constant interaction, and are connected in such ways that the effects produced together are broader and more thoroughgoing than effects that could be produced by any one. Values, beliefs, and practices that are culturally instantiated are derived from the macrosystem, but they are experienced in the microsystem. At the end of the day, a child's successful and continuing adjustment and adaptation depend on changing interactions between his or her individual attributes and the demands of his or her changing environments. In more faithful predictions of child development, environment and child are both important, and neither alone is an exclusive determinant.

We can best understand child development when we know more about the multiple ecologies in which children develop. The environment has been viewed as a setting within which the child learns appropriate patterns, as a source of stimulation, and as a context that provides the child with opportunities to practice skills. Environments include a wide range of biological, cognitive, and social influences, some of which affect whole populations, whereas others contribute to individual differences. Parents too offer children a range of environmental experiences, some of which are endured, some of which are rebuffed, and some of which are embraced (Goodnow, 1992; Lightfoot & Valsiner, 1992).

What is special about human beings, and in many ways the most significant characteristic of the species, is their long period of developmental plasticity, during which biological, mental, and social structures emerge in close attunement with their effective environments. This *neoteny* characterizes an organism capable of learning broad and flexible lessons. From this perspective, the relation between environment or experience and development is neither direct nor unidirectional. The structures that evolve as a result of interactions with the environment, even from a very early age, influence the types of information that the child may attend to and the interpretations the child places on that information.

Acknowledgments

This chapter summarizes selected aspects of my research, and portions of the text have appeared in previous scientific publications cited in the references. Supported by the Intramural Research Program of the NIH, NICHD.

References

Bee, H. L. et al. (1982). Prediction of IQ and language skill from perinatal status, child performance, family characteristics, and mother-infant interaction. *Child Development*, 53, 1134–1156.

Black, J. E., & Greenough, W. T. (1986). Induction of pattern in neural structure by experience: Implications for cognitive development. In M. E. Lamb, A. L. Brown, & B. Rogoff (Eds.), *Advances in developmental psychology*, pp. 1–50 (4th ed.). Hillsdale, NJ: Lawrence Erlbaum Associates.

Booth, C. L., Clarke-Stewart, K. A., Vandell, D. L., McCartney, K., & Owen, M. T. (2002). Childcare usage and mother-infant "quality time." *Journal of Marriage and Family*, 64, 16–26.

Bornstein, M. H. (1985). How infant and mother jointly contribute to developing cognitive competence in the child. *Proceedings of the National Academy of Sciences, USA*, 82, 7470–7473.

Bornstein, M. H. (Ed.). (1991). *Cultural Approaches to Parenting*. Hillsdale, NJ: Lawrence Erlbaum Associates.

Bornstein, M. H. (2002). Parenting infants. In M. H. Bornstein (Ed.), *Handbook of parenting*: Vol. 1. *Children and parenting*, pp. 3–43 (2nd ed.). Mahwah, NJ: Lawrence Erlbaum Associates.

Bornstein, M. H. (2006). Parenting science and practice. In K. A. Renninger, I. E. Sigel, W. Damon & R. M. Lerner (Eds.), *Handbook of child psychology*: Vol. 4. *Child psychology in practice*, pp. 893–949 (6th ed.). Hoboken, NJ: John Wiley & Sons Inc.

Bornstein, M. H. (2009). Toward a model of culture↔parent↔child transactions. In A. Sameroff (Ed.), *The Transactional Model of Development: How Children and Contexts Shape Each Other*, pp. 139–161. Washington, DC: American Psychological Association.

Bornstein, M. H. (Ed.). (2010). *The Handbook of Cultural Developmental Science*. Part 1. Domains of Development across Cultures. Part 2. Development in Different Places on Earth. New York: Psychology Press.

Bornstein, M. H., & Bradley, R. H. (Eds.) (2003). *Socioeconomic status, parenting, and child development*. Mahwah, NJ: Lawrence Erlbaum Associates.

Bornstein, M. H., Cote, L. R., Haynes, O. M., & Bakeman, R. (2012). Modalities of infant-mother interaction in Japanese, Japanese American immigrant, and European American dyads. *Child Development*.

Bornstein, M. H., & Sawyer, J. (2006). Family systems. In K. McCartney & D. Phillips (Eds.), *Blackwell handbook of early childhood development*, pp. 381–398. Malden: Blackwell Publishing.

Bornstein, M. H., & Tamis-LeMonda, C. S. (1989). Maternal responsiveness and cognitive development in children. *New Directions for Child Development*, 43, 49–61.

Bornstein, M. H., & Tamis-LeMonda, C. S. (1995). Parent-child symbolic play: Three theories in search of an effect. *Developmental Review*, 15, 382–400.

Bouchard, T. J., Lykken, D. T., McGue, M., Segal, N. L., & Tellegen, A. (1990). Sources of human psychological differences: The Minnesota study of twins reared apart. *Science*, 250, 223–228.

Bowlby, J. (1969). *Attachment and loss*: Vol. 1. *Attachment*. New York: Basic Books.

Bradley, R. H. (2010). The HOME Environment. In M. H. Bornstein (Ed.), *The handbook of cultural developmental science*: Part 2. *Development in different places on earth*, pp. 505–530. New York: Taylor & Francis Group.

Bradley, R. H., & Caldwell, B. M. (1984a). The HOME Inventory and family demographics. *Developmental Psychology*, 20, 315–320.

Bradley, R. H., & Caldwell, B. M. (1984b). The relation of infants' home environments to achievement test performance in first grade: A follow-up study. *Child Development, 55,* 803–809.

Bradley, R. H., Caldwell, B. M., & Rock, S. L. (1988). Home environment and school performance: A ten-year follow-up and examination of three models of environmental action. *Child Development, 59,* 852–867.

Bradley, R. H., Whiteside, L., Mundfrom, D. J., Casey, P. H., Kellher, K. J., & Pope, S. K. (1994). Early indications of resilience and their relation to experiences in the home environments of low birthweight, premature children living in poverty. *Child Development, 65,* 346–360.

Bronfenbrenner, U. (1994). Ecological models of human development. In T. Husen & T. N. Postlethwaithe (Eds.), *International encyclopedia of education.* Vol. 3, pp. 1643–1647. Oxford, UK: Pergamon.

Bronfenbrenner, U. (1999). Environments in developmental perspective: Theoretical and operational models. In S. L. Friedman & T. D. Wachs (Eds.), *Measuring environment across the life span: Emerging methods and concepts,* pp. 3–28. Washington, DC: American Psychological Association.

Bronfenbrenner, U., & Ceci, S. (1994). Nature-nurture reconceptualized in developmental perspective: A biological model. *Psychological Review, 101,* 568–586.

Bronfenbrenner, U., & Crouter, A. C. (1983). The evolution of environmental models in developmental research. In W. Kessen (Ed.), P. H. Mussen (Series Ed.), *Handbook of child psychology:* Vol. 1. *History, theory, and methods,* pp. 357–414. New York: Wiley.

Bronfenbrenner, U., & Morris, P. A. (1998). The ecology of developmental processes. In R. M. Lerner & W. Damon (Eds.), *Handbook of child psychology*: Vol. 1. *Theoretical models of human development,* pp. 993–1028 (5th ed.). Hoboken, NJ: John Wiley & Sons, Inc.

Bronfenbrenner, U., & Morris, P. A. (2006). The bioecological model of human development. In R. M. Lerner & W. Damon (Eds.), *Handbook of child psychology*: Vol. 1. *Theoretical models of human development,* pp. 793–828 (6th ed.). Hoboken, NJ: John Wiley & Sons, Inc.

Buss, A. H., & Plomin, R. (1984). *Temperament: Early developing personality traits.* Hillsdale, NJ: Lawrence Erlbaum Associates.

Carraher, T. N., Carraher, D., & Schliemann, A. D. (1985). Mathematics in the streets and in schools. *British Journal of Developmental Psychology, 3,* 21–29.

Chapman, B., Godecke, I., & Bonhoeffer, T. (1999). Development of orientation preference in the mammalian visual cortex. *Journal of Neurobiology, 41,* 18–24.

Chapman, B., & Stryker, M. P. (1993). Development of orientation selectivity in ferret visual cortex and effects of deprivation. *Journal of Neuroscience, 13,* 5251–5262.

Chugani, H. T. (1994). Development of regional brain glucose metabolism in relation to behavior and plasticity. In G. Dawson & K. W. Fischer (Eds.), *Human behavior and the developing brain,* pp. 153–175. New York: Guilford Press.

Cole, M., & Packer, M. (2011). Culture in development. In M. H. Bornstein & M. E. Lamb (Eds.), *Developmental science: An advanced textbook,* pp. 51–107 (6th ed.). New York: Psychology Press.

Collins, W. A., Maccoby, E. E., Steinberg, L., Hetherington, E. M., & Bornstein, M. H. (2000). Contemporary research on parenting: The case for nature and nurture. *American Psychologist, 55,* 218–232.

Damast, A. M., Tamis-LeMonda, C. S., & Bornstein, M. H. (1996). Mother-child play: Sequential interactions and the relation between maternal beliefs and behaviors. *Child Development, 67,* 1752–1766.

DeLoache, J. S. (1987). Rapid change in the symbolic functioning of very young children. *Science, 238,* 1556–1557.

DeLoache, J. S. (1989). Young children's understanding of the correspondence between a scale model and a larger space. *Cognitive Development, 4,* 121–139.

DeLoache, J. S. (2004). Scale errors by very young children: A dissociation between action planning and control. *Behavioral and Brain Sciences, 27,* 32–33.

Dube, E. F. (1982). Literacy, cultural familiarity, and "intelligence" as determinants of story recall. In U. Neisser (Ed.), *Memory observed: Remembering in natural contexts,* pp. 274–292. New York: Freeman.

Elardo, R., Bradley, R., & Caldwell, B. M. (1977). A longitudinal study of the relation of infants' home environments to language development at age three. *Child Development, 48,* 595–603.

Ellis, B. J., Boyce, W. T., Belsky, J., Bakermans-Kranenburg, M., & van IJzendoorn, M. H. (2011). Differential susceptibility to the environment: An evolutionary-neurodevelopmental theory. *Development and Psychopathology, 23,* 7–28.

Escalona, S. K. (1968). *The roots of individuality: Normal patterns of development in infancy.* Chicago: Aldine.

Evans, G. W. (2006). Child development and the physical environment. *Annual Review of Psychology, 57,* 423–451.

Fenichel, E. S., Lurie-Hurvitz, E., & Griffin, A. (1999). *Quality care for infants and toddlers.* Washington DC: National Child Care Information Center.

Ferguson, C. A. (1978). Learning to pronounce: The earliest stages of phonological development in the child. In F. D. Minifie & L. L. Llyods (Eds.), *Communicative and cognitive abilities: Early behavioral assessment,* pp. 273–297. Baltimore: University Park Press.

Garlick, D. (2002). Understanding the nature of the general factor of intelligence: The role of individual differences in neural plasticity as an explanatory mechanism. *Psychological Review, 109,* 116–136.

Garrett, P., Ng'andu, N., & Ferron, J. (1994). Poverty experiences of young children and the quality of their home environments. *Child Development, 65,* 331–345.

Goodman, R. (1991), Growing together and growing apart: The nongenetic forces on children in the same family. In P. McGuffin & R. Murray (Eds.), *The new genetics of mental illness,* pp. 212–224. Oxford, UK: Butterworth-Heinemann.

Goodnow, J. (1992). Parents' ideas, children's ideas: Correspondence and divergence. In I. Sigel, A. DeLisi, & J. Goodnow (Eds.), *Parental belief systems,* pp. 293–318. Hillsdale, NJ: Erlbaum.

Goodnow, J. J. (2010). Culture. In M. H. Bornstein (Ed.), *The handbook of cultural developmental science.* Part 1. *Domains of development across cultures,* pp. 3–19. New York: Taylor & Francis Group.

Goodnow, J. J., Cashmore, J. A., Cotton, S., & Knight, R. (1984). Mothers' developmental timetables in two cultural groups. *International Journal of Psychology, 19,* 193–205.

Gottfried, A. E., Gottfried, A. W., & Bathurst, K. (2002). Maternal and dual-earner employment status and parenting. In M. H. Bornstein (Ed.), *Handbook of parenting:* Vol. 2. *Biology and ecology of parenting,* pp. 207–229 (2nd ed.). Mahwah, NJ: Lawrence Erlbaum Associates.

Greenough, W. T. (1975). Experiential modification of the developing brain. *American Scientist, 63,* 37–46.

Greenough, W., Black, K., & Wallace, C. (1987). Experience and brain development. *Child Development, 58,* 539–559.

Greenough, W., Black, K., & Wallace, C. (1993). Experience and brain development. In M. Johnson (Ed.), *Brain Development and Cognition,* pp. 319–322. Oxford: Blackwell.

Harris, J. R. (1995). Where is the child's environment? A group socialization theory of development. *Psychological Review, 102,* 458–489.

Hart, B., & Risley, T. R. (1995). *Meaningful differences in the everyday experience of young American children.* Baltimore: Paul H. Brookes Publishing.

Harwood, R. L., Schölmerich, A., Schulze, P. A., & Gonzalez, Z. (1999). Cultural differences in maternal beliefs and behaviors: A study of middle-class Anglo and Puerto Rican mother-infant pairs in four everyday situations. *Child Development, 70,* 1005–1016.

Helburn, S. (Ed.) (1995.) *Cost, quality, and child outcomes in child care centers* (Technical Report). Denver: Department of Economics, Center for Research in Economic and Social Policy, University of Colorado at Denver.

Held, R. & Hein, A. (1963). Movement-produced stimulation in the development of visually guided behavior. *Journal of Comparative and Physiological Psychology, 56,* 872–876.

Hernandez, D. J. (1997). Child development and the social demography of childhood. *Child Development, 68,* 149–169.

Hewlett, B. S., & Lamb, M. E. (Eds.) (2005). *Hunter-gatherer childhoods: Evolutionary, developmental, and cultural perspectives.* New Brunswick, NJ: Aldine Transaction.

Hewlett, B. S., Lamb, M. E., Shannon, D., Leyendecker, B., & Scholmerich, A. (1998). Culture and early infancy among central African foragers and farmers. *Developmental Psychology, 34,* 653–661.

Hoff, E., Laursen, B., & Tardif, T. (2002). Socioeconomic status and parenting. In M. H. Bornstein (Ed.), *Handbook of parenting:* Vol. 2. *Biology and ecology of parenting,* pp. 231–252 (2nd ed.). Mahwah, NJ: Lawrence Erlbaum Associates.

Hoffman, L. (1991). The influence of the family environment on personality. *Psychological Bulletin, 110,* 187–203.

Howes, C., & Hamilton, C. E. (1993). The changing experience of child care: Changes in teachers and in teacher-child relationships and children's social competence with peers. *Early Childhood Research Quarterly, 8,* 15–32.

Howes, C., Matheson, C. C., & Hamilton, C. E. (1994). Maternal, teacher, and child care history correlates of children's relationships with peers. *Child Development, 65*, 264–273.

Hunt, J. M. (1961). *Intelligence and experience.* Oxford, UK: Ronald.

Hunt, J. M., & Paraskevopoulos, J. (1980). Children's psychological development as a function of the inaccuracy of their mothers' knowledge of their abilities. *Journal of Genetic Psychology, 136*, 285–298.

Kaplan, H., & Dove, H. (1987). Infant development among the Ache of Eastern Paraguay. *Developmental Psychology, 23*, 190–198.

Kolb, B. (1989). Brain development, plasticity, and behavior. *American Psychologist, 44*, 1203–1212.

Lamb, M., & Ahnert, L. (2006). Nonparental child care: Context, concepts, correlates, and consequences. In A. K. Renninger, I. E. Sigel, W. Damon, & R. M. Lerner (Eds.), *Handbook of child psychology*: Vol. 4. *Child psychology in practice*, pp. 950–1016 (6th ed.). Hoboken, NJ: John Wiley & Sons, Inc.

Lerner, R. M. (2002). *Concepts and theories of human development* (3rd ed.). Mahwah, NJ: Lawrence Erlbaum Associates.

Lerner, R. M., Lewin-Bizan, S., & Warren, A. E. A. (2011). Concepts and theories of human development. In M. H. Bornstein & M. E. Lamb (Eds.), *Developmental science: An advanced textbook*, pp. 3–49 (6th ed.). New York: Psychology Press.

Lightfoot, C., & Valsiner, J. (1992). Parental belief systems under the influence. In I. Sigel, A. DeLisi, & J. Goodnow (Eds.), *Parental belief systems*, pp. 393–414. Hillsdale, NJ: Erlbaum.

Luster, T., & Dubow, E. (1992). Home environment and maternal intelligence as predictors of verbal intelligence: A comparison of preschool and school-age children. *Merrill-Palmer Quarterly, 38*, 151–175.

Magnuson, K. A., & Duncan, G. J. (2002). Parents in poverty. In M. H. Bornstein (Ed.), *Handbook of parenting*: Vol. 4. *Social conditions and applied parenting*, pp. 95–121 (2nd ed.). Mahwah, NJ: Lawrence Erlbaum Associates.

McCartney, K., Harris, M. J., & Bernieri, F. (1990). Growing up and growing apart: A developmental meta-analysis of twin studies. *Psychological Bulletin, 107*, 226–237.

McLoyd, V. C., Aikens, N. L., & Burton, L. M. (2006). Childhood poverty, policy, and practice. In K. A. Renninger & I. E. Sigel (Ed.), W. Damon (Series Ed.), *Handbook of child psychology: Vol. 4. Child psychology in practice*, pp. 700–775 (6th ed.). Hoboken, NJ: Wiley.

McSwain, R. (1981). Care and conflict in infant development. *Infant Behavior and Development, 4*, 225–246.

Miller, S. (1988). Parents' beliefs about children's cognitive development. *Child Development, 59*, 259–285.

National Institute of Child Health and Human Development (NICHD) Early Child Care Research Network. (1996). Characteristics of infant child care: Factors contributing to positive caregiving. *Early Childhood Research Quarterly, 11*, 269–306.

Ninio, A. (1980). Picture-book reading in mother-infant dyads belonging to two subgroups in Israel. *Child Development, 51*, 587–590.

Olson, A. L., Bates, J. E., & Bayles, K. (1984). Mother-infant interaction and the development of individual differences in children's cognitive competence. *Developmental Psychology, 20*, 166–179.

Pike, A., McGuire, S., Hetherington, E., Reiss, D., & Plomin, R. (1996). Family environment and adolescent depressive symptoms and antisocial behavior. *Developmental Psychology, 32*, 590–604.

Plomin, R. (1989). Environment and genes: Determinants of behavior. *American Psychologist, 44*, 105–111.

Plomin, R., & Daniels, D. (1987). Why are children in the same family so different from each other? *Behavioral and Brain Sciences, 10*, 1–16.

Plomin, R., DeFries, J. G., & Loehlin, J. G. (1977). Genotype-environment interaction and correlation in the analysis of human behavior. *Psychological Bulletin, 84*, 309–322.

Pluess, M., & Belsky, J. (2010). Differential susceptibility to parenting and quality of child care. *Developmental Psychology, 46*, 379–390.

Putnam, S. P., Sanson, A. V., & Rothbart, M. K. (2002). Child temperament and parenting. In M. H. Bornstein (Ed.), *Handbook of parenting*: Vol. 1. *Children and parenting*, pp. 255–277 (2nd ed.). Mahwah, NJ: Lawrence Erlbaum Associates.

Quinn, N., & Holland, D. (1987). Culture and cognition. In D. Holland & N. Quinn (Eds.), *Cultural models in language and thought*, pp. 1–40. New York: Cambridge University Press.

Rogoff, B., & Gardner, W. (1984). Adult guidance of cognitive development. In B. Rogoff &

J. Lave (Eds.), *Everyday cognition: Its development in social context*, pp. 95–116. Cambridge, MA: Harvard University Press.

Rosenzweig, M. R. (1971). Effects of environment on development of brain and behavior. In E. Tobach (Ed.), *Biopsychology of development*, pp. 303–342. New York: Academic.

Rowe, D. (1994). *The limits of family influence.* New York: Guilford Press.

Rubin, K. H., Coplan, R., Chen, X., Bowker, J., & McDonald, K. L. (2011). Peer relationships in childhood. In M. H. Bornstein & M. E. Lamb (Eds.), *Developmental science: An advanced textbook*, pp. 519–570 (6th ed). New York: Psychology Press.

Sameroff, A. J. (1983). Developmental systems: Contexts and evolution. In P. H. Mussen (Series Ed.) & W. Kessen (Vol. Ed.), *Handbook of child psychology*: Vol. 1. *History, theory and methods*, pp. 237–244 (4th ed.). New York: Wiley.

Sameroff, A. J. (Ed.). (2009). *The transactional model of development: How children and contexts shape each other.* Washington, DC: American Psychological Association.

Scarr, S., & McCartney, K. (1983). How people make their own environments: A theory of genotype-environment effects. *Child Development, 54,* 424–435.

Schank, R. C., & Abelson, R. P. (1977). *Scripts, plans, goals and understanding: An inquiry into human knowledge structures.* Oxford, UK: Lawrence Erlbaum Associates.

Sengpiel, F., Stawinski, P., & Bonhoeffer, T. (1999). Influence of experience on orientation maps in cat visual cortex. *Nature Neuroscience, 2,* 727–732.

Serpell, R. (1979). How specific are perceptual skills? A cross-cultural study of pattern reproduction. *British Journal of Psychology, 70,* 365–380.

Snow, C. E. (1977). The development of conversation between mothers and babies. *Journal of Child Language, 4,* 1–22.

Sroufe, A. L., Egeland, B., Carlson, E. A., & Collins, W. A. (2005). *The development of the person: The Minnesota study of risk and adaptation from birth to adulthood.* New York: Guilford Publications.

Tamis-LeMonda, C. S., & Bornstein, M. H. (1989). Habituation and maternal encouragement of attention in infancy as predictors of toddler language, play, and representational competence. *Child Development, 60,* 738–751.

Tamis-LeMonda, C. S., & Bornstein, M. H. (1990). Language, play, and attention at one year. *Infant Behavior and Development, 13,* 85–98.

Tamis-LeMonda, C. S., & Bornstein, M. H. (1991). Individual variation, correspondence, stability, and change in mother and toddler play. *Infant Behavior and Development, 14,* 143–162.

Tamis-LeMonda, C. S., & McFadden, K. E. (2010). The United States of America. In M. H. Bornstein (Ed.), *Handbook of cultural developmental science*, pp. 299–322. New York: Psychology Press.

Thompson, L. (1996). Where are the environmental influences on IQ? In D. Detterman (Ed.), *Current topics in human intelligence:* Vol. 5. *The environment*, pp. 179–184. Norwood, NJ: Ablex.

Vibbert, M., & Bornstein, M. H. (1989). Specific associations between domains of mother-child interaction and toddler referential language and pretense play. *Infant Behavior and Development, 12,* 163–184.

Vygotsky, L. S. (1962). *Thought and language.* Oxford, UK: Wiley.

Wachs, T. D. (1995). Genetic and family influences on individual development: Both necessary, neither sufficient. *Psychological Inquiry, 6,* 161–173.

Wachs, T. D., & Chan, A. (1986). Specificity of environmental action, as seen in environmental correlates of infants' communication performance. *Child Development, 57,* 1464–1474.

Wachs, T. D., & Gandour, M. J. (1983). Temperament, environment, and six-month cognitive-intellectual development: A test of the organismic specificity hypothesis. *International Journal of Behavioral Development, 6,* 135–152.

Weisner, T. S. (2002). Ecocultural understanding of children's developmental pathways. *Human Development 45,* 275–281.

White, R. W. (1958). Motivation reconsidered: The concept of competence. *Psychological Review, 66,* 297–333.

Wiesel, T. N., & Hubel, D. H. (1974). Ordered arrangement of orientation columns in monkeys lacking visual experience. *Journal of Comparative Neurology, 158,* 307–318.

Yarrow, L. J. et al. (1982). Infants' persistence at tasks: Relationships to cognitive functioning and early experiencing. *Infant Behavior & Development, 5,* 131–141.

Yarrow, L. J., McQuiston, S., MacTurk, R. H., McCarthy, M. E., Klein, R. P., & Vietze, P. M. (1983). Assessment of mastery motivation during the first year of life: Contemporaneous and cross-age relationships. *Developmental Psychology, 19,* 159–171.

Yurgelun-Todd, D. (2002). Frontline interview "Inside the Teen Brain." Retrieved September 24, 2009. Available online: www.pbs.org/wgbh/pages/frontline/shows/teenbrain/interviews/todd.html

Zukow-Goldring, P. (2002). Sibling caregiving. In M. H. Bornstein (Ed.), *Handbook of parenting*: Vol. 3. *Being and becoming a parent*, pp. 253–286 (2nd ed.). Mahwah, NJ: Lawrence Erlbaum Associates.

CHAPTER 2

Risk and Adversity in Developmental Psychopathology

Progress and Future Directions

Jelena Obradović, Anne Shaffer, and Ann S. Masten

The study of risk in individual development played an instrumental role in the origin of contemporary developmental psychopathology and the emergence of resilience studies (Garmezy & Rutter, 1983; Gottesman, 1974; Masten, Best, & Garmezy, 1990; O'Dougherty & Wright, 1990; Rutter, 1979; Sameroff & Seifer, 1990). Historically, the concepts of risk and protection have roots in maritime insurance, as, centuries ago, merchants attempted to calculate the odds of losing a cargo in order to set insurance rates, and in public health, as communities attempted to prevent or contain disease outbreaks. The systematic study of risk in human development emerged much later, in the middle of the 20th century, as scientists attempted to understand the etiology of serious mental disorders and disabilities and the consequences of maternal deprivation (Anthony & Koupernick, 1974; Sameroff & Chandler, 1975). Identifying risk factors for a particular kind of problem was seen as a key step toward explaining causal processes and preventing or treating the problem. Scientists studying the etiology of schizophrenia, for example, observed that while schizophrenia occurred at base rates around 1 percent or less in the general population, it occurred at higher rates among individuals with a family history of the disorder (Gottesman, Shields, & Hanson, 1982). In order to study the onset and development of schizophrenia and learn ways to prevent or ameliorate it, investigators were confronted with a choice: begin with very large population samples or study a smaller group of people with a higher likelihood of developing the illness. A group of international investigators advanced the strategy of longitudinal studies of high-risk samples of children based on observations that children who had one or two biological parents with schizophrenia had much higher risk for developing the disorder than the general population (Garmezy, 1974; Watt, Anthony, Wynne, & Rolf, 1984). Other investigators identified a variety of "at risk" samples of children based on consistently observed correlates of developmental problems. Some of these risk factors were status variables (e.g., unmarried mother, minority race/ethnicity), while others represented specific events (e.g., death of a parent), conditions of living (e.g., poverty, homelessness, abusive parent), or biological measures (e.g., low birth weight).

When developmental investigators began to follow risk samples forward in time, they observed dramatic variations in pathways and outcomes and noted the multiplicity of ongoing individual-environment interactions that shaped the course of development. Understanding multiple pathways and the processes that gave rise to similar problems, as well as how analogous experiences could yield different developmental outcomes, became a central objective of developmental psychopathology (Cicchetti, 2006; Masten, 2006). Resilience studies emerged as a way to understand how some children manifested positive development despite their exposure to high levels of risk and adversity (Luthar, 2006; Masten & Obradović, 2006).

Over the next half-century, as the study of risk matured, attention shifted from a focus on single risk factors to cumulative risks, from static to more dynamic approaches, from cross-sectional to longitudinal studies, from global to more differentiated analyses, and from markers of risk to more direct measures of processes. Concomitantly, investigators wrestled with issues of conceptualizing, measuring, analyzing, and understanding risk, as they considered the implications and applications of their research findings, both for developmental theory and for interventions to promote healthier development in children. Early studies of risk for serious developmental problems in children were hampered by the limited tools available for direct measures of biological risk factors (e.g., genes, uterine environment, or brain functioning) and the statistical analysis for studying developmental trajectories or multifactorial interactions over time. That situation is rapidly changing (Masten, 2004); thus, it is timely to consider the current status of the field and future directions for risk research in developmental psychopathology.

The purpose of this chapter is to provide an overview of progress and ongoing issues encountered in the developmental study of risk and adversity. At the outset, we wish to clarify the distinction we make between "risk" and "adversity," since in the literature these terms are often used interchangeably. In the strictest sense, definitions of risk and risk factors imply statistical association between a risk factor and a specific outcome within a sample or a population; that is, the presence of a risk factor indicates an increased probability of a negative outcome. For example, obesity could be identified as a risk factor for type II diabetes in school-age children. However, it is important to note that the same status variable may be a risk factor for one outcome and an asset with respect to a different outcome. Having a young biological mother represents a risk for higher levels of behavior and emotional problems but is also related to a lower risk of having trisomy 21. In contrast, "adversity" is a term used to indicate that an individual has experienced or has been exposed to negative or stressful life experiences. Although the term is not defined with respect to a specific outcome, exposure to adversity can be conceived as one type of risk factor, as it challenges successful adaptation and often predicts a worse outcome on the aspect of adaptation under consideration. For example, a history of child maltreatment can increase the risk for a number of negative outcomes, including the development of psychopathology. While we recognize that these definitions are imperfect and plagued by many issues that are addressed later in the chapter, this simple distinction is meant to facilitate the organization of different considerations pertaining to measurement of risk factors and adversity exposure.

The chapter addresses different approaches for examining effects of risk and adversity on development. The first section discusses risk factors and cumulative risk indices, emphasizing environmental and sociodemographic status variables. The second section focuses on stressful life events and efforts to measure ongoing adversity exposure. The third section examines major issues in defining, measuring, and investigating developmental risk and adversity, while highlighting important new research directions. In the conclusion, we delineate promising areas for future consideration in theory and research.

Risk Factors and Cumulative Risk Index

Although early research on risk often focused on the role of one particular "risk factor" in developmental processes, investigators soon realized that risks often co-occur or pile up in the lives of children, and research shifted toward the study of cumulative risk and risk gradients and strategies for capturing the combined effects of multiple risks (Deater-Deckard, Dodge, Bates, & Pettit, 1998; Masten & Gewirtz, 2006; Stouthamer-Loeber, Loeber, Wei, Farrington, & Wikström, 2002). Researchers use cumulative or contextual risk indices to account for the array of environmental and sociodemographic risk factors that may be present in a child's life. Risk indices can be assembled in multiple ways: by capitalizing on available data, selecting the most powerful or salient risk variables, or attempting to represent multiple ecological levels (e.g., individual, family, community; Sameroff, 2006).

The most common strategy for constructing a risk index has been to count and sum risk factors, usually using well-established risk factors with an empirical record of validity for one or more specific outcomes being studied. This strategy emerged from the repeated observation that the aggregated *number* of such risk factors often seemed to matter more than the presence and variability of any particular risk factor (Deater-Deckard et al., 1998; Masten & Shaffer, 2006; Sameroff, 2006; Zeanah, Boris, & Larrieu, 1997). For example, in many classic studies of risk that focused on resilience in children who were identified as "high-risk," risk was defined in terms of multiple risk status (see Rutter, 1979; Werner & Smith 1982). Arnold Sameroff (2006), one of the pioneering investigators advocating multifactor risk indices, noted, "It is not any single factor in the child, the family, or the social surround that causes difficulties, but a set of factors that probabilistically contribute to the outcome" (p. 55). This idea has been revisited in various ways over the decades, as investigators attempt to refine their strategies for assessing risk.

Commonly, to create a cumulative risk index, investigators identify a list of risk factors and then count whether or not the risk factor is present in the child's life. Some risk factors are naturally dichotomous (present or absent), such as a single-parent household, but many common risk factors consist of continuous or dimensional variables, such as measures of parental years of education, degree of family discord, family income, age of mother at birth of child. In these cases, investigators typically transform continuous risk variables into binary (i.e., present/ absent) risk factors by dichotomizing the risk variable using a cutoff criterion. Ideally, defining the threshold of risk on such a variable would be objectively meaningful, established in reference to normative or other a priori methods. For example, researchers often define low parental education as less than a high school degree. However, cutoff points are sometimes established in reference to the research sample at hand, by dividing the sample at the median or at a specific percentile point. Sample-specific methods for dichotomizing data are often a less preferable alternative to normative standards, as a result of concerns regarding generalizability and replicability of the data; however, in the absence of normative standards for many psychosocial variables, sample-based criteria frequently cannot be avoided. Finally, not all cumulative risk indices sum dichotomous risk factors. There have been efforts to capture more variance in the severity of risk and covariance among sources of risk, for example, by averaging across standardized risk factor scores or conducting factor analyses to form composite risk scores (e.g., Burchinal, Roberts, Zeisel, Hennon, & Hooper, 2006; Deater-Deckard et al., 1998; Essex, Klein, Cho, & Kalin, 2002). These approaches, although statistically advantageous, have not been as popular as simple counts, perhaps because of replication issues, as noted earlier.

Use of a risk index affords multiple advantages. Theoretically, such composites more accurately depict the observed reality that any given risk factor rarely operates in isolation from other risk factors (Bronfenbrenner, 1994). For example, single-parent status and family income are often highly correlated, as households headed by single mothers are more likely to have family incomes in the lowest ranges compared with national averages (Seccombe, 2000). A risk index that aggregates factors operating in concert provides a more realistic picture of how these risk factors naturally occur. Moreover, risk indices are valued for their ability to measure cumulative risk exposure, by summing the total number of risks present, rather than assessing the relations of separate risk factors to outcomes. A cumulative risk index provides a statistically powerful way to detect relations between risk exposure and developmental outcomes, as a combination of multiple risk variables is more likely to account for a significant portion of the variance in adaptive functioning than any single risk variable (Rutter, 1979; Seifer et al., 1996). For example, the Rochester Longitudinal Study (RLS), begun in 1970, was one of the first large, longitudinal studies to utilize a multifactor risk index to predict developmental outcomes. In one of the earliest studies from the RLS, a 10-factor risk index emerged as a far more powerful predictor of child IQ than any risk factor considered in isolation (Sameroff, Seifer, Barocas, Zax, & Greenspan, 1987). Recently, we demonstrated that a childhood cumulative risk index significantly predicted outcomes in young adulthood, 20 years later (Obradović, Masten, & Shaffer, 2005).

The factors that cumulative risk indices comprise have varied significantly throughout the literature. Many studies designed to capture cumulative risk exposure include only family risk factors (e.g., Forehand, Biggar, & Kotchick, 1998; Smokowski, Mann, Reynolds, & Fraser, 2004), while others have expressly targeted multiple domains and ecological levels, responding to increased theoretical emphasis on understanding the influence of various contexts on development. Although community and neighborhood variables are notoriously difficult to study (Sampson, Morenoff, & Gannon-Rowley, 2002), some researchers have worked to include neighborhood-level variables in their risk indices (e.g., Evans, Kim, Ting, Tesher, & Shannis, 2007; Gerard & Buehler, 2004). A study of Philadelphia families is notable for its inclusion of community variables (e.g., census tract information, reports of neighborhood problems) and peer variables (e.g., association with antisocial/prosocial peers) as well as parenting and family-related variables in its cumulative risk index (Furstenberg, Cook, Eccles, Elder, & Sameroff, 1999). In addition to community and neighborhood level variables, researchers are increasingly measuring biomarkers of children's physiology and health in an effort to capture biological indicators of risk. Initially, identification of biological risk markers focused on indices of prematurity or serious medical illnesses in infants (Zeanah et al., 1997). However, concepts like allostatic load have in recent years drawn increasing attention in the risk literature. Allostatic load is conceptualized as a measure of the cumulative physiological burden due to chronic activation of the neurobiological stress response, which can be damaging to biological tissues and systems over time (McEwen & Wingfield, 2003). Allostatic load is generally measured using a composite index of neurobiological stress responses, such as activation of the hypothalamic-pituitary-adrenal (HPA) axis and autonomic nervous system (Seeman, McEwen, Rowe, & Singer, 2001). In this way, measures of allostatic load serve as physiological analogues to the previously reviewed indices of cumulative risk and adversity and are significant predictors of physical morbidity and mortality (Seeman et al., 2001). In fact, Evans and colleagues showed that physiological measures of allostatic load (e.g., overnight cortisol, norepinephrine and epinephrine; resting diastolic and systolic blood pressure) and psychosocial measures of cumulative risk are related in children and young adolescents living in rural, low-income environments (Evans, 2003; Evans et al., 2007).

With the mapping of the human genome, new technologies for imaging the human brain, and advances in the assessment of various biomarkers, there is also increasing attention to examining genes or endophenotypes as moderators of risk factors (Hanson & Gottesman, 2007; Rutter, 2006). Significant research in recent years has sought to identify candidate genes that may serve as risk factors, increasing individuals' susceptibility to variations in environmental contexts, as discussed in greater detail later in this chapter. Fewer studies have included genetic factors as components of cumulative risk indices, but as research in this area expands, it can be expected that future risk indices may include information regarding allelic variations or gene expression.

Despite the breadth and utility of cumulative risk indices, there are important drawbacks (Coie et al., 1993; Gerard & Buehler, 2004). Although these indices often are good predictors of developmental outcomes, little is learned about the underlying processes or specificity of any particular kind of risk or combination of risks. Such indices also mask interaction effects, and they assume that risk factors operate similarly for all individuals, despite findings regarding individual variability in the impact of risk factors. For example, Adler's research on the role of socioeconomic status (SES) as a risk factor has shown that the associations between SES and outcomes vary across different measures of SES (Adler, Epel, Castellazo, & Ickovics, 2000). Specifically, in a sample of adult women, psychological and physical health were more strongly correlated with subjective ratings of SES, in which participants were asked to compare their own SES to their surroundings, than with objective ratings of SES based on education level, income, and occupation. Although the subjective and objective measures of SES were moderately correlated, the significance of subjective SES for health outcomes over and above objective SES suggests that important aspects of individual variability can be lost by using only traditional, objective risk indices without consideration for how risk factors operate,

particularly in terms of their psychological impact (Adler et al., 2000).

A more nuanced examination of contextual risk requires an acknowledgment of the possibility that some domains or individual risks may be more influential than others in regard to a specific outcome. The use of cumulative risk indices can obscure this possibility by counting all risk factors in the same way, simply by computing the summed total of risks that are present (Gerard & Buehler, 2004). Moreover, valuable information can be lost when risk variables are dichotomized to create cumulative risk indices. For example, in one longitudinal study, Deater-Deckard et al. (1998) compared two different approaches to studying the effect of environmental risk exposure on externalizing behavior problems in middle childhood. Four domains of risk were assessed: child risk factors, sociocultural risk factors, parenting/caregiving risk factors, and peer-related risk factors. In addition to creating four sets of risk variables that were tested individually, Deater-Deckard and colleagues also created four cumulative risk indices, each representing the number of risks in each domain that each child had been exposed to, as well as the total cumulative risk index reflecting the total number of risks the child had experienced. The results revealed that each set of individual risk factors explained the unique variance of externalizing behaviors over and above the significant contribution of the other three sets of risk factors. Each cumulative risk index also uniquely predicted externalizing behaviors over and above the contribution of the other three cumulative risk indices; however, the percentage of explained variance was lower when compared to analyses using the sets of individual risk factors. Finally, each set of individual risk factors explained a significant amount of variance in externalizing behaviors, controlling for total cumulative risk exposure. While these findings demonstrate that predictive power is lost by artificially dichotomizing the individual differences of risk exposure, simultaneously examining the effect of multiple individual risk variables raises the issue of multicollinearity, as construct overlap between some indices of risk may render the contribution of individual risk variables nonsignificant. In addition, using continuous risk variables assumes that the probability of negative outcomes gradually grows with increased levels of risk exposure rather than that there are clearly defined deleterious levels of risk at the end of a continuum. Finally, studies with smaller sample sizes may not have enough power to test multiple risk variables using methods similar to Deater-Deckard et al. (1998), and thus may rely on cumulative risk indices to create a single variable that represents multiple risk processes. In this way, creating a cumulative risk index can also be seen as a data reduction strategy.

Researchers often explicitly set out to test the relations of cumulative risk indices to specific outcomes. Numerous studies, for example, have used indices of family risk to predict outcomes in single domains, such as behavior problems in children (Deater-Deckard et al., 1998; Jessor, van den Bos, Vanderrym, Costa, & Turbin, 1995; Williams, Anderson, McGee & Silva, 1990). Small and Luster (1994) found strong support for a cumulative risk model in predicting adolescent sexual behavior. Additionally, Evans et al. (2007) have used a cumulative risk variable to predict adolescent outcomes in terms of allostatic load, a physiological marker of response to chronic stress. Other studies use cumulative risk indices to predict a wider range of outcomes, such as measures of age-salient developmental tasks. Seifer and colleagues have noted that risk indices may indeed be best suited to identifying individuals who are at risk for a broad range of negative outcomes (Seifer et al., 1996), such as psychopathology, academic underachievement, poor health, and impaired social relationships. However, studies examining the specificity of risk indices across various measures of adaptive functioning are rare. In our longitudinal study of a community-based sample, a cumulative risk index reflecting a sum of eight childhood sociodemographic risk factors predicted academic achievement, conduct competence, work competence, civic engagement and externalizing

problems in young adulthood (Obradović et al., 2005). In contrast, the same index was not a long-term direct predictor of young adult self-worth, social and romantic competence, or internalizing symptoms, suggesting that it had less long-term significance for personal and interpersonal indices of young adult's adaptation.

There is an ongoing debate regarding whether cumulative risk indices show linear effects, as depicted by corresponding increases in negative outcomes with increases in risks, or if the effects are better captured by a threshold or curvilinear model of cumulative risk. The latter posits that significant decrement in adaptation occurs when a specific number of risk factors are present. The literature provides support for both sides of the argument. Multiple studies have demonstrated the power of a "risk gradient" approach to understanding these relations, where the likelihood of negative outcomes shows a linear increase with the addition of more risk factors (Masten & Obradović, 2006; Sameroff, 2006). Many studies of "SES gradients" show such linear patterns, where increases in socioeconomic status are associated with complementary increases in various measures of well-being, such as health status, across the entire continuum from low to high SES (Keating & Hertzman, 1999). On the other hand, multiple studies have provided evidence suggesting that cumulative risk may operate more as a threshold model, where the likelihood of negative outcomes increases exponentially after a certain number of risks are detected. Forehand et al. (1998) reported a steep increase in adolescent problem behaviors when number of family risk factors increased from three to four (out of total of five family risk factors), suggesting an exponential risk effect similar to the effect reported by Rutter (1979) in a classic cumulative risk analysis using data from the Isle of Wight. Biederman and colleagues (1995) have also reported evidence of threshold models of risk, where the likelihood of children meeting criteria for diagnoses of Attention Deficit/Hyperactivity Disorder increased exponentially for those who had more than three risk factors in their study. Greenberg and colleagues reported similar findings for diagnoses of conduct disorders in childhood (Greenberg, Speltz, DeKlyen, & Jones, 2001). Nevertheless, it is conceivable that unmeasured risk factors account for the apparent acceleration of risk in studies with nonlinear effects. The number of uncounted risks may grow as the counted number of risk factors increases, particularly in the case of major sociodemographic risks that tend to be correlated with other measured indicators of risk (Masten, 2001). Children in large, poor families headed by a single parent with little education are more likely to live in dangerous neighborhoods, with worse schools, more crime, higher exposure to toxic substances, deviant peer groups, negative role models of adult behavior, and a multitude of other risks associated with poverty and unstable housing, including domestic violence and homelessness.

Stressful Life Events and Adversity Exposure

An alternative approach to measuring environmental disadvantage involves examining specific negative life events that the child has experienced, such as child maltreatment or parental divorce. In this case, too, there has been an historical shift from the study of single stressful experiences to more cumulative or comprehensive indices of adverse conditions. Once again, it has become evident that major life events of this kind, such as divorce, actually represent a complex sequence of events or occur in the context of many other ongoing events and attendant risk factors (Masten et al., 1990). Investigators have responded to these findings by creating cumulative indices of adversity exposure and attempting to measure the adversity context with greater refinement or comprehensiveness, using multiple strategies. Indeed, efforts to assess multiple life events and combine them into indices of "stress" or "stressful life events" or "adversity" represent a variant of cumulative risk indices. In addition, many cumulative risk indices in

the literature (see Sameroff & Seifer, 1990; Werner & Smith, 1982) have included negative life experiences as a one of the risk factors linking the two approaches to measuring developmental disadvantage.

The most common strategy for assessing exposure to adverse experiences employs self-report instruments such as life event questionnaires, including inventories like the widely used 12-item Brugha List of Threatening Experiences (Brugha, Bebbington, Tennant, & Hurry, 1985). Adaptive outcomes tend to be poorer in the context of a history of multiple adversities (Dong et al., 2004; Taylor et al., 2008). The Adverse Childhood Experiences (ACE) study has repeatedly demonstrated that cumulative experiences of adversity, as measured by life experience questionnaires, are associated with increases in negative outcomes such as depression in adulthood (Chapman et al., 2004) and alcohol use in adolescence (Dube et al., 2006).

Brown and Harris (1978) championed the contextual life event interview strategy, whereby the circumstances surrounding an event could be taken into consideration. In Project Competence, we have created similarly complex measures of adversity exposure (see Gest, Reed, & Masten, 1999), using life history charts and rating scales modeled on early questionnaires initially designed by Holmes and Rahe (1967) and adapted for children by Coddington (1972a,b). First, all available information on potentially challenging life experiences was assembled from various informants and measures across multiple assessment time points onto a computerized life history chart, organized by chronological years. These life history charts could then be rated on adversity by clinical judges who were blind to the child's functioning and events in other periods. The level of exposure to stressful experiences during a given window of time was rated on the stressor scale from the DSM-III-R (American Psychiatric Association, 1987), using a 7-point scale ranging from minimal to catastrophic adversity (see Gest et al., 1999, for more details).

The life chart approach was designed to capture the severity of each event based on the participant's age and the context in which the event occurred. Only events deemed by independent observers to be universally stressful and either undesirable or ambiguous in desirability (e.g., pregnancy) were included in indices of global adversity (Gest et al., 1999). Daily hassles, chronic role strains, anticipated future events, and positive stressful events (e.g., job promotion) were excluded. Moreover, events that were almost certainly independent of the individual's adaptive functioning (e.g., parental unemployment) were examined separately from events that may have been confounded with the individual's behavior or psychological state (e.g., being arrested). Analysis of these global adversity composites revealed that exposure to adversities that could be influenced by a child's own behavior (non-independent scores) increased sharply in adolescence, as maladaptive youth with few coping resources tended to generate many more stressful life experiences than their peers (Gest et al., 1999).

In many early efforts to quantify adversity through life event inventories of these kinds, an effort was made to weigh the events, so that death of a parent, for example, was given more weight than moving to a new school. However, researchers have found it difficult to demonstrate that weighting systems improved the predictive validity of life event scores, perhaps because of the wide variation in circumstances in which events occurred. Thus, alternatives strategies were developed that accounted for context. In the most subjective approach, events were weighted by the reporter of the event according to their perceived stressfulness; however, this strategy raised issues of confounding the event with the outcome under investigation, such as the person's symptoms of psychological distress (Johnson, 1986; Masten, Neemann, & Andenas, 1994). A more objective approach, where the severity of adversity is weighted by an independent, clinical judge, has shown promise; judges' ratings of adversity have been found to predict variance in child adjustment problems over and above the frequency of adverse events as

determined by simple counts (Gest, Reed, & Masten, 1999).

In addition to examining the effects of cumulative adverse life events that occur over longer periods, researchers have studied how daily stressors and hassles affect adjustment and health of adolescents and adults. For this purpose, data collection methods known as experience sampling methods were developed in the 1970s and have increased in popularity since then (Csikszentmihalyi & Larson, 1987; Scollon, Kim-Prieto, & Diener, 2003). These methods utilize electronic paging devices or PDAs to signal participants, in their natural environments, to provide in-the-moment responses regarding their experiences over the course of a specified period. As compared to the macrolevel study of stressful life events, as represented by the life event questionnaires described earlier, these microlevel methods provide specificity in relating experiences to emotional or physiological reactions, For example, Adam (2006) has reported that adolescents experience greater increases in salivary cortisol levels when alone than with others. Moreover, Adam, Hawkley, Kudielka, and Cacioppo (2006) have shown that while experiences of sadness and loneliness predicted higher cortisol awakening response the following day in adults, higher awakening response was unrelated to negative feelings later that day. Experience sampling methods such as electronic diaries afford multiple advantages in measuring stressful events and emotional reactions in immediate and ecologically valid ways; however, these methods are also susceptible to the same social desirability biases inherent in all self-report methods (Scollon et al., 2003).

Methodological and Conceptual Issues

Despite the new methods of assessment and analytic approaches for studying risk and adversity in development, investigators still confront various conceptual, methodological, and ethical issues. Although a comprehensive review of all the concerns raised in the literature is beyond the scope of this chapter, we provide an overview of key issues that should be addressed by future research.

Definitions and Assessment of Risk

The term "risk" is used very generally in this chapter, and in much of the developmental and public health literature, to refer to an elevated probability of an undesirable outcome, with "risk factor" referring to a predictor of an undesirable outcome in a population. These terms refer to probabilities established by studying groups of people. If an individual is described as "at risk" it means that this person is a member of a group where research has shown an elevated probability of the negative outcome under consideration. Over the years, a number of issues have been raised about the meaning of risk terminology, with much recent discussion about sharpening the definitions of risk terms led by Helena Kraemer and her colleagues in a series of insightful articles (Kraemer et al., 1997; Kraemer, Stice, Kazdin, Offord, & Kupfer, 2001; Kraemer, Wilson, Fairburn, & Agras, 2002). This group has argued persuasively for distinguishing a causal risk factor from a correlational concomitant, by clearly establishing that the risk factor precedes the outcome. This is not an easy criterion to meet for many individual differences in human development where the onset of the problem is difficult to establish. A *causal* risk factor requires evidence that manipulating the factor changes the outcome, a standard that usually requires a randomized intervention trial approach, aiming to reduce risk, since it is unethical to add or increase risk in a child's life.

Another issue in the defining of risk has focused on continuous risk variables, such as SES or parenting quality, where a dimensional predictor is arbitrarily labeled as a risk factor when measured at one end of the continuum (such as low-quality parenting), when it could just as easily be called a "resource" or "asset" or "promotive factor" when measured at the opposite end of the same continuum (e.g., high

quality parenting; Masten, 2001; Rutter, 1990; Sameroff, 2006). Studies demonstrating significant relations between risk factors and developmental outcomes rarely examine whether it is one end of a risk distribution that is driving the significant relation or a general effect is present all along the continuum. Even with dichotomous risk factors, it is not often clear whether it is the presence or absence of risk that accounts for observed differences.

Certain factors can be conceptualized as exclusively risk related. Many of these risk factors constitute negative life experiences. For example, the experience of maltreatment is strongly and consistently associated with diverse indicators of maladaptive functioning and is widely viewed as a major risk marker for developmental problems (Cicchetti, 1996; Egeland, 1997; Masten & Wright, 1998). The absence of maltreatment, on the other hand, may not promote positive development. In contrast, certain environmental variables are continuously distributed, with a "good" and a "bad" end of the distribution; in these cases, the factor could be conceptualized as either a risk factor or a promotive factor (i.e., asset). For example, low SES can pose a risk for development, whereas high SES can be an advantage. Such variables may have functional effects all along the full range, although it is conceivable that the action is concentrated at the high or low end, as a curvilinear relation.

In many cases it is arbitrary to label a variable as a "risk factor" because the effective zone of action is unknown or presumed to be continuous. One might flip over a risk gradient and call it an "asset gradient" (Masten, Cutuli, Herbers, & Gabrielle-Reed, 2009). Indeed, many so-called risk gradients are actually a blend of counted risks and implicit resources. Some investigators and organizations (e.g., Search Institute) have chosen to focus on counting the positive factors (cf. "40 assets" measure created by the Search Institute), often in order to emphasize prevention targets, or resilience. In the Philadelphia family study mentioned previously, each risk dimension was redefined as a promotive factor by establishing the cutoff point at the top quartile for the sample, rather than the bottom quartile. These analyses revealed effects for promotive factors that were essentially the opposite of those for the risk factors, suggesting that the influence of these factors seems to be unidimensional (Sameroff, 2006). In another example from the maltreatment literature, Runyan et al. (1998) constructed a "resource index," as compared to the more common risk index described earlier, by summing the total number of social capital resources available to children who were part of the Longitudinal Studies of Child Abuse and Neglect Consortium (LONGSCAN) studies. These resources included having two parents in the home, high social support for the mother, regular church attendance, and high neighborhood support; notably, most of these resources could be conceptualized as risk variables when measured in the opposite direction.

Few researchers have attempted to delineate whether the effect of environmental variables on adaptation is specifically negative or positive. Stouthamer-Loeber and colleagues (2002) examined this issue by trichotomizing the distribution of each variable based on its effect on the development of persistent serious delinquency to see if effects were greater in a particular part of the distribution. Thus, three sections of any one variable's distribution were denoted as risk, neutral, and promotive factors. Some of their results have suggested that the "action" may be in the risk end rather than the promotive end of a distribution (Stouthamer-Loeber et al., 2002).

Another challenge to studying risk and adversity is the lack of a common definition for what constitutes mild, moderate, or severe exposure levels. The severity of risk and adversity is rarely quantified in general terms that can be compared across different populations and settings. Sample-specific methods for dichotomizing data are often a less preferable alternative to normative standards, as a result of concerns regarding generalizability and replicability of the data; however, in the absence of normative standards for many psychosocial variables, sample-specific criteria frequently cannot be avoided. Sameroff (2006) points out that while using the worst 25 percent as an appropriate cutoff for establishing high-risk conditions is "somewhat arbitrary and highly sample-specific, it generally works" (p. 59). But the worst 25 percent cutoff may translate to very different absolute levels of risk across various samples. In contrast, cutoff scores defining the "clinical range" of symptoms have been established for a number of behavior problem measures for children and adults (Lemery-Chalfant et al., 2007). Better standardization of risk and adversity measures might allow researchers to investigate how the effects of specific levels of risk and adversity and processes underlying those effects vary across different contexts and population.

Longitudinal Analyses of Risk and Adversity Effects

Most sources of risk and adversity are not static, but rather dynamic attributes and processes that can change over time. In particular, exposure to adverse events, such as domestic violence and homelessness, can wax and wane over time. Even sociodemographic risk indices such as maternal education, socioeconomic status, and number of siblings in a family can vary over time, although to a lesser extent. Thus, only studies with repeated measures of risk and adversity can identify processes contributing to continuity and change of risk and adversity and investigate how effects of risk and adversity vary across time and different developmental periods.

Currently, there is a paucity of studies investigating the growth of intraindividual adversity exposure or dynamic interplay between adversity exposure and indices of adaptation. However, there are a few notable exceptions in the field of developmental psychopathology. In a pioneering growth trajectory study, Ge and colleagues showed that in girls initial levels as well as rate of change of life stresses were significantly related to initial levels and growth of depressive symptoms (Ge, Lorenz, Conger, Elder, & Simons, 1995). Moreover, they showed that high levels of maternal warmth and support decreased the dynamic covariation between trajectories of life stressors and depressive symptoms. More recently, Ge, Natsuki, & Conger (2006) examined the influence of divorce and stressful life events on the growth of depressive symptoms in rural adolescents across 11 years of study. Adolescents whose parents divorced by age 15 were at significantly higher risk for experiencing depressive symptoms then their peers who come from intact families. However, the association between parental divorce and depressive symptomatology was mediated by the exposure to life stressors following divorce. In other words, most of the effect that divorce had on an adolescent's mental health was explained by adversity exposure within the two years following divorce.

The impact of risk and adversity effects can also change as a function of time and development itself. The significance of the same risk factor for subsequent or lasting problems may vary across different developmental periods (Masten & Gewirtz, 2006). For example, death of a parent or exposure to alcohol can have very different effects on a fetus, a preschooler, an adolescent, and a young adult. Similarly, sometimes the impact of an event (e.g., pregnancy) changes dramatically from adolescence to young adulthood, even though the nature of the event stays the same. This is presumably because the processes by which risk affects development are influenced by changes in the nature of the developing organism, relationships, and contexts.

The severity of certain types of adversity may also vary with development. For example, in the Project Competence study, the severity of physical adversity decreased with age as children's health became more robust and incidence of accidents decreased (Gest et al., 1999). In contrast, the severity of family and community adversity increased with age, as children transitioned into adolescence, tested family boundaries and ventured into the world on their own.

During transitions between different developmental periods, children and adolescents may be particularly vulnerable to effects of risk and adversity. For example, during the transition to early adolescence, African-American girls, especially early maturing ones, showed increased levels of risk for substance use (Ge et al., 2006). Interestingly, Obradović and Hipwell (2010) reported that the link between changes in pubertal status and internalizing symptoms in girls changes over time. Although advanced pubertal status was associated with increased symptoms between ages 9 and 12, this association was reversed after age 13, when most girls had reached advance stages of puberty. More studies need to consider developmental timing when measuring adverse life events and use this information to examine whether and how susceptibility to adverse events changes with development.

Among researchers who have explored the developmental timing of risk and adversity, the relative importance of early versus later experiences is a debated issue. Many researchers agree that early exposure to risk and adversity can have deleterious effects on development (Nelson, Zeanah, & Fox, 2007; O'Connor, 2006); however, only a few have examined the unique contribution of early risk and subsequent disadvantage. Researchers' understanding of the longitudinal stability of risk and adversity and whether early exposure augments the effect of later exposure or presents an independent influence is limited. For example, in a recent study of early childhood and middle childhood risk indices, both comprising family risks such as child maltreatment, interparental violence, family disruptions, maternal life stress, and socioeconomic status, the early childhood risk index emerged as a stronger predictor of adolescent psychopathology (Appleyard, Egeland, van Dulmen, & Sroufe, 2005). However, there is evidence that subsequent levels of risk can have an addition effect over and above previous levels of risk. Schoon and colleagues (2002) showed that after accounting for the concurrent association between socioeconomic risk and academic achievement, measures of early childhood, late childhood and adolescent socioeconomic risk also showed a significant time-lagged effect on achievement. This additional longitudinal effect of risk on achievement is noteworthy, given the strong stability of both domains across three developmental periods.

Issues of timing are also important for studies interested in examining how children may actively shape their experience of adversity. In a 6-year longitudinal study, Kim, Conger, Elder, & Lorenz (2003) reported significant reciprocal effects between repeated measures of stressful life events and behavior problems. In two separate models, stressful life events significantly predicted change in externalizing and internalizing symptoms, whereas internalizing and externalizing symptoms significantly predicted changes in stressful life events, controlling for the significant stability of both adversity and psychopathology. While reciprocal effects were significant between all consecutive assessment points, the size of the effect varied across development periods for externalizing symptoms. During early adolescence (between seventh and eighth grades), the effect of adversity on externalizing symptoms was stronger, whereas by late adolescence (between tenth and twelfth grades) the strength of the effect reversed, with levels of externalizing symptoms having a stronger effect on future adversity exposure.

Specificity and the Unique Contribution of Different Risk and Adversity Factors

Cumulative risk and adversity exposure indices, despite their longitudinal predictive power, can obscure more complex processes that occur between individual risk factors and development. The unique contribution of individual risk factors may emerge after controlling for the contribution of other conceptually related, but distinct risk factors. For example, using structural equation modeling, Keiley and colleagues examined the specificity of ten risk factors in predicting mother and teacher reports of pure externalizing, pure internalizing, and covarying externalizing-internalizing symptoms

(Keiley, Lofthouse, Bates, Dodge, & Pettit, 2003). Although each risk factor individually predicted symptoms, the specific contribution of different risk factors changed when all ten risk factors were included in the model. Across both informants, different sets of risk factors emerged as unique predictors of elevated internalizing behaviors, elevated externalizing behaviors and covarying symptoms. In addition, some risk factors emerged as unique predictors of only mother or teacher report of behavior problems. Similarly, Aikens and Barbarin (2008) sought to examine the relative contribution of family, socioeconomic, school, and neighborhood risk variables on the development of children's reading abilities over the first 4 years of school. While family and SES variables were most strongly predictive of reading abilities at the start of elementary school, the rates of reading achievement were best predicted by school and neighborhood variables rather than family and SES. Understanding the specificity of risk factors for different aspects of adaptive functioning and across different contexts (i.e., family and school) can promote more targeted intervention program designs.

Examining the unique contribution of individual risk and adversity variables can also reveal some surprising effects. Namely, the effect of traditional risk factors may change in the context of other sources of risk, and the outcomes of risk factors may be mediated or moderated by other contextual factors (Masten & Shaffer, 2006). For example, although the association between family income and children's adaptive functioning is well established (Brooks-Gunn & Duncan, 1997; Luthar, 1999; McLoyd, 1998), less is known about the specific underlying mechanisms linking the two. Recent studies posit that the effect of family income on children's development is indirect, mediated through processes that escalate parental level of stress, undermine the quality of parenting, or limit parental investment of resources in children (Guo & Harris, 2000; Linver, Brooks-Gunn, & Kohen, 2002; Mistry, Vandewater, Huston, & McLoyd, 2002). However, a recent study showed that the negative relation between family income and parental stress became positive when indicators of concurrent material hardship were included in the model (Gershoff, Aber, Raver, & Lennon, 2007). Follow-up analyses revealed that this initially counterintuitive finding was driven by families whose incomes fell right above the poverty threshold, which disqualified them from various government subsidies. Further, this study revealed interesting compensatory processes, in that high parental stress was linked to high parental investment once the effect of material hardship was considered. Even though material hardship was related to higher parental stress and lower parental investment, it was related to more positive parenting behaviors.

Although more complex developmental processes can emerge when different aspects of well-established risk factors are separately examined, researchers must be mindful of methodological issues surrounding such analyses. Kraemer and colleagues (2001) provide an important set of guidelines for testing the joint effects of multiple risk factors. Specifically, they suggest five possible analytic scenarios where (1) two risk factors operate independently, (2) one risk factor is a proxy for the other, (3) two risk factors have an overlapping effect, (4) one risk factors mediates the effect of the other, or (5) one risk factor moderates the effect of the other.

Interaction Effects between Different Sources of Risk and Adversity

Cumulative risk and adversity indices have also been employed in conjunction with single adversity or risk variables. Some researchers have tested whether the effects of cumulative risk indices vary as a function of single contextual risk factor. For example, Evans and colleagues (2007) considered the role of a single variable, maternal responsiveness, as a potential protective factor in moderating the effect of cumulative risk on physiological indicators of chronic stress and reported that the influence of cumulative risk is only significant in the

context of low maternal responsiveness. Other researchers have examined interaction effects between single indicators of environmental risk and adversity. In a study of inner-city boys, the history of childhood maltreatment predicted persistent serious juvenile delinquency over and above significant family risk factors (Stouthamer-Loeber, Wei, Homish, & Loeber, 2002). Follow-up analyses revealed significant interaction between maltreatment history and living with a single biological parent. Maltreated boys who also lived with a single biological parent were more likely to become persistent serious delinquents (51 percent) than those still living with both biological parents (22 percent).

Furthermore, the effects of specific risks and types of adversity may differ across various contexts and populations. The inclusion and examination of cultural differences in risk and adversity is a prominent area for consideration. For example, authoritarian parenting, which is high in strictness and parental control, has traditionally been viewed as a risk factor for children based on research conducted in primarily European American samples. However, this association has been challenged in research with other ethnic groups. Authoritarian parenting among Chinese families, for example, is consistent with cultural values regarding "training" and parental expectations, and higher levels of authoritarian parenting have been associated with improved academic achievement (Chao, 1994). Cultural norms have also been shown to moderate the association between physical punishment and child adjustment (Lansford et al., 2005). In the era of increased international immigration, it will be important to re-examine whether traditional risk and adversity factors operate in similar fashion among native populations and various generations of immigrants.

In addition to the interplay of different environmental factors, researchers have demonstrated that are behavioral, physiological, and genetic factors that make some children more susceptible to environmental effects than others (Obradović & Boyce, 2009). Infants and children who are prone to high levels of negative emotionality have been found to be at higher risk for developing behavioral problems than their temperamentally less reactive peers when both groups are exposed to maternal insensitivity, harsh parenting, and low-quality day care (Belsky, 2005; Morris et al., 2002; Pauli-Pott, Mertesacker, & Beckman, 2004). Similarly, children who show high autonomic or neuroendocrine reactivity to laboratory stressors have been found to be more susceptible to environmental effects; in comparison to less reactive children, they show higher levels of behavioral, cognitive, and health problems in the context of high family adversity (Boyce et al., 1995; Cummings, El-Sheikh, Kouros, & Keller, 2007; Obradović, Bush, Stamperdahl, Adler, & Boyce, 2010). Finally, recent methodological advances have enabled researchers to identify various genetic polymorphisms that render some children more genetically vulnerable to environmental risk and adversity. In landmark studies, Caspi and colleagues showed that allelic variation in the MAOA gene moderated the effect of childhood maltreatment on the development of later antisocial behavior (Caspi et al., 2002); whereas allelic variations in the 5-HTT gene moderated the effects of life stress on the development of depressive symptoms (Caspi et al., 2003). Work by Caspi and colleagues has been extended by a growing number of studies examining gene by environment interactions in children (cf. Cicchetti, Rogosch, & Sturge-Apple, 2007; Kaufman et al., 2004). For example, Brody and colleagues have found that an increased risk for substance abuse in adolescents among individuals with the short-allele serotonin transporter gene polymorphism was moderated by the presence of warm and supportive parenting practices (Brody et al., 2009). In addition, these studies have been informed and corroborated using experimental work with nonhuman primates. In a series of experiments with rhesus macaques, Suomi and colleagues have shown how different rearing environments can interact with genotypes to yield different behavioral outcomes (Champoux et al., 2002). For example, rhesus macaques with a short allele of the 5-HTTLPR gene were especially vulnerable to increased alcohol consumption when raised in more stressful peer-only rearing conditions, as compared to macaques raised by mothers (Barr et al., 2004).

Although genetically, physiologically, and behaviorally reactive children seem to be more vulnerable to deleterious effects of risk and adversity in their environments, several researchers have emphasized that these children may also be more susceptible to positive contextual influences (Belsky, Bakermans-Kranenburg, & Van IJzendoorn, 2007; Boyce & Ellis, 2005). For example, high negative emotionality has also been linked to better adjustment in the context of high quality care (Pluess & Belsky, 2009) and to greater behavioral and cognitive improvements in response to interventions (Klein Velderman, Bakermans-Kranenburg, Juffer, & van IJzendoorn, 2006). Likewise, in the context of low adversity, physiologically reactive children have been shown to have better adjustment than their less reactive peers (Ellis, Essex, & Boyce, 2005; Obradović et al., 2010). Finally, a genetic polymorphism (i.e., 7-repeat allele of DRD4), associated with higher externalizing symptoms in the context of early adversity, has also been linked to the largest decreases in externalizing symptoms in response to parenting intervention (Bakermans-Kranenburg, Van IJzendoorn, Pijlman, Mesman, & Juffer, 2008). Together these studies emphasize the importance of examining how multiple sources of risk and adversity interact across different levels of analysis in shaping the course of development.

The integration of fields such as behavior genetics and molecular genetics with the field of developmental psychopathology has yielded intriguing new findings, but also some misunderstandings. Rutter (2000) cautions against the misinterpretation of much behavior genetics research as "proving" that the cause of a particular characteristic or outcome is genetically based and thus impervious to psychosocial influences. Strong evidence of a genetic component does not mean that psychosocial processes are unimportant or epiphenomenal. For example, a risk factor such as low maternal IQ is obviously transmitted, to some degree, via direct genetic heritability to offspring. However, as Burchinal, Roberts, Hopper, and Zeisel (2000) observed, psychosocial processes also produce indirect effects of low maternal IQ on child development, via influences on caregiving or other environmental variables, as mothers with lower intelligence may not be able to obtain better paying jobs or manage the tasks of parenting as efficiently.

Moreover, the identification of candidate genes and specific gene by environment interactions as risk factors is a project still in its infancy, and recent metaanalyses provide cautionary messages about the need to replicate early and intriguing findings (Risch et al. 2009). However, exciting new frontiers are being opened by researchers who are starting to examine the processes by which social environments get under the skin to affect gene expression (Champagne & Mashoodh, 2009; Cole, 2009; Kim-Cohen & Gold, 2009). Emerging fields such as *social genomics*, which focuses on identifying socially regulated genes (Cole, 2009), have potential to transform our current understanding of processes moderating and mediating the effects of environmental risk and adversity on children's development.

Ethical Issues

Across the decades, a number of ethical issues have confronted researchers who study risk (Eddy, Smith, Brown, & Reid, 2005; Trickett, 1992). These issues are particularly salient in efforts to identify high-risk children for any purpose in which the status of the child might become known to parents, teachers, or the child himself or herself. Preventive interventions often involve the identification of risk groups, particularly in studies where there is screening for risk for an "indicated" intervention trial or when other judgments are made regarding the need of a particular group for services (Trickett, 1992). The concern is often focused on labeling effects, which might be described as the influence of "known risk" status, which could affect expectations, self-esteem, classroom

placement decisions, and many other aspects of human behavior. Hence the literature on "self-fulfilling prophecies" in education and concern among Institutional Review Boards (IRBs) approving human research protocols involving identification of risk groups. The ethical controversies related to risk identification are resurfacing with renewed vigor in the wake of the current surge of research involving the identification of specific genes as risk or vulnerability factors. To this end, it is important to reiterate that the concept of risk is often misunderstood when individuals are identified as members of a risk group. Risk is a population concept and cannot properly be applied to an individual. The higher probability of problems related to any risk factor or set of risk factors refers to elevated risk at the group level, although such probabilistic concepts are not easily translated for the general public.

The ethical issues involved in identifying "at-risk" groups are amplified in the use of randomized controlled trials (RCTs) to test the effectiveness of interventions that attempt to modify risk factors. The Moving to Opportunity for Fair Housing project undertaken by the Department of Housing and Urban Development is a striking example of how an RCT designed to modify neighborhood risk status can change children's developmental trajectories (Leventhal & Brooks-Gunn, 2004). In this study, families living in high-poverty, urban public housing were randomly assigned to one of three groups: a group that received assistance to move into private housing in low-poverty neighborhoods, a group that received assistance to move into private housing in neighborhoods of their choice, and a group that remained in public housing. As hypothesized by Leventhal and Brooks-Gunn (2004), household moves from high-poverty to low-poverty neighborhoods were associated with improved educational outcomes, particularly for adolescent males. However, randomized studies such as these require the equivalent of no-treatment control groups, raising ethical issues about the acceptability of assigning some families to stay in high-risk environments. Such dilemmas are long-standing in the clinical intervention literature, but it is important to be reminded of them as definitions of "interventions" expand to include the modification of contextual and biological risk factors. Furthermore, as more recent data from the Moving to Opportunity project have shown, it is important to consider the context of developmental risk. Altering only one risk factor, such as neighborhood poverty, may provide short-term effects that can diminish over time (Sanbonmatsu, Kling, Duncan, & Brooks-Gunn, 2006).

Another ethical dilemma in risk research on children is posed by the possibility of iatrogenic effects. One of the most important findings over decades of research on antisocial behavior in children is the possibility that well-intended programs that aggregate children at risk may actually worsen their behavior because of contagion effects or deviancy training by other children (Dishion, McCord, & Poulin, 1999). The possibility of iatrogenic effects is now routinely considered in weighing the risks and benefits of interventions, although probably with greater attention in research reviewed by IRBs than in practice or education.

Conclusion

There is clear progress in the study of risk in development, particularly in the methodology for studying risk and the processes that may account for risk effects at multiple levels of analysis. Nonetheless, many of the issues identified decades ago continue to confront investigators today as they attempt to understand the influences of psychosocial risk in development. Dramatic advances in measurement in molecular genetics and neuroscience have opened new opportunities for refining the study of risk; at the same time, these advances point to a need for better measures of individual differences in behavior, relationships, and contexts.

A large body of literature has accumulated on conditions of risk in childhood, including studies of maltreatment, neglect, war, disaster, immigration, poverty, homelessness, foster care, and many other adversities. This handbook itself affords evidence of the burgeoning literature on an ever-growing array of risks and hazards of childhood and the increasing sophistication of methods for this research. Similarly, a growing body of findings on resilience in children also speaks to the increasing knowledge about the processes that may prevent, mediate, or moderate risk effects (Lester, Masten, & McEwen, 2006; Luthar, 2006). Although some common risk and adversity factors emerge across different disadvantaged contexts and populations, each study of developmental risk and adversity should carefully identify relevant multilevel processes that may undermine adaptation, while considering issues such as developmental stage, cultural context, and other sources of interindividual variability in the specific sample being studied. Understanding adaptive systems implicated in the successful development of a particular population should be the first step in identifying risk and adversity factors that may compromise adaptation (Masten & Obradović, 2006).

At this juncture, there remain several promising areas for future research that can advance our current understanding of how risk operates in development. As discussed earlier, the conceptual work of defining risk factors still requires attention and increased clarity regarding the differences between risks and assets, and between markers of risk and experiences of adversity. In terms of methodology, researchers are encouraged to take advantage of newer statistical techniques that permit the study of dynamic processes of change in both risks and outcomes of interest, and to avail themselves of psychobiological or genetic data in order to incorporate multiple levels of analysis into the study of risk and adaptation. Moving away from the traditional conceptualization of risk and adversity factors may reveal more complex, curvilinear, context-dependent relations between individual, family, and societal characteristics. Finally, translational research is still needed to test theories about risk processes and how to prevent or reduce their effects, as well as to move empirical findings on risk processes into practice. Randomized clinical trials, as described earlier, offer compelling experimental tests of risk and protective processes.

There is a full agenda for future research on risk in development, but also a strong rationale for tackling this agenda. Practices or policies to prevent or ameliorate risk, or to promote positive development among high-risk children, require more delineated theories about risk processes, as well as the best ways to change the odds for development in more favorable directions (Masten & Gewirtz, 2006). In turn, experiments will test whether theory-driven interventions work, and will generate further theories about *how* they work, thus serving to advance the science on risk and resilience in child development.

Acknowledgments

Preparation of this chapter was supported in part by a National Institute of Mental Health (NIMH) predoctoral training grant (NRSA), a Killam Postdoctoral Research Fellowship from the University of British Columbia (UBC), and a research fellowship from the Canadian Institute for Advanced Research (CIFAR) to Jelena Obradović, and a grant from the National Science Foundation (NSF No. 0745643) to Ann S. Masten.

References

Adam, E. (2006). Transactions among adolescent trait and state emotion and diurnal and momentary cortisol activity in naturalistic settings. *Psychoneuroendocrinology, 31,* 664–679.

Adam, E. K., Hawkley, L. C., Kudielka, B. M., & Cacioppo, J. T. (2006). Day-to-day dynamics of experience–cortisol associations in a population-based sample of older adults. *Proceedings of the National Academy of Sciences, 103,* 17058–17063.

Adler, N. E., Epel, E. S., Castellazo, G., & Ickovics, J. R. (2000). Relationship of subjective and objective social status with psychological and physiological functioning: Preliminary data in healthy white women. *Health Psychology, 19,* 586–592.

Aikens, N. L., & Barbarin, O. (2008). Socioeconomic differences in reading trajectories: the contribution of family, neighborhood, and school contexts. *Journal of Educational Psychology, 100,* 235–251.

American Psychiatric Association (1987). *Diagnostic and statistical manual of mental disorders* (3rd ed., revised). Washington, DC: American Psychiatric Association.

Anthony, E. J., & Koupernick, C. (Eds.) (1974). *The child in his family: Children at psychiatric risk.* New York: Wiley.

Appleyard, K., Egeland, B., van Dulmen, M. H. M., & Sroufe, L. A. (2005). When more is not better: the role of cumulative risk in child behavior outcomes. *Journal of Child Psychology and Psychiatry, 46,* 235–245.

Bakermans-Kranenburg, M. J., Van IJzendoorn, M. H., Pijlman, F. T., Mesman, J., & Juffer, F. (2008). Experimental evidence for differential susceptibility: Dopamine D4 receptor polymorphism (DRD4 VNTR) moderates intervention effects on toddlers' externalizing behavior in a randomized controlled trial, *Developmental Psychology, 44,* 293–300.

Barr, C. S., Newman, T. K., Lindell, S., Shannon, C., Champoux, M., Lesch, K. P., Suomi, S. J., Goldman, D., & Higley, J. D. (2004). Interaction between serotonin transporter gene variation and rearing condition in alcohol preference and consumption in female primates. *Archives of General Psychiatry, 61,* 1146–1152.

Belsky, J. (2005). Differential susceptibility to rearing influence: An evolutionary hypothesis and some evidence. In B. Ellis & D. Bjorklund (Eds.), *Origins of the social mind: Evolutionary psychology and child development,* pp. 139–163. New York: Guilford.

Belsky, J., Bakermans-Kranenburg, M. J., & Van IJzendoorn, M. H. (2007). For better and for worse: Differential susceptibility to environmental influences. *Current Directions in Psychological Science, 16,* 300–304.

Biederman, J., Milberger, S., Faraone, S. V., Kiely, K., Guite, J., Mick, E., Ablon, S., Warburton, R., & Reed, E. (1995). Family-environment risk factors for attention-deficit hyperactivity disorder: A test of Rutter's indicators of adversity. *Archives of General Psychiatry, 52,* 464–470.

Boyce, W. T., Chesney, M., Alkon, A., Tschann, J. M., Adams, S., Chesterman, B., Cohen, F., Kaiser, P., Folkman, S., & Wara, D. (1995). Psychobiologic reactivity to stress and childhood respiratory illnesses: Results of two prospective studies. *Psychosomatic Medicine, 57,* 411–422.

Boyce, W. T., & Ellis, B. J. (2005). Biological sensitivity to context: An evolutionary-developmental theory of the origins and functions of stress reactivity. *Development and Psychopathology, 17,* 271–301.

Brody, G. H., Beach, S. R. H., Philibert, R. A., Chen, Y., Lei, M., Murry, V. M., & Brown, A. C. (2009). Parenting moderates a genetic vulnerability factor in longitudinal increases in youths' substance use. *Journal of Consulting and Clinical Psychology, 77,* 1–11.

Bronfenbrenner, U. (1994). Ecological models of human development. In T. Husten & T. N. Postlethwaite (Eds.), *International encyclopedia of education,* Vol. 3, pp. 1643–1647 (2nd ed.). New York: Elsevier Science.

Brooks-Gunn, J., & Duncan, G. J. (1997). The effects of poverty on children. *The Future of Children, 7,* 55–71.

Brown, G. W., & Harris, T. (1978). *Social origins of depression: A study of psychiatric disorder in women.* New York: Free Press.

Brugha, T., Bebbington, B., Tennant, C., & Hurry, J. (1985). The list of threatening experiences: A subset of 12 life event categories with considerable long-term contextual threat. *Psychological Medicine, 15,* 189–194.

Burchinal, M., Roberts, J. E., Hooper, S., & Zeisel, S. A. (2000). Cumulative risk and early cognitive development: a comparison of statistical risk models. *Developmental Psychology, 36,* 793–807.

Burchinal, M., Roberts, J. E., Zeisel, S. A., Hennon, E. A., & Hooper, S. (2006). Social risk and protective child, parenting, and child care factors in early elementary school years. *Parenting: Science and Practice, 6,* 79–113.

Caspi, A., McClay, J., Moffitt, T. E., Mill, J., Martin, J., Craig, I. W., Taylor, A., & Poulton, R. (2002). Role of genotype in the cycle of violence in maltreated children. *Science, 297,* 851–854.

Caspi, A., Sugden, K., Moffitt, T. E., Taylor, A., Craig, I. W., Harrington, H., McClay, J., Mill, J., Martin, J., Braithwaite, A., & Poulton, R. (2003). Influence of life stress on depression: moderation by a polymorphism in the 5-HTT gene. *Science, 301*(5631), 386–389.

Champagne, F. A., & Mashoodh, R. (2009). Genes in context: Gene-environment interplay and the origins of individual differences in behavior. *Current Directions in Psychological Science, 18,* 127–131.

Champoux, M., Bennett, A., Shannon, C., Higley, J. D., Lesch, K. P., & Suomi, S. J. (2002). Serotonin transporter gene polymorphism, differential early rearing, and behavior in rhesus monkey neonates. *Molecular Psychiatry, 7,* 1058–1063.

Chao, R. K. (1994). Beyond parental control and authoritarian parenting style: understanding Chinese parenting through the cultural notion of training. *Child Development, 65,* 1111–1119.

Chapman, D. P., Whitfield, C. L., Felitti, V. J., Dube, S. R., Edwards, V. J., & Anda, R. F. (2004). Adverse childhood experiences and the risk of depressive disorders in adulthood. *Journal of Affective Disorders, 82,* 217–225.

Cicchetti, D. (1996). Child maltreatment: implications for developmental theory and research. *Human Development, 39,* 18–39.

Cicchetti, D. (2006). Development and psychopathology. In D. Cicchetti & D. Cohen (Eds.), *Developmental Psychopathology:* Vol. 1. *Theory and method,* pp. 1–23 (2nd ed.). Hoboken NJ: Wiley.

Cicchetti, D., Rogosch, F. A., & Sturge-Apple, M. L. (2007). Interactions of child maltreatment and serotonin transporter and monoamine oxidase A polymorphisms: Depressive symptomatology among adolescents from low socioeconomic status backgrounds. *Development and Psychopathology, 19,* 1161–1180.

Coddington, R. D. (1972a). The significance of life events as etiologic factors in the diseases of children: I. A survey of professional workers. *Journal of Psychosomatic Research, 16,* 7–18.

Coddington, R. D. (1972b). The significance of life events as etiologic factors in the diseases of children. II. A study of a normal population. *Journal of Psychosomatic Research, 16,* 205–213.

Coie, J. D., Watt, N. F., West, S., Hawkins, J. D., Asarnow, J. R., Markman, H. J., Ramey, S. L., Shure, M. B., & Long, B. (1993). The science of prevention. *American Psychologist, 48,* 1013–1022.

Cole, S. W. (2009). Social regulation of human gene expression. *Current Directions in Psychological Science, 18,* 132–137.

Csikszentmihalyi, M., & Larson, R. (1987). Validity and reliability of the experience sampling method. *Journal of Nervous and Mental Disease, 175,* 526–537.

Cummings, M. E., El-Sheikh, M., Kouros, C. D., & Keller, P. S. (2007). Children's skin conductance reactivity as a mechanism of risk in the context of parental depressive symptoms. *Journal of Child Psychology and Psychiatry, 48,* 436–445.

Deater-Deckard, K., Dodge, K. A., Bates, J. E., & Pettit, G. S. (1998). Multiple risk factors in the development of externalizing behavior problems: group and individual differences. *Development and Psychopathology, 10,* 469–493.

Dishion, T. J., McCord, J., & Poulin, F. (1999). When interventions harm: peer groups and problem behavior. *American Psychologist, 54,* 755–764.

Dong, M., Anda, R. F., Felitti, V. J., Dube, S. R., Wiliiamson, D. F., Thompson, T. J., Loo, C. M., Giles, W. H. (2004). The interrelatedness of multiple forms of childhood abuse, neglect, and household dysfunction. *Child Abuse & Neglect, 28,* 771–784.

Dube, S. R., Miller, J. W., Brown, D. W., Giles, W. H., Felitti, V. J., Dong, M., & Anda, R. F. (2006). Adverse childhood experiences and the association with ever using alcohol and initiating alcohol use during adolescence. *Journal of Adolescent Health, 38,* 444.e1–444.e10.

Eddy, J., Smith, P., Brown, C., & Reid, J. (2005). A survey of prevention science training: Implications for educating the next generation. *Prevention Science, 6,* 59–71.

Egeland, B. (1997). Mediators of the effects of child maltreatment on developmental adaptation in adolescence. In D. Cicchetti & S. L. Toth (Eds.), *Developmental perspectives on trauma: Theory, research, and intervention,* pp. 403–434. Rochester, NY: University of Rochester Press.

Ellis, B. J., Essex, M. J., & Boyce, W. T. (2005). Biological sensitivity to context: II. Empirical explorations of an evolutionary-developmental theory. *Development and Psychopathology, 17,* 303–328.

Essex, M. J., Klein, M. H., Cho, E., & Kalin, N. H. (2002). Maternal stress beginning in infancy may sensitize children to later stress exposure: Effects on cortisol and behavior. *Biological Psychiatry, 52,* 776–784.

Evans, G. W. (2003). A multimethodological analysis of cumulative risk and allostatic load among rural children. *Developmental Psychology, 39,* 924–933.

Evans, G. W., Kim, P., Ting, A. H., Tesher, H. B., & Shannis, D. (2007). Cumulative risk, maternal responsiveness, and allostatic load among young adolescents. *Developmental Psychology, 43,* 341–351.

Forehand, R., Biggar, H., & Kotchick, B. A. (1998). Cumulative risk across family stressors: short- and long-term effects for adolescents. *Journal of Abnormal Child Psychology, 26,* 119–128.

Furstenberg, F. F., Cook, T., Eccles, J., Elder, G. H., & Sameroff, A. J. (1999). *Managing to make it: Urban families and adolescent success.* Chicago: University of Chicago Press.

Garmezy, N. (1974). Children at risk: The search for the antecedents to schizophrenia: Part II. Ongoing research programs, issues and intervention. *Schizophrenia Bulletin, 9,* 55–125.

Garmezy, N., & Rutter. M. (Eds.) (1983). *Stress, coping and development in children.* New York: McGraw-Hill.

Ge, X., Lorenz, F. O., Conger, R. D., Elder, G. H., & Simons, R. L. (1995). Trajectories of stressful life events and depressive symptoms during adolescence. *Developmental Psychology, 30,* 467–483.

Ge, X., Natsuki, M. N., & Conger, R. D. (2006). Trajectories of depressive symptoms and stressful life events among male and female adolescents in divorced and nondivorced families. *Development and Psychopathology, 18,* 253–273.

Gerard, J. M., & Buehler, C. (2004). Cumulative environmental risk and youth maladjustment: the role of youth attributes. *Child Development, 75,* 1832–1849.

Gershoff, E. T., Aber, J. L., Raver, C. C., & Lennon, M. C. (2007). Income is not enough: Incorporating material hardship into models of income associations with parenting and child development. *Child Development, 78,* 70–95.

Gest, S. D., Reed, M., & Masten, A. S. (1999). Measuring developmental changes in exposure to adversity: A life chart and rating scale approach. *Development and Psychopathology, 11,* 171–192.

Gottesman, I. I. (1974). Developmental genetics and ontogenetic psychology: Overdue détente and propositions from a matchmaker. In A. D. Pick (Ed.), *Minnesota symposium on child psychology,* Vol. 8, pp. 55–80. Minneapolis: University of Minnesota Press.

Gottesman, I. I., Shields, J., & Hanson, D. (1982). *Schizophrenia: The epigenetic puzzle.* Cambridge: Cambridge University Press.

Greenberg, M. T., Speltz, M. L., DeKlyen, M., & Jones, K. (2001). Correlates of clinic referral for early conduct problems: Variable- and person-oriented approaches. *Development and Psychopathology, 13,* 255–276.

Guo, G., & Harris, K. M. (2000). The mechanisms mediating the effects of poverty on children's intellectual development. *Demography, 37,* 431–447.

Hanson, D. R., & Gottesman, I. I. (2007). Choreographing genetic, epigentic, and stochastic steps in the dances of developmental psychopathology. In A. S. Masten (Ed.), *Multilevel dynamics in developmental psychopathology: Pathways to the future*, pp. 27–43. Mahwah, NJ: Erlbaum.

Holmes, T. H., & Rahe, R. H. (1967). The social readjustment rating scale. *Journal of Psychosomatic Research*, 11, 213–218.

Jessor, R., van den Bos, J., Vanderrym, J., Costa, F. M., & Turbin, M. S. (1995). Protective factors in adolescent problem behavior: Moderator effects and developmental change. *Developmental Psychology*, 31, 923–933.

Johnson, J. H. (1986). *Life events as stressors in childhood and adolescence*. Newbury Park, CA: Sage.

Kaufman, J. et al. (2004). Social supports and serotonin transporter gene moderate depression in maltreated children. *Proceedings of the National Academy of Sciences, USA*, 101, 17316–17421.

Keating, D. P., & Hertzman, C. (Eds.) (1999). *Developmental health and the wealth of nations: Social, biological and educational dynamics*. New York: Guilford.

Keiley, M. K., Lofthouse, N., Bates, J. E., Dodge, K. A., & Pettit, G. S. (2003). Differential risks of covarying and pure components in mother and teacher reports of externalizing and internalizing behavior across age 5 to 14. *Journal of Abnormal Child Psychology*, 31, 267–283.

Kim, K. J., Conger, R. D., Elder, G. H., & Lorenz, F. O. (2003). Reciprocal influences between stressful life events and internalizing and externalizing problems. *Child Development*, 74, 127–143.

Kim-Cohen, J., & Gold, A. L. (2009). Measured gene-environment interactions and mechanisms promoting resilient development. *Current Directions in Psychological Science*, 18, 139–142.

Klein Velderman, M., Bakermans-Kranenburg, M. J., Juffer, F., & van IJzendoorn, M. H. (2006). Effects of attachment-based interventions on maternal sensitivity and infant attachment: Differential susceptibility of highly reactive infants. *Journal of Family Psychology*, 20, 266–274.

Kraemer, H. C., Kazdin, A. E., Offord, D., Kessler, R. C., Jensen, P. S., & Kupfer, D. (1997). Coming to terms with the terms of risk. *Archives of General Psychiatry*, 54, 337–343.

Kraemer, H. C., Stice, E., Kazdin, A., Offord, D., & Kupfer, D. (2001). How do risk factors work together? Mediators, moderators, and independent, overlapping, and proxy risk factors. *American Journal of Psychiatry*, 158, 848–856.

Kraemer, H. C., Wilson, T., Fairburn, C. G., & Agras, W. S. (2002). Mediators and moderators of treatment effects in randomized clinical trials. *Archives of General Psychiatry*, 59, 877–883.

Lansford, J. E., Chang, L., Dodge, K. A., Malone, P. S., Oburu, P., Palmérus, K., Bacchini, D., Pastorelli, C., Bombi, A. S., Zelli, A., Tapanya, S., Chaudary, N., Deater-Deckard, K., Manke, B., & Quinn, N. (2005). Physical discipline and children's adjustment: cultural normativeness as a moderator. *Child Development*, 76, 1234–1246.

Lemery-Chalfant, K., Schreiber, J. E., Schmidt, N. L., Van Hulle, C. A., Essex, M. J., & Goldsmith, H. H. (2007). Assessing internalizing, externalizing, and attention problems in young children: Validation of the MacArthur HBQ. *Journal of the American Academy of Child and Adolescent Psychiatry*, 46, 1315–1323.

Lester, B., Masten, A. S., & McEwen, B. (Eds.) (2006). *Resilience in children*. New York Academy of Sciences, Vol. 1094. See http://www.nyas.org/Publications/Annals/Detail.aspx?cid=e0cba583-afcc-447f-94df-6c233a023204

Leventhal, T., & Brooks-Gunn, J. (2004). A randomized study of neighborhood effects on low-income children's educational outcomes. *Developmental Psychology*, 40, 488–507.

Linver, M. R., Brooks-Gunn, J., & Kohen, D. E. (2002). Family processes as pathways from income to young children's development. *Developmental Psychology*, 38, 719–734.

Luthar, S. S. (1999). *Poverty and children's adjustment*. Thousand Oaks, CA: Sage.

Luthar, S. S. (2006). Resilience in development: A synthesis of research across five decades. In D. Cicchetti & D. J. Cohen (Eds.), *Developmental psychopathology*: Vol. 3. *Risk, disorder, and adaptation*, pp. 739–795 (2nd ed.). New York: Wiley.

Masten, A. S. (2001). Ordinary magic: Resilience processes in development. *American Psychologist*, 56(3), 227–238.

Masten, A. S. (2004). Regulatory processes, risk and resilience in adolescent development. *Annals of the New York Academy of Sciences*, 1021, 310–319.

Masten, A. S. (2006). Developmental psychopathology: Pathways to the future. *International Journal of Behavioral Development*, 31, 46–53.

Masten, A. S., Best, K. M., & Garmezy, N. (1990). Resilience and development: Contributions from the study of children who overcome adversity. *Development and Psychopathology*, 2, 425–444.

Masten, A. S., Cutuli, J. J., Herbers, J. E., & Gabrielle-Reed, M. J. (2009). Resilience in development. In C. R. Snyder, & S. J. Lopez (Eds.), *The handbook of positive psychology*, pp. 117–131 (2nd ed.). New York: Oxford University Press.

Masten, A. S., & Gewirtz, A. (2006). Vulnerability and resilience in early child development. In K. McCartney & D. Phillips (Eds.), *Handbook of early childhood development*, pp. 22–43. Malden, MA: Blackwell.

Masten, A. S., Neemann, J., & Andenas, S. (1994). Life events and adjustment in adolescents: The significance of event independence, desirability, and chronicity. *Journal of Research on Adolescence*, 4, 71–97.

Masten, A. S., & Obradović, J. (2006). Competence and resilience in development. *Annals of the New York Academy of Sciences*, 1094, 13–27.

Masten, A. S., & Shaffer, A. (2006). How families matter in child development: reflections from research on risk and resilience. In A. Clarke-Stewart & J. Dunn (Eds.), *Families count: Effects on child and adolescent development*, pp. 5–25. Cambridge: Cambridge University Press.

Masten, A. S., & Wright, M. O. (1998). Cumulative risk and protection models of child maltreatment. *Journal of Aggression, Maltreatment, and Trauma*, 2, 7–30.

McEwen, B. S., & Wingfield, J. (2003). The concept of allostasis in biology and biomedicine. *Hormones and Behavior*, 43, 2–15.

McLoyd, V. C. (1998). Socioeconomic disadvantage and child development. *American Psychologist*, 53, 185–204.

Mistry, R. S., Vandewater, E. A., Huston, A. C., & McLoyd V. C. (2002). Economic well-being and children's social adjustment: the role of family process in an ethnically diverse low-income sample. *Child Development*, 73, 935–951.

Morris, A. S., Silk, J. S., Steinberg, L., Sessa, F. M., Avenevoli, S., & Essex, M. J. (2002). Temperamental vulnerability and negative parenting as interacting predictors of child adjustment. *Journal of Marriage and Family*, 64, 461–471.

Nelson, C. A., Zeanah, C. H., & Fox, N. A. (2007). The effects of early deprivation on brain-behavioral development: The Bucharest Early Intervention Project. In D. Romer & E. F. Walker (Eds.), *Adolescent psychopathology and the developing brain: integrating brain and prevention science*, pp. 197–215. New York: Oxford University Press.

Obradović, J., & Boyce, W. T. (2009). Individual differences in behavioral, physiological, and genetic sensitivities to contexts: Implications for development and adaptation. *Developmental Neuroscience*, 300–308.

Obradović, J., Bush, N. R., Stamperdahl, J., Adler, N. A., & Boyce, W. T. (2010). Biological sensitivity to context: The interactive effects of stress reactivity and family adversity on socioemotional behavior and school readiness. *Child Development*, 81, 270–289.

Obradović, J., & Hipwell, A. (2010). Psychopathology and social competence during transition to adolescence: The role of family adversity and pubertal development. *Development and Psychopathology*, 22, 621–634.

Obradović, J., Masten, A. S., & Shaffer, A. (April 2005). *Sorting out the significance of risks, adversity, and resources in childhood for success in adulthood*. Paper presented at the Society for Research in Child Development, Atlanta, GA.

O'Connor, T. G. (2006). The persisting effects of early experiences on psychological development. In D. Cicchetti & D. J. Cohen (Eds.), *Developmental psychopathology: Vol. 3. Risk, disorder, and adaptation*, pp. 202–234 (2nd ed.). Hoboken, NJ: Wiley.

O'Dougherty, M., & Wright, F. S. (1990). Children born at medical risk: Factors affecting vulnerability and resilience. In J. Rolf, A. S. Masten, D. Cicchetti, K. H. Nuechterlein & S. Weintraub (Eds.), *Risk and protective factors in the development of psychopathology*, pp. 120–140. New York: Cambridge University Press.

Pauli-Pott, U., Mertesacker, B., & Beckman, D. (2004). Predicting the development of infant emotionality from maternal characteristics. *Development and Psychopathology*, 16, 19–42.

Pluess, M., & Belsky, J. (2009). Differential susceptibility to rearing experience: The case of childcare. *Journal of Child Psychology and Psychiatry*, 50, 396–404.

Risch, N., Herrell, R., Lehner, T., Liany, K.-Y., Eaves, L., Hoh, J., Griem, A., Kovacs, M., Ott, J., & Merikangas, K. R. (2009). Interaction between the serotonin transporter gene (5-HTTLPR), stressful life events, and risk of depression: A meta-analysis. *Journal of the American Medical Association*, 301, 2462–2471.

Runyan, D. K. et al. (1998). Children who prosper in unfavorable environments: the relationship to social capital. *Pediatrics, 101*, 12–18.

Rutter, M. (1979). Protective factors in children's responses to stress and disadvantage. In M. W. Kent & J. E. Rolf (Eds.), *Primary prevention of psychopathology:* Vol. 3. *Social competence in children*, pp. 49–74. Hanover, NH: University Press of New England.

Rutter, M. (1990). Psychosocial resilience and protective mechanisms. In J. Rolf, A. S. Masten, D. Cicchetti, K. H. Nuechterlein & S. Weintraub (Eds.), *Risk and protective factors in the development of psychopathology*, pp. 181–214. New York: Cambridge University Press.

Rutter, M. (2000). Psychosocial influences: Critiques, findings, and research needs. *Development and Psychopathology, 12*, 375–405.

Rutter, M. (2006). How does the concept of resilience alter the study and understanding of risk and protective influences on psychopathology? *Annals of the New York Academy of Sciences, 1094*, 1–12.

Sameroff, A. (2006). Identifying risk and protective factors for healthy child development. In A. Clark-Stewart & J. Dunn (Eds.), *Families count: Effects on child and adolescent development*, pp. 53–76. Cambridge: Cambridge University Press.

Sameroff, A. J., & Chandler, M. J. (1975). Reproductive risk and the continuum of caretaking casualty. In F. D. Horowitz, M. Hetherington, S. Scarr-Salapatek, & G. Siegel (Eds.), *Review of child development research*, pp. 187–242. Chicago: University of Chicago Press.

Sameroff, A. J., & Seifer, R. (1990). Early contributors to developmental risk. In In J. Rolf, A. S. Masten, D. Cicchetti, K. H. Nuechterlein & S. Weintraub (Eds.), *Risk and protective factors in the development of psychopathology*, pp. 52–66. New York: Cambridge University Press.

Sameroff, A., J., Seifer, R., Barocas, B., Zax, M., & Greenspan, S. (1987). IQ scores of 4-year-old children: social-environmental risk factors. *Pediatrics, 79*, 343–350.

Sampson, R. J., Morenoff, J. D., & Gannon-Rowley, T. (2002). Assessing "neighborhood effects": Social processes and new directions in research. *Annual Review of Sociology, 28*, 443–478.

Sanbonmatsu, L., Kling, J. R., Duncan, G. J., & Brooks-Gunn, J. (2006). Neighborhoods and academic achievement: Results from the Moving to Opportunity experiment. *Journal of Human Resources, 61*, 649–691.

Schoon, I., Bynner, J., Joshi, H., Parsons, S., Wiggins, R. D., & Sacker, A. (2002). The influence of context, timing, and duration of risk experiences for the passage from childhood to mid-adulthood. *Child Development, 73*, 1486–1504.

Scollon, C. N., Kim-Prieto, C., & Diener, E. (2003). Experience sampling: Promises and pitfalls, strengths and weaknesses. *Journal of Happiness Studies, 4*, 5–34.

Seccombe, K. (2000). Families in poverty in the 1990s: Trends, causes, consequences, and lessons learned. *Journal of Marriage and the Family, 62*, 1094–1113.

Seeman, T. E., McEwen, B. S., Rowe, J. W., & Singer, B. H. (2001). Allostatic load as a marker of cumulative biological risk: MacArthur studies of successful aging. *Proceedings of the National Academy of Sciences, 98*, 4770–4775.

Seifer, R., Sameroff, A. J., Dickstein, S., Gitner, G., Miller, I., Rasmussen, S., & Hayden, L. C. (1996). Parental psychopathology, multiple contextual risks, and one-year outcomes in children. *Journal of Clinical Child Psychology, 25*, 423–435.

Small, S. A., & Luster, T. (1994). Adolescent sexual activity: an ecological, risk-factor approach. *Journal of Marriage and the Family, 56*, 181–192.

Smokowski, P. R., Mann, E. A., Reynolds, A. J., & Fraser, M. W. (2004). Childhood risk and protective factors and late adolescent adjustment in inner city minority youth. *Children and Youth Services Review, 26*, 63–91.

Stouthamer-Loeber, M., Loeber, R., Wei, E., Farrington, D. P., & Wikström, P. O. (2002). Risk and promotive effects in the explanation of persistent serious delinquency in boys. *Journal of Consulting and Clinical Psychology, 70*, 111–123.

Stouthamer-Loeber, M., Wei, E., Homish, D. L., & Loeber, R. (2002). Which family and demographic factors are related to both maltreatment and persistent serious juvenile delinquency? *Children's Services: Social Policy, Research, and Practice, 5*, 261–272.

Taylor, C. A., Boris, N. W., Heller, S. S., Clum, G. A., Rice, J. C., & Zeanah, C. H. (2008). Cumulative experiences of violence among high-risk urban youth. *Journal of Interpersonal Violence, 23*, 1618–1635.

Trickett, E. J. (1992). Prevention ethics: Explicating the context of prevention activities. *Ethics & Behavior, 2*, 91–100.

Watt, N. F., Anthony, E. J., Wynne, L. C., & Rolf, J. E. (1984). *Children at risk for schizophrenia: A longitudinal perspective*. New York: Cambridge University Press.

Werner, E. E., & Smith R. S. (1982). *Overcoming the odds: High risk children from birth to adulthood*. Ithaca, NY: Cornell University Press.

Williams, S., Anderson, J., McGee, R., & Silva, P. A. (1990). Risk factors for behavioral and emotional disorder in preadolescent children. *Journal of the American Academy of Child and Adolescent Psychiatry, 29,* 413–419.

Zeanah, C. H., Boris, N. W., & Larrieu, J. A. (1997). Infant development and developmental risk: A review of the past 10 years. *Journal of the American Academy of Child and Adolescent Psychiatry, 36,* 165–178.

CHAPTER 3

Maternal Care as the Central Environmental Variable

Marc de Rosnay and Lynne Murray

1. Introduction: Mothers in Focus

It is widely accepted in developmental psychology research that maternal care has a profound influence on infant and child development.[1] As a simple illustration, more than 850 publications since 2000 were cited in a search from PsycINFO using "mother-child relations," combined with "infant development" While this is but a crude and superficial index, it serves to show that the mother's role in infant development is a focused area of developmental psychological inquiry. But what is this role, and how should it be construed?

Within psychoanalytic theory, particularly that of the British Object Relations school (see Shuttleworth, 1993), the mother, or person filling her role, is no less than the primary environment for infant psychogenesis. In Winnicott's (1966) terms, the mother is the facilitating environment for mental development:

Infants come into being *differently according to whether the conditions are favourable or unfavourable. At the same time*

conditions do not determine the infant's potential. This is inherited, and it is legitimate to study this inherited potential of the individual as a separate issue, provided always that it is accepted that the inherited potential of an infant cannot become an infant unless linked to maternal care. *(Winnicott, 1966, p. 43)*

It is important to clarify here that, in Winnicott's view, mental development will occur irrespective of a mother's presence or conduct. The nature of maternal care, however, will be the major determinant of psychological well-being, which can be thought of in terms of the eventual structure of the individual's personality, and his or her capacity to engage in appropriate, empathic, and sustaining interpersonal and societal relations across the life span (Winnicott, 1966). Given such a focus, it is natural that much of Object Relations theory deals directly with the phenomenology of infant mental life, an aspect of development that is all but absent from mainstream developmental psychology. Nevertheless, the *relational contexts* supporting this putative mental life remain very much the focus of infancy research from the

perspectives of both social cognitive development and attachment theory. So, for example,
there has been a sustained and painstaking
research effort to establish the capacities for
social participation that are present in early
infancy, particularly from the point of view
of infant-mother interaction and communication (Braten, 1998; Bullowa, 1979; Field &
Fox, 1985; Lock, 1978). Indeed, the question
is no longer whether infants adopt an intentional stance with respect to persons but,
rather, how early we can be sure this is the
case, and what is the nature of the infant's
understanding of the mental attitudes of
others (Baldwin & Moses, 1996; Harris, 2006;
Tomasello, Carpenter, Call, Behne, & Moll,
2005). Thus, the view of the infant as a social
participant, and the dependencies that characterize such participation, which are firmly
articulated within Object Relations theory,
have proven remarkably durable.

In the sections that follow we first locate
the idea of maternal care within the theoretical tradition of psychoanalysis in which
it was initially elaborated. We then consider
development in infancy and early childhood
from the point of view of the infant growing toward independence within the context of maternal care. This discussion does
not focus on the nature and influence of
maternal care per se; rather, we provide a
portrait of the infant as an inherently social
participant whose development promotes,
and indeed requires, changing patterns of
parental care to facilitate its progress. Here,
we rely heavily on the work of Trevarthen
(1979), Tronick (1989), and Stern (1974, 1985),
and we also draw on attachment theory
and research (Ainsworth, Blehar, Waters, &
Wall, 1978; Bowlby, 1969/1997; Sroufe, 1995).
Finally, we consider research illustrating
the nature of the relation between maternal care and development. Because of the
enormous diversity of the literature dealing
with this relation, it is necessary to present
a selective account that yet speaks to a relatively broad developmental story, and to
this end we focus on the impact of mothers'
psychological well-being on the quality of
mother-infant interactions and their effects
on child development.

2. Maternal Care

What is the nature of maternal care? It is
helpful in the first instance to highlight those
features of maternal care that differentiate
it from other forms of care, as infants and
children may be cared for by many people.
In early infancy, maternal care implies immediate responsibility, both temporally and
proximally, and ultimate accountability
for an infant's well-being. The provision of
maternal care also needs to be understood
not merely in terms of what it means for the
infant at one moment or another, but what
it provides and implies for the infant over
time. That is, maternal care implies continuity, as is illustrated in the formation of differential patterns of attachment organization
between an infant and caregiver (Ainsworth
et al., 1978), and the relative resilience of
these patterns through development (Main,
Kaplan, & Cassidy, 1985). Maternal care is
thus best construed as the assumption of a
role, and while it is typically assumed by the
biological mother of the infant, others may
also assume the role.

Maternal care emerges in the context
of infantile dependence and is a manifestation of our evolutionary history (Bowlby
1969/1997), but this fact by no means diminishes its necessity for adaptive and healthy
psychological development. The biological
imperative of some form of maternal care
for the human infant's survival is nowhere
more apparent than in the psychoanalytic
theories of early infant psychic development. Though Freud (1926) himself devoted
relatively little attention to the particulars
of early maternal care, focusing primarily on
the formulation of the *economic* model and
the theory of infantile sexuality, he clearly
identified *infantile dependency* upon the
mother as a state of absolute dependence,
and one from which some of our most basic
interpersonal needs stem,

*The biological factor, then, establishes the
earliest situations of danger and creates
the need to be loved which will accompany the child through the rest of his life.
(p. 155)*

With the development of psychoanalytic practice with children it became important to address the nature of maternal care and its relation to infantile dependency, particularly insofar as failures of such care have the potential to impede the maturational process and undermine self-differentiation and, thus, ego development (e.g., A. Freud, 1968, 1973; Winnicott, 1966). In this way the early psychic experience of the infant in relation to the primary carer became the focus of sustained attention.[2] Leading the therapeutic and theoretical innovation was Klein, for whom the infant has a rich, albeit primitive, mental life arising from the meeting of instinctual activity and the environment. Within Klein's model of the mind, maternal care of the infant – both physical and psychological – constitutes the environment within which the infant can transform a nascent mentality constituted of fragmented part objects (e.g., the mother's breast) into a mental life inhabited by complete or whole objects (e.g., the mother) with external or objective integrity (e.g., a mother whose actions belong to her own subjective stance). *Objects*, in Klein's sense, are the objects of instinctual drives, and they are experienced as concrete psychic realities that do not initially cohere into a continuous mental experience (Segal, 1975; St. Clair, 1986).

For Klein (1975) and her contemporaries (e.g., Bion, 1962; Winnicott, 1966) the infant has a mental life that must be understood in order to explain clinical observations and experiences, particularly in very disturbed children, but also in adult psychoanalysis (A. Freud, 1973; Segal, 1975). Although a simplification, it is fair to say that this mental life is conceptualized as intense and immediate, a state of affairs that is intimately linked to the infant's sense of being *merged* or undifferentiated from his environment, which is primarily the mother and the care she provides.

Winnicott (1966) offers a relatively accessible rendition of this process from the point of view of typical development. Regarding the infant, Winnicott describes a movement from complete dependence, through relative dependence, toward independence

that occurs in the *holding* environment of maternal care (1966). The state of complete dependence in the infant is matched in the mother by the state of *primary maternal preoccupation*. During this time the infant is without ego resources, in psychoanalytic terms, so the impingements of the environment and bodily needs cannot be dealt with or integrated via ego mechanisms (A. Freud, 1973). Put in different terms, the infant needs a mother who can feel and think for him. As such, the environmental provision for the infant "is reliable in a way that that implies the mother's empathy" (Winnicott, 1966, p. 48). By way of illustration, Winnicott describes the most basic and fundamental act of physically holding the infant, which, if not empathically tailored to the infant's needs, can "quickly produce in the infant a sense of insecurity, and distressed crying" (p. 49). This early phase covers the first 2 to 3 months of the infant's life and, Winnicott argues, establishes the capacity for primitive (part) object relations, for which the infant must have some nascent sense of himself or herself as an autonomous *unit*.

Thus Winnicott describes a transition between this phase of early infancy, when the infant is *merged* with the mother, and the beginnings of independence, for which the infant must start to distinguish *me* from *not-me*. Such a distinction marks a profound transition in the infant's stance with respect to the world, which in the typical case is met by the mother's appreciation that the infant is now capable of signaling his needs: The mother is free to respond to, rather than anticipate, what her infant requires, precipitating the end of primary maternal preoccupation. The infant, on the other hand, having experienced empathic maternal care, has built memories or expectations about the environmental provision that form the foundation of a subjective, nonmerged, stance: The infant has become *aware of dependence* (Winnicott, 1966).

Two features of this early phase are particularly noteworthy. First, the maternal preoccupation described by Winnicott is a response to the infant's state of absolute dependence: The infant's state (in utero, as a neonate, etc.) *elicits* maternal preoccupation, which in most cases is taken for granted because it is appropriate to the infant's state and is willingly provided. Second, the end of merging is marked by a change in the infant, to which the mother responds. That is, the maturing capacity in the infant necessitates a different maternal attitude, one that respects the infant's *capacity to initiate*. In sum, the forces driving change in the structure of interpersonal relating are seen to lie in the infant's increasing maturational capacity to interact, a point to which we shall return later. Nevertheless, the provision of *good enough* care is essential if the infant is to emerge from maturational changes with an increasingly integrated and autonomous sense of self (Winnicott, 1966, 1982). An important feature of such care following the stage of absolute dependence is that the mother lessens her immediate adaptation to her infant's needs. This process results in inevitable frustrations for the infant, but Winnicott maintains that such experiences fortify his sense of autonomy and self because *he* is active in realizing his needs, so long as he experiences good-enough care.

The great thrust of Winnicott's (1966, 1982) writing on infancy concerns emotional *achievements* and the derailment of interpersonal functioning; indeed, this is true for the Object Relations school in general (see Shuttleworth, 1993). Within the framework sketched earlier, serious or sustained failures of the environmental provision do not allow merging to meet its natural end, and this is thought to have severe emotional consequences for the individual. But even when this critical period does not come to a satisfactory resolution, it is important to note that the infant does not cease to develop in other psychological respects: So, while such failures might mean that facets of the personality remain too rigidly grounded in early and, consequently, maladaptive modes of functioning, the child's capacity to understand and relate to the world in new ways continues to unfold. And so Winnicott's description of the older infant moves the discussion of emotional life into very different territory. In particular,

the emotional achievements set in motion by the infant's capacity to signal his need concern the emerging capacity to reconcile two overarching functions of the mother, "corresponding to the infant's quiet and exited state" (p. 266).

Winnicott, like others who have followed (e.g., Ainsworth et al., 1978; Sroufe, 1995; Stern, 1985), believed that the mother becomes known to the infant not just as a consequence of her distinctive voice, scent, or face, but also by the essential functions that she helps her infant enact, whether they be comforting, arousal/tension management, feeding, or communicating. Of course, such functions are achieved by the dyad, and as the infant's sense of self deepens, he also comes to form continuous expectations about the mother: the mother is becoming a *whole person*. Thus, Winnicott argues, the infant begins to realize that one and the same person is connected to heights of frustration (e.g., an unsuccessful feed) as well as the comfort that typically ensues (e.g., being held in a quiet state). In this period, the infant comes to feel that the purveyor of maternal care is a special person, someone whose absence, because she is sensed as the source of satisfaction and comfort, can be felt as a terrible specific loss; this is a theme that is clearly manifest in the attachment relationship by the end of the first year (Bowlby, 1969/1997, 1973/1997). Whereas the infant could previously experience the mother in a disembodied way, as a recipient of his impulses, frustrations, and needs, now the infant feels a rudimentary personal responsibility to the mother, with whom there is an ongoing and loving relationship: The infant has achieved, in Winnicott's (1966) terms, a *capacity for concern*.

The development of the capacity for concern is conceived as an emotional achievement, and it is fleshed out in terms of infant's psychic life in relation to the mother. Furthermore, the capacity for concern characterizes the initial *two-person* relationship, wherein the infant first appreciates the intentional orientation or subjective stance of the other person. Correspondingly, maternal awareness of this newly developing consciousness in the infant prompts further adjustments in caregiving. On the one hand, these include the mother's supporting the infant to manage his feelings of distress at the prospect of possible loss or failure, and, on the other, a more cooperative stance during reciprocal exchanges. Winnicott, who was a prodigious observer of infants and made extensive use of structured observation (i.e., the *set situation*, Winnicott, 1982),[3] links this phase to the infant's perfection of the game of *dropping* at about 9 months. Here, the infant draws another person into a reciprocal game of exchange, instantly recognizable to most parents, where, playfully, and at the infant's initiative and with maternal support, he experiences the loss and then the retrieval of the object.

Notably, Winnicott's rich assumptions about the social cognitive capacities of infants, which inform his portrait of what infants are actually thinking and feeling, have to a remarkable extent been borne out and clarified by subsequent empirical research (Harris, 2006; Trevarthen & Aitken, 2001). In a recent experimental study capitalizing on variants of a dropping game, Behne, Carpenter, Call, and Tomasello (2005) showed that, by 9 months, infants are sensitive to their play partner's intent: waiting patiently if their play partner appears to drop a desired object by accident but becoming agitated if the object is dropped deliberately. While it is unclear when infants first begin to realize that their actions have an impact on other people, a large body of research indicates that by 12 months infants point to make deliberate referential communicative gestures to direct others' attention (*protoimperative* gestures) and to share their interest (*prodeclarative* gestures; Bates, Camaioni, & Volterra, 1975; Trevarthen and Hubley, 1978; Carpenter, Nagell, & Tomasello, 1998; Liszkowski, Carpenter, Striano, & Tomasello, 2006; Liszkowski, Carpenter, & Tomasello, 2007). Relatedly, they engage in *affect sharing* with their caregivers about interesting events or objects (Waters, Wippman, & Sroufe, 1979). Thus, by 12 months infants seem to be treating others as intentional agents, at least in some contexts.

It is notable, however, that the psychic lives of infants, which enjoy such close scrutiny in the Object Relations tradition, do not really factor in many other contexts within developmental or clinical psychology. Contemporaneous theorists and researchers seem reluctant to entertain *what* infants think, phantasize, or hallucinate; perhaps they find the territory too difficult to subject to empirical inquiry, or perhaps they think it is unnecessary to make such speculations. Nevertheless, the focus on maternal care persists in empirical research, and a broad set of constructs has been advanced in order to characterize its nature. While differing in substantive ways, or in the contexts in which they are applicable, such constructs focus on the emotional qualities of dyadic interactions (or the relationship) and also place importance on the appropriate responsiveness of the caretaker to the infant's or young child's needs, whether physical or psychological. They include *affect attunement* (Stern, 1985), *sensitivity* (Ainsworth et al., 1978), *emotional availability* (Source & Emde, 1981), *mutually responsive orientation* (Kochanska, 1997), *reflective function* (Fonagy, Steele, Steele, Moran, & Higgit, 1991; Fonagy & Target, 1997), *mind-mindedness* (Meins, 1997), and *insightfulness* (Oppenheim & Koren-Karie 2002). Perhaps the most prominent of these global constructs is that of *sensitivity*, as used by Ainsworth and colleagues (Ainsworth, Bell, & Stayton, 1974; Ainsworth et al., 1978). From their behavioral rating scales, sensitivity is described as follows:

> *The optimally sensitive mother is able to see things from her baby's point of view. She is alert to perceive her baby's signals, interprets them accurately, and responds appropriately and promptly, unless no response is the most appropriate under the circumstances. She tends to give the baby what he seems to want, and when she does not she is tactful in acknowledging his communication. (Ainsworth et al., 1978, p. 142)*

Insensitivity, by contrast, is manifest when the contingency of maternal responding breaks down and is dictated by the mother's own ongoing concerns or preoccupations.

This typically takes the from either of intrusive responding, where the mother imposes her own agenda, regardless of the infant's behavior, or else she may also be nonsensitive in that she fails to respond at all.

The sensitivity construct is crucial to attachment theory in that it captures those aspects of maternal care underpinning important variations in dyadic emotion regulation, which in turn become organized as stable attachment relationships (Ainsworth et al., 1978; Sroufe, 1995). Indeed, while we cannot comment in depth on each of the constructs listed earlier, it is important to recognize that they all pertain to the provision of maternal care and generally rest on the assumption that the infant is an active social participant prior to the establishment of stable attachment patterns at the end of the first year. In the next section, we give further consideration to development in infancy and early childhood from the point of view of the infant's growing toward independence and note the accompanying alterations in maternal care that support them.

3. Mother and Child Moving toward Independence

In this section we provide an overview of research concerning the interpersonal nature of infant and toddler development. Rather than focussing on maternal care per se, we continue to elaborate relational competencies and themes in infancy. The structure of this section is broadly developmental. Although there are some fundamental psychological transitions in the infant and young child over this period, these achievements have been dealt with in detail elsewhere (Carpenter et al., 1998; Harris, 2006; Tomasello et al., 2005; Trevarthen & Aitken, 2001) and will only be referred to here selectively. Our focus is the infant's social participation and the mother's response to the infant's condition. We give particular attention to the first 3 months because of the importance placed on this period in establishing the terms of social engagement (e.g., Trevarthen, 1979; Tronick, 1989; Stern, 1985).

The First Three months

In the first few months, before manipulation is effective in exploring objects, an infant establishes the basis for a deep affectional tie to his mother and other constant companions. He does so by means of this delicate and specifically human system for person-to-person communication. (Trevarthen, 1979, p. 321)

If left to their own devices in a face-to-face interaction, a 2-month-old and his mother will very often arrive at a series of communicative exchanges that resembles a conversation without words, punctuated instead with expressive emotional signals and gestures. These exchanges are well organized in that each of the participants appears responsive to the other's communicative acts, and the rudiments of turn taking are clearly evident (Bateson, 1975; Mayer & Tronick, 1985; Stern, 1974; Trevarthen, 1979). Some features of such early *protoconversations* are particularly noteworthy. While there are great differences between individual infant-mother dyads, microanalytic techniques suggest that even at 2 months of age infants to a great extent respond to their mothers' turn yielding and, furthermore, the basic structure of the dyadic exchanges remains remarkably constant between 2 and 5 months (Mayer & Tronick, 1985). The mother is, of course, the dominant player in these exchanges, as she has a capacity to accommodate herself to the infant's changing needs (e.g., for sleep, food, containment) and an ability to assimilate spontaneous infant gestures and communications into an ongoing interaction, as well as respecting infant initiating and terminating signals (Trevarthen, 1979; Tronick, Als, & Adamson, 1979).

The infant's active participation in such affective communicative interactions, and his expectancies within such exchanges, has been most vividly illustrated in *perturbation* paradigms, pioneered by Tronick and colleagues (Tronick, Als, Adamson, Wise, & Brazelton, 1978; Tronick, Ricks, & Cohn, 1982). In one series of perturbations used with 6- to 12-week-old infants, Murray and Trevarthen (1985) showed that different kinds of disruption to normal face-to-face social engagement provoke distinct responses in the infant. Thus, the mother's presentation of an unresponsive, blank, or still face was followed first by infant signs of protest and then of distress, whereas when the contingency of maternal responses was disrupted via a double video replay link, with their form being meanwhile retained, a rapid shift in the infant to negative behaviors was provoked without apparent protest, and infants seemed, rather, puzzled or confused.[4] Finally, a condition comprising a naturalistic *interruption*, whereby a researcher engaged the mother in conversation and the infant was left out of the interaction, caused infants to become quiet and less positive, but not distressed or avoidant. These findings have been broadly confirmed by subsequent research (Nadel, Carchon, Kervella, Marcelli, & Reserbat-Plantey, 1999; Weinberg & Tronick, 1994, 1996; Legerstee & Markova, 2007) and attest both to the infant's capacity to apprehend the significance of distinct interpersonal contexts, as well as the strong motivation to maintain particular kinds of social engagement. The notable impact of the "unnatural" perturbations on the affective and behavioral responses of infants as young as 3 months suggests, moreover, that certain dimensions of maternal social engagement in this period, such as its contingent responsiveness and its emotional and interpersonal appropriateness, are likely to be of importance for optimal infant development.

Drawing on the rich description of early emotional communication, which is brought into focus by the influences of perturbation, Tronick has emphasized the importance of mutual emotional regulation in shaping the infant's *effectance* – his sense of what can and cannot be achieved – and overall mood (Tronick, 1989; Tronick et al., 1982). Stern (1985) also sees early mother-infant exchanges, in which communication is premised on the capacity to share emotion, as the bedrock of healthy emotional agency.

Trevarthen (1979) has, for more that 30 years, been steadfast in his view that human infants possess a special skill that gives them automatic access to the sharing of emotional states in the context of mutually regulated protoconversational exchanges, so-called primary intersubjectivity (Trevarthen & Aitken, 2001). Primary intersubjectivity is a kind of direct awareness of emotions and purposeful intent in others. Successful intersubjective exchanges rest on the ability "to exhibit to others at least the rudiments of individual consciousness and intentionality," which Trevarthen (1979) labels *subjectivity*. The organized emotional displays manifested in face-to-face interaction (e.g., Haviland & Lelwica, 1987; Weinberg & Tronick, 1994) are expressions of such subjectivity in Trevarthen's terms, in that they are intelligible actions: Their sensible apperception within the communicative setting is a function of the capacity for intersubjectivity.

The apparent innate readiness of infants for social interaction, along with their differential treatment of human and nonhuman stimuli (Brazelton, Koslowski, & Main, 1974; Legerstee & Markova, 2007), is consistent with research on neonatal imitation of human actions and expressions (Meltzoff & Moore, 1977, 1994) and early preference for human faces (Frantz, 1963; Morton & Johnson, 1991). Thus, a portrait of the infant emerges within the first 12 weeks as an inherently social being equipped for basic communicative exchanges. Braten (1987) captures such readiness with the notion of the *virtual other*, arguing that the nervous system is organized for the copresence of a complementary participant. Whether it should ultimately turn out that Trevarthen's strong nativist claims are correct, or some other version of biological preparedness should prevail, it is widely accepted that some system of mutual intelligibility must be established within the first 12 weeks and that the functioning of the system turns on, among other things, the direct communicability of emotional states (Hobson, 1995; Meltzoff, 2007; Tomasello et al., 2005).

Whereas Winnicott (1966) described this early period as one of *merging*, Stern (1985) writes of a sense of an *emergent self*. Stern draws heavily on the developmental literature and presents this period as one in which the infant experiences disconnected *islands* of organization. To a great extent, such organization stems from the infant's experience of his own body and movements, which rapidly cohere into larger organized products. However, the infant is also coming into being in a manner consistent with the observed capacity for interpersonal exchange. A mother might, for example, reflect back her infant's vocalization while moving her hands and head rhythmically and smiling brightly. According to Stern, the mother's behaviors coalesce and provide the infant with a sense of integrated experience contingent on the infant's initiating signal.[5] Stern describes such maternal responses as *vitality affects*, which can be differentiated from emotion in that they are not discrete (i.e., happy, sad), but, equally, they are not captured by general affective states or moods (e.g., distress, anxiety) and do not conform to notions of arousal and hedonic tone. Rather, vitality affects have contour and are best described by dynamic, kinetic terms (e.g., surging, deflating). In the course of ordinary interaction, Stern proposes, such vitality affects punctuate interpersonal responsivity and help sustain the infant's sense of personal continuity. In a further development of this line of thinking, Tronick notes that maternal responsiveness helps create shared, *dyadic* states of consciousness, whereby the infant's sense of self is both leant coherence and is enriched (Tronick, 2007).

Of course, mothers often communicate with their infants using expressive affective gestures in response to other kinds of infant behaviors. For example, when an infant experiences discomfort, a mother might stroke him while making soothing sounds, thereby organizing the infant's experience and calming him (Stern, 1985). Indeed, much of the time spent with her infant in the first phase has little to do with the communicative exchanges that have captured so much research attention. Periods of *alert inactivity*, during which such communicative exchanges are observed, are relatively infrequent (Shuttleworth, 1993; Tronick, 1989), and it is perhaps for this reason that many see this earliest phase as primarily one of physiological regulation and the provision

of smooth routines (Gianino & Tronick, 1988; Sander, 1962; Sroufe, 1995; Tronick, 2007). From an attachment perspective, infants clearly become familiar with their specific carer at this time, but stable attachment organization is not yet evident, and adoption studies indicate that adoption in the first 6 months is unlikely to lead to insecure attachment organization (e.g., Singer, Brodzinsky, Ramsay, Steir, & Waters, 1985). Sroufe (1995), however, emphasizes that this early period is of great importance for the mother, as her patterns of sensitive responding will assume increasing importance in the formation of stable attachment patterns over the ensuing year.

In the first 3 months, the infant is becoming a social participant and building a history of exchanges, of many kinds, with his mother and other constant companions. All the perspectives touched on here (Stern, 1985; Trevarthen & Aitken, 2001; Tronick, 1989; Winnicott, 1966) have a common emphasis on responsive, sensitive interactions, with a high degree of *mirroring* and/or affirmation of infant experience that imply an ability to "see things from her baby's point of view" (Ainsworth et al., 1978). In the following section we describe the emotional dialogue that occurs between infant and mother as the relationship grows.

Four to (about) Eight Months

At 32 weeks Tracy showed several other signs of willingness to share the fun of her play. She smiled conspiratorially while her mother watched her move an object, and she accepted replacement of objects of play by her mother more readily than before.... In spite of clear development in control of her actions ..., Tracey still failed to act reciprocally in giving objects to her mother's open hand. Except for her sharing of mood and humour, she still communicated as if contained within the circle of her own experience. (Trevarthen & Hubley, 1978, p. 199)

During this next phase the infant is in transition, increasingly able to coordinate both his acts on the world and his interpersonal communications, but not yet able to enter with the mother into shared psychological attitudes (Trevarthen & Hubley, 1978). Nevertheless, in the typical case, the infant comes to know the mother more fully as a reliable companion. Sroufe (1995) talks of the mother's role in regulating the infant's tensions, where *tension* denotes a full range of internal and relational states to which the infant can succumb (e.g., frustration, distress) but also has a role in initiating or maintaining (e.g., excitement). There are two main upshots of this regulation. First, the infant whose basic tensions are resolved is free to pursue his natural instinct to explore and seek psychological stimulation. Second, the infant is building his resilience with the aid of maternal care, and thus increasing his capacity to tolerate future challenges (Ainsworth et al., 1978; Brazelton et al., 1974; Fogel, 1982; 1993; Sroufe, 1995).

This tension-tolerance model describes a "big picture." The provision of stable maternal care, however, translates into countless moments of regulation, management and interaction, which must be worked through or *completed* (Winnicott, 1966). It is to these processes that we now turn because they are the stuff of which interpersonal experience is constituted in this period, and they form the basis of the sense of continuity and dependence in interpersonal relatedness that is so characteristic of the infant toward his first birthday (Ainsworth et al., 1978; Sroufe, 1995). In keeping with the tension-tolerance model, the function of the mother in this period is very much conceptualized in terms of regulation: She is in a position to accept the infant's affects, needs, and other states and respond in a manner that is appropriate to the infant's condition. As in all interpersonal relations there are times when this process goes awry. Furthermore, when this does happen, such situations often represent failures of mother-infant regulation and, if not repaired, result in negative affect, avoidance, and disengagement.

The nature of the mother-infant affective communication system, including its success, failure, and recovery, has been given considerable attention by Tronick and colleagues (Gianino & Tronick, 1988; Tronick,

1989; Weinberg & Tronick, 1994). In this conceptualization, the mundane comings and goings of everyday life present the dyad with challenges. When *interactive errors*, or *mismatches*, occur, the dyad has an opportunity to resolve them. As Gianino and Tronick (1988) point out, the occurence and resolution of such situations are connected with emotional consequences. Hence, when a frustrating failure of understanding is, with maternal support, transformed into a positive emotional experience an *interactive repair* occurs. Within Gianino and Tronick's view, infant emotional experience is inherently evaluative and communicative: Other-directed and self-directed behaviors are part of the normal repertoire for responding to such emotions and the situations to which they pertain. However, whereas self-directed behaviors (e.g., avoidance, self-soothing) cause the infant to disengage from overarousing events, other-directed behaviors present different opportunities, such as interactive repairs that might transform negative events to positive, manageable, ones. For Tronick and others (Izard & Harris, 1995), the continuity of care that an infant finds in his specific caregiver, and the emotional interactions and resolutions they share, are of tremendous significance for the infant's developing sense of well-being because such experiences are thought to accumulate and provide an affective backdrop that comes to color the infant's transactions with the environment as he develops. Thus,

> With the accumulation and reiteration of success and reparation, the infant establishes a positive affective core, with clear boundaries between self and other. (Tronick, 1989, p. 116)

It is important to emphasize that the processes described earlier explicitly require failures, misunderstandings, and misinterpretations between a mother and her infant. That such events occur is of far less significance than the manner in which they are resolved and assimilated to the infant's ongoing experience. The importance placed by Tronick and colleagues on interactive errors and repair sits comfortably with

Winnicott's (1966, 1982) notion of the *good enough* mother, who, beyond the phase of primary preoccupation, naturally provides a gradual deadaptation of herself to the infant. Such a state of affairs allows the infant to move toward independence and cultivate a sense of himself in relation to another autonomous being.

Between 3 and 8 months of age, Stern (1985) describes the emergence of the infant's *core self*, which comes into being because he experiences himself as an agent acting to fulfill goals, and he recognizes continuity in his own experiences, particularly when they are emotionally imbued ones. Although the accumulation of experiences into expectancies and memories can be conceptualized in various ways, Stern (1985) offers a clear account of the psychological condensation occurring within the infant during this period. He introduces the idea of representations of interactions that have been generalized (RIG) to describe reasonably stable psychological structures that "embody expectations about any and all interactions that can result in mutually created alterations in self-experience" (p. 115). RIGs of the infant-mother relationship allow the infant eventually to form an expectation of the mother even when she is absent (the *evoked companion*), much like the internal working models described in attachment theory (Bowlby, 1969/1997; Bretherton & Munholland, 1999). Whatever the mechanism might be, by the end of the eighth month the infant has formed firm expectations of a specific caregiver and, all being well, his own capacity to affect the environment. Such expectations become increasingly pertinent in a social world that is unfolding before his eyes.

Nine to Eighteen Months

At 40 weeks Tracey's mother became an acknowledged participant in actions. Tracey repeatedly looked up at her mother's face when receiving an object, pausing as if to acknowledge receipt. She also looked up to her mother at breaks in her play, giving the indication of willingness to share

experiences as she had never done before. (Trevarthen & Hubley, 1978, p. 200)

Somewhere around 8 or 9 months, a remarkable transition gets under way. Like Tracey, typically functioning infants start to take for granted that their subjective experiences can be shared with other people; in Trevarthen and Hubley's terms, they have achieved the foundations of *secondary intersubjectivity*. The early rudiments of this ability are probably manifest in the phenomenon of *stranger wariness*. By 18 months, infants can engage in genuine *social referencing*: here, they seek information from others that is normally marked out in terms of its emotional expressiveness in order to clarify its significance and their own relation to the world (Moses, Baldwin, Rosicky, & Tidball, 2001). In section 2 we described the infant's rapidly increasing comprehension of person-person-object relations, which is clearly manifest in the capacity for cooperation, and for joint attention as seen in pointing behaviors. Carpenter et al. (1998) summarize three domains in which the infant's joint attention matures in this period: Infants first *share* and *follow* attention, then they *direct* attention. How these capacities come into being is beyond the scope of this chapter, but it is noteworthy that while various influential accounts stress the necessity of social interaction (Tomasello et al., 2005; Trevarthen & Aitken, 2001), longitudinal research has only recently begun to focus on the specific qualities of maternal care that may be of importance for their emergence, such as teaching and conjoint action on a toy (Gaffan, Martins, Healey, & Murray, 2008).

We can ask, however, what this transition implies for maternal care. On the one hand, the mother no longer plays such an integrative or regulating role as we have described earlier. Instead, she is becoming more of a companion in cooperative endeavors, in keeping with the infant's rapidly developing capacity to see her as a social agent and explore the world independently (Sroufe, 1995; Stern, 1985). On the other hand, there is a sharp escalation in attachment behavior during this period; it seems that the very same developmental processes that allow the infant to grasp social agency bring into focus the need for a *secure base* (Ainsworth et al., 1978). Notably, this development broadly coincides with Winnicott's phase of the capacity for concern. In fact, the mother plays a profound role in emotional coregulation during this period, but unlike the preceding phases, mother and infant now have much more flexibility in the way that they respond to one another (Sroufe, 1995): Maternal care is no less important than in earlier periods, but the terms of the relationship have shifted. The nature of the dyad's relationship can be understood in various ways at this time, and it is useful to adopt different lenses to complement the infant's newfound capacities.

Consider the importance of the attachment relationship at this time. The function of the attachment behavioral system, as conceptualized by Bowlby (1969/1997), is to promote the protection and survival of the infant, and ultimately the species, via the maintenance of proximity with the primary caregiver. This is achieved through behaviors that put the caregiver into contact with the infant (e.g., crying, smiling), maintain contact (e.g., clinging), or, later on, put the infant in contact with the caregiver (e.g., locomotion). But a simple reading of attachment in terms of physical proximity soon breaks down. Indeed, attachment needs have to be balanced with the motivation to explore the environment at the very least. Thus, by 12 months attachment behaviors encompass substantial flexibility and may accommodate various degrees of proximity to the caregiver. For example, some environmental threats may cause the infant to require full physical contact, whereas others may simply require a reassuring glance. The attachment system as described here is fundamental in that it should be observed in all infants given the sustained availability of a caregiver. Bowlby's insights were profound and simple: The infant needs a primary attachment figure and, by this stage, it is typically the mother. She is the one to whom the infant instinctively turns in the face of threat and whose sustained absence

is felt as a terrible loss (Bowlby, 1973/1997; Tracy, Lamb, & Ainsworth, 1976).

Throughout this chapter we have focused on the broad developmental story of mother and infant moving toward independence and cooperation. In the attachment literature, however, great significance has been placed on qualitative differences in the organization of attachment relationships between dyads, both as a reflection on the parenting practices that lead to such variation and in terms of their longitudinal impact (Thompson, 1999; de Wolff & van IJzendoorn, 1997). Full treatment of maternal care and infant attachment organization is beyond the scope of this chapter, but some important points can be highlighted. The work of Ainsworth et al. (1978) and others (see Sroufe, 1995) has shown that by 12 months the great majority of infants have a coherent and stable pattern of attachment organization with a primary caregiver. Two forces appear to drive these patterns. First, infants need their caregivers when they experience attachment stress, such as when some environmental threat or period of separation is experienced. Second, infants have a remarkable embodied understanding, derived through countless interpersonal regulations and communications, of the ways in which their caregivers respond to them, particularly when they are emotionally aroused. Distinctive attachment patterns must accommodate these two realities. Thus, in the context of a history of sensitive care – as manifest by maternal awareness of infant signals and communications, reciprocity, and acceptance of infant states and needs – infants are generally *secure*, in that they take the availability of their caregiver for granted, call upon her in times of need without hesitation, and are able to find the comfort they require in order to restore their sense of wellbeing and return to exploration (Ainsworth et al., 1978).

In one of the two insecure attachment patterns, *avoidance*, there is an apparent paradox, where the infant will avoid direct contact with the caregiver precisely at the time when it is most needed. On the basis of the work of Mary Main, Cassidy (1994) proposed that the avoidant strategy represents a compromise between the infant's attachment needs and his embodied understanding, based on the dyad's specific history, that a direct emotional display will lead to rejection. In Gianino and Tronick's (1988) terms, avoidant children appear to employ self-directed regulatory behaviors at the very time a secure child would use an other-directed strategy: that is, seeking the mother. But it is important to note that both strategies ensure the maintenance of proximity to the caregiver at a time of attachment stress, albeit on different terms.

In this discussion we can see that, while Bowlby explained the attachment relationship in terms of a behavioral system, the particular properties of the system are largely mediated by the history of emotional interactions within dyads (Sroufe, 1995; Tronick, Ricks, & Cohn, 1982). Sroufe explains,

Attachment refers not to a set of behaviors or a trait of the infant, but to a special, emotional relationship between infant and caregiver. (p. 178).

During this period mother and infant are still often involved in moment-to-moment interactions that characterize the earlier periods, but the mother's role is shifting. The initiative to explore and engage belongs to the infant in a more profound sense, and the mother appears to provide a different kind of emotional support to facilitate her infant's experience of the world (Sander, 1962). Stern and colleagues (Stern, 1985; Stern, Hofer, Haft, & Dore, 1985) describe the infant as having a sense of a *subjective self,* and give careful consideration to the nature of affective exchanges during this period. In contrast to the strong emotional responses provoked in attachment paradigms, Stern et al. document a more subtle and continuous form of emotional scaffolding and sharing, namely *affect attunement.* Their research shows that in an ordinary play situation a mother will continuously provide affective matching that is appropriate to the infant's current state, but not a direct imitation of it. These instances are usually unmarked, in that the infant does not acknowledge them,

and, indeed, mothers themselves often fail to realize that they have done them.

To understand these processes better, Stern et al. (1985) used video feedback to train mothers to perturb such behaviors by inappropriately raising or lowering the intensity of their response to the infant. In keeping with their hypothesis, infants were put out by the discordant nature of these mis-attunements, which broke the rhythm of the infant's exploration. Affect attunement, then, is remarkable in its ordinariness, and when questioned on the function of such behaviors using video feedback, mothers most commonly say that they are *communing* with their infant: that is, being with them in an intimate and emotionally connected manner. Such conclusions are difficult to substantiate when one can only observe the outward behaviors of dyads, and accordingly the use of perturbation studies has been important in understanding early dyadic processes. But soon after this period toddlers begin to speak, and when they do it is clear that they want to communicate and expect to share their experience. They talk about how they feel and assume others will be interested, and they seek information about others' epistemic states. We turn briefly to this transition now.

Becoming a Conversational Partner

We have already noted that, during processes of social referencing, the infant is able to seek out the mother's emotional take on situations, which may then inform the infant's own response to them. This enhancement of the significance accorded to experience is dramatically elaborated with the emergence of language and conversational competence, when the nature of the mother-child relationship changes in important ways yet again; and these developments occur in an ever-widening social network. While we cannot do justice to this transition, it is helpful to consider some aspects of early mother-child conversational interaction, as they help elucidate the significance of the continuing relationship under different conditions.

In a pioneering study, Bretherton and Beeghly (1982) asked mothers to keep records on their toddlers' internal state language at 28 months, and the contexts in which they used it. Emotion related utterances were already common and, moreover, were used appropriately. Children used emotion words to label their own and others' current feelings; they asked questions about emotion (e.g., "You sad, Daddy?"); and they referred to past and present emotions (e.g., "Will it be scary?"). Furthermore, children produced causal utterances referring to emotion; they connect emotions with their (i) antecedent conditions (e.g., "It's dark. I'm scared"), (ii) consequences or contingent interventions (e.g., "I scared of the shark. Close my eyes."), and (iii) accompanying expressions (e.g., "I not cry now. I happy."). Subsequent research with conversational sampling and analyses of existing child language corpora similarly showed that discussions about emotion are highly relevant to young children; they seek to understand emotional events and share them with their mothers (Dunn, Bretherton, & Munn, 1987; Wellman, Harris, Banerjee, & Sinclair, 1995).

One finding emerging quite strongly is that mothers not only engage with young children on psychological topics, they also *foster* the development of such conversations (Dunn et al. 1987; Jenkins, Turrell, Kogushi, Lollis, & Ross, 2003; Ruffman, Slade, & Crowe, 2002). A similar pattern has been observed with causal/explanatory talk (Dunn & Brown, 1993). Furthermore, mothers are remarkably good at pitching their conversational input so that it is appropriate to their children's developmental level and helps them move forward (Taumoepeau & Ruffman, 2008). These studies capitalize on individual differences in the ways families converse and show continuities between measures of maternal conversational themes and young children's subsequent proclivity to engage in related topics. Furthermore, the findings strongly suggest that mothers who engage their young children in causally coherent psychological discourse engender their more advanced understanding of mind and emotion (see de Rosnay & Hughes, 2006,

for a review). Although the aforementioned studies deal only with typical variation in discourse, research on late signing deaf children (i.e., raised in nonsigning homes) goes further in showing that restricted access to early conversational interaction severely impedes children's capacity to understand others' mental states (Peterson & Siegal, 2000).

In sum, this research shows that access to conversational interaction promotes children's psychological understanding and, furthermore, the manner in which mothers speak to their children is of additional significance for children's psychological understanding. Specifically, psychological discourse that is coherent and appropriate seems to be particularly beneficial.

Summary

Thus far we have considered the first 2 years from the viewpoint of mother and infant growing toward independence, a prominent theme in the writings of Winnicott (1966, 1982) and other observers of infant socioemotional development (e.g., Sroufe, 1995; Stern, 1985; Tronick, 1989). At the same time, the nature of the infant's growing independence carries the possibility of cooperation – a theme emphasized by Trevarthen (Trevarthen and Hubley, 1978) and Tomasello (2005) – and, in Winnicott's view, of the capacity for concern. Although individual researchers emphasize different aspects of this period and elaborate distinct features of the mother-infant relationship, there are nonetheless noteworthy thematic continuities. From the infant's perspective, it is clear that he requires a caretaker who is sensitive to his needs and limitations, but who also recognizes from early on that he has the capacity to signal his needs. In Winnicott's terms, the mother's recognition of her infant's capacity to *initiate* precipitates the end of primary maternal preoccupation and marks the beginning of the gradual movement toward emotional independence. Furthermore, there is widespread recognition that infants have a remarkable orientation to persons and their communicative intent, particularly insofar as it is manifest in their emotional expressions. Indeed, Trevarthen's (1979) initial hypothesis concerning the innate capacity of primary intersubjectivity seems ever less radical as we learn more about the sociocognitive capacities and social sensitivities of young infants (e.g., Tomasello et al., 2005).

From the mother's viewpoint, the significance of her "environmental provision" continues to be emphasized. While the mother's role has been conceptualized in many terms, there is notable convergence in two domains. First, the idea of *continuity* in maternal care has proven durable. At one end of the spectrum, maternal care implies the provision of care in a reliable manner so that the infant's experiences of heightened distress and dysregulation are minimized and promptly ameliorated. At the other end, continuity in maternal care implies availability for reciprocal exchange and interaction around the activities that punctuate an infant's day, and for its own sake. Such reciprocity requires sensitivity to the infant's state and attunement to his emotional condition. The specific features of such care are naturally modified in line with the infant's increasing awareness of the care he receives and the stability of the mother who provides it, and we have discussed various ways in which this process might underpin his developing sense of himself. The second domain on which there is convergence is the need of the mother to accommodate herself to her infant's changing capacities and orientations. Thus, whereas the earliest months largely require anticipation of infant need, the middle of the first year is characterized by an escalation in the infant's initiative.

At the end of the first year, with the establishment of intentional communication, attachment research has shown that the infant's need for maternal care is no less significant, but the terms have changed from the *holding* environment characteristic of the first 6 months. The research of Ainsworth et al. (1978) and others (see Sroufe, 1995) shows that the mother's role is not to prevent the child from encountering stress or mild hazards, but rather to respond appropriately to the infant's signals when anxieties are felt or challenges become too great. While maternal care is still essential for optimal emotion regulation, and the infant has, by this stage, firm expectancies of the mother, the maternal role of companionship is of tremendous importance. Such companionship is seen, for example, in the ongoing intuitive facilitation and validation of the infant's experiences described by Stern (i.e., affect attunement), the shift to genuinely cooperative play (Trevarthen and Hubley, 1978), and is clearly manifest in the early conversations that occur between toddlers and their mothers with the onset of communicative competence.

In sum, continuity of maternal care and the accommodation of such care to the infant's changing capacities and orientations have emerged as consistent themes in the mother-infant relationship and have been consistently linked with socioemotional needs of the infant. Negative consequences of major failures in these domains are generally immediately apparent. Nevertheless, it is also informative to consider how variations in maternal care play out longitudinally. We next consider this issue, therefore, using clinical populations to elucidate this question.

4. The Relation between Maternal Care and Infant Development

Before addressing the question of how variation in maternal care is manifest longitudinally, some caveats are required. First, observers of early infancy have emphasized that most infants find what they need in the care they receive. Indeed, such a notion is inherent in Winnicott's idea of the *good enough* mother. In keeping with this observation, by 12 months the majority of infants are securely attached to their primary caregiver. But even for those who develop a less than optimal attachment organization (i.e., insecure-avoidant or insecure-resistant), most still experience a specific attachment relationship that largely meets their attachment needs (Cassidy, 1994; Sroufe, 1995).

Second, we have presented maternal care as a reasonably coherent, unified construct, despite the fact that the nature of provision changes with infant development. So, for example, in section 2 we identified various parenting constructs that share much in their conceptual underpinnings (*sensitivity, affect attunement, emotional availability*, etc). In practice, it seems likely that considerable convergence obtains in the expression of these dimensions of parenting; nevertheless, there are various conceptual challenges to reducing these constructs to a single variable, and importantly, there is virtually no existing empirical foundation for such a synthesis (see section 5, later). Studies of clinical populations can, however, help to elucidate more specific aspects of parenting, since disturbances in functioning may be selective. In the following, therefore, we briefly outline some of the accumulating research on the implications for infant and child development of the alterations in maternal care occurring in the context of two common clinical conditions, namely, depression and anxiety.

The Impact of Postnatal Depression and Maternal Anxiety

Considerable research has shown consistent associations between the occurrence of maternal depression in the postnatal months and beyond, and adverse infant and child outcomes (see review of Murray, Halligan, & Cooper, 2010): these include poor cognitive performance and learning, and a raised risk of behavior problems and insecure attachment. With regard to cognitive development, the relatively low level of *contingent maternal responsiveness* to the infant that is more common in depressed mothers appears to be a key mechanism underlying poor infant and child functioning. Here, it has been suggested that the depressed mother's low mood and preoccupations interfere with her ability to remain focused on the infant's experience and notice subtle infant cues; her consequent lack of responsiveness to him means that the infant does not have the usual opportunities to build

up a sense of effectance, and establish associations between his own behavior and events in the environment, a fundamental aspect of cognitive functioning and learning (e.g., Stanley, Murray & Stein, 2004). Within this overall reduction of contingency, the depressed mother's failure to adjust her behavior so as to maintain and sustain infant attention, particularly through vocal, intonational, modulations, has also been found to predict poor infant learning (e.g., Kaplan et al., 1999). In contrast, rather different processes appear to operate with regard to the development of behavior problems in postnatally depressed mothers' infants and children. Here, the lack of general *sensitivity*, or *emotional appropriateness* of depressed mothers' behavior, rather than the extent of responsiveness appears to be of particular importance, in all likelihood because insensitive maternal interactions (such as intrusive or hostile contacts) disrupt, or at the least fail to support, infant emotional and behavioral regulation (e.g., Field et al., 1988). Sensitivity of this kind is also relevant to promoting infant attachment security, as noted earlier (e.g., Tomlinson, Cooper & Murray, 2005). Research with wider populations indicates that, in addition to the mother's behavioral sensitivity, her capacity for understanding her infant's experience in term of his subjective psychological orientation (*mind-mindedness* or *reflective functioning*), is of particular importance in promoting secure attachments (Fonagy & Target, 1997; Meins, Fernyhough, Fradley, & Tuckey, 2001; van IJzendoorn, 1995); to date, this aspect of depressed mothers' care has been little researched, but it is a promising line of enquiry (see section 5).

With regard to maternal anxiety disorder, far less evidence is available concerning disturbances in early mother-infant interactions and their associated impact on infant and child development. Work with older children and anxious parents, however, has shown that maternal withdrawal and failure to support the child in managing challenges is associated with child anxiety (see review by Murray, Creswell, & Cooper, 2009). This has recently been demonstrated in anxious mothers in inter-action with their young infants, and such maternal behavior has even been found to show both concurrent and predictive rela-tions with the infant's own anxious behav-ior (Murray, Cooper, Creswell, Schofield, & Sack, 2007; Murray et al., 2008). In addi-tion, both experimental studies (Gerull & Rapee, 2002; de Rosnay, Cooper, Tsigaras, & Murray, 2006) and research with a clinical sample (Murray et al., 2008), has shown that mothers' own expressions of anxiety in the context of ambiguous or potentially fear-provoking stimuli serves, through processes of infant social referencing, to promote infant fearfulness. Such evidence indicates that the enhancement of significance that such maternal emotional signaling to the infant carries, presages, at a behavioral level, the *meaning-making* (Oppenheim, 2006) functions of later-emerging parent-child dis-course that have been found to be impor-tant in the transmission of parental anxiety (Barrett, Rapee, & Dadds, 1996; Dadds & Barrett, 1996).

In sum, the clear variations in maternal responsiveness to their infants that can be difficult to identify in nonclinical popula-tions help to elucidate the potential long-term effects of different aspects of maternal care. What emerges from this clinical liter-ature is that specific features of maternal care appear to have specific associations with later infant and child outcome. Thus, understanding such effects is likely to be of considerable value in enhancing the effec-tiveness of interventions to support moth-ers in providing *good enough* care for their infants. Despite the apparent importance of such variation in maternal responding within clinical contexts, and the existence of provocative animal models that also speak to the significance of the early caregiving environment for adaptive development in other species (Caldji, Tannenbaum, Sharma, Francis, Plotsky, & Meaney, 1998; Francis, Diorio, Liu, & Meaney, 1999), it would be premature to assert that the unfolding influ-ences of early maternal responding and dis-tinctive patterns of mother-infant interaction on child development are well understood.

In part, the limitations on our knowledge are arguably methodological in origin; whilst there has been sustained empirical interest in mother-infant interaction and its impact on child development, there is surpris-ingly little consensus, with the exception of attachment research (see Sroufe, 1995), on how the relationship should be studied, and what features of behavior are meaningful for analysis (e.g., Askan, Kochanska & Ortmann, 2006; Harrist & Waugh, 2002). There are, in fact, relatively few methods oriented to the study of maternal care that have been reli-ably and widely implemented across differ-ent research groups, and subjected to close scrutiny. Therefore, we turn to methodolog-ical considerations next.

5. Methodological Considerations in the Measurement of Maternal Care

In the preceding section it was evident that certain features of maternal care can be identified, measured, and associated with important aspects of child development. To establish the significance of the envi-ronmental provision afforded by maternal care, it is necessary to make such empirical connections between mother-infant interac-tions and child outcomes. To some extent, the importance of maternal care can be observed within short time frames. This is most clearly demonstrated in the perturba-tion studies reviewed earlier in this chap-ter (e.g., Murray & Trevarthen, 1985; Stern et al., 1985). For many researchers, prac-titioners and policy makers, however, the significance of maternal care needs to be demonstrated within a longitudinal context, such as we have discussed earlier in section 4 (e.g., Murray, Halligan, & Cooper, 2010). In this section, therefore, we initially outline the methodological merits of perturbation studies, or similarly motivated interven-tions, for understanding early mother-infant processes. We then consider other meth-odological approaches that have, generally speaking, been fruitful in establishing impor-tant associations between early features of maternal care and later child outcomes. This discussion is by no means exhaustive, and we do not address behavioral or representational measurement of attachment organization as this has been dealt with elsewhere in detail (see Cassidy & Shaver, 1999), and our attention has been largely on the first year. We end this section with a brief overview of methodological considerations.

We have already shown that meaningful links can be established between the mother's and the infant's behavior over short periods by disruption or modification of normal interactive processes. Indeed, perturbation is potentially a broad methodological approach of great utility; an infant's caregiver can be instructed to act or respond in ways that have a priori theoretical links with specific domains of infant functioning. So, for example, contrived maternal still face behavior has been successfully used to elucidate the influence of maternal postnatal depression on infant state regulation (see Tronick, 1989). More recently, de Ronsay et al. (2006) have shown that when nonanxious mothers are trained to behave in a socially anxious manner with a stranger, their infants, who witnessed these interactions, are more likely to adopt a wary mode of interacting with the same stranger themselves. Of course the findings from any kind of contrived or manipulated perturbation of maternal behavior need to be evaluated carefully against ecologically valid instances of similar behaviors. Thus, the findings of de Rosnay et al., for example, only take on particular importance if it can be shown that the same behaviors in mothers with clinical levels of social anxiety are systematically associated with similar responses in their infants (see Murray et al., 2008). If such a correspondence can be established, the use of deliberate manipulation of maternal behavior offers a methodological tool for better understanding the processes underpinning important relationship based behavioral phenomena. Also, in being process focused, it is also noteworthy that perturbation paradigms are likely to suggest possible modes of intervention when there is an interest in modifying maternal behavior.

Despite the empirical appeal of deliberately manipulating maternal behavior to elucidate salient relational processes, perturbation paradigms have been relatively underutilized in the study of maternal care. Rather, the focus of research on maternal care and infant development has come to encompass many *maternal factors* that have discernable associations with child development, or to attempt to distil naturally occurring features of the mother-child relationship that are of significance for the developing child. This orientation, of course, covers a broad array of empirical research concerned with relational predictors of child development and child socialization; including, for example, aspects of linguistic development, gender role identification, emotion coaching and discipline (see Maccoby, 1992, for an overview). Because this chapter is concerned with maternal care in a relatively narrow sense, connected with the historical origins of the construct, and it is anchored in a long-standing literature addressing the relation between the nature of the maternal provision and the socioemotional development of the child, we base our subsequent discussion of methodological considerations on aspects of maternal care already described in the earlier sections of this chapter. To put some order on the extant approaches to the measurement and operationalization of maternal care it is pragmatic, if not entirely accurate, to make some broad distinctions. In the first instance, a distinction can be made between wide ranging *relationship-based measures* that rely heavily on observations of qualitative aspects of mother-infant relating, on the one hand, and primarily *verbal measures* of the mother, or the mother and child, on the other hand. There is of course overlap between these categories.

Regarding relationship-based measures, there are many different approaches that to some extent vary as a function of the age of the infant under consideration. In early infancy, face-to-face global ratings of mother-infant interaction (Murray, Fiori-Cowley, Hooper, & Cooper, 1996) have been used in various forms and with diverse samples over a 20-year period (e.g., Murray et al., 2007; Murray, Hentges, Hill, Karpf, Mistry, Kreutz et al., 2008; Riordan, Appleby,

& Faragher, 1999; Tomlinson et al., 2005). In a similar vein, Belsky and colleagues (Belsky, Taylor, & Rovine, 1984; Isabella & Belsky, 1991) have described procedures for measuring mother-child interaction in the context of naturally occurring home observations at 3 and 9 months of age, and a range of methods exist to examine structured mother-infant play interactions (e.g., Stein, Woolley, Cooper, & Fairburn, 1994), or more naturalistic interactions in a home or laboratory setting between about 12 months and later toddlerhood, such as *emotional availability* (Biringen & Robinson, 1991; Bornstein, Tamis-LeMonda, Hahn, & Hayne, 2008; Volling, McElwain, Notaro, & Herrara, 2002).

While the specific features of these measurement procedures differ, there are a few recurrent, prominent themes. In particular, each method attempts to capture *responsiveness*, which entails perception and accurate interpretation of the infant's state, as well as an appropriate action or response, and is recognized as a positive influence on child outcomes (Eshel, Daelmans, Cabral de Mello, & Marines, 2006). The subtlety with which responsive parenting has been analyzed has depended on the orientation of the research in question. Whereas the synchrony (contingency or coordination) of mother-infant interactions has attracted sustained attention (see Harrist & Waugh, 2002, for a comprehensive review), the relation between synchronous dyadic responsiveness and affective (emotional) features of the mother-child interaction has been given differential treatment methodologically, with some researchers focusing quite narrowly on the synchrony or coordination of exchanges (e.g., Jaffe, Beebe, Feldstein, Crown, & Jasnow, 2001), while others have put explicit emphasis on warmth, acceptance, affect matching, mutuality, or attunement (e.g., Murray et al., 1996; Volling et al., 2002; De Wolff & van Ijzendoorn, 1997). Thus, despite the fact that synchronous interaction has a mutually rewarding quality (e.g., Isabella & Belsky, 1991), from a methodological point of view there are various reasons to assess the synchronous

and affective aspects of dyadic interactions separately during infancy (Harrist & Waugh, 2002; Murray et al., 2010).

In addition to synchronous and affective features of responsiveness, *intrusive* and *remote* (nonresponsive) patterns of maternal responding have also been reliably measured in the first year and linked with distinct child outcomes, such as insecure attachment organization (e.g., Isabella & Belsky, 1991; Tomlinson et al., 2005). Here too the continued, discrete measurement of such factors in the context of mother-infant interactions seems prudent. Indeed, attempts to create single measures or indices of mother-infant relationship quality, such as the sensitivity scale (see De Wolff & van Ijzendoorn, 1997, for a discussion), do not sit comfortably with the specificity of effects documented in the literature.

If we turn to methodologies that are primarily verbally based, a further distinction can be made between procedures that directly assess maternal language use or communicative features of the dyad, as we have discussed earlier in section 3 ("Becoming a Conversational Partner"), and methods that attempt to tap the underlying psychological orientation of the mother with respect to the infant or child (de Rosnay & Hughes, 2006). Regarding the latter, different research groups have independently arrived at a similar focus on the mother's proclivity or capacity to adopt the child's psychological perspective, and to reflect on psychological processes more generally. Thus, reflective functioning (Fonagy & Target, 1997), mind-mindedness (Meins, 1997), insightfulness (Oppenheim & Koren-Karie 2002), and parental meta-emotion philosophy (Gottman, Katz, & Hooven, 1997) all purportedly tap underlying maternal ways of thinking about the child's psychological experience. In a provocative study, Meins, Fernyhough, Wainright, Das Gupta, Fradley and Tuckey (2002) found that a mother's mind-mindedness, her proclivity to treat her 6-month-old infant as an independent psychological agent, predicted both mother-infant attachment at 1 year of age and the child's social cognitive understanding in early childhood. Mind-mindedness was measured by scoring the mother's appropriate mind-related verbal utterances in the context of a free play session. Importantly, as is suggested by Meins and colleagues' research, the psychological orientation of the mother is believed to underpin, to some extent at least, the responsive, sensitive interactions that are so painstakingly measured via coding of direct observations (Fonagy & Target, 1997; Meins et al., 2002). Should this turn out to be correct, it will represent both a methodological advance in the measurement of maternal care, and a theoretical advance regarding the psychological underpinnings of qualitative differences in mother-infant interaction.[6]

Though it may seem elegant to bypass direct assessment of dyadic interactions by focusing disproportionately on a mother's contribution to the mother-infant relationship – such as her conversational input or psychological orientation concerning the child – reluctance to engage methodologically with the nature of the mother-child relationship, even in the case of maternal mental illness, will almost certainly have inherent limitations: Indeed, it has been repeatedly argued (Hartup, 1989; Maccoby, 1992), and convincingly shown (e.g., Askan et al., 2006; Isabella & Belsky, 1991; Deater-Deckard & O'Connor, 2000) that many facets of the parent child relationship need to be understood in the relational context. How this relational context is to be construed, however, is not often given close scrutiny. Thus, even when an apparently maternal characteristic is measured (e.g., acceptance, warmth, intrusiveness, psychological discourse), the fact that it is measured in the relational context is taken for granted. It is seldom asked, for example, how a given mother or child would interact with a different partner (although see Jaffe et al., 2001). Paradoxically, it is also rare in the empirical literature to encounter genuinely dyadic measures of relationship functioning. It is deceptively easy to dismiss the need for such measures if one does not have them. As an illustration, consider the finding by Ruffman et al. (2002) that maternal

mental state discourse predicts child mental state understanding longitudinally, but the reverse relationship does not hold. The clear implication is that mothers set the tone for conversational exploration of psychological states. True though this may be, Ensor and Hughes (2008) have since shown that it is actually *connected* mental state conversations, in which partners respond appropriately to each other's contributions, that best predicts children's later mental state understanding.

In sum, despite the fact that there are not uniform methodological approaches to the measurement of maternal care, there is consensus on key features of maternal behavior and dyadic interaction that is of importance for concurrent and longitudinal child outcomes in the socioemotional domain. If the past is any indication, however, the future is likely to bring further specific relations between features of mother-infant dyadic interactions and child outcomes.

6. Concluding Remarks

While we have drawn briefly on research with clinical populations earlier, our discussion has focused on maternal care as it is commonly experienced. We have spoken of the infant's move toward independence, so vividly brought to life in the work of Winnicott, Trevarthen and others, and we have emphasized the cooperative interactions achieved and solidified by the mother-infant dyad during infancy and into toddlerhood. Insofar as maternal care can be cast as an environment, we have sought to highlight the themes of continuity of care, and accommodation of such care to the changing capacities and needs of the infant. However, there is another story to be told, on which we have only touched, about substantive failures of such continuity, or availability, and of maternal accommodation (for whatever reason). Compelling though this latter story may be, it too often eclipses the fact that most infants to a great extent receive *good enough* maternal care, a point Winnicott was keen to stress. Winnicott saw clearly that, beyond the phase of primary maternal preoccupation, one of the great tasks of maternal care is to allow the infant to encounter his environment with a degree of independence that is appropriate to his capacities and condition. Of course it follows that maternal *sensitivity* is a crucial feature of this process, but it is worth emphasizing that such sensitivity entails an appreciation and acceptance of the infant's agency, albeit in the context of profound dependence. Thus Winnicott (1966) describes a somewhat paradoxical situation in which the infant needs both a mother who perceives his signals and interprets them accurately, as exemplified by Ainsworth's notion of sensitivity, but also misunderstands his needs and misinterprets his signals precisely because he is acting independently. The tension between these positions is in part captured in Tronick's description of interactive error and repair, and helps us understand why the infant generally finds what he needs in a mother who is not "distorted by ill-health" or "environmental stress." As Winnicott (1966) explains:

> There is an idea for emphasis here, for the whole procedure of infant-care has as its main characteristic a steady presentation of the world to the infant. This is something that cannot be done by thought, nor can it be managed mechanically. It can only be done by continuous management by a human being who is consistently herself. There is no question of perfection here. Perfection belongs to machines; what the infant needs is just what he usually gets, the care and attention of someone who is going on being herself. This of course applies to fathers too. (pp. 87–88)

Notes

1   Given the focus on maternal care throughout this text, we adopt the masculine pronoun to refer to the infant for clarity and simplicity.

2   For a discussion see Shuttleworth (1993) and Brody (1982).

3   Symington (1986) reports that Winnicott conducted approximately 20,000 infant-mother sessions at the Paddington Green Children's Hospital, London.

4   To explore the mutuality involved in such interactions, Murray and Trevarthen (1986; Murray, 1998) also turned the tables, showing mothers a replay of noncontingent and nonresponsive infant behavior by means of the DV setup. Mothers found the episode distressing and quickly ceased to adopt verbal and prosodic features typical of mother-infant communication (Papousek & Papousek, 1987). They also tended to focus on their own response rather than the infants' becoming more demanding and directive.

5   Meltzoff and Moore (1994, 2007) offer a detailed discussion of the comprehensibility of complex multimodal human actions from early in infancy.

6   See van IJzendoorn (1995) for a closely related correspondence between mothers' attachment representations on the AAI and infant attachment organization; the so-called transmission gap.

References

Ainsworth, M. D. S., Bell, S. M., & Stayton, D. J. (1974). Infant-mother attachment and social development: "socialization" as a product of reciprocal responsiveness to signals. In M. P. M. Richards (Ed.), *The integration of a child into a social world*, pp. 99–135. Cambridge: Cambridge University Press.

Ainsworth, M. D. S., Blehar, M. C., Waters, E., & Wall, S. (1978). *Patterns of attachment: A psychological study of the Strange Situation*. Hillsdale, NJ: LEA.

Askan, N., Kochanska, G., & Ortmann, M. (2006). Mutually responsive orientation between parents and their young children: Towards methodological advances in the science of relationships. *Developmental Psychology*, 42(5), 833–848.

Baldwin, D. A. & Moses, L. J. (1996). The ontogeny of social information gathering. *Child Development*, 67, 1915–1939.

Barrett, P. M., Rapee, R. M., & Dadds, M. R. (1996). Family Treatment of Childhood Anxiety: A Controlled Trial. *Journal of Consulting and Clinical Psychology*, 64, 333–342.

Bates, E., Camaioni, L., & Volterra, V. (1975). The acquisition of performatives prior to speech. *Merrill-Palmer Quarterly*, 21, 205–224.

Bateson, M. C. (1975). Mother-infant exchanges: The epigenesis of conversational interaction. In D. Aaronson & R. W. Rieber (Eds.), *Developmental psycholinguistics and* communication disorders; *Annals of the New York Academy of Sciences*, Vol. 263, pp. 101–113. New York: New York Academy of Sciences.

Behne, T., Carpenter, M., Call, J., & Tomasello, M. (2005). Unwilling versus unable: Infants' understanding of intentional action. *Developmental Psychology*, 41(2), 328–337.

Belsky, J., Taylor, M., & Rovine, M. (1984). The Pennsylvania infant and family development project: II. Development of reciprocal interaction in mother-infant dyads. *Child Development*, 55, 718–722.

Bion, W. R. (1962). The psychoanalytic study of thinking: II. A theory of thinking. *International Journal of Psychoanalysis*, 43, 306–310.

Biringen, Z. & Robinson, J. (1991). Emotional availability in mother-child interactions: A reconceptualization for research. *American Journal of Orthopsychiatry*, 61, 258–271.

Bornstein, M. H., Tamis-LeMonda, C. S., Hahn, C., & Haynes, O. (2008). Maternal responsiveness to young children at three ages: Longitudinal analysis of a multidimensional, modular, and specific parenting construct. *Developmental Psychology*, 44(3), 867–874.

Bowlby, J. (1969/1997). *Attachment and loss, Vol. 1. Attachment* (2nd ed.). Sydney: Random House.

Bowlby, J. (1973/1997). *Attachment and loss, Vol. 2. Separation: Anxiety and anger* (2nd ed.). Sydney: Random House.

Braten, S. (1987). *Dialogic mind: The infant and the adult in proto conversation*. In M. Carvallo (Ed.), *Nature, cognition and systems*, pp. 187–205. Boston: D. Reidel.

Braten, S. (Ed.) (1998). *Intersubjective communication and emotion in early ontogeny*. Paris: Cambridge University Press.

Brazelton, T. B., Koslowski, B., & Main, M. (1974). The origins of reciprocity: The early mother-infant interaction. In M. Lewis & L. Rosenblum (Eds.), *The effect of the infant on its caregiver*, pp. 49–76. New York: Wiley.

Bretherton, I. & Beeghly, M. (1982). Talking about internal states: The acquisition of an explicit theory of mind. *Developmental Psychology*, 18(6), 906–921.

Bretherton, I. & Munholland, K. A. (1999). Internal working models in attachment relationships: A construct revisited. In J. Cassidy & P. R. Shaver (Eds.), *Handbook of attachment: Theory, research, and clinical applications*, pp. 89–111. New York: Guilford Press.

Brody, S. (1982). Psychoanalytic theories of infant development. *Psychoanalytic Quarterly*, 51, 526–597.

Bullowa, M. (Ed.) (1979). *Before speech: The beginning of interpersonal communication*. Melbourne: Cambridge University Press.

Caldji, C., Tannenbaum, B., Sharma, S., Francis, D., Plotsky, P. M., & Meaney, M. J. (1998). Maternal care during infancy regulates the development of neural systems mediating the expression of fearfulness in the rat. *Proceedings of the National Academy of Science of the United States of America*, 95(9), 5335–5340.

Carpenter, M., Nagel, K., & Tomasello, M. (1998). Social cognition, joint attention and communicative competence from 9 to 15 months of age. *Monographs of the Society for Research in Child Development*, 63(4), Serial No. 255.

Cassidy, J. (1994). Emotion regulation: Influences of attachment relationships. In N. A. Fox (Ed.), The development of emotion regulation: Biological and behavioral considerations, pp. 228–249. *Monographs for the Society for Research in Child Development*, 59(2–3), Serial No. 240.

Cassidy, J. & Shaver, P. R. (Eds.) (1999). *Handbook of attachment: Theory, research, and clinical applications*. London: Guilford Press

Dadds, M. R. & Barrett, P. M. (1996). Family processes in child and adolescent anxiety and depression. *Behavior Change*, 13, 231–239.

Deater-Deckard, K. & O'Connor, T. G. (2000). Parent-child mutuality in early childhood: Two behavioral genetic studies. *Developmental Psychology*, 36(5), 561–570.

de Rosnay, M., Cooper, P. J., Tsigaras, N., & Murray, L. (2006) Transmission of social anxiety from mother to infant: An experimental study using a social referencing paradigm. *Behavior Research and Therapy*, 44, 1165–75.

de Rosnay, M. & Hughes, C. (2006). Conversation and theory of mind: Do children talk their way to socio-cognitive understanding? *British Journal of Developmental Psychology*, 24(1), 7–37.

de Wolff, M. S. & van IJzendoorn, M. H. (1997). Sensitivity and attachment: A meta-analysis on parental antecedents of infant attachment. *Child Development*, 68(4), 571–591.

Dunn, J. & Brown, J. R. (1993). Early conversations about causality: Content, pragmatics and developmental change. *British Journal of Developmental Psychology*, 11, 107–123.

Dunn, J., Bretherton, I., & Munn, P. (1987). Conversations about feeling states between mothers and their young children. *Developmental Psychology*, 23(1), 132–139.

Ensor, R. & Hughes, C. (2008). Content or connectedness? Mother-child talk and early social understanding. *Child Development,* 79(1), 201–216.

Eshel, N., Daelmans, B., Cabral De Mello, M., & Martines J. (2006). Responsive parenting: Interventions and outcomes. *Bulletin of the World Health Organization,* 84(12), 992–998.

Fantz, R. L. (1963). Pattern vision in newborn infants. *Science,* 140, 296–7.

Field, T. M. & Fox, N. A. (Eds.) (1985). *Social perception in infants.* Norwood, NJ: Ablex Publishing Corporation.

Field, T., Healy, B., Goldstein, S., Perry, S. & et al. (1988). Infants of depressed mothers show "depressed" behavior even with nondepressed adults. *Child Development,* 59(6), 1569–1579.

Fogel, A. (1982). Affect dynamics in early infancy: affective tolerance. In Field, T. & Fogel, A. (Eds.), *Emotion and early interaction,* pp. 25–55. Hillsdale, NJ: Lawrence Erlbaum & Associates, Publishers.

Fogel, A. (1993). *Developing through relationships: Origins of communication, self, and culture.* Chicago: University of Chicago Press.

Fonagy, P., Steele, M., Steele, H., Moran, G. S. & Higgit, A. C. (1991). The capacity for understanding mental states: The reflective self in parent and child and its significance for security of attachment. *Infant Mental Health Journal,* 12(3), 201–218.

Fonagy, P. & Target, M. (1997) Attachment and the reflective function: Their role in self-organisation. *Development and Psychopathology,* 9, 679–700.

Francis, D., Diorio, J., Liu, D., & Meaney, M. J. (1999). Nongenomic transmission across generations of maternal behavior and stress responses in the rat. *Science,* 286(5442), 1155–1158.

Freud, A. (1968). *The ego and the mechanisms of defence.* London: Hogarth Press and the Institute of Psycho-Analysis.

Freud, A. (1973). *Normality and pathology in childhood: Assessments of development.* London: Hogarth Press and the Institute of Psycho-Analysis.

Freud, S. (1926). Inhibitions, Symptoms and Anxiety. *The Standard Edition of the Complete Psychological Works of Sigmund Freud:* Volume XX (1925–1926). *An Autobiographical Study, Inhibitions, Symptoms and Anxiety, The Question of Lay Analysis and Other Works,* 75–176. London: Hogarth Press.

Gaffan, E. A., Martins, C., Healey, S., & Murray L. (2010). Early social experience and individual differences in infants' joint attention. *Social Development,* 19(2), 369–393

Gerull, F. C. & Rapee, R. M. (2002). Mother knows best: Effects of maternal modelling on the acquisition of fear and avoidance behaviour in toddlers. *Behaviour Research and Therapy,* 40, 279–287.

Gianino, A. & Tronick, E. Z. (1988). The mutual regulation model: The infant's self and interactive regulation coping and defense. In T. Field, P. McCabe, & M. Schneiderman (Eds.), *Stress and coping,* pp. 47–68. Hillsdale, NJ: Earlbaum.

Gottman, J. M., Katz, L. F., & Hooven, C. (1997). *Meta-emotion: How families communicate emotionally.* Mahway, NJ: Lawrence Earlbaum.

Harris, P. L. (2006). Social cognition. In D. Kuhn and R. Siegler (Eds.), *Handbook of child Psychology* (6th ed.): Vol. 2. *Cognition, perception, and language,* pp. 811–868. New Jersey; John Wiley & Sons.

Harrist, A. W. & Waugh, R. M. (2002). Dyadic synchrony: Its structure and function in children's development. *Developmental Review,* 22, 555–592.

Hartup, W. W. (1989). Social relationships and their developmental significance. *American Psychologist,* 44, 120–126.

Haviland, J. & Lelwica, J. (1987). The induced affect response: 10-week-old infants' responses to three emotion expressions. *Developmental Psychology,* 23, 97–104.

Hobson, P. (1995). *Autism and the development of mind.* Hove, UK: LEA

Isabella, R. A. & Belsky, J. (1991). Interactional synchrony and the origins of infant-mother attachment: A replication study. *Child Development,* 62, 373–384.

Izard, C. & Harris, P. (1995) Emotional development and developmental psychopathology. In Cicchetti, D. & Cohen, D. (Eds.), *Developmental psychopathology:* Vol. 1. *Theory and methods,* pp. 467–503. Oxford, UK: John Wiley & Sons.

Jaffe, J., Beebe, B., Feldstein, S., Crown, C. L., & Jasnow, M. D. (2001). Rhythms of dialogue in infancy. *Monographs of the Society for Research in Child Development,* 66(2), Serial No. 265.

Jenkins, J. M., Turrell, S. L., Kogushi, Y., Lollis, S., & Ross, S. H. (2003). A longitudinal investigation of the dynamics of mental state talk in families. *Child Development,* 74(3), 905–920.

Kaplan, P. S., Bachorowski, J., & Zarlengo-Strouse, P. (1999). Child-directed speech produced by mothers with symptoms of depression fails to promote associative learning in 4-month-old infants. *Child Development* 70(3), 560–570.

Klein, M. (1975). *The psycho-analysis of children.* New York: Delta Books.

Kochanska, G. (1997). Mutually responsive orientation between mothers and their young children: Implications for early socialization. *Child Development,* 68(1), 94–112.

Legerstee, M. & Markova, G. (2007). Intentions make a difference: Infant responses to still-face and modified still-face conditions. *Infant Behavior and Development,* 30(2), 232–250.

Liszkowski, U., Carpenter, M., Striano, T., & Tomasello, M. (2006). 12- and 18-month-olds point to provide information for others. *Journal of Cognition and Development,* 7(2), 173–187.

Liszkowski, U., Carpenter, M., & Tomasello, M. (2007). Pointing out news, old news, and absent referents at 12 months of age. *Developmental Science,* 10(2), F1–F7.

Lock, A. (Ed.) (1978). *Action, gesture and symbol: The emergence of language.* London: Academic Press.

Maccoby, E. E. (1992). The role of parents in the socialization of children: An historical overview. *Developmental Psychology,* 28(6), 1006–1017.

Main, M., Kaplan, N., & Cassidy, J. (1985). Security in infancy, childhood and adulthood: a move to the level of representation. In I. Bretherton & E. Waters (Eds.), Growing points of attachment theory and research. *Monographs of the Society for Research in Child Development,* 50(1–2), 66–104, Serial No. 209.

Mayer, N. K. & Tronick, E. Z. (1985). Mothers' turn-giving signals and infant turn-taking in mother-infant interaction. In T. M. Field & N. A. Fox (Eds.), *Social perception in infants,* pp. 199–216. Norwood, NJ: Ablex Publishing Corporation.

Meins, E. (1997). Security of attachment and the social development of cognition. Hove, UK: Psychology Press.

Meins, E., Fernyhough, C., Fradley, E., & Tuckey, M. (2001). Rethinking maternal sensitivity: Mothers' comments on infants' mental processes predict security of attachment at 12 months. *Journal of Child Psychology and Psychiatry,* 42(5), 637–648.

Meins, E., Fernyhough, C., Wainwright, R., Das Gupta, M., Fradley, E., & Tuckey, M. (2002). Maternal mind-mindedness and attachment security as predictors of theory of mind understanding. *Child Development,* 73, 1715–1726.

Meltzoff, A. N. (2007). The "like me" framework for recognizing and becoming an intentional agent. *Acta Psychologica,* 124(1), 26–43.

Meltzoff, A. N. & Moore, M. K. (1977). Imitation of facial and manual gestures by human neonates. *Science,* 198, 75–78.

Meltzoff, A. N. & Moore, M. K. (1994). Imitation, memory, and the representation of persons. *Infant Behavior and Development,* 17, 83–99.

Moore, C. & Corkum, V. (1994). Social understanding at the end of the first year of life. *Developmental Review,* 14, 349–372.

Moore, C. & D'Entremont, B. (2001). Developmental changes in pointing as a function of attentional focus. *Journal of Cognition and Development,* 2(2), 109–129.

Morton, J. & Johnson, M. H. (1991). CONSPEC and CONLERN: A two-process theory of infant face recognition. *Psychological Review,* 98(2), 164–181.

Moses, L. J., Baldwin, D. A., Rosicky, J. G., & Tidball, G. (2001). Evidence for referential understanding in the emotions domain at twelve and eighteen months. *Child Development,* 72(3), 718–735.

Murray, L. (1998). Contributions of experimental and clinical perturbations of mother-infant communication to the understanding of infant intersubjectivity. In S. Braten (Ed.), *Intersubjective communication and emotion in early ontogeny,* pp. 127–143. Paris: Cambridge University Press.

Murray, L., Cooper, P., Creswell, C., Schofield, E., & Sack, C. (2007). The effects of maternal social phobia on mother-infant interactions and infant social responsiveness. *Journal of Child Psychology and Psychiatry,* 48(1), 45–52.

Murray, L., Creswell, C., & Cooper, P. J. (2009). The development of anxiety disorders in childhood: an integrative review. *Psychological Medicine,* 39, 1413–1423.

Murray, L., de Rosnay, M., Pearson, J., Bergeron, C., Schofield, E., Royal-Lawson, M. et al. (2008). Intergenerational transmission of social anxiety: The role of social referencing processes in infancy. *Child Development,* 79(4), 1049–1064.

Murray, L., Fiori-Cowley, A., Hooper, R., & Cooper, P. (1996) The impact of postnatal depression and associated adversity on early mother-infant interactions and later infant outcome. *Child Development,* 67, 2512–2526.

Murray L., Halligan, S. L., & Cooper, P. J. (2010). Effects of postnatal depression on mother-infant interactions, and child development. In G. Bremner & T. Wachs (Eds.), *The Wiley-Blackwell Handbook of Infant Development.* Chichester, West Sussex: Wiley-Blackwell.

Murray, L., Hentges, F., Hill, J., Karpf, J., Mistry, B., Kreutz, M. et al. (2008). The effect of cleft lip and palate, and the timing of lip repair on mother-infant interactions and infant development. *Journal of Child Psychology and Psychiatry*, 49(2), 115–123.

Murray, L. & Trevarthen, C. (1985). Emotional regulation of interactions between two-month-olds and their mothers. In T. M. Field & N. A. Fox (Eds.), *Social perception in infants*, pp. 177–197. Norwood, NJ: Ablex Publishing Corporation.

Murray, L. & Trevarthen, C. (1986). The infant's role in mother-infant communication. *Journal of Child Language*, 13, 15–29.

Nadel, J., Carchon, I., Kervella, C., Marcelli, D., & Reserbat-Plantey, D. (1999). Expectancies for social contingencies in 2-month-olds. *Developmental Science*, 2(2), 164–173.

Oppenheim, D. (2006). Child, parent, and parent–child emotion narratives: Implications for developmental psychopathology. *Developmental Psychology*, 18, 771–790.

Oppenheim, D. & Koren-Karie, N. (2002). Mothers' insightfulness regarding their children's internal worlds: The capacity underlying secure child-mother relationships. *Infant Mental Health Journal*, 23(6), 593–605.

Papousek, H. & Papousek, M. (1987). Intuitive parenting: A dialectic counterpart to the infant's integrative competence. In J. D. Osofsky (Ed.), *Handbook of infant development*, pp. 669–720 (2nd ed.). New York: Wiley.

Peterson, C. C. & Siegal, M. (2000) Insights into theory of mind from deafness and autism. *Mind and Language*, 15, 123–45.

Riordan, D., Appleby, L., & Faragher, B. (1999). Mother-infant interaction in postpartum women with schizophrenia and affective disorders. *Psychological Medicine*, 29, 991–995.

Ruffman, T., Slade, L., & Crowe, E. (2002). The relation between children's and mother's mental state language and theory-of-mind understanding. *Child Development*, 73(3), 734–751.

Sander, L. W. (1962). Infant and the caretaking environment: Investigation and conceptualization of adaptive behavior in a system of increasing complexity. In E. J. Anthony (Ed.), *Explorations in child psychiatry* (pp. 129–166). London: Plenum Press.

Segal, H. (1975). *Introduction to the work of Melanie Klein*. London: Hogarth Press and the Institute of Psycho-Analysis.

Shuttleworth, J. (1993). Psychoanalytic theory and infant development. In L. Miller, M. Rustin, M. Rustin, & J. Shuttleworth (Eds.), *Closely observed infants*, pp. 22–51. London: Duckworth.

Singer, L. M., Brodzinsky, D. M., Ramsay, D., Steir, M., & Waters, E. (1985). Mother-infant attachment in adoptive families. *Child Development*, 56(6), 1543–1551.

Source, J. F. & Emde, R. N. (1981). Mothers' presence is not enough: Effect of emotional availability on infant exploration. *Developmental Psychology*, 17(6), 737–745.

Sroufe, L. A. (1995). *Emotional development: The organization of emotional life in the early years.* Cambridge: Cambridge University Press

St. Clair, M. (1986). *Object relations and self psychology: An introduction.* Monterey, Ca: Brooks/Cole Publishing Company.

Stanley, C., Murray, L., & Stein, A. (2004). The effect of postnatal depression on mother-infant interaction, infant response to the Still-face perturbation and performance on an Instrumental Learning task. *Development and Psychopathology*, 16, 1–18.

Stein, A., Woolley, H., Cooper, S. D., & Fairburn, C. G. (1994). An observational study of mothers with eating disorders and their infants. *Journal of Child Psychology and Psychiatry*, 35(4), 733–748.

Stern, D. N. (1974). Mother and infant at play: The dyadic interaction involving facial, vocal and gaze behaviours. In M. Lewis & L. A., Rosenblum (Eds.), *The effect of the infant on its caregiver*, pp. 187–213. New York: Wiley.

Stern, D. N. (1985). *The interpersonal world of the infant: A view from psychoanalysis and developmental psychology.* New York: Basic Books.

Stern, D. N., Hofer, L., Haft, W., & Dore, J. (1985). Affect attunement: The sharing of feeling states between mother and infant by means of inter-modal fluency. In T. M. Field & N. A. Fox (Eds.), *Social perception in infants*, pp. 249–268. Norwood, NJ: Ablex Publishing Corporation.

Symmington, N. (1986). *The analytic experience: Lectures from the Tavistock.* London: Fress Association Books.

Taumoepeau, M. & Ruffman, T. (2008). Stepping stones to others' minds: Maternal talk relates to child mental state language and emotion understanding at 15, 24, and 33 months. *Child Development*, 79(2), 284–302.

Thompson, R. A. (1999). Early attachment and later development. In J. Cassidy & P. R. Shaver, *Handbook of attachment: Theory, research, and clinical applications*, pp. 265–286. London: Guilford Press.

Tomasello, M., Carpenter, M., Call, J., Behne, T., & Moll, H. (2005). Understanding and sharing intentions: The origins of cultural cognition. *Behavioral and Brain Sciences*, 28, 675–735.

Tomlinson, M., Cooper, P. & Murray, L. (2005) The mother-infant relationship and infant attachment in a South African peri-urban settlement. *Child Development*, 76(5), 1044–1054.

Tracy, R., Lamb, M., & Ainsworth, M. D. S. (1976). Infant approach behavior as related to attachment. *Child Development*, 47, 571–578.

Trevarthen, C. (1979). Communication and cooperation in early infancy: a description of primary intersubjectivity. In M. Bullowa (Ed.), *Before speech: The beginning of interpersonal communication*, pp. 321–347. Melbourne: Cambridge University Press.

Trevarthen, C. & Aitken, K. J. (2001). Infant intersubjectivity: Research, theory, and clinical approaches. *Journal of Child Psychology and Psychiatry*, 42(1), 3–48.

Trevarthen, C. & Hubley, P. (1978). Secondary intersubjectivity: Confidence, confiding and acts of meaning in the first year. In A. Lock (Ed.), *Action, Gesture and Symbol: The emergence of language*, pp. 183–229. London: Academic Press.

Tronick, E. Z. (1989). Emotions and emotional communication in infants. *American Psychologist*, 89 (February), 112–119.

Tronick, E. (2007). *The Neurobehavioral and social-emotional development of infants and children*. New York: Norton.

Tronick, E., Als, H., & Adamson, L. (1979). Structure of early face-to-face communicative interaction. In M. Bullowa (Ed.), *Before speech: The beginning of interpersonal communication*, pp. 349–372. Melbourne: Cambridge University Press.

Tronick, E., Als, H., Adamson, L., Wise, S., & Brazelton, B. (1978). The infant's response to entrapment between contradictory messages in face-to-face interaction. *Journal of the American Academy of Child Psychiatry*, 17(1), 1–13.

Tronick, E. Z., Ricks, M. & Cohn, J. F. (1982) Maternal and infant affective exchange: Patterns of Adaptation. In Field, T. & Fogel, A. (Eds.), *Emotion and early interaction*, pp. 83–100. London: LEA.

van Ijzendoorn, M. H. (1995). Adult attachment representations, parental responsiveness, and infant attachment: A meta-analysis on the predictive validity of the Adult Attachment Interview. *Psychological Bulletin*, 117(3), 387–403.

Volling, B. L., McElwain, N. L., Notaro, P. C., & Herrera, C. (2002). Parent's emotional availability and infant emotion competence: Predictors of parent-infant attachment and emerging self-regulation. *Journal of Family Psychology*, 16(4), 447–465.

Waters, E., Wippman, J., & Sroufe, L. A. (1979). Attachment, positive affect, and competence in the peer group: Two studies in construct validation. *Child Development*, 51, 821–829.

Weinberg, M. K. & Tronick, E. Z. (1994). Beyond the face: An empirical study of infant affective configurations of facial, vocal, gestural and regulatory behaviours. *Child Development*, 65(5), 1503–1515.

Weinberg, M. K. & Tronick, E. Z. (1996). Infant affective reactions to the resumption of maternal interaction after the still-face. *Child Development*, 67(3), 905–914.

Wellman, H. M., Harris, P. L., Banerjee, M., & Sinclair, A. (1995). Early understanding of emotion: Evidence from natural language. *Cognition and Emotion*, 9(2/3), 117–149.

Winnicott, D. W. (1966). *The maturational processes and the facilitating environment: Studies in the theory of emotional development*. New York: International Universities Press, Inc.

Winnicott, D. W. (1982). *Through paediatrics to psycho-analysis*. London: Hogarth Press and the Institute of Psycho-Analysis.

CHAPTER 4

Novel Assessment Techniques Aimed at Identifying Proximal and Distal Environmental Risk Factors for Children and Adolescents

Stacey B. Daughters, Jessica M. Richards, and Linda C. Mayes

Environmental risk factors have clearly been identified by prevention researchers as critical components in understanding poor child outcomes. These environmental factors are defined broadly across proximal (e.g., parent behavior, family dynamics, social networks) and distal (e.g., neighborhood crime, violence) environmental perspectives. Despite significant progress in identifying a myriad of environmental risk factors, the assessment of these risk factors has often relied on retrospective self-report assessments, which, despite their feasibility, are limited in their reliability (see Piasecki, Hufford, Solhan, & Trull, 2007 for a review). As one example, evidence indicates that current mood states and contextual cues affect the accuracy of memory recall (Kihlstrom, Eich, Sandbrand, & Tobias, 2000; Menon & Yorkston, 2000; Robinson & Clore, 2002). Further, the neighborhood context is a key factor in identifying environmental risks, and observational research in this area has been limited. As such, the goal of this chapter is to provide a discussion of novel assessment techniques that may strengthen our ability to identify

the environmental risks for children accurately and thoroughly. We begin with a discussion of assessment techniques aimed at identifying proximal risk factors such as parent behavior, family dynamics, and social networks, followed by a discussion of assessment techniques aimed at identifying more distal risk factors such as the neighborhood environment.

Assessment of Proximal Risk Factors

Ecological Momentary Assessment

Given the limitations of retrospective self-report measures, an assessment approach aimed at identifying the real-time everyday experiences of children and parents would be ideal for improving our understanding of proximal environmental risk and protective factors such as parental behavior, family dynamics, and social networks. A real-time assessment technique that has historically been used in basic research and clinical treatment settings are daily diaries (e.g., Scollon, Kim-Prieto, & Diener, 2003).

Researchers and clinicians find this approach advantageous because participants write down experiences at the time of the events, thereby minimizing the influence of memory deficits, recall bias, and subsequent events. Recent work has examined the relationship between real-time assessment and recall, with findings indicating notable discrepancies (Stone, Broderick, Shiffman, & Schwarz, 2004; Williams et al., 2004). As one example, patients with fibromyalgia were asked to report the degree of clinical pain they were experiencing with daily diaries, end-of-week reports, and monthly in-clinic reports (Williams et al., 2004). Findings indicated significant differences in the three methods, with the monthly reports producing the highest pain ratings and the diaries producing the lowest pain ratings. These findings highlight discrepancies among real-time and retrospective reports, thereby suggesting an advantage to real-time assessments.

Following the paper-and-pencil format of daily diaries was the development of an electronic version, often referred to as ecological momentary assessment (EMA; Stone & Shiffman, 1994). Although conceptually similar to the paper-and-pencil format of daily diaries, EMA devices are advantageous in that the timing and frequency of assessments can be controlled by the experimenter. There are currently a variety of implementation methods for EMA devices, which will undoubtedly continue to grow with advances in technology. The earliest and simplest versions are the pager and wristwatch that are programmed to signal the participant to fill out paper and pencil measures at certain times of the day (Broderick et al., 2003; Litt et al., 1998). Although clearly a methodological improvement, signaling alone is limited unless compliance is verified. For example, adults with chronic pain participated in a 24-day sampling protocol of three pain assessments per day in which participants were signaled with a programmed wristwatch to make an entry in their daily diaries (Broderick et al., 2003). Verified compliance was assessed with sensors that recorded when the diary was opened and closed. Self-reported compliance based on participants'

paper diaries was 85 percent and 91 percent for each of two groups, whereas verified compliance based on wristwatch data was 29 percent and 39 percent, highlighting the limitations in relying solely on signaling devices for real-time assessments. However, signaling did produce a significant increment in verified compliance when compared with an identical trial without signaling; suggesting that self-report dating of diary entries may mislead investigators about rates of compliance with diary protocols.

Given the limitations in relying solely on signaling with pagers and wristwatches, EMA techniques have advanced to include real-time assessments on personal digital assistants (PDAs). PDAs enable the researcher to program questionnaires onto the device so that the participant has to fill it out electronically, often following a programmed signal. Specifically, an audio cue emits at prescribed intervals and the participant then touches the screen to answer questions. Once the participant has answered a question, the data disappear from the PDA, thereby decreasing the likelihood that future responses are influenced by previous responses. Database software accompanies the device so that researchers can download data from the PDA, along with the time and date that information was filled out. As one example, ninth-grade adolescents with varying levels of anxiety were signaled to fill out diary entries on Palm III handheld computers every 30 minutes for 4 days to determine group differences in mood, activities, social settings, dietary intake, smoking, and alcohol use (Henker, Whalen, Jamner, & Delfino, 2002). Each assessment took approximately 1 minute for the adolescent to complete. If any adolescent did not fill out the diary before three reminder signals were emitted then the diary became inaccessible until the next signal. Participants also filled out one retrospective questionnaire, which was compared to the electronic diary data. Findings indicated that approximately 80 percent of the total possible daily diary entries were completed. Further, although both the daily diary and retrospective report differentiated the low vs high anxiety groups, sharper differentiations were apparent from the daily diary data. Taken together, although EMAs are subject to response biases similar to self-reports and are subject to participant burden from multiple reports, the advantage of assessing real-time data in natural environments provides an ideal next step in improving assessment techniques aimed at identifying proximal environmental risk and protective factors for children. The next sections highlight recent applications of this technology in identifying risk factors among school aged children and infants.

Utility of EMA with School Aged Children

Ecological momentary assessment (EMA) is ideally suited to provide rich data to improve our understanding of proximal environmental indices that effect child outcomes such as parent behavior, family dynamics, and social networks. Although not previously utilized to specifically assess environmental risk, previous research indicates that EMA technology is feasible with school aged children and early adolescents (Simonich et al., 2004; Whalen, Henker, Ishikawa, Jamner, Floro, Johnston et al., 2006; Whalen, Jamner, Henker, & Delfino, 2001). As one example, Whalen and colleagues (2006) used PDA diaries to examine the affective, cognitive, and social dimensions preceding challenging aspects of daily living among children with ADHD and their parents. Audio signals were used to prompt mothers and children to fill out their PDA every 30 minutes during non-school hours. Similar to Henker et al. (2002), three reminder signals were emitted at 1-minute intervals if the PDA was not activated and after 3 minutes the PDA became inaccessible until the next scheduled signal. When signaled, the mother and child specified their location, social context, current activity, ratings of child's symptomatic behaviors (e.g., impatient, restless) and moods (e.g., angry, good mood), and quality of their current interaction (e.g., having fun, getting along). The parents also rated their own mood. Results indicated high average rates of compliance for the mothers (91 percent) and children (89 percent), with all participants completing at least 71 percent of the prompted diaries and some completing 100 percent. Findings from this study indicated elevations in negative moods and maternal perceptions of lower parenting effectiveness and quality of life in the ADHD group. Further, differences in the contexts of maternal anger were salient, with mothers in the ADHD group more often angry when with their children and comparison mothers more often angry when not. These findings, in line with emerging data from other studies, highlight both the feasibility of this approach in difficult samples (e.g., ADHD) and the ability of this technology to identify individual difference variables.

Use of EMA to Identify Environmental Risks for Infants

In addition to evidence indicating that the use of EMA technology is feasible for school aged children, we must also address the environment of infants and toddlers, as this is a critical time period in child development. Given the inability of infants and toddlers to self-report their own mood, behavior, and social interactions, the use of EMA among parents may be a useful alternative. For example, findings suggest a strong genetic basis for infant emotionality, which, when paired with insensitive parenting, abuse, or neglect, leads to later problems with depression, poor impulse control, and externalizing/antisocial behaviors (Propper & Moore, 2006). Current assessment techniques aimed at identifying parental behaviors are limited to retrospective self-report questionnaires or data from government child protection agencies. For instance, neglect is a key environmental risk factor for infants and toddlers, as they are more likely to be victims of neglect than physical or sexual abuse (USDHHS, 2000). However, neglect is an understudied variable, despite the many negative consequences, potentially due to the difficulty in assessing omission of a behavior rather than a commission of behavior, as in the case of physical or sexual abuse (Connell-Carrick & Scannapieco, 2006). EMA technology may provide an ideal alternative in that parental report of basic infant needs can be monitored on an hourly basis. Specifically, parents could be signaled to indicate how often their infant eats, sleeps, spends time alone, is in the care of friends and relatives, and receives medical care. In addition, qualitative indicators such as the types of food the infant or toddler eats and those whom they spend their time with could provide even richer data. In addition to an assessment of parental neglect, important parental characteristics and behaviors that are known to lead to poor child outcomes can be monitored. For instance, parental stress is associated with higher rates of neglect and abuse (e.g., Éthier, Lacharité, & Couture, 1995). Utilizing EMA to track parent mood ratings and their response to infant cues (e.g., crying, irritability) over time may help identify at-risk parent-infant dyads for prevention and intervention programs aimed at reducing parental stress.

Methodological Considerations Use of EMA to Identify Environmental Risks for Infants

Although the appeal of EMA technology is an improvement over retrospective self-report questionnaires in that they are dependent on careful timing, include repeated observations, assess events as they occur, and occur in natural environments; a number of limitations and methodological issues should be addressed when designing a study using this technology. First, although advantages exist to real-time assessment, EMA remains a form of self-report and thus is subject to self-presentation biases and influences from response scales (Mazze et al., 1984). Second, issues of noncompliance continue to exist with EMA technology. In a recent study, participants were instructed to fill out paper and pencil diary cards at three time points during the day (Stone, Shiffman, Schwartz, Broderick, & Hufford, 2003). Unknown to the participants, each diary card also contained a sensor that signaled when the diary was opened and closed. When the participants turned in the diary cards at the end of the study, 90 percent appeared to have completed all of the diary cards. However, when the sensors in the diaries were examined, only 20 percent of the diary cards were completed within 90 minutes of the scheduled time. A comparison group was also used that utilized Palm technology to prohibit participants from filling out questionnaires, leading to a 94 percent completion rate within 30 minutes of each signal. This study highlights the importance of using technology that prevents participants from filling out forms at a later date. Finally, respondent burden becomes an issue with the use of EMAs because of the frequency of assessments. Thus, careful consideration needs to be taken when planning the assessment protocol. For example, if the aim is to assess parental stress, then requiring a high frequency of repeated assessments throughout the day may be necessary to identify the circumstances and behaviors surrounding increases in stress. If, however, the goal is to identify the frequency of substance use, a variable that does not change qualitatively throughout the day, then signaling every 30 minutes may be unnecessarily burdensome to the participant.

Taken together, EMA technology provides a novel approach to improving our understanding of the proximal environmental risk and protective factors for child outcomes, such as parental behavior, family dynamics, and social networks. However, EMA technology is still vulnerable to biases characteristic of other self-report scales; therefore, assessment strategies that provide an outsider's perspective of the home environment may be useful for decreasing bias and increasing measurement validity. As such, the following section reviews observational assessment approaches of home environments.

Assessment of Home Environment

Despite the utility of EMA technologies, maternal and child reports of their environment and behavior are still vulnerable to the same threats to validity present in self-report methods (Schwarz, 1999). For example, both mothers and children may want to portray themselves, their relationships, and their environments in a more favorable light than is necessarily true, or they may lack accurate insight into their own behaviors. It is crucial to employ the most valid, accurate methods of environmental assessment possible as current research in both high- and low-risk populations suggests that both positive parenting and home environments predict better child development outcomes and can serve as a buffer against high-risk environments (e.g., Connell & Prinz, 2002; Jones, Forehand, Brody, & Armistead, 2002). Therefore, additional assessment methods have been developed in order to provide an outsider's perspective of the home environment through direct observation and ratings by the researcher. In general, the two techniques that are used to assess the child's environment observationally are naturalistic assessments in the home environment and structured observations of parent-child interactions in a laboratory setting, with a recent emphasis on the use of a dynamic systems approach to analyze parent-child interactions.

The Home Observation for Measurement of the Environment (HOME)

The primary measure that is used in naturalistic observations of the home environment is the Home Observation for Measurement of the Environment inventory (HOME; Caldwell & Bradley, 1984). The HOME inventory was developed as a novel way of measuring the quality and quantity of stimulation and support available to a child in the early home environment. The inventory is completed during a 45- to 90-minute home visit scheduled during a time when the child of interest and the child's primary caregiver are both present and awake. The procedure is a semistructured observation and interview done in a way to minimize obtrusiveness and allow family members to act normally. Originally developed for use in infants and toddlers, additional versions of the HOME have been released for use in early childhood (ages 3–6; Bradley & Caldwell, 1988), middle childhood (ages 6–10; Caldwell &

Bradley, 1984), and early adolescence (ages 10–15; Bradley et al., 2000). Furthermore, a short form (HOME-SF) was created for use in the National Longitudinal Survey of Youth-Child Supplement (NLSY-CS; Baker & Mott, 1989).

The original Infant/Toddler HOME (HOME-IT) inventory contains 45 items presented as statements to be scored as YES or NO. Higher total scores on the HOME are indicative of an enriched home environment suitable for learning. Items are clustered into six subscales, the first three of which are scored primarily through observation: Emotional and Verbal Responsivity of Mother, defined as communicative and affective interactions between the caregiver and the child; Avoidance of Restriction and Punishment/Acceptance of Child, defined as how the adult disciplines the child; and Maternal Involvement with Child, defined as how the adult interacts physically with the child. The fourth subscale, Provision of Appropriate Play Materials, defined as the presence of several types of toys available to the child and appropriate for his/her age, is scored by noting play materials present in the home. The final two subscales, Organization of the Environment, defined as how the child's time is organized outside of the family house and what the child's personal space looks like; and Variety in Daily Stimulation, defined as the way the child's daily routine is designed to incorporate social meetings with people other than the mother, are scored primarily through interviewing the primary caregiver (see Totsika & Sylva, 2004 for a more detailed description of the subscales). Subscales derived through factor analysis have varied in number and scope on subsequent versions of the HOME.

For more than two decades, versions of the HOME have been utilized in a plethora of research studies examining the relationship between a child's early home environment and a number of outcome variables (e.g., for reviews see Bradley, 1993; Totsika & Silva, 2004). Some of the most commonly examined relationships are between scores on the HOME inventory and cognitive and behavioral outcomes. As would be expected, HOME scores are usually found to correlate positively with cognitive outcomes, and negatively with the development of behavioral problems, indicating that a higher quality, enriched home environment is associated with better cognitive development outcomes and reduced behavioral problems. Specifically, total HOME scores have been related to cognitive development (Barnard, Bee, & Hammond, 1984; Bee, Mitchell, Barnard, Eyres, & Hammond, 1984; Bradley, Caldwell et al., 1989; Gottfried & Gottfried, 1984), IQ (Bradley & Caldwell, 1976a; Bradley & Caldwell, 1976b; Bradley & Caldwell, 1980; Brooks-Gunn, Klebanov, & Duncan, 1996; Elardo, Bradley, & Caldwell, 1975; Epsy, Molfese, & DiLalla, 2001; Tong, Baghurst, Vimpani, & McMichael, 2007), infant executive capacity (Belsky, Garduque, & Hrncir, 1984), language development (National Institute of Child Health and Human Development Early Child Care Research Network, 2000), reading achievement (Zaslow et al., 2006), and later academic achievement (Bradley & Caldwell, 1984; Bradley, Caldwell, & Rock, 1988). The HOME has also been associated with a number of behavioral outcomes, including classroom behavior (Bradley, Caldwell, and Rock, 1988; Gottfried & Gottfried, 1988; Hammond et al., 1983), attentional ability (Dilworth-Bart, Khurshid, & Vandell, 2007), child attachment patterns (NICHD Early Child Care Research Network, 2001), adaptive social participation (Bakeman & Brown, 1980), and behavioral problems (Erickson, Sroufe, & Egeland, 1985), although correlations do not tend to be as strong as those between the HOME and cognitive development.

In addition, specific subscales of the HOME have been shown to differentially predict developmental outcomes, suggesting that specific aspects of the home environment may be more closely related to child development than others. Existing evidence indicates that the Learning Materials and Involvement subscales from the HOME for Infants/Toddlers (HOME-IT), as well as the Learning Materials and Variety subscales

from the HOME for Early Childhood (HOME-EC) yield the strongest relationship with intellectual and academic performance in later childhood (see Bradley & Tedesco, 1982; Kagan, 1984). One notable finding of this kind used the HOME-EC in a study of 31 methadone-treated and 27 matched non-drug-dependent mothers and found that children with higher General Cognitive Index scores at age 5 were from homes that scored higher on the Learning Stimulation and Responsivity HOME subscales (Strauss, Lessen-Firestone, Chavez, and Stryker, 1979). In a more recent study utilizing data from three longitudinal studies that used the HOME for Middle Childhood (HOME-MC), researchers found significant relationships between cognitive outcomes and several conceptually based HOME-MC subscales including Parental Warmth, Learning Stimulation, Access to Reading, and Outings/Activities (Han, Leventhal, & Linver, 2004). In regard to behavioral outcomes, Bradley, Caldwell, and Rock (1988) found that the Active Involvement and Family Participation subscales were moderately correlated with the Consideration and Task Orientation subscales of the Classroom Behavior Index (CBI) and with overall school adjustment, while the Responsivity subscale of the HOME was related to Consideration and Adjustment on the CBI. A more recent general report used data from 5 independent studies to examine the relationship between several conceptually based subscales of the HOME-EC and various cognitive and behavioral outcomes (Leventhal, Martin, & Brooks-Gunn, 2004). Subscales that most strongly predicted behavioral outcomes included Learning Stimulation and Access to Reading Materials.

Structured Parent-Child Interactions

When home visits are not possible, or the researcher's primary environmental interest is that of parental influence on the child's environment, structured parent-child interactions may be employed in the laboratory setting. Structured observations provide a standard context in which behaviors can be elicited that may not have been observed even during long naturalistic home observations. The challenges posed to families in these structured observational tasks illuminate specific aspects of parenting, such as the amount of emotional support shown toward the child and the effectiveness of the parent's teaching strategies, that may not be elicited in everyday interactions. However, structured laboratory observations are believed to be ecologically valid measures of average day-to-day parent-child interactions (Bronfenbrenner, 1977).

Structured laboratory observations of parent-child interactions tend to be videotaped sessions involving free play between parent and child, the completion of some kind of artificial task imposed by the researcher, or some combination thereof. It is often useful to employ a specific task during the structured laboratory session in order to efficiently elicit the behaviors of interest and to standardize the structured observation somewhat between subjects (Hughes & Haynes, 1978). Different tasks are used depending on the researcher's primary research question. For example, a task that might be used is the "Child's Game," in which parents are told to engage in joint play with their child, but to minimize their commands and follow the child's lead (Forehand & McMahon, 1981). Conversely, the Roberts & Powers (1988) "Compliance Test" encourages a more negative interaction by telling parents to have their child clean up the toys. Some researchers even use a combination of imposed laboratory tasks and free play sessions (e.g., Barkley, 1989). The tasks chosen for inclusion in the study are dependent upon the researcher's primary questions, as different tasks are expected to elicit different behaviors. For example, parents may be more controlling and children may be less compliant during clean-up tasks compared to free play; however, parents who are more controlling than average on one task are likely to be controlling in other tasks, and children who are noncompliant on one task are likely to be less compliant on other tasks (Gardner, 2000).

Following the completion of parent-child interactions in the laboratory, the variables of interest are usually quantified using a specific, validated coding system. A number of behavioral coding systems have been established and are widely used in parenting research. They range from relatively straightforward coding systems that code specific behaviors, such as the Dyadic Parent-Child Interaction Coding System (DPICS; Robinson & Eyberg, 1981), to more complex, specialized coding systems, such as the Living in Familial Environments coding system (LIFE; Hops, Davis, & Langoria, 1995), which is used to examine how maternal behavior toward the child changes with fluctuations in depressive symptoms; the System for Coding Interactions and Family Functioning (SCIFF; Lindahl & Malik, 1996); and the Interact system (Dumas, 1987), which examines patterns of elicitation, response, and control in parent-child interactions (Gardner, 2000). Coding systems vary considerably on which behaviors are coded and how often they are coded, depending on the primary research question of interest.

As one example of a well-established, widely used measure used to code parent-child interactions, Robinson & Eyberg (1981) developed the Dyadic Parent-Child Interaction Coding System (DPICS). A number of parent and child behaviors are observed continuously during a 5-minute parent-directed interaction (PDI) and a 5-minute child-directed interaction (CDI), resulting in total scores calculated by frequency of behaviors during each 5-minute interval. Examples of parent behavioral categories that are observed include direct commands, indirect commands, labeled praise, unlabeled praise, positive physical, negative physical, critical statements, descriptive statements, descriptive questions, acknowledgment, and irrelevant verbalization. In addition, observations of deviant child behaviors are noted (i.e., whining, crying, physical negatives, smart talk, yelling, and destructive behavior), as well as parental responses to the deviant behaviors (i.e., ignores or responds). Children are also coded on the basis of their response to parental commands (i.e., complies, does not comply, or no opportunity). Once all parent-child

interactions are coded, variables are created from the DPICS behavioral categories
including Total Praise, Total Deviants, Total
Commands, Command Ratio, Compliance
Ratio, and Noncompliance Ratio.

A number of parental behaviors have
been linked to child outcomes. Studies have
consistently reported that higher levels of
Maternal Responsivity, defined as a mother's
prompt, contingent, and appropriate behaviors in response to a child's actions, and
Paternal Sensitivity, or the degree to which
parents adapt to children's needs and abilities (Dodici, Draper, & Peterson, 2003), are
associated with more positive social, cognitive, and language outcomes (Barnard,
1997; Lamb-Parker, Boak, Griffin, Ripple, &
Peay, 1999; Landry, Smith, Miller-Loncar, &
Swank, 1997; Landry, Smith, Swank, Assel,
& Vellet, 2001). Positive parenting strategies,
such as positive comments, praise, smiles
and laughter, nurturing embraces or touches,
and limited negative comments and yelling
are associated with positive child outcomes
(Barnard, 1997). In addition, parental engagement, or the amount of time a parent is
mutually focused with the child on a single
object or task (Tomasello & Farrar, 1986), has
also been associated with a number of positive child outcomes such as language and skill
development (Dodici, Draper, & Peterson,
2003). Clearly, parental behaviors play a pivotal role in shaping the child's environment
and subsequent environmental outcomes;
therefore, structured laboratory observations of parent-child interactions may be a
useful tool for measuring different aspects of
parental behavior that may positively or negatively impact the child.

Dynamic Systems Approach to Assessing Parent-Child Interactions

More recently, researchers have begun to
employ a dynamic systems approach to
study parent-child interactions. While a
majority of methods for assessing parent-
child interactions focus on the content of
their interactions, the dynamic systems
approach is primarily focused on the structure of these interactions; that is, the relative

flexibility or rigidity of parent-child behavioral responses over the course of the interaction (Hollenstein, Granic, Stoolmiller, &
Snyder, 2004). Thus, variability of parent-
child responses serves as the primary factor
of interest, with greater variability indicating higher levels of behavioral flexibility.
Procedurally, the dynamic system approach
involves videotaping parent-child interactions and coding the behavioral responses of
both the parent and the child. Each coded
behavioral event is then collapsed into a
range of categories; for example, Granic,
Hollenstein, Dishion, & Patterson (2003)
categorized behaviors as hostile, negative, neutral, or positive. The responses are
then plotted on a state-space grid (SSG),
a hypothetical landscape of all possible
behavioral combinations, with the behavioral categories of the parent's responses
represented on the x-axis and the categories of the child's behavioral responses represented on the y-axis (Granic et al., 2003).
Thus, each point on the SSG represents a
two-event sequence (i.e., both the parental
response and the child response at a single point in time). Horizontal lines on the
SSG represent a parental movement from
one behavioral state to another, and vertical
lines represent the child's change from one
state to another. This temporally sensitive
approach to assessing parent-child interactions allows researchers to examine whether
behaviors remain clustered in a few cells or
spread out across many cells, as well as how
long the dyadic interaction remains in each
region of the SSG and how quickly it moves
to new regions. The amount of variability
across cells within the SSG is indicative
of the relative flexibility or rigidity of the
dyadic system.

Researchers have utilized this dynamic
systems approach to examine a number
of hypotheses. For example, Granic and
colleagues (2003) followed 149 boys longitudinally, assessing the structure of parent-
son interactions beginning at age 9–10 and
continuing every 2 years until age 18. The
dynamic systems approach showed relatively
stable parent-son interactions in preadolescence (i.e., ages 9–12), a phase of behavioral

reorganization marked by peak variability during early adolescence (ages 13–14), and restabilization of parent-son interactions in later adolescence (15–18), supporting their hypothesis that the developmental transition from childhood to adolescence is characterized by an increase in variability in the dyadic system. The structure of parent-child interactions has also been associated with a number of child outcome variables. For example, the dynamic systems approach has been used to distinguish children with purely externalizing behavioral problems from those with comorbid externalizing and internalizing problems (Granic & Lamey, 2002). Additionally, Hollenstein et al. (2004) assessed parent-child interactions in high-risk kindergarteners and found that rigidity in parent-child interactions was associated with externalizing behaviors at three different time points and a greater increase in these problems over time, as well as both concurrent and chronically high levels of internalizing problems. Further, in a study of early adolescent girls, lower dyadic flexibility during parent-daughter interactions was associated with a greater number of stressful events reported by the girls (Hollenstein & Lewis, 2006). Evidence also suggests that successful behavioral interventions can be effective at changing the structure of dyadic interactions. Specifically, researchers utilized a dynamic systems approach to examine changes in parent-child interactions following an intervention for child aggression and found that significant reductions in child externalizing behaviors following treatment were associated with increased emotional flexibility during a parent-child problem-solving interaction (Granic, O'Hara, Pepler, & Lewis, 2007). Taken together, findings suggest that greater flexibility in parent-child interactions, as assessed by a dynamic systems approach, is associated with more positive behavioral outcomes in children.

Methodological Considerations for Observational Assessments

While the HOME has proven to be a useful tool in predicting child intellectual and behavioral outcomes in a variety of racial, ethnic, and socioeconomic populations, there are some methodological issues to consider. First, because completion of the HOME is based on a single home visit, it is difficult to gauge behaviors that may occur erratically, thereby limiting the reliability and validity of some aspects of the data (Mott, 2004). In addition, ratings of some of the observation items can vary depending on the mood of the mother and child at the time of the visit, which reduces test-retest reliability, especially in children below the age of 4 (Mott, 2004). Additionally, inter-rater reliability can be hard to measure in live, unrecorded observations, and in many studies, raters were not required to maintain interrater reliability. The problem of poor interrater reliability is evidenced by a study by Tout, Zaslow, Mariner, and Halle (1998) in which they found poor interrater agreement for the HOME-SF.

Structured laboratory parent-child interactions may be one useful tool to use in conjunction with home observational measures. By using videotaped laboratory procedures, interrater reliability can be calculated and monitored, and behaviors can be elicited from the parent-child dyad that may not occur spontaneously even during lengthy home visits. However, structured laboratory observations have their limitations as well. First, parent-child interactions in a laboratory are contrived and may not be valid measures of day-to-day interactions between parent and child (e.g., see Gardner, 2000 for review). Second, it is well known that parents exhibit greater positive parenting when they are aware that they are being observed (e.g., Zegiob, Arnold, & Forehand, 1975; Zegiob & Forehand, 1978). Further, Zegiob, Forehand, and Resick (1979) showed that parents become habituated to an observer, with positive parenting behaviors decreasing across sessions, and then increasing significantly upon introduction of a new observer. Finally, staging parent-child interactions in a laboratory, videotaping the interaction, and training coders to quantify the interaction is a time consuming and costly endeavor; therefore, researchers must weigh the relative value of using observational data over less costly self-report methods.

Taken together, observational approaches to measuring the early home environment may be useful to improve our understanding of how proximal environmental factors such as parenting behaviors, cognitive stimulation, and family dynamics influence various developmental outcomes. However, these proximal determinants often interact with distal environmental factors such as the neighborhood environment. As such, the following section highlights novel approaches to assessing these distal environmental factors.

Assessment of Distal Risk Factors

In addition to the immediate home environment, another aspect of the child's experience that may serve as a risk or protective factor during development is the organization of the neighborhood environment. Over the past several decades, a growing body of research has emerged examining environmental factors that may influence different health outcomes, particularly for young people (Sampson, Morenoff, & Gannon-Rowley, 2002). From this research, several theories have emerged proposing that visual cues of disorder are the mediating mechanism underlying neighborhood disparities in a variety of negative social outcomes such as poverty, crime, and violence (Sampson & Raudenbush, 2004; Skogan, 1990; Taylor, 2001; Wilson & Keller, 1982). Disorder is generally broken down into two categories: social disorder and physical disorder. Social disorder refers to behavior, usually involving strangers, that is considered threatening, such as "hey honey" hassles, open solicitation for prostitution, public drug sales or drug use, public drunkenness, neighbors fighting or arguing in the streets, presence of homeless people and panhandlers, and rowdy groups of teenagers (especially young males) in public (Sampson & Raudenbush, 1999; Taylor, 2001). Signs of physical disorder include graffiti, abandoned cars, broken windows, garbage in the streets, discarded

crack pipes or syringes, abandoned houses and empty lots, and sidewalks and streets in need of repair (Sampson & Raudenbush, 1999; Taylor, 2001). Visual signs of disorder are of particular theoretical relevance as they are salient, symbolic factors that lead to specific inferences about a given public space. For example, according to the "Broken Windows" theory (Wilson & Kelling, 1982), minor forms of public disorder can lead to serious crime because visual disorder cues are presumed to attract criminal offenders who infer based on these cues that residents are indifferent to what goes on in the neighborhood (Sampson & Raudenbush, 2004). In addition to being related to both fear of crime and actual crime rates (Kelling & Coles, 1996; Skogan, 1990), research has also shown persistent correlations between perceived disorder and various mental health outcomes such as depression (Ross, 2000), psychological distress (Mitchell & LaGory, 2002), and perceived powerlessness (Geis & Ross, 1998), as well as mistrust, hostility, and conduct disorder (Aneshensel & Sucoff, 1996; Ewart & Suchday, 2002). Given the numerous negative outcomes associated with neighborhood disorder, the use of novel neighborhood assessments may be useful in studying the association between neighborhood environment and specific childhood development outcomes. As such, the following is a brief overview of two novel neighborhood assessment techniques.

Systematic Social Observation

One novel technique that is used to assess neighborhood environments is the use of Systematic Social Observation (SSO), which was introduced by Sampson and Raudenbush (1999) as a novel way to look at disorder in urban neighborhoods. Researchers drove down every street of an urban city at a rate of 5 miles per hour, observing and videotaping face blocks (portions of a street block that face the street). Researchers kept logs focusing on land use, traffic, the physical condition of buildings, and other evidence of physical disorder, which were then entered directly into their data files. The videotapes, however, first needed to be coded by trained raters. A random subset of face blocks was chosen and raters coded the videotapes based on the presence or absence of each indicator of disorder. The physical disorder scale utilized both the observer logs and the videotapes to rate the presence of 10 cues of physical disorder, including cigarettes or cigars in the street or gutter, garbage or litter on the street or sidewalk, empty beer bottles visible in the street, tagging graffiti, graffiti painted over, gang graffiti, abandoned cars, condoms on the sidewalk, needles/syringes on the sidewalk, and political message graffiti. The social disorder scale rated the presence of cues from the videotapes, including adults loitering or congregating, drinking alcohol in public, peer groups with gang indicators present, public intoxication, adults fighting or arguing in a hostile manner, selling drugs, and prostitutes on the street.

Findings indicated several correlations between disorder and various sociodemographic variables. Physical disorder was significantly associated with measures of predatory crime as measured by police recorded rates of homicide, robbery, and burglary. Further, physical disorder was significantly related to concentrated poverty and immigrant composition, with total disorder ratings accounting for 50 percent of the variance in both sociodemographic measures (Sampson & Raudenbush, 1999). Similar findings were also reported between social disorder and the various dependent variables. Given the strong relationship between disorder and various factors that themselves serve as risk factors for poor child development outcomes (i.e., poverty, crime, violence), more research is needed examining the relationships between neighborhood disorder and child outcomes such as cognitive development, academic achievement, and behavioral problems.

Geographic Information Systems (GIS) Technology

In addition to SSO, geographic information systems (GIS) technology has been developed to assess the environmental context, and allows researchers to identify spatial relationships between geographic locations frequented by teens, as well as the relative distances of the various locations from their homes. Using GIS technology, researchers can calculate linear distances between teens' homes and other locations that may serve as risk or protective factors in their lives. For example, Mason, Cheung, and Walker (2004) utilized GIS to examine the relationship between substance use, social networks, and geography in urban adolescents. They began by utilizing a structured interview to get a thorough description of each teen's daily activity locations, and descriptions of their various geographic environments. Teens were asked to identify locations that they frequent that are safe, defined to teens as safest place from harm, danger, or the likelihood of engaging in risky or dangerous activities; risky, defined as the place where you are most likely to engage in risky or dangerous activities, cause trouble, or do illegal activities; and important, defined as being the most meaningful and having the biggest impact on your life. In addition, teens identified members of their social network according to their specific geographic locations. GIS technology was then used to transform the information gained through these interviews into geographic coordinates, and the relative distances of the various places from each teen's home was calculated. In addition, GIS mapping images were used to count the relative number of additional locations within walking distance of a teen's home or school that may be risky (e.g., areas of condensed poverty, neighborhoods with high incidences of crime, and liquor stores) or protective (e.g., libraries and boys-and-girls clubs).

Using these techniques made available through GIS technology, findings indicated that the distance between the homes and safe places of substance-using teens were three times the distances between their homes and risky places (Mason, Cheung, & Walker, 2004). These early findings have profound implications for prevention in that

instead of making generic recommendations about constructing community centers
and other protective resources, researchers
and public policy administrators would be
able to identify specific neighborhoods that
are in need of these services. Furthermore,
physicians, psychologists, and other health
care professionals can use GIS technology
to identify protective resources that are
already available in close proximity to their
patients. Because of the limited research utilizing GIS with teens thus far, more research
is needed to better understand the relationship between geography and negative
outcomes such as substance use and HIV
risk behavior. In addition, further research
is needed to examine whether similar geographic relationships hold in suburban and
rural teens as well.

Methodological Considerations for Neighborhood Assessments

In utilizing these novel environmental
assessments of child neighborhoods, some
limitations should be considered. First,
SSO has only been utilized in Chicago
(Sampson & Raudenbush, 1999; Sampson,
Morenoff, & Raudenbush, 2005), illustrating the need for replication in additional locations, including suburban areas.
In addition, although the relationships
between neighborhood disorder and crime
have been consistent, longitudinal studies are needed to establish a causal direction of the effects. As for the GIS mapping
technology, future directions should focus
on tailoring the individualized nature of
the technology in order to make it more
accessible to a larger number of people in
order to truly maximize the potential preventative use of this technology (Walker,
Mason, & Cheung, 2006). Taken together,
the novel neighborhood assessment strategies discussed earlier appear to be promising avenues of research in order to more
fully understand the relationships between
the child's neighborhood environment and
future developmental and behavioral outcomes, and have profound implications for
prevention and intervention.

Summary and Conclusions

Taken together, traditional and emerging
novel assessment techniques aimed at identifying specific proximal and distal environmental risk factors are crucial to furthering
our understanding of risk, as well as the development of intervention and prevention programs specifically tailored to at-risk infants,
children, and adolescents. Advances in the
use of real-time assessment techniques from
daily diaries to portable electronic devices
now allow for strict controls on the timing
of mood and environmental context self-
reports. Future work utilizing EMA devices
to assess infant environments based on parental report will be useful in furthering our
understanding and identification of neglect,
an important and undertreated risk factor
for young children. A great deal of research
has been conducted examining the HOME
and parent-child interaction assessment
techniques. Although both techniques have
proven effective in identifying specific child
outcomes, future work utilizing the dynamic
systems approach in coordination with the
HOME may allow for a more comprehensive picture of the home environment.

The identification of proximal risk factors alone may be augmented by the assessment of distal neighborhood environmental
differences. Two recent techniques, SSO
and GIS, have been used to identify disorder
in environments, as well as the spatial proximity of risky and protective environmental structures. A novel assessment technique
that may add to the reliability of child and
teen report of movement in the neighborhood are Global Positioning Satellite (GPS)
devices. GPS devices allow for the real time
tracking of movement via satellite. Although
not readily applied to date, future work utilizing GPS technology to track the movement of children and parents, and map this
data onto neighborhood data gathered from
both SSO and GIS may provide a reliable
and comprehensive picture of the child's
risk for poor outcomes based on environmental exposure. As highlighted throughout
the chapter, novel assessment techniques are
continuing to be developed to improve the

reliability and validity of assessing both proximal and distal environmental risk factors. Future work combining these techniques into a comprehensive diagnostic system will be critical to our development of effective prevention and intervention programs.

References

Aneshensel, C. S. & Sucoff, C. A. (1996). The neighborhood context of adolescent mental health. *Journal of Health and Social Behavior*, 37, 293–310.

Bakeman, R., & Brown, J. V. (1980). Early interaction: Consequences for social and mental development at three years. *Child Development*, 51, 437–447.

Baker, P., & Mott, F. (1989). *NLSY child handbook 1989: A guide and resource document for the National Longitudinal Survey of Youth 1986 child data*. Columbus: Center for Human Resources Research, Ohio State University.

Barkley, R. A. (1989). Hyperactive girls and boys: Stimulant drug effects on mother-child interactions. *Journal of Child Psychology and Psychiatry*, 30, 379–391.

Barnard, K. E. (1997). Influencing parent-infant/toddler interactions for children at risk. In M. J. Guralnick (Ed.), *The effectiveness of early intervention*, pp. 249–270. Baltimore: Brookes.

Barnard, K. E., Bee, H. L., & Hammond, M. A. (1984). Home environment and cognitive development in a healthy, low-risk sample: The Seattle study. In A. Gottfried (Ed.), *Home environment and early cognitive development*, pp. 117–149. Orlando, FL: Academic Press.

Bee, H. L., Mitchell, S., Barnard, K., Eyres, S. J., & Hammond, M. A. (1984). Predicting intellectual outcomes: Sex differences in response to early environmental stimulation. *Sex Roles*, 10, 783–803.

Belsky, J., Garduque, L., & Hrncir, E. (1984). Assessing performance, competence and executive capacity in infant play: Relations to home environment and security of attachment. *Developmental Psychology*, 20, 406–417.

Bradley, R. H. (1993). Children's home environments, health, behavior, and intervention efforts: A review using the home inventory as a marker measure. *Genetic, Social, and General Psychology Monographs*, 119(4), 437–490.

Bradley, R. H., & Caldwell, B. M. (1976a). Early home environment and changes in mental test performance in children from 6 to 36 months. *Developmental Psychology*, 12, 93–97.

Bradley, R. H., & Caldwell, B. M. (1976b). The relation of infants' home environments to mental test performance at 54 months: A follow-up study. *Child Development*, 47, 1172–1174.

Bradley, R. H., & Caldwell, B. M. (1980). The relation of home environment, cognitive competence, and IQ among males and females. *Child Development*, 51(4), 1140–1148.

Bradley, R. H., & Caldwell, B. M. (1984). The relation of infants' home environments to achievement test performance in first grade: A follow-up study. *Child Development*, 55(3), 803–809.

Bradley, R., & Caldwell, B. (1988). Using the HOME Inventory to assess the family environment. *Pediatric Nursing*, 14, 97–102.

Bradley, R. H., Caldwell, B. M., & Rock, S. L. (1988). Home environment and school performance: A 10-year follow-up and examination of three models of environmental action. *Child Development*, 59, 852–867.

Bradley, R. H., Caldwell, B. M., Rock, S. L., Ramey, C. T., Barnard, K. E., Gray, C. et al. (1989). Home environment and cognitive development in the first 3 years of life: A collaborative study involving six sites and three ethnic groups in North America. *Developmental Psychology*, 25(2), 217–235.

Bradley, R. H., Corwyn, R. F., Caldwell, B. M., Whiteside-Mansell, L., Wasserman, G. A., & Mink, I. T. (2000). Measuring the home environments of children in early adolescence. *Journal of Research on Adolescence*, 10(3), 247–288.

Bradley, R. H., Rock, S. L., Caldwell, B. M., & Brisby, J. A. (1989). Uses of the HOME inventory for families with handicapped children. *American Journal of Mental Retardation*, 94, 313–330.

Broderick, J. E., Schwartz, J. E., Shiffman, S., Hufford, M. R., & Stone, A. A. (2003). Signaling does not adequately improve diary compliance. *Annals of Behavioral Medicine*, 26, 139–148.

Bradley, R. H., & Tedesco, L. (1982). Environmental correlates of mental retardation. In J. Lachenmeyer & M. Gibbs (Ed.), *The psychology of the abnormal child*, pp. 155–188. New York: Gardner Press.

Bronfenbrenner, U. (1977). Toward an experimental ecology of human development. *American Psychologist*, 32, 513–530.

Brooks-Gunn, J., Klebanov, P. K., & Duncan, G. J. (1996). Ethnic differences in children's intelligence test scores: Role of economic deprivation, home environment, and maternal characteristics. *Child Development, 67,* 396–408.

Caldwell, B., & Bradley, R. (1984). *Home observation for measurement of the environment.* Little Rock: University of Arkansas.

Connell, C., & Prinz, R. (2002). The impact of childcare and parent-child interactions on school readiness and social skills development for low income African-American children. *Journal of School Psychology, 40*(2), 177–193.

Connell-Carrick, K., & Scannapieco, M. (2006). Ecological Correlates of Neglect in Infants and Toddlers. *Journal of Interpersonal Violence, 21*(3), 299–316.

Dilworth-Bart, J., Khurshid, A., & Vandell (2007). Do maternal stress and home environment mediate the relation between early income-to-need and 54-month attention? *Infant and Child Development, 16,* 525 – 552.

Dodici, B. J., Draper, D. C., & Peterson, C. A. (2003). Early parent-child interactions and early literacy development. *Topics in Early Childhood Special Education, 23*(3), 124–136.

Dumas, J. E. (1987). INTERACT-A computer-based coding and data management system to assess family interactions. In R. J. Prinz (Ed.), *Advances in Behavioral Assessment of Children and Families, 3,* 177–203.

Elardo, R., Bradley, R. H., & Caldwell, B. M. (1975). The relation of infants' home environment to mental test performance from 6 to 36 months: A longitudinal analysis. *Child Development, 46,* 71–76.

Epsy, K. A., Molfese, V. J., & DiLalla, L. F. (2001). Effects of environmental measures on intelligence in young children: Growth curve modeling of longitudinal data. *Merrill-Palmer Quarterly, 47*(1), 42–73.

Erickson, M. E., Sroufe, L. A., & Egeland, B. (1985). The relationship between quality of attachment and behavior problems in a high risk sample. In I. Bretherton & E. Waters (Eds.), *Growing points of attachment theory and research.* Monographs of the Society for Research in Child Development 50, 147–166, Serial No. 209.

Éthier, L. S., Lacharité, C., & Couture, G. (1995). Childhood adversity, parental stress, and depression of negligent mothers. *Child Abuse & Neglect, 19*(5), 619–632.

Ewart, C. K., & Suchday, S. (2002). Discovering how urban poverty and violence affect health: Development and validation of a neighborhood stress index. *Health Psychology, 21,* 254–262.

Forehand, R., & McMahon (1981). *Helping the noncompliant child.* NY: Guilford Press.

Gardner, F. (2000). Methodological issues in the direct observation of parent-child interaction: Do observational findings reflect the natural behavior of participants? *Clinical Child and Family Psychology Review, 3*(3), 185–198.

Geis, K. J., & Ross, C. E. (1998). A new look at urban alienation: The effect of neighborhood disorder on perceived powerlessness. *Social Psychology Quarterly, 61,* 232–246.

Gottfried, A. E., & Gottfried, A. W. (1988). *Maternal employment and children's development: Longitudinal research.* New York: Plenum.

Gottfried, A. W., & Gottfried, A. E. (1984). Home environment and cognitive development in young children of middle-socioeconomic status families. In A. Gottfried (Ed.), *Home environment and early cognitive development,* pp. 57–115. Orlando, FL: Academic Press.

Granic, I., Hollenstein, T., Dishion, T. J., & Patterson, G. R. (2003). Longitudinal analysis of flexibility and reorganization in early adolescence: A dynamic systems study of family interactions. *Developmental Psychology, 39,* 606–617.

Granic, I., & Lamey, A. K. (2002). Combining dynamic systems and multivariate analyses to compare the mother–child interactions of externalizing subtypes. *Journal of Abnormal Child Psychology, 30,* 265–283.

Granic, I., O'Hara, A., Pepler, D., & Lewis, M. D. (2007). A dynamic systems analysis of parent-child changes associated with successful "real-world" interventions for aggressive children. *Journal of Abnormal Child Psychology, 35,* 845–857.

Hammond, M. A., Bee, H. L., Barnard, K. E., & Eyres, S. J. (1983). Child health assessment: Part IV. Followup at second grade (RO1 NU 00816). U.S. Public Health Service.

Han, W., Leventhal, T., & Linver, M. R. (2004). The home observation for measurement of the environment (HOME) in middle childhood: A study of three large-scale data sets. *Parenting: Science and Practice, 4*(2–3), 189–210.

Henker, B., Whalen, C. K., Jamner, L. D., & Delfino, R. J. (2002). Anxiety, affect, and activity in teenagers: Monitoring daily life with electronic diaries. *Journal of American Academy of Child and Adolescent Psychiatry, 41,* 660–670.

Hollenstein, T., Granic, I., Stoolmiller, M., & Snyder, J. (2004). Rigidity in parent-child interactions and the development of externalizing and internalizing behavior in early childhood. *Journal of Abnormal Child Psychology*, 32, 595–607.

Hollenstein, T., & Lewis, M. D. (2006). A state space analysis of emotion and flexibility in parent-child interactions. *Emotion*, 6(4), 656–662.

Hops, H., Davis, B., & Langoria, N. (1995). Methodological issues in direct observation: Illustrations with the Living in Familial Environments (LIFE) coding system. *Journal of Clinical Child Psychology*, 24, 193–203.

Hughes, H. M., & Hanes, S. N. (1978). Structured laboratory observation in the behavioral assessment of parent-child interactions: a methodological critique. *Behavior Therapy*, 9, 428–447.

Jones, D., Forehand, R., Brody, G., & Armistead, L. (2002). Positive parenting and child psychosocial adjustment in inner-city single parent African-American families: The role of maternal optimism. *Behavior Modification*, 26(4), 464–481.

Kagan, J. (1984). *The Nature of the Child*. New York: Basic Books.

Kelling, G., & Coles, C. (1996). *Fixing Broken Windows: Restoring order and reducing crime in our communities*. New York: Free Press.

Kihlstrom, J. F., Eich, E., Sandbrand, D., & Tobias, B. A. (2000). Emotion and memory: Implications for self-report. In A. A. Stone, J. S. Turkkan, C. A. Bachrach, J. B. Jobe, H. S. Kurtzman, & V. S. Cain (Eds.), *The science of self-report: Implications for research and practice*, pp. 81–99. Mahwah, NJ: Erlbaum.

Lamb-Parker, F., Boak, A. Y., Griffin, K. W., Ripple, C., & Peay, L. (1999). Parent-infant/toddler relationship, home learning environment, and school readiness. *School Psychology Review*, 28, 413–425.

Landry, S. H., Smith, K. E., Miller-Loncar, C. L., & Swank, P. R. (1997). Predicting cognitive language and social growth curves from early maternal behaviors in children and varying degrees of biological risk. *Developmental Psychology*, 33, 1040–1053.

Landry, S. H., Smith, K. E., Swank, P. R., Assel, M. A., & Vellet, S. (2001). Does early responsive parenting have a special importance for children's development or is consistency across early childhood necessary? *Developmental Psychology*, 37, 387–403.

Leventhal, T., Martin, A., & Brooks-Gunn, J. (2004). The EC-HOME across five national data sets in the 3rd and 5th year of life. *Parenting: Science and Practice*, 4(2–3), 161–188.

Lindahl, K. M., & Malik, N. M. (1996). System for Coding Interactions and Family Functioning (SCIFF). Unpublished manual, University of Miami, Miami, FL.

Litt, M. D., Cooney, N. L., & Morse, P. (1998). Ecological momentary assessment (EMA) with treated alcoholics: Methodological problems and potential solutions. *Health Psychology*, 17, 48–52.

Mason, M., Cheung, I., & Walker, L. (2004). Substance use, social networks, and the geography of urban adolescents. *Substance Use and Misuse*, 39(10–12), 1751–1777.

Mazze, R. S., Shamoon, H., Pasmantier, R., Lucido, D., Murphy, J., Hartmann, K., Kuykendall, V., & Lopatin, W. (1984). Reliability of blood glucose monitoring by subjects with diabetes mellitus. *The American Journal of Medicine*, 77, 211–217.

Menon, G., & Yorkston, E. A. (2000). The use of memory and contextual cues in the formation of behavioral frequency judgments. In A. A. Stone, J. S. Turkkan, C. A. Bachrach, J. B. Jobe, H. S. Kurtzman, & V. S. Cain (Eds.), *The science of self-report: Implications for research and practice*, pp. 63–79. Mahwah, NJ: Erlbaum.

Mitchell, C. U., & Lagory, M. (2002). Social capital and mental distress in an impoverished community. *City and Community*, 1, 195–215.

Mott, F. L. (2004). The utility of the HOME-SF scale for child development research in a large national longitudinal survey: The national longitudinal survey of youth 1979 cohort. *Parenting: Science and Practice*, 4, 259–270.

National Institute of Child Health and Human Development Early Child Care Research Network. (2000). The relation of child care to cognitive and language development. *Child Development*, 71, 960–980.

NICHD Early Child Care Research Network. (2001). Child care and family predictors of preschool attachment and stability from infancy. *Developmental Psychology*, 37, 847–862.

Piasecki, T. M., Hufford, M. R., Solhan, M., & Trull, T. J. (2007). Assessing clients in their natural environments with electronic diaries: Rationale, benefits, limitations, and barriers. *Psychological Assessment*, 19(1), 25–43.

Propper, C. & Moore, G. A. (2006). The influence of parenting on infant emotionality: A multi-level psychobiological perspective. *Developmental Review*, 26(4), 427–460.

Roberts, M. W. & Powers, S. W. (1988). The Compliance Test. *Behavioral Assessment, 10,* 375–398.

Robinson, E. A. & Eyberg, S. M. (1981). The dyadic parent-child interaction coding system: Standardization and validation. *Journal of Consulting and Clinical Psychology, 49*(2), 245–250.

Robinson, M. D. & Clore, G. L. (2002). Belief and feeling: Evidence for an accessibility model of emotional self-report. *Psychological Bulletin, 128,* 934–960.

Ross, C. E. (2000). Neighborhood disadvantage and adult depression. *Journal of Health and Social Behavior, 41,* 177–187.

Sampson, R. J., Morenoff, J. D., & Gannon-Rowley, T. (2002). Assessing "Neighborhood Effects": Social processes and new directions in research. *Annual Review of Sociology, 28,* 443–478.

Sampson, R. J., Morenoff, J. D., & Raudenbush, S. (2005). Social anatomy of racial and ethnic disparities in violence. *American Journal of Public Health, 95*(2), 224–232.

Sampson, R. J. & Raudenbush, S. W. (1999). Systematic social observation of public spaces: A new look at disorder in urban neighborhoods. *American Journal of Sociology, 105*(3), 603–651.

Sampson, R. J. & Raudenbush, S. W. (2004). Seeing disorder: Neighborhood stigma and the social construction of "Broken Windows." *Social Psychology Quarterly, 67*(4), 319–342.

Schwarz, N. (1999). Self-reports: How the questions shape the answers. *American Psychologist, 54,* 93–105.

Scollon, C. N., Kim-Prieto, C., & Diener, E. (2003). Experience sampling: Promises and pitfalls, strengths and weaknesses. *Journal of Happiness Studies, 4,* 5–34.

Simonich, H., Wonderlich, S., Crosby, R., Smyth, J. M., Thompson, K., Redlin, J. et al. (2004). The use of ecological momentary assessment approaches in the study of sexually abused children. *Child Abuse & Neglect, 28*(7), 803–809.

Skogan, W. G. (1990). *Disorder and Decline: Crime and the Spiral of Decay in American Neighborhoods.* Berkeley: University of California Press.

Stone, A. A., Broderick, J. E., Shiffman, S. S., & Schwartz, J. E. (2004). Understanding recall of weekly pain from a momentary assessment perspective: Absolute agreement, between- and within-person consistency, and judged change in weekly pain. *Pain, 107,* 61–69.

Stone, A. A., & Shiffman, S. (1994). Ecological momentary assessment (EMA) in behavioral medicine. *Annals of Behavioral Medicine, 16,* 199–202.

Stone, A. A., Shiffman, S., Schwartz, J. E., Broderick, J. E., & Hufford, M. R. (2002). Patient non-compliance with paper diaries. *British Medical Journal, 324,* 1193–1194.

Strauss, M. E., Lessen-Firestone, J. K., Chavez, C. J., & Stryker, J. C. (1979). Children of methadone-treated women at five years of age. *Pharmacology, Biochemistry and Behavior,* 2(Supplement), 3–6.

Taylor, R. B. (2001). *Breaking away from broken windows: Evidence from Baltimore neighborhoods and the nationwide fight against crime, grime, fear and decline.* New York: Westview Press.

Tomasello, M., & Farrar, M. J. (1986). Joint attention and early language. *Child Development, 57,* 1454–1463.

Tong, S., Baghurst, P., Vimpani, G., & McMichael, A. (2007). Socioeconomic position, maternal IQ, home environment, and cognitive development. *The Journal of Pediatrics, 151,* 284–288.

Totsika, V. & Sylva, K. (2004). The home observation for measurement of the environment revisited. *Child and Adolescent Mental Health, 9*(1), 25–35.

Tout, K., Zaslow, M. J., Mariner, C. L., & Halle, T. (1998). *Interviewer ratings of mother-child interaction and the home environment in the context of survey research: Contributions and concerns* (Methods Working Paper No. 98.5). Washington, DC: Child Trends.

U.S. Department of Health and Human Services. (2000). *Child maltreatment 1998.* Washington, DC: Government Printing Office.

Walker, L. R., Mason, M., & Cheung, I. (2006). Adolescent substance use and abuse prevention and treatment: Primary care strategies involving social networks and the geography of risk and protection. *Journal of Clinical Psychology in Medical Settings, 13*(2), 131–139.

Webster-Stratton, C. (1985). Mother perceptions and mother-child interactions: comparison of a clinic-referred and nonclinic group. *Journal of Clinical Child Psychology, 14*(4), 334–339.

Whalen, C. K., Henker, B., Ishikawa, S. S. et al. (2006). An electronic diary study of contextual triggers and ADHD: Get ready, get set, get mad. *Journal of the American Academy of Child & Adolescent Psychiatry, 45,* 166–174.

Whalen, C. K., Jamner, L. D., Henker, B., & Delfino, R. J. (2001). Smoking and moods in adolescents with depressive and aggressive dispositions: Evidence from surveys and electronic diaries. *Health Psychology*, 20, 99–111.

Williams, D. A., Gendreau, M., Hufford, M. R., Groner, K., Gracely, R. H., & Clauw, D. J. (2004). Pain assessment in patients with fibromyalgia syndrome: A consideration of methods for clinical trials. *Clinical Journal of Pain*, 20, 348–356.

Wilson, J. Q., & Kelling, G. (1982). The police and neighborhood safety: Broken windows. *Atlantic Monthly*, 127, 29–38.

Zaslow, M. J., Weinfield, N. S., Gallagher, M., Hair, E. C., Ogawa, J. R., Egeland, B., Tabors, P. O., & De Temple, J. M. (2006). Longitudinal prediction of child outcomes from differing measures of parenting in a low-income sample. *Developmental Psychology*, 42(1), 27–37.

Zegiob, L. E., Arnold, S., & Forehand, R. (1975). An examination of observer effects in parent child interactions. *Child Development*, 46(2), 509–512.

Zegiob, L. E., & Forehand, R. (1978). Parent-child interactions: observer effects and social class differences, *Behavior Therapy* 9, 118–23.

Zegiob, L. E., Forehand, R., & Resick, P. A. (1979). Parent-child interactions: Habituation and resensitization effects. *Journal of Clinical Child Psychology*, 8, 69–71.

Part II

CONTEMPORARY THEMES

CHAPTER 5

Beyond the Dyad

Michael Lewis

Historically, consideration of dyadic influences on children's development grows out of two distinct and fundamentally different models. The first is biological in nature and the second is educational. Both models have in common the strong belief that children's development, social as well as cognitive, is influenced primarily by dyadic interaction.

In the biological model, the emphasis on the mother-child dyad is predicated on the belief that this dyad constitutes a biological unit endowed with and possessing unique characteristics that are essential both for survival and for development. The dyad is conceived of as a biological imperative having evolutionary significance (Rosenblum & Moltz, 1983). It is often perceived as the critical factor in the young organism's development. Animal models, using nonhuman primates or other mammals, demonstrate the importance of the mother-child dyad and of the mother as the single most critical unit in the child's development. Adult males are either absent or uninterested in the young's development. Data from such studies are impressive in demonstrating the importance of a single

adult female's role in her offspring's development and the singularly unimportant role of the biological father. Nevertheless, such models and data often lose sight of the fact that the offspring's development, even though influenced by a mother, takes place in an environment in which there are large numbers of diverse conspecifics, including younger and older siblings, aunts, adult female and male strangers, and adult males and peers. In the last decade, the importance of other social figures in the child's life have been addressed, and although some might still argue for the primary importance of the mother, none would argue that others do not play some role in the child's development.

The teacher-pupil relationship also represents an important dyadic model, which focuses on information exchange and holds that the fundamental process through which information is disseminated is a dyadic one, defined as two people: a teacher and a learner. The model of the parent-child dyad owes much to the teacher-pupil model. The teacher-pupil model of learning focuses on interactions between two members. In the teacher-pupil dyad, it is the adult member, for the most part, who is believed to educate the pupil. Thus, the effects of learning – or in broader terms, the effects of socialization – occur (1) within the dyadic interaction and (2) as a direct consequence of what the adult member does to the child. The influences of the interaction are the influences of direct information and didactic techniques. These, in turn, cause the younger member to change or, in the specific teacher-pupil sense, to learn. Such models of learning, when translated into general dyadic models, clearly emphasize the didactic notion of change. In this view, one member directly influences the other member, and in the most prominent model, the older member influences the younger member. Thus, the dimensions thought important in the education of children vis-à-vis school are extended to the home and the family in observing mother-child learning situations. Moreover, both reflect, at least in part, the unidirectional feature, in which the teacher influences the pupil. Although recognizing that the dyad may be more interactive and multidirectional (Lewis & Rosenblum, 1974), such models, nevertheless, suggest that the primary mode of socialization is a dyadic one.

The teacher-pupil dyad model suffers from some of the same problems as are found in the mother-child dyad model. Let us explore some of the common difficulties. To begin with, the dyadic learning model neglects the fact that even in the teaching situation the teacher-pupil interaction occurs in the company of others: other students and, at times, even other adults. Thus, to think of the teacher-pupil dyad as the only significant source of information and, therefore, of learning is to negate the role of peers (either older or same-age peers) in the learning process. The classroom in which the teacher-pupil dyad is located is also filled with a multitude of dyads, including other teacher-pupil dyads as well as the pupils' interactions with each other.

A second problem occurs when we focus on the processes involved in either development or learning. Both dyadic models (or didactic effects) tend to focus on direct effects as the process inducing change. Although pupils learn directly from what they are given to read or from what their teachers say, there are other important forms of learning that are not didactic in nature. The existence of alternative forms of learning itself argues against dyadic interactions as the sole or even the predominant model of growth. Observational learning and imitation are examples of such forms of learning, which are not dyadic nor didactic. The process of imitation allows us the opportunity to explore the nondyadic processes that allow the child to imitate anyone it chooses, be it someone in a position of power or someone who acts and/or achieves in a fashion that the imitator wishes to emulate. The process of observational learning likewise allows children to learn from anyone, not just the person directly interacting with them. These alternative forms of learning are particularly important in that observing them allows us to consider units larger than two people and therefore allows for the consideration of interactions beyond the dyad.

The example of language acquisition can serve as a starting point. Most learning theories in the last 30 years have related the development of language to the mother-child dyad (Lewis & Rosenblum, 1977). Although these theories differ considerably in detail, the major model remains that of the mother's speaking to the child as it affects the child's language ability. However, if we embed the mother-child dyad within a family consisting of a father and an older sibling, the influence of the mother talking to the child becomes only one source of effect. In the family unit, there are at least two possible influences on the child's language acquisition: the mother's speech to the child and the impact of other dyads, which do not include the child directly, on the child's language acquisition. In a mother, father, and two children interactional system, besides the three dyads that directly include the child ($M \rightarrow C$;

F → C; S → C), there are other dyads that do not include the child: the mother-father dyad (M←→ F) and the parent-other-sibling dyad (M → S; F → S). Research on indirect effects suggests that the language interaction between the mother and the father may influence the child's language acquisition (Lewis & Feiring, 1982). Thus, measurement is made increasingly complex by the addition of more than two members and by indirect effects.

The focus on dyadic interactions enables the investigator to easily explore the direct consequences of the action of one member on the behavior of another. The ease of measurement of a dyadic interaction, in part, is one reason for its success. The measurement model, as applied to development, is surprisingly simple. One can simply measure how one member of the dyad behaves and measure, both concurrently and subsequently, how the other member behaves. Thus, children's language development can be studied by measuring some feature of maternal speech at one point in time and as it relates to infant and child speech both concurrently and subsequently. In this fashion, direct influences in a dyadic exchange can be viewed developmentally.

Before the early 1960s, mothers' behavior toward their children was measured primarily through clinical ratings or through observation and the use of scales. These scales consisted of categories of behavior believed important, and they were often selected on the basis of psychoanalytic as well as learning theory. Perhaps one of the earliest and most successful schemes of this sort grew out of the Fels Research Institute's longitudinal study and the work of Sontag and Baker (1958). Under the influence of the ethologists, such rating-scale procedures became outdated, and new techniques based on direct observation of particular behaviors were initiated. In part, the new systems of micromeasurement (see Cairns, 1979; Lamb, Suomi, & Stephenson, 1979; Lewis & Rosenblum, 1974) owe their origins to a discontent with the use of scales in assessing parent-child interaction. The use of a more behavior-oriented methodology resulted in the observation of a large number of maternal and child behaviors. Not only were methodologies that would allow for the accurate observation of such a set of behaviors developed, but statistical methodologies had to be devised so that the large number of data obtained from these observations could be treated. Although many of the difficulties of observation, data management, data analysis, and interpretation remain, many new techniques have emerged. Nevertheless, there are still difficulties in these microobservational systems. It is quite apparent that the attempt to measure all that occurs during a dyadic interaction is an impossible task because the number of possible behaviors is endless. Moreover, although more complex sequential-time-series analyses of data, in addition to simple counts of behaviors, are available, the use of these techniques, along with deciding what behaviors to measure, requires carefully articulated theories. Without these theories, what behaviors are to be observed and how the data are to be analyzed remain a problem.

The history of the measurement of dyadic interactions should immediately alert us to the major problems we face when we measure the more complete effect of the social environment on the child. However problematic, there has been much success in devising measurement systems for the dyad. This measurement success may act as a motive for the continuing use of the dyadic model as the major unit in development when, in fact, the need for other models has become increasingly clear. How a measurement system including more than two members would work is not fully articulated, although several suggestions have been made. Normally, when units larger than a dyad are considered, the measurement system used is restricted to a set of dyadic interactions. Thus, for example, in mother-child-father interaction, the separate mother-child, father-child, and mother-father dyads are each treated separately. Alternatively, the mother-child dyad has been compared when the mother-child dyad are alone versus when they are in the company of another (Pedersen, 1980). Although these observation systems carry us beyond the concept of the dyad, they nevertheless restrict their analyses to the dyad within the context of other dyads or individuals. Not until methodological issues are addressed will the study of units larger than the dyad become the rule.

Consideration of the social influences on the development of children from the perspective of units larger than the dyad is necessary. Few would argue (except perhaps those who advocate strong biological models or attachment theories) that the only unit of importance is the mother-child dyad. In studies beyond the dyad, three trends can be observed. The first is the recognition that one must go beyond the mother-infant or even the father-infant dyad in order to understand development. Such approaches suggest that a large number of other conspecifics need to be considered, including grandparents, uncles and aunts, cousins, siblings, and friends. Studies such as these at least point out that one dyad is insufficient in characterizing the child's development. The second trend in studying interaction is going beyond the dyad toward examining group interactions. Much of our social life, even in early childhood, takes place in groups. Group processes and their measurement allow for study of units larger than the dyad. Approaches that look at group processes do this in a variety of ways. The simplest model is to observe how a dyad is affected by other conspecifics, for example, how mother-child interaction is altered by the presence of the father. Although studies of this type are important, they have only limited application to the study of group interactions. The third trend involves studies of group processes that deal with indirect as well as direct effects. Lewis has suggested ways of studying more than two (Lewis & Feiring, 1981; Lewis & Weinraub, 1976).

A Classification of Extradyadic Social Influences

We consider *four* types of extradyadic social factors that are likely to influence infant behavior:

1. The physical presence of other people to form triads and larger groups (e.g., families and play groups).
2. The extent to which a dyad is isolated from or integrated within social networks.
3. The social experiences and relationships that each dyad partner has outside the dyad itself.
4. The ways in which others modify dyad partners' perceptions of each other, thus influencing dyadic interaction.

The Presence of Other People

The presence of additional individuals significantly affects social interaction through two major avenues. First, the new people can modify interaction within each dyad. Second, the presence of three or more individuals creates opportunities for higher-level interaction, as when several individuals converse together as a group. The entrance of a third person transposes the dyad into a triad, greatly altering the interactive structure. In triads, coalition formation is possible, as two individuals can ally in order to gain an advantage over the third. Indeed, interaction in three-person groups often results in coalition formation (Miller, 1981). Alliances are especially common between two lower-power actors who join forces to counter the more powerful actor, who would otherwise dominate the group and acquire most of the available rewards. Simmel (see Wolff, 1950) also suggests that when there is discord between two persons, the third individual may either act as a mediator to resolve the differences or take advantage of the rift in order to increase their own advantage. Indeed, the third person may actively drive a wedge between the other two.

Although the transition from dyad to triad is especially significant, the general issue of how group size influences interaction has also received much social psychological attention. As group size increases, the number of potential dyadic relationships increases. In an *n-member* group, the addition of one person increases the number of dyads by *n*. Furthermore, there is greater potential for simultaneous interaction among three or more people, as when group members work together on a common task. But larger group size is also correlated with decreased individual participation. An increase in group size decreases the average participation of each member in both adults' and children's groups (Bales & Borgatta, 1967).

Families and kinship networks provide important small-group interaction in all societies; even societies with the simplest social structure organize social life around kin-based groupings (Van den Berghe, 1978). Research on families has often focused on the distribution of power in families and conjugal relationships. Blood and Wolfe's (1960) study of how the husband-wife power balance is altered by the entry of children into the family system reflects an interest in how the presence of additional group members affects dyadic interaction (see also Lewis & Feiring, 1981).

Competing parents may each attempt to form a coalition with the child against the other parent (Broderick & Pulliam-Krager, 1979; Minuchin, 1974). Parents may confront the child with conflicting interpretations of situations (Sojit, 1971). In a somewhat different solution to family distress, parents may resolve their disagreement by forming an alliance with each other and scapegoating the child, who is then perceived as the source of marital discord (Vogel & Bell, 1960). The understanding of family interaction requires consideration not only of dyadic relationships but also of higher-level interaction and the interplay among dyads.

Information about extradyadic forces in infancy can be derived from earlier studies that were not explicitly directed toward such issues. Investigations of the effect of the mothers' proximity on infant-stranger interaction (Ainsworth, Blehar, Waters, & Wall, 1978; Campos, Emde, Gaensbauer, & Henderson, 1975; Feinman, 1980; Morgan

& Ricciuti, 1969) were, after all, concerned with the effect of a third person on dyadic interaction. The proximity of the mother increases the infant's comfort with the stranger. Investigations of the effects of birth order on caregiver-infant interaction have also considered extradyadic influences (Lewis & Kreitzberg, 1979). Mothers' less frequent interaction with later-borns than with firstborns is consistent with the small-group finding that the quantity of interaction per dyad decreases with increasing group size. Later-borns receive less attention because they are members of larger family groups than are firstborns. Similarly, the decrease of maternal attentiveness to and playfulness with firstborn offspring following the birth of a second infant reflects the effect of group size on dyadic interaction (Feiring & Lewis, 1982; Kendrick & Dunn, 1980). The finding that later-born infants spaced at least six years from the previous sibling receive about as much attention as do firstborns (Lewis & Kreitzberg, 1979) could be explained by the absence of older siblings from the household for the hours during which they are attending school. For about 6 hours each weekday, the distantly spaced later-born is a member of a smaller group and can receive more parental attention.

Research on indirect effects considers how the presence of one parent affects the infant's interaction with the other parent (Clarke-Stewart, 1978; Lamb, 1976, 1978; Lytton, 1979; Pedersen et al., 1980). Infants interact more frequently with a parent when alone with that parent than when both parents are present. Similarly, if one dyad in a three-person group does not interact, then interaction in the other two dyads should intensify. This pattern is reflected in the finding that infants interact more with each parent when the parents do not communicate with each other than when they do (Pedersen *et al.*, 1980). Similarly, 2-year-olds approach their mothers less often when in a triad of mother, infant, and older sibling than when with only the mother (Samuels, 1980). Infants between 10 and 14 months directed 36 percent more behaviors to peers and 174 percent more behaviors to peers' mothers when their own mothers were absent than when they were present (Field, 1979).

The Integration of the Dyad within Social Networks

The dyad's integration within or isolation from social networks of kinship, friendship, and community affects dyadic interaction in several ways. First, social connectedness enhances the probability that the dyad will be drawn into higher-level interaction. Second, social integration provides support and aid in everyday activities and in emergency situations. Individuals in socially isolated dyads do not have other people to call on when situational demands exceed the resources within the dyad. Third, extra-dyadic networks provide opportunities for social comparison, the process by which individuals evaluate their opinions and abilities through comparison with those of other people.

Connectedness with broader social networks can affect infant-caregiver dyads as well. Social ties provide information that can influence the caregiver's judgment of the appropriateness of particular interactive patterns with the child. Despite the nuclear family orientation of industrial societies, parents and children tend to be in contact with friends and relatives. For example, in the 1970s two-thirds of the elderly people surveyed in a study of six industrial societies reported that they lived either with a grown child or within 10 minutes of that household (Shanas, 1973). In addition to providing the infant with opportunities to interact within a wider social network, relatives and friends can be important sources of advice about child care (Weinraub, Brooks, & Lewis, 1977).

Social integration also facilitates support systems that supplement the dyad's capacity to cope with everyday demands. Social isolation and weaker ties with extended kin and the community are salient features of child-abusing parents (Garbarino, 1977; Parke & Collmer, 1975) and suggest that social isolation renders the dyad more vulnerable to stress. Garbarino and Sherman (1980)

found that children who resided in neighborhoods with higher rates of child abuse had fewer contacts with people beyond the nuclear family than did children in lower-risk neighborhoods. Lessened social integration appears to diminish the resources and the social support available to the dyad. Furthermore, socially integrated parents who abuse their children can learn, through social comparison, that their behavior is neither considered appropriate nor practiced by other people. The isolated child abuser lacks such opportunities. Within the realm of acceptable child care practices, parents who interact beyond the nuclear family have multiple bases for assessing their own and their infants' behavior because they can engage in comparative discussion and can also observe other infants.

The mother-infant dyad appears to be more socially integrated now than it was 20 years ago. As more mothers work outside the home, and more young children experience substitute care, they come to interact with new people and to develop opportunities for social support and social comparison. One result of recent alterations in the role of women in some industrial and industrializing societies seems to be the greater social integration of infants and mothers.

Social Experiences and Relationships outside the Dyad

Most individuals occupy more than one role in a society. A woman may be a mother, a wife, a carpenter, and a member of the local art guild. An infant may be a son or daughter, a sibling, a member of a day-care center, and a pediatric patient. What individuals do, how they are treated, and what they learn outside a particular dyad can affect their interaction within the dyad.

Because time clearly is limited, time devoted to interaction in one social position cannot be utilized in another. For example, employed mothers have less time than full-time ones to interact with their children and men who work long hours report having less time for their families. There may also be qualitative differences in how people interact as a function of the quantity of time available. Spouses in dual-career marriages appear to adapt to the smaller amount of nonwork time spent together by making adjustments that enable them to maintain affective bonds (Aldous, 1978). The results of the NICHD day care findings reveal that infant care alone does not affect the child's development. Rather, it is a complex interaction between time in the program and the quality of care along with maternal health. Similarly, the finding of less intense affect per dyad in loose-knit networks with many members than in close-knit networks with fewer individuals implies the existence of a finite amount of sociability (Granovetter, 1971).

The affective relationships that infants form with day-care providers do not appear to diminish affect for their parents (Lamb, 1982). On the other hand, infant-older-sibling antagonism (Abramovitch, Corter, & Lando, 1979) and the negative correlation between firstborns' affect to the mother and to the infant sibling (Dunn & Kendrick, 1981) may indicate that siblings compete over limited parental resources (Trivers, 1974). The decrement in mothers' interaction with firstborns once a second child is born (Kendrick & Dunn, 1980) and the diminished level of interaction between mother and later-borns compared with firstborns (Lewis & Kreitzberg, 1979) would suggest that the limits of mothers' time, if not affect, are being approached when they care for several children.

It is not particularly surprising to find that infants become friendlier with peers after having previous experience with same-age infants (Lewis, Young, Brooks, & Michalson, 1975). But infants also seem to generalize from learning in one social position to behavior in another. Infants' prior interaction with older children affects their later behavior with agemates (Snow, Jacklin, & Maccoby, 1981; Vandell, Wilson, & Whalen, 1981). Later-borns are less friendly than firstborns to peers, a finding suggesting that interaction with siblings may affect peer relationships. The generally agonistic quality of later-borns' interaction with older siblings

and, in particular, the tendency of older children to direct and dominate infants' behavior may diminish later-borns' enthusiasm for such interactions (Abramovitch et al., 1979). A disinclination for interaction with older children may generalize to infant peers as well, resulting in later-borns' lesser sociability with peers. Just as adults' work values may influence their child-rearing behavior, infants' experiences with older siblings may generalize to modify interaction with peers as well as with older children. Similarly, infants who had play-group experience with other infants interacted more actively with their parents (Vandell, 1979). While not detrimental at all, it may be that the more egalitarian nature of peer relationships carries over into the infants' expectations about interaction with adults as well.

The effect of social class on self-concept and perceived powerfulness would seem to be relevant to parent-infant interaction. It has been found that middle-class mothers engage in more distal interactions (e.g., vocalization) with their infants than did working-class mothers (Lewis & Wilson, 1972; Field & Pawlby, 1980). Similarly, middle-class mothers vocalized, attempted to entertain, and responded more often to their 10-month-olds (Tulkin & Kagan, 1972). Farran and Ramey (1980) report that lower-class mothers were less involved with their 6-month-olds. Thus, mothers' social class position within the society is correlated with their interaction with infants. It has been proposed that lower-class mothers are especially likely to perceive themselves as unable to effect changes in their infants' behavior (Tulkin & Kagan, 1972). Perhaps such beliefs stem from the general perceptions of ineffectiveness and poor self-image found in lower-class communities with regard to the world outside. The mother may view the infant as someone who controls her, rather than as a person whose behavior can be effectively modified. The position of "lower-class person" may lead mothers to adopt a less positive attitude toward themselves, which then affects their interactions with their infants.

Because an individual's multiple roles often possess conflicting expectations, using the behavioral norms for Position A while playing the role of Position B can be disturbing to role partners in the latter position. It is, of course, unreasonable to expect infants to be able to make sense of abstract concepts such as multiple roles and the division of labor. Yet infants do interact with people who possess differing interpersonal styles. The finding that year-old infants engage in more play with their fathers than with their mothers (Lamb, 1977) suggests that they distinguish among people not only according to physical features, but also with regard to behavioral style. Indeed, we have found that infants form differential expectations about various individuals or classes of people (see Edwards and Lewis, 1979; Lewis and Feiring, 1978).

Infants who have extensive social connections appear to be less vulnerable when one primary caregiver is absent. For example, the absence of alternative caregivers necessitates the placement of the children in residential nurseries when their mothers have to be hospitalized (Heinicke & Westheimer, 1966). If these children had lived within extended families with alternative caregivers, it is unlikely that they would have been separated from their homes and from other kin during the absence of a primary caregiver. Children who have multiple caregivers may, indeed, be less dependent on any one particular person for their physical and emotional needs (Lewis, 2005). When one person cannot care for the child, other caregivers are still available. Somewhat similarly, the accessibility of peers when rhesus monkey infants are isolated from their mothers appears to provide some substitute sources of affect – as in the together-together monkeys who become strongly attached to each other rather than to their absent mothers – and may even facilitate appropriate social development (Suomi & Harlow, 1975).

Experiences in one social position can also function as prerequisites or facilitators of effective performance in another role, rather than as functional alternatives. The mother's ability to interact effectively with her children may be strengthened by the father's provision of physical, financial, and emotional support to her (Parke, 1979). Adequate functioning of the mother-father relationship would then be a facilitator of effective interaction between mother and young child.

Social Influence on Perceptions of Dyadic partners: Social referencing

Dyadic interaction is greatly influenced by the perceptions that the dyadic partners have of each other. Because social influence often modifies individuals' responses to situations, it is reasonable to expect that perceptions of dyadic partners can be affected by others' opinions. Similarly, people evaluate their own abilities, opinions, and relationships through social comparison (Festinger, 1954). Other people and groups provide points of reference – hence the term *reference group* – by which individuals understand the world around them, and themselves as well. In particular, perceptions of one's dyadic partner can be shaped by the opinions expressed by people outside the dyad. Social influence, social comparison, and reference group phenomena have been termed *social referencing* – the request, receipt, and use of one's perception of other persons' interpretations of the situation to form one's own understanding of that situation (Feinman, 1982).

Although investigations of second-order effects (Clarke-Stewart, 1978; Lamb, 1978; Lewis & Feiring, 1981) have indicated that, for example, the mother's presence affects father-infant interaction, research has not focused on how the infant's perception of the father is influenced by the mother. Nor has the even more intriguing question of whether the infant's behavior toward another person influences the parent's interpretation of that person been considered. Nonetheless, there is evidence that suggests that the cognitive and social skills needed for social referencing develop during the second semester of the first year of life (Feinman, 1982; Klinnert, Campos, Sorce, Emde, & Svejda, 1983). Social referencing can occur if perception is based, at least in part, on constructionist activities involving interpretation of meaning or what has been called appraisal.

Infants often look toward their caregivers when encountering a new person or object (Feinman, 1980; Feinman & Lewis 1983; Haviland & Lewis, 1975). Such behavior could represent the request and receipt of information about the new event. Although very young infants do imitate familiar behaviors (Jacobson, 1979; Killen & Uzgiris, 1981; Lewis, 1979), the imitation of novel behaviors emerges later in the first year (Eckerman, Whatley, & McGhee, 1979). Beginning around 6 months, infants appear to distinguish among and react appropriately to emotional expressions (Charlesworth & Kreutzer, 1973). In light of infants' limited word comprehension, sensitivity to nonverbal affective cues is probably the major avenue through which social referencing can proceed during the second half-year.

Variation in the mothers' nonverbal affective cues modified the infants' interpretation of the stranger. Fifteen-month-olds were friendlier to a female stranger when the stranger had been seen interacting positively with the mother than when she had interacted with another person or with no one (Lewis & Feiring, 1981). The mother's favorable behavior to the stranger when the stranger was more positive to the mother may have influenced the infant's understanding of the stranger (Feiring, Lewis & Starr, 1984).

The Social Network

Imagine that one could invisibly watch a washday in a typical middle-class American home and watch a washday in a pretechnological Indian society in the Amazon basin. In the first scene, a mother and her 3-year-old child are alone in their home. The 3-year-old wants attention and would like to play with someone. The mother is busy collecting the laundry, putting it in the machine, and trying to straighten the house. The child is upset: there is no one to play with because the mother is busy. The mother is upset because she has work to do and because she would like to spend some time talking to her friend, Jane, with whom she has not spoken in several days.

Contrast this with a second scene. Picture an entire village down by the river. There, mothers and children are congregated, all doing their individual family tasks together. Mothers sit by the side of the river pounding their wash against large rocks and stumps of trees. The 3-year-olds play with their peers of the same age, and younger and older children play as their mothers work. The mothers work and at the same time are able to interact with other mothers, who also vary in age, some being older kin (their mothers or grandmothers), others being peers of varying age.

If we focus on the first scene, it becomes obvious that the social network of children is nearly restricted to their mothers. All functions that constitute good caregiving must be satisfied by a single person. The child's mother must be the nurturer, the teacher, the game player, the protector, the socializer, and the provider. At the same time, this adult female needs to derive most of her daily satisfaction from her young child. The network of the adult (mother) is as restricted as that of the child.

Not so for the Indian family. By the river, the 3-year-old has other children – kin, non-kin, older, and younger – with whom to play. Moreover, there are other adults, kin and nonkin, friends of the mother, and unfamiliar people. Likewise, the mother has a large array of other adults with whom to talk, to share, and even to play. For the most part, these are women; however, in this particular group, preadolescent boys and old men also wander down to the river. The network of the child, like the network of the mother, is a rich nexus, an interconnection of relationships. Within this nexus, the needs of both can be served, at times by each other, at times by others.

These two scenes serve to contrast the different social networks that are possible. In one, the American family, the child's network consists primarily of the mother-child dyad. In the Indian family, the child's network consists of many others, and the possible dyads are quite numerous. These two possible networks serve to contrast two opposite social milieus of which a young child may be a part. The differences in the social milieus point out the need to explore the nature of the child's network and point to the fact that even in the American family the mother-infant relationship needs to be considered only one of the possible dyads in a social network. Although the child in the American family is embedded in a social network that often includes mother, father, siblings, other kin (grandparents, aunts/ uncles, cousins), peers, adult friends of parents, and teachers, relatively little attention has been paid to these people and the role that they play in the child's social development (Lewis & Takahashi, 2005).

Social Network Systems Model

Systems in general and social systems in particular can be characterized by a number of features: (1) they have elements; (2) the elements are related; (3) the elements are nonadditive (i.e., the sum of the elements does not equal the total system); (4) the elements operate under a steady-state principle so that the elements have the ability to change and yet maintain the system; and (5) the systems are goal-oriented (Feiring & Lewis, 1978; Lewis, 1982; Lewis & Feiring, 1979, 1981).

ELEMENTS
Systems are composed of sets of elements. The influences of the social system elements in the young infant's life are not necessarily limited to the mother. The research literature indicates that the infant is embedded in a complex system of elements including mother, father, siblings, other relatives (especially grandparents, uncles, and aunts), and peers. Moreover, the infant is capable of interacting with these other people and of forming relationships with them. Some of these relationships may be attachments, some love without attachment, and some friendships. The constraints on these relationships probably rest on cultural factors.

Thus, the first requirement of a social network systems analysis is met: there is a multitude of possible elements.

INTERCONNECTION OF ELEMENTS
Systems are characterized not only by sets of elements but by a set of interrelated elements, that is, by elements that are influenced by each other (Monane, 1967). Within the family, the interaction of elements can be at several levels. At the simplest level, the infant affects its parents (Lewis & Rosenblum, 1974), the parents affect the infant, and the parents affect each other. Such effects come about through direct interactions among family members. Recall that elements are not restricted to individuals but may be dyads or even larger units. When larger elements are considered, the study of the interrelation of elements becomes more complex. For example, a child can affect not only each parent separately but also the parental interaction. The research on family size (number of children) and the age of the child shows that children affect marital satisfaction (Rollins & Galligan, 1978). Likewise, the father can influence the mother and the child individually, as well as the mother-child interaction. Many different effects of this complex nature have been observed. Pedersen (1975) and Feiring (1975) observed the parental relationship as it affects mother-child interactions, and investigators have studied the effect of the father on the mother-child relationship (Clarke-Stewart, 1978; Lamb, 1978; Lewis, Feiring, & Weinraub, 1981; Pedersen, Anderson, & Cain, 1977). Cicirelli (1975) looked at the influence of siblings on the mother-child relationship, and Dunn and Kendrick (1979) studied the effect of a newborn child (sibling) on the older-child-mother relationship.

NONADDITIVITY
Social systems also possess the quality of nonadditivity; that is, knowing everything about the elements that compose a system does not reveal everything about the operation of the whole. Any set of elements behaves quite differently within the system

from the way individual elements do in isolation. This rule holds for simple elements as well as for more complex ones. Within the family, how an individual person behaves alone can be quite different from how that person behaves in the presence of another. Observation of mothers, fathers, and children in dyadic (parent-child) and triadic (mother-father-child) interactions showed that the quantity and the quality of behavior in the isolated mother-child subsystem is changed when this dyad is embedded in the mother-father-child subsystem (Clarke-Stewart, 1978).

Moreover, whereas the father-husband frequently divides his behavior between the child and spouse in a three-person subsystem, the mother-wife spends much more time in dyadic interaction with the child than with her husband (Pedersen et al., 1977). The child also exerts influence on the parental system. Rosenblatt (1974) found that the presence of one or more children reduced adult-adult touching, talking, and smiling in selected public places such as the zoo, the park, and shopping centers. Lewis and Feiring (1982), looking at interactions at the dinner table, found that the number of children at the table affects the amount of mother-father verbal interaction and the amount of positive affect exhibited between the two. As the number of children in the family increases, the amount of positive affect between the parents decreases.

STEADY STATE

Social systems are characterized by steady states. The term *steady state* describes the process whereby a system maintains itself while always changing to some degree. A steady state is characterized by the interplay of flexibility and stability by which a system endeavors to maintain a viable relationship among its elements and its environment. Social systems are defined as goal-oriented, and steady-state processes are directed toward goal achievement. However, the same general goal may be served by different patterns of behavior as the system changes to adapt to its environment. Within development, such processes appear to be

essential because behavioral changes occur in the child as a function of age. The nature of the interactions between child and parent changes over the first 2 years of the child's life, although the function of maintaining a relationship, which these interactional behaviors serve, remains the same (Lewis & Ban, 1971).

GOALS

Social systems are also characterized by their purposeful quality. The family system is generally thought to exist in order to perform certain functions (or goal-oriented activities) that are necessary both to the survival of its members and to the perpetuation of the specific culture and society. The family's functions are often stated to be procreation and child rearing; thus, it is suggested that the family is the principal agent of these societal goals. Beyond this level of generality, there are numerous other ways of describing and defining family functions (Lewis & Feiring, 1978; Parsons & Bales, 1955).

The need to go beyond the dyad is clear if we are to understand the infant and child's social and emotional development. Most models of social development not only have restricted their conceptualization of the nature of the family relationships available to the young child by focusing more-or-less exclusively on the mother but also has limited its delineation of the types of activities or goals engaged in by the other family members. If only caregiving functions or goals are considered, then it may make some sense to study the mother as the most important (and only) element. However, other functions in the child's life – including, for example, play and teaching – may involve family members and even nonkin other than the mother. Once such considerations are taken, all the people in the child's network become important to study. Moreover, it is clear that in doing so we need to go beyond studying the dyad and to look at the complex interactions involving multiple people. This is the social environment that influences children's development.

References

Abramovitch, R., Corter, C., & Lando, B. (1979). Sibling interaction in the home. *Child Development, 50*, 1189–1196.

Ainsworth, M. D., Blehar, M. C., Water, E., & Wall, S. (1978). *Patterns of attachment.* Hillsdale, NJ: Lawrence Erlbaum.

Aldous, J. (1978). *Family careers: Developmental change in families.* New York: Wiley.

Bales, R. F., & Borgatta, E. F. (1967). Size of group as a factor in the interaction profile. In A. P. Hare, E. F. Borgatta, & R. F. Bales (Eds.), *Small groups.* New York: Knopf.

Blood, R. O., Jr., & Wolfe, D. M. (1960). *Husbands and wives: The dynamics of family living.* Glencoe, Ill.: Free Press.

Broderick, C. B., & Pulliam-Krager, H. (1979). Family process and child outcomes. In W. R. Burr, R. Hill, F. I. Nye, & I. Reiss (Eds.), *Contemporary theories about the family*, Vol. 1. New York: Free Press.

Cairns, R. B. (Ed.) (1979). *The analysis of social interactions: methods, issues, and illustrations.* Hillsdale, NJ: Lawrence Erlbaum.

Campos, J. J., Emde, R. N., Gaensbauer, T., & Henderson, C. (1975). Cardiac and behavioral interactions in the reactions of infants to strangers. *Developmental Psychology, 39*, 589–601.

Charlesworth, W. R., & Kreutzer, M. A. (1973). Facial expressions of infants and children. In P. Ekman (Ed.), *Darwin and facial expression.* New York: Academic Press.

Cicirelli, V. G. (1975). Effects of mother and older sibling on the problem solving behavior of the younger child. *Developmental Psychology, 11*, 749–756.

Clarke-Stewart, K. A. (1978). And daddy makes three: The father's impact on mother and young child. *Child Development, 49*, 466–478.

Dunn, J., & Kendrick, C. (1979). Interaction between young siblings in the context of family relationships. In M. Lewis & L. Rosenblum (Eds.), *The child and its family: The genesis of behavior*, Vol. 2. New York: Plenum Press.

Dunn, J., & Kendrick, C. (1981). Interaction between young siblings: Association with the interaction between mother and firstborn child. *Development Psychology, 17*, 336–343.

Eckerman, C. O., Whatley, J. L., & McGhee, L. J. (1979). Approaching and contacting the object another manipulates: A social skill of the 1 year old. *Developmental Psychology, 15*, 585–593.

Edwards, C. P., & Lewis, M. (1979). Young children's concepts of social relations: Social functions and social objects. In M. Lewis & L. A. Rosenblum (Eds.), *The child and its family.* New York: Plenum Press.

Farran, D. C., & Ramey, C. T. (1980). Social class differences in dyadic involvement during infancy. *Child Development, 51*, 618–628.

Feinman, S. (1980). Infant response to race, size, proximity, and movement of strangers. *Infant Behavior and Development, 51*, 187–204.

Feinman, S. (1982). Social referencing in infancy. *Merrill-Palmer Quarterly, 28*, 445–470.

Feinman, S., & Lewis, M. (1983). Social referencing at 10 months: A second order effect on infants' responses to strangers. *Child Development, 54*, 878–887.

Feiring, C. (1975). *The influence of the child and secondary parent on maternal behavior: Toward a social systems of early infant-mother attachment*, Doctoral dissertation, University of Pittsburgh.

Feiring, C., & Lewis, M. (1978). The child as a member of the family system. *Behavioral Science, 23*, 225–233.

Feiring, C., & Lewis, M. (1982). Early mother-child interaction: Families with only and first born children. In G. L. Fox (Ed.), *The child bearing decision.* Beverly Hills, Calif.: Sage.

Feiring, C., Lewis, M., & Starr, M. D. (1984). Indirect effects and infants' reactions to strangers. *Developmental Psychology, 20*, 485–491.

Festinger, L. A. (1954). A theory of social comparison processes. *Human Relations, 7*, 17–40.

Field, T. M. (1979). Infant behaviors directed towards peers and adults in the presence and absence of mother. *Infant Behavior and Development, 2*, 47–54.

Field, T. M., & Pawlby, S. (1980). Early face-to-face interaction of British and American working class and middle-class mother-infant dyads. *Child Development, 2*, 47–54.

Garbarino, J. (1977). The human ecology of child maltreatment: A conceptual model for research. *Journal of Marriage and the Family, 39*, 721–727.

Garbarino, J., & Sherman, D. (1980). High-risk neighborhoods and high-risk families: The human ecology of maltreatment. *Child Development, 51*, 188–198.

Granovetter, M. S. (1971). *Child-rearing, weak ties, and socialism: A conjecture.* Paper presented at the meeting of the American Sociological Association, Denver.

Haviland, J., & Lewis, M. (1975). *Infants' greeting patterns to strangers.* Paper presented at the meeting of Human Ethology Session of the Animal Behavior Society, Wilmington, NC.

Heinicke, C., & Westheimer, I. (1966). *Brief separations.* New York: International Universities Press.

Jacobson, S. W. (1979). Matching behavior in the young infant. *Child Development, 50,* 425–430.

Kendrick, C., & Dunn, J. (1980). Caring for a second baby: Effects on interaction between mother and first born. *Developmental Psychology, 16,* 303–311.

Killen, M., & Uzgiris, I. C. (1981). Imitation of actions with objects: The role of social meaning. *Journal of Genetic Psychology, 138,* 219–229.

Klinnert, M., Campos, J. J., Sorce, J., Emde, R. N., & Svejda, M. J. (1983). Social referencing: An important appraisal process in human infancy. In R. Plutchick & H. Kellerman (Eds.), *The emotions,* Vol. 2. New York: Academic Press.

Lamb, M. E. (1976). Twelve-month-olds and their parents: Interactions in a laboratory playroom. *Developmental Psychology, 12,* 237–244.

Lamb, M. E. (1977). Father-infant and mother-infant interaction in the first year of life. *Child Development, 48,* 167–181.

Lamb, M. E. (1978). The development of sibling relationships in infancy: A short-term longitudinal study. *Child Development, 49,* 1189–1196.

Lamb, M. E. (1978). Infant and social cognition and "second-order" effects. *Infant Behavior and Development, 48,* 167–181.

Lamb, M. E. (1982). Maternal employment and child development: A review. In M. E. Lamb (Ed.), *Nontraditional families: Parenting and childrearing.* Hillsdale, NJ.: Lawrence Erlbaum.

Lamb, M. E., Suomi, S. J., & Stephenson, G. R. (1979). *Social interaction analysis: Methodological issues.* Madison: University of Wisconsin Press.

Lewis, M. (1979). *Issues in the study of imitation.* Paper presented at the Biennial Meeting of the Society for Research in Child Development, San Francisco.

Lewis, M. (1982). The social network systems: Toward a general theory of social development. In T. Field (Ed.), *Review of human development,* Vol. 1. New York: Wiley Interscience.

Lewis, M. (2005). The child and its family: The social network model. *Human Development. Special Issue: Beyond the Dyad: Conceptualization of a Social Network, 48*(1–2), 8–27.

Lewis, M., & Ban, P. (1971). *Stability of attachment behavior: A transformational analysis.* Paper presented at a symposium on Attachment: Studies in Stability and Change, at the meeting of the Society for Research in Child Development, Minneapolis.

Lewis, M., & Feiring, C. (1978). The child's social world. In R. M. Lerner & G. B. Spanier (Eds.), *Child influences on marital and family interaction: A lifespan perspective.* New York: Academic Press.

Lewis, M., & Feiring, C. (1979). The child's social network: Social object, social functions and their relationship. In M. Lewis & L. Rosenblum (Eds.), *The child and its family: The genesis of behavior,* Vol. 2. New York: Plenum Press.

Lewis, M., & Feiring, C. (1981). Direct and Indirect Interactions in Social Relationships. In L. Lipsitt (Ed.), *Advances in infancy research,* Vol. 1. New York: Ablex.

Lewis, M., & Feiring, C. (1981). The father as a member of the child's social network. In M. Lamb (Ed.), *The role of the father in child development* (2nd ed.). New York: Wiley.

Lewis, M., & Feiring, C. (1982). Some American families at dinner. In L. Laosa & I. Sigel (Eds.), *The family as learning environments for children,* pp. 115–145, Vol. 1. New York: Plenum.

Lewis, M., Feiring, C., & Weinraub, M. (1981). The father as a member of the child's social network. In M. Lamb (Ed.), *The role of the father in child development* (2nd ed.). New York: Wiley.

Lewis, M., & Kreitzberg, V. S. (1979). Effects of birth order and spacing on mother-infant interaction. *Developmental Psychology, 15,* 617–625.

Lewis, M., & Rosenblum, L. (1974). *The effect of the infant on its caregiver: The origins of behavior,* pp. 15–24, Vol. 1. New York: Wiley.

Lewis, M., & Rosenblum, L. (1974). *The origins of fear: The origins of behavior,* Vol. 2. New York: Wiley.

Lewis, M., & Rosenblum, L. (1977). *Interaction, conversation, and the development of language: The origins of behavior,* pp. 1–8, Vol. 5. New York: Wiley.

Lewis, M., & Takahashi, K. (2005). Introduction: Beyond the dyad: Conceptualization of social networks. In M. Lewis & K. Takahashi (Eds.), *Human Development Special Issue, Beyond the Dyad: Conceptualizations of Social Networks,* pp. 5–7. Switzerland: Karger.

Lewis, M., & Weinraub, M. A. (1976). The father's role in the child's social network. In M. E. Lamb (Ed.), *The role of the father in child development.* New York: Wiley.

Lewis, M., & Wilson, C. D. (1972). Infant development in lower-class American families. *Human Development*, 15, 112–127.

Lewis, M., Young, G., Brooks, J., & Michalson, L. (1975). The beginning of friendship. In M. Lewis & L. A. Rosenblum (Eds.), *Friendship and peer relations*. New York: Wiley.

Lytton, H. (1979). Disciplinary encounters between young boys and their mothers and fathers: Is there a contingency system? *Developmental Psychology*, 15, 256–268.

Miller, C. E. (1981). Coalition formation in triads: Effects of liking and resources. *Personality and Social Psychology Bulletin*, 7, 296–301.

Minuchin, S. (1974). *Families and Therapy*. Cambridge, MA: Harvard University Press.

Monane, J. H. (1967). *A sociology of human systems*. New York: Appleton-Century-Crofts.

Morgan, G. A., & Ricciuti, H. N. (1969). Infants' responses to strangers during the first year. In B. M. Foss (Ed.), *Determinants of infant behavior*, Vol. 4. London: Methuen.

Parke, R. D. (1979). Conceptualization of the effects of fathers in infancy. In J. D. Osofsky (Ed.), *Handbook of infant development*. New York: Wiley.

Parke, R. D., & Collmer, C. W. (1975). Child abuse: An interdisciplinary analysis. In E. M. Hetherington (Ed.), *Review of child development research*, Vol. 5. Chicago: University of Chicago Press, 1975.

Parsons, T., & Bales, R. F. (1955). *Family socialization and interaction process*. Glencoe, Il: Free Press.

Pedersen, F. A. (1975). *Mother, father, and infant as an interactive system*. Paper presented at the meetings of the American Psychological Association, Chicago.

Pedersen, F. A. (Ed.) (1980). *The father-infant relationship: Observational studies in the family setting*. New York: Praeger.

Pedersen, F. A., Anderson, B. J., & Cain, R. L. (1977). *An approach to understanding linkups between the parent-infant and spouse relationship*. Paper presented at the Society for Research in Child Development meetings, New Orleans.

Pedersen, F. A., Anderson, B. J., & Cain, R. L., Jr. (1980). Parent-infant and husband-wife interaction at age five months. In F. A. Pedersen (Ed.), *The father-infant relationship*. New York: Praeger.

Rollins, B. C., & Galligan, R. (1978). The developing child and marital satisfaction of parents. In R. Lerner & G. Spanier (Eds.), *Child influences on marital and family interaction*. New York: Academic Press.

Rosenblatt, P. C. (1974). Behavior in public places: Comparisons of couples accompanied and unaccompanied by children. *Journal of Marriage and the Family*, 36, 750–755.

Rosenblum, L. A., & Moltz, H. (1983). *Symbiosis in parent offspring interaction*. New York: Plenum Press.

Samuels, H. R. (1980). The effect of an older sibling on infant locomotor exploration of a new environment. *Child Development*, 51, 607–609.

Shanas, E. (1973). Family-kin networks and aging in cross-cultural perspective. *Journal of Marriage and the Family*, 35, 505–511.

Snow, M. E., Jacklin, C. N. & Maccoby, E. E. (1981). Birth order differences in peer sociability at thirty-three months. *Child Development*, 52, 589–595.

Sojit, C. M. (1971). The double-blind hypothesis and the parents of schizophrenics. *Family Process*, 10, 53–75.

Sontag, L. W., Baker, C. T., & Nelson, U. L. (1958). Mental growth and personality development: A longitudinal study. *Monographs of the Society for Research in Child Development*, 23(68), 1–143.

Suomi, S. J., & Harlow, H. F. (1975). The role and reason of peer relationships in Rhesus monkeys. In M. Lewis & L. A. Rosenblum (Eds.), *Friendship and peer relations*. New York: Wiley.

Trivers, R. L. (1974). Parent-offspring conflict. *American Zoologist*, 14, 249–264.

Tulkin, S. R., & Kagan, J. (1972). Mother-child interaction in the first year of life. *Child Developmental Psychology*, 15, 379–385.

Vandell, D. L. (1979). Effects of a playgroup experience on mother-son and father-son interaction. *Developmental Psychology*, 15, 379–385.

Vandell, D. L., Wilson, K. S., & Whalen, W. T. (1981). Birth-order and social experience differences in infant-peer interaction. *Developmental Psychology*, 17, 379–385.

Van den Berghe, P. L. (1978). *Man in society* (2nd ed.). New York: Elsevier.

Vogel, E. F., & Bell, N. W. (1960). The emotionally disturbed child as a family scapegoat. In N. W. Bell & E. F. Vogel (Eds.), *A modern introduction to the family*. New York: Free Press.

Weinraub, M. A., Brooks, J., & Lewis, M. (1977). The social network: A reconsideration of the concept of attachment. *Human Development*, 20, 31–47.

Wolff, K. H. (1950). *The sociology of George Simmel*. New York: Free Press.

CHAPTER 6

Social Agents and Genes

Comments on the Ontogenesis of the "Social Genome"

Elena L. Grigorenko and Sarah Ward

Given how much has been written about genes and environments, it would appear rather difficult to say something new. Yet, taking into account how much the field has recently learned about the genes within a short period, it seems safe to assume that this new information must have and has changed the interpretation, meaning, and validity of those earlier writings. In fact, the whole field appears to be redefining itself. In this context, three comments should be made.

The first comment pertains to studies on the role of environmental factors as main effects. Researchers interested in individual differences in complex human behaviors and their etiology used to focus on environments and their characteristics as major measurable sources of these differences. For example, individual differences in school achievement were largely attributed to family characteristics (e.g., Alwin & Thornton, 1984); individual differences in social-emotional behavior were primarily attributed to social-economic status and parenting styles (e.g., McLoyd, 1998); individual differences in love and marriage outcomes were

thought to be closely linked to early parental attachment indicators (e.g., Goldberg, Muir, & Kerr, 1995). Thus, there have been multiple attempts to classify various types of environments and their influences with the goal of establishing causal relationships between them and "resulting" complex behaviors. Yet, in spite of the admitted dominance, although short-lived, of various environmental theories (as an illustration, see the discussion in DeGrandpre, 2000; Leigland, 2000), there have always been at least three major concerns about these theories. First, it appears that classifications of environments are much more difficult to generate than researchers first thought. In fact, there are so many permutations of various environments that it is easier and more accurate, probably, to consider pretty much any environmental indicator as continuously changing in time and cultural space. An illustration of this idea comes from a consideration of climate. Temperature is never discrete, although it might generate rather different qualitative weather states. Also, it changes as Earth ages and as human civilization influences it. Climate produces an infinite number of environmental states and their specific impacts on human development are difficult to quantify. Extreme temperature conditions can be harmful and even deadly, but the ultimate influences of these conditions depend on the presence of other factors in these environments, such as the availability of shelter, water, appropriate clothing, and so forth. Second, overall, the statistical effects of environmental factors have always been lower than those predicted by both experimentalists and theorists. In fact, the field has grown accustomed to small to moderate effects of environmental forces (e.g., Harris, 1995, 1998). Third, the effects of different environmental factors appear to be highly variable across the life span; the engagement and contribution of particular environmental factors appear to be dependent on the stage and quality of the developmental processes they influence. For example, the impact of early parenting appears to matter in a differential manner and at a different magnitude for time-proximal and time-delayed developmental outcomes, and for typically and atypically developing children. Thus, it appears that various types of moderating and mediating effects differentiate the impacts of the environment, and the complexities of this differentiation have been found to be so confounding that the enthusiasm for environmental theories and studies of environmental factors has been depleted. Although useful in earlier decades, in the late 20th and early 21st centuries environmental studies alone do not appear to provide satisfactory explanations for understanding individual differences in complex behaviors.

The second comment pertains to the growing interest in identifying and measuring genetic influences on human traits. It is important to note that, for many years, there was a trend to estimate, based on data from various types of genetically related family members, the contributions of environments and genes to individual differences in complex behavior traits, but these attempts pertained to dealing with decomposed (or modeled) components of variances, rather than with measured sources of variances. This

approach, known as a quantitative-genetic, biometrical, or behavior-genetic approach, has also been highly influential, especially in the later part of the 20th century, for its zeal in demonstrating, over and over again, that there are virtually no (or simply no) human traits for which genetic variance does not matter (DeFries, McGuffin, McClearn, & Plomin, 2000). In fact, it has increasingly became obvious that environmental variance itself is closely related to genetic variance so that, in some situations, such as SES family indicators, genes are *the* or at least *one* of the few sources of environmental variance (Plomin, Loehlin, & DeFries, 1985). However, although extremely successful in determining the boundaries of estimates of heritability and environmentality for complex behaviors, this approach is not well equipped to translate these estimates into measurable and manipulable environmental and genetic factors.

The issue of the relationships between genes and environments appeared to start redefining itself when the first results of the Human Genome Project (http://www.ornl.gov/sci/techresources/Human_Genome/project/progress.shtml) became available. With this resource, measures of genetic variation became readily accessible to researchers and this accessibility permitted extensive research into the genetic sources of individual differences. The interest, in part, was due to an impression that quantifying genetic difference was a solvable task. Unlike the endless number of combinations of various gradients of different quantitatively distributed environments, there are thought to be only ~24,500 discrete genes, and it is tempting to think that all of these genes can be characterized and that the actions of all or some of them can be associated with specific behaviors. This "quest" has been unfolding since 2003, and a substantial amount of progress has been made. However, similar to the "sobering" realizations that cooled the search for environmental determinants of behavior, genetic studies of complex traits have reached a number of anti-euphoric states of mind. First, with the rare special exception (related, primarily, to psychiatric conditions, e.g., Morrow et al., 2008; Walsh et al., 2008), the connections between genes and complex behaviors appear to be complex, although traceable (Baker, Taylor, & Hall, 2001; Caldu & Dreher, 2007). The genome seems to be wielding its influence on behavior by recruiting multiple genes of small effect into network that are difficult to disentangle. Second, although there is a limited number of genes, the number of proteins whose synthesis is controlled by these genes appears to be much larger than the number of genes; in fact, a gene can be regulated by other agents in such a way that multiple proteins can be synthesized from the information contained by that gene. Third, the action of "other agents" appears to be susceptible to, if not regulated by, various changes in environment. In sum, what was presented as a solvable problem only a few years ago quickly has spun into a much large problem of unknown complexity.

Finally, the third comment warranted by recent research relates to the accumulating data on how genes and environments coact homogeneously. Specifically, there are now a variety of classic examples in the literature capturing the essence of the existence of genomes in environments. These examples are numerous and come from studies of a variety of different organisms. Thus, there are illustrations (e.g., Foerstner, von Mering, Hooper, & Bork, 2005) of how distinct environments (ocean surface water, farm soil, an acidophilic mine drainage biofilm, and deep-sea whale carcasses) actively influence the content of the genome of complex microbial communities by restructuring its nucleotide compositions, specifically, its guanine and cytosine makeup (i.e., "GC content"). Another classic illustration is found in studies of the freshwater crustacean[1] *Daphnia*. Specifically, *Daphnia* mothers exposed to the chemical traces of a predator give birth to offspring with a protective defensive "helmet." However, if these offspring are in a predator-free environment, such a "helmet" becomes disadvantageous and these offspring lose in comparative success (Tollrian & Dodson, 1999). Yet another classic example comes from studies of vertebrates,

investigating if and how the environmental influences to which females are exposed during early development impact the growth and behavior patterns of their offspring. Specifically, if mothers, at their fetal state, experienced poor nutrition (i.e., if their mothers were food-restricted during the pregnancy), they tend to give birth to relatively light and small offspring, even though they themselves were reared with plenty of food (Huck, Labov, & Lisk, 1987).

These classic examples have been and continue to be further substantiated by recent research that has capitalized on opportunities connected to the availability of the draft of the human genome. In this chapter, we explore this new growing literature and offer a classification of the different types of coaction that can occur between environments and genes. Our main argument is that the coaction of genes and environments is unified, and that the heuristic of separating them into two classes of distinct forces, although helpful to the development of the field previously, might have outlived its usefulness. This coaction can be captured metaphorically in an image of a complex unfolding spiral that constantly increases in diameter, and in which each level of the spiral is derived from the previous one, but is larger in diameter as it incorporates new coacting factors. The main idea here is that there is a constant transaction between genes and environments, so that as soon as any single cell that is going to give rise to a larger organism comes into existence, the environment of that cell impacts its genome. Thus, its effects are incorporated into it, since the first division of that original single cell will be imprinted upon by the environment in which the division occurs, and henceforth the result of each subsequent division will be a unique outcome of this coaction and reflect both the genome and the environment inseparably. In other words, the "first" environment into which that first cell was "born" itself becomes a part of the genome, as at every subsequent stage of development, so that each larger turn of the developmental spiral is defined by the coaction of genes *and* environments.

Yet, as indicated earlier, genes and environments are many and they form multiple coacting structures. In this chapter, we are interested in surveying illustrations of such "unified coactions" by sampling from the genome and the matrix of environments. In particular, we focus on those coacting structures that include environments that are typically viewed as social agents. These illustrations, from our point of view, justify the view of ontogenesis as an example of the socialization of genes and the formation of the social genome.

Social Agents: What Are They, and How Do They Impact the Genome?

Viewing human development by connecting genes and environments with the term *and* rather than *versus* begs the task of understanding how that *and* works. How are genes and environments connected? What are some key illustrations of these connections? And, in particular, what are some illustrations of those environments that might be associated with the uniqueness of human individuals, that is, environments that reflect the social nature of human development?

The completion of the sequences for the human and other organisms' genomes has generated a wealth of information that stresses the complexity of their structure, but also the realization that there is a tremendous gap between the structure (now well understood) and the functioning (still understood only in the first approximation) of these genomes. Such mechanisms as the reuse of the same genetic structure over and over again to generate different proteins via ribonucleic acid (RNA) editing (Keegan, Gallo, & O'Connell, 2001) and/or alternative splicing (Maniatis & Tasic, 2002), and the transmission of heritable information by means other than deoxyribonucleic acid (DNA) (Rakyan, Preis, Morgan, & Whitelaw, 2001), along with others, extend our understanding of what the genome can do and does far beyond the central dogma of genetics (Henikoff, 2002). It is now thought that the understanding of the variety of the

functions associated with the genome can only be achieved by "placing the genome in context" (Sternberg, 2002, p. 156).

The view of the genome as a highly complex information-processing dynamic system that exists within a given environment and needs that environment for its existence (Fox Keller, 1999) leads, inevitably, to the recognition that the genotype-phenotype connection is highly nonlinear and nondeterministic (Strohman, 2002), regulated by causal mechanisms that, in spite the tremendous recent rapid progress in the genetic sciences, appear to be not less but more elusive and hard to fathom (Strohman, 2000). "The connection between genotype and phenotype is a many-to-one and one-to-many network of mappings, all of which are context-dependent" (Sternberg, 2002, p. 165).

And yet, the field now has much more information on how this connection works than even a year ago. Here we present bits and pieces of this knowledge, the majority of which was accumulated in studies of animal models. Thus, this knowledge may now be readily generalizable or might not be generalizable at all for the development of humans. Yet, it is a place to start (B. Bennett, Downing, Parker, & Johnson, 2006; N. H. Lee, 2007). So, although we may be wrong in some ways, we hope to be right with our main message: that the flexibility of the genome permits a relationship with social agents in which various mechanisms of the genome engage with the environment in ways that lead to the genome's contextualization and the formation of a "social genome." The social genome is thus formed within the context of its transactions with multiple social agents, which are channeled through society, family, school, and relationships with peers. Collectively, although not precisely, these social agents are referred to as *culture*.

In the many years that human development has been studied, developmentalists have been fascinated with the concept of culture and its role in the transformation of a single cell into a mature social individual. But what is culture? There are many definitions and interpretations of this concept; so many that we are not able to review them here comprehensively. For the discussion here an anthropological definition of the word *culture* is adequate: "the sum total of ways of living built up by a group of human beings and transmitted from one generation to another" (Webster's New Universal Unabridged Dictionary, 1996, p. 488). These cultural ways of living are captured later through discussions of ethnic cuisines, climates, lifestyles, schooling, and families. Here we argue that the exposure to all of these factors acculturate and contextualize the human genome, making it into a social genome. What is the genome's machinery that permits such a contextualization?

Diet

Diets differ across the globe and their differentiation corresponds in many (if not all) cases to cultural divides. To capture these differences, the term *ethnic cuisine* is used. Gastronomy, a field of inquiry into the relationship between culture and food, identifies, catalogs, classifies, and replicates cuisines of the world and connects them to the digestive system of the human body. Gastronomy has not traditionally been concerned, however, with individual differences among people with regard to their responses to the diets associated with various cuisines.

The importance of a healthy and tasty diet to living well, both somatically and emotionally, is well recognized. Throughout the emergence and transformations of various societies and regimes, humans have always paid a lot of attention to food, being concerned with it being plentiful, delicious, and nourishing. In addition, people have long been aware of preferences and tastes, as well as of health risks associated with certain diets.

According to recent advances in nutrigenomics,[2] it turns out that not everyone is suited to all ethnic cuisines, no matter how delicious they are, and that what might be good dietary advice for one person might be dangerous for another. The presence of a genetic polymorphism in isolation might not have a detrimental effect, but, when combined with a particular diet, a polymorphism could indeed be modulated by a distinct nutrient and result in a specific detrimental phenotype. Similarly, some diets might not present a risk by themselves, but they could put an individual at risk for a disorder, if that individual carries a particular genetic risk factor. Thus, interactions between (or various combinations of) diets and genetic polymorphisms might generate a variety of outcomes in individuals with respect to particular disorders. In one of his reviews of the field of nutrigenomics, Ordovas (2007) provides a number of illustrations of such interactions.

One example is from research on the relevance of various polymorphisms in genes that differentially impact the metabolism of lipids.[3] Cardiovascular disorders are characterized by a number of major risk factors, one of which is posed by plasma lipid concentrations. These levels are reported to account for significant population attributable risk (Yusuf et al., 2004). Adjusting these levels with pharmacological treatments is known to decrease the risk of disorder-related manifestations (Law, Wald, & Rudnicka, 2004; Robins & Bloomfield, 2006). The gene *LIPC* encodes hepatic triglyceride lipase, which is expressed in the liver. *LIPC* has the dual functions of hydrolasing triglyceride and serving as a mediating ligand/bridging factor for receptor-mediated lipoprotein uptake; both of these functions are important for high-density lipoprotein (HDL) metabolism. Low plasma concentration of HDL cholesterol (HDL-C) is one of the major risk factors for coronary artery disease. The *LIPC* gene has a number of polymorphisms, one of which is located in its promoter region and captures a substitution of C to T (-514C/T), where the T allele is associated with, among other factors, increased HDL-C concentration. An individual's HDL-C level is known to change as a function of a number of complex behaviors: it increases with physical activity, alcohol consumption, and the consumption of high saturated fatty acids (although these acids also increase low-density lipoprotein cholesterol, LDL-C), and it decreases with smoking and the substitution of dietary fat with carbohydrates. However, a large degree of heterogeneity of HDL-C levels was reported in response to manipulating levels of dietary fat; this differential profile of responses, obtained in conjunction with an administration of a uniform environmental factor (diet), suggested the presence of genetic influences. This hypothesis has been explored in a study of ~3,000 individuals, in which the interaction effects between the -514C/T *LIPC* polymorphism and dietary fat were investigated. It turned out that different genotypes at this polymorphism are associated with different predicted values of HDL-C at different total levels of dietary fat intake (Ordovas et al., 2002). Specifically, the T allele was associated with significantly greater HDL-C concentrations only in those participants who derived <30 percent of their energy from fat; when total fat intake was ≥30 percent of energy, mean HDL-C concentrations were lowest among those with the TT genotype, and there were no observed differences between CC and CT individuals. In other words, the TT genotype is associated with the highest HDL-C level in low-fat-intake diets and with the lowest HDL-C level with high-fat intake; no relationships were established between that genotype and HDL-C level in a moderate-fat intake diet indicating that the participants who carried the TT genotype appear to have difficulty with diets with higher animal fat diets, and, consequently, are characterized by higher levels of cardiovascular risk.

Another set of examples of these "intimate mechanisms" between genes and environments came out of studies of cancer. Many cancers are viewed as outcomes of destabilization and disorganization in the human genome, where levels of dysregulation and abnormality correlate with the degrees of the advancement of oncogenesis [for a review, see (Young, 2007)]. Furthermore, it appears that these levels are associated with the presence/absence and amount of specific environmental agents (both risk and protective, such as in lung, skin, cervix cancers) and broad indicators of lifestyle (again, both risk and protective, such as in gastric and colorectal cancers). Dietary factors are known to interact with the genome in both risk and protective fashions exerting direct (i.e., through gene expression regulation) and indirect (e.g., through DNA repair responses) influences. These influences can keep normal DNA stable, create a cellular environment that can slow the progress of oncogenesis, or trigger the process of genome self-stabilization through arresting cell-division, apoptosis or other mechanisms (Young, 2007). Specifically, a number of dietary factors have been shown to be protective in vivo. To illustrate, butyrate (or the salt of butyric acid, a substance present in dietary fiber and high-amylose maize starch), has been reported to be one such factor (Medina, Edmonds, Young, James, & et al., 1997); it acts by augmenting the colonic apoptotic response by affecting epigenetic mechanisms and, consequently, protecting against cancer (e.g., Cassidy, Bingham, & Cummings, 1994; Stephen & Cummings, 1980).

A major source of diet-related variation that captures the work of both environmental and genetic forces in unison is that of maternal health and, especially, the impact of the mother's well-being on the developing baby prenatally. There are observations regarding the impact of mismatches between birth and growing-up environments. Thus, individuals who were born small with weight indicators falling at the lower tail of the normal curve, but who subsequently grow up in affluent environments are at increased risk for developing coronary heart disease, type 2 diabetes, and hypertension (Gluckman & Hanson, 2004; Godfrey, Barker, Robinson, & Osmond, 1997; Vitzthum, 2003). On the contrary, individuals born as heavier babies and later raised in affluent environments have a substantially smaller risk for such disorders (Eriksson et al., 1999). The hypothesis that was generated on the basis of these findings suggests that the prenatal environment encountered by a woman carrying a child in poor nutritional environments might influence the developing fetus by preparing it for a harsh world and, possibly, modifying fetal metabolism so that the baby, prenatally and postnatally, has increased chances of coping with a shortage of food and nutrients. However, when the situation changes and a sufficient amount of food and nutrition become available, the marginal benefits of rapid growth for small babies may offset the costs, but they may also trigger health problems arising in later life (Bateson et al., 2004).

Climate

Cultural "ways of living" also depend on the climate conditions in which a culture "unfolds." It is hard to imagine Arabic culture without the heat of the desert, the waters of the Gulf, and the shades of palm oases; without a doubt, these climatic contexts impact cultures on the Arabian Peninsula. Similarly, the very word *Russia* triggers associations with snow, deep frost, taiga, and fur hats. And, of course, it is impossible to capture the essence of Russian culture without a reference to long cold winters and the celebration of their ends, marked by Maslennitsa, the essential feast of a calendar year, a blend of bliny (creps), caviar, and vodka, which warms up both the body and the soul.

In fact, there are many ways in which the genome responds to temperature. The transcriptional-translational machinery of the genome can be affected as it responds to temperature changes, through mechanisms such as ribosomal or other protein control. In such situations the control is exercised during transcription or in influencing already synthesized proteins. In addition, within the last few years, the field has learned about a variety of small RNA molecules related to messenger RNA (mRNA). These small molecules can sense changes in the temperature and various stimuli (e.g., metabolites) and then communicate this information to the genome, influencing gene expression. For example, a riboswitch is part of an mRNA molecule, a metabolite-sensing/temperature-sensitive RNA switch, which is capable of binding directly to a small target molecule such that, depending on the presence or absence of its target molecule, the mRNA can regulate its own activity. RNA thermosensors (Altuvia, Kornitzer, Teff, &

Oppenheim, 1989; Morita et al., 1999) are the simplest RNA switches, being composed of, for example, a loop RNA structure containing a ribosome binding site (RBS) and an initiation codon (Johansson et al., 2002). Correspondingly, when the temperature is lowered, RBS is masked by secondary elements and ribosome binding is prevented; thus, no translation can commence. When the temperature is raised, the secondary structures melt away, exposing RBS binds, and the translation of the mRNA is initiated. To illustrate, the entry of a pathogen *Listeria monocytogenes* into an animal host is characterized by a temperature increase; as a result, virulence-associated genes, typically silent at low temperatures, are transcribed. The mechanisms of this transcription initiation are due to the presences of a thermosensor in the 5' untranslated region (5'-UTR) of the *prfA* mRNA (Johansson et al., 2002). The literature contains a number of examples of how other simple (Chowdhury, Maris, Allain, & Narberhaus, 2006) and more complex RNA structures, including large *trans*-acting RNAs (Altuvia et al., 1989; Lybecker & Samuels, 2007; Morita et al., 1999; Shamovsky, Ivannikov, Kandel, Gershon, & Nudler, 2006) can participate in or control temperature-based responses (for a review, see Serganov & Patel, 2007).

When climatic pressure continues, the genome can evoke a system of responses referred to as "adaptive mutation" – beneficial mutations that arise in response to stress and environmental pressures on the phenotype (Hall, 1998; Rosenberg, 2001). This kind of climate-induced change occurs in bacteria in conditions of aerobic starvation; the many DNA changes stimulated by this starvation are aimed at the recovery of the ability to proliferate. For example, *Escherichia coli*, in response to aerobic starvation, engages a mechanism in which a DNA transposone[4] is activated through a number of steps (Lamrani et al., 1999) so that a fused (altered) protein coding sequence originates.

Having prokaryote and eukaryote models of response to thermoregulation, one can at least hypothesize that similar processes might be activated as humans regulate their reactions to changes in the temperature in response to prolonged climatic modulations such as seasonal changes (Sathish et al., 2007) or global warming (no human data just yet!), or to acute modulations such as those caused by heat shock (Bellyei et al., 2007) or strong emotions (Kreibig, Wilhelm, Roth, & Gross, 2007).

Lifestyles

One other dimension of culture that is of interest in this conversation is lifestyle. Lifestyle is typically defined as a way of life that reflects the attitudes, values, and common practices of a person or group.

For example, one of the main characteristics of the "younger" generation in the United States today is the so-called sedentary lifestyle (Hillman, Erickson, & Kramer, 2008). This style of inactivity has been reported to be associated with 2.4 percent of health-related expenditures in the United States (Colditz, 1999) and 2.5 percent in Canada (Katzmarzyk, Gledhill, & Shephard, 2000).

Similarly, metaanalytic research in 4- to 18- (Sibley & Etnier, 2003) and 6- to 90- (Etnier & al., 1997) year-olds has indicated the presence of an association between physical activity and cognitive performance. The effect sizes were reported to be larger for the younger group compared to the cross-life-span group, contributing to the point of view that early interventions are more cost- and outcome-effective (Heckman, 2007).

In addition to being associated with general "wellness," physical exercise is consistently reported to be related to cognitive performance. Metaanalytic appraisals of randomized control trials examining the impact of aerobic interventions on cognitive performance (Colcombe & Kramer, 2003; Etnier, Nowell, Landers, & Sibley, 2006; Heyn, Abreu, & Ottenbacher, 2004) also revealed a number of interesting effects. Although the number of such studies is limited and they are quite diverse in terms of their methodologies and designs, overall, they indicate that (1) the effects are significant although not substantial; (2) the effects appear to be larger on higher-level cognitive functions; and (3) the effects are differentiated by the duration and type of intervention as well as by the gender and age of the participants. There are also studies indicating that time spent on physical activities in the framework of a regular school curriculum does not take away from academic achievement (Ahamed & al., 2007; Castelli, Hillman, Buck, & Erwin, 2007; Kim & al., 2003).

In addition to these results, there are also findings indicating specific brain signatures across a variety of cognitive tasks characterizing more physically active individuals. These specifics include (1) P300[5] of larger amplitude and shorter latencies (Polich & Lardon, 1997); (2) apparently more effective, as detected by functional magnetic resonance imaging (fMRI) scans, modulation of areas of the brain engaged in tasks that are more taxing for the engagement of cognitive control, specifically, increased activation in the middle frontal gyrus and the superior parietal cortex, as well as decreased activation in the anterior cingulate cortex (Colcombe et al., 2004) and increased volume of cerebral blood in the dentrate gyrus of the hippocampus (Pereira et al., 2007); and (3) increased volumes of anterior white matter and prefrontal and temporal grey matter (Colcombe et al., 2006; Colcombe et al. 2004).

Although the importance of the findings presented earlier is obvious, the mechanisms behind the aerobic impacts on health and cognition are not clear, though there are data indicating what kinds of molecules might be involved in aerobic training – the health and brain connection. Brain-derived neurotrophic factor (BDNF) is required for the growth and maturation of new neurons and long-term potentiation (the neural basis of long-term memory formation). Serum and cortical concentrations of BDNF are diminished in Alzheimer's disease, Parkinson's disease, depression, anorexia, and a number of other complex human disorders. There is some evidence that selected cognitive and neural symptoms characteristic of these disorders can be prevented, by means of the increased regulation of BDNF secretion in response to aerobic activity (Adlard, Perreau, Pop, & Cotman, 2005; Cotman & Berchtold, 2002). Specifically, in rodents, exercise treatments are associated with levels of BNDF in the hippocampus, which are linked to enhanced learning and memory processes (Vaynman, Ying, & Gomez-Pinilla, 2004). In humans, serum concentrations of BDNF are increased after acute exercise regimens (Ferris, Williams, & Shen, 2007; Gold et al., 2003). In other words, although the molecular machinery behind the increases in BDNF in response to aerobic treatment is unclear, the observation that its secretion can be enhanced by physical exercise could be important (Hillman et al., 2008).

The concept of lifestyle typically includes multiple factors, both genetic and environmental. Of note is that environmental factors tend to be highly correlated with each other. For example, people with a healthy general lifestyle characterized by lack of excesses or abuses also tend to have other healthy habits (e.g., mind their diet, exercise, and take vitamins). Similarly, people with unhealthy lifestyles tend to have many unhealthy habits (e.g., develop alcohol and other abuse, have unhealthy diets). While such environmental indicators of risk have been found to correlate with each other (e.g., Smith et al., 2007), the large excess of the number of observed versus expected correlations between such factors indicates that these indicators tend to cluster. Quite on the contrary, it appeared that genetic risk factors are largely independent, based on the lack of excess of the number of observed versus expected correlations between genetic risk factors (Smith et al., 2007). Specific implications of these observations for public health are yet to be understood.

Schooling

Environments and environmental circumstances that facilitate social, cognitive, emotional, sensory, and/or motor stimulation are referred to as enriched.[6] School is one example of such enriched environments, where stimulation should be delivered in a systematic manner and warrant desired developmental outcomes. In addition, it should be noted that "being schooled" is the main activity in which developing children all over the world are engaged. Thus, understanding how schooling (enrichment) might work as a major genome socialization factor is important for defining the parameters of the impact of both current and future schools.

Animal studies have proven to be an extremely valuable source of information on the impact of enriched environments, specifically looking at animal models of neurodegeneration and brain disorders (for a review, see Nithianantharajah & Hannan, 2006). To summarize, these impacts can be categorized into genetic, cellular, molecular, brain, and behavioral outcomes. The findings attest to the presence of both short- and long-term effects of enrichment, although the magnitude and duration of these effects might differ.

At the genetic level, enrichment was reported to induce the expression of genes known to regulate neuronal structure, synaptic plasticity, and transmission (Rampon et al., 2000). Specifically, systematic exposure to an enriched environment increases the volume of the nerve growth factor (Torasdotter, Metsis, Henriksson, Winblad, & Mohammed, 1998), in particular, brain-derived growth factor and neurotrophin-3 (Ickes, Pham, Sanders, & Albeck, 2000), and the nerve growth factor receptors (Pham et al., 1999). Moreover, a number of proteins related to synaptic function (Frick & Fernandez, 2003; Lambert, Fernandez, & Frick, 2005; Nithianantharajah, Levis, & Murphy, 2004), synaptic strength (Naka, Narita, Okado, & Narita, 2005; Tang, Wang, Feng, Kyin, & Tsien, 2001), and synaptic plasticity (Duffy, Craddock, Abel, & Nguyen, 2001; Foster & Dumas, 2001) have been observed in higher volumes in the brains of rats exposed to enriched environments compared to those of unexposed or deprived animals.

At the cellular level, an enriched environment has been shown to stimulate neurogenesis (Kempermann, Kuhn, & Gage, 1997), when mediated by vascular endothelial growth factor (During & Cao, 2006), and T cells, and microglia (Ziv et al., 2006), and subsequently engage new neurons into existing neuronal networks (Bruel-Jungerman, Laroche, & Rampon, 2005).

With regard to the brain morphological outcomes, it has been reported that enrichment alters cortical weight and thickness (E. L. Bennett & Rosenzweig, 1976; E. L. Bennett, Rosenzweig, & Diamond, 1969; Diamond, Rosenzweig, Bennett, Lindner, & Lyon, 1972). An enriched environment, overall, stimulates neuronal growth (Faherty, Kerley, & Smeyne, 2003), specifically via an increased number of dendritic spines (Leggio et al., 2005), number and length of dendritic branches (Greenough & Volkmar, 1973), and number and size of synapses (Greenough, Hwang, & Gorman, 1985)

Finally, behaviorally, animals exposed to enriched environments demonstrate better performance on learning and memory tasks (E. H. Lee, Hsu, Ma, Lee, & Chao, 2003; Moser, Trommald, Egeland, & Andersen, 1997; Schrijver, Bahr, Weiss, & Wurbel, 2002) and more appropriate levels of emotional reactivity (Benaroya-Milshtein et al., 2004; Chapillon, Manneche, Belzung, & Caston, 1999), predisposing them for better learning outcomes.

Yet, although all these results are highly interesting, a key question that remains is how the environmental enrichment investigated in animals can be related to the variety of human life circumstances.

Humans tend to be quite similar in experiencing some major complex and ever-novel environments (e.g., schooling), yet, they vary widely in their levels of mental and physical stimulation and activity. There is some evidence that attempts to homogenize such variation by means of delivering early quality and enriched environments to all infants and children have formed more positive landscapes for long-term outcomes (Anderson et al., 2003). It has been argued that such early preventive investment is much more cost effective than the remediation of disorders post presentation (Heckman, 2007). Similarly, there is evidence that early deprivation and lack of cognitive stimulation are associated with a host of undesirable outcomes (Walker et al., 2007).

Family

Although family practices are influenced by culture, they arguably form a well-defined, significant layer in the loosely defined structure of translational circles describing the coaction of social agents and genes. One powerful representative of this translation is parenting.

The realization that the early experiences encompassed by parenting are extremely important for the well-being of developing children for the rest of their lives has been expressed in the literature for a long time (for a comprehensive review, see Bornstein, 2002). However, the mechanisms of such strong and profound impacts were not clear. Lately, though, a number of research groups working on understanding this mechanism have made tremendous progress in unfolding the genome-environment coaction encompassed by parenting, at least partially. This progress has been associated with the concept of epigenetics.

The term *epigenetics* (or a synthesis of *epigenesis* – the concept used in embryology to signify the differentiation of an initially homogeneous mass into a newly form complex organism) was coined by Conrad Waddington in the 1940s (Waddington, 1942). The essence of Waddington's term was the *epigenetic landscape* that contextualizes each organism through the establishment, maintenance, modification, and elimination of complex feedback and feedforward connections that occur between the genomic, nucleus, intracellular, intercellular, organismic, and external-to-the-organism environmental contexts (Waddington, 1957). The concept and the reality it captures, although initially well received, was somewhat pushed into the shadows by the discovery of the importance of DNA and its structural units, genes (Van Speybroeck, Van de Vijver, & De Waele, 2002). It has been recently brought out of its "shadowy" existence as the field has accumulated data on the importance of the genome's surrounding context to its own functioning.

Although multiple interpretations of the concept *epigenetic* exist (Jablonka & Lamb, 2002; Morange, 2002; Van Speybroeck, De Waele, & Van de Vijver, 2002), here we default to the one that defines epigenetic mechanisms as those that "confer long-term programming to genes and could bring about a change in gene function without changing gene sequence" (Szyf, Weaver, & Meaney, 2007, p. 10). It appears that these mechanisms are responsible for the utilization of "other" genetic information, different from and additional to that which is coded in the DNA; this "other" information is transmitted from a cell to its progeny and from an organism to its offspring. Among these mechanisms, there are mechanisms that involve the DNA[7] itself and its "context."[8]

There is a growing amount of evidence attesting to the importance of epigenetic mechanisms in accounting for the functional properties of the genome in various environmental contexts. The evidence ranges from attesting to the role of epigenetics in cancer by aberrant silencing of tumor suppressor genes by DNA methylation (Baylin et al., 2001; Feinberg & Tycko, 2004), to stressing the importance of highly dynamic DNA methylation patterns in neurons, so that the resulting methylation profiles play a central role in memory formation (Miller & Sweatt, 2007). This mounting evidence supports the early hypothesis that the balance between the methylation and demethylation of DNA is one possible mechanistic substrate for what is known as a statistically established gene-by-environment interaction (Ramchandani, Bhattacharya, Cervoni, & Szyf, 1999). One exemplification of this mechanism is in the connection between early rearing experiences in life and the brain gene-expression profile (Szyf et al., 2007).

This connection is captured by a number of brilliant studies. In these studies, it has been demonstrated that the quality of maternal care, exhibited either by a biological or fostering mother, has a long-term impact on the expression of the glucocorticoid receptor gene (Francis, Diorio, Liu, & Meaney, 1999; Liu et al., 1997) and hundreds of other genes (Weaver, Meaney, & Szyf, 2006) in the hippocampus of rat offspring. Specifically, this research demonstrated that high-quality (e.g., high levels of licking and grooming of pups by mother rats) parenting early in life is associated with elevated hippocampal expression of the glucocorticoid receptor, enhanced glucocorticoid feedback sensitivity, better regulated hypothalamic-pituitary-adrenal (HPA) axis response, and other indicators of more adaptive responsiveness to stress in offspring, compared to that of offspring reared in the conditions of poor (e.g., low levels of licking and grooming) parenting. It also demonstrated that maternal care engages changes in chromatin, DNA methylation, and transcription factor binding, thus, exemplifying a variety of epigenetic mechanisms. Whereas the specifics of the molecular machinery translating the social agent of parenting into long-term gene expression effects are not absolutely clear and are somewhat difficult to understand from a mechanistic point of view (Hatchwell & Greally, 2007), the charted pathway is hypothesized to involve (1) neurotransmitter-based signaling triggered by parenting behavior, (2) the activation of specific transcription factors, (3) the recruitment of histone-modifying enzymes, and (4) balancing the pattern of methylation-demethylation (Szyf et al., 2007).

Recently this research has been shown to be relevant to understanding the impact of early parenting on the human epigenome. Specifically, capitalizing on the literature indicating that childhood abuse alters HPA stress responses and increases the risk of suicide (Sfoggia, Pacheco, & Grassi-Oliveira, 2008), researchers (McGowan et al., 2009) investigated epigenetic profiles of the promoter of the neuron-specific glucocorticoid receptor gene using postmortem hippocampus samples collected from three different groups of adults: suicide victims with a history of childhood abuse, suicide victims with no childhood abuse, and deceased controls. The results indicated the decreased level of expression of the gene in the hippocampus in brain tissue samples from suicide victims with a history of childhood abuse compared with controls (victims of sudden, accidental death with no history of abuse). Of note also is that there were no differences in the glucocorticoid receptor gene expression between the two latter groups. The researchers concluded that these differences in the gene expression are associated with the presence/absence of history of abuse rather than presence/absence of suicide attempts.

There are some far-reaching conclusions that can be based on the relevant literature (for reviews, see Hatchwell & Greally, 2007; Szyf et al., 2007; Thieffry & Sánchez, 2002). First, there is now evidence that parenting can impact the epigenetic programming of offspring. This conclusion can be rephrased: social behavior can impact the epigenetics of the recipient of this behavior. Second, it appears that epigenetic programming can substantiate long-term cognitive, behavioral, and health outcomes. Third, epigenetic mechanisms can underlie individual differences among individuals with the same DNA structure. Fourth, it appears that epigenetic mechanisms remain important throughout life, constituting the foundation for changes in complex human phenotypes within developmental contexts such as maturation and aging and environmental changes. Fifth, epigenetic states appear to be able to sustain themselves, even after the removal of the particular social agent that triggered the formation of the state; moreover, these states can trigger subsequent regulatory interactions, generating other alterations in the genome's functioning.

An Emerging Picture: A Concluding Commentary

We conclude by commenting on the emerging picture of how the coaction of the genome and environments results in the manifestation of complex human behaviors. In this chapter we have attempted to "take the genome beyond its structure" and consider the various mechanisms through which social agents such as global cultural

characteristics can impact the function of the genome over and above that predetermined by its structure. The conclusion of this brief essay is that the relationships between the genome and behavior are complex and moderated by many factors, including those contextual factors of environments. Having exemplified various types of expression of the genome in particular environmental conditions, we would like to make a number of comments.

First, civilization's trend seems to move from severe infectious environmentally triggered diseases whose impact is great (deadly) to complex chronic noncommunicable diseases that appear to be emerging because of the vulnerability of the genome as it is immersed in a particular environment. These complex prevalent conditions now constitute, at least in the developed world, the major source of morbidity and mortality for the human race. One family of such common disorders is cancers. The International Agency for Research on Cancer (IARC) has collected quality-assured incidence data on various types of cancer (e.g., colon cancer, breast cancer, prostate cancer and non-Hodgkin lymphoma) from around the world (IARC, 2002). The differences in incidence range from 200-fold for prostate cancer to 13-fold for female non-Hodgkin lymphoma. Although these extreme values could be caused by small random variations, the highest incidence rates are representative of the level that is generally observed in developed countries. Analogously, the lowest rates closely represent the rates for the large Asian and African populations. These four types of cancer were selected because they are common in developed countries and they share few risk factors, except for age. A similar comparison for any type of cancer would show at least a 10-fold difference between the regions of low and high incidence. What is remarkable, however, is that there are no consistent trends that stratify incidences of cancer by country's income, geographic location, or any other indicators that could explain such a variation in incidences. The most apparent hypothesis is that this differentiation can be explained by emergent vulnerabilities of specific genomes placed in specific environments with resulting genomic dysregulation.

Second, the genome's capacity to generate complexity using a number of flexible regulatory mechanisms has been referred to as natural genetic engineering or genome reformatting (Shapiro, 2002); some of the "players" of this process have been discovered and understood, but, most likely, there are more of them yet to be identified. While researchers try to comprehend mechanisms of the emergence of such complexity, they survey lessons from the fields of artificial intelligence, self-adapting complex systems, and molecular cell biology. In addition to the mechanisms that open the genome to the environment for the sake of enhancing its complexity as described earlier, there are additional sources of multifunctionality and flexibility in the genome. One such "source" are mobile genetic elements (MGE; Britten, 1996; Brosius, 1999; McClintock, 1987). It is hypothesized that the mechanism here might be the targeting of specific MGEs to dispersed genomic regions encoding a suite of interacting proteins. Through a distribution of MGEs, a new regulatory system can emerge that can provide interacting proteins with new functions and new uses, for example, through shared novel activity domains. Through an insertion of the same MGEs into previously unrelated genomic locations, a new molecular machine associated with a completely novel function, can emerge. The activity of MGEs themselves also unfolds in a complex environmental context and, in turn, is itself regulated. In fact, "the genome is an interactive, semiotic, and super-sophisticated text that has, at this time, no other physical counterpart. It is a genomic book where, for instance, a sentence can take on a hundred related but different meanings, depending on the epigenetic context, all of which are compatible with the whole text. Furthermore, the genome-book contains many cryptic writings that, when transposed, rearranged, or read with an epigenetic decoder, reveal their meanings" (Sternberg, 2002, pp. 165–166). In short, although a first "read" of that text

is available, there is a substantial distance between understanding the letter structure of this text and the multiple images that it can create in its carrier, a human being.

Unfortunately, often the statement that behavior is complex does not necessarily generate much excitement among lay people. Specifically, the mass media has frequently been observed to misinterpret the results of genetic research, with a systematic bias toward overemphasizing the role of genetic factors (Condit, 2007; Conrad & Weinberg, 1996). It appears to be difficult for mass media and laypeople to switch from a "genes versus environments" to a "genes and environments" points of view (Horwitz, 2005), even in the presence of quickly accumulating evidence that the oppositional dichotomy of genes and environments has outlived its value, though it might have been a helpful concept at certain stages of our knowledge about development. Similarly, there is often much misunderstanding of the concepts of genetic variability. For example using 13 focus groups whose participants were recruited through nomination by U.S. multiracial community advisory boards, researchers (Bates, Templeton, Achter, Harris, & Condit, 2003) asked participants to answer the question "What does 'a gene for heart disease' mean?" The responses were coded and it turned out that ~28 percent interpreted this question to mean that a person with this gene will absolutely contract heart disease. Moreover, there are often implicit biases related to interpretations of specific concepts and terms. For example, the terms *mutation* and *mutant* are perceived negatively by laypeople (Condit, Dubriwny, Lynch, & Parrott, 2004), although in scientific discourse they simply refer to a change in DNA (Condit, Achter, Lauer, & Sefcovic, 2002).

Third, while considering different impacts of social agents on the genome, it is also important to consider "another source" of lack of determinism, which is the presence of stochastic factors that can also regulate the genome, but in an asystematic manner. For example, Hemminki and colleagues (Hemminki, Lorenzo Bermejo, &

Forsti, 2006) comparatively depicted survival curves of the control inbred Sprague–Dawley female rats (N = 150) in the aspartame bioassay (Soffritti et al., 2006) and of 34,439 British male smoking and non-smoking doctors, whose cause-specific mortality was followed for 50 years (Doll, Peto, Boreham, & Sutherland, 2004); the curves show survival when follow up was started at the age of 35 years (100 percent survival). The strikingly similar shapes of the curves indicate that interindividual differences that are observed for genetically identical rats housed in a standard environment are due to random stochastic processes.

Fourth, it is important to stress that most of the examples discussed in this chapter pertain to illustrations obtained from animal work. Our knowledge of the impacts of social agents on the human genome is quite limited. There are many reasons for this, of course, the main one being that the experimental approaches appropriated for use with animals are unacceptable for use in humans. Most of what we know with regard to the role of social factors in the functioning of the human genome comes from studies of statistical effects of gene-by-environment correlations/interactions, but many of the studies contributing to this literature have design imperfections (Andrieu, Dondon, & Goldstein, 2005; Kraft & Hunter, 2005), are uninformative (Hemminki et al., 2006), underpowered (Manolio, Bailey-Wilson, & Collins, 2006), or are not replicable (NCI-NHGRI Working Group on Replication in Association Studies et al., 2007). In addition, there are currently many sobering observations in the literature reporting on the higher rate of false positive results in studies of G × E and, even if true, questioning the biological significance of such statistical findings (Eaves, 2006).

Fifth, a substantial number of findings in the literature indicate that the nature of the environmental changes that are being imposed by humans through their "civilized" approach to nature might not necessarily always be beneficial for the genomes of humans themselves. As per Smithies, "My experiences during the course of this voyage into the field of multifactorial diseases lead me to emphasize the importance of looking for quantitative differences, as well as qualitative differences, when searching for genetic factors that determine individual risks for common disorders. Many quantitative differences have accumulated during human evolution – some easily seen as outward differences in our body proportions, some hidden in gene expression – that are without sufficient effects to have been fixed or eliminated by selection. These 'many little things' are a joyful source of our individuality. But they are probably also a source of the poorly understood differences in individual susceptibility to the damaging effects of an affluent society, and to the problems created by our surviving to ages to which our genomes are not adapted"(Smithies, 2005, p. 424). With the "progress" of civilization in our societies, are we pushing the limits of the human genome and where it can ultimately lead us?

Finally, as illustrated in the discussion earlier, the relationship between the genome and its environment can be characterized as (1) transactional, that is, one in which properties of one emerge only from interactions with the other and would not exist otherwise; (2) transcendent, that is, when something is created beyond the ordinary limits of either the genome or the environment, as they are considered separately; (3) transformational, that is, effecting necessary change; and (4) transubstantial, that is, blurring the "borders" between genome and environment, blending the two into one holistic dynamic system. These four "t(s)" are what elevate the interacting genome-environment system into a new whole with specific properties – the social genome.

In summary, here we have attempted to exemplify mechanisms through which social agents appear to impact the genome by upregulating, downregulating, or transforming its structural capacities. There is much to learn in the field, but the prospects are enticing; there is hope that we might generate key pieces of knowledge that will be influential for the delivery of environmental behavior and pharmacological therapies, whose goals are not to change the structure but alter the function of the genome.

Acknowledgments

Preparation of this chapter was supported by Grants TW006764–02 (PI: Grigorenko) from the National Institutes of Health Fogarty Program and R01 DC007665 as administered by the National Institute of Deafness and Communication Disorders (PI: Grigorenko). Grantees undertaking such projects are encouraged to express freely their professional judgment. Therefore, this article does not necessarily reflect the position or policies of the National Institutes of Health or the United States Agency for International Development, and no official endorsement should be inferred. We are thankful to Ms. Mei Tan for her editorial assistance.

Notes

1   A large group of arthropods, including animals, such as lobsters, crabs, shrimp, and crayfish.
2   A field of scientific inquiries (also referred to as nutritional genomics) which investigates molecular relationships between nutrition and structural variation in the genome.
3   Organic compounds (e.g., fats, oils, waxes, sterols, and triglycerides) that are insoluble in water but soluble in specific organic solvents.
4   A sequence of DNA that can move around to different positions within the genome of a single cell.
5   The P300 (EP300, P3) wave is an event related potential (ERP) which can be recorded via electroencephalography (EEG) as a positive deflection in voltage at a latency of roughly 300 ms in the EEG.
6   This concept is typically attributed to Donald Hebb, who observed and compared behaviors of caged rats and rats allowed to wander and explore their home environments; the "freely roaming" rats were reported to have done better on a number of behavioral learning tasks (Hebb, 1947). Since its introduction in the late 1940s, this paradigm has been widely used both in human and animal research.

7   For example, DNA methylation involves the addition of a methyl group to DNA with the effect of silencing gene expression. It is carried out by two mechanisms, direct (i.e., the introduction of a methyl residue in the recognition element of a transcription factor, so that the binding of the transcription factor results in the silencing of gene expression) and indirect (i.e., an attraction of methylated-DNA binding proteins, which, in turn, recruit other proteins to form a "closed" chromatin configuration hiding the gene from transcription).
8   In eukaryotes (i.e., animals, plants, fungi, and protists), DNA is tightly coiled into a nucleoprotein complex called chromatin, which has various structural levels. At the lowest level, the DNA, in runs of 147 bp, is wrapped around octameric complexes of histone proteins (termed H_1, H_2A/B, H_3, & H_4), together making up a nucleosome core particle; that histone octamer comprises a central $(H_3-H_4)_2$ tetramer flanked on either side by two H_2A-H_2B dimers. The next level is represented by the succession of nucleosomes, each separated from the rest by ~200 bp; nucleosomes are connected together as beads on a string, forming a 10-nm fiber of chromatin (Laskowski & Thornton, 2008). The N-terminal ends (or tails) of histone proteins are susceptible to modification via a variety of different mechanisms, such as methylation, phosphorylation, acetylation, and ubiquitination. The complex structure of chromatin allows it to change its own configuration from open to closed, i.e., to "expose" or "hide" specific regions of DNA, so that genes that are located in these regions are accessible and transcribed or inaccessible and silent.

References

Adlard, P. A., Perreau, V. M., Pop, V., & Cotman, C. W. (2005). Voluntary exercise decreases amyloid load in a transgenic model of Alzheimer's disease. *Journal of Neuroscience*, 25, 4217–4221.

Ahamed, Y. et al. (2007). School-based physical activity does not compromise children's academic performance. *Med Sci Sport Exerc*, 39, 371–376.

Altuvia, S., Kornitzer, D., Teff, D., & Oppenheim, A. B. (1989). Alternative mRNA structures of the cIII gene of bacteriophage lambda determine the rate of its translation initiation. *Journal of Molecular Biology*, 210, 265–280.

Alwin, D. F., & Thornton, A. (1984). Family origins and the schooling process: Early versus late influence of parental characteristics. *Sociological Review*, 49, 784–802.

Anderson, L. M., Shinn, C., Fullilove, M. T., Scrimshaw, S. C., Fielding, J. E., Normand, J. et al. (2003). Task Force on Community Preventive Services. The effectiveness of early childhood development programs: A systematic review. *American Journal of Preventive Medicine*, 24, 32–46.

Andrieu, N., Dondon, M. G., & Goldstein, A. M. (2005). Increased power to detect gene-environment interaction using siblings controls. *Annals of Epidemiology*, 15, 705–711.

Baker, B. S., Taylor, B. J., & Hall, J. C. (2001). Are complex behaviors specified by dedicated regulatory genes? Reasoning from Drosophila. *Cell*, 105, 13–24.

Bates, B. R., Templeton, A., Achter, P. J., Harris, T. M., & Condit, C. M. (2003). What does "a gene for heart disease" mean? A focus group study of public understandings of genetic risk factors. *American Journal of Medical Genetics*, 119, 156–161.

Bateson, P., Barker, D., Clutton-Brock, T., Deb, D., D'Udine, B., Foley, R. A. et al. (2004). Developmental plasticity and human health. *Nature*, 430, 419–421.

Baylin, S. B., Esteller, M., Rountree, M. R., Bachman, K. E., Schuebel, K., & Herman, J. G. (2001). Aberrant patterns of DNA methylation, chromatin formation and gene expression in cancer. *Human Molecular Genetics*, 10, 687–692.

Bellyei, S., Szigeti, A., Pozsgai, E., Boronkai, A., Gomori, E., Hocsak, E. et al. (2007). Preventing apoptotic cell death by a novel small heat shock protein. *European Journal of Cell Biology*, 86, 161–171.

Benaroya-Milshtein, N., Hollander, N., Apter, A., Kukulansky, T., Raz, N., Wilf, A. et al. (2004). Environmental enrichment in mice decreases anxiety, attenuates stress responses and enhances natural killer cell activity. *European Journal of Neuroscience*, 20, 1341–1347.

Bennett, B., Downing, C., Parker, C., & Johnson, T. E. (2006). Mouse genetic models in alcohol research. *Trends in Genetics*, 22, 367–374.

Bennett, E. L., & Rosenzweig, M. R. (1976). Effects of environment on morphology of rat cerebral cortex and hippocampus. *Journal of Neurobiology*, 7, 75–85.

Bennett, E. L., Rosenzweig, M. R., & Diamond, M. C. (1969). Rat brain: effects of environmental enrichment on wet and dry weights. *Science*, 163, 825–826.

Bornstein, M. H. (2002). *Handbook of parenting*. Hillsdale, NJ: Lawrence Erlbaum.

Britten, R. J. (1996). DNA sequence insertion and evolutionary variation in gene regulation. *Proceedings of the National Academy of Sciences of the United States of America*, 93, 9374–9377.

Brosius, J. (1999). RNAs from all categories generate retrosequences that may be exapted as novel genes or regulatory elements. *Gene*, 238, 115–134.

Bruel-Jungerman, E., Laroche, S., & Rampon, C. (2005). New neurons in the dentate gyrus are involved in the expression of enhanced long-term memory following environmental enrichment. *European Journal of Neuroscience*, 21, 513–521.

Caldu, X., & Dreher, J. C. (2007). Hormonal and genetic influences on processing reward and social information. *Annals of the New York Academy of Sciences*, 1118, 43–73.

Cassidy, A., Bingham, S. A., & Cummings, J. H. (1994). Starch intake and colorectal cancer risk: an international comparison. *British Journal of Cancer*, 69, 937–942.

Castelli, D. M., Hillman, C. H., Buck, S. M., & Erwin, H. (2007). Physical fitness and academic achievement in 3rd & 5th Grade Students. *J Sport Exerc Psychol*, 29, 239–252.

Chapillon, P., Manneche, C., Belzung, C., & Caston, J. (1999). Rearing environmental enrichment in two inbred strains of mice: 1. Effects on emotional reactivity. *Behavior Genetics*, 29, 41–46.

Chowdhury, S., Maris, C., Allain, F. H., & Narberhaus, F. (2006). Molecular basis for temperature sensing by an RNA thermometer. *EMBO Journal*, 25, 2487–2497.

Colcombe, S. J., Erickson, K. I., Scalf, P. E., Kim, J. S., Prakash, R., McAuley, E. et al. (2006). Aerobic exercise training increases brain volume in aging humans. *Journals of Gerontology Series A-Biological Sciences & Medical Sciences*, 61, 1166–1170.

Colcombe, S. J., & Kramer, A. F. (2003). Fitness effects on the cognitive function of older adults: a meta-analytic study. *Psychological Science*, 14, 125–130.

Colcombe, S. J., Kramer, A. F., Erickson, K. I., Scalf, P., McAuley, E., Cohen, N. J. et al. (2004). Cardiovascular fitness, cortical plasticity, and aging. *PNAS*, 101, 3316–3321.

Colditz, G. A. (1999). Economic costs of obesity and inactivity. *Med Sci Sport Exerc*, 31, 663–667.

Condit, C. M. (2007). How geneticists can help reporters to get their story right. *Nature Reviews Genetics, 8,* 815–820.

Condit, C. M., Achter, P. J., Lauer, I., & Sefcovic, E. (2002). The changing meanings of "mutation:" A contextualized study of public discourse. *Human Mutation, 19,* 69–75.

Condit, C. M., Dubriwny, T., Lynch, J., & Parrott, R. (2004). Lay people's understanding of and preference against the word "mutation." *American Journal of Medical Genetics, 130,* 245–250.

Conrad, P., & Weinberg, D. (1996). Has the gene for alcoholism been discovered three times since 1980? A news media analyses. *Social Problems, 8,* 3–25.

Cotman, C. W., & Berchtold, N. C. (2002). Exercise: a behavioral intervention to enhance brain health and plasticity. *Trends in Neuroscience, 25,* 295–301.

DeFries, J. C., McGuffin, P., McClearn, G. E., & Plomin, R. (2000). *Behavioral genetics* (4 ed.). New York: W H Freeman & Co.

DeGrandpre, R. J. (2000). A science of meaning: Can behaviorism bring meaning to psychological science? *Journal American Psychologist, 55,* 721–739.

Diamond, M. C., Rosenzweig, M. R., Bennett, E. L., Lindner, B., & Lyon, L. (1972). Effects of environmental enrichment and impoverishment on rat cerebral cortex. *Journal of Neurobiology, 3,* 47–64.

Doll, R., Peto, R., Boreham, J., & Sutherland, I. (2004). Mortality in relation to smoking: 50 years' observations on male British doctors. *BMJ, 328,* 1519.

Duffy, S. N., Craddock, K. J., Abel, T., & Nguyen, P. V. (2001). Environmental enrichment modifies the PKA-dependence of hippocampal LTP and improves hippocampus-dependent memory. *Learning & Memory, 8,* 26–34.

During, M. J., & Cao, L. (2006). VEGF, a mediator of the effect of experience on hippocampal neurogenesis. *Current Alzheimer Research, 3,* 29–33.

Eaves, L. J. (2006). Genotype × Environment interaction in psychopathology: Fact or artifact? *Twin Research and Human Genetics, 9,* 1–8.

Eriksson, J. G., Forsen, T., Tuomilehto, J., Winter, P. D., Osmond, C., & Barker, D. J. (1999). Catch-up growth in childhood and death from coronary heart disease: longitudinal study. *BMJ, 318,* 427–431.

Etnier, J. L. et al. (1997). The influence of physical fitness and exercise upon cognitive functioning: a meta-analysis. *J Sport Exerc Psychol, 19,* 249–274.

Etnier, J. L., Nowell, P. M., Landers, D. M., & Sibley, B. A. (2006). A meta-regression to examine the relationship between aerobic fitness and cognitive performance. *Brain Res Rev, 52,* 119–130.

Faherty, C. J., Kerley, D., & Smeyne, R. J. (2003). A Golgi-Cox morphological analysis of neuronal changes induced by environmental enrichment. *Brain Research Developmental Brain Research, 141,* 55–61.

Feinberg, A. P., & Tycko, B. (2004). The history of cancer epigenetics. *Nature Reviews Cancer, 4,* 143–153.

Ferris, L. T., Williams, J. S., & Shen, C. L. (2007). The effect of acute exercise on serum brain-derived neurotrophic factor levels and cognitive function. *Medicine & Science in Sports & Exercise, 39,* 728–734.

Foerstner, K. U., von Mering, C., Hooper, S. D., & Bork, P. (2005). Environments shape the nucleotide composition of genomes. *EMBO Reports, 6,* 1208–1213.

Foster, T. C., & Dumas, T. C. (2001). Mechanism for increased hippocampal synaptic strength following differential experience. *Journal of Neurophysiology, 85,* 1377–1383.

Fox Keller, E. (1999). Elusive locus of control in biological development: genetic versus developmental programs. *Journal of Experimental Zoology, 285,* 283–290.

Francis, D., Diorio, J., Liu, D., & Meaney, M. J. (1999). Nongenomic transmission across generations of maternal behavior and stress responses in the rat. *Science, 286,* 1155–1158.

Frick, K. M., & Fernandez, S. M. (2003). Enrichment enhances spatial memory and increases synaptophysin levels in aged female mice. *Neurobiology of Aging, 24,* 615–626.

Gluckman, P. D., & Hanson, M. A. (2004). The developmental origins of the metabolic syndrome. *Trends in Endocrinology & Metabolism, 15,* 183–187.

Godfrey, K. M., Barker, D. J., Robinson, S., & Osmond, C. (1997). Maternal birthweight and diet in pregnancy in relation to the infant's thinness at birth. *British Journal of Obstetrics & Gynaecology, 104,* 663–667.

Gold, S. M., Schulz, K. H., Hartmann, S., Mladek, M., Lang, U. E., Hellweg, R. et al. (2003). Basal serum levels and reactivity of nerve growth factor and brain-derived neurotrophic factor to standardized acute exercise in multiple sclerosis and controls. *Journal of Neuroimmunology, 138,* 99–105.

Goldberg, S., Muir, R., & Kerr, J. (Eds.) (1995). *Attachment theory: Social, developmental, and clinical perspectives.* Hillsdale, NJ: Analytic Press, Inc.

Greenough, W. T., Hwang, H. M., & Gorman, C. (1985). Evidence for active synapse formation or altered postsynaptic metabolism in visual cortex of rats reared in complex environments. *PNAS, 82,* 4549–4552.

Greenough, W. T., & Volkmar, F. R. (1973). Pattern of dendritic branching in occipital cortex of rats reared in complex environments. *Experimental Neurology, 40,* 491–504.

Hall, B. G. (1998). Adaptive mutagenesis: a process that generates almost exclusively beneficial mutations. *Genetica, 102–103,* 109–125.

Harris, J. R. (1995). Where is the child's environment? A group socialization theory of development. *Psychological Review, 102,* 458–489.

Harris, J. R. (1998). *The nurture assumption: Why children turn out the way they do.* New York: Free Press.

Hatchwell, E., & Greally, J. M. (2007). The potential role of epigenomic dysregulation in complex human disease. *Trends in Genetics, 23,* 588–595.

Hebb, D. O. (1947). The effects of early experience on problem-solving at maturity. *American Psychologist, 2,* 306–307.

Heckman, J. J. (2007). The economics, technology, and neuroscience of human capability formation. *Proceedings of the National Academy of Sciences of the United States of America, 104,* 13250–13255.

Hemminki, K., Lorenzo Bermejo, J., & Forsti, A. (2006). The balance between heritable and environmental aetiology of human disease. *Nature Reviews Genetics, 7,* 958–965.

Henikoff, S. (2002). Beyond the central dogma. *Bioinformatics, 18,* 223–225.

Heyn, P., Abreu, B. C., & Ottenbacher, K. J. (2004). The effects of exercise training on elderly persons with cognitive impairment and dementia: a meta-analysis. *Arch Phys Med Rehab, 84,* 1694–1704.

Hillman, C. H., Erickson, K. I., & Kramer, A. F. (2008). Be smart, exercise your heart: exercise effects on brain and cognition. *Nature Reviews Neuroscience, 9,* 59–65.

Horwitz, A. V. (2005). Media portrayals and health inequalities: a case study of characterizations of Gene × Environment interactions. *Journals of Gerontology Series B-Psychological Sciences & Social Sciences, 60,* 48–52.

Huck, U. W., Labov, J. B., & Lisk, R. D. (1987). Food-restricting first generation juvenile female hamsters (Mesocricetus auratus) affects sex ratio and growth of third generation offspring. *Biology of Reproduction, 37,* 612–617.

IARC (2002). *Cancer incidence in five continents.* Lyon, France: IARC.

Ickes, B. R., Pham, T. M., Sanders, L. A., & Albeck, D. S. (2000). Long-term environmental enrichment leads to regional increases in neurotrophin levels in rat brain. *Experimental Neurology, 164,* 45–52.

Jablonka, E., & Lamb, M. J. (2002). The changing concept of epigenetics. *Annals of the New York Academy of Sciences, 981,* 82–96.

Johansson, J., Mandin, P., Renzoni, A., Chiaruttini, C., Springer, M., & Cossart, P. (2002). An RNA thermosensor controls expression of virulence genes in Listeria monocytogenes. *Cell, 110,* 551–561.

Katzmarzyk, P. T., Gledhill, N., & Shephard, R. J. (2000). The economic burden of physical inactivity in Canada. *Can. Med. Assoc. J., 163,* 1435–1440.

Keegan, L. P., Gallo, A., & O'Connell, M. A. (2001). The many roles of an RNA editor. *Nature Reviews Genetics, 2,* 869–878.

Kempermann, G., Kuhn, H. G., & Gage, F. H. (1997). More hippocampal neurons in adult mice living in an enriched environment. *Nature, 386,* 493–495.

Kim, H.-Y. P. et al. (2003). Academic performance of Korean children is associated with dietary behaviours and physical status. *Asian Pac. J. Clin. Nutr., 12,* 186–192.

Kraft, P., & Hunter, D. (2005). Integrating epidemiology and genetic association: the challenge of gene–environment interaction. *Philosophical Transactions of the Royal Society of London – Series B: Biological Sciences, 360,* 1609–1616.

Kreibig, S. D., Wilhelm, F. H., Roth, W. T., & Gross, J. J. (2007). Cardiovascular, electrodermal, and respiratory response patterns to fear- and sadness-inducing films. *Psychophysiology, 44,* 787–806.

Lambert, T. J., Fernandez, S. M., & Frick, K. M. (2005). Different types of environmental enrichment have discrepant effects on spatial memory and synaptophysin levels in female mice. *Neurobiology of Learning & Memory, 83,* 206–216.

Lamrani, S., Ranquet, C., Gama, M. J., Nakai, H., Shapiro, J. A., Toussaint, A. et al. (1999). Starvation-induced   Mucts62-mediated coding sequence fusion: a role for ClpXP, Lon, RpoS and Crp. *Molecular Microbiology*, 32, 327–343.

Laskowski, R. A., & Thornton, J. M. (2008). Understanding the molecular machinery of genetics through 3D structures. *Nature Reviews Genetics*, 9, 141–151.

Law, M. R., Wald, N. J., & Rudnicka, A. R. (2004). Quantifying effect of statins on low density lipoprotein cholesterol, ischaemic heart disease, and stroke: systematic review and meta-analysis. *BMJ*, 326, 1423.

Lee, E. H., Hsu, W. L., Ma, Y. L., Lee, P. J., & Chao, C. C. (2003). Enrichment enhances the expression of sgk, a glucocorticoid-induced gene, and facilitates spatial learning through glutamate AMPA receptor mediation. *European Journal of Neuroscience*, 18, 2842–2852.

Lee, N. H. (2007). Physiogenomic strategies and resources to associate genes with rat models of heart, lung and blood disorders. *Experimental Physiology*, 92, 992–1002.

Leggio, M. G., Mandolesi, L., Federico, F., Spirito, F., Ricci, B., Gelfo, F. et al. (2005). Environmental enrichment promotes improved spatial abilities and enhanced dendritic growth in the rat. *Behavioural Brain Research*, 163, 78–90.

Leigland, S. (2000). On cognitivism and behaviorism. *American Psychologist*, 55, 273–274.

Liu, D., Diorio, J., Tannenbaum, B., Caldji, C., Francis, D., Freedman, A. et al. (1997). Maternal care, hippocampal glucocorticoid receptors, and hypothalamic-pituitary-adrenal responses to stress. *Science*, 277, 1659–1662.

Lybecker, M. C., & Samuels, D. S. (2007). Temperature-induced regulation of RpoS by a small RNA in Borrelia burgdorferi. *Molecular Microbiology*, 64, 1075–1089.

Maniatis, T., & Tasic, B. (2002). Alternative pre-mRNA splicing and proteome expansion in metazoans. *Nature*, 418, 236–443.

Manolio, T. A., Bailey-Wilson, J. E., & Collins, F. S. (2006). Genes, environment and the value of prospective cohort studies. *Nature Reviews Genetics*, 7, 812–820.

McClintock, B. (1987). *Discovery and characterization of transposable elements: The collected papers of Barbara McClintock*. New York: Garland.

McGowan, P. O., Sasaki, A., D'Alessio, A. C., Dymov, S., Labonte, B., Szyf, M. et al. (2009). Epigenetic regulation of the glucocorticoid receptor in human brain associates with childhood abuse. *Nature Neuroscience*, 12, 342–348.

McLoyd, V. C. (1998). Socioeconomic disadvantage and child development. *American Psychologist*, 53, 185–204.

Medina, V., Edmonds, B., Young, G. P., James, R. et al. (1997). Induction of caspase-3 protease activity and apoptosis by butyrate and trichostatin A (inhibitors of histone deacetylase): dependence on protein synthesis and synergy with a mitochondrial/cytochrome c-dependent pathway. *Cancer Research*, 57, 3697–3707.

Miller, C. A., & Sweatt, J. D. (2007). Covalent modification of DNA regulates memory formation. *Neuron*, 53, 857–869.

Morange, M. (2002). The relations between genetics and epigenetics: A historical point of view. *Annals of the New York Academy of Sciences*, 981, 50–60.

Morita, M. T., Tanaka, Y., Kodama, T. S., Kyogoku, Y., Yanagi, H., & Yura, T. (1999). Translational induction of heat shock transcription factor sigma32: evidence for a built-in RNA thermosensor. *Genes & Development*, 13, 655–665.

Morrow, E. M., Yoo, S. Y., Flavell, S. W., Kim, T. K., Lin, Y., Hill, R. S. et al. (2008). Identifying autism loci and genes by tracing recent shared ancestry. *Science*, 321, 218–223.

Moser, M. B., Trommald, M., Egeland, T., & Andersen, P. (1997). Spatial training in a complex environment and isolation alter the spine distribution differently in rat CA1 pyramidal cells. *Journal of Comparative Neurology*, 380, 373–381.

Naka, F., Narita, N., Okado, N., & Narita, M. (2005). Modification of AMPA receptor properties following environmental enrichment. *Brain & Development*, 27, 275–278.

NCI-NHGRI Working Group on Replication in Association Studies, Chanock, S. J., Manolio, T., Boehnke, M., Boerwinkle, E., Hunter, D. J. et al. (2007). Replicating genotype-phenotype associations. *Nature*, 447, 655–660.

Nithianantharajah, J., & Hannan, A. J. (2006). Enriched environments, experience-dependent plasticity and disorders of the nervous system. *Nature Reviews Neuroscience*, 7, 697–709.

Nithianantharajah, J., Levis, H., & Murphy, M. (2004). Environmental enrichment results in cortical and subcortical changes in levels of synaptophysin and PSD-95 proteins. *Neurobiology of Learning & Memory*, 81, 200–210.

Ordovas, J. M. (2007). Diet/genetic interactions and their effects on inflammatory markers. *Nutrition Reviews*, 65, S203-S207.

Ordovas, J. M., Corella, D., Demissie, S., Cupples, L. A., Couture, P., Coltell, O. et al. (2002). Dietary fat intake determines the effect of a common polymorphism in the hepatic lipase gene promoter on high-density lipoprotein metabolism: evidence of a strong dose effect in this gene-nutrient interaction in the Framingham Study. *Circulation, 106,* 2315–2321.

Pereira, A. C. et al. (2007). An in vivo correlate of exercise induced neurogenesis in the adult dentate gyrus. 104 (5638–5643).

Pham, T. M., Ickes, B., Albeck, D., Soderstrom, S., Granholm, A. C., & Mohammed, A. H. (1999). Changes in brain nerve growth factor levels and nerve growth factor receptors in rats exposed to environmental enrichment for one year. *Neuroscience, 94,* 279–286.

Plomin, R., Loehlin, J. C., & DeFries, J. C. (1985). Genetic and environmental components of "environmental" influences. *Developmental Psychology, 21,* 391–402.

Polich, J., & Lardon, M. (1997). P300 and long term physical exercise. *Electroencephalogr. Clin. Neurophysiol., 103,* 493–498.

Rakyan, V. K., Preis, J., Morgan, H. D., & Whitelaw, E. (2001). The marks, mechanisms and memory of epigenetic states in mammals. *Biochemical Journal, 356,* 1–10.

Ramchandani, S., Bhattacharya, S. K., Cervoni, N., & Szyf, M. (1999). DNA methylation is a reversible biological signal. *Proceedings of the National Academy of Sciences of the United States of America, 96,* 6107–6112.

Rampon, C., Jiang, C. H., Dong, H., Tang, Y. P., Lockhart, D. J., Schultz, P. G. et al. (2000). Effects of environmental enrichment on gene expression in the brain. *PNAS, 07,* 12880–12884.

Robins, S. J., & Bloomfield, H. E. (2006). Fibric acid derivatives in cardiovascular disease prevention: results from the large clinical trials. *Current Opinion in Lipidology, 17,* 431–439.

Rosenberg, S. M. (2001). Evolving responsively: adaptive mutation. *Nature Reviews Genetics, 2,* 504–515.

Sathish, P., Withana, N., Biswas, M., Bryant, C., Templeton, K., Al-Wahb, M. et al. (2007). Transcriptome analysis reveals season-specific rbcS gene expression profiles in diploid perennial ryegrass (Lolium perenne L.). *Plant Biotechnology Journal*(5).

Schrijver, N. C., Bahr, N. I., Weiss, I. C., & Wurbel, H. (2002). Dissociable effects of isolation rearing and environmental enrichment on exploration, spatial learning and HPA activity in adult rats. *Pharmacology, Biochemistry & Behavior, 73,* 209–224.

Serganov, A., & Patel, D. J. (2007). Ribozymes, riboswitches and beyond: regulation of gene expression without proteins. *Nature Reviews Genetics, 8,* 776–790.

Sfoggia, A., Pacheco, M. A., & Grassi-Oliveira, R. (2008). History of childhood abuse and neglect and suicidal behavior at hospital admission. *Crisis: Journal of Crisis Intervention & Suicide, 29,* 154–158.

Shamovsky, I., Ivannikov, M., Kandel, E. S., Gershon, D., & Nudler, E. (2006). RNA-mediated response to heat shock in mammalian cells. *Nature, 440,* 556–560.

Shapiro, J. (2002). Genome organization and reorganization in evolution formatting for computation and function. *Annals of the New York Academy of Sciences, 981,* 111–134.

Sibley, B. A., & Etnier, J. L. (2003). The relationship between physical activity and cognition in children: a meta-analysis. *Ped Exerc Sci, 15,* 243–256.

Smith, G. D., Lawlor, D. A., Harbord, R., Timpson, N., Day, I., & Ebrahim, S. (2007). Clustered environments and randomized genes: a fundamental distinction between conventional and genetic epidemiology. *PLoS Medicine, 4,* e352.

Smithies, O. (2005). Many little things: one geneticist's view of complex diseases. *Nature Reviews Genetics, 6,* 419–425.

Soffritti, M., Belpoggi, F., Degli Esposti, D., Lambertini, L., Tibaldi, E., & Rigano, A. (2006). First experimental demonstration of the multipotential carcinogenic effects of aspartame administered in the feed to Sprague-Dawley rats. *Environmental Health Perspectives, 114,* 379–385.

Stephen, A. M., & Cummings, J. H. (1980). Mechanism of action of dietary fiber in the human colon. *Nature* (284), 283–284.

Sternberg, R. V. (2002). On the roles of repetitive DNA elements in the context of a unified genomic–epigenetic system. *Annals of the New York Academy of Sciences, 981,* 154–188.

Strohman, R. C. (2000). Organization becomes cause in the matter. *Nature Biotechnology, 18,* 575–576.

Strohman, R. C. (2002). Maneuvering in the complex path from genotype to phenotype. *Science, 296,* 701–703.

Szyf, M., Weaver, I., & Meaney, M. J. (2007). Maternal care, the epigenome and phenotypic differences in behavior. *Reproductive Toxicology, 24,* 9–19.

Tang, Y. P., Wang, H., Feng, R., Kyin, M., & Tsien, J. Z. (2001). Differential effects of enrichment on learning and memory function in NR2B transgenic mice. *Neuropharmacology*, 41, 779–790.

Thieffry, D., & Sánchez, L. (2002). Alternative epigenetic states understood in terms of specific regulatory structures. *Annals of the New York Academy of Sciences*, 981, 135–153.

Tollrian, R., & Dodson, S. I. (1999). Inducible defenses in cladocera: Constraints, costs, and multipredator environments. In R. Tollrian & C. D. Harvell (Eds.), *The ecology and evolution of inducible defenses*, pp. 177–202. Princeton, NJ: Princeton University Press.

Torasdotter, M., Metsis, M., Henriksson, B. G., Winblad, B., & Mohammed, A. H. (1998). Environmental enrichment results in higher levels of nerve growth factor mRNA in the rat visual cortex and hippocampus. *Behavioural Brain Research*, 93, 83–90.

Van Speybroeck, L., De Waele, D., & Van de Vijver, G. (2002). Theories in early embryology: close connections between epigenesis, preformationism, and self-organization. *Annals of the New York Academy of Sciences*, 981, 7–49.

Van Speybroeck, L., Van de Vijver, G., & De Waele, D. (2002). Preface. *Annals of the New York Academy of Sciences*, 981, vii–x.

Vaynman, S., Ying, Z., & Gomez-Pinilla, F. (2004). Hippocampal BDNF mediates the efficacy of exercise on synaptic plasticity and cognition. *Eur. J. Neurosci*, 20, 1030–1034.

Vitzthum, V. J. (2003). A number no greater than the sum of its parts: the use and abuse of heritability. *Human Biology*, 75, 539–558.

Waddington, C. H. (1942). L'épigénotype. *Endeavour*, 1, 18–20.

Waddington, C. H. (1957). *The strategy of the genes.* London: Allen and Unwin.

Walker, S. P., Wachs, T. D., Gardner, J. M., Lozoff, B., Wasserman, G. A., Pollitt, E. et al. (2007). International Child Development Steering Group. Child development: risk factors for adverse outcomes in developing countries. *Lancet*, 369, 145–157.

Walsh, T., McClellan, J. M., McCarthy, S. E., Addington, A. M., Pierce, S. B., Cooper, G. M. et al. (2008). Rare structural variants disrupt multiple genes in neurodevelopmental pathways in schizophrenia. *Science*, 320, 539–543.

Weaver, I. C., Meaney, M. J., & Szyf, M. (2006). Maternal care effects on the hippocampal transcriptome and anxiety-mediated behaviors in the offspring that are reversible in adulthood. *Proceedings of the National Academy of Sciences of the United States of America*, 103, 3480–3485.

Webster's new universal unabridged dictionary (1996). New York: Barnes & Noble Books.

Young, G. P. (2007). Diet and genomic stability. *Forum of Nutrition*, 60, 91–96.

Yusuf, S., Hawken, S., Ounpuu, S., Dans, T., Avezum, A., Lanas, F. et al. (2004). INTERHEART Study Investigators. Effect of potentially modifiable risk factors associated with myocardial infarction in 52 countries (the INTERHEART study): case-control study. *Lancet*, 364, 937–952.

Ziv, Y., Ron, N., Butovsky, O., Landa, G., Sudai, E., Greenberg, N. et al. (2006). Immune cells contribute to the maintenance of neurogenesis and spatial learning abilities in adulthood. *Nature Neuroscience*, 9, 268–275.

CHAPTER 7

The Dynamic Systems Perspective

What Is the System?

Tom Hollenstein

Like biological determinism, an exclusively environmental explanation of behavior is a relic of the nature-nurture debate (DeWaal, 1999). The emergent developmental perspective of the 21st century has been characterized by such terms as *dynamic integration* (e.g., Susman & Rogol, 2004), *holistic interactionism* (e.g., Magnusson, 1999), or *probabilistic epigenesis* (e.g., Gottlieb & Willoughby, 2006) to reflect the dynamic interplay between endogenous and exogenous factors over the course of development. However, despite the mounting evidence in support of a more holistic view, the battle of nature versus nurture has not gone away (Oyama, Griffiths, & Gray, 2001; Pinker, 2004). Indeed, even the existence of the present volume indicates that the predilection to examine either nature or nurture separately is alive and well. Systems theorists argue that merely acknowledging the importance of both endogenous and exogenous factors is insufficient. Instead, the true metamorphosis of the nature-nurture debate is a paradigmatic shift in the way that developmental questions are even asked. That is, nature and nurture are functionally inseparable such

that the question should not be *whether* one or the other exerts more influence on a phenomenon of interest but *how* does that phenomenon emerge from a multitude of interdependent processes. Thus, this paradigm shift reflects a change of emphasis from factors to processes or, more abstractly, from nouns to verbs. What is required, therefore, is a theoretical and empirical approach that reflects this more integrated understanding of interdependent processes.

The dynamic systems (DS) approach to development is metatheoretical framework (Granic & Hollenstein, 2003; Lewis, 2000b; Witherington, 2007) that transcends the nature-nurture dichotomy by providing a comprehensive suite of explanatory mechanisms of developmental stability and change. From this perspective, "environmental context" is a structural level of organization *within* a system, the next most immediate level up in the system hierarchy. In the present chapter, I will outline this view by first describing DS principles and their relevance for the understanding of environmental context. The next section will focus on the definition of "the system" and how that definition reflects the researcher's or theorist's choice of the level of analysis. Several examples from my own work will be described to illustrate the DS perspective. In the final section, I will discuss the implications of the DS approach for the study of environmental contexts.

Systems Theories

Interest in more systemic or ecological approaches to development can be traced back to pioneers such as von Bertalanffy (1968). Inspired by cybernetic principles that emerged in 1940s and 1950s (e.g., Ashby, 1947; Weiner, 1950), von Bertalanffy's General Systems theory was an attempt to provide "models, principles, and laws that apply to generalized systems or their subclasses, irrespective of their particular kind, the nature of their component elements, and the relationships or 'forces' between them" (von Bertalanffy, 1968, p. 32). Thus, the goal is to explain complex behavior with a set of causal processes within a nested, hierarchical structure. This emphasis on the structure and processes of all open[1] systems, regardless of the specific elements of that system (i.e., content rather than structure), is the basis for all modern systems thinking. Indeed, the influence of General Systems theory can be found in most scientific disciplines, from microbiology to economics.

In developmental psychology, there have been several instantiations of a systemic approach, such as Ecological Systems theory (Bronfenbrenner, 1979), Developmental Systems theory (Ford & Lerner, 1992), the transactional perspective (Sameroff, 1983), and the probabilistic-epigenetic framework (Gottlieb, 2007). However, these models fall short of the goal set forth by von Bertalanffy for several reasons. First, some approaches provide only descriptive accounts of the system elements under consideration by recognizing the nested, hierarchical organization of the system (e.g., an individual within a family, neighborhood, and culture). From these perspectives, an environmental context is the next "higher" level of organization.

However, these highly inclusive structural models neglect the principles, laws, relationships, or forces (in von Bertalanffy's terms) among the elements within these nested structures. Hence, these models do not answer the "how" questions of development – again, in abstract terms, they provide elaborate lists of nouns with little concern for the verbs.

Some models (e.g., Gottlieb & Willoughby, 2006) do focus on the relations among system elements (i.e., the arrows in model figures). It is certainly a step in the right direction that these interactionist models (e.g., gene-environment interactions) include both top-down and bottom-up effects. However, these models stop short of identifying intrinsic system properties because of several limitations: (1) The bidirectional relations are additive – a sum of two unidirectional influences (X causes Y *and* Y causes X) that do not provide any further explanation of developmental processes beyond the unidirectional models upon which they are built. (2) Although several levels may be identified (e.g., genetic, neural, environmental), the relations are among only two at a time, thus neglecting how three or more factors or levels could be influential simultaneously. (3) Only the causal direction is stated but the mechanism or causal process is still not identified. (4) There are no generalized principles – each interaction has to be described in concrete terms unique to the phenomenon in question. Thus, these models posit systemlike properties of development without making the paradigmatic shift that a fully systemic approach requires. They still treat a round world as if it were flat.

Enter the DS approach.[2] Based on the properties of open systems identified by physicists and mathematicians, the DS approach provides a novel set of explanatory tools for developmental phenomena and is the realization of the goals of General Systems theory. Over the past 20 years, developmentalists have elaborated how processes of self-organizing systems can account for both stability and change across the life span (e.g., Granic & Patterson, 2006; Hollenstein, 2011; Lewis, 2000b, 2011; Thelen & Ulrich, 1991;

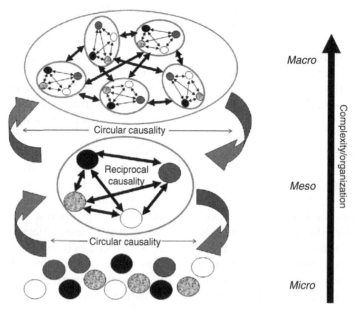

Figure 7.1. Illustration of a system at three levels of organization. The mesolevel emerges from the reciprocal interactions among system elements at the microlevel and in turn is constrained by the organization at the macrolevel via circular causality.

van Geert, 2011). Moreover, these accounts have provided unique, testable predictions that have guided diverse research designs. These DS principles will be reviewed next, before describing how a DS approach has been and can be used to understand environmental contexts.

The Dynamic Systems Approach

Simply stated, a dynamic system is a collection of elements that change over time (Thelen & Smith, 1998). Consistent with the previously reviewed systems theories, these elements are organized in a hierarchical structure of increasing complexity (e.g., cells within tissues within organs). However, unlike other systems models, the causal relations within and between levels are distinguished and elaborated. Within each level, elements interact reciprocally in a complex pattern of feedback processes; positive feedback amplifies variability in these interactions to instigate novelty while negative feedback dampens the variability to maintain stable patterns. Interactions between levels form the processes of circular causality:

Lower-order elements interact to form higher-order structures, while these higher-order structures are the elements at the next level of organization (see Figure 7.1). Consider an academic example. A given psychology department may be made up of a few dozen professors (microlevel) whose reciprocal interactions create the structure of the department (mesolevel). The psychology department is also one of many departments within the university (macrolevel) that provides resources and limitations to the departments of which it is composed. Thus, what is identified as the psychology department is a system and, as such, shares the properties of all open systems.

Relations among the micro-, meso-, and macroscales give rise to a number of other features of dynamic systems, particularly those that account for the development of a system in *time*: self-organization, attractors, and phase transitions. This emphasis on time is a cornerstone of the DS approach to development (Granic, 2005; Lewis, 2000b, 2005; Spencer, Clearfield, Corbetta, Ulrich, Buchanan, & Schoner, 2006). A deeper understanding of temporal processes allows

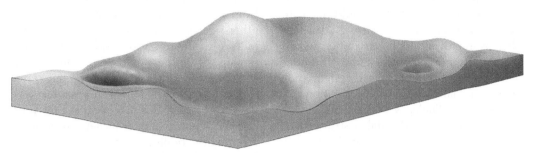

Figure 7.2. Hypothetical state space. The wells represent attractors.

developmentalists to begin to address some fundamental questions of stability and change across the life span. For DS developmentalists, the core research question is, How do *real-time* dynamics (i.e., moment-to-moment interactions) relate to patterns that emerge at a *developmental-time scale* (i.e., stable structures)? Thus, the DS approach to development goes beyond specifying a nested, hierarchical structure to account for how organisms become increasingly more complex over time as new structure emerges and stabilizes.

The first – and perhaps most important – DS principle to consider is the concept of self-organization. Over time, the structure of the system emerges as a product of the interactions among the systems elements. This is a radically different causal model than either deterministic or contextualist accounts provide. From a DS perspective, there is neither an endogenous (e.g., biological) cause nor an exogenous (e.g., environmental) cause of behavior. Instead, complex, adaptive, dynamic systems self-organize and the structure of these systems is an emergent property that is the result of both reciprocal and circular processes depicted in Figure 7.1. Thus, cause is not outside the system but a product of it.

Given the number of interactions among system elements, one might expect a nearly infinite number of states that could possibly occur. However, this is not the case. Dynamic systems settle into a small set of stable states called *attractors*. These are recurrent stable patterns that "pull" the system away from other states. Often attractors

are depicted as locations on a hypothetical landscape that represents the system's *state space* (an *n*-dimensional "space" of all possible states of a system). Figure 7.2 is a graphical depiction of a two-dimensional state space with several attractors wherein the current state of the system may be represented as a marble that is rolling around this landscape. It is highly probable that the marble will roll into one of the attractors represented as indentations on the state space and very unlikely that it will come to rest atop the peak. Once the system settles into one of these attractors, it requires a great deal of energy to emerge from that state. Furthermore, attractors vary in terms of their strength, reflected by the width and depth on the hypothetical state space. For example, this state space could represent an individual who suffers from depression. The attractor on the lower left of the state space could reflect a depressed state – a recurrent pattern from which it is difficult for the individual to emerge. However, other states are possible, such as the smaller attractor in the upper right corner of the state space, which could represent a more content state. Thus, the system remains dynamically variable as it moves from state to state but is also stable in that only relatively few states are available. That is, the structure of the system is constant but the behavior of the system fluctuates.

This distinction between structure and behavior permits a more parsimonious explanation of developmental change and stability. In real time, the trajectory of state changes (i.e., real-time variability) reveals the attractors in the system's state space. Relatively low variability would indicate the presence of fewer or strong attractors whereas relatively high variability would indicate the presence of a greater number of or weaker attractors. Thus, system variability is actually a signal of information and not just noise (Thelen & Ulrich, 1991) in that the dynamics reveal the stable structure of the system. The degree of this variability has also been interpreted as adaptive flexibility (Hollenstein, Granic, Stoolmiller, & Snyder, 2004; Lichtwarck-Aschoff, Kunnen, & van Geert, 2009), an index of the readiness of the system to adjust in the face of shifting situational demands. However, developing systems can also undergo periods of deep structural change where variability indicates alterations of the state space itself. In DS terms, change to this degree is a *phase transition*.

A phase transition is a period of temporary instability as a system moves from one stable structure to a new one. This is not simply a change in the current state of the system (i.e., stable levels of real-time variability) but a change in the underlying structure. Thus, the strength (i.e., width and depth) and location of the attractors on the state space are reorganized during a phase transition. In order for the old stable structures to break down and be replaced with the new ones, the system goes through a temporary period of increased variability and unpredictability – an earthquake on the landscape, if you will. The simplest and most illustrative example of a phase transition is the boiling of water. Interactions among the molecules (i.e., system elements) within a pot of cold water on the stove are relatively stable and there is not much movement. As heat is applied, the molecules begin to bounce around and bump into each other in a highly variable and unpredictable pattern. This jumbled pattern of interactions increases until the boiling point. This characteristic variability of a phase transition is the hallmark of a system in the process of change. Upon boiling, the water molecules once again return to a stable order except that now they move vertically in ordered

columns, rising up one side of the column from the heat and then falling again on the other side of the column as they cool. The molecules do not move side to side and remain within these narrow columns as long as the heat is sufficient for this boiling state. If you listen to water boil in your tea kettle, you will hear this process as the pitch or frequency of the simmering gets lower upon reaching the boiling point. In the same way, increased variability is a signal of change in all dynamic systems. As will be shown later, several studies have examined the variability of the system over time to detect developmental transitions.

Underlying both the real-time dynamics of systemic stability and the variability during the structural change of a phase transition are control parameters. These "agents of change" (Granic & Hollenstein, 2006) are mechanisms that affect real-time system dynamics in nonlinear ways. In the boiling water example earlier, heat is the control parameter. Within a narrow range, changes in the control parameter will result in relatively minor changes in the real-time variability – this is change in the energy of the system but not structural change. Thus, the water molecules will be relatively still or bang into each other at temperatures below the boiling point. Beyond a certain threshold, however, a control parameter can induce the structural change of a phase transition. For water, this threshold is 100 degrees Celsius.[3] Furthermore, control parameters regulate system dynamics *as part of the system* and are often difficult to identify, especially in psychology. One possible real-time control parameter, for example, may be anxiety that affects real-time behavior by narrowing the focus of attention and reducing variability (i.e., increased rigidity of behavior). Agents of developmental phase transitions can also be control parameters that pass critical maturation thresholds such as hormone concentrations, neuronal structures (i.e., synaptic pruning), or other physical characteristics. Hence, development from a DS perspective is a process by which system elements create stable structures over time and, when control parameters reach critical thresholds, these systems can achieve new stability and complexity through the reorganization of phase transitions.

In summary, the DS approach provides a set of mechanisms that can be used to understand how development transpires. In particular, processes of change and stability are understood in terms of self-organization and phase transitions. With these concepts in mind, we can now consider environmental context from a DS perspective. The primary means by which a researcher or theorist can adopt a DS approach to the study of environmental context is to answer the question "What is the system?"

What Is the System?

The primary assumption of the DS perspective is that the entire natural world, perhaps even the universe, is the "System" – atoms are nested within galaxies via a nested hierarchy of subsystems. This may seem a bit cosmic or metaphysical, but it is the natural conclusion of any systems perspective. As developmental researchers, however, we are interested in a much smaller subset of this all-inclusive system (e.g., children, families). Identifying the subsystem is based on the research question at hand and requires at least two sets of decisions: identifying the structural scale and the time scale.

Although it may not be explicit or conscious, every theory or research project has a level of analysis, typically determined by the scale of the dependent variable. The goal is to be able to make predictions or show associations with relevant (i.e., proximal) independent variables. A study on the development of the use of adverbs, for example, is not likely to include a child's height or the number of cars in the neighborhood as predictors but rather factors like the parent's use of adverbs and the amount of time spent reading. This is not a new or difficult idea. However, taking a DS approach extends the level of analysis decision to a more precise set of considerations. First, the focal level of analysis is always at the meso-level (Figure 7.1) within a nested

structure. This is the level of organization that the researcher or theorist is attempting to understand. Automatically, that decision then includes presumed macro- and microlevels. Thus, the system is defined by the mesolevel phenomena that have emerged from the microlevel interactions and are constrained by the macrolevel structures. Second, the macro- and microlevels need to be as proximal to the mesolevel as possible. More precisely, the microlevel components are the elements that create the mesolevel structure and the mesolevel components are the elements that create the macrolevel structure most directly. Therefore, for a DS developmentalist, the environmental context is not just any level higher up in the hierarchy but is the most immediate result of the interactions among the lower-order elements. For example, there may be a connection between SES and parent-child interactions, but the parent-child system is more proximally constrained by the immediate macrocontext (e.g., opportunities for interactions with a parent working two jobs) than by the more distal metrics of income or education.

Systems are not only nested in structure but also in time, thus the second consideration for defining the system of interest is the time scale. An individual's emotional behavior, for example, includes very rapid processing at the neuronal level (milliseconds), emotional states (seconds/minutes), and moods (minutes /hours), which are further nested within personality or temperament structures that emerge at the developmental time scale of months or years (see Lewis, 2000a for a detailed theoretical model of these temporal relations). Again, the phenomenon of interest should be considered at the meso time scale that emerged from the processes at the micro time scale and that simultaneously creates the process at the macro time scale. The direct implication, then, is that research designs must include multiple measurements within the time scale of interest in order to detect important dynamics of stability and change (Lavelli, Pantoja, Hsu, Messinger, & Fogel, 2006). However, incorporating analyses of real-time and developmental-time scales – even without adopting a systems view – is perhaps the most daunting endeavor of developmental research. Fortunately, with the advent of greater computing power, recent advances in measures and models of temporal relations have made this kind of analysis more accessible (for examples see Bergman, Magnusson, & El-Khouri, 2003; Collins & Sayer, 2001; Granic & Hollenstein, 2006; Moskowitz & Hershberger, 2002; van Geert & van Dijk, 2002). Here I will describe one such methodology, the state space grid technique, as it intuitively illustrates the relations between structural and temporal aspects of system dynamics.

State Space Grids

Based on the DS concept of a state space, state space grids (SSGs) are two-dimensional[4] matrices representing all the possible states of the system of interest (imagine an aerial view of Figure 7.2 with a grid matrix overlaid). With this technique, the states of the system are the joint intersection of one of the mutually exclusive and exhaustive categories from each dimension (i.e., axis). For example, the x-axis could represent parental affect (negative, neutral, or positive) and the y-axis could represent child affect (negative, neutral, or positive) to make a 3×3 state space of a parent-child dyad (see Figure 7.3). Because the categories within each dimension are mutually exclusive, each person could only be in one state (affect) at a time and therefore the system could only be in one joint state or cell on the grid at any moment. To depict a parent-child interaction on this space, a trajectory representing the sequence of joint states is plotted as dots in the cells connected by lines between those states that are adjacent in time. In the present example depicted in Figure 7.3, the size of the plot point represents the duration of a behavioral event (joint state) and the sequence of these events is depicted by the trace of the trajectory across the space. In this hypothetical example, the interpersonal dynamics of any parent-child system

can be plotted as a trajectory on this state space.

SSGs are not only visualizations, but a source of measures for capturing salient features of system dynamics. These measures range from simplistic and intuitive counts of the frequency or duration in the cells to more complex measures of return time and entropy. For example, several of the studies described in this chapter examine the variability of the system depicted on the SSG. The number of transitions (e.g., number of lines in the trajectory) and the dispersion across the state space (e.g., the number of cells visited by the trajectory) indicate greater variability, whereas the average of all the mean cell durations (e.g., the average size of the plot points) indicates lower variability. The next section of the chapter is devoted to reviewing various SSG studies that reveal critical aspects of system dynamics and structure. This review is organized in three sections so that the reader may more easily conceptualize his or her own data or research questions within this framework: real-time variability, perturbation, and longitudinal change and stability.

Predicting Developmental Outcomes with Real-time Variability

As mentioned before, the DS perspective is that variability is a signal and not noise. The critical inference then is to understand what individual differences in variability might mean within a developmental context. Once the system of interest is defined, it is not always clear what amount of variability is "normal" or "good" or "adaptive" – these evaluations will be able to be made more confidently only after many examinations of that system have been conducted. However, in the meantime, *relative* variability can be used to distinguish differences between individuals in a sample. Here I will describe a couple of studies that have examined dyadic variability in novel ways.

One possible interpretation of real-time variability is flexibility or, conversely, rigidity (Hollenstein et al., 2004; Lichtwarck-Aschoff et al., 2009). A flexible system is ready to adapt

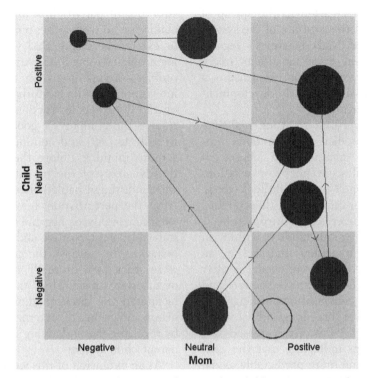

Figure 7.3. Example SSG of a mother-child interaction. The interaction sequence begins with the open circle in the mother-positive/child-negative cell. The lines with arrows depict the direction of change to the next state, and the sizes of the plot points represent the duration of each event. (Image created using GridWare; Lamey, Hollenstein, Lewis, & Granic, 2004.)

to shifting contextual demands, whereas a rigid system is unprepared for change and is less adaptive. For example, Hollenstein et al. (2004) examined whether affective flexibility in parent-child dyads was associated with the development of psychopathology in early childhood. Parents and kindergarten children were observed for a continuous hour on each of two separate occasions while engaged in various tasks (e.g., playing a game, talking, doing math problems). The affective states of the parent and child were used to make a dyadic SSG, where the individual cells represented simultaneous or joint states (e.g., mother anger, child defensive). Thus, the system of interest for this study was the dyad (mesolevel), composed of the affective states of the individuals (microlevel), and analyzed across contexts and occasions (macrolevel). Because of the

varied tasks and the duration of observation, affect was expected to vary as the parent and child played, squabbled, and struggled with challenging tasks. Limited variability in this case would indicate a limited affective repertoire or a more rigid system. The measure of rigidity in this study was a combination of the number of transitions between dyadic states (reversed) and the average of the mean durations in each dyadic state. Because of the design, test-retest reliability was examined in order to validate this new measure. Correlations across the two sessions were moderately high, especially for observational measures: .6 for transitions and .4 for average mean durations. Most importantly, greater dyadic rigidity predicted teacher reports of concurrent externalizing behavior, concurrent internalizing behavior, and the growth in externalizing behavior from fall of kindergarten to the spring of first grade. Thus, the *structure* of the system (the parent-child dyad) dynamics – regardless of the content or specific affects (micro level) and across diverse contexts (macro) – was associated with the early development of problem behavior.

A second approach to using real-time variability to predict developmental outcomes was to measure the degree of entropy in adolescent peer conversations (Dishion, Nelson, Winter, & Bullock, 2004). Derived from an information theory index (Shannon & Weaver, 1949), entropy reflects the amount of predictability within an action-reaction transition matrix (i.e., an SSG where one axis is one event lag after the other axis). In this case, the actions and reactions were conversations among adolescent males over three longitudinal waves (ages 14, 16, and 18). Entropy decreased over these age groups indicating that the conversations became more predictable as the boys matured. The most interesting result, however, was an interaction between age 14 entropy and age 14 "deviant peer process" (e.g., talking about breaking rules, doing drugs) – an interaction between structure and content – to predict antisocial behavior *10 years later*. Those with low entropy and high deviant peer process at age 14 engaged in the highest amount of antisocial behavior at age 24. Thus, as with the previous study on rigidity, low variability appears to be a risk factor for the development of problem behaviors and psychopathologies. Further work is necessary in this area to examine how structure and content can best be combined for improving early detection of problem behavior.

Perturbing the System

Relative variability can also be used to make comparisons across contexts. One of the best ways to determine the structure of a system is to perturb it and observe changes (or lack thereof). In other words, compare the variability of the system before and after the perturbation. Granic and Lamey (2002), for example, examined the underlying structure of parent-child interactions with children who were either pure externalizers or externalizers comorbid with internalizing problems using SSGs. After 4 minutes of problem-solving discussion, the dyads were interrupted by the perturbation (a knock on the door and instructions to "wrap up, resolve the conflict for good, and end on friendly terms") and continued talking for 2 more minutes. Before the perturbation, the dynamics of the parent-child systems were indistinguishable between the groups. After the perturbation, however, the pure externalizing dyads became stuck in dyadic states of parent positive and child negative behaviors. In contrast, the comorbid dyads were stuck in a mutually negative region of the state space. Thus, the perturbation facilitated the discrimination of heterogeneous subgroups of externalizing children by revealing the underlying structure of the parent-child system.

As an extension of this work, several DS studies have explored the results of perturbations using the classic A-B-A design (Granic, O'Hara, Pepler, & Lewis, 2007; Hollenstein & Lewis, 2006). This design allows for a more specific examination of system behavior at two or more time scales. First, there is the real-time variability within each segment of the design (i.e., before, during, and after perturbation). Second, there is the change from A to B and back to A again, which can be examined as an index of the adaptability of the system. These two time scales may also be nested within a third time scale in a longitudinal design (e.g., Hollenstein, 2005). In general, the A-B-A design is well suited to DS analyses of the effect of perturbations. For example, Granic et al. (2007), compared the variability of parent-child interactions between those dyads that improved (IMPs) and did not improve (NIMPs) after a 12-week parent management training and child cognitive-behavioral therapy program. Before and after the treatment program, the dyads' affect was coded during (A) a fun conversation (e.g., winning the lottery or planning a party), (B) a conflict discussion, and (A) another fun conversation on a different topic. Using variability measures derived from dyadic SSGs, the IMP dyads were significantly more flexible during the conflict discussion than the NIMPs. Moreover, following treatment, the IMP dyads were able to "repair" (return to the positive region of the SSG) in the discussion following the conflict, whereas the NIMP dyads could not flexibly adjust to the change in context and continued to express negative affect during the fun discussion. Thus, in this study, flexibility was examined at two different time scales. The real-time variability measures indicated the flexibility of the parent-child dyads while engaged in a conflict discussion. At the slightly longer time scale, the ability to affectively adjust to a shift in the emotional valence of the conversational topic was also associated with successful treatment change.

In a more direct examination of the relations between negative emotion and flexibility, Hollenstein and Lewis (2006) used a similar A-B-A design with mother-daughter dyads. Early adolescent girls' and their mothers' affects were coded during positive, conflictual, and positive discussions. As expected, negative emotion was highest during the conflict discussions and flexibility was lowest during conflict. The dyads were also split into low and high stress groups based on self-reported stressful events to examine the effect of stress on flexibility. There were no differences in the amount of negative emotion expressed by the dyads in each group across the three discussions; however, the high-stress group had a flatter profile of flexibility across the three discussions whereas the low-stress group showed dramatic changes in flexibility from A to B to A. Hence, stress appeared to reduce the ability for these dyads to flexibly adjust to changes in topic.

Longitudinal Change and Stability

As the previous studies have demonstrated, the structure of a dynamic system can be revealed by real-time variability. However, systems can change in structure and this is most evident in the nonlinear, qualitative shifts that developing organisms undergo as they progress to maturity. As explained earlier, this is change at a deep, fundamental level of underlying organization that is different from typical fluctuations and is called a phase transition (Granic & Hollenstein, 2003; Thelen & Ulrich, 1991). One of the most prominent characteristics of a phase transition is a temporary increase in variability – an imminently testable feature of human systems. Thus, the developmental phase transition hypothesis predicts that transition periods between consecutive developmental stages will be relatively more variable than the stable periods before and after. Specifically, the profile of variability across transition periods is expected to be a quadratic peak. This hypothesis has been tested at two critical developmental transitions: early adolescence (Granic, Hollenstein, Dishion, & Patterson, 2003) and the 18–20-month transition (Lewis, Zimmerman, Hollenstein, & Lamey, 2004).

In the Granic et al. (2003) study, adolescent boys and their parents were observed during conflict discussions across five longitudinal waves, when the boys were 9–10, 11–12, 13–14, 15–16, and 17–18. The hypothesized transition period was at age 13–14, when the boys just entering early adolescence. Variability (number of cells and transitions on the SSG) peaked, as expected, at the third wave. This pattern of results is consistent with the long-standing conceptualization of adolescence as a developmental transition. In the Lewis et al. (2004) study, toddlers' socioemotional habits were coded along two dimensions: attention to a frustrating toy (e.g., broken jack-in-the-box) and attention to mother. The toddlers were observed once a month from age 14 months to 25 months. Changes on the SSGs from month to month revealed that the period of most frequent change in the SSG patterns was from 18 to 20 months, as predicted. Taken together, these studies are consistent with a DS view of developmental change and stability and suggest a fruitful line of inquiry for understanding developmental processes (for a more detailed discussion of developmental change using SSGs see Hollenstein, 2007).

Summary

Depicting, measuring, and analyzing system dynamics with SSGs is one way to incorporate a DS perspective into developmental research easily. In the examples provided, the nested, hierarchical organization of all open dynamic systems has been used as a framework for understanding various aspects of developmental processes. In addition to the structural relations among the micro-, meso-, and macroscales, these examples showed how a system's behavior changes and stabilizes at several time scales. However, work in this area has only just begun.

Conclusions

In this chapter, I have argued that the treatment of the environment as a separable entity from systems of interest is not consistent with a DS perspective. Instead, the environment is a macrolevel within a system's organization. Thus, integrating "environmental effects" into research and theory is a problem of interacting scales. For a developmentalist, these scales are both structural (i.e., nested hierarchies) and temporal (i.e., real time vs. developmental time). The challenge of the 21st century is to figure out how to measure and model the interaction processes within and between these scales so as to facilitate a greater understanding of developmental phenomena. This may seem like a daunting task for those less familiar with this approach. However, there are a few relatively simple things that could be more commonly incorporated into developmental research that would move the field forward to a more integrated approach.

First, the bounds of the "environment" of interest must be precisely defined with respect to the focal level of analysis. Ideally, the variables of a particular study or model are immediately nested within each other, but this is not always possible. Nevertheless,

it is still possible to define these variables in terms of the structural or temporal proximity to the focal level variable(s). For example, a parent is a person within a family system who has many different attributes that contribute to and that are the product of that system. Within the context of a child's development, there are myriad ways that a parent's contributions and products can be defined depending on the focus. If the focus is on parent-child affect, as depicted in some of the examples earlier, then the parent is actually an integral part of the level of analysis as a dyad member. If the focus is on a child's eating habits, parental attitudes and affect are certainly part of the system but only insofar as these moderate the actual food the child consumes. Thus, in this case the parent is a more distal (i.e., macro) part of the system. In a study of a child's language use in the classroom, the parent would be even more distal.

This may seem to be a rather banal or even pedantic delineation of parental effects. However, fully acknowledging the structure of the system has clear implications. Self-organizing system processes – positive and negative feedback, circular and reciprocal causality – are immediate, proximal mechanisms. Thus, the more distal factors *must* act at the level of interest through more proximal means. SES is a vague proxy or correlate for the day-to-day experiences of a child, for example. On the road to the more fully integrated or holistic account of development espoused by the DS approach, one accessible step forward is to move levels of explanation as close to the proximal as possible. This can be achieved through considering the dynamics of reciprocally or circularly causal processes that might give rise to the behavior within the system of interest. If the variables at hand are too distal, it will be impossible to specify such processes without including a more proximal variable.

Change and stability are the cornerstones of developmental science, yet we have barely scratched the surface of understanding these seemingly countervailing forces. A second, slightly more difficult, way that developmental research can approach a more integrated, systemic perspective is through more explicitly incorporating time into models and analyses (Granic, 2005; Lewis, 2000b, 2005; Spencer et al., 2006; Witherington, 2007). For research designs, this means taking relatively frequent measurements within the typical period in which change transpires (e.g., Lavelli et al., 2006). Thus, different ages require different time frames. For example, individual differences in the typical emergence of new developmental behaviors in infancy can occur within a time window of weeks or months (e.g., reaching with grasping), but behaviors that emerge at later ages may occur within a wider age range (e.g., parent-adolescent conflict). Measurement periods within designs should correspond to these typical ranges.

The more difficult part of incorporating time is the analysis. Time series analysis has traditionally been focused on more continuous or very long time series data (e.g., heart rate, economic trends); often developmental research cannot meet the assumptions of such analysis. Aside from the methods derived from the general linear model described earlier (e.g., repeated-measures ANOVA), there are some recent advances in the analysis of developmental continuity and change (e.g., Bergman et al., 2003; Collins & Sayer, 2001; Moskowitz & Hershberger, 2002; van Geert & van Dijk, 2002). Paul van Geert has provided many useful methods that can be used with both simulated and empirical data (e.g., van Geert & van Dijk, 2002). Event history analysis (a variant of cox regression, also called hazard analysis) is a promising but relatively untested tool for examining real-time dynamics (Snyder, Stoolmiller, Wilson, & Yamamoto, 2003; Stoolmiller & Snyder, 2006). There are many others but listing them is beyond the scope of this chapter (see Granic & Hollenstein, 2003, 2006 for reviews).

In conclusion, the DS approach provides an escape from the nature-nurture debate into a more integrated focus on developmental processes. It will no doubt take some time to make the necessary shifts in our theories and methods – and perhaps most importantly in our thinking. Forty years after von Bertalanffy's (1968) call for a general systems theory, the foundations are in place and ready to be applied.

Notes

1 Open systems are those in which energy can flow through or be transferred between subsystems, in contrast to closed systems, in which the energy is contained. Closed systems rarely occur in nature.

2 Note that I use terms such as "approach," "perspective," or "framework" to maintain the emphasis on the metatheoretical status of developmental dynamic systems "theory."

3 These nonlinear thresholds in response to changes in control parameters are best described with catastrophe models and the concept of hysteresis, but this is beyond the scope of the present chapter (see Granic & Hollenstein, 2006 or Guastello, 1995).

4 State spaces can certainly be more than two dimensions. In this first decade of the existence of the SSG technique, they have been two-dimensional because this is most easily represented visually. Efforts to extend the SSG method into three or more dimensions are in progress and new software will be available in the next few years.

References

Ashby, W. R. (1947). Principles of the self-organizing dynamic system. Journal of General Psychology, 37, 125–128.

Bergman, L. R., Magnussen, D., & El-Khouri, B. M. (2003). Studying individual development in an interindividual context: A person-oriented approach. Mahwah, NJ: Lawrence Erlbaum Associates.

Bronfenbrenner, U. (1979). The ecology of human development: Experiments by nature and design. Cambridge, MA: Harvard University Press.

Collins, L. M., & Sayer, A. G. (2001). New methods for the analysis of change. Washington DC: APA.

de Waal, F. B. M. (1999). The end of nature versus nurture. Scientific American, 281, 94–99.

Dishion, T. J., Nelson, S. E., Winter, C. E., & Bullock, B. M. (2004). Adolescent friendship as a dynamic system: Entropy and deviance in the etiology and course of male antisocial behavior. *Journal of Abnormal Child Psychology*, 32(6), 651–663.

Ford, D. H., & Lerner, R. M. (1992). *Developmental systems theory: An integrative approach.* Newbury Park, CA: Sage.

Gottlieb, G. (2007). Probabilistic epigenesis. *Developmental Science*, 10, 1–11.

Gottlieb, G., & Willoughby, M. T. (2006). Probabilistic epigenesis of psychopathology. In D. Cicchetti & D. J. Cohen (Eds.), *Developmental psychopathology: Theory and method*, vol. 1 (2nd ed.). New York: Wiley.

Granic, I. (2005). Timing is everything: Developmental psychopathology from a dynamic systems perspective. *Developmental Review*, 25(3–4), 386–407.

Granic, I., & Hollenstein, T. (2003). Dynamic systems methods for models of developmental psychopathology. *Development and Psychopathology*, 15(3), 641–669.

Granic, I., & Hollenstein, T. (2006). A survey of dynamic systems methods for developmental psychopathology. In D. Cicchetti & D. J. Cohen (Eds.), *Developmental Psychopathology*, pp. 889–930. New York: Plenum Press.

Granic, I., Hollenstein, T., Dishion, T. J., & Patterson, G. R. (2003). Longitudinal analysis of flexibility and reorganization in early adolescence: A dynamic systems study of family interactions. *Developmental Psychology*, 39(3), 606–617.

Granic, I., & Lamey, A. V. (2002). Combining dynamic systems and multivariate analyses to compare the mother-child interactions of externalizing subtypes. *Journal of Abnormal Child Psychology*, 30(3), 265–283.

Granic, I., O'Hara, A., Pepler, D., & Lewis, M. D. (2007). A dynamic systems analysis of parent-child changes associated with successful "real-world" interventions for aggressive children. *Journal of Abnormal Child Psychology*, 35(5), 845–857.

Granic, I., & Patterson, G. R. (2006). Toward a comprehensive model of antisocial development: a dynamic systems approach. *Psychological Review*, 113(1), 101–131.

Guastello, S. J. (1995). *Choas, catastrophe, and human affairs: Applications of nonlinear dynamics to work, organizations, and social evolution.* Mahwah, NJ: Lawrence Erlbaum Associates.

Hollenstein, T. (2005). *Socioemotional development across the early-adolescent transition*, Unpublished Doctoral Thesis, University of Toronto, Canada.

Hollenstein, T. (2007). State space grids: Analyzing dynamics across development. *International Journal of Behavioral Development*, 31(4), 384–396.

Hollenstein, T. (2011). Twenty years of dynamic systems approaches to development: Significant contributions, challenges, and future directions. *Child Development Perspectives*, 5, 256–259.

Hollenstein, T., Granic, I., Stoolmiller, M., & Snyder, J. (2004). Rigidity in parent-child interactions and the development of externalizing and internalizing behavior in early childhood. *Journal of Abnormal Child Psychology*, 32(6), 595–607.

Hollenstein, T., & Lewis, M. D. (2006). A state space analysis of emotion and flexibility in parent-child interactions. *Emotion*, 6(4), 656–662.

Lamey, A., Hollenstein, T., Lewis, M. D., & Granic, I (2004). GridWare (Version 1.1). [Computer software]. http://statespacegrids.org

Lavelli, M., Pantoja, A. P. F., Hsu, H.-c., Messinger, D., & Fogel, A. (2006). Using microgenetic designs to study change processes. In D. M. Teti (Ed.), *Handbook of research methods in developmental science.* London: Blackwell Publishers.

Lewis, M. D. (2000a). Emotional self-organization at three time scales. In M. D. Lewis & I. Granic (Eds.), *Emotion, development, and self-organization: Dynamic systems approaches to emotional development*, pp. 37–69. New York: Cambridge University Press.

Lewis, M. D. (2000b). The promise of dynamic systems approaches for an integrated account of human development. *Child Development*, 71(1), 36–43.

Lewis, M. D. (2005). Bridging emotion theory and neurobiology through dynamic systems modeling. *Behavioral and Brain Sciences*, 28(2), 169–245.

Lewis, M. D. (2011). Dynamic systems approaches: Hot enough? Cool enough? *Child Development Perspectives*, 5, 279–285.

Lewis, M. D., Zimmerman, S., Hollenstein, T., & Lamey, A. V. (2004). Reorganization in coping behavior at 1½ years: Dynamic systems and normative change. *Developmental Science*, 7(1), 56–73.

Lichtwarck-Aschoff, A., Kunnen, S., & van Geert, P. (2009). Here we go again. A dynamic systems perspective on emotional rigidity across parent-adolescent conflicts. *Developmental Psychology*, 45, 1364–1375.

Magnusson, D. (1999). Holistic interactionism: A perspective for research on personality development. In L. A. Pervin and O. John (Eds.), *Handbook of personality: Theory and research*, pp. 219–247. New York: Guilford Press.

Moskowitz, D. S., & Hershberger, S. L. (2002). *Modeling intraindividual variability with repeated measures data: Methods and applications.* Mahwah, NJ: Lawrence Erlbaum Associates.

Oyama, S., Griffiths, P. E., & Gray, R. D. (2001). *Cycles of contingency: Developmental systems and evolution.* Boston, MA: MIT Press.

Pinker, S. (2004). Why nature and nurture won't go away. *Daedalus*, 133, 5–17.

Sameroff, A. J. (1983). Developmental systems: Contexts and evolution. In W. Kessen (Ed.), *History, theory, and methods*, pp. 237–294, Vol. 1. (4th ed.). New York: Wiley.

Shannon, C. E., & Weaver, W. (1949). *The mathematical theory of communication.* Urbana: University of Illinois Press.

Snyder, J., Stoolmiller, M., Wilson, M., & Yamamoto, M. (2003). Child anger regulation, parental responses to children's anger displays, and early child antisocial behavior. *Social Development*, 12(3), 335–360.

Spencer, J. P., Clearfield, M., Corbetta, D., Ulrich, B., Buchanan, P., & Schoner, G. (2006). Moving toward a grand theory of development: In memory of Esther Thelen. *Child Development*, 77(6), 1521–1538.

Stoolmiller, M., & Snyder, J. (2006). Modeling heterogeneity in social interaction processes using multilevel survival analysis. *Psychological Methods*, 11(2), 164–177.

Susman, E. J., & Rogol, A. (2004). Puberty and psychological development. In R. M. Lerner & L. Steinberg (Eds.), *Handbook of Adolescent Psychology*, pp. 15–44 (2nd ed.). Hoboken, NJ: John Wiley & Sons.

Thelen, E., & Smith, L. B. (1998). Dynamic systems theories. In W. Damon (Ed.), *Dynamic systems theories*, pp. 563–634, Vol. 1. Hoboken, NJ: John Wiley & Sons.

Thelen, E., & Ulrich, B. D. (1991). Hidden skills: A dynamic systems analysis of treadmill stepping during the first year. *Monographs of the Society for Research in Child Development*, 56(1), 30–35, Serial No 223.

Van Geert, P. (2011). The contribution of complex dynamic systems to development. *Child Development Perspectives*, 5, 273–278.

van Geert, P. & van Dijk, M. (2002). Focus on variability: New tools to study intraindividual variability in developmental data. *Infant Behavior & Development*, 25, 340–374.

von Bertalanffy (1968). *General system theory: Foundations, development, applications*, New York: George Braziller

Weiner, N. (1950). *The human use of human beings: Cybernetics and society.* Boston: Houghton Mifflin.

Witherington, D. C. (2007). The dynamic systems approach as metatheory for developmental psychology. *Human Development*, 50(2–3), 127–153.

CHAPTER 8

New Approaches to the Notion of "Environmental Risk"

Aliza W. Pressman, Pamela K. Klebanov,
and Jeanne Brooks-Gunn

Introduction

The research literature on risks has spanned an impressive three decades. Although most of the earlier research has focused upon adult health outcomes, some of the more recent work has emphasized its effects upon early childhood developmental outcomes. While much is known about the deleterious effects of risk, less is known about the nature of risks, whether the effects of risks are relatively stable across early childhood, and whether risk trajectories can be altered. In fact, oddly, there is no agreed upon operational definition of risk (Sameroff, 2006). Risks are often broadly defined as biological and environmental conditions that increase the likelihood of negative outcomes. Biological factors that often have been considered risks include low birth weight, intrauterine growth retardation, low Apgar scores; economic factors include family poverty and unemployment; human capital includes parental education and welfare receipt; psychological factors include parental mental health, stress, and social support. Studies often examine a somewhat different set of variables. In this chapter, we delineate the different classifications of risks and summarize the research findings for children's development, present the findings from the primary research model used to examine risks, examine some of the pressing issues facing research, and discuss some new approaches to understanding environmental risks.

Classification of Different Types of Risks

In this section we present the research pertaining to six different types of risks and address these risks in the context of Bronfenbrenner's Ecological Systems theory (Bronfenbrenner & Morris, 1998). Bronfenbrenner theorized that there are four levels of a child's environment that shape a child's development ranging from immediate factors that occur in a child's home to the more distal factors that occur within the child's larger community. Along these lines, we begin by examining the more proximal risks in the child's environment and move to discuss the broader,

NEW APPROACHES TO THE NOTION OF "ENVIRONMENTAL RISK"   153

more distal risks. Specifically, we examine the following environmental risks directly related to the child: (1) demographic characteristics; (2) parenting practices, attitudes, and beliefs; (3) maternal mental health; (4) home environment, as well as aspects of the child's environment that connect the child to the broader community, such as (5) neighborhood; and finally, to a broader exposure to risk through (6) environmental toxins. The implications for children's health, cognitive performance, and behavioral problems are discussed.

Demographics

Demography, specifically, family structure, economic status, and educational status can all pose a significant risk on child outcomes.

Family structure is particularly important in the context of poverty because there is such a strong link between single-parent homes and poverty. For example, an increase in divorce rates in the United States since the 1960s and nonmarital childbearing result in fewer resources for a child (McLanahan, 2004). Census data shows that children brought up in single-parent homes are 4.5 times more likely than children from dual-parent homes to live in poverty (The Brookings Institution, 2007; U.S. Census Bureau, 2007).

Poverty is associated with a range of negative outcomes for children including cognitive and social and emotional deficits (Brooks-Gunn & Duncan, 1997; Brooks-Gunn & McLanahan, 2005). Currently, more than one in three children live in low-income families in the United States (Douglas-Hall & Chau, 2007; U.S. Census Bureau, 2007). Growing up in a poor household poses greater risk for child outcomes when taking into account that single parenthood, maternal depression, low social support, economic stress, and stressful life events and high maternal parity all appear at higher rates in poor families and are linked with negative parenting behaviors (Brooks-Gunn, Klebanov, & Liaw, 1995).

Children who come from families with low educational attainment are also more likely to be poor. The National Center of Children in Poverty indicates that four out of five children with parents who have less than a high school diploma live in low-income households. Further, children of parents with low educational attainment are also more likely to have cognitive deficits (Haveman & Wolfe, 1994).

Family demography is the most proximal of risk factors, representing the characteristics of the child and families themselves. Growing up in a single-parent, poor, and low educational attainment household is associated with many of the risks discussed later.

Parenting Practices, Attitudes, and Beliefs

Parenting practices, attitudes, and beliefs are important aspects of the child's home environment. Parental education, ethnicity parental stimulation, marital status, parental mental health, and disciplinary practices such as spanking, all have an impact on child outcomes. Parenting practices are largely a function of cultural and ethnic associations with particular parenting styles (Bradley et al., 2001). However, poor parents have the added burden of stress connected with economic hardship (Bradley et al., 2001; McLoyd, 1990). The combination of negative parenting behaviors with these multiple risk factors may be particularly destructive (Brooks-Gunn et al., 1995). For example, spanking is more prevalent in poor homes than in nonpoor homes in the United States (Bradley et al., 2001). Given the added stress and dangers of living in poverty, it is not surprising that poor parents discipline more harshly than nonpoor parents. Across all ethnic groups, nonpoor mothers are more likely to exhibit verbal and physical affection than their poor counterparts. Teenage parents are also less likely to exhibit warmth, controlling for ethnicity and SES (Brooks-Gunn et al., 1995). Literature suggests that parental affection facilitates positive child adjustment and positive behavioral outcomes (Gray & Steinberg, 1999; Ispa et al., 2004).

Certain parenting styles are associated with children's behavior problems. For example, high levels of maternal behavioral control (i.e., defining clear lines of appropriate behavior to the child) are associated with fewer behavioral problems (Aunola & Nurmi, 2005). Further, research suggests that parenting styles help explain ethnic and racial gaps in school readiness (Brooks-Gunn & Markman, 2005). In fact, when controlling for parenting differences, the gaps in school readiness close by 25–50 percent (Brooks-Gunn & Markman, 2005). Ethnic and racial differences do persist on the following parenting domains: nurturance, discipline, teaching, language, monitoring, management, and materials. Brooks-Gunn and Markman (2005) found that black mothers have lower scores than white mothers in parenting domains that are traditionally associated with school readiness (Brooks-Gunn & Markman, 2005).

Beyond parenting style, parental attitudes and knowledge related to child rearing influence the quality of the home environment and child cognitive and behavioral outcomes (Benasich & Brooks-Gunn, 1996). Maternal knowledge about developmental abilities may influence the mother's design of a stimulating environment for the child (Brooks-Gunn, Klebanov, & Liaw, 1995). Mothers who scored higher on maternal knowledge (mother's knowledge of developmental milestones) had children with higher Stanford-Binet IQ scores at 36 months. Overall, measures of maternal knowledge of child development were found to predict home environment, behavioral outcomes, and child IQ at 36 months. Future research is warranted to show whether similar findings exist for Caucasian families. What is clear is that there are links among parental knowledge about child development, home environment, and cognitive and behavioral outcomes, though this may vary across ethnicities (Benasich & Brooks-Gunn, 1996).

The frequency and quality of mother-child interactions represent another influence on child outcomes, with an impact on cognitive abilities, specifically verbal abilities. Poverty puts children at risk for slower vocabulary development because poor children have different language experiences (Hoff, 2003). Hoff (2003) found that maternal speech is the mediating variable that helps explain the mechanism by which SES affects child vocabulary development. SES may have an effect on maternal child speech interactions because poverty imposes stressors that may remove the leisure time associated with longer verbal interactions, as well as account for different beliefs and values about what is appropriate when talking to children (Hoff, 2003). On average, children from more advantaged homes display better language skills than their less advantaged counterparts (Hoff, 2003), and the reasons for this disparity may include maternal child language interactions. In a study investigating maternal correlates of growth in toddler vocabulary, Pan, Rowe, Singer, and Snow (2005) analyzed mother-child communication in poor families. By examining number of words spoken, word types, and pointing, Pan et al. (2005) found that diversity of word types was a stronger predictor of child vocabulary acquisition than maternal talkativeness. Also, pointing was positively correlated with child vocabulary construction, which suggests that the gesture of pointing may go along as a helpful explanation when giving directions to children (Pan et al., 2005).

Maternal Mental Health

It is well documented that maternal mental health, specifically maternal depression, has an impact on various aspects of child development including motor skills, cognitive development, and behavioral outcomes (Dodge, 1990; Petterson & Albers, 2001; Rutter & Quinton, 1984). Apart from genetic transmissions, symptoms of maternal depression such as lack of warmth and engagement, mixed messages, and poor communication can lead to a poor parenting environment. Such family disruptions are associated with maladaptive outcomes in children (Dodge, 1990). Also important to note is that the child's response to the mother also contributes to maternal engagement so when the mother is disengaged, the child is more likely to be disengaged and thus the cycle of maladaptive behaviors continues (Hammen, Burge, & Stansbury, 1990)

Maternal depression can have an impact on early motor and cognitive development in the child (Petterson & Albers, 2001). Given the already high risk for poor motor and cognitive outcomes that children in poverty are exposed to, the added risk of poverty can be associated with maternal depressive symptoms and lower self-esteem that puts an added burden on the disadvantaged child (Brody & Flor, 1997).

Using the IHDP data set, Liaw and Brooks Gunn (1994) found that 28 percent of poor mothers compared to 17 percent of their more economically advantaged counterparts reported high rates of maternal depression. The interaction between poverty and maternal depression exacerbates the maladaptive effects on already at-risk children (Petterson & Albers, 2001). Petterson and Albers (2001) also found that more chronic maternal depression had more deleterious effects on child outcomes than more temporary maternal depression. While income tends to temper the impact of accumulative environmental risks, Petterson and Albers (2001) found that affluent girls also scored worse on measures of cognitive development than their counterparts with nondepressed mothers. In one study, investigators found that maternal depression slowed toddler vocabulary production (Pan et al., 2005).

Overall, maternal depression has particularly deleterious consequences for child outcomes regardless of socioeconomic status, though poor children of depressed mothers are at much greater risk of maladjustment and developmental deficits than more advantaged children of depressed mothers.

Home Environment

Although there is little research examining the effects of housing conditions on the mental health of occupants, the evidence that does exist suggests such associations (Evans, Well, & Moch, 2003). Home environment impacts social contacts and support, feelings of isolation, sense of place, sense of control, and other dimensions that may be linked with mental health outcomes. Poor housing quality has been associated with greater childhood behavioral problems and psychological distress (Evans et al., 2003). If the home is a place where children can presumably feel safe and escape the chaos and uncertainty of the school and neighborhood, especially within low-income neighborhoods, it is reasonable to pursue further efforts to understand the associations of housing and mental health (Evans et al., 2003).

One study looking at short-term associations between household order and child development found a link between household order and the reading abilities of 5- and 6-year-olds (Johnson, Martin, Brooks-Gunn, & Petrill, 2008). In a study examining the long-term effects of household order and cleanliness, Dunifon and colleagues (2001) found that people who are motivated to keep a clean and organized home environment are not only more likely to maintain organization in other aspects of their lives such as parenting and work, but also to have children who may be more likely to be successful at schoolwork (Dunifon, Duncan, & Brooks-Gunn, 2001).

The child's home environment has potential for providing enriching materials such as books as well as providing a physical space that lends itself to cleanliness and organization, and a sense of safety. Poverty decreases the likelihood that children will be exposed to enriching materials in the home (Bradley, Corwyn, McAdoo, & Coll, 2001). For example, nonpoor children are likely to have at least ten more developmentally appropriate books in the home than their poor counterparts. Additionally, poor homes are more likely to have clutter and be judged as "dark and monotonous" than nonpoor homes (Bradley et al., 2001). Being poor affects every aspect of the child's daily home environment.

The home environment is also linked with children's early motor and social development, vocabulary development, cognitive achievement, and behavior problems (Bradley et al., 2001). Learning stimulation is moderately associated with early motor and social development, language competence, and achievement in varying ethnic groups for both poor and nonpoor children (Bradley et al., 2001). Consistent with previous research, the physical environment of the home is linked with language competence and behavioral outcomes, especially in poor children (Bradley et al., 2001).

The stability (e.g., residential stability and parental stability) of the child's home environment is also a factor in influencing child well-being (Adam, 2004). Specifically, moves from one home to another, is a disruptive event for children. Adam (2004) found that the number of moves that a child made was associated with more adjustment problems. Similarly, living with different parental figures and separating from these figures is also very disruptive to children. Such instability can cause anxiety, a loss of social support and a loss of security associated with consistency in living with the same parental figures (Adam, 2004). Family instability is characterized by chronically disordered and erratic family environments (Ackerman, Kagos, Youngstrom, Schoff, & Izard, 1999). In a longitudinal study examining family instability, child variables and behavioral adjustment, Ackerman et al. (1999) found that there is a unique relationship between family instability and child adjustment for poor families. Cumulative measures of instability, that is, multiple changes in a child's life, can have deleterious effects on child outcomes. Finally, children in poor homes are less likely to have physically safe home environments.

Neighborhood

The neighborhoods in which families reside have a significant impact on the physical and emotional health of children (Caspi, Taylor, Moffitt, & Plomin, 2000; Evans, 2004; Xue, Leventhal, Brooks-Gunn, & Earls, 2005). Poor children are exposed to more violence and crime within their own neighborhood than their more advantaged peers (Evans, 2004). Neighborhood disadvantage is also associated with less utilization of community resources, less organizational participation, and less frequent interactions with

a social network (Evans, 2004; Xue et al., 2005). This exacerbates the effect of poverty by undermining the social support system and social capital associated with positive outcomes (Evans, 2004).

Low-income neighborhoods also often lack the infrastructure to manage such elements as garbage collection, police and fire protection, and retail and service merchants (Evans, 2004). For example, low-income neighborhoods have fewer large chain supermarkets that tend to stock healthier food options than do higher-income neighborhoods (Moreland, Wing, Diez-Roux, Poole, 2001; Powell, Slater, Mirtcheva, Bao, & Chaloupka, 2006). Not only do these lower-income neighborhoods provide fewer opportunities for healthy food consumption, they provide up to three times more opportunities for alcohol purchases because of a higher number of stores and bars per capita than in more advantaged neighborhoods (Evans, 2004; Laveist & Wallace Jr., 2000).

Poor neighborhoods are also less physically safe than nonpoor neighborhoods (Evan, 2003). Not only are children's lives in danger by virtue of proximity to chronic violence, but they are also exposed to clinical amounts of stress as a result of this exposure (Osofsky, 1995). Preschool children may be less likely to do developmentally appropriate exploring of their environment while school age children often experience sleep disturbances, nightmares, and anxiety associated with chronic exposure to violence (Osofsky, 1995). As neighborhood safety decreases, instances of Oppositional Defiant Disorder and Conduct Disorder increase among school age children and adolescents (Aneshensel & Sucoff, 1996).

Childhood obesity is another consequence associated with dangerous neighborhoods and the lack of safe play spaces for children (Evans, 2003). Children in poor neighborhoods have higher rates of obesity, in part due to the lack of physical activity, which may be partially attributable to a lack of safe places to play (Molner, Gortmaker, Bull, & Buka, 2004; Powell, Slater, Chaloupka, & Harper, 2006). Neighborhood interventions to increase safety may also increase rates of physical activity while decreasing prevalence of obesity (Molner et al., 2004).

Environmental Toxins

Children in poverty are at high risk of exposure to environmental toxins including air pollution, pesticides, tobacco smoke, and lead (Braun et al., 2006; Landrigan et al., 1999). Children are more likely to absorb environmental toxins because of their biological vulnerabilities as a result of their immature immune systems; their use of hands to play and explore, crawl, and likely put things into their mouths and potential in utero and early postnatal exposure (Landrigan et al., 1999; National Research Council, 1993).

Children living in overcrowded and inadequate housing associated with poverty also have a higher likelihood of direct exposure to legal and illegal chemicals used to alleviate problems such as vermin and roaches common in urban environments. A report by the National Research Council concluded that early exposure to pesticides can cause disease later in life such as neurological and behavioral dysfunction, cancer, reproductive anomalies, and immune system disorders (Landrigan et al., 1999; National Research Council, 1993). Children are exposed to pesticides through home, school, day care, parks, and drinking water (Landrigan et al., 1999). Because of their young age, children have more time to be chronically exposed to these toxins. Additionally, if a child's development is in any way retarded by these toxins, there is little way to repair the actual damage. There are emerging data that suggest that prenatal, infant, and child exposure to two of the most common pesticides used in inner cities, chlorpyrifos and pyrethroids, may pose a threat to neurochemical and behavioral outcomes as well as the reproductive development of the exposed fetus, infant, or child (Landrigan et al., 1999).

Children's exposure to lead is another environmental toxin linked to poor behavioral outcomes. Lead is more common in poor neighborhoods as a result of inadequate building and school maintenance and old paint. In fact, lead levels in poor children are four times higher than in nonpoor children (Brody et al., 1994). In the aforementioned study of environmental toxins and Attention Deficit Hyperactivity Disorder (ADHD), a significant association was found between high childhood exposure to lead and ADHD (Braun et al., 2006). This study indicated that 290,000 cases of ADHD in the United States are in part attributable to exposure to lead (Braun et al., 2006).

While the threat of tobacco smoke has decreased in United States households, it is still a hazard for children. Poor children are more than twice as likely as non-poor children to live in a household with someone who smokes in the home. Specifically, 32 percent of poor children and 12 percent of non-poor children are exposed to secondhand tobacco smoke in their home (Seith & Isakson, 2011).One of the most common childhood disorders related to tobacco smoke exposure is ADHD, with a prevalence of 3–8 percent (Milberger, Biederman, Faraone, Chen, & Jones, 1997). Studies have linked prenatal exposure to tobacco smoke to ADHD (Braun et al., 2006; Ernst et al. 2001; Mick et al., 2002; Milberger et al., 1997). A recent study (Braun, 2006) suggests that prenatal exposure to tobacco accounted for up to 270,000 more cases of ADHD in U.S. children. Further investigation to children's exposure to tobacco is necessary.

In addition, children's prenatal exposure to airborne PAH (polycyclic aromatic hydrocarbon), which includes tobacco smoke as well as automobile emissions, has been associated with lower cognitive scores at age 3 (Bayley MDI; see Perera, Rauh, Whyatt, Tsai, Tang, Diaz et al. (2006). This prospective study of nonsmoking African American and Dominican mothers who resided in New York City found that children exposed prenatally to high levels of PAH were about three times more likely than children who were unexposed to suffer cognitive delays at age 3 (i.e., have a MDI score <85, about 1 standard deviation below the mean. This is the first study of prenatal exposure to airborne PAH, and thus the results require confirmation.

Poverty is inextricably linked with the worst outcomes for children exposed to the previously discussed risk factors. Thus, having presented the most commonly considered individual risk factors that are associated with negative outcomes for children and families, we turn now to the current research model of how the accumulation of risks impact children.

The Effects of Risk on Child Development: Cumulative Risk Model

The earliest research on risk has been epidemiological research on risk factors in heart disease. In the Framingham study researchers found that by accumulating risk variables, the predictive efficiency of understanding heart disease increased. Mortality and morbidity rates increase with the accumulation of risk factors. Similar findings were also reported by Rutter (1979) and by Sameroff and colleagues in the Rochester Longitudinal Study (Sameroff, Seifer, Baldwin, & Baldwin, 1993; Sameroff, Seifer, Barocas, Zax, & Greenspan, 1987), thus laying the foundation for future risk research.

A cumulative risk model of development posits that adverse developmental outcomes can be better predicted by combinations of risk factors than by single risk factors (Sameroff et al., 1993). The premise is that the accumulation of risks, rather than individual risk factors, accounts for developmental delays. The best example of research using a cumulative risk model has been by Sameroff and colleagues (Sameroff et al., 1987, 1993). The Rochester Longitudinal Study examined the cognitive and socioemotional outcomes of children from families where there was a high level of maternal psychopathology. While the study found that maternal psychopathology and family SES were individually important correlates of children's outcomes, the unique set of circumstances in which the child lived were important to understanding his or her development. Sameroff and colleagues came up with a set of 10 environmental conditions that were related to the family's economic

circumstances but more broadly captured a child's living environment: (1) maternal mental illness, (2) high maternal anxiety, (3) rigid beliefs about child development, (4) few positive interactions with infant, (5) head of household in unskilled occupation, (6) low maternal education, (7) ethnic minority status, (8) single parenthood, (9) stressful life events, and (10) large family size. The cumulative effects of ten socioeconomic and environmental risk factors on young children's IQ scores were examined. Sameroff, Seifer, Zax, and Barocas (1987) found that the 4-year-old children with no risks scored 2 standard deviations higher on IQ tests than children who were considered high-risk (eight or more risk factors). Generally, each risk factor was associated with a decrease of 4 IQ points.

The cumulative risk model has been employed in numerous studies (although most studies have focused upon the effects of risk for health outcomes), and its findings have been replicated for children's cognitive (Burchinal, Roberts, Zeisel, & Rowley, 2008) and behavioral outcomes over the years (Atzaba-Pori, Pike, & Deater-Deckard, 2004; Burchinal et al., 2008; Forehand, Biggar, & Kotchick, 1998; Gerard & Buehler, 2004; see Sameroff 2006 for a brief overall review). The model has had its share of criticism. Some critics of the risk index believe that it may be less able to predict children's outcomes because data are reduced when risk variables are dichotomized and tallied, compared to the examination of individual risk factors (Burchinal, Roberts, Hooper, & Zeisel, 2000). Even when a risk index is predictive, it is not clear which risks produce the negative outcomes (Deater-Deckard, Dodge, Bates, & Pettit, 1998). Moreover, others have questioned the basic assumption that all risks are weighted equally (Foster, 2012). However, the examination of individual risk variables is also problematic since variables may be highly intercorrelated and the number of variables considered may be limited by small sample sizes (Burchinal et al., 2000).

A complete discussion of the cumulative risk model is beyond the scope of this chapter. Instead, we focus upon four basic questions that merit further examination in the risk literature. Data from the Infant Health and Development Program (IHDP) are used to supplement our knowledge in addressing each question. First, which groups of children and families are more greatly affected by risks? Second, are the effects of cumulative risks similar across early childhood? Third, does the quantity of risks or the quality of risks drive the overall cumulative risk model? Fourth, do early childhood interventions such as the IHDP moderate the effects of risks? The IHDP is an eight-site randomized clinical trial designed to evaluate the efficacy of a comprehensive early-intervention program for LBW premature infants (Gross, Spiker & Haynes, 1997).

Which Children Are More Negatively Affected by Risks?

The cumulative risk approach may have important implications for the most vulnerable children. Some recent studies have found that children who are more vulnerable may be more negatively affected by risks (Appleyard, Egeland, van Dulmen, & Sroufe, 2005; Burchinal et al., 2008; Gerard & Buehler, 2004). Adolescents at-risk may be particularly vulnerable since normative tension already induces common stress as all teenagers face puberty and identity formation among the huge changes in their development. Using a national sample of 5,070 youth ages 11–18 from the National Longitudinal Study of Adolescent Health, Gerard and Buehler (2004) found that while some youth attributes provide limited protection, they do not protect children who are exposed to multiple risks across life domains. Another study looking at cumulative risk and adolescent behavioral outcomes confirms that the cumulative risk model does in fact predict poorer behavioral outcomes for adolescents and that these risks at a young age predict teen behavioral outcomes (Appleyard et al., 2005). A third study found that black children were more vulnerable to risks during the adjustment to

middle school (Burchinal et al., 2008). These researchers also found that the effects of risk were moderated by children's language skills. Risks were not associated with achievement scores when children's language skills were strong but were negatively associated with achievement when language skills were weak. However, Deater-Deckard, Dodge, Bates, and Pettit (1998) found that the externalizing behavior of white children may be more negatively affected by the presence of risks than the behavior of black children.

In addition, the IHDP is one of the few studies that have examined specifically how the cumulative effects of multiple risks are experienced by LBW children. IHDP data was used to examine whether risk factors were equally important in predicting children's developmental outcomes for poor families and nonpoor families (Liaw & Brooks-Gunn, 1994). Thirteen risk factors similar to those examined by Sameroff et al. (1993) were accumulated and collapsed into a risk index. Risk by poverty interactions were examined separately for children's cognitive test scores and behavior problems at age 3. A significant interaction was found for cognitive test scores. The effect of risk on IQ was similar for poor and non poor children when they experience few risks, but when children were exposed to a large number of risks (more than five) the IQ scores of nonpoor children dropped almost 20 points and converged with those of poor children. The interaction between risk and poverty was nonsignificant for behavior problems. A second IHDP study examined the effects of risks on children's home environments for poor and nonpoor families separately (Brooks-Gunn et al., 1995). Compared to nonpoor families, poor families experienced multiple risk factors and had lower home environment scores. However, the number of risk factors was associated with less stimulating home environments, in both poor and nonpoor families. Although differential negative effects of risk on nonpoor children were found only for their cognitive test scores, but not for behavior problems or the home environment, these findings have prompted some researchers to examine the effects of risk separately for poor and nonpoor families. These findings are inconclusive about the direction of differential effects. While some have found greater effects of risk upon more vulnerable children, while others have not, nor have the results been consistent by ethnicity or across outcome domains.

Are the Effects of Cumulative Risks Similar across Childhood?

Few studies have examined this question directly. While past research has pinpointed specific risk factors and their impacts on child outcomes, the cumulative risk model allows for an understanding of how these risk factors operate over time and the extent to which they increase the negative effects of risk on child outcomes. In terms of Sameroff and Rosenblum (2006) and findings for adolescents (Forehand et al., 1998), similar slopes for levels of risk by IQ were expected across time. Less, however, is known about behavior problems, although one study (Forehand et al., 1998) did not find concurrent but only delayed associations between risks and behavior problems.

Recent analyses of the IHDP data, based on a subsample of 228 poor families with heavier LBW children, examined whether the effects of cumulative risks are similar across early childhood (Klebanov & Brooks-Gunn, 2006). Nine risk factors measured at birth or 1 year of age, representing human capital, demographic, psychological, and parenting conditions were considered. Human capital risks included maternal unemployment, welfare receipt, and less than a high school education. Psychological risks included depressive symptoms, stressful life events (four items related to illness and residential instability), and low social support. High risk was defined as having a score higher than the highest 25 percent for depressive symptoms and stressful life events and the lowest 25 percent for social support. Demographic risks included teenage motherhood, father absence, and four or more children in the household. The dichotomized nine individual risk factors were summed into a single cumulative risk

factor and collapsed into the following categories: zero to one risk (22 percent), two to three risks (34 percent), four to five risks (34 percent), and six or more risks (10 percent). Children's Stanford-Binet IQ scores at age 3 (Terman & Merrill, 1973), Wechsler Preschool and Primary Scale of Intelligence (WPPSI; Wechsler, 1989) were used at age 5 years, and the Wechsler Intelligence Scale for Children-III (WISC-III; Wechsler, 1991) was used at age 8.

Was the accumulation of these early risk factors linked to cognitive test scores similarly at ages 3, 5, and 8 years? All analyses controlled for the effects of site, gender, neonatal health, ethnicity, and whether the mother was born in the United States. Greater risks were associated with worse cognitive scores at all times. However, more importantly, at all three ages, children with few or no risks scored 3/4 to almost a full standard deviation higher on IQ tests than children who were considered high risk (six or more risk factors). There were similar slopes for risk and IQ scores at ages 3, 5, and 8. Although the negative effect of having two to three risks, compared to having little or no risk, was somewhat greater for 3-year-old children than for 5- or 8-year-old children (see figure 1 of Klebanov & Brooks-Gunn, 2006).

The same analyses are now extended to children's behavior problems at ages 3, 5, and 8. Behavioral functioning at age 3 was measured by the Child Behavior Checklist for Ages 2–3 (CBCL/2–3; Achenbach, Edelbrock, & Howell 1987). At ages 5 and 8, mothers provided reports of their child's behavior using the Achenbach Child Behavior Checklist for ages 4–16 (Achenbach & Edelbrock, 1984). Similar to the findings for IQ scores, the effects of risk and behavior problems were significant and were similar across time. At all three ages, there was no difference in behavior between having zero to one risk and having two to three risk. However, at all three ages, children having two to three risks displayed fewer behavior problems than children having four to five risks. Two other studies (Forehand et al., 1998; Rutter, 1979) also found a sharp increase in negative behavior when risks increased from three to four. Interestingly, there was a leveling off of behavior problems beyond four risks (i.e., no difference in behavior problems between four to five risks and six or more risks; the study by Forehand et al. [1998] focusing on family stress risks such as divorce, family conflict, health problems, depression, and parent-teen relationship problems). Thus, in general, there was no detectable difference in the effects of risk upon children's outcomes assessed at ages 3, 5, and 8.

Of further interest to researchers is the larger question of how risks measured at different times are associated with children's outcomes. Few studies have assessed risks at multiple periods. While the expectation is that assessments closer in time to the measurement of children's outcomes would be stronger, two studies have not found it to be the case. Burchinal and colleagues (2008) found that both earlier and concurrent risks were similarly associated with black middle school children's achievement and behavioral outcomes. A second study found the opposite. Appleyard and colleagues (2005) have found stronger associations between risks experienced earlier in childhood (before age 5) and adolescent behavior problems than between risks experienced later in childhood (from first to sixth grade) and adolescent behavior problems. Such findings merit replication by other researchers.

Does the Quality of Risks versus the Quantity of Risks Drive the Risk Model?

Most of the research focus has been upon how the quantity of risks affects children and families. One issue that has received less direct attention has concerned the quality of risk factors. Are all risk factors created equal? Sameroff and colleagues have examined whether one risk factor was "driving" the results. A cluster analysis of risk factors produced five clusters of risk, however, none of the clusters was associated with worse outcomes for children (Sameroff, 2006).

Scholars disagree as to whether human capital or psychological capital risk factors have stronger associations with child

outcomes. Those arguing for the human capital model (Haveman & Wolfe, 1994) believe that parents who lack educational and employment resources are likely to have children with lower cognitive outcomes. There has been a considerable amount of research on the association between human capital resources of parents upon their children's outcomes (Peters & Mullis, 1997; Teachman, Paasch, Day, & Carver, 1997). Our own prior research with individual risk factors found that parental education is one of the stronger predictors of child cognitive outcomes (Duncan & Brooks-Gunn, 1997; Smith, Brooks-Gunn, & Klebanov, 1997).

Relying upon IHDP data, we examine the effects of two qualitatively different sets of risk factors – human capital and psychological capital –on children's IQ scores. On the basis of the research by Alderson and colleagues (2008), the three human capital risk variables are examined for our IHDP subsample of poor heavier birth weight children: maternal employment during pregnancy, maternal education at the child's birth, and maternal welfare status at 12 or 24 months. The least disadvantaged mothers were those who worked, had a high school degree, and were not on welfare at 12 or 24 months (27 percent). The most disadvantaged mothers were those who did not work, had less than a high school degree, and received welfare at 12 or 24 months (22 percent). The moderately disadvantaged mothers were those who were neither least disadvantaged nor highly disadvantaged (51 percent).

The three maternal psychosocial risk variables were maternal life events, social support, and depression. High risk for each measure was defined as the highest 25 percent of the sample, similar to our previous research and that of Sameroff and colleagues (1987; 1993). More than a third (37 percent) did not have any psychosocial risks; 38 percent had one risk, and 25 percent of the sample had two or three risks.

The effects of each risk model upon children's cognitive test scores at ages 3, 5, and 8 were examined separately (controlling for the same set of variables in the previous risk analyses). Our expectation is that human capital risk factors will be more highly associated with IQ than psychological resources. Greater human capital disadvantage was associated with children's IQ scores at ages 3, 5, and 8 (Klebanov & Brooks-Gunn, 2006; see Table 1). Children who were not disadvantaged scored more than a half to more than a full standard deviation higher on IQ tests than children who were considered highly disadvantaged. In contrast, psychosocial risks were not associated with decrements in children's IQ scores at ages 3 through 8 (Klebanov & Brooks-Gunn, 2006). There was only a 1/6 to 1/3 standard deviation difference in IQ scores between children who had no psychosocial risks and children who had two to three risks. Next, the proportion of variance in children's cognitive test score accounted for by each set of risks is compared to determine which set of risks is more explanatory of children's cognitive development. When the effects of both human capital and psychosocial risks are examined in the same regression model, we find overwhelming support for the importance of human capital risks (human capital risks account for more than 80 percent of the variance). Moreover, there is only a very negligible 3 percent increase in the explanatory value of adding psychosocial risks (Klebanov & Brooks-Gunn, 2006).

When these analyses are extended to children's behavior problems, neither model accounts for much of the variance in children's behavior. However, as expected, of the two models, psychosocial risks fare better than human capital risks. Human capital risks are not associated with behavior problems at ages 3, 5, and 8 (adjusted R squares of 0.00 to 0.07). Psychosocial risks are marginally associated with greater behavior problems at age 5 (adjusted R square of 0.06, $p < .06$) and significantly at age 8, but not at age 3 (adjusted R squares of 0.08 and 0.00, respectively). When both models are examined together in the regression model, neither model is significant at age 3 (adjusted R square of 0.00); psychosocial risks are marginally significant (adjusted R square of 0.06, $p < .07$) and human capital risks are nonsignificant at age 5 (adjusted R square

of 0.04), and both models are significant at age 8 (adjusted R squares of 0.08 and 0.07, respectively). Taking into consideration the adjusted R squares of each of the models, it appears that the psychosocial model best accounts for children's behavior problems.

Although the model with both human capital and psychosocial risks account for the greatest amount of variance in children's test scores, human capital risks accounts for most of the overall variance in test scores. Thus, the findings based on IHDP data reveal that human capital risk factors – maternal employment, welfare receipt, and level of education – are more highly associated with children's cognitive outcomes than maternal psychosocial factors and may be the most important contributors to the overall cumulative risk effect. As for children's behavior problems, while the model with both human capital and psychosocial risks accounts for the greatest amount of variance behavior problems at ages 3, 5 and 8, psychosocial risks account for most of the overall variance in behavior. Thus, quality of risks, rather than the quantity of risks, prevails. These findings are similar to those of the NICHD Research Network on Child and Family Well-Being (2000), which found that of the three general types of risks examined (socioeconomic, psychosocial, and sociocultural, which examined single-parent status and ethnicity) socioeconomic risks were associated with children's vocabulary scores at ages 2 and 3, while psychosocial risks were associated with children's behavior problems (CBCL) at these ages.

Are Interventions Such as the IHDP Effective for At-Risk Children?

Children who have a greater number of risks fare more poorly than children who do not. Does the presence of such risks influence the effectiveness of early childhood education (ECE) programs? One previous study of the IHDP (Liaw & Brooks-Gunn, 1994) has found that when risks are low, the cognitive test scores of poor children are enhanced from the receipt of the intervention. However, when risks are high, there is no effect of treatment for poor children's test scores. Recall that in the IHDP, LBW infants and their families received comprehensive center-based ECE and extensive home visitation from birth through age 3. When the intervention ended, children who received the treatment had significantly higher cognitive test scores than children in the follow-up group. The intervention was especially efficacious for heavier low birth weight children.

More recently, whether human capital risks and psychosocial risks moderate the effect of treatment upon children's IQ scores were examined (controlling for the same variables used in Klebanov & Brooks-Gunn, 2006). No treatment by psychosocial risk interactions were found for poor heavier birth weight children's IQ – the differences between treatment and follow-up groups were significant for each level of risk. However, interactions between treatment and human capital risks (maternal education, welfare receipt, and employment) were found for children's IQ scores at ages 5 and 8. The effect of the intervention was greater for the moderately disadvantaged group. For example, the effect of the intervention upon cognitive test scores at age 5 was 8 points higher for the moderately disadvantaged group (more than half a standard deviation), compared to 3 points higher for the least disadvantaged group and 3 ½ points lower for the most disadvantaged group (less than a fifth of a standard deviation). However, the interaction was not significant at age 3; the effect of treatment was significant at each level of risk.

These same analyses are now extended to children's behavior problems at ages 3, 5, and 8. No significant interactions between treatment and human capital risks and between treatment and psychosocial risks for children's behavior problems at any of these ages (results available from authors upon request). While the results do not conclusively support the notion that risks impede the effectiveness of ECE programs such as the IHDP, not surprisingly, treatment effects may not often exist for families who experience high levels of risk.

Directions for Future Research and Policy Implications

In this section, we consider three promising avenues for future risk research: (1) the use of statistical methods such as recursive partitioning to examine nonlinear effects, (2) resilience or the ability of children to thrive despite the presence of risks, and (3) the role of gene-environment interaction in understanding risk.

Recursive Partitioning

The statistical method of analyzing the effects of risks, namely, the use of multiple linear regression, has come under greater scrutiny (Bronfenbrenner & Morris, 1998). The examination of nonlinear relationships and interactions may be better suited using other statistical techniques. One alternative method to examining risk involves the use of Classification and Regression Tree (CART) models. CART uses a set of explanatory variables to subset a sample into homogenous groups based on the minimization of impurities. These subdivisions are depicted as a tree diagram, with the total set of observations depicted as the root, each subgroup depicted as branches, and at successive levels as leaves of the tree. Branches closest to the root contribute the most explanatory value (i.e., are the most powerful predictors). Although such models have been used in medicine for purposes of classification and segmentation (Fonarow, Adams, Abraham, Yancy, & Boscardin, 2005; Harper & Winslett, 2006; Toschke, Beyerlein, & von Kries, 2005), these techniques seldom have been used by social scientists (see Foster, 2012, and Gruenewald, Mroczek, Ryff, & Singer, 2008, for exceptions). Such data analyses, though guided by the researcher in the choice of variables to consider, allow the data "to speak for themselves" (Foster, 2012) concerning which risks are most predictive of children's outcomes. Thus, the use of CART may make a unique contribution to our understanding of the differential impact of risk factors.

In this chapter we present some preliminary results of CART models run using

SPSS AnswerTree software. Using the nine risk factors identified earlier (Klebanov & Brooks-Gunn, 2006; but now also including maternal receptive vocabulary), we examine which of these risks are most important to IHDP children's cognitive test scores and behavior problems at age 3. Rather than arbitrarily dichotomizing our risk variables at the 25th or 75th percentile as is often done in studies examining cumulative risks, we allow the program to determine the actual division on the basis of maximizing the homogeneity of subgroups. A p value of 0.05 was chosen as the alpha for splitting groups; thus, all branches are statistically significant. We present the results for the entire sample of children in the IHDP.

Figure 8.1 displays the tree diagram generated for children's IQ at age 3. Mother's welfare status constitutes the first branch on the tree. Children whose mothers received welfare at 12 months had lower IQ scores than children whose mothers did not receive welfare at 12 months (12 points or ¾ SD lower). Of children whose mothers received welfare, the number of children in the household was the next predictor. Only children or those with one sibling had higher IQ scores than children with more than one sibling (7 points, or almost ½ SD higher). For children who had at most one sibling, maternal depression was the next predictor, with children whose mothers reported greater depressive symptoms having higher IQ scores than children whose mothers reported lower levels of depressive symptoms (6 ½ points higher). No other branch was generated for children with more than one sibling.

Of children whose mothers did not receive welfare, maternal education emerged as the next predictor. Children whose mothers had a college degree had higher IQ scores than children whose mothers had either graduated high school or had some college (15 points, or almost 1 SD higher) or than children whose mother had not graduated from high school (26 points, or almost 1 ½ SD higher). Although no other branch was generated for children whose mothers had not graduated from high school, branches

were generated for the other two maternal education groups. Of children whose mothers were high school graduates or had some college, maternal receptive vocabulary scores was the next predictor. Children whose mothers had higher receptive vocabulary scores had higher IQs (more than 16 and 14 points higher, respectively, about 1 SD). Of children whose mothers had a college degree or more, family stress emerged as the next predictor. Children whose families had a stressor had lower IQ scores than those children whose families did not have a stressor (about 7 points, or almost 1/2 SD).

This model confirms the importance of human capital and demographic risk factors to children's IQ scores. Welfare status emerged as the most important predictor of children's IQ at age 3, followed by maternal education and household density, and later by maternal receptive vocabulary, stress, and depressive symptoms (although not in the expected direction for the latter). However, somewhat different paths were generated, based on maternal welfare status. For mothers not on welfare, maternal education was next in importance, whereas for mothers on welfare, it was the number of children in the household.

The model for children's behavior problem scores at age 3 (Figure 8.2) also supports the overall importance of human capital and demographic risk factors to children's developmental outcomes. Maternal education constitutes the first branch of the tree. Children with more educated mothers had lower reported behavior problems: Behavior problems of children whose mothers had less than a high school education were 7 points higher than children whose mothers graduated from high school or had some college and 14 points higher than children whose mothers were college educated. Of children whose mothers had the least education, maternal receptive vocabulary emerged as the next predictor. Children whose mothers had receptive vocabulary scores of less than 64 (less than 2 SD below the mean) had behavior problem scores that were 8 points higher than children whose mothers had scores greater than 64. Mothers who

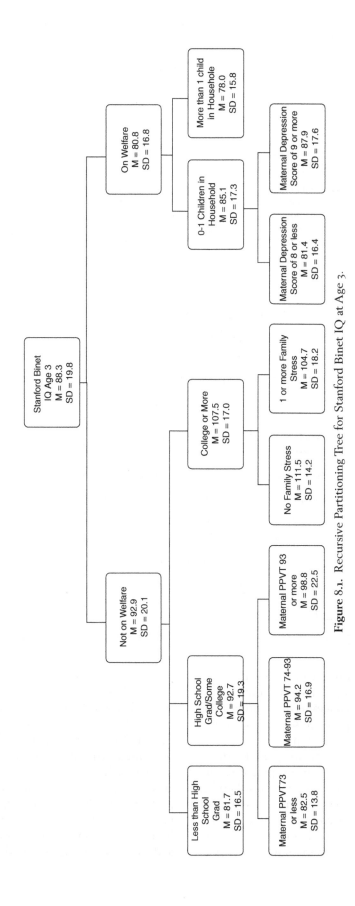

Figure 8.1. Recursive Partitioning Tree for Stanford Binet IQ at Age 3.

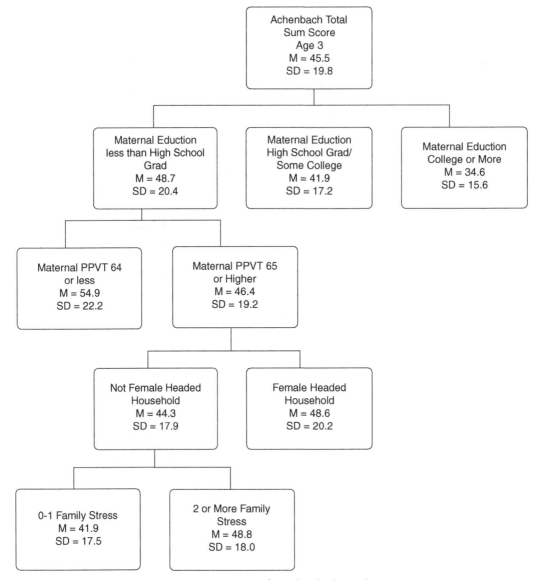

Figure 8.2. Recursive Partitioning Tree for Achenbach Total Sum Score at Age 3.

had higher receptive score were then further subdivided by female headship status. Children from female-headed families had higher behavior problem scores that were 4 points higher than children from two-parent families. Children from two-parent families were then subdivided into separate groups by family stress, with children whose families had at most one stressor having fewer behavior problems than children whose families had more than one stressor (7 points lower). The path to predicting children's behavior

problems was more nuanced when mothers had less than a high school education, than when mothers had graduated or gone beyond high school. For the children of less educated mothers, maternal characteristics (e.g., maternal education, receptive vocabulary, female headship) and stress emerged as strong predictors of children's behavior problems. While these results are preliminary, they underscore the importance of human capital and demographic risk factors and suggest that different pathways exist in better understanding children's cognitive and behavioral outcomes.

Resilient Children

Given that children exposed to adversity have worse developmental outcomes, (e.g., poor children fare worse in school and children of mothers with mental illnesses have an increased likelihood of poor mental health), researchers have had a growing interest in those children who thrive despite these risk factors (Sameroff, 2005). The capacity for children to function and thrive in the face of adversity is a construct known as resilience (Luthar, Cicchetti, & Becker, 2003). Positive adaptation is reflected in markers of developmental success that include mental health, satisfactory social relationships, and educational success (Sameroff, 2005). While much is known about the support mechanisms that enhance resilience, its underlying psychological and biological origins are unclear (Zandonella, 2006). Identifying these processes can further promote resilience in higher functioning, at-risk children as well as help increase resilience in less competent children (Sameroff, 2005). In fact, researchers emphasize that resilience is not a single trait of an individual, but rather, a complex mixture of various assets that may include personal, environmental and familial attributes (Luthar, 2005). This area of research has significant policy implications for ECE programs. The potential exists for ECE programs to promote resilience by timing interventions to windows of opportunity to have the strongest impact on childhood outcomes. Such programs may help shield children from future adversity by promoting this resilience in early childhood.

Most recently, researchers are looking at the role of biology in resilience and vulnerability (Luthar, 2005). For example, Caspi, Sugden, Moffitt, Taylor, Craig, and Harrington (2003) found that children exposed to maltreatment had less of a chance of future mental illness in the presence of a genotype that enables transport of serotonin. The interaction between genes and environment may make it possible to reveal whether children who appear resilient in the face of adversity actually show different brain patterns in response to stressful events than their lower functioning peers.

The implications for how the interplay between gene and environment affect one another have enormous implications for child development. Traditionally, the effects of genes and environment on human behavior were assumed to be independent (Plomin, 1977; Scarr & McCartney, 1983). More recently, research suggests that in fact genes influence the development and maintenance of certain environments while certain environments influence the expression of genes (Dickens, 2005; Rutter, 2005). Although only in its infancy, research on gene-environment interaction suggests that certain environmental outcomes produce deleterious effects only in the presence of certain genes and that certain genes only display adverse effects in the presence of certain environmental risks (Moffitt, Caspi & Rutter, 2005). Social scientists can now revisit previous assumptions about the impact of adverse environments (e.g., the risks discussed in this chapter) and determine whether some risks are understated or overstated depending on the genetic contributions to protecting or promoting specific risk (Rutter, 2005).

Concluding Remarks

This is an exciting time for risk research. Improvements in statistical analyses and especially recent advancements in the area of gene by environment interactions have elevated the examination of risks to an entirely new level. Future research will provide confirmation of the biochemical effects of risks and illuminate how individual differences in response to stress and risk are manifested by differences in brain patterns of resilient individuals. Such research can monitor changes in stress hormones and brain functioning over time and examine how the plasticity of the developing brain responds to early childhood interventions to reduce risk. Together both research methodologies will enhance our understanding of the cumulative impact these risks have upon children and families and upon the processes by which risks affect us.

Acknowledgments

Brooks-Gunn and Klebanov supported in part by research Grant No. 12-FY06–233 from the March of Dimes Foundation.

References

Achenbach, T. M., & Edelbrock, C. S. (1984). Psychopathology of childhood. *Annual Review of Psychology, 35,* 227–256.

Achenbach, T. M., Edelbrock, C. S., & Howell, C. T. (1987). Empirically-based assessment of the behavioral/emotional problems of 2- and 3-year-old children. *Monographs of the Society for Research in Child Development, 46.*

Ackerman, B. P., Kogos, J., Youngstrom, E., Schoff, K., & Izard, C. E. (1999). Family instability and the problem behaviors of children from economically disadvantaged families. *Developmental Psychology, 35,* 258–268.

Adam, E. K. (2004). Beyond quality: Parental adjustment and residential stability and children's adjustment. *Current Directions in Psychological Science, 13(5),* 210–213.

Alderson, D. P., Gennetian, L. A., Dowsett, C. J., Imes, A. E., & Huston, A. C. (2008). Economic, child care and child outcome effects of employment-based programs by prior levels of family disadvantage. *Social Services Review, 82,* 361–394.

Aneshensel, C. S., & Sucoff, C. A. (1996). The neighborhood context of adolescent mental health. *Journal of Health and Social Behavior, 37,* 293–310.

Appleyard, K., Egeland, B., van Dulmen, M. H. M., & Sroufe, L. A. (2005). When more is not better: The role of cumulative risk in child behavior outcomes. *Journal of Child Psychology and Psychiatry, 46,* 235–245.

Atzaba-Poria, N., Pike, A., & Deater-Deckard, K. (2004). Do risk factors for problem behavior act in a cumulative manner? An examination of ethnic minority and majority children through an ecological perspective. *Journal of Child Psychology and Psychiatry, 45,* 707–718.

Aunola, K., & Nurmi, J. E. (2005). The role of parenting styles in children's problem behavior. *Child Development, 76,* 1144–1159.

Benasich, A. A., & Brooks-Gunn, J. (1996). Maternal attitudes and knowledge of child rearing: Associations with family and child outcomes. *Child Development, 67,* 1186–1205.

Bradley, R. H., Corwyn, R. F., McAdoo, H., & Coll, C. (2001). The home environments of children in the United States: Part I. Variations by age, ethnicity, and poverty status. *Child Development, 72,* 1844–1867.

Braun, J., Kahn, R. S., Froehlich, T., Auinger, P., & Lanphear, B. (2006). Exposures to environmental toxicants and attention deficit hyperactivity disorder in US children. *Environmental Health Perspectives.* Doi:10.1289/ehp.9478, available at http://dx.doi.org/.

Brody, G. H., & Flor, D. (1997). Maternal psychological functioning, family processes, and child adjustment in rural, single parent, African-American families. *Developmental Psychology, 33,* 1000–1011.

Brody, G. H., Stoneman, Z., Flor, D., McCrary, C., Hastings, L., & Conyers, O. (1994). Financial resources, parental psychological functioning, parent co-giving, and early adolescent competence in rural two-parent African American families. *Child Development, 65,* 590–605.

Bronfenbrenner, U., & Morris, P. (1998). The ecology of developmental processes. In R. M. Lerner & W. Damon (Eds.), *Handbook of child psychology: Theoretical models of human development,* pp. 993–1028, Vol. 1 (5th ed.). New York: John Wiley & Sons.

The Brookings Institution. (2007). *Poverty and Income in 2006: A look at the new census data and what the numbers mean for children and families (Proceedings).* Paper presented at the Center on Children and Families Briefing, Washington, DC: Brookings Institution.

Brooks-Gunn, J., & Duncan, G. J. (1997). The effects of poverty on children. *Future of Children, 7,* 55–71.

Brooks-Gunn, J., Klebanov, P. K., & Liaw, F. (1995). The learning, physical, and emotional environment of the home in the context of poverty: The Infant Health and Development Program. *Children and Youth Services Review, 17,* 251–276.

Brooks-Gunn, J. & Markman, L. (2005). The contribution of parenting to ethnic and racial gaps in school readiness. *The Future of Children, 15,* 138–167.

Burchinal, M. R., Roberts, J. E., Hooper, S., & Zeisel, S. A. (2000). Cumulative risk and early cognitive development: A comparison of statistical risk models. *Developmental Psychology*, 36, 793–807.

Burchinal, M. R., Roberts, J. E., Zeisel, S. A., & Rowley, S. J. (2008). Social risk and protective factors for African American children's academic achievement and adjustment during the transition to middle school. *Developmental Psychology*, 44, 286–292.

Caspi, A. K., Sugden, T. E., Moffitt, A., Taylor, L. W., Craig, H., & Harrington, H. (2003). Influence of life stress on depression: moderation by polymorphism in the 5-HTT gene. *Science*, 301, 386–189.

Caspi, A., Taylor, A., Moffitt, T., & Plomin, R. (2000). Neighborhood deprivation affects children's mental health: Environmental risks identified in a genetic design. *Psychological Science*, 11, 338–342.

Cohen, J. B., & Lazarus, R. S. (1977). *Social support questionnaire*. Berkeley: University of California.

Deater-Deckard, K., Dodge, K., Bates, J. E., & Pettit, G. S. (1998). Multiple risk factors in the development of externalizing behavior problems: Group and individual differences. *Development and Psychopathology*, 10, 469–493.

Dickens, W. T. (2005). Genetic differences and school readiness. *The Future of Children*, 15(1): 55–90.

Dodge, K. A. (1990). Developmental psychopathology in children of depressed mothers. *Developmental Psychology*, 26, 3–6.

Douglas-Hall, A., & Chau, M. (2007). *Basic facts about low-income children: Birth to age 18*. New York: National Center for Children and Poverty, Mailman School of Public Health, Columbia University. Document Number.

Duncan, G. J., & Brooks-Gunn, J. (1997). Income effects across the lifespan: Integration and interpretation. In G. J. Duncan & J. Brooks-Gunn (Eds.), *Consequences of growing up poor*, pp. 596–610. New York: Russell Sage Foundation.

Dunifon, R., Duncan, G. J., & Brooks-Gunn, J. (2001). As ye sweep, so shall ye reap. *American Economic Review*, 91, 150–154.

Ernst, M., Moolchan, E. T., & Robinson, M. L. (2001) Behavioral and neural consequences of prenatal exposure to nicotine. *Journal of the American Academy of Child and Adolescent Psychiatry*, 40, 630–641.

Evans, G. W. (2003). A multimethodological analysis of cumulative risk and allostatic load among rural children. *Developmental Psychology*, 39, 924–933.

Evans, G. W. (2004). The Environment of childhood poverty. *American Psychologist*, 59, 77–92.

Evans, G. W., Wells, N. M., & Moch, A. (2003). Housing and mental health: a review of the evidence and a methodological and conceptual critique. *Journal of Social Issues*, 59, 475–500.

Fonarow, G. C., Adam, K. F. Jr., Abraham, W. T., Yancy, C. W., & Boscardin, W. J. (2005). Risk stratification for in-hospital mortality in acutely decompensated heart failure: Classification and regression tree analysis. *JAMA*, 293, 572–580.

Forehand, R., Biggar, H., & Kotchick, B. A. (1998). Cumulative risk across family stressors: Short- and long-term effects for adolescents. *Journal of Abnormal Child Psychology*, 26, 119–128.

Foster, E. M. (2012). Are risk factors cumulative? New insights from data mining. Unpublished manuscript.

Fried, P. A., & Matkind, J. E. (1987). Neonatal behavioral correlates of prenatal exposure to marihuana, cigarettes and alcohol in a low risk population. *Neurotoxical Teratol*, 9, 1–7.

Gerard, J. M., & Buehler, C. (2004). Cumulative environmental risk and youth maladjustment: The role of youth attributes. *Child Development*, 75, 1832–1849.

Goldberg, D. (1978). *Manual of the general health questionnaire*. London: NFER Publishing Company.

Gray, M. R., & Steinberg (1999). Unpacking authoritative parenting: Reassessing a multidimensional construct. *Journal of Marriage and the Family*, 61, 574–587.

Gross, R., Spiker, D., & Haynes, C. W. (Eds.) (1997). *Helping low birthweight, premature babies: The Infant Health and Development Program*. Stanford, CA: Stanford University Press.

Grunewald, T. L., Mroczek, D. K., Ryff, C. D., & Singer, B. H. (2008). Diverse pathways to positive and negative affect in adulthood and later life: An integrative approach using recursive partitioning. *Developmental Psychology*, 44, 330–343.

Hammen, C., Burge, D., & Stansbury. (1990). Relationship of mother and child variables to child outcomes in a high-risk sample: a causal modeling analysis. *Developmental Psychology*, 26(1): 24–30.

Harper, P. R., & Winslett, D. J. (2006). Classification trees: A possible method for maternity risk grouping. *European Journal of Operational Research, 169*, 146–156.

Haveman, R., & Wolfe, B. (1994). Succeeding generations: On the effects of investment in children. New York: Russell Sage Foundation.

Hoff, E. (2003). The specificity of environmental influence: Socioeconomic status affects early vocabulary and development via maternal speech. *Child Development, 74*, 1368–1378.

Ispa, J. M., Fine, M. A., L. C. Halgunseth, Harper, S., Robinson, J., Boyce, L., Brooks-Gunn, J. et al. (2004). Maternal intrusiveness, maternal warmth, mother-toddler relationship outcomes: Variations across low-income ethnic and acculturation groups. *Child Development, 6*, 1613–1631.

Johnson, A., Martin, A., Brooks-Gunn, J., & Petrill, S. (2008). Order in the house! Associations among household chaos, the home literacy environment, maternal reading ability, and children's early reading. *Merrill-Palmer Quarterly, 54*, 445–472.

Klebanov, P. K., & Brooks-Gunn, J. (2006). Cumulative, human capital, and psychological risk in the context of early intervention: Links with IQ at ages 3, 5, and 8. *Ann. N.Y., Acad. Sci., 1094*, 63–82.

Landrigan, P. J., Claudio, L., Markowitz, S., Berkowitz G., Brenner, B. L., Romero, H., et al. (1999). Pesticides and inner-city children: exposures, risks and prevention. *Evironmental Health Perspectives, 107*(3), 431–437.

LaVeist, T. A., & Wallace, J. M. (2000). Health risk and inequitable distribution of liquor stores in African American neighborhood. *Social Science and Medicine, 51*, 613–617.

Liaw, F., & Brooks-Gunn, J. (1994). Cumulative familial risks and low birth weight children's cognitive and behavioral development. *Journal of Clinical Child Psychology, 23*, 360–372.

Lupien, S. (2000). Child's stress hormone levels correlate with mother's socioeconomic status and depressive state. Biological Psychiatry, issue 48, 976–980.

Luthar, S. (2005). Resilience at an early age and its impact on child psychological development. In R. E. Tremblay, R. G. Bar, R. DeV. Peters (Eds.), *Encyclopedia on early childhood development*, 1–6. Montreal: Centre of excellence for early childhood development. Available online at http://www.excellence-earlychildhood.ca/documents/LutharANGxp.pdf.

Luthar, S., Cicchetti, D., & Becker, B. (2003). The construct of resilience: A critical evaluation and guidelines for future work. *Child Development, 71*, 543–562.

McLanahan, S. (2004). Diverging destinies: How children are faring under the second demographic transition. *Demography, 41*, 607–627.

McLoyd, V. C. (1990). The impact of economic hardship on black families and development. *Child Development, 61*, 311–346.

Meaney, M. J. (2001). Maternal care, gene expression, and the transmission of individual differences in stress reactivity across generations. *Annual Review of Neuroscience 24*, 1161–1192.

Mick, E., Biederman, J., Faraone, S. V., Sayer, J., & Kleinman, S. (2002). Case-control study of attention-deficit hyperactivity disorder and maternal smoking, alcohol use and drug use during pregnancy. *Journal of the American Academy of Child & Adolescent Psychiatry, 41*(4), 378–385.

Milberger, S., Biederman, J., Faraone, S. Chen, L., & Jones, J. (1997). Is maternal smoking during pregnancy a risk factor for attention deficit hyperactivity disorder in children? *Obstetrical & Gynecological Survey, 52*(4), 213–214.

Moffitt, T. E., Caspi, A., & Rutter, M. (2005). Strategy for investigating interactions between measured genes and measured environments. *Arch Gen Psychiatry, 62*, 473–481.

Molner, B. E., Gortmaker, S. L., Bull, F. C., & Buka. S. L. (2004). Unsafe to play? Neighborhood disorder and lack of safety predict reduced physical activity among urban children and adolescents. *American Journal of Health Promotion, 18*, 378–386.

Moreland, K., Wing, S., Diez-Rioux, A., & Poole, C. (2002). Neighborhood characteristics associated with the location of food stores and food services place. *American Journal of Preventative Medicine, 22*, 23–29.

National Research Council. Pesticides in the Diets of Infants and Children. Washington, DC: National Academy Press, 1993.

NICHD Early Child Care Research Network (2000). The interaction of child care and family risk in relation to child development at 24 and 36 months. *Applied Developmental Science, 6*, 144–156.

Osofsky, J. (1995). He effects of exposure to violence on young children. *American Psychologist, 50*, 782–788.

Pan, B. A., Rowe, M. L., Singer, J. D., & Snow, C. E. (2005). Maternal correlates of growth in toddler vocabulary production in low income families. *Child Development, 76*, 763–782.

Perera, F. P., Rauh, V., Whyatt, R. M., Tsai, W-Y., Tang, D., Diaz, D. et al. (2006). Effect of prenatal exposure to airborne polycyclic aromatic hydrocarbons on neurodevelopment in the first 3 years of life among inner-city children. *Environmental Health Perspectives*, 114, 1287–1292.

Peters, H. E., & Mullis, N. C. (1997). The role of family income and sources of income in adolescent achievement. In G. J. Duncan & J. Brooks-Gunn (Eds.), Consequences of growing up poor, pp. 340–381. New York: Russell Sage.

Petterson, S. M. & Albers, A. B. (2001). Effects of poverty and maternal depression on early child development. *Child Development*, 72, 1794–1813.

Plomin, R. (1977). Genotype-environment interaction and correlation in the analysis of human behavior. *Behavior Genetics*, 7, 83.

Powell, L. M., Slater, S., Chaloupka, F. J., & Harper, D. (2006) Availability of physical activity-related facilities and neighborhood demographic and socioeconomic characteristics: A national study. *American Journal of Public Health*, 96(9), 1676–1680.

Powell, L. M., Slater, S., Mirtcheva, D., Bao, Y. & Chaloupka, F. J. (2006). Food store availability and neighborhood characteristics in the United States. *Preventive Medicine*, doi:10.1016/j.ymwd.2006.08.008.

Rouse, C., Brooks-Gunn, J., & McLanahan, S. (2005). Introducing the issue, "School readiness: Closing racial and ethnic gaps." *The Future of Children*, 15, 5–14.

Rutter, M. (1979). Protective factors in children's responses to stress and disadvantage. In M. W. Kent & J. E. Rolf (Eds.), *Primary prevention of psychopathology*: Vol. 3. *Social competence in children*, pp. 49–74. Hanover, NH: University Press of New England.

Rutter, M. (2005). Environmentally mediated risks for psychopathology: Research strategies and findings. *Journal of the American Academy of Child and Adolescent Psychiatry*, 44, 3–18.

Rutter, M., & Quinton, D. (1984). Parental psychiatric disorder: effects on children. *Psychological Medicine*, 14, 853–880.

Sameroff, A. (2005). The science of infancy: academic, social and political agendas. *Infancy*, 7, 219–242.

Sameroff, A. (2006). Identifying risk and protective factors for healthy youth development. In A. Clarke-Stewart, & J. Dunn, *Families count: Effects on child and adolescent development*, pp. 53–76. Cambridge: Cambridge University Press.

Sameroff, A., & Rosenblum, K. L. (2006). Psychological constraints on the development of resilience. *Annals New York Academy of Science*, 1094, 116–124.

Sameroff, A. J., Seifer, R., Baldwin, A. & Baldwin, C. (1993). Stability of intelligence from preschool to adolescence: The influence of social and family risk factors. *Child Development*, 64, 80–97.

Sameroff, A. J., Seifer, R., Barocas, R., Zax, M., & Greenspan, S. (1987). Intelligence quotient scores of 4-year-old children: Social environmental risk factors. *Pediatrics*, 79, 343–350.

Sampson, R. J., Raudenbush, S. W., & Earls, F. (1997). Neighborhoods and violent crime: a multilevel study of collective efficacy. *Science*, 277, 918–924.

Scarr, S., & McCartney, K. (1983). How people make their own environments: a theory of genotype-environment effects. *Child Development*, 54, 424–435.

Seith, D., & Isakson, E. A. (2011). Who are America's poor children?: Examining health disparities among children in the United States. National Center for Children in Poverty, Columbia University Mailman School of Public Health.

Smith, J. R., Brooks-Gunn, J., & Klebanov, P. K. (1997). The consequences of living in poverty for young children's cognitive and verbal ability and early school achievement. In G. J. Duncan & J. Brooks-Gunn (Eds.), *Consequences of growing up poor*, pp. 132–189. New York: Russell Sage.

Suomi, S. J. (1999). Attachment in rhesus monkeys. In J. Cassidy & P. Shaver (Eds.), *Handbook of attachment: Theory, research and clinical implications*, pp. 181–197. New York: Guilford Press.

Suomi, S. J. (2003). Gene–environment interactions and the neurobiology of social conflict. *Annals of the New York Academy of Sciences*, 1008, 132–139.

Teachman, J. D., Paasch, K. M., Day, R. D., & Carver, K. P. (1997). Poverty during adolescence and subsequent educational attainment. In G. J. Duncan & J. Brooks-Gunn (Eds.), *Consequences of growing up poor*, pp. 382–418. New York: Russell Sage.

Terman, L. M., & Merrill, M. A. (1973). *Stanford-Binet intelligence scale: Manual for the third revision, form L-M*. Boston: Houghton Mifflin.

Toschke, A. M., Beyerlein, A., & von Kries, R. (2005). Children at high risk for overweight: A classification and regression trees analysis approach. *Obesity Research*, 13, 1270–1274.

U.S. Census Bureau. (2007). America's Families and Living Arrangements: 2006. U.S. Census Bureau, available online at http://www.census.gov/population/www/socdemo/hh-fam/cps2006.html.

Wandersman, A., & Nation, M. (1998). Urban neighborhoods and mental health. *American Psychologist, 53,* 647–656.

Wechsler, D. (1989). *Wechsler preschool and primary scale of intelligence.* San Antonio, TX: Psychological Corporation.

Wechsler, D. (1991) *WISC-III: Wechsler Intelligence Scale for Children manual* (3rd ed.). San Antonio, TX: Psychological Corporation.

Xue, Y., Leventhal, T., Brooks-Gunn, J. & Earls, F. (2005). Neighborhood residence and mental health problems of 5–11-year-olds. *Archives of General Psychiatry, 62,* 1–10.

Zandonella, C. (2006). Resilience in Children Conference: National Academy of Science available online at http://www.nyas.org/ebriefreps/main.asp?intEBriefID=490.

CHAPTER 9

Environment across Time

Ronald Seifer

Students of human development reserve their attention to developmental phenomena as it is expressed in the organism. With very rare exceptions, environment is viewed as a contributor to organismic development, but itself is not the focus of developmental analysis. To be sure, the dynamic interplay of organismic development and environmental context is in sharp focus (Bronfenbrenner & Morris, 2006; Sameroff et al., 2004), but the latter is viewed more as a coconspirator, rather than a developing entity in and of itself. Historically, this disciplinary attitude emanates from the dominant influence of psychological science as the foundation for understanding individual human development. As such, my organization of this chapter will have three main components. First, I will expand on the many ways that components of the environment may be conceptualized when human development is the focus. Second, I will discuss issues relevant to how time has been conceptualized in this field. Third, I will integrate this material in a developmental perspective, which simultaneously considers stability, change, and transformation in both organism and context. Finally, I will provide a series of integrative conclusions. *Environment across time* (the title of this chapter) may be viewed as having two distinct but interrelated meanings: (1) environmental influences over the course of an individual's development and (2) the developmental history of the environments themselves, perhaps affected by the individual. My ultimate goal in this chapter is to build upon existing perspectives to arrive at an integrated approach to understanding environment across time.

Environment as Ecology

The large majority of published empirical studies in the human development literature consider environment from the perspective of individual life histories. Questions are often of the form: how is the individual's developmental trajectory influenced by (for example) parenting practices within his or her family (Bornstein, 2002), peer influences (Prinstein & Dodge, 2008), exposure to media (Huesmann & Taylor, 2006), overwhelming or traumatic events

(Goenjian et al., 2005), or socioeconomic factors (Sameroff et al., 1993)? Such questions, however, represent only a portion of how individual development and environment might be conceptualized.

This generic form of question does not consider many related areas of inquiry, all of which may be brought to bear on issues of individual human development:

What Is the Organization of the Environment?

Developmentally relevant (from the organismic perspective) components of the environment are not randomly distributed. Instead, these components of the environment have distinct structure, much like the biological and psychological components of the developing organism. Thus, questions could address how the structure of environments affects development of individuals.

What Is the Animate Character of the Environment?

Because environments are complex and structured, consideration of fundamental characteristics of the component of the environment under study is useful. One critical characteristic is whether focus is on human or nonhuman components of environment. For example, parenting is a largely human activity, while physical infrastructure is largely nonhuman. Both may have important associations with individual developmental trajectories, but may differ dramatically on the degree to which they interact with other components of the environment or their susceptibility to change.

How Does the Environment Change over Time?

This, of course, is not a single or simple question. Given that environments have structure and components differ in their degree of human influence, change may occur very differently in different parts of the environment. Features of these changes might include rapidity of change, regularity of change, and predictability of change.

How Does an Individual Affect His or Her Environment?

Central to integrated theories of individuals in environmental context is the notion that individuals identify an adaptive niche within their environment. Individuals, however, are not passive recipients and occupiers of their niches; they actively create their niches by exerting changes to their immediate environments.

Development of the Environment: Ecological View

As readers of the questions earlier may recognize, these issues enumerated earlier are fundamental to the discipline of ecology. A simple definition of ecology is: (1) a branch of science concerned with the interrelationship of organisms and their environments; (2) the totality or pattern of relations between organisms and their environments (Merriam-Webster, 2008). Modern human development theory certainly embraces these two elements of the definition. Where human developmentalists and ecologists differ is where they focus their developmental questions. Human developmentalists, as noted earlier, focus on the organism; ecologists focus their questions on the environment.

A visit to an academic ecology setting (journal, Web site, encyclopedia) will invariably present the viewer with pictures (mental or graphical) of fields, forests, mountains, wetlands, rivers, or other sensitive physical environments. And, there will also be the occasional picture of a factory with smokestacks, an agricultural enterprise, or a waste site. Such human activities are viewed as settings for the development of the environments under consideration. Much like the human developmentalists' lack of emphasis on developments within the environment, ecologists treat the human actors in this equation more as static agents, rather than dynamically developing systems.

The ecological perspective has, however, been of great benefit to human developmentalists. Bronfenbrenner's (1979; Bronfenbrenner & Morris, 2006) ecological model has become a mainstay of developmental theory (although not as frequently a source of specific hypotheses for empirical studies). The feature of Bronfenbrenner's approach that has garnered the most attention has been the representation of nested levels of environmental organization, virtually always depicted by a series of concentric circles. These components, moving from most proximal to most distal, are *microsystem* (e.g., a child's family or classroom), *mesosystem*, or two microsystems in interaction (e.g., family and classroom), *exosystem* (e.g., parental workplace), *macrosystem* (e.g., social, political, or cultural context); in recent treatments the last system has also been termed the *macrochronosystem*, adding the temporal feature of change or patterning of environmental events.

This multiple level of analysis perspective, fundamental to ecology, provides a starting point for designing and interpreting empirical work in human development. The companion component is identification of critical features of the environmental-levels by organism interplay where developmental processes are especially sensitive. Within this ecological framework, environments are not collections of disconnected influences. Rather, there is some degree of structure, and this structure provides insight as to how specific components of the environment might exert direct or indirect effects on individuals.

Most work within this framework has focused on environment structured at levels external and distal to the child (with family typically the most proximal). There are other microsystem environments articulated in this model, but rarely studied under the rubric of ecological theory. Although counterintuitive at first glance, individual biological factors may also be viewed as microsystem environments. Stated a bit more specifically, there are biological processes that serve as microenvironments in which behavior is expressed and the social/physical world is experienced. For example, neurohormonal state (such as HPA axis activation) may condition the organism to experience events in a particular manner, or predispose biases in behavioral repertoires. Similarly, a child with a chronic illness carries around a set of environmental factors and constraints. In the case of asthma or diabetes, where family management of illness is integrated with daily life, the environmental factors associated with medications (or nonadherence to medication regimens) are ubiquitous.

Interactions among Structural Components of Environment.

Human ecology theory has emphasized the importance of mesosystem, or interactions among different microsystems. At first, this form of analysis would suggest that large groups of individuals might be affected in common ways by such interacting forces. This is not the case, however, as individuals bring to this equation a set of unique microsystems, in which they are dynamic contributors. For example, virtually all children are affected by the mesosystem described by the interaction of family and school. This is, however, a highly individual set of environmental effects. The variety of factors that characterize an individual family (e.g., parental presence, intergenerational presence, siblings, cultural practices, behavior control styles) are combined with school characteristics (e.g., class size, educational philosophy, distance from family home, daily schedule), as well as the interface of the family and school (e.g., child academic ability, parent involvement, parent-teacher personality match, child-teacher personality match, child's peer group) to generate highly individualistic interactions.

The status of this individual mesosystem is also subject to change over time. The structure of each component might change. Families change compositions, schools change administrators or teachers, children participate in different classrooms each year, families may move to a new school district, and so on.

Environment and Development

Now that structural components of the environment have been described, attention can focus on the core issue of conceptualizing environment across time. This last phrase immediately raises two questions. First, what is meant by time? And second, what do we want to understand about the environment within this conceptualization of time.

Structure of Time

The answer to the first question has multiple components, all of which center around the size and pattern of the time interval being considered. A large portion of the research literature focuses on very short time intervals. In particular, studies that include experimental manipulations, usually in laboratory studies, often occur over the course of just a few minutes. By their very nature, experiments include researcher-driven manipulations of environment over these short time frames. In most cases, however, it is not these specific interactions of individuals with their environments that are of interest. Rather, these experiments are meant to be analogs of processes that occur across much larger time frame outside the constrained laboratory setting. This is not to say that there are no instances where such short time frames are not the core interest – as studies employing microanalytic processes exemplify. At the other end of the spectrum, environments are often considered as they affect long-term developmental life course. In such cases, the time intervals in question may be decades in duration (Elder & Shanahan, 2006).

In between these extremes, there are many smaller intervals relevant to various types of developmental questions. These various time frames constrain the type of analysis of environments that may be conducted. For very short intervals, analysis of the environment is typically constrained to that which is immediately proximal to the individual. As time frames get longer, there is more opportunity to identify more varied components of the environmental structure, and to examine interactions among the different ecological components. The flip side of this richness in analyzing the structure of the environment is that the depth of exploration of each component is relatively limited.

The final point to make about time is that it is not simply a linear dimension that is segmented into chunks of different size. Time also has structural properties that are important to consider. The temporal structure most apparent in daily life is the periodicity associated with diurnal cycles (Refinetti, 2006). The linear period of 7 days considered in simple sequential fashion is fundamentally different from the same chunk of time reorganized into critical circadian features (most simply 7 days and 7 nights). Other structures of time include more regular variants such as seasonality, annual schedules (e.g., school years, holiday periods), and less regular historical periods (e.g., Republican control of Congress, active wars in the Persian Gulf region, era of No Child Left Behind). In subsequent discussion, I will refer to these as *nonlinear time structures*.

Development of the Environment Temporal Structures

The immediately preceding discussion of the structure of time is intentionally missing the issues to be considered regarding the temporal structures; I now turn to explicating these general themes.

STABILITY
One important feature environment and time is consistency. There are many examples of environmental stability, well documented in the research literature and in daily life experience. The buildings in an individual's residence neighborhood exhibit high levels of stability – destruction or construction of buildings is a relatively rare event. Presence and characteristics of social partners may also exhibit substantial stability. Parental presence in a child's household is relatively stable, as are the general parenting practices they employ.

CHANGE

In contrast, the reciprocal feature of importance is change in environments. Some examples of environmental changes are change of residence (particularly when the move is to a new neighborhood), change in family structure such as parental separation, or annual changes in classroom that typically occur for children (which usually entails a new teacher and perhaps many new peers).

FLUCTUATION

Environments may also exhibit periods of relatively nonsystematic stability and change. A simple example is periods of sun and clouds in many geographic regions; some days are sunny and some are cloudy, with relatively little predictability to more than a few days in the future. More relevant to psychological development, social acceptance in peer groups, parent affective state (especially when parents have mood disorders), difficulty of school-related tasks are examples of fluctuations in microsystem environments.

STRUCTURED CHANGE

Periods of change and stability in environments may be more predictable and structured than the fluctuations described earlier. Perhaps the best example of this is reinforcement contingencies in an individual's environment. On the one hand, there are periods of stability, when environments are consistent in being neutral vis-à-vis reward structure for an individual. On the other, there are periods when the environment changes to positive (or negative) reward structure for an individuals. What distinguishes structured change from fluctuation is the relative predictability of the change (in this case, contingent on the behavior of the individual).

Ecological Analysis of Environment across Time

When integrating the elements described in the preceding sections, the conceptual task is essentially to overlay the structure of time

on the structure of environments, with particular emphasis on their human ecological importance. The following material will be organized by temporal structures, integrating the components of environment and development in the integrative discussion. Studies representative of different manifestations of environment across time will be presented to exemplify the many ways that developmentalists have addressed this issue. This organization does not include a developmental chronology (i.e., what environments are most operative at what stages of development), as this is addressed in many other places; instead the focus is on areas that exemplify a substantive analysis of the person-environment-time ecology.

Development in the Moment: Microanalytic Analysis of Child and Environment

SOCIAL INTERACTION

The nature of environment across time is fundamental in the body of work that examines in detail social interaction in continuous time, often designated as microanalysis (Cohn & Tronick 1987; Fogel 1977, Coan & Gottman, 2007). Social interactions are, of course, dyadic at a minimum and involve mutual, reciprocal influences. For each individual social agent, his or her social partner(s) may be viewed as a component of the microsystem environment. These studies lend themselves to addressing questions about average behavior across the period of the observations (sometimes as short as a few minutes). Where these studies provide unique information, however, is in their ability to provide information about sequential patterns within the behavior stream, as well as contingencies in the behaviors of the social partners (Bakeman & Quera, 1995).

Stability of the microsystem may be reflected in behavioral averages of a social partner (when they are representative of the totality of the observation period), as in the example of affective states (such as positive, negative, neutral). Stability may also be identified in behavioral sequences, as when a social partner regularly follows a verbal prompt with a physical intervention during toy play. Change in the microsystem is most clearly indicated in sequential analyses focused in contingencies across social partners. Increasing interpersonal conflict over the course of an interaction can be indicative of mutual negative reinforcement, characteristic of a coercive process (Patterson, 1982; Burke et al., 2008). In a more experimental mode, the well studied still-face procedure manipulates the environment (by asking mothers of infants to engage in socially unexpectable behavior) in order to observe subtypes of change in the microsystem (Tronick, 1989).

PHYSIOLOGY

Another microsystem of interest is the internal environment indicated by physiologic parameters. Through the course of daily life, or in experimentally contrived situations, individuals face an ever-changing series of challenges, ranging from minor (e.g., a teacher greets a child) to substantial (a 12-month-old is separated from parent at child care dropoff). Internally, there a multiple rapid physiologic changes to these challenges, many of which are believed to affect behavioral responses. Two such physiologic processes that have received substantial attention are cardiac physiology and hypothalamic-pituitary-adrenal (HPA) axis activity indexed by cortisol levels.

Activation of the sympathetic branch (heart rate, pre-ejection period) and parasympathetic branch (heart rate variability) are thought to be indicative of behavioral reactivity and regulation respectively (Grossman & Taylor, 2007; Porges, 1995); these reactions are immediately detectable. HAP axis activity is less immediately detectable. Synthesis and secretion of corticotrophin releasing hormone (CRH) in the hypothalamus, often in response to environmental challenge, begins a cascade that results in cortisol synthesis and release in the adrenal cortex. Cortisol, in turn, can have acute and chronic effects on neurotransmitter (serotonin) and structural (hippocampus) brain systems, with downstream behavior

implications. Furthermore, there are multiple effects of cortisol outside the nervous system, including short-term energy increase, immune response, and decreased pain sensitivity (Sapolsky et al., 2000).

These behaviorally relevant physiologic microsystem changes are, in fact, indicative of interactions of multiple microsystems. That is, the physiologic responses are not random, but are conditioned on the challenges in the individual's immediate external environment. Thus, the interplay of these external challenges and internal physiologic changes reflect a prototypical example of Bronfenbrenner's description of mesosystems. To be sure, physiology is typically viewed as a constitutional/biologic process, but with respect to behavioral expressions may in fact be most appropriately conceived as a behaviorally relevant environment changing across short periods.

HPA axis activity, indicated by cortisol levels, is not only a process that plays out in linear time. Cortisol levels are also one of the well-studied circadian processes. Individuals display a strongly organized diurnal pattern of cortisol secretion, with increasing secretion during nighttime sleep, peaking shortly after awakening, declining over the course of the day, and reaching a nadir during the night. This association of neurohormonal environment to the circadian temporal structure has two important implications for the current discussion. First, the interpretation of cortisol levels must be embedded in the known circadian pattern of cortisol secretion. Second, the moment-to-moment patterns of cortisol secretion may also have longer-term consequences (which will be discussed later in this chapter).

Some might question the use of the term development in the context of microanalytic studies. In the human development literature, the term development is often reserved for changes of an enduring nature, particular those that represent systemic transformations (Sameroff, 1983). These large-impact developmental transformations do not, however, occur in a vacuum. Instead, they emanate from the type of individuals' interplay with the environment across time discussed herein. This focus on microan-alytic processes is akin to analysis in the political realm, embodied in former House Speaker Tip O'Neill's famous statement that "all politics are local." Without the local microanalytic processes, the organism-wide developments would not occur.

Development within Regular Contexts

For lack of a better term (and the field of human development has no particular term it uses), *regular contexts* will be used to indicate environments that are relatively stable, but do undergo changes over lon-ger intervals of time (more on the order of year-to-year than day-to-day). These regular contexts are mostly microsystems that indi-viduals interact with directly. Some of the environmental features discussed later are obvious, but some are less often considered when discussing environment and human development.

SOCIAL CONTEXTS: FAMILIES AND PEERS
Family contexts are one regular envi-ronment for developing children. From a structural perspective, events such as parental separation, birth of a new sibling, or death of a family member are relatively rare events. Parenting refers to behavior of individuals within families, whereas family functioning refers to behavior of the overall family unit. Issues such as overall levels of conflict and accomplishment of the tasks of daily living (Moos & Moos, 1981, Dickstein et al., 1998). Parenting styles show relatively little change over time (Lerner et al., 2002). Levels of conflict within families as well as overall family functioning are also quite consistent over time (Cummings & Davies, 1994; Seifer et al., 2008). In terms of envi-ronmental effects on human development, there may be more literature with respect to family and parenting processes than any other environmental component (Bornstein, 2002). The predictive utility for child com-petence of authoritative parenting, sensitive parenting, scaffolding, and positive affectiv-ity has been widely supported (Steinberg & Silk, 2002).

As children grow older, peers become an increasingly important social environ-ment. As in the case of parenting and fam-ily function, peers exert strong influence on developing children, and there is substan-tial stability in these peer environments. Quality of friendships, degree of same-sex and opposite-sex peer group participation, exposure to deviant peer group influences are among the features relevant to children's development, which may have time-varying environmental characteristics (Prinstein & Dodge, 2008).

SCHOOLS AND NEIGHBORHOOD INSTITUTIONS
Many neighborhood institutions are regular contexts for individual child development (schools, churches, community groups). Each of these has many characteristics that endure over time, including physical infrastructure, adult leadership (principals, clergy, CBO administrators), adult staffing (teachers, vol-unteers, line staff), philosophy (school cur-ricula, religious practices, community group programming), and general resource levels (annual budgets, wealth level in the church community). In the human development literature, most of what we know about the effects of churches and community organi-zations is at the level of presence or absence as influences in a child's life (King & Furrow, 2004; Kim, 2008). Schools, in contrast, have a wealth of literature on factors that influ-ence children's development. These factors include school size, class size, experience of teachers, and financial resources (Englehart, 2007; Lee & Wong, 2004).

There are also some vexing questions about characterizing school environments. There are many characteristics of schools that may be little more than proxies for the general social and economic circumstances of the larger community, which makes it dif-ficult to tease apart the components of the environment that are operative in develop-ment of individual children. Wealthier com-munities generally have higher per-pupil budgets, which in turn translate into smaller class size, more experienced teachers, and more varied academic and extracurricular programs. Implicit in this comment is that multiple levels of the environment interact in the ecology of individual development within schools. That is, schools do not exist in a vacuum; the microsystem of a school operated in the macrosystem of economic milieu of a community.

Another conceptual problem when thinking about schools is how to ascribe stability and change in certain circumstances. Many inner-city school districts and preschool settings are characterized by high rates of teacher turnover, high dropout rates and otherwise transient student populations, frequent disruptions because of student behavior and infrastructure failures, and administrative changes in response to poor student performance. Is it most advantageous to characterize the school environments as having a high level of *change*? Or is it more advantageous to identify the chaos as an element of *stability* in the school environment? Put another way, is unpredictability that endures over time best thought of as change or as stability?

MEMORY

We generally think of memory as an individual function; the main connection with the environment is that the remembered events occurred in a specific time and place. It is also widely recognized, however, that memory is a constructive process (Piaget, 1972). Recent studies also document that environmental factors are integral to how we remember. In the simplest case, we know that factors such as affective arousal and specific contextual clues affect salience of specific events. For example, providing cues about the race of an individual's resume alters what respondents remember about that individual (Frazier & Wiersma, 2001). These are examples of environmental influence, but with no meaningful time dimension.

More germane to the topic of environment across time is the twin phenomena of recovered memory and false memory. In each case, a series of environmental events and changes is necessary to produce these outcomes. In the case of recovered memory (Elliott, 1997), an environmental setting

of overwhelming input sets the stage for memory suppression (e.g., abuse, combat, imprisonment), and a subsequent series of environmental events serve to bring the memories to consciousness (e.g., psychotherapy, revisiting a salient site or individual). In the case of false memory, innocuous environmental events result in relatively nonsalient memories; when followed by environmental events that support reconstruction of those events including nonveridical information (intentional deception used in laboratory studies, unintentional suggestion occurring in clinical or forensic settings) memories can be reconstructed that are not accurate reflections of past events (Davis & Loftus, 2007; Loftus & Davis, 2006). In these cases of repressed, recovered, and false memories, the structure of the environment across time (sometimes very long periods) affect individual recall of past events.

NATURAL AND MAN-MADE DISASTERS

Disastrous events, whether natural or resulting from human action, have rapid onset and represent a major environment change. Recent examples include hurricane Katrina and the airplane attacks of 9/11/2001. The rapidity and depth of change of the events themselves are matched by the stability of the aftereffects that endure over time. For those directly affected, some individuals suffer the ultimate consequence when there are fatalities. For those who survive (or who have close associations with those who were directly affected), the disaster can have far-reaching effects on multiple components of developmental ecology. Some examples from the case of hurricane Katrina include immediate consequences such as loss of a family member, loss of residence, loss of other property, move to a new region, disruption in employment, and separation from close family members. Each of these, in turn, can lead to additional environmental changes. These include more permanent family dissolution, transition to poverty, changes in peer group, decline in social supports, loss of religious affinity, removal from familiar culture, and change in schooling. Most striking is these lists is the sheer number and variety of changes in environment across the transition defined by the disaster. A more academic view is that all levels of ecology are affected – multiple microsystems, exosystems of family members, and macrosystems in which daily life is experienced. Developmental effects include increased levels of behavior problems, psychopathology, and perhaps academic achievement (Scheeringa & Zeanah, 2008).

Development within Enduring Contexts

As with the term *regular contexts*, there is no standard in the field for what I am calling *enduring contexts*. This term is meant to designate environmental components that are highly resistant to change, with those changes often at the level of generation to generation (or even less frequent). The environments in question are typically at the macrosystem level, reflecting systems in which the individuals of interest do not directly participate.

CULTURAL INSTITUTIONS AND PRACTICES
Culture may be found in either brick-and-mortar or social practices. In a multicultural society such as the United States, individuals may participate in one or more among a diverse set of cultural institutions. Some have become indigenous to the United States, while others have been brought by recent immigrants. Cultural institutions can condition a wide range of activities affecting individual development.

Within families, the most obvious relation to social practices is in parenting styles. For example, it is well established that African-American families more frequently exhibit authoritarian styles than their European-American counterparts, and these styles may be more successful in this subgroup (Ceballo & McLoyd, 2002).

Family supports of children's education and learning are also influenced by cultural background. Different cultures view learning and participation in schooling in very different ways. Chinese families, for example, highly value respect for teachers, individual work/effort, and maximizing achievement

as fundamental to the educational process (Li, 2006). Parental involvement in school is also related to cultural practices. Beliefs such as those described earlier for Chinese families may serve to reduce their motivation to engage with their children's teachers. Furthermore, for families where recent immigration results in language barriers in communication with school personnel, there is reduced probability that parents will be involved with their children's schools (Garcia Coll et al., 2002). These are again prototypical examples of mesosystem interactions among multiple microsystems in which children directly participate. Qualities of families and qualities of schools (as well as the match or mismatch of these factors) likely place meaningful constraints on children's academic potential.

RACE AND ETHNICITY
Much of the environment of race and ethnicity is subsumed under cultural practices. But, there remains environmental variation after those cultural factors are considered. The two environmental factors of most importance are discrimination and segregation. America has a long history of discrimination based on race and ethnicity. Although the most egregious manifestations (such as slavery) are no longer operative, there remain many more subtle discriminatory practices. Access to jobs, housing, schooling, social networks, and health care are all affected by discriminatory practices. Within these microsystems, discrimination can affect individuals' functioning within them, as when teachers behave differently with children based on race or ethnicity or in health care disparities (Saft & Pianta, 2001; Murray & Murray, 2004; McGuire et al., 2008)

American culture remains highly segregated along racial and ethnic lines. Residential patterns, which in turn affect school patterns, are highly determined by racial and ethnic factors. Even within settings where social integration is feasible, individuals frequently self-select into social groups segregated along racial and ethnic lines (Wahl et al., 2007). Such segregation is manifest in a society where decades of evidence indicate that separate is not equal (Jencks, 1972). Thus, children remain at a disadvantage owing to race and ethnicity in a microsystem highly immune to change.

SOCIAL/ECONOMIC CIRCUMSTANCES

Perhaps the strongest predictor of major life outcomes of children is socioeconomic status (Sameroff et al., 1993). Affluence and poverty macrosystems can have pervasive effects on individual development. One important consideration is that environmental characteristics associated with culture and immigration (discussed earlier) have substantial covariation with social and economic status. There is also strong intergenerational stability in these status characteristics. In early 20th century America, there was meaningful improvement of individuals' economic circumstances across their development, more so than in current American culture. Even so, major change in status most often occurred across generations.

The other consideration for the social and economic macrosystem is the overall performance of the economic system. During flush economic times (such as in the mid-1990s to mid-2000s) many families are able to achieve social and economic goals associated with home purchases in high quality neighborhoods (e.g., residential infrastructure, quality schooling, safe neighborhoods, positive peer influences). When the economic cycle reverses and families are more distressed financially, home purchases and existing home ownership may be affected. More families either move to less desirable locations, or perhaps can no longer afford home ownership. Thus, the temporal characteristics of the macrosystem affect the environments of large numbers of developing children.

As noted earlier, effects of economic status, particularly poverty, are pervasive. The list includes academic failure, aggressive social interactions, substance use, delinquent behavior, psychopathology, and limited occupational success (McLoyd et al., 2006). The ultimate question in the field of human development is the specific processes in microsystems that account for these large and consistent effects.

CHRONIC ILLNESS

As with physiologic processes, chronic illness is not typically considered as an environmental structure. There are, however, several ways that chronic illness serves as an environment for psychological development. This is true even when conditions with direct psychological influences are not considered (e.g., Down syndrome, autistic spectrum disorders).

Environments are created around children with chronic illness. When identifiable to peers and other adults (e.g., visits to school nurse, use of medications such as inhalers, visible symptoms of illness), social behavior is potentially altered (Bijstra et al., 2000). Although not technically a chronic illness, childhood obesity may create very similar environments for children. Physical limitations may also be associated with chronic illness that preclude certain types of activities (e.g., breathing or motor problems limit participation in sports activities).

The treatment of chronic illness also creates characteristic environments for children. Most obviously, when medications or procedures are part of the treatment regimen, the side effects of those treatments are part of the developing child's environment. Complementary to the direct impact of treatments is the environment structured to implement those treatments. The most common chronic conditions, asthma and diabetes, both have treatment regimens that require active family management on a daily basis (McQuaid et al., 2003, Stark et al., 1987).

From a more cognitive/experiential perspective, children and their families may structure their understanding and memory of development in terms of the chronic illness. For example, time blocks might include "before my daughter was diagnosed with asthma" or "after I started needing insulin every day." Such structuring of time and experience can affect individual cognition and behavior, as well as interpersonal dynamics.

Many chronic illnesses do not substantially remit over time, and thus these environments would be considered highly stable. Unlike some of the other enduring contexts described earlier, chronic illness primarily is manifest as alterations in micro-systems, and these environments do have systematic effects on children's development. Academic performance is impaired, quality of social development is affected, and family functioning may be impacted (Currie, 2005).

Development and Environments with Nonlinear Time Structures

Previous sections addressed issues of environments that varied with respect to time duration and degree of stability and change. In the following material, attention is on the nonlinear time structures discussed earlier.

PHYSIOLOGY AND CIRCADIAN PROCESSES
Function of the HPA axis in response to stress was described earlier. This stress response in and of itself is only one part of the story, however. The diurnal secretion of cortisol also is important and interaction with chronically challenging environments can alter the circadian process. In particular, when the HPA axis is activated in response to chronic challenge, there can be a general down-regulation of the system. This is manifest as low early morning levels or cortisol and dampened decline across the daytime hours (Boyce & Ellis, 2005). This pattern has been linked to alterations in gene expression in animal studies (Meaney, 2001), and to a variety of maladaptive processes (such as relationship disturbance and conduct problems) in human studies (Gunnar & Vasquez, 2001; Murray-Chase et al., 2008). Even though direction of effect is unclear, there is a likelihood that some portion of this variance is attributable to environmental influence.

SLEEP ORGANIZATION
The behavior most associated with circadian temporal structure is sleep. The environment surrounding the diurnal pattern of sleep has become a focus of attention, processes often referred to as sleep hygiene. Environmental

features such as allowing sufficient time in bed, minimizing distractions (such as television) in the sleep environment, management of bedtime resistance and night waking, and minimizing weekday-weekend variation in sleep duration are among the components of sleep hygiene. Family-managed sleep hygiene, in addition to more intrinsic components of sleep efficiency, can contribute to varying degrees of daytime sleepiness. Sleepiness and performance during the day are intrinsically linked, important for academic performance, cognitive processing, and emotion regulation (Wolfson & Carskadon, 2003; Crossin et al., 2008).

There are special considerations regarding sleep and circadian timing in the first years of life. Newborn infants have no particular circadian patterning to their sleep (even though close to 85 percent of time is spent asleep). Circadian patterning emerges in the first months of life, yet it is still discordant with the more mature human pattern of sleep organization in that night waking is the norm. Similar challenges occur when preschoolers begin to give up their daytime naps (Crossin et al., 2008). Thus, the adaptation of family environments to accommodate the immature sleep timing is critical to maintaining optimal developmental contexts for young infants (Seifer et al., 2000).

The transitions during infancy and early childhood are not the only changes in the sleep environment across time. There are also circadian changes the co-occur with puberty, where the interaction of changes in intrinsic circadian period interact with other microsystems to produce the end result of sleepiness during the morning hours at precisely the developmental period when current cultural practices demand high levels of performance because of early school start times (Wolfson & Carskadon, 2003).

SOCIAL NOVELTY AND SHYNESS
Circadian periods are highly regular and predictable (cycling once every 24 hours). Other nonlinear time structured environments are far less regular. One that is particularly important to a subgroup of children is the presence of novel social situations

(Kagan et al., 1989, Fox et al., 2001). Many of these events are not highly predictable, such a family acquaintances visiting a home, shopping in new places, eating at a restaurant. Others are more predictable, such as the beginning of a new school year. In either event, the temporal structure of the environment for children who are dispositionally shy is defined by the onset of the relatively nonpredictable events. Exposure to these environments can produce high levels of distress, perhaps reinforcing nonadaptive behaviors. Such behaviorally inhibited children are may be more prone to developing anxiety and other behavior problems (Rosenbaum et al., 1988; Biederman et al., 2001).

Development within Reliably Changing Contexts: Developmental Transitions

Similar to the nonlinear time structures discussed immediately earlier, there are numerous well-established transitions in developmental context. These differ from the prior set in that they are not repeating, but instead are generally one-time occurrences that occur regularly across most individuals. Some examples discussed later include puberty, school transitions, acculturation. In some ways the hallmark of these transitions is the changing nature of the environment across time.

PUBERTY

Puberty has clear internal and external manifestations. Internally, there is a large increase in the presence of sex hormones, as well as more subtle changes in other physiologic systems such as the HPA axis and intrinsic circadian period. Externally, there are distinctive signs of puberty – growth spurts, secondary sex characteristics, and voice changes. Thus, the internal environment relevant to behavioral development and the external social environment in response to the external characteristics are both in flux. Furthermore, many social institutions are specifically adapted to pubertal transitions (e.g., schools, marketplaces, media).

Negotiating this set of changes presents unique challenges to adolescents. On the one hand, there is excitement associated with autonomy, emerging privileges of adulthood, sexuality, and mobility. On the other, there are the uncertainties of identity formation, novel social situations, complex organizations, and assumption of responsibilities. These contextual changes, combined with biological changes, set the stage for a highly vulnerable period (Dahl, 2004).

ACCULTURATION

Immigration presents substantial challenges to children and families. By definition, acculturation involves a substantial change in the environment at multiple levels. Macrosystems of nationality, government, and culture are substituted; along with these are changes in the multiple microsystems that individuals inhabit. The adaptation to these changes (particularly the degree to which individuals accommodate to new practices and assimilate features of the new culture) are termed acculturation.

In immigrant families, each family member individually (as well as collectively with other family members) negotiates these acculturation processes. As with transitions to puberty, transition to new cultures presents a developmental context promoting vulnerability (Duarte et al., 2008). Furthermore, it is not only individual acculturation, but patterns of acculturation within families (including discordance among individual family members in degree of acculturation) that best predict these vulnerabilities (Duarte et al., 2008; Schofield et al., 2008). Thus, the changing environment across a period of years, conditioned by individual construction of those environments, within the microsystem contexts of family and school illustrate the complexity of the person-context-time system that characterizes the ecological analysis.

Concluding Remarks

Where are we in the study of environments across time in the field of human development? The most optimistic view is that we have many exciting research opportunities. The current theoretical and empirical base includes (1) some good ideas about structural components of the environment, (2) some limited appreciation of temporal change and stability of environments, and (3) theoretical appreciation that there is dynamic interplay in the person-environment-time system. There are many real limitations in our current understanding as well, including (1) limited research in the development of the environments themselves over time, and (2) limited empirical testing of the dynamic person-environment-time hypotheses that our most advanced theoretical appreciation would generate.

How do we move forward? As in most behavioral research agendas, methods are required to address the known complexity of the phenomena under study. Thus, we need to move from (1) static to dynamic measurement of the environment, (2) concurrent measurement of multiple levels of environment in individual studies, (3) use of measurement tools sensitive to environmental change, and (4) implementation of research designs that allow for testing of complex person-environment-time interactions. There are not easy tasks, but they are tasks that represent some future directions of human development research.

References

Bakeman, R., & Quera, V. (1995). *Analyzing interaction: Sequential analysis with SDIS and GSEQ*. Cambridge: Cambridge University Press.

Biederman, J., Hirshfeld-Becker, D. R., Rosenbaum, J. F., Hérot, C., Friedman, D., Snidman, N., Kagan, J., & Faraone, S. V. (2001). Further evidence of association between behavioral inhibition and social anxiety in children. *American Journal of Psychiatry, 158,* 1673–1679.

Bijstra, J. O., Mellenbergh, G. J., & Wolters, W. H. G. (2000). Social functioning in children with a chronic illness. *Journal of Child Psychology and Psychiatry, 41,* 309–317.

Blair, C., Granger, D., Razza, R. P. (2005). Cortisol reactivity is positively related to executive function in preschool children attending Head Start. *Child Development, 76,* 554–567.

Bornstein, M. (Ed.) (2002). *Handbook of parenting* (2nd Ed.). Mahwah, NJ: Lawrence Erlbaum.

Boyce, W. T., & Ellis, B. J. (2005). Biological sensitivity to context: I. An evolutionary-developmental theory of the origins and functions of stress reactivity. *Development and Psychopathology, 17,* 271–301.

Bronfenbrenner, U. (1979). *The ecology of human development*. Cambridge, MA: Harvard University Press.

Bronfenbrenner, U. & Morris, P. M. (2006). The bioecological model of human development. In R. M. Lerner (Ed.), *Handbook of child psychology* (6th ed.): Vol. 1. *Theoretical models of human development,* pp. 793–828. New York: Wiley.

Burke, J. D., Pardini, D. A., & Loeber, R. (2008). Reciprocal relationships between parenting behavior and disruptive psychopathology from childhood through adolescence. *Journal of Abnormal Child Psychology, 36,* 679–692.

Ceballo, R., & McLoyd, V. C. (2002). Social support and parenting in poor, dangerous neighborhoods. *Child Development, 73,* 1310–1321.

Coan, J. A., & Gottman, J. M. (2007). The Specific Affect Coding System (SPAFF). In J. A. Coan & J. B. Allen (Eds.), *Handbook of emotion elicitation and assessment,* pp. 267–285. New York: Oxford University Press.

Cohn, J. F., & Tronick, E. Z. (1987). Mother infant face-to-face interaction: The sequence of dyadic states at 3, 6, and 9 months. *Developmental Psychology, 23,* 68–77.

Crossin, R., Seifer, R., Carskadon, M. A., & LeBourgeois, M. K. (2008). Nap deprivation effects on emotion regulation in preschool children. Paper presented at the American Sleep Disorders Association/Sleep Research Society meeting, Baltimore.

Cummings, E. M., & Davies. (1994). *Children and marital conflict: The impact of family dispute and resolution*. New York: Guilford.

Currie, J. (2005). Health disparities and gaps in school readiness. *The Future of Children, 15,* 117–138.

Dahl, R. E. (2004). Adolescent brain development: A period of vulnerabilities and opportunities. *Annals of the New York Academy of Sciences, 1021,* 1–22.

Davis, D., & Loftus, E. F. (2007). Internal and external sources of misinformation in adult witness memory. In M. P. Toglia, J. D. Read, D. F. Ross, & R. C. Lindsay (Eds.), *The handbook of eyewitness psychology*: Vol. 1. *Memory for events*, pp. 195–237. Mahwah, NJ: Lawrence Erlbaum.

Dickstein, S., Seifer, R., Hayden, L. C., Schiller, M., Sameroff, A. J., Keitner, G., Miller, I., Rasmussen, S., Matzko, M., & Dodge-Magee, K. (1998). Levels of family assessment: II. Impact of maternal psychopathology on family functioning. *Journal of Family Psychology*, 12, 23–40.

Duarte, C. S., Bird, H. R., Shrout, P. E., Wu, P., Lewis-Fernandéz, R., Shen, S., & Canino, G. (2008). Culture and psychiatric symptoms in Puerto Rican children: longitudinal results from one ethnic group in two contexts. *Journal of Child Psychology and Psychiatry*, 49, 563–572.

Elder, G. H., & Shanahan, M. J. (2006). The life course and human development. In R. M. Lerner (Ed.), *Handbook of child psychology* (6th ed.): Vol. 1. *Theoretical models of human development*, pp. 665–715. New York: Wiley.

Elliott, D. M. (1997). Traumatic events: Prevalence and delayed recall in the general population. *Journal of Consulting and Clinical Psychology*, 65, 811–820.

Englehart, J. M. (2007). The centrality of context in learning from further class size research. *Educational Psychology Review*, 19, 455–467.

Fogel, A. (1977). Temporal organization in mother-infant face-to-face interaction. In H. R. Schaffer (Ed.), *Studies in mother-infant interaction*, pp. 119–152. New York: Academic.

Fogel, A., & Thelen, E. (1987). Development of early expressive and communicative action: Reinterpreting the evidence from a dynamic systems perspective. *Developmental Psychology*, 23, 747–761.

Fox, N. A., Henderson, H. A., Rubin, K. H., Calkins, S. D., & Schmidt, L. A. (2001). Continuity and discontinuity of behavioral inhibition and exuberance: Psychophysiological and behavioral influences across the first four years of life. *Child Development*, 72, 1–21.

Frazer, R. A., & Wiersma, U. J. (2001). Prejudice versus discrimination in the employment interview: We hire equally, but or memories harbor prejudice. *Human Relations*, 54, 173–191.

García Coll, C. T., Akiba, D., Palacios, N., Silver, R., DiMartino, L., Chin, C., & Bailey, B. (2002). Parental Involvement in Children's Education: Lessons from Three Immigrant Groups. *Parenting: Science and Practice*, 2, 303–324.

Goenjian, A. K., Walling, D., Steinberg, A. M., Karayan, I., Najarian, L. M., & Pynoos, R. (2005). A prospective study of posttraumatic stress and depressive reactions among treated and non-treated adolescents 5 years after a catastrophic disaster. *American Journal of Psychiatry*, 162, 2302–2308.

Gottman, J. M., & Wilson, B. J. (1997). A theory of meta-emotion, parenting, and emotion regulation. In J. M. Gottman (Ed.), *Meta-emotion: How families communicate emotionally*, pp. 90–129. Hillsdale, NJ: Lawrence Erlbaum.

Gunnar, M. R., & Vazquez, D. M. (2001). Low cortisol and a flattening of expected daytime rhythm: Potential indices of risk in human development. *Development and Psychopathology*, 13, 515–538.

Grossman, P., & Taylor, E. W. (2007). Toward understanding respiratory sinus arrhythmia: Relations to cardiac vagal tone, evolution and biobehavioral functions. *Biological Psychology*, 74, 263–285.

Harvey, A. G. (2008). Sleep and circadian rhythms in bipolar disorder: Seeking synchrony, harmony, and regulation. *American Journal of Psychiatry*, 165, 820–829.

Huesmann, L. R., & Taylor, L. D. (2006) The role of media violence in violent behavior. *Annual Review of Public Health*, 27, 393–415.

Jencks, C., Smith, M., Acland, H., Mane, M. J., Cohen, D., Gintis, H., Heyns, B., & Michelson, S. (1972). *Inequality: A reassessment of the effect of family and schooling in America*. New York: Basic Books.

Kagan, J., Resnick, J. S., & Gibbons, J. (1989). Inhibited and uninhibited types of children. *Child Development*, 60, 838–845.

Kim, J. (2008). The protective effect of religiosity on maladjustment among maltreated and non-maltreated children. *Child Abuse & Neglect*, 32, 711–720.

King, P. E., & Furrow, J. L. (2004). Religion as a resource for positive youth development: Religion, social capital, and moral outcomes. *Developmental Psychology*, 40, 703–713.

Lee, J., & Wong, K. K. (2004). The impact of accountability on racial and socioeconomic equity: Considering both school resources and achievement outcomes. *American Educational Research Journal*, 41, 797–832.

Lerner, R. M., Rothbaum, F., Boulos, S., & Castellino, D. R. (2002). Developmental systems perspective on parenting. In M. Bornstein (Ed.), *Handbook of parenting*, pp. 315–344, Vol. 2 (2nd ed.). Mahwah, NJ: Lawrence Erlbaum.

Li, J. (2006). Self in learning: Chinese adolescents' goals and sense of agency. *Child Development*, 77, 482–501.

Loftus, E. F., & Davis, D. (2006). Recovered memories. *Annual Review of Clinical Psychology, 2*, 469–498.

McGuire, T. G., Ayanian, J. Z., Ford, D. E., Henke, R. E., Rost, K. M., Zaslavsky, A. M. (2008). Testing for statistical discrimination by race/ethnicity in panel data for depression treatment in primary care. *Health Services Research, 43*, 531–551.

McLoyd, V. C., Aikens, N. L., & Burton, L. M. (2006). Childhood poverty, policy, and practice. In K. A. Rettinger & I. E. Sigel (Eds.), *Handbook of child psychology* (6th ed.): Vol. 4. *Theoretical models of human development*, pp. 700–775. New York: Wiley.

McQuaid, E. L., Kopel, S. J., Klein, R. B., & Fritz, G. K. (2003). Medication adherence in pediatric asthma: Reasoning, responsibility, and behavior. *Journal of Pediatric Psychology, 28*, 323–333.

Meaney, M. J. (2001). Maternal care, gene expression, and the transmission of individual differences in stress reactivity across generations. *Annual Review of Neuroscience, 24*, 1161–1192.

Merriam-Webster OnLine Dictionary (2008). www.merriam-webster.com/dictionary.

Moos, R. H., & Moos, B. S. (1981). *Family environment scale manual*. Palo Alto, CA: Consulting Psychologists Press.

Murray, C., & Murray, K. M. (2004). Child level correlates of teacher-student relationships: An examination of child demographic characteristics, academic orientations and behavioral orientations. *Psychology in the Schools, 41*, 751–762.

Murray-Chase, D., Han, G., Cicchetti, D., Crick, N. R., & Rogosch, F. A. (2008). Neuroendocrine regulation and physical and relational aggression: The moderating roles of child maltreatment and gender. *Developmental Psychology, 44*, 1160–1176.

Patterson, G. R. (1982). *A social learning approach to family intervention*. Eugene, OR: Castalia.

Piaget, J. (1972). *The psychology of intelligence*. Totowa, NJ: Littlefield Adams.

Porges, S. W. (1995). Orienting in a defensive world: Mammalian modifications of our evolutionary heritage: A polyvagal theory. *Psychophysiology, 32*, 301–318.

Prinstein, M. J., & Dodge, K. A. (2008). *Understanding peer influence in children and adolescents*. New York: Guilford.

Refinetti, R. (2006). *Circadian Physiology* (2nd ed.). Boca Raton, FL: CRC Press.

Rosenbaum, J. F., Biederman, J., Gersten, M., Hirshfeld, D. R., Meminger, S. R., Kagan, J.,

Reznick, J. S., & Snidman, N. (1988). Behavioral inhibition in children of parents with panic disorder and agoraphobia. *Archives of General Psychiatry, 45*, 463–470.

Saft, E. W., & Pianta, R. C. (2001). Teachers' perceptions of their relationships with students: Effects of child age, gender, and ethnicity of teachers and children. *School Psychology Quarterly, 16*, 125–141.

Sameroff, A. J. (1983). Developmental systems: contexts and evolution. In W. Kessen (Ed.), *Handbook of child psychology: History, theories and methods*, pp. 237–294 (4th ed.). New York: Wiley.

Sameroff, A. J., Peck, S. C., & Eccles, J. S. (2004). Changing ecological determinants of conduct problems from early adolescence to early adulthood. *Development and Psychopathology, 16*, 873–896.

Sameroff, A. J., Seifer, R., Baldwin, A., & Baldwin, C. P. (1993). Stability of intelligence from preschool to adolescence: The influence of social and family risk factors. *Child Development, 64*, 80–97.

Sapolsky, R. M., Romero, L. M., & Munck, A. U. (2000). How do glucocorticoids influence stress responses? Integrating permissive, suppressive, stimulatory, and preparative actions. *Endocrine Reviews, 21*, 55–89.

Scheeringa, M. S., & Zeanah, C. H. (2008). Reconsideration of harm's way: Onsets and comorbidity patterns of disorders in preschool children and their caregivers following hurricane Katrina. *Journal of Clinical Child and Adolescent Psychology, 37*, 508–518.

Thomas J. Schofield, T. J., Parke, R. D., Kim, Y., & Coltrane, S. (2008). Bridging the acculturation gap: Parent-child relationship quality as a moderator in Mexican American families. *Developmental Psychology, 44*, 1190–1194.

Seifer, R., Dickstein, S., Sameroff, A. J. (2008). Providence Family Study, unpublished data.

Seifer, R., Dickstein, S., Wachtel, K., & Belair, R. (2000). Infant sleep and mother symptoms: Actigraph monitoring of infants, mother appraisal of sleep, and mother depression and anxiety. Paper presented at the International Conference on Infant Studies, Brighton, England.

Stark, L. J., Dahlquist, L. M., & Collins, F. L. (1987). Improving children's compliance with diabetes management. *Clinical Psychology Review, 7*, 223–242.

Steinberg, L., & Silk, J. S. (2002). Parenting adolescents. In M. Bornstein (Ed.), *Handbook of parenting*, pp. 103–134, Vol. 1 (2nd ed.). Mahwah, NJ: Lawrence Erlbaum.

Tronick, E. Z. (1989). Emotions and emotional communication in infants. *American Psychologist, 44,* 112–119.

Wahl, A. G., Breckenridge, R. S. & Gunkel, S. E. (2007). Latinos, residential segregation and spatial assimilation in micropolitan areas: Exploring the American dilemma on a new frontier. *Social Science Research, 36,* 995–1020.

Wolfson, A., & Carskadon, M. A. (2003). Understanding adolescents' sleep patterns and school performance: a critical appraisal. *Sleep Medicine Review, 7,* 491–506.

Part III

ENVIRONMENTS

CHAPTER 10

Parental Care and Attachment

Michelle Sleed and Peter Fonagy

The Significance of Parenting for Personality Development

Maccoby (2000) pointed out that there are three primary agents of socialization, at least for children in Western society: families, peer groups, and day care centers or schools. For the best part of the past century both professional and cultural emphasis has been on the family, in other words, the parents, as agents of socialization. Common sense psychological views, as embodied in media messages and legislation, were in agreement with psychological theories in pointing to the quality of parenting as pivotal in shaping an individual's values, beliefs, and character, as well as dysfunctions in adaptation.

There is a wealth of empirical data gathered over the first 100 years of psychology that support the view that the quality of parenting is strongly related to personality development and psychopathology. Throughout the latter part of the last century, it became increasingly well accepted that an association existed between perceptions of parenting, on the one hand, and personality development and levels of psychopathology, on the other (e.g., Parker, 1982; Parker, Barrett, & Hickie, 1992). A range of research methods pointed to the same conclusion: negative parenting was a major contributing factor in the development of individual vulnerability, thus the possible development of mental disorders. The notion that parental rearing behavior might have long-lasting and profound effects on psychosocial development reaches back far before Freud to the educational philosophy of Locke (1693) and Jean-Jacques Rousseau and his writings on educational method (Rousseau, 1762). More systematic interest focusing on developmental aspects dates back to the early 20th century and was linked with the rise of interest in early learning and the influence of early experience. This was attributable, probably in roughly equal measure, to the rise of psychoanalytic theory and the emphasis on learning processes in the psychology of Pavlov, Watson, Skinner, and many others, based on Lockean conceptions.

Early theories and studies based on them tended to adopt strong models of linear causality seeking to identify point-to-point correspondence between parental behaviors and developmental outcomes for the child. The undue emphasis placed upon early training of the child in the process of socialization was then critically scrutinized from conceptual (Swanson, 1961) and empirically based viewpoints (Clarke & Clarke, 1976; Maccoby & Martin, 1983). Here we will briefly summarize some of the more robust classical findings in order to identify conceptual and methodological difficulties with these early investigations. We will also provide a background for current, more theoretically driven perspectives on the ways in which the parenting environment might impact on child development, focusing on the area of research where the influence of parenting has been most reliably demonstrated: the relationship between attachment and parental care.

Patterns of Parenting

It is a reliable observation, for example, that overdependent, fearful, and emotionally labile children are more likely to have had mothers described as overly attentive to dependency needs and punitive for independent actions (Parker, 1983). By contrast, hostile, punitive, shaming, rejecting or overcontrolling parenting techniques have again and again been shown to be more likely to be observed in parents of children manifesting various forms of aggression. This was first identified reliably in the work of Sears and colleagues (1957) but has been replicated across many studies of conduct disorder. For example, in studies of parenting associated with persistent trajectories of physical aggression (Cote et al., 2007), parenting quality was found to mediate the relationship between consistent aggression throughout childhood and qualities of family environment typically associated with aggression (low income, low maternal education, single parenting, young maternal age, maternal depression). The Canadian accelerated longitudinal study of more than 10,000 children was one of many studies to show that developmental trajectories

where aggression remains high between 2 and 11 years of age, rather than desisting trajectories, were associated with fewer positive parent-child interactions, less consistent parenting, less effective family functioning, and above all, parenting that was observed to be both hostile and ineffective (Cote, Vaillancourt, LeBlanc, Nagin, & Tremblay, 2006; see also NICHD Early Child Care Research Network, 2004; Shaw, Gilliom, Ingoldsby, & Nagin, 2003; Tremblay et al., 2004). Although these are recent studies, cross-cultural evidence linking hostile, punitive parenting to childhood aggression goes back to the 1980s (Ekblad, 1988). The flip side of these observations concerns family environments that are warm, positive, and democratic, which have similarly repeatedly been shown to promote intellectual growth, creativity, and motivation in children (Wachs & Gruen, 1982).

Baumrind (1991) offered more systematic classifications in relation to parenting based on natural observations as well as laboratory structural interactions. She identified three main patterns that turned out to be enduring descriptions of key dimensions of parenting style. The first pattern, associated with the most favorable outcomes for children of both genders, was characterized by firm, loving, demanding, and understanding parenting. The second pattern observed in parents of dysphoric, disaffiliated children who often went on to demonstrate antisocial behavior patterns was seen to be punitive, extremely firm, and lacking in affection. Finally, dependent, immature children experienced parenting that lacked control and was only moderately loving, and in which fathers showed ambivalence and a lax attitude. These classical observations have been confirmed with studies repeatedly showing that parental support for the child's autonomy predicts adjustment and achievement, with maternal involvement often found to be specifically predictive of achievement, confidence, and adjustment. Children in families where control is lacking and ambivalence towards the child is marked are more at risk. The observations made in the 1950s by, for example, Sears, Maccoby, and

Lewin on the basis of independent ratings of detailed interviews concerning parenting practices of mothers of kindergarten children, were followed up when these children were in their 40s (Franz, McClelland, & Weinberger, 1991; McClelland & Franz, 1992). Maternal warmth at age 5 was associated with high levels of conventional social accomplishments at age 41. These individuals had long and happy marriages and were more likely to have children, less likely to be divorced or separated, and more involved with close friends outside their marriage. These findings are consistent with the famous Harvard longitudinal studies of Vaillant (1977). Interestingly, in the Sears and Maccoby sample, warm fathers at age 5 predicted that a child would become a generative, hardworking, affectionate, and communicative adult. A striking finding, not frequently replicated, was that parental agreement and parental warmth predicted social accomplishments and adjustment to a greater extent for men than for women (Franz et al., 1994).

In summary, there exists a substantial body of longitudinal data indicating that parenting that is firm, punitive, and hostile is associated with problem behaviors in the child that persist into adulthood, and a parenting environment that lacks control and is only moderately loving may also carry risks, particularly of persistent dependence and relative immaturity. A cold environment has been shown to be associated with low self-esteem and low accomplishment. Most consistently, a pathogenic parenting style appears to be one that combines low care and high protection (Parker, 1990). Families characterized by lack of affection, lack of warmth and closeness, overprotectiveness, intrusiveness and excessive control have been found to be closely linked with negative outcomes. There have been only a limited number of studies where parenting experience was objectively studied at the time of childhood and the child was followed up and systematically assessed in adulthood. The strongest body of literature that speaks to this key empirical domain is attachment theory, and we will review some longitudinal studies carried out within this theoretical framework in the next sections.

Parenting versus Genetics

The optimism in relation to the influence of relational environments gave way to an almost nihilistic attitude as findings from behavior genetic studies increasingly implicated genetic transmission and deemphasized the importance of gross measures of parenting environments. Twin and adoption studies repeatedly demonstrated that most individual difference attributes, including normal personality and various psychological disorders, were best understood as genetically determined. For some time toward the end of the last century it appeared as if research in genetics had all but entirely eclipsed classical socialization theories and refuted all theories that advocated a key role for early family experience (Scarr, 1992). For example, the behavioral geneticist Rowe (1994) wrote that "parents in most working to professional class families may have little influence on what traits their children may eventually develop as adults" (p. 7). He went on to say that he was skeptical that undesirable traits manifested by children could be substantially modified by his or her parents' actions.

There were six key findings that behavioral genetics brought to the table in relation to parenting. These were:

1) The connection between early parenting and socialization outcomes is in general very weak and most observed associations are better interpreted in terms of reverse causality, that is, the child's emerging disorder causes family dysfunction (e.g., Hooley & Richters, 1995).

2) Correlations between early parenting and later child behavior may be seen as arising out of the child's genetic characteristics, which determine differences in parental responses. For example, adoption studies suggest that the parent's report of warmth and negativity and the

child's report of achievement orientation appear to be genetically rooted. The genes that determine parental warmth also cause achievement orientation and a lack of pathology (Deater-Deckard, Fulker, & Plomin, 1999; Losoya, Callor, Rowe, & Goldsmith, 1997). There is increasing evidence that there are substantial genetic influences on parenting, both as reported by parents themselves and as directly observed (Fearon et al., 2006; Neiderhiser, Reiss, & Hetherington, 2007; Spinath & O'Connor, 2003).

3) When variability in a trait is apportioned to genetic effects and environmental effects, environment has been reported to account for around 40 percent of the variability. For example, the heritability estimates for ADHD range between 54 percent and 82 percent, leaving little room for environmental variability, including the parenting environment (Eaves et al., 1997). Even influences that all would expect to be environmental, such as parental reading with a child to accelerate literacy acquisition or the adverse influences of parental divorce, turned out to be genetically mediated (O'Connor, Caspi, DeFries, & Plomin, 2003; Rowe, 1994). Environmental influences associated with parenting that could be confirmed by genetic studies turned out to be nonshared. In twin studies, if a trait under scrutiny is determined by a shared environment, then both monozygotic and dizygotic twins should be correlated on the trait. If the environmental influence is nonshared, then siblings would not be expected to be correlated. Behavior genetic studies repeatedly yield findings suggesting that a shared environment to which both siblings are exposed, such as parental characteristics, account for little or no variability. Plomin (1994) put the general finding quite elegantly: "So often we have assumed that the key influences on children's development are shared: their parents' personality and childhood experiences, the quality of their parents' marriage relationship,

children's educational background, the neighborhood in which they grow up, and their parents' attitude to school or to discipline. Yet to the extent that these influences are shared, they cannot account for the differences we observe in children's outcomes" (p. 23).

4) Finally, it has even been suggested that nonshared environmental effects, that is, the specific ways in which children are treated differently by a parent, may also be best understood as having genetic origins. It is possible that genetically influenced aspects of a child's behavior are responsible for provoking specific responses from a parent, and a sibling without the same genetic predisposition does not cause the parent to behave in that way. For example, studies of adopted children have reported that authoritarian parenting does not cause oppositional behaviors but rather is elicited by them (Ge, Conger, Cadoret, Neiderhiser, & Yates, 1996).

In sum, the lay public as well as scientists have gradually shifted their implicit accounts of developmental problems from those focusing on parents to explanations centered on genetics and brain chemistry. How can we understand this rapid and dramatic shift in our understanding of socialization? The excitement and lure of technological advance and scientific discovery must be part of any account, but perhaps there is more that we should take on board. The reduction of mind to brain chemistry was appealing even to Freud. Whilst our conscious experiences, our genuine experience of free will, and our general sense of subjectivity may be our most treasured possession, our phenomenological world is also the source of all our sadness, misery and pain. The move from parents as causes of disturbance may represent a progressive step in relation to the absurdly parent-blaming, naïve environmental accounts that repeatedly surfaced during the course of the last century. However, the abandonment of social determination of mind in preference for biological models of causation may also be more comfortable for us. Just as blaming parents created a convenient, if unjust, shorthand for understanding misery, so biological reductionism may be a self-serving disservice on our part that disempowers and shifts causality to an inappropriate domain.

The Current Case for Socialization

Methodological improvements in studies of socialization, both in terms of breadth and depth of measurement, have been helpful in creating an effective counterpoint to the behavior genetics influence. For example, there is increasing support for the hypothesis that the influence of macrosocial factors such as socioeconomic disadvantage may be mediated by distortions in intrafamilial relationships, particularly the relationship between the child and the parent. For example, a large scale study of 9,000 children in the United Kingdom involving various family configurations found that the degree of negativity in the children's relationship with their caregiver was related to adjustment outcome regardless of the degree of biological relationship between child and caregiver (Dunn, Deater-Deckard, Pickering, O'Connor, & Golding, 1998). Better controlled studies (see Maccoby, 2000) have produced a number of robust findings on parenting influence, even in genetically informed studies. The influence of parenting is highlighted by studies showing that: (1) parents' childhood relationship experiences with their own parents, influenced child outcomes, with adverse early experiences increasing the likelihood of family conflict and divorce (O'Connor, Thorpe, Dunn, & Golding, 1999); (2) economic and social disadvantage made itself felt on childhood via poorer parenting practices (Hughes, Deater-Deckard, & Cutting, 1999); (3) a parent's selection of a partner with a history of deprivation and disadvantage had a negative impact that was increased by the parent's own history of adverse early experience (Krueger, Moffitt, Caspi, Bleske, & Silva, 1998); (4) the length of time parents spent in their current family setting predicted the quality of their relationship with their child (NICHD Early Child Care Research Network, 2004); (5) biological relatedness enhanced emotional relatedness between parent and child, suggesting an alternative social account of behavioral genetic adoption studies (Dunn, Davies, O'Connor, & Sturgess, 2000); (6) the influence of siblings on development highlights the importance of a systemic perspective and the centrality of a systemic family-wide account moving beyond parenting (Dunn et al., 1998; East & Khoo, 2005).

The strongest evidence for the importance of parenting comes from experimental studies. In both treatment and prevention of psychiatric disorders of childhood it has become increasingly clear that the treatment of parents as well as children is essential for effectiveness. For example, parent training has been shown to have a substantial effect on the outcomes of children with oppositional defiant disorder (Roth & Fonagy, 2005). Some of the most successful long-term treatment prevention programmes have focused attention on parents who were at high risk of providing inadequate parental support to their children, with highly variable results. The parent-nurse partnership has been shown in 3 large scale RCTs to have long term beneficial effects in reducing the risk of criminality and delinquency (Olds, Sadler, & Kitzman, 2007). Recent trials that entail targeting a common vulnerability across parental psychopathology and poor parenting have been particularly encouraging. One study focused on feelings of powerlessness in family relationships experienced by some mothers living in economically difficult circumstances, particularly in the presence of children with difficult temperament. These mothers showed greater levels of stress-induced hormones and behaved in ways that independent observers considered abusive (Martorell & Bugental, 2006). Interventions focused on modifying social cognitions of powerlessness and distress intolerance have been particularly effective in improving child care as well as enhancing the mothers' sense of self-efficacy (Bugental & Schwartz, 2009). Similarly, interpersonal therapy, which targets maternal depression and the challenges the mother experiences engaging with her child, was shown to have a powerful impact on both mother and child. In our own work, we have found parent-infant psychotherapy, focusing simultaneously on the mother's problems and the child's state of mind, to be a potent method for enhancing the child's cognitive development as measured by standardized tests (Fonagy, Sadie, & Allison, 2002).

What we hope the earlier overview has highlighted is the need for a sophisticated understanding, borne out of a relatively complex framework, of the impact of the parenting environment on the child. We have identified four components critical to study of this relationship: (1) a theoretical framework that explains the way parenting may potentially influence child development; (2) an adequate measure of the parenting environment; (3) the availability of longitudinal studies linking parenting to adult behavior; (4) behavior genetics data that precludes a genetic interpretation of the environmental findings. In our view, attachment theory and research provides the most appropriate frame of reference for explaining the relationship between the parenting environment and child development.

Attachment Theory

Attachment theory provides an integrated framework through which parent-child environments and developmental processes can be understood. The attachment relationship between parent and child is thought to provide a template for the child's current and later social and emotional functioning. This relationship is believed to lay the essential foundations upon which self-understanding and understanding of the social world – as well as the patterns or systems that will structure the individual's behavior during interpersonal situations – are later constructed. Furthermore, the quality of the attachment relationship that parents had during their own early experiences with their caregivers is thought to be a crucial factor in determining the quality of the parenting environment they provide to their own children. Attachment theorists have therefore developed techniques that have been used by clinicians and researchers to examine parent-child relationships, to classify the various parenting styles exhibited in these relationships, and to study the effect of these various styles in facilitating or inhibiting a young child's emotional development. In the next sections we will show how attachment theory can be used to assess and understand the parenting environment.

Individual Differences in Patterns of Infant Attachment in Infancy and Preschool

The pioneer of attachment theory, John Bowlby (1958), posited that human infants have developed an adaptive system of parent-directed behaviors that elicit the adult's care and protection. The direct effect of this system, of course, is to improve the infant's immediate chances of physical survival. However, the (for the most part) selective exhibition of such behaviors towards a recognized and consistent caregiver also acts as the basis for the attachment relationship between parent and child, and this relationship provides further emotional and intellectual advantages. Bowlby posited a reciprocal caregiving behavioral system as a complement to this system in the child: an organized system of goal-corrected behaviors that function to provide protection, care, and comfort for the child (Bowlby, 1969; George & Solomon, 2008a). According to attachment theory, infants will form an attachment to a caregiver when they receive some form of regular contact and care from that individual, and it is the child's level of confidence in the availability of the caregiver, and the quality of the care the child receives, that will determine the organization of the infant's attachment system. The Strange Situation Procedure (SSP; Ainsworth, Blehar, Waters, & Wall, 1978) has become the gold standard by which the organization of the infant's attachment to the caregiver is assessed. The procedure involves a series of separations and reunions between the infant and caregiver, sometimes in the presence of an unknown adult, the "stranger." These separations are designed to induce mild levels of fear in the infant, such that the infant's attachment system becomes activated. Trained observers study the infant's behavior during these separations and then use an assessment protocol to classify the infant's attachment patterns.

Three patterns of attachment that infants exhibit towards their caregivers, particularly at the reunion stages of the procedure, were initially observed and described (Ainsworth et al., 1978). The first category, termed *secure*, is characterized by protesting at separation, and proximity seeking and a reduction in negative affect upon reunion with the caregiver. Secure children typically play freely and will engage with the stranger when their caregiver is in the room but show distress in the absence of their caregiver. Upon the caregiver's return, they seek comfort, are easily and quickly soothed and are soon able to resume exploration and play. The second category is insecure- avoidant. These infants typically show no signs of distress during separation and do not seek proximity to the caregiver following reunion. Their overall level of play and exploration is relatively low throughout the assessment. The third category is insecure ambivalent. These infants are distressed when the caregiver leaves the room but upon reunion they demonstrate ambivalence, showing anger and a reluctance to warm to the caregiver and return to play.

Later, in a review of a large number of cases, Main and Solomon (1986, 1990) noted a group of infants whose behavior did not seem to fall into any of the originally identified behavioral categories. This led them to posit a fourth category of *disorganized* attachment. In these cases the infants displayed a perplexing array of often contradictory and inexplicable behaviors such as proximity seeking followed by avoidance or freezing, avoidance coupled with expressions of strong distress; undirected, misdirected, incomplete, or interrupted movements or expressions; asymmetrical movements; mistimed movements; anomalous postures; freezing; stilling; and slowed movement.

A modified version of the Strange Situation and a number of projective measures for assessing older children's attachment representations have been developed (e.g., Bretherton, Ridgeway, & Cassidy, 1990; Cassidy, 1988; Cassidy & Marvin, 1992; George & Solomon, 1990/1996/2000; Green, 2000; Hodges, 1992; Hodges, Hillman, & Steele, 2007; Kaplan, 1987; Slough & Greenberg, 1990). All of these methods of assessment are based on the attachment prototypes described earlier. Although an individual's attachment-related behavior will change as s/he develops over time, regardless of his or her attachment style, the goal of that behavior always remains the same (George & Solomon, 2008a): to elicit protection, care, and comfort from the attachment figure with the goal of achieving a sense of safety on the part of the child.

Internal Working Models of Attachment

In humans, the evolutionary purpose of the attachment relationship is more than merely to secure protection for vulnerable infants: this relationship also provides a medium for the transmission of essential skills, cultural knowledge and values from one generation to the next. According to attachment theorists, the bond between an infant and his or her caregiver plays an important role in facilitating the infant's early psychological, social, emotional, and personality development, and the experience of this early bond will continue to exert an important influence on an individual's development, not only in the immediately subsequent stages of childhood but across the life span. Indeed, research has shown that a great deal of stability exists in an individual's attachment organization from infancy through to adulthood (Main, Hesse, & Kaplan, 2005; Sroufe, 2005). Bowlby (1973) argued that the early attachment relationship furnishes the infant with an important framework for understanding him- or herself and others, and provides a template for subsequent interpersonal relationships. According to Bowlby, the mental representations that individuals develop of themselves and others, termed "internal working models", consist of systems of beliefs, expectations, thoughts, memories, and emotions that are first fashioned during infancy, and shaped by caregiver responses to the infant's behaviors. The internal working models impact on the individual's perceptions of events and behaviors in interpersonal interactions. They enable the individual to understand and predict social encounters. Although the early experiences of an infant with their caregiver form the original basis for these mental representations, they are flexible and can change in response to new experiences; in fact, an individual's internal working models will continue to develop into adulthood and across the life span. They play an important part in determining an individual's understanding of and behavior in other close relationship with peers, romantic partners, and their own children (Bretherton & Munholland, 2008).

Internal working models can be thought of as schematic representations of interpersonal relationship expectations. If attachment in early infancy has an impact on later social, emotional and interpersonal functioning, it is likely that the mediation is via relationship expectations. Internal working models of attachment are thought to account for the continuity in attachment behaviors throughout development and for the influence that early attachment organization appears to have on adult functioning.

Longitudinal Studies of Early Attachment Patterns

Several longitudinal studies of attachment have elucidated some of the outcomes of infant attachment security, insecurity and disorganization in later childhood and adulthood (Bosquet & Egeland, 2006; Carlson, 1998; Dutra, Bureau, Holmes, Lyubchik, & Lyons-Ruth, 2008; Kobak, Cassidy, Lyons-Ruth, & Ziv, 2006; Lyons-Ruth, Alpern, & Repacholi, 1993; Lyons-Ruth, Dutra, Schuder, & Bianchi, 2006; Lyons-Ruth, Easterbrooks, Davidson Cibelli, & Bronfman, 1995 (April); Sroufe, 2005; Sroufe, Egeland, Carlson, & Collins, 2005; Warren, Huston, Egeland, & Sroufe, 1997). In this section, we will illustrate some of these longitudinal findings with a few recent studies.

Secure attachment in infancy has been consistently associated with positive psychological and behavioral outcomes in later years. In the Minnesota Study of Risk & Adaptation from Birth to Adulthood (Bosquet & Egeland, 2006; Sroufe, 2005; Sroufe et al., 2005; Warren et al., 1997), children were recruited in infancy with their families and followed up to age 28; early secure attachment was found to be significantly associated with emotional health, self-esteem, a sense of agency, self-confidence, positive affect, ego resiliency and social competence in childhood and adolescence. Secure attachment style in infancy has also been shown to be a protective factor against later psychopathology (Belsky & Fearon, 2002; Greenberg, 1999). For example, Dallaire and Weinraub (2007) found that attachment security at 15 months may protect children from developing symptoms of anxiety under conditions of high family stress during the preschool years. Although many individuals with histories of insecure attachment do not go on to develop serious behavior problems or psychiatric disturbance later on in life, insecure infant attachment has been shown to be one risk factor for the development of such problems (Sroufe, 2005), and some studies have reported that insecure-avoidant infants are the most vulnerable – relative to infants with all other attachment classifications – to the development of behavioral difficulties and impairments in social competence when exposed to negative contextual and environmental influences (Belsky & Fearon, 2002). In the Minnesota longitudinal study, infants with resistant attachment patterns were found to be significantly more likely than infants with secure or avoidant attachments to be diagnosed with anxiety disorders as adolescents, even when controlling for differences in temperament (Bosquet & Egeland, 2006; Sroufe, 2005; Sroufe et al., 2005; Warren et al., 1997). Children in secure attachment relationships have been found to be better at emotional self-regulation than those with insecure relationships (Thompson & Meyer, 2007). Finally, the following positive outcomes have been shown to be consistently associated with secure infant attachment in a whole series of studies: more positive social relationships, more positive self-concepts, enhanced emotional understanding and social cognition, conscience development, and, possibly even improved memory (see Thompson, 2008 for a review).

Infant disorganized attachment – indicated in the Strange Situation by bizarre infant behavior during reunions with the caregiver, and characterized by controlling and sometimes pseudoparenting types of behavior during middle childhood – has arguably generated the greatest clinical interest compared to other categories of attachment style. Most attachment theorists understand disorganized attachment to be the result of a child's experiences of seeking comfort and reassurance from the very person responsible for causing the fear that activated the attachment system in the first place. The child who is maltreated by adults may feel both an intense need to be comforted by, but also a deep fear of contact with, any adult linked to the abuser by an associative process, for example, gender and appearance. Obviously this is most marked when the attachment figure is him- or herself the abuser.

It is hardly surprising that the long-term outcomes of the disorganized classification have identified this group as most at risk. A number of investigators have found disorganized attachment to be strongly predictive of later psychopathology. For example, Carlson (1998) found that disorganized infants, in comparison to those not classified as disorganized, exhibited significantly more behavior problems, internalizing problems, dissociation, and general psychopathology throughout their development up to age 19. Other longitudinal research has confirmed that early disorganized attachment is associated with an increased risk of later psychopathology relative to nondisorganized attachments (Dutra et al., 2009; Dutra & Lyons-Ruth, 2005; Kobak et al., 2006; Lyons-Ruth et al., 2006; MacDonald et al., 2008; Ogawa, Sroufe, Weinfield, Carlson, & Egeland, 1997; Sroufe, 2005; Sroufe et al., 2005).

The internal working models that are created in early childhood and updated and modified by later experience are thought to be the most likely vehicles through which the early infant-caregiver relationship exerts its long-term influence. The influence and continuity of internal working models make the assessment of these hypothetical structures in later adulthood an important goal in the study of attachment.

Assessing the Working Model of Attachment

In the last two decades, a great deal of interest has been directed towards the assessment of adult attachment representations or internal working models. This has mostly followed from the development of the Adult Attachment Interview (George, Kaplan, & Main, 1985). The AAI is a semistructured interview aimed at assessing an adult's current state of mind regarding their childhood relationship with their caregiver(s). In the interview, adults are asked to provide attachment-related memories from their early childhood and to evaluate these memories from their current perspective. The AAI coding system in its original form, developed by Mary Main and colleagues (Main & Goldwyn, 1993), uses the quality and coherence of the interviewee-delivered narrative, rather than the content of the narrative per se, to classify interviewees' attachment style. Interviewees are grouped into three major categories: autonomous, dismissing, and preoccupied. Those classified as having an autonomous attachment style are distinguished by their largely coherent narratives; the narratives of those with a dismissing attachment style tend to be sparse and patchy and are sometimes explicitly denigrating towards attachment; and the narratives of preoccupied individuals are full of angry and blaming descriptions of early relationships. These categories are roughly analogous, respectively, to the categories of secure, insecure-avoidant, and insecure-ambivalent attachment used with infants. Individuals can also be classified as *unresolved/disorganized*, in addition to one of the other three classifications, if part of their narrative encompasses an episode of loss or abuse, and the description of the episode is qualitatively different from the rest of their account in certain ways, showing lapses in monitoring of reasoning and/or discourse. Hesse and Main (2006) have proposed that individuals who have unresolved experiences of loss or trauma (such as abuse) may become overwhelmed by thinking about the trauma itself or by fragmented memories of the experience, and that this can result in a sudden shift or alteration in the quality of the discourse when such frightening and/or overwhelming feelings are elicited.

A metaanalysis of more than 200 studies that used the AAI on a total of more than 10,000 individuals has recently been carried out (van IJzendoorn & Bakermans-Kranenburg, 2009). This study has confirmed the validity of the AAI, showing that its classifications are largely independent of gender, language, and country of origin, and that it is able to discriminate between different clinical groups. Notwithstanding the very different measurement approaches in the AAI and the Strange Situation, studies have demonstrated a remarkable continuity between early attachment classification using the Strange Situation Procedure and classification of attachment in young adulthood using the AAI. In the absence of major life events, secure attachment behavior observed in infancy translates to coherent adult verbal responses in as many as 80 percent of cases (Hamilton, 2000; Sroufe, 2005; Waters, Merrick, Treboux, Crowell, & Albersheim, 2000; Weinfield, Whaley, & Egeland, 2004). Thus, the AAI can retrospectively provide a measure of the quality of attachment relationships an adult is likely to have experienced in childhood.

The Intergenerational Transmission of Attachment

The AAI has also turned out to be an extraordinarily reliable predictor of the next generation's attachment environment. Soon after the introduction of the AAI 20 years ago, it was shown to be capable of predicting the quality of an infant's attachment to their caregiver even before the birth of the infant (Benoit & Parker, 1994; Fonagy, Steele, & Steele, 1991, 1996; Steele, Steele, & Fonagy, 1996). A secure adult attachment classification seems to provide an indication of the adult's capacity to provide an attachment environment that will engender a secure internal working model in their infant, at least as indicated by the Strange Situation.

In 1995, van IJzendoorn carried out a metaanalysis on a number of studies that had assessed infant and parent attachment status. His metaanalysis revealed a very high correlation between parental adult attachment classification using the AAI and infant attachment classification using the Strange Situation Procedure, where correlation was defined as analogous classification. The two-way classifications (secure/autonomous versus nonsecure/autonomous) corresponded in 75 percent of the 854 parent-infant dyads, and the three-way classifications (all categories except unresolved/disorganized) corresponded in 70 percent of the cases. The correspondence between unresolved status on the AAI and infant disorganization was slightly lower, but still significant.

This impressive continuity of attachment representation/behavior from one generation to the next has stimulated a proliferation of research that has aimed to examine the processes underlying and associated with the intergenerational transmission of attachment patterns. This research is important not only for what it reveals about the means of transmission itself, but also because these processes tell us something about the nature and quality of the parenting environment and the child's everyday lived experiences. Clearly what the research cited earlier seems to demonstrate is that something about an adult's attachment style indexes, or even determines, the attachment environment that their child will experience. If we can understand the exact nature of this influence, and the mechanisms underlying intergenerational transmission, we will also understand a key aspect of how a child develops specific working models and patterns of attachment and how these impact on individual functioning throughout development. In other words, what characteristics of the attachment environment that the parent provides exert an influence on the infant's evolving representations of themselves and of their interpersonal relationships? To answer this question, we will first consider the evidence for genetic transmission and attachment. We will then describe the behavioral and cognitive aspects of parenting that appear to mediate the link between the parent's internal working model of attachment and that of the child. Finally, additional aspects of the parenting environment that may disrupt or indeed increase the likelihood that attachment security will be engendered will be considered.

Genetic Factors Mediating the Intergenerational Transmission of Attachment

The observation of intergenerational transmission clearly raises the question of genetic causation. Several studies have looked at the concordance rate for attachment security in groups differing in biological relatedness. O'Connor and Croft (2001), studied a sample of 57 monozygotic and dizygotic twin pairs and reported concordance rates of 70 percent for monozygotic and 64 percent for dizygotic twins. Bokhorst and colleagues (2003) reported slightly lower concordance rates for monozygotic than dizygotic (56 versus 60 percent). Caspers et al. (2007) reported comparable concordance rates for unrelated, nonbiological and biological siblings. Thus, biological relatedness seems to

have little influence. The impact of genes may be more subtle than behavior genetic studies suggest. It is possible that looking at a molecular genetics level, certain polymorphisms may exist that index an infant's openness to environmental influence. In a review of studies of the behavioral and molecular genetics of attachment, Bakermans-Kranenburg & van IJzendoorn (2007) reported an association between the DRD4 7-repeat polymorphism and an increased risk for disorganized attachment, but only when combined with environmental risk. The studies revealed more negative outcomes for genetically susceptible children in unfavorable environments, but also positive outcomes for susceptible children in favorable environments. Furthermore, it has been reported that infants with the short allele of the *5HTTLPR* gene are more likely to be insecure if their mothers show little sensitivity. Those with the long allele of this gene are equally likely to develop attachment security, regardless of maternal characteristics (Barry, Kochanska, & Philibert, 2008). The impact of the parental environment is likely to be moderated by genetics, with some children apparently impervious to environmental influence, whilst the development of others is affected by the quality of the parenting they receive.

Environmental Factors Mediating the Intergenerational Transmission of Attachment

Attachment and Parental Behavior

Perhaps unsurprisingly, researchers have considered that parents' behavior and responses to their child are the most direct means by which intergenerational transmission of attachment occurs. Very early on in the development of attachment theory, Mary Ainsworth suggested that certain parental behaviors and attributes play a key role in determining the type of attachment style that a child will develop, highlighting a parent's capacity sensitively to interpret the child's cues and communications and respond appropriately as vital for promoting healthy child attachment (Ainsworth, 1976). A large number of studies have subsequently examined this hypothesis, and research has consistently shown a modest link between maternal sensitivity and infant security (see De Wolff & van IJzendoorn, 1997 for a metaanalytic review). Longitudinal studies have also highlighted the importance of parental behavior beyond early infancy. In the Minnesota Study of Risk and Adaptation from Birth to Adulthood (Bosquet & Egeland, 2006; Warren et al., 1997; Sroufe 2005), the power of secure infant attachment status to predict positive adult outcomes was enhanced when indicators of the quality of subsequent care were factored into the calculation. In the study, as the children grew older, the effects of early security became more and more subject to mediation/moderation by subsequent relational influences.

The development of the AAI has led researchers to investigate the link between parental attachment status on the AAI and parental behavioral sensitivity towards infants. A large number of studies have found an association between autonomous AAI classifications and optimal parental behaviors. Specifically, mothers classified as autonomous have been found to be more responsive, sensitive, warm, attuned, perceptive, and willing to provide help and support to their infants and toddlers than nonautonomous parents (Adam, Gunnar, & Tanakar, 2004; Crowell & Feldman, 1988; DeOliveira, Moran, & Pederson, 2005; Grossman, Fremmer-Bombik, Rudolph, & Grossman, 1988; Macfie, McElwain, Houts, & Cox, 2005; Ward & Carlson, 1995).

In his metaanalysis of the intergenerational transmission of attachment, van IJzendoorn (1995) investigated the role of maternal sensitivity in relation to both adult and infant attachment. He found that parental sensitive responsiveness could explain a modest amount of the concordance between parent and child attachment, but not all. He termed the protective and risk factors that play a part in the intergenerational transmission of attachment patterns but were not accounted for by most indices

of parental sensitivity the "transmission gap." The association between maternal sensitivity and infant attachment is far less robust in clinical and lower SES samples (De Wolff & van IJzendoorn, 1997; True, Pisani, & Oumar, 2001; Ward & Carlson, 1995), and it is less useful in explaining the association of parental unresolved loss or trauma and infant disorganized attachment patterns (van IJzendoorn, Scheungel, & Bakermans-Kranenburg, 1999).

More recent research into higher-risk populations has led to the identification of a wider range of behaviors that are now thought to link less optimal parental attachment representations and infant attachment, and are particularly helpful in accounting for the association between the unresolved/disorganized category in parents and disorganized attachment in the next generation. Main and Hesse (1990; 1992) hypothesized that parents who have experienced trauma or loss, and whose traumatic experiences remain unresolved, are prone to fleeting frightening, frightened, and/or dissociated behaviors in their interactions with their child. They termed these behaviors "FR" behaviors (Hesse & Main, 1999), and they argued that these temporary FR behaviors that occur during unresolved parents' behavioral interactions with their children echo the temporary manifestations of partially dissociated frightening ideation that occur during an unresolved adult's performance on the AAI. According to Hesse and Main, since the attachment figure is also normally the one who provides comfort and protection for the child during times of heightened arousal, and since this is how the attachment figure is perceived by the child themselves, when an unresolved parent exhibits FR behavior towards the child he or she is experienced by the child as simultaneously the source of fear and the provider of the means by which that fear is regulated. This paradox is thought to impede the child's ability to form an organized attachment system.

Lyons-Ruth and colleagues outlined other behaviors that they hypothesized were associated with both parental and infant attachment disorganization (Bronfman, Parsons, & Lyons-Ruth, 1999; Lyons-Ruth, 2001; Lyons-Ruth & Jacobvitz, 2008). They hypothesized that, in addition to frightened, frightening and dissociated behavior, parents with unresolved attachment may display contradictory or competing caregiving strategies towards their infants, which parallel the contradictory behaviors displayed by infants classified as disorganized in the strange situation. Concrete examples of these lapses, which they termed "affective communication errors," include incongruent physical and verbal behaviors, missed cues, or inappropriate responses to infant cues. In addition, these authors emphasize the importance of the parent's overall ability to regulate infant arousal under stressful conditions in facilitating secure infant attachment. They suggest that parental withdrawal or role-reversing behaviors, especially during times of heightened attachment arousal, would also hinder the parent's capacity adequately to regulate and respond to their child. Lyons-Ruth and colleagues have developed a coding system to classify and rate the parental behaviors of unresolved parents, which they call the Atypical Maternal Behavior Instrument for Assessment and Classification (AMBIANCE; Bronfman et al., 1999).

The parental behaviors described by Main and Hesse and Lyons-Ruth and colleagues have been shown to be consistently associated with both parental unresolved status and infant disorganization (Abrams, Rifkin, & Hesse, 2006; Goldberg, Benoit, Blokland, & Madigan, 2003; Jacobvitz, Leon, & Hazen, 2006; Lyons-Ruth, Bronfman, & Parsons, 1999; Madigan, Moran, & Pederson, 2006; Madigan, Moran, Schuengel, Pederson, & Otten, 2007; Schuengel, Bakermans-Kranenburg, & van IJzendoorn, 1999; Schuengel, Bakermans-Kranenburg, van IJzendoorn, & Blom, 1999; True et al., 2001). Hesse and Main's hypothesis that FR behavior is the main mediator between parental unresolved status and infant disorganization was not fully borne out by the data: a metaanalysis by (Madigan, Bakermans-Kranenburg et al., 2006) found that FR behavior only partially explained the association between parental unresolved

status and infant attachment disorganization, accounting for 42 percent of the variance. A handful of studies have found that unresolved parents who have a secondary classification as secure demonstrate less frightened or frightening behavior towards their infants and/or are less likely to have infants classified as disorganized (Heinicke et al., 2006; Hesse, 2008; Jacobvitz et al., 2006; Schuengel, Bakermans-Kranenburg, & van IJzendoorn, 1999), suggesting that a parent's underlying secure-autonomous state of mind with respect to attachment may be a protective factor for the child when the parent is also unresolved in relation to loss or trauma.

Some advances have been made in our understanding of the parenting environment in relation to both adult and child attachment. It has been shown that parental secure-autonomous attachment representations and subsequent sensitive and responsive behavior towards the child is important for the child's development of a secure attachment. Conversely, insecure and particularly unresolved attachment representations, in conjunction with insensitive and/or frightened, frightening, dissociated, withdrawn, or role reversed behavior, are likely to lead to less optimal and possibly disorganized attachments in the child. Table 10.1 summarizes the features of the parenting environment typically associated with these two streams of attachment transmission (secure versus insecure attachment and disorganized attachment). Despite these theoretical advances, the transmission gap cannot be fully explained in terms of observed parental behavior.

Parent-child Attachment Representations

Following the advent of the AAI, a wave of research began to examine internal working models of attachment and methods of assessing such representations, and eventually some of this research began to focus on the more direct representational processes of current parent-child relationships. It is now recognized that the parenting environment cannot be defined in behavioral

Table 10.1: **Features of Parenting Behavior Associated with Infant Attachment Classifications**

Secure vs. Insecure	Disorganized
• Sensitivity to infant cues	• Frightening behavior
• Responsiveness to infant cues	• Frightened behavior
• Contingency of response	• Dissociation
• Structuring/ support	• Withdrawal
• Noninstrusiveness	• Role reversal
• Nonhostility	• Treats child as sexual partner
• Synchrony	• Contradictory signals to infant
• Mutuality	• Nonresponsiveness to infant
• Cooperation	cues
• Physical contact/ stimulation	• Inappropriate responses to
• Positive attitude	infant cues or needs

Sources: Biringen, Robinson, & Emde, 1993, 2000; Biringen, Robinson, & Emde, 2008; Bronfman et al., 1999; De Wolff & van IJzendoorn, 1997; Hesse & Main, 2006.

terms alone and that a representational intersubjective link must also be considered when the emotional environment of the young child is being evaluated. Edward Tronick was perhaps the first to bring research results together that pointed to a coconstructed consciousness between parent and child (Tronick, 2001, 2003, 2005). These ideas have much in common with Kochanska's notion of mutually responsive orientation: a positive, mutually binding, and mutually cooperative relationship between parent and child (Kochanska, 1997; Kochanska, Aksan, Prisco, & Adams, 2008). From this perspective, the child's environment is best conceptualized as a combination of the physical and the psychological, where the latter is thought about in terms of the correspondence between the caregiver and child's psychological awareness of each other. What is crucial to the evaluation of this environment is the parents' awareness of the child as a psychological being, and of themselves as parents relating to that individual's experience.

A number of theorists have developed methods for assessing parents' representations of themselves as parents and of their relationship with their child (see George & Solomon, 2008a for a review). Most of these have structured their understanding

of parental representations in parallel to the infant and adult attachment classifications from the SSP and AAI, that is, by categorizing individuals into the four attachment groups. In Table 10.2 we have summarized the characteristics of the various parental representations belonging to each of the four categories, as elicited or revealed by the Working Model of the Child Interview (Zeanah, Benoit, Hirshberg, Barton, & Regan, 1994), the Insightfulness Assessment (Koren-Karie, Oppenheim, Dolev, Sher, & Etzion-Carasso, 2002; Oppenheim, Koren-Karie, & Sagi, 2001), and the Caregiving Interview (George & Solomon, 1996; Solomon & George, 1996).

In an attempt to elaborate our understanding of the process by which adult attachment is related to next generation parent-child relationships, it has been proposed that parents' capacity for mentalization, or their Reflective Functioning (RF) is an important mediating factor (Fonagy, Steele, Moran, Steele, & Higgitt, 1991). These ideas emerged from a study of parental attachment during pregnancy and subsequent child attachment. It was found that the extent to which parents were able to understand their childhood relationships in terms of their own and their caregivers' mental states, as elucidated during the AAI,

Table 10.2: Features of Parental Representations Associated with Infant Attachment Classifications

Secure	Avoidant	Resistant	Disorganized
• Emotional warmth • Acceptance • Sensitivity to infant needs • Expresses a broad range of emotions • Mutual enjoyment • Trust • Reflective • Positive and negative behaviors and emotions acceptable	• Minimizing of affect • Idealization • Distancing • Rejection of child's needs • Rational problem solving • Value child's independence • Superficial descriptions • Pseudoattachment	• Confusion/ uncertainty • Anxiety • Overwhelmed by child's needs • Heightened arousal • Blurred boundaries (mild role reversal) • Difficulty balancing child's needs with own	• Mixed representations • Helplessness • Frightening content • Power struggles • Role reversal • Abdication from caregiving role

Sources: George & Solomon, 2008b; Koren-Karie et al., 2002; Oppenheim & Koren-Karie, 2002; Oppenheim et al., 2001; Zeanah et al., 1993; Zeanah et al., 1994.

predicted child attachment security even more strongly than parental attachment security. RF refers to an essential human capacity to understand behavior in terms of underlying mental states and intentions. The capacity to mentalize is intrinsic to the ability to form productive social relationships as well as to affect regulation, and failures in the development of mentalizing capacity have been associated with later psychopathology (Fonagy, Gergely, Jurist, & Target, 2002; Fonagy, Steele, Moran et al., 1991; Fonagy, Stein, Allen, & Fultz, 2003; Fonagy, Target, Steele, & Steele, 1998).

Recent findings from neuroimaging studies have suggested that humans have a fundamental capacity to envision and understand others as psychological, intentional beings who can evaluate, anticipate and decide on a course of action (Buccino et al., 2001; Decety, Chaminade, Grezes, & Meltzoff, 2002; Gallese, 2005; Gallese, Fadiga, Fogassi, & Rizzolatti, 1996; Iacoboni et al., 2005; Rizzolatti & Craighero, 2004). One study found that the anterior insular in the brain is activated in the same way when one directly experiences disgust or feelings of rejection as it is when one observes these feelings in others via visible emotional displays (Eisenberger, Lieberman, & Williams, 2003; Wicker et al., 2003). Such findings

suggest, as one author asserted, that "human brains are built for intersubjectivity, or the ability to understand other people and to imagine interactions with them through embodied (and experiential) simulation" (Bretherton & Munholland, 2008, p. 110).

Assessment of parental reflective functioning has been extended beyond the methods employed in the Fonagy study (in which adults' representations of their childhood relationships with their parents were investigated) and recent studies have targeted parental representations of their current relationships with their own children. Slade and colleagues, most notably, have developed a parent-child relationship representation-based RF coding system in conjunction with a new instrument, the Parent Development Interview, which is used to elicit these representations (PDI; Aber, Slade, Berger, Bresgi, & Kaplan, 1985; Slade, 2005; Slade, Aber, Bresgi, Berger, & Kaplan, 2004; Slade, Bernbach, Grienenberger, Levy, & Locker, 2004) by adapting the childhood-relationship representation-based RF coding system employed in the Fonagy study (Fonagy, Steele, Steele, & Target, 1997). This important methodological innovation by Slade et al. has enabled a more direct assessment of a parent's capacity to reflect on the child's internal experience, a parental skill that is considered important in promoting not only infant secure attachment, but also a range of other positive developmental outcomes in the child, including the acquisition of mentalizing capacities (Fonagy, Gergely et al., 2002; Sharp & Fonagy, 2008; Sharp, Fonagy, & Goodyer, 2006; Slade, 2005).

A series of studies of parental RF have highlighted its importance in determining the quality of the parenting environment, and particularly in the intergenerational transmission of attachment. Slade and colleagues (Slade, Grienenberger, Bernbach, Levy, & Locker, 2005) carried out a preliminary investigation into the role of parental RF, assessed with the PDI, in mediating the so-called transmission gap between adult and child attachment. They found that parental RF was related to both adult attachment (measured in pregnancy) and infant attachment (measured at 14 months). In addition, their findings suggested that parental reflective functioning may play a crucial role in mediating the transmission of attachment across generations. Another study of the same sample (Grienenberger, Kelly, & Slade, 2005) examined the link between parental RF, parental behavior measured on the AMBIANCE (described earlier), and child attachment. Findings from this study showed that maternal behavior on the AMBIANCE mediated the link between parental RF and child attachment. In other words, an association between low levels of parental RF and less optimal, especially disorganized, attachment in the child could be accounted for by the mother's affective communication errors and frightened, frightening, dissociated, withdrawn, or role-reversed behavior toward the child.

A number of other theorists have developed methods for assessing parental representations that focus on the capacity to consider their child's and their own thoughts, feelings and intentions (see Sharp & Fonagy, 2008 for a review). Despite slight differences of approach, these have all been shown to relate to the infant's capacity to form a secure attachment. For example, the Insightfulness Assessment (Koren-Karie et al., 2002; Oppenheim, Goldsmith, &

Koren-Karie, 2004; Oppenheim, Koren-Karie, Dolev, & Yirmiya, 2009; Oppenheim, Koren-Karie, Etzion-Carasso, & Sagi-Schwartz, 2005; Oppenheim et al., 2001) assesses the parent's capacity to understand their own and their child's emotions and intentions while talking about a recently video-recorded interaction between them and their child. This is in contrast to the more generalized working models that an interview such as the PDI taps. "Mind-mindedness" (Meins & Fernyhough, 1999; Meins, Fernyhough, Fradley, & Tuckey, 2001; Meins, Fernyhough, Russel, & Clark-Carter, 1998; Meins et al., 2003; Meins et al., 2002), in contrast, is assessed by looking at the parent's use of mental state language during an interaction with the child. This approach lies more in the realm of behavioral interaction than the representational working models, but we believe that it is related to the same underlying processes. Bowlby proposed two modes by which parental internal working models of attachment relationships are passed on to the child: through the quality of behavioral interaction, and through caregivers providing verbal discussions of emotions and relationships (Bowlby, 1973, 1988; Bretherton & Munholland, 2008). It is probably the latter that the mind-mindedness concept relates to. Using a similar interview method to that of the PDI, the Meta-Emotion Interview (Katz & Gottman, 1986; Katz, Gottman, Shapiro, & Carrere, 1997) is used to assess a parent's awareness of their own and their child's emotions, and of their descriptions of coaching child emotions. This concept of "metaemotion philosophy" has, as with the other concepts described earlier, been linked with parental attachment (DeOliveira et al., 2005) and parent-child interaction (Gottman, Katz, & Hooven, 1997; Hooven, Gottman, & Katz, 1995).

We are beginning to uncover converging lines of evidence that the quality of the parent's cognitive and emotional representations of the child's mind directly translate into the child's own self-representations. If we assume that the child is learning about themselves, and particularly about how their mind functions, not through a simple process of internal self-recognition but instead through an intersubjective process, then it becomes clear why the quality of maternal representations of the child's mind might make such a big difference. Recently, developmental theorists have turned to the ideas of human pedagogy and attachment as a framework for understanding this intersubjective development of the self.

The Pedagogical Stance, Attachment, and the Parenting Environment

The theory of human pedagogy (Csibra & Gergely, 2006; Gergely & Csibra, 2005) provides one framework to explore and illuminate the role that mentalization, as well as particular aspects of caregiving behavior, play in a child's social-cultural and self-development. Pedagogy refers to the collaborative process by which information is transmitted from a knowledgeable figure to an ignorant figure or group. According to the theory of human pedagogy, this process is biologically hard-wired to occur between infants and caregivers, triggered by a primary cognitive system that then facilitates the process and allows it to be performed efficiently (Csibra & Gergely, 2006; Gergely & Csibra, 2006). The caregiver is biologically directed to act in the role of the "teacher"/pedagogue, and to make use of pedagogical communicative cues that the infant is biologically conditioned to receive. These "ostensive cues" made by the caregiver signal to the infant that the adult has an overt communicative intent that is specifically addressed to him or her. Ostensive cues, which are usually made in conjunction with the establishment of eye-contact (which is in itself an ostensive cue), include the raising of the eyebrows, the brief widening or shrinking of the eyes, the tilting of the head slightly forward towards the infant, the calling of the infant's name, and the adoption of the speech intonation pattern of "motherese" or baby-talk. Infants have an innate sensitivity to and preference for these ostensive cues (Gergely & Csibra, 2005), and these cues trigger them to adopt the "pedagogical

stance." This specific receptive attentional and interpretive attitude is characterized by the awareness that new and relevant knowledge is about to be communicated and also that the communication is specifically addressed to the infant.

The pedagogical process that occurs between infants and caregivers serves as more than a means for the transfer of knowledge about the external world: it also transfers knowledge about the internal world. Through a kind of pedagogical process, according to the theory, a child learns to envision a subjective self and to construct second-order representations of their own internal states (Fonagy, Gergely, & Target, 2007). A number of developmental theorists have proposed that infants, rather than being introspectively aware of their differential emotional states from birth, instead only learn over time to differentiate the internal patterns that characterize different feelings, and that this learning process takes place through caregiver interactions, as the caregiver facially and vocally mirrors the infant's feelings/internal states back to them and thereby provides the infant with objective signifiers by which these internal states can be differentiated and coded (Gergely & Watson, 1996, 1999; Legerstee & Varghese, 2001; Meltzoff, 1990; Mitchell, 1993; Schneider-Rosen & Cicchetti, 1991). By consistently and accurately mirroring the baby's internal states, as revealed by their automatic emotion-expressive displays, the caregiver provides the baby with the tools to develop introspectively accessible second-order representations of their primary emotional states (Gergely & Watson, 1996). By making that mirroring contingent on and directly responsive to the infant's emotional states over time, moreover, the caregiver furnishes the infant with the experience of having his or her emotions responded to directly, and in a sense, influenced and managed; the infant is made to experience having their emotions externally regulated, and this experience facilitates the development of later emotional *self*-regulation (Fonagy, Gergely et al., 2002). As with the transfer of knowledge about the external world, this transfer of knowledge about the internal world (and how to manage it) is facilitated by infant-directed ostensive cues, which in this case are given in conjunction with the acts of affective mirroring. In this case, however, the infant is directed by these ostensive cues to adopt a pedagogical stance that is partially inward-directed: the object to which the caregiver's instruction refers is the infant's own subjective self-states, and the skills the infant is taught involve acting on these subjective self-states, either by constructing second-order representations of these states or by actively regulating and manipulating them.

A parent's acts of affective mirroring must satisfy a number of criteria if they are to effectively enable the infant to understand and regulate his or her emotions. Firstly, mirroring must be *contingent* to the state of the infant so that, noticing the parallel transformations between internal state and mirroring act, the infant will be able to make the inference that they are associated (Gergely, Koós, & Watson, 2002). Secondly, the mirroring must be *congruent* so that the caregiver accurately mirrors the infant's mental state. Finally, though mirroring must be broadly congruent with the infant's mental state, it must at the same time be "marked," whereby the caregiver expresses an affect and at the same time indicates that it is not his or her own mental state being expressed (Gergely & Watson, 1996, 1999). Marking can be considered a special kind of ostensive cuing: it employs many of the same cues (such as the establishment of eye contact, the raising of the eyebrows, the narrowing or widening of the eyes, the tilting forward of the head) that are characteristic of human pedagogy. The "marked" form of the parent's mirrored emotional expression and the other ostensive cues enable the infant to distinguish it from expressions of the parent's own emotion state. As the parent's eye gaze will be focused on the infant while displaying marked affect mirroring, the infant, in the pedagogical stance, will direct his attention to his own physical self, rather than the world at large, as the locus of meaning to which the caregiver's

communications refer. In this way the child gradually comes to be able to symbolize his own mental states and to develop the capacity to regulate these.

The development of the theory of human pedagogy and the recent shift towards viewing social-cognitive and self-development as intersubjective processes have highlighted the significance of early attachment relationships and the parenting environment for the child's development (Gergely & Unoka, 2008). It has been suggested that, from an evolutionary perspective, infants may be more prepared to respond to overt pedagogical cues when these are from a known and trusted adult with whom they have an attachment bond (Fonagy et al., 2007). It has also been suggested, and largely accepted, that the nature of both a parent's behavior and the representational model they have constructed of their child play a crucial role in determining their capacity to perform effective (in the sense of developmentally facilitative) marked affect mirroring. Maternal sensitivity is conceptualized as a mother's accuracy in perceiving and interpreting her infant's cues (congruence) and her ability to react to them in a timely and appropriate manner (contingency) (Ainsworth et al., 1978). Thus, the defining features of a sensitive parenting environment are also characteristic of effective marked affect mirroring. Additionally, by definition, congruence in parental affect mirroring depends on the parent's capacity to accurately interpret the infant's mental state, that is, to mentalize. Expressions of affective responses by the parent that are not contingent to or congruent with the infant's affect will undermine the infant's capacity to establish introspectively accessible second-order representations for their internal states, and the result is that these states will remain confusing and will be experienced as unsymbolized and hard to regulate. This may be the reason why attachment security, which has been empirically shown to be associated with a sensitive parenting environment where parents are able to reflect on their child's thoughts and feelings, appears also to be a protective factor against contextual risk and later internalizing and externalizing symptoms (Belsky & Fearon, 2002; Dallaire & Weinraub, 2007; Greenberg, 1999; Sroufe et al., 2005) and emotion dysregulation (Thompson & Meyer, 2007). The fact that maternal sensitivity is also likely to be associated with more effective pedagogical strategies for teaching the infant may also account for the broad and generic intellectual benefits that have been associated with attachment security. The combination of the human infant's dependence on the caregiver for information about the world and their need for physical welfare and comfort has created an alignment of cultural (cognitive) and emotional development. The caregiver's sensitivity creates a sense of being known that in turn generates an epistemic trust in the child towards the specific adult from whom knowledge can be safely acquired. As we have seen, this necessarily embraces knowledge about the world as well as knowledge about the self.

The intergenerational transmission of more extreme impairments in social cognitive development and affect regulation and of attachment disorganization can also be understood in light of this theoretical framework. An adult whose early experiences were with a parent who was not able to effectively understand and re-present to them their thoughts, feelings and emotions, may not have been able to develop the strategies to effectively regulate their affective states under conditions of heightened arousal. When this adult becomes a parent, disruptions in their capacity to regulate their own states of arousal may impinge on their capacity to provide the marked affect mirroring that the infant needs when the attachment and caregiving systems are activated. As the parent has not developed the second order, symbolized representations of their own emotional states that would enable them to regulate their emotions effectively, they may experience their infant's expressions of dysregulated negative affective states in a manner that is undifferentiated from their own

arousal states. This would mean that their mirrored expressions towards the infant would lack the marking that would enable the infant to distinguish between the parent's affect and their own. In the presence of such a caregiver, affective stimulation will not provide the infant with the opportunity of learning to form second-order representations of their internal states, or of developing a sense of control over those states, but will merely trigger ever-increasing affective arousal. The infant will therefore, over time, develop the same impairments as the parent, and by the same process will cause such impairments to develop in their own children.

This theory offers us a way to understand the observed frightened, frightening and dissociated parenting behavior associated with disorganized attachment relationships (Hesse & Main, 1999; Hesse & Main, 2006; Lyons-Ruth & Jacobvitz, 2008); unmarked affective responses to infant fear will place the infant in a disorganizing attachment position of seeking comfort from somebody who is simultaneously a source of fear. In addition, it is proposed that the lapses of monitoring in reasoning associated with unresolved classifications on the AAI are caused by dysregulation, especially around fearful affect (Hesse & Main, 2000; Main & Hesse, 1990). It is likely that a process of mutual dysregulation at times of arousal is the disorganizing element for both parent and child. This theoretical framework also enables us to comprehend the feelings of helplessness that parents of disorganized infants tend to exhibit in their attachment-related representations (George & Solomon, 1999; George & Solomon, 2008a; Lyons-Ruth, Bronfman, & Atwood, 1999; Lyons-Ruth, Yellin, Melnick, & Atwood, 2005; Solomon & George, 1999a), which may relate to memories of unprocessed states of arousal and the parent's lack of effective strategies to regulate either her baby's emotions or her own. Furthermore, the extreme role-reversal seen in the parental behavior (Lyons-Ruth & Jacobvitz, 2008) and representations (George & Solomon, 2008b; Macfie et al., 2005; Solomon &

George, 2006) of disorganized attachment relationships may relate to the limited capacity of both caregiver and child to differentiate between the internal states of self and other.

Factors Moderating the Intergenerational Transmission of Attachment

We have described certain mechanisms that have been proposed to explain how attachment in early infancy continues to influence the individual throughout the life span and into the next generation. We will now turn to two further features of the parenting environment that are relevant in the investigation of early attachment and development: parental psychopathology and the parental couple relationship.

Parental Psychopathology

As we have outlined earlier, insecure and especially disorganized patterns of attachment in infancy are associated with psychopathology in adulthood. Adult attachment classifications have also been associated with different forms of psychopathology. For example, insecure adults are more likely to experience depressive symptoms; preoccupied and unresolved adults are more likely to have internalizing disorders (e.g., borderline personality disorders); dismissing and preoccupied status has been shown to correlate with diagnosis of externalizing disorders (e.g., antisocial personality disorders); and identification of unresolved loss or trauma with the AAI has been shown to correlate with history of abuse and posttraumatic stress (van IJzendoorn & Bakermans-Kranenburg, 2009). Since, therefore, it can be assumed that certain patterns of *parental* attachment and certain kinds of *parental* psychopathology co-occur, it seems reasonable to hypothesize that they may function together in establishing particular patterns in the quality of the parenting environment. We will present two recent studies that illustrate the impact of parents'

psychological and emotional well-being in the attachment relationship.

Parental attachment status has been shown to relate to both adult emotional well-being and the quality of parenting behavior. There is also substantial evidence to suggest that parental emotional well-being is directly related to quality of parenting. Adam and colleagues (Adam et al., 2004) carried out a study of how these three factors (adult attachment status, adult emotion, and parenting quality) interact. They were particularly interested in exploring whether adult attachment style and quality of parenting were independently related, or if this association was mediated or moderated by adult emotional state. They found that preoccupied individuals both demonstrated greater levels of anger and intrusiveness towards their infants, and tended to have higher levels of emotional distress than parents with other attachment classifications. Despite this, the parent emotion variables did not mediate the relationship *between* adult attachment and the quality of parenting behavior. In other words, the association between adult attachment and angry/intrusive parenting was independent of maternal emotion. They did, however, find that parents with a dismissing attachment classification and moderate to high levels of depression showed less warmth and responsiveness to their infants. The results of this study indicate that parental emotion is not likely to be the primary mechanism by which adult attachment status impacts parental behavior and, by extension, parent-child interaction quality, but that some aspects of parents' internal working models and emotional states may have a cumulative effect on the quality of the parenting environment. Further studies are still required in clinical and high-risk populations so that the interactions between high levels of parental psychopathology and attachment disorganization can be fully explored.

In another study, this one carried out with a higher-risk sample, Hughes and colleagues (Hughes, Turton, Mcgauley, & Fonagy, 2006) prospectively followed mothers who had experienced a miscarriage through to, and over the first year following, a subsequent pregnancy. They reported a significant association between unresolved status in relation to the miscarriage (or in relation to some other trauma) and disorganization of the infant. Interestingly though, unresolved mothers whose children were not classified as disorganized reported significantly higher levels of depression and of intrusive thoughts during pregnancy, and showed higher levels of intrusive thoughts when the infant was 1 year old, than unresolved mothers of disorganized infants. To explain this somewhat counterintuitive finding, the authors suggested that depression, and the experiencing of painful intrusive thoughts, may protect the mother from the dissociated state of mind that leads to infant disorganization. Thus, maternal depression may actually constitute an adaptive emotional strategy in cases of maternal trauma, one that serves to minimize subsequent risk to the infant.

The Parental Couple Relationship

According to a number of attachment theorists, the quality of the relationship between parents will influence the quality of care that the parents provide to their children (Bowlby, 1969; Gable, Belsky, & Crnic, 1992). The parental couple relationship has been shown in some studies to influence the effect of parental attachment on the parenting environment and on child attachment. For example Cohn, Cowan, Cowan, & Pearson (1992) found that mothers of preschoolers whose partners were secure tended to be warmer and better able to provide structure to their child than those whose partners were insecure, even if the mother herself was classified as insecure. These findings indicate that the risk posed by insecure parental attachment status in relation to parenting quality is more pronounced when both parents are insecure. Das Eiden, Teti, & Corns (1995) examined the effects of marital adjustment on the relation between parental and child attachment security. They found that children of insecure mothers who reported good levels of marital adjustment were more likely to have a secure

attachment than those of insecure mothers with poor marital adjustment. Other aspects of the parental relationship that have been found to be important for the child's attachment and parenting environment include level of cooperativeness between parents, and the predisposition of parents to cancel out or override each other's insensitivity as it arises (Cowan, Bradburn, & Cowan, 2005; Edwards, Eiden, & Leonard, 2006; Solomon & George, 1999b). The findings of the studies cited earlier indicate more specifically, as do the findings of the Das Eiden study, that certain positive qualities of the marital relationship can act as a protective factor against the potentially negative effects of parental attachment insecurity.

In summary, there is some evidence to indicate that both parental psychopathology and the quality of the parental couple relationship can influence the effect of the parent-child attachment relationship on the developing child, and that disturbances in the emotional well-being of parents, or in the quality of the romantic partnership between parents, can distort the child's attachment relationship with them because these difficulties may distort the functioning of the attachment system in the parent. Conflict between two parents, by creating a temporary disorganization of their romantic attachment relationship, might, for example, undermine the attachment system in one or both of them and activate insecure aspects of their internal working models, which will in turn have an effect on the interactions between these parents and their children. The caregiving behavioral system, which works in tandem with the child's attachment system, is only one of several organized behavioral systems that influence adult behavior. For example, caregivers have relationships and affiliations with other children, friends, jobs, and partners, all of which have a different set of goals and different organizations that underpin behavior, and that at times may be in competition with each other (George & Solomon, 2008a). Disruptions in the romantic partnership system may therefore disrupt the caregiving behavioral system.

Summary and Conclusion

In this chapter we have presented a brief historical background to how the parenting environment has been understood and we have outlined some of the most recent knowledge that contemporary attachment theory and research has elucidated. Despite various technological and epistemological advances, attachment theory has continued to provide the strong theoretical framework that encapsulates human development across the life span, the rigorous observational methods, and the flexibility that is required to expand our understanding of the parenting environment and human development.

We have described some of the mechanisms that have been hypothesized to underlie and shape the parenting environment – structures including working models of attachment and attachment-related behavioral systems. The empirical work in this area has shown that the eventual acquisition of healthy and flexible internal working models (regarding both interpersonal relationships and the self) depends, in large part, on the existence of early secure attachments with sensitive caregivers. The security of a child's early attachment, in turn, depends on their caregiver's internal working model of their child, which depends in large part on the caregiver's own internal working model of attachment, based on their experiences throughout their own development. We have shown that the parenting environment is shaped by both behavioral and cognitive factors, and that they can communicate with the child from a very early stage by the pedagogic stance. Attachment theory has provided us with some insight into how early intersubjective experiences in the parenting environment are linked with a broad range of developmental outcomes, and how, for example, impingements in the attachment relationship can have a deleterious effect on social-cognitive development. We are just beginning to recognize the importance of social cognition for adaptive social and emotional functioning, and how disruptions

in the development of these capacities can be linked to some psychological disorders (Fonagy & Sharp, 2008). It seems, though, that if there are no impingements on a parent's capacity to hold the child's mind in mind, if parents are able to respond sensitively to their child's emotional displays and to use a pedagogical stance effectively, the environmental prerequisites for developing a sense of self are present. The quality of the attachment relationship that exists between parent and infant is determined by the quality of the intersubjective connection between them. The infant is able to discover the world and its culture-specific and almost infinitely variable features through their relationship with a trusted adult who provides reliable emotional and cognitive information with which they can construct a representation of their external, physical and interpersonal, as well as internal psychological and embodied worlds. The quality of the early environment and the quality of key early social relationships determines the extent to which the child feels open to learning about that environment. An individual's degree of openness, as they become adults, may, as we have seen, determine their pedagogical proficiency with their own children, passing on knowledge as well as a mentalizing stance from generation to generation.

References

Aber, J. L., Slade, A., Berger, B., Bresgi, I., & Kaplan, M. (1985). The parent development interview. Unpublished manuscript.

Abrams, K., Rifkin, A., & Hesse, E. (2006). Dissociative "FR" parental behavior observed in a laboratory play session predicts infant disorganization. *Development and Psychopathology*, 18, 345–361.

Adam, E. K., Gunnar, M. R., & Tanakar, A. (2004). Adult attachment, parent emotion, and observed parenting behavior: Mediator and moderator models. *Child Development*, 75(1), 110 – 122.

Ainsworth, M. D. S. (1976). *System for rating maternal-care behavior*. Princeton, NJ: Princeton University Press.

Ainsworth, M. D. S., Blehar, M. C., Waters, E., & Wall, S. (1978). *Patterns of attachment: A psychological study of the Strange Situation.* Hillsdale, NJ: Erlbaum.

Bakermans-Kranenburg, M. J., & IJzendoorn, M. H. v. (2007). Research review: Genetic vulnerability or differential susceptibility in child development: the case of attachment. *Journal of Child Psychology and Psychiatry, 48*(12), 1160–1173.

Barry, R. A., Kochanska, G., & Philibert, R. A. (2008). G × E interaction in the organization of attachment: mothers' responsiveness as a moderator of children's genotypes. *Journal of Child Psychology and Psychiatry, 49*(12), 1313–1320.

Baumrind, D. (1991). Parenting styles and adolescent development. In J. Brooks-Gunn, R. Lerner & A. C. Petersen (Eds.), *The encyclopedia on adolescence,* pp. 746–758. New York: Garland.

Belsky, J., & Fearon, R. M. (2002). Infant-mother attachment security, contextual risk, and early development: A moderational analysis. *Development and Psychopathology, 14,* 293–310.

Benoit, D., & Parker, K. (1994). Stability and transmission of attachment across three generations. *Child Development, 65,* 1444–1457.

Biringen, Z., Robinson, J. L., & Emde, R. N. (1993). Emotional Availability Scales. Boulder: University of Colorado, Health Science Center.

Biringen, Z., Robinson, J. L., & Emde, R. N. (2000). Emotional Availability Scales (3rd ed.). *Attachment and Human Development, 2,* 257–270.

Biringen, Z., Robinson, J. L., & Emde, R. N. (2008). Emotional Availability Scales (4th ed.). University of Colorado.

Bokhorst, C., Bakermans-Kranenburg, M., Fearon, P., Van ijzendoorn, M., Fonagy, P., & Schuengel, C. (2003). The importance of shared environment in mother-infant attachment security: A behavioral genetic study. *Child Development, 74*(6), 1769–1782.

Bosquet, M., & Egeland, B. (2006). The development and maintenance of anxiety symptoms from infancy through adolescence in a longitudinal sample. *Dev Psychopathol, 18*(2), 517–550.

Bowlby, J. (1958). The nature of the child's tie to his mother. *International Journal of Psychoanalysis, 39*(5), 350–373.

Bowlby, J. (1969). *Attachment and loss:* Vol. 1. *Attachment.* London: Hogarth Press and the Institute of Psycho-Analysis.

Bowlby, J. (1973). *Attachment and loss:* Vol. 2. *Separation: Anxiety and anger.* London: Hogarth Press and Institute of Psycho-Analysis.

Bowlby, J. (1988). *A secure base: Clinical applications of attachment theory.* London: Routledge.

Bretherton, I., & Munholland, K. A. (2008). Internal working models in attachment relationships: Elaborating a central construct in attachment theory. In J. Cassidy & P. R. Shaver (Eds.), *Handbook of attachment: Theory, research, and clinical applications* (2nd ed.). New York: Guilford Press.

Bretherton, I., Ridgeway, D., & Cassidy, J. (1990). Assessing internal working models of the attachment relationship: An attachment story completion task. In M. T. Greenberg, D. Cicchetti & E. M. Cummings (Eds.), *Attachment in the preschool years: Theory, research and intervention,* pp. 273–308. Chicago: University Chicago Press.

Bronfman, E., Parsons, E., & Lyons-Ruth, K. (1999). *Atypical Maternal Behavior Instrument for Assessment and Classification (AMBIANCE): Manual for coding disrupted affective communication, version 2.* Unpublished manuscript. Cambridge, MA: Harvard Medical School.

Buccino, G., Binkofski, F., Fink, G. R., Fadiga, L., Fogassi, L., Gallese, V. et al. (2001). Action observation activates premotor and parietal areas in a somatotopic manner: an fMRI study. *Eur J Neurosci, 13*(2), 400–404.

Bugental, D. B., & Schwartz, A. (2009). A cognitive approach to child mistreatment prevention among medically at-risk infants. *Dev Psychol, 45*(1), 284–288.

Carlson, E. A. (1998). A prospective longitudinal study of attachment disorganization/disorientation. *Child Development, 69,* 1107–1128.

Caspers, K., Yucuis, R., Troutman, B., Arndt, S., & Langbehn, D. (2007). A sibling adoption study of adult attachment: the influence of shared environment on attachment states of mind. *Attach Hum Dev, 9*(4), 375–391.

Cassidy, J. (1988). Child-mother attachment and the self in six-year-olds. *Child Development, 59,* 121–134.

Cassidy, J., & Marvin, R. S. (1992). Attachment organization in preschool children: Coding guidelines. Seattle: MacArthur Working Group on Attachment. Unpublished Coding Manual. Seattle, WA.

Clarke, A. M., & Clarke, A. D. B. (1976). *Early experience: Myth and evidence.* London: Open Books.

Cohn, D., Cowan, P., Cowan, C., & Pearson, J. (1992). Mothers' and fathers working models of childhood attachment relationships, parenting style, and child behavior *Dev Psychopathol*, 4, 417–431.

Cote, S. M., Boivin, M., Nagin, D. S., Japel, C., Xu, Q., Zoccolillo, M. et al. (2007). The role of maternal education and nonmaternal care services in the prevention of children's physical aggression problems. *Arch Gen Psychiatry*, 64(11), 1305–1312.

Cote, S. M., Vaillancourt, T., LeBlanc, J. C., Nagin, D. S., & Tremblay, R. E. (2006). The development of physical aggression from toddlerhood to pre-adolescence: A nation wide longitudinal study of Canadian children. *Journal of Abnormal Child Psychology*, 34, 68–82.

Cowan, P. A., Bradburn, I., & Cowan, C. P. (2005). *Parents' working models of attachment: The intergenerational context of parenting and childrens' adaptation to school.* Mahwah, NJ: Erlbaum.

Crowell, J. A., & Feldman, S. S. (1988). Mothers' internal models of relationships and children's behavioral and developmental status: A study of mother-child interaction. *Child Development*, 59, 1273–1285.

Csibra, G., & Gergely, G. (2006). Social learning and social cognition: The case for pedagogy. In M. H. Johnson & Y. M. Munakata (Eds.), *Processes of change in brain and cognitive development: Attention and Performance*, pp. 249–274, Vol. XXI. Oxford: Oxford University Press.

Dallaire, D. H., & Weinraub, M. (2007). Infant-mother attachment security and children's anxiety and aggression at first grade. *Journal of Applied Developmental Psychology*, 28, 477–492.

Das Eiden, R., Teti, D. M., & Corns, K. M. (1995). Maternal working models of attachment, marital adjustment, and the parent-child relationship. *Child Development*, 66, 1504–1518.

De Wolff, M. S., & van IJzendoorn, M. H. (1997). Sensitivity and attachment: A meta-analysis on parental antecedents of infant attachment. *Child Development*, 68, 571–591.

Deater-Deckard, K., Fulker, D. W., & Plomin, R. (1999). A genetic study of the family environment in the transition to early adolescence. *Journal of Child Psychology and Psychiatry*, 40, 769–795.

Decety, J., Chaminade, T., Grezes, J., & Meltzoff, A. N. (2002). A PET exploration of the neural mechanisms involved in reciprocal imitation. *Neuroimage*, 15(1), 265–272.

DeOliveira, C. A., Moran, G., & Pederson, D. R. (2005). Understanding the link between maternal adult attachment classifications and thoughts and feelings about emotions. *Attachment & Human Development*, 7(2), 153–170.

Dunn, J., Davies, L. C., O'Connor, T. G., & Sturgess, W. (2000). Parents' and partners' life course and family experiences: links with parent-child relationships in different family settings. *J Child Psychol Psychiatry*, 41(8), 955–968.

Dunn, J., Deater-Deckard, K., Pickering, K., O'Connor, T. G., & Golding, J. (1998). Children's adjustment and prosocial behaviour in step-, single-parent, and non-stepfamily settings: findings from a community study. Avon Longitudinal Study of Pregnancy and Childhood (ALSPAC) Study Team. *J Child Psychol Psychiatry*, 39(8), 1083–1095.

Dutra, L., Bureau, J., Holmes, B., Lyubchik, A., & Lyons-Ruth, K. (2009). Quality of early care and childhood trauma: Prospective study of developmental pathways to dissociation. *J Nerv Ment Dis*, 197(6), 383–390.

Dutra, L., & Lyons-Ruth, K. (2005). Maltreatment, maternal and child psychopathology, and quality of early care as predictors of adolescent dissociation. In J. Borelli (ed.), *Interrelations of attachment and trauma symptoms: A developmental perspective.* Paper presented at the Symposium conducted at the biennial meeting of the Society for Research in Child Development.

East, P. L., & Khoo, S. T. (2005). Longitudinal pathways linking family factors and sibling relationship qualities to adolescent substance use and sexual risk behaviors. *Journal of Family Psychology*, 19(4), 571–580.

Eaves, L. J., Silberg, J. L., Meyer, J. M., Maes, H. H., Simonoff, E., Pickles, A. et al. (1997). Genetics and developmental psychopathology: 2. The main effects of genes and environment on behavioral problems in the Virginia Twin Study of Adolescent Behavioral Development. *J Child Psychol Psychiatry*, 38(8), 965–980.

Edwards, E. P., Eiden, R. D., & Leonard, K. E. (2006). Behaviour problems in 18- to 36-month old children of alcoholic fathers: secure mother-infant attachment as a protective factor. *Dev Psychopathol*, 18(2), 395–407.

Eisenberger, N. I., Lieberman, M. D., & Williams, K. D. (2003). Does rejection hurt? An FMRI study of social exclusion. *Science*, 302(5643), 290–292.

Ekblad, S. (1988). Influence of child-rearing on aggressive behavior in a transcultural perspective. *Acta Psychiatrica Scandinavica*, 344(Supplement), 133–139.

Fearon, P., van IJzendoorn, M. H., Fonagy, P., Bakermans-Kranenburg, M. J., Schuengel, C., & Bokhorst, C. L. (2006). In search of shared and nonshared environmental factors in security of attachment: A behavior-genetic study of the association between sensitivity and attachment security. *Developmental Psychology*, 42(6), 1026–1040.

Fonagy, P., Gergely, G., Jurist, E., & Target, M. (2002). *Affect regulation, mentalization and the development of the self*. New York: Other Press.

Fonagy, P., Gergely, G., & Target, M. (2007). The parent-infant dyad and the construction of the subjective self. *Journal of Child Psychology and Psychiatry*, 48, 288–328.

Fonagy, P., Sadie, C., & Allison, E. (2002). *The Parent-Infant Project (PIP) Outcome Study*. London: Anna Freud Centre.

Fonagy, P., & Sharp, C. (2008). Treatment outcome of childhood disorders: The perspective of social cognition In C. Sharp, P. Fonagy & I. Goodyer (Eds.), *Social cognition and developmental psychology*. Oxford: Oxford University Press.

Fonagy, P., Steele, H., Moran, G., Steele, M., & Higgitt, A. (1991). The capacity for understanding mental states: The reflective self in parent and child and its significance for security of attachment. *Infant Mental Health Journal*, 13, 200–217.

Fonagy, P., Steele, H., & Steele, M. (1991). Maternal representations of attachment during pregnancy predict the organization of infant-mother attachment at one year of age. *Child Development*, 62, 891–905.

Fonagy, P., Steele, H., & Steele, M. (1996). Associations among attachment classifications of mothers, fathers, and their infants: Evidence for a relationship-specific perspective. *Child Development*, 67, 541–555.

Fonagy, P., Steele, M., Steele, H., & Target, M. (1997). *Reflective-Functioning Manual, version 4.1, for Application to Adult Attachment Interviews*. London: University College London.

Fonagy, P., Stein, H., Allen, J., & Fultz, J. (2003). The relationship of mentalization and childhood and adolescent adversity to adult functioning. Paper presented at the Biennial Meeting of the Society for Research in Child Development, Tampa, FL.

Fonagy, P., Target, M., Steele, H., & Steele, M. (1998). *Reflective-Functioning Manual, version 5.0, for Application to Adult Attachment Interviews*. London: University College London.

Franz, C. E., McClelland, D. C., & Weinberger, J. (1991). Childhood antecedents of conventional social accomplishment in midlife adults: A 36-year prospective study. *Journal of Personality and Social Psychology*, 60, 586–595.

Franz, C. E., McClelland, D. C., Weinberger, J. & Peterson, C. (1994). Parenting antecedents of adult adjustment: A longitudinal sudy. In C. Perris, W.A. Arrindell, M. Eisemann (Eds). *Parenting and Psychopathology*, pp. 127–124. New York: Wiley.

Gable, S., Belsky, J., & Crnic, K. (1992). Marriage, parenting, and child development: Progress and prospects. *Journal of Family Psychology*, 5, 276–294.

Gallese, V. (2005). Embodied simulation: From neurons to phenomenal experience. *Phenomenology and the Cognitive Sciences*, 4(23–48).

Gallese, V., Fadiga, L., Fogassi, L., & Rizzolatti, G. (1996). Action recognition in the premotor cortex. *Brain*, 119 (Pt 2), 593–609.

Ge, X., Conger, R. D., Cadoret, R., Neiderhiser, J., & Yates, W. (1996). The developmental interface between nature and nurture: a mutual influence model of child antisocial behavior and parent behavior. *Developmental Psychology*, 32, 574–589.

George, C., Kaplan, N., & Main, M. (1985). The Adult Attachment Interview. Unpublished manuscript, Department of Psychology, University of California at Berkeley.

George, C., & Solomon, J. (1990/1996/2000). Six-year attachment doll play classification system. Unpublished manuscript. Oakland, CA: Mills College.

George, C., & Solomon, J. (1996). Representational models of relationships: Links between caregiving and attachment. *Infant Mental Health Journal*, 17, 198–216.

George, C., & Solomon, J. (1999). The development of caregiving: A comparison of attachment and psychoanalytic approaches to mothering. *Psychoanalytic Inquiry*, 19, 618–646.

George, C., & Solomon, J. (2008a). The caregiving behavioral system: A behavioral system approach to parenting In J. Cassidy & P. Shaver (Eds.), *Handbook of attachment:*

Theory, research, and clinical application (2nd ed.). New York: Guilford Press.

George, C., & Solomon, J. (2008b). Internal Working Models of Caregiving Rating Manual. Unpublished manuscript. Oakland, CA: Mills College.

Gergely, G., & Csibra, G. (2005). The social construction of the cultural mind: Imitative learning as a mechanism of human pedagogy. *Interaction Studies*, 6, 463–481.

Gergely, G., & Csibra, G. (2006). Sylvia's recipe: Human culture, imitation, and pedagogy. In N. J. Enfield & S. C. Levinson (Eds.), *Roots of human sociality: Culture, cognition, and human interaction*, pp. 229–255. Berg Press: London.

Gergely, G., Koós, O., & Watson, J. S. (2002). Contingency perception and the role of contingent parental reactivity in early socio-emotional development [Perception causale et role des comportements imitatifs des parents dans le développement socio-émotionnel précoce]. In J. Nadel & J. Decety (Eds.), *Imiter pour découvrir l'human: Psychologie, neurobiology, robotique et philosophie de l'esprit*, pp. 59–82. Paris: Presses Universitaires de France.

Gergely, G., & Unoka, Z. (2008). Attachment, affect regulation and mentalization: The developmental origins of the representational affective self. In C. Sharp, P. Fonagy & I. Goodyer (Eds.), *Social cognition and developmental psychology*. Oxford: Oxford University Press.

Gergely, G., & Watson, J. (1996). The social biofeedback model of parental affect-mirroring. *International Journal of Psycho-Analysis*, 77, 1181–1212.

Gergely, G., & Watson, J. (1999). Early social-emotional development: Contingency perception and the social biofeedback model. In P. Rochat (Ed.), *Early social cognition: Understanding others in the first months of life*, pp. 101–137. Hillsdale, NJ: Erlbaum.

Goldberg, S., Benoit, D., Blokland, K., & Madigan, S. (2003). Atypical maternal behavior, maternal representations, and infant disorganized attachment. *Dev Psychopathol*, 15(2), 239–257.

Gottman, J. M., Katz, L. F., & Hooven, C. (1997). *Meta-emotion: How families communicate emotionally*. Mahwah, NJ: Lawrence Erlbaum.

Green, J. (2000). A new method of evaluating attachment representations in young school-age children: The Manchester Child Evaluation Story Task. *Attachment and Human Development*, 2(1), 48–70.

Greenberg, M. T. (1999). Attachment and psychopathology in childhood. In J. Cassidy & P. R. Shaver (Eds.), *Handbook of attachment: Theory, research, and clinical applications*, pp. 469–496. New York: Guilford.

Grienenberger, J. F., Kelly, K., & Slade, A. (2005). Maternal reflective functioning, mother-infant affective communication, and infant attachment: exploring the link between mental states and observed caregiving behavior in the intergenerational transmission of attachment. *Attach Hum Dev*, 7(3), 299–311.

Grossman, K., Fremmer-Bombik, E., Rudolph, J., & Grossman, K. E. (1988). Maternal attachment representations as related to patterns of infant-mother attachment and maternal care during the first year. In R. A. Hinde & J. Stevenson-Hinde (Eds.), *Relationships within families: Mutual influences*, pp. 241–260. Oxford, UK: Clarendon Press.

Hamilton, C. E. (2000). Continuity and discontinuity of attachment from infancy through adolescence. *Child Development*, 71(3), 690–694.

Heinicke, C. M., Goorsky, M., Levine, M., Ponce, V., Ruth, G., Silverman, M. et al. (2006). Pre- and post-natal antecedents of a home visiting intervention and family developmental outcome. *Infant Mental Health Journal*, 27, 91–119.

Hesse, E. (2008). The Adult Attachment Interview: Protocol, method of analysis, and empirical studies. In J. Cassidy & P. R. Shaver (Eds.), *Handbook of attachment: Theory, research, and clinical applications*, pp. 552–598 (2nd ed.). New York: Guilford Press.

Hesse, E., & Main, M. (1999). Second-generation effects of unresolved trauma in nonmaltreating parents: Dissociated, frightened, and threatening parental behavior. *Psychoanalytic Inquiry*, 19, 481–540.

Hesse, E., & Main, M. (2000). Disorganized infant, child, and adult attachment: Collapse in behavioral and attentional strategies. *Journal of the American Psychoanalytic Association*, 48(4), 1097–1127.

Hesse, E., & Main, M. (2006). Frightened, threatening, and dissociative parental behavior in low-risk samples: Description, discussion, and interpretations. *Dev Psychopathol*, 18(2), 309–343.

Hodges, J. (1992). Little Piggy Story Stem Battery. Unpublished manuscript.

Hodges, J., Hillman, S., & Steele, M. (2007). Story Stem Assessment Profile Rating Manual. Unpublished Document.

Hooley, J. M., & Richters, J. E. (1995). Expressed emotion: a developmental perspective. In D. Cicchetti & S. L. Toth (Eds.), *Emotion, cognition and representation*, Vol. VI. Rochester, NY: University of Rochester Press.

Hooven, C., Gottman, J. M., & Katz, L. F. (1995). Parental meta-emotion structure predicts family and child outcomes. *Cognition and Emotion*, 9, 229–264.

Hughes, C., Deater-Deckard, K., & Cutting, A. (1999). "Speak roughly to your little boy?" Sex differences in the relations between parenting and preschoolers' understanding of mind. *Social Development*, 8, 143–160.

Hughes, P., Turton, P., Mcgauley, G. A., & Fonagy, P. (2006). Factors that predict infant disorganization in mothers classified as U in pregnancy *Attachment & Human Development*, 8(2), 113–122.

Iacoboni, M., Molnar-Szakacs, I., Gallese, V., Buccino, G., Mazziotta, J. C., & Rizzolatti, G. (2005). Grasping the intentions of others with one's own mirror neuron system. *PLoS Biol*, 3(3), e79.

Jacobvitz, D., Leon, K., & Hazen, N. (2006). Does expectant mothers' unresolved trauma predict frightened/frightening maternal behavior? Risk and protective factors. *Dev Psychopathol*, 18(2), 363–379.

Kaplan, N. (1987). *Individual differences in 6-year-olds thoughts about separation: Predicted from attachment to mother at age 1*. Berkeley: University of California.

Katz, L. F., & Gottman, J. M. (1986). The meta-emotion interview. Unpublished manual, Seattle: University of Washington.

Katz, L. F., Gottman, J. M., Shapiro, A. F., & Carrere, S. (1997). The meta-emotion interview for parents of toddlers. Unpublished manual, University of Washington, Seattle.

Kobak, R., Cassidy, J., Lyons-Ruth, K., & Ziv, Y. (2006). Attachment, stress and psychopathology: A developmental pathways model. In D. Cicchetti & D. J. Cohen (Eds.), *Development and psychopathology:* Vol. 1. *Theory and method*, pp. 334–369 (2nd ed.). New York: Wiley.

Kochanska, G. (1997). Mutually responsive orientation between mothers and their young children: Implications for early socialization. *Child Development*, 68(1), 94–112.

Kochanska, G., Aksan, N., Prisco, T. R., & Adams, E. E. (2008). Mother-child and father-child mutually responsive orientation in the first 2 years and children's outcomes at preschool age:

mechanisms of influence. *Child Development*, 79(1), 30–44.

Koren-Karie, N., Oppenheim, D., Dolev, S., Sher, S., & Etzion-Carasso, A. (2002). Mother's insightfulness regarding their infants' internal experience: Relations with maternal sensitivity and infant attachment. *Developmental Psychology*, 38, 534–542.

Krueger, R. F., Moffitt, T. E., Caspi, A., Bleske, A., & Silva, P. A. (1998). Assortative mating for antisocial behavior: developmental and methodological implications. *Behav Genet*, 28(3), 173–186.

Legerstee, M., & Varghese, J. (2001). The role of maternal affect mirroring on social expectancies in 2–3 month-old infants. *Child Development*, 72, 1301–1313.

Locke, J. (1693). Some thoughts concerning education. In P. Gay (Ed.), *John Locke on Education*. New York: Bureau of Publications, Teacher's College, Columbia University (1964).

Losoya, S. H., Callor, S., Rowe, D. C., & Goldsmith, H. H. (1997). Origins of familial similarity in parenting: a study of twins and adoptive siblings. *Developmental Psychopathology*, 33, 1012–1023.

Lyons-Ruth, K. (2001). The two-person construction of defenses: Disorganised attachment strategies, unintegrated mental states, and hostile/helpless relational processes. *Newsletter of the Division of Psychoanalytic Psychology of the American Psychological Association*.

Lyons-Ruth, K., Alpern, L., & Repacholi, B. (1993). Disorganized infant attachment classification and maternal psychosocial problems as predictors of hostile-aggressive behavior in the preschool classroom. *Child Development*, 64, 572–585.

Lyons-Ruth, K., Bronfman, E., & Atwood, G. (1999). A relational diathesis model of hostile-helpless states of mind: Expressions in mother-infant interaction. In J. Solomon & C. George (Eds.), *Attachment disorganization*, pp. 33–70. New York: Guilford Press.

Lyons-Ruth, K., Bronfman, E., & Parsons, E. (1999). Atypical attachment in infancy and early childhood among children at developmental risk: IV. Maternal frightened, frightening, or atypical behavior and disorganized infant attachment patterns. In J. Vondra & D. Barnett (Eds.), *Typical patterns of infant attachment: Theory, research and current directions*, pp. 67–96 Vol. 64. Monographs of the Society for Research in Child Development.

Lyons-Ruth, K., Dutra, L., Schuder, M. R., & Bianchi, I. (2006). From infant attachment disorganization to adult dissociation: relational adaptations or traumatic experiences? *Psychiatr Clin North Am*, 29(1), 63–86, viii.

Lyons-Ruth, K., Easterbrooks, M. A., Davidson Cibelli, C. E., & Bronfman, E. (April 1995). Predicting school-age externalising symptoms from infancy: Contributions of disorganised attachment strategies and mild mental lag. Paper presented at the biennial meeting of the Society for Research in Child Development, Indianapolis.

Lyons-Ruth, K., & Jacobvitz, D. (2008). Attachment disorganization: Genetic factors, parenting contexts, and developmental transformation from infancy to adulthood. In J. C. P. Shaver (Ed.), *Handbook of Attachment* (2nd ed.). New York: Guilford Press.

Lyons-Ruth, K., Yellin, C., Melnick, S., & Atwood, G. (2005). Expanding the concept of unresolved mental states: hostile/helpless states of mind on the Adult Attachment Interview are associated with disrupted mother-infant communication and infant disorganization. *Dev Psychopathol*, 17(1), 1–23.

Maccoby, E. E. (2000). Parenting and its effects on children: On reading and misreading behaviour genetics. *Annual Review of Psychology*, 51, 1–27.

Maccoby, E., & Martin, J. A. (1983). Socialisation in the context of the family: Parent-child interaction. In E. M. Hetherington (Ed.), *Handbook of child psychology: Socialization, personality and social development* (Vol. 4). New York: Wiley.

MacDonald, H. Z., Beeghly, M., Grant-Knight, W., Augustyn, M., Woods, R. W., Cabral, H. et al. (2008). Longitudinal association between infant disorganized attachment and childhood posttraumatic stress symptoms. *Dev Psychopathol*, 20(2), 493–508.

Macfie, J., McElwain, N. L., Houts, R. M., & Cox, M. J. (2005). Intergenerational transmission of role reversal between parent and child: dyadic and family systems internal working models. *Attach Hum Dev*, 7(1), 51–65.

Madigan, S., Bakermans-Kranenburg, M. J., Van Ijzendoorn, M. H., Moran, G., Pederson, D. R., & Benoit, D. (2006). Unresolved states of mind, anomalous parental behavior, and disorganized attachment: a review and meta-analysis of a transmission gap. *Attach Hum Dev*, 8(2), 89–111.

Madigan, S., Moran, G., & Pederson, D. R. (2006). Unresolved states of mind, disorganized attachment relationships, and disrupted interactions of adolescent mothers and their infants. *Dev Psychol*, 42(2), 293–304.

Madigan, S., Moran, G., Schuengel, C., Pederson, D. R., & Otten, R. (2007). Unresolved maternal attachment representations, disrupted maternal behavior and disorganized attachment in infancy: links to toddler behavior problems. *J Child Psychol Psychiatry*, 48(10), 1042–1050.

Main, M., & Goldwyn, R. (1993). *Adult Attachment Classification System*. University of California, Berkeley.

Main, M., & Hesse, E. (1990). Parents' unresolved traumatic experiences are related to infant disorganized attachment status: Is frightened and/or frightening parental behavior the linking mechanism? In M. Greenberg, D. Cicchetti & E. M. Cummings (Eds.), *Attachment in the preschool years: Theory, research and intervention*, pp. 161–182. Chicago: University of Chicago Press.

Main, M., & Hesse, E. (1992). Disorganized/disoriented infant behaviour in the Strange Situation, lapses in the monitoring of reasoning and discourse during the parent's Adult Attachment Interview, and dissociative states. In M. Ammaniti & D. Stern (Eds.), *Attachment and Psychoanalysis*, pp. 86–140. Rome: Gius, Latereza and Figli.

Main, M., Hesse, E., & Kaplan, M. (2005). Predictability of attachment behavior and representational processes at 1, 6 and 19 years of age. In K. E. Grossmann, K. Grossmann & E. Waters (Eds.), *Attachment from infancy to adulthood: The major longitudinal studies*. New York: Guilford.

Main, M., & Solomon, J. (1986). Discovery of an insecure-disorganized/disoriented attachment pattern. In T. B. Brazelton & M. W. Yogman (Eds.), *Affective Development in Infancy*, pp. 95–124. Norwood, NJ: Ablex.

Main, M., & Solomon, J. (1990). Procedures for identifying infants as disorganized/disoriented during the Ainsworth Strange Situation. In M. Greenberg, D. Cicchetti & E. M. Cummings (Eds.), *Attachment during the preschool years: Theory, research and intervention*, pp. 121–160. Chicago: University of Chicago Press.

Martorell, G. A., & Bugental, D. B. (2006). Maternal variations in stress reactivity: implications for harsh parenting practices with very young children. *Journal of Family Psychology*, 20(4), 641–647.

McClelland, D. C., & Franz, C. E. (1992). Motivational and other sources of work accomplishments in mid-life. *Journal of Personality*, 60, 679–707.

Meins, E., & Fernyhough, C. (1999). Linguistic acquisitional style and mentalising development: The role of maternal mind-mindedness. *Cognitive Development*, 14, 363–380.

Meins, E., Fernyhough, C., Fradley, E., & Tuckey, M. (2001). Rethinking maternal sensitivity: Mothers' comments on infants mental processes predict security of attachment at 12 months. *Journal of Child Psychology and Psychiatry*, 42, 637–648.

Meins, E., Fernyhough, C., Russel, J., & Clark-Carter, D. (1998). Security of attachment as a predictor of symbolic and mentalising abilities: a longitudinal study. *Social Development*, 7, 1–24.

Meins, E., Fernyhough, C., Wainwright, R., Clark-Carter, D., Das Gupta, M., Fradley, E. et al. (2003). Pathways to understanding mind: construct validity and predictive validity of maternal mind-mindedness. *Child Dev*, 74(4), 1194–1211.

Meins, E., Fernyhough, C., Wainwright, R., Das Gupta, M., Fradley, E., & Tuckey, M. (2002). Maternal mind-mindedness and attachment security as predictors of theory of mind understanding. *Child Development*, 73, 1715–1726.

Meltzoff, A. N. (1990). Foundations for developing a concept of self: The role of imitation in relating self to other and the value of social mirroring, social modeling and self practice in infancy. In D. Cicchetti & M. Beeghly (Eds.), *The self in transition: Infancy to childhood*. Chicago: University of Chicago Press.

Mitchell, R. W. (1993). Mental models of mirror self-recognition: Two theories. *New Ideas in Psychology*, 11, 295–325.

Neiderhiser, J. M., Reiss, D., & Hetherington, E. M. (2007). The Nonshared Environment in Adolescent Development (NEAD) project: a longitudinal family study of twins and siblings from adolescence to young adulthood. *Twin Res Hum Genet*, 10(1), 74–83.

NICHD Early Child Care Research Network. (2004). Type of child care and children's development at 54 months. *Early Childhood Research Quarterly*, 19(2), 203–230.

O'Connor, T. G., Caspi, A., DeFries, J. C., & Plomin, R. (2003). Genotype–environment interaction in children's adjustment to parental separation. *Journal of Child Psychology and Psychiatry*, 44(6), 849–856.

O'Connor, T. G., & Croft, C. M. (2001). A twin study of attachment in preschool children. *Child Dev*, 72(5), 1501–1511.

O'Connor, T. G., Thorpe, K., Dunn, J., & Golding, J. (1999). Parental divorce and adjustment in adulthood: findings from a community sample. The ALSPAC Study Team. Avon Longitudinal Study of Pregnancy and Childhood. *J Child Psychol Psychiatry*, 40(5), 777–789.

Ogawa, J. R., Sroufe, L. A., Weinfield, N. S., Carlson, E. A., & Egeland, B. (1997). Development and the fragmented self: Longitudinal study of dissociative symptomatology in a nonclinical sample. *Development and Psychopathology*, 9, 855–879.

Olds, D. L., Sadler, L., & Kitzman, H. (2007). Programs for parents of infants and toddlers: recent evidence from randomized trials. *J Child Psychol Psychiatry*, 48(3–4), 355–391.

Oppenheim, D., Goldsmith, D., & Koren-Karie, N. (2004). Maternal insightfulness and preschoolers' emotion and behavior problems: Reciprocal influences in a therapeutic preschool program. *Infant Mental Health Journal*, 25(4), 352–367.

Oppenheim, D., & Koren-Karie, N. (2002). Mothers' insightfulness regarding their children's internal worlds: The capacity underlying secure child-mother relationships. *Infant Mental Health Journal*, 23, 593–605.

Oppenheim, D., Koren-Karie, N., Dolev, S., & Yirmiya, N. (2009). Maternal insightfulness and resolution of the diagnosis are associated with secure attachment in preschoolers with autism spectrum disorders. *Child Development*, 80(2), 519–527.

Oppenheim, D., Koren-Karie, N., Etzion-Carasso, A., & Sagi-Schwartz, A. (April 2005). Maternal insightfulness but not infant attachment predicts 4 year olds' theory of mind (poster). Paper presented at the Biennial meeting of the Society for Research in Child Development, Atlanta, Georgia.

Oppenheim, D., Koren-Karie, N., & Sagi, A. (2001). Mothers' empathic understanding of their preschoolers' internal experience: Relations with early attachment. *International Journal of Behavioral Development*, 25, 16–26.

Parker, G. (1982). Re-searching the schizophrenogenic mother. *Journal of Nervous and Mental Disease*, 170(8), 452–462.

Parker, G. (1983). *Parental overprotection: a risk factor in psychosocial development*. New York: Grune & Stratton.

Parker, G. (1990). The Parental Bonding Instrument: A decade of research. *Soc Psychiatry Psychiatr Epidemiol*, 25(6), 281–282.

Parker, G. B., Barrett, E. A., & Hickie, I. B. (1992). From nurture to network: examining links between perceptions of parenting received in childhood and social bonds in adulthood. *Am J Psychiatry*, 149(7), 877–885.

Plomin, R. (1994). *Genetics and Experience: The interplay between nature and nurture.* Thousand Oaks, Ca: Sage Publications.

Rizzolatti, G., & Craighero, L. (2004). The mirror-neuron system. *Annu Rev Neurosci, 27,* 169–192.

Roth, A., & Fonagy, P. (2005). *What works for whom? A critical review of psychotherapy research* (2nd ed.). New York: Guilford Press.

Rousseau, J. J. (1762). *Emile, or Education* (translated by B. Foxley). London: J. M. Dent and Sons (1948).

Rowe, D. (1994). *The limits of family influence: Genes, experience and behaviour.* New York: Guilford Press.

Scarr, S. (1992). Developmental theories for the 1990s: Development and individual differences. *Child Development, 63,* 1–19.

Schneider-Rosen, K., & Cicchetti, D. (1991). Early self-knowledge and emotional development: Visual self-recognition and affective reactions to mirror self-image in maltreated and non-maltreated toddlers. *Developmental Psychology, 27,* 481–488.

Schuengel, C., Bakermans-Kranenburg, M., & van IJzendoorn, M. (1999). Frightening maternal behaviour linking unresolved loss and disorganised infant attachment. *Journal of Consulting and Clinical Psychology, 67,* 54–63.

Schuengel, C., Bakermans-Kranenburg, M. J., van IJzendoorn, M. H., & Blom, M. (1999). Unresolved loss and infant disorganisation: Links to frightening maternal behavior. In J. Solomon & C. George (Eds.), *Attachment Disorganization,* pp. 71–94. New York: Guilford.

Sears, R. R., Maccoby, E. E., & Levin, H. (1957). *Patterns of child-rearing.* Evanston, IL: Row Peterson.

Sharp, C., & Fonagy, P. (2008). The parent's capacity to treat the child as a psychological agent: Constructs, measures and implications for developmental psychopathology. *Social Development,* 17(3), 737–754.

Sharp, C., Fonagy, P., & Goodyer, I. (2006). Imagining your child's mind: Psychosocial adjustment and mothers' ability to predict their children's attributional response styles. *British Journal of Developmental Psychology,* 24(1), 197–214.

Shaw, D. S., Gilliom, M., Ingoldsby, E. M., & Nagin, D. S. (2003). Trajectories leading to school-age conduct problems. *Dev Psychol,* 39(2), 189–200.

Slade, A. (2005). Parental reflective functioning: an introduction. *Attachment and Human Development,* 7(3), 269–281.

Slade, A., Aber, J. L., Bresgi, I., Berger, B., & Kaplan, M. (2004). *The Parent Development Interview – Revised.* Unpublished protocol. New York: The City University of New York.

Slade, A., Bernbach, E., Grienenberger, J., Levy, D., & Locker, A. (2004). Addendum to Fonagy, Target, Steele, & Steele reflective functioning scoring manual for use with the Parent Development Interview. Unpublished Manuscript. New York: The City College and Graduate Center of the City University of New York.

Slade, A., Grienenberger, J., Bernbach, E., Levy, D., & Locker, A. (2005). Maternal reflective functioning, attachment, and the transmission gap: a preliminary study. *Attachment and Human Development,* 7(3), 283–298.

Slough, N. M., & Greenberg, M. T. (1990). 5-year-olds' representations of separations from parents: Responses from the perspective of self and other. *New Directions for Child Development, 48,* 67–84.

Solomon, J., & George, C. (1996). Defining the caregiving system: Toward a theory of caregiving. *Infant Mental Health Journal,* 17, 183–197.

Solomon, J., & George, C. (1999a). The caregiving behavioral system in mothers of infants: A comparison of divorcing and married mothers. *Attachment & Human Development,* 1, 171–190.

Solomon, J., & George, C. (1999b). The development of attachment in separated and divorced families. Effects of overnight visitation, parent and couple variables. *Attach Hum Dev,* 1(1), 2–33.

Solomon, J., & George, C. (2006). Intergenerational transmission of dysregulated maternal caregiving: Mothers describe their upbringing and child rearing. In O. Mayseless (Ed.), *Parenting representations: Theory, research, and clinical implications,* pp. 265–295. New York: Cambridge University Press.

Spinath, F. M., & O'Connor, T. G. (2003). A behavioral genetic study of the overlap between personality and parenting. *J Pers,* 71(5), 785–808.

Sroufe, L. A. (2005). Attachment and development: a prospective, longitudinal study from birth to adulthood. *Attach Hum Dev*, 7(4), 349–367.

Sroufe, L. A., Egeland, B., Carlson, E., & Collins, W. A. (2005). *The development of the person: The Minnesota study of risk and adaptation from birth to adulthood.* New York: Guilford.

Steele, H., Steele, M., & Fonagy, P. (1996). Associations among attachment classifications of mothers, fathers, and their infants. *Child Development*, 67, 541–555.

Swanson, G. E. (1961). Determinants of the individual's defense against inner conflict: Review and reformation. In J. C. Glidwell (Ed.), *Parental Attitudes and Child Behavior*, pp. 5–41. Springfield, Ill.: Thomas.

Thompson, R. (2008). Early Attachment and later development: Familiar questions, new answers. In J. Cassidy & P. R. Shaver (Eds.), *Handbook of attachment: Theory, research, and clinical applications*, pp. 348–365 (2nd ed.). New York: Guilford Press.

Thompson, R., & Meyer, S. (2007). The socialization of emotion regulation in the family. In J. Gross (Ed.), *Handbook of emotion regulation*, pp. 249–268. New York: Guilford Press.

Tremblay, R. E., Nagin, D. S., Seguin, J. R., Zoccolillo, M., Zelazo, P. D., Boivin, M. et al. (2004). Physical aggression during early childhood: Trajectories and predictors. *Pediatrics*, 114(1), e43–50.

Tronick, E. Z. (2001). Emotional connection and dyadic consciousness in infant-mother and patient-therapist interactions: Commentary on paper by Frank M. Lachman. *Psychoanalytic Dialogue*, 11, 187–195.

Tronick, E. (2003). "Of course all relationships are unique": How co-creative processes generate unique mother-infant and patient-therapist relationships and change other relationships. *Psychoanalytic Inquiry*, 23, 473–491.

Tronick, E. Z. (2005). Why is connection with others so critical? The formation of dyadic states of consciousness: Coherence governed selection and the co-creation of meaning out of messy meaning making. In J. Nadel & D. Muir (Eds.), *Emotional Development*, pp. 293–315. Oxford: Oxford University Press.

True, M., Pisani, L., & Oumar, F. (2001). Infant-mother attachment among the Dogon in Mali. *Child Development*, 72(5), 1451–1466.

Vaillant, G. E. (1977). *Adaptation to life.* Boston, MA: Little Brown.

van IJzendoorn, M. H. (1995). Adult attachment representations, parental responsiveness, and infant attachment: A meta-analysis on the predictive validity of the Adult Attachment Interview. *Psychological Bulletin*, 117, 387–403.

van IJzendoorn, M., & Bakermans-Kranenburg, M. J. (2009). The first 10,000 adult attachment interviews: Distributions of adult attachment representations in clinical and non-clinical groups. *Attachment and Human Development*, 11(3), 223–263.

van IJzendoorn, M., Scheungel, C., & Bakermans-Kranenburg, M. J. (1999). Disorganized attachment in early childhood: Meta-analysis of precursors, concomitants and sequelae. *Development and Psychopathology*, 22, 225–249.

Wachs, T. D., & Gruen, G. E. (1982). *Early experiences and human development.* New York: Plenum Press.

Ward, M. J., & Carlson, E. A. (1995). Associations among adult attachment representations, maternal sensitivity, and infant-mother attachment in a sample of adolescent mothers. *Child Development*, 66, 69–79.

Warren, S. L., Huston, L., Egeland, B., & Sroufe, L. A. (1997). Child and adolescent anxiety disorders and early attachment. *Journal of the American Academy of Child and Adolescent Psychiatry*, 36, 637–644.

Waters, E., Merrick, S. K., Treboux, D., Crowell, J., & Albersheim, L. (2000). Attachment security from infancy to early adulthood: a 20 year longitudinal study. *Child Development*, 71(3), 684–689.

Weinfield, N. S., Whaley, G. J., & Egeland, B. (2004). Continuity, discontinuity, and coherence in attachment from infancy to late adolescence: sequelae of organization and disorganization. *Attach Hum Dev*, 6(1), 73–97.

Wicker, B., Keysers, C., Plailly, J., Royet, J. P., Gallese, V., & Rizzolatti, G. (2003). Both of us disgusted in *My insula*: the common neural basis of seeing and feeling disgust. *Neuron*, 40(3), 655–664.

Zeanah, C. H., Benoit, D., Barton, M., Regan, C., Hirshberg, L. M., & Lipsitt, L. P. (1993). Representations of attachment in mothers and their one-year-old infants. *Journal of the American Academy of Child and Adolescent Psychiatry*, 32, 278–286.

Zeanah, C. H., Benoit, D., Hirshberg, L., Barton, M. L., & Regan, C. (1994). Mothers' representations of their infants are concordant with infant attachment classifications. *Developmental Issues in Psychiatry and Psychology*, 1, 1–14.

CHAPTER 11

Understanding the Developmental Influences of the Family Environment

Sharon Landesman Ramey and Craig T. Ramey

Introduction: Taxonomy as a Framework for Advancing Knowledge about Family Influences on Child Development

Taxonomy is the branch of science devoted to the study of classification and the discovery of basic principles that govern the grouping of individual elements into meaningful sets. There has been no taxonomy of children's family environments, despite extensive research on the association between many family variables and children's development (e.g., Borkowski, Ramey, & Bristol-Powers, 2002). In this chapter, we advocate that developmental science is well positioned to engage in systematic investigation that will create a taxonomy of family environments with the explicit goal of understanding how different types of family environments contribute to the lifelong development of individual children.

Developmental science had a major breakthrough four decades ago when investigators reconceptualized the construct of "influence" across the generations as being inherently bidirectional, rather than unidirectional – that is, parents influence children and children also influence parents (cf. Bell, 1968; Lewis & Rosenblum, 1979). This idea of bidirectionality soon was replaced by a more complex conceptualization captured by the term *transactional* (cf. Lewis & Feinman, 1991; Sameroff, 1983, 2009), in which the dynamic exchanges between parents and their children, or between environments and children, became characterized as a chainlike series of changes *over time* that demonstrated potential differential outcomes that reflect individual differences of the participants and how they respond to the events that occur. This appreciation for the duality that environments both shape and are shaped by the people in them now serves as a fundamental axiom in developmental science and human ecology. Yet how to apply this axiom adequately in longitudinal inquiry about the family environment has remained challenging and largely elusive.

The family has long been a central interest in the fields of psychology, sociology, and anthropology. Increasingly the need to understand family and the environment family members create is considered vital to the success of the educational and clinical systems that serve children. The greatest challenge for developmental science is how to organize and synthesize what amounts to a vast array of widely scattered findings about parenting practices, parent-child relationships, family size and structure, parent qualities, family income, and the home environment. Can we construct a cohesive and informative framework about family environments that will increase our understanding developmental processes at the level of the individual child? What basis can be used to inform a taxonomy of family environments, particularly given the well-known fact that families are profoundly affected by culture, cohort, and community norms and resources? How can we use the most robust findings from previous studies of families and children to generate a more cohesive knowledge framework?

Formally, taxonomy refers to "the theoretical study of classification, including its bases, principles, procedures, and rules" (Simpson, 1961, p. 11). Often developmental scientists lament the lack of "taxonomy" in the field of children's home environments. Contextual analysis of this lament indicates they mean a method for classifying or a comprehensive inventory (catalog) of the phenomena they study, rather than formal taxonomy. For example, Magnusson (1981) long recognized "the problem of taxonomy of situations," using taxonomy as a synonym for a classification scheme.

In this chapter, taxonomy proper is distinguished from the actual activity and products (e.g., specific categorization schemes, keys, typologies) of classifying. Classification involves the ordering of elements into groups, based on rules such as contiguity and similarity. As such, the subject of classification consists of the individual elements (e.g., environments, behavioral acts) and what is known about them. In contrast, the subject of taxonomy proper is classification, including its processes, its products, and its implications for scientific study within a given field.

To date, most research in child development is driven by either the developmental

domain of interest (e.g., children's cognitive, language, moral, social, or emotional development) or by a pressing clinical or educational issue (e.g., children with learning disabilities, autism spectrum disorders, chronic health conditions, behavioral problems, poor academic achievement, risk for school dropout), decisions concerning what data to collect about parents and the family environment are guided by the central topic. A longitudinal study of young children's language development, for instance, understandably might concentrate on measuring language transactions between parents and their children and the language competence of parents, rather than engage in a broad study of the entire family environment. Variables such as the relationship between mothers and fathers, family spiritual practices, and stability of family resources would seem remote or relatively esoteric to include in such a study. Similarly, research on children's emerging comprehension of emotions and their own social-emotional competence is likely to select those aspects of the family environment and parental characteristics that appear to have highest relevance, such as the mental health status of the parents and how parents explicitly and implicitly teach children about emotions and emotional expressiveness.

Interestingly, many studies concerning clinical groups of children have cast a wide net in terms of what they measure about families and the home environment. Clinically focused studies often seek to answer one of two key questions: How does having a child with this condition influence the family (e.g., parental relationships, impacts of the mental and physical health of parents and siblings, financial and employment effects)? or How do families of children with this condition differ from families with typically developing children or children with other conditions (e.g., stress levels, resilience, marital stability, parenting practices, parenting practices, attention to siblings)? The findings from these divergent family studies may be interesting, but they seldom permit major new insights about the family environment that transcends the particular topic of initial investigation. This leaves the field of developmental science lacking a broad and integrated foundation for establishing and refining the taxonomy of family environments.

How can this situation be shifted? We propose that the taxonomy of family environments start with a focus on the primary purposes of families, the perspectives of individuals who are close to and care about families, and findings about families across cultures and cohorts that affirm important dimensions of the family environment related to supporting child development. Briefly, families are the units of society most closely linked to childbearing, child rearing, and transmission of intergenerational resources, values, and practices. From a child's perspective, he or she has a family (and sometimes more than one family) that provides the environment(s) where the child lives and grows up. Similarly, from the perspective of parents and other adults in the family, they assume responsibility for creating the family environment(s) and, over time, adjusting that environment to meet the needs of and take advantage of opportunities that appear for individual family members, while balancing the needs of the family unit as a whole. For family members, the family environment is multidimensional and engaged in supporting all aspects of development. The family environment can be described in terms of features such as the family's physical and financial resources, parents' direct caregiving practices, their social interactions within and outside the home environment, as well as the reflections and memories exchanged or withheld by family members about the family and, over time, the stability and responsiveness of the family to major life events, including normative and unexpected or sudden events. A family environment taxonomy must embrace such breadth of environmental characteristics, and be grounded in basic assumptions about human environments.

Taxonomy provides an opportunity to organize existing knowledge and to develop guidelines for categorizing environments and experiences. As George Gaylord Simpson (1961), founder of modern animal taxonomy, observed, "The necessity for aggregating things into classes is a completely general characteristic of living things" (p. 3). Taxonomy provides alternatives for arranging complex data into forms that may serve theory, inform data collection, or provide ideas for clinical practice or interventions. Classification can yield tremendous efficiencies in conveying large amount of relevant information; further, classification can be heuristic, such as suggesting ways in which knowing about the type of family environment could generate innovative ideas about how to help families or children when certain problems arise. Clinicians and educators alike often endorse the adage that "a one size solution does not fit all," yet they usually lack evidence-based strategies to guide the individual tailoring of treatments and educational plans that truly takes into account the family environment is rarely available. A family environment taxonomy may facilitate identifying distinctive approaches for different types of family that could yield similar benefits. Conversely, the same behavior enacted in different types of family environments may have different meaning and consequences.

Simpson recognized the delicate balance essential to maintain classification schemes that are up-to-date with scientific knowledge yet remain stable enough to serve their vital role in fostering communication and comparison of findings across studies and over time. We endorse Simpson's advocacy for consistency in classification and nomenclature, narrowing changes to a published classification scheme only when these are essential for alignment with known facts and accepted principles.

Defining the Family and the Family Environment

We define the family environment as something that encompasses the home but is distinguished by many features that transcend where the family resides. We recognize that the home environment expresses many things about the family, including resources, valued activities, organization, and aesthetics. The home can provide an environment that facilitates or hinders aspects of family functioning and individual development. For children, their home provides a base that acquires emotionally laden attributes associated with their family and the memories of what occurred at home as well as what was missing. Families distinguish themselves by their salient activities, relationships, and the emotional tone of how the family functions as a whole, and how subunits within the family operate. The family home also acquires a history, often recalled by children as though the home had a personality of its own. Children's words about their home convey almost person-like attributes, along a continuum from positive (e.g., warm, inviting, fun, interesting, well stocked, sunny, clean, and safe) to negative (e.g., cold, dark, dirty, noisy, silent, frightening, dangerous, and disorganized). A taxonomy of family environments thus must consider how to incorporate both the objective and subjective features of the family and the home(s) where the family lives.

Home as part of a larger social ecology. The family home environment is surrounded by a larger ecological context with critical physical and social dimensions that can affect what occurs in the home. Issues such as whether the family's home is congruent with and supported by the neighborhood and community, and typically show considerable congruence with the positive or negative features of the surrounding homes and activities, although atypically may be characterized as an outlier. The practical and psychological consequences of certain family features could differ tremendously as a function of whether these features are viewed as normative and desirable versus deviant and harmful. The norms for families as well as the ideals promoted for a family vary tremendously across cultures, communities, and cohorts. Although in theory some structural and physical characteristics of families may afford nearly universal advantages or disadvantages, many aspects of the family environment are relativistic, rather than absolute, in terms of their merit or risk. Family features are subject to interpretation by each family member; we hypothesize that this subjective appraisal (i.e., what families think about themselves and their environments) may exert a substantial effect on the degree to which certain features exert a developmental impact. For instance, the impact of a family event such as divorce, with consequences for the family's environment, may be mediated considerably by the family's perception of the reasons for and the possible consequences of the divorce on the family's everyday functioning and its ability to achieve its child rearing function.

Fundamental Assumptions and Definitions

Any exploration of the concept of the family environment or "home" leads to several general conclusions.

First, families and home environments do not exist apart from human beings who occupy them and live there, respectively. This means that assessing directional influences or causality is very difficult. If a certain environment is associated with a particular pattern of human behavior, we cannot discern whether the environment fostered the behavior or whether the people who created or entered that kind of environment were predisposed to behave that way, or at least to structure their environment in ways that would support particular kinds of behavior. Fundamentally, the line that separates environments from the people who design, use, and evaluate them is arbitrary and conventional, not absolute.

Second, families and home environments may be described and analyzed at many levels. These levels of description and analysis range from the proximal and day-to-day level of functioning and allocation of resources to increasingly global level. Level of analysis is a well-recognized axiom in social ecology, but rarely have theories of the family environment per se been developed sufficiently to postulate what these levels represent in terms of the creation, functional integrity, and influence of a family environment on its members or community.

Third, families and home environments include many diverse features and elements. Environments are at least as complex and problematic to delineate and to measure as are individuals. Deductively, environments ought to be even more complex than individuals are, because environments contain both individuals and inanimate components and all the relationships among these social and physical components. These features include the structural organization and membership of a family, the physical and financial resources, the explicit and implicit rules and expectations about the family's appearance and functioning both within and outside the home, and how the family's attributes compare to those of other families in their community or in their intergenerational history.

Fourth, families and home environments are dynamic, not static. This necessitates monitoring the key features or variables of families and homes over time. Theoretically, this dynamic nature of an environment, including changes associated with internal and external factors, is an important dimension of the environment. Single or static assessment of environments thus ignores a central quality of environments and yields, by definition, an incomplete picture.

Fifth, families and home environments may be considered in terms of objective and subjective terms. Many environmental and developmental psychologists (Lewin, 1935; Stokols, 1982; Ramey, Ramey, & Lanzi, 2006) discuss the distinctions between external, geographical, objectively observed, or "actual" environments on the one hand and behavioral, immediate, subjective, or "perceived" environments on the other. These different perspectives can yield markedly different conclusions about the relative significance of particular environmental variables. Further, the subjective experience or phenomenology of a given family environment almost certainly will vary across family members, depending on their role, age, temperament, and actual experiences with the family environment; and we lack

a standardized approach to creating a composite or balanced summary picture of this subjective diversity.

Sixth, and finally, families and home environments can be responded to as a whole as well as to its individual forms. That is, the total impression (gestalt) of environments is hypothesized to be more than the collection of many separate characteristics, resources, relationships, and activities. This conclusion is not at odds with the fact that some features of environments are more important than are others; neither does this imply that individuals fail to dimensionalize their own environments or to perceive some elements as distinctive within the total environment. To those collecting multilevel, dynamic, subjective, and objective data about a family environment, how to create this gestalt or total description has been highly problematic. Yet remarkably, almost every child when queried seems to have a pretty good idea of "what my family is like" and "how we are different or the same as other families" (Reid, Landesman, Jaccard, & Treder, 1989; Reid, Ramey, & Burchinal, 1990). Thus, the composite idea of "my family" is likely to exert an influence that is distinct from any standard or weighted sum of individual elements.

The Family: A Unit or a Changing Collection of Subunits?

One dilemma investigators encounter when studying an individual's development within the family environment is how to treat the construct of family. How can family be studied as a unit without negating the significance of specific dyadic relationships and subunits within it? To what extent do family members, including young children, have a concept of "family" or a collective "we" that is distinct from their independent relationships with individual family members? And how does this notion of "family" influence the experiences of individual family members and their behavior?

In a review of anthropological attempts to derive a "scientific, correct, and useful definition of the family," Yanagisako (1979) concluded that we should abandon efforts to discover "the irreducible core of the family and its universal definition" and instead "seek out the functions of the family in each society" (p. 200). Accordingly, in our conceptual framework, we define the family as follows:

> The family is a collection of individuals who have a perceived long-term commitment to the general well-being of one another, who label themselves a "family," and who are recognized in their community as an integral unit with designated responsibilities within society.

This definition is sensitive to the many structural and demographic changes in families across cultures, countries, religions, and cohorts. It implicitly recognizes that criteria such as legal establishment of the adult partners' relationship, the biological relatedness between adults and children, a common place of residence, actual or likely long-term stability of the unit, and focus on childrearing activities are inadequate for purposes of identifying the heterogeneity of families today. Because our primary interest is how families function and what aspects of the family environment have significant and pervasive effects on children and their society, we strongly endorse this nonrestrictive definition of the family. In fact, this definition permits the possibility that individuals may belong to more than one family at a time and some family members may include (or exclude) one another in their own definition of their family's membership (Landesman, 1986).

Is the home environment different from the family? Yes, because the idea of a home or a physical place where the family lives can be delineated in space and time; and this home serves many practical purposes for the family as a whole and for the individual family members. Families may move and/or change their home environments; further, for children who spend time with parents who do not live together, they may have more than one home environment. Some families are nomadic, others homeless, at

periods and to varying degrees in their family's history. Thus, an independent definition of the home environment is worthwhile, recognizing that one of the universal functions of a family is to create a home environment that can facilitate its role in promoting the well-being of family members and the family as a stable societal unit. We thus define the home environment as follows:

The home environment is defined as

> the physical place the family considers its primary base, often coinciding with its primary residence, and where the family conducts much of its private and interpersonal activity that helps the family fulfill its own purpose and societal responsibility.

Generally, the home environment in many societies is considered essential for healthy survival and important for promoting within-family activities and nurturing of individual family members. The home environment serves as a natural expression of the family's sense of identity or "self," through its accumulation of resources, its display of values and preferences, and its internal organization. The home environment is influenced by the family unit, the status and control of individual family members, and the relationship of the family to its surrounding society. The home environment has the potential to transcend the physical reality of the home; that is, the home environment can become an internalized representation for family members, although its physical existence may convey influences beyond those directly linked to the family, such as environmental risks and affordances associated with the physical structure and the neighborhood.

In the study of child development, the terms *family* and *home* have been used interchangeably without consistent delineation. We advocate differentiating these terms, in part, because the family is a far more pervasive entity than the home environment, continuing to exist even when family members disperse to live elsewhere (temporarily or permanently) and when the home environment changes or becomes unstable. As scientific inquiry into families adopts an increasingly longitudinal framework, coinciding with the expansion of life span studies of individual children, and incorporates measures that permit understanding dynamic changes, the value of a family taxonomy in which the family home environments are classified in standard ways with adequate specificity (e.g., when and where these homes existed as the family's primary base of operation) becomes more compelling. In societies and periods characterized by high mobility rates, disruption, and/or disaster, this ability to differentiate precisely regarding the continuities and discontinuities in the family and in the home environment will be exceptionally valuable.

Level of Analysis

Within a family, at least three levels of analysis are possible: (1) analysis at the level of individuals, (2) analysis at the level of social subunits (all combinations of two or more individuals), and (3) analysis at the level of the group as a whole. Ideally, an analysis of how a family functions would incorporate all three. In this conceptual framework, a family is described at the individual level by examining all family members' behavior, as well as their individual goals, strategies, resources, and experiences that pertain to family functioning. At the individual level of analysis, the family is equated with the composite obtained by considering each family member separately (i.e., the family equals the sum of its parts).

At the social subunit level, the nature of each dyad, triad, etc. is considered, including quantitative and qualitative descriptions of the similarities and differences of family members in each subunit. The subunits are viewed as having a valid existence that is distinct from data concerning individuals. For example, when considering the parental dyad, a mother may have different goals or aspirations for her children than does the father. Or both parents may share the same goals, but select alternative strategies to help achieve them. For a given subunit, when family members have differing goals, strategies, resources, and/or individual experiences, these can be characterized as "conflicting" (i.e., the attainment of one person's goals would prevent the attainment of the other person's goals), "nonimplicative" (i.e., one person's goals, if realized, would not affect the achievement of another's goals), or "complementary" (i.e., success in reaching one person's goals fosters the attainment of the other person's goals). We hypothesize that social subunits have effects on how the family actually behaves, above and beyond those attributable to the individuals within these subunits. These effects represent relativistic or relational properties that theoretically have significant social influences in their own right. Two mothers from different families, for example, may have identical goals, similar strategies for attaining them, comparable resources, and equivalent individual life experiences relevant to their functioning as mothers. Yet, these maternal variables may have significantly different meaning and consequences in the two families depending on the degree to which other family members have goals that are similar, conflicting, nonimplicative, or complementary to the mother's.

At the level of the family as a whole, the goal is to describe the family as a single unit. To achieve this, our approach involves a contextual analysis that simultaneously considers the goals, strategies for attaining goals, resources, and individual life experiences profiles of all family members. This then yields a single characterization of the entire family unit. A second approach treats the family as a single subject or single unit for analysis. For instance, an investigator might observe the activities of family members, which then are converted to a single code to describe the entire family. Similarly, judgments can be made about a family's overall or collective strategies to achieve goals. Finally, a third approach is to use "family" as a conceptual entity. This approach recognizes that most family members have and use a concept of the collective unit (i.e., "we are a family"), which may mediate aspects of their behavior. Theoretically, the collected statements and ratings by family members about their perceptions of their family "as a whole" may not be a simple function of component analyses at the individual and subunit levels. In essence, an abstracted conception of "family" can be created, by a variety of empirical methods, and used to study changes over time and effects of the "family" on children's outcomes.

Although we emphasize the importance of assessing each family member's goals, strategies, resources, and individual life experiences, we do not assume that the profiles of family members are independent of one another. For example, the goals of individual family members frequently emerge through discussions and interactions with other family members. The elements of a broad spanning system of describing the family are viewed as inherently dynamic and interdependent.

Family Behavior and Functional Domains

We propose a model in which family behavior is defined as the overt behavior of family members, generally enacted so as to realize the goals for the family unit. The behavior of family members outside the family realm is not included in this definition, although this can affect family functioning. For instance, a child's school adjustment is not considered part of family behavior, even though this may influence the family. Similarly, a parent's activities at work are not viewed as family behavior, but these may influence the parent's behavior toward other family members or may change the parent's goals or resources related to the family.

We categorize family behavior into six major functional domains:

(1) physical development and health,
(2) emotional development,
(3) social development,
(4) cognitive and intellectual development,
(5) moral and spiritual development, and
(6) cultural and aesthetic development.

These domains correspond to a combination of how societies and communities organize their resources and institutions and how adult family members invest in the nurturance of individuals during periods of dependence and natural growing up. We recognize that alternative domains could be identified, and that there is overlap in these functional areas. In terms of a hierarchy, the assurance of healthy physical development and health is undeniably part of the universal role of a family – to ensure survival of the next generation and beyond. For families in high resource, relatively safe communities, issues like survival and provision of basic shelter, food, and clothing often are scarcely addressed as a goal or an issue, because there is little that threatens achieving this goal. Yet even apparently advantaged families can be challenged in ways that are unexpected and sometimes sudden, such as when a family members becomes acutely ill or permanently disabled or when a natural disaster or economic crisis destroys the resources that the family had taken for granted as being invariably available. For the majority of families worldwide, the goal of achieving health and safety for all family members is a highly prominent one, and can exert a pervasive influence on how the family functions in the other domains. Table 11.1 provides a general description of these goal-related domains of the family. For each domain, there are features in the home environment that conceptually can be linked to these areas of family functioning.

For a given family or family member, the relative emphasis on different goal-related domains is determined, in part, by variables such as the ages of family members (e.g., relatively more emphasis may be placed by the parent on physical development and health when children are infants than when they are adolescents), the family's value system (e.g., parents who value formal education highly are likely to spend more time and resources related to cognitive development than parents who do not), and the society in which the family lives (e.g., a family in a communal or cooperative society may be more concerned about social and moral development than would a typical family in an individually competitive society).

Table 11.1: Proposed Major Goal-directed Domains of Family Functioning

Domain 1: Physical development and health. This domain concerns meeting basic needs for survival, such as providing food, housing, and clothing; promoting good health (medical and dental care, good nutrition, personal hygiene); arranging for child care (responsible adult supervision when children do not have minimal self-care skills); and ensuring safety (protection from potential physical or social harm, procedures for handling emergencies).

Domain 2: Emotional development and well-being. This refers to acquiring emotional self-regulation, fostering positive expression of emotional states, encouraging constructive ways to deal with emotions (especially negative states), developing the capacity to give and receive love (both within and outside the family context), learning to assess the emotional needs of other people, and maintaining good mental health.

Domain 3: Social development. This domain focuses on developing the types of effective interaction skills the family and its individual members need to initiate and maintain relationships, acquiring the ability to avoid and/or resolve social conflict, and recognizing the role of the individual in group contexts, both within and outside the family unit.

Domain 4: Cognitive development. Encompasses activities that foster intelligence and academic skills (e.g., formal education), daily living skills (e.g., money management, transportation use), and future vocational competence; learning to think critically and creatively, and understanding how to evaluate one's own thought processes.

Domain 5: Moral and spiritual development. This domain includes efforts to help family members acquire beliefs and values about ethical behavior and a philosophy of life. Examples of activities that foster the acquisition of such beliefs and values are religious education and practices, discussion of basic values, and reasoning about moral dilemmas.

Domain 6: Cultural and aesthetic development. This domain includes activities that foster an appreciation of one's own and others' cultural heritage, folklore, and traditions, as well as help one develop a personal sense of beauty, art, recreation, and entertainment.

Families also differ in how much family members agree with one another regarding the relative priorities for these broad developmental domains.

The necessity for multidimensional appraisal of families. Because we hypothesize that families are likely to vary in how skillfully or effectively they function across the six behavioral domains, we view any attempt to generate a global or unidimensional assessment of a family (e.g., as more or less "successful," "supportive," "normal," or "cohesive") as limited in value and likely to be misleading. Multidimensional study, in contrast, permits identifying a family's domain-specific strengths and weaknesses and could contribute to creating a family "profile" suitable for making predictions about the effects of family environments on selected aspects of individual development. Different combinations of environmental variables may facilitate or hinder "success" (i.e., achievement of goals) in the functional domains. Family behavior is expected to

change over time and across situations, as a direct result of shifts in the family's goals, strategies and plans, resources, and individual experiences of its members relative to the six functional domains. We further recognize the potential for cross-domain conflicts or cross-domain enhancement in family functioning. That is, a family's behavior at a given time may serve multiple functions: An activity that enhances functioning in one domain may also advance or restrict functioning in other domains. Similarly, individuals or subunits within the family may benefit from certain behavioral decisions or activities, while others within the same family may be adversely affected.

The Creation of a Family Environment and Home

For the purpose of taxonomy, we seek to describe the family environment broadly, encompassing the family's behavior and the combined goals, strategies, resources, and individual life experiences of family members. This definition includes physical and behavioral features of the environment, as well as the subjective experiences and emotions of family members. In this framework, the family and the home environment are not thought of as "influences," but as an evolving set of behaviors, perceived opportunities and risks, and observable changes that can serve as signs to the family members, as well as society, as to how effectively the family is functioning. This framework does not seek to separate family behavior from its environment but acknowledges their interdependency and codetermination over time. What becomes central to scientific inquiry about child development is how different aspects of the family and home environment relate to one another (e.g., how goals relate to family behavior; how family behavior affects a family member's emotions or moods, how the biological propensities or life histories of family members contribute to the ways they allocate time and financial resources) and, in turn, how these jointly contribute to child and family outcomes of interest (e.g., educational attainment, self-sufficiency, creative contributions, parenting competence for the next generation, positive physical and mental health).

Moving from All-encompassing Conceptual Frameworks to Difficult Choices about Empirical Inquiry

At a practical level, not all research about children will seek to generate a full profile of the family environment or the home life of the child. Yet a thorough grounding in a theory of or conceptual framework about the family environment, *which includes the mission of supporting multiple domains of functioning simultaneously*, may yield a new level of consensus about what aspects of the family and home environment are important to measure, and at what level. A research project that initially appears to be highly focused on a single topic, such as studying the promotion of healthy eating in preschool-age children or preventing negative consequences of risk-taking behavior in adolescents, may benefit from exploring aspects of the family environment that impinge upon a wider range of choices, priorities, and behavior. For example, the domain of moral and spiritual development may exert markedly different types and amounts of influence depending on whether the outcome of interest is healthy eating or preventing risk taking in teenage children.

We have entered a new era of public science, in which all publicly supported studies of human development are required to make their data sets publicly available within a reasonable period. This creates an unprecedented opportunity for cross-study comparisons and validation regarding basic principles of human development. To the extent that the families and home environments are intertwined with children's development over time, then a commitment to collecting a core set of descriptors about the family and the home environment could be highly efficient and scientifically productive. The current limits relate to the lack of a standard set of terms with operational definitions about the family and home environment, and the diversity of tools for capturing family behavior. Developmental science as a socially guided, collective endeavor has the ability to convene groups that will seek to reach consensus about a core set of descriptors, and through our institutions (funding agencies, universities and their Institutional Review Boards that seek to protect the well-being of study participants and promote ethical conduct and scientific integrity, and our national organizations) we could begin to implement requirements about collecting and storing minimal family descriptors. Only a few decades ago the child development research literature had no standards regarding the collection or reporting of the gender and ethnic and racial characteristics of study participants. When we realized that these variables assumed a potentially major role in interpreting the findings of a given study and comparing results across multiple studies, then we required all scientific publications to include these variables. We think the rationale is strongly compelling

Table 11.2: Dimensions for a Core Set of Standard Family Descriptors and Optional Additional Information (Adapted to Study Purposes and Resources) at Each Time of Data Collection

1. Family Creation: Dates when primary family began; family's description of the type of adult/ parent relationships in family; dates and types of major changes in legal and living arrangements prior to study start date
2. Family Composition: Number and current roles of individuals in family; identification of which members live in family home
3. Individual Family Members: Birth dates and gender of each family member; children's status in family (e.g., biological, adoptive, foster child; other relative) history of adults in terms of prior family units and their outcomes (e.g., death, divorce, separation, abandonment); educational level, employment status, and occupation for all adult family members; identification of major disability and serious physical, mental health, and addiction conditions affecting family members
4. Family Financial Resources: Sources and amount of annual income (cash and in-kind goods); stability estimate of income; availability of cash reserves and assets
5. Family Home: Type of residence (e.g., single-family home, multifamily home, apartment/condo, transient setting, homeless), whether parents are primary individuals in charge of residence or whether others are (e.g., grandparents, relatives, friends), neighborhood descriptors and geocoding, duration in home, family's perception of adequacy of the home for current overall needs
6. Family Goals and Values (optional)
7. Parenting Practices, Knowledge, and Behavior (optional)
8. Children's Perspectives on their Family and Parents (optional)
9. Family Strategies to Achieve Goals and Adaptability and Agreement among Adults about how Family Functions (optional)
10. Availability, Use, and Perceptions about Outside Resources to Assist Family in Childrearing and Overall Functioning (optional)
11. Quality of Within-Family Relationships (optional); Parental relationship, Parent-child dyadic relationships, Sibling relationships, other sub-units
12. Relationship of Family Unit to Extended Kinship Network and Relatives (optional)

that information about the family and home environment is needed as well. Indeed, the ideas for this edited book – a handbook focused on the environment per se – could be joined with social actions in our leading professional organizations to promote more vigorous and systematic measurement of the human environments that coexist with the life course of individuals. In Table 11.2, we outline core elements nominated for standard descriptors of the family for all children in developmental research, along with optional areas that will be relevant for many studies. This preliminary list would then need specification and refinement informed by experts from diverse disciplines, with guidelines for ways to collect and code the data. Many ongoing studies could supplement their extant databases with relatively modest investment to collect missing information. The wide availability of diverse longitudinal databases with standard family environment data would provide a timely and vastly expanded scientific opportunity for advancing the taxonomy of family environments.

Family Outcomes and the Identification of "Successful" Families

Family success in a general way is determined by how well a family functions relative to achieving family goals. The family goals used in judging success may be identified either by family members (i.e., self-defined) or by external sources (e.g., community, investigator). In this framework, the merits of particular parenting beliefs, values, and practices or the effects of different family resources are evaluated by measuring the degree to which these foster or hinder achieving particular family goals. We do not endorse establishing an a priori notion of what constitutes optimal family functioning or an ideal family environment, except to state generally that "successful" or "effective" families will engage in activities that will tend to increase the probability of realizing specified family goals or child outcomes. Conclusions about how successfully a family functions in particular domains may differ depending on whether a family's own criteria or external standards are used. Further, simple or formulaic measures, such as counting the number of achieved goals or calculating a ratio of met goals to unmet goals, convey only limited information, because families differ in the number of goals they set, how explicit their goals are, the proportion of goals shared or recognized by family members, the degree to which priorities are set and stable about these goals, and whether their goals are long- versus short-term.

The definition of family "success" as the achievement of (or satisfactory progress toward) family goals places the concept of "optimal family functioning" within a relativistic framework. For one family member, the family might be highly "successful," whereas for another family member, it may not be. If a father places high priority on the goal that his child be religious, and if the child is not, then from the father's perspective, a "problem" exists (in this case, in the moral and spiritual development domain). In contrast, the mother may be indifferent about the religiosity of her child, and the fact that the child is not religious does not constitute a family failure from her perspective.

External and Demographic Influences on the Family Environment

Sociologists and psychologists have studied extensively the impact on child development of such variables as social class, family size, birth order, parental age and education, religion, and life transitions (cf. Borkowski, Ramey, & Bristol-Powers, 2002). Although

this research has yielded important findings, it has failed to identify adequately the important variables that mediate and moderate the influence of these variables on child development. In our view, it is not sufficient to say, for example, that family income or birth order "influences" the intelligence of the child. Rather, we want to obtain a better understanding of why such variables are related and the processes that account for the relationship. The environmental framework we have proposed is designed to identify combinations of variables that, over time and in certain sequences, may be reliable associated with certain life trajectories. The traditional models of causality thus are replaced with relativistic probability models and with creation of alternative pathway models that serve to identify the most critical environmental features that can promote or hinder particular developmental processes. The fact (axiom) that the children's development has helped to increase or decrease the probability of certain family environmental features being present or absent is no longer a focus of debate; rather, the likelihood of these joint probabilities and pathways and the circumstances associated with exceptional or deviant pathways become the focus of investigation. Thus, differences in children's intelligence or mental health "outcomes" associated with the "static" demographic variables would be related instead to identifiable differences in family behavior and in the goals, strategies for attaining goals, resources, and individual life experiences for differing types of families.

Examples of Research Focused on the Family Environment

We wrote this chapter to help frame the basic topic of the family and home environment as central to understanding child development. By far, most scientific study of developmental processes has occurred without adequately studying the variation in the family contexts where children are living and growing up. For investigators who study basic developmental topics, rather than at-risk or clinical populations, they have tended to rely on samples of convenience, primarily children from relatively healthy, stable, high-resource family and community settings. Accordingly, variations among these families do not seem to be likely sources of influence that could account for major differences in the development of the children being studied. Issues about the generalizability of findings about development from these samples of convenience are seldom even considered. In contrast, scientists who study highly vulnerable children, such as those living in extremely impoverished environments, children who have been abused or neglected, children with serious health conditions and/or disabilities, are far more likely to hypothesize that the family environment can and often does contribute to different courses of development among the children. Indeed, these studies now routinely seek to identify family "strengths" and "resilience" pathways along with delineating the correlates of multiple risk factors.

In our own research, we have conducted longitudinal studies in which we collect extensive background information about each child's family and home environment at the time of study enrollment. We then gather prospective data about the family environment from a variety of sources. Typically, we seek to collect at least two independent measures of each major aspect of the family environment, relying on different informants whenever possible. In the Washington Family Behavior Study, for example, we conducted similar interviews with both mothers and fathers (regardless of whether the households were headed by a single mother or two parents living together) (e.g., Wan, Jaccard, & Ramey, 1996); directly observed and scored dimensions of the family home, including quantitative coding (in person and video-based) of parent-child interactions and family dinners (e.g., Ramey & Juliusson, 1998); and having dialogues with children (ages 4 and older) about their perceptions of their family and activities within the family context (e.g., Reid, Landesman, Treder, & Jaccard, 1989).

(For an overview of the construction of the child measures that use a Vygotskian-style dialogue approach to having children provide reliable and valid data about their family, see Reid, Ramey, & Burchinal, 1990.) In addition, we always seek to obtain time-distributed multiple measures to both increase our confidence in the adequacy of the data to depict important dimensions of the home environment, and to monitor for changes over more extended periods.

One of the most interesting methodological findings we have detected, but that we unfortunately have not emphasized adequately in our published findings, is something we have come to label as variation in a family's "baseline self-reflection or self-awareness level." We uncovered this finding on several occasions when we readministered many of the same interview and self-administered tools twice – within a 3-week period – to a cohort of 400 middle-class African American and white/non-Hispanic families in the Seattle Family Behavior Study. Initially, we sought simply to establish updated or missing short-term test-retest reliability estimates for these tools. We also were curious as to whether differences between mothers and fathers, for example, about aspects of their family life were any larger than within-person differences that might occur when asked a parent responds to the same set of questions in a short period (i.e., a period when things about their family were unlikely to have changed much). We originally planned to use the multiply collected data by averaging the responses of a family member to the same questions, reasoning that this would probably yield a more robust estimate of the respondent's perceptions or a more complete report about family events and activities. Instead, what we learned is that there were two fairly distinct subgroups of families: (1) those who provided fairly stable answers on both occasions to the same items, regardless of the construct being studied (e.g., quality of the marital relationship, family values, perceptions of the parent-child relationship, family satisfaction, and personal life satisfaction) and (2) another group for whom their answers differed significantly on the two occasions. For this latter group, we explored how well their responses corresponded with some of the child or family outcomes of interest (e.g., child success in school, perceptions of parenting stress) – in other words, we considered the concurrent or predictive validity of the tools by comparing use of (i) the first round of answers only, (ii) the averaged or combined data from two assessment sessions, and (iii) the second round of data only. We found that using the second set of data yielded findings that were significantly much clearer, with stronger associations (e.g., higher correlation coefficients or far more variance accounted for in the proposed models of family functioning), than those based on either the first set of data alone or the combined or averaged scores. Although we attended to this finding to inform the statistical models we generated for subsequent data analyses, we essentially overlooked considering what this finding might be revealing about families in a more substantive way. Over time, we have developed the hypothesis that families may vary considerably along a continuum that corresponds to the degree to which they naturally reflect about themselves and their family environment (i.e., when not prompted by a research study or clinician to provide information about their family's home, values, parenting practices, problems, etc.). For families in which the adults or the adults and children engage in frequent self-appraisal and perhaps discussion or even formal therapy about their family, the responses family members provide to items on the standardized research tools may provide a valid and reliable portrayal of their family on the first administration of these tools. For other families that do engage in similar levels of self-reflection and/or discussion about these matters, their first set of responses may provide a less complete, accurate, or coherent set of data, in large part because this may be the first time they are considering their feelings or observations about certain aspects of their family and relationships within the family. We hypothesize that for the less naturally self-reflective families the

first administration of the tools may stimulate some new thinking about these family matters; and the, when provided a second opportunity to answer the same questions, the family members may reveal information that is more indicative of their "informed" opinions or newly stimulated awareness about certain aspects of their family life. In fact, we have pondered whether a brief tool about the extent to which family members engage in reflection about the family as a unit, seek out information about parenting, and compare themselves to others or to their own "ideal" standards might be interesting. (We have not found such a tool, nor created one yet.)

We propose that the earlier and unexpected finding raises a central question for those studying the family environment: To what extent are one-time only assessments about many of the important dimensions of the family environment adequate in terms of accuracy, sensitivity, and predictive validity? This goes beyond the convenient psychometric appraisal about internal consistency of items to tap a subscale or factor and would necessitate systematic investigation about methods across a heterogeneous group of families, at different stages in their evolution, with different types of parents and children. To continue to accept measures of the family environment that are fairly brief and fail to tap many central issues will leave the field of developmental environmental science in its current and underdeveloped stage. Such methodological inquiry will benefit from theory and empirical findings, and from including clinicians, educators, and families themselves in contributing to a more refined set of tools to capture dimensions such as family goals, values, strategies, and perceived problems and their consequences for children's development.

Diversity among Families Living in Poverty: An Illustration of How Typologies Can Be Applied in Studying Children's Developmental Trajectories

For more than three decades, we have been studying children who live in poverty, often in the very lowest resource communities with multiple intra- and extrafamilial risks. One of the most established relationships is that poverty is strongly linked to many adverse childhood outcomes, yet the majority of children growing up poor still do relatively well (Ramey, Ramey, & Lanzi, 2006). To study variation among poverty families, we began to apply cluster analytic strategies to develop and refine a typology of families (Ramey, Yeates, & MacPhee, 1984), using families from two randomized controlled trials (N = 175) of early educational intervention. Children from families with young single mothers whose formal education and tested intelligence levels were low had very high risk for both social and cognitive problems by school entry. Conversely, poverty-level children from families with older mothers with higher education and tested IQs were at relatively low risk. We demonstrated that the family types defined by demographic factors were strongly associated with patterns of parenting and the quality of stimulation in the home environment.

We later expanded our approach using a national longitudinal, multisite, randomized trial of 5,406 former Head Start children and their families – the National Head Start–Public School Early Childhood Transition Demonstration project-NTDP (Ramey, Ramey, & Lanzi, 1998; Ramey, Ramey, & Lanzi, 2004). We generated a family typology based on 13 readily available variables about families: (1) maternal education, (2) father presence in the home, (3) maternal age, (4) number of children in the home, (5) number of adults in the home, (6) household annual income, (7) mother's employment status, (8) maternal U.S. citizenship, (9) whether the family was homeless in the last year, (10) whether the mother reported someone else assisted with parenting responsibilities in the home, (11) presence of maternal chronic physical and/or mental health problems, (12) receipt of public cash assistance, and (13) whether English was spoken in the home. (For details about the analytic techniques, including split-half randomization of the sample and validation before finalizing the family typology, see Ramey, Ramey, & Lanzi,

1998, 2004.) Table 11.3 summarizes the six major family types we identified, after following a series of theory-driven tests to realize the best solution for the typology. These largely confirmed the same types of families identified in our research decades earlier, with the exception of new types of foreign-born and families that were homeless or did not have a mother living with the child.

Figure 11.1 displays how the family typology related strongly to children's school entry scores on the Peabody Picture Vocabulary Test, which we include to illustrate that the composite of these family environmental variables often contain more information that typically one or two variable analyses. Further, in-depth analyses of these longitudinal data set indicated that the family types had strong association with many behavioral and planning aspects of the family and the supports it provided (or failed to provide) for the child as he or she entered public school. Further, the typology predicts many aspects of the children's progress in the first 4 years of public school, across multiple domains of development. Subsequently, we have used these typologies to guide training and professional development for those plan and implement programs for families in poverty, to study the stability of family "types" over time and the likely processes associated with major changes in the family environment, and to consider tailoring of services and programs for children whose families differ functionally in their resources, values, strengths, and challenges.

Conclusion

We propose that the time is right to advance the systematic study of how to classify and organize complex information about the family and home environments that support the growth and development of children, from before birth until adulthood. There is a large and scattered literature that could be reviewed with this objective. Consensus among scientists and clinicians about key variables to add as part of almost all longitudinal scientific investigations could provide

Table 11.3: A Family Typology: Diversity of Families with Incomes below Poverty Level

Family Type A: Traditional Family. This family type represents 30% of the former Head Start families. Fathers are present in almost 90%; nearly 95% have at least two adults regularly care for their child. Mothers have an average high school education and were typically 24 or 25 years old when their child was born. This traditional family type living in poverty has the highest average income, although still below poverty. (*Note*: In describing each family type. it is important to recognize that there are some families that vary in terms of some characteristics; e.g., for Family Type A, about 10% do not have fathers present in the homes and some mothers have less than a high school education.)

Family Type B: Single Unemployed Mother with Larger Family Size. This group represents the next largest family type (29%). Typically, the father is not present and the is not employed. Overwhelmingly, mothers received public assistance (92%). Virtually all mothers were born in the United States, spoke English at home, and did not self-report chronic health problems. Mothers averaged less than high school completion (11.3 years) and these families were the largest in terms of number of children living at home.

Family Type C: Working Mother, Usually Single, Smaller Family, The third major family type represents 24% of the families and may be primarily distinguished by high rates of maternal employment (72%) and by corresponding much lower rates of receiving AFDC (18%). All of the mothers were born in the United States, and the fathers are present in 24% of these families. The average number of children is 2.5 per family, smaller than any other family type. All of these families speak English at home, and the mothers have no chronic maternal health problems.

Family Type D: Traditional, Foreign Born, Non-English-Speaking at Home. The most important feature that differentiates this family type is that more than 99% do not speak English as their primary language at home. and 80% of the mothers were not born in the United States. Fathers are present in 70% of these families, although only 57% of the mothers report that they have someone who helps them in major parenting duties. These mothers report having the least amount of formal schooling (average years of schooling = 10). This group represents 10% of the sample participating in the NTDP.

Family Type E: Chronic Maternal Health Problems, Older Mothers. This family type represents only 3% of the study families. In all of these families, the mother has chronic major health problems. These mothers are, on the average, 2 to 4 years older than are mothers in the other family types, and their family incomes are very low. Fathers are present in 39% of these homes, although 69% of the mothers report that someone else in their home helps them with childrearing. The mothers in this group have an average educational level of 11.6 years.

Family Type F: Homeless in Last Year, Unemployed. This family type represents 3% of the study sample. All of these families were homeless at least some time in the past 12 months. On the average, they have more than three children, and most mothers are not employed (unemployment rate is 74%). AFDC is received by 60% of these families. Only 8% do not speak English as their first language at home. These mothers have less than a high-school education, on the average (11.5 years).

Taken as a whole, the six clusters or family types accounted for 99% of participating families. Three of these six clusters are highly similar to clusters from the North Carolina sample: (1) The Traditional Nuclear Family (30% vs. 15%), (2) The Single Unemployed Mother with Multiple Children (29% vs. 23%), and (3) The Single, Working Mother with One or Two Children (24% vs. 17%). Thus these three clusters together account for 83% of the families studied in the HTDP. In addition to these prominent clusters, we have identified three clusters that occurred with lesser frequency: Traditional Nuclear, Foreign Born Mothers from Non-English-speaking homes (10%); Older Mothers with Chronic Health Problems (3%); and Mothers Who Have Been Homeless in the Past Year and Unemployed (3%).

an accelerated way to understand the important descriptive elements vital to understanding how children, parents, and environments mutually influence one another over time. An explicit goal includes the need to better individualize family and child interventions for those at-risk or with identified special needs. Increasingly, however, there are crises

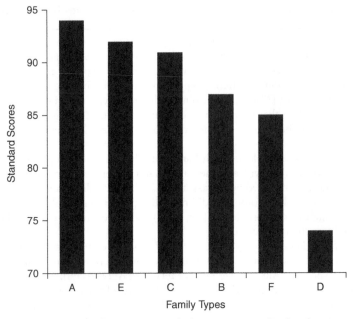

Figure 11.1. Peabody Picture Vocabulary Test scores by family type.

among what have been considered healthy and normative families. The availability of family environmental data, conjoined with other information about outside influences, could facilitate this next step of individualizing interventions based on systematic empirical evidence.

The family environment is inherently multidimensional, dynamic, and complex. The responses of children to their families, and the contribution children make to the functioning of their families, have been related to many variables, ranging from microbehavioral observations of interaction patterns to broad classes of exogonous factors. To create a cohesive picture of the role of the family environment in the development of children, from birth on, we have proposed the use of a conceptual framework that is designed to be multipurpose. Specifically, we have defined the family as a functional unit of individuals identified by two features: their self-definition as a "family" within their culture and their commitment to the general well-being of family members. This commitment may be dimensionalized into broad domains of family functioning that operate concurrently and apply to all

family members: (1) physical development and health, (2) emotional development, (3) social development, (4) cognitive development, (5) moral and spiritual development, and (6) cultural and aesthetic development. A fundamental axiom in this framework is that family environments are not inherently good or bad, but that select aspects of the environment potentially have differential effects on each domain of family functioning. Accordingly, multivariate assessment of the family environment is needed to account for the complex child outcomes observed, and to provide data relevant to understanding the processes that mediate both child and family outcomes.

Despite the logistical and statistical difficulties inherent in treating the family as a single unit (although continuing to recognize the potential contribution of individuals and dyads), we are optimistic about the merit of developing procedures to permit contextual and relativistic assessment of family environments. Abstract judgments of family "success" and family "problems" must be related to family goals and priorities. These may be defined from multiple perspectives (e.g., family members, the investigator, society). Theoretically, these different perspectives are hypothesized to lead to different conclusions about the significance of particular family environment variables.

We have presented a framework for analyzing family functioning as well as for understanding family and child outcomes. We describe the family environment as the product of four major classes of variables – family goals, strategies and plans for attaining goals, social and physical resources, and individual life experiences. We believe it is important to consider each class of variables when evaluating family outcome measures. At the very least, an investigator who studies a single type of variable (e.g., emotions) should recognize that its effects will operate, in natural contexts, in combination with the other classes of variables specified in our framework. To ignore these other variables may result in a failure to understand key aspects of how a single or a few variables influence family outcomes. We hope investigators will find our framework useful in that we provide a multidimensional context within which research findings can be interpreted. More importantly, potential mediating and moderating variables are identified in a manner that facilities understanding how one or two variables may impinge on child development or family functioning. Thus, our intent has been to explicate a framework that can guide data collection efforts and can serve as a useful diagnostic tool for analyzing the effects of a wide array of distal (external) and proximal (internal) variables on family and child outcomes.

References

Beavers, W. R., & Voeller, M. N. (1983). Family models: Comparing and contrasting the Olson Circumplex Model with the Beavers Systems Model. *Family Process*, 22, 85–98.

Becker, W., & Krug, R. (1965). Parent attitude research instrument: A research review. *Child Development*, 36, 329–365.

Bell, R. Q. (1968). A reinterpretation of the direction of effects in studied of socialization. *Psychological Review*, 75, 81–95.

Belsky, J. (1981). Early human experience: A family perspective. *Developmental Psychology*, 17, 3–23.

Bertalanffy, Von L. (1968). *General systems theory*. New York: Braziller.

Borkowski, J.G., Ramey, S.L., & Bristol-Powers, M. (Eds.) (2002). *Parenting and the child's world: Influences on academic, intellectual, and social-emotional development*. Mahwah, NJ: Erlbaum Publishers.

Bronfenbrenner, U. (1979). *The ecology of human development*. Cambridge, MA: Harvard University Press.

Brownell, A., & Shumaker, S. (1984). Social support: An introduction to a complex phenomenon. *Journal of Social Issues*, 40, 1–10.

Cattell, R. (1965). *The scientific analysis of personality*. Baltimore: Penguin.

Cauce, A. M., Reid, M., Landesman, S., & Gonzales, N. (1990). Social support in young children: Measurement, structure, and behavioral impact. In I. G. Sarason, B. R. Sarason, & G. R. Pierce (Eds.), *Social Support: An Interactional View*, pp. 64–94. New York: John Wiley & Sons.

Chan, D., Ramey, S. L., Ramey, C. T., & Schmitt, N. (2000). Modeling intraindividual changes in children's social skills at home and at school: A multivariate latent growth approach to understanding between-settings differences in children's social skill development. *Multivariate Behavioral Research*, 35, 365–396.

Clarke-Stewart, K. A. (1978). And daddy makes three: The father's impact on mother and young child. *Child Development*, 49, 466–478.

Daly, E., Lancee, W., & Polivy (1983). A conical model for the taxonomy of emotional expression. *Journal of Personality and Social Psychology*, 45, 443–457.

Dunn, J. (1983). Sibling relationships in early childhood. *Child Development*, 54, 787–811.

Elder, G. H. (1984). Families, kin, and the life course: A sociological perspective. In R. D. Parke (Ed.), *Review of child development research*: Vol. 7. *The family*, pp. 80–136. Chicago: University of Chicago Press.

Epstein, N. B., & Bishop, D. S. (1981). Problem centered systems therapy of the family. *Journal of Marital and Family Therapy*, 7, 23–31.

Epstein, N. B., Bishop, D. 5., & Baldwin, L. M. (1982). McMaster model of family functioning: A view of the normal family. In F. Walsh (Ed.), *Normal family processes*, pp. 115–141. New York: Guilford.

Feinman, S., & Lewis, M. (1984). Is there social life beyond the dyad?: A social-psychological view of social connections in infancy. In M. Lewis (Ed.), *Beyond the dyad*, p. 1341. New York: Wiley.

Feiring, C., & Lewis, M. (1984). Changing characteristics of the U.S. family: Implications for family networks, relationships, and child development. In M. Lewis (Ed.), *Beyond the dyad*, pp. 59–89. New York: Plenum Press.

Gottlieb, B. (1981). *Social networks and social support*. Beverly Hills, CA: Sage.

Gottman, J. M., & Levinson, R. W. (1986). Assessing the role of emotion in marriage. *Behavioral Assessment, 8*, 31–48.

Grotevant, H. D., Scarr, S., & Weinberg, R. A. (1977). Intellectual development in family constellations with adopted and natural children: A test of the Zajonc and Markus model. *Child Development, 48*, 1699–1703.

Gurman, A. S., & Kniskern, D. P. (Eds.) (1981). *Handbook of family therapy*. New York: Brunner(Mazel.

Holman, 1. B., & Burr, W. R. (1980). Beyond the beyond: The growth of family theories in the 1970s. *Journal of Marriage and the Family, 42*, 729–741.

Jaccard, J., & Choi, W. (1986). Cross-cultural methods for the study of behavioral decision making. *Journal of Cross-Cultural Psychology, 17*, 123–149.

Jaccard, J., & Wood, G. (1986). An idiothetic analysis of behavioral decision making. In D. Brinberg & R. Lutz (Eds.), *Methodological perspectives in consumer behavior*, pp. 67–106. New York: Springer-Verlag.

Jackson, D. (1967). *Personality research form manual*. Goshen, NY: Research Psychologists Press.

Lamb, M. E. (Ed.), *The role of the father in child development*. New York: Wiley.

Landesman, S. (1986). Toward a taxonomy of home environments. In N. R. Ellis & N. W. Bray (Eds.), *International review of research in mental retardation*, pp. 259–289, Vol. 14. New York: Academic Press.

Landesman, S., Jaccard, J., & Gunderson, V. (1991). The family environment: The combined influence of family behavior, goals, strategies, resources, and individual experiences. In M. Lewis & S. Feinman (Eds.), *Social influences and socialization in infancy*, pp. 63–96. New York: Plenum Press.

Lewin, K. (1935). *A dynamic theory of personality*. New York: McGraw-Hill Book Company.

Lewis, M. (1982). The social network systems model: Toward a theory of social development. In T. Field, A. Huston, H. C. Quay, L. Troll, & G. E. Finley (Eds.), *Review of human development*, pp. 180–214. New York: Wiley.

Lewis, M. (1984). *Beyond the dyad*. New York: Plenum Press.

Lewis, M., & Feinman, S. (1991). *Social influences and socialization in infancy*. New York: Plenum Press.

Lewis, M., & Feiring, C. (1979). The child's social network: Social object, social functions and their relationship. In M. Lewis & L. A. Rosenblum (Eds.), *The child and its family*, pp. 9–27. New York: Plenum Press.

Lewis, M., & Feiring, C. (1981). Direct and indirect interactions in social relationships. In L. Lipsitt (Ed.), *Advances in infancy research*, pp. 131–161, Vol. 1. New York: Ablex.

Lewis, M., & Michalson, L. (1983). *Children's emotions and moods*. New York: Plenum Press.

Lewis, M., & Rosenblum, L. A. (Eds.) (1974). *The effect of the infant on its caregiver*. New York: Wiley.

Lewis, M., & Rosenblum, L. A. (Eds.) (1979). *The child and its family*. New York: Plenum Press.

Maccoby, E. E., & Martin, J. A. (1983). Socialization in the context of the family: Parent child interaction. In P. H. Mussen (Ed.), *Handbook of child psychology*, pp. 1–101, Vol. 4 (4th ed.). New York: Wiley.

MacDonald, K., & Parke, R. D. (1984). Bridging the gap: Parent-child play interaction and peer interactive competence. *Child Development, 55*, 1265–1277.

Magnusson, D. (1981) *Toward a psychology of situations: An interactional perspective*. Hillsdale, NJ: Erlbaum.

Malpass, R. (1977). Theory and method in cross-cultural psychology. *American Psychologist, 32*, 1069–1079.

Mancuso, J. c., & Handin, K. H. (1983). Prompting parents toward constructivist caregiving practices. In I. Sigel and L. Laosa (Eds.), *Changing families*, pp. 167–202. New York: Plenum Press.

Miller, J. G. (1965). Living systems: Basic concepts. *Behavioral Sciences, 10*, 193–237.

Minuchin, S. (1974). Families and family therapy. Cambridge, MA: Harvard University Press.

Norman, W. (1963). Toward an adequate taxonomy of personality attributes: Replicated factor structure in peer nomination personality ratings. *Journal of Abnormal and Social Psychology, 66*, 574–583.

Nye, F. I., & Berardo, F. M. (Eds.) (1966). *Emerging conceptual frameworks in family analysis*. New York: Macmillan.

Olson, D. H. (1985). Commentary: Struggling with congruence across theoretical models and methods. *Family Process, 24*, 203–207.

Olson, D. H., Russell, C. S., & Sprenkle, D. H. (1983). Circumplex model of marital and family systems: VI. Theoretical update. *Family Process, 22*, 69–83.

Olson, D. H., Sprenkle, D. H., & Russell, C. S. (1979). Circumplex model of marital and family systems: I. Cohesion and adaptability dimensions, family types, and clinical applications. *Family Process, 18*, 3–28.

Parke, R. D., Power, T. G., & Gottman, J. M. (1979). Conceptualizing and quantifying influence patterns in the family triad. In M. E. Lamb, S. J. Suomi, & G. R. Stephenson (Eds.), *Social interaction analysis: Methodological issues*, pp. 231–252. Madison: University of Wisconsin.

Pattee, H. H. (Ed.) (1973). *Hierarchy theory: The challenge of complex systems*. New York: Braziller.

Patterson, G. R. (1982). *Coercive family process*. Eugene, OR: Castalia.

Poortinga, Y. (1975). Some implications of three different approaches to intercultural comparisons. In J. Berry & W. Lonner (Eds.), *Applied cross-cultural psychology*, pp. 327–332. Amsterdam: Swets & Zeitlinger.

Ramey, C. T., MacPhee, D., & Yeates, K. O. (1983). *Preventing developmental retardation: A general systems model*. Hanover, NH: University Press of New England.

Ramey, C. T., & Ramey S. L. (1993). Home visiting programs and the health and development of young children. *The Future of Children, 3*, 129–139.

Ramey, C. T., Ramey, S. L., Gaines, R., & Blair, C. (1995). Two-generation early intervention programs: A child development perspective. In I. Sigel (Series Ed.) and S. Smith (Vol. Ed.), *Two-generation programs for families in poverty: A new intervention strategy: Vol. 9. Advances in applied developmental psychology*, pp. 199–228. Norwood, NJ: Ablex.

Ramey, C. T., Ramey, S. L., & Lanzi, R. G. (1998). Differentiating developmental risk levels for families in poverty: Creating a family typology. In M. Lewis, & C. Feiring (Eds.), *Families, risk, and competence*, pp. 187–205. Hillsdale, NJ: Erlbaum.

Ramey, C.T., Ramey, S.L., & Lanzi, R.G. (2006). Children's health and education. In I. Sigel & A. Renninger (Eds.), *The handbook of child psychology*. Vol. 4 (pp. 864–892). Hoboken, NJ: Wiley & Sons.

Ramey, C.T., Yeates, K.O., & MacPhee, D. (1984). Risk for retarded development among disadvantaged families: A systems theory approach to preventive intervention. In B. Keogh (Ed.), *Advances in special education*, pp. 249–272. Greenwich, CT: JAI Press.

Ramey, S. L. (2002). The science and art of parenting. In J. G. Borkowski, S. L. Ramey, & M. Bristol-Power (Eds.), *Parenting and the child's world: Influences on academic, intellectual, and social-emotional development*, pp. 47–71. Mahwah, NJ: Erlbaum.

Ramey, S. L., Gaines, R., Phillips, M., & Ramey, C. T. (1998). Perspectives of former Head Start children and their parents on the transition to school. *Elementary School Journal, 98*, 311–328.

Ramey, S. L., & Juliusson, H. (1998). Family dynamics at dinner: A natural context for revealing basic family processes. In M. Lewis, & C. Feiring (Eds.), *Families, risk, and competence*, pp. 31–52. NJ: Erlbaum.

Ramey, S. L., & Keltner, B. R. (1996). Family adaptation and challenges: Multiple perspectives. *Current Opinion in Psychiatry, 9*, 322–327.

Ramey, S. L., Krauss, M. W., & Simeonsson, R. J. (1989). Research on families: Current assessment and future opportunities. *American Journal of Mental Retardation, 94*, ii–vi.

Ramey, S.L., Ramey, C.T., & Lanzi, R.G. (2004). The transition to school: Building on preschool foundations and preparing for lifelong learning. In E. Zigler & S.J. Styfco (Eds.), *The Head Start debates*, pp. 397–413. Baltimore: Paul H. Brookes.

Reid, M., Landesman, S., Treder, R., & Jaccard, J. (1989). "My Family and Friends": Six to twelve-year-old children's perceptions of social support. *Child Development, 60*, 896–910.

Reid, M., Ramey, S. L., & Burchinal, M. (1990). Dialogues with children about their families. In I. Bretherton & M. Watson (Eds.), *Children's perspectives on their families: New directions for child development*, pp. 5–28. San Francisco: Jossey-Bass.

Reiss, D. (1971a). Varieties of consensual experience: 1. A theory for relating family interaction to individual thinking. *Family Process, 10*, 1–27.

Reiss, D. (1971b). Varieties of consensual experience: II. Dimensions of a family's experience of its environment. *Family Process, 10*, 28–35.

Robinson, N. M., Lanzi, R. G., Weinberg, R. A., Ramey, S. L., & Ramey, C. T. (2002). Family factors associated with high academic competence in former Head Start children at third grade. *Gifted Child Quarterly, 46,* 281–294.

Robinson, N. M., Weinberg, R. A., Redden, D., Ramey, S. L., & Ramey, C. T. (1998). Family factors associated with high academic competence among former Head Start children. *Gifted Child Quarterly, 42,* 148–156.

Sameroff, A. J. (1983). Contexts and development: The systems and their evolution. In W. Kessen (Ed.), *History, theories and methods,* pp. 237–294, Vol. 1 of P. H. Mussen (Ed.), *US handbook of child psychology.* New York: Wiley.

Sameroff, A. J. (Ed.) (2009). *The transactional model of development: How children and contexts shape each other.* Washington, DC: American Psychological Association.

Schaefer, E. (1965). Children's reports of parental behavior: An inventory. *Child Development, 36,* 413–424.

Sigel, I. E. (1982). The relationship between parental distancing strategies and the child's cognitive behavior. In L. M. Laosa & I. E. Siegel (Eds.), *Families as learning environments for children,* pp. 47–86. New York: Plenum Press.

Sigel, I. E., & Laosa, L. (1983). Changing families. New York: Plenum Press.

Simpson, G. G. (1961). *Principles of animal taxonomy.* New York: Columbia University Press.

Sternberg, R. J. (1986). *Beyond IQ: A triarchic theory of human intelligence.* New York: Cambridge University Press.

Stokols, D. (1982). The environmental context of behavior and well-being. In D. Perlman P. Cozby (Eds.), *Social psychology: A social issues perspective.* New York: Holt, Rinehart, & Winston.

Terkelson, K. G. (1980). Toward a theory of the family life cycle. In E. A. Carter & M. McGoldrick (Eds.), *The family life cycle: A framework for family therapy,* pp. 21–52. New York: Gardner.

Tinsley, B., & Parke, RD. (1984). Grandparents as support and socialization agents. In M. Lewis (Ed.), *Beyond the dyad,* pp. 161–194. New York: Plenum Press.

Turnbull, A., Summers, J. D., & Brotherson, M. J. (1986). Family life cycle: theoretical and empirical implications and future directions for families with mentally retarded members. In J. Gallagher & P. Vietze (Eds.), *Families of handicapped persons: Research, programs, and policy issues,* pp. 45–65. Baltimore: Paul H. Brookes.

Wan, C. K., Jaccard, J., & Ramey, S. L. (1996). The relationship between social support and life satisfaction as a function of family structure: An analysis of four types of support. *Journal of Marriage and the Family, 58,* 502–513.

Washington, W. N., Ramey, S. L., Calhoun, J., Bost, K., & Vaughn, B. E. (1997). Attributes of children's character and behavior valued by African-American parents: A study across socioeconomic boundaries and across time. *Family Science Review, 10,* 244–257.

Yanagisako, S. J. (1979). Family and household: The analysis of domestic groups. *Annual Review of Anthropology, 8,* 161–205.

Zajonc, R. B. (1976). Family configuration and intelligence. *Science, 192,* 227–236.

Zajonc, R. B. (1983). Validating the confluence model. *Psychological Bulletin, 93,* 457–480.

Zajonc, R. B., & Markus, G. B. (1975). Birth order and intellectual development. *Psychological Review, 82,* 74–88.

Zajonc, R. B., Markus, H., & Markus, G. B. (1979). The birth order puzzle. *Journal of Personality and Social Psychology, 37,* 1325–1341.

CHAPTER 12

Measuring the Environments of Early Care, Education, and Intervention Programs for Children in Poverty

Walter S. Gilliam and Laura Stout Sosinsky

Early care and education settings are primary early environments for the majority of young children in the United States today. Data from the 2005 National Household Education Survey indicates that 60 percent of children from birth through age 5 and not yet in kindergarten were in at least one weekly nonparental care arrangement (Iruka & Carver, 2006). Seventy-three percent of 3- to 5-year-olds were in nonparental care and 78 percent of those were in a center-based arrangement. Many programs are targeted to children considered at risk by virtue of living in poor families. In 2005, Head Start, the federal preschool education program for children from lower-income families, was serving 13 percent of 3- to 5-year-olds on a weekly basis (Iruka & Carver, 2006). Of the 38 states that funded prekindergarden programs in 2007, serving another 22 percent of 4-year-olds, 27 states had an income requirement (Barnett, Hustedt, Friedman, Boyd, & Ainsworth, 2007).

The theoretical foundation for targeting early care and education programs to lower-income or otherwise at-risk children rests on the idea that early experience strongly influences development in many domains, and that the lower availability of enriching and stimulating experiences to poor children leaves them behind their more-advantaged peers even before they have begun elementary education. Some high-risk children do "overcome the odds" and grow into competent, confident, caring young adults. Researchers employing a longitudinal birth-cohort study that followed children exposed to both biologic and psychosocial risk factors found that the quality of the rearing environment predicted the outcome of virtually every biological risk condition, and that positive, caring and supportive adult relationships with a parent or another significant adult, such as a mentor or teacher, protected children against the effects of risk factors (Werner, 1994).

Research on the effects of early care and education programs on poor children demonstrates that high-quality early care and education can disrupt the intergenerational effects of poverty on children's academic skills and behaviors (Bowman, Donovan, & Burns, 2001). The first model programs provided a strong evidence base for the promise and potential of early care and education, which contributed in part to the creation and expansion of federal and state early care and education programs. Evaluations of these large-scale programs also have shown positive results but to a lesser degree, and facilitated examination of the mechanisms of program effects (Zigler, Gilliam, & Jones, 2006).

The positive effects of early care and education on child development vary by a number of factors, including characteristics of an ECE program as directly experienced by children, as well as characteristics of a program in interaction with the child's broader ecology. Program characteristics that are related to effects on child development include program quality, most specifically the quality of teacher-child interactions, plus the duration, quantity, and setting of the program. Program interactions with a child's broader ecology include two-generation programs aimed at changing parental behavior or familial circumstances (e.g., parental income, employment, mental health). Programs employing these designs follow a mediational model, proposing that positive changes in these mediators will indirectly transmit benefits to children. A related conceptualization of program effects suggests that high-quality early care and education programs may directly affect child outcomes but may also indirectly do so by removing children from "toxic" environments, at least for some hours of the day.

In this chapter, we first describe the disadvantages faced by children from poverty and the gap in outcomes between poor and nonpoor children in all domains of development, illustrating how the risks poor children are exposed to are often confounded and that their effects are cumulative. Then, we review the research evidence for direct effects of early care and education programs on the development of poor children, including a discussion of the mechanisms that transmit effects and interaction of program characteristics with child and family characteristics. Third, we discuss two-generation programs and indirect effects on child outcomes via changes in the family and home environment. Finally, we describe several instruments used to measure the environments where early child care, education, and intervention occur.

Poverty, School Readiness, and Later Educational Achievement

Children from poverty have less favorable physical, cognitive, and social-emotional health and developmental outcomes compared with their more advantaged peers. Research has extended understanding to include the processes that account for these associations as well as the role of the timing and duration of poverty. Much of this knowledge has come from research on early intervention and early education programs targeted to children from poverty. By garnering findings from a body of rich correlational and experimental longitudinal examinations of children and their changing contexts, our understanding of the effects of poverty on child development can grow, and, perhaps more importantly, guide current and future prevention and intervention efforts to help maximize the developmental potential of children from poverty.

Family income is associated with children's cognitive development, educational achievement, and social behavior from the early years throughout elementary school and beyond (Brooks-Gunn, 2003; Duncan & Brooks-Gunn, 1997, 2000; Lee & Burkman, 2002; Pagani, Boulerice, Vitaro, & Tremblay, 1999; Smith, Brooks-Gunn & Klebanov, 1997). The adverse effects of poverty on children's development are apparent by 18 to 24 months of age, with the developmental gap between poor and nonpoor children increasing over time (McCall, 1979). By preschool age, children living in persistent poverty already show pronounced effects on their intelligence test scores and vocabulary (Brooks-Gunn & Duncan, 1997; Brooks-Gunn, Klebanov, Liaw, & Spiker, 1993; Duncan, Brooks-Gunn, & Klebanov, 1994; Klebanov, Brooks-Gunn, McCarton, & McCormick, 1998; McLoyd, 1998). Later, they are more likely to suffer academic failure and grade retention (Bendersky & Lewis 1994; Brooks-Gunn & Duncan, 1997; Pagani, Boulerice, & Tremblay, 1997) and school drop-out (Cairns, Cairns, & Neckerman 1989). Childhood poverty is also associated with poor social development and with adverse outcomes that include low self-esteem, underachievement, and antisocial behavior (Huston, 1994; McLoyd, 1989; National Research Council & Institute of Medicine, 2000; Ramey & Campbell, 1991; Yoshikawa, 1995). The unique importance of early childhood experiences is underscored by the finding that family income during the preschool and early childhood years, but not later years, is associated positively with rates of high school completion (Duncan, Brooks-Gunn, Yeung, & Smith, 1998).

The processes that account for the association of poverty and poor outcomes are complex and interactive. Risk factors within the child covary with poverty. For example, poor children have disproportionately high rates of prenatal and early negative health environments and consequences and developmental delays and disabilities and are less likely to receive adequate care for these conditions. Family processes that relate to the association of poverty and poor child outcomes and are found at higher rates in poor families include more negative parental behaviors and parent-child interaction, higher rates of single-headed households, lower levels of support and stimulation available in the home, negative psychosocial characteristics of the parent and greater exposure to negative life events and stressors, lower levels of parental involvement in their child's education, and smaller amounts of time available to spend with children (Costello, Compton, Keeler, & Angold, 2003; NICHD Early Child Care Research Network, 2001; McLoyd, 1998; Robinson & Emde, 2004). Moreover, these risk factors often coexist, and the effects of multiple risk factors appear to be cumulative rather than additive (Burchinal, Roberts, Hooper, & Zeisel, 2000).

The role that genetic and neurobiological factors play in mediating the observed association between environment and outcomes is an area of ongoing debate and exploration (Caspi, Taylor, Moffitt, & Plomin, 2000; Plomin & Bergeman, 1991, 1994). Recent research has also moved beyond the main effects of poverty to demonstrate that persistent or chronic poverty is more deleterious than transitory poverty (Costello et al., 2003; McLoyd, 1998; NICHD Early Child Care Research Network, 2005), although there is evidence that concurrent poverty may be just as detrimental (Ackerman, Brown, & Izard, 2004a, 2004b). Movements in and out of poverty are associated with respective declines and improvements in the home environment (Garrett, Ng'andu, & Ferron, 1994; Votruba-Drzal, 2003). Potential differential effects on the basis of specific timing of transient poverty (e.g., during infancy versus during the preschool years) remain an issue for further research, with studies showing conflicting evidence (NICHD Early Child Care Research Network, 2005). Further, income is not linearly associated with children's environments and development. The harmful effects on children of deep or extreme poverty, often defined as income levels at half the federal poverty line, are more pronounced compared with children just above them but still poor (Bradley, Corwyn, Pipes McAdoo, & Garciã-Coll, 2001; Duncan, Yeung, Brooks-Gunn, & Smith, 1998; Garrett et al., 1994; Votruba-Drzal, 2003).

Effects of Early Care and Education

Poverty places children at risk of beginning school without the skills they need for success, setting them up for early school failure (Bowman, Donovan, & Burns, 2001; Dauber, Alexander, & Entwisle, 1993; May & Kundert, 1997, Morrison, Griffith, & Alberts, 1997; National Research Council & Institute of Medicine, 2000), lower educational achievement, and higher delinquency rates (Reynolds, Temple, Robertson, & Mann, 2001). After about half a century of research on early education and intervention programs, it is clear that, when delivered at high quality, they can positively impact the educational achievement of low-income children (Bowman et al., 2001; Brooks-Gunn, 2003; National Research Council and Institute of Medicine, 2000). With good physical health being critical to school readiness (Zigler & Trickett, 1978), these programs also have been successful in providing broader services to improve children's nutrition and access to medical and dental care (Barnett & Brown, 2000; Fosburg, Goodrich, & Fox, 1984; Hale, Seitz, & Zigler, 1990; O'Brien, Connell, & Griffin, 2004).

Evidence from Model Programs

Several longitudinal, prospective, randomized controlled trials of the benefits of high-quality early childhood educational interventions for children from low-income, high-risk families have demonstrated the promise of these programs. The High/Scope Perry Preschool Program provided a high-quality part-day preschool program with home visits to 58 low-income African-American 3- and 4-year-old children in Ypsilanti, Michigan, from 1962 through 1967, who showed significantly better outcomes over 40 years in comparison to the 70 children in the control group on educational, cognitive, and literacy measures; economic performance, employment, and use of social services, as well as arrest and incarceration rates; and some health and family indicators (Schweinhart, 2004). Cost-benefit analysis shows that by age 40 Perry saved $12.90 for every $1 invested in the program in terms of lower special education service use, higher tax revenues, lower welfare payments, and lower criminal justice system expenditures (the largest source of program benefits; Belfield, Nores, Barnett, & Schweinhart, 2006).

The Abecedarian program was similar to Perry, with some notable differences in service provision. Abecedarian was an intensive, all-day, year-round early care and education program that lasted from birth through age 5. Between 1972 and 1977, 112 children from high-risk families were randomly enrolled in a high-quality child care program (with low child-staff ratios, in-service training, low

teacher turnover, etc.) or to a no-treatment control group. By the age 15 follow-up, treatment-group children's intelligence and achievement scores remained higher than control-group children's (Campbell, Pungello, Miller-Johnson, Burchinal, & Ramey, 2001). By young adulthood, the treatment group continued to score higher on intellectual and academic measures, had attained more years of education and were more likely to attend a 4-year college, and showed a reduction in teen pregnancy (Campbell, Ramey, Pungello, Sparling, & Miller-Johnson, 2002). Cost-benefit analyses showed a different pattern of effects than in the Perry Preschool program, although both programs showed benefits greater than costs, with the Perry program showing a benefit – cost ratio of 9:1, and Abecedarian of 2.5:1 (Barnett & Masse, 2007). Differences in costs included the higher expense of providing full-day, year-round child care in the Abecedarian study. Differences in benefits included greater impact of Abecedarian on grade repetition and any use of special education, but a greater impact of Perry on the number of years spent in special education with its associated high educational costs, as well as the lack in Abecedarian of the criminal justice system savings seen in Perry, possibly due to differences in the cities of the populations served (Barnett & Masse, 2007).

Evidence from Large-Scale Programs

Model program studies show stronger and longer-lasting benefits than do larger-scale community-based early care and education programs. Programs such as community-based child care, the federal Head Start program, and state-funded prekindergarten programs present thorny research challenges. The programs vary greatly in terms of their focus, delivery methods and program intensity, classrooms and programs vary from site to site even within the same program, and the populations served are much more varied and it is difficult to control for selection bias. However, even when the large-scale programs are examined in randomized controlled trials or with other rigorous study designs, results are seldom as strong as seen in the Perry and Abecedarian studies of model interventions (Love et al., 2005; U.S. Department of Health and Human Services, Administration for Children and Families, 2005).

Head Start, the federally funded prekindergarten program aimed at closing the school readiness gap between low-income children and their more-advantaged peers, has been in operation since 1965. But the most comprehensive research examination of its effects has been done much more recently, starting in the 1990s and including two large-scale studies. The Head Start Family and Child Experiences Survey (FACES) began in 1997 and included a nationally representative sample of 3,200 3- and 4-year-old children and their families in 40 Head Start programs, with an additional 2,800 children and families in 43 different Head Start programs in the 2000 cohort. There is no non–Head Start comparison group; rather, assessment measures with national norms are employed to permit comparisons between sample children and age-similar norming samples. Results indicated that Head Start children made gains during the Head Start year toward the national averages in preacademic skills like vocabulary knowledge and early writing skills, although rates of gain were steeper for children who began with lower levels of knowledge and skill.

The Head Start Impact Study is a congressionally mandated study of approximately 5,000 newly entering children applying for Head Start who were randomly assigned to either a Head Start group that had access to Head Start program services or to a non–Head Start group that could enroll in available community non–Head Start services selected by their parents. For children in the 3-year-old group, preliminary results from the first year of data collection demonstrated small to moderate effects favoring the children enrolled in Head Start for cognitive skills (prereading and prewriting skills, letter identification, and vocabulary skills), social-emotional development (lower frequency and severity of parent-reported problem behavior), and, for children in both age groups, health indicators (greater receipt of dental care; U.S. Department of Health and Human Services, Administration for Children and Families, 2005).

Positive effects have also been documented for large scale interventions for infants and toddlers. The Early Head Start program (EHS), a federal program begun in 1995 and designed to promote parental caregiving and child development among low-income women and their families with infants and toddlers, was evaluated through a randomized trial of more than 3,000 families in 17 programs. Overall, EHS demonstrated positive effects on children's cognitive, language and social-emotional development compared with those of control children (Love et al., 2005).

The Chicago Child-Parent (CPC) Preschool Program employed a quasi-experimental design to examine differential effects of CPC, a large-scale publicly funded center-based early education program, on 3- and 4-year-old CPC children born in 1979–80 from families in high-poverty neighborhoods, compared with children from randomly selected schools in low-income neighborhoods who participated in non-CPC government-funded early childhood programs such as full-day kindergarten intervention programs and/or Head Start. Findings indicate significant associations between CPC participation and higher school achievement, lower rates of grade retention, dropout, and higher rates of high school completion and college attendance by age 22 (Ou & Reynolds, 2006). Benefit-cost analysis of the CPC program demonstrates a societal benefit of $10.15 returned for every dollar invested (Reynolds & Temple, 2008).

The accumulating evidence of the developmental and economic benefits of good early care and education programs has supported the expansion of preschool access and the explosion of state-funded prekindergarten programs for 3- and 4-year-olds (Gilliam & Zigler, 2001). Although these programs primarily serve children at risk (with the notable exceptions of universal programs in Oklahoma and Georgia), participants typically are more heterogeneous in regards to family income, race and ethnicity than those in the previously discussed programs. Benefit-cost analyses have not yet been conducted on state-funded prekindergarten programs, but effect sizes from evaluations of these programs indicate a positive and meaningful though small impact on school readiness. Evaluations of programs in 13 states up to 1998 had several methodological flaws, but the pattern of overall findings offers modest support for positive effects on children's competencies, later school attendance and performance, and subsequent grade retention (Gilliam & Zigler, 2001), with an average effect size of 0.36 standard deviation in six states and the District of Columbia (Reynolds & Temple, 2008).

Despite the more modest impacts of large-scale community programs, many researchers critique the Perry Preschool and Abecedarian programs on grounds of poor generalizability due to their small sample sizes and the provision of a level of quality that cannot be duplicated in an ordinary preschool program (e.g., in Perry, teachers were paid public school salaries plus a 10 percent bonus for working in a special program; Schweinhart, 2004). Although the effects may be smaller than those demonstrated for model programs, the large number of children benefiting from the program argues for meaningful aggregate impacts (McCartney & Rosenthal, 2000). Nevertheless, the vanguard programs set the bar and demonstrate that it is possible for a high-quality early care and education program to have a significant, life-long, meaningful impact on the development of children from poverty as well as for society in terms of tax-dollars saved.

Processes of ECE Program Effectiveness

Teacher-child Interactions and Relationships

Follow-up research on community-based early care and education programs has gone beyond evaluations of the model programs by examining the processes and moderators at work much more rigorously. From this body of research, one overarching message is that the strongest mechanism through which early care and education programs directly impact child outcomes is via proximal processes, or the quality of teacher-child interactions and relationships. This is consistent with theoretically driven expectations that the proximal, face-to-face experiences of children in these programs will convey a program's effects (Bronfenbrenner & Morris, 2006). Further, a bioecological perspective on early care and education suggests that teaching approaches that integrate cognitive learning and social development might have the greatest impact.

Research supports the importance of teacher-child interactions and relationships for child development in a variety of ECE programs including state-funded prekindergarten programs, Head Start programs, and community child care programs. In both preschool and child care settings, close teacher-child relationships and higher-quality classroom practices were related to higher social skills of preschoolers (Howes et al., 2008; Peisner-Feinberg & Burchinal, 1997). Teachers who provided positive communication, warm affection and opportunities for children to be in charge were more likely to have preschoolers with high levels of social skills such as completing work, tolerating frustration, and interacting positively with peers (Brophy-Herb, Lee, Nievar, & Stollak, 2007). The impact of close teacher-child relationships in preschool and kindergarten appears to last beyond the child's time in that classroom, predicting lower levels of internalizing problems such as anxiety, depression, and social withdrawal in first grade (Pianta & Stuhlman, 2004). Similarly, problematic teacher-child interactions have been linked with poorer developmental outcomes over time. High teacher-child conflict in kindergarten and first grade was associated with lower social skills in the areas of responsibility, cooperation, self-control, and assertion in first grade (Pianta & Stuhlman, 2004).

Teacher-child interactions and relationships are also associated with academic skills. Further, practices and approaches that integrate cognitive learning and social development are reinforced by the evidence base. From research with 2,500 children (47 percent poor) in 671 state-funded pre-kindergarten (pre-K) classrooms in 11 states with large, well-established pre-K programs (serving about 80 percent of the children in the country who attended state pre-K programs), higher-quality instructional interactions were positively associated with all measures of academic or language skills, and higher-quality emotional interactions were associated with some ratings of higher social competence and lower problem behaviors (Mashburn et al., 2008). Research from the same multisite study of state-funded prekindergarten programs also demonstrated that preschoolers who have close relationships with teachers tend to know more letters and have higher math scores and advanced language and literacy skills while in preschool (Howes et al., 2008). These positive effects of teacher-child interaction on preacademic skills are similar to findings from child care classrooms (Peisner-Feinberg & Burchinal, 1997).

Program Characteristics

Various programmatic characteristics such as duration, timing, and program delivery method also contribute to associations between ECE programs and changes in child outcomes. There was modest evidence from the CPC program that children who attended for more than one year had greater peer social skills in early adolescence compared with those with only one year of participation (Niles, Reynolds, & Roe-Sepowitz, 2008). This was similarly supported by evidence from FACES that children who graduated after 2 years of Head Start made greater gains from entry to graduation than children who spent only one year in Head Start (Zill et al., 2006). Results from comparisons of effects of EHS participation on child development by service-delivery approach (center-based, home-based, or a mixed approach) demonstrated that children in the mixed-approach group showed higher performance in cognitive and language functioning (Love et al., 2005).

Child and Family Characteristics

ECE program effects may be moderated by various child and family factors. Regarding child characteristics, most children appeared to benefit equally from the CPC program, although males benefited more than did females on acting-out behaviors and high school completion, and there was modest support for the prediction that children experiencing a large number of family risk factors are more likely to benefit from program participation (Niles et al., 2008; Ou & Reynolds, 2006). In the Head Start Impact Study, positive impacts of Head Start were stronger for children whose primary language was English. But by race/ethnicity, positive program effects across several domains were stronger for African-American and Hispanic children but only for those in the 3-year-old group; in the 4-year-old group, fewer positive effects were observed for minority children, particularly for Hispanic children (U.S. Department of Health and Human Services, Administration for Children and Families, 2005).

Some have hypothesized that the strength of effects might be greater for children experiencing greater social risk. This is based in part on the idea that the discrepancy between the quality of a good early care and education setting and the home environment might be greater for at-risk children, and that poverty may moderate the impact of program quality on child outcomes. Although this implies that initiating positive changes for higher-risk children may require overcoming more obstacles, it also may mean that a program's positive impact may be felt more strongly by higher-risk children. This is based on the concept that the family settings of children living in poverty often lack sufficient early learning opportunities, and that sensitive, responsive and stimulating interactions with caregivers or teachers and exposure to stimulating experiences will enhance the development of these children more than children from more-advantaged family settings.

There is limited support for this hypothesis. For example, most children appeared to benefit equally from the CPC program, but children experiencing a large number of family risk factors evidenced a somewhat greater benefit (Niles et al., 2008). However, EHS showed a much clearer pattern of favorable outcomes by risk, but with the greatest impact on families with a moderate number or risks, not families with high or low risk (U.S. Administration for Children and Families, 2002). Also, the quality of early education programs remains a significant predictor of program effect, even when the degree of developmentally appropriate home stimulation is controlled (Bryant, Burchinal, Lau, & Sparling, 1994).

From community child care programs, there may be more support for the simpler concept that responsive, developmentally appropriate care will enhance development similarly for all children (Lamb, 1998). Research with community child care showed that higher-quality care and better teacher-child relationships were modestly but significantly related to children's social, language, and academic development for all children, poor or not, although for children of color, child care quality was differentially more important for language development (Burchinal, Peisner-Feinberg et al., 2000). The lack of a strong or consistent pattern of greater program effects on poor children does not discount the importance of targeted programs or diminish the meaning of potential effects. These are the children who need high-quality early care and education programs most (or at least just as much as all other children) yet are the most likely to need help accessing them (Kagan & Neuman, 1997).

A similar question pertains to whether ECE programs have differential impact on children depending on their level of problems and competencies, and whether early education programs will have stronger effects on children with greater problems. Children in the Head Start FACES study sample who entered Head Start with the lowest levels of social skills and/or highest levels of problem behaviors gained the most during their time in Head Start, although they did not close the gap with other children (Zill et al., 2006). However, early education programs can only benefit children with behavioral challenges when they actually attend the program. In one nationally representative study of state-funded prekindergarten programs, children were expelled for behavior problems at three times the rate of children in K–12 (Gilliam, 2005), highlighting the need for teacher support and mental health consultation (Gilliam & Shahar, 2006).

Effects of Two-Generation Programs

High-quality early care and education programs can have a positive impact on poor children's developmental outcomes, especially when teacher-child relationships and interactions support children's social skills and emotional relationships and integrate cognitive learning and social development. However, early childhood programs alone cannot be expected to alleviate fully the toxic effects of poverty (Brooks-Gunn, 2003). First, parenting and the home environment are the most consistent and strong predictors of all child outcomes (Zill et al., 2006). In one comparison of effect sizes, parenting was about twice as strong a predictor of development in all domains as child care quality (NICHD Early Child Care Research Network, 2006). Further, we know that program effects are moderated by or interact with the home environment. For example, children who had close teacher-child relationships in preschool and a structured and disciplined environment at home had higher reading skills than children whose parents were not as firm (Mashburn et al., 2008). Infants at risk for an insecure attachment to their mother due to low maternal sensitivity and responsiveness were more likely to be securely attached when child care quality was high, although there was no main effect of child care experience on attachment security (NICHD Early Child Care

Research Network, 1997). Similarly, analyses of data from two of the 17 EHS sites that included more intensive measurement of maternal depression indicated that EHS program effects on parent-child interaction and on child cognition and language were strongest for women at the highest level of risk for depression (Robinson & Emde, 2004).

Given the importance of the home environment and the interaction among home and educational environments, many programs take a two-generational approach. These programs emerge from a bioecological perspective and the premise that program effectiveness is dependent not only on the ability to change child development directly, but also strengthened by the capacity to change the environment in which the child lives, especially given the greater number of risks faced by children from poverty and evidence that risks tend to accumulate and interact to effect children's development (Bronfenbrenner & Morris, 2006; Brooks-Gunn, Berlin, & Fuligni, 2000; Smith & Zaslow, 1995). Two-generation programs may address several classes of familial outcomes, such as parent education, employment, or self-sufficiency, parent mental health, parent-child interaction and relationship quality, quality of the home environment, and/or child maltreatment (Brooks-Gunn et al., 2000). Some begin in infancy or even prenatally, while others begin later. They may include a home visiting component, a center-based component, or a combination of both.

Effects on Parent Education, Employment, and Self-Sufficiency

The model early education program Abecedarian did not provide direct parenting education or other similar services, but did provide a very valuable service to parents in the form of 5 years of free, full-time educational child care. This did have a positive effect on mothers' educational change and employment, with post–high school education when their children were age 15 higher among treatment-group mothers compared with control mothers,

and the highest among treatment-group mothers who were adolescents at the time of their child's birth (80 percent) compared with adolescent control-group mothers (28 percent; Ramey et al., 2000). There were also small but consistent effects of the EHS program on parents' employment and enrollment in education or job training (Love et al., 2005).

Effects on Parent Mental and Physical Health

The Nurse-Family Partnership had positive effects on maternal depression, although this improvement did not mediate positive outcomes in parent-child interaction or child development, suggesting that maternal depression and behavior might be correlated, but treatment for each might be helped by different aspects of an intervention (Olds et al., 1998; Robinson & Emde, 2004). The EHS program did not find any positive program effects on maternal depression by the end of the program at age 3. However, a reduction in maternal depressive symptoms was found 2 years later (Love et al., 2005). This possible "sleeper effect" was confirmed and elucidated by analyses demonstrating that the EHS intervention's improvements in parenting, the parent-child relationship, and child behavior when children were 2 and 3 years old did, over time, lead to improvements in parent well-being (Chazan-Cohen et al., 2007). In fact, the earlier impacts on children, specifically their abilities and communication skills, were the strongest mediators of the later reduction in depression, which speaks to the importance of approaching early care and education and intervention programs from a two-generational, dynamic, ecological perspective.

Effects on Parent-Child Interaction, Relationship Quality, and the Home Environment

Head Start has as one of its four pillars a focus on parents as their child's first teacher, recognizing that the involvement of parents is critical for school readiness. As a precursor program to Head Start, Early Head Start has shown significant positive impact on parental emotional support and support for language and learning, with modest effect sizes ranging from .10 to .15. Compared with control families, EHS parents showed higher levels of responsiveness to and positive regard for the child and lower rates of spanking, plus higher rates of daily book reading and higher ratings of the support and stimulation available in the home (Love et al. 2005). As with effects on child development, the effects on parenting were greater for EHS families in mixed-approach programs (Love et al., 2005). Home visiting programs utilizing a nurse-family partnership model showed positive effects in terms of more sensitive, supportive, and positive parenting behaviors for parents receiving the randomized treatment compared with control families (Olds, Sadler, & Kitzman, 2007). Findings from both age cohorts of the Head Start Impact Study show that Head Start had a small positive impact on the extent to which parents reported reading to their children, exposing them to a variety of cultural enrichment activities (e.g., trips to a museum or zoo), and using less physical discipline compared with children in the non–Head Start group (U.S. Department of Health and Human Services, Administration for Children and Families, 2005). Early education and intervention programs may also help reduce the impact of risk factors associated with child maltreatment (Asawa, Hansen, & Flood, 2008). The Nurse-Family Partnership trials demonstrate reductions in harsh or negative parenting behaviors for parents receiving the treatment compared with control parents (Olds et al., 2007), leading to considerable current interest in large-scale replication of home visiting programs (Haskins, Paxson, Brooks-Gunn, 2009).

Measuring the Early Care, Education, and Intervention Environments

As described earlier in this chapter, there are several processes that appear responsible for the effects of early care, education, and intervention settings on young children's

development. Overall, these areas of program quality address the degree to which these settings provide care for young children that is safe; health promoting, in terms of being clean, sanitary, and nutritional; developmentally appropriate, in terms of cognitive, linguistic, physical, creative, and socially stimulated; positive, in terms of interactions between caring adults and children; encouraging of emotional developmental and independence; and facilitative of positive relationships with peers (Cryer, 1999, 2003). Indeed, much of the research on the effectiveness of the programs on facilitating young children's development has tied effectiveness specifically to the quality of the program.

Although various aspects of structural quality (e.g., the amount of services, the qualifications of the teachers, the ratio of children to staff) are more amenable to regulation than process quality (e.g., teacher-child interactions, environmental stimulation, etc.), their worth is that they may create conditions where process quality may be maximized (Phillipsen, Burchinal, Howes, & Cryer, 1997). Measures of program process quality are collected through direct observation of the child care, education, or intervention setting and are often used to predict effectiveness. Although structural quality indicators are important for understanding program effects, their collection is typically straightforward and often achieved by surveying program directors and teachers or collecting the information from public sources (e.g., child care licensing agencies). Therefore, this discussion focuses on the measure of process quality, which is far more labor intensive but also more directly related to child outcomes.

A recent review by the National Research Council (2008) provides a very useful description of the most commonly used measures of program quality. These measures typically require a trained and reliable rater to observe a typical set of activities and interactions in the program and rate the presence of certain indicators of quality or their impression of how well certain program aspects were implemented. The amount of observation required to complete these measures varies from as little as 1 hour to as much as 5 to 6 hours. All of the measures require at least some degree of rater training and practice prior to administration, and, because of the subjective nature of observational ratings, specific procedures for computing interrater reliability are often included. Some of the more commonly used measures of program quality – the majority of which have been developed during the past decade – are listed later.

Most measures focus on global aspects of quality across a wide array of dimensions. These measures include the Assessment Profile for Early Childhood Programs (APECP; Abbot-Shinn & Sibley, 1992); Classroom Assessment Scoring System (CLASS; Pianta, La Paro, & Hamre, 2007); Early Childhood Classroom Observation Measure (ECCOM; Stipek & Byler, 2004); Observation Record of the Caregiving Environment (ORCE; NICHD Early Child Care Research Network, 2000); Preschool Program Quality Assessment (PQA; High/Scope, 2003); and the family of environment rating scales, Early Childhood Environment Rating Scale-Revised Edition (ECERS-R; Harms, Clifford, & Cryer, 1998), Early Childhood Environment Rating Scale-Extension (ECERS-E; Sylva, Siraj-Blatchford, & Taggart, 2003), Family Child Care Environment Rating Scale-Revised Edition (FCCERS-R; Harms, Cryer, & Clifford, 2007), and Infant and Toddler Environment Rating Scale-Revised (ITERS-R; Harms, Cryer, & Clifford, 1990).

Additional measures focus on more specific dimensions, such as teacher-child interaction (Caregiver Interaction Scale (CIS; Arnett, 1989)), program features associated with accreditation (e.g., Classroom Practices Inventory (CPI; Hyson, Hirsh-Pasek, & Rescorla, 1990), A Developmentally Appropriate Practices Template (ADAPT; VanHorn & Ramey, 2004)), and general and specific areas of academic foci, such as Early Language and Literacy Classroom Observation (ELLCO; Smith & Dickinson, 2002); Emerging Academics Snapshot (EAS; Ritchie, Howes, Kraft-Sayre, & Weiser, 2001); Observation Measure of Language and Literacy Instruction (OMLIT; Abt Associates, 2006); Preschool Classroom Mathematics Inventory (PCMI; National Institute for Early Education Research, 2007); Supports for Early Literacy Assessment (SELA; Smith, Davidson, Weisenfield, & Katsaros, 2001); and Supports for English Language Learners Classroom Assessment (SELLCA; National Institute for Early Education Research, 2005).

Conclusions

Overall, several conclusions can be drawn about the impact of preschool programs for disadvantaged children. First, high quality programs clearly have the potential of improving the school readiness of disadvantaged children and can often lead to remarkable long-term effects in terms of improved functioning in school, work, and life. Second, the impacts of these programs may vary for different groups of children. Therefore, more clearly needs to be known about which types of programs are effective for which types of children (Guralnick, 1997). Third, significant effects can be obtained for large-scale programs implemented on a national or state-wide level. However, much remains to be learned about the pathways by which these programs reduce risk and place children in poverty on a better pathway toward school and later life success. Given the massive public investment in these programs, specifically those aimed at children from disadvantaged families and communities, understanding *how* these programs work may lead to more cost-effective models of intervention and improved methods of ensuring program quality and measurable outcomes.

References

Abbot-Shinn, M., & Sibley, A. (1992). Assessment profile for early childhood programs: Research version. Atlanta: Quality Assist.

Abt Associates Inc. (2006). *Observation training manual: OMLIT early childhood.* Cambridge, MA: Author.

Ackerman, B. P., Brown, E. D., & Izard, C. E. (2004a). The relations between persistent poverty and contextual risk and children's behavior in elementary school. *Developmental Psychology*, 40, 367–377.

Ackerman, B. P., Brown, E. D., & Izard, C. E. (2004b). The relations between contextual risk, earned income, and the school adjustment of children from economically disadvantaged families. *Developmental Psychology*, 40, 204–216.

Arnett, J. (1989). Caregivers in day-care centers: Does training matter? *Journal of Applied Developmental Psychology*, 10, 541.

Asawa, L. E., Hansen, D. J., & Flood, M. F. (2008). Early childhood intervention programs: Opportunities and challenges for preventing child maltreatment. *Education & Treatment of Children*, 31, 73–110.

Barnett, W. S., & Brown, K. C. (2000). *Issues in children's access to dental care under Medicaid. Dental Health Policy Analysis Series.* Chicago: American Dental Association.

Barnett, W. S., Hustedt, J. T., Friedman, A. H., Boyd, J. S., & Ainsworth, P. (2007). *The state of preschool: 2007 state preschool yearbook.* New Brunswick, NJ: The National Institute for Early Education Research, Rutgers, The State University of New Jersey.

Barnett, W. S., & Masse, L. N. (2007). Comparative benefit-cost analysis of the Abecedarian program and its policy implications. *Economics of Education Review*, 26, 113–125.

Belfield, C. R., Nores, M., Barnett, W. S., & Schweinhart, L. J. (2006). The High/Scope Perry Preschool Program: Cost–benefit analysis using data from the age-40 followup. *Journal of Human Resources*, XLI(1), 162–190.

Bendersky, M., & Lewis, M. (1994). Environmental risk, biological risk, and developmental outcome. *Developmental Psychopathology*, 30, 484–494.

Bowman, B. T., Donovan, M. S., & Burns, M. S. (Eds.) (2001). *Eager to learn: Educating our preschoolers.* Washington, DC: National Academy Press.

Bradley, R. H., Corwyn, R. F., Pipes McAdoo, H., & Garciã-Coll, C. (2001). The home environments of children in the United States: Part I. Variations by age, ethnicity, and poverty status. *Child Development*, 72, 1844–1867.

Bronfenbrenner, U., & Morris, P. A. (2006). The bioecological model of human development. In R. M. Lerner, W. Damon, R. M. Lerner & W. Damon (Eds.), *Handbook of child psychology* (6th ed.): Vol. 1. *Theoretical models of human development*, pp. 793–828. Hoboken, NJ: John Wiley & Sons Inc.

Brooks-Gunn, J. (2003). Do you believe in magic? What we can expect from early childhood intervention programs. *Social Policy Report*, 17, 3–14.

Brooks-Gunn, J., Berlin, L. J., & Fuligni, A. S. (2000). Early childhood intervention programs: What about the family? In J. P. Shonkoff & S. J. Meisels (Eds.), *Handbook of early childhood intervention*, pp. 549–588 (2nd ed.). New York: Cambridge University Press.

Brooks-Gunn, J., & Duncan, G. J. (1997). The effects of poverty on children. *Future of Children*, 7, 55–71.

Brooks-Gunn, J., Klebanov, P. K., Liaw, F., & Spiker, D. (1993). Enhancing the development of low birth weight, premature infants: Changes in cognition and behavior over the first three years. *Child Development*, 64, 736–753.

Brophy-Herb, H. E., Lee, R. E., Nievar, M. A., & Stollak, G. (2007). Preschoolers' social competence: Relations to family characteristics, teacher behaviors and classroom climate. *Journal of Applied Developmental Psychology*, 28, 134–148.

Bryant, D. M., Burchinal, M., Lau, L. B., & Sparling, J. J. (1994). Family and classroom correlates of Head Start children's developmental outcomes. *Early Childhood Research Quarterly*, 9, 289–309.

Burchinal, M. R., Peisner-Feinberg, E., Bryant, D. M., & Clifford, R. (2000). Children's social and cognitive development and child-care quality: Testing for differential associations related to poverty, gender, or ethnicity. *Applied Developmental Science*, 4, 149–165.

Burchinal, M. R., Roberts, J. E., Hooper, S., & Zeisel, S. A. (2000). Cumulative risk and early cognitive development: A comparison of statistical risk models. *Developmental Psychology*, 36, 793–807.

Cairns, R. B., Cairns, B. D., & Neckerman, H. J. (1989). Early school dropout: Configurations and determinants. *Child Development*, 60, 1437–1452.

Campbell, F. A., Pungello, E. P., Miller-Johnson, S., Burchinal, M., & Ramey, C. T. (2001). The development of cognitive and academic abilities: Growth curves from an early childhood educational experiment. *Developmental Psychology*, 37, 231–242.

Campbell, F. A., Ramey, C. T., Pungello, E., Sparling, J., & Miller-Johnson, S. (2002).

Early childhood education: Young adult outcomes from the Abecedarian Project. *Applied Developmental Science, 6,* 42–57.

Caspi, A., Taylor, A., Moffitt, T. E., & Plomin, R. (2000). Neighborhood deprivation affects children's mental health: Environmental risks identified in a genetic design. *Psychological Science, 11,* 338–342.

Chazan-Cohen, R., Ayoub, C., Pan, B. A., Roggman, L., Raikes, H., McKelvey, L. et al. (2007). It takes time: Impacts on Early Head Start that lead to reductions in maternal depression two years later. *Infant Mental Health Journal, 28,* 151–170.

Colen, C. G., Geronimus, A. T., Bound, J., James, S. A. (2006). Maternal upward socioeconomic mobility and black-white disparities in infant birthweight. *American Journal of Public Health, 96,* 2032–2039.

Costello, E., Compton, S. N., Keeler, G., & Angold, A. (2003). Relationships between poverty and psychopathology: A natural experiment. *JAMA: Journal of the American Medical Association, 290,* 2023–2029.

Cryer, D. (1999). Defining and assessing early childhood program quality. *Annals of the American Academy of Political and Social Science, 563,* 39–55.

Cryer, D. (2003). Defining program quality. In D. Cryer & R. M. Clifford (Eds.), *Early childhood education and care in the USA*, pp. 31–46. Baltimore: Paul H. Brookes.

Dauber, S. L., Alexander, K., & Entwisle, D. R. (1993). Characteristics of retainees and early precursors for retention in grade: Who is held back? *Merrill-Palmer Quarterly, 39,* 326–343.

Duncan, G. J., & Brooks-Gunn, J. (1997). Income effects across the lifespan: Integration and interpretation. In G. J. Duncan & J. Brooks-Gunn (Eds.), *Consequences of growing up poor*, pp. 596–610. New York: Russel Sage.

Duncan, G. J., & Brooks-Gunn, J. (2000). Family poverty, welfare reform, and child development. *Child Development, 71,* 188–196.

Duncan, G. J., Brooks-Gunn, J., & Klebanov, P. K. (1994). Economic deprivation and early-childhood development. *Child Development, 65,* 296–318.

Duncan, G. J., Yeung, W. J., Brooks-Gunn, J., & Smith, J. R. (1998). How much does childhood poverty affect the life chances of children? *American Sociological Review, 63,* 406–423.

Fosburg, L. B., Goodrich, N., & Fox, M. (1984). *The effects of Head Start health services: Report of the Head Start Health Evaluation.* Cambridge, MA: Abt Associates.

Garrett, P., Ng'andu, N., & Ferron, J. (1994). Poverty experiences of young children and the quality of their home environments. *Child Development, 65,* 331–345.

Gilliam, W. S. (2005). *Prekindergarteners left behind: Expulsion rates in state prekindergarten systems.* New Haven, CT: Yale University Child Study Center.

Gilliam, W. S., & Shahar, G. (2006). Preschool and child care expulsion and suspension: Rates and predictors in one state. *Infants and Young Children, 19,* 228–245.

Gilliam, W. S., & Zigler, E. F. (2001). A critical meta-analysis of all evaluations of state-funded preschool from 1977 to 1998: Implications for policy, service delivery and program evaluation. *Early Childhood Research Quarterly, 15,* 441–473.

Guralnick, M. J. (Ed.) (1997). *The effectiveness of early intervention.* Baltimore: Brookes.

Hale, B., Seitz, V., & Zigler, E. (1990). Health services and Head Start: A forgotten formula. *Journal of Applied Developmental Psychology, 11,* 447–458.

Haskins, R., Paxson, C., & Brooks-Gunn, J. (Fall 2009). Social science rising: A tale of evidence shaping public policy. *The Future of Children Policy Brief.*

Harms, T., Cryer, D., & Clifford, R. (1990). *Infant/toddler environment rating scale.* New York: Teachers College Press.

Harms, T., Cryer, D. R., & Clifford, R. M. (2007). *Family Child Care Environment Rating Scale – Revised Edition.* New York: Teachers College Press.

Harms, T., Clifford, R., & Cryer, D. (1998). *Early childhood environment rating scale* (rev. ed.). New York: Teachers College Press.

High/Scope. (2003). *Preschool program quality assessment* (2nd ed.). Ypsilanti, MI: High/Scope Press.

Howes, C., Burchinal, M., Pianta, R., Bryant, D., Early, D., Clifford, R. et al. (2008). Ready to learn? Children's pre-academic achievement in pre-kindergarten programs. *Early Childhood Research Quarterly, 23,* 27–50.

Hoy, E. A., & McClure, B. G. (2000). Preschool experience: A facilitator of very low birthweight infants' development? *Infant Mental Health Journal, 21,* 481–494.

Huston, A. C. (1994). Children in poverty: Designing research to affect policy. *Social Policy Report, 8,* 1–12.

Hyson, M., Hisrch-Pasek, K., & Rescorla, L. (1990). The classroom practices inventory: An observation instrument based on NAEYC's guidelines for developmentally appropriate practices for 4- and 5-year old children. *Early Childhood Research Quarterly, 5,* 475–494.

Iruka, I. U., & Carver, P. R. (2006). *Initial results from the 2005 NHES Early Childhood Program Participation Survey.* (No. NCES 2006–075). Washington, DC: U.S. Department of Education National Center for Education Statistics.

Kagan, S. L., & Neuman, M. (1997). Defining and implementing school readiness: Challenges for families, early cra ena deducation, and schools. In R. R. Weissberg (Ed.), *Establishing preventive services,* pp. 61–96. Thousand Oaks, CA: Sage.

Klebanov, P. K., Brooks-Gunn, J., McCarton, C., & McCormick, M. C. (1998). The contribution of neighborhood and family income to developmental test scores over the first three years of life. *Child Development, 69,* 1420–1436.

Lamb, M. E. (1998). Nonparental child care: Context, quality, correlates, and consequences. In W. Damon, I. E. Sigel & K. A. Renniger (Eds.), *Handbook of child psychology:* Vol. 4. *Child psychology in practice,* pp. 73–133 (5th ed.). New York: Wiley.

Love, J. M., Kisker, E. E., Ross, C., Raikes, H., Constantine, J., Boller, K. et al. (2005). The effectiveness of Early Head Start for 3-year-old children and their parents: Lessons for policy and programs. *Developmental Psychology, 41,* 885–901.

Mashburn, A. J., Pianta, R. C., Hamre, B. K., Downer, J. T., Barbarin, O. A., Bryant, D. et al. (2008). Measures of classroom quality in pre-kindergarten and children's development of academic, language, and social skills. *Child Development, 79,* 732–749.

May, D. C., & Kundert, D. K. (1997). School readiness practices and children at-risk: Examining the issue. *Psychology in the Schools, 34,* 73–84.

McCall, R. (1979). The development of intellectual functioning in infancy and the prediction of later I.Q. In J. D. Osofsky (Ed.), *Handbook of infant development,* pp. 707–741. New York: Wiley.

McCartney, K., & Rosenthal, R. (2000). Effect size, practical importance, and social policy for children. *Child Development, 71,* 173–180.

McLoyd, V. C. (1989). Socialization and development in a changing economy: The effects of paternal job and income loss on children. *American Psychologist, 44,* 293–302.

McLoyd, V. C. (1998). Socioeconomic disadvantage and child development. *American Psychologist, 53,* 185–204.

Morrison, F. J., Griffith, E., & Alberts, D. (1997). Nature-nurture in the classroom: Entrance age, school readiness, and learning in children. *Developmental Psychology, 33,* 254–262.

National Institute for Early Education Research. (2007). *Preschool classroom mathematics inventory.* New Brunswick, NJ: Author.

National Institute for Early Education Research. (2005). *Support for English language learners classroom assessment.* New Brunswick, NJ: Author.

National Research Council, Committee on Developmental Outcomes and Assessments for Young Children. (2008). Measuring quality in early childhood environments. In C. E. Snow and S. B. Van Hemel (Eds.), *Early childhood assessment: Why, what, and how,* pp. 145–177. Washington, DC: National Academies Press.

National Research Council and Institute of Medicine. (2000). *From neurons to neighborhoods: The science of early childhood development.* Committee on Integrating the Science of Early Childhood Development. J. P. Shonkoff & D. A. Phillips (Eds.). Board on Children, Youth, and Families, Commission on Behavioral and Social Sciences and Education. Washington, DC: National Academy Press.

NICHD Early Child Care Research Network. (1997). The effects of infant child care on infant-mother attachment security: Results of the NICHD study of early child care. *Child Development, 68,* 860–879.

NICHD Early Child Care Research Network. (2000). The relationship of child care to cognitive and language development. *Child Development, 71,* 960–980.

NICHD Early Child Care Research Network. (2001). Nonmaternal care and family factors in early development: An overview of the NICHD Study of Early Child Care. *Journal of Applied Developmental Psychology, 22,* 457–492.

NICHD Early Child Care Research Network. (2005). Duration and developmental timing of poverty and children's cognitive and social development from birth through third grade. *Child Development, 76,* 795–810.

NICHD Early Child Care Research Network. (2006). Child-care effect sizes for the NICHD Study of Early Child Care and Youth

Development. *American Psychologist, 61,* 99–116.

Niles, M. D., Reynolds, A. J., & Roe-Sepowitz, D. (2008). Early childhood intervention and early adolescent social and emotional competence: Second-generation evaluation evidence from the Chicago Longitudinal Study. *Educational Research, 50,* 55–73.

O'Brien, R. W., Connell, D. B., & Griffin, J. (2004). Head Start's efforts to improve child health. In E. Zigler & S. Styfco (Eds.), *The Head Start debates,* pp. 161–178. Baltimore: Paul H. Brookes.

Olds, D., Henderson, C., Jr., Kitzman, H., Eckenrode, J., Cole, R., & Tatelbaum, R. (1998). The promise of home visitation: Results of two randomized trials. *Journal of Community Psychology, 26,* 5–21.

Olds, D. L., Sadler, L., & Kitzman, H. (2007). Programs for parents of infants and toddlers: Recent evidence from randomized trials. *Journal of Child Psychology and Psychiatry, 48,* 355–391.

Ou, S.-R., & Reynolds, A. J. (2006). Early childhood intervention and educational attainment: Age 22 findings from the Chicago Longitudinal Study. *Journal of Education for Students Placed at Risk, 11,* 175–198.

Pagani, L., Boulerice, B., Vitaro, F., & Tremblay, R. E. (1999). Effects of poverty on academic failure and delinquency in boys: A change and process model approach. *Journal of Child Psychology and Psychiatry, 40,* 1209–1219.

Peisner-Feinberg, E. S., & Burchinal, M. R. (1997). Relations between preschool children's child-care experiences and concurrent development: The Cost, Quality, and Outcomes Study. *Merrill-Palmer Quarterly, 43,* 451–477.

Pianta, R. C., La Paro, K. M., & Hamre, B. K. (2007). *Classroom assessment scoring system.* Baltimore: Brookes.

Pianta, R. C., & Stuhlman, M. W. (2004). Teacher-child relationships and children's success in the first years of school. *School Psychology Review, 33,* 444–458.

Phillipsen, L. C., Burchinal, M. R., Howes, C. & Cryer, D. (1997). The prediction of process quality from structural features of child care. *Early Childhood Research Quarterly, 12,* 281–303.

Plomin, R., & Bergeman, C. S. (1991). The nature of nurture: Genetic influence on "environmental" measures. *Behavioral and Brain Sciences, 14,* 373–427.

Plomin, R., & Bergeman, C. S. (1994). More on the nature of nurture. *Behavioral and Brain Sciences, 17,* 751–752.

Ramey, C. T., & Campbell, F. A. (1991). Poverty, early childhood education, and academic competence: The Abecedarian experiment. In A. Huston (Ed.), *Children reared in poverty,* pp. 190–221. New York: Cambridge University Press.

Ramey, C. T., Campbell, F. A., Burchinal, M., Skinner, M. L., Gardner, D. M., & Ramey, S. L. (2000). Persistent effects of early childhood education on high-risk children and their mothers. *Applied Developmental Science, 4,* 2–14.

Reynolds, A. J., & Temple, J. A. (2008). Cost-effective early childhood development programs from preschool to third grade. *Annual Review of Clinical Psychology, 4,* 109–139.

Reynolds, A. J., Temple, J. A., Robertson, D. L., & Mann, E. A. (2001). Long-term effects of an early childhood intervention on educational achievement and juvenile arrest: A 15-year follow-up of low-income children in public schools. *Journal of the American Medican Association, 285,* 2339–2346.

Ritchie, S., Howes, C., Kraft-Sayre, M., & Weiser, B. (2001). *Emerging academic snapshot.* Los Angeles: University of California.

Robinson, J., & Emde, R. N. (2004). Mental health moderators of Early Head Start on parenting and child development: Maternal depression and relationship attitudes. *Parenting: Science and Practice, 4,* 73–97.

Schweinhart, L. J. (2004). *The High/Scope Perry Preschool Study through age 40: Summary, conclusions, and frequently asked questions.* Ypsilanti, MI: High/Scope Press.

Smith, J. R., Brooks-Gunn, J., & Klebanov, P. K. (1997). The consequences of living in poverty for young children's cognitive and verbal ability and early school achievement. In G. J. Duncan & J. Brooks-Gunn (Eds.), *Consequences of growing up poor,* pp. 132–189. New York: Russell Sage.

Smith, M., & Dickinson, D. (2002). *User's guide to the early language and literacy classroom observation toolkit.* Baltimore: Brookes.

Smith, S., Davidson, S., Weisenfield, G. & Katsaros, S. (2001). *Supports for early literacy assessment (SELA).* New York: New York University School of Education, Child and Family Policy Center.

Smith, S., & Zaslow, M. (1995). Rationale and policy context for two-generation

interventions. In S. Smith (Ed.), *Two generation programs for families in poverty: A new
intervention strategy*, pp. 1–35. Westport, CT:
Ablex Publishing.

Stipek, D., & Byler, P. (2004). The early childhood classroom observation measure. *Early
Childhood Research Quarterly, 19*, 375–397.

Sylva, K., Siraj-Blatchford, I., & Taggart, B. (2003).
*Assessing quality in the early years: Early
childhood environment rating scale-extension
(ECERS-E): Four curricular subscales.* Stoke-on
Trent, UK: Trentham Books.

U. S. Department of Health and Human Services,
Administration for Children and Families.
(2002). *Making a difference in the lives of infants
and toddlers and their families: The impacts of
Early Head Start:* Volume I. *Final technical
report.* Washington, DC: Administration for
Children and Families, U.S. Department of
Health and Human Services.

U.S. Department of Health and Human Services,
Administration for Children and Families.
(2005). *Head Start Impact Study: First year
findings.* Washington, DC.

Van Horn, M., & Ramey, S. (2004). A new measure for assessing developmentally appropriate practices in early elementary school, a
developmentally appropriate practice template. *Early Childhood Research Quarterly, 19*,
569–587.

Votruba-Drzal, E. (2003). Income changes and
cognitive stimulation in young children's
home learning environments. *Journal of
Marriage and Family, 65*, 341–355.

Werner, E. E. (1994). Overcoming the odds.
*Journal of Developmental & Behavioral
Pediatrics, 15*, 131–136.

Yoshikawa, H. (1995). Long-terms effects of early
childhood programs on social outcomes and
delinquency. *The Future of Children, 5*(3),
51–75.

Zigler, E., Gilliam, W. S., & Jones, S. M. (2006).
A vision for universal preschool. New York:
Cambridge University Press.

Zigler, E., & Trickett, P. (1978). IQ, social competence, and evaluation of early childhood
intervention programs. *American Psychologist,
33*, 789–798.

Zill, N., Resnick, G., Kim, K., O'Donnell, K.,
Sorongon, A., Ziv, Y. et al. (2006). *Head Start
Performance Measures Center Family and Child
Experiences Survey (FACES 2000) technical
report.* Washington, DC: U.S. Department of
Health and Human Services, Administration
for Children and Families, Office of Planning,
Research and Evaluation.

CHAPTER 13

School Influences on Human Development

Jacquelynne S. Eccles and Robert W. Roeser

Schools hold a central place in the socialization of children in almost all nations. They are the most well organized and extensive extrafamilial context for children and adolescents: From the time they first enter school until they complete their formal schooling, children and adolescents spend more time in schools than any other place outside their homes. Consequently, educational institutions play a central role in both promoting children's acquisition of knowledge and shaping the ways in which they learn to regulate their attention, emotions, and behavior. In this chapter, we focus on the ways in which schools either promote children's developmental competence or reinforce developmental difficulties. In this chapter, we build on our previous theoretical work (see Eccles & Roeser, 1999) to offer an overview of what one should study if one wants to understand the role that schools play in shaping human development. Drawing extensively on our 1999 chapter, we describe schools as multilevel contexts that influences children's social-emotional and behavioral development through organizational, social, and instructional processes that operate at several different levels. To understand the influence of schools on human development fully, researchers need to think about these multiple levels interact and then measure aspects of each of the levels in order to study these interactive processes.

Drawing on Bronfennbrenner's ecological view of the child nested within concentric circles of ever expanding realms of influence, we conceptualize the school context as a series of concentric spheres of influence that begin with the face-to-face interactions between students and teachers and move out to a series of more distal systems (such as schoolwide policies set by the principal, districtwide policies set by the school board, and national educational policies that, in turn, influence the social organization of the entire school community) that affect human development through their impact on immediate daily experiences of children and adolescents within their classrooms and their school buildings. As we go through these descriptions, we focus on measurable constructs at each of the many levels. Well-developed measures are available for most of these constructs in the studies that we review. The most glaring omission in the existing body of research on schools as contexts is the scarcity of more comprehensive studies that look at these multiple levels simultaneously. It is our hope that our conceptualization of school environments and the availability of the measures in the studies we review will stimulate more comprehensive research on the impact of schools on human development.

A Multilevel Theoretical Perspective on Schools as Contexts

Assumptions in Our Approach

In our 1999 discussion of schools as a multilevel system, we assumed that (1) schools are systems characterized by multiple levels of regulatory processes (organizational, social, and instructional in nature); (2) these processes are interrelated across levels of analysis; (3) such processes are usually dynamic in nature, sometimes being worked out each day among the various social actors (e.g., teachers and students); (4) these processes "develop" or change as children move through different school levels (elementary, middle, and high school); and (5) it is these processes that regulate children's cognitive, social-emotional, and behavioral development.

Assumption 1. From the location of the school within macroregulatory systems characterized by laws and educational policies of the nation, state, and local school district "down" to the miniregulations that involve an individual teacher's eye contact and body language in relation to a particular child, schools are a system of complex, multilevel, regulatory processes. Processes at each of these levels impact children's development. In this chapter, we begin our discussion of the many ways in which schools influence human development with those processes most directly related to the day-to-day interactions children have with their teachers. We then move out from the child in a hierarchically ordered set of steps to discuss processes located increasingly more distal from the child's immediate experiences

to those processes related to the nature and design of tasks and instruction, the nature and structure of classroom activities and groups, the classroom structure and social ethos, academic tracks, the school organizational structure and ethos, linkages between schools and other institutions in the local community (home, community-based organizations), and finally to district, state, and national governance policies that influence what goes on in schools on a day-to-day basis.

Assumption 2. In 1999, we proposed that in any given school setting, the multilevel processes are interwoven with one another. Relations between different levels of organization in the school may be complementary or contradictory, and may influence children either directly or indirectly. For instance, a principal may decide to mandate certain techniques such as cooperative learning (school level) that the teachers are supposed to implement at the class level. If done well, children within specific classrooms in this school would be seen working in groups (group level) on fairly complex, conceptual problems for which cooperative techniques were designed (task level). Such a well-implemented school policy could indirectly lead to increases in self-esteem, interethnic relationships, and achievement among children, especially those of low ability or status (Stevens & Slavin, 1995). In contrast, if done poorly, chaos could result, leading to far less positive outcomes at the student level.

Alternatively, consider the possible indirect negative effects of school-level mandates to enhance student performance on achievement tests. Mandated testing often leads to the use of particular classroom instructional methods such as drill and practice on test-like items; these practices are often at odds with teachers' own instructional goals and strategies (Ball, 2002). This discrepancy can lead to a dampening of teacher enthusiasm, which, in turn, could undermine students' motivation, effort, and learning (Wigfield et al., 2006). In this example, a well-intended mandate from the nation, state, or district could inadvertently undermine students' performance through its effect on teacher beliefs and practices.

Assumption 3. In 1999, we proposed that it is the processes associated with the different levels of school interacting dynamically with each other, rather than static resources or characteristics of the curriculum, teachers, or school per se, that influence children. In addition, children's own constructions of meaning and interpretation of events within the school environment are the critical mediators between school characteristics and children's feelings, beliefs, and behaviors.

Assumption 4. Finally, we proposed that these different school-related processes change across the course of children's development as they progress through elementary, middle, and high school. That is, not only are children developing, but so too is the whole nature of the schools that they attend. For example, Eccles and her colleagues (1993) have found that of organizational, social, and instructional processes in schools change as children move from elementary to middle school. These changes are associated with declines in many children's motivational beliefs and behaviors. Understanding the interaction of different school features on children at different ages of development is a critical component of understanding the role of schooling in children's development.

In the next section, we describe each of the major contextual levels we outlined in 1999 and discuss how their associated processes can influence children's academic and social-emotional functioning. We also summarize what we know about developmental changes in these contextual processes as children progress through different school types (elementary, middle, and high school) and how such contextual changes influence children's development. We point to particularly good studies of each of the processes we outline. We italicize those references that include particularly good measures of the constructs being discussed or good methods for studying the processes being described. We also note which constructs and processes are in need of more refined measurement strategies.

Levels of Organization in Schools: Level 1: Academic Tasks and Instruction

Academic work is at the heart of the school experience. It is here that students most directly confront what they are supposed to learn. Two aspects of academic tasks are important: the content of the curriculum and the design of instruction. The nature of academic content has an important impact on the regulation of children's attention, interest, and cognitive effort. Academic work that is meaningful to the historical and developmental reality of children's experience promotes sustained attention, high investment of cognitive and affective resources in learning, and strong identification with educational goals and aims (Dewey, 1902). Content that provides meaningful exploration is critical given that boredom in school, low interest, and perceived irrelevance of the curriculum are associated with poor attention, diminished achievement, disengagement, and finally, alienation from school (Jackson & Davis, 2000; NRC/IOM, 2004). Curricula that represent the "voices," images, and historical experiences of traditionally underrepresented groups are particularly important (Ball, 2002; *Romo & Falbo, 1996*). The disconnection of traditional curricula from the experiences of these groups can explain the alienation of some group members from the educational process, sometimes eventuating in school dropout (Ball, 2002; Fine, 1991). By and large, the research on this aspect of academic work has been qualitative in nature and so no well validated quantitative measures exist.

The design of instruction also influences children's self-regulation of attention, cognition, motivation, learning, and investment in school (Ball, 2002; Blumenfeld, 1992; Brophy, 2004; Deci & Ryan, 2002; Dewey, 1902). Choosing materials that provide an appropriate level of challenge for a given class, designing learning activities that require diverse cognitive operations (e.g., opinion, following routines, memory, comprehension), structuring lessons so they build on each other in a systematic fashion, using multiple representations of a given problem, and explicitly teaching children strategies that assist in learning are but a few of the design features that can "scaffold" learning and promote effort investment, interest in learning, and achievement among children. The best work in this area is being done in the learning sciences by scholars interested in curriculum design and evaluation (e.g., Blumenfeld et al., 2000).

From a developmental perspective, there is evidence that the nature of academic work does not change over time in ways that are concurrent with the increasing cognitive sophistication, diverse life experiences, and identity needs of children and adolescents as they move from the elementary into the secondary school years (see Eccles et al., 1998). As one indication of this, Larson and his colleagues have used the *Experience Sampling Method* to study students' emotions during class. They found that middle school children report the highest rates of boredom when doing schoolwork, especially passive work (e.g., listening to lectures) and in particular classes such as social studies, mathematics, and science (*Larson & Richards*, 1989; Larson, 2000). Academic work becomes less, rather than more, complex in terms of the cognitive demands as children move from elementary to junior high school (see Eccles et al., 1998). There is also evidence that the content of the curriculum taught in schools does not broaden to incorporate either important health or social issues that become increasingly salient as children move through puberty and deal with the identity explorations associated with adolescence (Carnegie Council, 1989; Jackson & Davis, 2000; Romo & Falbo 1996). It may be that declines in children's motivation during the transition to secondary school in part reflect academic work that lacks challenge and meaning commensurate with children's cognitive and emotional needs (Brophy, 2004; Eccles et al., 1998; Jackson & Davis, 2000; *Lee & Smith*, 2001).

The impact of instructional materials on students' emotions is just one of the many ways in which experiences at school influence emotions. Much more work on the impact of experiences in classrooms and schools

on students' and teachers' emotional well-being needs to be. Recent work by Pekrun and his colleagues has greatly extended our knowledge of ways in which experiences in the classroom influence students' emotional reactions in school (Pekrun, 2006; Pekrun, Goetz, Titz, & Perry, 2002). Their techniques and measures are appropriate for many of the topics we discuss throughout this chapter. We encourage the readers to use these techniques to investigate the many ways in which experiences at school at multiple levels influence the emotional well-being of students.

Level 2: Activity Structures and Groups

The next level of school influence concerns the structure of activities in the classroom. Classroom instruction is delivered through different activity structures, including whole-group instruction, individualized instruction, and small-group instruction. Groups are often formed based on children's ability level; alternatively, groups are sometimes formed from students representing a diverse array of abilities brought together in a cooperative work arrangement (e.g., Oakes, 2005; Stevens & Slavin, 1995). These different activity structures communicate quite different implicit messages about social relationships and children's abilities – messages that, in turn, influence children's perceptions of both their own academic competence and their social acceptability. These group structures also elicit different patterns of teacher behaviors and peer group associations. Because much of this work is experimental in nature, the methods are available but not specific scales.

The use of either whole-class instruction or within-class ability groups can highlight ability differences and lead to both increased social comparison and differential teacher treatment of high and low achievers in the classroom (Eccles et al., 1998; *Mac Iver & Reuman*, 1988; Oakes, 2005). When this happens, these structures promote achievement status hierarchies, differentiated competence beliefs between low and high achievers, and friendship selection patterns based primarily on similarities in academic abilities. Consequently, low-ability children come to feel increasingly less competent, worthy, or valued precisely because their relatively lower ability is made salient (Rosenholtz & Simpson, 1984; Oakes, 2005). These low-ability children also come to be perceived by their peers as less desirable friends than their high-achieving classmates; that, in turn, can increase their social isolation.

The use of collaborative or cooperative groups is a popular alternative to either whole group, ability-grouped, or individualized instruction at the elementary school level. *Stevens and Slavin* (1995) concluded that cooperative learning techniques in which students work in small groups and receive rewards or recognition based on group performance lead to increases in student achievement, self-esteem, and social acceptance among students of different social statuses and racial/ethnic backgrounds. With proper instruction in the social skills necessary for group work, cooperative groups can provide numerous "niches" for students with different strengths to participate in the learning process, can increase the amount of social support and reinforcement available in the classroom for learning complex material, and can increase contact among students of different abilities and thus can foster a broader network of friendship patterns in the classroom and fewer instances of social isolation (Stevens & Slavin, 1995).

From a developmental perspective, the use of whole-group and within-class ability-grouped instruction increases in frequency as children progress from elementary to middle and high school. Within class ability grouping in reading is wide spread even in the early grades; the use of between-class ability grouping in mathematics, English, and science classes increases dramatically as children move into, and through, secondary school (Eccles et al., 1998; NRC/IOM, 2004). At the same time, the use of both individualized instruction and cooperative grouping declines. We discuss the implications of these grade-related trends later when we discuss the transition into junior high school.

Level 3A: Teacher Beliefs

The next level of school contextual processes is most closely associated with the teacher. In this section, we discuss three examples of processes at this level: teacher beliefs, instructional practices, and teacher-student relationships. Although these three contextual features are typically studied independently and by different sets of researchers, it is important to remember that they always operate interdependently in the classroom and, are, thus, likely to have interactive effects on children. More research is needed on the ways in which these three different sets of beliefs interact that either facilitate or undermine the motivation and well-being of students.

Teachers' General Sense of Efficacy. Teachers' general expectations for their students' performance (i.e., their sense of teaching efficacy) is an important belief that has received a great deal of research attention over the last 15 years. When teachers hold high generalized expectations for student achievement and students perceive these expectations, students achieve more, experience a greater sense of esteem and competence as learners, and resist involvement in problem behaviors during both childhood and adolescence (Calderhead, 1996; Eccles et al., 1998; Lee & Smith, 2001; *Midgley, Feldlaufer, & Eccles,* 1988, 1989a; NRC/IOM, 2004; *Roeser, Eccles, & Sameroff,* 1998). Such expectations, when communicated to the child, become internalized in positive self-appraisals that enhance feelings of worth and achievement. Similarly, teachers who feel they are able to reach even the most difficult students, who believe in their ability to affect students' lives, and who believe that teachers are an important factor in determining developmental outcomes above and beyond other social influences tend to communicate such positive expectations and beliefs to their students. Thus, a high sense of teacher efficacy can enhance children's own beliefs about their ability to master academic material, thereby promoting effort investment and achievement (*Ashton,* 1985; *Midgley, Feldlaufer, & Eccles,*

1989b). On the other hand, low feelings of teacher efficacy can lead to behaviors likely to reinforce feelings of incompetence in the child, potentiating both learned helpless responses to failure in the classroom and the development of depressive symptoms (NRC/IOM, 2004). More research is now needed on the ways in which the kinds of more distal level school cultures and practices discussed later affect individual teachers' general expectations for success and the ways in which teachers can be trained or school building cultures can be changed to support higher levels of general expectations for the promise of all students.

Differential Teacher Expectations. Equally important are the differential expectations teachers often hold for various individuals within the same classroom and the differential treatment practices that sometimes accompany these expectations. Most of the studies linking differential teacher expectations to either their own behaviors or to their students' achievement and motivation have been done under the rubric of teacher expectancy effects. A great deal of the work on teacher expectancy effects has focused on differential treatment related to gender, race/ethnic group, and/or social class. Most of this work has investigated the potential undermining effects of low teacher expectations on girls (for mathematics and science), on minority children (for all subject areas), and on children from lower social class family backgrounds (again for all subject areas) (Ball, 2002; Eccles et al. 1998; Jussim et al., 1996; Romo & Falbo, 1996). More recently, researchers such as Steele and Aronson (Aronson & Steele, 2005; Aronson, Fried & Good, 2002) have linked this form of differential treatment, particularly for African American students, to school disengagement and disidentification (the separation of one's self-esteem from all forms of school-related feedback). Steele and Aronson argue that African American students become aware of the fact that teachers and other adults have negative stereotypes of African American children's academic abilities. This awareness increases their anxieties, which, in turn, lead them to disidentify with the school

context to protect their self-esteem (see also Burchinal, Roberts, Zeisel, & Rowley, 2008; Wong, Eccles & Sameroff, 2003).

Recent work, however, suggests that teacher expectancy effects may not always be as negative as once believed. For the effect to be of great concern, one needs to demonstrate that it has a negative biasing effect (i.e., that teachers' expectations lead to changes in motivation and performance over time beyond what would be expected given knowledge of the characteristics of the specific students (Jussim et al., 1996; Jussim et al., 2000; Madon et al., 2001)). Evidence for such negative biasing effects is minimal. Much of the association between teacher expectations for individual students and subsequent student motivation and performance reflects the "accurate" association between teacher expectations and student characteristics like prior achievement levels and behavioral patterns (Jussim et al., 1996; Madon et al., 2001). In addition, not all teachers respond to their expectations with behaviors that undermine the motivation and performance of the low expectancy students. Some teachers respond to low expectations with increased instructional and motivational efforts for particular students and succeed in increasing both their motivation and their learning (Goldenberg, 1992). This work suggests that teacher-expectancy effects depend on whether teachers structure activities for, and interact, differently with, high and low expectancy students and on whether the students perceive these differences (Brophy, 1988; Jussim, Eccles, & Madon, 1996; Parsons, Kaczala, & Meece, 1982; Rosenthal, 1969; Rist, 1970; Weinstein, 1989). Future research needs to focus on how to enable teachers to use their perceptions of differential competence levels in ways that support the intellectual growth of all students.

Nonetheless, small but consistent teacher expectancy effects over time can have a large cumulative effect on both motivation and achievement (Jussim et al., 1996; Smith, Jussim & Eccles, 1999), particularly if these effects begin in kindergarten and the first grade (Entwisle & Alexander, 1993). Finally,

Jussim et al. (1996) found that girls, low-SES students, and minority students are more susceptible to these effects than European American, middle-class boys.

Teachers' Beliefs Regarding the Nature of Ability. Both developmental and educational psychologists have become interested in teachers' beliefs regarding the nature of abilities. Some individuals conceive of intellectual abilities as stable and largely inherited potentials; others conceive of intellectual abilities as acquired skills. Dweck (2000) refers to this distinction as an entity versus an incremental view of intelligence. Recently, educational psychologists have begun to investigate the implications of such beliefs for student and teacher behaviors. Ames (1992), *Maehr and Midgley (1996)*, and Midgley (2002) hypothesize that these beliefs affect the goals both teachers and students have for learning; these goals, in turn, affect both the teachers' instructional practices and the students' learning behaviors. (The intervention and evaluation methodology used by Maehr and Midgley, 1996, and the PALS measurement battery developed by Midgley, Pintrich, and their colleagues are particularly impressive [see Midgley, 2002].) These researchers focus on two particular achievement goals, performance versus mastery goals, and hypothesize that these two goals are linked to two different patterns of instruction: the first pattern called an "ability-goal orientation," emphasizes relative ability, social comparison, and competition. Grouping by ability, differential rewards for high achievers, public evaluative feedback, academic competitions, and other practices can promote the notion that academic success means outperforming others and proving one's superior ability. Unfortunately, most youth, by definition, are not "the best" and thus may not receive rewards and recognition in a classroom that emphasize relative ability. We know that in ability-oriented classrooms, children are more likely to use low-level strategies to learn, experience more anxiety and negative affect, and devote attentional resources to making themselves look smarter or avoiding looking dumber than other students rather than learning the material (Midgley, 2002). Children who lack confidence in their academic competence are particularly vulnerable in such environments. Learned helpless responses to academic failure, the avoidance of engaging in work, and negative emotional experience are more likely to beset low-ability students in ability-focused environments (Dweck, 2000).

In contrast, teachers who hold an incremental view of intelligence tend to adopt a "task-goal orientation" in their instructional practices. Such an orientation stresses self-improvement and effort as the major hallmarks of academic success. These teachers acknowledge individual effort and improvement regardless of a child's current ability level, provide choice and collaborative work, and emphasize to their students that mastering new content, learning from mistakes, and continuing to try are all highly valued hallmarks of success. Such practices reduce children's concerns about their ability relative to peers and the feelings of self-consciousness, anxiety, or disenfranchisement that often accompany such concerns (Maehr & Midgley, 1996; Midgley, 2002; NRC/IOM, 2004). In these mastery-focused environments, children use deeper processing strategies to learn, report more positive and less negative affective states, and seem less concerned with their current ability and more concerned with task mastery, understanding, and self-improvement.

The association of teachers' mastery versus performance goals to teachers' behaviors, classroom culture, and student outcomes is well established. Future research needs to focus on how to change such beliefs and how to support teachers' implementation of more mastery based teaching practices, particularly in the face of increased standardized testing and No Child Left Behind national school policies.

Developmental Changes in Teachers' Beliefs. Grade-level changes have been documented for all of these types of teacher beliefs. For example, grade-level differences have also been identified for teachers' endorsement of mastery versus ability goals. For example, Midgley and her colleagues (Anderman,

Maehr & Midgley, 1999; Midgley, 2002; Midgley, Anderman, & Hicks, 1995; *Roeser, Midgley, & Maehr,* 1994) found that, as children progress from elementary to middle school, both teachers and students think that their school environment is becoming increasingly focused on competition, relative ability, and social comparison. These changes occur during a time when adolescents are particularly vulnerable to social comparison with peers. They are beginning to differentiate ability from effort and also are starting to view ability more as a "fixed capacity" than on incremental skill. Not measuring up to one's peers in terms of academic ability in school settings that increasingly emphasize ability differences is very likely to undermine many adolescents' self-esteem and academic motivation (Juvonen, 2007; Juvonen et al., 2004; Roeser & Eccles, 2000; Roeser, Eccles, & Strobel, 1998; Roeser, Strobel, & Quihuis, 2002).

Finally, there are grade-level differences in teachers' sense of their own efficacy (i.e., their ability to teach and influence all of the students in their classes). For example, Midgley, Feldlaufer, & Eccles (1989a) found large differences in teachers' efficacy between elementary school and junior high school teachers: Teachers in junior high school environments feel less efficacious than their colleagues who teach in elementary school settings. These results are not surprising because of the larger number of students, the lack of extended contact with students during the day, and the content-focused educational training that secondary teachers experience in comparison to their elementary school colleagues. Nonetheless, this decline in teacher efficacy can have a major impact on many of the children's development, particularly the low performing children. Future research needs to focus on how such grade related changes in teachers' beliefs can be changed

Level 3B: Instructional Practices

Instructional practices and teacher discourse convey both implicit and explicit messages concerning: children's moral, social, and

intellectual capacity, the goals and purposes of learning, and the different reasons for engaging in academic activities. Children's interpretation of these messages, in turn, influences the quality of their academic and social-emotional functioning (Ball, 2002; Roeser et al., 1996; Deci & Ryan, 2002). Motivational researchers have been particularly interested in practices related to classroom climate and classroom management.

Classroom Climate and Emotional Support. Historically, most studies of teacher practice effects focused on the impact of their personal characteristics and teaching style on children's overall achievement, motivation, satisfaction, and self-concept (Eccles et al., 1998). This research assumed that general teacher characteristics (like warmth) and practices (like directness) would enhance student satisfaction, persistence, curiosity, and problem-solving capability through their impact on general classroom climate. Research has supported this assumption (Eccles et al., 1998) and many measures of such teacher characteristics and practices have been developed (e.g., Trickett & Moos, 1973).

More recent examinations of the effect of classroom climate have disentangled factors such as teacher personality and warmth from teacher instruction and managerial style. This research has shown that effects of "climate" depend on its association with other aspects of the teachers' beliefs and practices. For instance, Moos and his colleagues found that student satisfaction, personal growth, and achievement are maximized only when teacher supportiveness is accompanied by efficient organization, stress on academics, and provision of focused goal-oriented lessons (Trickett & Moos, 1973, 1974; Moos, 1987). Furthermore, these practices are more common among teachers who believe they can influence their students' performance and future achievement potential (NRC/IOM, 2004).

Classroom Management. Work related to classroom management has focused on issues of orderliness predictability, accountability, and responsibility and control/autonomy. As one would expect, students learn more and are better behaved in classrooms that orderly and well managed (NRC/IOM, 2004). In addition, children value success more, see themselves as more competent and learn more in classrooms where they are held accountable for work (NRC/IOM, 2004).

Control/Autonomy. Classroom practices related to the structure of authority are also important for the development of children's regulation of their achievement behavior and for aspects of their emotional adjustment. According to Deci and Ryan's Self-Determination Theory (Deci & Ryan, 2002), intrinsic motivation is good for learning and classroom environments that are overly controlling and do not provide an adequate amount of autonomy undermine intrinsic motivation, mastery orientation, ability self-concepts and expectations, and self-direction, and induce, instead, a learned helpless response to difficult tasks. Support for this hypothesis has been found in both laboratory and field-based studies (e.g., Grolnick et al., 2002; Jackson & Davis, 2000; NRC/IOM, 2004): In classroom settings where children are given opportunities to make choices, pursue their interests, and contribute to classroom discussions and decisions, a sense of autonomous, self-determined behavior in relation to school work is inculcated. This sense of autonomy is related to children's intrinsic valuing of school, quality of cognitive and affective engagement with learning, performance, and feelings of esteem and personal control (Deci & Ryan, 2002; NRC/IOM, 2004). In contrast, in classrooms where few provisions for self-determined behavior are granted and where external rewards, punishments, and praise are frequently used to induce achievement behavior, children are more likely to feel their behavior is being controlled by factors outside themselves. This feeling is associated with children's extrinsic motivation, external locus of control, and shallower engagement with learning activities (Ryan & Deci, 2002; Pintrich & De Groot, 1990; Maehr & Midgley, 1996).

The challenge for future research is studying the interface between support for autonomy and adequate provision of structure. Both are needed and the proper balance is likely to change with grade level and subject matter. Furthermore, the best strategies for supporting autonomy likely vary across subject areas. Finally, the balance between support for autonomy, the relevance of the curriculum for future goals, and the need to prepare all students for certain levels of literacy in different subject areas need to be studied. How do we train teachers so that they have sufficient self-confidence, sufficient pedagogical knowledge (trade craft) and sufficient subject matter content knowledge so that they can achieve the right balance in classrooms inhabited by many students with different levels of current competence, motivation, and self-regulation.

Developmental Changes in Control Strategies. Contrary to what one might expect to happen given the increasing developmental maturity of the children, middle and junior high school teachers, compared to elementary school teachers, use more control-oriented strategies, enforce stricter discipline, and provide fewer opportunities for student autonomy and decision-making in the classroom (Juvonen et al., 2004; Midgley, 2002; Midgley & Feldlaufer, 1987; Midgley, Feldlaufer, & Eccles, 1988). Apparently, as children move from elementary to middle and junior high school environments, their teachers believe that they are less trustworthy and need to be controlled more. To explain this pattern, Willower and Lawrence (1979) suggested that, as children grow older, bigger, and more mature, and as peer subcultures become stronger during adolescence, teachers increasingly see students as a threat to their authority and thus respond with more control and discipline. Stereotypes about adolescents as unruly and out of control are also likely to reinforce such beliefs and strategies. Recent high-profile school violence cases are likely to have increased teachers' concerns about their own safety as well as the safety of other school personnel and students, leading to even tighter controls over high school students' behaviors (Elliott et al., 1998; Lee & Smith, 2001). Finally, the demands of secondary school environments, in which teachers have to deal with many students, may predispose them to using more controlling strategies as a way of coping with large numbers of students.

More Integrated Approaches to General Practices and Beliefs. The work reviewed thus far is based on studies focused on only one or two belief systems and/or contextual characteristics at a time. There has been a shift to a more global, integrated view of the impact of learning contexts on motivation. Among the first such efforts, Rosenholtz and Simpson (1984) suggested a cluster of teaching practices (e.g., individualized versus whole group instruction; ability grouping practices; and public quality of feedback) that should affect motivation because these practices make ability differences in classroom especially salient to students. These researchers assumed that these practices affect the motivation of all students by increasing the salience of extrinsic motivators and ego-focused learning goals, leading to greater incidence of social comparison behaviors, and increased perception of ability as an entity state rather than an incremental condition. All of these changes should reduce the quality of children's motivation and learning. The magnitude of the negative consequences of these shifts, however, should be greatest for low-performing children: As these children become more aware of their relative low standing, they are likely to adopt a variety of ego-protective strategies that, unfortunately, undermine learning and mastery. Research evidence has supported all of these hypotheses (Covington, 1992; Eccles et al., 1998; Maehr & Midgley, 1996; Midgley, 2002).

The work on understanding group differences in achievement and achievement choices is another example of an attempt to identify a broad set of classroom characteristics related to motivation. The work on girls and mathematics is one example of this approach. There are sex differences in children's preference for different types of learning contexts that likely interact with subject area to produce sex differences in interest in different subject areas (Eccles,

2007; Hoffmann, 2002). Females appear to respond more positively to mathematics and science instruction if it is taught in a cooperative or individualized manner rather than a competitive manner, if it is taught from an applied/person centered perspective rather than a theoretical/abstract perspective, if it is taught using a hands-on approach rather than a "book learning" approach, and if the teacher avoids sexism in its many subtle forms. The reason given for these effects is the fit among the teaching style, the instructional focus, and females' value, goals, motivational orientation, and learning styles. The few relevant studies support this hypothesis (see Eccles et al., 1998; Hoffmann, 2002; Meece, Glienke, & Burg, 2006). If such classroom practices are more prevalent in one subject area (e.g., physical science or mathematics) than another (e.g., biological or social science), then one would expect gender differences in motivation to study these subject areas. In addition, however, mathematics and physical science do not have to be taught in these ways; more "girl-friendly" instructional approaches can be used. And when they are, girls, as well as boys, are more likely to continue taking courses in these fields and to consider working in these fields when they become adults.

The girl-friendly classroom conclusion is a good example of Person-Environment Fit. Many investigators have suggested that children will be maximally motivated to learn in situations that fit well with their interests, current skill level, and psychological needs, so that the material is challenging, interesting, and meaningful (e.g., Eccles, Midgley et al., 1993; Krapp, Hidi, & Renninger, 1992; NRC/IOM, 2004). Variations on this theme include aptitude by treatment interactions and theories stressing cultural match or mismatch as one explanation for group differences in school achievement and activity choices (e.g., Burchinal et al., 2008; Eccles, 2009; Fordham & Ogbu, 1986).

Level 3C: Teacher-Student Relationships

The last aspect of classroom life discussed in this section concerns the relationships that teachers and students share with one another. Research has demonstrated that quality teacher-student relationships provide the affective underpinnings of academic motivation and success (Eccles et al., 1998; NRC/IOM, 2004). Teachers who are trusting, caring, and respectful of students provide the social-emotional support that children and adolescents need to approach, engage, and persist on academic learning tasks and to develop positive achievement-related self-perceptions and values (*Goodenow*, 1993; Midgley, Feldlaufer, & Eccles, 1989b; Midgley, 2002). Correlational studies with adolescents also show that students' perceptions of caring teachers enhance their feelings of self-esteem, school belonging, and positive affect in school (*Roeser & Eccles*, 1998; *Roeser et al.*, 1996).

In addition to enhancing motivation, several authors have noted that in a highly complex society, teachers represent one stable source of nonparental role models for adolescents. Teachers not only teach, they can provide guidance and assistance when social-emotional or academic problems arise, and may be particularly important in promoting developmental competence when conditions in the family and neighborhood do not (Eccles, Lord, & Roeser, 1996; Mortimer, Shanahan & Ryu, 1994; Simmons & Blyth, 1987; Staff, Mortimer, & Uggen, 2004). Evidence from a variety of sources suggest that the quality of teacher-student relationships that allow such guidance and assistance to occur decrease dramatically with the transition from elementary school into secondary school – at a time when young adolescents are in particular need for close, nonfamilial relationships (Eccles et al., 1993; Juvonen et al., 2004; *Roeser & Midgley*, 1997).

Level 3: Summary

In summary, these studies of classroom level influences suggest that development is optimized when students are provided with challenging tasks in a mastery-oriented environment that provides good emotional and cognitive support, meaningful material

to learn and master, and sufficient support for their own autonomy and initiative. Deci and Ryan (2002) proposed that humans have three basic needs: to feel competent, to feel socially attached, and to have autonomous control in one's life. Further, they hypothesized that individuals develop best in contexts that provide opportunities for each of these needs to be met. Clearly, the types of classroom characteristics that emerge as important for both socioemotional and intellectual development would provide such opportunities.

Over the last 15 years Connell and his colleagues have developed a whole school high school reform effort based on these ideas (Connell & Klem, 2000). This reform, First-things-first, includes the following components: small learning communities, team teaching, close relationships between students and teachers, supports for autonomy, and curricular supports so that all students can succeed. These features were selected because they are known to increase feelings of belonging and attachment between teachers and students, feelings of competence for both teachers and students, and a mastery focus and high expectations for all students. Initial evaluations of this reform model have been very promising (Connell & Klem, 2000).

Level 4: Academic Tracks/Curricular Differentiation

The next level of influences is that of academic tracks or "curriculum differentiation policies." These terms refer to the regularities in the ways in which schools structure sets of learning experiences for different types of students. The process of providing different educational experiences for students of different ability levels is a widespread yet very controversial practice in American schools. Tracking takes different forms at different grade levels. It includes within-class ability grouping for different subject matters or between-class ability grouping in which different types of children are assigned to different teachers. Within-classroom ability grouping for reading and mathematics is quite common in elementary school. In the middle and high school years, between-class tracking becomes both more widespread and more broadly linked to the sequencing of specific courses for students bound for different post secondary school trajectories (college prep, general, vocational). Differentiated curricular experiences for students of different ability levels structure experience and behavior in two major ways: First, tracking determines the quality and kinds of opportunities to learn the child receives (Oakes, 2005) and, second, it determines exposure to different peers and thus, to a certain degree, the nature of social relationships that youth form in school (Fuligni, Eccles, & Barber, 1995).

Despite years of research on the impact of tracking practices, few strong and definitive answers have emerged (Fuligni et al., 1995). The results of these studies vary depending on the outcome assessed, the group studied, the length of the study, the control groups used for comparison, and the specific nature of the context in which these practices are manifest. The research situation is complicated by the fact that conflicting hypotheses about the likely direction and the magnitude of the effects of tracking emerge depending on the theoretical lens one uses to evaluate the practice. The best justification for tracking practices derives from a person-environment fit perspective. Children will be more motivated to learn if their educational materials and experiences can be adapted to their current competence level. There is some evidence consistent with this perspective for children placed in high ability classrooms, high within-class ability groups, and college tracks (Fuligni et al., 1995; Gamoran & Mare, 1989; Kulik & Kulik, 1987; Pallas et al., 1994).

In contrast, when long-term effects are found for children placed in low-ability and noncollege tracks, they are usually negative primarily because these children are typically provided with inferior educational experience and support (e.g., Jackson & Davis, 2000; Lee & Smith, 2001; *Pallas et al.,* 1994; Vanfossen, Jones, & Spade, 1987). Low-track placements have been related to poor

attitudes toward school, feelings of incompetence, and problem behaviors both within school (nonattendance, crime, misconduct) and in the broader community (drug use, arrests) as well as to educational attainments (Oakes, 2005). But whether or not academic tracks promote such outcomes or reflect preexisting differences remains a matter of considerable debate. It is also important to note that these negative effects result from the stereotypically biased implementation of ability-grouping programs. A different result might emerge for the low-competence students if the teachers implemented the program more in keeping with the goals inherent in the person-environment fit perspective – that is, by providing high-quality instruction and motivational practices tailored to the current competence level of the students.

Social comparison theory leads to a different prediction regarding the effect of ability grouping and tracking on one aspect of development: ability self-concepts. People often compare their own performance with the performances of others to determine how well they are doing (Marsh et al., 2007; Marsh, Trautwein, Lüdtke & Brettschneider, 2008). They typically conclude they are doing well, and that they have high-ability, if they are doing better those around them. In turn, this conclusion should bolster their confidence in their ability to master the material being taught. Ability grouping should narrow the range of possible social comparisons in such a way as to lead to declines in the ability self-perceptions of higher-ability individuals and to increases in the ability self-perceptions of lower-ability individuals. The few existing studies support this hypothesis. For example, Reuman, found that being placed in a low-ability mathematics class in the seventh grade led to an increase in self-concept of mathematics ability and a decrease in test anxiety; and conversely being placed in a high-ability mathematics class led to a decrease in self-concept of mathematics ability (Reuman, 1989).

The impact of these changes on other aspects of development likely depends on a variety of individual and contextual factors. For example, in his original achievement motivation theory, Atkinson (1957) provided strong evidence that the engagement of highly motivated individuals is maximized when the probability of success is .5. If the net result of the big-fish–little-pond effect is to bring both low and high performers closer to the .5 probability level, then ability grouping should have a positive impact on all of the students in both ability groups who are highly motivated and a negative impact on all of the individuals in both ability groups who have low motivation to succeed. Theories focused on the importance of challenging material in a supportive environment suggest an increase in motivation for everyone provided that the quality of instruction leads to equally challenging material for all ability levels. Conversely, if the social comparison context also increases the salience of an entity view rather than an incremental view of ability (see earlier discussion of teacher's views about intellectual ability; Dweck, 2000), then the decline in ability self-concepts of the high ability individuals might lead them to engage in more failure avoidant and ego-protective strategies.

Yet another way to think about the impact of ability grouping on development is in terms of its impact on peer groups: Between-classroom ability grouping and curricular differentiation promotes continuity of contact among children and adolescents with similar levels of achievement and engagement with school. For those doing poorly in school, such practices can structure and promote friendships among students who are similarly alienated from school and are more likely to engage in risky or delinquent behaviors (Dryfoos, 1990). The "collecting" of children with poor achievement or adjustment histories also places additional burdens on teachers who teach these classes (Oakes, 2005).

Tracking and ability grouping can also lead to the concentration of children with similar behavioral vulnerabilities. For instance, Kellam, Rebok, Wilson, and Mayer (1994) found that rates of moderate to severely aggressive children ranged from 7–8 percent to 63 percent among two different first-grade classrooms in the same elementary school. They found that these differing rates were a direct result of between-class ability grouping policies. As a result of this policy, children in these two classrooms were exposed to very different environments: one in which aggression was deviant (only 7–8 percent of students are aggressive) and one in which it was pretty much the norm (63 percent aggressive students). It seems likely that aggressive behavior would not necessarily lead to peer rejection in the classroom with high rates of aggression. To the contrary, in such an environment, aggression might confer status and social rewards among peers and thus be reinforced. By placing children with similar vulnerabilities in the same environment, both the reinforcement of negative behavior and promotion of friendships among similarly troubled children are more likely.

In summary, between-class ability grouping and curriculum differentiation provide examples of how school policy, teacher beliefs and instruction, and student characteristics can all conspire to create maladaptive transactions that perpetuate poor achievement and behavior among low-ability children. The placement of many low-ability children in a low track classroom may cause some teachers to feel overwhelmed and inefficacious. This might translate into poor instruction, low expectations, and use of controlling strategies on the part of such teachers. These factors, in turn, can fuel student disengagement (Kagan, 1990), which then feeds back into the teachers' beliefs and practices. Eventually, academic failure of certain low-ability children can result from these reciprocal processes.

Another important and controversial aspect of curriculum differentiation involves how students get placed in different classes and how difficult it is for students to move between class levels as their academic needs and competencies change once initial placements have been made. These issues are important both early in a child's school career (Entwisle & Alexander,

1993) and later in adolescence when course placement is linked directly to the kinds of educational options that are available to the student after high school. Dornbusch (1994) described the impact of tracking on a large, ethically diverse sample of high school students in northern California. Analyzing the data course by course, Dornbusch found that 85 percent of his sample stayed in the same track during high school – there was little mobility. Furthermore, Dornbusch found that many average students were incorrectly assigned to lower track courses. This mistake had long-term consequences for these students, in effect putting them on the wrong path toward meeting the requirements for getting into California's higher educational system. Of particular concern was the fact that these youth and their parents, who were more likely to be of color and poor, were never informed of the potential consequences of course decisions made by school personnel during the child's early high school career. Thus, curricular differentiation and school-home communication practices exerted a profound influence over the life paths of these average students who, though able, were placed in lower ability classrooms in high school.

Level 5: Schools as Organizations

Schools also function as formal organizations. These aspects of the whole school environment impact children's intellectual, social-emotional, and behavioral development. Important school organizational factors include student characteristics and fiscal resources (Lee et al., 1993; Lee & Smith, 2001), school climate and sense of community (Bryk, Lee, & Holland, 1993; Goodenow, 1993; Lee & Smith, 2001), and such school-wide practices as start time (Carskadon, 1997).

School Resources. Certainly student composition issues such as the number of low-ability students or the percent of minority students can affect both the internal organization and the climate of the school, which, in turn, can impact the educational and behavioral outcomes of the students

(Rutter et al., 1979). School resources in terms of adequate materials, a safe environment, and continuity of teaching staff are also important for adolescents' learning and well-being. School district level variations in such school resources are likely a major contributor to the continuing inequity in educational outcomes for several minority groups in the United States. Thirty-seven percent of African American youth and 32 percent of Hispanic youth, compared to 5 percent of European American and 22 percent of Asian youth are enrolled in the 47 largest city school districts in this country; in addition, African American and Hispanic youth attend some of the poorest school districts in this country. Twenty-eight percent of the youth enrolled in city schools live in poverty, and 55 percent are eligible for free or reduced cost lunch, suggesting that class may be as important (or more important) as race in the differences in achievement that emerge. Teachers in these schools report feeling less safe than teachers in other school districts, drop out rates are highest, and achievement levels at all grades are the lowest (Lee & Smith, 2001). Finally, schools that serve these populations are less likely than schools serving more advantaged populations to offer either high quality remedial services or advanced courses and courses that facilitate the acquisition of higher order thinking skills and active learning strategies. Even adolescents who are extremely motivated may find it difficult to perform well under these educational circumstances.

School Size. Early studies of schools focused primarily on objective characteristics of schools such as school size, teacher-student ratios, number of books in the library, and per-pupil expenditures (Barker & Gump, 1964). School size emerged as one of the most important of these structural characteristics: Both children and their teachers scored better on a wide variety of indicators of successful development if they were in small schools rather than large schools. Recent work by Elder and his colleagues (Elder & Conger, 2000) has confirmed these results. In their studies of adolescents in Iowa, small school size emerged as a major predictor of healthy adolescent develop-ment and high school achievement. Most likely these results reflect the increased opportunities provided by small schools for close teacher-student relationships, active monitoring of student progress and student difficulties, student involvement in a wide variety of extracurricular activities, and high levels of parent involvement.

The complexity of the school size issue, however, has been complicated lately by the emergence of schools within schools (Maroulis & Gomez, 2008; Ready & Lee, 2008; Wyse, Keesler, & Schneider, 2008). In an effort to create smaller learning commu-nities within existing school buildings, many school districts have been implementing a schools-within-schools plan. In high schools this often consists of creating several theme based learning communities that occupy different regions of the school buildings and that stay together over the 3–4 years of high school. The challenge is how to prevent such theme based programs from becom-ing yet another form of curricular track-ing that ends up sorting the students into social class based groups and creates the same problems we discussed in the earlier section on tracking. The few existing stud-ies suggest that there is a strong tendency for exactly this to happen unless the school principal guards carefully against it (Ready & Lee, 2008). Recent studies further sug-gest that the students themselves are happy to sort into themes that recreate the older tracking systems loosely labeled college prep and vocational training (Ready & Lee, 2008). Together these policy experiments and the early results illustrate the complex-ity of school reform in ways that support autonomy and increase academic relevance without recreating social class stratification. Future research is needed on how to achieve the right balance once again.

General Social Climate. Recently, research-ers have become interested in the social climate of entire school. These researchers suggest, and provide some evidence, that schools, like communities, vary in the cli-mate and general expectations regarding stu-dent potential (e.g., Bryk et al., 1993; Comer,

1980; Lee & Smith, 2001). They suggest that general climate affects the development of both teachers and students in very funda-mental ways. For example, in a preliminary evaluation of a school intervention based on these principles, *Cauce, Comer, and Schwartz* (1987) demonstrated a clear impact on chil-dren's confidence in their academic abilities. Similarly, in their analysis of higher achieve-ment in Catholic schools, Bryk et al. (1993) discuss how the culture within Catholic schools is fundamentally different from the culture within most public schools in ways that positively affect the motivation of students, parents, and teachers. This cul-ture (school climate) values academics, has high expectations that all children can learn, and affirms the belief that the business of school is learning (see also Lee & Smith, 2001). Similarly, Bandura and his colleagues documented between-school differences in the general level of teachers' personal effi-cacy beliefs (Bandura, 1994) and have argued that these differences translate into teaching practices that undermine the motivation of many students and teachers in the school. Mac Iver, Reuman, and Main (1995) discuss how many schools limit students' access to learning opportunities and evaluate them in ways that undermine their motivation and achievement (see also Midgley, 2002; NRC/IOM, 2004).

School Academic and Social Climate. *Maehr and Midgley (1996)* argued that just as classroom practices give rise to certain achievement goals, so too do schools as a whole through particular policies and prac-tices (see also Midgely, 2002). A school-level emphasis on different achievement goals creates a school psychological environ-ment that affects students' academic beliefs, affect, and behavior (Midgley, 2002; Roeser, Midgley, & Urdan, 1996; Urdan & Roeser, 1993). For example, schools' use of public honor rolls and assemblies for the highest achieving students, class rankings on report cards, differential curricular offerings for students of various ability levels, and so on are all practices that emphasize relative abil-ity, competition, and social comparison in the school ("school ability orientation"). On the other hand, through the recognition of academic effort and improvement, rewards for different competencies that extend to all students, and through practices that emphasize learning and task mastery (block scheduling, interdisciplinary curricular teams, cooperative learning) schools can promote a focus on discovery, effort and improvement, and academic mastery ("school task orientation"). Maehr and Midgley (1996) spent three years working with one middle school to test these ideas. Although it was quite difficult to actually change the school's practices, student motivation did increase as the school became more task focused and less ability focused (see also NRC/IOM, 2004).

The academic goal focus of a school has important implications for students' mental health. In a series of studies, we found that middle school adolescents' beliefs that their school is ability-focused was associated with declines in their educational values, achievement, and self-esteem, and increases in their anger, depressive symptoms, and school truancy from seventh to eighth grade. These effects were found after controlling for prior levels of each adjustment outcome, adolescents' prior academic ability, and their demographic background (race, gender, family income; Roeser & Eccles, 1998; Roeser, Eccles, & Sameroff, 1998). These results support the idea that schools that emphasize ability are likely to alienate a significant number of students who cannot perform at the highest levels leading to anxiety, anger, disenchantment, and self-selection out of the school environment (Finn, 1989; Maehr & Midgley, 1996; Midgley, 2002). In contrast, schools that emphasize effort, improvement, task mastery, and the expectation that all students can learn appear to enfranchise more children in the learning process, promote adaptive attributions (e.g., achievement is based on effort and is therefore malleable), reduce depression, and decrease the frustration and anxiety that can be generated in achievement settings.

One final note on school level academic goal emphases: they are strongly correlated with adolescents' perceptions of the school social climate. Adolescents who perceive a task-orientation in their school also report that their teachers are friendly, caring, and respectful. These factors, in turn, predict an increased sense of belonging in school among adolescents (Goodenow, 1993; Midgley, 2002; Roeser et al., 1996). In contrast, perceptions of a school ability-orientation are negatively correlated with adolescents' perceptions of caring teachers (Roeser et al., 1996). From the adolescents' perspective, a de-emphasis on comparison and competition and an emphasis on effort and improvement are intertwined with their view of caring teachers.

School Start and End Time. School start time is yet another example of how regulatory processes associated with schools can interact with individual regulatory processes, here biological ones, to influence development. Research conducted by Carskadon (1990, 1997) has shown that, as children progress through puberty they actually need more, not less sleep. During this same period, as children move through elementary to middle and high school, schools typically begin earlier and earlier in the morning, necessitating earlier rise times for adolescents (Carskadon, 1990, 1997). In concert with other changes, such as the later hours at which adolescents go to bed, the earlier school start times of the middle and high school create a "developmental mismatch" that can both promote daytime sleepiness and undermine adolescents' ability to make it to school on time, alert, and ready to learn.

The time when school ends also has implications for child and adolescent adjustment. In communities where few structured opportunities for after-school activities exist, especially impoverished communities, children are more likely to be involved in high-risk behaviors such as substance use, crime, violence, and sexual activity during the period between 2 and 8 p.m. Providing structured activities either at school or within community organizations after school when many children have no adults at home to supervise them is an important consideration in preventing children and adolescents from engaging in high-risk behaviors (Carnegie Council, 1989; Eccles & Templeton, 2002).

School Calendar. American schools typically are in session from September into June. This calendar reflects the historical need for students to be available to work on family farms during the summer. Such need is no longer typical for the vast majority of America's students. What is the consequence of this calendar for learning? This question has become very salient in educational policy discussions as a result of increasing evidence that social class differences in school achievement result in large part because of social class differences in the "summer learning gap." Most recently, the work by Alexander, Entwisle, and their colleagues showed that much of the social class differential in school achievement reflects differences that already exist when the students enter kindergarten and differences that accumulate over the elementary school years in learning over the summer vacations. On average, children living in poor families learn less and forget more over the summer vacation than children living in middle-class and upper-social class families, in part because these families are able to provide their children with a variety of structured learning experiences over the summer (Alexander, Entwisle, & Olson, 2007). When they compared the actual rate of learning over the course of the school year across social class lines in the Baltimore school district, Alexander and his colleagues found little if any social class difference; in contrast, they found a substantial difference over the summer time. Work on summer schools has shown that well designed summer school programs can help ameliorate this social-class differential (Alexander et al., 2007).

Level 6: School Home/Community Linkages

Home-school Linkage. Parent involvement in their child's schooling has consistently emerged as an important factor in promoting both academic achievement and socioemotional well-being (Comer, 1980; Eccles & Harold, 1993). Parent involvement in the form of monitoring academic activities and homework, providing assistance with homework, engaging children in educational enrichment activities outside of school, and active participation in classroom activities and in school organizations (e.g., governance, parent-teacher associations) all represent different forms of involvement (Epstein, 1992). Such parental involvement communicates positive educational expectations, interest, and support to the child. Parent involvement also helps to establish a "safety net" of concerned adults (parents and teachers) that can support children's academic and social-emotional development and assist children if adjustment problems should arise (see Jackson & Davis 2000; NRC/IOM, 2004).

Evidence also suggests that home-school connections are relatively infrequent during the elementary years and become almost nonexistent during the middle and high school years (e.g., Carnegie, 1989; Eccles & Harold, 1993; Epstein, 1992; Stevenson & Stigler, 1992). This lack of involvement has been attributed to few efforts on the part of schools to involve parents, especially as children transition out of neighborhood-based elementary schools into the larger, more impersonal middle and high school environments (Eccles & Harold, 1993). The cultural beliefs that teachers are in charge of children's learning also contribute to the low levels of parent involvement in schools in the United States (Stevenson & Stigler, 1992). Other characteristics and experiences of parents that reduce involvement include a lack of time, energy, and/or economic resources, lack of knowledge, feelings of incompetence, failure to understand the role parents can play in education, or a long history of negative interactions of parents with the schools are also important factors in explaining low levels of parent involvement in school (Eccles & Harold, 1993; NRC/IOM, 2004).

School-Community Linkages. Comer (1980) stressed the importance of school-community links: He argued that schools are a part of the larger community and that they will be successful only to the extent that they are well integrated into that community at all levels. For example, schools need to be well connected to the communities' social services so that schools can play a cooperative role in furthering children's and their family's well-being. Conversely, communities need to be invested in their schools in ways that stimulate active engagement across these two societal units. For example, when the business community is well connected to the school, there are likely to be increased opportunities for students to develop both the skills and knowledge necessary to make a smooth transition from school into the world of work. Such opportunities can range from frequent field trips to various employment settings, to apprenticeships, to direct involvement of employees in the instructional program of the school

Concern about a stronger link between communities and schools has lead to a recent increase in opportunities for students to be involved in community service learning opportunities. In 1989, the Turning Points report (Carnegie, 1989) recommended that every middle school include supervised youth service in the community or school as part of the core academic curriculum. Today 25 percent of elementary schools, 38 percent of middle schools, and 46 percent of all high schools have students participating in either mandatory or voluntary service-learning activities (National Center for Education Statistics NCES, 2004).

Evidence for a positive impact of service learning on various indicators of child and adolescent development is accumulating (NRC/IOM, 2004). For example, participants in well designed service-learning programs do better than comparison groups on measures of problem-solving ability, reading and mathematics achievement, and course failure (Eyler, Root & Giles, 1998; Fisher, 2001; Melchior & Bailis, 2002; Moore & Allen, 1996). Participation in service learning programs is also linked to positive social assets, civic engagement, community involvement, and increased social and personal responsibility (Kahne, Chi, & Middaugh, 2002; Scales, Blyth, Berkas, & Kielsmeier, 2000; Youniss, McLellan, & Yates, 1997), empathetic understanding (Scales et al., 2000), improved attitudes toward diverse groups in society

(Yates & Youniss, 1996), altruistic motivation (Scales et al., 2000), closer communication with one's parents (Scales et al., 2000), more positive or mastery orientated motivation for school work (Scales et al., 2000), greater commitment to academic learning (Scales et al., 2000), increased feelings of personal efficacy and self-esteem (Kahne et al., 2002; Yates & Youniss, 1996), and a better sense of oneself (Hamilton & Fenzel, 1988). Finally, service learning has also been related to reductions in problem behaviors. In a review of programs aimed at reducing adolescent pregnancy and unprotected sex, Kirby (2002) concluded that service learning is an effective approach. Additional support linking service learning to decreases in problem behavior include: lower course failure, school suspension, and school dropout (Allen, Philliber, Herrling & Kuperminc, 1997); fewer discipline problems (Calabrese & Schumer, 1986); and reduced absenteeism (Melchior & Balis, 2002).

Closer ties between schools and communities may be especially important in high-risk neighborhoods. Both researchers and policy makers have become concerned with the lack of structured opportunities for youth after school (e.g., Carnegie Corporation, 1989; Eccles & Gootman, 2002; Eccles & Templeton, 2002). In most communities, adolescents finish their schoolday by 2 or 3 in the afternoon. Also in most communities there are few structured activities available for these youth other than work. And typically, their parents are working until early evening – leaving the adolescents largely unsupervised. Such a situation is worrisome for two reasons: First, communities are missing an opportunity to foster positive development through meaningful activities and, second, adolescents are most likely to engage in problem behaviors during this unsupervised period. A closer collaboration between communities and schools could help solve this dilemma. At the most basic level, school buildings could be used as activity centers. At a more cooperative level, school and community personnel could work together to design a variety of programs to meet the multiple needs of their youth. More research is needed on these types of partnerships can be effectively created and sustained.

Conclusions

In this chapter, we have summarized the many ways in which schools can influence development. We began by pointing out how the multiple levels of school organization interact to shape the day-to-day experiences of children and teachers. We stressed how one must think of schools as complex organizations to understand how decisions and regulatory processes at each level impact on schools as a context for development. We also stressed the interface of schools as complex changing institutions with the developmental trajectories of individuals. To understand how schools influence development, one needs to understand change at both the individual and the institutional level. The stage-environment fit theory provides an excellent example of the linking of these two developmental trajectories. Imagine two trajectories: one at the school level and one at the individual level. Schools change in many ways over the grade levels. The nature of these changes can be developmentally appropriate or inappropriate in terms of the extent to which they foster continued development toward the transition into adulthood and maturity. (The changes can also be developmentally irrelevant but we will not discuss these types of changes.) Children move through this changing context as they move from grade to grade and from school to school. Similarly, children develop and change as they get older. They also have assumptions about their increasing maturity and the privileges it ought to afford them. We believe optimal development occurs when these two trajectories of change are in synchrony with each other – that is, when the changes in the context mesh well with, and perhaps even slightly precede, the patterns of change occurring at the individual level. Furthermore, we summarized evidence that the risk of negative developmental outcomes is increased when these two trajectories are out of synchrony – particularly when the context changes in a developmental regressive pattern.

Another way to think about school contexts is in terms of their relative ability to meet human needs. As we noted earlier, Connell and Wellborn (1991) suggested that individuals develop best in contexts that provide opportunities to feel competent, to feel socially connected and valued, and to exercise control over one's own destiny. If this is true, then individuals ought to be drawn toward those contexts that provide these opportunities in developmentally appropriate doses. Variations across contexts on these characteristics could explain why individuals come to prefer one context over another – for example, adolescents who are not doing well in school or who are having difficulty getting along with their parents might turn to their peer group to find a sense of sense of competence and positive self-esteem. Essentially, we are arguing that when individuals have some choice over where to spent their time, they will choose to spend the most time in those social contexts that best fulfill their needs for a sense of competence, high quality social relationship, for respect from others for their autonomy and individuality, and for a sense of being valued by one's social partners. If they can fulfill these needs within social contexts that reinforce normative behavior, they are likely to do well in school and other culturally valued institutions. If they can not fulfill their needs in these types of social contexts, they are likely to seek out other social contexts, which, in turn, may reinforce more norm breaking and problematic behaviors. Thus, if we want to support positive, normative developmental pathways for our children and adolescents, it is critical that we provide them with ample opportunities to fulfill their basic human needs in social contexts that reinforce positive normative developmental pathways. Schools provide a unique opportunity to provide such developmentally appropriate social contexts. Unfortunately, we often fall short of this goal, in part because of the complexity of multilevel systems underlying the daily experiences children and adolescents have in their schools. Future research needs to embrace this complexity so that comprehensive policy strategies can be developed and assessed.

References

Alexander, K. L., Entwisle, D. R. & Olson, L. S. (2007). Lasting consequences of the summer learning gap. *Sociology of Education*, 72, 167–180.

Allen, J. P., Philliber, S., Herrling, S., & Kuperminc, G. P. (1997). Preventing teen pregnancy and academic failure: Experimental evaluation of a developmentally-based approach. *Child Development*, 64, 729–742.

Ames, C. (1992). Classrooms: Goals, structures, and student motivation. *Journal of Educational Psychology*, 84, 261–271.

Anderman, E. M., Maehr, M. L., & Midgley, C. (1999). Declining motivation after the transition to middle school: Schools can make a difference. *Journal of Research and Development in Education*, 32, 131–147.

Aronson, J., Fried, C. B., & Good, C. (2002). Reducing the effects of stereotype threat on African American college students by shaping theories of intelligence, *Journal of Experimental Social Psychology*, 38, 113–125.

Aronson, J., & Steele, C. M. (2005). Stereotypes and the fragility of academic competence, motivation, and self-concept. In A. J. Elliot & C. S. Dweck (Eds.), *Handbook of competence and motivation*. New York: Guilford.

Ashton, P. (1985). Motivation and the teacher's sense of efficacy. In C. Ames & R. Ames (Eds.), *Research on motivation in education*: Vol. 2. *The classroom milieu*, pp. 141–171. Orlando, FL: Academic Press.

Atkinson, J. W. (1957). Motivational determinants of risk taking behavior. *Psychological Review*, 64, 359–372.

Ball, A. F. (2002), Three decades of research on classroom life: Illuminating the classroom communicative lives of America's at-risk students. In W. G. Secada (Ed.), *Review of Research in Education*, 26, pp. 71–112. Washington, DC: American Educational Research Association Press.

Bandura, A. (1994). *Self-efficacy: The exercise of control*. New York: W. H. Freeman.

Barker, R., & Gump, P. (1964). *Big school, small school: High school size and student behavior.* Stanford, CA: Stanford University Press.

Blumenfeld, P. C. (1992). Classroom learning and motivation: Clarifying and expanding goal theory. *Journal of Educational Psychology*, 84, 272–281.

Blumenfeld, P., Fishman, B. J., Krajcik, J, Marz, R. W., & Soloway, E. (2000). Creating usable innovations in systemic reform: Scaling up technology-embedded project-based science in urban schools. *Educational Psychologist*, 35, 149–164. DOI: 10.1207/S15326985EP3503_2

Boggiano, A. K., & Katz, P. (1991). Maladaptive achievement patterns in students: The role of teacher's controlling strategies. *Journal of Social Issues*, 47, 35–51.

Brophy, J. (1988). Research linking teacher behavior to student achievement: Potential implications for instruction of Chapter 1 students. *Educational Psychologist*, 23, 235–286.

Brophy, J. E. (2004). *Motivating students to learn* (2nd ed.). Mahwah, NJ: Erlbaum.

Bryk, A. S., Lee, V. E., & Holland P. B. (1993). *Catholic schools and the common good*. Cambridge, MA: Harvard University Press.

Burchinal, M. R., Roberts, J. E., Zeisel, S. A., & Rowley, S. J. (2008). Social risk and protective factors for African American children academic achievement and adjustment during the transition to middle school. *Developmental Psychology*, 44(1), 286–292.

Calabrese, R., & Schumer, H. (1986). The effects of service activities on adolescent alienation. *Adolescence*, 21(83), 675–687.

Calderhead, J. (1996). Teachers, beliefs, and knowledge. In D. C. Berliner & R. C. Calfee (Eds.), *Handbook of Educational Psychology*, pp. 709–725. New York: Simon & Schuster Macmillan.

Carnegie Council on Adolescent Development (1989). *Turning points: Preparing American youth for the 21st century*. New York: Carnegie Corporation.

Carskadon, M. A. (1990). Patterns of sleep and sleepiness in adolescents. *Pediatrician*, 17, 5–12.

Carskadon, M. A. (1997, April). *Adolescent sleep: Can we reconcile biological needs with societal demands?* Lecture given at Stanford University, April 21, 1997.

Cauce, A. M., Comer, J. P., & Schwartz, D. (1987). Long term effects of a systems oriented school prevention program. *American Journal of Orthopsychiatric Association*, 57, 127–131.

Comer, J. (1980). *School Power*. New York: Free Press.

Connell, J. P. (2003). *Getting off the dime: First steps toward implementing First Things First*. Reported prepared for the US Department of Education. Philadelphia: Institute for Research and Reform in Education.

Connell, J. P. & Klem, A. M. (2000). You can get there from here: Using a theory of change approach to plan urban education reform. *Journal of Educational and Psychological Consultation*, 11, 93–120.

Connell, J. P., & Wellborn, J. G. (1991). Competence, autonomy, and relatedness: A motivational analysis of self-system processes. R. Gunnar & L. A. Sroufe (Eds.), *Minnesota symposia on child psychology*, pp. 43–77, Vol. 23. Hillsdale, NJ: Lawrence Erlbaum Associates.

Covington, M. V. (1992). *Making the grade: A self-worth perspective on motivation and school reform.* New York: Cambridge University Press.

Deci, E. L., & Ryan, R. M. (2002). Self-determination research: Reflections and future directions. In E. L. Deci & R. M. Ryan (Eds.), *Handbook of self-determination theory research*, pp. 431–441. Rochester, NY: University of Rochester Press.

Dewey, J. (1902/1990). *The child and the curriculum.* Chicago: University of Chicago Press.

Dornbusch, S. M. (1994). *Off the track.* Presidential address at the biennial meeting of the Society for Research on Adolescence, San Diego, CA.

Dryfoos, J. G. (1990). *Adolescents at risk: Prevalence and prevention.* Oxford: Oxford University Press.

Dweck, C. S. (2000). *Self-theories: Their role in motivation, personality, and development.* Philadelphia: Psychology Press.

Eccles, J. S. (2007). Where are all the women? Gender differences in participation in physical science and engineering. In S. J. Ceci & W. M. Williams (Eds.), *Why aren't more women in science? Top researchers debate the evidence*, pp. 199–210. Washington, DC: American Psychological Association.

Eccles, J. S. (2009). Who am I and what am I going to do with my life? Personal and collective identities as motivators of action. *Educational Psychologist*, 44(2), 78–89.

Eccles, J. S., & Gootman, J. A. (Eds.) (2002). *Community programs to promote youth development.* Washington, DC: National Academy Press.

Eccles, J. S., & Harold, R. D. (1993). Parent-school involvement during the early adolescent years. *Teachers' College Record*, 94, 568–587.

Eccles, J., Lord, S., & Roeser, R. (1996). Round holes, square pegs, rocky roads, and sore feet: The impact of stage/environment fit on young adolescents' experiences in schools and families. In D. Cicchetti, & S. L. Toth (Eds.), *Rochester Symposium on Developmental Psychopathology:* Vol. VIII. *Adolescence: Opportunities and Challenges*, pp. 47–93. Rochester NY: University of Rochester Press.

Eccles, J. S., Midgley, C., Wigfield, A., Buchanan, C. M., Reuman, D., Flanagan, C., & MacIver, D. (1993). Development during adolescence: The impact of stage-environment fit on adolescents' experiences in schools and families. *American Psychologist*, 48, 59, 90–101.

Eccles, J. S., & Roeser, R. (1999). School and community influences on human development. In M. Bornstein and M. Lamb (Eds.), *Developmental psychology: An advanced textbook*, pp. 503–554 (4th ed.). Mahwah, NJ: Lawrence Erlbaum Associates Press.

Eccles, J. S., & Templeton, J. (2002). Extracurricular and other after-school activities for youth. In W. S. Secada (Ed.), *Review of Educational Research*, pp. 113–180, Vol. 26. Washington, DC: American Educational Research Association Press.

Eccles, J. S., Wigfield, A., & Schiefele, U. (1998). Motivation. In N. Eisenberg (Ed.), *Handbook of child psychology*, pp. 1017–1095, Vol. 3 (5th ed.). New York: Wiley.

Elder, G. H., & Conger, R. D. (2000). *Children of the land.* Chicago: University of Chicago Press.

Elliott, D. S., Hamburg, B. A., & Williams, K. R. (1998). *Violence in American schools.* Cambridge: Cambridge University Press.

Entwisle, D. R., & Alexander, K. L. (1993). Entry into school: The beginning school transition and educational stratification in the United States. *Annual Review of Sociology*, 19, 401–423.

Epstein, J. L. (1992). School and family partnerships. In M. Alkin (Ed.), *Encyclopedia of educational research*, pp. 1139–1151, New York: MacMillan.

Eyler, J., Root, S., & Giles, D. E., Jr. (1998). Service-learning and the development of expert citizens: Service-learning and cognitive science. In R. Bingle and D. Duffey (eds.), *With service in mind.* Washington, DC: American Association of Higher Education.

Feldlaufer, H., Midgley, C., & Eccles, J. S. (1988). Student, teacher, and observer perceptions of the classroom environment before and after the transition to junior high school. *Journal of Early Adolescence*, 8, 133–156.

Fine, M. (1991). *Framing dropouts: Notes on the politics of an urban public high school.* Albany: State University of New York Press.

Finn, J. D. (1989). Withdrawing from school. *Review of Educational Research*, 59, 117–142.

Finn, J. D. (2006). *The adult lives of at-risk students: The roles of attainment and engagement in high school*. Report to National Center of Educational Statistics, Washington, DC: U.S. Department of Education NCES 2006–328.

Fisher, D. (2001). "We're moving on up": Creating a schoolwide literacy effort in an urban high school. *Journal of Adolescent & Adult Literacy*, 45(2), 92–101.

Fordham, S., & Ogbu, J. U. (1986). Black students' school success: Coping with "the burden of 'acting white.'" *The Urban Review*, 18, 176–206.

Fuligni, A. J., Eccles, J. S., & Barber, B. L. (1995). The long-term effects of seventh-grade ability grouping in mathematics. *Journal of Early Adolescence*, 15(1), 58–89.

Gamoran, A., & Mare, R. D. (1989). Secondary school tracking and educational inequality: Compensation, reinforcement, or neutrality? *American Journal of Sociology*, 94, 1146–1183.

Goldenberg, C. (1992). The limits of expectations: A case for case knowledge about teacher expectancy effects. *American Educational Research Journal*, 29, 517–544.

Goodenow, C. (1993). Classroom belonging among early adolescent students: Relationships to motivation and achievement. *Journal of Early Adolescence*, 13(1), 21–43.

Grolnick, W. S., Gurland, S. T., Jacob, K. F., & Decourcey, W. (2002). The development of self-determination in middle childhood and adolescence. In A. Wigfield & J. S. Eccles (Eds.), *Development of achievement motivation*, pp. 147–171. San Diego: Academic Press.

Hamilton S. F., & Fenzel, L M. (1988). The impact of volunteer experience on adolescent social development: Evidence of program effects. *Journal of Adolescent Research*, 3 (1), 65–80.

Hoffmann, L. (2002). Promoting girls' interest and achievement in physics classes for beginners. *Learning and Instruction*, 12, 447–465.

Holland, A., & Andre, T. (1987). Participation in extracurricular activities in secondary school: What is known, what needs to be known? *Review of Educational Research*, 57, 437–466.

Hunt, D. E. (1975). Person-environment interaction: A challenge found wanting before it was tried. *Review of Educational Research*, 57, 437–466.

Jackson, A. W., & Davis, G. A. (2000). *Turning points 2000: Educating adolescents in the 21st century*. New York: Teachers College Press.

Jussim, L., Eccles, J. S., & Madon, S. (1996). Social perception, social stereotypes, and teacher expectations: Accuracy and the quest for the powerful self-fulfilling prophecy. In L. Berkowitz (Ed.), *Advances in experimental social psychology*, pp. 281–388. New York: Academic Press.

Jussim, L., Palumbo, P., Chatman, C., Madon, S., & Smith, A. (2000). Stigma and self-fulfilling prophecies. In T. F. Heatherton, R. E. Kleck, M. R. Hebl, & J. G. Hull (Eds.), *The social psychology of stigma*, pp. 374–418. New York: Guilford Press.

Juvonen, J. (2007). Reforming middle schools: focus on continuity, social connectedness, and engagement. *Educational Psychologist*, 42(4), 197–208.

Juvonen, J., Le, V. N., Kaganoff, T., Augustine, C., & Constant, L. (2004). *Focus on the wonder years: Challenges facing the American middle school*. Santa Monica, CA: Rand Co.

Kagan, D. M. (1990). How schools alienate students at risk: A model for examining proximal classroom variables. *Educational Psychologist*, 25, 105–125.

Kahne, J., Chi, B. and Middaugh, E. (2002), CityWorks Evaluation Summary. Surdna Foundation and Mills College.

Kellam, S. G., Rebok, G. W., Wilson, R., & Mayer, L. S. (1994). The social field of the classroom: Context for the developmental epidemiological study of aggressive behavior. In R. K. Silbereisen & E. Todt (Eds.), *Adolescence in context: The interplay of family, school, peers, and work in adjustment*, pp. 390–408. New York: Springer-Verlag.

Kirby, D. B. (2002). Effective approaches to reducing adolescent unprotected sex, pregnancy, and childbearing. *The Journal of Sex Research*, 39, 51–57.

Krapp, A., Hidi, S. & Renninger, K. A. (1992). Interest, learning and development. In K. A. Renninger, S. Hidi & A. Krapp (Eds.), *The role of interest in learning and development*, pp. 3–25. Hillsdale, NJ: Erlbaum.

Kulik, J. A., & Kulik, C. L. (1987). Effects of ability grouping on student achievement. *Equity & Excellence*, 23, 22–30.

Larson, R. W. (2000). Toward a psychology of positive youth development. *American Psychologist*, 55, 170–183.

Larson R. & Richards, M. (Eds.) (1989). *The changing life space of early adolescence Journal of Youth and Adolescence* (Special Issue) 501–626.

Lee, V. E., Bryk, A. S., & Smith, J. B. (1993). The organization of effective secondary schools. In L. Darling-Hammond (Ed.), *Review of*

Research in Education, pp. 171–267, Vol. 19. Washington, DC: American Educational Research Association.

Lee, V. E. & Smith, J. (2001). *Restructuring high schools for equity and excellence: What works.* New York: Teacher's College Press.

Mac Iver, D. J., Reuman, D. A., & Main, S. R. (1995). Social structuring of school: Studying what is, illuminating what could be. In M. R. Rosenzweig & L. W. Porter (Eds.), *Annual review of psychology*, Vol. 46. Palo Alto, CA: Annual Reviews Inc.

Mac Iver, D., & Reuman, D. A. (April 1988). Decision-making in the classroom and early adolescents' valuing of mathematics. Paper presented at the annual meeting of the American Educational Research Association, New Orleans.

Madon, S., Smith, A., Jussim, L., Russell, D. W., Eccles, J. Palumbo, P., & Walkiewicz, M. (2001). Am I as you see me or do you see me as I am? Self-fulfilling prophecies and self-verification. *Personality and Social Psychological Bulletin*, 27, 1214–1224.

Maehr, M. L., & Midgley, C. (1996). *Transforming school cultures to enhance student motivation and learning.* Boulder, CO: Westview Press.

Maroulis, S., & Gomez, L. M. (2008). Does "connectedness" matter? Evidence from a social network analysis within a small-school reform. *The Teachers College Record*, 100, 1901–1929.

Marsh, H. W., Trautwein, U., Lüdtke, O., Baumert, J., & Köller, O. (2007). The big-fish-little-pond effect: Persistent negative effects of selective high schools on self-concept after graduation. *American Educational Research Journal*, 44, 631–669.

Marsh, H. W., Trautwein, U., Lüdtke, O., & Brettschneider, W. (2008). Social comparison and big-fish-little-pond effects on self-concept and other self-belief constructs Role of generalized and specific others. *Journal of Educational Psychology*, 100, 510–524.

Meece, J. L., Glienke, B. B., & Burg, S. (2006). Gender and motivation. *Journal of Social Psychology*, 44, 351–373.

Melchior, A., & Bailis, L. N. (2002). Impact of service-learning on civic attitudes and behaviors of middle and high school youth: Findings from three national evaluations. In A. Furco & S. H. Billig (Eds.), *Service-learning: The essence of the pedagogy*, pp. 201–222. Greenwich, CT: Information Age.

Midgley, C. M. (2002). *Goals, Goal Structures, and Patterns of Adaptive Learning.* Mahwah, NJ: Erlbaum.

Midgley, C. M., Anderman, E., & Hicks, L. (1995). Differences between elementary and middle school teachers and students: A goal theory approach. *Journal of Early Adolescence, xx,* 90–113.

Midgley, C. M., & Feldlaufer, H. (1987). Students' and teachers' decision-making fit before and after the transition to junior high school. *Journal of Early Adolescence*, 7, 225–241.

Midgley, C. M., Feldlaufer, H., & Eccles, J. S. (1988). The transition to junior high school: Beliefs of pre- and post-transition teachers. *Journal of Youth and Adolescence*, 17, 543–562.

Midgley, C. M., Feldlaufer, H., & Eccles, J. S. (1989a). Changes in teacher efficacy and student self- and task-related beliefs during the transition to junior high school. *Journal of Educational Psychology*, 81, 247–258.

Midgley, C. M., Feldlaufer, H., & Eccles, J. S. (1989b). Student/teacher relations and attitudes toward mathematics before and after the transition to junior high school. *Child Development*, 60, 981–992.

Moore, C., & Allen, J. P. (1996). The effects of volunteering on the young volunteer. *Journal of Primary Prevention*, 17, 231–258.

Moos, R. H. (1987). Person-environment congruence in work, school, and health care settings. *Journal of Vocational Behavior*, 31, 231–247.

Mortimer, J. T., Shanahan, M., & Ryu, S. (1994). The effects of adolescent employment on school-related orientation and behavior. In R. K. Silbereisen & E. Todt (Eds.), *Adolescence in context: The interplay of family, school, veers, and work in adjustment*, pp. 304–326. New York: Springer-Verlag.

National Center for Education Statistics (2004). Washington, DC: http://nces.ed.gov/surveys/frss/publications/1999043/5.asp

National Research Council and Institute of Medicine (NRC/IOM) (2004). *Engaging Schools.* Washington, DC: National Academies Press.

Oakes, J. (2005). *Keeping track: How schools structure inequality* (2nd ed.). New Haven: CT: Yale University Press.

Pallas, A. M., Entwisle, D. R., Alexander, K. L., & Stluka. M. F. (1994). Ability-group effects: Instructional, social, or institutional? *Sociology of Education*, 67, 27–46.

Parsons, J. S., Kaczala, C. M., & Meece, J. L. (1982). Socialization of achievement attitudes and beliefs: Classroom Influences. *Child Development*, 53, 322–339.

Pekrun, R. (2006). The control-value theory of achievement emotions: Assumptions, corollaries, and implications for educational research and practice. *Educational Psychology Review, 18*, 315–341.

Pekrun, R., Goetz, T., Titz, W., & Perry, R. P. (2002). Academic emotions in students' self-regulated learning and achievement: A program of qualitative and quantitative research. *Educational Psychologist, 37*, 91–105.

Pintrich, P. R., & de Groot, E. V. (1990). Motivational and self-regulated learning components of classroom academic performance, *Journal of Educational Psychology, 82*, 33–40. DOI: 10.1037/0022-0663.82.1.33

Ready, D. D., & Lee, V. E. (2008). Choice, equity, and schools-within-schools reform. *Teachers College Record, 110*(9), 1930–1958.

Reuman, D. A. (1989). How social comparison mediates the relation between ability-grouping practices and students' achievement expectancies in mathematics. *Journal of Educational Psychology, 81*, 178–89.

Rist, R. C. (1970). Student social class and teacher expectations: The self-fulfilling prophecy in ghetto education. *Harvard Educational Review, 40*, 411–451.

Roeser, R. W., & Eccles, J. S. (1998). Adolescents' perceptions of middle school: Relation to longitudinal changes in academic and psychological adjustment. *Journal of Research on Adolescence, 88*, 123–158.

Roeser, R. W., & Eccles, J. S. (2000). Schooling and mental health. A. J. Sameroff, M. Lewis, & S. M. Miller (Eds.), *Handbook of developmental psychopathology*, 135–156 (2nd ed.). New York: Plenum.

Roeser, R. W., Eccles, J. S., & Sameroff, J. (1998). Academic and emotional functioning in early adolescence: Longitudinal relations, patterns, and prediction by experience in middle school. *Development and Psychopathology, 10*, 321–352.

Roeser, R. W., Eccles, J. S. & Strobel, K. (1998). Linking the study of schooling and mental health: Selected issues and empirical illustrations at the level of the individual. *Educational Psychologist, 33*, 153–176.

Roeser, R. W., & Midgley, C. M. (1997). Teachers' views of aspects of student mental health. *Elementary School Journal, 98*(2), 115–133.

Roeser, R. W., Midgley, C. M., & Maehr, M. L. (February 1994). *Unfolding and enfolding youth: A development study of school culture and student well-being.* Paper presented at the Society for Research on Adolescence, San Diego.

Roeser, R. W., Midgley, C., & Urdan, T. C. (1996). Perceptions of the school psychological environment and early adolescents' psychological and behavioral functioning in school: The mediating role of goals and belonging. *Journal of Educational Psychology, 88*, 408–422.

Roeser, R. W., Strobel, K. R., & Quihuis, G. (2002). Studying early academic motivation, social-emotional functioning, and engagement in learning: Variable- and person-centered approaches. *Anxiety, Stress, and Coping, 15*(4), 345–368.

Romo, H. D., & Falbo, T. (1996). *Latino high school graduation.* Austin, TX: University of Texas Press.

Rosenholtz, S. J., & Simpson, C. (1984). The formation of ability conceptions: Developmental trend or social construction? *Review of Educational Research, 54*, 301–325.

Rosenthal, R. (1969). Interpersonal expectations effects of the experimenter's hypothesis. In Rosenthal & R. L. Rosnow (Eds.), *Artifact in behavioral research*, pp. 182–279. New York: Academic Press,

Rutter, M., Maughan, B., Mortimore, P., & Ouston, J. (1979). *Fifteen thousand hours: Secondary schools and their effects on children.* Cambridge, MA: Harvard University Press.

Scales, P. C., Blyth, D. A., Berkas, T. H., & Kielsmeier, J. C. (2000). The effects of service-learning on middle school students' social responsibility and academic success. *Journal of Early Adolescence, 20*(3), 332–358.

Simmons, R. G., & Blyth, D. A. (1987). *Moving into adolescence: The impact of pubertal change and school context.* Hawthorn, NY: Aldine de Gruyler.

Smith, A. E., Jussim, L., & Eccles, J. S. (1999). Do self-fulfilling prophecies accumulate, dissipate, or remain stable over time? *Journal of Personality and Social Psychology, 77*, 548–565.

Staff, J., Mortimer, J. T., & Uggen, C. (2004). Work and leisure in adolescence. In R. L. Lerner & L Steinberg (2004). *Handbook of Adolescent Psychology*, pp. 429–450, (2nd ed.). Hoboken, NJ: Wiley & Sons.

Steinberg, L., Fegley, S., & Dornbusch, S. M. (1993). Negative impact of part-time work on adolescent adjustment: Evidence from a longitudinal study. *Developmental Psychology, 29*, 171–180.

Stevens, R. J., & Slavin, R. E. (1995). The cooperative elementary school: Effects on students' achievement, attitudes, and social relations.

American Educational Research Journal, 32, 321–351.

Stevenson, H. W., & Stigler, J. W. (1992). *The learning gap: Why our school are failing and what we can learn from Japanese and Chinese education.* New York: Summit Books.

Trickett, E. J., & Moos, R. H. (1973). The social environment of junior high and high school classrooms. *Journal of Educational Psychology,* 65, 93–102.

Trickett, E. J., & Moos, R. H. (1974). Personal correlates of contrasting environments: student satisfaction in high school classrooms. *American Journal of Community Psychology, 2,* 1–12.

Urdan, T. C., & Roeser, R. W. (1993, April). *The relations among adolescents' social cognitions, affect, and academic self-schemas.* Paper presented at the annual meeting of the American Educational Research Association, Atlanta.

Vanfossen, B. E., Jones, J. D., & Spade, J. Z. (1987). Curriculum tracking and status maintenance. *Sociology of Education,* 60, 104–122.

Weinstein, R. (1989). Perceptions of classroom processes and student motivation: Children's views of self-fulfilling prophecies. In C. Ames & R. Ames (Eds.), *Research on motivation in Education*: Vol. 3. *Goals and cognitions,* pp. 13–44. New York: Academic Press.

Wigfield, A., Eccles, J. S., Schiefele, U., Roeser, R., & Davis-Kean, P. (2006). Motivation. In N. Eisenberg (Ed.), *Handbook of child psychology,* pp. 933–1002, Vol. 3 (6th ed.). New York: Wiley.

Willower, D. J., & Lawrence, J. D. (1979). Teachers' perceptions of student threat to teacher status and teacher pupil control ideology. *Psychology in the Schools,* 16, 586–590.

Wong, C. A., Eccles, J. S., & Sameroff, A. J. (2003). The influence of ethnic discrimination and ethnic identification on African-Americans adolescents' school and socioemotional adjustment. *Journal of Personality,* 71, 1197–1232.

Wyse, A. E., Keesler, V., & Schneider, B. (2008). Assessing the effects of small school size on mathematics achievement: A propensity score-matching approach. *Teachers College Record,* 110(9), 1879–1900.

Yates, M., & Youniss, M. (1996). A developmental perspective on community service in adolescence. *Social Development,* 5(1), 85–111.

Youniss, J., McLellan, J. A., & Yates, M. (1997). What we know about engendering civic identity. *American Behavioral Scientist,* 40, 619–630.

CHAPTER 14

Siblings and Peers in the Adult-Child-Child Triadic Context

Sybil L. Hart

Relationships among siblings and peers entail a range of events; those characterized by cooperation and collaboration are harmonious while others are colored by enmity and conflict (Arsenio & Lemerise, 2004; Dunn, 1985; Hay & Ross, 1982; C. U. Shantz & Hobart, 1989). Agonistic events can be rare and of low intensity, but they can also be frequent and hostile (Garcia, Shaw, Winslow, & Yaggi, 2000; Hay & Ross, 1982; Ishikawa & Hay, 2006; Lussier, Deater-Deckard, Dunn, & Davies, 2002; Rubin, Bukowski, & Parker, 2006). The wide disparities in behaviors and levels of adjustment have been addressed through inquiry into a number of child characteristics, such as gender, temperament, and birth order (Bates & Pettit, 2007; Downey & Condron, 2004; Maccoby, 2004; D. W. Shantz, 1986). In this chapter we will explore sibling and peer relationships in light of contextual events, particularly those that include parents and caregivers. Since an attachment figure's presence is more likely to occur among younger children, we will focus on children at the toddler and preschool stages.

Parallels and Distinctions between Sibling and Peer Relationships

Parallels between children's social functioning in sibling and peer relationships have been sought in a number of studies (Volling, Youngblade, & Belsky, 1997). Recent findings on sibling relationship quality as a predictor of conflict in later peer relationships (Bank, Patterson, & Reid, 1996; Garcia et al., 2000; Patterson, Reid, & Dishion, 1998) has led to renewed interest in consistencies across contexts, and the process through which these occur. Indeed, following works in which sibling conflict was found to be more frequent and more intense than peer conflict (Abramovitch, Corter, Pepler, & Stanhope, 1986; Furman & Buhrmester, 1985; Stauffacher & DeHart, 2005), newer works using school-age children, adolescents (Fagan & Najman, 2003; Richmond, Stocker, & Rienks, 2005; C. M. Stocker, Burwell, & Briggs, 2002; Williams, Conger, & Blozis, 2007; Yeh & Lempers, 2004), as well as younger children (Cote, Vaillancourt, Barker, Nagin, & Tremblay, 2007; Criss & Shaw, 2005; Garcia et al., 2000; Ingoldsby, Shaw, & Garcia, 2001) show that children's internalizing and externalizing behaviors are predicted by earlier difficulties within the sibling relationship. Findings on physical aggression have also been complemented by findings on relational aggression (Stauffacher & DeHart, 2006). Research across multiple contexts (Ostrov, Crick, & Stauffacher, 2006) reported that a younger sibling's use of physical aggression with peers was predicted by degree of exposure to an older sibling's physical aggression. In a similar vein, a younger sibling's use of relational aggression toward peers was predicted by exposure to relational aggression by an older sibling.

Some evidence suggests that prosocial behaviors may too be generalizable from sibling to peer contexts. One source has been data from large-scale epidemiological research (Baydar, Hyle, & Brooks-Gunn, 1997; Downey & Condron, 2004; Richman, Stevenson, & Graham, 1982). Follow-up of children in the National Longitudinal Survey of Youth Study revealed that after an initial period of adjustment following the transition from status of only child to older sibling, children show some signs of heightened maturity (Baydar et al., 1997). Other provocative research (Downey & Condron, 2004) using nationally representative samples of teacher reports on 20,649 kindergarteners in the Early Childhood Longitudinal Study suggests modest advantages to peer relationships among children who have siblings, with greatest advantages appearing among children with one or two siblings rather than three or more.

Evidence that children's relationships with peers may be predicted by earlier events with siblings has stimulated interest in mechanisms responsible for sibling-peer linkages but these are still poorly understood (DeHart, 1999; Kramer & Kowal, 2005; Steinmetz, 1977). The fact that sibling relationships tend to precede peer relationships, especially among firstborn children, has led theorists to draw on social learning frameworks (Dunn & Sherrod, 1988; MacKinnon-Lewis, Starnes, Volling, & Johnson, 1997; Rubin, Bukowski, & Parker, 2006; Stauffacher & DeHart, 2005; Teti, 2002). It has been

suggested that through interactions with siblings, children acquire interaction patterns, social skills, and social understanding abilities that generalize to relationships with peers (Brody, 1998; Criss & Shaw, 2005; Dunn, 1983, 1993; Parke, 2004; Rubin, Bukowski, & Parker, 2006). Because of the more numerous interactive experiences afforded by the more constant presence of siblings, children with siblings have greater opportunities to encounter situations that call for conflict management and perspective-taking, emotion regulation, and empathy, among other attributes and competencies that have been found conducive to friendship.

These opportunities notwithstanding, studies that have drawn direct comparisons between child-sibling and child-friend or child–unfamiliar peer relations have failed to explain the manner through which early and numerous experiences with siblings exert influence on peer relationships (Downey & Condron, 2004; Parke, 2004; Polit & Falbo, 1988; Teti, 2002). Some (Vandell & Wilson, 1987) have observed that infants' greater turn-taking exchanges with a peer correspond with greater levels of such behavior exhibited with an older sibling. In a similar vein, children's performance on tasks of emotional understanding has been found superior among children with siblings (McAlister & Peterson, 2006; Ruffman, Perner, Naito, Parkin, & Clements, 1998). Others, however, reported that a toddler's prosocial behavior toward a peer was less likely to occur if the toddler had a sibling (Demetriou & Hay, 2004; Vandell, Wilson, & Whalen, 1981). Still others (Abramovitch et al., 1986; McElwain & Volling, 2005) reported that when children were observed separately with a sibling and a friend during different kinds of activities, few overlaps of any kind were uncovered.

The inconsistent evidence of social skills' transfer from sibling to peer contexts has pointed to fundamental differences between the two systems. Distinctions have been noted in terms of background, temperament, expectancies, and the extent to which entry into the relationship is voluntary (Dunn, 1993; Parke, 2004). Emphasizing differences stemming largely from birth order and spacing, peer relationships have often been characterized as entailing greater reciprocity due to their involving greater symmetry or similarity in terms of age, physical size, and skills (Brody, 1998; DeHart, 1999; Dunn, 1983; Laursen, Hartup, & Koplas, 1996; Ross, Cheyne, & Lollis, 1988). Yet, the importance of these types of factors has received weak support from studies in which contrasts between sibling and peer competencies have included some controls for inequalities stemming from age differences among siblings, as in research using twins (Pike & Atzaba-Poria, 2003; Vandell, Owen, Wilson, & Henderson, 1988).

Parental Involvement in Children's Relationships

Insight into sibling-peer overlaps may be gleaned through inquiry into contributions of parental involvement in sibling and peer interactions (Criss & Shaw, 2005; Howe, Aquan-Assee, & Bukowski, 2001). The literatures on sibling and peer relationships have included attention to the contributions of parental involvement, yet treatments in the two literatures have entailed somewhat distinctive types of approaches and implicit aims. The long held and still unchallenged view that parents and caregivers play a key role in shaping the often problematic nature of their children's sibling relationships (Dunn, 1985; Furman & Lanthier, 2002; Teti, 2002) has generated a body of research that focuses largely on child-rearing concerns, and methods for mitigating antipathy (Furman & Giberson, 1995; Howe et al., 2001). Contrasting with this tradition, the bulk of works on parental involvement in peer relationships has tended to focus on friendship, and parents' use of direct and indirect strategies for facilitating prosocial behavior.

Parents among Siblings

Positive sibling relationships have been found associated with protective influences,

such as parental warmth and positive marital relationship quality (Brody, Stoneman, & Burke, 1987; Hetherington & Clingempeel, 1992; Stocker, Dunn, & Plomin, 1989; Volling, McElwain, & Miller, 2002). They have also been explored in relation to attachment security. When distressed by mother's departure, toddlers have been found more likely to receive comfort from an older sibling who was securely rather than insecurely attached (Teti & Ablard, 1989). Responses to parents' differential treatment have been mixed. Compared with securely attached toddlers, insecurely attached toddlers have been found more likely to exhibit aggression toward a sibling or their mother (Teti & Ablard, 1989), though this has not been found consistently (Volling et al., 2002).

Efforts to identify specific aspects of parental involvement that account for beneficial effects on sibling relationships have highlighted the positive influence of mothers discussing children's feeling states and intentions, social rules, and consequences (Dunn, Bretherton, & Munn, 1987; Dunn & Munn, 1986). Such conversations are often stimulated by sibling disputes. Illustrating the high priority that parents place on teaching their children the importance of sharing property, such as toys, parents are most likely to intervene in children's conflicts in instances where sharing had been disrupted, and have then justified their position by endorsing sharing (Ross, 1996). Parental interventions are also more common in instances where children's conflicts are more intense (Steinmetz, 1977). In these situations they have been found associated with reductions in the intensity level of animosity and with children's enhanced reasoning and perspective-taking skills (Dunn & Munn, 1986). Generally, the correlational nature of studies has made it difficult to ascertain whether parental involvement in sibling conflict serves to improve sibling compatibility, perhaps by modeling conflict resolution skills and settling disputes before they escalate, or if it leads to intensified conflict, perhaps by rewarding aggression or by precluding opportunities for children to acquire conflict resolution skills for themselves (Kramer, Perozynski, & Chung, 1999; Vandell & Bailey, 1992).

Some clarity has been emerging from work (Perlman & Ross, 1997) that drew comparisons between quarrelling sibling dyads in which parents did or did not intervene and between children's conflict-related behaviors before and immediately following parental involvement. Supporting earlier reports (Dunn & Munn, 1986), parental involvement was found associated with children engaging in more sophisticated negotiations and using fewer power strategies. Further, these results help establish that parental involvement serves as a causal influence on sibling compatibility. Follow-up work (Perlman, Garfinkel, & Turrell, 2007) highlighted the separate influences of parental involvement as well as older siblings' conflict resolution skills to younger siblings' superior abilities to assert themselves. Encouraging findings have also emerged from studies that explore parents' use of positive and negative disciplinary practices and socialization techniques that have been incorporated in interventions for the improvement of parenting skills (Denham et al., 2000; Gardner, Shaw, Dishion, Burton, & Supplee, 2007). Recent treatments incorporate training on methods of mediating sibling disputes (J. Smith & Ross, 2007). Observations of sibling interactions following parent training revealed that the children exhibited less negativity in recurrent conflicts, better understanding of the role of interpretation in assessing blame, and better knowledge of their siblings' perspectives. Other interventions (Kramer, 2004) have succeeded in fostering improved sibling relationships and heightened perspective taking through a program of social skills training.

In addition to research that is narrowly focused on parental involvement as a response to sibling conflict, parental influences have sometimes been observed within a wider range of situations. Longitudinal research (Howe et al., 2001) identified pairs of young siblings who were initially categorized as hostile, nonhostile, or cooperative, and followed-up two years later, at which point outcomes were explored in terms of

parenting styles. These were characterized as either controlling, in which case mothers tended to initiate behavior or provide direct verbal or physical management; interactive, where mothers actively monitored and were jointly engaged in children's play; or anticipatory, a less direct style marked by mothers' conversations pertaining to a sibling's feelings, desires, and abilities. Findings revealed that the effectiveness of any parenting style differed with characteristics of the sibling dyad. Use of a controlling style was found more helpful to social behavior among children who had initially been hostile, but least helpful to children who had been nonhostile. Conversely, anticipatory and interactive styles were found beneficial to siblings who had been initially nonhostile, but disadvantageous to those who had been hostile. The investigators interpreted the results as supporting suggestions (Hinde, 1987) that positive outcomes over time require behavioral meshing between complex aspects of behaviors of social partners.

Parental involvement among siblings has also been explored in situations where, in general, it is not construed as occurring in response to sibling behavior, neither positive nor negative. These include works in which sibling behavior has been found to differ with the extent to which parental involvement entails differential treatment of siblings. Such treatment has a long history of being considered pivotal to triggering negative behavior that is widely known in such contexts as sibling rivalry (Freud, 1916–1917; Levy, 1937). Unequal treatment can entail differences in parents' distribution of affection, praise, privileges, or possessions (Bryant & Crockenberg, 1980; Dunn, 1985; Vandell & Bailey, 1992). It can be necessary and appropriate, if not inevitable, as in instances where age differences between children are large or when a child is ill or in danger. At other times, however, it may be unwarranted. Sometimes referred to in such instances as favoritism, these instances of differential treatment are often considered especially egregious.

The task of identifying conditions under which differential treatment is fair and appropriate poses a dilemma, and since it can remain problematic throughout the experience of child rearing, it can also be among the most continuous challenges to parenting in households with more than one child (Buhrmester, 1992; Furman & Lanthier, 2002). Difficulties with definition are compounded by the sense that conditions that appear reasonable to a parent and one child may not seem so to another child (Furman & Buhrmester, 1985). Perceptions and concerns about favoritism have been associated with problematic sibling relationships (McHale, Sloan, & Simeonsson, 1986). Yet, the validity of such perceptions cannot be assumed. In research with infant twins (Vandell & Bailey, 1992) maternal behavior with each twin was rated objectively by independent observers. Findings revealed that even though maternal attention was equally distributed between infants, each rater was of the opinion that the infant that she had observed had actually received less attention relative to its twin (Vandell & Bailey, 1992).

With a remarkable degree of consistency, parents' differential treatment of siblings has been associated with children's deteriorated social behavior (Brody et al., 1987; Bryant & Crockenberg, 1980; Stocker et al., 1989). Detrimental effects of differential treatment have been observed when it occurs at the hand of fathers (Brody, Stoneman, McCoy, & Forehand, 1992), and when exhibited among children of varying ages, (Hetherington, Pasley, & Ihinger-Tallman, 1987). It has also been observed in trying situations where it would be considered warranted by one child's greater needs, as in cases where one child's greater demands result from behavioral difficulties or a disability (McHale & Harris, 1992; McHale et al., 1986; Webster-Stratton & Eyberg, 1982).

Linkages between differential treatment and deteriorated sibling behavior are poorly understood. Given that differential treatment can, like other instances of parental involvement, operate as either a cause or result of sibling conflict, correlational studies have been of limited use in tracking the nature of the pathway between differential treatment and siblings' diminished

prosocial behavior. Experimental research that manipulated parental attention among young siblings (Teti & Ablard, 1989; Volling et al., 2002) reported that a target child's protests and distress were increased when parental attention was directed toward his sibling. These works established parental behavior as a causal influence on children's deteriorated behavior. However, further research with added controls for absolute amounts of received attention is necessary in order to clarify whether children's negative behavior may be viewed as attributable to differential treatment or parental unresponsiveness. Such refinement would then call for deeper inquiry into complex issues, such as the perplexing observation (Bryant & Crockenberg, 1980) that differential maternal attention is associated with diminished sociability among siblings that is due to negative behaviors exhibited not only by the unfavored child, but by the favored one as well.

Another context that entails parental involvement that has consistently been found detrimental to sibling behavior involves the introduction of a newborn infant to the family (Dunn, Kendrick, & MacNamee, 1981; Legg, Sherick, & Wadland, 1974; Nadelman & Begun, 1982; Stewart, Mobley, Van Tuyl, & Salvador, 1987). Individual differences in a firstborn's adjustment can differ widely, and for some children the transition is highly disturbing (Campbell, 2006; Volling, 2005). Though disturbances in this context were documented several decades ago, surprisingly little has been learned about their origins. In part, a newborn's arrival may be stressful to a firstborn because of its coinciding with maternal separation during hospitalization for childbirth (Field & Reite, 1984). A second contributing factor may be deterioration in the quality of interactions between mother and firstborn child following the newborn's arrival (Dunn & Kendrick, 1981). A related issue may be destabilization in the quality of attachment in the mother-firstborn dyad, which for some children entails transition from secure to insecure (Touris, Kromelow, & Harding, 1995). Another explanation stems from observations that a firstborn child's misbehavior is more likely to occur when her mother is preoccupied with the newborn (Dunn & Kendrick, 1981). This observation has led to suggestions that firstborns' negativity may be precipitated by perceptions of differential treatment that, in turn, trigger rivalry (Dunn, 1985; Vandell & Bailey, 1992).

Yet another possible explanation for an older sibling's disturbances is that jealousy is elicited, but not by favoritism, perceived favoritism, or differential treatment. Rather, it may be triggered simply by exposure to loss of exclusivity in an attachment relationship. Research in which infants and toddlers have been ignored as their mothers attended to a toy baby (actually a lifelike baby doll) or a musical story book found that they were more upset by the toy baby condition (Hart & Carrington, 2002; Hart, Field, Del Valle, & Letourneau, 1998a). Since these manipulations were conducted within episode lasting merely 60 seconds, it appears, as illustrated in Figures 14.1a and 14.1b, that children can be disturbed by even momentary instances of loss of exclusivity. Given the brevity of these episodes, it hardly seems precise for child disturbance to be construed as attributable to differential treatment. It may be that for children, as for adults (White & Mullen, 1989), sharing *any* amount of an attachment figure's love and intimate attention can be disturbing (Hart, 2010a).

Parents and Caregivers among Peers

The large body of work documenting the importance of peer relationships to children's mental health and social adjustment has stimulated considerable interest in the foundations of peer friendships (Fabes, Gaertner, & Popp, 2006; Hay, Payne, & Chadwick, 2004; Ladd, 2005; Rubin, Bukowski, & Parker, 2006; Rubin, Coplan, Chen, Buskirk, & Wojslawowicz, 2005; Vandell, Nenide, & Van Winkle, 2006) and theoretical underpinnings of social behavior (Dovidio, Piliavin, Schroeder, & Penner, 2006; Tremblay, Hartup, & Archer, 2005). Friendships differ on a range of qualities,

such as constructiveness, closeness, symmetry, and affective substrates, some of which carry advantages while others are developmentally disadvantageous (Hartup, 1996; Parker, Rubin, Erath, Wojslawowicz, & Buskirk, 2006). Regardless of whether alliances are geared toward pro- or antisocial endeavors, children are attracted to individuals that are not dissimilar from themselves (Rubin, Bukowski, & Parker, 2006).

Peer sociability has been associated with parental characteristics, such as warmth and mental health status (Chen, Li, Li, Li, & Liu, 2000; Diener & Kim, 2004). Others have explored children's peer relationships in relation to parent-child attachment. These have often found secure mother-child attachment associated with toddlers' superior social competencies and more harmonious relationships (Erickson, Sroufe, & Egeland, 1985; Fagot, 1997; Howes, Rodning, Galluzzo, & Myers, 1988; LaFreniere & Sroufe, 1985; Waters, Wippman, & Sroufe, 1979; Youngblade & Belsky, 1992) although there have been exceptions that instead found associations between peer sociability and teacher-child attachment (Howes, Hamilton, & Phillipsen, 1998; Howes, Matheson, & Hamilton, 1994). Modest associations have also been found between children's peer acceptance and father-child attachment (Schneider, Atkinson, & Tardif, 2001).

Following works that uncovered linkages between peer sociability and styles of child rearing, such as authoritative parenting (Dekovic & Janssens, 1992), investigators have focused on specific methods that account for differences in child behavior among peers (Fabes et al., 2006). The repertoire of parenting practices includes direct as well as more subtle, indirect practices (Bornstein, 2002; Ladd & Pettit, 2002; Rubin, Bukowski, & Parker, 2006). Indirect influences have been identified in works noting that parents model and reinforce social behavior (Eisenberg et al., 1992). They select, provide, and structure opportunities for social contact and play, and then maintain the social exchanges through monitoring and scaffolding (Ladd & Hart, 1992; Ladd &

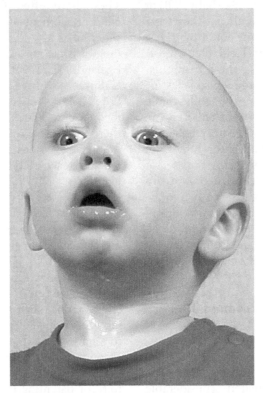

Figure 14.1. A firstborn 1-year-old displays heightened vigilance. (Photo by Kenny Braun, courtesy of Sybil L. Hart, Texas Tech University).

Pettit, 2002; Power, 2004). Parents incorporate inductive reasoning and explicit instructions on matters pertaining to the handling of social situations involving playmates (Hart, De Wolf, & Burts, 1992). Through conversation, they provide rules about property rights and ownership, methods for resolving disputes, conventional wisdom on matters such as turn-taking, and lessons in etiquette (Colwell, Mize, Pettit, & Laird, 2002; Diener & Kim, 2004; Parke et al., 2002; Siegler, DeLoache, & Eisenberg, 2003).

Parental involvement is often precipitated by children's squabbles, frequently about sharing property and toys (Hay, 2006; Lollis, Ross, & Tate, 1992). Newer works have also been exploring nonphysical instances of aggression, as in relational aggression among peers (Ostrov & Crick, 2006; Pellegrini & Roseth, 2006). Parents respond distinctively to children's physical and relational aggression (Werner, Senich, & Przepyszny, 2006). Children's use of both relational and physical aggression have been found associated with parents' reports of their own and their partner's parenting style, psychological control behaviors, as well as indicators of the quality of attachment relationship (Casas et al., 2006).

Parental involvement among peers also occurs in instances where it is not precipitated by conflict. Some interesting and unexpected results emerged from rare studies that manipulated maternal presence among peers. In a naturalistic study (Field, 1979) of 12-month-olds in a parents' cooperative nursery, each mother was present on a rotating basis. Findings revealed that whereas toddlers' peer-directed vocalizations, positive affect, and offers of toys were more frequent while mother was absent, crying and snatching toys from peers occurred more frequently during maternal presence. Mother-toddler dyads have also been observed at home along with the toddler's friend, either alone or with his mother (Rubenstein, Howes, & Pedersen, 1982). Peer-directed positive affect and higher-level reciprocal play were exhibited more frequently by friends during periods in which their mothers were absent than those during which their mothers were present. A follow-up study (E. W. Smith & Howes, 1994) explored individual differences in preschoolers' reactions to maternal presence and absence while volunteering at the child's cooperative preschool. In line with previous findings (Field, 1979; Rubenstein et al., 1982), toddlers exhibited less frequent, less complex, and less positively valenced peer-directed behaviors during mothers' presence than absence. Another unexpected result was

failure to uncover evidence that secure attachment serves as a protective influence in this context as it does in other types of peer contexts (Erickson et al., 1985; Fagot, 1997; Howes et al., 1988; LaFreniere & Sroufe, 1985; Waters et al., 1979; Youngblade & Belsky, 1992).

To interpret these results, Smith and Howes (1994) suggested that maternal presence among peers inhibits sociability by acting as a stressor (E. W. Smith & Howes, 1994). Extending this suggestion, we would submit that under conditions that include peers, parental presence is stressful because the context is one that inherently entails loss of mother's exclusive attention and differential treatment, which, in turn, precipitate jealousy. Indeed, Field (1979) noted that if his own mother was absent, a crying toddler would approach another child's mother for comfort. Smith and Howes (1994) observed that children would become especially upset when their mother would leave the room with another child in order to take him to the restroom, and would sometimes remain standing by the door anxiously until her return. Some support for this interpretation of mothers' detrimental effect on peer sociability may be derived from laboratory research in which a preschooler was ignored by his mother as she read a story to a peer who was seated on her lap or one in which she was reading aloud to herself (Bauminger, 2010; Bauminger, Chomsky-Smolkin, Orbach-Caspi, Zachor, & Levy-Shiff, 2008). As in works in which children were observed as their mothers attended to a toy baby (Hart & Carrington, 2002; Hart et al., 1998a), the episode in which the mother held a peer led to greater disturbances, which were interpreted as jealousy.

Indirect Effects on the Child's Relationships and Social Competencies

A large body work on children's relationships and social competencies have focused on contexts that are dyadic and where the child's involvement is active and reciprocal.

It has been observed that friendship is inherently dyadic (Parker et al., 2006), as are attachment relationships (Bowlby, 1980), yet these dyadic relationships occur in multiples and they coexist, often profitably, within the larger social environments in which they are embedded (Lewis, 2005). Indeed, the social network that is rich in attachment relationships and friends is one that is potentially rich in companionship, support, intimacy, and affection. Though recognized for its importance, the network has been enigmatic to investigators largely as a result of the scarcity of methodological approaches that can feasibly tap the dynamic process through which interdependent dyadic relationships, both attachment and affiliative, evolve, but not in parallel (Vandell & Wilson, 1987), rather as they emerge simultaneously and in concert with one another.

Toward the overarching goal of unraveling the complex social network, a number of studies have examined child development in triadic environments where third parties have sometimes been construed as exerting influences that are "indirect" (Feiring, Lewis, & Starr, 1984; Lewis & Feiring, 1981). These studies have tended to explore the manner in which a child is influenced by being present among two adults, either mother and father, or mother and stranger, as they interact directly with each other. Less is known about the indirect effects of being among peers and adults, especially if the adult happens to be a figure of attachment. Inquiry into this environment stands to offer much toward understanding the nature of socioemotional development and how it unfolds, not in isolation, and not simply against a blurry backdrop of other relationships that are assumed to be of lesser value, and more or less equivalent to one another. While it may be the case that some aspects of friendship are inherently dyadic, it is actually rare for children to have friends all to themselves (Parker, Kruse, & Aikins, 2010). As intimate and reciprocal as a child's relationships may be, her friends and attachment figures often have relationships with individuals other than herself. With the understanding that peer relationships operate against a backdrop that is filled with friends and caregivers who have other relationships, including some that are of great value to them, we call for investigative attention to the question, how is the child affected by such an environment?

A pivotal issue pertains to the interpretation of findings that may seem contrary to those on indirect effects in studies where children were present among mothers who were interacting with fathers or strangers. Generally, these have found that the sensitive mother's positive affectivity toward the social partner was paralleled by her child, who would show positive bids as well (Feiring, Lewis, & Starr, 1984; Lewis & Feiring, 1981). In light of the numerous studies that had observed the child's parallel pattern of prosocial behavior toward third parties, Field (1979) was perplexed to find that peer contacts were facilitated by maternal absence rather than presence. In a similar vein, Smith and Howes (1994) were surprised to find that in peer contexts that include mothers, secure attachment does *not* entail benefits to peer sociability. These findings lead to suggesting that whether the indirect effects of parental involvement exert protective influences depend on the object of the parent's attention. If it is another child, the indirect effects of parental presence seem to be negative (Hart, 2010b). This, of course, does not mesh with current ways of understanding parental involvement. Can a mother who leaves her child anxiously clinging by the classroom door be considered unresponsive if her departure is necessitated by the more immediate needs of another child? Is it reasonable for a parent to be deemed unresponsive if her toddler is disturbed as he watches her smile at a baby *and* if her smiling infant fails to be the recipient of her immediately contingent attention? These questions raise dilemmas that are age old; they also call for some willingness to expand and reframe understanding of constructs, such as sensitivity, that have thus far been defined on the basis of research that has been confined to the dyadic, caregiver-child environment.

In the process of redefining constructs that pertain to caregivers, those that pertain to the child may also call for some clarification. Notions about social competencies such as, sociability, empathy, and social understanding are likely to be advanced, if not reshaped dramatically, by augmenting attention to the child's social functioning in caregiver-child-child contexts. Moreover, productive work would factor in the effects of parents and peers, not in the foreground where they operate as direct influences, but in the background where they may prove to operate, albeit indirectly, as profound influences. Taken together, it may not be premature to assert that environmental influences are powerful and that the validity of any conclusions about a child's social functioning should be considered questionable unless the indirect influence of factors in the social environment are taken fully into account.

Implications for Future Research

Though it has often been asserted that the sibling relationship serves as a foundation of later relationships with peers, strong evidence of direct carryover of interaction styles from child-sibling to child-peer relationships has been illusive. This has been attributed to the moderating influences of birth order effects as well as the lesser reciprocity and voluntariness, and greater disparities in temperament, background, and role expectations of the sibling relationship (Dunn, 1993; Rubin, Bukowski, & Parker, 2006). Certainly these factors are not inconsequential but after accounting for differences in environments where the interactions are observed, especially conditions that entail the presence and involvement of attachment figures, the impact of birth order and voluntariness may be found to be relatively circumscribed. In naturalistic studies where peer sociability has been assessed during maternal presence (Field, 1979; Rubenstein, Howes, & Pedersen, 1982; E. W. Smith & Howes, 1994) as well as laboratory research (Bauminger, 2010; Bauminger et al., 2008; Hart et al., 1998a, Hart & Carrington, 2002), findings reveal that maternal involvement can be disturbing to peers, and it appears

to occur here much as it does among siblings. Thus, it would appear that in order to establish sibling-to-peer carryover, findings on the elicitation and management of disturbances stemming from maternal presence among siblings must be compared with those involving similar events among peers. Similarities across sibling and peer environments in children's responses to differential treatment and their ensuing coping mechanisms will be essential toward understanding the translation of social behavior from the familial to the extrafamilial environment, and to then informing understanding of the manner and extent to which other differences between sibling and peer environments, such as age and temperament, moderate carryover.

Findings on continuity of relational and physical aggression (Crick et al., 2006) across sibling and peer social relationships and across time suggest that a child's aggressive response to loss of exclusivity may extend to other contexts and different forms of provocation. Thus, we might speculate that inquiry into overlaps between sibling and peer relationships may be especially productive if efforts are directed at exploring the stability of aggressive behavior and strategies for resolving triadic conflict. The wide individual differences in children's reactions to loss of exclusivity include highly intense levels of anger. Several studies (Bauminger et al., 2008; Cummings, Zahn-Waxler, & Radke-Yarrow, 1981; Miller, Volling, & McElwain, 2000) observed aggressive responses, such as pushing and shoving, being directed toward the rival. Aggression toward mother has been more rare but not unheard of; at least one report (Teti & Ablard, 1989) besides our own work with toddlers reported attacks on mother. Thus, paradigms that entail loss of exclusivity may afford fresh opportunity to unearth origins of aggression. As investigators recognize that the sibling relationship is indeed the training ground for peer aggression we would argue that investigative attention into early peer aggression through attention to peer conflict over sharing toys and property would be complemented by efforts that inquire into the manner through which peers, perhaps like siblings, express and regulate anger when faced with an environment in which they are being asked to share an attachment figure's exclusive attention.

References

Abramovitch, R., Corter, C., Pepler, D. J., & Stanhope, L. (1986). Sibling and peer interaction: A final follow-up and a comparison. *Child Development*, 57(1), 217–229.

Arsenio, W. F., & Lemerise, E. A. (2004). Aggression and moral development: Integrating social information processing and moral domain models. *Child Development*, 75(4), 987–1002.

Bank, L., Patterson, G. R., & Reid, J. B. (1996). Negative sibling interaction patterns as predictors of later adjustment problems in adolescent and young adult males. In G. H. Brody (Ed.), *Sibling relationships: Their causes and consequences*, pp. 197–229. Westport, CT: Ablex Publishing.

Bates, J. E., & Pettit, G. S. (2007). Temperament, parenting, and socialization. In J. E. Grusec & P. D. Hastings (Eds.), *Handbook of socialization: Theory and research*, pp. 153–177. New York: Guilford Press.

Bauminger, N. (2010). Jealousy in autism spectrum disorders (ASD). In S. L. Hart & M. Legerstee (Eds.), *Handbook of jealousy: Theory, research, and multidisciplinary approaches*, pp. 267–292. Malden, MA: Wiley-Blackwell.

Bauminger, N., Chomsky-Smolkin, L., Orbach-Caspi, E., Zachor, D., & Levy-Shiff, R. (2008). Jealousy and emotional responsiveness in young children with ASD. *Cognition and Emotion*, 22(4), 595–619.

Baydar, N., Hyle, P., & Brooks-Gunn, J. (1997). A longitudinal study of the effects of the birth of a sibling during preschool and early grade school years. *Journal of Marriage & the Family*, 59(4), 957–965.

Bornstein, M. H. (2002). Parenting infants. In M. H. Bornstein (Ed.), *Handbook of parenting: Vol. 1. Children and parenting*, pp. 3–43 (2nd ed.). Mahwah, NJ: Lawrence Erlbaum Associates Publishers.

Bowlby, J. (1980). *Attachment and loss*. New York: Basic Books.

Brody, G. H. (1998). Sibling relationship quality: Its causes and consequences. *Annual Review of Psychology*, 49, 1–24.

Brody, G. H., Stoneman, Z., & Burke, M. (1987). Child temperaments, maternal differential behavior, and sibling relationships. *Developmental Psychology*, 23(3), 354–362.

Brody, G. H., Stoneman, Z., McCoy, J. K., & Forehand, R. (1992). Contemporaneous and longitudinal associations of sibling conflict with family relationship assessments and family discussions about siblings problems. *Child Development*, 63(2), 391–400.

Bryant, B. K., & Crockenberg, S. B. (1980). Correlates and dimensions of prosocial behavior: A study of female siblings with their mothers. *Child Development*, 51(2), 529–544.

Buhrmester, D. (1992). The developmental courses of sibling and peer relationships. In F. Boer & J. Dunn (Eds.), *Children's sibling relationships: Developmental and clinical issues*, pp. 19–40. Hillsdale, NJ: Lawrence Erlbaum Associates, Inc.

Campbell, S. B. (2006). Maladjustment in preschool children: A developmental psychopathology perspective. In K. McCartney & D. Phillips (Eds.), *Blackwell handbook of early childhood development*, pp. 358–377. Malden, MA: Blackwell Publishing.

Casas, J. F., Weigel, S. M., Crick, N. R., Ostrov, J. M., Woods, K. E., Jansen Yeh, E. A. et al. (2006). Early parenting and children's relational and physical aggression in the preschool and home contexts. *Journal of Applied Developmental Psychology*, 27(3), 209–227.

Chen, X., Li, D., Li, Z., Li, B., & Liu, M. (2000). Sociable and prosocial dimensions of social competence in Chinese children: Common and unique contributions to social, academic, and psychological adjustment. *Developmental Psychology*, 36, 302–314.

Colwell, M. J., Mize, J., Pettit, G. S., & Laird, R. D. (2002). Contextual determinants of mothers' interventions in young children's peer interactions. *Developmental Psychology*, 38(4), 492–502.

Cote, S. M., Vaillancourt, T., Barker, E. D., Nagin, D., & Tremblay, R. E. (2007). The joint development of physical and indirect aggression: Predictors of continuity and change during childhood. *Development and Psychopathology*, 19(1), 37–55.

Crick, N. R., Ostrov, J. M., Burr, J. E., Cullerton-Sen, C., Jansen-Yeh, E., & Ralston, P. (2006). A longitudinal study of relational and physical aggression in preschool. *Journal of Applied Developmental Psychology*, 27(3), 254–268.

Criss, M. M., & Shaw, D. S. (2005). Sibling relationships as contexts for delinquency training in low-income families. *Journal of Family Psychology*, 19(4), 592–600.

Cummings, E. M., Zahn-Waxler, C., & Radke-Yarrow, M. (1981). Young children's responses to expressions of anger and affection by others in the family. *Child Development*, 52(4), 1274–1282.

DeHart, G. B. (1999). Conflict and averted conflict in preschoolers' interactions with siblings and friends. In W. A. Collins & B. Laursen (Eds.), *Relationships as developmental contexts*, pp. 281–303. Mahwah, NJ: Lawrence Erlbaum Associates Publishers.

Dekovic, M., & Janssens, J. M. A. M. (1992). Parents' child-rearing styles and child's sociometric status. *Developmental Psychology*, 28, 925–932.

Demetriou, H., & Hay, D. F. (2004). Toddlers' reactions to the distress of familiar peers: The importance of context. *Infancy*, 6(2), 299–318.

Denham, S. A., Workman, E., Cole, P. M., Weissbrod, C., Kendziora, K. T., & Zahn-Waxler, C. (2000). Prediction of externalizing behavior problems from early to middle childhood: The role of parental socialization and emotion expression. *Development and Psychopathology*, 12(1), 23–45.

Diener, M. L., & Kim, D.-Y. (2004). Maternal and child predictors of preschool children's social competence. *Journal of Applied Developmental Psychology*, 25(1), 3–24.

Dovidio, J. F., Piliavin, J. A., Schroeder, D. A., & Penner, L. (2006). *The social psychology of prosocial behavior*. Mahwah, NJ: Lawrence Erlbaum Associates Publishers.

Downey, D. B., & Condron, D. J. (2004). Playing well with others in kindergarten: The benefit of siblings at home. *Journal of Marriage and Family*, 66(2), 333–350.

Dunn, J. (1983). Sibling relationships in early childhood. *Child Development*, 54(4), 787–811.

Dunn, J. (1985). *Sisters and brothers*. Cambridge, MA: Harvard University Press.

Dunn, J. (1993). *Young children's close relationships: Beyond attachment*. Thousand Oaks, CA: Sage Publications, Inc.

Dunn, J., Bretherton, I., & Munn, P. (1987). Conversations about feeling states between mothers and their young children. *Developmental Psychology*, 23(1), 132–139.

Dunn, J., & Kendrick, C. (1981). The arrival of a sibling: Changes in patterns of interaction between mother and first-born child. *Annual Progress in Child Psychiatry & Child Development*, 362–379.

Dunn, J., Kendrick, C., & MacNamee, R. (1981). The reaction of first-born children to the birth of a sibling: Mothers' reports. *Journal of Child Psychology and Psychiatry*, 22(1), 1–18.

Dunn, J., & Munn, P. (1986). Sibling quarrels and maternal intervention: Individual differences in understanding and aggression. *Journal of Child Psychology and Psychiatry*, 27(5), 583–595.

Dunn, J., & Sherrod, L. (1988). Changes in children's social lives and the development of social understanding. In E. M. Hetherington, R. M. Lerner & M. Perlmutter (Eds.), *Child development in life-span perspective*, pp. 143–157. Hillsdale, NJ: Lawrence Erlbaum Associates, Inc.

Eisenberg, N., Fabes, R. A., Carlo, G., Trover, D., Speer, A. L., & Karbon, M. (1992). The relations of maternal practices and characteristics to children's vicarious emotional responsiveness. *Child Development*, 63, 583–602.

Erickson, M. F., Sroufe, L. A., & Egeland, B. (1985). The relationship between quality of attachment and behavior problems in preschool in a high-risk sample. *Monographs of the Society for Research in Child Development*, 50(1), 147–166.

Fabes, R. A., Gaertner, B. M., & Popp, T. K. (2006). Getting along with others: Social competence in early childhood. In K. McCartney & D. Phillips (Eds.), *Blackwell handbook of early childhood development*, pp. 297–316. Malden, MA: Blackwell Publishing.

Fagan, A. A., & Najman, J. M. (2003). Sibling influences on adolescent delinquent behaviour: An Australian longitudinal study. *Journal of Adolescence*, 26(5), 546–558.

Fagot, B. I. (1997). Attachment, parenting, and peer interactions of toddler children. *Developmental Psychology*, 33(3), 489–499.

Field, T. M. (1979). Infant behaviors directed toward peers and adults in the presence and absence of mother. *Infant Behavior & Development*, 2(1), 47–54.

Field, T. M., & Reite, M. (1984). Children's responses to separation from mother during the birth of another child. *Child Development*, 55(4), 1308–1316.

Feiring, C., Lewis, M., & Starr, M. D. (1984). Indirect effects and infants' reaction to strangers. *Developmental Psychology*, 20(3), 485–491.

Freud, S. (1916–1917). *Introductory lectures on psycho-analysis* (translated by J. Strachey). New York: Liveright.

Furman, W., & Buhrmester, D. (1985). Children's perceptions of the personal relationships in their social networks. *Developmental Psychology*, 21(6), 1016–1024.

Furman, W., & Giberson, R. S. (1995).Identifying the links between parents and their children's sibling relationships. In S. Shulman (Ed.), *Close relationships and socioemotional development*, pp. 95–108. Westport, CT: Ablex Publishing.

Furman, W., & Lanthier, R. (2002). Parenting siblings. In M. H. Bornstein (Ed.), *Handbook of parenting:* Vol. 1. *Children and parenting*, pp. 165–188 (2nd ed.). Mahwah, NJ: Lawrence Erlbaum Associates Publishers.

Garcia, M. M., Shaw, D. S., Winslow, E. B., & Yaggi, K. E. (2000). Destructive sibling conflict and the development of conduct problems in young boys. *Developmental Psychology*, 36(1), 44–53.

Gardner, F., Shaw, D. S., Dishion, T. J., Burton, J., & Supplee, L. (2007). Randomized prevention trial for early conduct problems: Effects on proactive parenting and links to toddler disruptive behavior. *Journal of Family Psychology*, 21(3), 398–406.

Hart, C. H., De Wolf, D. M., & Burts, D. C. (1992). Linkages among preschoolers' playground behavior, outcome expectations, and parental disciplinary strategies. *Early Education & Development*, 3, 265–283.

Hart, S. L. (2010a). A theoretical model of the development of jealousy: Insight through inquiry into jealousy protest. In S. L. Hart & M. Legerstee (Eds.), *Handbook of jealousy: Theory, research, and multidisciplinary approaches* (pp. 331–361) Malden, MA: Wiley-Blackwell.

Hart, S. L. (2010b). The ontogenesis of jealousy in the first year of life: A theory of jealousy as a biologically-based dimension of temperament. In S. L. Hart & M. Legerstee (Eds.), *Handbook of jealousy: Theory, research, and multidisciplinary approaches* (pp. 58–82). Malden, MA: Wiley-Blackwell.

Hart, S., & Carrington, H. (2002). Jealousy in 6-month-old infants. *Infancy*, 3(3), 395–402.

Hart, S., Field, T., Del Valle, C., & Letourneau, M. (1998a). Infants protest their mothers' attending to an infant-size doll. *Social Development*, 7(1), 54–61.

Hart, S., Field, T., Letourneau, M., & Del Valle, C. (1998b). Jealousy protests in infants of depressed mothers. *Infant Behavior & Development*, 21, 137–148.

Hart, S. L., Carrington, H. A., Tronick, E. Z., & Carroll, S. R. (2004). When infants lose exclusive maternal attention: Is it jealousy? *Infancy*, 6(1), 57–78.

Hartup, W. W. (1996). The company they keep: Friendships and their developmental significance. *Child Development*, 67(1), 1–13.

Hay, D. F. (2006). Yours and mine: Toddlers' talk about possessions with familiar peers. *British Journal of Developmental Psychology*, 24(1), 39–52.

Hay, D. F., Payne, A., & Chadwick, A. (2004). Peer relations in childhood. *Journal of Child Psychology and Psychiatry*, 45(1), 84–108.

Hay, D. F., & Ross, H. S. (1982). The social nature of early conflict. *Child Development*, 53(1), 105–113.

Hetherington, E. M., & Clingempeel, W. G. (1992). Coping with marital transitions: A family systems perspective. *Monographs of the Society for Research in Child Development*, 57(2), 1–242.

Hetherington, E. M., Pasley, K., & Ihinger-Tallman, M. (1987). Family relations six years after divorce. In *Remarriage and stepparenting: Current research and theory*, pp. 185–205. New York: Guilford Press.

Hinde, R. A. (1987). *Individuals, relationships and culture: Links between ethology and the social sciences*. New York: Cambridge University Press.

Howe, N., Aquan-Assee, J., & Bukowski, W. M. (2001). Predicting sibling relations over time: Synchrony between maternal management styles and sibling relationship quality. *Merrill-Palmer Quarterly*, 47(1), 121–141.

Howes, C., Hamilton, C. E., & Phillipsen, L. C. (1998). Stability and continuity of child-caregiver and child-peer relationships. *Child Development*, 69(2), 418–426.

Howes, C., Matheson, C. C., & Hamilton, C. E. (1994). Maternal, teacher, and child care history correlates of children's relationships with peers. *Child Development*, 65(1), 264–273.

Howes, C., Rodning, C., Galluzzo, D. C., & Myers, L. (1988). Attachment and child care: Relationships with mother and caregiver. *Early Childhood Research Quarterly*, 3(4), 403–416.

Ingoldsby, E. M., Shaw, D. S., & Garcia, M. M. (2001). Intrafamily conflict in relation to boys' adjustment at school. *Development and Psychopathology*, 13(1), 35–52.

Ishikawa, F., & Hay, D. F. (2006). Triadic interaction among newly acquainted 2-year-olds. *Social Development*, 15(1), 145–168.

Kramer, L. (2004). Experimental interventions in sibling relationships. In R. D. Conger, F. O. Lorenz & K. A. S. Wickrama (Eds.), *Continuity and change in family relations: Theory, methods, and empirical findings*, pp. 345–380. Mahwah, NJ: Erlbaum.

Kramer, L., & Kowal, A. K. (2005). Sibling relationship quality from birth to adolescence: the enduring contributions of friends. *Journal of Family Psychology*, 19(4), 503–511.

Kramer, L., Perozynski, L. A., & Chung, T.-Y. (1999). Parental responses to sibling conflict: The effects of development and parent gender. *Child Development*, 70(6), 1401–1414.

Ladd, G. W. (2005). *Children's peer relations and social competence: A century of progress*. New Haven, CT: Yale University Press.

Ladd, G. W., & Hart, C. H. (1992). Creating informal play opportunities: Are parents' and preschoolers' initiations related to children's competence with peers? *Developmental Psychology*, 28(6), 1179–1187.

Ladd, G. W., & Pettit, G. S. (2002). Parenting and the development of children's peer relationships. In M. H. Bornstein (Ed.), *Handbook of parenting: Vol. 5. Practical issues in parenting*, pp. 269–309 (2nd ed.). Mahwah, NJ: Lawrence Erlbaum Associates Publishers.

LaFreniere, P. J., & Sroufe, L. A. (1985). Profiles of peer competence in the preschool: Interrelations between measures, influence of social ecology, and relation to attachment history. *Developmental Psychology*, 21(1), 56–69.

Laursen, B., Hartup, W. W., & Koplas, A. L. (1996). Towards understanding peer conflict. *Merrill-Palmer Quarterly*, 42(1), 76–102.

Legg, C., Sherick, I., & Wadland, W. (1974). Reaction of preschool children to the birth of a sibling. *Child Psychiatry & Human Development*, 5(1), 3–39.

Levy, D. M. (1937). Studies in sibling rivalry. *Research Monographs, American Orthopsychiatric Association*(2), 96–96.

Lewis, M., & Feiring, C. (1981). Direct and indirect interactions in social relationships. *Advances in Infancy Research*, 1, 129–161.

Lewis, M., & Takahashi, K. (2005). Beyond the dyad: Conceptualization of social networks. *Human Development*, 48(1), 5–7.

Lollis, S. P., Ross, H. S., & Tate, E. (1992). Parents' regulation of children's peer interactions: Direct influences. In R. D. Parke & G. W. Ladd (Eds.), *Family-peer relationships: Modes of linkage*, pp. 255–281. Hillsdale, NJ: Lawrence Erlbaum Associates, Inc.

Lussier, G., Deater-Deckard, K., Dunn, J., & Davies, L. (2002). Support across two generations: Children's closeness to grandparents following parental divorce and remarriage. *Journal of Family Psychology*, 16(3), 363–376.

Maccoby, E. E. (2004). Aggression in the context of gender development. In M. Putallaz & K. L.

Bierman (Eds.), *Aggression, antisocial behavior, and violence among girls: A developmental perspective*, pp. 3–22. New York: Guilford Publications.

MacKinnon-Lewis, C., Starnes, R., Volling, B., & Johnson, S. (1997). Perceptions of parenting as predictors of boys' sibling and peer relations. *Developmental Psychology*, 33(6), 1024–1031.

McAlister, A., & Peterson, C. C. (2006). Mental playmates: Siblings, executive functioning and theory of mind. *British Journal of Developmental Psychology*, 24(4), 733–751.

McElwain, N. L., & Volling, B. L. (2005). Preschool children's interactions with friends and older siblings: relationship specificity and joint contributions to problem behavior. *Journal of Family Psychology*, 19(4), 486–496.

McHale, S. M., & Harris, V. S. (1992). Children's experiences with disabled and nondisabled siblings: Links with personal adjustment and relationship evaluations. In F. Boer & J. Dunn (Eds.), *Children's sibling relationships: Developmental and clinical issues*, pp. 83–100. Hillsdale, NJ: Lawrence Erlbaum Associates, Inc.

McHale, S. M., Sloan, J., & Simeonsson, R. J. (1986). Sibling relationships of children with autistic, mentally retarded, and non-handicapped brothers and sisters. *Journal of Autism and Developmental Disorders*, 16(4), 399–413.

Miller, A. L., Volling, B. L., & McElwain, N. L. (2000). Sibling jealousy in a triadic context with mothers and fathers. *Social Development*, 9(4), 433–457.

Nadelman, L., & Begun, A. (1982). The effects of the newborn on the older sibling: Mothers' questionnaires. In M. E. Lamb & B. Sutton-Smith (Eds.), *Sibling relationships: Their nature and significance across the lifespan*, pp. 13–38. Hillsdale, NJ: Erlbaum.

Ostrov, J. M., & Crick, N. R. (2006). How recent developments in the study of relational aggression and close relationships in early childhood advance the field. *Journal of Applied Developmental Psychology*, 27(3), 189–192.

Ostrov, J. M., Crick, N. R., & Stauffacher, K. (2006). Relational aggression in sibling and peer relationships during early childhood. *Journal of Applied Developmental Psychology*, 27(3), 241–253.

Parke, R. D. (2004). Development in the family. *Annual Review of Psychology*, 55, 365–399.

Parke, R. D., Simpkins, S. D., McDowell, D. J., Kim, M., Killian, C., Dennis, J. et al. (2002). Relative contributions of families and peers to children's social development. In P. K. Smith &

C. H. Hart (Eds.), *Blackwell handbook of childhood social development*, pp. 156–177. Malden, MA: Blackwell Publishing.

Parker, J. G., Rubin, K. H., Erath, S. A., Wojslawowicz, J. C., & Buskirk, A. A. (2006). Peer relationships, child development, and adjustment: A developmental psychopathology perspective. In D. Cicchetti & D. J. Cohen (Eds.), *Developmental psychopathology: Vol. 1. Theory and method*, pp. 419–493 (2nd ed.). Hoboken, NJ: John Wiley & Sons Inc.

Parker, J. G., Kruse, S. M., & Aikins (2010). When friends have other friends: Friendship jealousy in childhood and early adolescence. In S. L. Hart & M. Legerstee (Eds.), *Handbook of jealousy: Theory, research, and multidisciplinary approaches* (pp. 516–546). Malden, MA: Wiley-Blackwell.

Patterson, G. R., Reid, J. B., & Dishion, T. J. (1998). Antisocial boys. In J. M. Jenkins, K. Oatley & N. L. Stein (Eds.), *Human emotions: A reader*, pp. 330–336. Malden, MA: Blackwell Publishing.

Pellegrini, A. D., & Roseth, C. J. (2006). Relational aggression and relationships in preschoolers: A discussion of methods, gender differences, and function. *Journal of Applied Developmental Psychology*, 27(3), 269–276.

Perlman, M., Garfinkel, D. A., & Turrell, S. L. (2007). Parent and sibling influences on the quality of children's conflict behaviours across the preschool period. *Social Development*, 16(4), 619–641.

Perlman, M., & Ross, H. S. (1997). The benefits of parent intervention in children's disputes: An examination of concurrent changes in children's fighting styles. *Child Development*, 68(4), 690–700.

Pike, A., & Atzaba-Poria, N. (2003). Do sibling and friend relationships share the same temperamental origins? A twin study. *Journal of Child Psychology and Psychiatry*, 44(4), 598–611.

Polit, D. F., & Falbo, T. (1988). The intellectual achievement of only children. *Journal of Biosocial Science*, 20(3), 275–285.

Power, T. G. (2004). Stress and coping in childhood: The parents' role. *Parenting: Science and Practice*, 4(4), 271–317.

Richman, N., Stevenson, J., & Graham, P. J. (1982). Pre-school to school: A behavioural study. *Behavioural Development: A Series of Monographs*, 1–228.

Richmond, M. K., Stocker, C. M., & Rienks, S. L. (2005). Longitudinal associations between sibling relationship quality, parental differential treatment, and children's adjustment. *Journal of Family Psychology*, 19(4), 550–559.

Ross, H. S. (1996). "Negotiating principles of entitlement in sibling property disputes". *Developmental Psychology*, 32(1), 90–101.

Ross, H. S., Cheyne, J. A., & Lollis, S. P. (1988). Defining and studying reciprocity in young children. In S. Duck, D. F. Hay, S. E. Hobfoll, W. Ickes & B. M. Montgomery (Eds.), *Handbook of personal relationships: Theory, research and interventions*, pp. 143–160. Oxford, UK: John Wiley & Sons.

Ross, H. S., Cheyne, J. A., Lollis, S. P., Duck, S., Hay, D. F., Hobfoll, S. E. et al. (1988). Defining and studying reciprocity in young children. In *Handbook of personal relationships: Theory, research and interventions*, pp. 143–160. Oxford, UK: John Wiley & Sons.

Rubenstein, J. L., Howes, C., & Pedersen, F. A. (1982). Second order effects of peers on mother-toddler interaction. *Infant Behavior & Development*, 5(2), 185–194.

Rubin, K. H., Bukowski, W. M., & Parker, J. G. (2006). Peer interactions, relationships, and groups. In N. Eisenberg, W. Damon & R. M. Lerner (Eds.), *Handbook of child psychology: Vol. 3. Social, emotional, and personality development*, pp. 571–645 (6th ed.). Hoboken, NJ: John Wiley & Sons.

Rubin, K. H., Coplan, R., Chen, X., Buskirk, A. A., & Wojslawowicz, J. C. (2005). Peer relationships in childhood. In M. H. Bornstein & M. E. Lamb (Eds.), *Developmental science: An advanced textbook* (5th ed.), pp. 469–512. Mahwah, NJ: Lawrence Erlbaum Associates Publishers.

Ruffman, T., Perner, J., Naito, M., Parkin, L., & Clements, W. A. (1998). Older (but not younger) siblings facilitate false belief understanding. *Developmental Psychology*, 34(1), 161–174.

Schneider, B. H., Atkinson, L., & Tardif, C. (2001). Child-parent attachment and children's peer relations: A quantitative review. *Developmental Psychology*, 37(1), 86–100.

Shantz, C. U., & Hobart, C. J. (1989). Social conflict and development: Peers and siblings. In T. J. Berndt & G. W. Ladd (Eds.), *Peer relationships in child development*, pp. 71–94. Oxford, UK: John Wiley & Sons.

Shantz, D. W. (1986). Conflict, aggression, and peer status: An observational study. *Child Development*, 57(6), 1322–1332.

Siegler, R., DeLoache, J., & Eisenberg, N. (2003). *How children develop*. New York: Worth Publishers.

Smith, E. W., & Howes, C. (1994). The effect of parents' presence on children's social interactions in preschool. *Early Childhood Research Quarterly*, 9(1), 45–59.

Smith, J., & Ross, H. (2007). Training parents to mediate sibling disputes affects children's negotiation and conflict understanding. *Child Development*, 78(3), 790–805.

Stauffacher, K., & DeHart, G. B. (2005). Preschoolers' relational aggression with siblings and with friends. *Early Education and Development*, 16(2), 185–206.

Stauffacher, K., & DeHart, G. B. (2006). Crossing social contexts: Relational aggression between siblings and friends during early and middle childhood. *Journal of Applied Developmental Psychology*, 27(3), 228–240.

Steinmetz, S. K. (1977). The use of force for resolving family conflict: The training ground for abuse. *The Family Coordinator*, 26(1), 19–26.

Stewart, R. B., Mobley, L. A., Van Tuyl, S. S., & Salvador, M. A. (1987). The firstborn's adjustment to the birth of a sibling: A longitudinal assessment. *Child Development*, 58(2), 341–355.

Stocker, C., Dunn, J., & Plomin, R. (1989). Sibling relationships: Links with child temperament, maternal behavior, and family structure. *Child Development*, 60(3), 715–727.

Stocker, C. M., Burwell, R. A., & Briggs, M. L. (2002). Sibling conflict in middle childhood predicts children's adjustment in early adolescence. *Journal of Family Psychology*, 16(1), 50–57.

Teti, D. M. (2002). Retrospect and prospect in the psychological study of sibling relationships. In J. P. McHale & W. S. Grolnick (Eds.), *Retrospect and prospect in the psychological study of families*, pp. 193–224. Mahwah, NJ: Lawrence Erlbaum Associates Publishers.

Teti, D. M., & Ablard, K. E. (1989). Security of attachment and infant-sibling relationships: A laboratory study. *Child Development*, 60(6), 1519–1528.

Touris, M., Kromelow, S., & Harding, C. (1995). Mother-firstborn attachment and the birth of a sibling. *American Journal of Orthopsychiatry*, 65(2), 293–297.

Tremblay, R. E., Hartup, W. W., & Archer, J. (2005). *Developmental origins of aggression*. New York: Guilford Press.

Vandell, D. L., & Bailey, M. D. (1992). Conflicts between siblings. In C. U. Shantz & W. W. Hartup (Eds.), *Conflict in child and adolescent development*, pp. 242–269. New York: Cambridge University Press.

Vandell, D. L., Nenide, L., & Van Winkle, S. J. (2006). Peer relationships in early childhood. In K. McCartney & D. Phillips (Eds.), *Blackwell handbook of early childhood development*, pp. 455–470. Malden, MA: Blackwell Publishing.

Vandell, D. L., Owen, M. T., Wilson, K. S., & Henderson, V. K. (1988). Social development in infant twins: Peer and mother-child relationships. *Child Development*, 59(1), 168–177.

Vandell, D. L., & Wilson, K. S. (1987). Infant's interactions with mother, sibling, and peer: Contrasts and relations between interaction systems. *Child Development*, 58(1), 176–186.

Vandell, D. L., Wilson, K. S., & Whalen, W. T. (1981). Birth-order and social-experience differences in infant-peer interaction. *Developmental Psychology*, 17(4), 438–445.

Volling, B. L. (2005). The transition to siblinghood: a developmental ecological systems perspective and directions for future research. *Journal of Family Psychology*, 19(4), 542–549.

Volling, B. L., McElwain, N. L., & Miller, A. L. (2002). Emotion regulation in context: The jealousy complex between young siblings and its relations with child and family characteristics. *Child Development*, 73(2), 581–600.

Volling, B. L., Youngblade, L. M., & Belsky, J. (1997). Young children's social relationships with siblings and friends. *American Journal of Orthopsychiatry*, 67(1), 102–111.

Waters, E., Wippman, J., & Sroufe, L. A. (1979). Attachment, positive affect, and competence in the peer group: Two studies in construct validation. *Child Development*, 50(3), 821–829.

Webster-Stratton, C., & Eyberg, S. M. (1982). Child temperament: Relationship with child behavior problems and parent-child interactions. *Journal of Clinical Child Psychology*, 11(2), 123–129.

Werner, N. E., Senich, S., & Przepyszny, K. A. (2006). Mothers' responses to preschoolers' relational and physical aggression. *Journal of Applied Developmental Psychology*, 27(3), 193–208.

White, G. L., & Mullen, P. E. (1989). *Jealousy: Theory, research, and clinical strategies*. New York: Guilford Press.

Williams, S. T., Conger, K. J., & Blozis, S. A. (2007). The development of interpersonal aggression during adolescence: The importance of parents, siblings, and family economics. *Child Development*, 78(5), 1526–1542.

Yeh, H.-C., & Lempers, J. D. (2004). Perceived sibling relationships and adolescent development. *Journal of Youth and Adolescence*, 33(2), 133–147.

Youngblade, L. M., & Belsky, J. (1992). Parent-child antecedents of 5-year-olds' close friendships: A longitudinal analysis. *Developmental Psychology*, 28(4), 700–713.

CHAPTER 15

Neighborhood Environments

A Multimeasure, Multilevel Approach

Ross D. Parke, Shoon Lio, Thomas J. Schofield, Louis Tuthill, Eric Vega, and Scott Coltrane

For the past 20 years, psychologists, sociologists, geographers and economists have paid increasing attention to neighborhoods as an important context for both parent and child well-being (Bamaca, Umana-Taylor, Shin & Alfaro, 2005; Booth & Crouter, 2001; Brooks-Gunn, Kebanov & Sealand, 1993; Elliott, Menard, Rankin, Elliott, Wilson & Huizinger, 2006; Furstenberg, Cook, Eccles, Elder, & Sameroff, 1999; Shinn & Toohey, 2003). The overall aim of this chapter is to assess recent progress in the social sciences regarding the conceptualization and measurement of neighborhoods as environments of human development.

The study of neighborhoods has a long history in social science, as evidenced by the early Chicago studies by Park, Burgess, and McKenzie (1925) and Shaw and McKay (1942). A renewed interest in neighborhood effects was spurred by Wilson (1987), who argued that concentrated poverty isolates the urban poor from social resources and job networks available to the middle class (Wilson, 1996; Small & Newman, 2001). Empirical research on neighborhood effects has focused on a range of outcomes including

crime rates (Gardner & Brooks-Gunn, 2009), use of controlled substances (Bierut, Strickland, Thompson, Afful, & Cottler, 2008; Hawkins, Catalano, & Arthur, 2002,), antisocial behavior (Trentacosta, Hyde, Shaw, & Cheong, 2009), cognitive development (Caughy, & O'Campo, 2006), mental health (Burke, O'Campo, Salmon & Walker, 2009; Buu et al., 2009), and educational attainment (Ainsworth, 2002; Harding, 2011; Roscigno, Tomaskovic-Dewey & Crowley, 2006). Much of this work has focused on implications for child and adolescent development (Leventhal & Brooks-Gunn, 2000; Leventhal, Dupéré, & Brooks-Gunn, 2009).

To the extent that neighborhood research is intended to inform policy and prevention science, identification of the processes linking neighborhood attributes to developmental outcomes is crucial (Roosa, Jones, Tein, & Cree, 2003). Accordingly, in addition to early and often descriptive studies focused on hypothesized main effects of neighborhoods, a recent and growing literature has addressed mediating or moderating processes linking neighborhoods to child and adolescent development (Avenilla &

Singley 2001; Hart, Atkins, Markey, & Youniss, 2004, Mrug & Windle, 2009; Roosa et al., 2005; Small 2004). This increased focus on *process* is consistent with our ecological-developmental perspective that recognizes that human development is shaped by both the dynamic social nature of neighborhoods as well as their physical characteristics (Bronfenbrenner, 1989). From this viewpoint, neighborhoods are contexts in which a variety of social influences are nested, such as formal institutions (e.g., social services, legal and police agencies, work settings, schools, religious organizations) and informal systems (e.g., families, peers, and social networks).

The first goal of this chapter is to review the literature on archival-based assessments of neighborhoods (e.g., various measures of census-based units) and to compare and contrast these measures with subjective respondent-based indices (e.g., interviews, questionnaires, ethnographies) as well as observer-based methods. We view these approaches as useful for addressing different research and policy questions. Second, we highlight the strengths and weaknesses of each type of data. Third, we review newer methods for assessing neighborhoods such as spatial mapping approaches and policy-based experimental studies of neighborhood relocation. Fourth, we address a variety of remaining problems in the measurement of these contexts. Finally, we note the policy implications of recent work on measurement of neighborhoods. We begin with a preliminary overview of how researchers have defined neighborhoods in prior work.

Defining the Neighborhood: It Depends Whom You Ask

A standard conceptualization of neighborhoods has not been achieved, and the variety of definitions of neighborhood remains a problem for the field (Chaskin, 1997; Nicotera, 2007; Sampson, Morenoff, & Gannon-Rowley, 2002; Roosa, Jones, Tein, & Cree, 2003). Neighborhoods may be conceived as physical or geographic sites, as social contexts involving social networks and social organization, and as social constructions based on residents' subjective perceptions (Burton, Price-Spratlen, & Spencer, 1997; Settersten, Jr. & Andersson, 2002). Adding to the problem, the conceptualization and operationalization of neighborhood effects tend to vary systematically by disciplinary focus. Criminologists, sociologists, and demographers frequently use putatively more objective measures of neighborhood structural attributes (e.g., census-based data) while psychologists and ethnographers more often rely on putatively more subjective measures (e.g., respondent-based data). The outcome variables used in neighborhood research also tend to vary by discipline. For example, while sociologists, demographers, and criminologists may focus on crime, class, gender, and race issues, psychologists and educational researchers may study mental health and education outcomes that often make cross-study comparisons difficult because of differences in definitions, levels of analysis, and outcomes of interest. The sample of neighborhoods in a given data set can also vary across disciplinary focus, with some researchers utilizing only data specifically intended for neighborhood research, and other researchers merging neighborhood data post hoc onto a data set originally designed for other purposes (Leventhal et al., 2009). Unless the post hoc sample of neighborhoods is sufficiently heterogeneous, attempting neighborhood-based analyses on data sets not intended to test for neighborhood effects may result in a restriction of range in neighborhood characteristics such as socioeconomic status (SES), residential mobility, or ethnic composition. This can result in attenuation of correlations between neighborhood attributes and outcomes of interest. Intradisciplinary clustering in approaches to the study of neighborhoods occurs in other respects as well, which may contribute to repetition of errors. Attempts to mediate neighborhood effects via more proximal (e.g., family) variables are frequently weakened due an over-reliance on respondent reports, because any mediation could be partially due to shared method variance. Alternatively, attempts to demonstrate the salience of neighborhood context above and beyond family characteristics are frequently weakened by an over-reliance on family demographics (e.g., SES, marital status) instead of more meaningful constructs.

Defining Boundaries and Characteristics of Neighborhoods

A critical issue in assessing the effects of neighborhoods on development is to define their boundaries (Coulton, Korbin, Chan & Su, 2001; Shinn & Toohey, 2003). As one researcher put it, "identifying 'true' neighborhood differences also requires identifying 'true' neighborhoods" (Subramanian, 2003, p. 1965). Two major approaches have been taken to defining neighborhood boundaries, namely, researcher-defined boundaries (e.g., census and administrative data) or participant-derived boundaries (e.g., surveys; ethnographies). Census-based approaches view neighborhoods as geographic sites that vary in terms of socioeconomic milieu (e.g., poverty levels, racial composition, crime rates) and physical characteristics (e.g., environmental toxins and pollutants, noise, and crowding). In contrast, participant-based measures focus on the social construction/perception of neighborhoods (e.g., dangerousness, social support) and seek to assess the meanings associated with different aspects of the neighborhood context (Lee & Campbell, 1997; Lofland, 1994). This distinction between objective and subjective approaches is, of course, not absolute because census-based units (e.g., tracts, block groups, blocks) are based in part on social consensus as well as objective physical markers. Moreover much of the data collected by the Census are based on interviews that are susceptible to biases and measurement error. Similarly, ethnographic methods often involve not only subjective interviews but also often "objective" observer-based ratings of various physical and social aspects of the neighborhood. Notwithstanding this conceptual overlap, we employ this distinction

in organizing our review and end by exploring ways in which these various approaches can be used together in mixed methods strategies (Elliott et al., 2006; Furstenberg et al., 1999; Weisner, 2005).

Census-Based Approaches to Boundaries and within-Neighborhood Processes

Operationalizing the neighborhood using census boundaries and other administrative data such as city boundaries, school districts, and police jurisdictional areas allows one to analyze structural neighborhood conditions (Linney, 2000; Nicotera 2007). In this approach, the boundaries of the neighborhood are defined by census units such as blocks, block groups, tracts or tract groups, and zip code areas. Census block is the smallest geographic unit for which the Census Bureau tabulates data (though release of such data is often restricted to ensure that individual households are not identifiable). In urban areas, blocks correspond to city blocks; in rural areas they may include many square miles and have boundaries that are not streets (U.S. Census Bureau Geography Division, 2011). A census block group is a cluster of census blocks generally containing between 600 and 3,000 people with an optimal size of 1,500 people. Most block groups are delineated by local participants as part of the U.S. Census Bureau Participant Statistical Areas Program. Census tracts contain between 3,000 and 8,000 individuals, and a census place corresponds roughly to a city or a town. Studies of neighborhoods have used combinations of multiple census units that can be aggregated into larger clusters; for example, in the Project on Human Development in Chicago Neighborhoods, Sampson, Raudenbush, and Earls (1997) combined 865 census tracts into 343 neighborhood clusters with an average of 2.5 tracts and 8,000 persons in each cluster. The use of census, police and other types of administrative data (e.g., child abuse reports, health and crime statistics, school-based data) can provide important details about the structural conditions that would impact child development such as levels of crime and violence, percentages of homeowners and renters, numbers of single headed households, residential stability, and other SES indices (income and education), levels of public assistance, racial and ethnic diversity (Coulton et al., 2001; Nicotera, 2007). Such data readily lend themselves to analytic techniques such as hierarchical linear modeling (HLM), which permit cross-neighborhood comparisons as well as calculation of within context variability. By geocoding family addresses to corresponding census units (i.e., blocks, tracts, etc.) household-level characteristics can be combined with the census data to test for both mediators and moderators of neighborhood effects (Toro et al. 2009).

Advantages of the Census Level Approach

There are several advantages to the census level approach. First, the data are readily available to researchers for secondary analyses. Census data can be combined with national, multisite, city, or regional studies of individuals and families to transform these studies into investigations of neighborhoods. National studies include the Panel Study of Income Dynamics, the National Longitudinal Study of Youth-Child Supplement, and the Infant Health and development program (see Brooks-Gunn, Duncan & Aber, 1997 for a review). Multisite studies include the Conduct Problems Prevention Research Group (Greenberg, Lengua, Coie, Pinderhughes et al., 1999) and the NICHD Early Child Care Research Network (Clarke-Stewart, Vandell, & Parke et al., 2007) while city and regional studies include the Promotion of Academic Competence study in Atlanta (Spencer, McDermott, Burton, & Swanson, 1997) and the Los Angeles County Study (Aneshensel & Sucoff, 1996). With nationally representative samples, a full range of neighborhoods can be included, making these data sets well suited for examining between-neighborhood differences. Second, census data have been collected over a 70-year period

at 10-year intervals and readily allow cross-time analyses. Third, census data afford researchers with minimal financial resources the opportunity to conduct neighborhood research. Fourth, census data offer a source of neighborhood data independent of other variables that may be present in an analysis, enabling the researcher to avoid shared-method variance problems that frequently arise with respondent reports of neighborhood characteristics. Clearly this approach has been valuable, is the most frequently used approach, and has and will continue to yield important insights into neighborhood differences and effects on children and families (see Leventhal et al., 2009 for a recent review of the effects of neighborhoods on adolescents and their families).

Limitations and Disadvantages of a Census-Level Approach

There are several limitations associated with using census data to analyze neighborhood effects. First, the use of aggregated data such as census tracts is not nuanced enough to capture the variability within a particular geographic space or the micro neighborhoods that coexist within census tracts (Burton & Jarrett, 2000; Harding, 2011; Hipp, 2007). Second, while census approaches are useful for providing economic and demographic profiles of neighborhoods, they do a poor job of capturing the social fluidity and the dynamics critical to understanding the interactions in that social space and between it and other social spaces (Small, 2004). Third, people's subjective definitions of their neighborhood boundaries do not necessarily conform to census boundaries (Shinn & Toohey, 2003). This issue of validity of neighborhood boundaries has been addressed recently by Elliott et al. (2006), who asked participants in Denver and Chicago, "when you think about your neighborhood, are you thinking about the block or street you live on (census block), this block or street and several blocks or streets in each direction (a census block group), the area within a 15-minute walk from your

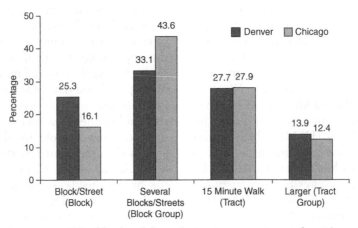

Figure 15.1. Neighborhood boundaries: a comparison of resident perceptions and census-based units. Reproduced by permission from Elliott et al. (2006) *Good kids from bad neighborhoods.* New York; Cambridge University Press, p. 18.

house (a census tract), or an area larger than this (a census area)?" As Figure 15.1 shows, most respondents identified their neighborhood as a geographical area involving a single block or block group, while only 15 percent viewed their neighborhood as being as large as a census tract. Moreover almost 60 percent provided consistent definitions over a 1-year period and among those who changed, most shifted toward a more restricted geographical space rather than a larger one. This suggests that census data may not capture the areas that are meaningful to residents and used by them on a regular basis. Fourth, the use of census data as a proxy for patterns of neighborhood use does not account for the fact that individuals may interact in neighborhoods beyond the neighborhood of residence identified by the census data (Nicotera, 2007). Fifth, decisions about level of aggregation (block, block group, tract, etc.) can vary widely, with methodological choices influencing the observed magnitude of neighborhood effects. Hipp (2007) illustrated that failure to measure aggregate effects at the proper unit of analysis may explain why some contextual effects appear to be small (Liska, 1990). Sixth, some argue that census data may have limited value for understanding minority groups due to reporting and sampling biases (Burton &

Price-Spratlen). Seventh, while census data is of value in tracking long-term historical patterns of change in economic and demographic characteristics of neighborhoods (Hernandez, 1994), short-term changes are difficult to assess.

Systematic Social Observations

In order to assess the physical as well as the social dimensions of neighborhoods, several approaches have been used including windshield surveys, walk-throughs, and videotaping of neighborhood conditions (e.g., Burton et al., 1997; Caughy et al., 2001; Cook Shagle, & Degirmencioglu, 1997; Diez-Roux et al., 2001; Kingston, Mitchell, Florin, & Stevenson, 1999). All of these approaches involve systematic social observations that can be tallied or coded to provide a portrait of the physical and social qualities of the neighborhood. Measures can include physical disorder (e.g., presence or absence of cigarettes, garbage, liquor bottles, graffiti, abandoned cars), physical conditions of housing (e.g., vacant houses, burned out buildings, poorly maintained parks), alcohol- and smoking-related influences (e.g., tobacco and liquor ads, bars, liquor stores), social disorder (e.g., presence or absence of adults, loitering, public drinking, intoxication, fighting, prostitution), and normative social activity (e.g., adult socializing, children playing). (Sampson, Morenoff, & Gannon-Rowley, 2002). For example, O'Neil, Parke, and McDowell (2001) used a windshield survey method to assess a variety of physical characteristics such as speed bumps, public lighting, potholes, and abandoned buildings/cars with a rating system completed by an observer who drove through the neighborhood. Perhaps the most ambitious effort to document both the physical and social aspects of neighborhoods was the Project on Human Development in Chicago Neighborhoods (Sampson, Raudenbush, & Earls, 1997; Sampson & Raudenbush, 1999). Research assistants drove slowly through every street of a sample of Chicago neighborhoods and used videotape and trained observers to capture both the physical and the social activities of the blocks. By using blocks, data can be aggregated to various levels of analysis (e.g., block, tract, etc.) to describe the physical and social aspects of these contexts (Hipp, 2007; Sampson & Raudenbush, 2004).

Advantages of Systematic Social Observations

The systematic social observation approach provides data regarding the current physical state of neighborhoods, which is only indirectly inferred from census data. As with census data, it also has the advantage of being independent from other variables in a given study. It has the capacity to generate a highly standardized, reliable set of metrics to assess neighborhood physical attributes. Moreover, it is sensitive to the temporal shifts in neighborhood environments because data can be collected at different times of the day or night. Finally, it offers data on current behaviors of neighborhood residents and current neighborhood characteristics, which can only be inferred from census data and may provide an outdated profile especially as the time after the census is completed increases.

Disadvantages of Systematic Social Observations

On the negative side, both videotaped and live observations are expensive and time intensive, and it can be even more time consuming to code the tapes and establish reliability between raters (Zenk et al., 2007). Sampson et al. (2002) suggest using field interviewers who are conducting surveys to also rate the physical features of neighborhoods as a less expensive alternative. A second problem with systematic social observations is that the salience of an environmental cue like graffiti or litter may vary between a neighborhood researcher and a neighborhood resident (Sampson and Raudenbush, 2004). Finally, these types of methods are restricted to observable aspects of neighborhoods and therefore are best used in combination with other methods to obtain a wider range of neighborhood characteristics.

Perceptions of Residents as Measures of Neighborhood Boundaries and Features

Resident perceptions are frequently employed to define neighborhood boundaries and explore key aspects of neighborhoods such as danger or social support. Perceptions capture the cognitive maps of residents and offer a better characterization of the functional boundaries of the neighborhood space that residents actually utilize (Matei, Ball-Rokeach, & Quiu, 2001). Questionnaire-based approaches are the primary source of subjective neighborhood data (Lee & Campbell, 1997). In addition, focus groups and interviews are used to assess the subjective perspective regarding neighborhoods. In family studies focused on neighborhood effects, parents are the most frequently solicited source of neighborhood perceptions. One issue that emerges with the use of parent reports of neighborhood characteristics is possible discrepancy between mother and father reports. The vast majority of studies use mother reports of neighborhood quality, so systematic comparison of the relative predictive power of mother versus father reports using multiple samples has not yet been attempted.

In addition to parent reports, child reports have been used. Notwithstanding the existence of parent reports of children's experiences (Prezza, Alparone, Cristallo, & Luigi, 2005), child perceptions have allowed the examination of children's own views about boundaries (Burton & Price-Spratlen, 1999), risks (Bamaca et al., 2005), and satisfaction with neighborhoods (O'Leary & Covell, 2002). Children, adolescents, and adults view boundaries differently. Burton and Price-Spratlen found that 56 percent of children and adolescents had different and smaller "functional neighborhood" boundaries than adults. When asked to describe the boundaries of their neighborhood, Kevin, an 8-year-old African American boy and his mother offered different descriptions. Kevin commented:

> Well my neighborhood is where all my best friends live. Eric lives on the corner of Anderson, Devon lives in the middle of the block on Tyree Street, and Jason lives at the end of the street on Beacon.... My neighborhood doesn't go past those streets either way. That's my neighborhood.

In contrast, Kevin's mother provided this description of her son's neighborhood:

> I would say that the neighborhood is an area that is about 8 blocks north, 5 blocks south, to the west by the river, and to the east by the railroad tracks. I call this Kevin's neighborhood because that's as far as he can walk and be safe without me. (Burton & Price-Spratlen, 1999, p. 85).

Clearly adult and child perspectives are unique and both merit consideration. Moreover, adolescents may have access to several neighborhoods or "neighborhoods of sociability" (Burton & Graham, 1998) due to their increased mobility, and consequently using their neighborhood of residence as a social address may fail to capture the full range of their neighborhood experience. For instance, a child may live part-time with a parent in one neighborhood and part-time

with a grandparent who resides in a different neighborhood. Connections with other neighborhoods make it more difficult to attribute neighborhood effects to a single context such as the neighborhood of residence (Small, 2004; Maher, 2004; Newman, 1999). As with definitions of neighborhood boundaries, adults and children have different perceptions of the qualities of their neighborhoods, like the level of danger. For example, a recent study showed that Mexican American children see their neighborhood as less dangerous than do their fathers (Coltrane, Melzer, Vega, & Parke, 2005).

At what age can children make valid and reliable judgments of their neighborhoods? While adolescent samples (above 10 years of age) have generally shown convergent validity with parent assessments and census data (Ceballo, McLoyd, & Toyokawa, 2004), concerns have arisen in studies using younger samples (Holaday, Swan, & Turner-Henson, 1997; O'Neil et al., 2001; Shumow, Vandell, & Posner, 1999). However, several studies show reports from children as young as first and second grades correlate significantly with census data (Silk, Sessa, Morris, Steinberg, & Avenevoli, 2004) and function well as indicators of neighborhood characteristics (Bubier, Drabick, & Breiner, 2009). Other studies have shown adolescent self-reports of neighborhood quality to predict salient developmental outcomes (Byrnes, Chen, & Miller, 2007; Daly, Shin, Thakral, Selders, & Vera, 2009; Romero, 2005; Salzinger, Ng-Mak, Feldman, Kan, & Rosario, 2006; Wilson, Syme, Boyce, Battistich, & Selvin, 2005).

Of particular relevance for measurement of neighborhoods is the finding that the definition of boundaries varies with the type of question (Elliott et al., 2006). For example, if the issue is institutional resources, residents use a broader definition of neighborhood than if the topic is social networks or educational opportunities, for which a smaller boundary is identified. Elliott and colleagues found that both socioeconomic status and race matter as well. African Americans select smaller neighborhood units (a block or block group) than whites (census tracts).

Hispanic Americans select either a single block or a multitract area. Lower SES residents choose blocks or block groups; higher SES respondents perceive their neighborhood as block groups or tracts.

Questionnaire data can also be used to create neighborhood level variables from sources independent from study participants using a community survey approach. These approaches allow evaluation of important constructs that are not readily derived from census data such as social cohesion, collective socialization, behavioral norms (Ahern, Galea, Hubbard, & Syme, 2009) and collective efficacy (Sampson et al., 1997). While these are sometimes measured at the individual level (for an example, see Deng et al., 2006), these variables are commonly conceptualized as neighborhood-level constructs, and are measured by asking a group of respondents in a neighborhood, and combining their reports into a single neighborhood score (Brisson & Usher, 2005; Caughy & Franzini, 2005; Sampson, Raudenbush, & Earls, 1997). Another approach is to ask "neighborhood experts" such as religious, political, business, or social leaders, under the assumption that their opinion reflects an objective assessment that can be used as a proxy for the average scores of the neighborhood residents themselves. These scores can be used as neighborhood level measures that serve as mediating or moderator variables linking census or police data with individual level outcomes. Since the target individuals were not part of the community survey, the two levels of analysis are independent.

To illustrate the value of this community survey approach, consider the construct of collective efficacy (Bandura, 1996), which describes "the extent of social connections in the neighborhood and the degree to which residents monitor the behavior of others in accordance with socially accepted practices and with the goal of supervising children and maintaining public order" (Leventhal & Brooks-Gunn, 2000, p. 326). Some evidence suggests a negative link between collective efficacy and community violence (Morenoff, Sampson, & Raudenbush, 2001), although

more detailed examination of this multifaceted construct suggests that some components of collective efficacy may be more important than others (see Elliott et al., 2006). Moreover, the content around which collective efficacy is organized is important as well. Elliott and colleagues found neighborhoods that were socially organized around a drug culture, gang activities or individualism and privacy were not related to positive youth outcomes. Clearly, social organizational features of neighborhoods cannot be divorced from the content of the activities that are endorsed.

Advantages of Perception-Based Assessments

There are several advantages to perception-based assessments. First, subjective reports are more likely to assess the elements of a neighborhood that are perceived as salient to participants. Second, perception-based measures may be better suited than more "objective" measures to capture the nuances of resident's everyday experience. For example, Nicotera (2008) employed a mixed methodology to examine the associations and discrepancies between a census measure of neighborhood and a qualitative measure of children's perceptions of their neighborhood. She found that children perceived high levels of resources and neighbor affiliations that were not apparent using census-based measures of social resources. Third, if developmentalists seek to track change across time, subjective reports can be taken as often as needed, and are readily turned into time-varying predictors, while census data changes less frequently, making it less amenable to longitudinal research (Ingoldsby et al., 2006). A fourth advantage of perception-based measures is that they offer unique support for the construct validity of neighborhood effects. While a concern in the past has been that subjective reports include too much common method variance with child or family outcomes, some of the strongest support for neighborhood effects comes from subjective report-based neighborhood effects predicting outcomes, after controlling for family level variables reported by the same participants (e.g., Meyers & Miller, 2004). While census data run the risk of geographically defining the neighborhood very differently from residents, that risk is much lower with subjective reports. Fifth, subjective measures of neighborhood attributes enable neighborhood researchers to "grow past" demographic data: that is, to hypothesize and test a much wider range of factors that could mediate or moderate the link between neighborhood attributes and child outcomes such as individual level factors (e.g., perceptions of neighborhood dangerousness) or neighborhood level variables (e.g., collective efficacy). Subjective measures can also be useful for researchers who generally conceptualize neighborhood effects in more distal terms (e.g., neighborhood level SES, residential mobility), because the strongest evidence for such an objective neighborhood effect would be testing for it after controlling for "subjective" measures. Detailed review of these mediating and moderating variables is beyond the scope of this chapter (see Elliott et al., 2006; Furstenberg et al., 1999; Leventhal et al., 2009; Sampson et al., 2002 for reviews of direct and indirect models of neighborhood influence). Suffice it to note that several studies have found that within neighborhood effects on individual families and children are often explained by variations in parental child rearing practices and management strategies across families in the same neighborhood (Coltrane et al., 2005; Furstenberg et al., 1999; Letiecq & Koblinsky, 2004; O'Neil et al., 2001). An increasing amount of research is emerging on the link between objective and subjective reports of neighborhood attributes (Latkin, German, Hua, & Curry, 2008; Roosa et al., 2009). For example, Schofield, Conger, and Conger (2009) sought to identify factors that would explain additional variance in adolescent reports of neighborhood dangerousness, after controlling for census and observer assessments. They found that after controlling for census- and observer-based assessments of neighborhood dangerousness,

additional variance in adolescent reports of neighborhood dangerousness was explained by the number of times the adolescent has been physically attacked in the neighborhood, the degree to which the adolescent has access to illegal substances in the neighborhood, and the degree to which the adolescent's mother reports engaging in deviant behavior. This suggests that information unique to respondent reports may in fact represent valid information about the neighborhood, and not simply measurement bias. More investigations of this sort will help determine the degree to which mismatch between objective and subjective reports of neighborhood attributes are due to respondents' having an awareness of their neighborhood that is unavailable with census-based or observation-based data. For questions concerning individual differences in how neighborhoods are perceived and adapted to in terms of family practices, this is clearly the method of choice but it is less well suited for evaluating between neighborhood effects.

Disadvantages of Perception-Based Assessments

Subjective reports are useful supplements to census data, but the degree of convergence across respondents may vary and merits consideration when planning research. Clearly, more work needs to be done comparing mother, father, and child reports of neighborhood quality, and careful consideration should be given to who will answer questions about different neighborhood characteristics. While parents may be more knowledgeable about safety, children and adolescents may know more about the availability of illegal drugs and gang activities. Since both parent and child descriptions of neighborhood quality have shown unique predictive power in our data, we recommend inclusion of both if possible. A further problem is that different participants within a neighborhood may vary in the geographic bounds they assign to the same neighborhood. A possible solution would be to ask participants to define the boundaries of their neighborhood, and confirm that reported areas are acceptably homogenous. A participant who defines a neighborhood as an area twice as large as another participant from the same neighborhood could give very different estimates of cohesion, crime, or other neighborhood variables. Respondent reports highlight the potential discrepancies between census level definitions as well as within neighborhood variability in boundary estimates. Finally, when the same reporters offer both neighborhood perception data as well as information on moderating, mediating, or outcome variables the resulting shared-method variance will need to be addressed (Duncan & Raudenbush, 2001a).

Ethnographic Approaches to Neighborhood Assessment

In addition to questionnaire-based self-reports completed by either the parent or the child, some studies employ an ethnographic methodology combining both subjective and observational assessments (Anderson, 1999; Burton, Garrett-Peters & Eaton, 2009; Burton & Stack, 2010). Ethnographers use intensive, in depth investigative and analytic strategies (e.g., life history interviews, participant observation, focus groups, field observation) to gather and analyze data on the shared definitions, beliefs, practices, and behaviors of individuals within a specific social context or culture (Burton & Price-Spratlen, 1999; Burton et al., 2009). Ethnographic researchers are able to identify and understand the neighborhood dynamics and social processes that influence children's lives through direct observation and participation in the routine activities of children and adults (Weisner, 1997; Heath, 1996). Neighborhoods are not merely geographically bound territories but are social constructions named and bounded differently by different individuals (Lee, Oropesa, & Kanan, 1994; Lee & Campbell 1997). This conceptualization stresses how children, adults and institutional elites socially construct the boundaries of neighborhoods and

define the range of possible identities, social roles, parenting practices, and the meaning of motherhood and fatherhood (Edin & Kefalas 2005; Kaplan 1997; Lareau, 2003; MacLeod 1995; Villenas, 2001). Therefore, the conceptual and methodological payoff of a more differentiated social geography based on ethnographic research is a better understanding of the boundaries, structures, functions, and problems of social territories (Kusenbach 2006; Lofland 1994).

Advantages of Ethnographic Approaches

An underlying assumption of an ethnographic approach is an emphasis on strengths as well as limitations of families in disadvantaged contexts as well as modes of successful adaptations. This approach enables one to analyze how children, adolescents, and adults create, organize, and navigate their own social worlds within and across the various social settings and institutional contexts of their neighborhood (Lopez, 2003; Pollock, 2008). For example, poverty might be a condition met with participation in illicit markets and an underground economy as an adaptive strategy to ensure survival in difficult economic circumstances (Venkatesh, 2006). Ethnographers have described the lives of resilient adolescents and families who managed to overcome the risk factors of family and neighborhood poverty (Delgado-Gaitan, 2001; Holleran & Waller, 2003; Jarrett, 1997; Villenas, 2001). This approach describes various parental strategies and practices used to control adolescents' exposure to neighborhood risks such as drugs, gang violence, deviant peer groups, and premature sexuality. For instance, parents use strategies to monitor or supervise their children's time, space and friendships within the neighborhood (Anderson, 1989; Fordham, 1988; Heath, 1983; Jarrett, 1998). By participating in the everyday life of families, ethnographers are able to see how parents enhance their children's life chances through establishing ties with the various institutions and resources in and outside of the neighborhood (Delgado-Gaitan, 2001; Jarrett 1997). Second, ethnographic research can capture short-term changes that may go undetected in census-based neighborhood research. Third, neighborhoods have temporal use patterns that vary by time of day and time of week (Burton & Graham, 1998). For example, children might run free in a given neighborhood during the day while drug dealers might control the streets in the early evening hours. Fourth, compared to census measures, ethnographic approaches are better suited to track the fluidity of family structure due to marriage, divorce, child-bearing, death, familial excommunication, and other unfolding interpersonal processes (Burton, 2001). Fifth, ethnographic research has also demonstrated how neighborhoods are dynamic and heterogeneous (Moore & Pinderhughes, 1993; Pattillo-McCoy 1999; Small & Newman, 2001). Small's study of a subsidized housing complex in Boston's South End showed how some of its residents were highly integrated in middle-class networks at the same time that others were profoundly isolated from mainstream society. Such approaches are also able to reveal temporal variability, as when neighborhoods experience high community participation followed by prolonged periods of apathy and alienation.

Although Elliott et al. (2006) found that institutional resources have a small but positive effect on child and adolescent outcomes, the mere presence of institutional resources is not sufficient to achieve benefits for children and youth. It is critical that these resources be of high quality, accessible and utilized by residents. Moreover, some economic resources may have negative effects such as an abundance of liquor stores, pawn shops or check cashing outlets (Korbin, 2001). Ethnographies can illuminate the quality and availability of institutional resources (schools, religious institutions, recreational facilities, local businesses, etc.) within a neighborhood, as well as residents' perception of their accessibility and usage (Delgado-Gaitan, 2001; Small & McDermott, 2006; Phillips, 1983; Small, 2006; Venkatesh, 2006).

Disadvantages of Ethnographic Approaches

The ethnographic approach has several limitations, including the likelihood of interviewer/observer bias, and lower external validity. Another disadvantage is that the ethnographically derived definitions of neighborhood boundaries may be idiosyncratic to particular respondents, which makes inter-neighborhood and cross-respondent comparisons difficult (Small & Newman, 2001). Another limitation of ethnographic research is that ethnographers may overlook the heterogeneity of the neighborhoods they are studying because their findings have been structured by existing theories.

New Designs and Measurement Strategies: GIS and Spatial Analysis of Neighborhoods

Geographical Information Systems (GIS) and spatial analysis are often used synonymously to describe mapping and statistical software packages, qualitative and quantitative analysis of social space, and theorizing about the use of space. GIS refers to the computer software packages capable of mapping (or geocoding), integrating, analyzing, editing, and presenting georeferenced information (See footnote 1). GIS and spatial analysis technologies allow users to produce maps that show concentrations of spatially based data including crime levels, concentrations of poverty, retail outlets (grocery stores, liquor stores, restaurants, fast food outlets), and institutional resources (e.g., day care centers, after school programs, medical services) within a particular geographic area. In addition to creating visual representations of spatial data, these technologies allow the linkage of multiple data sources to a physical place (Burrough & McDonnell, 1998; Matei, Ball-Rokeach & Quiu, 2001; Skinner, Matthews & Burton, 2005). Thus, GIS and spatial analysis can integrate social, economic, environmental and individual data with geographic information to produce a detailed portrait

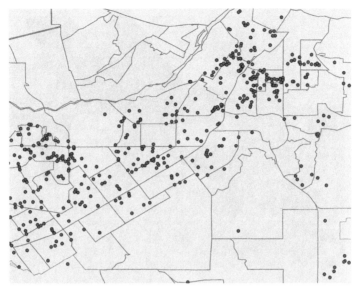

Figure 15.2. Concentration of service calls reporting domestic violence using point referenced data.

of the nested ecology of risk and protection (Mason, Cheung, & Walker, 2004).

One of the primary uses of this technology is to identify first-order effects, or mapping data across a physical space. Examples of such descriptive analyses include demonstrating that nations that are geographical neighbors have more similar IQs than nations that are far apart (Gelade, 2008), that psychosocial health service clinics are isolated from needy populations (Han & Stone, 2007; Moreno et al., 2008), and that almost half of registered sex offenders violate the law by living within 1,000 feet of a school (and that this violation cannot be attributed to lack of affordable housing outside the restriction zone; Grubesic, Mack, & Murray, 2007).

A second use of GIS data is to examine second-order effects, or the degree to which variations in hotspots (high concentrations of a particular behavior or event) predict outcomes of interest. Examples of such predictive analyses include demonstrating that construction of a freeway results in residents shrinking their definition of "their neighborhood" as well as reporting a lower sense of community (Lohmann & McMurran 2009), that changes over time

in density of retail alcohol outlets predict changes in violence rates (Gruenewald & Remer, 2006), that family ethnicity moderates the associations between census-tract level predictors and child maltreatment (Freisthler, Bruce, & Needell, 2007), and that relocation of low-income public housing developments predicts a subsequent relocation of hotspots for aggravated assaults (Suresh & Vito, 2007).

There are two major types of mapped data – point referenced (also called disaggregated) data and field referenced (also called aggregated) data. Point referenced data occur at a single geographic point (e.g., a school), whereas field referenced data is generally a geographic unit (e.g., census tract). The two maps later show the same domestic violence calls for service by point referenced data (Figure 15.2) and by population-normalized census track data (Figure 15.3).

The primary method of examining point referenced data has been to examine the level at which these points cluster together. Using a G statistic (Getis & Ord, 1992), one can create clusters to determine areas of high and low frequency. Examples of this work include crime mapping (Boba,

Figure 15.3. Concentration of service calls reporting domestic violence using population-normalized census.

2005), police perceptions of criminal areas vs. real criminal areas (Ratcliffe, 2001) and citizen perceptions of crime (Groff, 2005). Additionally, this type of information can assist in decisions about the placement of support services or interventions. Finally, point pattern analysis has been used in geographic profiling, a process by which a map that estimates the likelihood of areas where the potential offender might be hiding is produced (Canter et al., 2000; Taylor, Bennell, & Snook, 2002). Current work with point referenced data includes exploring improved clustering techniques to deal with intermediate cases and outliers (Grubesic, 2006).

The second map illustrates the rate of domestic violent events using the same data as the first map. As in point pattern analysis, we can examine the significant clustering of events at the field level using the LISA (Local Indicator of Spatial Autocorrelation) statistic (Anselin, 1995). This tool permits the display of such spatial relationships while normalizing for rates. One could also examine things such as the proportion of alcohol outlets to rates of juvenile delinquency and violent crimes (Lapham, Gruenwald, Remer

& Layne, 2004; Alaniz, Cartmill, & Parker, 1998). Additionally, using spatial statistics, researchers can examine spatial relationships among these field units in a way similar to running linear regression, or analysis of variance (ANOVA), to examine relationships among and across individuals. The standard statistic used to measure the statistical strength among aerial units is Moran's I (Moran 1950), a measure of spatial autocorrelation similar to Pearson's r correlation statistic for independent samples. Thus, a positive measure of spatial autocorrelation would indicate that nearby spatial units are similar and rates of events are alike. Conversely, a negative measure would indicate that rates of an event, or the number of objects, are dissimilar across spatial units. Using these statistical measures one could also measure spatial lag and spatial error (see footnote 2).

Spatially based analytic approaches are not exempt from the basic assumptions of parametric analyses including equality of variance (Bailey & Gatrell, 1995), and non-independence. HLM approaches to spatial analyses can be particularly important as field-referenced data are often dependent (e.g., census tracts are generally not independent) or when point-referenced data are not independent (e.g., crime rates generally cluster around hotspots). Researchers seeking to discuss generalizability also have to consider that census fields like tracts or block groups are rarely randomly sampled (Stoker & Bowers, 2002). There are spatial statistical tools that can measure spatiotemporal autoregressive (STAR) models (Pace, Barry, Clapp, & Rodriguez, 1998) and spatial hierarchical linear regressive (spatial HLM) models (Raudenbush & Bryk, 2002) to examine change over time or nested data, respectively (see Banerjee, Carlin, & Gefland, 2004; Schabenberger & Gotway, 2005 for discussion of statistical modeling practices for the advanced user).

Advantages of GIS Approaches

A major advantage is the provision of a visual representation of the spatial distribution of neighborhood socioeconomic conditions, the availability of services and institutional resources in relation to outcomes of interest such as crime, abuse, and child development. For instance, Small and McDermott (2006) used GIS technology to test Wilson's theory of social disorganization that argues that poor neighborhoods lack organizational resources for basic day-to-day living. They found that availability of resources was contingent upon population density, the proportion of blacks and foreign-born, and the poverty rate of the neighborhood. Small and Stark (2005) used geocoded data on licensed child care centers and neighborhood poverty level and found that the probability of presence of a child care center does not decrease as poverty level of a neighborhood increases. Second, spatial data allows distance from an event or object to be used as an explanatory variable with greater precision than other approaches. Third, these quantitative data can be linked to qualitative data that allow researchers to assess the meaning that people attach to observed activities. For example, Matei, Ball-Rokeach, & Quiu (2001) compared people's fear of places where

they thought violent crime occurs with actual crime rates. In this way, spatial analysis is one of the tools that contributes to multimethod practices.

Disadvantages of GIS Approaches

Some problems have plagued GIS approaches. First, there may be mismatching between the maps and the census derived geographical unit. Much of the work on neighborhoods uses the U.S. Census and/or some other type of administrative boundary to define "neighborhood," such as police department beat or voting district. There are several mathematical ways to address such issues (Lapham et al., 2004), but these are only approximations. As noted earlier, there are several problems with reliance on census data and its fixed measurement categories. First, a census block group (about 39 blocks, with an average of 1,500 people per group) is the smallest unit of measurement publicly reported in most neighborhood research and as one moves up to larger units (tracts, or various aggregate statistical areas like SMSAs, zip codes, cities, or counties), these numbers become even larger. The problem is that with each field unit there is likely internal variability that may confound results.

A second problem is that results can change when analysts aggregate to different regions like block-group or census tract. This problem is not unique to GIS approaches; it is a problem with census data as well. More detailed explanations for the aggregation level chosen for our analyses would be a helpful step toward addressing this problem

Another issue raised by spatial analysis (though not unique to spatial analysis) is that neighborhoods are often analyzed as static rather than dynamic; therefore, spatial theorizing often does not account for the dynamic processes that create and maintain neighborhoods. One of the challenges posed by urban ethnographers is how to incorporate cross-time spatial theorizing into GIS mapping approaches (Skinner, Matthews, & Burton, 2005).

Beyond Description of Neighborhoods: Experimental Demonstration Studies as an Approach to Understanding Causal Processes

Throughout this chapter, our focus has been on measurement strategies for describing qualities of neighborhoods and their links with child adaptation. While we have reported results of studies suggesting that child outcomes vary with neighborhood features, the causal role of neighborhoods in producing changes in child adaptation remains unclear. Only by systematically altering children's neighborhood environments through experimentally planned change can firm statements concerning the causal role of neighborhoods on shifts in children's developmental outcomes be ascertained. In spite of the increasing sophistication of our statistical models such as cross time causal modeling and growth curve analyses, experimental intervention remains the "gold standard" for testing causal hypotheses.

Government policies that involve relocating families to less impoverished neighborhoods provide opportunities to evaluate the impact of change in neighborhood on family and individual outcomes. Since the families in these studies were assigned to conditions (move to new setting or stay in original neighborhood) and were not self-selected, these experimental policy based studies provide unique opportunities to examine neighborhood effects while avoiding the problem of self-selection bias that plagues most work in this area. Two notable projects illustrate both the potential of this approach and at the same time offer a cautionary tale about the difficulties inherent in field experimental studies. The earliest and best known study was the Gautreaux Project (Rubinowitz & Rosenbaum, 2000) a quasi-experimental study based on a 1976 court order to desegregate Chicago housing. Low-income African American families in public housing or on the waiting list were permitted to move to private housing throughout the greater Chicago area (to areas within the city as well as the suburbs) with the aid of vouchers. This was done in a quasi-random manner dependent on the availability of housing rather than on the basis of housing preferences. After 10 years, children who moved to the suburbs were more likely to complete high school and continue to college than children who continued to live in poorer city neighborhoods (Rosenbaum, 1995). More recently, a more ambitious five-city experiment – the Moving to Opportunity for Fair Housing Demonstration (MTO) – was undertaken in which low-income families with children were randomly assigned to one of three conditions: (1) the low poverty voucher group received vouchers and assistance in moving to private housing in low poverty neighborhoods, (2) the voucher-only group who received unrestricted vouchers that allowed them to move to neighborhoods of their choice, and (3) a control group who stayed in low-income public housing. The results have been mixed or modest at best. Although early reports from the New York City site after 2 1/2 years (Leventhal & Brooks-Gunn, 2004) in the voucher/low poverty neighborhood group indicated that boys had higher reading and math achievement scores, later reports at 5 years failed to find positive effects. Specifically, at the New York site (Leventhal, Fauth, & Brooks-Gunn, 2005) the earlier effects were not sustained; male and female adolescents in low poverty neighborhoods had lower grades and lower levels of school engagement than those in the high poverty neighborhoods (control group). Moreover, the results from the five-city study after 5 years were similar, with limited effects on educational outcomes across groups. There was no evidence that reading or math scores improved; nor did behavior problems or school engagement change significantly (Sanbonmatsu, Brooks-Gunn, Duncan, & Kling, 2006). In some analyses only girls benefited from the move to low poverty neighborhoods while boys did not (Kling, Liebman & Katz, 2007).

Advantages of Experimental Demonstration Studies

The major strength of the demonstration approach is the ability to make causal inferences about the effects of neighborhoods on child outcomes without the interpretative problems associated with self-selection effects. Second, there is the opportunity to explore variations in experimental conditions to more clearly determine those aspects of neighborhood that are most critical to development by examining moves that do or do not result in shifts in social networks or changes in schools. Third, as implied earlier, experimental studies offer unique opportunities to evaluate theory-based processes. Fourth, field experiments of this type have high levels of ecological validity and if successful would be a persuasive basis for guidance of policy.

Disadvantages of Experimental Demonstration Studies

Field experimental studies often encounter problems of selective attrition, failure to comply with the program aims (e.g., some families move back to high-poverty areas as a result of economic problems or continue to send their children to their old schools), or unexpected secondary effects such as the stress associated with relocation (e.g., loss of peer networks and changing schools) that may offset the benefits of upward residential mobility. The MTO project encountered many of these problems. Although this design is a useful and persuasive approach, implementation problems clearly limit its widespread utility.

Combination Designs Using Mixed Methods

One of the major lessons from recent research is to recognize the value of utilizing a variety of methods in the same project (see Weisner, 2005 for a review of mixed method research). As Huston (2005) notes, by viewing quantitative and qualitative methods as a continuum of approaches rather than a dichotomy, resistance to the use of mixed methods is less likely to occur. The ecological validity of subjective reports

of neighborhood attributes can be bolstered by including objective reports (i.e., census-, crime-, or observer-based data), and vice versa. Several studies have combined different types of neighborhood data and illustrate how these approaches can be mutually reinforcing. For example, Kling, Ludwig, and Katz (2005) combined qualitative methods and quantitative assessments in the Boston site of the MTO project. By conducting in depth open ended interviews with a subsample they generated several themes (e.g., neighborhood violence, safety and health concerns) that were not included in the original data collection plan, but were then included in the quantitative surveys administered to all study participants. Another example is a study by Hill and Herman-Stahl (2002) that identified maternal depression as a mediator between neighborhood safety and maternal disciplinary strategies. By including both mother- and observer-based reports of neighborhood safety, they were able to avoid the common reporter problem and demonstrate that the mediation effect was meaningful and not merely artifactual.

Another example is the combined use of ethnography and GIS technology (Skinner, Matthews & Burton, 2005). They used ethnographic material to construct patterns of neighborhood service usage and then represented these patterns as maps using GIS technology. The major value of this approach beyond the impact of the visual image is that maps can highlight neighborhood problems that would not have been evident but can be followed up using ethnographic methods. For example, "GIS can quickly identify families who are more isolated, have fewer supports and fewer outside resources and services ... or how far families have to go for different types of services" (Skinner et al., 2005, p. 235). In addition, new insights that were not evident from the ethnographic record alone can emerge from GIS mapping. For example, cross site differences and within site variations due to SES or ethnicity are often revealed more clearly through the combined use of these methods. Investigators with the Three City Project, an ethnographic study of poor children and

Table 15.1: Advantages and Disadvantages of Different Approaches to Neighborhood Measurement

Source of Information	Type of Question	Advantages	Disadvantages
Census	– Defining boundaries – Sociodemographic information	– Inexpensive – Readily available – Can be used to create neighborhoods – Permits cross-time historical comparisons	– Definition of boundaries may be discrepant – Distal. Provides very limited information about important processes – Comparatively few constructs available
Systematic Social Observations	– Distribution of institutional resources – Physical features of neighborhoods – Social features of neighborhoods (age, ethnicity of residents) – Trace patterns of use	– Reliable, objective assessment – Videotape allows for secondary coding	– High cost/time intensive for observer training, data collection & coding – Limited to observable aspects of neighborhoods
Participant Reports/ perceptions	– Resident-based perceptions of boundaries – Process information (e.g., individual, dyadic, family, efficacy, etc.) – Perception of important neighborhood features	– Capture participant perspectives on important aspects of neighborhoods – Standardized/close-ended responses – Easily scorable	– Expensive, time intensive – Reporter biases and inaccuracies – Often not independent from other variables in study – Idiosyncratic definitions that make comparisons difficult
Ethnographic Method	– Captures "meanings" of neighborhood characteristics – Sensitive to dynamic aspects of neighborhoods (e.g., family changes, temporal rhythms) – Physical aspects of neighborhood via observation – Parental practices and neighborhood interaction practices – Describe patterns of use of neighborhood resources	– Hypothesis generating capability – Aid in interpretation of quantitative data – Capture "meanings" of neighborhood features – Capture microlevel interactions and practices – Capture subjective definition of neighborhood boundaries	– Expensive, time intensive – Observer biases and inaccuracies – Distortions due to participant observations – Idiosyncratic definitions that vary across reporter – Lack of standardization of instruments
Spatially based approaches	– Plotting spatial distribution of neighborhood residents and resources	– Provides visual display – Allows distance to be used as a variable in analyses	– Mismatch between census units and maps based on census units/ administrative data such as police jurisdiction, school districts, etc

Source of Information	Type of Question	Advantages	Disadvantages
	– Map the ecology of risk and protection	– Can be applied to various types of neighborhood data, statistical techniques – Allows quantification of spatial distributions	– Most software not user-friendly – Of limited value without other measures
Demonstration Experiments	– Residential relocation – SES changes – Shifts in physical condition of neighborhoods	– Causal inference – Allows comparison across conditions	– Avoids selection effects – Noncompliance (e.g., move, but stay in same school district) – Difficult to manipulate single changes, rather than clusters – Interpretation of effects are difficult
Mixed Methods	– Wide range of social/ physical variables	– Allows use of multiple assessments and therefore compare full range of effects	– Coordination of personnel with different training skills and biases – Costly – Difficulty of coordinating & combining different methods

families, are developing a virtual ethnography prototype for (Burton & Price-Spratlen, 1999) that will allow the integration of context data (e.g., demographic, SES data, crime patterns) with content data (e.g., ethnographic field notes and project specific data). The availability of such programs will greatly enhance the feasibility of using this type of mixed method strategy.

The need for multiple assessments of neighborhood attributes cannot be overstated, as variation across studies in the conceptual and operational definitions of neighborhoods and communities make cross study comparisons difficult (Chaskin, 1997; Nicotera, 2007; Sampson, Morenoff, & Gannon-Rowley, 2002). Some studies find for a given analysis a significant association between their outcome variable and neighborhood context indexed by putatively more objective measures (i.e., census or observer reports) but no effect using parent or child reports (e.g., Ceballo, McLoyd,

& Toyokawa, 2004). Other studies find the opposite pattern of results (e.g., Chung & Steinberg, 2006; Caughy & Franzini, 2005). Yet others find both census and respondent reports to be significant unique predictors (Ingoldsby et al., 2006; Soubhi, Raina, & Kohen, 2004). This inconsistency continues in more recent work on mediators and moderators of neighborhood effects (e.g., Silk et al., 2004). For example, a study of adolescent conduct problems by Zalot, Jones, Kincaid, and Smith (2009) found the patterns of moderation between adolescent attributes (i.e., hyperactivity, impulsivity, and inattention) and neighborhood context to vary depending on whether they used the census- or mother-based assessments of neighborhood. Future reviews of neighborhood effects will benefit greatly from the utilization of multiple sources of data in current studies. For a summary of our discussion of alternative methods for measurement of neighborhoods, turn to Table 15.1. As this table underscores, each of the alternative strategies have value depending on the aim of the research question.

Continuing Problems in the Measurement of Neighborhoods

Despite recent progress, a number of challenges remain in assessing neighborhood effects. Methodological and theoretical issues including capturing the dynamic quality of neighborhoods, selection bias, measurement error due to omitted variables, the need to focus on affluent as well as poor neighborhoods, and the need to move beyond single variable to process models. Without more attention to these issues, drawing definitive conclusions about the causal role of neighborhoods in development will be difficult (Sampson, 2001; Duncan & Raudenbush, 1999; Winship & Morgan, 1999).

Measurement of Neighborhoods as Dynamic Contexts

Despite evidence of the perpetuation of socioeconomic positions across generations including continued disparities in the presence and quality of community resources, educational funding and abilities of disadvantaged residents to move out of undesirable neighborhoods (Wilson, 1987), most researchers adopt dynamic approaches to neighborhoods. In our globalized society (Sassen, 2000), people move more frequently; in the last 20 years there has been a massive migration of people in the United States to the South and Southwest of the country.

Among the most notable demographic factors that illustrate the dynamic nature of neighborhoods is the growth in the number and diversity of recent immigrants to the United States, which has created new challenges for measurement of neighborhoods where they reside. Ethnically diverse and immigrant diverse contexts have different patterns of social organization and resource

utilization than homogeneous areas and are in states of dynamic flux as new waves of immigrants enter these neighborhoods (Kingston, 2005; Small & McDermott, 2006). Description and tracking of these patterns of change in immigrant neighborhoods is a major challenge (Coltrane et al., 2005; Moore & Pinderhughes, 1993).

A related manifestation of the dynamic nature of neighborhoods is evident from historical analyses of neighborhood change (von Hoffman, 2003) that have resulted from a variety of racial and demographic shifts over the last century. Not only are neighborhoods defined differently than previously, but some scholars argue that the role of neighborhoods in our lives has changed as well. As Elliott and colleagues suggest, "with the introduction of television, the widespread ownership of cars and telephones and the development of mass transportation systems and other conveyers of mass culture, the sociodemographic neighborhood of today may be less important as a developmental context than it was prior to the 1950s" (2006, p. 94). Tracing the relative importance of neighborhoods for child and adolescent development across historical time is an important challenge for future investigators (Leventhal & Brooks–Gunn, 2011).

Selection Bias

How do we know whether particular outcomes are the result of neighborhood factors rather than the differential selection of adolescents or their families into certain neighborhoods? Are there particular family or individual level characteristics such as family values, concerns about safety, or educational aspirations that are associated with choice of particular neighborhoods? We cannot adequately specify these characteristics and therefore these often are unrecognized or unmeasured. Moreover the same set of family and individual characteristics may affect both children's outcomes and the choice of neighborhood that, in turn, makes inferences about pure neighborhood effects problematic (Leventhal & Brooks-Gunn, 2000; Sampson et al., 2002). Nor are selection effects restricted to initial neighborhood selection, but are relevant to issues of mobility as well. If the poorest or least capable remain in a particular neighborhood while the more resourceful move to other contexts, this would lead to an overestimation of the negative effects of neighborhoods. On the other hand, if resourceful individuals choose to stay and try to improve the neighborhood this could exaggerate the positive profile of a neighborhood. A neglected aspect of this issue is the role of children in the selection and relocation decision processes. Although children – especially young children – are not usually direct participants in the choice of neighborhoods, the extent to which their needs are actively considered or ignored by parents in their deliberations about neighborhood location could be important mediators or moderators of the impact of neighborhoods on children's outcomes. The extent to which children's voices are part of the family decision making process regarding choice of neighborhood probably changes across development. For example, adolescents may be more active participants than younger children by articulating their concerns about moving to a new neighborhood that may involve loss of friendship networks and shifts in school district. In a real sense, testimony to children's power is evidenced by the increase in residential mobility of families after children complete high school. Selection bias can result from differential participation rates in neighborhood assessments. Immigrants are less likely to enroll in research projects and/or employ avoidant strategies regarding interviews or questions about themselves, their family, or their friends, during recruitment efforts. When immigrants do participate, financial hardship and limited mobility negatively impact their continued involvement (Parke et al., 2004). On a more positive note, Sampson and Sharkey (2008) in an analysis of the Chicago neighborhood study found that omitted variables such as maternal depression, motivation or level of personal organization were unrelated to measures of neighborhood selection. In spite of this encouraging report, continued attention to this issue is warranted. To accomplish this goal, Leventhal et al. (2009) have outlined various strategies for addressing selection effects, including comparison of siblings and first cousins to hold family characteristics constant, instrumental variable analyses as a way of reducing the impact of unmeasured covariation between characteristics and child /adolescent outcomes, behavior genetic models to assess genetic versus environmental effects, and propensity scores, which permit matching of participants who do or do not live in different types of neighborhoods.

The Omitted Variable Problem

Several investigators (Duncan & Raudenbush, 2001b; Elliott et al., 2006; Hipp, 2007) have cautioned about the hazards involved in choosing the wrong measures or omitting important indices of neighborhood functioning. For example, poverty is often the major variable used to represent neighborhood disadvantage, but as Elliott et al. (2006) recently found, residential instability is an equally important index as poverty in predicting adjustment. This is the kind of variable that is often either unobserved or omitted but is likely to influence parent and child outcomes. This may result in misappropriations about the weight of particular parent/family characteristics that create misunderstandings about the relative effects of neighborhoods and family processes. There are statistical approaches to control for these omitted or unobserved family factors accounting for the potential endogamy of neighborhood characteristics. To the extent that these variables are time invariant, family units or individual respondents can be used as their own control by regressing changes in outcomes on changes in neighborhood characteristics. Another strategy is to collect more extensive and reliable data on children, parents, and families. Improvements in measuring key variables (e.g., parental cognitive skills, attitudes towards child development, and family dynamics) can reduce the problem of neighborhood endogamy (Duncan and Raudenbush, 1999).

Beyond Poor/Urban Neighborhoods

To date the bulk of the work on neighborhoods has involved poor urban settings with much less attention to other kinds of neighborhoods. More work is needed to document the effects of affluent neighborhoods on children and youth development. The early work by Medrich, Roizen, Rubin, and Buckley (1982) illustrates how affluent settings in which houses are widely separated and that have few sidewalks shape children's peer contacts; these children have fewer friends and travel longer distances to make contact and their friendship patterns were more formal and rigid. In contrast children in neighborhoods with little distance and few barriers between houses reported a higher number of friends and more spontaneous play patterns, a reminder that affluence is not necessarily a route to better social relationships. Similarly more work on suburban and rural neighborhoods that vary in the level of poverty would aid in sorting out the effects of SES and neighborhood physical organization on children's outcomes. More attention to variations in social capital and collective efficacy in different types of neighborhoods would be worthwhile. For example, commuter/bedroom and gated neighborhoods may have less social integration among residents, less collective efficacy and sense of shared neighborhood (Low, 2004; Wilson-Doenges, 2000, p. 69). The lack of a shared values and shared responsibility for the social activities of residents, especially children, may be a factor in the externalizing and internalizing behavior problems of some children in affluent settings (Ansary & Luthar, 2009; Currie, 2005; Luthar, 2003). Clearly, poor neighborhoods are not always problematic for children's development nor are affluent ones always good for children. As Elliott et al. (2006) noted, "It depends on their organizational, cultural and physical characteristics. The quality of the neighborhood is not fixed or determined by its level of socioeconomic advantage or disadvantage/poverty" (p. 278).

Beyond Single Processes or Single Neighborhood Characteristics

Just as multiple levels of assessment are necessary for an understanding the effects of neighborhoods on children's development, multiple sets of processes are also required to capture neighborhood effects. As we have noted, physical characteristics of neighborhoods, social organization and opportunities each make measurable contributions to neighborhood effects, but different features may have stronger or weaker effects in some neighborhoods than others. For example, good schools have a greater buffering effect in disadvantaged neighborhoods while ethnicity has more negative effects on development in disadvantaged contexts (Elliott et al., 2006). More attention to the bundling or clustering of neighborhood elements is needed as is the specification of whether the clusters are similar across different types of neighborhoods (Hipp, 2007). Finally more work on mediating processes such as family-level variables is needed to help specify the pathways through which neighborhoods achieve their effects. A variety of family processes need attention including disciplinary strategies, family rituals and routines, values and expectations, and regulatory strategies such as monitoring and supervision. Clearer theoretical guidelines are needed to prioritize family processes that are most likely to be important mediating processes in neighborhood research.

Policy Implications of Neighborhood Research

One value of basic research and theory about measurement and conceptualization of neighborhoods is to provide guidelines for intervention and prevention policy programs. Our review suggests that interventions need to be conceptualized as multilevel and multidetermined enterprises. It is clear that there is no simple or single intervention that can be recommended. Instead the issue is which components are most likely to yield payoff for children and families, which neighborhoods are most likely to benefit, and to whom should resources within neighborhoods be targeted? First, the focus should be on disadvantaged neighborhoods even though many residents in these contexts are able to cope and raise well functioning children. In these neighborhoods, targeting fundamental issues of safety, residential stability and improved resources (e.g., social services, retail outlets, adequate public transportation and recreational opportunities) are a reasonable starting point. Second, to be effective, interventions need to include more than just neighborhood level efforts in light of the fact that other levels of social organization such as families, peers, schools as well as employment opportunities operate in concert with neighborhoods to produce and sustain good developmental outcomes. A special focus on family processes within neighborhoods would be worthwhile since the evidence suggests that within neighborhood variation is disproportionately due to differences in the effectiveness of families. Third, some individuals are more vulnerable to the effects of neighborhoods and therefore need to be targeted for assistance. While children of all ages are vulnerable, adolescents who are less constrained and influenced by family rules and regulations are more susceptible to extrafamilial influences such as peers and non family member adults in their neighborhoods, and are therefore profitable intervention targets. Similarly, ethnic minority youth are more susceptible to the negative effects of disadvantaged neighborhoods than nonminority youth. Careful tailoring of programs that are sensitive to the needs and values of various ethnic groups is critical if interventions are to succeed (Coltrane et al., 2005). Building on strengths of different ethnic groups such as a strong sense of familism

in Mexican American families (Parke & Buriel, 2006) or the high level of social support from extended family or neighbors in Mexican American and African American families (Burton & Jarrett, 2000; Coltrane et al., 2005) is likely to produce more effective interventions.

Conclusions

The measurement of neighborhoods has evolved over the past decade into a more theoretically based and methodologically and statistically sophisticated enterprise. At the same time it is clear that a decontextualized treatment of neighborhoods as separate entities is an unproductive strategy. Instead neighborhoods need to be viewed as part of a larger set of ecological systems that not only influence other subsystems such as families, schools and peers in both positive and negative ways and, in turn, are influenced by these other subsystems but operate together to influence development. By using this ecological perspective to guide our quest to better understand neighborhoods, we will be better able to define the unique role of neighborhoods in development and to develop policies to improve these contexts to better serve children and families. More attention needs to be given to the positive features of neighborhoods in the lives of children and their families (Dupere, Leventhal, Crosnoe, & Dion, 2010). Finally our review suggests that multiple levels of analysis and multiple methods are necessary for progress in disentangling neighbourhood positive and negative effects.[1]

Notes

1   For GIS and spatial analysis technology novices, there are several helpful online Web sites including the Center for Spatial Integrated Social Sciences (www.csiss.org), ESRI (www.esri.com), and Spatial Analysis Laboratory (sal.uiuc.edu). There are also useful software programs that one may want to consider investing in or downloading free from the

Internet, such as ArcGIS (ESRI), CrimeStat (Levine, 2002), GeoDa (Anselin, 1995, 2006), and Spatial Statistical Systems.

2　The novice user might want to try GeoDa freeware from Luc Anselin at sal.uiuc.edu, which can perform LISA and Moran's I measures, and has some sample maps to work with as well.

References

Ahern, J., Galea, S., Hubbarde, A., & Syme, S. L. (2009). Neighborhood smoking norms modify the relation between collective efficacy and smoking behavior. *Drug and Alcohol Dependence*, 100, 138–145.

Ainsworth, J. W. (2002). Why does it take a village? The mediation of neighborhood effects on educational achievement. *Social Forces*, 81, 117–152.

Alaniz, M. L., Cartmill, R. S., & Parker, R. N. (1998). Immigrants and violence: The importance of neighborhood context. *Hispanic Journal of Behavioral Sciences*, 20, 155–174.

Anderson, E. (1989). Sex codes and family life among inner-city youths. *Annals of the American Academy of Political and Social Sciences*, 501, 59–78.

Anderson, E. (1999). *Code of the street: Decency, violence, and the moral life of the inner city* (1st ed.). New York: W. W. Norton.

Aneshensel, C. S., & Sucoff, C. A. (1996). The neighborhood context of adolescent mental health. *Journal of Health and Social Behavior*, 37, 293–310.

Ansary, N. S., & Luthar, S. S. (2009). Distress and academic achievement among adolescents of affluence: A study of externalizing and internalizing problem behaviors and school performance. *Development and Psychopathology*, 21, 319–341.

Anselin, L. (1995). The local indicators of spatial association – lisa. *Geographical Analysis*, 27, 93–115.

Anselin, L. (2006). Spatial econometrics. In T.C. Mills and K. Patterson (Eds.), *Handbook of econometrics: Vol. 1. Econometrics theory*, pp. 901–941, Basingstoke, UK: Palgrave Macmillan.

Avenilla, F., & Singley, S. (2001). Neighborhood effects on child and adolescent development: Assessing today's knowledge for tomorrow's villages. In A. Booth & A. C. Crouter (Eds.), *Does it take a village? Community effects on children, adolescents, and families*, pp. 229–243. Mahwah, NJ: Lawrence Erlbaum Associates, Publishers.

Bailey, T. C., & Gatrell, A. C. (1995). *Interactive spatial data analysis*. Essex, UK: Longman Group Limited.

Bamaca, M. Y., Umana-Taylor, A. J., Shin, N., & Alfaro, E. C. (2005). Latino adolescents' perceptions of parenting behaviors and self-esteem: Examining the role of neighborhood risk. *Family Relations*, 54, 621–632.

Bandura, A. (1996). *Self efficacy: The exercise of control*. New York: Freeman.

Banerjee, S., Carlin, B. P., & Gelfand, A. E. (2004). *Hierarchical modeling and analysis for spatial data*. Boca Raton, Fl: Chapman & Hall/CRC.

Bierut, L. J., Strickland, J. R., Thompson, J. R., Afful, S. E., & Cottler, L. B. (2008). Drug use and dependence in cocaine dependent subjects, community-based individuals, and their siblings. *Drug and Alcohol Dependence*, 95, 14–22.

Boba, R. (2005). *Crime analysis and crime mapping*. Thousand Oaks, CA: Sage Publications.

Booth, A., & Crouter, A. C. (Eds.) (2001). *Does it take a village? Community effects on children, adolescents, and families*. Mahwah, NJ: Lawrence Erlbaum Associates, Publishers.

Brisson, D. S., & Usher, C. L. (2005). Bonding social capital in low-income neighborhoods. *Family Relations: Interdisciplinary Journal of Applied Family Studies*, 54, 644–653.

Bronfenbrenner, U. (1989). Ecological systems theory. In R. Vasta (Ed.), *Annals of child development*, pp. 187–249, Vol. 6. Greenwich, CT: JAI Press.

Brooks-Gunn, J., Duncan, G. J., & Aber, J. l. (Eds.) (1997). *Neighborhood poverty: Vol. 1. Context and consequences for children*. New York: Russell Sage Foundation.

Brooks-Gunn, J., Duncan, G. J., Klebanov, P. K., & Sealand, N. (1993). Do neighborhoods influence child and adolescent development. *American Journal of Sociology*, 99, 353–395.

Bubier, J. L., Drabick, D. A. G., & Breiner, T. (2009). Autonomic functioning moderates the relations between contextual factors and externalizing behaviors among inner-city children. *Journal of Family Psychology*, 23, 500–510.

Burke, J., O'Campo, P., Salmon, C., & Walker, R. (2009). Pathways connecting neighborhood influences and mental well-being: Socioeconomic position and gender differences. *Social Science and Medicine*, 68, 1294–1304.

Burrough, P. A., & McDonnell, R. A. (1998). *Principles of geographical information system.* New York: Oxford University Press.

Burton, L. (2001). One step forward and two steps back: Neighborhoods, adolescent development, and unmeasured variables. In A. Booth & A. C. Crouter (Eds.), *Does it take a village? Community effects on children, adolescents, and families*, pp. 149–159. Mahwah, NJ: Lawrence Erlbaum Associates, Publishers.

Burton, L., & Graham, J. E. (1998). Neighborhood rhythms and the social activities of adolescent mothers. In A. C. Crouter & R. Larson (Eds.), *Temporal rhythms in adolescence: Clocks, calendars, and the coordination of daily life. New directions for child and adolescent development.* Monograph no. 82, pp. 7–22. San Francisco, CA: Jossey-Bass.

Burton, L., & Price-Spratlen, T. (1999). Through the eyes of children: An ethnographic perspective on neighborhoods and child development. In A. S. Masten (Ed.), *Cultural processes in child development. The Minnesota symposia on child psychology*, pp. 77–96. Mahwah, NJ: Lawrence Erlbaum Associates Publishers.

Burton, L., Price-Spratlen, T., & Spencer, M. B. (1997). On ways of thinking about measuring neighborhoods: Implications for studying context and developmental outcomes for children. In J. Brooks-Gunn, G. J. Duncan, & J. L. Aber (Eds.), *Neighborhood poverty: Policy implications in studying neighborhoods*, pp. 132–144, Vol. 2. New York: Russell Sage Foundation.

Burton, L. M., Garrett-Peters, R., & Eaton, S. C. (2009). "More than good quotations": How ethnography informs knowledge on adolescent development and context. In R. M. Lerner, & L. Steinberg (Eds.), *Handbook of adolescent psychology*, pp. 55–91. Hoboken, NJ: Wiley.

Burton, L. M., & Jarrett, R. L. (2000). In the mix, yet on the margins: The place of families in urban neighborhood and child development research. *Journal of Marriage and Family*, 62, 1114–1135.

Burton, L.M. & Stack, C.B. (2010) *Ethnography: A method that "rocks" our soul.* National Council on Family Relations (NCFR) Reports, vol. 55 no. F5-F8

Buu, A., DiPiazza, C., Wang, J., Puttler, L. I., Fitzgerald, H. E., & Zucker, R. A. (2009). Parent, family, and neighborhood effects on the development of child substance use and other psychopathology from preschool to the start of adulthood. *Journal of Studies on Alcohol and Drugs*, 70, 489–498.

Byrnes, H. F., Chen, M., Miller, B. A., & Maguin, E. (2007). The relative importance of mothers' and youths' neighborhood perceptions for youth alcohol use and delinquency. *Journal of Youth and Adolescence*, 36, 649–659.

Canter, D., Coffey, T., Huntley, M., & Missen, C. (2000). Predicting serial killers' home base using a decision support system. *Journal of Quantitative Criminology*, 16, 457–478.

Caughy, M. O., & Franzini, L. (2005). Neighborhood correlates of cultural differences in perceived effectiveness of parental disciplinary tactics. *Parenting: Science and Practice*, 5, 119–151.

Caughy, M. O., & O'Campo, P. J. (2006). Neighborhood poverty, social capital, and the cognitive development of African American preschoolers. *American Journal of Community Psychology*, 37, 141–154.

Caughy, M. O., O'Campo, P. J., & Patterson, J. (2001). A brief observational measure for urban neighborhoods. *Health Place*, 7, 225–236.

Ceballo, R., McLoyd, V., & Toyokawa, T. (2004). The influence of neighborhood quality on adolescents' educational values and school effort. *Journal of Adolescent Research*, 19, 716–739.

Chaskin, R. J. (1997).Perspectives on neighborhood and community: A review of the literature. *Social Service Review*, 71, 521–547.

Chung, H., & Steinberg, L. (2006). Relations between neighborhood factors, parenting behaviors, peer deviance, and delinquency among serious juvenile offenders. *Developmental Psychology*, 42, 319–331.

Clarke-Stewart, K. A., Vandell, D. L., Parke, R. D., & NICHD Early Child Care Research Network. (2007). Location, location, location: Neighborhood effects on psychological problems in third grade children. Unpublished manuscript, University of California, Irvine.

Coltrane, S., Melzer, S., Vega, E., & Parke, R. D. (2005). Mexican American fathering in neighborhood context. In W. Marsiglio, K. Roy & G. L. Fox (Eds.), *Situated fathering: A focus on physical and social spaces.* Lanham, MD: Rowman & Littlefield Publishers, Inc.

Cook, T. D., Shagle, S. C., & Degirmencioglu, S. M. (1997). Capturing social process for testing mediational models of neighborhood effects. In J. Brooks-Gunn, G. J. Duncan & L. Aber (Eds.), *Neighborhood poverty: Context and consequences of children* (Vol. 2). New York: Russell Sage Foundation.

Coulton, C. J., Korbin, J., Chan, T., & Su, M. (2001). Mapping residents' perceptions of neighborhood boundaries: A methodological note. *American Journal of Community Psychology, 29*, 371–383.

Currie, E. (2005). The road to whatever: Middle-class culture and the crisis of adolescence. New York: Henry Holt & Company.

Daly, B. P., Shin, R. Q., Thakral, C., Selders, M., & Vera, E. (2009). School engagement among urban adolescents of color: Does perception of social support and neighborhood safety really matter? *Journal of Youth and Adolescence, 38*, 63–74.

Delgado-Gaitan, C. (2001). *The power of community: Mobilizing for family and schooling.* Lanham, MD: Rowman & Littlefield Publishers.

Deng, S., Lopez, V., Roosa, M. W., Ryu, E., Burrell, G. L., Tein, J. et al. (2006). Family processes mediating the relationship of neighborhood disadvantage to early adolescent internalizing problems. *Journal of Early Adolescence, 26*, 206–231.

Diez-Roux, A. V., Kiefe, C. I., Jacobs, D. R., Haan, M., Jackson, S. A., Nieto, F. J. et al. (2001). Area characteristics and individual-level socioeconomic position indicators in three population-based epidemiologic studies. *Annual Review of Epidemiology, 11*, 395–405.

Duncan, G. J., & Raudenbush, S. W. (1999). Assessing the effects of context in studies of child and youth development. *Educational Psychologist, 34*, 29–41.

Duncan, G. J., & Raudenbush, S. W. (2001a). Getting context right in studies of child development. In A. Thornton (Ed.), *The well-being of children and families: Research and data needs*, pp. 356–383. Ann Arbor: University of Michigan Press.

Duncan, G. J., & Raudenbush, S. W. (2001b). Neighborhoods and adolescent development: How can we determine the links? In A. Booth & A. C. Crouter (Eds.), *Does it take a village? Community effects*, pp. 105–136. Mahwah, NJ: Lawrence Erlbaum Associates, Publishers.

Dupere V., Leventhal, T., Crosnoe, R. & Dion, E. (2010). Understanding the positive role of neighborhood socioeconomic advantage in achievement: The contribution of the home, child care and school environments. *Developmental Psychology, 46*, 1227–1244.

Edin, K., & Kefalas, M. (2005). *Promises I can keep: Why poor women put motherhood before*

marriage. Berkeley: University of California Press.

Elliott, D. S., Menard, S., Rankin, B., Elliott, A., Wilson, W. J., & Huizinga, D. (2006). *Good kids from bad neighborhoods: Successful development in social context.* New York: Cambridge University Press.

Fordham, S. (1988). Racelessness as a factor in black students' school success: Pragmatic strategy or pyrrhic victory? *Harvard Educational Review, 58*, 54–84.

Freisthler, B., Bruce, E. & Needell, B. (2007). Understanding the geospatial relationship of neighborhood characteristics and rates of maltreatment for Black, Hispanic, and White children. *Social Work, 52*, 7–16.

Furstenberg Jr., F. F., Cook, T. D., Eccles, J., Elder Jr., G. H., & Sameroff, A. (1999). *Managing to make it: Urban families and adolescent success.* Chicago and London: University of Chicago Press.

Gardner, M., & Brooks-Gunn, J. (2009). Adolescents' exposure to community violence: Are neighborhood youth organizations protective? *Journal of Community Psychology, 37*, 505–525.

Gelade, G. A. (2008). The geography of IQ. *Intelligence, 36*, 495–501.

Getis, A., & Ord, J. K. (1992). The analysis of spatial association by use of distance statistics. *Geographical Analysis, 24*, 189–206.

Greenberg, M. T., Lengua, L. J., Coie, J., Pinderhughes, E. E., & The Conduct Problems Prevention Research Group. (1999). Predicting developmental outcomes at school entry using a multiple-risk model: Four American communities. *Developmental Psychology, 35*, 403–417.

Groff, E. R., Kearley, B., Fogg, H., Beatty, P., Couture, H., & Wartell, J. (2005). A randomized experimental study of sharing crime data with citizens: Do maps produce more fear? *Journal of Experimental Criminology, 1*, 87–115.

Grubesic, T. H. (2006). On the application of fuzzy clustering for crime hot spot detection. *Journal of Quantitative Criminology, 22*, 77–105.

Grubesic, T. H., Mack, E., & Murray, A. T. (2007). Geographic exclusion: Spatial analysis for evaluating the implications of Megan's Law. *Social Science Computer Review, 25*, 143–162.

Gruenewald, P. J., & Remer, L. (2006). Changes in outlet densities affect violence rates. *Alcoholism: Clinical and Experimental Research, 30*, 1184–1193.

Han, M., & Stone, S. (2007). Access to psycho-social services among pregnant and parenting teens: Generating questions using youth reports and GIS mapping techniques. *Child & Youth Care Forum, 36,* 213–224.

Harding, D. J. (2011). Rethinking the cultural context of schooling decisions in disadvantaged neighborhoods: From deviant subculture to cultural heterogeneity. *Sociology of Education, 84,* 322–339.

Hart, D., Atkins, R., Markey, P., & Youniss, J. (2004). Youth bulges in communities: The effects of age structure on adolescent civic knowledge and civic participation. *Psychological Science, 15,* 591–597.

Hawkins, J. D., Catalano, R. F., & Arthur, M. W. (2002). Promoting science-based prevention in communities. *Addictive Behaviors, 27,* 951–976.

Heath, S. B. (1983). *Ways with words: Language, life, and work in communities and classrooms.* Cambridge: Cambridge University Press.

Heath, S. B. (1996). Ruling places: Adaptation in development by inner-city youth. In R. Jessor, A. Colby & R. A. Shweder (Eds.), *Ethnography and human development: Context and meaning in social inquiry,* pp. 225–251. Chicago and London: University of Chicago Press.

Hernandez, D. J. (1994). *America's children.* New York: Russell Sage Foundation.

Hill, N. E., & Herman-Stahl, M. A. (2002). Neighborhood safety and social involvement: Associations with parenting behaviors and depressive symptoms among African-American and Euro-American mothers. *Journal of Family Psychology, 16,* 209–219.

Hipp, J. R. (2007). Block, tract, and levels of aggregation: Neighborhood structure and crime and disorder as a case in point. *American Sociological Review 72,* 659–680.

Holaday, B., Swan, J. H., & Turner-Henson, A. (1997). Images of the neighborhood and activity patterns of chronically ill school age children. *Environment and Behavior, 29,* 348–373.

Holleran, L., & Waller, M. A. (2003). Sources of resilience of Chicano/a youth: Forging identities in the borderlands. *Child and Adolescent Social Work Journal, 20,* 335–350.

Huston, A. C. (2005). Mixed methods in studies of social experiments for parents in poverty: Commentary. In T. S. Weisner (Ed.), *Discovering successful pathways in children's development: New methods in the study of childhood and family life,* pp. 305–316. Chicago: University of Chicago Press.

Ingoldsby, E. M., Shaw, D. S., Winslow, E., Schonberg, M., Gilliom, M., & Criss, M. M. (2006). Neighborhood disadvantage, parent-child conflict, neighborhood peer relationships, and early antisocial behavior problem trajectories. *Journal of Abnormal Child Psychology, 34,* 303–319.

Jarrett, R. L. (1997). Resilience among low-income African American youth: An ethnographic perspective. *Ethos, 25,* 218–229.

Jarrett, R. L. (1998). African American children, families, and neighborhoods: Qualitative contributions to understanding developmental pathways. *Applied Developmental Science, 2,* 2–16.

Kaplan, E. B. (1997). *Not our kind of girl: Unraveling the myths of black teenage motherhood.* Berkeley: University of California Press.

Kingston, B. (2005). The effects of the neighborhood context on adolescent delinquency and drug use. Boulder, CO: University of Colorado Press.

Kingston, S., Mitchell, R., Florin, P., & Stevenson, J. (1999). Sense of community in neighborhoods as a multi-level construct. *Journal of Community Psychology, 27,* 681–694.

Kling, J. R., Liebman, J. B., & Katz, L. F. (2007). Experimental analysis of neighborhood effects. *Econometrica, 75,* 83–119.

Kling, J. R., Ludwig, J., & Katz, L. F. (2005). Neighborhood effects on crime for female and male youth: Evidence from a randomized housing voucher experiment. *Quarterly Journal of Economics, 120,* 87–130.

Korbin, J. (2001). Context and meaning in neighborhood studies of children and families. In A. Booth & A. C. Crouter (Eds.), *Does it take a village? Community effects on children, adolescents, and families,* pp. 79–86. Mahwah, NJ: Lawrence Erlbaum Associates, Publishers.

Kusenbach, M. (2006). Patterns of neighboring: Practicing community in the parochial realm. *Symbolic Interaction, 29,* 279–306.

Lapham, S. C., Gruenwald, P. J., Remer, L., & Layne, L. (2004). New Mexico's 1998 drive-up liquor window closure: Study I. Effects on alcohol-involved crashes. *Addiction, 99,* 598–606.

Lareau, A. (2003). *Unequal childhoods: Class, race, and family life.* Berkeley: University of California Press.

Latkin, C. A., German, D., Hua, W., & Curry, A. D. (2008). Individual-level influences on perceptions of neighborhood disorder: A multilevel analysis. *Journal of Community Psychology*, 37, 122–133.

Lee, B. A., & Campbell, K. E. (1997). Common ground? Urban neighborhoods as survey respondents see them. *Social Science Quarterly*, 78, 922–936.

Lee, B. A., Oropesa, R. S., & Kanan, J. W. (1994). Neighborhood context and residential mobility. *Demography*, 31, 249–270.

Letiecq, B., & Koblinsky, S. A. (2004). Parenting in violent neighborhoods: African American fathers share strategies for keeping children safe. *Journal of Family Issues*, 25, 715–734.

Leventhal, T., & Brooks-Gunn, J. (2000). The neighborhoods they live in: The effects of neighborhood residence on child and adolescent outcomes. *Psychological Bulletin*, 126, 309–337.

Leventhal, T., & Brooks-Gunn, J. (2004). A randomized study of neighborhood effects on low-income children's educational outcomes. *Developmental Psychology*, 40, 488–507.

Leventhal, T. & Brooks-Gunn, J. (2011). Changes in neighborhood poverty from 1990 to 2000 and youth's problem behaviors. *Developmental Psychology*, 47, 1680–1698.

Leventhal, T., Dupéré, V., & Brooks-Gunn, J. (2009). Neighborhood influences on adolescent development. In R. M. Lerner, & L. Steinberg (Eds.), *Handbook of adolescent psychology*: Vol. 2. *Contextual influences on adolescent development*, pp. 411–443 (3rd ed.). Hoboken, NJ: Wiley.

Leventhal, T., Fauth, R. C., & Brooks-Gunn, J. (2005). Neighborhood poverty and public policy: A 5-year follow-up of children's educational outcomes in the New York City moving to opportunity demonstration. *Developmental Psychology*, 41, 933–952.

Levine, N. (2002). CrimeStat II: A Spatial Statistics Program for the Analysis of Crime Incident Locations (version 2.0). Ned Levine & Associates, TX/National Institute of Justice, Houston, Washington, D.C.

Linney, J. A. (2000). Assessing ecological constructs and community context. In J. Rappaport, & E. Seidman (Eds.), *Handbook of community psychology*, pp. 647–668. Dordrecht, Netherlands: Kluwer Academic Publishers.

Liska, A. E. (1990). The significance of aggregate dependent variables and contextual independent variables for linking macro and micro theories. *Social Psychology Quarterly* 53, 292–301.

Lofland, L. H. (1994). Observations and observers in conflict: Field research in the public realm. In S. E. Cahill & L. H. Lofland (Eds.), *The community of the streets*, pp. 19–32. Greenwich, CT.: JAI.

Lohmann, A. & McMurran, G. (2009). Resident-defined neighborhood mapping: Using GIS to analyze phenomenological neighborhoods. *Journal of Prevention & Intervention in the Community*, 37, 66–81.

Lopez, N. (2003). *Hopeful girls, troubled boys: Race and gender disparity in urban education.* New York: Routledge.

Low, S. (2004). *Behind the gates: Life, security, and the pursuit of happiness in fortress America.* New York: Routledge.

Luthar, S. (2003). The culture of affluence: Psychological costs of material wealth. *Child Development*, 74, 1581–1593.

MacLeod, J. (1995). *Ain't no makin' it: Aspirations and attainment in a low-income neighborhood.* Boulder, CO: Westview.

Maher, K. H. (2004). Borders and social distinction in the global suburb. *American Quarterly*, 56, 781–806.

Mason, M., Cheung, I. & Walker, L. (2004). Substance use, social networks, and the geography of urban adolescents. *Substance Use & Misuse*, 39, 1751–1777.

Matei, S., Ball-Rokeach, S., & Quiu, J. L. (2001). Fear and misperception of Los Angeles urban space: A spatial-statistical study of communication-shaped mental maps. *Communication Research*, 28, 429–463.

Medrich, E. A., Roizen, J., Rubin, V., & Buckley, S. (1982). *The serious business of growing up: A study of children's lives outside of school.* Berkeley: University of California Press.

Meyers, S. A., & Miller, C. (2004). Direct, mediated, moderated, and cumulative relations between neighborhood characteristics and adolescent outcomes. *Adolescence*, 39, 121–144.

Moore, J., & Pinderhughes, R. (1993). *In the barrios: Latinos and the underclass debate.* New York: Russell Sage Foundation.

Moran, P. A. P. (1950). Notes on continuous stochastic phenomena. *Biometrika*, 37, 17–23.

Moreno, B., García-Alonso, C. R., Hernández, Miguel A. N., Torres-González, F., & Salvador-Carulla, L. (2008). Spatial analysis to identify hotspots of prevalence of schizophrenia. *Social Psychiatry and Psychiatric Epidemiology*, 43, 782–791.

Morenoff, J. D., Sampson, R. J., & Raudenbush, S. W. (2001). Neighborhood inequality, collective efficacy, and the spatial dynamics of urban violence. *Criminology*, 39, 517–560.

Mrug, S., & Windle, M. (2009). Mediators of neighborhood influences on externalizing behavior in preadolescent children. *Journal of Abnormal Child Psychology*, 37, 265–280.

Newman, K. S. (1999). *No shame in my game: The working poor in the inner city*. New York: Knopf and the Russell Sage Foundation.

Nicotera, N. (2007). Measuring neighborhood: A conundrum for human service researchers and practitioners. *American Journal of Community Psychology*, 40, 26–51.

Nicotera, N. (2008). Children speak about neighborhoods: Using mixed methods to measure the construct neighborhood. *Journal of Community Psychology*, 36, 333–351.

O'Leary, J., & Covell, K. (2002). The tar ponds kids: Toxic environments and adolescent well-being. *Canadian Journal of Behavioral Science*, 34, 34–43.

O'Neil, R. L., Parke, R. D., & McDowell, D. J. (2001). Objective and subjective features of children's neighborhoods: Relations to parental regulatory strategies and children's social competence. *Applied Developmental Psychology*, 22, 135–155.

Pace, R. K., Barry, R., Clapp, J. M. & Rodriguez, M. (1998). Spatiotemporal autoregressive models of neighbourhood effects. *Journal of Real Estate Finance and Economics*, 17, 15–33.

Park, R., Burgess, E. W., & McKenzie, R. D. (1925). *The city*. Chicago: University of Chicago Press.

Parke, R. D., & Buriel, R. (2006). Socialization in the family: Ethnic and ecological perspectives. In N. Eisenberg, W. Damon & R. M. Lerner (Eds.), *Handbook of child psychology: Vol. 3. Social, emotional, and personality development*, pp. 429–504. Hoboken, NJ: John Wiley & Sons Inc.

Parke, R. D., Coltrane, S., Duffy, S., Buriel, R., Dennis, J., Powers, J., French, S., & Widaman, K. (2004) Economic stress, parenting and child adjustment in Mexican American and European American families. *Child Development*, 75, 1632–1656.

Pattillo-McCoy, M. (1999). Black picket fences: Privilege and peril among the black middle-class. Chicago: University of Chicago Press.

Philips, S. U. (1983). *Invisible culture: Communication in classroom and community on the warm springs Indian reservation*. Prospect Heights, IL: Waveland Press.

Pollock, M. (2008). From shallow to deep: Toward a thorough cultural analysis of school achievement patterns. *Anthropology & Education Quarterly*, 39, 369–380.

Prezza, M., Alparone, F. R., Cristallo, C., & Luigi, S. (2005). Parental perception of social risk and of positive potentiality of outdoor autonomy for children: The development of two instruments. *Journal of Environmental Psychology*, 25, 437–453.

Ratcliffe, J. H., & McCullagh, M. J. (2001). Chasing ghosts? Police perception of high crime areas. *British Journal of Criminology*, 41, 330–341.

Raudenbush, S. W., & Bryk, A. S. (2002). *Hierarchical linear models: Applications and data analysis methods* (2nd ed.). Thousand Oaks, CA: Sage.

Romero, A. J. (2005). Low-income neighborhood barriers and resources for adolescents' physical activity. *Journal of Adolescent Health*, 36, 253–259.

Roosa, M. W., Deng, S., Ryu, E., Lockhart Burrell, G., Tein, J. Y., Jones, S., Lopez, V., & Crowder, S. (2005). Family and child characteristics linking neighborhood context and child externalizing behavior. *Journal of Marriage and Family*, 67, 515–529.

Roosa, M. W., Jones, S., Tein, J.-Y., & Cree, W. (2003). Prevention science and neighborhood influences on low-income children's development: Theoretical and methodological issues. *American Journal of Community Psychology*, 31, 55–72.

Roosa, M. W., White, R. M. B., Zeiders, K. H., & Tein, J. (2009). An examination of the role of perceptions in neighborhood research. *American Journal of Community Psychology*, 37, 327–341.

Roscigno, V. J., Tomaskovic-Dewey, D., & Crowley, M. (2006). Education and the inequalities of place. *Social Forces*, 84, 2121–2145.

Rosenbaum, J. E. (1995). Changing the geography of opportunity by expanding residential choice: Lessons from the Gautreaux program. *Housing Policy Debate*, 6, 231–269.

Rubinowitz, L. S., & Rosenbaum, J. E. (2000). *Crossing the class and color lines: From public housing to white suburbia*. Chicago: University of Chicago Press.

Salzinger, S., Ng-Mak, D., Feldman, R., Kam, C., & Rosario, M. (2006). Exposure to community violence: Processes that increase the risk for inner-city middle school children. *Journal of Early Adolescence*, 26, 232–266.

Sampson, R. J. (2001). How do communities undergird or undermine human development? Relevant contexts and social mechanisms. In A. Booth & A. C. Crouter (Eds.),

Does it take a village? Community effects on children, adolescents, and families, pp. 3–30. Mahwah, NJ: Lawrence Erlbaum Associates, Publishers.

Sampson, R. J., Morenoff, J. D., & Gannon-Rowley, T. (2002). Assessing "Neighborhood effects": Social processes and new directions in research. *Annual Review of Sociology*, 28, 443–478.

Sampson, R. J., & Raudenbush, S. W. (1999). Systematic social observation of public spaces: A new look at disorder in urban neighborhoods. *American Journal of Sociology*, 105, 603–651.

Sampson, R. J., & Raudenbush, S. W. (2004). Seeing disorder: Neighborhood stigma and the social construction of "broken windows." *Social Psychology Quarterly*, 67, 319–342.

Sampson, R. J., Raudenbush, S. W., & Earls, F. (1997). Neighborhoods and violent crime: A multilevel study of collective efficacy. *Science*, 277, 918–924.

Sampson, R. J., & Sharkey, P. (2008). Neighborhood selection and the social reproduction of concentrated racial inequality. *Demography*, 45, 1–29.

Sanbonmatsu, L., Kling, J. R., Duncan, G. J., & Brooks-Gunn, J. (2006). Neighborhoods and academic achievement: Results from moving to opportunity experiment, *NBER Working Paper No. W11909*: NBER.

Sassen, S. (2000). *Cities in a world economy* (2nd ed.). Thousand Oaks, Ca: Pine Forge Press.

Schabenberger, O., & Gotway, C. A. (2005). *Statistical methods for spatial data analysis*. Boca Raton, FL: Chapman & Hall/CRC.

Schofield, T. J., Conger, K. J., & Conger, R. D. (2009). Observer, census, mother, and pre-adolescent reports of neighborhood quality: Does nonoverlap signal spuriousness? Paper presented at the biennial meeting for the Society for Research in Child Development, Denver, CO.

Settersten Jr., R. A., & Andersson, T. E. (2002). Moving and still: Neighborhoods, human development, and the life course. *Advances in Life Course Research*, 7, 197–227.

Shaw, C. R., & McKay, H. D. (1942). *Juvenile delinquency and urban areas, a study of rates of delinquents in relation to differential characteristics of local communities in American cities*. Chicago: University of Chicago Press.

Shinn, M., & Toohey, S. M. (2003). Community contexts of human welfare. *Annual Review of Psychology*, 54, 427–459.

Shumow, L., Vandell, D. L., & Posner, J. (1999). Risk and resilience in the urban neighborhood: Predictors of academic performance among low-income elementary school children. *Merrill-Palmer Quarterly*, 45, 309–331.

Silk, J., Sessa, F. M., Sheffield Morris, A., Steinberg, L., & Avenevoli, S. (2004). Neighborhood cohesion as a buffer against hostile maternal parenting. *Journal of Family Psychology*, 18, 135–146.

Singh, S. (2009). Neighborhood: The "outside" space for girls in urban India. *International Journal of Social Welfare*, 18, 1–9.

Skinner, D., Matthews, S., & Burton, L. (2005). Combining ethnography and GIS to examine constructions of developmental opportunities in contexts of poverty and disability. In T. Weisner (Ed.), *Discovering successful pathways in children's development: New methods in the study of childhood and family life*, pp. 223–239. Chicago: University of Chicago Press.

Small, M. L. (2004). *Villa Victoria: The transformation of social capital in a Boston barrio*. Chicago: University of Chicago Press.

Small, M. L. (2006). Neighborhood institutions as resource brokers: Childcare centers, interorganizational ties, and resource access among the poor. *Social Problems*, 53, 274–292.

Small, M. L., & McDermott, M. (2006). The presence of organizational resources in poor urban neighborhoods: An analysis of average and contextual effects. *Social Forces*, 84, 1697–1724.

Small, M. L., & Newman, K. S. (2001). Urban poverty after "The truly disadvantaged": The rediscovery of the family, the neighborhood, and culture. *Annual Review of Sociology*, 27, 23–45.

Small, M. L., & Stark, L. (2005). Are poor neighborhoods resource deprived? A case study of childcare centers in New York. *Social Science Quarterly*, 86, 1013–1036.

Soubhi, H., Raina, P., & Kohen, D. (2004). Neighborhood, family, and child predictors of childhood injury in Canada. *American Journal of Health Behavior*, 28, 397–409.

Spencer, M. B., McDermott, P. A., Burton, L. M., & Kochman, T. J. (1997). An alternative approach to assessing neighborhood effects on early adolescent achievement and problem behavior. In J. Brooks-Gunn, G. J. Duncan, & J. L. Aber (Eds.), *Neighborhood poverty: vol. 2. Policy implications in studying neighborhoods*, pp. 145–163. New York: Russell Sage Foundation.

Stoker, L. & Bowers, J. (2002). Designing multi-level studies: Sampling voters and electoral contexts. *Electoral Studies, 21*, 235–267.

Subramanian, S. V. (2004). The relevance of multilevel statistical models for identifying causal neighborhood effects. *Social Science and Medicine, 58*, 1961–1967.

Suresh, G., & Vito, G. F. (2007). The tragedy of public housing: Spatial analysis of hotspots of aggravated assaults in Louisville, KY (1989–1998). *American Journal of Criminal Justice, 32*, 99–115.

Taylor, P. J., Bennell, C., & Snook, B. (2002). Problems of classification in investigative psychology. In K. Jajuga, A. Sokolowski, & H.-H., Bock (Eds.), *Classification, clustering, and data analysis: Recent advances and applications*, pp. 479–487. Vertlag, Heidelberg: Springer.

Toro, R. I., Parke, R. D., Coltrane, S., Schofield, T. J., & Tuthill, L. (2009). Neighborhood ethnic composition as a moderator of the association between neighborhood risk and preadolescent externalizing. Paper presented at the biennial meeting for the Society for Research in Child Development, Denver, CO.

Trentacosta, C. J., Hyde, L. W., Shaw, D. S., & Cheong, J. (2009). Adolescent dispositions for antisocial behavior in context: The roles of neighborhood dangerousness and parental knowledge. *Journal of Abnormal Psychology, 118*, 564–575.

U.S. Census Bureau, Geography Division (2011). *Topologically Integrated Geographic Encoding and Referencing system*. Washington, DC: US Census Bureau.

Venkatesh, S. A. (2006). *Off the books: The underground economy of the urban poor*. Cambridge, MA: Harvard University Press.

Villenas, S. (2001). Latina mothers and small-town racisms: Creating narratives of dignity and moral education in North Carolina. *Anthropology & Education Quarterly, 32*, 3–28.

Von Hoffman, A. (2003). *House by house, block by block: The rebirth of America's urban neighborhoods*. New York: Oxford University Press.

Weisner, T. S. (1997). The ecocultural project of human development: Why ethnography and its findings matter. *Ethos, 25*, 177–190.

Weisner, T. S. (Ed.) (2005). *Discovering successful pathways in children's development: Mixed methods in the study of childhood and family life*. Chicago: University of Chicago Press.

Wilson, N., Syme, S. L., Boyce, W. T., Battistich, V., & Selvin, S. (2005). Adolescent alcohol, tobacco, and marijuana use: The influence of neighborhood disorder and hope. *American Journal of Health Promotion, 20*, 11–19.

Wilson, W. J. (1987). *The truly disadvantaged: The inner city, the underclass, and public policy*. Chicago: University of Chicago Press.

Wilson, W. J. (1996). *When work disappears: The world of the new urban poor*. New York: Knopf.

Wilson-Doenges, G. (2000). An exploration of sense of community and fear of crime in gated communities. *Environment and Behavior, 32*, 597–611.

Winship, C., & Morgan, S. L. (1999). The estimation of causal effects from observational data. *Annual Review of Sociology, 25*, 659–706.

Zalot, A., Jones, D. J., Kincaid, C., & Smith, T. (2009). Hyperactivity, impulsivity, inattention (HIA) and conduct problems among african american youth: The roles of neighborhood and gender. *Journal of Abnormal Child Psychology, 37*, 535–549.

Zenk, S. N., Schulz, A. J., Mentz, G., House, J. S., Gravlee, C. C., & Miranda, P. Y. (2007). Interrater and test-retest reliability: Methods and results for the neighborhood observational checklist. *Health and Place, 13*, 452–465.

CHAPTER 16

Rural versus Urban Environments

Robert H. Bradley

Introduction

Population migration in almost every country has resulted in the gradual concentration of population in or near metropolitan areas. Although the operational definitions used by the U.S. Department of Commerce for metropolitan and non metropolitan areas have shifted somewhat through time, the pattern of births, deaths, and migration in the United States over the past several decades has led to increasingly lower percentages of the population in areas considered as rural (www.census.gov/population/www/cen2000/briefs.html). The most recent (2003) definition of rural used by the U.S. Bureau of the Census is an area that comprises open country with fewer than 2,500 residents. Using this definition, most counties in the United States contain a combination of urban and rural areas. Urban areas are of two types: (1) urbanized areas – wherever there is an urban nucleus of 50,000 or more, with a core population density of at least 1,000 per square mile. An urban cluster requires the same core population density but a cluster pertains to situations where

there are several closely situated population nuclei of 2,500 to 49,999 people; (2) rural areas – open country and settlements with less than 2,500 residents. Even though almost two-thirds of the counties in the United States are categorized as rural under these criteria, only about 17 percent of the population lives in a rural county (www.ers.usda.gov/briefing/ rurality/NewDefinitions).

The definition of urban and rural settings used by the U.S. Census Bureau, the Office of Management and Budget, and the U.S. Department of Agriculture in the United States essentially characterizes an urban-rural continuum based on population density and proximity to metropolitan areas. Other countries use cut points and definitions that vary somewhat from the official U.S. definition. Moreover, social scientists often include in their conceptualization and operational definitions ideas pertaining to social dynamics together with geographic features of the environment (e.g., differentiation, segmentation, segregation, and marginalization) (Marsella, 1998). Accordingly, there is some degree of fragmentation in the literature of urban and rural life even though the primary definition essentially revolves around population density.

Although there is value connected to technical definitions of urban and rural, the notion of what constitutes an urban or a rural place is not fully realized in such technical definitions. Perceptions about places devolve from both cultural constructions and realistic appraisals about what those environments afford (Nairn, Panelli, & McCormack, 2003). In most societies rural life has been idealized, often sentimentalized, its meaning shaped by cultural discourse. It is the nature of cultural discourse to purify (i.e., simplify) ideas pertaining to place, even as most people inhabiting particular places can point to numerous exceptions to such ideas and may, in fact, be living lives that stand somewhat at variance to those idealized notions. In a national survey conducted in 2001, the majority of Americans perceived rural America as serene, a setting that is friendlier and more relaxed than urban America, a place where there is strong commitment to community and self-reliance (WW Kellogg Foundation, 2003). Rural America was viewed as a safe place to raise children in a country that is otherwise focused on materialism and moral decline. Most Americans also worried that rural America is in jeopardy of being overtaken by corporate giants and urban sprawl. Those living in rural areas also expressed concerns about lack of access to good health care, high-quality education, and opportunities for professional advancement.

There is a tendency for cultural constructions about places to change more slowly than the conditions in those places change. For example, the majority of Americans think of rural America as being based largely on agriculture despite the fact that only 12 percent of the rural economy actually is. Likewise, even though there is a common perception that urban environments are unsafe, the majority of urban youth find numerous places to hang out and have fun, places where the rates of injury and victimization are quite low. Whatever the perceptions, and whatever their tie to reality, the complex features that are contained in any place are encountered with variable frequency by those who inhabit the place. In rural areas, those who live on farms and those who do not tend to have different experiences and, consequently, different points of view. Likewise, there tend to be differences between those who live in the inner city and those who live in the suburbs. Critically, young people do not always valorize the presumed benefits or risks of living in a particular rural or urban place as do adults. Because there is also broad access to media, urban life penetrates into the consciousness of those living in rural areas, and vice versa. In effect, what it means to live in an urban versus a rural environment varies a great deal, both for residents in those environments and members of society generally.

The perceptions of rural life in America revealed in the Kellogg survey are similar to those reported by rural families living in other developed countries. For example, in a study of rural families in Scotland and northern England, parents reported that a rural community provided the ideal environment in which to rear children because of the access to nature, sense of freedom and safety, access to neighbors, and reciprocal help in time of need (Mauther, McKee, & Strell, 2001). By the same token, parents described limitations in terms of access to steady, high-paying employment and specialty health services. They also pointed to lack of recreational opportunities for adolescents. Employment for both men and women tended to be insecure and low paying, but it also had aspects of flexibility that allowed them to attend to their children's needs. Both men and women often worked nonstandard and restricted hours to meet the combination of economic and family obligations. This had the effect that both mothers and fathers were involved in caretaking in ways that run counter to historic roles.

In this chapter, I consider four questions as regards life in rural versus urban environments: (a) How different is daily life in urban and rural communities? (b) What does it mean for adults? (c) What does it mean for children? and (d) What does it mean for family adaptation and parenting? I conclude with some general thoughts about the implications of urban-rural differences as regards behavior and development.

How Different Is Daily Life in Urban and Rural Communities?

Access to nature. Research shows that spending time in nature has social, cognitive, emotional, and physiologic benefits (Hartig, Mang, & Evans, 1991; Sullivan, 2004; Wells, 2000). Hence, there is a general worry that growing up in the inner city means having little access to open, green spaces and that having access only to barren spaces could limit activity and compromise development (Wells & Evans, 2003). However, a study of 64 urban public housing outdoor spaces revealed considerable variability in access to green spaces with more than half having considerable vegetation (Sullivan, 2004; Taylor, Wiley, Kuo, & Sullivan, 1998). Of the 262 children observed, most (73 percent) were involved in meaningful play, and the vast majority (87 percent) were supervised to some degree. That said, involvement of adults was less in the more barren spaces and the play of children was less creative. Moreover, surveys done with housing project residents indicated that good maintenance of trees and grass in nearby space increased the perception of safety and reduced the level of crime (Kuo & Sullivan, 2001). Other studies have shown that natural landscaping encouraged greater use of outdoor areas and attracted a more diverse group to the space (Coley, Sullivan, & Evans, 1997; Kuo, Bacaicoa, & Sullivan, 1998). Among older inner city adults, the use of green outdoor common spaces played a role (small) in the formation and maintenance of social ties (Kweon, Sullivan, & Wiley, 1998). For children residing in poor urban environments, having natural green spaces nearby has a restorative effect. Children who moved to homes with much higher levels of greenness had the highest levels of cognitive functioning after the move. For rural children in grades 3–5, having high levels of nature

nearby reduced the impact of life stress (Wells & Evans, 2003).

Sense of Community and Social Isolation. A number of factors affect people's sense of community and level of involvement within the community (Funk, Allan, & Chappell, 2007). These include access to natural features and open spaces but also the overall layout of the community. Also at issue are perceived safety and perceived stress (Kim & Kaplan, 2004). With regard to using (or being in) certain urban spaces, a key factor in perceived danger pertains to how one perceives the opportunity to escape danger should it arise (Blobaum & Hunecke, 2005). Accordingly, for most urban spaces there is not a strong sense of fear. In a recent poll done in Pennsylvania, people in Philadelphia and Allegheny County expressed greater concerns about safety than people in other parts of the state. However, there was little in the way of difference in expressed concerns regarding safety for those in the suburbs in the large metropolitan areas, more remote suburbs, and small towns (Taylor, 2005).

The factors that bear upon sense of community vary somewhat depending on what area of a community one lives in. For suburbanites, higher satisfaction was related to the amount of participation in the community and level of privacy afforded (Wilson & Baldassare 1996). In more densely populated central city areas, perceptions of crowding were salient, but the perception of crowding was tied to the sociodemographic diversity of residents and spatiophysical features of the area (Bonnes, Bonaiuto, & Escolani, 1991).

There is a long tradition of social theory suggesting that urban life may be detrimental to the quality and quantity of social relationships, and there is evidence that people living in urban areas are less likely to extend help to strangers (Amato, 1993). However, the negative consequences of urban life seem largely situated in dense, inner city neighborhoods, often with high concentrations of poor minority families (Tigges, Browne, & Green, 1998). Residents in such communities are often socially isolated and report higher levels of incivilities from others (Reisig & Cancino, 2004). Sociologists have identified a number of meaningful indicators of social isolation for adults: (1) whether there is another adult in the household, (2) whether there is someone outside the household who functions as a regular partner for communication, (3) whether there is a close connection with someone who is employed, (4) whether there is a close connection to someone with a college education. Living in a neighborhood with a high concentration of households below the poverty line (i.e., > 30 percent in the neighborhood) decreases the likelihood of all such connections. Adults who are socially isolated have less access to social resources or social capital. They tend to function outside the mainstream and have weak connections to institutions of work, education, church, or government. They are less likely to know someone who can help them find employment and less likely to know someone who manifests the virtues and benefits of adherence to the broader norms of society (Reisig & Cancino, 2004). Indeed, people living in urban ghettos are often subjected to the kinds of social and economic conditions that foster an oppositional culture to success in mainstream society.

Although the precepts of social disorganization theory tend to apply to those living in dense urban ghettos, relations between area of residence and various types of social behaviors appear more complex. For example, Nation, Fortney, and Wandersman (2010) observed little difference among urban, suburban, and rural dwellers as regards the amount of time spent with neighbors. What did differ is how they interacted with neighbors. Rural dwellers were more likely to lend money to or borrow money from a neighbor. Urban and suburban dwellers were more likely to discuss problems with them. Moreover, the differences in engagements with neighbors varied by race.

Subcultural theory suggests that social ties for rural dwellers may depend more on circumstances: that is, whom one lives near and has routine contact with (family, coworkers, members of social organizations). By contrast, social ties for urban and suburban dwellers may be more a matter of choice: that is, those who share one's interests, lifestyles, or values. Consistent with this proposition, Amato (1993) found that urbanites received more help from friends, whereas rural dwellers received more help from family members. There also tended to be more reciprocity within urbanite networks. The exception was the urban elderly who were more socially isolated.

To a degree the social networks of rural dwellers tend to be more enduring, as they are more a matter of circumstance than choice. However, the nature of such ties can be something of a mixed blessing. Specifically, although one can count on receiving various forms of instrumental and emotional support from the social network, it entails an obligation to provide such support as well, often at considerable cost (Seeman, 1996).

Geographic Isolation. It is not as clear whether living in a poor rural area produces the level of social isolation observed in urban ghettos, albeit access to social resources is more limited in high-poverty rural areas as well. In rural communities, having access to dependable transportation is often key to accessing social networks, engaging in social institutions (e.g., church, community organizations), and obtaining everyday necessities (including food and health care). A large survey done with older adults in Alabama found that geographic isolation was critical to many health outcomes (Locher, Ritchie, Roth, Baker, Bodner, & Allman, 2005). Being poor and socially isolated, which often means having limited access to dependable transportation, were significant factors in nutritional risk.

Interestingly, farm families (who often live at some distance from their neighbors) tend to have fairly strong social networks and tend to be strongly connected to social institutions in their communities (Coleman, Ganong, Clark, & Madsen, 1989). Perhaps because these social networks are largely taken for granted, farm families who were surveyed regarding their child rearing goals more often emphasized intellectual and emotional development as contrasted to social development. This distinguished them from urban families, who emphasized social development more.

Caring for Children. To some extent macrolevel environmental conditions and maternal employment have become the great equalizers in daily life for children in the United States. For both urban and rural families, the ability of mothers to engage in outside employment depends on having access to child care. Generally speaking, there is very little difference in patterns of nonparental child care for rural and urban families (Smith, 2006). Preschool-age children of working mothers from rural areas spend an average of 37 hours per week in nonparental care. This compares to an average of 35 hours per week for working mothers living in urban areas. Informal nonrelative care is a little more common in rural areas than urban areas (25 percent vs. 20 percent). By contrast, organized, center-based care is slightly less common in rural communities (31 percent vs 33 percent).

Grandparents play a very significant role in the lives of children in rural, suburban, and urban areas, a greater role than is often realized in that they are major providers of child care. of all grandparents 30 percent provide routine care for their grandchildren when their daughters are employed outside the home; 19 percent are the primary providers of care. If they live within 1 hour of their daughter, 40 percent routinely provide care for grandchildren (U.S. Census Bureau, 2008). Notably, many also live with their grandchildren, but there are differences depending on whether grandparents live in rural, suburban, or urban areas. of grandparents who live in urban areas 9.74 percent live with their grandchildren (6.56 percent provide a home for their children and grandchildren). The corresponding figures for suburban grandparents are 6.91 percent and 4.13 percent, and for rural grandparents are 6.99 percent and 5.52 percent (Fields, 2003).

What Does Living in a Rural versus an Urban Environment Mean for Adults?

Educational Attainment. Results from the National Opinion Research Center's General Social Survey indicated that people living in central cities and suburbs of large metropolitan areas in the United States have significantly higher levels of educational attainment than those in smaller cities and rural areas (Sander, 2006). The reasons for this include migration of more highly educated individuals to large metropolitan areas and family background factors that are more favorable to higher levels of educational attainment in large urban areas. It is also shown that although urban advantages in schooling for respondents at age 16 have declined over time, urban advantages for respondents when they are older have increased. For years of schooling at age 16, the data indicate that respondents from suburbs acquire the most schooling, followed by respondents from big cities and small cities. Respondents from farms and other rural areas acquired the least schooling. The same pattern exists in the data for years of schooling by current location. Respondents from suburbs acquire the most schooling followed by respondents from cities. Data on college graduation rates indicate a similar pattern in the data. Respondents who grew up in suburbs or who live in suburbs of the largest cities are the most likely to have acquired a college degree followed by respondents from cities and respondents from large suburbs. There is a slight difference in the pattern in the data on high school dropouts. Although respondents who either live in a suburb now or grew up in a suburb have the lowest dropout rates, respondents living in the largest cities have a relatively high dropout rate – higher than respondents living in other cities but not as high as the rural dropout rate.

Some of the educational advantage that large metropolitan areas have is a result of migration of more educated respondents to these areas. Family background factors are also more favorable to higher levels of educational attainment in large urban areas. The result is that college graduates are increasingly concentrated in the largest metropolitan areas.

Health and Physical Activity. Rural areas are generally thought of as safer (meaning one is less likely to be victimized) than urban areas. A study of intentional deaths by firearms showed relatively little difference between urban and rural areas (an odds ratio of only 1.03 favoring rural areas). More critically, the most rural counties experienced 1.54 times the adjusted firearm suicide rate of the most urban; the most urban counties experienced 1.90 times the adjusted firearm homicide rate of the most rural. Similar opposing trends were not found for nonfirearm suicide or homicide (Branas, Nance, Elliott, Richmond, & Schwab, 2004). By contrast, the rate of unintentional injury is higher in rural areas (Boland, Staines, Fitzpatrick, & Scallan, 2005). The national death rates from trauma are higher in rural areas, partly owing to higher rates of serious injury (Chapital, Harrigan, Davis, Easa, Withy, Yu, & Takanishi 2007). The rates of nonfatal injuries were also higher. Compared with large urban counties, small urban counties experienced 8 percent higher injury odds; suburban counties 20 percent higher injury odds; and rural counties 30 percent higher injury odds after adjusting for age, gender, marital status, education, and health insurance (Tiesman, Zwerling, Peek-Asa, Sprince, & Cavanaugh, 2007). Data from the National Survey of America's Families indicated that 13.1 percent of adults living in rural areas rated themselves as being in fair to poor health, as contrasted to 9.6 percent in urban areas and 9.0 percent in areas adjacent to urban areas (Ormond, Zuckerman, & Lhila, 2000).

According to the National Health Information Survey, rates of cardiovascular disease and diabetes are higher in rural areas (Slifkin, Goldsmith, & Ricketts, 2000). Part of this disparity reflects the fact that adults living in rural areas tend to be older, poorer, and less well educated, which is connected to poorer nutritional status and less physical activity (Mainous & Kohrs, 1995). Adults living in rural areas also tend to have

somewhat different health beliefs and practices compared to adults living in urban and suburban areas (Long, 1993; Morgan, 2002). For example, women living in rural areas are less likely to get mammograms (Slifkin et al., 2000). However, the poorer health status of rural adults also reflects the fact that rural residents have more limited access to health insurance and specialty medical care (Ormond et al., 2000). That said, there was greater availability of nursing home beds in rural versus urban areas (66.7 beds per 1,000 older rural residents versus 51.9 beds per 1,000 older urban residents) (Dalton, Slifkin, & Walsh, 2003).

In contrast to the data on cardiovascular illness, research has shown higher rates for some forms of cancer among urban dwellers. Specifically, there is a higher incidence of head and neck cancers among those living in some urban areas compared with those living in neighboring rural communities owing to atmospheric pollution (Wake, 2007). Indeed, life expectancy is actually greater in rural areas, especially for adults living in poverty, perhaps owing to greater access to social networks among rural residents (Geronimus, Bound, Colen, Ingber, & Shchet, 2004). Finally, it should be noted that whatever generalizations might be made about rurality and health status, the generalization does not appear to fit all regions and countries. In a study of rural and regional residence on the health of older adults in the United States, negative health effects of rural residence were found only in the South region (Ziembroski, & Breiding, 2006). Positive health effects of rural residence were found only in the Midwest region. There are no observed health risks associated with rural or regional residence across group. In developing countries where there is rapid migration of poor people into urban areas, it is often the case that newcomers live in squalid, high-density housing areas where there are frequent exposures to environmental toxins and infectious agents, leading to high rates of morbidity and mortality (Pruss, Kay, Fewtrell, & Bartram, 2002).

Consistent with findings pertaining to health status, research on physical activity among adults also points to problems with health-related behavior for rural residents. In a national sample of women older than 40, 56 percent of rural women were classified as sedentary, compared to 49 percent of urban women (Wilcox, Castro, King, Hoursmann, & Brownson, 2000). Likewise, only 8.5 percent were classified as being regularly active, versus 10.2 percent of urban women. The two groups identified different barriers as regards engaging in regular physical activity. Urban women said that they were too tired or had too little time to exercise regularly. By contrast, rural women said others discouraged them from exercising, they were afraid of being injured, they had too many caregiving duties and they had no safe place to exercise.

The differential rates of leisure-time physical activity observed for women older than 40 were mirrored in younger women as well and were even more pronounced for men (CDC, 1996). The Centers for Disease Control conducted a nation-wide survey of more than 100,000 households. The overall prevalence of leisure-time physical inactivity was lowest (27.4 percent) in central metropolitan areas and highest (36.6 percent) in rural areas. Data were stratified by age, sex, level of education, and household income and analyzed within each stratum across urban-rural categories. Inverse relations between physical inactivity and degree of urbanization remained consistent in most strata, although the pattern was weaker in some strata of education, lower income levels, and older age groups.

Mental Health and Addiction. Information from surveys done in the United States and other developed countries paints a very complicated picture of relations between area of residence and socioemotional well-being. In the 1988 National Survey of Families and Households, rural adults described themselves as being less happy than adults in metropolitan areas; but middle-aged and older adults were generally better off on six other indicators of well-being (Eggebeen & Lichter, 2009). Data from the 2002–2004 National Surveys on Drug Use compared residents in three county types: rural, urbanized

metropolitan, and metropolitan (Gfroerer, Larson, & Colliver, 2007). Findings showed that rural adults had generally lower rates of illicit drug use than metropolitan adults, but adults in rural and urbanized nonmetropolitan areas had higher rates of methamphetamine use than those in metropolitan areas. Rural adults had higher rates of tobacco use but lower rates of alcohol use.

Results from the National Co-morbidity Study in the United States showed that rural men had more mood and anxiety disorders than urban men, perhaps owing to loss of jobs and financial strain for white men (Diala & Muntaner, 2003). Although women generally exhibit higher levels of mood and anxiety disorders than men, it did not prove to be the case among rural residents.

A large European study found that residents (especially male residents) in urban areas had higher rates of mood disorders, but differences varied by country (Kovess-Masfety, Alonso, de Graff, & Demyttenaere, 2005). However, rates of alcohol disorders were no different. Importantly, many of the rural-urban differences disappeared after controlling for marital status. Until 1980, suicide rates in urban areas tended to surpass those in rural areas. Since then rates of suicide among young adults living in rural areas have escalated, especially among women 15–24, so that they are now equal to or greater than suicide rates in urban areas (Middleton, Gunnell, Frankel, Whitley, & Dorling, 2003). In England and Wales suicide rate among inner-city dwellers was high, as was suicide rate among adults living in the more remote areas (Middleton, Sterne, & Gunnell, 2006). The marked increase in rural areas probably reflects declining economic opportunities, long-term battles with illness, and continuing reluctance of those in rural areas to seek help for stress and mental health problems. It was also particularly high in single-person households, suggesting possible social fragmentation.

A second study done in Europe revealed that living in an urban area increases the risk of psychosis (Peen & Dekker, 2004). The prevalence of psychiatric disorders gradually increased over five levels of urbanization (Peen, Dekker, Schoevers, Have, de Graaf, & Beekman, 2007). There was suggestive evidence that people with genetic vulnerabilities who grow up in urban areas may be more likely to express psychiatric symptoms than similar people who grow up in rural areas; however, the difference between urban and rural rates was not clear. Urban compared to rural birthplace was associated with both increased risk of adult-onset psychoses and other nonaffective psychoses (Harrison, Fouskakis, Rasmussen, Tynelius, Sipos, & Gunnell, 2003). It was especially strong for those born in winter months. The relation was not mediated by educational attainment. One partial explanation offered for the rural-urban difference was differential migration into urban areas.

The idea that mobility to urban areas rather than place of residence per se explains urban-rural differences in prevalence rates for psychiatric problems has been noted before. A review of the worldwide literature on the topic of urbanization and mental health revealed little consistency in findings, partly owing to different methodologies for sampling and assessing mental health and partly owing to different ways of defining rural and urban residence (Marsella, 1998). Data from the National Co-Morbidity Study showed little in the way of consistent difference in the rates of either lifetime or 12-month rates of mental illness for urban and rural residents (Hartley, Bird, & Dempsey, 1999).

In the past, the argument was put forth that there were fewer mental health problems in rural areas because those living in rural areas had more ready access to supportive social ties. Such ties were assumed both to foster a sense of well-being directly and to serve to protect people from life's stresses. However, research on social ties indicates that relations are not uniform for all subgroups. There is suggestive evidence, for instance, that social connections may paradoxically increase levels of mental illness in women who live in conditions of limited resources (Kawachi & Berkman, 2001). All in all, place of residence may have less to do with mental health status than other socioeconomic and demographic factors.

What Does Living in Rural versus Urban Environments Mean for Children?

Academic Achievement. A larger percentage of rural public school students in the fourth and eighth grades scored at or above the proficient level on the National Assessment of Educational Progress (NAEP) reading, mathematics, and science assessments in 2005 than did public school students in central cities at these grade levels. However, smaller percentages of rural public school students than suburban public school students scored at or above the proficient level in reading and mathematics. In 2004, the high school status dropout rate (i.e., the percentage of persons not enrolled in school and not having completed high school) among 16- to 24-year-olds in rural areas was higher than in suburban areas, but lower than in cities. Interestingly, children from farm families had greater academic success than children from nonfarm families living in rural areas (Russell & Elder, 1997). The differences were largely owing to strong parental involvement and high levels of integration into the local community. Current public school expenditures per student were higher in rural areas in 2003–4 than in any other locale after adjusting for geographic cost differences.

A study done in North Carolina, using data from the 2006–7 school year, indicated that the state dropout rate was 5.24 (Haley, Harder, & Lea, 2008). Dropout rates tend to vary little between rural and mixed rural counties (5.23 to 5.65), regardless of integration with a micropolitan or metropolitan area. However, the difference in dropout rates between urban metro and mixed urban metro counties is significant. Urban metro counties recorded a dropout rate of 5.9, the highest among all categories, whereas mixed urban metro recorded the lowest (4.3).

While there are relatively modest differences in school attendance in the United States, there are often quite substantial differences in poor, less technologically advanced societies. In almost all cases, attendance rates are greater in urban areas, partly owing to socioeconomic circumstances and access to schools (Ingram, Wils, Carrol, & Townsend, 2006; Reilly & Al-Samarrai, 2000).

Health and Physical Activity. Infant mortality rates are higher for all races in rural areas according to data from the National Health Interview Survey (Slifkin, Goldsmith, & Ricketts, 2000). Childhood mortality rates in general are higher, with drowning, motor vehicle accidents, firearm injuries, and farm machinery accidents as the leading causes (Cherry, Huggins, & Gilmore, 2007). Living in an urban area was also associated with a lower body mass index (BMI) for children ages 2 through 11 (Oliver & Hayes, 2008). However, the association appears more complex than the simple rural-urban distinction, as studies done in other countries do not always reveal urban-rural differences in prevalence rates of overweight or obesity (Ara, Moreno, Leiva, Guitin, & Casajus, 2007; Ismailov & Leatherdale, 2010). When data from the National Longitudinal Study of Adolescent Health were analyzed using diverse measures of residential neighborhoods, adolescents living in newer suburbs were less likely to be overweight than those in rural working-class, exurban, and mixed-race urban neighborhoods, independent of individual SES, age, and race/ethnicity (Nelson, Gordon-Larsen, Song, & Popkin, 2006). Adolescents living in older suburban areas were more likely to be physically active than residents of newer suburbs. Those living in low-SES inner-city neighborhoods were more likely to be active, though not significantly so, compared to mixed-race urban residents. These findings demonstrate disadvantageous associations between specific rural and urban environments and behavior, illustrating important effects of the neighborhood on health and the inherent complexity of assessing residential landscapes across the United States. Simple classical urban-suburban-rural measures mask these important complexities.

Residing in an urban area is associated with higher rates of asthma (Wong & Chow, 2008). Consistent findings of a markedly lower prevalence of asthma in children and adults who have been raised in a farming environment clearly indicate the importance of environmental influence of asthma development. Although the exact protective environmental factors in the rural region remain to be defined, there have been many studies suggesting that early exposure to microbes or microbial products may play a role in modulating the immune system so as to reduce the future risk of asthma and allergies.

Rural children with special health care needs are less likely to be seen by a pediatrician than urban children (Skinner & Slifkin, 2007). They are more likely to have unmet health care needs due to transportation difficulties or unavailability of care in the area; there were minimal other differences in barriers to care. Families of rural children with special health care needs are more likely to report financial difficulties associated with their children's medical needs and more likely to provide care at home for their children.

Although urban children tend to live in closer proximity to health care providers, they also tend to live in closer proximity to traffic congestion, construction sites, and other sources of noise pollution. Research shows that chronic exposure to noise can lead to various forms of stress reactivity and has negative consequences for physiologic response (Evans, Bullinger, & Hygge, 1998).

According to data developed by the World Health Organization (1995), about 12 million children below age 5 still die each year, mostly from causes related to their living environments. The problems may be greatest in the "urban slums" of underdeveloped nations. Many children living in dense urban areas do not have ready access to clean water or good sanitation; consequently, they are subject to numerous serious illnesses (Bartlett, 1999; Evans, Lepore, Shejwal, & Palsane, 1998). These children often have to carry water for the family, which can lead to damage to the head, neck, and spine, not to mention a general drain on energy (Thompson, Porras, Wood, Tumwine, Mujwahauzi, & Katui-Katua, 2000). The overcrowding and poor ventilation that characterizes many of their homes exposes them to many airborne pollutants and respiratory infections as well. Living in crowded urban areas also tends to expose children to many dangers that can cause injuries, including unprotected stairways, elevated walkways, kerosene heaters, debris, and busy roadways. Children often do not have the understanding to avoid such pitfalls (Bartlett, 1999). That said, one has to be careful to making gross distinctions between what it means to live in urban versus rural environments as there are enormous differences within each broad category. For example, a careful evaluation of sanitary quality in Salvador, Brazil showed considerable variation in the environmental conditions present and the load of parasitic infections among children living in 30 selected districts within the city (Milroy, Borja, Barros, & Barreto, 2001).

Mental Health and Substance Use. Because inner-city urban children are more often exposed to crime and violence, there has been concern about the negative consequences for their mental health (Berman, Jurtines, Silverman, & Serafini, 1996; Fitzpatrick, 1993; Gorman-Smith, & Tolan, 1998; Schwab-Stone, Ayers, Dasprow, Voyce, Barone, Shriver, & Weissberg 1995). Unfortunately, most population-based studies of children's mental health do not break down urban and rural areas in such a way as to document these relations. Accordingly, to date there is little evidence that place of residence per se is strongly implicated in development of psychiatric problems for children (Costello, Keeler, & Angold, 2001; Marsella, 1998). Although the data on children is not as good as the data on adults, there is no consistent pattern of urban-rural differences and it appears that some of the observed differences may reflect different patterns of outmigration and various demographic confounds. Moreover, even though there may be less exposure to crime and violence in rural areas generally speaking, that does not mean that the there are not other risk factors

present in rural environments. Interestingly, in a study of fears among children in fourth to sixth grades in Tennessee, rural children exhibited higher levels of fear than did urban children when the urban children did not live in dense urban neighborhoods (Davidson, White, Smith & Poppen, 2001).

There is evidence that alcohol consumption (especially heavy drinking) is higher in rural areas (Donnermeyer & Park, 1995; Kenny & Schreiner, 2009; Martino, Ellickson & Mc Caffrey, 2008; Rountree & Clayton, 1999). The urban-rural difference appears to reflect higher levels of cumulative risk for rural youth (e.g., parent history of substance abuse and low educational attainment). It also suggests the changing work and family environment in many rural areas: that is, factors that used to be protective against drug and alcohol use (e.g., tight family bonds, church attendance, strong social ties) are not as operative today. It is especially likely that rural youth will use drugs if they live in an area that includes a town of at least medium size. The higher rate of alcohol consumption among rural adolescents is associated with higher rates of injury (Jiang, Boyce, & Pickett, 2008). Recently, marijuana use increased at a higher rate among youth living in micropolitan and metropolitan areas as contrasted to youth living in sparsely populated areas, partly as a function of residential instability and drug availability (Martino et al., 2008).

Findings pertaining to urban-rural differences in substance use and psychiatric problems for children have to be interpreted with caution in that studies vary considerably with regard to the methods used. Moreover, there have been generational drifts in patterns of findings, reflective of broader societal shifts in both urban and rural areas.

What Does Living in Rural versus Urban Environments Mean for Parenting and Family Relationships?

There is little in the way of theory or research to support the notion that living in an urban, suburban or rural setting in an of itself affects the general quality of family functioning independent of the socioeconomic or demographic factors that are associated with living in such surroundings. The social ties of urban and rural dwellers tend to be a little different. For example, there is a weak trend showing that urbanites receive more help from friends than do rural dwellers and they get less from relatives. These differences are mainly due to the demographic composition of the two areas and because urban dwellers tend to live further from relatives (Amato, 1993).

There is a substantial literature showing that socioeconomic and demographic factors affect the adaptive functioning of all family members and helps determine how parents parent (Bradley & Corwyn, 2002; Conger & Donnellan, 2007). Low socioeconomic status tends to be associated with more violence, a more disorganized and chaotic family environment, and poorer quality parenting, irrespective of place of residence. The impact of chronic adversity and trauma appears to depend on how parents structure the environment (routines, organization and management of daily life, designation of roles for family members, norms and expectations, monitoring of children), the quality of relationships among family members, and the coping strategies used (Krenichyn, Saegert, & Evans, 2001). Parent involvement, parent-child conflict, and parental monitoring have been shown to be associated with externalizing behavior of 6- to 10-year-old inner-city boys (Wasserman, Miller, Pinner, & Jaramillo, 1996). Each contributes independently and they may be more an issue for vulnerable boys. Having a tight family structure, using positive approaches to discipline, and having access to positive male adult role models appear to reduce the likelihood of externalizing behavior in inner-city boys ages 10 to 15 (Florsheim, Tolan, & Gorman-Smith, 1998). Parental monitoring appears to moderate the impact of living in an urban (not restricted to inner city) environment for African American boys and girls, reducing the likelihood of delinquency, drug use and aggressiveness. The combination of having a close, warm relationship between parent and child plus strong monitoring and supervision reduced the likelihood of both health compromising behaviors and violence throughout adolescence for both males and females (Richards, Miller, O'Donnell, Wasserman, & Colder, 2004; Vazsonyi, Pickering, & Bolland, 2006).

There is evidence for both white and black youth that part of the value of responsive parenting and careful supervision is that it reduces the likelihood of affiliating with deviant peers. By contrast, harsh and unsupportive parenting exacerbated the impacts of traumatic exposure on physiological reactivity and adjustment (Evans & English, 2002). In general, using a coping strategy that is coherent and positive and that deals with children's emotional responses in ways that move them toward emotional control appears to help mitigate exposures to trauma and adversity (Kiser & Black, 2005). Studies done with rural African American families attest to the value of active coping and positive parent-child relationships (Brody & Flor, 1997; Bynum & Brody, 2005). That said, a study done on inner-city Hispanic fourth and fifth graders found that the benefit of parental monitoring was reduced as exposure to violence became greater and greater (Ceballo, Ramirez, Hearn, & Malatese, 2003). Moreover, there was evidence from a study of inner-city African American and Latino youth that being reared in families that were less cohesive, provided less supervision and had less supportive family relationships increased the likelihood of being exposed to more community violence than youth from the same neighborhoods who were reared in better functioning families (Gorman-Smith, Henry, & Tolan, 2004). These factors, although more often studied in inner-city families, also appear to be operative among poor rural families as well. For example, following a decline in the local rural economy, community disorganization undermined effective parenting via reduced social support, increased negative life events, and felt distress (Simons, Johnson, Conger, & Lorenz, 1997).

One of the challenges faced by poor parents who live in dangerous areas is how to arrange for nonparental caregiving and how to management movement and leisure activities. If social networks of kith and kin are available in the area, it makes is easier for parents to obtain care while they are at work or involved in other pursuits where they cannot take their children. Such networks are also often a source for structuring leisure time activities, as kin can help arrange and monitor children's activities. If parents are fearful, they often confine their children with extended family and use them to chaperone the child's activities. To some degree this allows the children access to mainstream activities when otherwise they would not have the opportunity. It also allows parents a means of keeping children out of harm and away from undesirable places and peers (Outley & Floyd, 2002). On the other hand, as children age, they find such confinement and control bothersome – such are the challenges of parents in both urban and rural areas.

Very few studies that have looked at the context of parenting and its impact on child well-being have made direct comparisons between urban and rural families. In the few instances when such comparisons have been made, results have tended to be similar, with perhaps an occasional exception (Pinderhughes, Nix, Foster, Jones, & the Conduct Problems Research Group, 2001). For example, Imig (1983) reported that rural fathers had a greater tendency to disengage in the face of stress than did urban fathers; but the sample was small and the study occurred more than three decades ago. A more recent study in which relations between family factors and adolescent substance abuse was examined for rural, suburban, and urban 11th graders found that the threat of family sanctions, the quality of parent-child communication, and the level of family involvement in school worked to reduce the likelihood of substance abuse about equally well in all three groups (Sheer, Borden, & Donnermeyer, 2000).

Final Considerations

Life in rural, suburban, and urban America is both diverse and dynamic. So, too, is life in rural, suburban, and urban areas throughout the globe. The degree of heterogeneity and pace of change varies from place to place – so, even though there tend to be average differences in the physical and social affordances present in rural, suburban, and urban areas – it is difficult to characterize adequately what it means to be urban or rural. Because urban areas differ greatly in terms of their physical characteristics, the resources generally available to residents that inhabit them, and the social networks residence are members of, it is difficult to characterize what it means to be "urban" beyond some banal particulars – the same can be said of what it means to be "rural." A number of factors make it difficult to draw clear conclusions about what living in a rural versus living in an urban environment implies human behavior and human development, including the difficulties attendant to defining what constitutes a rural versus an urban or a suburban environment. Different estimates of rurality "effects" have emerged depending on precisely what geographic areas are defined as being rural or metropolitan and the like, including how different geographic areas are aggregated to represent rural, urban, or suburban environments. Different estimates are also obtained depending on how one addresses problems of endogeneity (i.e., what controls for spuriousness one utilizes). Likewise, it is difficult to disentangle the effect being in a place may have on human behavior and development from the reasons people have for inhabiting those places (i.e., people choose to migrate as a consequence of economic need, employment opportunity, the need for particular services, and the desire to separate oneself from current social networks or geographic surroundings); that is, there are a number of selection biases one must consider when trying to determine the effect of living in a particular area (Marsella, 1998; Weber, Jensen, Miller, Mosley, & Fisher, 2005). Any effort to define what belongs in any sort of abstract geographic spatial category is rife with conceptual and operational difficulties. As well, real places are complex and dynamic composites of particular physical and social conditions (living in a remote Inuit village in Alaska is likely to be quite different from living in a remote vacation hideaway in the Caribbean or a living in a cabin in the Appalachians). As dynamic systems theory would predict, the amalgam of conditions present in any one locale can contain offsetting processes related to a given outcome; and they can contain multiple conditions that all converge to facilitate or prevent a particular outcome (Ford & Lerner, 1992). Not surprisingly, at present there is little convincing evidence that living in a rural as opposed to an urban area per se accounts for most of the differences in behavior and development observed for those inhabiting places described as rural or urban. Rather, most of the evidence points to particular economic or social or physical environmental factors as being more likely determiners of the behavior and development of those who inhabit particular places. Thus, research aimed at understanding how living in particular urban or rural settings may affect the lives of those who live there needs to include a consideration of the specific social, physical, and economic conditions present in those settings.

References

Amato, P. R. (1993). Urban-rural differences in helping friends and family members. *Social Psychology Quarterly*, 56, 249–262.

Ara, I., Moreno, L. A., Leiva, M. R. Gutin, B., & Casajus, J. A. (2007). Adiposity, physical activity, and physical fitness among children from Aragón, Spain. *Obesity*, 15, 1918–1924.

Bartlett, S. (1999). Children's experience of the physical environment in poor urban settlements and the implications for policy and practice. *Environment & Urbanization*, 11, 63–73.

Berman, S. L., Kurtines, W. M., Silverman, W. K., & Serafini, L. T. (1996). The impact of exposure to crime and violence on urban youth. *American Journal of Orthopsychiatry*, 6, 329–336.

Blobaum A., & Hunecke, M. (2005). Perceived danger in public space. *Environment & Behavior*, 37, 465–486.

Boland, M., Staines, A., Fitzpatrick, P., & Scallan, E. (2005). Urban-rural variation in mortality and hospital admission rates for unintentional injury in Ireland. *Injury Prevention*, 11, 38–42.

Bonnes, M., Bonaiuto, M., & Escolani, A. P. (1991). Crowding and residential satisfaction in the urban environment. *Environment & Behavior*, 23, 531–552.

Bradley, R. H., & Corwyn, R. F. (2002). SES and child development. *Annual Review of Psychology*, 53, 371–399.

Branas, C. C., Nance, M. L., Elliott, M. R., Richmond, T. S., & Schwab, W. (2004). Urban-rural shifts in intentional firearm death: Different causes, same results. *American Journal of Public Health*, 94, 1750–1755.

Brody, G. H., & Flor, D. L. (1997). Maternal psychological functioning, family processes, and child adjustment in single-parent, African American families. *Developmental Psychology*, 33, 1000–1011.

Bynum, M. S., & Brody, G. H. (2005). Coping behaviors, parenting, and perceptions of children's internalizing and externalizing problems in rural African American mothers. *Family Relations*, 54, 58–71.

CDC. (1996). *Physical activity and health: a report of the Surgeon General*. Atlanta: US Department of Health and Human Services, Public Health Service.

Ceballo, R., Ramirez, C., Hean, K. D., & Malatese, K. L. (2003). Community violence and children's psychological well-being: Does parental monitoring matter? *Journal of Clinical Child & Adolescent Psychology*, 32, 586–592.

Chapital, A. D., Harrigan, R. C., Davis, J., Easa, D., Withy, K., Yu, M., & Takanishi, D. M. (2007). Traumatic brain injury: Outcomes from rural and urban locations over a 5-year period. *Hawaii Medical Journal*, 66, 318–321.

Cherry, D. C., Huggins, B., & Gilmore, K. (2007). Children's health in the rural environment. *Pediatric Clinics of North America*, 54, 121–133.

Coleman, M., Ganong, L. H., Clark, J. M., & Madsen, R. (1989). Parenting perceptions in rural and urban families: Is there a difference? *Journal of Marriage & Family*, 51, 329–335.

Coley, R. L., Sullivan, W. C., & Evans, G W. (1997). Where does community grow? *Environment & Behavior*, 29, 468–494.

Conger, R. D., & Donnellan, M. B. (2007). An interactionist perspective on the socioeconomic context of human development. *Annual Review of Psychology*, 58, 175–199.

Costello, E. J., Keeler, G. P., & Angold, A. (2001). Poverty, race/ethnicity, and psychiatric disorder: A study of rural children. *American Journal of Public Health, 91,* 1494–1498.

Dalton, K., Slifkin, R., & Walsh, J. (2003). *Background paper: Rural and urban differences in nursing home and skilled nursing supply.* Chapel Hill, NC: North Carolina Rural Health Research and Policy Analysis Program, Working Paper No. 74. Available online at www.shepcenter.unc.edu/research_programs/rural_program.

Davidson, P. M., White, P. N., Smith, D. J., & Poppen, W A. (2001). Content and intensity of fears in middle childhood among rural and urban boys and girls. *Journal of Genetic Psychology, 150,* 51–58.

Diala, C. C., & Muntaner, C. (2003). Mood and anxiety disorders among, rural, urban, and metropolitan residents in the United States. *Community Mental Health Journal, 39,* 239–252.

Donnermeyer, J. F., & Park, D. S. (1995). Alcohol use among rural adolescents: Predictive and situational factors. *International Journal of the Addictions, 30,* 459–479.

Eggebeen, D. J., & Lichter, D. T. (2009). Health and well-being among rural Americans: Variations across the life course. *Journal of Rural Health, 9,* 86–98.

Evans, G. W., Bullinger, M., & Hygge, S. (1998). Chronic noise exposure and physiological response: A prospective study of children living under environmental stress. *Psychological Science, 9,* 75–77.

Evans, G. W., & English, K. (2002). The environment of poverty: Multiple stressor exposure, psychophysiological stress, and socioemotional adjustment. *Child Development, 73,* 1238–1248.

Evans, G. W., Lepore, S. J., Shejwal, B., & Palsane, M. N. (1998). Chronic residential crowding and children's well-being: An ecological perspective. *Child Development, 69,* 1514–1523.

Fields, J. (2003). *Children's living arrangements: March 2002.* Current Population Reports, P20–547. U. S. Census Bureau, Washington, DC.

Fitzpatrick, K. M (1993). Exposure to violence and presence of depression among low-income, African American youth. *Journal of Clinical & Consulting Psychology, 61,* 528–531.

Florsheim, P., Tolan, P., & Gorman-Smith, D. (1998). Family relationships, parenting practices, and the availability of male family members, and the behavior of inner-city boys in single-mother and two-parent families. *Child Development, 69,* 1437–1447.

Ford, D. H., & Lerner, R. M. (1992). *Developmental systems theory, an integrative approach.* Newbury Park, CA: Sage.

Funk, L. M., Allan, D. E., & Chappell, N. L. (2007). Testing the relationship between involvement and perceived neighborhood safety. *Environment & Behavior, 39,* 332–351.

Geronimus, A. T., Bound, J., Colen, C G., Ingber, L. B., & Shocket, T. (2004). Urban/rural differences in excess mortality among high poverty populations: Evidence from the Harlem Health Survey and Pitt County Hypertension Study. ERIU Working Paper 44. Available online at www.umich.edu/ eriu/pdf/wp44.pdf.

Gfroerer, J. C., Larson, S. L., & Colliver, J. D. (2007). Drug use patterns and trends in rural communities. *The Journal of Rural Health, 23* (Supplement 10–5).

Gorman-Smith, D., Henry, D. B., & Tolan, P. H. (2004). Exposure to community violence and violence perpetration: The protective effect of family functioning. *Journal of Clinical Child & Adolescent Psychology, 33,* 439–449.

Gorman, Smith, D., & Tolan, P. (1998). The role of exposure to community violence and developmental problems among inner-city youth. *Developmental Psychopathology, 10,* 101–116.

Haley, M., Harder, C., & Lea, A. (2008). *A new lens for understanding rural-urban integration.* North Carolina Dept. of Commerce, Division of Policy, Research and Strategic Planning. Retrieved July 11, 2008.

Harrison, G., Fouskakis, D., Rasmussen, R., Tynelius, P., Sipos, A., & Gunnell, D. (2003). Association between psychotic disorder and urban place of birth is not mediated by obstetric complications or childhood socioeconomic status: A cohort study. *Psychological Medicine, 33,* 723–731,

Hartig, T., Mang, M., & Evans, G. W. (1991). Restorative effects of natural environment experience. *Environment & Behavior, 23,* 3–26.

Hartley, D., Bird, D., & Dempsey, P. (1999). Rural mental health and substance abuse. In T. C. Ricketts III (Ed.), *Rural health in the United States,* pp. 159–178. New York: Oxford University Press.

Imig, D. R. (1983). Urban and rural families: A comparative study of the impact of stress on family interaction. *Rural Education, 1,* 43–46.

Ingram, G., Wills, A., Carrol, B., & Townsend, F. (2006). *How public-private partnerships can advance education for all.* Washington, DC: Education Policy Data Center, U.S.

Agency for International Development. Available on at http://www.epdc.org/static/UntappedOpportunity.pdf.

Ismailov, R., & Leatherdale, S. (2010). Rural-urban differences in overweight and obesity among a large sample of adolescents in Ontario. *International Journal of Pediatric Obesity*, 5, 351–360.

Jiang, X., Li, D., Boyce, W., & Pickett, W. (2008). Alcohol consumption and injury among Canadian adolescents: Variations by urban-rural geographic status. *Journal of Rural Health*, 24, 143–147.

Kawachi, I., & Berkman, L. (2001). Social ties and mental health. *Journal of Urban Health: Bulletin of the New York Academy of Medicine*, 78, 458–467.

Kenny, D., & Schreiner, I. (2009). Predictors of high-risk alcohol consumption in young offenders on community orders: Policy and treatment implications. *Psychology, Public Policy & Law*, 15, 54–79.

Kim, J., & Kaplan, R. (2004). Physical and psychological factors in sense of community. *Environment & Behavior*, 36, 313–340.

Kiser, L. J., & Black, M. M. (2005). Family process in the midst of urban poverty: What does the trauma literature tell us? *Aggression & Violent Behavior*, 10, 715–730.

Kmet, L., & Macarthur, C. (2006). Urban-rural differences in motor vehicle crash fatality and hospitalization rates among children and youth. *Accident Analysis & Prevention*, 38, 122–127.

Kovess-Masfety, V., Alonso, J., de Graff, R., & Demyttenaere, K. (2005). A European approach to rural-urban differences in mental health: The ESEMeD 2000 comparative study. *Canadian Journal of Psychiatry*, 50, 926–936.

Krenichyn, K., Saegert, S., & Evans, G. W. (2001). Parents as moderators of psychological and physiological correlates of inner-city children's exposure to violence. *Journal of Applied Developmental Psychology*, 22, 581–602.

Kuo, F. E., Bacaicoa, M., & Sullivan, W. C. (1998). Transforming inner-city landscapes. *Environment & Behavior*, 30, 28–59.

Kuo, F. E., & Sullivan, E. C. (2001). Environment and crime in the inner city: Does vegetation reduce crime? *Environment & Behavior*, 33, 343–355.

Kweon, B-S., Sullivan, W. C., & Wiley, A. R. (1998). Green common spaces and the social integration of inner-city older adults. *Environment & Behavior*, 30, 832–858.

Locher, J. L., Ritchie, C. S., Roth, D. L., Baker, P. S., Bodner, E. V., & ALlman, R. M. (2005). Social isolation, support, and capital and nutrition risk in an older sample: Ethnic and gender differences. *Social Science & Medicine*, 60, 747–761.

Long, K. A. (1993). The concept of health. *Rural Nursing*, 28, 123–130.

Macpherson, A. K., To, T. M., Parkin, P. C., Moldofsky, B., Wright, J. G., Chipman, M. L., & Macarthur, C. (2003). Urban/rural variation in children's bicycle-related injuries. *Accident Analysis & Prevention*, 36, 649–654.

Mainous, A. G., & Kohrs, F. P. (1995). A comparison of health status between rural and urban adults. *Journal of Community Health*, 20, 423–431.

Marsella, A. J. (1998). Urbanization, mental health, and social deviancy: A review of issues and research. *American Psychologist*, 53, 624–634.

Martino, S. C., Ellickson, P. L., & McCaffrey, D. R. (2008). Developmental trajectories of substance use from early to late adolescence: A comparison of rural and urban youth. *Journal of Studies on Alcohol and Drugs*, 69, 43–440.

Mauther, N., McKee, L., & Strell, M. (2001). *Work and family life in rural communities*. York, UK: Joseph Rountree Foundation.

Middleton, N., Gunnell, D., Frankel, S., Whitley, E., & Dorling, D. (2003). Urban-rural differences in suicide trends in young adults: England and Wales, 1981–1998. *Social Science & Medicine*, 57, 1183–1194.

Middleton, N., Sterne, J. A., & Gunnell, D. (2006). The geography of despair among 15–44-year-old men in England and Wales: Putting suicide on the map. *Journal of Epidemiology & Community Health*, 60, 1040.

Milroy, C. A., Borja, P. C., Barros, F. R., & Barreto, M. L. (2001). Evaluating quality and classifying urban sectors according to environmental conditions. *Environment & Urbanization*, 13, 235–255.

Morgan, A. (2002). A national call to action: CDC's 2001 urban and rural chartbook. *Journal of Rural Health*, 18, 382–383.

Nairn K., Panelli, R., & McCormack, J. (2003). Destabilizing dualisms, Young people's experiences of rural and urban environments. *Childhood*, 10, 9–42.

Nation, M., Fortney, T., & Wandersman, A. (2010). Race, place, and neighboring: Social ties among neighbors in urban, suburban, and rural contexts. *Environment and Behavior*, 42, 581–596.

National Council for Education Statistics (2007). *Status of education in rural America* (NCES 2007040). Washington, DC.

Nelson, M. C., Gordon-Larsen, P., Song, Y., & Popkin, B. M. (2006). Built and social environments associations with adolescent overweight and activity. *American Journal of Preventive Medicine, 31,* 109–117.

Oliver, L. N. & Hayes, M. V. (2008). Effects of neighbourhood income on reported body mass index: an eight year longitudinal study of Canadian children. *BMC Public Health, 8,* 16.

Ormond, B. A., Zuckerman, S., & Lhila, A. (2000). *Rural/urban differences in health care are not uniform across states.* Washington, DC: Urban Institute, No. B-11. Available online at www. urban.org/publications/309533.html.

Outley, C. W., & Floyd, M. F. (2002). The home they live in: Inner city children's views on the influence of parenting strategies on their leisure behavior. *Leisure Science, 24,* 161–179.

Peen, J., & Dekker, J. (2004). Is urbanicity an environmental risk-factor for psychiatric disorders? *The Lancet, 363,* 2012–2013.

Peen, J., Dekker, J., Schoevers, R. A., Have M. T., de Graaf, R., & Beekman, A. T. (2007). Is the prevalence of psychiatric disorders associated with urbanization? *Social Psychiatry and Psychiatric Epidemiology, 42,* 984–989.

Pinderhughes, E. E., Nix, R., Foster, E. M., Jones, D., & the Conduct Problem Research Group. (2001). Parenting in context: Impact of neighborhood poverty, residential stability, public services, social networks, and danger on parental behaviors. *Journal of Marriage & Family, 63,* 941–953.

Pruss, A., Kay, D., Fewtrell, L., & Bartram, J. (2002). Estimating the burden of disease from water, sanitation, and hygiene at a global level. *Environmental Health Perspectives, 110,* 537–542.

Reilly, B., & AL-SamarraI, S. (2000). Urban and rural differences in primary school attendance: An empirical study for Tanzania. *Journal of African Economies, 9,* 232–244.

Reisig, M. D., & Cancino, J. M. (2004). Incivilities in nonmetropolitan communities: The effects of structural constraints, social conditions, and crime. *Journal of Criminal Justice, 32,* 15–29.

Richards, M. H., Miller, R. V., O'Donnell, P. C., Wasserman, M. S., & Colder, C. (2004). Parental monitoring mediates the effect of age and sex on problem behavior among African American urban young adolescents. *Journal of Youth & Adolescence, 33,* 221–233.

Rountree, P. W., & Clayton, R. R. (1999). A contextual model of adolescent alcohol use across the rural-urban continuum. *Substance Use & Misuse, 34,* 495–520.

Russell, S., & Elder, G. H. (1997). Academic success in rural America: Family background and community integration. *Childhood, 4,* 169–181.

Sander, W. (2006). Educational attainment and residential location. *Education & Urban Society, 38,* 307–326.

Scheer, S. D., Borden, L. M., & Donnermeyer, J. F. (2000). The relationship between family factors and adolescent substance use in rural, suburban, and urban settings. *Journal of Child & Family Studies, 9,* 105–115.

Schwab-Stone, M. E., Ayers, T. S., Dasprow, W., Voyce, C., Barone, C., Shriver, T., & Weissberg, R. P. (1995). No safe haven: A study of community violence exposure in an urban community. *Journal of the American Academy of Child & Adolescent Psychiatry, 34,* 1343–1352.

Seeman, T. E. (1996). Social ties and health: The benefits of social integration. *Annals of Epidemiology, 6,* 442–451.

Simons, R. L., Johnson, C., Conger, R. D., & Lorenz, R. O. (1997). Linking community context to quality of parenting: A study of rural families. *Rural Sociology, 62,* 207–23.

Skinner, A. C., & Slifkin, R. T. (2007). Rural/urban differences in barriers to and burden of care for children with special health care needs. *Journal of Rural Health, 23,* 150–157,

Slifkin, R., Goldsmith, L., & Ricketts, T. (2000). Race and place: Urban-rural differences in health for racial and ethnic minorities. *NC RHRP Working Paper Series,* No. 66.

Smith, K. (2006). *Rural families choose home-based child care for the preschool-aged children.* Durham: Carsey Institute, University of New Hampshire. Policy Brief No 3.

Sullivan, W. C. (2004). The fruit of urban nature. *Environment & Behavior, 36,* 678–700.

Taylor, A. F., Wiley, A., Kuo, F. E., & Sullivan, W. C. (1998). Growing up in the inner city: Green spaces as places to grow. *Environment & Behavior, 30,* 3–27.

Taylor, R. (2005). Where and how does place matter in Pennsylvania? Available online at mpip. temple.edu/mpip/attitudes.html.

Thompson, J., Porras, I. T., Wood, E., Tumwine, J. K., Mujwahuzi, M. R., & Katui-Katua, M. (2000). Waiting at the tap: Changes in urban water use in East Africa over three decades. *Environment & Urbanization, 12,* 37–52.

Tiesman H., Zwerling C., Peek-Asa C., Sprince N., & Cavanaugh J. E. (2007). Non-fatal injuries among urban and rural residents: the National Health Interview Survey, 1997–2001. *Injury Prevention, 13,* 115–119.

Tigges, L. M., Browne, I., & Green, G. P. (1998). Social isolation of the urban poor: Race, class, and neighborhood effects on social resources. *Sociological Quarterly, 39,* 53–77.

U.S. Census Bureau. (2008). *Who's minding the kids? Child care arrangements: Spring 2005.* Washington, DC.

U.S. Department of Agriculture, Economic Research Service. (2003). Measuring rurality, New definitions in 2003. Available online at www.ers.usda.gov/briefing/rurality/NewDefinitions.

U.S. Department of Commerce, U.S. Census Bureau (2011). *Population distribution and change 2000 to 2010. Census 2010 Brief (C2010BR–01).* Available online at www.census.gov/population/www/cen2010/briefs.html.

Vazsonyi, A. T., Pickering, L. E., & Bolland, J. M. (2006). Growing up in a dangerous developmental milieu: The effects of parenting processes on adjustment in inner-city African American adolescents. *Journal of Community Psychology, 34,* 47–73.

Wake, M. (2007). The urban/rural divide in head and neck cancer – the effect of atmospheric pollution. *Clinical Otolaryngology & Allied Sciences, 18,* 298–302.

Wasserman, G. A., Miller, L S., Pinner, E., & Jaramillo, B. (1996). Parenting predictors of early conduct problems in urban-high-risk boys. *Journal of the American Academy of Child & Adolescent Psychiatry, 35,* 1227–1235.

Weber, B., Jensen, L., Miller, K., Mosley, J., & Fisher, M. (2005). A critical review of rural poverty literature: Is there truly a rural effect? *Discussion Paper No. 1309–05.* Institute for Research on Poverty, University of Wisconsin, Madison, WI. Available online at www.irp.wisc.edu.

Wells, N. M. (2000). At home with nature. *Environment & Behavior, 32,* 775–795.

Wells, N. M., & Evans, G. W. (2003). Nearby nature. *Environment & Behavior, 35,* 311–330.

WHO (1995). *The world health report 1995: Bridging the gap.* Geneva, Switzerland: World Health Organization

Wilcox, S., Castro, C., King, A. C., Housemann, R., & Brownson, R. C. (2000). Determinants of leisure time physical activity in rural compared with urban older and ethnically diverse women in the United States. *Journal of Epidemiology and Community Health, 54,* 667–672.

Wilson, G., & Baldassare, M. (1996). Overall "sense of community" in a suburban region. *Environment & Behavior, 28,* 27–43.

Wong, G. W., & Chow, C. M. (2008). Childhood asthma epidemiology: insights from comparative studies of rural and urban populations. *Pediatric Pulmonology, 43,* 107–116,

WW Kellogg Foundation. (2003). *Perceptions of America.* Available online at www.wkkf.org/pubs/FoodRur/pub2973.pdf.

Ziembroski, J. S., & Breiding, M. J. (2006). The cumulative effect of rural and regional residence on older adults. *Journal of Aging & Health, 18,* 631–659.

CHAPTER 17

Poverty

Current Research and New Directions

Stephanie M. Jones, Monica Yudron, Aelesia Pisciella, and Hadas Eidelman

Young children just entering school from the lowest quintile of family income score at about the 30th percentile of their cohort's academic achievement; while those from the top quintile of income enter school scoring at about the 70th percentile. Disadvantages arise early in life, and poorer children do not arrive at the school door as prepared for academic learning.

(Phillips & Whitebook, 2007, p. 1)

It is clear from a decade of research on the influence of environments on children's development that child and family poverty has a discernable and significant impact not only on children's cognitive development and their achievement in school, but also on their social and behavioral skills and their mental health (e.g., Aber, Jones, & Cohen, 2000; Duncan & Brooks-Gunn, 2000; Luthar, 1999; McLeod & Shanahan, 1993; 1996; McLoyd, 1998). Moreover, the few studies that have been conducted with children below the age of 6 suggest that economic conditions and associated risks are particularly strong determinants

of children's developmental paths during childhood (Brooks-Gunn & Duncan, 1997; Duncan & Brooks-Gunn, 2000; Guo, 1998). This should not surprise us, as children in poverty are more likely to be exposed to multiple ecological risks such as residential instability, higher levels of neighborhood and family violence, greater psychological distress among adult caregivers, and a range of other "cofactors" that appear to place their development in jeopardy (Brooks-Gunn, Duncan, & Aber, 1997; Linver, Brooks-Gunn, & Kohen, 2002). Despite the now-vast literature underscoring the links between poverty and its cofactors and child and family functioning, we have made comparatively little progress in effecting change: in both reducing the prevalence of poverty and in mitigating its direct impact on children and families.

In our view, the challenge for the field and the most promising new directions emerging from it involve the movement from individually focused theories, measures, and intervention strategies to environmentally focused, place-based orientations, conceptualizations, and prevention/intervention strategies. In this chapter we describe a set of new directions in our understanding of how poverty and poverty-related individual and environmental risks influence children and families by summarizing work in three areas: (1) definitions of poverty and of the environment, (2) new and emerging multidiscipline research on the links between poverty and child and family outcomes with an emphasis on mechanisms, and (3) innovations in prevention and intervention efforts both to change poverty itself and to interrupt the links between poverty and poor child and family outcomes.

Definitions of Poverty and of the Environment

Despite our current knowledge of the pernicious and multiple negative impacts of poverty on children and families (e.g., Aber, Jones & Cohen, 2000; Gershoff, Aber & Raver, 2002; McLoyd 1990, 1998), poverty as a construct remains difficult to define. Indeed, various definitions of poverty have been used in both research studies and public policy analysis over the last several decades. We begin this section with a short review of how poverty is typically operationalized in research.

Income Poverty

The measurement of income poverty in the United States is based upon an absolute measure, the federal poverty threshold (FPT), developed in 1963 by the Department of Agriculture. The FPT roughly determines "poverty" to be any level of sustenance below the cost of the Department of Agriculture's economy food plan times a factor of 3, with the economy food plan representing the least expensive budget a household could devote to food and still receive adequate nutrition (Orshansky, 1963). Thresholds are adjusted annually in concurrence with the Consumer Price Index (Fisher, 1997). For the year 2002, the federal poverty guidelines (a simplification of the FPT used for administrative purposes, such as determining

assistance eligibility) defined the poverty line for a family of four at the income level of $18,100 (DHHS, 2002).

Although this definition of poverty is employed in scores of settings, its limitations have been well documented. For example, since its development, it has not been adjusted for change in the proportion of total income devoted to food expenditures. Moreover, adjustments are not made for real differences in the cost of living in different geographic areas, and the standard definition ignores the increasing tax burden experienced by many lower-income families (Edin & Lein, 1997; Citro & Michael, 1995). Using a fixed-ratio definition does not allow other material costs to rise more rapidly than food (e.g., housing costs); nor does it account for other basic necessities such as transportation and child care. In addition, the FPT operates at an individual or family level and therefore cannot address larger contributing factors such as regional unemployment, job loss, or broader economic downturn (Aber et al., 2000; Gershoff et al., 2002).

It is broadly understood that the negative impact of poverty is not limited to those children living below 100 percent of the federal poverty threshold. Empirical studies document that living near the poverty threshold (variously defined as income between 100 and 185 percent or income below 200 percent of the federal poverty line) has also been linked to poor outcomes for children (Bolger, Patterson, Thompson & Kupersmidt, 1995; Bradley & Whiteside-Mansell, 1997; Duncan, Brooks-Gunn, Yeung, & Smith, 1998; Hernandez & Myers, 1993; Gilman & Collins, 2000). Thus, any estimates of poverty's impact that fail to include children living near the poverty threshold are likely to underestimate the scope of the problem grossly.

The practice of research suggests that measures of family income and socioeconomic status (typically an index of parental education, occupation, and income) may be adequate proxies for poverty in studies that are not specifically interested in understanding and identifying strategies for intervention (Aber, Jones & Raver, 2007; Gershoff,

Raver, Aber & Lennon, 2007; Nelson & Sheridan, 2011). For those who intend to examine poverty and its consequences as a first step toward designing and evaluating interventions to offset its impacts or reduce its prevalence, a more complex, multiply determined operationalization is necessary.

Despite its traditional view of poverty as a static, monolithic phenomenon, we know *poverty* reflects a complex set of interacting and dynamic characteristics that are present at multiple levels of an individual's ecology. Poverty is not just a matter of insufficient income, or relatively low income, but rather a state defined by the interaction of income status and the sum total of ecological, social, and biological risks present in an individual or family context. While definitions of poverty abound, few go beyond measures of income or material wealth (or its absence) to construct a definition that echoes the complex and varied nature of the contexts that truly define poverty. For example, a simple income-only definition of poverty ignores how varied child outcomes can be among children in any income band. Outcomes vary widely because income only potentiates the contexts in which the child is raised, increasing the probability of being exposed to additional risks such as income drops. It is these risks and the risk saturation of the ecological contexts in which the child is raised that most likely underlie the causal pathways through which low family income results in poor child outcomes. It is the interaction of family income with environment that may serve as a more accurate and predictive operationalization of poverty.

Poverty and Cooccurring Environmental Risk

A considerable amount of research has described the cooccurrence of poverty and multiple familial and ecological risk factors, such as teen and single parenthood, negative life events, violence exposure, marital distress, and parent psychopathology (e.g., Aber et al., 1999; Brooks-Gunn, Klebanov & Liaw, 1995; Luthar, 1999; McLeod & Kessler, 1990; Sameroff, Bartko, Baldwin,

Baldwin & Seifer, 1998). Some have argued that poverty's deleterious impact on child development may be due in part to exposure to these family and ecological risks, which, both individually and in combination, have been associated with negative outcomes for children and youth (e.g., Sameroff et al., 1998). For example, for children living in poverty, family factors including maternal psychological distress, such as high depression and anxiety (McLeod & Shanahan, 1993; McLoyd, Jayaratne, Ceballo & Borquez, 1994; McLoyd & Wilson, 1990, Sameroff & Chandler, 1975); low external resources in terms of social networks and the support they provide (Leventhal & Brooks-Gunn, 2003; Hashima & Amato, 1994; Jackson, 2000); and high negative life events and other demographic risks (Ackerman, Kogos, Youngstrom, Schoff & Izard, 1999; Ackerman, Schoff, Levinson, Youngstrom & Izard, 1999; Burchinal, Roberts, Hooper & Zeisel, 2000; Sameroff et al., 1998) have all been associated with poor child outcomes. Bradley and Whiteside-Mansell (1997) have referred to these collective factors as "poverty cofactors." The authors call our attention to the methodological and analytical complexity underpinning the relationships among poverty, its cofactors, and child development. For example, any particular outcome may be driven by poverty, a specific cofactor, a combination of the two, or a third variable that influences all three.

More recently, psychological research has begun to identify measures of socioeconomic status that assess psychological aspects of poverty, rather than relying solely on external or distal conceptualizations of poverty. Social exclusion refers to the degree to which poor children and families are excluded from situations and activities that are considered to be a normal or desirable part of life (Aber, Jones & Raver, 2007). Roosa and colleagues (2005), building on the work of Aber, Gershoff, and Brooks-Gunn (2002), propose social exclusion as an alternative specification of relative poverty (relative poverty is determined contextually and is contingent upon the assessment of the income of a particular population relative to other populations in the society), which captures the degree to which people are unable to participate in activities and events accessible to those of moderate and high income. The authors acknowledge that the problematic nature of this definition rests in its vagueness; it rests on the sociopolitical context in which the family is living, which may vary over time within a given country or across nations within a given time and may differ from region to region of a specific country in any given time. Operationalizing this concept in a study of poverty may mean taking on the challenge of normalizing the measure for each population studied, with the potential resulting benefit of a more precise representation of a key social mechanism through which low-income children experience different environments. Bask (2010), when studying immigrants within Sweden, considers a person to be socially excluded if "he or she suffers from at least two of the following six welfare problems: chronic unemployment, economic problems, health problems, experiences of threat or violence, crowded housing and lack of interpersonal relationships" (p. 1).

To move toward a conceptualization of poverty as environmental we need new tools that will enable us to reflect the multifaceted, fluid, and dynamic nature of poverty and it's ecological cofactors, which are themselves dynamic (e.g., family mobility, job instability) and multilevel (e.g., the safety of neighborhoods and the kinds of resources and services available in local communities). Operationalizing poverty in multiple manners, at both proximal and distal contextual levels and within and across time, allows poverty to be considered as a pervasive life experience that exists and influences children and families in multiple ways and at multiple levels of their own ecologies. As such, developmental contextual models (e.g., Bronfenbrenner, 1979; Cicchetti & Aber, 1998), which recognize and incorporate the importance of contextual effects for both healthy and psychopathological development, are particularly useful for poverty researchers. Such an ecological approach allows for the identification of multiple contexts important to development and can encompass both objective and subjective dimensions (Aber et al., 2000; Bronfenbrenner & Morris, 1998; Cicchetti & Rogosh, 2002; Jessor, 1993).

While various disciplines are focused on understanding poverty's impact on children and families, a lack of consensus still exists concerning what constitutes poverty or rather what threshold of environmental risk truly constitutes the poverty state versus nonpoverty. Nevertheless, there seems to be some convergence in academic inquiry across fields into how income interacts with various aspects of an individual's or family's environment to alter outcomes.

New and Emerging Multidiscipline Research on the Effects of Poverty

Because there is a point at which financial resources are inadequate to protect a family from external stressors and are insufficient to provide access to social, cultural, and other important physical resources that might help buffer the impacts of harmful and/or stressful life events, income is an important indicator of poverty. Nevertheless, as noted earlier, poverty impacts human welfare and particularly child development through its impact on the contexts in which the family lives. As we broaden the way in which we conceptualize poverty, it is imperative that we also benefit from the breadth of work currently being conducted across fields that targets one or several aspects of this new conceptualization of poverty. Already, there is some convergence in the view that environments or contexts have profound impacts on individual outcomes. Main findings across disciplines indicate that the timing and persistence of a child's experience in the kinds of high-risk environments common for low-income families matter a great deal.

In the following section we summarize the current state of the evidence emerging from the basic sciences (e.g., neuroscience), psychology, sociology, and economics. For the social sciences, in addition to considering new substantive findings, we consider how innovative data analytic techniques allow us to fit observational and experimental data with models that more closely approximate environmental composition as well as allow us to test hypotheses about causal mechanisms.

Basic Sciences

In the last two decades, biological fields of inquiry have made great strides in uncovering the structural and biochemical impact of adversity throughout the life course. First with animal models such as rat and nonhuman primates and then with humans, specialists in various biology fields have begun to uncover the causal pathways through which severe adversity such as physical and sexual abuse and exposure to chronic stress impact brain development throughout the life course.

After conception, a cascade of events is begun in the embryo (then fetus) that, while largely governed in the beginning by genetics, is highly sensitive to the environment in which the individual is developing. This sensitivity plays out in a number of ways with both short- and long-term impacts. Characteristics of the environment impact child development for a number of reasons, which ultimately are centered in the nature of development itself such that an individual's skills and abilities are potentiated by nature (the unique genetic and biochemical composition of the individual) but determined by the interaction of nature with the specific contextual characteristics of the environment into which the individual is born and continues to develop throughout the life course (Fox & Sheridan, in press; Sameroff, 2010). As noted earlier, a person's environment includes relational, psychosocial, and physical contexts. Poverty impacts development to the degree to which it alters these contexts. For example, adversity that influences the language experiences of a child in the first years of life influences the way that neurons are pruned in key language centers of the developing brain and may alter the language trajectory of the child in ways that are more difficult to change later

in life (Fox, Levitt, & Nelson, 2010). And because brains are built over time, environmental deprivation associated with poverty and, more important, chronic stress associated with living in the high-risk contexts most commonly associated with poverty act to shape development throughout the life course. A specific finding around which there is agreement: Children exposed to adverse experiences such as abuse have increased stress reactivity and higher and more sustained levels of stress hormones such as glucocorticoides than their peers. This exposure impacts learning, memory, immunity, and more (Danese et al., 2009; Lupien, McEwan, Gunnar & Heim 2009; Shonkoff, Boyce & McEwen, 2009). More controversial, but an important consideration in the context of poverty research, is the finding that social threat, the feeling of being inferior, may also bring about these same conditions, particularly if this feeling of social threat is chronic and permeates a child's social experience (Fox & Sheridan, in press). While there is not yet agreement around what constitutes chronic stress (that is, there is little agreement around what constitutes the lower bound of this term), chronic stress experienced in early life – the kind of stress that may be experienced by a child living in an unstable environment where parents or other caregivers are unable to provide critical buffering against other environmental stressors such as a dangerous or chaotic neighborhood – leads to alterations in parts of the brain associated with memory and learning (the hippocampus) and complex cognitive functions (the prefrontal cortext) (Fox, Levitt, & Nelson, 2010). Children who experience chronic stress in childhood are also at elevated risk for a number of health issues that manifest later in life such as cardiovascular disease and depression (Danese, et al., 2009). In addition, evidence of these effects may not be noticeable until later in life (Fox & Sheridan, in press; Shonkoff, Boyce & McEwen, 2009). Essentially, neuroscience is providing insight into some of the causal mechanisms underlying disparities due to poverty that arise. This evidence points directly to environmental effects and the importance of how poverty alters the environment and the nature of the experiences children in poverty have.

Overall basic science research has made great strides in uncovering how early adversity and long-term exposure to stress – both of which are salient characteristics of contexts of poverty – alter developmental trajectories and put normative development at risk. At the same time as basic science is raising alarms at the severity of the danger of doing nothing in the face of the heightened risks associated with childhood poverty, evidence is also accumulating that intervention even after the early stages of life have passed is possible. The rallying call for continued efforts at intervention in childhood and beyond is supported by the notion that the human brain remains plastic – malleable throughout the life course – and though larger and more consistent inputs are needed the older the person, change is possible. Propensity toward disease can be reduced, and learning difficulties and regulatory delays can be offset with carefully targeted interventions for the vast majority of children who experience adversity early in life (Fox, Lupien, Levitt, 2010; Nelson & Sheridan, 2011; National Scientific Council on the Developing Child, 2010).

Psychology, Sociology, Economics

The social sciences have always struggled with conceptualizing poverty. Recently, social scientists have begun working across disciplines to refine and standardize the manner in which poverty is investigated. Beyond simple definitions of poverty as income or socioeconomic status (SES), new measures include material hardship, food insecurity, housing instability, and others (e.g., Gershoff, Raver, Aber & Lennon, 2007). Most innovative is the increasing use of geographical information systems (GIS) technologies to understand and model specific environmental characteristics of the physical world in which families live such as frequency and seriousness of violent crime in the neighborhood; access to key resources within the community such as parks, police stations, grocery stores, and health clinics; stability of residency in neighborhood; neighborhood poverty rate; and access to public transportation. While many of these resources do not play an important role in the lives of children until adolescence, for the parents or other adult caregivers, these characteristics define the world in which they live and are key ingredients in the nature and degree of the stressors in their lives. And as a child's development is really nested in the context of the caregiver's well-being, these elements of the broader environment are important to determining the risk of exposure to chronic stress the child has.

SOCIOLOGY

While time poverty and social exclusion are concepts largely used in Europe to describe ways in which poverty disrupts the broader psychosocial context in which children and families live, they are not commonly used in by researchers in the United States. Recent studies looking at the impact of poverty on very specific domains of child development use measures that approximate these measures. Time poverty refers to the fact that, particularly among working poor families, time is a limited resource that is generally invested in income-generating activities at the expense of time spent with children. Time poverty, particularly when school-age and younger children are involved, impacts key developmental processes such as language development and self-regulatory skills.

Family structure is a concept linked to the structure of the family in which one originates and the probability that you yourself will end up in a family of a particular structure in the future. Family structure is seen as a key predictor of poverty status, and single-parent or divorced families tend to be thought of as risk factors for children growing up in poverty because of the increased instability of income and housing. Shocks in a single-income family tend to have more immediate and severe impacts because there is no second income earner to step in if hours are cut, salaries slashed, jobs lost, or children all of a sudden need medical attention, for instance (Rowlingston & McKay, 2005; Walker, Crawford & Taylor, 2008; Edin & Kissane, 2010).

ECONOMICS

New methodological techniques, such as regression discontinuity analysis, propensity score analysis, rising prevalence of instrumental variables analysis, neighborhood effects, more than just labor and employment move beyond the simple parental investment models of poverty. Studies of neighborhood effects, such as those made possible by the Moving to Opportunity demonstration, have highlighted some unexpected effects (Edin & Kissane, 2010). The interest is turning from just adult outcomes and relationships of individual characteristics to a deeper investigation of how the setting of the adult – access to employment, policy environment in which the individual is embedded – really matters.

PSYCHOLOGY

The notion of stress as a causal pathway through which poverty impacts child outcomes is becoming common in the social sciences, primarily in psychology. For example, Dearing (2009) highlights the constraints poverty places on the physical and psychosocial environments of children, which, in turn, act to increase a child's exposure to stress and limit exposure to normative stimulation. Family stress models emphasize the impact of stress on parenting.

Innovation in Prevention and Intervention

Some of the most innovative poverty reduction or alleviation interventions are place- or setting-based, seeking to infuse entire communities or settings with resources meant to reduce the prevalence or impact of one or more poverty-related risks. One category of these interventions have elements similar to prior income supplementation interventions in that they deliver additional funds to families who meet certain predetermined criteria. Whereas prior income supplement programs (such as Temporary Assistance for Needy Families (TANF), welfare, and Women, Infants and Children (WIC)) which are linked strictly to earnings of the family system required little of the recipients, current and emerging income supplementation interventions are based on families' fulfilling specific obligations prior to receipt of the cash. One such conditional cash transfer that is quite common in the United States is the provision of child care subsidies to poor mothers who have young children. Even prior to entering the waiting list for a child care subsidy, mothers must prove employment as well as economic need. Brooks (2002) found that these subsidies, while unsuccessful in facilitating a family's move out of poverty, prevented recipient families from remaining very poor. Brooks (2002) argues that this is most likely due to the greater ease with which mothers were able to retain employment and pursue training opportunities, thereby maintaining a steady, albeit meager, income.

Another trend in poverty alleviation and reduction interventions can be seen in conditional cash transfer programs such as Mexico's Oportunidades (called Bolsa Familia or Escola in Brazil and piloted as Opportunity New York in New York City). Not only does this program require families to fulfill certain requirements before receiving income supplementation; it also takes a multisetting approach to curtailing poverty-related disruption. That is, this intervention attempts to alleviate the impacts and prevent the deepening of poverty for families by requiring that existing resources available to poor families such as health care and education are utilized before the family receives the income supplement. Additionally, when the income supplement is delivered, it is the mother who is given control of the funds in an effort of the government not only to increase the probability that the money will be invested in the children but also with the most likely unintended impact of changing the distribution of power in the family. This program sought to increase enrollment and persistence in receiving health care and education for poor children by removing some of the need that families have to place children in income earning positions. There was additional effort made to increase participation in schooling among female children by making the amount of supplementation for girls larger than that received for boys. A recent reauthorization of Oportunidades extended the age through which children are eligible to receive support so that children who remain in school through the end of secundario are able to receive small monthly deposits to a bank account that can later be used to pay for job training or postsecondary education. As a result of participation in Progresa (the forerunner of Oportunidades) or Oportunidades, children of both genders were found to remain in school longer and experience an 8 percent increase in wages earned as adults (Shultz, 2004). Female children, particularly those who were the second or third born, benefited in markedly larger ways.

In Opportunity New York, a pilot program in New York City modeled on Progresa, poor families in five high-poverty neighborhoods were offered income supplements based on a set of criteria similar to those of Progresa/Oportunidades (access to health care services, attendance in school), which were adapted to the particular U.S. context that New York City represents. Adaptations included a requirement that parents attend job training programs. Preliminary findings for Opportunity New York are mixed but skewed toward increases in educational attainment for the program participants compared to the control group (Miller, Riccio, & Smith, 2009; Riccio, Dechausey, Greenberg, Miller, Rucks, & Verma, 2010). In a commentary written in 2009, Aber suspects that the original complexity of the design and the insistence by New York City government to roll out the entire program at once in a short period may have curtailed the kinds of effects visible in the program. Yet, one clear innovation of efforts such as this are their infusion of resources and services into entire settings in which poverty is occurring. In Oportunidades, entire villages are provided with access to resources, changing the broader context in which poor families navigate and conduct their daily lives. In Opportunity New York, the entire neighborhood is given access to the program resources, and although uptake was lower than in Mexico, the intention was to change the communitywide experience of poverty.

Another income supplementation program, microfinance, seeks to ease the burden of poverty by providing poor families, generally those led by single mothers, with small, short-term, low-interest loans meant to be used for job training or other activities and investments that ultimately would help the families transition out of poverty. Studies of such programs in developing countries like Bangladesh have found that female participants are more likely to be self-employed, use health care services, and have more autonomy in family decision making (Mahmud, 2003). Similar programs are in place in several U.S. states such as California, yet little is known about the effects of these programs in increasing income and housing stability or the probability that recipient families make the move out of poverty (Bhatt & Tang, 2002).

As a form of income supplementation, Head Start services have provided poor and near-poor families with subsidized or free child care and education services for more than 40 years. A recent review of the impact of Head Start services reveals that while initial gains are high, they dissipate as a child progresses in public elementary schools (U.S. DHHS, 2010). Likely culprits for the attenuation of these effects are lack of continuity of services across settings in which poor children live as well as a lack of continuity in the quality of educational and care services available to children as they transition from Head Start centers into formal education settings.

Summary and Conclusions

Building upon innovative efforts of current and emerging programs, future interventions seeking to alleviate poverty or buffer the effects of poverty ought to consider the following general guidelines. First, poverty as a contextual or environmental characteristic must be addressed in the setting in which it is occurring, be it a community, neighborhood, or family. At each level, saturation can be achieved only by acknowledging how poverty changes the landscape in which poor families must live. Access to health care facilities, grocery stores, safe outdoor spaces, and opportunities for civic engagement can be provided to entire communities with targeted income supplementation for the poorest families in order to shift the set of probable outcomes toward those normally reserved for middle- to high-income families such as a predictable income that is sufficient for supporting the family, stable and safe housing, and access to high-quality educational opportunities. Second, interventions and prevention programs that address child and family risks with high prevalence among poor families yet still experienced by families of all income levels, such as parental mental health disturbances, social isolation, and substance abuse, ought to be offered universally to alleviate further the stressors of living in poverty. By offering components that are universally beneficial, a broader support base for the targeted portions of the intervention may be accessed. Finally, future interventions must include processes by which poor families and children can become strong and effective advocates for their own needs, thereby assuring that they are able to access and utilize support services beyond the purview of the intervention and for as long as needed regardless of the intervention's length.

References

Aber, J. L., Gershoff, E. T., & Brooks-Gunn, J. (2002). Social exclusion of children in the United States: Identifying potential indicators. In A. J. Kahn & S. B. Kamerman (Eds.), *Beyond child poverty: The social exclusion of children*, pp. 245–286. New York: Columbia University.

Aber, J. L., Jones, S. M., & Cohen, J. (2000). The impact of poverty on the mental health and development of very young children. In C. H. Zeanah (Ed.), *Handbook of infant mental health*, pp. 113–128 (2nd ed.). New York: Guilford.

Aber, J. L., Jones, S. M., & Cohen, J. (2000). The impact of poverty on the mental health and development of very young children. In C. H. Zeanah, Jr. (Ed.), *Handbook of infant mental health*, pp. 113–128 (2nd ed.). New York, NY: Guilford Press.

Aber, L. (2009). Experiments in 21st century anti-poverty policy. *Public Policy Research*, 16(1), 57–63.

Aber, L. Jones, S. M., & Raver, C. C. (2007). Poverty and child development: New perspectives on a defining issue. In L. Aber, D. Phillips, S. M. Jones, and K. McLearn (Eds.) *Child development and social policy: Knowledge for action*, pp. 149–166. Washington, DC: APA Publications.

Ackerman, B. P., Izard, C. E., Schoff, K., et al. (1999). Contextual risk, caregiver emotionality, and the problem behaviors of six- and seven-year-old children from economically disadvantaged families. *Child Development*, 70(6), 1415–1427.

Ackerman, B. P., Kogos, J., Youngstrom, E., Schoff, K., & Izard, C. (1999). Family instability and the problem behaviors of children from economically disadvantaged families. *Developmental Psychology*, 35, 258–268.

Albert, V. (2009). Citizenship status, poverty, and government transfers for families with children. *Journal of Social Service Research*, 35(2), 135–148.

Axford, N. (2009). Developing congruent children's services to improve child well-being. *Child & Family Social Work*, 14(1), 35–44.

Ayoub, C., O'Connor, E., Rappolt-Schlictmann, G., Vallotton, C., Raikes, H., & Chazan-Cohen, R. (2009). Cognitive skill performance among young children living in poverty: Risk, change, and the promotive effects of early head start. *Early Childhood Research Quarterly*, 24(3), 289–305.

Bask, M. (2010). Increasing inequality in social exclusion occurrence: The case of Sweden during 1979–2003. *Social Indicators Research*, 97(3), 299–323.

Bhatt, N., & Tang, S. (2002). Determinants of repayment in microcredit: Evidence from programs in the United States. *International Journal of Urban and Regional Research*, 26, 360–76.

Bradley, R. H., & Whiteside-Mansell, L. (1997). Children in Poverty. In R. T. Ammerman & M. Hersen (Eds.), *Handbook of prevention and treatment with children and adolescents: Intervention in the real world context*, pp. 13–58 Hoboken, NJ: John Wiley & Sons.

Bronfenbrenner, U. (1979). *The ecology of human development: Experiments by nature and design*. Cambridge, MA: Harvard University Press.

Bronfenbrenner, U., & Morris, P. A. (1998). The ecology of developmental process. In W. Damon & R. M. Lerner (Eds.), Handbook of child psychology: Vol. I, *Theoretical models of human development*, pp. 993–1028 (5th ed.). Hoboken, NJ: John Wiley & Sons.

Brooks, F. (2002). Impacts of child care subsidies on family and child well-being. *Early Childhood Research Quarterly*, 17(4), 498–511.

Burchinal, M. R., Roberts, J. E., Hooper, S., & Zeisel, S. A. (2000). Cumulative risk and early cognitive development: A comparison of statistical riskmodels. *Developmental Psychology*, 6, 793–807.

Cicchetti, D., & Aber, J. L. (1998). Contextualism and developmental psychopathology. *Development and Psychopathology*, 10, 137–141.

Cicchetti, D., & Rogosch, F. A. (2002). A developmental psychopathology perspective on adolescence. *Journal of Consulting and Clinical Psychology*, 70, 6–20.

Collins, J. W. J., Wambach, J., David, R. J., & Rankin, K. M. (2009). Women's lifelong exposure to neighborhood poverty and low birth weight: A population-based study. *Maternal & Child Health Journal*, 13(3), 326–333.

Conroy, S., & Marks, M. N. (2003). Maternal psychological vulnerability and early infant care in a sample of materially disadvantaged women. *Journal of Reproductive & Infant Psychology*, 21(1), 5.

Copeland, W., Shanahan, L., Costello, E. J., & Angold, A. (2009). Configurations of common childhood psychosocial risk factors. *Journal of Child Psychology and Psychiatry*, 50(4), 451–459.

Criss, M. M., Shaw, D. S., Moilanen, K. L., Hitchings, J. E., & Ingoldsby, E. M. (2009). Family, neighborhood, and peer characteristics as predictors of child adjustment: A longitudinal analysis of additive and mediation models. *Social Development*, 18(3), 511–535.

Cunha, F., & Heckman, J. (2007). The technology of skill formation. *American Economic Review*, 97(2), 31–47.

Danese, A., Moffitt, T. E., Harrington, H., Milne, B. J., Polanczyk, G., Pariante, C. M. et al. (2009). Adverse childhood experiences and adult risk factors for age-related disease. *Archives of Pediatrics and Adolescent Medicine*, 163(12), 1135–1143.

Dearing, E., McCartney, K., & Taylor, B. A. (2009). Does higher quality early child care promote low-income Children's math and reading achievement in middle childhood? *Child Development*, 80(5), 1329–1349.

Duncan, G. J., & Brooks-Gunn, J. (2000). Family poverty, welfare reform, and child development. *Child Development*, 71(1), 188–196.

Eamon, M. K., Wu, C., & Zhang, S. (2009). Effectiveness and limitations of the earned income tax credit for reducing child poverty in the United States. *Children and Youth Services Review*, 31(8), 919–926.

Edin, K., & Kissane, R. J. (2010). Poverty and the American family: A decade in review. *Journal of Marriage & Family*, 72(3), 460–479.

Evans, G. W. (2004). The environment of childhood poverty. *American Psychologist*, 59(2), 77–92.

Evans, G. W., & Schamberg, M. A. (2009). Childhood poverty, chronic stress, and adult working memory. *PNAS Proceedings of the National Academy of Sciences of the United States of America*, 106(16), 6545–6549.

Fernald, L. C., Gertler, P. J., & Neufeld, L. M. (2009). 10-year effect of Oportunidades, Mexico's conditional cash transfer programme, on child growth, cognition, language, and behaviour: A longitudinal follow-up study. *Lancet*, 374(9706), 1997–2005.

Fox, S. E., Levitt, P., & Nelson, C. a. (2010). How the timing and quality of early experiences influence the development of brain architecture. *Child development*, 81(1), 28–40. doi:10.1111/j.1467-8624.2009.01380.x

Frankel, H., & Frankel, S. (2006). Family therapy, family practice, and child and family poverty: Historical perspectives and recent developments. *Journal of Family Social Work*, 10(4), 43–80.

Gershoff, E. T., Raver, C. C., Aber, J. L., & Lennon, M. C. (2007). Income is not enough: Incorporating material hardship into models of income associations with parenting and child development. *Child Development*, 78(1), 70–95.

Goodson, B. D., Layzer, J. I., St. Pierre, R. G., Bernstein, L. S., & Lopez, M. (2000).

Effectiveness of a comprehensive, five-year family support program for low-income children and their families: Findings from the comprehensive child development program. *Early Childhood Research Quarterly*, 15(1), 5–39.

Greenberg, N., Carr, J. A., & Summers, C. H. (2002). Causes and consequences of stress. *Integrative and Comparative Biology*, 42(3), 508–516.

Hashima, P. Y., & Amato, P. R. (1994). Poverty, social support, and parental behavior. *Child Development*, 65, 394–403.

Jessor, R. (1993). Successful adolescent development among youth in high-risk settings. *American Psychologist*, 48(2), 117–126.

Kishiyama, M. M., Boyce, W. T., Jimenez, A. M., Perry, L. M., & Knight, R. T. (2009). Socioeconomic disparities affect prefrontal function in children. *Journal of Cognitive Neuroscience*, 21(6), 1106–1115.

Leventhal, T., & Brooks-Gunn, J. (2003). *Moving to opportunity: An experimental study of neighborhood effects on mental health.* American Public Health Association.

Lieberman, A., & Merrick, J. (2009). Comorbidity of poverty among adolescents. *International Journal of Child and Adolescent Health*, 2(1), 1–2.

Lupien, S. J., McEwew, B. S., Gunnar, M. R., & Heim, C. (2009). Effects of stress throughout the lifespan on the brain, behavior and cognition. *Nature Reviews Neuroscience*, 10, 434–445.

Luthar, S. S. (1999). Poverty and children's adjustment. Thousand Oaks, CA: Sage.

Mahmud, S. (2003). Actually how empowering is microcredit. *Development and Change*, 34, 577–605.

McAllister, C. L., Thomas, T. L., Wilson, P. C., & Green, B. L. (2009). Root shock revisited: Perspectives of early head start mothers on community and policy environments and their effects on child health, development, and school readiness. *American Journal of Public Health*, 99(2), 205–210.

Merritt, D. H. (2009). Child abuse potential: Correlates with child maltreatment rates and structural measures of neighborhoods. *Children and Youth Services Review*, 31(8), 927–934.

Miller, C., Riccio, J., & Smith, J. (2009). A preliminary look at early educational results of the Opportunity NYC-Family Rewards Program: A research note for funders. Retrieved October 20, 2009, from http://www.mdrc.org/publications/525/overview.html.

Mistry, R. S., Biesanz, J. C., Chien, N., Howes, C., & Benner, A. D. (2008). Socioeconomic status, parental investments, and the cognitive and behavioral outcomes of low-income children from immigrant and native households. *Early Childhood Research Quarterly*, 23(2), 193–212.

Moon, S. S., Hegar, R. L., & Page, J. (2009). TANF status, ethnicity, and early school success. *Children and Youth Services Review*, 31(8), 854–863.

Mrug, S., & Windle, M. (2009). Mediators of neighborhood influences on externalizing behavior in preadolescent children. *Journal of Abnormal Child Psychology: An Official Publication of the International Society for Research in Child and Adolescent Psychopathology*, 37(2), 265–280.

Nelson, C. A., & Sheridan, M. A. (2011). Lessons from neuroscience research for understanding causal links between family and neighborhood characteristics and educational outcomes. In Greg J. Duncan & Richard J. Murnane (Eds.), *Whither Opportunity? Rising Inequality, School, and Children's Life Chances* pp. 27–46. Boston: Russell Sage Foundation.

Philipsen Hetzner, N., Johnson, A. D., & Brooks-Gunn, J. (2010). Poverty, effects of on social and emotional development. In Penelope Peterson, Eva Baker, & Barry McGaw (Eds.), *International encyclopedia of education*, pp. 643–652. Oxford: Elsevier.

Radey, M., & Brewster, K. L. (2007). The influence of race/ethnicity on disadvantaged mothers' child care arrangements. *Early Childhood Research Quarterly*, 22(3), 379–393.

Rappolt-Schlichtmann, G., Willett, J. B., Ayoub, C. C., Lindsley, R., Hulette, A. C., & Fischer, K. W. (2009). Poverty, relationship conflict, and the regulation of cortisol in small and large group contexts at child care. *Mind, Brain, and Education*, 3(3), 131–142.

Raver, C. C., Jones, S. M., Li-Grining, C., Zhai, F., Metzger, M. W., & Solomon, B. (2009). Targeting children's behavior problems in preschool classrooms: A cluster-randomized controlled trial. *Journal of Consulting and Clinical Psychology*, 77(2), 302–316.

Riccio, J., Dechausey, N., Greenberg, D., Miller, C., Rucks, Z., & Verma, N. (2010). *Toward poverty across generations: Early findings from New York City's conditional cash transfer program.* MDRC. New York.

Riley, A. W., Coiro, M. J., Broitman, M., Colantuoni, E., Hurley, K. M., Bandeen-

Roche, K. et al. (2009). Mental health of children of low-income depressed mothers: Influences of parenting, family environment, and raters. *Psychiatric Services*, 60(3), 329–336.

Roosa, M. W., Deng, S., Nair, R. L., & Burrell, G. L. (2005). Measures for studying poverty in family and child research. *Journal of Marriage and Family*, 67(4), 971–988.

Roosa, M. W., Deng, S., Ryu, E., Burrell, G. L., Tein, J., Jones, S. et al. (2005). Family and child characteristics linking neighborhood context and child externalizing behavior. *Journal of Marriage & Family*, 67(2), 515–529.

Rouse, H. L., & Fantuzzo, J. W. (2009). Multiple risks and educational well being: A population-based investigation of threats to early school success. *Early Childhood Research Quarterly*, 24(1), 1–14.

Rowlingston, K., & McKay, S. (2005). Lone motherhood and socio-economic disadvatage: Insights from quantitative and qualitative evidence. *Sociological Review*, 53(2), 30–49.

Sameroff, A. (2010). A Unified Theory of Development: A Dialectic Integration of Nature and Nurture. *Child Development*, 81(1), 6–22.

Sameroff, A. J., Bartko, W. T., Baldwin, A., Baldwin, C., & Seifer, R. (1998). Family and social influences on the development of child competence. In M. Lewis & C. Feiring (Eds.), *Families, risk, and competence*, pp. 161–186. Mahwah, NJ: Erlbaum.

Shonkoff, J. P., Boyce, W. T., & McEwen, B. S. (2009). Neuroscience, molecular biology, and the childhood roots of health disparities. *Journal of the American Medical Association*, 301(21), 2252–2259.

Summers, C. H. (2002). Social interaction over time, implications for stress responsiveness. *Integrative and Comparative Biology*, 42(3), 591–599.

Timberlake, J. M. (2009). Effects of household and neighborhood characteristics on children's exposure to neighborhood poverty and affluence. *Social Science Research*, 38(2), 458–476.

U.S. Department of Health and Human Services, Administration for Children and Families (2010). *Head Start Impact Study: Final report*. Washington, DC.

Walker, J., Crawford, K., & Taylor, F. (2008). Listening to children: Gaining a perspective of the experiences of poverty and social exclusion from children and young people of single-parent families. *Health & Social Care in the Community*, 16(4), 429–436.

Williams Shanks, T. R. (2007). The impacts of household wealth on child development. *Journal of Poverty*, 11(2), 93–116.

Winsler, A., Tran, H., Hartman, S. C., Madigan, A. L., Manfra, L., & Bleiker, C. (2008). School readiness gains made by ethnically diverse children in poverty attending center-based childcare and public school pre-kindergarten programs. *Early Childhood Research Quarterly*, 23(3), 314–329.

CHAPTER 18

Social Networks

Mary J. Levitt

Social networks can be broadly conceptualized as complex relational systems that are primary environmental contexts for human development. Sociologists and anthropologists have long used network analysis to describe social environments, but interest in social networks is a relatively recent trend in developmental psychology, initiated with the publication of seminal papers by Cochran and Brassard (1979), Lewis (Lewis & Feiring, 1979; Lewis, 1982), and Kahn and Antonucci (1980). Research on the development of social networks has continued sporadically over the ensuing decades, accruing a relatively small, but significant body of work on the topic.

The aims for this chapter are threefold: (1) to review existing theory and associated research on the development of social networks, (2) to provide an overview of conceptual and methodological issues in the study of social network development, and (3) to note unique and emerging trends in network research. Each of these topics is addressed in the following sections of the chapter, followed by a brief summary note with suggestions for future research.

I. Theoretical Perspectives and Research on Network Development

The preeminent developmental theory of social relationships has been the Bowlby-Ainsworth attachment theory (Bowlby, 1969/1997; Ainsworth, Blehar, Waters, & Wall, 1978). Bowlby drew on ethology and psychoanalysis in formulating this theory focused initially on the infant's relationship with a primary caregiver. According to Bowlby, early interactions with the caregiver establish within the child a cognitive-affective "working model" of the self in relation to the caregiver, engendering expectations that carry over into subsequent relationships. Ainsworth enriched this theory in two ways, first, by introducing the idea that attachment figures provide the infant with a secure base from which to engage both the social and nonsocial worlds and second, by developing a means to assess individual differences in patterns of attachment, creating a typology of secure and insecure patterns of attachment-related behaviors.

Attachment theory has had powerful heuristic value among developmental psychologists, generating volumes of research findings over the years and spawning attempts to extend the theory to social relationships outside those with caregivers and beyond infancy (Ainsworth, 1989, Antonucci, 1976; Hazan & Shaver, 1987). However, there is now relatively widespread acknowledgement of the limitations of attachment theory as a general developmental theory of social relations (see articles and commentary in a recent special issue of *Human Development* edited by Lewis and Takahashi [2005]). Thus, there is a need to articulate a more encompassing theory to account for the development of relationships with the broader network of figures encountered in the individual's social sphere across the life span.

Theoretical views of social network development offered to date include those of Bryant (1985), Cochran (1990a,b; Cochran & Brassard, 1979), Tietjen (1989, 1994), Furman and Buhrmester (1985, 1992), Hinde and Stevenson-Hinde (1987), Lewis (1982, 2005), Takahashi (1990, 2005), and Kahn and Antonucci (1980; Antonucci, 1986). Following is a brief overview of each of these viewpoints and research on network development generated by these authors. Findings specifically reflecting age-related trends in network development are presented here. Additional research related to these views is cited in later sections.

Bryant: Autonomy and Connectedness

Bryant (1985) conceptualized the social network in terms of resources available in the child's neighborhood that support a balance of social connection and autonomous functioning. She developed a "neighborhood walk" procedure to assess the availability and utilization of sources of support in middle childhood (ages 7 to 10) from the child's perspective, reasoning that children would be best able to identify support resources as they were encountered in a walk around the neighborhood. Potential sources included other persons (in peer, parent, and grandparent generations), pets; intrapersonal resources, such as hobbies or fantasies; and

environmental sources, such as organizations and formal or informal meeting places.

Bryant's (1985) findings were among the first to identify a potential developmental trend, with 10-year-olds perceiving more elaborated sources of support than 7-year-olds and support being related more strongly to socioemotional functioning at age 10 than at age 7. She also affirmed that children could be interviewed reliably about their social networks as young as age 7.

Cochran: The Ecology of Extrafamilial Social Networks

Cochran (Cochran, 1990a,b; Cochran & Brassard, 1979) has offered a perspective on social networks related to Bronfenbrenner's (1986) ecological systems model. Bronfenbrenner described the context of development as a set of inclusive systems. Children interact directly with microsystem influences (parents, peers, schools, etc.), nested within macrosystem influences (parents' jobs, local economies, etc.) that are nested within broader exosystem (culture, global economic forces, etc.) and chronosystem (historical trends in child rearing, etc.) influences. Bronfenbrenner used the term mesosystem to refer to linkages between microsystem settings (e.g., between parents and schools). Cochran (1990a) defines social networks as consisting of relations among people that transcend specific settings.

Whereas most researchers consider immediate family members to be part of children's networks, Cochran and Brassard (1979) conceptualized the social network as "those people outside the household who engage in activities and exchanges of an affective and/or material nature with the members of the immediate family" (p. 601). This network is thought to mediate exosystem influences on the family and to have both direct and indirect (through the parent) influences on the child.

According to Cochran and Brassard (1979), social networks can be characterized in terms of relational, structural, and positional properties. Relational properties include the content (functions) of dyadic relationships within the network (exchange of goods and services, sharing of information, recreation, and emotional support), the degree of intensity and reciprocity in these relationships, and the strength and patterning of relational influences within the network. Structural properties include the size of the network, the interconnectedness of its members, and the diversity of network members (in terms of their personal characteristics and their role in relation to the child). Positional properties include the location of network members in space (their geographic proximity to the family) and the continuity of network members and network characteristics over time. These properties are similar to those specified in other social network models (Kahn & Antonucci, 1980; Lewis, 2005; Marsden, 2005).

Cochran and his colleagues conducted a multisite international investigation of families' social networks (Cochran, Larner, Riley, Gunnarson, & Henderson, 1990), in which mothers reported on their children's social networks by listing adults and children (outside the immediate family) the child "cares about or sees a couple of times a month" and those the child "knows or plays with." Mothers also indicated, for each network member, the activities engaged in with the child. However, the study was focused on assessing network characteristics across differing ecological contexts, rather than on age-related trends in network development.

Tietjen: Social Networks and Cultural Competence

Tietjen (1989, 1994) was also influenced by Bronfenbrenner's ecological framework. In her view, differing sociocultural ecologies lead to networks with diverse forms and functions. The overriding function of the network, according to Tietjen, is to provide support that promotes the development of competence within the individual's culture. An important consideration is the number of roles represented within the network (parents, siblings, extended family, peers, unrelated adults, etc.), as persons in different roles provide different kinds of support,

interact in different ways, and model different activities and skills. Other relevant characteristics include the number of people within each role, the frequency and extent of contact with network members, the longevity of relationships with network members, and their interconnectedness. Content dimensions include esteem, informational, instrumental, and companionship support. According to Tietjen, these network characteristics are likely to be relevant across cultures, but will vary in emphasis within particular cultures. Of most importance developmentally is the match between ecological demands and available support.

Tietjen's empirical work has been focused primarily on personal and ecological influences on children's networks, rather than on developmental trends. In a study of the social networks of 2nd and 3rd grade children in Sweden, based on child interviews, she did find some indication of grade level differences suggesting an age-related move toward closer friendship ties and less family involvement (Tietjen, 1982).

Furman and Buhrmester: Network of Relationships and Social Provisions

In formulating their view of social network development, Furman and Buhrmester, (1985, 1992; Furman, 1989) drew on Sullivan's interpersonal relations theory and Weiss's relational provisions theory. According to Furman and Buhrmester, individuals seek support from members of their social networks in the form of reliable alliance, enhancement of self-worth, instrumental assistance, companionship, affection, and intimacy. Relations with network members may also be characterized in terms of the network member's power relative to the individual, experiences of conflict and satisfaction in the relationship, and the importance of the relationship to the individual.

Furman and Buhrmester (1985) devised the Network of Relationships Inventory (NRI) to assess variations in support provision, power, conflict, satisfaction, and importance across network relations (mothers, fathers, siblings, grandparents, friends, and teachers) from the child's perspective. Furman and Buhrmester (1992) later assessed cross-sectional grade level (fourth, seventh, and tenth, and college) differences on these dimensions, adding nurturance of other and punishment in a revision of the NRI. In this study, parents were the most important sources of support for the younger children. Same sex friends were equal to parents in supportiveness for seventh graders and exceeded parents as support providers for tenth graders. Romantic partners became increasingly important providers across adolescence and were equal in importance to parents and friends by college age. Grade level differences were also reported along the other dimensions of the NRI. In general, the NRI has proven to be a useful measure, with good psychometric properties, for assessing individuals' relations with specific network members.

Hinde and Stevenson-Hinde: Levels of complexity

Hinde and Stevenson-Hinde (1987; Hinde, 1992) have proposed an ethologically based view of social interactions and relationships as successive layers in a multilevel system. A dialectic process operates across levels: Individuals engage in interactions, which create relationships, which constitute social groups and generate social norms; social groups and norms affect relationships, which govern interactions, which affect individuals. Relationships can be characterized along a number of dimensions, ranging from molecular to molar, and including the content of interactions, the diversity of interactions, the qualities of several types of interaction, qualities based on the patterning of interactions, reciprocity versus complementarity, intimacy, interpersonal perception, and commitment.

Empirically, these authors have focused primarily on exploring the individual-relationship interface. Individuals bring certain characteristics to a relationship, some of which are distinctly properties of the individual (e.g., physical characteristics), some of which may vary moderately across relationships (e.g., temperament) and some of which are clearly properties of the relationship (e.g., relationship satisfaction).

Lewis: The Social Matrix

Drawing on general systems theory, Lewis (1982, 2005) proposes that infants are embedded in a social network from birth onward. As the child's network develops, different relational systems emerge relatively independent of one another (rather than stemming from caregiver-infant attachment), because different relations (elements of the system) provide different functions to satisfy different needs and have different evolutionary origins. The system is flexible and adaptive, yet goal-oriented and governed by processes that strive to maintain a steady state while adapting to changing conditions.

Lewis represents the social network graphically as a matrix of relationships, with network members spaced along the vertical axis and network functions along the horizontal axis. Early functions include protection, caregiving, nurturance, play, exploration/learning, and affiliation. Persons and functions, along with the relative importance of specific persons and functions, may change over time. Thus, for example, children may add more peers to their networks and peers may become more important providers of network functions as the child develops.

Different relations within the network affect the child through both direct and indirect interactions in a holistic nonadditive way. Thus, interactions involving the child that include mother, father, and sibling are different in nature than interactions between the child and mother, father, or sibling alone and interactions among network members that do not directly include the child may still affect the child. For example, Lewis (2005) notes that dinner table conversations are associated with children's interactive behavior and IQ scores, even when the children are not directly involved in the conversations. At the same time, because relational domains within the network are relatively independent, a problem in one domain will not necessarily cause problems in another domain. For example, a child might have a poor relationship with a parent, but good relations with peers.

Lewis and Feiring conducted a longitudinal study of changes in the social networks of children who were age 3, 6, or 9 at the beginning of the research, using a combination of maternal and child interviews (Lewis, Feiring, & Kotsonis, 1984; Feiring & Lewis, 1988, 1989, 1991a, 1991b). Children had diverse networks of immediate and extended family, peers and nonrelated adults, even at age 3. Involvement with peers, particularly same sex peers, increased with age while kin contacts declined.

Takahashi: The Affective Relationships Model

Takahashi (1990, 2005) focuses on the network of affectively close relationships satisfying the individual's need for emotional interactions with significant others. Specific needs/functions include proximity, emotional support, reassurance, encouragement/help, sharing information/experience, and giving nurture. Affective networks include multiple persons in a hierarchical structure, with focal figures, who provide more functions, at the top and those who provide fewer functions below. Network members are selected by the individual in the context of cultural expectations related to age and gender.

Takahashi has developed two measures to assess the extent to which persons provide specific functions, one used with children (the Picture Affective Relationships Test [PART]) and the other with adolescents and adults (the Affective Relationships Scale [ARS]). On the basis of her work with these measures, she proposes that networks evolve over the life span through several periods, beginning with the simultaneous emergence of multiple affective relationships in infancy (with mother, father, grandparents, etc.) already differentiated to some extent by function. The second period involves rapid extension of the network in early childhood. The third period, school age, is marked by socialization of affective behaviors within formal organizations, with age mates playing a significant role. The fourth period, adolescence to young adulthood, is characterized by the emergence of an "existential focus" on a primary support figure. Subsequent periods of transformation occur in response to major life transitions or age-related changes in support needs. In general, networks change throughout the life span as individuals encounter more suitable providers, re-evaluate existing figures, or replace figures lost through death, mobility, or other circumstances. However, new experiences are mediated by previous relational experiences, promoting relative stability in network characteristics.

Individual variation in network structure and function is defined in terms of the focal figure(s) at the top of the hierarchy. Takahashi has identified three types of networks, family focused, friend focused, and lone wolf, based on which focal persons provide the most functions. These variations are found across age levels and are seemingly persistent over time. Family focused and friend focused individuals are equally well adjusted and better adjusted than lone wolf types, who receive few provisions and are lacking in a focal figure. However, being family or friend focused may facilitate or inhibit adaptation depending on the context. For example, Takahashi has found that friend focused types adjust more easily across the transition to college (Takahashi, 2005).

Kahn and Antonucci: The Convoy Model

Building on theories of attachment and social roles, Kahn and Antonucci (1980; Antonucci, 1986) proposed a model of social network development across the life span. They adopted the term convoy to capture both the protective function and the dynamic nature of the social network as it moves with the individual through the life cycle. The social convoy is viewed as emerging developmentally from a core of attachment relations in infancy and expanding to include other important relationships as the child engages a broader social milieu.

Attachment relations throughout the life span can be seen as comprising a small, relatively stable, and highly influential subset of convoy relations (Levitt, 1991). The convoy functions optimally to afford the exchange of support in the form of affective support, self-affirmation, and direct aid, although negative aspects of convoy relations (conflict, excessive demands, etc.) are also addressed (Antonucci, Akiyama, & Lansford, 1998; Levitt, Silver, & Franco, 1996). Following the construct of secure attachment, supportive interchanges between social convoy members are viewed as providing a secure base for individual functioning (Antonucci & Jackson, 1987).

Structural and functional properties of the individual's convoy develop through the coaction of personal and situational characteristics, which affect the individual's perceived need for support and capacity to obtain needed support. Convoys change as normative and nonnormative transitions in personal situations and social roles occur over the life span, necessitating the construction of posttransition networks adequate to meeting support needs. Examples of normative transitions leading to convoy change are marriage, when in-law relations may be incorporated into the individual's convoy (Santos & Levitt, 2007) or retirement, when work relations may be lost (Bosse, Aldwin, Levenson, Workman-Daniels, & Ekerdt, 1990). A nonnormative transition known to precipitate convoy change is international migration, when new relationships are formed in the host country and relationships in the country of origin may be disrupted (Levitt, Lane, & Levitt, 2005).

The convoy is defined empirically as consisting of relations that are close and important in the individual's life, conceptualized as a hierarchy of three concentric circles surrounding the individual. Inner circle relations are those to whom the individual feels so close that life cannot be imagined without them. Persons less close, but still important are found in the middle circle and those not as close as the others, but still important in the individual's life occupy the outermost circle. Support for the convoy model

has been found in cross-sectional research and short-term longitudinal studies with adult populations (Antonucci & Akiyama, 1987; Antonucci, Akiyama, & Takahashi, 2004; Bosse et al., 1990; Guiaux, Van Tilburg, & Van Groenou, 2007; Levitt, 1991; Levitt, Weber, & Guacci, 1993; Levitt, Coffman, Guacci-Franco, & Loveless, 1994).

In a study addressing network development in childhood and adolescence, Levitt, Guacci-Franco, and Levitt (1993) measured convoy structure and function in an ethnically diverse cross-sectional sample (age 7, 10, and 14) with a children's convoy mapping procedure based on the adult procedure described by Antonucci (1986). With adults, interviewers write the names of persons nominated by participants in a concentric circle diagram with the participant represented at the center and convoy members distributed hierarchically into the three circles according to their perceived closeness and importance to the participant. Modifications introduced in this study included the use of circular stickers to represent network members and some language simplification. For example, the authors used a standard probe asking for placement of persons according to "closeness and importance," but added "people you really love or like and people who really love or like you." To assess support functions, they asked the children to indicate people "you talk to about things that are important to you," "who make you feel better when something bothers you or you are not sure about something," "who would take care of you if you are sick," "who help you with homework or other work that you do for school," "who like to be with you and do fun things with you," and "who make you feel good about yourself."

Close family members were most likely (but not always) to be found in the inner circle, with extended family and friends in the outer circles. There were age-related differences in convoy composition and function, with most variation found in the outer circles of the convoy. Participants reported larger networks and more support overall at ages 10 and 14 than at age 7. They included more extended family in their convoys at age 10 than at age 7 or 14, and more friends at age 14 than at the other ages. More support was received from close family members than from friends or extended family at all ages. Extended family support exceeded friend support at age 10, but, at age 14, friend support exceeded extended family support and approached the level of close family support.

In a subsequent study, Franco and Levitt (1997) interviewed preschool (age 4–5) children with a measure based conceptually on the convoy model, but simplified to accommodate cognitive limitations. Figure drawings of various age persons from Takahashi's PART measure were used to represent potential network members. Children were first asked to name all of the people who love them, people who live in their house, and their best friends, and then to indicate who provides each of five functions (playing fun games, care when sick, making the child feel better when sad, making the child feel happy, and showing the child how to do things). All of the children included parents and friends in their networks, most included siblings, more than half included extended family members, and a quarter included other persons (teachers, etc.). Children differentiated their network members by function, with parents viewed as the main providers, except for "playing fun games" where friends took the lead.

Levitt and colleagues have also conducted short-term longitudinal studies addressing convoy development over the transitions from middle childhood to adolescence (Levitt, 2001; Levitt, Levitt, Bustos, Crooks, Santos, Telan, Hodgetts-Barber, & Milevsky, 2005) and adolescence to adulthood (Levitt & Silver, 1999a,b). As in prior research with the convoy model, change occurred most often in the peripheral circles of the convoy. However, these studies revealed multiple patterns of change and related adaptations across these transitions.

In an attempt to capture some of this variation, Levitt et al. (2005) performed cluster analyses of the amount of support provided to children by close family, extended family, and friends at ages 9 and 11, with follow-up

at ages 11 and 13. Three clusters emerged, including one in which participants received most support from close family members and friends, one involving support primarily from close and extended family members, and one in which support was received primarily from close family members alone. Children with multiple sources of support were better adjusted, regardless of the specific sources of support. These findings, along with those of Takahashi (2005), indicate the potential utility of a typological approach to the study of social network development.

II. Conceptual and Methodological Issues

Issues common to research on network development include problems of definition, informant selection, reliability and validity, setting network boundaries, the relevance of specific network characteristics, assessing network functions and providers, the effects of personal and contextual factors, the role of cognition, specification of change processes, and articulating network research with other research on the development of social relationships. Although these issues are considered separately here, they are not necessarily orthogonal in nature. For example, decisions about definition guide and constrain the choice of research informants, setting of network boundaries, and so on.

The following overview draws on a number of sources providing more extensive treatment of these issues. Marsden (2005) offers an excellent account of basic methodological issues and recent developments with respect to the measurement of social networks. General issues regarding network support functions are considered in seminal works by Cohen and Syme (1985), Cohen and Wills (1985), Hall and Wellman (1985), and Sarason, Sarason, and Pierce (1990). Issues in the study of social networks in childhood and adolescence have been covered by Belle (1989a), Cauce and her colleagues (Cauce, Mason, Gonzales, Hiraga, & Liu, 1994; Cauce, Reid, Landesman, & Gonzales, 1990), Cochran (1990a), Tietjen (1989), van

Aken, Coleman, and Cotterell (1994), and Wolchik, Beals, and Sandler (1989).

Problems of Definition

Most authors discussing definitional problems in the study of social networks note the importance of distinguishing between the terms "social network" and "social support" (Cochran, 1990a: Hall & Wellman, 1985; Wolchik et al., 1989). Social networks are configurations of individuals bearing some relation to each other (people who work together, children who "hang out with each other" in school [Cairns & Cairns, 1994; Kindermann, 1993], or people who are "close and important" to an individual [Antonucci, 1986], for example). Social support is typically defined in terms of the provision of emotional, self-enhancing, informational, and/or tangible resources to an individual. Support is often viewed as a function of social networks and is one way, but only one way, of defining a network (as those who provide or exchange support). Even then, it must be recognized that persons composing social support networks may often behave in ways that are not supportive (Antonucci, Akiyama, & Lansford, 1998; Cochran, 1990a; Hall & Wellman, 1985).

Another fundamental distinction is between defining social networks as whole networks versus personal, egocentric networks (Cochran, 1990a; Marsden, 2005). Whole network analysis assesses the interrelations among all individuals in a defined network. Within developmental psychology, this approach has been use primarily to define peer networks in schools. Researchers interested in broader networks mostly study personal networks, in which network information is gathered relative to a focal individual. This is sometimes for pragmatic reasons, as it is more feasible to collect data from multiple individuals in a constrained setting (e.g., children in school) than in an open field context (e.g., all persons who exchange support). However, it is also the case that personal networks may be of more interest to developmental psychologists than to those in other fields employing network

analysis (sociology, anthropology, and organizational psychology, for example), given the focus of the field on intraindividual development. Even when whole network data are gathered, the focus of research is often on personal outcomes. An example is Kindermann's (1993) analysis of change in children's school motivation in relation to the motivational characteristics of their peer groups.

Thus, in general, social networks can be defined in numerous ways. The selection of a particular definition will depend on the goals of the researcher.

Choice of Informants and Reliability and Validity Issues

The gathering of social network information is fraught with questions regarding the reliability and validity of informants' accounts and all network identification methods are subject to some degree of bias (Marsden, 2005). Whole network analysis often entails collecting information from all potential network members. Ennett and Bauman (1996), for example, asked all 9th graders in five schools to identify their friends in order to detect the social organization inherent in their schools (cliques, liaisons, or isolates). Kindermann (1993, 1996), however, describes a procedure for collecting similar data through interviews with a subset of potential network members that yields comparable information. Egocentric network analysis typically employs the focal person as the informant, although when young children have been the focus, researchers have sometimes engaged mothers as informants (Cochran & Riley, 1990; Feiring & Lewis, 1988, 1991b).

Methods used to identify network members typically involve recognition, wherein informants select network members from lists of potential members (class lists, for example) or free recall, in which the informant must draw on memory. Recognition tasks require the researcher to preidentify potential network members, which imposes constraints on informant responding. For example, asking children to identify friends based on class lists excludes information regarding children's friendships outside of class. Free recall formats afford more flexibility, but are subject to informant forgetfulness. Other sources of error include "expansiveness bias" (for example, over-nominating classmates as friends), interpretive bias with respect to relational cues (for example, the meaning of "friend" or "important person in your life" may vary across informants), and variations across interviewers or contexts that may affect informant response (Marsden, 2005).

One issue that often arises in discussions of egocentric network analysis is the use of single versus multiple informants. Although direct comparisons have been rare, the few studies comparing network information elicited through focal "insider" accounts to that obtained from outsiders suggest that insider accounts may have greater validity (Antonucci & Israel, 1986; Franco & Levitt, 1997). It is, after all, likely to be the individual's own perceptions of network characteristics that govern related affective and behavioral outcomes. (See Furman, 1984 for a general discussion of insider versus outsider perspectives on social relationships.)

In the Franco and Levitt (1997) preschool study, for example, information about child networks was also obtained from mothers with the standard adult convoy mapping procedure. The extent to which child or mother reports were associated with teacher and peer preference ratings was then assessed. As in prior studies (Godde & Engfer, 1994; Zelkowitz, 1989), mother reports tended to include more distant family members and nonkin, compared to child reports. Franco and Levitt found additionally that those included in mother, but not child, reports tended to be those with whom the child had little contact. Furthermore, child reports were associated more strongly than maternal reports with the teacher and peer ratings, suggesting the validity of insider reports even from young children.

The Franco and Levitt (1997) preschool network measures yielded good test-retest reliability coefficients, as did the measures obtained with the Levitt, Guacci-Franco, and Levitt (1993) Children's Convoy Mapping Procedure. Other measures with good test-retest reliability are the "My Family and Friends" instrument developed for use with children age 4–15 (Reid, Landesman, Treder, & Jaccard, 1989) and Bryant's (1985) neighborhood walk indices. For the most part, though, researchers have not addressed this issue (Cauce, Reid, Landesman, & Gonzales, 1990; Marsden, 2005). Reliability assessments are especially crucial for developmental studies focused on change in networks over time, to rule out the possibility that apparent network change is the result of error variance. Test-retest periods should be relatively short, however, to ensure that variation across assessments is not reflecting actual changes in the network (Marsden, 2005).

Network Boundary Issues

As suggested by the familiar phrase "six degrees of separation" (the probability that any individual could connect with any other individual in the world through an average of six intermediate contacts), social networks could potentially be almost limitless. Thus, any study of social networks must define the bounds of the network to be assessed. Setting network boundaries typically involves trade-offs, in that boundaries make the research manageable, but information about network ties outside the bounds is lost. For example, delimiting the network as all persons who are "close and important" to an individual (Antonucci, 1986) often leaves out work associates (for adults) or teachers (for children) who may affect the individual, even though they fall outside the defined bounds of the network. As noted previously, when peer network assessments are limited to school relationships, researchers forego information about out-of-school networks.

Ideally, decisions about boundaries would be theory-driven and limitations ensuing from these decisions would be acknowledged. Cochran (1990a), for example, indicated that his admittedly controversial decision to view nuclear family members as focal, and network members as persons outside the nuclear family, was guided by the view that social-ecological factors impinging on the family from outside are theoretically significant and qualitatively different from within-family dynamics.

Relevance of Specific Network Characteristics

Social networks embody a number of characteristics that might potentially be assessed. Structural factors include such properties as network size (number of persons in the network), density/interconnectedness (number known to each other), age, gender, and specific roles of network members (parent, friend, etc.), diversity of roles represented in the network, proximity to and frequency of contact with network members, and duration of relationships with network members. Functional or relational characteristics may include the amount of support received from the network and/or from specific individuals or groups (family, friends, etc.) within the network, the amount of support provided to network members, the amount of conflict experienced with network members, measures of relationship satisfaction or quality in reference to network members, or other functions and characteristics of interest.

The researcher's decision to assess specific network characteristics should be guided by the goals of the research and based, to the extent possible, on available information regarding the costs and benefits of assessment. As Marsden (2005) notes, gathering extensive information about a range of network members is quite demanding of informant time and cognitive energy. Analytic complexity also increases as more characteristics are added. Thus, researchers often need to set limits on the information obtained.

Assessing Network Functions and Providers

Although peer network analysts have addressed potentially negative effects of network involvement on developmental outcomes (lower school motivation, heightened aggression, risky behavior, etc.), developmental researchers have most often focused on the support functions of personal social networks. Support function effects might be represented in a number of ways. For example, researchers might calculate the total number of functions provided by all persons in the network to arrive at a total support score and/or adjust for variations in the number of persons available in the network by calculating a proportional score (amount of support divided by the number in the network). However, proportional scores may underestimate the individual's support availability, as support amounts are related to the number of potential support providers. In our own work, we have found few practical differences in research outcomes resulting from the use of total versus proportional scores.

Support functions might also be assessed independently, with separate calculations for amounts of different types of support. For example, researchers might sum separately the number of persons providing emotional, instrumental, companionship, and esteem support (or average ratings across providers for each type of support, if rating scales are used). Alternatively, researchers might focus separately on the providers of support, by calculating the amount of support received from particular providers or provider categories (for example, family or friends). In general, factor analyses have yielded greater differentiation of support by providers than by functions (Cauce et al., 1994; Levitt, Guacci-Franco, & Levitt, 1993; Wolchik et al., 1989), perhaps because core members of personal networks tend to provide several types of support.

A related issue is the extent to which social network members are interchangeable with respect to the functions they fulfill within the network. Theoretically, a number of authors have argued for relative specificity with regard to the functions provided by different relationships (Cochran, 1990b; Furman & Buhrmester, 1985; Lewis, 1982, 2005; Takahashi, 1990, 2005; Tietjen, 1994), although most recognize that some relations provide multiple functions and some functions are provided by multiple relations. As Cauce et al. (1990) have observed, support providers may be "generalists" or "specialists." Parents, for example, tend to be generalists, providing many types of support, whereas teachers may function singularly to provide informational support. However, some theorists point to commonalities, as well as divergence, of functions across relationships (Kindermann, 2003: Levitt, 2005). Baumeister and Leary (1995) argue that relationships are potentially interchangeable, so long as they fulfill the individual's basic "need to belong."

Another way of conceptualizing this issue is to ask whether one relationship may compensate for the absence of another relationship within the individual's network. Can emotional support from a friend or sibling, for example, compensate for lack of emotional support from a parent? Although some researchers have explored compensation across specific relationships (Milevsky & Levitt, 2005; Stocker, 1994), this important question has rarely been addressed at the network level. A notable exception is a study by van Aken and Asendorpf (1997) on compensation across relationships (mother, father, classmate, sibling, nonschool peer, grandparent, other adult, and young child) in the social networks of preadolescents, with self-esteem as the outcome variable. Support provision effects were relatively specific to relationship categories. Lack of support from a parent, for example, was compensated only by support from the other parent and sibling support did not compensate for low support from classmates. The authors did note, however, that greater substitutability might be present across core members of the social network (for example, support from an older sibling or close friend in the child's inner circle might compensate for low parent support), although they were not able to test this proposition within the study.

To the extent that important network functions are relationship specific, it follows that multiplexity or diversity with respect to the relationships within the network would be advantageous (Bryant, 1985; Cauce et al. 1994; Cochran, 1990a; Lewis, 2005; Levitt, 2005; Tietjen, 1989). Empirically, Bryant (1985) determined that children with broad-based networks exhibited better socioemotional functioning. Franco and Levitt (1997) reported a link between social acceptance and the presence of both siblings and extended kin in the networks of preschool children and, in their prospective analysis of children in transition to adolescence, Levitt et al. (2002: Levitt, 2005) found that having more diverse inner circle relations was associated with better adjustment. In a study by Laursen, Furman, and Mooney (2006), adolescents reporting high levels of support from a combination of close friends, mothers, and romantic partners had higher self-esteem and social competence than did adolescents with low support from mothers and friends and no romantic involvement. Those with low maternal and friend support who had a romantic partner had intermediate scores on the adjustment measures, suggesting that the romantic relationship may have compensated to some extent for the lack of parent and friend support.

Personal and Contextual Influences

As Kindermann (2003) notes, the study of development is the study of changing individuals in changing contexts. Social networks operate at the microlevel of contextual influences involving direct interactions with the developing individual. Networks are themselves affected by macrolevel contexts, including such factors as geography, population distributions, economic conditions, and culture. For example, friendship networks typically expand in size and functional significance as children develop from infancy to adolescence, but both the size and significance of the network may depend on personal characteristics of the child and the characteristics and interrelations of persons in the network, which are, in turn, affected by other microlevel conditions and by macrolevel forces. Thus, more sociable children may tend to develop more expansive friendship networks, but this tendency may be tempered by the extent to which parents control access to peers at the microlevel. Friendship networks may also be constrained by school demographics that limit the available pool of potential friends or by risky neighborhood conditions that lead parents to restrict peer access. At the macrolevel, friendship networks may be limited by cultural values that emphasize the significance of family over friendship ties.

The remainder of this section is devoted to a brief review of some personal and contextual factors that have been studied in relation to network characteristics. Personal factors include gender, personality/temperament, and network building skills/capacity. Contextual influences at the microlevel include family structure and socioeconomic, school, and neighborhood factors. Macrolevel influences include historical time and cultural effects. In line with the foregoing discussion, however, it is important to keep in mind that these factors do not operate independently of each other.

Personal factors. There has been little empirical research on linkages between personal characteristics and social network development. Gender is one characteristic that has been assessed with mixed results. Not all researchers have found gender differences in social network structure or function (Levitt et al., 1993; van Aken & Asendorpf, 1997). However, Bost, Vaughn, Boston, Kazura, and O'Neal (2004) found preschool African-American girls to have larger networks overall than boys and Feiring and Lewis (1991b) reported larger friendship networks for adolescent girls than for boys. When consistent gender differences are found, they tend to be in qualitative measures of support function, rather than in structural network indices (Belle, 1989b), in the direction of females reporting greater intimacy in their friendships and more reliance on familial support compared to males (Belle, 1989b; Bryant, 1985; Furman & Buhrmester, 1992; Tietjen, 1982). The roots of such gender differences are likely to be found in the socialization of gender roles, but little is known about the pervasiveness or developmental origins of these differences.

Asendorpf and van Aken (2003) addressed the association of personality traits to the supportiveness of social networks from age 12 to 17. Core (Big Five) personality traits predicted changes in support from parents and peers, and parent and peer support predicted changes in surface traits (self-worth, peer acceptance, loneliness). Van Aken and Dubas (2004) also reported differential support patterns from family members and friends across adolescents classified as having resilient, overcontrolled, or undercontrolled personalities. Thus, network characteristics may develop in part as a function of temperamental or personality characteristics of the child.

Other researchers have cited network building capacity (Berndt, 1989; Cochran, 1990c; Stanton-Salazar, 2001; Thompson, Flood, & Goodvin, 2006) as a personal characteristic leading to variations in social network development. Based on studies of adolescents in low-income families of Mexican origin in California, Stanton-Salazar (2001) reported variations in network orientation among youth that partially governed their ability to develop supportive networks. He described a condition of "alienated embeddedness" whereby an adolescent might have a social network, but be personally ambivalent or averse toward seeking or accepting support. Immigrant youth, for example, may be reluctant to seek support from parents or other network members whom they perceive as lacking knowledge or understanding regarding the demands of adapting to a U.S. school environment. Coffman and Ray (1999, 2002) also observed, in a qualitative study of unwed pregnant women, that the extent to which support is provided by the social network depends in part on the readiness of the potential recipient to garner and accept support from network members.

Microlevel Contextual Factors: Family Structure and Socioeconomic, School, and Neighborhood Characteristics. With respect to family structure, Tietjen (1982) found that children in grades 2–3 from father absent homes had smaller peer networks and spent less time with family members. On the other hand, Noack, Krettek, and Walper (2001) did not find major effects of family structure on peer relations in children age 10–20 who resided in nuclear, stepparent, or single-parent families. In Bryant's (1985) study, children's networks varied in relation to family size, with those in larger families tending to be more involved with peers and with individuals in the grandparent generation.

Socioeconomic and neighborhood constraints have also been addressed, in some cases interacting with ethnic minority status. Cochran (1990b) recognized that both personal initiative and contextual constraints affect the development of social networks, but he argued that contextual factors outweigh personal factors, as when poor neighborhoods constrain personal initiative by reducing opportunities for social interaction. Cochran et al. (1990) estimated that 40–50 percent of the support available to parents in their sample was related to their education, employment, and neighborhood characteristics.

Specifically, Cochran et al. (1990) found that children with less educated mothers had smaller networks and, as part of the Cochran et al. study, Cross (1990) found that black children and mothers in single-parent families had the smallest networks in the sample. Black mothers in general had smaller networks than white mothers, and mothers reported black children to have fewer school contacts than white children. Cross suggested that these size differentials may reflect relatively lower numbers of blacks available as network members within the mid-sized community studied. A similar point regarding differential availability was made by Hirsch, Engel-Levy, DuBois, and Hardesty (1990) with respect to black adolescents reporting fewer out-of-school contacts with school friends, but greater contact with nonschool friends in their neighborhoods.

In terms of two studies in the California area, Stanton-Salazar (2001) indicated that, because of segregation trends and economic conditions, poor minority youth often tend to be embedded in small, homogeneous, geographically bounded networks that lack the social capital or ability to engage institutional support needed to overcome barriers of race, class, and gender that may diminish developmental opportunity. Similarly, Cooper and her colleagues have written extensively about the need for immigrant youth from ethnic minority groups to navigate within and across multiple social worlds in order to pursue their dreams of achievement and a better life (Cooper, Domínguez, & Rosas, 2005; Cooper, Jackson, Azmitia, & Lopez, 1998).

Macrolevel Contextual Factors: Historical Time and Culture. Harevan (1989) described historical changes that may have altered the nature of children's social networks, including increases in longevity leading to more stable networks, the rise of blended families, age-graded institutions, fertility changes, nuclear family isolation, and changing economic conditions. Otherwise, very little attention has been given to historical time effects.

Culture is a primary macrolevel context for the development of social networks (Antonucci & Akiyama, 1994; Azmitia, Ittel, & Brenk, 2006; Cauce et al., 1990; Cochran, 1990c; Lewis, 2005; Tietjen, 1994; Weisner, 1989, 2005). Cultures are sources of norms, values, beliefs, and social-ecological constraints and opportunities likely to play a significant role in the structuring and functional attributes of social networks emerging within them.

Weisner (1989), for example, discusses a number of factors varying across cultures that impact on social network development in childhood, including the distribution of caregiving responsibilities, the physical health and safety of families, the availability of kin and nonkin to provide support, persons with whom children interact on a daily basis, peer characteristics, and caregiver beliefs about parental roles and desirable developmental outcomes. In his work with the Abaluyia of Kenya, he has observed aspects of support in childhood that seem to be relatively culture specific, including work participation as a source of support, support accompanied with teasing and aggression, indirect reciprocity (reciprocating support from one person by providing support to a different person), attending to the support needs of others, the use of food as a means of providing support, and seeking support from peers. Wenger (1989) also observed high levels of age-mate support among the Giriama of Kenya.

Hammer and Sutton (1988) studied the social networks of Yoruba children in Nigeria, observing a cultural preference for large extended kin networks, with much cross-household fostering of children, as a means of socializing kin obligation and of providing children with access to education and other opportunities. High levels of kin fostering have also been observed in the networks of Haitian children (Gutwirth-Winston, 1988).

In considering the effects of culture on social networks, researchers have tended to focus on variations in the value placed by cultures on personal autonomy versus social interdependence. A related issue is the relative value assigned by different cultures to family connections (familism) versus involvement with nonkin peers or others outside the family (Azmitia et al., 2006). Some research has been conducted across nations or across subcultural groups in the United States thought to represent these differing values, but the findings do not offer a unified portrait of the role played by autonomous/individualistic versus interdependent/collectivist cultural orientations in the development of social networks (Takahashi, Antonucci, Akiyama, & Ohara, 2002). As an example, French, Bae, Pidada, and Okhwa (2006) tested the hypothesis that individuals in collectivist cultures (Indonesia and South Korea) would report less extensive but more intimate friendship networks than those in an individualistic culture (the United States). The hypothesis received support with respect to the friendship patterns of South Korean, but not Indonesian college students.

The most consistent finding appears to be that social networks of individuals from cultures thought to be collectivist or familistic do appear to be more family oriented.

Employing functional measures based on the Convoy Model, Antonucci and Akiyama (1994) found more concern with intergenerational familial obligation in Japan than in the United States. In a cross-national study using the Network of Relationships Inventory, French and his colleagues found that Indonesian children and adolescents, compared to a U.S. sample, reported receiving relatively more companionship support from family members and less from friends (French, Rianasari, Pidada, Nelwan, & Buhrmester, 2001). They also reported more satisfaction with family members and less with friends, compared to their U.S. counterparts. In another cross-national comparison based on the NRI, DeRosier and Kupersmidt (1991) found that fourth- and sixth-grade Costa Rican children viewed family members as more important, relative to friends, than did those in a U.S. sample. However, in line with observations of greater heterogeneity within, than across, cultures (Azmitia et al., 2006: Gjerde, 2004), Harrison, Stewart, Myambo, and Clarkston (1997) found that the extent to which the networks of Zimbabwean adolescents were family oriented depended on whether they lived in traditional rural or modern urban families.

Within the United States, in research based on the Convoy Model, children and adolescents in both Hispanic-American and African-American families included relatively more family members versus friends in their networks than did those in Anglo/European-American families (Levitt et al., 1993). In a study of the social networks of three generations of adult women with Anglo-European versus Hispanic cultural origins, Levitt, Weber, and Guacci (1993) found higher proportions of family members and fewer friends in the networks of the Hispanic women. MacPhee, Fritz, and Miller-Heyl (1996) used the convoy mapping procedure to compare social networks of American Indian, Hispanic, and Anglo parents of young children. American Indian and Hispanic parents had more interconnected networks, while Anglos had more diffuse, less kin-focused networks.

Azmitia et al. (2006) drew on four studies of adolescent friendship in noting that family relationships are central to Latino-American adolescents (especially for immigrants, whose parents are more likely to restrict access to local peers). However, local friendship networks were also found to be more important to both Latino- and African-Americans, as adolescents in these groups were more concerned about losing these friends in the transition to college than were European-American adolescents. Bost et al. (2004) found extended kin to be central in the networks of African-American preschoolers.

In general, these studies illustrate some of the complexity involved in attempting to establish generalities regarding the role of culture in social development. As Gjerde (2004) observes, culture is a moving target for researchers – ever evolving and subject to economic, political, and historical forces, heterogeneous and defiant of neat categorization, and impossible to analyze objectively absent the limitations of the researchers' own cultural worldviews. Furthermore, even at a single point in time and space, cultural effects are confounded with those of other contextual variables, such as social class, economic conditions, minority or majority status, migration patterns, and geographic location. Thus, it is unlikely that we will find social network characteristics to be easily classifiable by culture.

In addition, methodological issues involved in cross-cultural research are formidable. Problems are likely to be encountered with respect to finding and recruiting samples that are culturally representative, translation of materials, establishing an acceptable degree of measurement equivalence, and drawing inferences about results. A combination of quantitative and qualitative approaches will likely be needed to make any headway in understanding the role of culture in the development of social relationships (Azmitia et al., 2006; Azmitia, Ittel, & Radmacher, 2005; Stanton-Salazar, 2001). Although essential, the challenge of assessing culturally divergent and culturally transcendent aspects of social network development is quite daunting.

The Role of Cognition

When researchers gather data on personal social networks through interview or survey methods (the most common procedures), they are in fact assessing perceptual-cognitive representations of these networks, constrained by the specific methodology used to elicit network member information. As already noted, personal network representations have been found to be more salient with respect to adjustment than outsider perspectives. However, very little is known regarding how these representations evolve and how they affect other aspects of development.

Disparate models regarding social perception have been proposed within the social psychological literature. One model suggests that social schemas emerge from central prototypes to which new instances are compared (Fiske & Taylor, 1991). Once a prototypic representation is in place, it tends to bias further perception. Bowlby's conception of working relationship models is consistent with this view. Interactions with a primary caregiver are viewed as central to working model formation early in development and perceptions of new relations are filtered through this prototype. Thus, research from this perspective has focused primarily on assessing associations between the security of the infant's relationship with the mother, or later representations of this relationship, and the qualities of other relationships (with peers, marital partners, etc.).

Alternatively, social schemas may be formed from specific exemplars, without a central prototype (Smith & Zarate, 1992). From this perspective, expectations about new relations would be based on the degree of similarity between the new relation and those with whom the individual has interacted in the past in specific contexts (Levitt et al., 1994; Levitt, 2005). Consistent with this view, van Ijzendoorn and Sagi (1999) have suggested that working models integrate experiences with different caregivers and that carryover from these experiences may be domain-specific, noting that infant security with nonparental caregivers in an Israeli kibbutz was more predictive of socioemotional competence in kindergarten than was security with either parent. In their study of preschool social networks, Franco and Levitt (1997) also reported domain specific effects. Teacher acceptance was related to perceived support from extended family members, whereas peer acceptance was linked to the child's perceptions of friend support.

Andersen and Chen (2002) also favor an exemplar model, reviewing evidence suggesting that adults have multiple representations of "relational selves" that are invoked in new interpersonal encounters, depending on the extent to which the newly encountered person and context are similar to existing exemplars. These authors also share the view expressed by Levitt (1991) that role-based expectations are included in the cognitive-affective structure of working models; that is, expectations regarding relationship partners emerge both from past and present experiences and from cultural norms regarding role performance.

Change Processes and Problems of Measuring Change

Much of the research on social network development has been descriptive and relatively little attention has been given to understanding how, when, or why social networks undergo change over time. Larner (1990) addressed this issue empirically by tracking changes in maternal networks over time in the Cochran et al. (1990) study. As in research based on the Convoy Model, she found that the most important primary/kin ties were the most stable. Network turnover was highest for single mothers, who generally experienced greater life stress and had fewer kin ties. When asked to give reasons for the departure of network members, participants cited predominantly changes in their own lives, changes in network members' lives (such as moving away), and changes in the quality of the relationship with the network member.

Feld, Suitor, and Hoegh (2007) have outlined potential foci for studies of change in personal networks, including individual versus whole network change, whether specific social ties are added or lost in the network, and whether and how changes occur in continuing ties within the network. Thus, understanding the development of social networks will require a model explaining how significant social ties are formed, maintained, and attenuated throughout development. A hypothetical model proposed by Levitt and colleagues (Levitt, 1991; Levitt et al., 1994) builds on cognitive expectancy models (e.g., Bowlby, 1969/1997; Lamb & Malkin, 1986; Lewis & Goldberg, 1969) and incorporates aspects of the literature on social exchange and social support. In brief, contingent interactions with familiar social network members have affective consequences that provide a basis for the development of social attachments (Watson, 1972). Interactions are a primary source of interpersonal expectations, but, with maturation, relationship expectations are also influenced by social norms governing interpersonal roles. Thus, for example, we expect our parents to love us and care for us, not only because of our interactions with them, but also because that is what parents are meant to do normatively. Role-based expectations are often life stage related and culture specific.

As cognitive capacity increases with development, social expectancies can be held for very long time periods and are resistant to change in the absence of a clear violation. Life transitions represent periods of heightened vulnerability with respect to relationships, as support needs increase and expectations regarding support provision are tested. Transitions that involve changes in roles may also usher in new expectations or create conflicting expectations between relationship partners, as, for example, when children acculturate faster than parents following migration to a new country. Relationships may then be enhanced when a partner's behavior exceeds expectations, maintained at current levels when expectations are met, and threatened when expectations are violated. Support for this model has been found with respect to marital quality outcomes following the childbirth transition (Levitt et al., 1994).

Articulation with Other Research on Relationships

Research on social relationships has a relatively long history in developmental psychology, but relationships that are often highly interconnected in the individual's social milieu have been studied largely in isolation. Separate lines of research have been established for the study of parent-child relationships, sibling relationships, peer relationships, teacher-child relationships, romantic relationships, and so on. How these relationships function together in the life of the individual has rarely been considered (Furman & Buhrmester, 1992; Levitt, 1991, 2005). Furthermore, some important relationships have been largely neglected, including grandparent-grandchild relations and relations with other extended family members.

As many researchers have now observed, social network systems models have the potential to integrate these diverse relationship literatures and to organize research on the variety of social influences involved in development (Cairns & Cairns, 1994; Cochran & Brassard, 1979; Furman & Buhrmester, 1992; Hinde & Stevenson-Hinde, 1987; Kahn & Antonucci, 1980; Lamb, 1977, 2005; Lewis, 1982; Levitt, 1991; Takahashi, 1990). However, despite mounting evidence that the organization and functioning of multiple relationships in the child's social sphere matter with respect to developmental outcomes, the mainstream has been slow to adopt a network perspective. Research on social networks is rarely presented in child development texts and, remarkably, the index of the most recent edition of the *Handbook of Child Psychology: Social and Emotional Development* (Eisenberg, 2006) contains only a single entry on social networks (indexing a brief reference to peer networks). Questions regarding commonalities, differences, and developmental synergies that may exist across social relationships remain unanswered.

Practically speaking, reluctance to endorse a network approach may reflect the absence to date of a consensually agreed upon conceptual and methodological paradigm that is able to capture the complexity of social network systems, yet be accessible to mainstream researchers. Although advances in statistical analysis are promising with respect to handling complex research designs, further work remains to be done, both theoretically and empirically, to realize fully the potential for a network systems model to integrate the study of developing relationships.

III. Unique and Emerging Trends in Network Research

This section provides a brief glimpse of unique trends and emerging work on social networks. This includes work on social network closure, observational studies, specialized populations, cyberspace networks, and interventions.

Social Network Closure

Recent work on social network closure addresses a potentially important network characteristic, interconnectedness (the number of network members who know each other or are connected to each other in some way) which has received little attention from developmental researchers. Fletcher, Newsome, Nickerson, and Bazley (2001) studied closure with respect to the friends and parents of fourth-grade children, by first mapping the children's peer groups at school, and then assessing closure, through parent interviews, as the extent to which each child's parents were socially connected to the parents of the child's friends. More closure was related to higher achievement and variations in closure were associated with behavioral adjustment, although the direction of the latter effect differed by ethnicity. Feiring and Lewis (1992) also found greater social and moral competence and less risk behavior in adolescents as a function of the extent to which their mothers knew their opposite sex friends.

Observational Studies

Most analyses of network relationships have employed self-report, but a few researchers have ventured into the more difficult territory of observation. Observations by Lewis and Feiring of families interacting at dinner have already been noted (Lewis, 2005). More recently, Gjerde (1986) observed family interaction patterns in parent-adolescent dyads and triads, finding that the extent to which parents exhibited sex-role differentiated and differentiating behavior depended on whether they were observed together or alone with the adolescent. Gavin and Furman (1996) combined self-report and observational methods in assessing the harmony of adolescent girls' relationships with their mothers and their best friends. Relationship harmony was linked to matches of personal characteristics and needs across dyads and observations were concordant with the self-report measures. These studies begin to address observationally the complex dynamics inherent in network systems.

Specialized Populations

Studies of specialized populations are potentially useful, as they may lead to an understanding of social network development under nonnormative conditions. Kazak and Wilcox (1984) found the networks of families with a disabled (spina bifida) child to be smaller and denser than those of matched families. McHale and Gamble (1988) found no differences in network characteristics of children with or without a mentally disabled sibling, but mothers of disabled children received more support from relatives and professionals. Woodgate (2006) assessed support systems in a qualitative study of adolescent cancer patients. Primary support sources were immediate family members, best friends, and health care team members. These studies are generally consistent with observations regarding the importance of a match between support needs and the capacity of the social network to provide the needed support (Cohen & Wills, 1985). Although professional service providers are not typically cited as important network members, they tend to become more important when coping with severe illness or disability.

Another specialized population that has received some attention is homeless street children, who might be expected to have networks dramatically different from those of children who live in families. The limited research available, however, suggests that the networks of these children may not be so unique. Based on a review of studies of street children in a number of developing nations, Ennew (1994) concluded that these children have relationships with both peers and adults and that they often maintain ties with family members. Similar findings were reported recently by Johnson, Whitbeck, and Hoyt (2005) in a large scale study of homeless and runaway adolescents in the United States. These adolescents had heterogeneous networks consisting of both home and street relationships and including family, nonrelated adults, and peers.

Cyberspace Networks

We are currently witnessing the rapid emergence of a phenomenon whereby social networks are formed and/or perpetuated through wireless and Web-based technologies. This likely represents a significant historical and cultural shift in the nature of social systems. As Gjerde and Cardilla (2005) note, technology now allows individuals to maintain contact with network members on a global scale. These authors state, "Virtual social networks – whether based on the Internet or mobile phones – can reach across town or across the world" (p. 99) and "cyberspace makes up a new and increasingly important living space for children and youth" (p. 100). Indeed, a recent estimate indicates that social networking sites, such as Facebook and MySpace, have more than 100,000,000 users (Subrahmanyam & Greenfield, 2008). The proliferation of cyberspace networks creates fertile ground for developmental researchers interested in this phenomenon.

Although still quite scarce, studies of online networking are beginning to appear in the literature. Preliminary findings with emerging adults suggest that online and offline network members tend to overlap and that individuals may use online communication to maintain or enhance their offline relationships (Subrahmanyama, Reich, Waechter, & Espinoza, 2008). Developmental implications of online social networking are considered in a recent special issue of the *Journal of Applied Developmental Psychology* (Subrahmanyam & Greenfield, 2008).

In contemplating the potential for social networking technology to promote human connection, I am reminded of a storyline in Kurt Vonnegut's 1976 novel *Slapstick.* The principal character is elected president after campaigning on a proposal to create artificial family networks by randomly assigning a flower or fauna name (Daffodil, Chipmunk, etc.) to each individual in the country. Those with the same assigned name would then become family members, with all of the normative rights and responsibilities expected of family (a place to stay when in town, etc.). The campaign slogan was "Lonesome No More." Tongue-in-cheek as this proposal was, computer-generated networks are already becoming part of our social landscape, as network technology enables the formation of social networks based on common interests and goals, with the potential to turn strangers into friends. An example is the use of online networking in the 2008 U.S. presidential campaign to recruit volunteers and bring them together in both cyberspace and real-space. The extent to which virtual social networks might, in the future, help us to be "lonesome no more" remains to be seen.

Intervention/Mentoring

Nowhere is an understanding of social network development more critical than in the area of intervention. In general, attempts to compensate for deficiencies in natural social networks have not been very successful. The topic is too extensive to cover within the limits of this chapter, but Thompson et al. (2006) provide a thoughtful overview of issues involved in the study of social support

in relation to developmental psychopathology, with a focus on intervention. Rhodes and DuBois (2007) describe similar issues with respect to youth mentoring programs. The literature linking social network characteristics to both child and adult adjustment is extensive, but intervention requires a much deeper understanding of these characteristics and how they function to foster or inhibit individual adaptation.

IV. Summary and Future Research Directions

Theoretically, social networks are generally viewed as complex systems with multiple levels that cannot be understood as the sum of the dyadic relations between the individual and specific members of his or her social network. Networks have holistic structural and functional properties that transcend these individual relationships. Describing these properties as they evolve over time and assessing their meaning for personal development are primary research goals. However, a number of conceptual and methodological issues must be navigated to approach a thorough understanding of network development.

Empirical research supports the theoretical view that, from infancy onward, individuals interact with a diverse social network that expands and changes functionally as they develop across the life span. In U.S. samples, extended family relations seem to become increasingly important in middle childhood, with peer relations achieving greater significance in adolescence. However, there is personal and contextual variation in the structure and function of developing networks, both within and across cultures, that we are only beginning to define. Thus, another important goal for researchers is to establish a typology that captures meaningful variation in network characteristics.

Another area in need of attention is the functions served by network members. Network members are more than just support providers. They are role models, sources of both positive and negative feedback, transmitters of social norms and values, and often engaged in day-to-day interactions with the individual. The present data are insufficient to draw conclusions about what functions might be needed from what relationships at what points in development, how different relationships function together, or the extent to which relationships are interchangeable. The issue of network member interchangeability is critically important, both theoretically, and with respect to determining potential avenues of intervention for children deficient in support or other network functions. Resolving this issue satisfactorily will require an understanding of the reasons for apparent specificity, as well as the adaptive processes required to attain important functions outside normative channels (as in the case of intervention).

In conclusion, research on social network development is still in a formative stage. There are many unanswered questions about the origins, developmental paths, patterning, and consequences of variations in network relationships. However, as the field continues to acquire the conceptual and methodological tools needed to master the development of complex person-environment systems, achieving an understanding of the social relational context of development is increasingly within reach.

Acknowledgments

Thank you to the many authors who provided information regarding their work related to the development of social networks, including Toni Antonucci, Jens Asendorpf, Margarita Azmitia, Karl Bauman, Deborah Belle, Thomas Berndt, Kelly Bost, Duane Buhrmester, Rand Conger, Catherine Cooper, David DuBois, Candace Feiring, Wyndol Furman, Per Gjerde, Kurt Johnson, Thomas Kindermann, Michael Lamb, Michael Lewis, David MacPhee, Molly Reid, Ricardo Stanton-Salazar, Keiko Takahashi, Ross Thompson, Marcel van Aken, Les Whitbeck, Sharlene Wolchik, and Phyllis Zelkowitz.

References

Ainsworth, M. D. S. (1989). Attachments beyond infancy. *American Psychologist*, 44, 709–716.

Ainsworth, M. D. S., Blehar, M. C., Waters, E., & Wall, S. (1978). *Patterns of attachment: A psychological study of the Strange Situation*. Hillsdale, NJ: Erlbaum.

Andersen, S. M., & Chen, S. (2002). The relational self: An interpersonal social-cognitive theory. *Psychological Review*, 109, 619–645.

Antonucci, T. C. (1976). Attachment: A life span concept. *Human Development*, 19, 135–142.

Antonucci, T. C. (1986). Hierarchical mapping technique. *Generations*, 10, 10–12.

Antonucci, T. C., & Akiyama, H. (1994). Convoys of attachment and social relations in children, adolescents, and adults. In F. Nestmann, & K. Hurrelmann (Eds.), *Social networks and social support in childhood and adolescence*, pp. 37–52. New York: Walter de Gruyter.

Antonucci, T. C., & Akiyama, H. (1987). Social networks in adult life and a preliminary examination of the convoy model. *Journal of Gerontology*, 42, 519–527.

Antonucci, T. C., Akiyama, H., & Lansford, J. E. (1998). Negative effects of close relations. *Family Relations*, 47(4), 379–384.

Antonucci, T. C., Akiyama, H., & Takahashi, K. (2004). Attachment and close relationships across the life span. *Attachment and Human Development*, 6, 353–370.

Antonucci, T. C., & Israel, B. (1986). Veridicality of social support: A comparison of principal and network members' responses. *Journal of Consulting and Clinical Psychology*, 54, 432–437.

Antonucci, T. C., & Jackson, J. S. (1987). Social support, interpersonal efficacy, and health: A life course perspective. In L. L. Carstensen, & B. A. Edelstein (Eds), *Handbook of clinical gerontology*, pp. 291–311. Elmsford, NY: Pergamon Press.

Asendorpf, J. B., & van Aken, M. A. G. (2003). Personality–relationship transaction in adolescence: Core versus surface personality characteristics. *Journal of Personality*, 71, 629–666.

Azmitia, M., Ittel, A., & Brenk, C. (2006). Latino-heritage adolescents' friendships. In X. Chen, D. C. French & B. H. Schneider (Eds.), *Peer relationships in cultural context*, pp. 426–451. Cambridge: Cambridge University Press.

Azmitia, M., Ittel, A., & Radmacher, K. (2005). Narratives of friendship and self in adolescence. *New Directions for Child and Adolescent Development*, no. 107, pp. 23–39.

Baumeister, R. F., & Leary, M. R. (1995). The need to belong: Desire for interpersonal attachments as a fundamental human motivation. *Psychological Bulletin*, 117, 497–529.

Belle, D. (1989a). Studying children's social networks and social supports. In D. Belle (Ed.), *Children's social networks and social supports*, pp. 1–12. New York: Wiley.

Belle, D. (1989b). Gender differences in children's social networks and supports. In D. Belle (Ed.), *Children's social networks and social supports*, pp. 173–188. New York: Wiley.

Berndt, J. J. (1989). Obtaining support from friends during childhood and adolescence. In D. Belle (Ed.), *Children's social networks and social supports*, pp. 308–331. New York: Wiley.

Bosse, R., Aldwin, C. M., Levenson, M., Workman-Daniels, K., & Ekerdt, D. J. (1990). Differences in social support among retirees and workers: Findings from the Normative Aging Study. *Psychology and Aging*, 5, 41–47.

Bost, K. K., Vaughn, B. E., Boston, A. L., Kazura, K. L., & O'Neal, C. (2004). Social support networks of African-American children attending Head Start: A longitudinal investigation of structural and supportive network characteristics. *Social Development*, 13, 393–412.

Bowlby, J. (1969/1997). *Attachment and loss*: Vol. 1. *Attachment*. London: Pimlico/Random House, UK.

Bronfenbrenner, U. (1986). Ecology of the family as a context for human development: Research perspectives. *Developmental Psychology*, 22, 723–742.

Bryant, B. K. (1985). The neighborhood walk: Sources of support in middle childhood. *Monographs of the Society for Research in Child Development*, 50(3), Serial No. 210.

Cairns, R. B., & Cairns, B. D. (1994). *Lifelines and risks: Pathways of youth in our time*. Cambridge: Cambridge University Press.

Cauce, A. M., Mason, C., Gonzales, N., Hiraga, Y., & Liu, G. (1994). Social support during adolescence: Methodological and theoretical considerations. In F. Nestmann, & K. Hurrelmann (Eds.), *Social networks and social support in childhood and adolescence*, pp. 89–108. New York: Walter de Gruyter.

Cauce, A. M., Reid, M., Landesman, S., & Gonzales, N. (1990) Social support in young children: Measurement, structure, and behavioral impact. In B. R. Sarason, I. G. Sarason, & G. R. Pierce (Eds.), *Social support: An interactional view*, pp. 64–94. New York: Wiley.

Cochran, M. (1990a). Personal networks in the ecology of human development. In M. Cochran, M. Larner, D. Riley, L. Gunnarson, & C. Henderson (Eds.), *Extending families: The social networks of parents and their children*, pp. 3–34. New York: Cambridge University Press.

Cochran, M. (1990b). The network as an environment for human development. In M. Cochran, M. Larner, D. Riley, L. Gunnarson, & C. Henderson (Eds.), *Extending families: The social networks of parents and their children*, pp. 3–34. New York: Cambridge University Press.

Cochran, M. (1990c). Environmental factors constraining network development. In M. Cochran, M. Larner, D. Riley, L. Gunnarson, & C. Henderson (Eds.), *Extending families: The social networks of parents and their children*, pp. 277–296. New York: Cambridge University Press.

Cochran, M., & Brassard, J. (1979). Child development and personal social networks. *Child Development*, 50, 609–616.

Cochran, M., Larner, M., Riley, D., Gunnarson, L., & Henderson, C. (1990). *Extending families: The social networks of parents and their children*. New York: Cambridge University Press.

Cochran, M., & Riley, D. (1990). The social networks of six-year-olds: Context, content and consequence. In M. Cochran, M. Larner, D. Riley, L. Gunnarson, & C. Henderson (Eds.), *Extending families: The social networks of parents and their children*, pp. 154–178. New York: Cambridge University Press.

Coffman, S., & Ray, M. A. (1999). Mutual intentionality: A theory of support processes in pregnant African American women. *Qualitative Health Research*, 9, 479–492.

Coffman, S., & Ray, M. A. (2002). African-American women describe support processes during high-risk pregnancy and postpartum. *Journal of Obstetric, Gynecologic, and Neonatal Nursing*, 31, 536–544.

Cohen, S., & Syme, S. L. (1985). Issues in the study and application of social support. In S. Cohen, & S. L. Syme (Eds.), *Social support and health*. Orlando: Academic Press.

Cohen, S., & Wills, T. A. (1985). Stress, social support, and the buffering hypothesis. *Psychological Bulletin*, 98, 310–357.

Cooper, C. R., Domínguez, E., & Rosas, S. (2005). Soledad's dream: How immigrant children bridge their multiple worlds and build pathways to college. In C. R. Cooper, C. Garcia

Coll, T. Bartko, H. Davis, & C. Chatman (Eds.), *Developmental pathways through middle childhood: Rethinking context and diversity as resources*, pp. 236–259. Mahwah, NJ: Erlbaum.

Cooper, C. R., Jackson, J. F., Azmitia, M., and Lopez, E. M. (1998). Multiple selves, multiple worlds: Ethnically sensitive research on identity, relationships, and opportunity structures in adolescence. In V. C. McLoyd and L. Steinberg (Eds.), Studying *Minority adolescents: Conceptual, methodological and theoretical issues*, pp. 111–126. Mahwah, NJ: Erlbaum.

Cross, W. E., Jr. (1990). Race and ethnicity: Effects on social networks. In M. Cochran, M. Larner, D. Riley, L. Gunnarson, & C. Henderson (Eds.), *Extending families: The social networks of parents and their children*, pp. 67–85. New York: Cambridge University Press.

DeRosier, M. E., & Kupersmidt, J. B. (1991). Costa Rican children's perceptions of their social networks. *Developmental Psychology, 27*, 656–662.

Eisenberg, N. (Ed.) (2006). *Handbook of child psychology: Social and emotional development*, Vol. 3 (6th ed.). New York: Wiley.

Ennett, S. T., & Bauman, K. E. (1996). Adolescent social networks: School, demographic and longitudinal considerations. *Journal of Adolescent Research, 11*, 194–215.

Ennew, J. (1994). Parentless friends: A cross-cultural examination of networks among street children and street youth. In F. Nestmann, & K. Hurrelmann (Eds.), *Social networks and social support in childhood and adolescence*, pp. 409–426. New York: Walter de Gruyter.

Feiring, C., & Lewis, M. (1988). The child's social network from three to six years: The effects of age, sex, and socioeconomic status. In S. Salzinger, J. Antrobus, & M. Hammer (Eds.), *Social networks of children, adolescents, and college students*, pp. 93–112. Hillsdale, NJ: Erlbaum.

Feiring, C., & Lewis, M. (1989). The social networks of girls and boys from early through middle childhood. In D. Belle (Ed.), *Children's social networks and social supports*, pp. 119–150. New York: Wiley.

Feiring, C., & Lewis, M. (1991a). The transition from middle childhood to early adolescence: Sex differences in the social network and perceived self-competence. *Sex Roles, 24*, 489–509.

Feiring, C., & Lewis, M. (1991b). The development of social networks from early to middle childhood: Gender differences and the relation to school competence. *Sex Roles, 25*, 237–253.

Feiring, C., & Lewis, M. (1992). Do mothers know their teenagers' friends? Implications for individuation in early adolescence. *Journal of Youth and Adolescence, 22*, 337–353.

Feld, S. L., Suitor, J., & Hoegh, J. G. (2007). Describing changes in personal networks over time. *Field Methods, 19*, 218–236.

Fiske, S. T., & Taylor, S. E. (1991). *Social Cognition*. New York: McGraw-Hill.

Fletcher, A. C., Newsome, D., Nickerson, P., & Bazley, R. (2001). Social network closure and child adjustment. *Merrill-Palmer Quarterly, 47*, 500–531.

Franco, N., & Levitt, M. J. (1997). The social ecology of early childhood: Preschool social support networks and social acceptance. *Social Development, 6*, 292–306.

French, D. C., Bae, A., Pidada, S., & Okhwa, L. (2006). Friendships of Indonesian, South Korean, and U.S. college students. *Personal Relationships, 13*, 69–81.

French, D. C., Rianasari, M., Pidada, S., Nelwan, P., & Buhrmester, D. (2001). Social support of Indonesian and U.S. children and adolescents by family members and friends. *Merrill-Palmer Quarterly, 47*, 377–394.

Furman, W. (1984). Some observations on the study of personal relationships. In J. C. Masters, & K. Yarkin-Levin (Eds.), *Boundary areas in social and developmental psychology*, pp. 15–42. New York: Academic Press.

Furman, W. (1989). The development of children's social networks. In D. Belle (Ed.), *Children's social networks and social supports*, pp. 151–172. New York: Wiley.

Furman, W., & Buhrmester, D. (1985). Children's perceptions of the personal relationships in their social networks. *Developmental Psychology, 21*, 1016–1022.

Furman, W., & Buhrmester, D. (1992). Age and sex differences in perceptions of networks of personal relationships. *Child Development, 63*, 103–115.

Gavin, L., & Furman, W. (1996). Adolescent girls' relationships with mothers and best friends. *Child Development, 67*, 375–386.

Gjerde, P. F. (1986). The interpersonal structure of family interaction settings: Parent-adolescent relations in dyads and triads. *Developmental Psychology, 1986, 22*, 297–304.

Gjerde, P. F. (2004). Culture, power, and experience: Toward a person-centered cultural psychology. *Human Development, 47*, 138–157.

Gjerde, P. F. & Cardilla, K. (2005). Social network research in the era of globalization: Moving beyond the local. *Human Development, 48,* 95–101.

Godde, M., & Engfer, A. (1994). Children's social networks and the development of social competence: A longitudinal analysis. In F. Nestmann, & K. Hurrelmann (Eds.), *Social networks and social support in childhood and adolescence,* pp. 191–216. New York: Walter de Gruyter.

Guiaux, M., Van Tilburg, T., & Van Groenou, M. B. (2007). Changes in contact and support exchange in personal networks after widowhood. *Personal Relationships, 14,* 457–473.

Gutwirth-Winston, L. (1988). Domestic and kinship networks of some American-born children of Haitian immigrants. In S. Salzinger, J. Antrobus, & M. Hammer (Eds.), *Social networks of children, adolescents, and college students.* Hillsdale, NJ: Erlbaum.

Hall, A., & Wellman, B. (1985). Social networks and social support. In S. Cohen, & S. L. Syme (Eds.), *Social support and health.* Orlando, fl: Academic Press.

Hammer, M., & Sutton, C. (1988). The social world of the Yoruba child. In S. Salzinger, J. Antrobus, & M. Hammer (Eds.), *Social networks of children, adolescents, and college students,* pp. 285–304. Hillsdale, NJ: Erlbaum.

Harevan, T. K. (1989). Historical changes in children's networks in the family and community. In D. Belle (Ed.), *Children's social networks and social supports,* pp. 15–36. New York: Wiley.

Harrison, A. O., Stewart, R., Myambo, K., & Clarkston, T. (1997). Social networks among early adolescent Zimbabweans extended families. *Journal of Research on Adolescence, 7,* 153–172.

Hazan, C., & Shaver, P. R. (1987). Romantic love conceptualized as an attachment process. *Journal of Personality and Social Psychology, 52,* 511–524.

Hinde, R. A. (1992). Developmental psychology in the context of other behavioral sciences. *Developmental Psychology, 28,* 1018–1029.

Hinde, R. A., & Stevenson-Hinde, J. (1987). Interpersonal relationships and child development. *Developmental Review, 7,* 1–21.

Hirsch, B. J., Engel-Levy, A., DuBois, D. L., & Hardesty, P. H. (1990). The role of social environments in social support. In B. R. Sarason, I. G. Sarason, & G. R. Pierce (Eds.), *Social support: An interactional view,* pp. 367–393. New York: Wiley.

Johnson, K. D., Whitbeck, L. B., & Hoyt, D. R. (2005). Predictors of social network composition among homeless and runaway adolescents. *Journal of Adolescence, 28,* 231–248.

Kahn, R. L., & Antonucci, T. C. (1980). Convoys over the life course: Attachment, roles, and social support. In P. B. Baltes & O. G. Brim (Eds.), *Life span development and behavior,* pp. 253–286, Vol. 3. San Diego, CA: Academic Press.

Kazak, A. E., & Wilcox, B. L. (1984). The structure and function of social support networks in families with handicapped children. *American Journal of Community Psychology, 12,* 645–661.

Kindermann, T. A. (1993). Natural peer groups as contexts for individual development: The case of children's motivation in school. *Developmental Psychology, 29,* 970–977.

Kindermann, T. A. (1996). Strategies for the study of individual development within naturally-existing peer groups. *Social Development, 5,* 158–173.

Kindermann, T. A. (2003). Children's relationships and development of person-context relations. In J. Valsiner & K. J. Connolly (Eds.), *Handbook of developmental psychology,* pp. 407–430. Thousand Oaks, CA: Sage.

Lamb, M. E. (1977). A re-examination of the infant's social world. *Human Development, 20,* 65–85.

Lamb, M. E. (2005). Attachments, social networks, and developmental contexts. *Human Development, 48,* 108–112.

Lamb, M. E., & Malkin, C. M. (1986). The development of social expectations in distress-relief sequences: A longitudinal study. *International Journal of Behavioral Development, 9,* 235–249.

Larner, M. (1990). Changes in network resources and relationships over time. In M. Cochran, M. Larner, D. Riley, L. Gunnarson, & C. Henderson (Eds.), *Extending families: The social networks of parents and their children,* pp. 181–204. New York: Cambridge University Press.

Laursen, B., Furman, W., & Mooney, K. S. (2006). Predicting interpersonal competence and self-worth from adolescent relationships and relationship networks: Variable-centered and person-centered perspectives, *Merrill-Palmer Quarterly, 52,* 572–600.

Levitt, M. J. (1991). Attachment and close relationships: A life span perspective. In J. L. Gewirtz, & W. F. Kurtines (Eds.), *Intersections with attachment,* pp. 183–205. Hillsdale, NJ: Erlbaum.

Levitt, M. J. (2001, May). *Social networks and school adaptation in middle childhood and early adolescence*. Final report to The Spencer Foundation.

Levitt, M. J. (2005). Social relations in childhood and adolescence: The Convoy Model perspective. *Human Development, 48*, 28–47.

Levitt, M. J., Bustos, G. L., Crooks, N. A., Hodgetts, J., Milevsky, A., & Levitt, J. L. (August 2002). *Multiple attachments and well-being in middle childhood and adolescence*. Presented at the meeting of the American Psychological Association, Chicago.

Levitt, M. J., Coffman, S., Guacci-Franco, N., & Loveless (1994). Attachment relations and life transitions: An expectancy model. In M. B. Sperling, & W. H. Berman (Eds.), *Attachment in adults: Clinical and developmental perspectives*, pp. 232–255. New York: Guilford.

Levitt, M. J., Guacci-Franco, N., & Levitt, J. L. (1993). Convoys of social support in childhood and early adolescence: Structure and function. *Developmental Psychology, 29*, 811–818.

Levitt, M. J., Lane, J. D., & Levitt, J. L. (2005). Immigration stress, social support, and adjustment in the first post-migration year: An intergenerational analysis. *Research in Human Development, 2*, 159–177.

Levitt, M. J., Levitt, J. L., Bustos, G. L., Crooks, N. A., Santos, J. D., Telan, P., Hodgetts-Barber, J., & Milevsky, A. (2005). Patterns of social support in the middle childhood to early adolescent transition: Implications for adjustment. *Social Development, 14*, 398–420.

Levitt, M. J., & Silver, M. E. (1999a, June). *Late adolescents in transition: Temperament, stress, and social support*. Final report to the National Science Foundation.

Levitt, M. J., & Silver, M. E. (1999b, September). *Late adolescents in transition: Temperament, stress, and social support*. Final report to the W. T. Grant Foundation.

Levitt, M. J., Silver, M. E., & Franco, N. (1996). Troublesome relationships: A part of human experience. *Journal of Social and Personal Relationships, 13*, 523–536.

Levitt, M. J., Weber, R. A., & Guacci, N. (1993). Convoys of social support: An intergenerational analysis. *Psychology and Aging, 8*, 323–326.

Lewis, M. (1982). The social network systems model: Toward a theory of social development. In T. Field (Ed.), *Review of human development*, pp. 180–213, Vol. 1. New York: Wiley.

Lewis, M. (2005). The child and its family: The social network model. *Human Development, 48*, 8–27.

Lewis, M. & Feiring, C. (1979). The child's social network: Social objects, social functions, and their relationship. In M. Lewis & L. Rosenblum (Eds.), *The child and its family: The genesis of behavior*, pp. 9–27, Vol. 2. New York: Plenum.

Lewis, M., & Feiring, C. (1992). Indirect and direct effects of and family interaction at dinner. In S. Feinman (Ed.), *Social referencing and the social construction of reality in infancy*, pp. 111–134. New York: Plenum.

Lewis, M., Feiring, C., & Kotsonis, M. (1984). The social network of the young child: A developmental perspective. In M. Lewis (Ed.), *Beyond the dyad: The genesis of behavior*, pp. 129–160, Vol. 4. New York: Plenum.

Lewis, M., & Goldberg, S. (1969). Perceptual-cognitive development in infancy: A generalized expectancy model as a function of the mother-infant interaction. *Merrill-Palmer Quarterly, 15*, 81–100.

Lewis, M., & Takahashi, K. (2005). Beyond the dyad: Conceptualization of social networks. *Human Development, 48*, 28–47.

MacPhee, D., Fritz, J., & Miller-Heyl, J. (1996). Ethnic variations in personal social networks and parenting. *Child Development, 67*, 3278–3295.

Marsden, P. V. (2005). Recent developments in network measurement. In P. J. Carrington, J. Scott & S. Wasserman (Eds.), *Models and methods in social network analysis*. Cambridge: Cambridge University Press.

McHale, S. M., & Gamble, W. C. (1988). The social networks of children with disabled and non-disabled siblings. In S. Salzinger, J. Antrobus, & M. Hammer (Eds.), *Social networks of children, adolescents, and college students*, pp. 149–168. Hillsdale, NJ: Erlbaum.

Milevsky, A. M., & Levitt, M. J. (2005). Sibling support in early adolescence: Buffering and compensation across relationships. *European Journal of Developmental Psychology, 2*, 299–320.

Noack, P., Krettek, C., & Walper, S. (2001). Peer relations of adolescents from nuclear and separated families. *Journal of Adolescence, 24*, 535–548.

Reid, M., Landesman, S., Treder, R., & Jaccard, J. (1989). My family and friends: Six to twelve year old children's perceptions of social support. *Child Development, 60*, 896–910.

Rhodes, J. E., & DuBois, D. L. (2007). Understanding and facilitating the youth mentoring movement. *Social Policy Report*, 20(3). Society for Research in Child Development.

Santos, J. D., & Levitt, M. J. (2007). Intergenerational relations with in-laws in the context of the social convoy: Theoretical and practical implications. *Journal of Social Issues*, 63, 827–843.

Sarason, B. R., Sarason, I. G., & Pierce, G. R. (1990). Traditional views of social support and their impact on adjustment. In B. R. Sarason, I. G. Sarason, & G. R. Pierce (Eds.), *Social support: An interactional view*, pp. 9–25. New York: Wiley.

Smith, E. R., & Zarate, M. A. (1992). Exemplar-based model of social judgment. *Psychological Review*, 99, 3–21.

Stanton-Salazar, R. D. (2001). *Manufacturing hope and despair: The school and kin support networks of U.S.-Mexican youth*. New York: Teachers College Press.

Stocker, M. S. (1994). Children's perceptions of relationships with siblings, friends, and mothers: Compensatory processes and links with adjustment. *Journal of Child Psychology and Psychiatry*, 35, 1447–1459.

Subrahmanyam, K., & Greenfield, P. M. (2008). Virtual worlds in development: Implications of social networking sites. (Editorial introduction to special issue). *Journal of Applied Developmental Psychology*, 29, 417–419.

Subrahmanyama, K. Reich, S. M., Waechter, N., & Espinoza, G. (2008). Online and offline social networks: Use of social networking sites by emerging adults. *Journal of Applied Developmental Psychology*, 29, 420–433.

Takahashi, K. (1990). Affective relationships and their lifelong development. In P. B. Baltes, D. L. Featherman, & R. M. Lerner (Eds.), *Life-span development and behavior*, pp. 1–27, Vol. 10. Hillsdale, NJ: Erlbaum.

Takahashi, K. (2005). Toward a life span theory of close relationships: The Affective Relationships Model. *Human Development*, 48, 48–66.

Takahashi, K., Antonucci, T. C., Akiyama, H., & Ohara, N. (2002). Commonalities and differences in close relationships among the Americans and Japanese: A comparison by the individualism/collectivism concept. *International Journal of Behavioral Development*, 26, 453–465.

Thompson, R. A., Flood, M. F., & Goodvin, R. (2006). Social support and developmental psychopathology. In D. Cicchetti, & D. Cohen (Eds.), *Developmental psychopathology:* Vol. 3. *Risk, disorder, and adaptation*, pp. 1–37 (2nd ed.). New York: Wiley.

Tietjen, A. M. (1982). The social networks of preadolescent children in Sweden. *International Journal of Behavioral Development*, 5, 111–130.

Tietjen, A. M. (1989). The ecology of children's social support networks. In D. Belle (Ed.), *Children's social networks and social supports*, pp. 37–69. New York: Wiley.

Tietjen, A. M. (1994). Supportive interactions in cultural context. In F. Nestmann, & K. Hurrelmann (Eds.), *Social networks and social support in childhood and adolescence*, pp. 395–407. New York: Walter de Gruyter.

van Aken, M. A. G. & Asendorpf, J. B (1997). Support by parents, classmates, friends, and siblings in preadolescence: Covariation and compensation across relationships. *Journal of Social and Personal Relationships*, 14, 79–93.

van Aken, M. A. G., Coleman, J. C., & Cotterell, J. C. (1994). Issues concerning social support in childhood and adolescence. In F. Nestmann & K. Hurrelmann (Eds.), *Social networks and social support in childhood and adolescence*, pp. 429–441. New York: Walter de Gruyter.

van Aken, M. A. G., & Dubas, J. S. (2004). Personality type, social relationships, and problem behaviour in adolescence. *European Journal of Developmental Psychology*, 1, 331–348.

van IJzendoorn, M. H., & Sagi, A. (1999). Cross-cultural patterns of attachment: universal and contextual dimensions. In J. Cassidy & P. R. Shaver (Eds.), *Handbook of attachment*, pp. 713–734. New York: Guilford Press.

Watson, J. S. (1972). Smiling, cooing, and "the game." *Merrill-Palmer Quarterly*, 18, 323–341.

Weisner, T. S. (1989). Cultural and universal aspects of social support for children: Evidence from the Abaluyia of Kenya. In D. Belle (Ed.), *Children's social networks and social supports*, pp. 1–12. New York: Wiley.

Weisner, T. S. (2005). Attachment as a cultural and ecological problem with pluralistic solutions. *Human Development*, 48, 89–94.

Wenger, M. (1989). Work, play, and social relationships among children in a Giriama community. In D. Belle (Ed.), *Children's social networks and social supports*, pp. 91–115. New York: Wiley.

Wolchik, S. A., Beals, J., & Sandler, I. N. (1989). Mapping children's support networks. In

D. Belle (Ed.), *Children's social networks and social supports*, pp. 191–220. New York: Wiley.

Woodgate, R. L. (2006). The importance of being there: Perspectives of social support by adolescents with cancer. *Journal of Pediatric Oncology Nursing, 23,* 122–134.

Zelkowitz, P. (1989). Parents and children as informants concerning children's social networks. In D. Belle (Ed.), *Children's social networks and social supports*, pp. 221–237. New York: Wiley.

CHAPTER 19

Marital Health

E. Mark Cummings and Lauren M. Papp

Partner relationships, including marriage, serve as a central context for *adult and child* health and development (National Institute of Child Health and Human Development, 2006) and as a benchmark of overall family functioning (Greeff, 2000). Parental benefits related to happy partnerships include better health and higher life satisfaction (Dush & Amato, 2005; Lillard & Waite, 1995). Furthermore, family characteristics are generally stronger, more consistent predictors of youth functioning across multiple domains than other developmental environments, including early child care experiences (National Institute of Child Health and Human Development Early Child Care Research Network, 2002). Attention to fathers' and mothers' relationship functioning in relation to children's developmental adaptations, including cognitive, social, and emotional developmental trajectories, is warranted (Cummings, Davies, & Campbell, 2000). Although family researchers have often focused on the parent-child relationship as a family influence, many other relationships within the family also influence the children.

In recent years particular attention has been called to the influence of the interparental relationship on children's development, including the impact of marital conflict. Derived from the traditional focus on parenting as a family influence, some researchers initially assumed that any influence of the marital relationship would be mediated through parenting (Erel & Burman, 1995). However, a considerable body of research now indicates that children are also affected by exposure to interparental relations, with the quality of how parents resolve everyday disputes a particularly strong predictor of children's functioning (Cummings, Goeke-Morey, & Papp, 2004).

The health and quality of the marital relationship are thus important aspects of the family to consider as environments for child development. A key component of family systems theory is the notion that all family members and relationships among them are closely interconnected (Cox & Paley, 1997, 2003). As such, children's development occurs in the context of multiple interrelated family relationships: marital relationships, parent-child relationships, oftentimes sibling relationships, and grandparent and other extended kinships. With regard to the marital relationship, findings from a wide variety of research literatures and perspectives support marital health as a critical developmental environment, including child psychology and psychiatry, child clinical psychology, developmental psychology, and developmental psychopathology (Davies & Cummings, 2006).

Associations between the quality of the marital relationship and child development outcomes have long been demonstrated (Cummings & Davies, 1994). However, recent advances in defining marital health, assessing it, and putting the role of marital functioning in a broader context as an environment for child development encourage an updated review of the area and current implications for future work. Thus, at the outset, we consider the definition of marital health. Next, we focus on explicating the components of marital health, including distinctions between destructive and constructive interparental conflict from the children's perspective. Findings are then reviewed concerning pathways of the effects of marital health on children, including influences following from (a) exposure to marital functioning (i.e., direct effects), and (b) changes in family functioning, illustrated by parenting, linked with qualities of marital functioning (i.e., indirect effects). Additional interrelated family contexts associated with marital health are then examined, including parental psychological adjustment, and divorced and divided families as well as blended families. Finally, we present future directions for understanding marital health as a developmental context for child development.

Defining Marital Health

Marital health – a construct used to encompass broadly defined characteristics of the relationship between committed romantic partners – includes numerous indicators and components. Satisfaction with marital health reported by the partners reflects

agreement about issues, clear communication, and overall positive feelings about their partner and relationship, whereas low satisfaction or relationship distress is marked by partners' high conflict levels or frequent disagreements, ineffective problem solving skills, and general relational negativity (Funk & Rogge, 2007). Although these components are interrelated, research strongly underscores the particular significance of how couples handle their conflicts and disagreements to both child and marital outcomes (Cummings & Davies, 1994; Emery, 1982; Hawkins, Carrère, & Gottman, 2002).

Recent research has undertaken to improve measurement of marital health, through statistical and methodological improvements. Notably, to refine the concept of marital relationship quality, Funk and Rogge (2007) utilized an item-response theory approach to refine relationship satisfaction measurement. At same time, methodological improvements in the measurement of conflict have advanced from checklists of behaviors that might have occurred in past year (e.g., Conflict Tactics Scale) to examination of specific conflict expressions (e.g., behaviors and emotions) at the level of momentary expressions (Driver & Gottman, 2004) or instances of disagreement (e.g., Waldinger & Schulz, 2006). In particular, recent studies have advanced assessments of specific components of marital conflict, including emotional and behavioral responses, (a) during problem-solving discussions in laboratory settings (Sturge-Apple, Davies, & Cummings, 2006) and (b) by having partners complete diary reports of actual conflict instances that occur in naturalistic settings (Cummings, Goeke-Morey, Papp, & Dukewich, 2002).

Refining methods of measurement of marital health, including marital conflict, permits detailed investigation of the role of conflict expressions in parental well-being and family functioning. As an example, a recent study by Papp, Kouros, and Cummings (2009) utilized a parent-reported diary to advance understanding of demand-withdraw communication during marital conflict, a behavior pattern in which one partner attempts to discuss a problem, while the other avoids the issue or ends the discussion (Christensen, 1988). The demand-withdraw communication pattern has been identified through laboratory-based studies of discussions or partners' self-reported questionnaires as one of the most maladaptive ways of handing interspousal differences, associated with a high likelihood of issues recurring. For example, findings from laboratory-based studies suggested that the wife demand-husband withdraw pattern was more common than husband demand-wife withdraw. By contrast, results based on both spouses' diary reporting indicated that the two patterns occurred nearly equally (Papp et al., 2009). On the other hand, the findings based on the diary method supported laboratory-based results in that demand-withdraw communication in the home predicted other maladaptive conflict expressions and conflicts remaining unresolved, and further related husband demand-wife withdraw pattern to spouses' elevated depressive symptoms, highlighting the connection of specific conflict tactics to partners' psychological functioning (Papp et al., 2009).

Fincham (2003) underscored the familywide importance of marital conflict in a seminal review: "The attention given marital conflict is understandable when we consider its implications for mental, physical, and family health" (p. 23). Marital conflict, controlling for general marital distress, accounts for unique variance in mental health of parents (Papp, Goeke-Morey, & Cummings, 2007) and child adjustment problems (see review in Cummings & Davies, 1994). The present review thus focuses on marital conflict as an indicator of overall marital health, consistent with its documented significance in family and child functioning, and describes our recent and ongoing research projects.

Components of Marital Health from the Children's Perspective

The developmental psychopathology perspective provides further support for considering children's development in the context of interparental relations (Cummings et al., 2000). According to this perspective, disruptions and conflict in the marital subsystem of the family are both inevitable (if not commonplace) and potentially distressing for children and their developmental outcomes. Of these various indicators, interparental conflict warrants particular attention as a context for child development. As conceptualization of marital conflict was refined (see Cummings, 1998a), its components and characteristics emerged as particularly consistent indicators of children's emotional and behavioral adjustment. Studies show marital conflict to serve as a better predictor of children's developmental outcomes than other measures of marital relations, such as marital dissatisfaction and marital quality (see Cummings & Davies, 1994; Emery, 1982). Figure 19.1 presents a framework for elements and aspects to consider regarding relations between marital conflict and child adjustment over time from a process-oriented perspective.

Thus, attention should be given to specific expressions of marital differences to explicate correlates and outcomes related to positive and negative child adjustment. Associations between interparental conflict and disruptions in children's emotional and behavioral adjustment, social and interpersonal problems, and impairments in cognitions have all been reliably documented (reviewed in Cummings & Davies, 1994; Cummings & Davies, 2002). Interrelations between marital conflict and physiological and psychological regulation in affecting child development have also been identified. For example, Cummings, El-Sheikh, Kouros, and Keller (2007) found that skin conductance level reactivity to marital conflict and other stressors moderated longitudinal relations between parental dysphoria and children's internalizing, externalizing and social adjustment problems. These findings thus begin to address gaps in the study of individual differences in children's characteristics as moderators of risk, and in the consideration of physiological processes underlying the risk for adjustment problems in the context of family stressors (see review in Cummings, El-Sheikh, Kouros, & Buckhalt, 2009). Finally, notions stemming from the developmental psychopathology perspective would lead us to expect that both positive and negative conflict and conflict resolution styles warrant attention (see Figure 19.1). Considerable research indicates that qualities of marital conflict are particularly important indicators of marital health (see Cummings & Davies, 1994). Further, multiple dimensions of conflict have been found to be differentially related to children's responding to conflict and to broader adjustment levels (e.g., Cummings et al., 2002; Cummings, Goeke-Morey, & Papp, 2003; Cummings et al., 2004) (see Figure 19.1).

Furthermore, the health of the marital relationship has been directly linked with child development. That is, a substantial literature has documented the direct effects of exposure to dimensions of marital conflict on children's emotional, social and cognitive functioning, including laboratory studies carefully controlling for alternative interpretations. For example, these laboratory controls eliminate multiple otherwise plausible alternative interpretations for children's reactions, such as (a) simply exposure to interadult interactions or (b) any emotional interactions between adults, (c) the order of presentation of interactions, (d) the personal characteristics of actors (e.g., appearance, voice), as well as (e) indirect effects that may occur in the home, including pathways reflecting the effects of marital conflict on parenting or sibling relations (see reviews in Cummings & Davies, 1994, 2002). Moreover, recent work has demonstrated pathways of relations between exposure to marital conflict and children's adjustment, including studies identifying processes mediating these relations over time, such as patterns of social, emotional or cognitive responding (Davies, Harold, Goeke-Morey, & Cummings, 2002; Grych, Harold, & Miles, 2003; Rhoades, 2008). However, marital conflict is not a homogeneous stimulus. Thus, it is important to differentiate the effects of specific forms of marital conflict on children's functioning, including any possible positive effects of healthy ways of negotiating or resolving conflicts (see Figure 19.1).

Destructive Marital Conflict

The focus of much research has been on marital discord and negative marital conflict resolution processes (see Figure 19.1). In terms of identifying specific dimensions of destructive marital conflict processes, there can be no doubt that exposure to physical violence between the parents is related to negative reactions by children and increased risk for psychopathology. Experiencing physical violence and aggression between spouses poses serious risks for children, including the risk of overlapping occurrence between interpartner and parent-child aggression (Cummings, 1998b). Studies show husbands' marital violence is linked with child internalizing behavior problems and conduct problems, controlling for general marital discord, parents' aggression toward children, and wives' marital violence (McDonald, Jouriles, Norwood, Ware, & Ezell, 2000; O'Leary, Slep, & O'Leary, 2000). Concern is increased by evidence reported by Hutchison and Hirschel (2001) showing that a majority of husband-to-wife spousal abuse cases responded to by police were witnessed by at least one child below the age of 18. Specifically, 66.8 percent of the cases involved females victims' own child or children living at home, and 75.6 percent involved children when youth who did not live at the house full-time (e.g., stepchildren, nieces, and nephews) were considered. Although the characteristics of the witnessing children, such as age and gender, were not obtained for each dispute, nearly half of the women in the sample had at least one child below the age of 6. These findings underscore the troubling potential for children being exposed to significant forms of marital conflict, even at a very young age (Hutchison & Hirschel, 2001).

Additional interparental conflict behaviors have been identified as destructive from the children's perspective, that is, increase children's risk probabilistically for adjustment problems and heightened negative reactivity

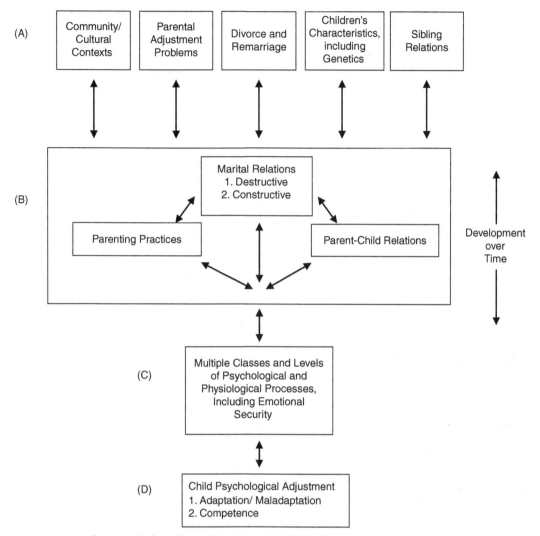

Figure 19.1. A framework for relations between marital health and child adjustment. (Adapted from Cummings and Davies, 2002.)

(Cummings, 1998a). Among these behaviors in the context of marital conflict that elicit negative reactions from children are verbal and nonverbal hostility (Grych & Fincham, 1993; Johnston, Gonzales, & Campbell, 1987); threat (Goeke-Morey, Cummings, Harold, & Shelton, 2003; Laumakis, Margolin, & John, 1998); defensiveness (Cummings et al., 2003; Goeke-Morey et al., 2003); stonewalling, silent treatment, sulking, or withdrawal (Cummings, Ballard, & El-Sheikh, 1991; Jenkins & Smith, 1991; Katz & Woodin, 2001; Kerig, 1996); parents' negative emotionality during conflict (Cummings et al., 2002); and

child-related conflict, encompassing themes of child rearing and child behavior (Davies, Myers, & Cummings, 1996; Grych, 1998; Grych & Fincham, 1993; Jouriles, Bourg, & Farris, 1991).

Constructive Conflict

Although notions of constructive conflict have long been discussed, only recently has this notion been subjected to empirical study, including conceptualizing of how to evaluate whether conflicts are constructive as opposed to destructive (see Figure 19.1).

For example, Goeke-Morey et al. (2003) employed an analogue methodology to examine the responses of 11- and 12-year-olds to video presentations of marital conflict vignettes. In this method, children were presented with recordings of male and female actors representing their parents engaging in a range of conflict tactics during scenarios of dealing with everyday sources of interparental conflict (e.g., a messy house, purchasing a television). The situations were described in detail so children could vividly imagine the actors were their parents. Following each video clip, children answered a series of questions to assess their responses to each behavior as if it occurred at home (e.g., "How did that make you feel?" "What would you do if you were in the room with your parents?").

Children's responses formed the basis of classifying marital conflict expressions, with behaviors resulting in more positive than negative emotional and behavioral responses by children categorized as "constructive," on the basis of the principle that increased positivity indicated well-being, and therefore emotional security was increased by exposure to these behaviors during conflict (see also Cummings & Davies, 2002). By contrast, behaviors eliciting significantly more negative than positive responses by children were classified as "destructive," on the basis of the notion that exposure reduced children's sense of emotional security based on the preponderant negative reactivity shown by the children to these behaviors. Notably, applying these criteria, support, problem solving, and affection were identified as highly constructive behaviors from the children's perspective by Goeke-Morey et al. (2003). That is, even when presented in the context of otherwise negative and conflictual interactions between the parents, children indicated having primarily positive emotional responses to the parents' interactions following exposure to these conflict behaviors.

Towards further exploring these issues, children's reactions to expressions of actual marital conflict behaviors in the home were examined in a series of studies based on parental diaries about specific incidents of marital conflicts (e.g., Cummings et al., 2002, 2003). These studies also addressed issues of the external validity, by testing whether responses to marital conflict behaviors in the home elicited similar reactions as in the laboratory. On the basis of children's reactions, affection, support, and calm discussion were again identified as constructive behaviors during everyday conflicts in the home (Cummings et al., 2003). In addition, parents' positive emotionality emerged as a constructive conflict behavior in terms of children's highly positive emotional responding (Cummings et al., 2002). More recently, the value of codes reflecting the overall constructiveness of marital conflict resolution interactions has also been demonstrated (Cummings, Faircloth, Mitchell, Cummings, & Schermerhorn, 2008).

The ways in which interparental conflict is resolved (or not resolved) are predictive of children's responding to marital conflict, with a series of laboratory studies demonstrating that marital conflict resolution reduces children's negative emotional reactivity to interparental conflict (Cummings et al., 1991; Cummings, Simpson, & Wilson, 1993; Cummings, Vogel, Cummings, & El-Sheikh, 1989; Davies, Myers, Cummings, & Heindel, 1999). Further advancing this issue, Goeke-Morey, Cummings, and Papp (2007) recently provided tests of relations between conflict resolution and children's responses based on actual marital conflicts in the home, with parallel tests of responding to specific forms of conflict resolution in the laboratory. Specifically, mothers' diary home reports of marital conflict resolution and children's responses were examined, along with the reactions of children to analog presentations of these same conflict endings in the laboratory. The significance of specific conflict endings, including the emotionality of conflict endings, was indicated, demonstrating these relations for the first time in the home, with laboratory results generally confirming findings based on responding in the home (Goeke-Morey et al., 2007). In this study, children's responses strongly supported the highly ameliorative effects of tactics of conflict resolution and positive emotionality during conflict ending on children's responses to interparental conflicts in the home. Moreover, children's happy or positive emotional responses were substantially elevated by the introduction of conflict resolution in both the home and laboratory, supporting the conclusion that children's emotional security is increased by observing the resolution of conflicts by the parents. Thus, these results support that conflict resolution merits classification as a highly constructive conflict behavior from the children's perspective. By contrast, lack of resolution was linked with children's elevated negative emotional reactions, and other responses reflective of emotional insecurity about these interactions, for example, children's desire to mediate or intervene in the parents' conflicts. Accordingly, lack of resolution can be seen as destructive from the children's perspective. Finally, children's responses to conflict endings were related to their adjustment, with negative emotionality in response to unresolved marital conflict related to children's internalizing and externalizing problems (Goeke-Morey et al., 2007).

Direct and Indirect Pathways: Marital Health and Child Outcomes

Marital conflict offers one mechanism by which marital health directly impacts children's development, that is, a direct pathway of influence. By comparison, the notion of parenting as a mediator is described as an indirect pathway. There is considerable evidence that both pathways are pertinent to understanding relations between marital health and child outcomes (see Cummings & Davies, 2010).

Direct Pathways

The assumption of direct effects models is that children are affected by exposure to marital conflict as a result of the influence of conflict on children's functioning (e.g., emotional, social, or behavioral), which,

in turn, increases, or decreases, their risk for adjustment problems, depending on whether children are exposed to destructive or constructive conflict, respectively (see Figure 19.1). Notably, the proposition of direct effects models is not simply a pathway from marital conflict to child adjustment, but a pathway from marital conflict to some mediating process (e.g., emotional security; severity or chronicity of stress; modeling processes) to child adjustment. In this paper we will focus on emotional security theory (EST) as a prominent theoretical model towards conceptualizing mediating processes that may explain how and/or why exposure to marital conflict affects children's adjustment (Cummings & Davies, 2010; Davies & Cummings, 1994) (see Figure 19.1).

EST posits that children evaluate marital conflict in terms of the set-goal of emotional security, with the emotional security behavioral system activated if that set-goal is threatened (Davies et al., 2002). Moreover, if the desired or set-point level of security is violated, children are hypothesized to be motivated to respond towards regaining emotional security, with the emotional security response system serviced, in particular, by component regulatory systems of emotional reactivity, behavioral action tendencies, and cognitive appraisals. These responses thus function as regulatory response systems for maintaining or regaining the set goal of emotional security (see Bowlby, 1969), and also serve to reveal children's emotional security about marital conflict in specific contexts (see Cummings & Davies, 2010). Davies and Sturge-Apple (2007) have recently proposed that social defense is another goal in the regulation of children's responding to marital conflict.

The emotional security response system thus regulates, organizes, and motivates a child's responses to interparental discord. Moreover, emotional security can be thought of as a bridge between the child and the world. When the marital relationship is high functioning, a secure base is provided for the child. Similarly to a structurally sound bridge, positive marital relationships support the child's optimal functioning in the context of potentially threatening conditions, fostering exploration and confident relationships with others. When destructive marital conflict erodes the bridge, children become hesitant to move forward and lack confidence, or may move forward in a dysfunctional way, failing to find the best footing in relations with others or within themselves.

Several longitudinal studies in recent years support relations between marital conflict, processes implicated by emotional security theory and child adjustment. For example, Cummings, Schermerhorn, Davies, Goeke-Morey, and Cummings (2006) longitudinally tested models of emotional security as an explanatory mechanism for relations between interparental discord and child maladjustment in two studies, based on independent samples of families with children between 9 and 18 years of age (Study 1) and between 5 and 7 years of age (Study 2), respectively. Despite the differences in samples and age periods, consistent support was found for the EST model for relations between interparental discord, emotional security, and child adjustment. That is, emotional security was identified as an explanatory mechanism for children's adjustment, for children ranging in age from kindergarten through adolescence. Moreover, the pattern of results indicated emotional security related to the explanation of both internalizing and externalizing problems in children.

At the same time, whereas destructive conflict acts to undermine children's emotional security about marital relations, observing constructive conflict between parents may serve to increase children's confidence in the safety and security of marital functioning by showing that even difficult, challenging, and potentially threatening matters such as interparental conflicts can be effectively handled by the parents. Consequently, EST posits that exposure to constructive conflict may increase children's sense of emotional security and thereby their socioemotional functioning. At the same time, little work has systematically or longitudinally addressed whether children do, in

fact, benefit from exposure to constructive conflict, although speculation in the literature is that children's positive social skills may be advanced by exposure to constructive marital conflict.

To address this significant gap in the literature, based on a three-wave longitudinal study, McCoy, Cummings, and Davies (2009) examined relations between constructive and destructive conflict, children's emotional security, positive parenting (i.e., couples' warm parenting), and children's prosocial behavior. Even after controlling for prior levels of children's prosocial behavior, children's elevated emotional security acted as an intervening variable between constructive marital conflict and children's increased prosocial behavior over time. The results of Cummings et al. (2006) and McCoy et al. (2009) thus both support pathways of direct effects and advance a theoretical model for the processes accounting for these effects over time (see also Davies & Cummings, 1998; El-Sheikh, Cummings, Kouros, Elmore-Staton, & Buckhalt, 2008).

Indirect Pathways

This terminology is rooted in the basic presumption that marital conflict can increase child risk for maladaptive coping and maladjustment *indirectly* through associations with disruptions in parent-child and family relationship dynamics. Marital conflict has been indirectly tied to child development via other family processes, including parents' mental health, parent-child relationship (e.g., attachment security) and parenting practices (e.g., parental responsiveness; Cummings et al., 2000; Davies & Cummings, 1994; see Figure 19.1). Focusing on parenting here, results from metaanalyses show significant and positive association between quality of the marital relationship and quality of the parent-child relationship (Erel & Burman, 1995), with interparental conflict and marital quality negatively related (Krishnakumar & Buehler, 2000). Sturge-Apple, Davies, and Cummings (2006) found that increased parental emotional unavailability with children was a key explanatory mechanism linking prior histories of destructive marital conflict with subsequent child adjustment problems (also see Schoppe-Sullivan, Schermerhorn, & Cummings, 2007).

Studies simultaneously assessing indirect and direct pathways within models of child psychological adjustment confirm the operation of both pathways. For example, Davies et al. (2002) found that emotional insecurity in the interparental and parent-child relationships each mediated the link between marital conflict and adolescent internalizing and externalizing symptoms. Using a multimethod, longitudinal design, Sturge-Apple, Davies, Winter, Cummings, and Schermerhorn (2008) reported that parent-child relationship processes and children's insecure internal representations of the interparental relationship were each intervening mechanisms in the link between marital conflict and teacher reports of children's emotional and classroom difficulties.

At the same time, little progress has been made towards identifying the processes that account for why parenting problems in high conflict homes increase child vulnerability to psychological difficulties. At the same time, support has emerged for an EST model: that is, parenting operates by disrupting children's sense of security in multiple family relationships (Davies et al., 2002; Harold, Shelton, Goeke-Morey, & Cummings, 2004). Moreover, Cummings and Davies (2010) have recently advanced a specific conceptualization for the role of children's emotional security in accounting for indirect pathways between marital conflict, parenting, and child adjustment, including analysis of the EST explanation in relation to other theoretical accounts for the indirect effects of marital conflict.

Broader Environmental Contexts: Relations between Marital Health and Child Adjustment

In addition to influences associated with contexts of marital conflict, how marital health is expressed and associated with child development depends upon broader contextual factors and environments. Specifically, mental health, divorce and remarriage, and cultural considerations warrant attention: Each has been demonstrated to be related to marital health and thus can be viewed as pertinent for how marital health serves as a developmental context for children.

Mental Health of Parents: Parental Adjustment Problems

Linkages between marital relations and psychological functioning of parents are well established (Cummings et al., 2000). Empirical and theoretical accounts indicate bi-directional associations between marital relationships and mental health, particularly depression (e.g., Beach, Whisman, & O'Leary, 1994; Karney, 2001) (see Figure 19.1). Moreover, the interplay of the two predicts environments for children beyond the effects of the two independently. Accumulating evidence suggests that considering parents' psychological adjustment (e.g., mental health, substance use) and relationship functioning jointly improves our understanding of child development (Nomura, Wickramaratne, Warner, Mufson, & Weissman, 2002; see also Suchman and DeCoste, Chapter 20, "Parental Psychopathology").

Parental depression and alcohol use are specific psychological indicators that have received attention in this area. Children of depressed parents are several times more likely than children of nondepressed parents to have diagnosable disorders, especially depression and other internalizing problems (e.g., Avenevoli, Stolar, Li, Dierker, & Merikangas, 2001; Hammen, 1991). Marital health has long been identified as a pathway for the effects of parental depression on children (see review in Cummings & Davies, 1994). Recent work has increasingly implicated marital health as a pathway of transmission and further specifies bases for these relations. For example, specific negative interparental conflict styles (e.g., depressive conflict styles), insecure attachment relationships between the parents, and children's emotional insecurity each may contribute to the associations linking maternal and paternal depression to child maladjustment (Cummings, Keller, & Davies, 2005; Du Rocher Schudlich & Cummings, 2003, 2007).

Parental problematic drinking behaviors are also associated with higher levels of marital discord and lower levels of conflict resolution, in the context of other family processes (e.g., parenting problems, Keller, Cummings, & Davies, 2005). Furthermore, parental drinking behaviors have been interrelated with other parental risk factors in longitudinally predicting child adjustment problems over time, even with rigorous controls for initial levels of child adjustment problems (Keller, Cummings, Davies, & Mitchell, 2008). Moreover, El-Sheikh and Flanagan (2001) found the associations between mothers' and fathers' problem drinking behaviors and child behavior problems were mediated by maternal depression and interparental conflict, underscoring the complexity of relations among these family processes.

Recent investigations of mothers' and fathers' psychological distress along multiple dimensions (depression, anxiety, hostility) further supports consideration of a broad assessment of parents' mental health in relation to their marital functioning and children's adjustment. As an example, Papp, Cummings, and Schermerhorn (2004) utilized data drawn from a community sample of parents with older children (8 to 16 years) to model pathways among marital distress, mothers' and fathers' psychological symptoms, and child adjustment problems. Two related models were tested towards explicating directions of pathways among these family processes: In the first, maternal and paternal psychological symptoms were hypothesized to mediate the association between marital distress and child adjustment problems, and in the second, marital distress was expected to mediate the association between parental psychological symptoms and child adjustment problems. Both models were supported by the data: In the first model, both mothers' and fathers' symptoms mediated positive links between marital distress and child adjustment problems. In the second model, the association between fathers' symptoms (but not mothers') and child adjustment was mediated by marital distress, suggesting potentially different processes for mothers and fathers linking marital functioning and parental symptoms to child adjustment. Thus, taken together, these recent investigations indicate multiple dimensions of mothers' and fathers' mental health (i.e., depression, alcohol use, and global psychological distress) are related in complex ways to marital functioning and child adjustment.

Divorce and Remarriage

A growing number of children in the United States are affected by parental divorce and remarriage. Research has examined a range of concurrent and subsequent child functioning indicators following parental divorce. Reviews of published studies report that children of divorce have poorer outcomes compared to children of nondivorced parents on numerous outcomes, including school achievement, externalizing problems, internalizing problems, self-esteem, social adjustment, and parent-child relationships (Kelly, 2000; Reifman, Villa, Amans, Rethinam, & Telesca, 2001). However, many children of divorced parents eventually fare as well as those from intact families (Hetherington & Kelly, 2002), especially if interparental conflict declines following the divorce (see Kelly, 2000).

A potential mitigating factor is parental levels of conflict. Using a large-scale national sample of young American children, Morrison and Coiro (1999) examined the effects of divorce on children from low- and high-conflict marriages along with outcomes of children whose parents remained in high conflict marriages. Findings revealed that while children whose parents separated and divorced (at both high and low levels of conflict) displayed higher than average levels of behavior problems (indexed by internalizing and externalizing symptoms), children of high-conflict parents who remained together evidenced even greater increases in behavior problems. Thus, conflict emerges as a reliable indicator of children's adjustment problems across marital relationship status (i.e., remain together, separate or divorce).

Following divorce, interparental relationship health remains important and continues to serve as an environment for child development. Accumulating evidence suggests that systematic programs designed to manage or alleviate negative interparental communication are effective in reducing children's problematic outcomes (Emery, Kitzmann, & Waldron, 1999; Shifflett & Cummings, 1999). Accordingly, participation in mediation programs during and after a divorce is recommended as an effective way to address parenting issues and protect children from the potentially harmful outcomes related to divorce (Emery, 1994).

The developmental context of marital health for children expands to include additional marital relationships when their parents remarry. Relatively few studies have focused on the impact of marital health in the context of remarriage, but study of this environment for child development is likely to grow in the future as a result of the increasing number of children in such situations (Coleman, Ganong, & Fine, 2004). Cox and Paley's (1997) review indicated that becoming part of a stepfamily was related to positive changes, especially mothers' marital satisfaction and overall happiness, and higher family income. Parent-child relationships also tended to become more positive, but children demonstrated higher behavior problems. Cox and Paley noted different linkages among relationships as a function of different family contexts; for example, parental increases in marital satisfaction had different implications and meaning for children in stepfamilies compared to children in nondivorced families. Further, Cox and Paley pointed to evidence that younger children typically fared better in stepfamilies than older children, particularly when the stepfather was warm and accepting and the previous divorce was not linked to increased child behavior problems. The evidence suggested that adolescents may have more difficulty adapting to new roles in stepfamilies,

demonstrating more negativity toward stepfathers and greater disengagement from both parents. In sum, transitions such as divorce or remarriage influence all family members and associations among them. Requiring change and adaptation, these transitions are likely related to both negative and positive child developmental outcomes, depending on many factors but especially on the child's age. At the same time, the detrimental effects of these transitions may subside over time as family members in these systems adapt to new circumstances (Cox & Paley, 2003).

Finally, Amato (2006) described results drawn from a prospective study, a nationally representative investigation of married adults in United States in 1980. Interviews were conducted with adult offspring, including three types of families: married with low discord, married with high discord, and divorced. Notably, analyses controlled for many potential confounding variables. Children whose parents divorced compared to children from low discord married homes, had less education, lower psychological adjustment, less close relationships with mothers and fathers, and more disrupted intimate relationships themselves (e.g., when married had higher marital discord). Thus, divorce during childhood was linked with numerous maladaptive outcomes for adult children. Similar, yet fewer, problematic outcomes were found for children from discordant but still married parents. That is, compared to children from low discord homes they had lower psychological adjustment, less perceived social support, less close to fathers, and higher marital discord when married. The effect size for psychological distress was similar for children from divorced and high discord homes, but father relationship impairment was greater among divorced families.

Child Characteristics

There is some indication that the implications of marital health vary as a function of children's characteristics, such as gender, or developmental context, age, among other child individual differences (see

Figure 19.1). Studies have documented children's distressed responding to others' conflictual interactions as early as 1 year of age (Cummings, Zahn-Waxler, & Radke-Yarrow, 1981). Mahoney, Jouriles, and Scavone (1997) reported that among 4- to 9-year-old children seeking treatment for behavior problems, the negative associations between marital adjustment and child internalizing and externalizing problems were stronger for younger children relative to older children. Davies and Lindsay (2004) reported that adolescent girls evidenced greater internalizing problems in relation to interparental conflict compared with boys, explained in part through girls' higher tendencies to be affectively or emotionally linked to family members or others. The positive associations between interparental conflict and externalizing problems were not moderated by child gender. Essex, Klein, Cho, and Kraemer (2003) assessed family stressors when children were toddlers, subsequently rating behavior problems in kindergarten. Boys evidenced higher levels of externalizing problems, and girls showed higher levels of internalizing problems in the face of family stressors such as marital conflict and maternal depression.

Parents may express conflict at different levels of intensity based on child characteristics. Specifically, Kerig (1998) reported that girls and boys (ages 8 to 11) did not respond differentially to interparental conflict tactics; however, parents of boys reported using more verbal aggression during conflict than parents of girls. Other studies, however, do not document such differences. For example, O'Hearn, Margolin, and John (1997) found no difference in exposure to daily conflict for boys versus girls. Cummings, Davies, and Simpson (1994) also found no differences in this regard for families with boys versus girls (children 9 to 12 years old). Correlation analyses showed overt conflict to relate in positive direction to internalizing and externalizing problems for boys and girls.

Cultural and Community Contexts

To reflect the changing cultural landscape of United States, a small but growing number of studies focus on culture and ethnicity and strive for diversity and representation of families from multiple cultural and ethnic backgrounds (see McLoyd, Harper, & Copeland, 2001; also see Harkness and Super, Chapter 24, "The Cultural Organization of Children's Environment"). In a review of marital functioning research conducted with families from Asian American, African American, and Latino backgrounds, McLoyd, Cauce, Takeuchi, and Wilson (2000) noted that Asian American marriages and families are particularly underinvestigated. Studies reviewing African American samples showed that African American couples tended to report lower marital satisfaction than those from European American samples. In addition, marital research conducted with Latino families has been limited mostly to conceptual contributions, particularly those focused on men and women's gender roles within the family context. In general, compared to samples of European American youth, children from underrepresented ethnic families may be less distressed in relation to exposure to interparental conflict, perhaps because of their stronger ties to extended family members and higher cultural connectedness, although these conclusions await further investigation and replication (McLoyd et al., 2000).

Researchers have posited that developmental course and timing of marital and family processes may differ among various ethnic groups. For example, elevated rates of teenage childbearing documented in a study of multigenerational African American families may reflect a shorter expected life course for African American men and women (Burton, 1990). Furthermore, adaptive processes for one culture may not serve as protective factors or promote positive development in another culture. As an example, recent findings indicate that participating in shared activities with parents delayed sexual initiation for non-Latino/a white adolescents, but not for Latino/a or African American youths (Pearson, Muller, & Frisco, 2006).

Observed levels of family processes (e.g., marital health indicators, child adjustment) may differ among families from various backgrounds. For example, Parke et al. (2004) found in a study of families with fifth-grade children that higher levels of marital problems were reported among European American families than Mexican American families, while maternal and paternal hostility were higher in Mexican American families than in European American families. The findings also showed that pathways through which family processes are linked may differ among families from various backgrounds: Hostile parenting predicted child adjustment problems in European American families, whereas marital problems were more strongly linked to adjustment problems in Mexican American children. These initial reviews and findings provide a foundation for additional work that is needed to examine ethnic and cultural factors in relation to marital health as an environment for child development.

Future Directions in Marital Health as a Context for Child Development

To understand marital health as a context of child development fully, additional factors warrant consideration, including sibling relationships within the family, joint contributions of genetic and environmental influences, and longitudinal research designs. Each of these directions is in a relatively early stage of development or has been the subject of relatively few studies, so much future study is needed.

Sibling Relationships

Concurrent sibling relationships in the family system covary with marital health: Associations between marital conflict and less warmth and more conflict and rivalry in sibling relationships have been documented (Brody, Stoneman, & Burke, 1987; Stocker & Youngblade, 1999) (see Figure 19.1). Marital functioning also has implications for the differential adjustment and development of siblings within a family. As an example, using a sample of 112 sibling pairs (aged 8 and older)

and mothers currently residing in domestic violence shelters, Skopp, McDonald, Manke, and Jouriles (2005) found that the sibling pair member who reported feeling more threatened by or more to blame for interparental conflict displayed higher levels of behavior problems than the other. Along similar lines, findings from intact, community-based families indicate that children who are exposed to higher levels of conflict and feel more to blame for marital conflict than their siblings report higher levels of depressive symptoms and behavioral problems (Richmond & Stocker, 2003).

In addition, marital health during childhood has implications for subsequent sibling relationships during adulthood. In one of the few studies to assess these relations directly, Panish and Stricker (2001) found that adult siblings' perceptions of interparental conflict during childhood were linked with sibling relationships during adulthood. Interestingly, findings also revealed ratings of marital conflict to be more closely linked than marital intactness to sibling closeness and conflict in adulthood. Clearly, siblings' development and relationships are associated with the health and functioning of the marital relationship and warrant additional study (also see Hart chapter).

Siblings may also be sources of support for each other in the context of marital conflict. In one of the few observational studies of this question, Cummings and Smith (1993) reported that expressions of positive affect increased among female siblings when exposed to interadult conflict whereas prosocial behavior greatly increased among male siblings following conflict resolution. Jenkins, Smith, and Graham (1989) found that seeking contact with a sibling was a commonly reported strategy in coping with interadult conflict. Moreover, there is evidence that siblings may support each other when family relationships are strained (Tucker, McHale, & Crouter, 2001) and positive sibling relationships may mediate relationships between stressful life events and child adjustment (Gass, Jenkins, & Dunn, 2007). At the same time, the possible role of sibling relationships in coping with interparental conflict requires much more study,

Considering Family Environment and Genetics Together

Recent studies examining both marital health factors and their associations with child development have utilized behavioral genetics designs as attempts to disentangle genetic and family environmental influences (e.g., D'Onofrio et al., 2006; Jenkins, Simpson, Dunn, Rasbash, & O'Connor, 2005; Rice, Harold, Shelton, & Thapar, 2006; Spotts, Prescott, & Kendler, 2006; see also Grigorenko and Ward, Chapter 6, "Social Agents and Genes: Comments on the Ontogenesis of the 'Social Genome'"). For example, researchers have explored differences in men and women's marital quality levels as a function of genetic and environmental sources of influence (Spotts et al., 2006). Results indicated that both genetic and nonshared environmental influences are associated with marital quality levels, with men and women showing potentially different heritability levels for relationship warmth and conflict (Spotts et al., 2006).

Along similar lines, research designs are increasingly accounting for genetic predispositions together with family environment in the prediction of child adjustment (see Figure 19.1). As an example, Rice et al. (2006) utilized a longitudinal twin design (consisting of 934 twin dyads) to assess genetic and environmental influences on children's depressive symptoms. The authors noted that genetic risk for depression would be evidenced if a child's cotwin had a depression score above clinical cutoff levels as rated by mothers on the Mood and Feelings Questionnaire (Costello & Angold, 1988). Findings revealed that average levels of family conflict were not higher among children with genetic risk for depression. However, children's genetic risk interacted with their environments (i.e., family conflict) such that those children at risk for depression who were also from environments of high family conflict evidenced higher depressive symptomatology (Rice et al., 2006).

D'Onofrio and colleagues (2006) employed a "children of twins" behavioral genetic design to further specify the cause (i.e., genetic transmission or environmental stressor) of elevated rates of multiple types of problems among children who experienced a parental divorce during childhood. By examining rates and levels of problems of children of both monozygotic and dizygotic twin pairs, with some of the children's parents having divorced and others' not, the analyses were able to disentangle effects of divorce (i.e., an environmental stressor or genetic confounds). Results indicated that the environmental stressor of parental divorce had a causal role in predicting the majority of the problematic outcomes of interest, including earlier sexual activity, increased emotional problems, more problematic education outcomes, higher depressed mood, and elevated suicidal ideation, whereas genetic predispositions were associated with increased risk for cohabitation and earlier start of drug use. On the basis of a genetically sensitive design, Natsuaki, Ge, Reiss, and Neiderhiser (2009) recently reported evidence for the unique contribution of sibling aggression in understanding changes in externalizing problems during adolescence. Feinberg, Button, Neiderhiser, Reiss, and Hetherington (2007) found, using sophisticated and careful measurement and analytic methods, evidence that parenting moderated the effects of genotype on antisocial behavior. Results from these initial family process behavior-genetics investigations support continued consideration of both genetic and environmental processes when studying children's developmental environments.

Longitudinal Designs and Methodological Variety

Investigations of marital health that employ multiple methodologies and longitudinal designs have promise to advance our understanding of children's development in the context of marital environments (see Cummings, Goeke-Morey, & Dukewich, 2001; also see Seifer, Chapter 9, "Environment across Time"). Multiple levels of assessment and analysis are needed to fully capture the marital and family processes described in the present chapter. Methodologies used to investigate marital health and child development are varied and include self-report questionnaires, laboratory methods, analog methods (Goeke-Morey et al., 2003), and home diary methodologies. The diary methods in particular have shed light on the context of marital health by providing information about children's experiences of marital conflict in the home (Cummings et al., 2003, 2004). Advances in methodology elucidate marital conflict topography, what happens in families' homes, as well as specific dimensions of conflict relating to children's responding and adjustment.

Reflecting the importance of multimethod approaches, multiple carefully conducted laboratory studies have reported that marital conflicts are less destructive in the presence of the children. However, this question was rarely examined in the home, so it was uncertain whether findings generalized to home environments. Addressing this gap, Papp, Cummings, and Goeke-Morey (2002) used a diary methodology to test marital conflict characteristics and expressions as a function of whether children were present or not during interparental conflict in the home. Contrary to the findings of laboratory research, both mothers and fathers reported that they and their spouse displayed more negative emotions and behaviors during conflict in the home in which children were present. In addition, children's presence predicted the topic of conflict being about the children, which has been shown to relate to children's feelings of insecurity about family relationships and their role in family disagreements.

Added to the complexity of interrelationships among family members is that developmental or longitudinal designs are critical for understanding growth and change in children in relation to their developmental contexts, including the multiple aspects of marital health described here. Fortunately, ongoing advances in theoretical and practical implications of analyzing data collected from dyads and families facilitate investigation of marital health as a context of child development (see Burchinal, Nelson, & Poe, 2006; Kenny, Kashy, & Cook, 2006). Moreover, to accomplish these aims related to using multiple data sources and longitudinal designs, family scientists have encouraged secondary analyses of existing large-scale data sets (i.e., National Longitudinal Survey of Youth) to understand marital health processes such as marital conflict and divorce better (e.g., Houseknecht & Hango, 2006). In sum, by considering these future directions when designing studies of marital health and child development, research efforts will continue to explicate the role of marital health as a context for child development.

Conclusions

This brief review provides an overview of different pathways and processes through which marital health serves as an environmental influence on pathways of children's emotional, social, and cognitive development. The evidence support that all studies of children's developmental health should take into account marital health, given the overwhelming findings of support for children's environments both in normal families and families challenged by adversity and psychopathology (Cummings & Davies, 2010). Parenting and family researchers have sometimes neglected marital functioning in studies of family influences on child development, or assigned these influences a secondary status as family context variables, with the assumption that marital functioning affects children only indirectly through parenting (Erel, Margolin, & John, 1998; Fauber & Long, 1991). As we have seen, there is considerable evidence that exposure to marital conflict has direct effects on children's functioning and that direct pathways due to exposure to marital conflict and indirect pathways through other family processes are both significant influences. At the same time, marital and family conflict processes are also relevant to understanding the effects of many other contexts of development (e.g., divorce and remarriage) and are influenced by broader environmental contexts. For example, relations among community violence, marital health, parenting, and child adjustment have been identified, indicating that marital health is also influenced by broader environmental contexts (e.g., Cummings, Goeke-Morey, Schermerhorn, Merrilees, & Cairns, 2009). What is minimally needed is a valid and effective measure of marital conflict, distinguishing the occurrence of constructive as well as destructive conflict. In addition, measures of children's emotional security or other processes of responding to marital conflict are desirable, since these measures typically are even more powerfully reflective of the impact of marital conflict and are even more closely linked with child outcomes (see Cummings & Davies, 2010, for examples of such assessments). Thus, additional sophistication is needed both for the inclusion of marital health in broader models of environmental influences on children and for marital researchers to be aware of the broader environmental influences that may be in play in the impact of marital health on the children.

References

Amato, P. R. (2006). Marital discord, divorce, and children's well-being: Results from a 20-year long study of two generations. In A. Clarke-Stewart & J. Dunn (Eds.), *Families count: Effects on child and adolescent development*, pp. 179–202. New York: Cambridge University Press.

Avenevoli, S., Stolar, M., Li, J., Dierker, L., & Merikangas, K. R. (2001) Comorbidity of depression in children and adolescents: Models and evidence from a prospective high-risk family study. *Biological Psychiatry*, 49, 1071–1081.

Beach, S. R. H., Whisman, M. A., & O'Leary, K. D. (1994). Marital therapy for depression: Theoretical foundations, current status, and future directions. *Behavior Therapy*, 25, 345–371.

Bowlby, J. (1969). *Attachment and loss: Attachment* (Vol. 1). New York: Basic.

Brody, G. H., Stoneman, Z., & Burke, M. (1987). Family system and individual child correlates of sibling behavior. *American Journal of Orthopsychiatry*, 57, 561–569.

Burchinal, M. R., Nelson, L., & Poe, M. (2006). Growth curve analysis: An introduction to various methods for analyzing longitudinal data. In K. McCartney, M. Burchinal, & K. L. Bub (Eds.), *Best Practices in Quantitative Methods for Developmentalists. Monographs of the Society for Research on Child Development*, 71(1), 65–87, Serial No. 285.

Burton, L. M. (1990). Teenage childbearing as an alternative life-course strategy in multigenerational black families. *Human Nature*, 1, 123–143.

Christensen, A. (1988). Dysfunctional interaction patterns in couples. In P. Noller & M. A. Fitzpatrick (Eds.), *Perspectives on marital interaction*, pp. 31–52. Philadelphia, Multilingual Matters.

Coleman, M., Ganong, L., & Fine, M. (2004). Communication in stepfamilies. In A. L. Vangelisti (Ed.), *Handbook of Family Communication*, pp. 215–232. Mahwah, NJ: Lawrence Erlbaum Associates.

Costello, E. J., & Angold, A. (1988). Scales to assess child and adolescent depression: Checklists, screens, and nets. *Journal of the American Academy of Child and Adolescent Psychiatry*, 27, 726–737.

Cox, M. J., & Paley, B. (1997). Families as system. *Annual Review of Psychology*, 48, 243–268.

Cox, M. J., & Paley, B. (2003). Understanding families as systems. *Current Directions in Psychological Science*, 12, 193–196.

Cummings, E. M. (1998a). Children exposed to marital conflict and violence: Conceptual and theoretical directions. In G. W. Holden, B. Geffner, & E. N. Jouriles (Eds.), *Children exposed to marital violence: Theory, research, and applied issues*, pp. 55–94. Washington, DC: American Psychological Association.

Cummings, E. M. (1998b). Stress and coping approaches and research: The impact of marital conflict on children. *Journal of Aggression, Maltreatment, and Trauma*, 2, 31–50.

Cummings, E. M., Ballard, M., & El-Sheikh, M. (1991). Responses of children and adolescents to interadult anger as a function of gender, age, and mode of expression. *Merrill-Palmer Quarterly*, 37, 543–560.

Cummings, E. M., & Davies, P. T. (1994). *Children and marital conflict: The impact of family dispute and resolution*. New York and London: Guilford Press.

Cummings, E. M., & Davies, P. T. (2002). Effects of marital conflict on children: Recent advances and emerging themes in process-oriented research. *Journal of Child Psychology and Psychiatry, 43*, 31–63.

Cummings, E. M., & Davies, P. T. (2010). *Marital conflict and children: An emotional security perspective*. New York and London: Guilford Press.

Cummings, E. M., Davies, P. T., & Campbell, S. B. (2000). *Developmental psychopathology and family process: Theory, research, and clinical implications*. New York and London: Guilford Press.

Cummings, E. M., Davies, P. T., & Simpson, K. S. (1994). Marital conflict, gender, and children's appraisal and coping efficacy as mediators of child adjustment. *Journal of Family Psychology, 8*, 141–149.

Cummings, E. M., El-Sheikh, M., Kouros, C. D., & Buckhalt, J. A. (2009) Children and violence: The role of children's regulation in the marital aggression-child adjustment link. *Clinical Child and Family Psychology Review, 12*, 3–15.

Cummings, E. M., El-Sheikh, M., Kouros, C. D., & Keller, P. S. (2007). Children's skin conductance reactivity as a mechanism of risk in the context of parental depressive symptoms, *Journal of Child Psychology and Psychiatry, 48*, 436–445.

Cummings, E. M., Faircloth, B. F., Mitchell, P. M., Cummings, J. S., & Schermerhorn, A. C. (2008). Evaluating a brief prevention program for improving marital conflict in community families. *Journal of Family Psychology, 22*, 193–202.

Cummings, E. M., Goeke-Morey, M. C., & Dukewich, T. L. (2001). The study of relations between marital conflict and child adjustment: Challenges and new directions for methodology. In J. H. Grych & F. D. Fincham (Eds.), *Child development and interparental conflict: Theory, research, and applications*, pp. 39–63. Cambridge, MA: Cambridge University Press.

Cummings, E. M., Goeke-Morey, M. C., & Papp, L. M. (2003). Children's responses to everyday marital conflict tactics in the home. *Child Development, 74*, 1918–1929.

Cummings, E. M., Goeke-Morey, M. C., & Papp, L. M. (2004). Everyday marital conflict and child aggression. *Journal of Abnormal Child Psychology, 32*, 191–202.

Cummings, E. M., Goeke-Morey, M. C., Papp, L. M., & Dukewich, T. L. (2002). Children's responses to mothers' and fathers' emotionality and conflict tactics during marital conflict in the home. *Journal of Family Psychology, 16*, 478–492.

Cummings, E. M., Goeke-Morey, M. C., Schermerhorn, A. C., Merrilees, C. E., & Cairns, E. (2009). Children and political violence from a social ecological perspective: Implications from research on children and families in Northern Ireland. *Clinical Child and Family Psychology Review, 12*, 16–38.

Cummings, E. M., Keller, P. S., & Davies, P. T. (2005). Towards a family process model of maternal and paternal depressive symptoms: Exploring multiple relations with child and family functioning. *Journal of Child Psychology and Psychiatry, 46*, 479–489.

Cummings, E. M., Schermerhorn, A. C., Davies, P. T., Goeke-Morey, M. C. & Cummings, J. S. (2006). Interparental discord and child adjustment: Prospective investigations of emotional security as an explanatory mechanism. *Child Development, 77*, 132–152.

Cummings, E. M., Simpson, K. S., & Wilson, A. (1993). Children's responses to interadult anger as a function of information about resolution. *Developmental Psychology, 29*, 978–985.

Cummings, E. M., & Smith, D. (1993). The impact of anger between adults on siblings' emotions and social behavior. *Journal of Child Psychology and Psychiatry, 34*, 1425–1433.

Cummings, E. M., Vogel, D., Cummings, J. S., & El-Sheikh, M. (1989). Children's responses to different forms of expression of anger between adults. *Child Development, 60*, 1392–1404.

Cummings, E. M., Zahn-Waxler, C., & Radke-Yarrow, M. (1981). Young children's responses to expressions of anger and affection by others in the family. *Child Development, 52*, 1274–1282.

Davies, P. T., & Cummings, E. M. (1994). Marital conflict and child adjustment: An emotional security hypothesis. *Psychological Bulletin, 116*, 387–411.

Davies, P. T., & Cummings, E. M. (1998). Exploring children's emotional security as a mediator of the link between marital relations and child adjustment. *Child Development, 69*, 124–139.

Davies, P. T., & Cummings, E. M. (2006). Interparental discord, family process, and developmental psychopathology. In D. Cicchetti & D. Cohen (Eds.), *Developmental psychopathology:* Vol. 3. *Risk, disorder, and adaptation*, pp. 86–128 (2nd ed.). New York: John Wiley & Sons.

Davies, P. T., Harold, G. T., Goeke-Morey, M. C., & Cummings, E. M. (2002). Children's emotional security and interparental conflict. *Monographs of the Society for Research on Child Development*, 67(3), Serial No. 270.

Davies, P. T., & Lindsay, L. L. (2004). Interparental conflict and adolescent adjustment: Why does gender moderate early adolescent vulnerability? *Journal of Family Psychology*, 18, 160–170.

Davies, P. T., Myers, R. L., & Cummings, E. M. (1996). Responses of children and adolescents to marital conflict scenarios as a function of the emotionality of conflict endings. *Merrill-Palmer Quarterly*, 42, 1–21.

Davies, P. T., Myers, R. L., Cummings, E. M., & Heindel, S. (1999). Adult conflict history and children's subsequent responses to conflict. *Journal of Family Psychology*, 13, 610–628.

Davies, P. T., & Sturge-Apple, M. L. (2007). Advances in the formulation of emotional security theory: An ethologically based perspective. *Advances in Child Development and Behavior*, 35, 87–137.

D'Onofrio, B. M., Turkheimer, E., Emery, R. E., Slutske, W. S., Heath, A. C., Madden, P. A., & Martin, N. G. (2006). A genetically informed study of the processes underlying the association between parental marital instability and offspring adjustment. *Developmental Psychology*, 42, 486–499.

Driver, J. L., & Gottman, J. M. (2004). Daily marital interactions and positive affect during marital conflict among newlywed couples. *Family Process*, 43, 301–314.

Du Rocher Schudlich, T. D., & Cummings, E. M. (2003). Parental dysphoria and children's internalizing symptoms: Marital conflict styles as mediators of risk. *Child Development*, 74, 1663–1681.

Du Rocher Schudlich, T. D., & Cummings, E. M. (2007). Parental dysphoria and children's adjustment: Marital conflict styles, children's emotional security, and parenting as mediators of risk. *Journal of Abnormal Child Psychology*, 35, 627–639.

Dush, C. M. K., & Amato, P. A. (2005). Consequences of relationship status and quality for subjective well-being. *Journal of Social and Personal Relationships*, 22, 607–627.

El-Sheikh, M., Cummings, E. M., Kouros, C. D., Elmore-Staton, L., & Buckhalt, J. A. (2008). Marital psychological and physical aggression and children's mental and physical health:

Direct, mediated, and moderated effects. *Journal of Consulting and Clinical Psychology*, 78, 138–148.

El-Sheikh, M., & Flanagan, E. (2001). Parental problem drinking and children's adjustment: Family conflict and parental depression as mediators and moderators of risk. *Journal of Abnormal Child Psychology*, 29, 417–432.

Emery, R. E. (1982). Interparental conflict and the children of discord and divorce. *Psychology Bulletin*, 92, 310–330.

Emery, R. E. (1994). *Renegotiating family relationships: Divorce, child custody, and mediation*. New York and London: Guilford Press.

Emery, R. E., Kitzmann, K. M., & Waldron, M. (1999). Psychological interventions for separated and divorced families. In E. M. Hetherington (Ed.), *Coping with divorce, single parenting, and remarriage: A risk and resiliency perspective*, pp. 323–344. Mahwah, NJ: Erlbaum.

Erel, O., & Burman, B. (1995). Interrelatedness of marital relations and parent-child relations: A meta-analytic review. *Psychological Bulletin*, 118, 108–132.

Erel, O., Margolin, G., & John, R. S. (1998). Observed sibling interaction: links with the marital and the mother-child relationship. *Developmental Psychology*, 34, 288–298.

Essex, M. J., Klein, M. H., Cho, E., & Kraemer, H. C. (2003). Exposure to maternal depression and marital conflict: gender differences in children's later mental health symptoms. *Journal of the American Academy of Child and Adolescent Psychiatry*, 42, 728–737.

Fauber, R. L., & Long, N. (1991). Children in context: The role of the family in child psychotherapy. *Journal of Consulting and Clinical Psychology*, 59, 813–820.

Feinberg, M. E., Button, T. M. M., Neiderhiser, J. M., Reiss, D. & Hetherington, E. M. (2007). Parenting and adolescent antisocial behavior and depression: Evidence of genotype × parenting environment interaction. *Archives of General Psychiatry*, 64, 457–465.

Fincham, F. D. (2003). Marital conflict: Correlates, structure and context. *Current Directions in Psychological Science*, 12, 23–27.

Funk, J. L., & Rogge, R. D. (2007). Testing the ruler with item response theory: Increasing precision of measurement for relationship satisfaction with the Couples Satisfaction Index. *Journal of Family Psychology*, 21, 572–583.

Gass, K., Jenkins, J. M., & Dunn, J. (2007). Are sibling relationships protective?: A longitudinal study. *Journal of Child Psychology and Psychiatry*, 48, 167–175.

Goeke-Morey, M. C., Cummings, E. M., Harold, G. T., & Shelton, K. H. (2003). Categories and continua of destructive and constructive marital conflict tactics from the perspective of Welsh and US children. *Journal of Family Psychology*, 17, 327–338.

Goeke-Morey, M. C., Cummings, E. M., & Papp, L. M. (2007). Children and marital conflict resolution: Implications for emotional security and adjustment. *Journal of Family Psychology*, 21, 744–753.

Greeff, A. P. (2000). Characteristics of families that function well. *Journal of Family Issues*, 21, 948–962.

Grych, J. H. (1998). Children's appraisals of interparental conflict: Situational and contextual influences. *Journal of Family Psychology*, 12, 1–17.

Grych, J. H., & Fincham, F. D. (1993). Children's appraisals of marital conflict: Initial tests of the cognitive contextual framework. *Child Development*, 64, 215–230.

Grych, J. H., Harold, G., & Miles, C. (2003). A prospective investigation of appraisals as mediators of the link between interparental conflict and child adjustment. *Child Development*, 74, 1176–1193.

Hammen, C. (1991). *Depression runs in families: The social context of risk and resilience in children of depressed mothers.* New York: Springer-Verlag.

Harold, G. T., Shelton, K. H., Goeke-Morey, M. C., & Cummings, E. M. (2004). Marital conflict and child adjustment: Prospective longitudinal tests of the mediating role of children's emotional security about family relationships. *Social Development*, 13, 350–376.

Hawkins, M. W., Carrère, S., & Gottman, J. M. (2002). Marital sentiment override: Does it influence couples' perceptions? *Journal of Marriage and Family*, 64, 193–201.

Hetherington, E. M., & Kelly, J. B. (2002). *For better or worse.* New York: Norton.

Houseknecht, S. K., & Hango, D. W. (2006). The impact of marital conflict and disruption on children's health. *Youth and Society*, 38, 58–89.

Hutchison, I. W., & Hirschel, J. D. (2001). The effect of children's presence on woman abuse. *Violence and Victims*, 16, 3–17.

Jenkins, J. M., Simpson, A., Dunn, J., Rasbash, J., & O'Connor, T. G. (2005). Mutual influences of marital conflict and children's behavior

problems: Shared and nonshared family risk. *Child Development*, 76, 24–39.

Jenkins, J. M., & Smith, M. A. (1991). Marital disharmony and children's behavioral problems: Aspects of a poor marriage which affect children adversely. *Journal of Child Psychology and Psychiatry*, 32, 793–810.

Jenkins, J. M., Smith, M. A., & Graham, P. J. (1989). Coping with parental quarrels. *Journal of the American Academy of Child and Adolescent Psychiatry*, 28, 182–189.

Johnston, J. R., Gonzales, R., & Campbell, L. E. G. (1987). Ongoing postdivorce conflict and child disturbances. *Journal of Abnormal Child Psychology*, 15, 493–510.

Jouriles, E. N., Bourg, W. J., & Farris, A. M. (1991). Marital adjustment and child conduct problems: A comparison of the correlation across subsamples. *Journal of Consulting and Clinical Psychology*, 59, 354–357.

Karney, B. R. (2001). Depressive symptoms and marital satisfaction in the early years of marriage: Narrowing the gap between theory and research. In S. R. H. Beach (Ed.), *Marital and family processes in depression: A scientific foundation for clinical practice*, pp. 45–68. Washington, DC: American Psychological Association.

Katz, L. F., & Woodin, E. M. (2001). *Hostility, hostile-detachment, and conflict engagement in marriages: Effects on child and family functioning.* Paper presented at the meeting of the Society for Research on Child Development, Minneapolis, MN.

Keller, P. S., Cummings, E. M., & Davies, P. T. (2005). The role of marital discord and parenting in relations between parental problem drinking and child adjustment. *Journal of Child Psychology and Psychiatry*, 46, 943–951.

Keller, P. S., Cummings, E. M., Davies, P. T., & Mitchell, P. M. (2008). Longitudinal relations between parental drinking problems, family functioning, and child adjustment. *Development and Psychopathology*, 20, 195–212.

Kelly, J. B. (2000). Children's adjustment in conflicted marriage and divorce: A decade review of research. *Journal of American Academy of Child and Adolescent Psychiatry*, 39, 963–973.

Kenny, D. A., Kashy, D. A., Cook, W. L. (2006). *Dyadic data analysis.* New York and London: Guilford Press.

Kerig, P. K. (1996). Assessing the links between interpersonal conflict and child adjustment:

The conflict and problem-solving scale. *Journal of Family Psychology, 4,* 454–473.

Kerig, P. K. (1998). Moderators and mediators of the effects of interparental conflict on children's adjustment. *Journal of Abnormal Child Psychology, 26,* 199–212.

Krishnakumar, A., & Buehler, C. (2000). Interparental conflict and parenting practices: A meta-analysis. *Family Relations, 49,* 25–44.

Laumakis, M. A., Margolin, G., & John, R. S. (1998). The emotional, cognitive, and coping responses of preadolescent children to marital conflict. In G. W. Holden & R. Geffner (Eds.), *Children exposed to marital violence: Theory, research and applied issues,* pp. 257–288. Washington, DC: American Psychological Association.

Lillard, L. E., & Waite, L. J. (1995). 'Til death do us part: Marital disruption and mortality. *American Journal of Sociology, 100,* 1131–1156.

Mahoney, A., & Jouriles, E. N., & Scavone, J. (1997). Marital adjustment, marital discord over childrearing and child behavior problems: Moderating effects of child age. *Journal of Clinical Child Psychology, 26,* 415–423.

McCoy, K., Cummings, E. M., & Davies, P. T. (2009). Constructive and destructive marital conflict, emotional security, and children's prosocial behavior. *Journal of Child Psychology and Psychiatry, 50,* 270–279.

McDonald, R., Jouriles, E. N., Norwood, W., Ware, H. S., & Ezell, E. (2000). Husbands' marital violence and the adjustment problems of clinic-referred children. *Behavior Therapy, 31,* 649–665.

McLoyd, V. C., Cauce, A. M., Takeuchi, D., & Wilson, L. (2000). Marital processes and parental socialization in families of color: A decade review of research. *Journal of Marriage and the Family, 62,* 1070–1093.

McLoyd, V. C., Harper, C. I., & Copeland, N. L. (2001). Ethnic minority status, interparental conflict, and child adjustment: Theory, research, and application. In J. H. Grych & F. D. Fincham (Eds.), *Interparental conflict and child development: Theory, research, and applications,* pp. 98–125. New York: Cambridge University Press.

Morrison, D. R., & Coiro, M. J. (1999). Parental conflict and marital disruption: Do children benefit when high-conflict marriages are dissolved? *Journal of Marriage and the Family, 61,* 626–637.

National Institute of Child Health and Human Development (October 18, 2006). Marriage and couple relationships. Retrieved December 12, 2006, from http://www.nichd.nih.gov/about/org/cpr/dbs/prog_dem/marriage.cfm.

National Institute of Child Health and Human Development Early Child Care Research Network (2002). The interaction of child care and family risk in relation to child development at 24 and 36 months. *Applied Developmental Science, 6,* 144–156.

Natsuaki, M. N., Ge, X., Reiss, D., Niderhiser, J. M. (2009). Aggressive behavior between siblings and the development of externalizing problems: Evidence from a genetically sensitive study. *Developmental Psychology, 45,* 1009–1018.

Nomura, Y., Wickramartne, P. J., Warner, V., Mufson, L., & Weissman, M. M. (2002). Family discord, parental depression, and psychopathology in offspring: Ten-year follow-up. *Journal of American Academy of Child and Adolescent Psychiatry, 41,* 402–409.

O'Hearn, H. G., Margolin, G., & John, R. S. (1997). Mothers' and fathers' reports of children's reactions to naturalistic marital conflict. *Journal of the American Academy of Child and Adolescent Psychiatry, 36,* 1366–1373.

O'Leary, K. D., Slep, A. M. S., & O'Leary, S. G. (2000). Co-occurrence of partner and parent aggression: research and treatment implications. *Behavior Therapy, 31,* 631–648.

Panish, J., & Sticker, G. (2001). Parental marital conflict in childhood and influence on adult sibling relationships. *Journal of Psychotherapy in Independent Practice, 2,* 3–16.

Papp, L. M., Cummings, E. M., & Goeke-Morey, M. C. (2002). Marital conflict in the home when children are present versus absent. *Developmental Psychology, 38,* 774–783.

Papp, L. M., Cummings, E. M., & Schermerhorn, A. C. (2004). Pathways among marital distress, parental symptomatology, and child adjustment. *Journal of Marriage and Family, 66,* 368–384.

Papp, L. M., Goeke-Morey, M. C., & Cummings, E. M. (2007). Linkages between spouses' psychological distress and marital conflict in the home. *Journal of Family Psychology, 21,* 533–537.

Papp, L. M., Kouros, C. D., & Cummings, E. M. (2009). Demand-withdraw patterns in marital conflict in the home. *Personal Relationships, 16,* 285–300.

Parke, R. D., Coltrane, S., Duffy, S., Buriel, R., Dennis, J., Powers, J., French, S., & Widaman, K. F. (2004). Economic stress, parenting, and child adjustment in Mexican American and European American families. *Child Development*, 75, 1632–1656.

Pearson, J., Muller, C., & Frisco, M. (2006). Parental involvement, family structure and adolescent sexual decision making. *Sociological Perspectives*, 49, 67–90.

Reifman, A., Villa, L. C., Amans, J. A., Rethinam, V. R., & Telesca, T. Y. (2001). Children of Divorce in the 1990s: A meta-analysis. *Journal of Divorce and Remarriage*, 36, 27–37.

Rhoades, K. A. (2008). Children's responses to interparental conflict: A meta-analysis of their associations with child adjustment. *Child Development*, 79, 1942–1956.

Rice, F., Harold, G. T., Shelton, K. H., & Thapar, A. (2006). Family conflict interacts with genetic liability in predicting childhood and adolescent depression. *Journal of the American Academy of Child and Adolescent Psychiatry*, 45, 841–848.

Richmond, M. K., & Stocker, C. M. (2003). Sibling's differential experiences of marital conflict and differences in psychological adjustment. *Journal of Family Psychology*, 17, 339–350.

Schoppe-Sullivan, S. J., Schermerhorn, A. C., & Cummings, E. M. (2007). Marital conflict and children's adjustment over time: Testing parental behavioral control, psychological autonomy, and warmth as mediators. *Journal of Marriage and Family*, 69, 1118–1134.

Shifflett, K., & Cummings, E. M. (1999). A program for educating parents about the effects of divorce and conflict on children. *Family Relations*, 48, 79–98.

Skopp, N. A., McDonald, R., Manke, B., & Jouriles, E. N. (2005). Siblings in domestically violent families: Experiences of interparent conflict and adjustment problems. *Journal of Family Psychology*, 19, 324–333.

Spotts, E. L., Prescott, C. A., & Kendler, K. S. (2006). Examining the origins of gender differences in marital quality: A behavior genetic analysis. *Journal of Family Psychology*, 20, 605–613.

Stocker, C. M., & Youngblade, L. (1999). Marital conflict and parental hostility: Links with children's sibling and peer relationships. *Journal of Family Psychology*, 13, 598–609.

Sturge-Apple, M. L., Davies, P. T., & Cummings, E. M. (2006). Hostility and withdrawal in marital conflict: Effects on parental emotional unavailability and inconsistent discipline. *Journal of Family Psychology*, 20, 227–238.

Sturge-Apple, M. L., Davies, P. T., & Cummings, E. M. (2006). The impact of hostility and withdrawal in interparental conflict on parental emotional unavailability and children's adjustment difficulties. *Child Development*, 77, 1623–1641.

Sturge-Apple, M. L., Davies, P. T., Winter, M. A., Cummings, E. M., & Schermerhorn, A. C. (2008). Interparental conflict and children's school adjustment: The explanatory role of children's internal representations of interparental and parent-child relationships. *Developmental Psychology*, 44, 1678–1690.

Tucker, C. J., McHale, S. M., & Crouter, A. C. (2001). Conditions of sibling support in adolescence. *Journal of Family Psychology*, 15, 254–271.

Waldinger, R. J., & Schulz, M. S. (2006). Linking hearts and minds in couple interactions: Intentions, attributions, and overriding sentiments. *Journal of Family Psychology*, 20, 494–504.

CHAPTER 20

Parental Psychopathology

A Developmental Perspective on Mechanisms of Transmission

Nancy E. Suchman and Cindy DeCoste

Introduction

It has been well established that human psychopathology, including depression, anxiety disorders, substance use disorders, eating disorders, attention deficit disorders and schizophrenia, aggregates within families and occurs across generations (Goodman & Gotlib, 1999; Moore, Whaley, & Sigman, 2004; Murray & Johnston, 2006; Turner, Beidel, Roberson-Nay, & Tervo, 2003; Waugh & Bulik, 1999). Very little is understood, though, about the mechanisms of transmission by which parental psychopathology is "passed on" to children. Recent research, particularly research focusing on parental depression, suggests that pathways of influence are dynamic, multiple and complex. The influence of parental psychopathology on child development can be understood as a function of its own dynamic or fluctuating nature. That is, the nature of adult psychopathology inevitably varies in terms of timing, duration, chronicity, symptom constellation and severity, occurrence of single vs. multiple episodes, and comorbidity. These fluctuations are, in turn, likely to

cause variation in consequences for children. Parental psychopathology can also influence child development by any number of direct and indirect pathways. Direct pathways can include genetic or hereditary mechanisms that predate the child's birth, biological mechanisms occurring during pregnancy and social interactive mechanisms that begin at birth and continue throughout childhood. More complex and indirect pathways can involve the occurrence of subclinical affects, cognitions or behaviors in a parent that may bring about related subclinical features in a child that, in turn, increase the child's vulnerability to develop a psychiatric disorder. Alternatively, indirect pathways can involve processes of mediation and moderation. Parental psychopathology may predispose a parent to presentations or behaviors that may, in turn, trigger a series of mediating factors that then influence child development. Alternatively, parental psychopathology may be directly influenced by distal (e.g., socioeconomic background, cultural milieu, or physical environment) or proximal (e.g., family configuration, marital relationship, availability of social and emotional support, or child characteristics) environmental factors that then moderate its influence on child development.

The developmental trajectories of both child and parent may also influence parental psychopathology and moderate its influence on child development. Parental psychopathology may best be understood within a developmental framework that is sensitive to the normative maturational tasks that a child is attempting to master at the time of exposure (Goodman & Gotlib, 1999). Parental psychopathology may influence subclinical and clinical phenomena in the child differentially across infancy, toddlerhood, school-age and adolescent years as stage-salient child developmental tasks change. These influences may occur as a result of one-way or reciprocal interactive processes between parent and child.

The developmental framework must also take into account the normative tasks and transitions that the parent is negotiating in his or her role as parent at the time of occurrence. Beginning with the first pregnancy and continuing through each child's progression to adulthood, a parent also transitions through developmental stages characterized by requisite parenting challenges and tasks commensurate with the child's stage of physical, psychological and social development.

The aim of this chapter is to review existing evidence about the influence of parental psychopathology and its implications for child development from the perspective that parental psychopathology is a *dynamic process* (rather than a static factor) that can adopt any number of potential direct, indirect, and multidirectional pathways outlined earlier. Perhaps the most attention in the psychopathology literature during the last 20 years has been given to parental depression, although, more recently, studies examining parental anxiety disorders, eating disorders and substance use disorders have been important contributions to the parenting literature. Far less has been published on parental attention deficit disorder, obsessive-compulsive disorder, personality disorder, psychotic disorders, and schizophrenia.

In this chapter, findings from review articles and reports of individual investigations, alike, are drawn on for evidence of the proposed mechanisms outlined earlier.

The chapter begins with a focus on broad considerations regarding the nature of parental psychopathology. The focus then shifts toward examining direct pathways of influence, starting with genetic pathways initiated prior to a child's birth, followed by biological pathways that are salient during pregnancy, and ending with psychosocial pathways following a child's birth. Findings pertaining to psychosocial pathways of influence are considered within a developmental framework that takes into account stages of child and parental development. Finally, evidence for more complex mediating and moderating psychosocial processes of influence are presented.

Substance use disorders are unique among psychiatric disorders because they involve the ingestion of alcohol or drugs that have specific neuropharmacological effects for the parent and, when ingested during pregnancy, the child. The use of illicit drugs (e.g., marijuana, cocaine and heroin) and the misuse of prescription drugs also entail participation in illegal activities related to the procurement and ingestion of drugs. These activities have placed parents with substance-using disorders at odds with societal norms. Each of these important aspects of parental drug use has profound implications for parental functioning and child development. The topic is therefore addressed in a separate section following the review of other parental psychiatric disorders.

A majority of studies to date have focused on maternal (versus paternal) psychopathology. In referring to parental psychopathology throughout the main body of the chapter, we are most often reporting on findings pertaining to maternal psychopathology unless otherwise noted. Although a new body of literature on paternal psychopathology is emerging, it has continued to receive less attention than maternal psychopathology in research. Findings from recent studies examining effects of paternal psychopathology for children both in relation to maternal psychopathology as well as alone are summarized in a separate section. The chapter ends in the *Conclusions* section with a focus on areas yet to be addressed in the parental psychopathology literature, including psychopathology in foster and adoptive parents, pros and cons of parental absenteeism during treatment, and implications of parental psychopathology for caregiving in the next generation.

The Fluctuating Nature of Parental Psychopathology

Timing of Episode

The timing of a parent's psychopathology episode may be a strong predictor of its effect on child development. Early exposure to parental psychopathology, for example, may interfere with development of regulatory functions in the infant (Goodman & Gotlib, 1999). Systems that are relevant to the regulation of arousal (e.g., HPA system and parasympathetic regulation) are functionally immature at birth and mature gradually over the first years of life. Cortical inhibitory controls over arousal also emerge gradually during infancy. Maternal regulation of arousal is therefore needed most in the first year of life. The child's social and emotional development that builds on the foundation of regulation is almost entirely contingent upon the relationship with the caregiver during the first years. Psychopathology that interferes with maternal capacity to regulate arousal (e.g., postpartum depression and anxiety) may render mothers incapable of providing regulatory guidance. The potential for parental mental illness to have the greatest impact on a child's adjustment, then, would likely be greatest during early childhood, when children are most dependent on the caregiver (Seifer, 2003).

Research on parental depression suggests that the timing of a parent's psychopathology episode – especially the first episode – in a child's lifetime may be the strongest determinant of the nature and magnitude of its effect on the child's subsequent development and vulnerability to developing a psychological disorder (Goodman & Gotlib, 1999). Research on maternal depression has also suggested that exposure to maternal psychopathology during infancy may be more difficult for an infant to recover from because of potentially lost ground in normal development due to effects of maternal depression on the infant's regulatory capacities. Thus, the negative effects could continue through later periods of child development when the child may additionally acquire peer status (rejected or neglected) or dysfunctional patterns (e.g., cognitive sets) that are difficult to alter (Goodman & Gotlib, 1999).

Chronicity and Recurrence

Parental psychopathology is not usually a single time-limited event. Many mental illnesses are chronic or recurrent over long periods that coincide with the unfolding of the parent-child relationship and the child's development (Goodman & Gotlib, 1999; Seifer, 2003). Moreover, patterns of chronicity and recurrence are likely to affect the timing of psychopathology episodes. For example, new mothers are most vulnerable to increased depressive symptoms following their first pregnancy but these symptoms usually diminish over time (Seifer, 2003). Taking timing and chronicity of parental psychopathology into account, the older a child is at the time of exposure to parental psychopathology, the more likely it is that behavioral systems will have matured and the child will be less vulnerable to adverse effects and will have developed competencies that prepare him / her for successful coping (Goodman & Gotlib, 1999).

A chronic course of psychopathology may be likely to have more negative effects for children than a single episode. Chronicity of depression, for example, has been associated with poorer mother-infant interactions, child hostility at school and at home, lower adaptive functioning and higher rates of psychopathology in children and adolescents (Goodman & Gotlib, 1999; Seifer, 2003). Increases in parental depression over time have also predicted more internalizing and externalizing problems in children and lower social competence in adolescents (Zahn-Waxler, Duggal, & Gruber, 2002).

Even when parental psychopathology remits, it is not clear whether the impact on children also subsides. For example, there is some evidence that infants of mothers whose postpartum depression abated ceased to be symptomatic at 12 months. Other studies have shown that, regardless of parental recovery, children whose parents were depressed during infant or toddler years continue to show behavior problems, lower cognitive functioning, internalizing problems, mood symptoms, and somatic complaints during school-age and adolescent years (Goodman & Gotlib, 1999).

Situational versus Global Psychopathology

Parental psychopathology can be thought of as situational, emerging in response to a specific stressor, or global, maintaining a constant presence regardless of the ebb and flow of stressors in an individual's life. This is particularly evident in research on parental anxiety disorders that emerge in response to external stressors and trauma. For example, there is some evidence that separation anxiety in parents may be a function of a parent's appraisal of resources or strain in relevant situations. Hsu (2004) found that maternal apprehension about separation from infants was specifically related to parenting hassles that were child-related (e.g., scheduling child activities) or work-related (e.g., finding child care) rather than global and nonspecific. In another study, Wijnorks (1999) found that anxiety precipitated by premature birth predicted intrusive maternal behavior at 6 months post partum.

The stress precipitated by exposure to precipitating events can also impact parental psychological functioning. Community violence, for example, has been found to affect the ability of parents to respond to the needs of their children negatively because of higher levels of parental emotional distress, lower levels of parenting efficacy, and diminished self-esteem. As a result, children

exposed to community violence may be unable to derive feelings of safety and security from distressed and possibly traumatized parents (Aisenberg & Ell, 2005). Preexisting psychological vulnerability is also a major risk factor for more extreme and sustained negative reactions to external stressors or traumas, particularly those identified with posttraumatic stress (Phillips, Featherman, & Liu, 2004).

Children's responses to external stressors and traumas (e.g., war, terrorism, community violence) can also affect the parent's psychological functioning. For example, parents who perceived more distress in their children following the 9/11 attacks remained twice as likely to feel threatened as parents who did not encounter distressed children for 1 year following the attacks (Phillips et al., 2004). Children's aggressive response to community violence may likewise diminish a parent's sense of self-efficacy and self-esteem and increase a parent's emotional distress and sense of powerlessness (Aisenberg & Ell, 2005). The psychological well-being of parents may therefore be placed at greater risk by their exposure to and responsibility for children who are struggling with parallel fears and insecurities in response to a traumatic event (Phillips et al., 2004).

A child illness can also trigger parental posttraumatic stress symptomatology in parents, although social contextual factors can help buffer the severity of symptoms. In one study with 72 mothers of children (ages 5 to 23) who had successfully completed cancer treatment, Manne and colleagues (2000) reported that perceived social support (a sense of belonging to a social network) and perceived social constraints (comfort expressing cancer-related thoughts and feelings to friends and family) appeared to play a key role in mothers' long-term adjustment to their children's illness.

Contextual factors may also protect children from parental psychopathology. For example, in a study examining attachment and traumatic stress in female holocaust child survivors and their daughters,

Sagi-Schwartz and colleagues (2003) reported that, even after 50 years, survivors showed more unresolved loss on the Adult Attachment Interview and displayed more anxiety and traumatic stress than a matched comparison group. The daughters of the survivors, however, did not differ from the comparison group in their attachment representations, anxiety, traumatic stress reactions, or maternal behavior toward their infants. The authors suggest that the child survivors were able to protect their social lives and family relationships from being influenced by their Holocaust experiences.

The Mediating Role of Parental Psychopathology

Parental psychopathology may also mediate effects of external stressors and traumas on children. Studies of people living in war zones, for example, have confirmed that the level of emotional upset and anxiety displayed by parents, not the war conflict itself, is the most important factor in predicting children's response (Aisenberg & Ell, 2005). Maternal distress has also been shown to be a mediator of child behavior problems, reducing the direct effect of community violence by at least 50 percent (see Aisenberg & Ell, 2005).

Diagnosis

Psychiatric diagnosis, and commensurate characteristics of a disorder, appear to play a role in differentiating among parenting difficulties. For example, compared with mothers with affective disorders, schizophrenic mothers are more remote, insensitive, intrusive, and self-absorbed, less likely to maintain contact, show sensitivity or responsiveness, less affectively involved, and likely to provide a poorer home environment and less maintenance of routine care (Zahn-Waxler et al., 2002).

Personality disorder classifications have also been linked with variations in parenting styles. For example, schizoid and paranoid personality disorders, both characterized by highly restricted involvement with others,

have each been linked with a lack of involvement with children. Dependent personality disorder, characterized by an excessive need to be taken care of and fear of separation, has been associated with overinvolved parenting. Avoidant personality, characterized by social inhibition, feelings of inadequacy, and hypersensitivity to criticism, has been linked with unavailable or underinvolved parenting. Antisocial personality disorder, characterized by a marked absence of conscience or concern about others, has been associated with maternal unresponsiveness to child emotional cues and distress (for a review, see Zahn-Waxler, 2002).

Perhaps the starkest example of the salience of psychiatric diagnosis involves the parental diagnosis of borderline personality disorder. Based on borderline personality disorder characteristics, children of parents with borderline personality disorder are likely to be exposed to dramatic behaviors (e.g., recurrent suicidal behavior, gestures, threats, self-mutilating behavior, impulsivity) that can be frightening and traumatic. Children are also likely to be at risk for becoming targets of their parent's projections and distortions of reality, given the characteristic extreme preoccupation the parent is likely to have with being abandoned and with the his or her own needs. Children may be viewed by the parent as a stressor on a fragile intimate relationship and treated with covert or overt hostility. Children may, alternatively, be viewed as a source of stability and support for the parent, which may overburden the child with adult concerns and a sense of responsibility for the parent's well-being. The parent's difficulty with controlling anger may increase physical and emotional abuse. Reactivity of parent's mood may be confusing and frightening (Zahn-Waxler et al., 2002).

Symptom Constellation, Severity and Comorbidity

The specific cluster of symptoms may be a better determinant of parental psychopathology effects than overall diagnosis. For example, positive symptoms of schizophrenia (vs negative symptoms) are associated with parental unresponsiveness, absence of positive affect, understimulation, and hostility, whereas schizophrenic mothers with psychotic symptoms are more likely to exhibit infant neglect (Zahn-Waxler et al., 2002).

Symptom severity is also likely to predict worsened parenting. In mothers of infants, low levels of separation anxiety have been found to promote optimal parenting behavior whereas excessive separation anxiety may be maladaptive and disruptive to the normal development of the mother-child relationship (Hsu, 2004). Greater severity of eating disorders has generally been associated with a higher frequency of perinatal complications (Waugh &Bulik, 1999).

A combination of disorders may increase a child's exposure to one or both disorders. For example, the common co-occurrence of depression and personality disorders increases the probability for parenting problems. Children are also more likely to be exposed to parental depressive symptoms when an underlying personality disorder is also present. Other common co-occurrences of mental disorders include depression and anxiety disorders, eating disorders with depression or anxiety, and antisocial personality disorder with substance abuse. The latter has been linked with aggravated affect toward children (Zahn-Waxler et al., 2002).

Pathways of Influence Prior to the Birth of the Child

Genetic Pathways

The first pathway by which parental psychopathology may influence child development involves the transmission of a genetic predisposition of a disorder or vulnerability to the disorder by way of DNA. In other words, children of parents with the disorder inherit DNA that is different than that inherited by children of parents without the psychiatric disorder. Evidence for this pathway lies in the high level of aggregation of similar disorders within families. Depression, for example, has been found to be 25 percent heritable (Goodman & Gotlib, 1999).

For depression, DNA appears to also regulate the biological mechanism that either increases or decreases a child's vulnerability to the disorder (Goodman & Gotlib, 1999). For anxiety, though, there is some evidence that age-specific environmental factors may switch anxiety "on" or "off" (Woodruff-Borden, Morrow, Bourland, & Cambron, 2002). Heritability of eating disorder symptoms (e.g., body dissatisfaction, eating and weight concerns, and abnormal eating behaviors such as binge eating and vomiting) has been found to range from 32 to 72 percent, though a large proportion of variance remains unexplained by genetic factors, implying that environmental contributions are also very important (Park, Senior, & Stein, 2003). Eating disorders may share genetic transmission with other psychiatric disorders, particularly major depression and obsessive-compulsive disorder, although there is also evidence of independent genetic effects. Some eating abnormalities associated with eating disorders may be activated at puberty and mediated by ovarian hormones (Park et al., 2003).

The severity of psychiatric disorders transmitted from parents to children may be linked with a genetic predisposition for that disorder. For example, for depression in children of mothers diagnosed with major depression, 78 percent of variance has been linked with genetic effects and family environment appears to play a small role. Depression in children of mothers with subclinical symptoms of depression is more likely to be a function of environmental factors (Goodman & Gotlib, 1999).

Evidence of a genetic factor linked to the transmission of psychiatric disorders has also been found in comparisons of individuals with specific disorders with and without family histories of that disorder. For example, women with higher familial incidence of depression are more likely to experience postpartum depression in response to normal challenges of pregnancy and child birth. Offspring of mothers who experienced depression before age 20 or post partum are more likely to carry higher heritability for depression than offspring whose mother's depression occurred after age 20 and was not post partum. Higher familial incidence of depression has been linked with an onset of depression before age 20. Genetic transmission of risk for depression plays an important role in child and adolescent onset of depression as well (Goodman & Gotlib, 1999). Evidence of a genetic factor has also been found in research examining implications of the presence versus absence of specific genetic risk factors. Van IJzendoorn and Bakermans-Kranenburg (2006) also found that transmission of maternal unresolved loss to the next generation of infants as evidenced in their disorganized attachment status was moderated by the presence of a genetic risk factor associated with inefficient re-uptake of the dopamine neurotransmitter. It took this combination of a parenting environmental factor and a genetic risk factor to develop the most anxious type of attachment in infants.

Children may also inherit vulnerabilities to personality traits, cognitive or interpersonal styles that increase risk for developing a psychiatric disorder (e.g., temperament, affect, self-esteem, shyness or outgoingness). For example, high reactivity in 4-month old infants (high motor and cry activity in response to novel stimuli) has been associated with behavioral inhibition later (quiet withdrawal in response to novel inanimate stimuli and strangers), which has been found to be more prevalent among children of anxious and panic disordered parents. Behavioral inhibition has been found to be more prevalent in children of parents with panic disorder than children of parents without psychopathology and also a strong predictor of later anxiety disorder (Warren, Gunnar, Kagan, Anders et al., 2003). Behavioral inhibition, a temperament characteristic commonly found in toddlers of anxious parents, appears to have a genetic basis for predisposition as well (Kaitz and Maytal, 2005).

Biological Pathways

A second potential pathway for parental psychopathology involves the interaction of innate dysfunctional neuroregulatory mechanisms in the mother with the fetus via biological pathways during pregnancy (Goodman & Gotlib, 1999). This kind of transmission is restricted to infants born to mothers who experienced episodes of the disorder during pregnancy or suffered an episode prior to the pregnancy that caused biological changes to the mother from which she did not recover. The child is then born with a dysfunctional neuroregulatory mechanism that is a direct effect of abnormal fetal developments caused by mother's disorder during pregnancy. The dysfunction could result from exposure to neuroendocrine alterations associated with the disorder, abnormal blood flow to fetus, poor maternal health behaviors caused by the disorder, or use of psychotropic medication for the disorder. At birth, abnormal fetal developments manifest as behavioral traits or tendencies to react to certain events with a particular response style (i.e., behavioral or affective response). These behaviors and responses are thought to suggest neuroregulatory dysfunction because they occur too close to birth to reflect infant responses to the mother's disorder. The behaviors are also thought to increase the infant's vulnerability to development of subsequent disorder.

Within a few days of birth, for example, infants of depressed mothers have shown poorer performance on Brazelton Neonatal Behavioral Assessment Scale for orientation and depressive clusters, minimal response to inanimate or social stimuli, decreased motor tone and lower activity levels, less robustness and endurance, and excessive crying and inconsolability (Goodman & Gotlib, 1999). Likewise, the hypothalamic-pituitary-adrenal (HPA) axis and elevations in levels of salivary cortisol have been described as activated in response to conditions of fear, anxiety and threat. Although higher levels of salivary cortisol have not been consistently associated with anxiety disorders in children, per se, they have been associated with risk for internalizing symptoms (Warren et al., 2003). It is feasible, then that elevated salivary cortisol in infants may be an indicator for higher arousal or arousability, signifying a vulnerability to developing an anxiety disorder that would be a function of parental disorder, occurring too early to be a response to the parenting environment. Behavioral inhibition, a characteristic among many toddlers of anxious mothers, also appears to have a physiological as well as genetic basis for predisposition (Kaitz & Maytal, 2005).

Women with eating disorders have an increased rate of fertility problems (Park et al., 2003). Active eating disorder symptoms during pregnancy increase risk of miscarriage as well as physiological complications for infants after birth, including obstetric complications, prematurity, low birth weight, congenital malformations, growth impairment, and higher perinatal mortality. Even when other symptoms remit, a fundamental, pathognomonic ambivalence toward weight gain in mothers with anorexia nervosa appears to inhibit them from achieving essential weight gain during pregnancy that, in turn, is reflected in their children's lower birth weight (Park et al., 2003; Waugh & Bulik, 1999). Case reports of infants of mothers diagnosed with anorexia nervosa have indicated prematurity, perinatal mortality, obstetric complications, lower Apgar Scores in newborns, and congenital abnormalities (Park et al., 2003). Case reports of infants born to mothers with bulimia nervosa have shown increased rates of intrauterine growth impairment, obstetric complications and congenital malformations as well. Serotonin dynamics may also be disturbed in women with eating disorders, even on recovery (Park et al., 2003).

Prebirth Psychological Characteristics

A third and perhaps more elusive pathway involves the link between prenatal psychological characteristics and postnatal parental adjustment. For the prospective parent, the period of pregnancy to birth involves a symbiotic phase characterized by the formation and reformation of images of what is to come, including birth and parenthood, with the central parenting tasks being the preparation for the parenting role, for relationship changes, and the formation of feelings and impressions of the baby (Galinsky,

1981). There is evidence that a broad spectrum of critical postnatal parenting tasks, including responding to the needs of the infant, teaching and exposing children to new cognitive experiences, and promoting children's autonomy, are predicted by prebirth psychosocial characteristics of the individual (Heinicke, 2002). These parenting tasks, in turn, are related to postnatal infant development in many areas of competence, security, and autonomy. Prebirth parental characteristics that are critical to postnatal parental functioning include (1) personality functioning (operationalized as ego strength, emotional stability, adaptation-competence, absence of task-related anger, and flexible approaches to problem solving); (2) ego-development (operationalized as autonomy and confidence as opposed to insecurity in visualizing oneself as a parent); (3) capacity for positive sustained relationships (operationalized as a coherent and balanced internal working model, an absence of serious conflict in relationships with others, sensitivity to others' needs, and trust in interpersonal relationships); (4) prebirth experience of partnerships (operationalized as openness to communication, consensus on mutual roles, satisfaction with relationship, expressing negative affects and persistence with conflict resolution); and (5) experience of support from family and friends, including instrumental (or concrete) and emotional support (Heinicke, 2002). Each of these domains, as will be discussed later in this chapter, is likely to be influenced and altered by the presence of psychopathology. Thus, prebirth personality and psychosocial functioning, within the context of psychopathology, are critical factors that must be considered in terms of their influence on postnatal parental functioning, including their impact on parenting behaviors, cognitions, affect, and the distal and proximal parenting environment.

Pathways of Influence after the Birth of the Child

Although heritability and biological predisposition clearly play a role in the transmission of psychopathology from parent to child, there is strong evidence that these influences are moderate and that psychosocial mechanisms also play an important role in the transmission (Turner et al., 2003). A primary pathway for the transmission of parental psychopathology after the birth of the baby generally involves social or interactive mechanisms occurring within the context of the parent-child relationship. The first leg of the social mechanism involves the impact of psychopathology on the parent's own parental attributions, parental cognitions and parenting behavior. Parental attributions, cognitions and behaviors that are altered by psychopathology may then influence the child's physical health or psychosocial adjustment. Alternatively, they may trigger a new series of mother-child interactions that can place dyadic adjustment in jeopardy. In this section, findings are presented based on their relevance to each of these possible patterns of influence.

The psychosocial effects of parental psychopathology on children is likely to be influenced by the developmental task most salient to the child at the age of exposure as well as the most salient coinciding developmental and psychological tasks of the parent (e.g., managing separation and connection, resolving images of what could have been versus how things turned out to be, Galinsky, 1981). The effects of parental psychopathology via pathways of social interaction will therefore be considered within the context of the child's developmental continuum (i.e., from infancy to adolescence) as well as within the coinciding developmental spectrum of the parent.

Parental Psychopathology during Infancy

For the parent, from the child's birth until the child is 2 years of age, the parenting tasks center on the parent's role as nurturer and the negotiation of physical and emotional separateness and connectedness. The central new tasks of this phase include becoming attached to the infant, determining how much time to devote to the infant, and reconciling discrepancies between earlier expectations and present realities (Galinsky, 1981).

The primary developmental tasks of infancy that are supported by the parent-infant relationship involve fostering a secure attachment relationship, facilitating the development of the infant's capacity for self-regulation, and the infant's development of neuroregulatory mechanisms. The parenting tasks during infancy that promote the infant's development in these areas involve showing sensitivity and responsiveness to infant cues, and providing adequate stimulation.

Parental psychopathology and parenting behavior during infancy. Parental psychopathology has been linked with numerous deficits in parenting behaviors with infants, including parental insensitivity, intrusiveness, overcontrol, and emotional negativity, all of which likely interfere with parental fostering of infant regulatory functions.

Parental depression has been associated with less maternal sensitivity, a slower response time, less contingent response, lower synchronicity, less reciprocal vocalization, less affectionate contact, an absence of use of "motherese" when speaking to infants, and more feeding difficulties (Goodman & Gotlib, 1999; Lovejoy, Graczyk, O'Hare, & Neuman, 2000; Seifer, 2003).

Parental anxiety during infancy has been linked with feeding difficulties, maternal unresponsiveness, intrusiveness, overprotection, overcontrol and insensitivity (Kaitz & Maytal, 2005; Seifer, 2003; Zahn-Waxler, 2002). The behavior of anxious mothers with infants has been described in terms that reflect exaggerated, ill-timed, and often-inappropriate responses to the infant (Kaitz & Maytal, 2005). Perceptual distortion of 9-month-old infants have also been found in parents with anxiety disorders (Zahn-Waxler et al., 2002).

Panic disorder has been found to be associated with lower levels of maternal sensitivity toward infants. Panic disordered mothers observed during interactions with their infants have appeared distracted and less attentive to infant emotions and signals than mothers with no psychiatric diagnosis

(Warren et al., 2003). Maternal panic disorder has also been associated with problematic parenting related to putting infants to sleep (e.g., putting infants to sleep after feeding rather than awake, having infants sleep in same room or bed as mother, and having infant spend more time out of his/her own bed, Warren et al., 2003).

A mother's exposure to trauma during early childhood has also been studied in terms of its potential impact on parenting and child development. Mothers who were exposed to trauma as children have been thought to be "unresolved" or "still traumatized" in terms of their attachment status. These attachment classifications, in turn, have been linked with frightened and/or frightening maternal behavior (including withdrawal, dissociation, hostility, and aggression) with infants (Turton, Hughes, Fonagy, & Fainman, 2004). In one longitudinal study, Jacobvitz and colleagues (2006) found that women classified as having an unresolved/disorganized attachment status during pregnancy were more likely to engage in frightened or frightening behavior with their infants at 8 months postpartum than mothers who were classified as secure/autonomous, dismissing, or preoccupied. Interestingly, the two groups did not differ in terms of maternal sensitivity during interactions with infants. Moreover, mothers who had lost a parent during childhood were more likely to display frightening and frightened behavior with their infants regardless of attachment status. These findings suggest that other psychological processes, in addition to unresolved and disorganized representations are involved in both moderating and mediating effects of trauma on parenting.

The postpartum period has been identified as a time of potential vulnerability to the onset and exacerbation of eating disorder pathology in clinical and community samples of women. Residual change in body weight and shape resulting from pregnancy are likely to be partly responsible for the postpartum increase in body shape and weight concern (Park et al., 2003). Eating disordered mothers have shown more difficulty

reading infant cues and setting aside their own concerns during their infant's mealtime (e.g., prioritizing their own needs for cleanliness over their infant's need for autonomous feeding), more intrusive and less facilitating behavior, and more expressed negative emotion and conflict with their infants than control mothers (Park et al., 2003; Waugh & Bulik, 1999). Women with eating disorders have reported more difficulties with and reluctance about breast feeding (possibly because of heightened self-awareness and self-consciousness about their bodies), which often result in early introduction of their infants to formula (Park et al., 2003; Waugh & Bulik, 1999; Zahn-Waxler, 2002). Several clinical case studies have reported tense and cool atmospheres between mothers and children at mealtime. Mothers diagnosed with anorexia nervosa are more likely to underfeed their children in a variety of ways starting with dilution of bottle feeds in early childhood. Mothers with eating disorders have also been found to feed their infants on a less regular schedule for non-nutritive purposes (e.g., to reward or calm offspring, Park et al., 2003). The constant focus on attending to infant feeding during infancy may in itself trigger loss of control, binges, and other eating disorder symptoms in mothers. At the same time, eating disorder symptomatology may improve during the postpartum period in response to regulating effects of lactation and weaning (Park et al., 2003).

Schizophrenic mothers, in comparison with mothers with no mental illness, have shown more negative and less positive affect, less responsiveness, involvement, spontaneity, and expressiveness, and little sensory or motor stimulation with their children during infancy (Zahn-Waxler et al., 2002).

Parental attributions and parenting behavior during infancy. Differences in parental attributions of infants associated with parental psychopathology may also play an important role in determining how parents will interact with their infants. Depressed mothers are more likely to see their infants as fussy, hungry and demanding in comparison with mothers without a psychiatric disorder (Seifer, 2003). Anxious mothers who perceive their infants as having low intentionality interact less sensitively with them (Seifer, 2003). Anxious maternal behavior may be guided by negative cognitions and perceptions that are strong correlates of anxiety and considered by some to be at anxiety's core (see Kaitz & Maytal, 2005). Similarly, anxious parents are prone to put a more negative slant on events and items than nonanxious parents, which may, in turn, impact their appraisal of infant signals, such that benign signals receive prompt attention and infants are seen as more vulnerable and prone to distress. These actions may, in turn, help explain the overprotection and intrusive behaviors of some anxious mothers with infants (Kaitz & Maytal, 2005). A negative skew in self-perceptions as inadequate parents unworthy of infant attention may also lead to overactive parenting among anxious mothers (Kaitz & Maytal, 2005). In one study, maternal general separation anxiety (e.g., global apprehension, worry, and guilt about separating from the infant) was found to be associated with higher responsiveness to infant negative signals but lower responsiveness to infant positive signals. The author of this study proposed that this counterintuitive finding may be an indication that maternal mood directs the mother's attention toward similar mood states and suppresses her attention toward opposite mood states (Hsu, 2004).

Mothers with eating disorders have not shown misperceptions of their infant's shape and size, although they have expressed concerns about infants becoming fat and children being unnaturally greedy, even when their children are within a normal weight range (Park et al., 2003).

Parental psychopathology and infant adjustment. Generally, infants of mentally ill parents show small but consistent trends toward difficulties with the development of self-regulatory capacities. Affective responsiveness of infants to their parents is less well organized among infants of mentally ill parents. Insecure and disorganized attachment classifications are more prevalent. Infant cognitive and motor development is generally less affected (except in the case of schizophrenia where infant motor development seems to be affected as well, Seifer, 2003).

Infants of depressed mothers are particularly likely to develop insecure attachment styles and the stable or chronic presence of maternal depressive symptoms as well as depression severity have been associated with disorganized attachment in infants (Goodman & Gotlib, 1999; Seifer, 2003; Zahn-Waxler, 2002). Infants of depressed mothers have also shown delayed development of the autonomic regulatory system at 6 months (indicated by low vagal tones), reduced left-frontal brain activity (indicated by lower approach-related behavior), dysregulated emotion, and lower motor and mental development (Goodman & Gotlib, 1999; Zahn-Waxler, 2002).

Findings on maternal anxiety and infant adjustment suggest that some risk is present, although the associations are complex and not uniform across samples and conditions (see Kaitz & Maytal, 2005). In comparison with infants of mothers with no psychiatric disorders, infants of mothers with anxiety disorders have generally been found to be less involved and more distressed during mother-infant interactions, at greater risk for lack of security and emotional dysregulation, driven to alternative and likely ineffective means for coping with discomfort and distress, and engaging in less exploratory behavior and less secure attachment relationships with caregivers at 1 year (Kaitz & Maytal, 2005; Zahn-Waxler, 2002).

Infants of panic-disordered mothers have been observed as having higher levels of salivary cortisol (indicating higher levels of arousal) at 4 months, sleep disturbances at 8 months (Warren et al., 2003), but no significant differences from infants of control mothers in A B C or D attachment classifications at 14 months (Warren et al., 2003). Infants of mothers who experienced unresolved loss and manifested an unresolved attachment status (e.g., demonstrated unmonitored, incompatible thoughts and behaviors) in response to the Adult Attachment Interview, have shown a disorganized attachment status (e.g., approach / avoidance responses to reunions with the mother after separation [Turton et al., 2004]).

Some studies of infants whose mothers have symptoms of anxiety have reported infants as having an ambivalent attachment style, characterized by a mixture of withdrawal and avoidance that seems to reflect concurrent drives to seek out the mother as a potential source of comfort and escape the stress that she elicits (Kaitz & Maytal, 2005). A mixture of infant withdrawal and avoidance may be an indication of the infant's efforts both to approach the mother for security and avoid the mother's harmful interactions. It may also indicate genuine confusion in response to the mother's erratic and simultaneous conveyance of positive and anxious affect (Kaitz & Maytal, 2005). Any of the aforementioned infant responses to anxious parents are unlikely to mitigate the distress and dysregulation that their interactions incur and are thus likely to prolong insecure attachment relationships with mothers and predispose infants for psychiatric distress during childhood and adolescence (Kaitz & Maytal, 2005).

Disorganized infant attachment behaviors, characterized by an absence of systematic attempts to seek proximity to the mother, have been found among infants whose mothers were clinically diagnosed with anxiety disorders and with histories of exposure to trauma during childhood (Kaitz & Maytal, 2005). Interestingly, in one study of 60 parents who had suffered serious traumatic loss and whose infants had high levels of disorganized attachment, Turton and colleagues (2004) found no significant association between maternal PTSD symptoms and infant disorganized attachment. They suggest that child disorganized attachment may be more a function of parental dissociation and unresolved state of mind resulting from the traumatic loss rather than conscious and troubling phenomenon associated with PTSD. It is also possible that only severe maternal PTSD symptoms are associated with disorganized attachment in children whereas mild to moderate maternal PTSD symptoms are associated with insecure attachment styles (Bomgardner, 2005).

Differences in birth weight have been observed in newborn infants of mothers with eating disorders but these differences have not persisted after 6 weeks nor have any delays been observed in the achievement of primary developmental milestones of early infancy (Waugh & Bulik, 1999). Infants of mothers with eating disorders have been found to be smaller in terms of weight and length, less cheerful during mealtimes and play times than infants of comparison mothers (Waugh & Bulik, 1999; Zahn-Waxler, 2002). Infants of mothers with eating disorders have shown higher rates of suckling at 2 and 4 weeks and have weaned from bottle feeding later and with more difficulty than controls (Park et al., 2003).

Infants and young children of schizophrenic parents have generally shown a range of disturbance in social, emotional, cognitive, physical, physiological, anatomical, and neurological domains – as well as greater risk for psychiatric disorder and psychological symptoms later in life (Zahn-Waxler et al., 2002). In terms of their neurophysiology, infants of schizophrenic parents have shown reduced physiological arousal, brain abnormalities and other neurobehavioral deficits (Zahn-Waxler et al., 2002). In terms of attachment, they have shown more anxious attachment than infants of parents without psychopathology as well as an absence of fear of strangers in the first year (Zahn-Waxler et al., 2002).

Parental psychopathology and dyadic adjustment during infancy. Dyadic adjustment in mother-infant pairs where mothers have mental illnesses have also been characterized by problems in synchronicity and mutual regulation. Interactions of dyads involving a depressed mother have been marked by less contingency, less frequently matched positive affect, more frequently matched negative affect, and longer delays in repairing interactional errors than is characteristic of interactions of typical dyads. Infants of depressed mothers have been observed responding to their mother's depressed affect with negative affect in facial expressions and gestures, and this response may be an early indication of the infant's attempt to get the mother to regulate her own negative affect and to engage in self-directed regulatory behavior. Infants of depressed mothers who behave intrusively have been observed looking away during intrusive interactions whereas infants of withdrawn depressed mothers have been observed protesting and appearing distressed (Goodman & Gotlib, 1999). Infants of depressed mothers have also appeared to resonate with their mothers' negative behavior whereas infants of nondepressed mothers have been more responsive to their mothers' positive behaviors (see Kaitz and Maytal, 2005).

Dyadic interactions of anxious mothers with their infants have been much less extensively studied than interactions involving depressed mothers and findings have been mixed. In some studies, no robust findings have been established regarding the synchrony or affect matching of anxious mothers with their infants. In other studies, covert maternal anxiety has been linked with lower levels of dyadic harmony (see Kaitz & Maytal, 2005). In response to the arousal, frustration, and anger-provocation that are likely entailed during interactions with anxious mothers, infants have shown active avoidance of mother, gaze aversion, rejecting-type behavior, protest and distancing. Infant's avoidance has been particularly noted during interactions where mothers are intrusive and overcontrolling, a common behavior observed in anxious mothers. These infant behaviors may indicate attempts to reduce proximity to a potentially distress-inducing and harmful stimulus, to establish self-regulation by achieving a "time out" from the stimulus or circumstances, or to signal distress or disinterest to the parent (Kaitz & Maytal, 2005).

Some dyads involving anxious mothers exhibit hypersynchrony – an overly tight coordination between mother and infant whereby some anxious mothers "adamant in their efforts to control their infants' behavior and state and intolerant of their infants' disengagement – force mutuality upon the dyad, albeit not with the same positive affect that usually accompanies the moments of mutuality experienced in typical dyads." (Kaitz & Maytal, 2005, p. 583). Increased dyadic coordination has also been linked to novel conditions and marital distress in adults, and may indicate a "mutual interactive vigilance" in the service of countering uncertainty and increasing predictability of uncertain situations. This tight coordination of behavior and affect may "induce a sense of togetherness that is bound up in negative feelings, frustration, and dysregulation that does not afford mother or infant the mutual regulation this the byproduct and a primary benefit of well-managed interactions" (Kaitz & Maytal, 2005, p. 583).

Some infants of anxious mothers have shown indications of withdrawal from the mother rather than avoidance, manifested by little initiative during interactions, restricted affect, irritability, frequent self-soothing, and either avoidance of eye contact, glazed focus, or persistent monitoring and, in more extreme cases, freezing of posturing or motility. Withdrawal may predispose infants of anxious parents to the challenge of having a parent who may be limited in capacity to maintain a level of responsiveness and affect within a range that is comfortable and appropriate for the infants. It may also be difficult for anxious mothers to provide the infants sufficient space to "come out of their shell" (Kaitz & Maytal, 2005).

Maternal PTSD also appears to influence dyadic adjustment in mother-infant pairs. In a qualitative study conducted with six women who reported clinically significant PTSD after birth, Ayers and colleagues (2006) reported that mother-baby bonds were seriously affected, with nearly all women reporting initial feelings of rejection towards the baby (although these feelings changed over time). Long-term, women seemed to have either avoidant or anxious attachments with their children.

An emerging literature on stressful or traumatic experiences of parents related to pregnancy and childbirth has shown that between 1 and 6 percent of parents develop PTSD symptoms as a result of childbirth

(Ayers, Eagle, & Waring, 2006; Ayers, Wright, and Wells, 2007; Beck, 2006). The implications of child-birth related to PTSD are not yet clear, with some findings pointing to consequences for maternal sensitivity (e.g., Coppola, Cassibba, & Constantini, 2007), maternal reverie (Mendelsohn, 2005), affect regulation of the child and relational and attachment processes (e.g., Thiel-Bonney, C., & Cierpka, M., 2004) and other findings showing that parents' PTSD symptoms resulting from childbirth were unrelated to parent-baby bond at 9 weeks (Ayers et al., 2007).

For infants of mothers with eating disorders, mother-infant conflict during mealtime has been the strongest predictor of infant weight. Mother-infant interactions that are relatively smooth and harmonious have been shown to predict higher infant weight at 12 months than interactions characterized by conflict (Park et al., 2003; Zahn-Waxler, 2002).

Infants of schizophrenic mothers have shown a lack of positive interaction with the mother upon reunion after separation. Although mechanisms of influence are so far unclear, the increased level of deficits in infants born to schizophrenic mothers may increase the hardship of caring for the infants (Zahn-Waxler et al., 2002).

Dyadic interactions between infants and mothers diagnosed with antisocial personality disorder have shown higher levels of maternal unresponsiveness and infant passivity when the mother's disorder was more severe (Zahn-Waxler et al., 2002).

Parental Psychopathology during Toddlerhood and Preschool Years

In his theory of parental development, Galinsky (1981) proposed that, as the infant enters the years of development and growth as a toddler (at age 2) and continuing to age 5, the parent enters the parallel Authority Stage, during which the parent is primarily engaged in determining how he or she will manage control and power in relation to the child. The central new parenting tasks during this stage of the child's development include selecting and enforcing limits, fostering autonomy (versus shielding and protecting), managing conflicts and power struggles with the child, and working out conflicts and power struggles with others who deal with child (Galinsky 1981).

The primary developmental tasks for a child during toddlerhood and preschool years involve movement toward recognizing emotional states, separation and individuation, socialization, cognitive development and development of social competence with peers and adults. Parents help children meet the challenges of these tasks by providing external support for understanding social and emotional situations, using language to convey understanding and expression of emotions, guiding behavior during social referencing, facilitating relationships with peers and other adults, and scaffolding upward movement across levels of cognitive and social functioning (Heinicke, 2002).

Parental psychopathology and parenting behavior during toddlerhood and preschool years. Parenting behavior deficits associated with parental psychopathology during toddlerhood and preschool years are not as well documented as they are among parents with infants. Identified parenting behavior problems include emotional negativity or withdrawal, restrictions in fostering autonomy, and other deficits in the development of a social partnership. Depressed parents of toddlers have shown less time engaged with them in mutually shared activity, a lack of encouragement of their toddler's sustained attention to objects or tasks, avoidance of confronting their children's resistance (e.g., dropping original demands or failing to achieve compromises), and engagement in mutual coercive interactions (e.g., retaliations and revenge, Goodman & Gotlib, 1999). Depressed parents have been reported to attribute problem behaviors of their preschool children to stable, controllable causes personal to the child rather than universal to children of that age (Zahn-Waxler et al., 2002). Different symptom configurations seem to result in the depressed parent being a different type of social partner for the child such that parents whose depression manifests as anger tend to engage in distracting and restless behavior with their young children whereas parents whose depression manifests as withdrawal have shown pervasive sadness and rumination during interactions with their young children (Goodman & Gotlib, 1999).

Mothers with panic disorders have reported less effective disciplinary parenting behaviors and greater tendencies toward displaying anger toward their children in disciplinary situations than parents with no psychiatric disorders. These parenting behaviors may be a function of underlying emotional regulatory difficulties experienced by the mothers (Warren et al., 2003).

There is some evidence that interactive behaviors of eating disordered mothers with toddlers can be compromised during mealtimes (Waugh & Bulik, 1999). Among mothers with eating disorders, no evidence has been found of dissatisfaction with toddlers' or preschoolers' appearance or shape in comparison with control mothers (Waugh & Bulik, 1999). Moreover, there is no evidence of gross deficiencies in the diets of young children of eating disordered mothers, although the nature of interactions observed during mealtimes are concerning. There is some evidence that mothers with eating disorders are more likely to restrict their toddlers' food intake and avoid cooking for them, although this evidence comes from only a handful of studies (Waugh & Bulik, 1999). Mothers with eating disorders may also experience exacerbation of their own psychological distress related to eating (e.g., fears about proximity to food or binging) during their toddlers' mealtimes (Waugh & Bulik, 1999).

Mothers with aneroxia nervosa may reduce the amount of food available in the home, confine food to mealtimes, forbid sweets, or discourage children's requests for second helpings in later childhood (Park et al., 2003). Case studies have reported that mothers with bulimia nervosa also have difficulty feeding their children and often do not keep food in the house (Park et al., 2003). Eating disordered mothers observed interacting during mealtimes with their children

ages 1 to 4 have shown an absence of positive comments about food, avoidance of eating in front of their children, disengagement from interaction, and an absence of appreciation for the taste of food or experience of eating, indicating a discomfort with food that may inhibit them from providing modeling of food intake (Waugh & Bulik, 1999).

Parental psychopathology and toddler and preschooler adjustment. Adjustment among toddlers and preschoolers cared for by mentally ill parents has also received less attention than adjustment in infants. Generally, developmental problems have centered on areas of social competence, autonomy and emotional and behavioral regulation.

Young children of depressed parents have been observed as having cognitive and emotional problems parallel to infants, including less effective self-regulation strategies, high levels of anxiety during mildly stressful situations, and negative reactions to stress. In terms of social competence, toddlers of depressed parents have demonstrated fewer interpersonal skills in interactions with their peers, a lack of social competence as evidenced by tendencies toward aggression, withdrawal, other inappropriate behaviors toward peers and disturbances in the development of functional autonomy (Seifer, 2003; Zahn-Waxler, 2002). With regard to cognitive development, toddlers and preschoolers of depressed parents have shown shorter attention spans to objects during spontaneous play, and poorer school readiness, expressive language and verbal comprehension (Goodman & Gotlib, 1999; Seifer, 2003; Zahn-Waxler, 2002).

Young children (ages 18 – 59 months) of mothers with anxiety disorders have shown higher rates of insecure attachment (Warren et al., 2003; Zahn-Waxler, 2002). Antenatal maternal anxiety has also been associated with behavior problems, especially hyperactivity and inattention in 4 year old boys (Leverton, 2003).

When young children are exposed, along with their parents, to traumatic events, parents' own vulnerability to PTSD may be exacerbated. Dyadic adjustment in 3 examples of mother-toddler pairs exposed to extreme violence in Kosavo, for example, indicated that children's increased attachment behavior and posttraumatic symptoms functioned as a trigger for posttraumatic symptoms in the mother, damaged internal representations (of self and the mother-child relationship), and disengagement in the caregiving system (Almqvist & Broberg, 2003).

Generally, young children of mothers with eating disorders are more likely to have feeding problems than young children of control mothers (Park et al., 2003). Although in some studies, no differences have been found in parenting, children of mothers with eating disorders have shown more negative affect such as sadness, crying and irritability, suggesting that other interactive mechanisms involving affect and modeling may also mediate the impact of maternal eating disorders on young children (Park et al., 2003). The independent eating behaviors of young children of women with eating disorders have also identified dieting behavior and frank eating disorders (Waugh & Bulik, 1999). Early childhood feeding problems may also be associated with the development of eating disorders in later childhood (Park et al., 2003).

Parental psychopathology and dyadic adjustment during toddlerhood and preschool years. Problems in dyadic adjustment have generally reflected earlier deficits in mutual regulation and attachment organization as well as emerging deficits in negotiations centered around autonomy.

Toddlers of depressed parents have been observed engaging in self-soothing behaviors in response to their parent's distress (Goodman & Gotlib, 1999).

In one sample of mothers who experienced high rates of loss and abuse as children, mothers' experiences of parental death in childhood and unresolved states of mind in attachment interviews were independently related to infant disorganization at 12 months (with severity of trauma controlled). When infants were 18 months, maternal Hostile-Helpless (but not unresolved) state of mind strongly predicted infant disorganization and mediated effects of parental loss on infant disorganization. The authors

suggest that findings may indicate that the influence of maternal trauma on infant attachment may become more prominent at 18 months as the infant makes the transition to toddlerhood. For mothers who have been exposed to violence and abuse, infants' increased mobility and agency may trigger mothers' feelings of helplessness and hostility related to past abuse (Lyons-Ruth, Yellin, Melnick, & Atwood, 2003).

Parents diagnosed with borderline personality disorder may have difficulty with developmental periods when a child is working toward greater autonomy (toddler and adolescent years). Inability to model emotional regulation may cause child to think emotions are overwhelming and frightening (Zahn-Waxler et al., 2002).

Parental Psychopathology during School-age and Adolescent Years

In his theory of parental development, Galinsky (1981) proposed that, as children enter their school-aged years (ages 6 to 12), their parents enter a parallel Interpretive Stage, during which they are primarily engaged in interpreting the world to their child, interpreting themselves to children, interpreting their children's self-concept, answering their children's questions, providing access to skills and information, and helping their children form values. Then, as children enter adolescent years (ages 13 to 16), Galinsky (1981) proposes that parents enter a parallel Interdependent Stage that involves interacting with the "new" child, renegotiating relationships, and handling new issues (Galinsky, 1981).

The primary developmental tasks for school-aged children and adolescents focus on establishing capacities for autonomy and self-discipline in preparation for functioning independently, social competence with peers, and cognitive and intellectual growth. Parental tasks include providing social and emotional support, buffering effects of stress, supporting cognitive and intellectual development, supporting adaptation to the social environment, monitoring behavior and supporting self-discipline, and providing appropriate discipline and limits (Heinicke, 2002).

Parental psychopathology and parenting behaviors with school-age and adolescent children. In general, parental psychopathology during children's school-age and adolescent children has been associated with problems with parental communication, monitoring and discipline, excessively negative, critical, harsh and overbearing parenting behaviors, and an absence of empathy and tolerance. Depressed parents rearing school-aged and adolescent children are more likely than parents with no psychopathology to use negative appraisal, criticism, punishment and to show lower tolerance in response to their children's problematic behavior (Goodman & Gotlib, 1999). Depressed parents have been observed to be more impatient, less responsive, less effective communicators and more likely to use directives in guiding their children's behavior (Lovejoy et al., 2000). Depressed parents are also more likely to suppress their own dysphoric affect in response to their children's aggression (Goodman & Gotlib, 1999).

Observations of anxious mothers' interactions with their school-aged and adolescent children have indicated a tendency to catastrophize and criticize their children more, to grant less autonomy (e.g., solicit children's opinion, tolerate differences in opinion), and to display less warmth than mothers with no psychopathology when discussing areas of conflict and anxiety with their children (Whaley, Pinto, & Sigman, 1999).

When engaged in mildly stressful tasks (e.g., creating a speech, solving unsolvable anagrams) with their 6–12 year old children, anxious mothers have been observed to be more withdrawn and disengaged from tasks with children, less likely at agree with or praise and more likely to ignore their children than mothers with no psychopathology (Woodruff-Borden et al., 2002). When participating in more play-oriented activities that involve some physical risk with their children (e.g., climbing and balancing), anxious parents have not differed from nonanxious parents in their attempts to direct or control their children's behavior or to criticize their children's behavior. However, anxious parents have reported higher levels of apprehension about their children's involvement in the activities and are more reluctant to engage in the riskier activities themselves. Anxious parents have also reported significantly more concern about "every day" events such as separation from parents, riding skateboards, going to overnight camp, particularly when these activities are undertaken beyond close proximity (Turner et al., 2003). It may be that parental anxiety is transmitted to children in these instances by more vicarious means. This interpretation is supported by research on family environment showing that overt expression of feeling tends to be lower in families with an anxious parent (Turner et al., 2003). It may also be that the focus of parental anxiety helps to determine whether it is overtly transmitted to children.

Parental stress disorders may trigger a distortion in parental perceptions of children's wellbeing. In one study, parents reporting symptoms of acute stress disorder (ASD) were more likely to overrate ASD symptoms in their children (ages 8 to 17 years). Interestingly, parents in this study who did not have an acute stress disorder were more likely to underrate ASD in their children (Kassam-Adams, Garcia-Espana, Miller, & Winston, 2006).

Mothers with ADHD, in comparison with mothers without ADHD, have shown no differences in positive parenting strategies (e.g., affection and praise) by their own and their children's reports. However, mothers diagnosed with ADHD have been found to monitor their school-aged and adolescent children's behavior less, to use inconsistent or lax discipline practices in comparison with mothers without ADHD and to show a weaker response on parental problem solving tasks than mothers without ADHD Importantly, these findings held even after taking comorbid psychopathology into account, which suggests that ADHD alone has a unique influence on parenting (Murray & Johnston, 2006).

Children of mothers diagnosed with anorexia nervosa have been found to have abnormally low weight and growth – in one study by as much as 30 percent in comparison with control children (see Park et al., 2003). Anorexic mothers of underweight children have been shown low levels of concern about their children's weight or about giving their children too little food. Some anorexic mothers have been found to adopt extreme methods to ration their children's food intake behavior based on apparent concerns that their children might become fat (Park et al., 2003).

Parents diagnosed with antisocial personality have demonstrated ineffective, harsh, and inconsistent discipline practices, little positive parental involvement, poor monitoring and supervision, and less empathy and understanding with their school-aged and adolescent children (Zahn-Waxler et al., 2002).

Parental psychopathology and school-age and adolescent children's adjustment. Problems of adjustment for school-age and adolescent children cared for by parents with psychopathology have generally been in the areas of behavioral regulation, social competence, academic performance, substance abuse, self-efficacy and self-acceptance. School-age and adolescent children of depressed mothers have shown adjustment problems in terms of their popularity and relationships with peers, as reported by their teachers (Goodman & Gotlib, 1999; Zahn-Waxler, 2002). Clinical problems with anxiety, and disruptive behavior disorders and cognitive difficulties related to poor school performances have also been reported in children of depressed mothers (Zahn-Waxler et al., 2002). Depressed adolescents of depressed mothers have been found to have more impaired social functioning in social domains – particularly in relationships with other family members, elevated rates of interpersonal and conflict life events, dysfunctional cognitions about their social selves and worlds, fewer friends and social activities, by their own reports, and less secure and more dismissing and fearful cognitions about relationships than depressed adolescents of nondepressed mothers (Hammen & Brennan, 2001).

If characteristics of behavioral inhibition found in toddlers of mothers with anxiety disorders remain stable, shyness and anxiety disorders can develop during childhood and adolescence (Kaitz & Maytal, 2005). Children of mothers with anxiety disorders have shown lower perceptions of control over risk along with greater fear and anxiety than children of mothers with no psychopathology (Zahn-Waxler et al., 2002). Lower perceptions of control then predispose school-aged and adolescent children for anxiety or depressive disorders (Zahn-Waxler et al., 2002). Children of anxious parents have scored higher on internalizing and externalizing indices of the CBCL (Woodruff-Borden et al., 2002). Parental agoraphobia and mixed phobia have also been linked with behavioral and anxiety problems in school-aged and adolescent children (Woodruff-Borden et al., 2002).

Research has also shown that children are affected when their parents were exposed to violence and trauma. In a sample of 23 children (ages 4–7) of violence-exposed mothers with PTSD, trauma-related responses on story completion task related to responses on a drawing task indicating insecure and disorganized attachment (Schechter, Zygmunt, Trabka, Davies, Colon, Kolodji, & McCaw, 2007). In another sample of 60 African American children ages 6 to 12 growing up an urban community, children whose parents had been victimized by community violence showed higher levels of psychiatric distress symptoms (at the borderline of clinical significance) than children whose parents had not been victimized (Dulmus & Wodarski, 2000). In a third study, children whose mothers had a betrayal trauma history and dissociation symptoms were more likely to also have dissociation symptoms (Chu & DePrince, 2006). In a fourth study, adolescent children of fathers who are Vietnam veterans with PTSD were at risk for a broad range of emotional and behavioral problems, including elevated levels of hostility, clinically elevated scale scores on the Minnesota Multiphasic Personality Inventory (MMPI), elevated numbers of PTSD symptoms, illegal drug use, and behavior problems (Beckham, Braxton, Kudler, Feldman, Lytle, & Palmer, 1997)

School-aged children (as young as nine years old) of eating disordered mothers have been found to harbor desires for thinness and motivation to diet regardless of their actual weight. High levels of dietary restraint have also been reported in nine and ten year old daughters of eating disordered mothers (Park et al., 2003).

School-aged and adolescent children of schizophrenic parents have also suffered with a range of problems, including adverse emotional illnesses and conflicting emotions, impaired interpersonal relationships and social competence, increased propensity for antisocial behavior, and, paradoxically, assumption of adult-like responsibilities (e.g., providing for their own physical care, Zahn-Waxler et al., 2002).

Parental psychopathology and dyadic adjustment with school-age and adolescent children. Research on dyadic adjustment involving parents caring for school-age and adolescent children has shown that parents with psychopathology can have strong negative reactions to their children's difficult or challenging behavior. A number of dyadic interaction patterns have been identified between depressed mothers and their school-aged and adolescent children. Depressed mothers have shown high levels of aversive response to children's resistance whereas, in response to their children's aggressive behavior, depressed mothers have shown a suppression of dysphoric affect (Goodman & Gotlib, 1999). In response to their depressed mothers' aggressive behaviors, children have shown aggressive behaviors. Dysfunctional communication initiated by depressed mothers has been associated with negative self-concept and interactional behavior in children (Goodman & Gotlib, 1999). When depressed mothers engage in overt conflict with their children, their children are more likely to exhibit behavioral problems (Seifer, 2003).

Whereas maternal anxiety status most strongly predicts lack of maternal warmth and positivity toward school-aged children, during discussions focused on conflict and stress, children's anxiety status has been found to predict more strongly lower levels of maternal granting of autonomy (Whaley, 1999). Low maternal warmth and positivity associated with maternal anxiety disorder has also shown positive associations with child anxiety (Zahn-Waxler et al., 2002).

Children of mothers with eating disorders may end up being neglected or abandoned at times when mothers are preoccupied with binging or vomiting (Park et al., 2003). Some children have been reported as feeling responsible for their mothers' symptoms and older children have been reported as taking over the caretaker role within the relationship. Three patterns of mother-child dyadic interactions have emerged in the literature including overprotection and enmeshment, role reversals in which children become caretakers, and distant relationships in which the mother uses emotional control (Park et al., 2003).

Social Learning and the Acquisition of Subclinical Cognitions, Affect and Behavior

Goodman & Gotlib (1999) have suggested that the process of social learning and modeling – a process that includes but goes beyond the simple transmission of psychopathology from parent to child – increases the risk for children of developing psychopathology. Through the process of being exposed to and actively learning from parental behaviors, cognitions and affects of psychiatrically disordered parents, children's development across multiple domains is altered, disrupted, or heightened. These alterations become apparent in specific characteristics of children's own cognitions, affect, and behavior that may be asymptomatic precursors to later development of mental illnesses.

Parental cognitions, affect and behaviors. The social cognitions of depressed parents, for example, tend to be more negative than those of parents without psychopathology. Depressed mothers tend to have lower perceived self-efficacy, which translates to lower competence interacting with their children. Depressed mothers with lower internal loci of control behave in a more controlling manner with their children whereas depressed mothers with higher illusory control have more insecurely attached infants (Seifer, 2003).

Depressed parents' attributions about their children also tend to be more negative and their affect toward children has been characterized by aggravation and disappointment (Goodman & Gotlib, 1999; Seifer, 2003; Zahn-Waxler et al., 2002). Negative events are often attributed to internal, stable, and global causes and problem behaviors in preschool children have been attributed by depressed parents to stable, controllable causes personal to the child rather than universal to children of that age (Zahn-Waxler et al., 2002). However, depressed mothers who view their children as "a good match" temperamentally to their family environment may be more likely to interact sensitively with their children who, in turn, may be more likely to exhibit social and emotional competence (Seifer, 2003).

Findings regarding depressed parents' parenting behaviors in general reflect a concerning array of maladaptive parenting styles that include low nurturance and sensitivity, intrusiveness, anger-driven, and negative and retaliatory behaviors. As well, depressed parents are more likely to use harsh, hostile, and negative discipline that can be interspersed with lax undercontrol, use of psychological and coercive control, anxiety and guilt induction, more critical and unsupportive statements to their children and ineffective conflict resolution (Zahn-Waxler et al., 2002).

Anxious parents can often display a persistent fear or anxious reaction. Anxious parents have also been found to have limited social skills as well as deficient skills for modeling constructive problem solving and coping (Woodruff-Borden et al., 2002). Mothers with separation anxiety have also been found to attribute higher levels of intentionality to their infants, which may be an indication of oversensitivity to infants' signals of distress (Feldman & Reznick, 1996).

Mothers with significantly disturbed eating habits and attitudes have been reported to have children with feeding disorders. Mothers with clinical eating disorders also often report their offspring developing problems similar to their own. Several maternal eating disorder symptoms have been found to predict child eating behaviors during the first 5 years: Maternal disinhibition, hunger, body dissatisfaction, and bulimic symptoms have been found to predict the emergence of secretive eating in children whereas maternal restraint and drive for thinness have been found to predict emergence of overeating. Case studies have reported that even at an early age, children imitate their mother's eating disorder behaviors (e.g., retching when eating, refusing or "wolfing down" food, or purging in similar ways to their mother). At a later age, children have been found to model their mothers' attitudes around eating, particularly daughters of mothers with anorexia nervosa who expressed desires to be as thin as their mothers (Park et al., 2003). It may be that children adopt some of the abnormal eating habits of their mothers through social processes such as modeling.

Subclinical cognitions, affect and behavior in children. Subclinically symptomatic children often acquire cognitions, affect and behaviors characteristic of the parental psychiatric disorder and their deficient skills and styles place them at risk for developing the disorder. Children of depressed parents, for example, can manifest a range of asymptomatic cognitive, affective and behavioral characteristics that resemble those of their depressed parents. Infants of depressed mothers, for instance, have been observed as less active, less responsive, and less content with flatter affect and fewer cues of distress during separation from their caregivers (Goodman & Gotlib, 1999). Toddlers of depressed mothers have exhibited heightened emotionality when exposed to conflict, and paradoxically suppressed emotions when coping with stress. School-aged and adolescent children of depressed parents have exhibited more negative cognitive styles, more self-criticism and blame for negative outcomes, tendencies to attribute negative events to internal, stable, and global causes, lower self-esteem, and poorer peer relations and relational skills (Goodman & Gotlib, 1999; Zahn-Waxler et al., 2002).

Infants of withdrawn anxious mothers can have a tendency to model or mirror their mothers' withdrawn behavior and restricted affect, which may increase the frequency and duration of shared affect and attention in the dyad, but not with the same expansive positive affect that often characterizes shared affect of typical dyads (Kaitz & Maytal, 2005). Children of anxious parents may also adopt more cautious and fearful stance based on observing their parents' responses (Woodruff-Borden et al., 2002).

Goodman & Gotlib (1999) present evidence of social learning by children from their parents with psychopathology through dyadic interactions. Infants of depressed mothers, for example, have been observed matching their mothers' negative emotional state. Toddlers of depressed mothers have been observed matching their lower rates of speech and decreasing the length of attention as their mother's distraction level increases. In mother-toddler dyads, mutually negative affect has been observed more often and mutually positive affect less often when the mother was depressed. In dyads involving school-aged children, negative tone of maternal comments has been found to match children's negative self-schemas, and maternal criticism during tasks related to the child have been matched to children's self-critical comments and self-blaming styles (Goodman & Gotlib, 1999).

Gender also seems to play a role in social learning in the context of parental psychopathology. For example, mothers appear to be stronger models of dysphoric affect for girls than for boys (Goodman & Gotlib, 1999). Daughters appear more likely than sons to suppress their own aggression to comfort a depressed parent and to become overinvolved in their mothers' depression (e.g., experience feelings of guilt and responsibility for the mother's mood and responsibility to care for the mother, Zahn-Waxler et al., 2002). Daughters of mothers

with eating disorders are also more likely to be at greater risk of being underweight, having concerns about thinness regardless of their actual weight, and engaging in dieting behavior than sons (Park et al., 2003).

Infants of depressed parents have shown multiple characteristics that are known risk factors for later psychiatric disorders. These characteristics include less optimal neurological development, low vagal tone, high cortisol levels, fewer facial emotional reactions and expressions, limited capacity for self-soothing. Inability to suppress vagal tone at 9 months also predicted behavioral problems at 3 years of age. Negative affect observed in infants has also been linked with later learning problems. (Goodman & Gotlib, 1999).

By 2 years of age, some infants of anxious parents show a clear pattern of quiet, withdrawn behavior in the face of novel and arousing stimuli or strangers, which has been termed "behavioral inhibition" (Kaitz & Maytal, 2005). Children of parents with panic disorder are more likely to have a temperament characterized by behavioral inhibition than children of parents with no psychopathology. Children characterized as behaviorally inhibited at 21 months and followed to age 7 were found to have higher rates of anxiety disorders compared with children without this temperament trait. Thus, early inhibition may be an early reflection of anxiety-proneness (Woodruff-Borden et al., 2002). For school-aged children, negative cognitions and attributions have been linked with subsequent depression (Goodman & Gotlib, 1999). Sleep disturbances, which are often antecedents to psychopathology, have been found in 8 month old infants and 15–16 month old toddlers of mothers with panic disorder (Warren et al., 2003). Toddlers of depressed parents have also been observed manifesting early anxiety that later led to child depression (Zahn-Waxler et al., 2002).

School-aged children of mothers with separation anxiety have reported higher levels of fear and anxiety and lower perceived control over risks than children of parents with no psychopathology. The high probability to continue perceiving events as beyond one's control may predispose school-aged children for anxiety and depressive disorders later in their lives (Zahn-Waxler et al., 2002). Sleep disturbance is also more common in school-aged and adolescent children whose parents have anxiety disorders than in children whose parents have no psychopathology. Sleep disturbance in young children may be an indication of increased difficulties with arousal/arousability and create greater risk for developing anxiety disorder or other psychopathology later in their lives (Warren et al., 2003).

Moderating and Mediating Factors

Moderating effects of the environment. Parental psychopathology generally occurs within the context of other related environmental risk factors that are less likely to be present for parents without psychopathology. Parental depression, for example, occurs more often within a context of poverty, financial burden, vocational problems, marital discord and divorce, family conflict and other social or interpersonal stressors, family conflict (Goodman & Gotlib, 1999; Leverton, 2003; Seifer, 2003; Zahn-Waxler et al., 2002). The presence of added environmental risks, in turn, places children at greater risk for psychosocial problems and possibly psychopathology.

Parental anxiety has been associated with lower perceived social support and marital satisfaction (Hsu, 2004; Zahn-Waxler et al., 2002). Children of anxiety-disordered parents have described the family environment as less cohesive, more conflictual, less autonomy fostering, and more controlling (Zahn-Waxler et al., 2002). Mothers experiencing greater separation anxiety experience greater role strain and conflict and also receive lower levels of instrumental and emotional support (Hsu, 2004). The availability of instrumental and emotional support also likely serves as a buffer for interactions involving anxious mothers and their children (Kaitz & Maytal, 2005).

Parents with ADHD are more likely to be single, have lower levels of formal education, have a comorbid anxiety or depressive disorder, and higher rates of substance abuse than parents without ADHD (Murray & Johnston, 2006). Children of parents with borderline personality disorder are more likely to be exposed to unstable adult relationships and other parent figures who have little investment in caring for children (Zahn-Waxler et al., 2002).

The combination of environmental stressors and parental psychopathology has not been well studied and thus effects of parental psychopathology may be overestimated. There is some evidence, though, that stressful contexts associated with parental psychopathology impact children's well-being. For example, the presence of marital discord appears to increase negative effects of maternal depression on child functioning. Children whose depressed mothers were divorced have shown lower ego resiliency, poor behavioral control, and conduct disorders. Heightened marital anger has also been found to moderate the impact of parental depression on children's psychosocial functioning (Goodman & Gotlib, 1999). Depressed parents who have low social and marital support have been found to be less likely to invest in care for their children (Seifer, 2003). Marital discord may also prevent depressed mothers from responding to psychological intervention (Zahn-Waxler et al., 2002). Causal patterns among parental psychopathology and environmental stressors can also be bidirectional. For example, marital discord and maternal depression likely perpetuate each other (Zahn-Waxler et al., 2002). Children of depressed mothers are more likely to have adjustment problems if their mothers are financially poor than children of depressed mothers who are not financially burdened. The presence of chronic environment stress has been found to increase the impact of parental depression on child psychiatric diagnoses and behavioral problems (Goodman & Gotlib, 1999).

Although sociocultural influences play a significant role in the emergence of eating problems in children (particularly adolescent girls), no studies to date have reported on possible moderating effects of social environment on parenting among eating disordered parents (Park et al., 2003). It seems likely that mothers with eating disorders in particular have been influenced in their eating and parenting behaviors by strong societal norms for thinness and dieting.

Moderating effects of child characteristics. Characteristics of children can also influence the impact of parental psychopathology on children's well-being. For example, infant negativity has been found to moderate associations between maternal depression and parenting sensitivity such that higher levels of infant negativity are associated with lower maternal sensitivity (Seifer, 2003). Other child characteristics, including temperament, gender, intellectual capacities, social competence, and cognitive skills have all been found to influence effects of maternal depression (Goodman & Gotlib, 1999).

There is a host of infant-related factors that can contribute to the dyadic process of infants and their anxious mothers. Infants who are temperamentally easy (i.e., predictable, adaptable, not irritable), for example, are likely to be more easily regulated and more proficient at self-regulating than infants with more difficult temperaments. Anxious mothers are also more likely to have an easier time reading the cues of easy infants and keeping their interactions within comfortable bounds whereas infants who are more difficult to regulate may evoke feelings of inadequacy about parenting in anxious mothers (see Kaitz & Maytal, 2005). Infant temperamental negativity as perceived by mothers and in behavioral measures of infant reactivity and regulation in response to mild stress has been linked with higher levels of child-related maternal separation anxiety, even when maternal personal and contextual characteristics have been taken into account (Hsu, 2004).

Children's psychological states can also have a profound effect on parenting behaviors. Because children's psychological status is not always taken into account, many of the links between parental psychopathology and parenting behavior may be overestimated. Moore and colleagues (2004), for example, replicated earlier work of Whaley and colleagues (1999) on respective associations of

maternal behavior with maternal and child anxiety symptoms, and found that variations in maternal warmth and overcontrol that were previously attributed to maternal anxiety were more strongly associated with children's anxiety levels. In other words, children who were anxious appeared to elicit maternal responses characterized by more overcontrol and less warmth than children who were not anxious (Moore et al., 2004). Mothers experience higher levels of separation anxiety when their infants suffer colic, night waking, and health-related vulnerabilities (Hsu, 2004).

Birth order may also affect the impact of parental anxiety disorders. First children of parents with anxiety disorders have been found more likely to experience social, emotional, and behavior problems than children born second or later (Zahn-Waxler et al., 2002).

Moderating effects of gender. Parent gender is another proximal factor that seems to influence effects of parental psychopathology. In general, maternal psychiatric disorders have been linked with externalizing, internalizing, emotional, behavioral, and substance abuse problems in children whereas paternal psychiatric disorder has been linked with externalizing and behavioral problems and substance abuse in children (Leverton, 2003). Major depression in fathers has also more strongly predicted conduct disorder in children whereas major depression in mothers is more strongly linked with risk for substance abuse in children Major depressive disorders in mothers may be a stronger predictor of major depressive disorders in male children whereas major depressive disorders in fathers may be a stronger predictor of major depressive disorders in female children (Leverton, 2003).

Parental psychopathology may also have different meanings for different genders. Fathers' separation anxiety, for example, has been found to be predicted by wives' separation anxiety whereas mothers' separation anxiety has been predicted by contextual stressors (e.g., child- and work-related concerns, Hsu, 2004). Fathers may be responding to maternal (rather than their own) responsivity to environmental stressors that may interfere with caring for children.

Mediating effects of parental behavior. Growing evidence suggests that relations between parental mental illness and child adjustment are mediated by parent behaviors. In general, the social-emotional differences in children of parents with mental illnesses versus children of parents with no mental illness are observed within the context of patterns of parental behaviors, including parental affect dysregulation, distorted cognitions (especially cognitions about the child), less involvement with the child, and less supportive interaction patterns (Seifer, 2003). In the case of maternal depression, maternal sensitivity to child cues has been found to mediate the impact of maternal depression on child's attachment status (Seifer, 2003).

The impact of maternal anxiety disorders on child anxiety symptoms has also been shown to be mediated by a constellation of behaviors that include catastrophizing, criticizing, limited granting of autonomy, lower warmth and lower positivity, and level of sensitivity manifested by mothers (Dallaire & Weinraub, 2005; Zahn-Waxler et al., 2002). Behaviors of anxious mothers observed during interactions with their school-aged children (e.g., catastrophizing, criticizing, less granting of autonomy, and absence of warmth and positivity) have more strongly predicted development of child anxiety than maternal diagnostic status (Whaley et al., 1999). Dallaire and Weinraub (2005) found that, although maternal separation anxiety was significantly associated with child separation anxiety in 6 year old children, this association disappeared after accounting for infant-mother attachment security and maternal sensitivity. Post hoc testing of a mediation model revealed that the impact of maternal separation anxiety on children's separation anxiety was almost entirely mediated by maternal sensitivity. Warren and colleagues (2003) found that 8-month old infants of mothers diagnosed with panic disorder were more likely to have sleep problems and sleep disorders than infants of mothers without panic disorder.

Mothers with panic disorders were also more likely to feed their infants during the night rather than put the infants to bed awake and to share a bed or room with their infants rather than having them sleep in a separate room. These maternal behaviors of mothers with panic disorder were found to mediate effects of maternal diagnosis on infant sleep disturbance (Warren et al., 2003).

Schwerdtfeger & Goff (2007) found that expectant mothers who reported a history of interpersonal trauma had more impaired prenatal attachments to their fetuses (measured with a narrative interview) than expectant mothers with no history of interpersonal trauma. Although not directly examined, the influence of impaired prenatal attachments on parenting behavior and infant attachment after birth has been documented elsewhere (see Cannella, 2005)

Although no studies to date have examined the comparative effects of maternal eating disorders and maternal behavior on children's eating behaviors, direct comments about children's weight appear to be a strong predictor of child weight and shape concerns (Park et al., 2003).

Parental Substance Abuse: A Unique Psychiatric Disorder

Substance abuse disorders are unique among psychiatric disorders because they involve the ingestion of alcohol or drugs that have specific neuropharmacological effects for the parent and, when ingested during pregnancy, the child. For the parent, these effects most often involve immediate changes in mood, mental state, and behavior. Repeated ingestion can also result in addiction, which manifests as an intense desire for the substance with an impaired ability to control the urges to take that drug, even at the expense of serious adverse consequences (Volkow & Li, 2004). Substance-induced changes in neuropsychiatric symptoms can vary in type, rapidity and severity based on many factors, including the type, amount, combination, potency and purity of substances ingested; the mode of ingestion; the rate of drug metabolism and the severity of withdrawal. Some drugs with addictive potential (e.g., nicotine) are not associated with significant interpersonal behavioral effects, whereas other drugs (e.g., heroine, PCP, amphetamines and hallucinogens) have pronounced social effects such as withdrawal, isolation, and diminished social self-efficacy (Dunn, Tarter, Mezzich, Vanyukov, Kirisci, & Kirillova, 2002).

Impairment in parental functioning also appears to vary according to the nature and type of ingested drugs although the mechanisms of influence are not yet clear. Women who use cocaine, PCP, amphetamines and heroine have generally had children placed out of home more frequently as a result of abandonment, neglect and abuse. Women who use opiates and alcohol, on the other hand, have shown stronger tendencies to neglect rather than abuse their children (Dunn et al., 2002). Adults who use cannabis have demonstrated an increased risk for marital break-up and postponement of parenthood but have also shown a greater likelihood to stop using cannabis within one year of pregnancy (Dunn et al., 2002). In comparison with alcohol-abusing and non-drug-abusing fathers, fathers with drug abuse disorders have shown more physical violence, reported more marital conflict, and engaged in more dysfunctional disciplinary practices and less monitoring of their children. The mediating effects of these parenting deficits on child internalizing and externalizing have also been found to be stronger for drug abusing than alcohol abusing fathers (Fals-Stewart, Kelley, Fincham, Golden, & Logsdon, 2004).

Contextual Factors

Sociodemographic context. Many parents with substance abuse disorders face extreme poverty, residential instability, and unemployment, resorting to pawning possessions and prostitution as a means of financial support. Diversion of family fiscal resources to the procurement of alcohol and drugs can also deplete limited family resources (Dunn et al., 2002). Substance using women are not likely to have help of partners in caring for their children (McMahon, Winkel, Suchman, & Rounsaville, 2007; Stewart, Gossop, & Trakada, 2007). Children of substance-using mothers are twice as likely to be exposed to a given sociodemographic risk factor in comparison with children of nonaddicted parents. It is also likely that the cumulative rather than individual effect of these risk factors contributes to developmental problems for children (Conners, Bradley, Mansell, Liu, Roberts, Burgdorf, & Herrell, 2004). Substance abusing parents who have low SES backgrounds, nonwhite ethnicity, are unmarried, poorly educated, and unemployed are more likely to come to the attention of child welfare (Grella & Greenwell, 2006). This disadvantaged population may therefore be overrepresented in research on parenting problems of substance users.

The societal context of addiction. Despite accumulating evidence suggesting that addiction is a disease of the brain (see Volkow & Li, 2004 for discussion), societal views still characterize parents with substance use disorders as "weak" and "lacking moral judgment" (McMahon et al., 2007). Social isolation and marginalization are likely consequences of these strong social biases (Dunn et al., 2002). Substance using parents' strong feelings of guilt and denial and fears of losing children may also, in part, be a response to social stigmatization. Confronting the problems of addiction can become more difficult because of insufficient resources and treatment programs available to substance-abusing parents. As a consequence, parents tend to withdraw from health care and social systems until their situation become so difficult that their children are taken into custody (Pajulo, Savonlahti, & Piha, 1999).

In contrast to societal stereotypes, there is evidence to the contrary that, while struggling with addiction, fathers and mothers have made attempts to conceive and parent their children in a socially responsible manner (McMahon et al., 2007). In one study of 331 mothers and fathers entering drug treatment, Collins and colleagues (2003) reported that a majority (57 percent mothers and 51 percent fathers) were highly involved with their children. Despite the "absent father" stereotype, McMahon and colleagues (2007) found in a sample of 50 methadone-maintained fathers that nearly half (47 percent) shared joint legal guardianship of their minor children with the children's mothers and nearly a third (29 percent) reported seeing their children daily. Nearly three quarters (70 percent) were legal guardians of their youngest children and 82 percent reported providing financial support to their youngest child.

Chaotic lifestyle and caregiving discontinuity. An individual's lifestyle and functioning and his or her family's routines often become profoundly disrupted by addiction. Impaired functioning often results in unemployment (regardless of social status; Dunn et al., 2002; McMahon et al., 2007). Procuring substances can incur excessive cost and time (Dunn et al., 2002). Illegal activities associated with procurement and ingestion of illicit drugs often lead to multiple arrests, convictions, and incarcerations. The consequences of illegal activity for children can include exposure to illegal activity and extended periods of separation during incarceration (McMahon et al., 2007).

Familial and social context. Parents with substance use disorders usually have experienced many conflictual relationships and communication difficulties within their families of origin. Marital and partner relationships are also usually conflicted, abusive and violent with little support for pregnancy or parenting (McMahon et al., 2007, Pajulo et al., 1999). Spousal relationships often end in separation or divorce (McMahon et al., 2007). Caregiver interpersonal support that may ordinarily buffer parenting against child neglect is typically insufficient (Dunn et al., 2002). Instead, pregnant and parenting parents who are drug users tend to congregate with family and friends who are also drug users (Derauf, LaGasse, Smith, Grant, Shah, Arria et al., 2007). Efforts toward effective parenting diminish, resulting in a home environment that is frequently chaotic and unpredictable (Dunn et al., 2002). Parental absenteeism is also common as a result of time spent procuring and consuming drugs, in treatment, and serving jail sentences (Dunn et al., 2002). Child care responsibilities are often delegated to partners or other family members who serve as parenting surrogates when a substance-using parent is absent (Stewart et al., 2007).

Recent legislation has required that children removed from the home by child welfare services have permanent placements within two years of removal and that substance-abusing parents with welfare entitlements return to work and forfeit benefits within a prescribed time period. These policies place pressure on parents with substance use disorders either to complete their recovery and address parenting and employment issues or permanently forfeit parental rights. More than any other psychiatric disorder, parental substance abuse results in child placement out of home and permanent adoption of children out to foster homes (Marcenko, Kemp, & Larson, 2000).

Parental Substance Abuse and Pathways of Influence

Developmental and timing considerations. The age at which a parent started using drugs is important in that it can determine how the parent's developmental history will impact the development of his or her offspring. Timing of drug use (e.g., before, during, or after pregnancy) will also likely affect the ways it influences children's development. A child's age during periods of parental use, abstinence, relapse and treatment can also influence the impact of substance use disorders on current and later development.

Genetic pathways. Substance use disorders cluster in families. Risk for a substance use disorder doubles for individuals who have alcohol abusing relatives and triples for those who have drug abusing relatives in comparison with those with no family history of substance use. Several genes have been implicated in the transmission of alcohol and substance use (Pears, Capaldi, & Owen, 2007). Children of alcoholic parents may inherit a predisposition for lower serotonergic functioning, which has been associated with impulsive and aggressive behavior in adults and children that, in turn, are precursors to the development of antisocial alcoholism in adulthood (Twitchell, Hanna, Cook, Fitzgerald, Little, & Zucker, 2000).

Biological pathways. A majority of children born to mothers with addiction problems are prenatally exposed to alcohol, other drugs, and cigarette smoke. A mother's physical health during pregnancy can also be diminished during episodes of substance use and thereby affect her baby's health. General hygiene, diet, and nutrition are often compromised during episodes of use. Alcohol-abusing mothers often have more complications during pregnancy and labor, which can worsen their own somatic condition (Pajulo et al., 1999). Nearly a quarter of drug- and alcohol-exposed children have health problems at birth (Connors, Bradley, Mansell, Liu, Roberts, Burgdorf, & Herrell, 2004). Alcohol use during pregnancy can result in fetal alcohol effects and withdrawal symptoms in infants after delivery that, in turn, can make them difficult to handle and comfort (Pajulo et al., 1999). Somatic problems of children exposed to maternal drug use include premature birth and retarded growth (Dunn et al., 2002). Almost all babies exposed to maternal opiate use in utero evidence narcotics abstinence syndrome (NAS), which makes them hypersensitive and irritable and therefore more difficult to handle and soothe (Pajulo et al., 1999).

During the neonatal period, drug-exposed infants can show deficient growth (including brain development), and a variety of neurobehavioral impairments such as hypoactive reflexes, poor motor coordination, inability to sustain orientation to visual and auditory stimuli, and poor regulation of affect, arousal and attention. Following the neonatal period, children of cocaine-exposed children have shown small stature and hypertonia. Infant attempts to shut out external stimulation in response to hypertonia and to send other interactive messages to the parent may be perceived by parents as a personal rejection (Dunn et al., 2002; Pajulo et al., 1999). Although biological effects of paternal substance use at conception on infant growth and development have not been studied, paternal biological contributions during conception are also possible.

Comorbid psychopathology. Substance use disorders often co-occur with other psychiatric disorders in adult women and men, in part because of a higher prevalence of exposure to trauma (Burgdorf, Chen, Walker, Porowski, & Herrell, 2004). Research on parenting and addiction has focused primarily on comorbidity with affective disorders, anxiety disorders, and personality disorders (particularly antisocial personality disorder). In general, findings have shown that the presence of comorbid psychiatric disorders such as depression or antisocial personality disorder increases the likelihood that parenting will be impaired and that children will have emotional and behavioral problems. Eiden and colleagues (1999), for example, found that several risk factors associated with paternal alcoholism, including parental depression, antisocial behavior, and aggression, were associated with lower paternal sensitivity with infants. Luthar and Sexton (2007) reported that comorbidity (presence of affective or anxiety disorder) in methadone-maintained mothers was associated with higher levels of maladjustment in their school-age and adolescent children than substance use disorders alone or the absence of any psychiatric diagnosis. Interestingly, they found no difference in child maladjustment between children of mothers in the latter two groups. Other studies controlling for other psychiatric disorders have shown a direct effect between substance abuse and severity of child neglect (Dunn et al., 2002).

Substance abusing women are more likely to exhibit early-onset antisocial behavior and criminality, characterized by low levels of empathy, inability to maintain enduring attachments to friends and sexual partners, poor marital quality, deficient parenting, and recurrent violent confrontations with others (Dunn et al., 2002). Hans and colleagues (1999) reported that the association between maternal opiate dependence and poor parenting (unresponsiveness and negative behaviors) was largely explained by the effects of comorbid maternal psychopathology, particularly symptoms of antisocial and related personality disorders. Comorbidity with antisocial personality disorder has also been associated with higher levels of externalizing in children of alcoholic parents (Puttler & Zucker, 1998). Conceiving of comorbid psychiatric disturbance as "parental internalizing and externalizing," Burstein and colleagues (2006) found that both were associated with affective problems in school-age and adolescent children and that "parental externalizing" alone was associated with child anxiety.

Parenting Behavior and Dyadic Adjustment

Many of the effects of prenatal drug and alcohol exposure on children's cognitive and emotional development are mediated by the quality of the childrearing environment (Chasnoff, 1997). Parental substance abuse has been linked with poor discipline skills (use of coercive control, harsh discipline, and failure to follow through), limited or absent parental monitoring, ineffective control of children's behaviors, and problems regulating aggression (Keller, Cummings, & Davies, 2005; Pears et al., 2007; Smyth, Miller, Mudar, & Skiba, 2003). Parental substance abuse has also been linked with lower levels of engagement or involvement, poorer synchrony, and more negative behaviors (Pears et al., 2007). In one study involving mothers enrolled in an inner-city methadone program, the parenting style most often represented was uninvolved (other styles included authoritarian, authoritative and indulgent). When mothers in the study desired involvement with their children, the author observed them interacting with their children as friends more so than as parents (Copeland, 2007). Among mothers and fathers with addiction disorders, those who are more involved with their children have lower levels of addiction severity, psychological severity, fewer symptoms of psychological distress, and higher self-efficacy in the parenting role (Collins, Grella, & Hser, 2003).

The most common form of child maltreatment among substance-abusing parents is neglect (Dunn et al., 2002; Mezzich, Bretz, Day, Corby, Kirisci, Swaney, Cornelius, & Weyant, 2007). Child abuse is most commonly associated with paternal alcoholism (Peiponen, Laukkanen, Korhonen, Hintikka, & Lehtonen, 2006). Importantly, neglect has been documented as having more severe adverse effects on developmental outcomes than child abuse, placing children of substance-abusing parents at higher risk for psychiatric problems and social dysfunction (Dunn et al., 2002).

As a result of a parent's substance abuse, children may manifest disturbances that require enhanced parental investment of effort and resources. Health problems, difficult temperament characteristics and deviations from developmental milestones, in the context of parental substance use disorders, augment risk for maladaptive parenting (Dunn et al., 2002). Maladaptive parenting can also be exacerbated by child characteristics associated with genetic and phenotypic components of risk for a substance use disorder (Dunn et al., 2002). Genetic factors, for example, may contribute to a parent-child similarity of temperament (e.g., emotionality) in substance-using families that exacerbates reciprocal negative influences at the behavioral level. Substance using mothers at risk for maltreating their children have exhibited high levels of negative emotionality (hostility, distress, and sadness) in response to images of infants in distress, and low empathy with the infants. The mothers and children in this example appeared to mirror each other in a process of emotional contagion (Milner, Halsey, & Fultz, 1995).

Parenting behavior and dyadic adjustment with infants. Some mothers with substance use disorders enter pregnancy with unrealistically high expectations of themselves as mothers and, when they fail to fulfill them, fall back into substance use and abandon their children (Pajulo et al., 1999). Other mothers who idealize the prospects of parenthood become hostile to their children and attribute intentionality to behaviors typical of high-risk newborns, such as irritability, negative affect, and low adaptability (Dunn et al., 2002). Many others attend to their children's physical needs, but have difficulty accepting and satisfying their emotional needs. Substance using mothers generally seem to derive less joy from their children's development than do non-substance-abusing mothers (Pajulo et al., 1999).

Development during the first year of life may be seriously disturbed if the mother cannot adapt to and support her baby's signals and needs (Pajulo et al., 1999). Substance-using mothers have been observed as having a tendency toward rigidity and overcontrol in their interactions with infants, a lack of enjoyment and pleasure in relating to infants, and limited emotional involvement or responsiveness in their interactions (Burns, Chethik, Burns, & Clark, 1991; Eiden et al., 1999). An overall reduction in reciprocity, mutual enjoyment, and regulation of interaction between mother and infant has also been observed (Burns et al., 1991). Heightened infant irritability often makes it more frustrating and difficult for a mother to bond with her newborn and soothe its distress (Dunn et al., 2002; Pajulo et al., 1999). Babies may also need intensive care after delivery and be separated from the mother for a considerable time. This may disturb natural bonding and cause distorted interaction patterns between mother and child (Pajulo et al., 1999).

Insecure attachment in offspring of substance-abusing parents appears to be among the earliest adverse developmental outcomes and a salient mechanism of continuity in maladaptive psychosocial functioning from infancy to early childhood (Dunn et al., 2002). When mothers continue to use drugs postnatally, insecure attachment is stable from infancy into early childhood and the security or insecurity of attachment does not depend on the particular drug abused by the mother but rather on the quality of the postnatal rearing environment (Howard, Beckwith, & Rodning, 1989). Consequent to emotional unavailability and physical absence, insecure attachment is more frequent in children of substance-using mothers than children of non-substance-using

mothers (Dunn et al., 2002; Howard et al., 1989). Alcohol-using fathers have also been observed as having lower sensitivity and higher negative affect in their interactions with their infants than nonalcoholic fathers (Eiden et al., 1999).

Parenting behavior and toddler adjustment. Findings regarding maladaptive parenting and adverse developmental outcomes for children beyond infancy are less consistent. Moreover, whether toddler adjustment reflects genetic, environmental, or combined effects has also not yet been well-established. Drug-exposed, insecurely attached toddlers obtain significantly lower scores on developmental tests than secure high-risk preterm or full-term infants who were not exposed to drugs in utero (Howard et al., 1989).

Studies have also shown an association between prenatal exposure to alcohol and lower verbal and memory capacity at age 2, lower IQ scores at ages 3–7, and disruptive and disorganized play patterns (Dunn et al., 2002). Maternal substance use has also been linked with anxious regressive behavior and with deficits in reflective behavior (deliberate and careful actions) in 2-year-old children (Dunn et al., 2002). Parental alcohol use problems have also been linked with behavior problems, externalizing behavior, and internalizing problems in preschool age children (Puttler & Zucker, 1998).

In several studies, toddlers and preschool-age children of alcoholic fathers have shown greater impulsivity and more problems with effort control and attention than control children (Eiden et al., 2004; Fitzgerald et al., 1993). Parental alcoholism has also been linked to lower maternal and paternal warmth toward female toddlers and lower paternal warmth toward male toddlers. Parental warmth, in turn, has mediated associations between parental alcoholism and effortful control in 2-year-old boys and girls. Each of these deficits places children at greater risk for later alcohol abuse (Eiden et al., 2004). Fathers' alcoholism has been positively linked with deficits in their 2- to 3-year-old sons' emotional and attentional control, which, in turn, mediate effects of paternal alcoholism on later child externalizing (Loukas, Fitzgerald, Zucker, & von Eye, 2001).

Parental behavior and adjustment in school-age and adolescent children. Very little has been published in the research literature about substance-using parents' behavior with older children. In one study of families with a drug-dependent parent, poor parental monitoring was associated with rule-breaking behavior in school-age and adolescent children (Stanger, Dumenci, Kamon, & Burstein, 2004). In another study, family cohesion was lower in families with an alcoholic parent than control families, and lower cohesion was associated with lower self-esteem among adolescents (Bijttebeier, Goethals, & Ansoms, 2006). In another study, higher family conflict was a risk factor for adolescent drug use whereas higher parental disapproval was a protective factor (Lam, Cance, Eke, Fishbein, Hawkins, & Williams, 2007). In third study, alcohol-abusing parents of African American ethnicity showed less authoritative parenting styles (balancing authority and nurturing) and less inclination to use reasoning so that their adolescent children could learn the meaning behind decisions than nonalcoholic parents. Mothers with alcohol use disorders were more inclined to yell and fuss when their children misbehaved whereas alcohol-abusing fathers were more inclined to use punishment and less inclined to talk with their adolescent children than non-alcohol-abusing fathers (Mupier, Rodney, & Samuels, 2002).

Early development of alcohol use during adolescence may, in turn, have a negative influence on parental attachment. In one longitudinal study, van der Vorst and colleagues (2006) reported that younger adolescent consumers of alcohol were more likely to perceive attachment relationships with their parents as weaker. Greater numbers of parenting disruptions in families affected by parental substance use have been linked with a higher probability of delinquent behavior in early adolescents (age 14) (Keller, Catalano, Haggerty, & Fleming, 2002).

Data regarding psychosocial adjustment in older children suggest that developmental difficulties in infancy and early childhood, including lack of adaptability, insecure attachment, neurocognitive deficits and conduct disorder continue to be exhibited in middle and late childhood. These disturbances become generalized to other agents and contexts of socialization such as school and peers. In addition to higher levels of psychopathology, developmental outcomes during late childhood reflect failures to resolve developmental tasks relevant to this time period, such as social competence outside the family context, school adjustment, and academic performance (Dunn et al., 2002).

In one study, after controlling for parental IQ, children of alcoholic parents had poorer intellectual functioning than children of nonalcoholic parents as early as elementary school. Children of antisocial alcoholic parents were at particular risk for lower Full Scale IQ scores than children of nonantisocial alcoholic parents, although mean IQ scores for both groups fell within normal limits. In the same study, differences in academic achievement between children of alcoholic and nonalcoholic parents appeared as early as first and second grade (Poon, Ellis, Fitzgeral, & Zucker, 2000).

Substance use in parents has been associated with psychological dysregulation (cognitive, affective and behavioral) in 10–12-year-old children (Dunn et al., 2002). School age children of alcoholic parents have also been found to have more behavior problems (e.g., hyperactivity, truancy, lying and stealing), school social adjustment problems, externalizing behavior, and internalizing problems (e.g., anxiety and depression) (Dunn et al., 2002; Fals-Stewart, Kelley, Fincham, Goldon, & Longsdon, 2004; Keller et al., 2005; Puttler & Zucker, 1998). Importantly, parental alcoholism has been found to predict internalizing and externalizing behaviors and drug use in adolescents, above and beyond the general effects of family stress and disruption (Dunn et al., 2002).

Although fathers are underrepresented in research on parental substance abuse and infant adjustment, many studies conducted on parental substance abuse and adjustment of school age and adolescent children focus on mother-father comparisons or fathers' parenting. Peiponen and colleagues (2006), for example, reported that maternal alcohol abuse problems were associated with daughters' internalizing and externalizing problems whereas paternal alcohol abuse was associated with domestic violence and adolescent boys' bullying. In another study, Collins and colleagues (2003) found that lower levels of addiction severity in parents (particularly fathers) was associated with higher levels of involvement with children. In a third study, Fals-Stewart and colleagues (2004) reported that, although school age children of drug and alcohol abusing fathers showed higher levels of internalizing and externalizing behavior problems than children of non-substance-using fathers, the *T-scores* for behavioral problems for both groups fell within normal limits, suggesting adequate levels of adjustment in both groups. In fourth study, Loukas and colleagues (2003) reported that parental alcohol abuse was associated with higher levels of disruptive behavior problems in boys, starting in preschool and continuing through early adolescence. Paternal alcoholism explained unique variance in boys' disruptive behavior, even after maternal alcoholism, parent antisocial personality disorder, and family conflict were taken into account.

School-age boys of substance-using fathers may be at greatest risk for psychosocial maladjustment. In one study, Moss and colleagues (1999) found decreased salivary cortisol response to anticipated stress in preadolescent sons of substance-abusing fathers. These lower levels of cortisol were associated with regular monthly cigarette smoking and marijuana use during adolescence. Longitudinal research has shown that psychological dysregulation is more common in male children (age 10–12) of substance-using fathers (Dunn et al., 2002). In a different study, paternal history of substance abuse was associated with deviant peer affiliations in sons ages 10 to 12. This association was mediated by difficult temperament in fathers and sons, sons' intelligence, sons'

acceptance of deviant peer behavior as normative, and sons' mesomorphy (Blackson, Tarter, Loeber, Ammerman, & Windle, 1996).

Paternal Psychopathology: An Underrepresented Area of Research

Although, in the last 15 years, there has been growing recognition and research activity examining the role of fathers in children's psychosocial adjustment (Connell & Goodman, 2002), fathers have consistently been underrepresented in research on parental psychopathology (Cassano, Adrian, Veits, & Zeman, 2006; Phares, Fields, Kamboukos, & Lopez, 2005). This unfortunate omission is likely to leave a large portion of variance in child outcomes unaccounted for, or worse, incorrectly attributed solely to mothers (Connel & Goodman, 2002). Many barriers have precluded the inclusion of fathers in parenting research, including a societal emphasis on the mother as the sole caregiver, a higher prevalence of researched psychological disorders (e.g., depression and anxiety) among women, and biases in developmental theories that place most emphasis on the mother's role in a child's normal and abnormal psychological development (for a discussion, see Connell & Goodman, 2002).

Studies examining associations between paternal psychopathology and child adjustment have generally shown significant findings, although the magnitude of these findings has been questionable in some cases. Phares and Compas (1992) have reported a consistent pattern linking paternal depression with a range of negative child outcomes and paternal alcoholism, substance abuse and antisocial behaviors linked with higher rates of externalizing in children. Paternal psychopathology has also been found to contribute independently to development of BPD in persons constitutionally predisposed to the disorder (Helgeland & Torgersen, 2004). However, in a metaanalysis of 32 studies examining paternal depression, Kane & Garber (2004) found that depression in fathers was significantly positively associated with internalizing and externalizing symptoms in children but that the proportion of variance explained by paternal depression was modest.

One approach to studying paternal psychopathology has been to compare it with maternal psychopathology in relation to child emotional and behavioral disorders. This research design takes into account the presence of both parents as potential influences on children's well-being and on each other's adjustment. Some studies have reported cumulative unique effects of maternal and paternal psychopathology. Sareen and colleagues (2005), for example, found that paternal and maternal psychopathology had independent significant associations on offspring development of diagnosable disorder in adulthood. Likewise, Marmorstein and colleagues (2004) found that paternal and maternal depression had an additive effect on youth externalizing symptoms. In a metaanalysis of 134 studies comparing effects of maternal and paternal psychopathology in relation to children's internalizing and externalizing symptoms, Connell and Goodman (2002) found that children's externalizing symptoms were equally associated with psychopathology in mothers and fathers, whereas children's internalizing symptoms were more closely related to the presence of psychopathology in mothers. However, the magnitude of this difference was small and further examination of variation in effect size across studies indicated that variation was due largely to methodological differences across studies. Connell & Goodman (2002) also found that depression in fathers was less closely related to children's internalizing than depression in mothers and that alcoholism and substance abuse disorders in fathers were less closely related to children's externalizing than the same disorders in mothers. They suggested that this finding may reflect children's increased exposure to biological influences of maternal (vs. paternal) psychopathology during pregnancy.

Other findings have indicated interdependence between maternal and paternal psychopathology. For example, Marmorstein and colleagues (2004) found that depressed mothers tended to partner with antisocial fathers. Brennan and colleagues (2002) found that maternal depression interacted with both paternal depression and paternal substance abuse in predicting youth depression. Stewart and colleagues (2007) found that paternal psychopathology played less of a role in child maladjustment in the presence (versus absence) of maternal antisocial personality disorder.

Connell and Goodman (2002) examined, in their metaanalysis, whether paternal and maternal psychopathology influenced children differently across time. They found that maternal psychopathology (particularly depression) was more closely related to emotional and behavioral problems in younger children, whereas paternal psychopathology (particularly alcoholism and depression) was more closely related to emotional behavior and problems in samples of older children. These differences remained significant after potentially confounding moderator variables were controlled. The authors suggested that this finding may reflect different levels of involvement for mothers and fathers across periods of child development with mothers' involvement higher during early years and fathers' involvement higher during adolescent years. The authors also suggested that these findings are more likely to reflect a bidirectional rather than causal influence of parental psychopathology. That is, the presence of emotional and behavioral problems in young children likely exacerbates maternal psychopathology whereas the presence of emotional and behavioral problems during adolescence likely exacerbates paternal psychopathology.

The mechanisms by which paternal psychopathology potentially influences children's adjustment has received more limited attention. Kane and Garber (2004) reported findings from their metaanalysis that effects of paternal depression on child internalizing and externalizing were partially mediated by conflict in the father-child relationship. They suggested that conflict may be linked with externalizing and internalizing through inappropriate modeling of coercive and hostile behavior, feelings of helplessness and loss of control or emotional dysregulation. The strength of a father's investment in caregiving may moderate the impact of paternal psychopathology on children's adjustment. Stewart and colleagues (2007) have suggested that quality of marital relations and certainty about paternity might influence a father's investment and subsequently the quality of relations with children but no empirical findings to date have supported this claim.

Conclusions

In this chapter, parental psychopathology and its potential implications for child maladjustment were examined within a developmental context. That is, the impact of parental psychopathology was considered within the context of salient developmental tasks for children and parents, as children progress from infancy to adolescence. Parental psychopathology was also considered a dynamic factor whose influence on child development varies depending on its timing, chronicity, recurrence, symptom constellation, severity, vehicle (e.g., DNA vs neuroregulatory vs psychosocial pathways), environmental context (distal and proximal) and influence on mediating factors.

In general, of all the considered ways that parental psychopathology can fluctuate, timing appears to be the most critical factor. The presence of parental psychopathology during infancy may represent the greatest risk because of an infant's complete dependence on the parent for physical, cognitive, social and emotional well-being and because any developmental compromises during infancy are likely to affect subsequent development. One caveat related to this conclusion, though, is that it may, in part, reflect a stronger emphasis in recent research on infancy. As more studies focus on parental psychopathology and associated parenting behaviors and dyadic adjustment issues from toddlerhood through adolescence, risks related to exposure during these periods may become more apparent and our understanding of their mechanisms more refined.

The nature of risk to children's normal development also appears to vary depending on the nature of the parent's psychiatric illness. That is, rather than there being an underlying process that is universal to the occurrence of parental psychopathology, the particular nature of mental illness seems to play a determining role in the specific patterns of parenting behavior, child responses, and dyadic interactions, which may, in turn, serve as adaptations to the specific nature of the parent's mental illness. At the time this chapter was written, a majority of published studies on parenting and psychopathology focused on the impact of maternal depression for children, and a substantial minority focused on maternal anxiety disorders and eating disorders, indicating a necessary shift toward examining a broader range of adult disorders. Surprisingly little has been reported in the empirical literature on parental personality disorders and their implications for parenting behavior, child adjustment and dyadic interactions. Given the enduring and pervasive nature of personality disorders and their particular implications for disturbance in interpersonal relationships, there is a marked need for carefully designed studies examining pathways of potential influence on children's social and emotional development and their interaction with contextual and mediating factors. One caveat related to this conclusion is that research focused on the implications of a specific type of parental psychopathology (e.g., anxiety, eating disorders) often examines child adjustment domains that are expected to be associated with the specific type of psychopathology (e.g., eating behavior in children of parents with eating disorders). Whereas strengths in this approach include its close adherence to principles of positivistic science (e.g., generating and testing hypotheses versus simply exploring), it may be that more general and global effects of parental psychopathology can be found in examining similar domains of child adjustment across many types of psychopathology. Studies of infant attachment are one example of how research can transcend this barrier to identify similar patterns of infant disorganization that occur as a general consequence of parental psychopathology.

Aside from a handful of gender effects reported in this chapter, very few studies have examined the implications of paternal versus maternal psychopathology for children's psychosocial development. Social trends toward a more equitable division of parenting and financial responsibilities in heterosexual parenting couples and civil unions between same-sex parents in the United States suggest that more children may be reared primarily by a father in the next 10 years. Largely absent in the empirical literature on parenting are studies reporting on child outcomes in families where a male adult is the primary caregiver, and little is known how changing social pressures and contexts might interact with psychopathology in primary caregiving fathers.

Another topic that has received little attention in the parenting and abnormal psychology literature is the impact of paternal psychopathology on adoptive and foster parents. Adoptive and foster parenting are both unique and changing forms of parenting. Adults become adoptive and foster parents for many reasons, the most common being the desire to help a child in need, the wish to do something for one's community, and the interesting having children (Haugaard & Hazan, 2002). Adoptive and foster parents begin their route to parenting by becoming engaged with adoptive and foster family services. Their parenting roles involve ongoing relationships with these services and can also involve relationships with biological parents or, at the very least, consideration of the biological parent's influence on the child. How these unique and complex aspects of the parenting role interact with parental psychopathology to affect children's development is an important area for future research.

Another important area for future research is the benefit versus cost of parental absence to children during episodes of a parent's psychological treatment. The severity of parental psychopathology, the length and number of absences, the timing of absences in relation to the child's developmental tasks, the availability of ancillary parental support, the negotiation of separations and reunions are a few factors to be considered when examining effects of parental absenteeism.

A fourth topic to be considered in future studies is the long-term influence of parental psychopathology. How will the well-documented effects of parental psychopathology on children's adjustment play out in parental and dyadic function and child adjustment in the next generation? In this chapter, we have reported some evidence (primarily from literature on parental exposure to trauma) that a parent's own early childhood experiences have direct implications for children's adjustment but also that parents exposed to trauma have been able to protect their children from transmission of traumatic symptoms. Further longitudinal research on the transition from adolescence to young adulthood to parenthood in individuals who were exposed to parental psychopathology during their childhood will help address this current gap. In this research, it will be important to weigh the effects of the parenting environment against other influential factors (e.g., social and familial support, availability of resources). It will also be important to identify potential antecedents to parental function and dysfunction in prospective and retrospective studies of individuals exposed to their parents' mental illness.

Finally, evidence presented in this chapter underscores the need for systematic development and evaluation of parenting interventions that target parenting deficits known to be associated with specific psychiatric disorders. Interventions that focus on specific areas of risk for parent-child interactions and child maladjustment are far more likely to be efficient and cost-effective than more generic and global approaches to parent training. Treatment providers who know what risks to look for in psychiatrically impaired adults and their children are also far more likely to intervene earlier and in ways that are more beneficial to children's developmental needs.

Acknowledgments

Preparation of the manuscript was funded by grants from the National Institutes of Health (R01DA017294).

References

Aisenberg, E., & Ell, K. (2005). Contextualizing community violence and its effects: An ecological model of parent-child interdependent coping. *Journal of Interpersonal Violence, 20*, 855–871.

Almqvist, K., & Broberg, a. G. (2003). Young children traumatized by organized violence together with their mothers – the critical effects of damaged internal representations. *Attachment and Human Development, 5*, 367–380.

Ayers, S., Eagle, A., & Waring, H. (2006). The effects of childbirth-related post-traumatic stress disorder on women and their relationships: A qualitative study. *Psychology, Health and Medicine, 11*, 389–398.

Ayers, S., Wright, D. B., & Wells, N. (2007). Symptoms of post-traumatic stress disorder in couples after birth: Association with the couple's relationship and parent-baby bond. *Journal of Reproductive and Infant Psychology, 25*, 40–50.

Banyard, V. L., Williams, L. M., & Siegel, J. A. (2003). The impact of complex trauma and depression on parenting: An exploration of mediating risk and protective factors. *Child Maltreatment, 8*, 334–349.

Beck, C. T. (2006). The anniversary of birth trauma: Failure to rescue. *Nursing Research, 55*, 381–390.

Beckham, J. C., Braxton, L. E., Kudler, H. S., Feldman, M. E., Lytle, B. L., & Palmer, S. (1997). Minnesota Multiphasic Personality Inventory profiles of Vietnam combat veterans with posttraumatic stress disorders and their children. *Journal of Clinic Psychology, 53*, 847–852.

Bijttebeier, P., Goethals, E., & Ansoms, S. (2006). Parental drinking as a risk factor for children's maladjustment: The mediating role of family environment. *Psychology of Addictive Behaviors, 20*, 126–130.

Blackson, T. C., Tarter, R. E., Loeber, R., Ammerman, R. T., & Windle, M. (1996). The influence of paternal substance abuse on difficult temperament in fathers and sons on sons' disengagement from family to deviant peers. *Journal of Youth and Adolescence, 25*, 389–411.

Bomgardner, A. L. (2005). Mild to moderate PTSD I mothers: Consequences and interventions for children's attachment security. *Dissertation Abstracts International: Section B: The Sciences and Engineering, 66*(6-B), 3398.

Brennan, P. A., Hammen, C., Katz, A. R., & LeBrocque, R. M. (2002). Maternal depression, paternal psychopathology, and adolescent diagnostic outcome. *Journal of Consulting and Clinical Psychology, 70*, 1075–1085.

Burgdorf, K., Chen, Xiaowu, Walker, T., Porowski, A., & Herrell, J. M. (2004). The prevalence and prognostic significance of sexual abuse in substance abuse treatment of women. *Addictive Disorders and their Treatment, 3*, 1–13.

Burns, K., Chethik, L., Burns, W. J., & Clark, R. (1991). Dyadic disturbances in cocaine-abusing mothers and their infants. *Journal of Clinical Psychology, 47*, 316–319.

Burstein, M., Stanger, C., Kamon, J., & Dumenci, L. (2006). Parent psychopathology, parenting, and child internalizing problems in substance-abusing families. *Psychology of Addictive Behaviors, 20*, 97–106.

Cannella, B. L. (2005). Maternal-fetal attachment: An integrative review. *Journal of Advanced Nursing, 50*, 60–68.

Cassano, M., Adrian, M., Veits, G., & Zeman, J. (2006). The inclusion of fathers in the empirical investigation of child psychopathology: An update. *Journal of Clinical Child and Adolescent Psychology, 35*, 583–589.

Chasnoff, I. J. (1997). Prenatal exposure to cocaine and other drugs: is there a profile? In P. J. Accardo, B. K. Shapiro, & A. J. Capute (Eds.), *Behavior belongs in the brain*, pp. 311–321. Baltimore: York.

Chu, A., & DePrince, A. P. (2006). Development of dissociation: Examining the relationship between parenting, maternal trauma and child dissociation. *Journal of Trauma and Dissociation, 7*, 75–89.

Collins, C. C., Grella, C. E., & Hser, Y. (2003). Effects of gender and level of parental involvement among parents in drug treatment. *American Journal of Drug and Alcohol Abuse, 29*, 237–261.

Connell, A. M., & Goodman, S. H. (2002). The association between psychopathology in fathers versus mothers and children's internalizing and externalizing behavior problems: a meta-analysis. *Psychological Bulletin, 128*, 746–773.

Conners, N. A., Bradley, R. H., Mansell, L. W., Liu, J. Y., Roberts, T. J., Burgdorf, K., & Herrell, J. M. (2004). Children of mothers with serious substance abuse problems: An accumulation of risks. *The American Journal of Drug and Alcohol Abuse, 30*, 85–100.

Copeland, E. E. (2007). Relationship of substance abusing women's parenting styles to their children's problem behaviors. *Dissertation Abstracts International Section A: Humanities and Social Sciences, 67*(8-A), 3179.

Coppola, G., Cassibba, R., & Constantini, A. (2007). What can make the difference? Premature birth and maternal sensitivity at 3 months of age: The role of attachment organization, traumatic reaction and baby's medical risk. *Infant Behavior and Development, 30*, 679–684.

Dallaire, D. H., & Weinraub, M. (2005). Predicting children's separation anxiety at age 6: The contributions of infant-mother attachment security, maternal sensitivity, and maternal separation anxiety. *Attachment and Human Development, 7*(4), 393–408.

Derauf, C., LaGasse, L. L., Smith, L. M., Grant, P., Shah, R., Arria, A., Huestis, M., Haning, W., Strauss, A., Grotta, S. D., Liu, J., & Lester, B. M. (2007). Demographic and psychosocial characteristics of mothers using methamphetamine during pregnancy: Preliminary results of the infant development, environment, and lifestyle study (IDEAL). *American Journal of Drug and Alcohol Abuse, 33*, 281–280.

Dulmus, C. N., & Wodarski, J. S. (2000). Trauma-related symptomatology among children of parents victimized by urban community violence. *American Journal of Orthopsychiatry, 70*, 272–277.

Dunn, M. G., Tarter, R. E., Mezzich, A. C., Vanyukov, M., Kirisci, L., & Kirillova, G. (2002). Origins and consequences of child neglect in substance abuse families. *Clinical Psychology Review, 22*, 1063–1090.

Eiden, R. D., Chavez, F., & Leonard, K. E. 1999). Parent-infant interactions among families with alcholic fathers. *Development and Psychopathology, 11*, 745–762.

Eiden, R. D., Edwards, E. P., & Leonard, K. E. (2004). Predictors of effortful control among children of alcoholic and non-alcoholic fathers. *Journal of Studies on Alcohol, 65*, 309–319.

Fals-Stewart, W., Kelley, M. L., Finchman, F. D., Golden, J., & Logsdon, T. (2004). Emotional and behavioral problems of children living with drug-abusing fathers: Comparisons with children living with alchol-abusing and non-substance-abusing fathers. *Journal of Family Psychology, 18*, 319–330.

Feldman, R., & Reznick, J. S. (1996). Maternal perception and infant intentionality at 4 and 8 months. *Infant Behavior and Development, 19*, 483–496.

Fitzgerald, H. E., Sullivan, L. A., Ham, H. P., Zucker, R. A., Bruckel, S., Schneider, A. M. et al. (1993). Predictors of behavior problems in 3-year-old sons of alcoholics: Early evidence for the onset of risk. *Child Development, 64*, 110–123.

Galinsky, E. (1981). *Between generations: The six stages of parenthood.* New York: Berkeley.

Goodman, S. H., & Gotlib, I. H. (1999). Risk for psychopathology in the children of depressed mothers: A developmental model for understanding mechanisms of transmission. *Psychological Review, 106*(3), 458–490.

Grella, C. E., & Greenwell, L. (2006). Correlates of parental status and attitudes toward parenting among substance-abusing women offenders. *Prison Journal, 86*, 89–113.

Hammen, C., & Brennan, P. A. (2001). Depressed adolescents of depressed and nondepressed mothers: Tests of an interpersonal impairment hypothesis. *Journal of Consulting and Clinical Psychology, 69*(2), 284–294.

Hans, S. L., Bernstein, V. J., & Henson, L. G. (1999). The role of psychopathology in the parenting of drug-dependent women. *Development and Psychopathology, 11*, 957–977.

Haugaard, J., & Hazan, C. (2002). Foster parenting. In M. Bornstein (Ed.), *Handbook of parenting,* (2nd ed.): Vol. 5. *Children and parenting,* pp. 313–327. Mahwah, NJ: Erlbaum.

Heinicke, C. M. (2002). The transition to parenting. In M. Bornstein (Ed.), *Handbook of Parenting:* Vol. 3. *Being and becoming a parent,* pp. 363–388 (2nd ed.). Mahwah, NJ: Lawrence Erlbaum Associates.

Helgeland, M. I., & Torgersen, S. (2004). Developmental antecedents of borderline personality. *Comprehensive Psychiatry, 45*, 138–147.

Howard, J., Beckwith, L., & Rodning, C. (1989). The development of young children in substance abusing parents: insights from seven years of intervention and research. *Zero to Three: Bulletin of the National Center for Clinical Infant Programs, 9*, 8–12.

Hsu, H. (2004). Antecedents and consequences of separation anxiety in first-time mothers: Infant, mother, and social-contextual characteristics. *Infant Behavior and Development, 27*, 113–133.

Jacobvitz, D., Leon, K., & Hazen, N. (2006). Does expectant mothers' unresolved trauma predict frightened/frightening maternal behavior? Risk and protective factors. *Development and Psychopathology, 18*, 363–379.

Kaitz, M., & Maytal, H. (2005). Interactions between anxious mothers and their infants: An integration of theory and research findings. *Infant Mental Health Journal, 26*(6), 570–597.

Kane, P., & Garber, J. (2004). The relations among depression in fathers, children's psychopathology, and father-child conflict: A meta-analysis. *Clinical Psychology Review, 24*, 339–360.

Kassam-Adams, N., Garcia-Espana, J. F., Millar, V. A., & Winston, F. (2006). Agreement regarding children's acute stress: The role of parent acute stress reactions. *Journal of the American Academy of Child and Adolescent Psychiatry, 45*, 1485–1493.

Keller, P. S., Cummings, E. M., & Davies, P. T. (2005). The role of marital discord and parenting in relations between parental problem drinking and child adjustment. *Journal of Child Psychology and Psychiatry, 46*, 943–951.

Keller, T. E., Catalano, R. F., Haggerty, K. P., & Fleming, C. B. (2002). Parent figure transitions and delinquency and drug use among early adolescent children of substance abusers. *American Journal of Drug and Alcohol Abuse, 28*, 399–427.

Lam, W. K. K., Cance, J. D., Eke, A. N., Fishbein, D. H., Hawkins, S. R., & Williams, J. C. (2007). Children of African-American mothers who use crack cocaine: Parenting influences on youth substance use. *Journal of Pediatric Psychology, 32*, 877–887.

Leverton, T. J. (2003). Parental psychiatric illness: the implications for children. *Current Opinion in Psychiatry, 16*, 395–402.

Loukas, A., Fitzgerald, H. E., Zucker, R. A., & von Eye, A. (2001). Parental alcoholism and co-occurring antisocial behavior: Prospective relationships to externalizing behavior problems in their young sons. *Journal of Abnormal Child Psychology, 29*, 91–106.

Loukas, A., Zucker, R. A., Fitzgerald, H. E., & Krull, J. L. (2003). Developmental trajectories of disruptive behavior problems among sons of alcoholics: Effects of parent psychopathology, family conflict, and child undercontrol. *Journal of Abnormal Psychology, 112*, 119–131.

Lovejoy, M. C., Graczyk, P. A., O'Hare, E., & Neuman, G. (2000). Maternal depression and parenting behavior: A meta-analytic review. *Clinical Psychology Review, 20*(5), 561–2000.

Luthar, S., & Sexton, C. C. (2007). Maternal drug abuse versus maternal depression: Vulnerability and resilience among school-age and adolescent offspring. *Development and Psychopathology, 19*, 205–225.

Lyons-Ruth, K., Yellin, C., Melnick, S., & Atwood, G. (2003). Childhood experiences of trauma and loss have different relations to maternal unresolved and Hostile-Helpless states of mind on the AAI. *Attachment and Human Development, 5*, 330–352.

Manne, S., DuHamel, K., & Redd, W. H. (2000). Association of psychological vulnerability factors to post-traumatic stress symptomatology in mothers of pediatric cancer survivors. *Psycho-Oncology, 9*, 372–384.

Marcenko, M. O., Kemp, S. P., & Larson, N. C. (2000). Childhood experiences of abuse, later substance use, and parenting outcomes among low-income mothers. *American Journal of Orthopsychiatry, 70*, 316–326.

Marmorstein, N. R., Malone, S. M., & Iacono, W. G. (2004). Psychiatric disorders among offspring of depressed mothers: Associations with paternal psychopathology. *American Journal of Psychiatry, 161*, 1588–1594.

McMahon, T. J., Winkel, J. D., Suchman, N. E., & Rounsaville, B. J. (2007). Drug-abusing fathers: Patterns of pair bonding, reproduction, and parental involvement. *Journal of Substance Abuse Treatment, 33*, 295–302.

Mendelsohn, A. (2005). Recovering reverie: Using infant observation in interventions with traumatized mothers and their premature babies. *Infant Observation, 8*, 195–208.

Mezzich, A. C., Bretz, W. A., Day, B., Corby, P. M., Kirisci, L., Swaney, M., Cornelius, J. R., & Weyant, R. J. (2007). Child neglect and oral health problems in offspring of substance-abusing fathers. *American Journal on Addictions, 16*, 397–402.

Milner, J. S., Halsey, L. B., & Fultz, J. (1995). Empathic responsiveness and affective reactivity to infarct stimuli in high- and low-risk for physical child abuse mothers. *Child Abuse and Neglect, 19*, 767–780.

Moore, P. S., Whaley, S. E., & Sigman, M. (2004). Interactions between mothers and children: Impact of maternal and child anxiety. *Journal of Abnormal Psychology, 113*(3), 471–476.

Moss, H. B., Vanyukov, M., Yao, J. K., & Kirillova, G. P. (1999). Salivary cortisol responses in prepubertal boys: The effects of parental substance abuse on association with drug use behavior during adolescence. *Biological Psychiatry*, 45, 1293–1299.

Mupier, R., Rodney, H. E., & Samuels, L. A. (2002). Difference in parenting style between African American alcholoic and non-alcholic parents. *Families in Society*, 83, 604–610.

Murray, C., & Johnston, C. (2006). Parenting in mothers with and without attention-deficit/hyperactivity disorder. *Journal of Abnormal Psychology*, 115(1), 52–61.

Pajulo, M., Savonlahti, E., & Piha, J. (1999). Maternal substance abuse: Infant psychiatric interest: A review and a hypothetical model of interaction. *American Journal of Drug and Alcohol Abuse*, 25, 761–769.

Park, R. J., Senior, R., & Stein, A. (2003). The offspring of mothers with eating disorders. *European Child and Adolescent Psychiatry* 12(Supplement 1), 110–119.

Pears, K., Capaldi, D. M., & Owen, L. D. (2007). Substance use risk across three generations: The roles of parent discipline practices in inhibitory control. *Psychology of Addictive Behaviors*, 21, 373–386.

Peiponen, S., Laukkanen, E., Korhonen, V., Hintikka, U. & Johannes, L. (2006). The association of parental alchol abuse and depression with severe emotional and behavioral problems in adolescents: A clinical study. *International Journal of Social Psychiatry*, 52, 395–406.

Phares, V., & Compas, B. E. (1992). The role of fathers in child and adolescent psychopathology: Make room for daddy. *Psychological Bulletin*, 111, 387–412.

Phares, V., Fields, S., Kamboukos, D., & Lopez, E. (2005). Still looking for poppa. *American Psychologist*, 60, 735–736.

Phillips, D., Featherman, D. L., & Liu, J. (2004). Children as an evocative influence on adults' reactions to terrorism. *Applied Developmental Science*, 8, 195–210.

Poon, E., Ellis, D. A., Fitzgerald, H. E., & Zucker, R. A. (2000). Intellectual, cognitive, and academic performance among sons of alcoholics during the early school years: Differences related to subtypes of familial alcohol. *Alcoholism: Clinical and Experimental Research*, 24, 1020–1027,

Puttler, L. I., & Zucker, R. A. (1998). Behavioral outcomes among children of alcoholics during the early and middle childhood years: Familial subtype variations. *Alcoholism: Clinical and Experimental Research*, 22, 1962.

Sagi-Schwartz, A., van IJzendoorn, M. H., Grossman, K. E., Joels, T., Grossman, K.,

Scharf, M., Koren-Karie, N., & Alkalay, S. (2003). Attachment and traumatic stress in female holocaust child survivors and their daughters. *American Journal of Psychiatry*, 160, 1086–1092.

Sareen, J., Fleisher, W., Cox, B. J., Hassard, S., & Stein, M. B. (2005). Childhood adversity and perceived need for mental health care: Findings from a Canadian community sample. *Journal of Nervous and Mental Disease*, 193, 396–404.

Schechter, D. S., Zygmunt, A., Trabka, K. A., Davies, M., Colon, E., Kolodji, A., & McCaw, J. E. (2007). Child mental representations of attachment when mothers are traumatized: The relationship of family-drawings to story-stem completion. *Journal of Early Childhood and Infant Psychology*, 3, 119–140.

Schwerdtfeger, K. L., & Goff, B. S. N. (2007). Intergenerational transmission of trauma: Exploring mother-infant prenatal attachment. *Journal of Traumatic Stress*, 20, 39–51.

Seifer, R. (2003). Young children with mentally ill parents: Resilient developmental systems. In S. S. Luthar (Ed.), *Resilience and vulnerability: Adaptation in the context of childhood adversities*, pp. 29–49. New York: Cambridge University Press.

Smyth, N. J., Miller, B. A., Mudar, P. J., & Skiba, D. (2003). Protecting children: Exploring differences and similarities between mothers with and without alcohol problems. *Journal of Human Behavior in the Social Environment*, 7, 37–58.

Stanger, C., Dumenci, L., Kamon, J., & Burstein, M. (2004). Parenting and children's externalizing problems in substance-abusing families. *Journal of Clinical Child and Adolescent Psychology*, 33, 590–600.

Stewart, D., Gossop, M., & Trakada, K. (2007). Drug dependent parents: Childcare responsibilities, involvement with treatment services, and treatment outcomes. *Addictive Behaviors*, 32, 1657–1668.

Thiel-Bonney, C., & Cierpka, M. (2004). Birth as a stressful experience of parents with newborns and infants showing regulatory disorders. [Belastungserfahrun bei eltern von sauglingen mit selbstregulationsstorungen.] *Praxis der Kinderpsychologie und Kinder Psychiatrie*, 53, 601–622.

Turner, S. M., Beidel, D. C., Roberson-Nay, R., & Tervo, K. (2003). Parenting behaviors in parents with anxiety disorders. *Behaviour Research and Therapy*, 41, 541–665.

Turton, P., Hughes, P., Fonagy, P., & Fainman, D. (2004). An investigation into the possible overlap between PTSD and unresolved responses following stillbirth: An absence of linkage with only unresolved status predicting infant disorganization. *Attachment and Human Development*, 6(3), 241–253.

Twitchell, G. R., Hanna, G. L., Cook, E. H., Fitzgerald, H. E., Little, K. Y., & Zucker, R. A. (2000). Serotonergic function, behavioral disinhibition, and negative affect in children of alcoholics: The moderating effects of puberty. *Alcoholism: Clinical and Experimental Research*, 24, 972–979.

Van der Vorste, H., Engels, R. C. M. E., Meeus, W., Dekovic, M., & Vermulst, A. (2006). Parental attachment, parental control, and early development of alcohol use: A longitudinal study. *Psychology of Addictive Behaviors*, 20, 107–116.

Van IJzendoorn, M. H., & Bakermans-Kranenburg, M. J. (2006). DRD4 7-repeat polymorphism moderates the association between maternal unresolved loss or trauma and infant disorganization. *Attachment and Human Development*, 8, 291–307.

Volkow, N. D., & Li, T. (2004). Drug addiction: the neurobiology of behavior gone awry. *Nature Reviews Neuroscience*, 5, 963–970.

Warren, S. L., Gunnar, M. R., Kagan, J., Anders, T. F., Simmens, S. J., Rones, M., Wease, S., Aron, E., Dahl, R. E., & Sroufe, L. A. (2003). Maternal panic disorder: Infant temperament, neurophysiology, and parenting behaviors. *Journal of the American Academy of Child and Adolescent Psychiatry*, 42(7), 814–825.

Waugh, E., & Bulik, C. M. (1999). Offspring of women with eating disorders. *International Journal of Eating Disorders*, 25(2), 123–133.

Whaley, S. E., Pinto, A., & Sigman, M. (1999). Characterizing interactions between anxious mothers and their children. *Journal of Consulting and Clinical Psychology*, 67(6), 826–836.

Wijnorks, L. (1999). Maternal recollected anxiety and mother-infant interaction in preterm infants. *Infant Mental Health Journal*, 20, 393–409.

Woodruff-Borden, J., Morrow, C., Bourland, S., & Cambron, S. (2002). The behavior of anxious parents: Examining mechanisms of transmission of anxiety from parent to child. *Journal of Clinical Child and Adolescent Psychology*, 31(3), 364–374.

Zahn-Waxler, C., Duggal, S., & Gruber, R. (2002). Parental psychopathology. In M. H. Bornstein (Ed.), *Handbook of parenting*, pp. 295–327. Mahwah, NJ: Lawrence Erlbaum Associates.

CHAPTER 21

The Environment of Children of Illicit Drug Users

Its Conceptualization, Examination, and Measurement

Jessica F. Magidson and Stacey B. Daughters

Children of illicit drug users are at heightened risk for poor psychosocial outcomes resulting from exposure to a drug-using environment, thus necessitating a further examination of the context in which many of these outcomes begin to develop. Accordingly to ecological theory (Belsky, 1993), environmental risks children of illicit drugs users face are multifaceted and cut across numerous domains, including those proximal (e.g., effects of parenting) and distal (e.g., neighborhood characteristics). For example, risks range from in utero exposure (Schempf, 2007) to factors related to parenting behaviors (Lam, Cance, Eke, Fishbein, Hawkins, Williams, 2007), familial context (Gruber & Taylor, 2006), social/peer network (Mason, Cheung, & Walker, 2004), and the neighborhood (Luthar & Cushing, 1999). Further, ecological theory posits that the assessment of these factors cannot exist in isolation given that they interact and influence each other to impact child development (Belsky, 1993). Existing research specific to children of illicit drug users rarely captures a comprehensive depiction of the proximal and distal factors comprising the environment for these youth, despite work that has advocated for the need to better understand the interaction and interplay of these numerous risk factors (i.e., Suchman, McMahon, Slade, & Luthar, 2005). A better understanding and assessment of crucial environmental factors may facilitate improved screening for at-risk children of illicit drug users to be targeted for prevention and intervention programs. Further, this increased understanding may serve to clarify the necessary components of such programs, and where in the environmental context interventions may be most effective.

Distinguishing Illicit Drug versus Alcohol Using Environments

Research pertaining to children of substance-abusing parents has disproportionately focused on children of alcoholics (COAs) over children of illicit drug users (Johnson & Leff, 1999; Peleg-Oren & Teichman, 2006), and reviews of such studies typically group drug and alcohol using parents together (Austin & Prendergast, 1991; Johnson, 1991).

However, children of illicit drug users face unique and often intensified risk factors that should be distinguished from COAs, particularly in the discussion of environmental context (Hogan, 1998; Johnson, 1991) and higher rates of psychopathology and functional impairment than COAs (Wilens, Biederman, Bredin, Hahesy, Abrantes et al., 2002).

Children of illicit drug users are most commonly distinguished from children of alcoholics based on specific physiological risks and negative outcomes resulting from in utero drug exposure (Schempf, 2007). Further, the environmental risks faced by children of illicit drug users, regardless of in utero exposure, are often intensified by the drug lifestyle (Hogan, 1998). The distinct nature of the drug versus alcohol using lifestyle derives most fundamentally from the illegality of drug use versus alcohol use. This contributes greatly to the increased denial, secrecy, and maladaptive communication patterns characteristic of drug users' family context (McCrady & Epstein, 1995; O'Farrell & Fals-Stewart, 2000). Illicit drug users have to pursue much more extensive measures to acquire drugs than alcoholics, contributing to the common association of drug use with other illegal behaviors and ultimately manifesting in higher rates of incarceration and thus parental absenteeism (Hogan, 1998; Dunn, Tarter, Mezzich, Vanyukov, Kirisci, & Kirillova, 2002). Also resulting from the illegal status of drug use, scarce social and community support typically exists for drug users (Kumpfer & Bluth, 2004). Neighborhood factors are also often unique for children of illicit drug users, as illicit drug use is more common in urban, impoverished environments, while alcohol use is prevalent across socioeconomic statuses (Hogan, 1998). In such environments, children of illicit drug users also face more severe health risks, particularly in the context of exposure to intravenous (IV) drug use (ie., HIV, hepatitis; McCoy, Lai, Metsch, Messiah, & Zhao, 2004), higher rates of crime and violence (Lam et al., 2007; Turner & Lloyd, 2003), and juvenile delinquency and substance use (Griffin, Botvin, Scheier, Doyle, & Williams, 2003).

A discussion of the environmental context of illicit drug users must take into account the key differences that distinguish their environment from that of COAs, particularly when studies may not distinguish these two groups. In this chapter, we highlight research pertaining to children of illicit drug users or substance users (i.e., the term substance use in this case referring to parents using both alcohol and illicit drugs). In line with this understanding, this chapter aims to provide an in-depth examination of how proximal and distal environmental factors for children of illicit drug users are conceptualized and measured, as well as how our understanding and methodology can be improved.

Parenting

Parenting can dictate many aspects of the early environment for a child, and specific practices can mold a child's developmental pathway (Bowlby, 1988). Negative parenting patterns of drug users, while defined in multiple ways in the literature, most commonly relate to deficient monitoring, maladaptive discipline practices, scarce parental involvement, abuse, and neglect, and such practices are associated with a host of negative outcomes for children (Suchman & Luthar, 2000; Dunn et al., 2002; Bays, 1990). Illicit drug-using parents consistently demonstrate higher rates of negative parenting behaviors than non-drug-using parents (see Mayes & Truman, 2002 for a review), the consequences of which manifest in a direct impact on their child's initiation of substance use (Kumpfer & Bluth, 2004), internalizing symptoms (Stanger, Higgins, Bickel, Elk, Grabowski, Schmitz et al., 1999), and externalizing behaviors (Stanger, Dumenci, Kamon & Burstein, 2004). Thus, investigating the conceptualization and assessment of relationship between illicit drug use and parenting and the subtleties of the parent-child relationship are crucial to fully understand the impact of parental illicit drug use on child outcomes (Kumpfer & Bluth, 2004). Although the majority of the extant literature relates to mothers' parenting practices, there is some literature on the role of drug abusing fathers in relation to children's outcomes (see McMahon & Rounsaville, 2002 for a review). In this section, we will review findings related to both drug abusing mothers' and fathers' parenting practices (when available), and their effects on child outcomes.

Maladaptive Infant Interactions: Abuse and Neglect

Characteristic of the mother-child relationship of an illicit drug-using mother is an inability for the mother to accurately interpret her infant's cues, fueling a cycle of neglect and abuse (Davis, 1990). Cocaine-exposed infants often demonstrate increased reactivity as compared to noncocaine exposed infants (Lester, Tronick, LaGasse, Seifer, Bauer, Shankaran et al., 2002), and these behaviors (e.g., excessive crying, irritability, jitteriness, tone abnormalities, and attention problems) can be considered particularly distressing to drug-using mothers (Papousek & von Hofacker, 1998; Porter & Porter, 2004; Nair, Schuler, Black, Kettinger, & Harrington, 2003). The increased parenting stress in response to these infantile cues can be associated with hostile and punitive behavior (Miller, Smyth, & Mudar, 1999) and other forms of abuse (Nair et al., 2003).

In addition to visible or audible cues that may trigger stress in mothers, an absence of certain cues in cocaine-exposed infants (e.g., times of lethargy, unresponsiveness, lack of enjoyment during play) can also contribute to increased guilt and frustration (Porter & Porter, 2004; Nair et al., 2003). Mothers may experience stress from cues related to premature birth characteristics (e.g., low birth weight), and these can foster maternal cognitions of failure, inadequacy, or guilt (Suchman & Luthar, 2001). These maternal reactions are associated with increased unresponsiveness to and neglect of infant needs, as well as decreased motivation to seek external care giving assistance or resources for the child (Hans, Bernstein, & Henson, 1999; Pajulo, Savonlahti, Sourander, Ahlqvist, Helenius, & Piha, 2001; Davis, 1990; Suchman

& Luthar, 2001). In turn, physical and emotional neglect are associated with poor child outcomes (e.g., developmental delays, externalizing and internalizing symptoms) particularly if parental neglect continues into childhood (Dunn et al., 2002).

Assessment of Parent-Child Interactions and Maternal Perceptions

The maternal-child interaction is typically assessed using coded live observations or videotaped footage such as the Parent-Child Early Relational Assessment (ERA; Clark, 1985) or the Parent Child Observations Guides for Program Planning (PCOG; Bernstein, Percansky, & Hans, 1987), which assess dimensions of care giving such as "sensitive responsiveness" (i.e., emotional engagement, prompt response to child's needs) and "encouragement/guidance" (i.e., positive and active role in teaching, limit-setting). Observations usually consist of a clip of a feeding interaction and/or play behavior. Researchers have also adapted previously used child style rating scales (Cowan & Cowan, 1992) to specifically assess at-risk, urban, minority populations (i.e., Hutcheson et al., 1997; Schuler, Nair, Black, & Kettinger, 2000). Self-report measures are typically utilized to assess maternal perceptions of infant temperament (i.e., the Infant Behavior Questionnaire, IBQ; Rothbart, 1981) and parental stress (i.e., Parenting Stress Index, PSI; Abidin, 1986). These measures can also be supplemented with objective information regarding infant behavior through behavioral assessments (i.e., NICU Network Neurobehavioral Scale, Neonatal Behavioral Assessment Scale; Lester & Tronick, 2001).

Parenting Behaviors: An Overview of Risk and Protective Factors

Beyond infancy, children of illicit drug users are exposed to a range of risk and protective factors related to parental characteristics

(Luthar, Cushing, Merikangas, & Rounsaville, 1998). Various studies have identified parental behaviors typical of illicit drug-using parents that can positively or negatively impact child outcomes. Most commonly studied behaviors include parenting skill-related factors such as involvement, monitoring, and discipline, as well as parental abuse and neglect. These main areas are most predictive of early substance use (Lam et al., 2007), internalizing (Burstein, Stanger, Kamon, & Dumenci, 2006) and externalizing psychopathology (Stanger et al., 2004; Stanger et al., 1999).

Further, although parental substance use is associated with more negative parenting practices, addicted parents are not necessarily deficient in all areas of parenting behavior (Suchman & Luthar, 2000). Thus, it is crucial to have a clear understanding of which parental practices are directly related to parental substance use, as well as which practices are associated with negative child outcomes, for crafting substance use–specific interventions for substance-using parents to affect child outcomes optimally.

Parental Involvement, Monitoring, and Discipline

Parental involvement with children has been demonstrated to be directly affected by substance use (Suchman & Luthar, 2000). As opposed to other substance-using parents' practices (i.e., discipline, autonomy) that can be better explained by environmental factors, parental involvement has been demonstrated to be a direct result of parental addiction (Suchman & Luthar, 2000); further, parental involvement, defined as expressed interest in child's lives and activities, as well as the capacity to connect with children, has significant implications for child development. Lower levels of positive parental involvement have been associated with increased externalizing symptoms and other behavioral problems in children of illicit drug users (Suchman & Luthar, 2000). Furthermore, high levels of positive parental involvement moderates the relationship between parental externalizing symptoms

and child internalizing symptoms (Burstein et al., 2006). Thus, level of positive parental involvement is a crucial environmental variable to consider as both a risk and protective factor in environments of children of illicit drug users.

Parental monitoring and inconsistent discipline are two additional negative parenting domains frequently associated with substance-using families. For example, in assessing the relationship between parental monitoring, inconsistent discipline, and child externalizing symptoms among 399 children with a treatment seeking drug-depending parent, lower rates of parental monitoring predicted rule-breaking behavior, and inconsistent discipline predicted rule-breaking, attention problems, and aggressive/oppositional behavior (Stanger et al., 2004). Similar findings have also been reported elsewhere (Tarter, Blackson, Martin, Loeber, & Moss, 1993; Stanger et al., 1999). Parental monitoring may be particularly crucial in low-income, urban, drug-using environments given the higher rates of potential exposure to illegal behavior for youth (Hogan, 1998). In addition to parental monitoring, discipline practices have also been demonstrated to function as crucial protective factors for youth (Kumpfer & Bluth, 2004), particularly with regard to outcomes such as substance use prevention, academic failure, and delinquent behaviors (Ary, Duncan, Biglan, Metzler, Noell, & Smolkowski, 1999).

Specific to fathering, Fals-Stewart, Kelley, Fincham, Golden, & Logdson (2004) compared functioning of school aged children of drug-abusing fathers to children with fathers that abused alcohol as well as those with non-substance-abusing fathers. Children with drug-abusing fathers demonstrated higher rates of internalizing and externalizing psychopathology compared to the other two groups using self-report assessment (parent and child) as well as teacher report. Further, in answering *why* this relationship existed, one mediator identified was parenting. Specifically, fathers in the drug-abusing families had more inconsistent and dysfunctional discipline practices as well as lower rates of parental monitoring than the two other groups. Interestingly, mothers' parenting practices did not differ among the three groups, which may further suggest the importance of focusing on fathers' behaviors (Fals-Stewart et al., 2004). To further isolate the effect of father characteristics on child outcomes, Fals-Stewart, Kelley, Cooke, & Golden (2003) controlled for two crucial variables: prenatal drug exposure and postnatal maternal drug use. They examined postnatal predictors of outcomes in school-aged children of substance users without prenatal drug exposure and restricted their sample to households with non-substance-using mothers. Specific to paternal characteristics, higher frequency of substance use, higher psychological distress, and a diagnosis of ASPD were associated with poorer youth psychosocial functioning (Fals-Stewart et al., 2003).

Assessment of Parenting Practices

To assess both monitoring and discipline, the Alabama Parenting Questionnaire (APQ; Frick, 1991) is frequently utilized, which is a parental self-report measure assessing (1) positive involvement, defined as frequency of praise and positive reinforcement for prosocial child behavior, parental interest and positive interactions with the child; (2) negative/ineffective discipline, defined as inconsistent discipline, fulfilling parental responsibilities, and punishment; and (3) deficient monitoring, defined as parental supervision of child activities (Hinshaw, Owens, Wells, Kraemer, Abikoff, Arnold et al., 2000; Shelton, Frick, & Wooton, 1996). To specifically assess parenting monitoring, studies may also use the Parental Monitoring Scale (PM; Blank, Forgatch, Patterson & Fetrow, 1993), which is a 12-item instrument that assesses parental knowledge of children's activities. Self-report instruments regarding parents' perceptions of their relationships with their children are also utilized to assess parenting, such as the Parent-Child Relationship Questionnaire (PCRQ; Furman & Giberson, 1995) and the Parent-Child Relationship Inventory (PCRI;

Gerard, 1994). The PCRI, for example, is a 78-item measure with seven subscales, four of which address parenting behaviors: (1) communication (capacity to talk with and connect with child); (2) involvement (demonstration of interest in child's activities); (3) limit setting (provision of appropriate discipline); and (4) autonomy (promotion of child's independence). Parental involvement has been defined by combining the communication and involvement subscales, and parental monitoring has been defined by combining the limit setting and autonomy subscales (Suchman & Luthar, 2000). Parenting can also be assessed using child ratings or parental behavior (i.e., using the Children's Report of Parental Behavior Inventory, CRPBI; Schaefer, 1965).

Abuse

Beyond parenting styles or practices that can be maladaptive for children of illicit drug users, parents with lifetime histories of illicit drug use are more likely to engage in child abuse, likely because of increased anger reactivity and decreased frustration tolerance common in chronic drug users (Ammerman, Kolko, Kirisci, Blackson, & Dawes, 1999). Physical and sexual child abuse is associated with a host of poor outcomes, including internalizing and externalizing problems, particularly depression, conduct disorder, academic underachievement, cognitive impairment, social problems, and early substance use (Chaffin, Kelleher, & Hollenberg, 1996; Johnson, Kotch, Catellier, Winsor, Dufort, Hunter, & Amaya-Jackson, 2002; Molnar, Buka & Kessler, 2001; Malinosky-Rummell & Hansen, 1993; Manly, Cicchetti, & Barnett, 1994). The majority of research on physical or sexual abuse relies on reports from professional or governmental agencies (Straus, Hamby, Finkelhor, Moore, & Runyan, 1998). However, these reports do not capture all incidents of physical or sexual abuse, and additional methods are needed to screen for physical abuse and child maltreatment (Straus et al., 1998).

An alternative to relying on self-report or government reports is the use of the Child

Abuse Potential Inventory (CAPI; Milner, 1986), a measure of propensity for abuse. As opposed to assessing history, this assessment incorporates aspects of parenting that often predict abuse. Various studies have demonstrated the utility of the CAPI in reliably identifying abusive parents (see Milner, 1994 for a review), as well as the association between high CAPI scores and other behavioral measures of negative parenting, such as observational coding of negative verbalizations indicating annoyance and criticism and harsh physical behaviors (ie., slapping a child's hand or taking a toy away; Haskett, Scott & Fann, 1995).

Neglect and Absenteeism

A lack of parental action is a key concern in understanding the environment of children of illicit drug users. Various researchers have examined "parental absenteeism" in drug-using parents, driven primarily as a result of criminal activity and resulting periods of incarceration, time spent in residential drug treatment, and the cumulative time spent procuring, seeking, consuming, and withdrawing from drugs (Dunn et al., 2002; Kumpfer, 1987). Parental absenteeism is problematic for young children, as it is associated with decreased parental supervision, and an increased likelihood for abuse and neglect (Dunn et al., 2002). While the direct drug-related time of absenteeism is harder to quantify, researchers can measure absenteeism based on time spent incarcerated or in residential drug treatment (Kumpfer, 1987).

Even when drug-using parents are present in the home, parental absenteeism can exist in the form of neglect. Research has demonstrated higher rates of neglect in drug-using parents, and 80–90 percent of cases of neglect reported to Child Protective Services (CPS) are of caregivers who use substances (Bays, 1990; Famularo, Kinscherff, & Fenton, 1992; Dunn et al., 2002). Neglect has been defined and examined according to three main areas: failure to satisfy basic child needs (Dubowitz, Black, Starr, & Zuravin, 1993), infliction of harm on children (Trocme,

1996), and inadequate parental supervision (Manly, Cicchetti, & Barnett, 1994). Neglect has been associated with serious negative outcomes in children of illicit drug users, which manifests through social, emotional, cognitive, and behavioral problems throughout a child's development (Dunn et al., 2002), notably internalizing and externalizing problems as well as increased likelihood for substance use (see Kaplan, Pelcovitz, & Labruna, 1999 for a review).

The reliance on reported cases of child neglect has overly defined neglect categorically, rather than dimensionally in terms of specific parental behaviors, contributing to an underestimation of the prevalence of neglect (Kaufman, Jones, Stieglitz, Vitulano, & Mannerino, 1994) and lack of uniformity in defining neglect (Dunn et al., 2002). In moving away from a categorical perspective or utilization of CPS cases, researchers have used the Diagnostic Interview Schedule (DIS). For example, the 4 items of the DIS that assess neglect (e.g., leaving young children unattended, inadequately feeding children, inadequately caring for children, or having a statement from a professional that children were neglected) have been used to identify parents who engage in varying degrees of neglect (Kelleher, Chaffin, Hollenberg, & Fischer, 1994). Researchers have also identified neglect by asking parents about their levels of supervision and time spent with children (e.g., Tarter et al., 1993).

Family Environment

Given that parenting style only accounts for a moderate level of variance in child outcomes in most studies (e.g., Burstein et al., 2006), it is crucial to identify other factors that may account for poor child outcomes. In particular, family functioning in illicit drug-using families can serve as a risk or protective factor (Burstein et al., 2006), and the processes underlying dysfunctional family environments can contribute to poor future outcomes (Kumpfer & Bluth, 2004). Thus, an understanding of the family environment is crucial for inter-vention-related research, as the ability to change the family environment has been considered the most feasible method to reduce overall risk for children of substance users (Kumpfer, 1999). First and foremost, drug activity in the household often dictates the family environment led by drug-using parents, leading to modeling of drug use and other illegal behaviors (Gruber & Taylor, 2006; Catalano, Gainey, Fleming, Haggerty, & Johnson, 1999). Additional characteristics of substance-using families emerge as being consistently predictive of positive and neg-ative child outcomes: conflict, communi-cation, and cohesion (Kumpfer, 1999). The interaction of these components can dictate an environment of cumulative risk or pro-tection for children of substance users.

Modeling Drug Use Behavior and Attitudes

Parents' ongoing drug use and lifestyle choices place children at a higher risk for poor outcomes (Derauf, LaGasse, Smith, Grant, Shah, Arria et al., 2007). The level of drug use, therefore, is an important vari-able to consider when examining the envi-ronmental context of children of illicit drug users; for some parents drug use is social or recreational, and for others, it is part of a cha-otic, violent lifestyle, filled with crime and other illegal behaviors (Nair et al., 2003; Lam et al., 2007). High-risk behaviors performed by parents expose children to more nega-tive social contexts and the associated ille-gal behaviors and violence (Hequembourg, Mancuso, & Miller, 2006), as well as put chil-dren at higher-risk for HIV (McCoy et al., 2004). In addition to modeling drug use behaviors from parents, as well as siblings, children may be forced to be involved in drug-related activities for parents or siblings (e.g., buying drugs; Kumpfer & Bluth, 2004) or be pressured or tempted to engage in drug use with parents or siblings (Kandel & Andrews, 1987; Jackson, 1997). Reviews of relevant literature have suggested that a con-sistent, standardized approach to measure

the degree of parental substance use is lack-ing (Kumpfer, 1999) and the strength of the association between parental substance use and child maltreatment may vary based on how parental substance use is assessed (Ammerman et al., 1999). Further, model-ing of drug use behavior is typically assessed based upon the severity of parental or sib-ling substance use (e.g., Jackson, 1997; Ary, Tildesley, Hops, & Andrews, 1993), rather than an assessment of the degree of drug use modeling itself. While clearly severity of use can impact the degree of modeling of drug use behaviors, other factors should also be considered, such as time spent with the parent, parental efforts to hide use, or a child's susceptibility towards modeling behaviors.

Just as parental behaviors can be mod-eled and transmitted to children, attitudes can also easily be conveyed (Ary, Tildesley, Hops, & Andrews, 1993). Children may model antisocial, moral, and trust-related values, as well as substance use-related atti-tudes from drug-using parents (Kandel & Andrews, 1987; Lam et al., 2007). Expressed parental disapproval of substance use is a particularly salient protective factor typ-ically absent in illicit drug-using families (Lam et al., 2007). Researchers have devel-oped self-report measures to target these substance-use related expectancies in chil-dren (ie., Dunn & Goldman, 1998), as this cognitive area may be a crucial point for intervention (Kumpfer, 1999).

Conflict, Communication, and Cohesion

Beyond actual involvement in substance use as a key element of the family envi-ronment for children of drug users, conflict resulting from drug use-related behaviors, for instance marital conflict and conflict between other family members, commonly defines the family environment (Gruber & Taylor, 2006). Family conflict in substance-using households is associated with a wide variety of negative consequences for youth, including internalizing and externalizing symptoms (Pilowsky, Zybert, & Vlahov, 2004), physical health issues (e.g., increased illnesses, abuse-related injuries; Repetti, Taylor, & Seeman, 2002), and increased substance use (Lam et al., 2007). In a study discussed earlier that examined the relationship between fathers' parenting practices and poor child outcomes, Fals-Stewart and colleagues (2004) identified an additional mediator of this relationship: interparental conflict. Specifically, children with drug-abusing fathers experienced higher rates of physical violence and witnessed more marital conflict than households with alcohol-using or non-substance-using fathers, and this was found to mediate the relationship between fathers' substance-abusing status and child psychosocial functioning. Similar findings have also been demonstrated elsewhere (Fals-Stewart et al., 2003).

A lack of parental response to family conflict also tends to be problematic in substance-using families, and maladaptive family problem-solving and avoidance of familial conflict has been associated with reinforcement of substance use behavior (McCrady & Epstein, 1995; O'Farrell & Fals-Stewart, 2000). Underlying the communication pattern in families of drug users are avoidance and denial, which prevents a discussion of important moral or behavioral lessons throughout childhood; further, this may also demonstrate avoidant coping strategies to children starting at an early age (McCrady & Epstein, 1995; Denton & Kampfe, 1994). Modeling avoidant coping for youth has significant long-term outcomes, as avoidant coping has been linked to externalizing and delinquent behavior such as substance use (Fromme & Rivet, 1994; Wills, Sandy, & Yaeger, 2001), risky sexual behavior (Semple, Patterson, & Grant, 2000) and conduct disorder (Hastings, Anderson, & Hemphill, 1997), as well as internalizing symptoms (Ollendick, Langley, Jones, & Kephart, 2001). Although negative communication styles within the household commonly may be a risk factor for poor developmental outcomes for children, positive communication (i.e., in the form of open, honest communication,

and communication specifically regarding parental expectations and goals for children) can also act as important protective factor, particularly with regard to substance-use related outcomes and delinquency (Fors, Crepaz, & Hayes, 1999; Vakalahi, 2001).

The presence of cohesion in the family environment, typically defined as family bonding and engagement in shared activities, is also an important protective factor for children of substance users, although research has demonstrated that drug dependent mothers often report a lack of cohesion in their family environment (Suchman et al., 2005). Cohesion has been operationalized in multiple ways in the literature. For example, cohesion has been defined based on the number of family meetings (regarding fun activities, family problems, drug use, and household chores), family bonding activities, and the existence of household rules (Catalano et al., 1999), as well as the number of family rituals (ie., meals, holidays, vacations; Werner, Joffe, & Graham, 1999). Interrupted family cohesion is associated with increased substance use risk in children, while increased family bonding and engagement of activities together, particularly when there is an open style of communication and expression, is associated with decreased risk for engagement in substance use (Hawkins, Catalano & Miller, 1992; Johnson, Bryant, Collins, Noe, Strader & Berbaum, 1998; Johnson & Pandina, 1991; Werner et al., 1999). Further, these three components of the family environment are also interactive; for instance, evidence indicates that family cohesion is compromised in the presence of high levels of conflict), and cohesive efforts are not as effective when not accompanied by open communication (Johnson & Pandina, 1991).

Assessment of Conflict, Communication, and Cohesion

Typically conflict, communication, and cohesion are assessed together using self-report measures of the overall family environment, either from the child or parent's perspective (i.e., the Moos Family Environmental Scale, FES, Moos, 1974; the Conflict-Tactic Scales, CTS, Straus, 1990). The FES includes 10-item scales for family conflict, family cohesion, and family communication, and has been demonstrated to be a sensitive outcomes measure for family-based interventions (Kumpfer, 1998). To target more specific constructs, such as the child's level of exposure to interparental conflict, self-report instruments such as the O'Leary-Porter Scale (OPS; Porter & O'Leary, 1980) assess parental perception of the frequency of marital conflict in the presence of the child. This captures not only the frequency of marital conflict, but also the perceived frequency of instances in which the child was directly affected.

Social Network

The social network is an important factor in understanding the environment of children of illicit drug users. In addition to exposure to inappropriate role modeling from parents using drugs, children of illicit drug users are often exposed to inadequate role modeling from relatives and siblings in such families (Pivnick, Jacobson, Eric, Doll, & Drucker, 1994; Ary et al., 1993). Further, as a result of increased social isolation in substance-using families, children may not have access to external role models and community support resources (Bays, 1990; Dawe, Harnett, Staiger, & Dadds, 2000). The lack of social support for parents also serves to perpetuate or exacerbate many negative parenting practices, thereby contributing to negative child outcomes via parenting stress and social alienation (Powis, Gossop, Bury, Payne, & Griffiths, 2000; Dunn et al., 2002). Research has also suggested that level of social support may not be most predictive of negative parenting practices and/or negative outcomes among children of illicit drug users, but rather the *perceived* level of social support may directly affect parents' caregiving abilities (Suchman et al., 2005) and can serve to distinguish resilient from nonresilient youth (Pilowsky et al., 2004).

Parent's Social Network

A parental social network, when positive, has been shown to buffer many negative parenting practices or parental stressors involved in caretaking (Crnic & Greenberg, 1990; Crnic & Booth, 1991). For illicit drug users, however, their social networks may revolve around drug use or involvement in other illegal activities (Knowlton, Buchanan, Wissow, Pilowsky & Latkin, 2008), which serves to perpetuate parental drug use (Latkin, Knowlton, Hoover, & Mandell, 1999; Schroeder, Latkin, Hoover, Curry, Knowlton, & Celentano, 2001) and further expose children to drug use behavior (Pivnick et al., 1994). Degree of drug use in a parental social network is also associated with immediate negative outcomes in children, particularly externalizing problems (Knowlton et al., 2008). However, a positive adult influence within or outside of a parent's social network can also serve as a crucial protective factor for at-risk youth (Garmezy, 1993), as the presence of a non-drug-using adult enables a child to be exposed to healthy behaviors, and children may model actions not involved with drug use or illegal behavior (Furstenberg & Hughes, 1997).

Assessment of a Parent's Social Network

A parent's social network is typically defined by the number of substance users or frequency of substance use in the network. For example, a parent's "deviant peer network" has been defined as the proportion of parent's four closest friends who used illegal drugs and engaged in illegal activities (Catalano et al., 1999). Other studies have used self-report assessments in the form of a "network inventory" in which subjects report important individuals. This data is reported based on total number of people named, characteristics of network members, relations within the network, and social resources (e.g., social support and ties to employed individuals; Williams & Latkin, 2007). The degree of drug influence in the network is also assessed through various dimensions: encouragement of drug use, number of drug users in social network, and number of daily users in the network (Williams & Latkin, 2007). In addition to an individualistic perspective of a social network, sociometric techniques that aggregate data from interviews of all members of a social network can be used to analyze a broader social impact (Valente, Gallaher, & Mouttapa, 2004).

Child's Social Network

A negative parental social network can also serve to directly influence a child's choice to associate with drug-using peers (Knowlton et al., 2008). Regardless of the influence of a parent's social network, children living in urban environments are exposed to higher rates of juvenile delinquency and substance use among youth (Griffin, Botvin, Scheier, Doyle, & Williams, 2003). Extensive research has demonstrated the link between peer influence and substance use, both in terms of age of initiation, continuation, and severity (Simons-Morton & Chen, 2006). Peers may also influence engagement in criminal activity, as research has demonstrated that criminal offending among youth most often occurs with a peer living in close proximity (Reiss & Farrington, 1991). However, peers may also act as protective factors, which becomes particularly vital when the household of a child is tainted with substance use and associated unrest (Simons-Morton, Haynie, Crump, Eitel, & Saylor, 2001). Children who have demonstrated resiliency in such environments have been shown to proactively construct a positive social network for themselves (Wolin & Wolin, 1993).

Assessment of Peer Social Network

Similar to assessing parental social networks, the peer social network is frequently assessed through self-report on multiple domains, such as the number of substance users in a social network, pressure to use substances, types of activities performed together, percentage of members of network who know each other or are in same domain, satisfaction with network, frequency of contact, and perceived closeness (Mason, Chueng, & Walker, 2004). As discussed in the assessment of the parental social network, sociometric techniques can be utilized to get information from an entire community or other sources to assess a peer social network (Valente et al., 2004). For example, a peer social network analysis including the variables social embeddedness, social status, and social proximity to substance users significantly predicted risk and protective factors for adolescent substance use, such that low social embeddedness but high status and social proximity to peer substance users predicted substance use, and high embeddedness, middle status levels, and fewer substance-using friends acted as protective factors (Ennett, Bauman, Hussong, Faris, Foshee, Cai et al., 2006).

Another approach to examining the overall social network for high-risk children includes an assessment of "social capital" (e.g., Runyan et al., 1998). A social capital index is formed by assigning one point to various social network-related criteria, such as two parents or parental figures in the household, social support for the maternal caregiver, a family size of less than or equal to 2 children, neighborhood support, and regular church attendance; in one study, maternal social support was assessed using self-report information regarding access to social support in seven areas (e.g., I can talk to someone regarding family problems), and neighborhood support was defined based on self-report information regarding how much neighbors help each other, watch out for each other's children, and are reliable (Runyan et al., 1998). An understanding of social capital has also been useful in understanding child outcomes related to other risk factors in substance-using families, such as family violence and neglect (Zolotor & Runyan, 2006).

Social Network: Conclusion

Although research has consistently demonstrated the role of peers and dynamics of a social network in the development of various child outcomes, particularly substance use, less research has put this directly in the context of children of substance users (i.e., how is the role of peer influence unique for children of substance users?). Research has shown that children are likely to experience a discrepancy between parental and peer norms (Barnes & Windle, 1987), particularly when children are able to surround themselves with positive peer influences (Wolin & Wolin, 1993). The ability for children to associate themselves with positive versus negative peer influences may be a function of the overall neighborhood or community characteristics, and what types of peers are accessible to the child; however, further research is needed to examine these relationships specifically for children of substance users.

Neighborhood

Crime, Violence, and Poverty

In addition to parental behavior, family dynamics, and social networks, other factors may distinguish low-income, urban neighborhood settings where illicit drug use takes place. In particular, impoverished neighborhoods suffer from higher unemployment rates, poor housing situations, crowding, crime, violence, and poverty (Roosa, Jones, Tein, & Cree, 2003; Sampson, Morenoff, & Gannon-Rowley, 2002). Minority youth in urban areas are disproportionately exposed to neighborhood stressors such as witnessing domestic and community violence, drug use, illegal activities, and racism (Lam et al., 2007; Turner & Lloyd, 2003). For example, children in disadvantaged neighborhoods were more than 5 times more likely to have been offered cocaine compared to children living in less disadvantaged areas (Crum, Lillie-Blanton, & Anthony, 1996). Interestingly, this association was not as strong for tobacco or alcohol exposure, thus suggesting a particularly unique vulnerability towards illicit drug use in urban neighborhoods. Further, exposure to substance use in the home and in the neighborhood has been shown to be a direct correlate of child-exposure to violence (Ondersma, Delaney-Black, Covington, Nordstrom, & Sokol, 2006).

Assessment of Neighborhood Risk

Neighborhood risk factors are often assessed through self-report from the perspective of the child or the mother. For example, data pertaining to the degree of drug exposure was assessed via interviews with middle school children living in an urban area (Crum et al., 1996) and by asking mothers whether their family had been victimized by violent crime (e.g., mugging, assault, burglary, break-in; Jaffee, Caspi, Moffitt, Polo-Tomás, & Taylor, 2007). Exposure to violence can also be assessed using child self-report, even in children as young as age 6. For example, Ondersma et al. (2006) used 11 items from the Things I have Seen and Heard (TSH) scale (Richters & Martinez, 1993) to examine child report of exposure to violence, which includes items such as "I have seen somebody get shot" or "somebody threatened to kill me." Although not specific to violence, other items tap child report of exposure to illicit drugs in their environment, including "I have seen drug deals and I have seen drugs in my home" as well as more general questions such as "I feel safe at home." Child report has been shown to offer incremental validity in predicting psychosocial impairment (e.g., Augustyn, Frank, Posner, & Zuckerman, 2002).

While a more individual account of the degree of crime or drug use a child is exposed to can be meaningful, less subjective assessments are critical to increase reliability of reporting. A more objective technique includes using census tract data and crime reports. As one example, neighborhood characteristics were defined as the concentration of low-income residents, presence of successful employed adults, and area crime rates using census tracts (Luthar & Cushing, 1999). Concentration of poor residents was assessed using the percentage of low-income households (i.e., annual income < 10,000) and the rates of successful working adults (i.e., the percentage of people employed in a management position or higher). Crime in the community was assessed using crime report data from local police departments. The reports include annual incidents of FBI index crimes, including murder, rape, robbery, aggravated assault, burglary, larceny, and automotive theft, and the rate is determined by the total number of annual offenses committed in a town divided by the town's population. This method of assessing crime rates has been useful in past research as well to assess community-based crime (e.g., Coulton, Korbin, Su, & Chow, 1995; Gephart, 1997).

Although not specifically pertaining to the environments of children of drug users, other studies that have more generally examined neighborhood characteristics associated with drug use utilize census data for a given neighborhood have focused on the following neighborhood-level variables: percentage living in poverty and receiving public assistance, rates of unemployment, low education levels, percentage female-headed households, and median household income, as well as creating a composite neighborhood disadvantage measure (Williams & Latkin, 2007).

Discussion and Future Directions

Taken together, evidence indicates that a myriad of environmental risk and protective factors across parenting behaviors, family environment, social context, and the neighborhood play a role in determining outcomes for children of illicit drug users. Although the identification of these risk and protective factors are an important step in developing intervention and prevention programs, a number of new directions also will be necessary to improve our understanding of the dynamics among risk factors.

Cumulative Risk Model

Although the isolation of specific risk and protective factors is important in targeting interventions, the interaction of these individual factors within larger domains is what contributes to substance use outcomes (Pires & Jenkins, 2007; Sameroff, Seifer, Barocas, Zax, & Greenspan, 1987). Research attempting to pinpoint specific risk or protective factors may overemphasize the role of these factors in isolation (Szapocznik & Coatsworth, 1999; Mason, Cheung, & Walker, 2004), thus preventing a more cumulative understanding of environmental risk.

As such, research has suggested the need to examine environmental risk based upon the summation of specific environmental factors, such as using a cumulative index, in line with the understanding that it may be the cluster of risk factors a child is exposed to that predicts child outcomes rather than specific factors alone (Liaw & Brooks-Gunn, 1994; Sameroff et al., 1987). As one example, the cumulative risk model (Sameroff et al., 1987) creates a summation score of a number of risk factors, which include low income (i.e., household income less than $10,000), single parent with no caregiving support from another adult, family size (more than five), caregiver with less than a high school education, and minority status. Using this model, cumulative environmental risk has been shown to account for more variance in the developmental outcomes of children than individual risk factors alone (i.e., prenatal drug exposure; Carta, Atwater, Greenwood, McConnell, McEvoy, & Williams, 2001), supporting the need to utilize a more comprehensive assessment strategy when identifying environmental risk specific to the environment of children of drug users.

Environmental Context-Specific Factors

In conjunction with utilizing a cumulative index, it remains important to continue efforts to specify risk factors within unique environmental contexts. Using parenting behavior and urbanicity as an example, in lower SES households, a parent is more likely to restrict a child's autonomy (Suchman & Luthar, 2000); although restricted autonomy is often considered a negative parenting practice and associated with negative child outcomes, this practice may be adaptive in urban, low-income neighborhoods given the violence and substance use often existent in such neighborhoods (Chilcoat, Dishion, & Anthony, 1995; Suchman & Luthar, 2000). Additionally, deficient monitoring has been shown to have a more significant negative impact on child outcomes for urban African American youth than those growing up in rural environments (Armistead, Forehand, Brody, & Maguen, 2002). Such findings demonstrate the importance of incorporating the unique features of the urban environmental context when assessing parental behavior, or other social influences, to understand effects on the child.

Age and Gender

A comprehensive understanding of the environment of children of illicit drug users must also incorporate a developmental perspective. Risk and protective factors are optimally understood according to the specific developmental stage in which they are most applicable, as types of risk or protective factors inevitably shift with age (Sobeck, Abbey, Agius, Clinton, & Harrison, 2000). Risk factors related to parenting are particularly salient examples of how types of risk factors can shift based on age, and especially for children of illicit drug users, a developmental perspective is crucial to understand at which point negative parenting most affects the children.

As one example, research has demonstrated that low parental involvement is the primary indicator of externalizing behavior during adolescence (Frick, Christian, & Wootton, 1999); however, for younger children, punishment is more strongly associated with externalizing behavior than parental involvement (Frick et al., 1999), suggesting that parental practices that are deemed risk factors may differ according to developmental time points. Thus, assessment should not only focus on the age at which children are most vulnerable to develop negative

outcomes, but also the type of parental practice that is most damaging for that specific age group.

This consideration is particularly important for research related to children of illicit drug users, as significant gaps exist in the developmental research of this particular group. Research predominantly focuses on either end of the child development spectrum, with the majority of research on children of illicit drug users pertaining to the postnatal and infant periods (Johnson & Leff, 1999) or adolescence (Hogan 1998). There is a scarcity of research pertaining to school aged children of illicit drug users, and a focus on this age group is crucial to have a comprehensive understanding of developmental outcomes.

Gender may also influence a developmental model of environmental risk. For example, research has suggested a differential effect of certain neighborhood risk and protective factors based on gender. Male children have been shown to have worse outcomes than girls in lower-income neighborhoods with high crime rates, and girls have been shown to have better outcomes than boys with a greater presence of professional adults in the community (Luthar & Cushing, 1999). This understanding of distinct susceptibilities to environmental risk factors based on gender may guide future directions for assessment. Finally, gender differences may also need to be taken into account in the interpretation of assessment instruments, particularly related to adolescent drug abuse and psychosocial factors (Botzet, Winters, & Stinchfield, 2006).

Assessment Technique

Overall, the assessment of environmental factors for children of illicit drug users utilizes a range of self-report measures from both the child and parental perspectives (in particular to address factors related to parenting practices, the family context, social networks), government or professional agency reports (most commonly to assess abuse, neglect, and neighborhood factors such as crime and poverty), and observational coding (predominately for maternal-infant interaction assessment). The environmental context is most often measured using self-report, which is problematic, particularly in this population. Self-report poses unique limitations for substance-using mothers; substance-using mothers have been shown to deny or underreport child-related problems (Hennigan et al., 2006) and also experience significant guilt and shame regarding use (Ehrmin, 2001), which may serve to further perpetuate potential biases in self-report assessment. Child reports may have similar limitations, as children of substance users may deny or minimize their parents' dysfunction as a result of shame about their parents' behavior or fear of forced removal from the household (Kumpfer, 1999).

Despite the potential biases of self-reported assessment in this population, behavioral assessments are underutilized for older children (Kumpfer, 1999). The assessment of parenting of older children and family context would be enhanced by using observational coding, either video-based or live observation. In the laboratory, structured interaction tasks can be utilized to measure parent-child functioning for older children and adolescents (Samoulis, Hogue, Dauber, & Liddle, 2005). This assessment technique has been shown to be effective in assessing parent-adolescent functioning for urban adolescents with substance use and externalizing behaviors and can be supplemented with self-report information regarding parenting style and family conflict (Samoulis et al., 2005). Self-report information can also be enhanced through the incorporation a third-party perspective (e.g., assessments from teachers, other family members, neighbors) to increase reliability of assessments. Additionally, particularly with regards to the modeling of drug use behavior or other illegal activities, assessments tend to be based solely upon the association between the degree of such behaviors and child outcomes (e.g., Jackson, 1997; Ary et al., 1993) rather than an assessment of modeling such behaviors. A technique to better measure the actual degree

to which children witness such behaviors or are involved in such activities may increase accuracy of assessments.

Assessments regarding neighborhood characteristics have extended beyond self-report limitations through the common utilization of census data. While clearly using census data can have numerous advantages to self-report, there have also been methodological controversies surrounded census-based data, particularly in the demarcation of neighborhoods, which has been subjective and ambiguous in the literature, particularly for urban areas with developed local transportation (Furstenberg & Hughes, 1997; Weiss, Ompad, Galea, & Vlahov, 2007). In response to such difficulties, researchers have investigated neighborhoods prior to relying on census data. For example, the Inner-City Mental Health Study Predicting HIV/AIDS, Club and Other Drug Transitions (IMPACT) (Weiss et al., 2007) used a multistep neighborhood assessment process that included developing census group maps, reviewing census tract data and land use, and conducting field visits and observations of designated communities in order to delineate and identify neighborhoods to study optimally.

An accurate assessment of neighborhood characteristics may need to also extend beyond census data. For example, geographic information systems (GIS) can be used to analyze spatial relationships and linear distances between locations where adolescents are most active, how they rate these locations, and objective environmental risk data pertaining to these areas. The objective environmental risk data may include locations of liquor stores, libraries, boys and girls clubs, parks, as well as locations of crimes committed. In one study among substance-using adolescents, the distance between their homes and identified safe places was three times the distance between their home and identified risky places. The substance-using teens also reported higher levels of depression, stress, and engagement in negative activities with substance-using peers (Mason, Cheung, & Walker, 2004). This utilization of GIS-derived data in combination with self-report information exemplifies the integration of subjective and objective data.

Taken together, a comprehensive understanding of the environment of children of illicit drug users must exist as a larger conceptual model and incorporate a developmental as well as ecological perspective. Targeting high-risk children cannot solely rely on degree of parental drug use; we need to increase utilization of cumulative environmental risk factors in line with a developmental understanding to better identify those at high-risk (Pires & Jenkins, 2007). Further, we need to add breadth to our assessment repertoire by increasing the number of behavioral and observational measures to safeguard against limitations inherent in self-reports. In order to begin to better understand the environmental context for children of illicit drug users, we need to study the interactive and cumulative effects of parenting, family functioning, social network, and neighborhood-related factors on child outcomes.

References

Abidin, R. R. (1986). *Parenting stress index.* Charlottesville, VA: Pediatric Psychology Press.

Ammerman, R. T., Kolko, D. J., Kirisci, L., Blackson, T. C., & Dawes, M. A. (1999). Child abuse potential in parents with histories of substance use disorder. *Child Abuse & Neglect,* 23, 1225–1238.

Armistead, L., Forehand, R., Brody, G., & Maguen, S. (2002). Parenting and child psychosocial adjustment in single-parent African American families: Is community context important? *Behavior Therapy,* 33, 361–375.

Ary, D. V., Duncan, T. E., Biglan, A., Metzler, C. W., Noell, J. W., & Smolkowski, K. (1999). Development of adolescent problem behavior. *Journal of Abnormal Child Psychology,* 27, 141–150.

Ary, D. V., Tildesley, E., Hops, H., & Andrews, J. (1993). The influence of parent, sibling, and peer modeling and attitudes on adolescent use of alcohol. *Int J Addict,* 28, 853–880.

Augustyn, M., Frank, D. A., Posner, M., & Zuckerman, B. (2002). Children who witness violence and parent report of children's behavior. *Arch Pediatr Adolesc Med,* 156, 800–803.

Austin, G., & Prendergast, M. (1991). Young children of substance abusers. *Prevention Research Update,* 8, 1–69.

Barnes, G., & Windle, M. (1987). Family factors in adolescent alcohol and drug abuse. *Pediatrician,* 14, 13–18.

Bays, J. (1990). Substance abuse and child abuse. *Pediatric Clinics of North America,* 37, 881–904.

Belsky, J. (1993). Etiology of child maltreatment: A developmental ecological analysis. *Psychological Bulletin,* 114, 413–434.

Bernstein, V. J., Percansky, C., & Hans, S. L. (1987). Screening for social-emotional impairment in infants born to teenage mothers. Paper presented at the biannual meeting of the Society for Research in Child Development, Baltimore.

Blank, L., Forgatch, M. S., Patterson, G. R., & Fetrow, R. A. (1993). Parenting practices of single mothers: Mediators of negative contextual factors. *Journal of Marriage and the Family,* 55, 371–384.

Botzet, A. M., Winters, K. C., & Stinchfield, R. (2006). Gender differences in measuring adolescent drug abuse and related psychosocial factors. *Journal of Child and Adolescent Substance Abuse,* 16, 91–108.

Bowlby, J. (1988). A secure base: Parent-child attachment and healthy human development. New York: Basic Books.

Bradley, R. H., Whiteside, L., 1, Casey, P. H., Kelleher, K. J., & Pope, S. K. (1994). Contribution of early intervention and early caregiving experience to resilience in low birthweight premature children living in poverty. *Journal of Clinical Child Psychology,* 23, 425–434.

Brooks-Gunn, J., Duncan, G. J., Klebanov, P. K., & Sealand, N. (1993). Do neighborhoods influence child and adolescent development? *American Journal of Sociology,* 99, 353–395.

Burstein, M., Stanger, C., Kamon, J., & Dumenci, L. (2006). Parent psychopathology, parenting, and child internalizing problems in substance-abusing families. *Psychol Addict Behav,* 20, 97–106.

Burton, L. M., Price-Spratlen, T., & Spencer, M. B. (1997). On ways of thinking about measuring neighborhoods: Implications for studying context and developmental outcomes for children. In J. Brooks-Gunn, G. J. Duncan, & J. L. Aber (Eds.), *Neighborhood Poverty:* Vol. II. *Policy implications in studying neighborhoods,* pp. 132–144. New York: Russell Sage.

Carta, J. J., Atwater, J. B., Greenwood, C. R., McConnell, S. R., McEvoy, M. A., & Williams, R. (2001). Effects of cumulative prenatal substance exposure and environmental risks on children's developmental trajectories. *J Clin Child Psychol*, 30, 327–337.

Catalano, R. F., Gainey, R. R., Fleming, C. B., Haggerty, K. P., & Johnson, N. O. (1999). An experimental intervention with families of substance abusers: One-year follow-up of the focus on families project. *Addiction*, 94, 241–254.

Chaffin, M., Kelleher, K., & Hollenberg, J. (1996). Onset of psychical abuse and neglect: psychiatric, substance abuse, and social risk factors from prospective community data. *Child Abuse & Neglect*, 20, 191–203.

Chilcoat, H. D., Dishion, T. J., & Anthony, J. C. (1995). Parent monitoring and the incidence of drug sampling in urban elementary school children. *Am J Epidemiol*, 141, 25–31.

Clark, R. (1985). *The Parent-Child Early Relational Assessment: Instrument and manual*. University of Wisconsin Medical School, Department of Psychiatry.

Coulton, C. J., Korbin, J. E., Su, M., & Chow, J. (1995). Community level factors and child maltreatment rates. *Child Development*, 66, 1262–1276.

Cowan, P., & Cowan, C. (1992). *School children and their families project: Description of childstyle ratings*. Berkeley: University of California at Berkeley, Department of Psychology.

Crnic, K. A., & Booth, C. L. (1991). Mothers' and fathers' perceptions of daily hassles of parenting across early childhood. *Journal of Marriage and the Family*, 53, 1042–1050.

Crnic, K. A., & Greenberg, M. T. (1990). Minor parenting stresses with young children. *Child Development*, 61, 1628–1637.

Crum, R. M., Lillie-Blanton, M., & Anthony, J. C. (1996). Neighborhood environment and opportunity to use cocaine and other drugs in late childhood and early adolescence. *Drug and Alcohol Dependence*, 43, 155–161.

Davis, S. K. (1990). Chemical dependency in women: a description of its effects and outcome on adequate parenting. *Journal of Substance Abuse Treatment*, 7, 225–232.

Dawe, S., Harnett, P. H., Staiger, P., & Dadds, M. R. (2000). Parenting training skills and methadone maintenance: Clinical opportunities and challenges. *Drug Alcohol Depend*, 60, 1–11.

Denton, R. E., & Kampfe, C. M. (1994). The relationship between family variables and adolescent substance abuse: A literature review. *Adolescence*, 29, 475–495.

Derauf, C., LaGasse, L. L., Smith, L. M., Grant, P., Shah, R., Arria, A. et al. (2007). Demographic and psychosocial characteristics of mothers using methamphetamine during pregnancy: Preliminary results of the infant development, environment, and lifestyle study (IDEAL). *Am J Drug Alcohol Abuse*, 33, 281–289.

Dubowitz, H., Black, M., Starr, R. H., & Zuravin, S. (1993). A conceptual definition of child neglect. *Criminal Justice and Behavior*, 20, 8–26.

Dunn, M. E., & Goldman, M. S. (1998). Age and drinking-related differences in the memory organization of alcohol expectancies in 3rd-, 6th-, 9th-, and 12th-grade children. *J Consult Clin Psychol*, 66, 579–585.

Dunn, M. G., Tarter, R. E., Mezzich, A. C., Vanyukov, M., Kirisci, L., & Kirillova, G. (2002). Origins and consequences of child neglect in substance abuse families. *Clin Psychol Rev*, 22, 1063–1090.

Ehrmin, J. T. (2001). Unresolved feelings of guilt and shame in the maternal role with substance-dependent African American women. *J Nurs Scholarsh*, 33, 47–52.

Ennett, S. T., Bauman, K. E., Hussong, A., Faris, R., Foshee, V. A., Cai, L., & DuRant, H. (2006). The peer context of adolescent substance use: Findings from social network analysis. *Journal of Research on Adolescence*, 16, 159–186.

Fals-Stewart, W., Kelley, M. L., Cooke, C. G., & Golden, J. C. (2003). Predictors of the psychosocial adjustment of children living in households of parents in which fathers abuse drugs: The effects of postnatal parental exposure. *Addictive Behaviors*, 28, 1013–1031.

Fals-Stewart, W., Kelley, M. L., Fincham, F. D., Golden, J., & Logsdon, T. (2004). Emotional and behavioral problems of children living with drug-abusing fathers: Comparisons with children living with alcohol-abusing and non-substance-abusing fathers. *Journal of Family Psychology*, 18, 319–330.

Famularo, R., Kinscherff, R., & Fenton, T. (1992). Parental substance abuse and the nature of child maltreatment. *Child Abuse & Neglect*, 16, 475–483.

Fors, S. W., Crepaz, N., & Hayes, D. M. (1999). Key factors that protect against health risks in youth: Further evidence. *Am J Health Behav*, 23, 368–380.

Frick, P. J. (1991). *The Alabama Parenting Questionnaire*. Birmingham: University of Alabama.

Frick, P. J., Christian, R. E. & Wootton, J. M. (1999). Age trends in the association between parenting practices and conduct problems. *Behavior Modification*, 23, 106–128.

Fromme, K., & Rivet, K. (1994). Young adults' coping style as a predictor of their alcohol use and response to daily events. *Journal of Youth & Adolescence*, 23(1), 85–97.

Furman, W., & Giberson, R. S. (1995). Identifying the links between parents and their children's sibling relationships. In S. Shuman (Ed.), *Close relationships in social-emotional development*, pp. 95–108. Norwood, NJ: Ablex

Furstenberg, F. F., & Hughes, M. E. (1997). The influence of neighborhoods on children's development: a theoretical perspective and a research agenda. In J. Brooks-Gunn, G. J. Duncan, & J. L., Aber (Eds.), *Neighborhood Poverty*: Vol. II. *Policy implications in studying neighborhoods*, pp. 23–47. New York: Russell Sage Foundation.

Garmezy, N. (1993). Children in poverty: Resilience despite risk. *Psychiatry*, 56, 127–136.

Gephart, M. A. (1997). Neighborhoods and communities as contexts for development. In J. Brooks-Gunn, G. J. Duncan, and J. L. Aber (Eds.), *Neighborhood poverty:* – Vol. 1. *Context and consequences for children*, pp. 1–43. New York: Russell Sage Foundation.

Gerard, A. B. (1994). *Parent-Child Relationship Inventory (PCRI) manual.* Los Angeles: Western Psychological Services.

Griffin, K. W., Botvin, G. J., Scheier, L. M., Doyle, M. M., & Williams, C. (2003). Common predictors of cigarette smoking, alcohol use, aggression, and delinquency among inner-city minority youth. *Addict Behav*, 28, 1141–1148.

Gruber, K. J. & Taylor, M. F. (2006). A family perspective for substance abuse implications from the literature. *Journal of Social Work Practice in the Addictions*, 6, 1–29.

Hans, S. L., Bernstein, V. J., & Henson, L. G. (1999). The role of psychopathology in the parenting of drug-dependent women. *Dev Psychopathol*, 11, 957–977.

Haskett, M. E., Scott, S. S., & Fann, K. D. (1995). Child abuse potential inventory and parenting behavior: Relationships with high-risk correlates. *Child Abuse Negl*, 19, 1483–1495.

Hastings, T., Anderson, S. J., & Hemphill, P. (1997). Comparisons of daily stress, coping, problem behavior, and cognitive distortions in adolescent sexual offenders and conduct-disordered youth. *Sexual Abuse: A Journal of Research and Treatment*, 9, 29–42.

Hawkins, J. D., Catalano, R. F., & Miller, J. Y. (1992). Risk and protective factors for alcohol and other drug problems in adolescence and early adulthood: Implications for substance abuse prevention. *Psychological Bulletin*, 112, 64–105.

Hennigan, K. M., O'Keefe, M., Noether, C. D., Rinehart, D. J., & Russell, L. A. (2006). Through a mother's eyes: Sources of bias when mothers with co-occurring disorders assess their children. *J Behav Health Serv Res*, 33, 87–104.

Hequembourg, A., Mancuso, R., & Miller, B. (2006). A comparative study examining associations between women's drug-related lifestyle factors and victimization within the family. *Violence Vict*, 21, 231–246.

Hinshaw, S. P., Owens, E. B., Wells, K. C., Kraemer, H. C., Abikoff, H. B., Arnold, L. E. et al. (2000). Family processes and treatment outcome in the MTA: Negative/ineffective parenting practices in relation to multimodal treatment. *Journal of Abnormal Child Psychology*, 28, 555–568.

Hogan, D. M. (1998). Annotation: the psychological development and welfare of children of opiate and cocaine users: Review and research needs. *J Child Psychol Psychiatr*, 39, 609–620.

Hutcheson, J., Black, M. M., Talley, M., Dubowitz, H., Berenson-Howard, J., Starr, R., & Thompson, B. (1997). Risk status and home intervention among children with failure-to-thrive: Follow-up at age 4. *Journal of Pediatric Psychology*, 22, 651–668.

Jackson, C. (1997). Initial and experimental stages of tobacco and alcohol use during late childhood: Relation to peer, parent, and personal risk factors. *Addict Behav*, 22, 685–698.

Jaffee, S. R., Caspi, A., Moffitt, T. E., Polo-Tomás, M., & Taylor, A. (2007). Individual, family, and neighborhood factors distinguish resilient from non-resilient maltreated children: A cumulative stressors model. *Child Abuse & Neglect*, 31, 231–253.

Johnson, J. (1991). Forgotten no longer: An overview of research on children of chemically dependent parents. In T. M. Rivinus (Ed.), *Children of chemically dependent parents*, pp. 29–54. New York: Brunner.

Johnson, J. L., & Leff, M. (1999). Children of substance abusers: Overview of research findings. *Pediatrics*, 102, 1085–1099.

Johnson, K., Bryant, D. D., Collins, D. A., Noe, T. D., Strader, T. N., & Berbaum, M. (1998). Preventing and reducing alcohol and other drug use among high-risk youths by increasing family resilience. *Social Work*, 43, 297–308.

Johnson, R. M., Kotch, J. B., Catellier, D. J., Winsor, J. R., Dufort, V., Hunter, W., & Amaya-Jackson, L. (2002). Adverse behavioral and emotional outcomes from child abuse and witnessed violence. *Child Maltreatment*, 7, 179–186.

Johnson, V., & Pandina, R. J. (1991). Effects of the family environment on adolescent substance use, delinquency, and coping styles. *American Journal of Drug and Alcohol Abuse*, 17, 71–88.

Kandel, D. B., & Andrews, K. (1987). Process of adolescent socialization by parents and peers. *International Journal of Addictions*, 22, 319–342.

Kaplan, S. J., Pelcovitz, D., & Labruna, V. (1999). Chile and adolescent abuse and neglect research: a review of the past 10 years: Part I. physical and emotional abuse and neglect. *Journal of the American Academy of Child and Adolescent Psychiatry*, 38, 1214–1222.

Kaufman, J., Nones, B., Stieglitz, E., Vitulano, L., & Mandarino, A. (1994). The use of multiple informants to assess children's maltreatment experiences. *Journal of Family Violence*, 9, 227–248.

Kelleher, L., Chaffin, M., Hollenberg, J., & Fischer, E. (1994). Alcohol and drug disorders among physically abusive and neglectful parents in 9 community-based samples. *American Journal of Public Health*, 84, 1586–1590.

Kelley, M. L., & Fals-Stewart, M. (2004). Psychiatric disorders of children living with drug-abusing, alcohol-abusing, and non-substance abusing fathers. *Journal of the American Academy of Child & Adolescent Psychiatry*, 43, 621–628.

Kettinger, L. A., Nair, P., & Schuler, M. E. (2000). Exposure to environmental risk factors and parenting attitudes among substance-abusing women. *Am J Drug Alcohol Abuse*, 26, 1–11.

Kettinger, L. A., Nair, P., & Schuler, M. E. (2000). Exposure to environmental risk factors and parenting attitudes among substance-abusing women. *American Journal of Drug and Alcohol Abuse*, 26, 1–11.

Knowlton, A., Buchanan, A., Wissow, L., Pilowsky, D. J., & Latkin, C. (2008). Externalizing behaviors among children of HIV seropositive former and current drug users: Parent support network factors as social ecological risks. *J Urban Health*, 85, 62–76.

Kumpfer, C. L. (1987). Special populations: etiology and prevention of vulnerability to chemical dependence in children of substance abusers: In B. S. Brown, & A. R. Mills (Eds.), *Youth at high risk for substance abuse*, pp. 1–71. Washington, DC: NIDA, DHHS.

Kumpfer, K. L. (1998). Selective prevention approaches for drug use prevention: Overview of outcome results from multi-ethnic replications of the Strengthening Families Program. In R. Ashery, E. Robertson, & K. L. Kumpfer (Eds.), *Family intervention research for the prevention of drug use in youth*. Rockville, MD: National Institute on Drug Abuse.

Kumpfer, K. L. (1999). Outcome measures of interventions in the study of children of substance-abusing parents. *Pediatrics*, 103, 1128–1144.

Kumpfer, K. L., & Bluth, B. (2004). Parent/child transactional processes predictive of resilience or vulnerability to "substance use disorders." *Subst Use Misuse*, 39, 671–698.

Lam, W. K., Cance, J. D., Eke, A. N., Fishbein, D. H., Hawkins, S. R., & Williams, J. C. (2007). Children of African-American mothers who use crack cocaine: Parenting influences on youth substance use. *Journal of Pediatric Psychology*, 32, 877–887.

Latkin, C. A., Knowlton, A. R., Hoover, D., & Mandell, W. (1999). Drug network characteristics as a predictor of cessation of drug use among adult injection drug users: A prospective study. *Am J Drug Alcohol Abuse*, 25, 463–473.

Lester, B. M., & Tronick, E. Z. (2001). Behavioral Assessment Scales: The NICU Network Neurobehavioral Scale, the Neonatal Behavioral Assessment Scale, and the assessment of the preterm infant's behavior. In L. T. Singer, P. S. Zeskind (Eds.), *Biobehavioral Assessment of the Infant*, pp. 363–380. New York: Guilford Press.

Lester, B. M., Tronick, E. Z., LaGasse, L., Seifer, R., Bauer, C. R., Shankaran, S. et al. (2002). The maternal lifestyle study: Effects of substance exposure during pregnancy on neurodevelopmental outcome in 1-month old infants. *Pediatrics*, 110, 1182–1192.

Liaw, F. R., & Brooks-Gunn, J. (1994). Cumulative familial risks and low-birthweight children's cognitive and behavioral development. *Journal of Clinical Child Psychology*, 23, 360–372.

Luthar, S. S. & Cushing, G. (1999). Neighborhood influences and child development: a prospective study of substance abusers' offspring. *Dev Psychopathol*, 11, 763–784.

Luthar, S. S., Cushing, G., Merikangas, K. R., & Rounsaville, B. J. (1998). Multiple jeopardy: Risk and protective factors among addicted mothers' offspring. *Dev Psychopathol*, 10, 117–136.

Malinosky-Rummell, R., & Hansen, D. J. (1993). Long-term consequences of childhood physical abuse. *Psychological Bulletin*, 114, 68–79.

Manly, J. T., Cicchetti, D., & Barnett, D. (1994). The impact of subtype, frequency, chronicity, and severity of child maltreatment on social competence and behavior problems. *Development and Psychopathology*, 6, 121–143.

Mason, M., Cheung, I., & Walker, L. (2004). Substance use, social networks, and the geography of urban adolescents. *Subst Use Misuse*, 39, 1751–1777.

Mayes, L., & Truman, S. (2002). Substance abuse and parenting. In M. Bornstein (Ed.), *Handbook of parenting*: Vol. 4. *Social conditions and applied parenting*, pp. 329–359. Mahwah, NJ: Lawrence Erlbaum Associates.

McCoy, C. B., Lai, S., Metsch, L. R., Messiah, S. E., & Zhao, W. (2004). Injection drug use and crack cocaine smoking: Independent and dual risk behaviors for HIV infection. *Ann Epidemiol*, 14, 535–542.

McCrady, B. S., & Epstein, E. E. (1995). Theoretical bases of family approaches to substance abuse treatment. In F. Rotger, D. S. Kekker, & J. Morganstern (Eds.), *Treating substance abuse: Theory and technique*, pp. 117–142. New York: Guilford Press.

McMahon, T. J. & Rounsaville, B. J. (2002). Substance abuse and fathering: Adding poppa to the research agenda. *Addiction*, 97, 1109–1115.

Miller, B. A., Smyth, N. J., & Mudar, P. J. (1999). Mothers' alcohol and other drug problems and their punitiveness toward their children. *J Study Alcohol*, 60, 632–642.

Milner, J. S. (1986). *The Child Abuse Potential Inventory: Manual* (2nd ed.). Webster, NC: Psytec.

Milner, J. S. (1994). Assessing child abuse risk: The Child Abuse Potential Inventory. *Clinical Psychology Review*, 14, 547–583.

Molnar, B. E., Buka, S. L., & Kessler, R. C. (2001). Child sexual abuse and subsequent psychopathology: results from the National Comorbidity Survey. *American Journal of Public Health*, 91, 753–760.

Moos, R. (1974). *Family environment scale*. Palo Alto, CA: Consulting Psychologists Press.

Nair, P., Schuler, M. E., Black, M. M., Kettinger, L., & Harrington, D. (2003). Cumulative environmental risk in substance abusing women: Early intervention, parenting stress, child abuse potential and child development. *Child Abuse Negl*, 27, 997–1017.

Nair, P., Schuler, M. E., Black, M. M., Kettinger, L., & Harrington, D. (2003). Cumulative environmental risk in substance abusing women: early intervention, parenting stress, child abuse potential and child development. *Child Abuse and Neglect*, 27, 997–1017.

O'Farrell, T. J., & Fals-Stewart, W. (2000). Behavioral couples therapy for alcoholism and drug abuse. *Journal of Substance Abuse Treatment*, 18, 51–54.

Ollendick, T. H., Langley, A. K., Jones, R. T., & Kephart, C. (2001). Fear in children and adolescents: Relations with negative life events, attributional style, and avoidant coping. *Journal of Child Psychology and Psychiatry*, 42, 1029–1034.

Ondersma, S. J., Delaney-Black, V., Covington, C. Y., Nordstrom, B., & Sokol, R. J. (2006). The association between caregiver substance abuse and self-reported violence exposure among young urban children. *Journal of Traumatic Stress*, 19, 107–118.

Pajulo, M., Savonlahti, E., Sourander, A., Ahlqvist, S., Helenius, H., & Piha, J. (2001). An early report on the mother-baby interactive capacity of substance-abusing mothers. *Journal of Substance Abuse Treatment*, 20, 143–151.

Papousek, M., & von Hofacker, N. (1998). Persistent crying in early infancy: a non-trivial condition of risk for the developing mother-infant relationship. *Child Care Health Dev*, 25, 395–424.

Peleg-Oren, N., & Teichman, M. (2006). Young children of parents with substance use disorders (SUDs): A review of the literature and implications for social work practice. *Journal of Social Work in the Addictions*, 6, 49–61.

Pilowsky, D. J., Zybert, P. A., & Vlahov, D. (2004). Resilient children of injection drug users. *Journal of the American Academy of Child & Adolescent Psychiatry*, 43, 1372–1379.

Pires, P., & Jenkins, J. M. (2007). A growth curve analysis of the joint influences of parenting affect, child characteristics and deviant peers on adolescent illicit drug use. *Journal of Youth and Adolescence*, 36, 169–183.

Pivnick, A., Jacobson, A., Eric, K., Doll, L., & Drucker, E. (1994). AIDS, HIV infection, and illicit drug use within inner-city families and social networks. *American Journal of Public Health*, 84, 271–274.

Porter, B., & O'Leary, K. D. (1980). Marital discord and childhood behavior problems. *Journal of Abnormal Child Psychology*, 8, 287–295.

Porter, L. S., & Porter, B. O. (2004). A blended infant massage-parenting enhancement program for recovering substance-abusing mothers. *Pediatric Nursing, 30,* 363–401.

Powis, B., Gossop, M., Bury, C., Payne, K., & Griffiths, P. (2000). Drug-using mothers: Social, psychological and substance use problems of women opiate users with children. *Addiction & Treatment, 19,* 171–180.

Reiss, A. J., & Farrington, D. P. (1991). Advancing knowledge about co-offending: Results from a prospective longitudinal survey of London males. *Journal of Criminal Law and Criminology, 82,* 360–395.

Repetti, R. L., Taylor, S. E., & Seeman, T. E. (2002). Risky families: Family social environments and the mental and physical health of offspring. *Psychol Bull, 128,* 330–366.

Richters, J. E., & Martinez, P. (1993). The NIMH community violence project: I. Children as victims of and witnesses to violence. *Psychiatry, 56,* 7–21.

Roosa, M. W., Jones, S., Tein, J. Y., & Cree, W. (2003). Prevention science and neighborhood influences on low-income children's development: Theoretical and methodological issues. *American Journal of Community Psychology, 31*(1–2), 55–72.

Rothbart, M. K. (1981). Measurement of temperament in infancy. *Child Development, 52,* 569–578.

Runyan, D. K., Hunter, W. M., Socolar, R. R., Amaya-Jackson, L., English, D., Landsverk, J. et al. (1998). Children who prosper in unfavorable environments: The relationship to social capital. *Pediatrics, 101,* 12–18.

Sameroff, A. J., Seifer, R., Barocas, R., Zax, M., & Greenspan, S. (1987). Intelligence quotient scores of 4-year-old children: Social environmental risk factors. *Pediatrics, 79,* 343–350.

Samoulis, J., Hogue, A., Dauber, S., & Liddle, H. A. (2005). Autonomy and relatedness in inner-city families of substance abusing adolescents. *Journal of Child & Adolescent Substance Abuse, 15,* 53–86.

Sampson, R. J., Morenoff, J. D., & Gannon-Rowley, T. (2002). Assessing "neighborhood effects": Social processes and new directions in research. *Annual Review of Sociology, 28,* 443–478.

Sampson, R. J., Raudenbush, S. W., & Earls, F. (1997). Neighborhoods and violent crime: A multilevel study of collective efficacy, *Science, 277,* 918–924.

Schaefer, E. S. (1965). Children's reports of parental behavior: An inventory. *Child Development, 36,* 413–424.

Schempf, A. (2007). Illicit drug use and neonatal outcomes: A critical review. *Obstetrical & Gynecological Survey, 62,* 749–757.

Schroeder, J. R., Latkin, C. A., Hoover, D. R., Curry, A. D., Knowlton, A. R., & Celentano, D. D. (2001). Illicit drug use in one's social network and in one's neighborhood predicts individual heroin and cocaine use. *Ann Epidemiol, 11,* 389–394.

Semple, S. J., Patterson, T. L., & Grant, I. (2000). Psychosocial predictors of unprotected anal intercourse in a sample of HIV positive gay men who volunteer for a sexual risk reduction intervention. *AIDS Educ Prev, 12,* 416–430.

Shelton, K. K., Frick, P. J., & Wooton, J. (1996). Assessment of parenting practices in families of elementary school-age children. *Journal of Clinical Child Psychology, 25,* 317–329.

Simons-Morton, B., & Chen, R. S. (2006). Over time relationships between early adolescent and peer substance use. *Addict Behav, 31,* 1211–1223.

Simons-Morton, B., Haynie, D. L., Crump, A. D., Eitel, S. P., & Saylor, K. E. (2001). Peer and parent influences on smoking and drinking among early adolescents. *Health Educ Behav, 28,* 95–107.

Sobeck, J., Abbey, A., Aguis, E., Clinton, M., & Harrison, K. (2000). Predicting early adolescent substance use: do risk factors differ depending on age of onset? *J Subst Abuse, 11,* 89–102.

Stanger, C., Dumenci, L., Kamon, J., & Burstein, M. (2004). Parenting and children's externalizing problems in substance-abusing families. *J Clin Child Adolesc Psychol, 33,* 590–600.

Stanger, C., Higgins, S. T., Bickel, W. K., Elk, R., Grabowski, J., Schmitz, J., Amass, L., Kirby, K. C., & Seracini, A. M. (1999). Behavioral and emotional problems among children of cocaine- and opiate-dependent parents. *J Am Acad Child Adolesc Psychiatry, 38,* 421–428.

Straus, M. A. (1990). The Conflict Tactics Scale and its critics: An evaluation and new data on validity and reliability. In M. A. Straus, & R. J. Gelles (Eds.), *Physical violence in American families,* pp. 49–73. New Brunswick, NJ: Transaction Publishers.

Straus, M. A., Hamby, S. L., Finkelhor, D., Moore, D. W., & Runyan, D. (1998). Identification of child maltreatment with the parent-child conflict tactics scales: Development and psychometric data for a national sample of American parents. *Child Abuse & Neglect, 22,* 249–270.

Suchman, N. E., & Luthar, S. S. (2000). Maternal addiction, child maladjustment and socio-demographic risks: Implications for parenting behaviors. *Addiction*, 95, 1417–1428.

Suchman, N. E., & Luthar, S. S. (2001). The mediating role of parenting stress in methadone-maintained mothers' parenting. *Parenting: Science and Practice*, 1, 285–315.

Suchman, N. E., McMahon, T. J., Slade, A., & Luthar, S. S. (2005). How early bonding, depression, illicit drug use, and perceived support work together to influence drug-dependent mothers' caregiving. *Am J Orthopsychiatry*, 75, 431–445.

Szapocznik, J., & Coatsworth, D. (1999). An ecodevelopmental framework for organizing the influences on drug abuse: A developmental model of risk and protection. In M. D. Glanz, & C. R. Hartel (Eds.), *Drug abuse: Origins and interventions*, pp. 331–366. Washington, DC: American Psychological Association.

Tarter, R. E., Blackson, T., Martin, C., Loeber, R., & Moss, H. B. (1993). Characteristics and correlates of child discipline practices in substance abuse and normal families. *Addiction & Treatment*, 2, 18–25.

Trocme, N. (1996). Development and preliminary evaluation of the Ontario child neglect index. *Child Maltreatment*, 2, 145–155.

Turner, R. J., & Lloyd, D. A. (2003). Cumulative adversity and drug dependence in young adults: Racial/ethnic contrasts. *Addiction*, 98, 305–315.

Vakalahi, H. F. (2001). Adolescent substance use and family-based risk and protective factors: A literature review. *J Drug Educ*, 31, 29–46.

Valente, T. W., Gallaher, P., & Mouttapa, M. (2004). Using social networks to understand and prevent substance use: A transdisciplinary perspective. *Subst Use Misuse*, 39, 1675–1712.

Weiss, L., Ompad, D., Galea, S., & Vlahov, D. (2007). Defining neighborhood boundaires for urban health research. *Am J Prev Med*, 32, S154–S159.

Werner, M. J., Joffe, A., & Graham, A. V. (1999). Screening, early identification, and office-based intervention with children and youth living in substance-abusing families. *Pediatrics*, 103, 1099–1112.

Wilens, T. E., Biederman, J., Bredin, E., Hahesy, A. L., Abrantes, A., Neft, D., Millstein, R., & Spencer, T. J. (2002). A family study of the high-risk children of opioid and alcohol dependent parents. *American Journal on Addiction*, 11, 41–51.

Williams, C. T., & Latkin, C. A. (2007). Neighborhood socioeconomic status, personal network attributes, and use of heroin and cocaine. *Am J Prev Med*, 32, S203–S210.

Wills, T. A., Sandy, J. M., Yaeger, A., & Shinar, O. (2001). Family risk factors and adolescent substance use: Moderation effects for temperament dimensions. *Dev Psychol*, 37, 283–297.

Wolin, S. J., & Wolin, S. (1993). *Bound and Determined: Growing Up Resilient in a Troubled Family*. New York: Villard Press.

Zolotor, A. J., & Runyan, D. K. (2006). Social capital, family violence, and neglect. *Pediatrics*, 117, 1124–1131.

CHAPTER 22

Early Exposure to Trauma

Domestic and Community Violence

Patricia Van Horn and Alicia F. Lieberman

The idea that young children must be understood in the context of their environments is not new. Donald Winnicott's observation that there is no such thing as a baby, only a baby and someone who cares for the baby (Winnicott, 1952/1958), sparked a tradition of intervention in which the relationship between infants and their caregivers is accepted as the most parsimonious and effective port of entry for treatment when the infant's mental health is at risk (Fraiberg, Adelson, & Shapiro, 1975; Stern, 1995; Lieberman & Van Horn, 2008).

There is also a consensus that even very young infants must be understood through a broader relational lens than the merely dyadic, as infants develop essentially different relationships with both parents (McHale, 2007; Pruett, 2000) and with a hierarchy of attachment figures (Bowlby, 1969). The eco-logical-transactional developmental model (Bronfenbrenner, 1979, 1986; Cicchetti & Lynch, 1993) is based on the premise that children grow and develop in complex inter-action with their families and with the larger social and cultural environment that sup-ports, neglects, or places traumatic stressors on the family. Indeed, Winnicott later spe-cifically recognized that this broader frame was essential to understanding the baby, stating that "A baby is a complex phenom-enon that includes the baby's potential *plus* the environment" (Winnicott, 1969/1989, at 253, italics in original).

It is also generally accepted that this is not a one-way interaction with children being acted on by their families and larger envir-onments. Babies are born with the capacity to be relational, and are full partners with their caregivers in shaping patterns of inter-action among them (Brazelton & Cramer, 1990; Stern, 1985). Infants and very young children influence and shape the environ-ments in which they develop because chil-dren's behavior shapes parents' responses. Children's individual needs also affect the ways in which their parents interact with broader societal and cultural forces.

Violence in a child's environment is an especially salient variable in the complex interaction of effects among child, fam-ily, and broader world. In this chapter, we examine the impact of violence and trauma on young children's development through an environmental lens, beginning with the child's internal psychophysiological environment. We consider the ways in which children's physiologies are regulated by the relationships that guide their growth and dysregulated by trauma, and demonstrate that parallel processes occur in the child's caregiving environment as caregivers and family are regulated and strengthened by social and cultural environments that nurture them and dysregulated when those environments are neglectful and dangerous. Through an environmental lens, we see that violence and trauma lead to a range of outcomes for children, from internal dysregulation through external behavior changes that cause perturbations and disturbances in relationships. We see as well that parents' own response to violence in their environments changes they way they think about and behave toward their children, shaping their children's development in ways that can persist into the next generation.

The Scope of the Problem: Exposure and Risk

Exposure to Stress and Violence

Childhood trauma has been characterized as an urgent public health problem (Harris, Putnam & Fairbank, 2006) and the largest single preventable cause of mental illness (Sharfstein, 2006), with alarming numbers of children at risk for serious trauma. There are 3 million yearly reports of child abuse and neglect, with cases substantiated at the rate of 1 million per year (USDHHS, 2005). Young children are also disproportionately the direct victims of this violence and neglect. During the first year of life, more children are physically abused and die as the result of the abuse than at any other 1-year period (Zeanah & Scheeringa, 1997). Extrapolating from data from 40 states reported to the National Center on Child Abuse and Neglect in 1995, the National Research Council and Institute of Medicine (2000) found that more than one third of victims of substantiated reports to child protection agencies were under age 5,

and 77 percent of the children killed were under age 3.

Young children are also frequent witness to violence between the adults who care for them. Nearly 15.5 million children are exposed to domestic violence annually, including 7 million children exposed to severe violence in their homes (McDonald, Jouriles, Ramisetty-Mikler, Caetano & Green, 2006); these children are 158 percent more likely to be victimized by violence themselves than children from nonviolent homes (Mitchell & Finkelhor, 2001), and children under age 5 are more likely than older children to be present in homes where domestic violence occurs (Fantuzzo, Brouch, Beriama, & Atkins, 1997). In a nationally representative sample of children age 2 to 17, Finkelhor (2008) found that 71 percent of the children and youth surveyed had experienced at least one incident of victimization in the previous year, and that among the victimized children the average number of victimizations in the prior year was 3, with the range extending to 15.

Young children are also frequently exposed to community violence. Forty-seven percent of the mothers surveyed in the waiting room of the Boston Medical Center pediatric clinic reported that their children under 6 had heard gunshots, and 94 percent of this subset of mothers reported more than one such episode. In addition, 10 percent of the children had witnessed a knifing or a shooting, and nearly 20 percent had witnessed an episode of hitting, kicking, or shoving between adults (Taylor, Zuckerman, Harik & Groves, 1994). Shahinfar (1997) interviewed parents and their children aged 3 and 4 who were enrolled in Head Start programs near Washington DC and found that 78 percent of the children and 67 percent of the parents reported that the child had witnessed or been the victim of at least one violent event in the community.

In addition to exposure to intentional violence, very young children are routinely exposed to a range of additional stressors. We discuss these here because they potentially have an impact similar to acts of intentional violence on the child's developing nervous system. In a pediatric sample of 305 children between ages 2–5, 52.5 percent of the children had experienced a severe traumatic stressor in their lifetimes. Although the older children had a higher incidence of these experiences, 42 percent of the 2-year-olds had suffered from at least one severe stressor. As a group, 20.9 percent experienced the loss of a loved adult; 16 percent had been hospitalized; 9.9 percent had been in a motor vehicle accident; 9.5 percent had a serious fall, and 7.9 percent had been burned. There was a strong association between the number of stressors experienced by a child and the likelihood of DSM-IV emotional or behavioral disorders, with 17.4 percent of the children showing such a disorder (Egger & Angold, 2004). Children under 5 are hospitalized and die from drowning and submersion, burning, falls, suffocation, choking, and poisoning more frequently than children in any other age group (Grossman, 2000). Violence and other traumatic stressors affect a vast number of children each year, and society bears the burden of the developmental challenges that these children face. Even as we ponder optimal treatment strategies, the importance of public policies designed to decrease the pervasiveness of violence as well as to prevent and ameliorate the impact of violence once it occurs cannot be overstated (Harris, Lieberman & Marans, 2007).

Environmental Risk Factors for Exposure to Violence

The co-occurrence of multiple types of threat and risk immerses affected children in atmospheres of violence and makes it virtually impossible to tease out the unique impact of any one stressor. Finkelhor (2008) proposes a term, "developmental victimology," to encompass harm that comes to children at the hands of human actors that violate social norms. Consistent with the philosophy of this volume, Finkelhor notes the common cooccurrence of risk factors and proposes that the fragmentation that follows the parsing of childhood victimization into exposure to particular types of violence engenders incomplete understanding

of the problem and may therefore obstruct the finding of enduring solutions.

Risk for childhood victimization, whether it is due to violence sustained or witnessed by the child, is complex and multidetermined. For example, Lynch (2006) notes that a combination of child characteristics (male gender, ethnic minority status, and adolescent age), family characteristics (poverty, father absence, family conflict, and poor parenting practices), and social characteristics (economic disadvantage at the neighborhood level) place children at risk for exposure to community violence. It is accumulation of these risk factors that is especially toxic (Evans, 2004; Felitti et al., 1998; Rutter, 2000).

Regulatory Processes and the Child's Internal Environment

Even the infant's internal environment is essentially relational. Humans can be conceptualized as open systems, receiving information from the surrounding environment and from other people, and using that information to inform and regulate their own responses (Lewis, Armini & Lannon, 2001; Tronick, 2007). This is particularly true of infants, who have little independent capacity to self-regulate, and who are dependent on regulating behavior from others, most commonly caregivers, to sustain even such basic homeostatic processes as body temperature, sleep-wake cycles, digestion, and motor stability (National Research Council Institute of Medicine, 2000). Infants and young children subjected to traumatic stressors such as violence are met with additional challenges as they develop and strive to attain increasing independence in their physiological and emotional regulation: they must cope as well with stress response systems that are dysregulated by overactivation.

The Development of the Normal Stress Response

Newborns secrete high levels of stress hormones, including cortisol, in response to such environmental challenges as blood sampling, cortisol elevations that are positively associated with crying. Healthy newborns also have the capacity to withdraw into quiescent states associated with lower levels of stress hormone secretion, a demonstration of early attempts at self-regulation. Healthy babies habituate to stress crying less over time and secreting less stress hormones in response to the same levels of stimulation. Less healthy babies are less able to regulate their hormone levels by withdrawal, and so habituate less readily. In these infants, crying is not an accurate index of their stress levels because they continue to have high cortisol levels even after they have been soothed. It is possible that less healthy babies will remain more physiologically vulnerable to stress as they develop, requiring less intense stimulation to trigger a full-blown stress response (Gunnar, 1992).

Healthy newborns' habituation to stress becomes more sophisticated as they develop and as caregiving patterns help them achieve some measure of physiological regularity. By three months, infants' pattern of cortisol production is related to the sleep-wake cycle, with levels highest in the morning and declining throughout the day (White, Gunnar, Larson, Donzella, & Barr, 2000). Cortisol is controlled by a system of negative feedback loops with high levels, such as are seen in stressful or frightening situations, triggering a shutdown in production (Jacobson & Sopolsky, 1991). Older infants secrete stress hormones on separation from their caregivers or in novel situations, but also evidence a growing capacity to use caregivers to help them modulate their response, at least if their attachment relationships are secure (Gunnar, 2005). When they are with their attachment figures, insecure toddlers, but not secure ones, show elevations in cortisol to distressing events (Gunnar & Donzella, 2002). As they grow into the school years, children who deploy moderate cortisol levels in response to stress are more competent with peers, more cooperative, and more realistic in their appraisals of a stressful situation. Elevations in cortisol do not automatically signal stress or anxiety, but may index children's active attempts to cope both with the stressor and with their emotional responses to it (Gunnar, 1992; McEwen, 1999). These findings suggest that children who develop in "good enough" environments of care become increasingly able to self-regulate in the face of stress, first using their caregivers, and then appraising and responding to stress with growing independence. Vagal tone, an index of parasympathetic nervous system influences on heart rate variability, serves as another marker of emotion regulation, with a greater ability to buffer vagal tone in response to environmental challenge believed to protect children from negative outcomes (Beauchine, 2001; Katz & Gottman, 1995; Porges, 1995).

internal Environments in the Presence of Stress and Trauma

The body responds to highly stressful stimuli with a dynamic process that involves multiple neurotransmitter systems, including the catecholamine, serotonin, and dopamine systems as well as multiple neuroendocrine axes, including the hypothalamic-pituitary-adrenal (HPA) axis, which produces cortisol (Lipschitz, Rasmusson, & Southwick, 1998; McEwen, 1999). We focus here on the HPA axis because it is the most thoroughly studied stress-response system, and because it is implicated in both fear conditioning and the production of stress hormones in response to fear (Yehuda, Giller, Levengood, Southwick, & Siever, 1995).

The essence of a traumatic event is that visual, auditory, olfactory, tactile and kinetic stimuli from the environment join with a rapidly accelerating cascade of feelings from within to overwhelm the traumatized person's capacity to appraise and cope with the danger. Infants and young children are too cognitively immature to carry out the appraisal function. Similarly, their burgeoning capacities for self-regulation are overwhelmed by less intense stimuli than would be required to overwhelm an older and better-regulated child or an adult. When infants and young children experience such catastrophic events, they experience as well a failure of their developmentally appropriate expectations that their caregivers will protect them from such dangers, a protection that goes to the heart of the security of the child's attachment (Pynoos, Steinberg, & Piacentini, 1999). When the parents fail in their protective function, often in spite of noble effort, the failure reverberates within the parent as well as the child. The child's pain and fear has meaning for the parent, and the parent's response mediates the child's own response to the event. One study of children under 4 who experienced severe burns demonstrated a direct path linking the stressor of children's pain to parental distress about the pain, which was in turn linked to acute stress symptoms in the children (Shalev, Peri, Canetti, & Schreiber, 1966). This circuit of distress demonstrates how complex the environmental impact of child trauma can be. As we show later, the experience of traumatic stress changes the child's internal environment. It may also, however, change the caregiving environment, as parents may respond to their children's stress with withdrawal of care, placing the security of the child's attachment at risk and making the parent a less effective partner in the child's developmental striving toward self-regulation (Strathearn, 2007; Weinfield, Sroufe, & Egeland, 2000).

When a trauma occurs, the terrifying external sensory information is processed by the brain in two separate pathways: a rapid path to the amygdala, a bilateral structure located in the limbic brain whose function is to assess the aversive emotional significance of the sensory stimulus and set in motion the fear response, and a slower one to the sensory prefrontal cortex, the seat of analysis, planning and executive function (LeDoux, 1996, 1998). Survival is dependent upon the rapid physiological response to danger that is made possible by the shorter pathway to the amygdala. When the amygdala and its related structures assess a situation as dangerous, the sympathetic nervous system discharges, mobilizing a set of physiological changes that the brain perceives as part of a global situation of danger (Southwick, Yehuda, & Morgan, 1995). In response to both the external and internal stimuli, the amygdala activates the HPA axis, resulting in the release of high levels of corticosteroids, including cortisol (LeDoux, 1995). If, after initial activation of the HPA response, the individual continues to assess the event as dangerous, the assessment interferes with the negative feedback loop that, under conditions of mild or moderate stress, halts the production of cortisol. In situations of ongoing stress and danger, the body continues to produce large quantities of cortisol.

Although the nervous system may habituate even to predictably high levels of stress over time, such habituation appears not to occur in childhood if stresses are severe, unpredictable, uncontrollable, or novel. In these conditions, high levels of stress hormones will continue to be secreted even in response to stimuli that are not inherently traumatic. It is as if the switch that controls the production of stress hormones is recalibrated and reset to a position where less frightening stimuli are sufficient to activate it (Yehuda, Giller, Southwick, Lowy, & Mason, 1991). In most studies, traumatized children show higher levels of cortisol than matched nontraumatized controls (DeBellis et al., 1999a; Carrión, 2006). A pattern of hypo-responsiveness in the HPA axis and low levels of cortisol is most frequently observed in adult trauma survivors, however (Yehuda, Giller, Levengood, Southwick, & Siever, 1995), leading to the hypothesis that the body makes a long-term adaptation to trauma because it cannot sustain the hyper-secretion of cortisol that is triggered in childhood by extreme stress and trauma (DeBellis et al. 1999a; Gunnar & Vazquez, 2001).

Recent research suggests not only that physiological adaptations to stress take place over time but also that they may be intergenerational. Radtke and colleagues (2011) studied children and adolescents 10 through 19 years of age (mean age 14.1 years), collecting retrospective data from the mothers concerning whether they had sustained intimate partner violence during their pregnancies with the subject children. They found that the methylation status of the glucocorticoid receptor (GR) gene, a major regulator of the

HPA axis, in the children was associated with exposure *in utero* to intimate partner violence. Interestingly, there was no relationship between methylation status of the GR gene and intimate partner violence experienced by the mother either before her pregnancy or after the birth of the subject child. Witnessing violence between parents was thought, therefore, not to be associated with changes in this gene. Rather, the impact came from violence sustained by the mother during pregnancy when she literally shares a physiological environment with her unborn baby.

There is also empirical evidence of changes in brain structure and volume following trauma (DeBellis et al., 1999b; Carrión, 2006; Carrión et al., 2001; Carrión, Weems, and Reiss, 2007), associated with earlier age and longer duration of maltreatment, and greater severity of PTSD symptoms. These changes in brain structure are associated with limitations in cognitive functioning, including capacity for abstract reasoning and executive function that are positively correlated with total brain volume and negatively correlated with duration of maltreatment (Beers and DeBellis, 2002; DeBellis et al., 1999b).

Investigators have also observed that traumatized children's perceptions are altered in ways that may affect their post-trauma relationships and ability to learn. In laboratory settings, traumatized children attended selectively to negative emotions and negative situations (Pollack, Cicchetti, Klorman, & Brumaghim, 1997). Such preferential attention to negative stimuli might be adaptive in chronically dangerous environments, but in less threatening situations it is likely to interfere with traumatized children's ability to process emotionally neutral information both in learning situations and in relationships that may be helpful in restoring their feelings of safety.

Children's Outcomes: Mediators, Moderators, and Context

There is broad empirical support for the proposition that children exposed to violence in their families and communities have a variety of behavioral, cognitive, emotional and psychiatric difficulties, although outcomes vary (Evans, Davies, & DiLillo, 2008; Kitzmann, Gaylord, Holt, & Kenny, 2003; Proctor, 2006; Wolfe, Crooks, Lee, McIntyre-Smith, & Jaffe, 2003). Most commonly, children exposed to violence in their homes and communities have been found to suffer from increased internalizing and externalizing behavior problems, increased symptoms of posttraumatic stress disorder and diminished cognitive functioning when compared to nonexposed children (for a review see Van Horn & Lieberman, 2011). Researchers have moved from that simple comparison to a range of questions consistent with the environmental approach taken by this volume, investigating environmental risk factors for exposure, mediators and moderators of outcome, and the interactions of contextual and risk factors. This new generation of research demonstrates beyond doubt that a variety of factors interacting with one another work together to mediate and moderate exposed children's negative outcomes.

Children's Internal Environments

The central nervous system and information processing changes described earlier have demonstrated effects on outcome, with emotional dysregulation and social information processing both mediating the association between violence exposure and behavior problems (Schwartz & Proctor, 2000), positive play (Leary and Katz, 2004), and negative peer group interactions (Katz, Hessler, & Annest, 2007). Children's appraisals of violence also influence their outcomes. Children who feel more threatened by the violence, or who blame themselves for it experience more depression, anxiety, and social adjustment problems (Skopp, McDonald, & Manke, 2005; Grych, Fincham, Jouriles, & McDonald, 2000).

Parenting Factors

In families where there is domestic violence, the violence between parents is associated with negative changes in parenting behavior; the violence affects children directly by frightening them, and indirectly by changing for the worse they ways in which their parents interact with them. Domestic violence has been associated with elevations in parenting stress (Holden & Ritchie, 1991; Levendosky & Graham-Bermann, 1998), hostility toward children (Gordis, Margolin & John, 1997; Margolin & John, 1997), as well as negative affect toward children and decreases in empathy (Margolin, Grodis, & Oliver, 2004; Margolin, John, Ghosh, & Gordis, 1997). These negative parenting behaviors have generally been found to explain unique variance in children's negative outcomes over and above the impact of violence exposure. Positive parenting, especially warmth (Skopp et al., 2005) and attunement to children's emotional responses (Johnson & Lieberman, 2007) are protective, however, even in violent families.

Parent functioning and general well-being also affect the outcomes of children exposed to a variety of types of violence. The behavior problems of children exposed to community violence are mediated by maternal distress, even after maternal socioeconomic status and family aggression (Linares, Heeren, Bronfman, Zuckerman, Augustyn, & Tronick, 2001). In another study, maternal psychological functioning and family cohesion predicted the longitudinal adjustment of Israeli preschoolers whose homes were damaged by SCUD missiles during the Gulf War (Laor, Wolmer & Cohen, 2001). As in cases where children are exposed to domestic violence, the presence in the child's life of protective factors, particularly in the form of a close emotional relationship with a supportive adult, can ameliorate the impact of adversity and promote a positive developmental outcome (Lynch & Cicchetti, 1998).

Parents affect children's outcomes in a third way, more subtle than the direct impact of their overt behavior or the indirect impact of their global functioning. All parents make attributions, global beliefs about the children's existential cores, to their children. These attributions are internalized by children and shape their development (Lieberman, 1997). When parents have suffered violence at the hands of others, either in their own childhoods or as adults, there is a risk that their views of relationships with others, including their children, will be colored by those traumatic experiences such that they will anticipate aggression and victimization in their relationships (Janoff-Bulmann, 1992; Pynoos, 1997). A parent's expectations of aggression, internalized by the child as an attribution that he is violent by nature, will shape the child sense of self. He will come to believe that he is violent, will identify with the parent's attribution, and behave in violent ways. The child's internal self-identification and external aggressive behavior will, in turn, change the shape of the child's environment. Family members and peers may respond to the child with hostility, aggression, or rejection, causing the child to feel isolated and vulnerable to abandonment by people who are important to him. Fear of abandonment and aggressive acting out will then mark the growing child's relationships both in the present and the future. Thus, parental expectations and attributions not only shape the child's present sense of self but become a vehicle for the intergenerational transmission of violence.

Bidirectional Effects of Parent and Child Behavior and Functioning

There is empirical evidence in support of the principle that children affect their environments just as their environment shape them. In one study of school-age children and their mothers in a battered women's shelter, researchers studied the complex relationships among a number of variables: extent of interparental physical violence; children's PTSD symptoms, behavior problems, and intervention in violence between parents; and mothers' depression, anxiety, and anger (Jarvis, Gordon, & Novaco, 2005). The findings demonstrated the bi-directional impact of children and parents on one another, consistent with the ecological-transactional model. Children's PTSD symptoms were associated with the amount of physical violence that occurred; their behavioral problems, however, were related to maternal anxiety and anger. Mother's depression was associated with child intervention in episodes of violence and the quality of the mother-child relationship; anxiety was related to witnessing child abuse, child age and child internalizing behaviors; anger was associated with violence-related injuries, violence frequency, and children's internalizing behaviors.

Intergenerational Patterns of Transmission

Parent's attributions to their children are one potential path for the intergenerational transmission of violence and trauma when the attribution is internalized by the child. There is also evidence that parent's own childhood experience of violence and trauma may be a path for intergenerational transmission. Noll and her colleagues (Noll, Trickett, Harris, & Putnam, 2008) performed a multigenerational study that compared females with substantiated childhood sexual abuse and nonabused comparison females. Both groups were assessed at six points spanning 18 years in a prospective, longitudinal study. Although this study did not examine mediational models or cumulative risk, it did find, consistent with earlier literature, that the children of the sexually abused women were more likely than the children of comparison women to be born to a teen mother, to be born preterm, and to be involved in protective services. The abused women themselves, however, had more troubled histories than the nonabused women, including higher rates of school drop-out and higher rates of psychiatric problems, substance abuse, and domestic violence. It is possible that, had these factors been analyzed as mediators, they would have been found to be more responsible than the history of sexual abuse itself for the higher risk to the abused women's offspring. Studies that examined the impact of maternal child abuse (Collishaw et al., 2007) and maternal history of highly stressful life events (Lieberman, Van Horn, & Ozer, 2005) on children's emotional-behavioral outcomes found that those associations were mediated by such factors as maternal psychiatric disturbance, quality of the mother-child relationship, parental hostility, and family type.

Other Family Factors

Children's responses to community violence are moderated by a number of family factors in addition to parenting behaviors and parents' well-being. Perceived social support within the family, the family's general well-being and cohesion, family size and composition, and family socioeconomic status are all moderators of the impact of children's exposure to community violence on their emotional and behavioral functioning. In keeping with the ecological-transactional model, the most predictive models test the impact of multiple variables (Proctor, 2006)

Broader Cultural Factors

Cultural practices, beliefs, and norms shape children's identity from the earliest months of their lives, mediated by family practices and relationships, by parents' values, beliefs and goals, and by interactions between the child and the parent (Tamminen, 2006). A culture's experience with violence is part of the system of beliefs and values that are passed from parent to child, and multiple levels of cultural influences determine an individual's response to trauma (Lewis and Ghosh Ippen, 2004).

When the individual is part of a minority cultural group, the first level of influence is often the set of supports, policies, and institutional responses that the dominant/host culture has in place to support the individual struggling with a traumatic event. A second level of influence has to do with how the individual's culture of origin responds the event: what meanings are ascribed to it and how the caregiving environment transmits those meanings to the child through daily interactions, shaping the child's response. Levels of acculturation and assimilation into the host culture are important, as is the culture of origin's group experience of trauma. Such group experiences (for example, the Holocaust, the internment of Japanese-Americans during World War II, and slavery)

provide lenses through which the traumatized group views later experience, shaping
its response to violence and trauma across
generations (Lewis and Ghosh Ippen, 2004).
This group response is made more complex
by the layering on, for each family, of lenses
on the world that are provided by the family's personal set of experiences. The values,
beliefs, and norms that grow from both
group and personal experiences are passed
on to the children, shaping their development and worldview.

Conclusion: Assessing Exposure and Intervening to Restore Children's Positive Developmental Trajectories

Assessment. Because exposure to violence
is so pervasive in early childhood and has
such a potentially devastating impact on
children's development, clinicians should
always assess for exposure to violence even
in cases where exposure is not the reason for
the referral. As we have seen, the etiology
of children's symptoms may be multiply
determined. If, however, a child for whom
parents are seeking treatment is violence
exposed and the clinician does not ask the
pertinent questions, the strength of societal
taboos about victimization, violence, and
trauma may prevent children and parents
from disclosing exposure, leaving clinicians
in the dark about important potential causes
of the child's difficulties.

There are a number of excellent measures
that clinicians can use to assess whether and
to what degree children are exposed to violence. Richters and Martinez (1993) developed two forms of a Children's Exposure
to Community Violence Questionnaire, one
to be completed by parents and the other,
by children themselves. Both questionnaires inquire about the level of children's
exposure to a variety of kinds of violence
in the home and community. The Traumatic
Events Screening Inventory (TESI: Ghosh
Ippen et al., 2002) is a parent report measure
that assess violence exposure and a range
of other kinds of adverse events, including
involuntary separation from a parent, the
death of someone close, and living with a

parent who is mentally ill or addicted to
substances. The Violence Exposure Scale for
Children-Revised (Fox & Leavitt, 1995) is a
self-report measure of violence exposure in
the home, community, and school for children aged four to ten. Where sexual assault
is suspected, clinicians can use instruments
such as the Checklist of Sexual Abuse
and Related Stressors (Spaccarelli, 1995)
to measure level of exposure to a range of
events associated with sexual abuse and its
sequelae.

Intervention. Violence shapes who children are by effecting changes in their physiology. Surrounding this basic change is
a cascade of other effects in the way the
child understands the motives of others
and behaves toward others, affecting in turn
the way in which others view and behave
toward the child. These effects shape who
the child will become across time. In this
complex network of intention and interaction, no relationships are as determinant
of the developing children's trajectories as
their relationships with parents and other
caregiving figures. If we hope to succeed in
restoring children exposed to violence to
positive developmental trajectories, interventions must be designed to shift their
internal environments by restoring a sense of
inner calm and belief that relationships are
predictable and benign. Interventions must
also tend to children's caregiving environments, improving parents' well-being and
capacity to care for and protect their children in ways that include and respect the
family's cultural norms and beliefs. Reviews
of efficacious interventions for maltreated
and violence-exposed children confirm that
the interventions that are most effective in
changing children's symptoms are those that
include parents (e.g., Cohen, Mannarino,
Murray, & Ingelman, 2006).

Parents may be included in interventions
for a variety of reasons. Some interventions seek to improve child wellbeing by
coaching the parent to behave differently
toward the child. Others seek to enhance
the parent's capacity to understand and
empathize with the child's perceptions of
traumatic experiences. We advocate early

relationship-focused interventions such as child-parent psychotherapy (Lieberman, Van Horn & Ghosh Ippen, 2005; Lieberman, Ghosh Ippen & Van Horn, 2006; Toth, Maughan, Manly, Spagnola, & Cicchetti, 2002) that focus on the parent's mental health as well as the child's and that promote healthy developmental outcomes by enhancing the child's primary attachment relationships, thus shifting the dynamic interplay between constitutional strength or vulnerability and environmental stress. There is emerging evidence that interventions that focus on enhancing children's primary caregiving relationships also improve their physiological reactivity (Dozier et al., 2006). The promise that relationship-based interventions may succeed in restoring greater physiological balance has important clinical implications because of the sometimes dramatic and enduring impact of traumatic stress on brain development.

Violence affects children's environments at every level, from the internal to the cultural. Efforts to help children must target not only child behaviors and symptoms but the caregiving environments that sustain children and shape the trajectories of their development.

References

Beauchine, T. P. (2001). Vagal tone, development, and Gray's motivational theory: Toward an integrated model of autonomic nervous system functioning in psychopathology. *Development and Psychopathology*, 13, 183–214.

Beers, S. R., & De Bellis, M. D. (2002). Neuropsychological function in children with maltreatment-related posttraumatic stress disorder. *American Journal of Psychiatry*, 159, 483–486.

Bowlby, J. (1969). *Attachment and loss*: Vol. 1. *Attachment*. New York: Basic books.

Brazelton, T. B., & Cramer, B. G. (1990). *The earliest relationship: Parents, infants, and the drama of early attachment*. Reading, MA: Perseus Books.

Bronfenbrenner, U. (1979). *The ecology of human development: Experiments by nature and design*. Cambridge, MA: Harvard University Press.

Bronfenbrenner, U. (1986). Ecology of the family as a context for human development: Research perspectives. *Developmental Psychology*, 22, 723–742.

Carrión, V. G (2006). Understanding the effects of early life stress on brain development. In A. F. Lieberman and R. DeMartino (Eds.), *Interventions for children exposed to violence*. New York: Johnson & Johnson Pediatric Institute.

Carrión, V. G., Weems, C. F., Eliez, S., Patwardhan, A., Brown, W., Ray, R. D., & Reiss, A. L. (2001). Attenuation of frontal asymmetry in pediatric posttraumatic stress disorder. Biological Psychiatry, 50, 943–951.

Carrión, V. G., Weems, C. F., & Reiss, A. L. (2007). Stress predicts brain changes in children: A pilot longitudinal study on youth stress, PTSD and the hippocampus. *Pediatrics*, 119, 509–516.

Cicchetti, D., & Lynch, A. (1993). Toward an ecological/transactional model of community violence and child maltreatment: Consequences for children's development. *Psychiatry*, 56, 96–118.

Cohen, J. A., Mannarino, A. P., Murray, L. K., & Ingelman, R. (2006). Psychosocial interventions for maltreated and violence-exposed children. *Journal of Social Issues*, 62, 737–766.

Collishaw, S., Dunn, J., O'Connor, T. G., Golding, J., & Avon Longitudinal Study of Parents and Children Study Team (2007). Maternal childhood abuse and offspring adjustment over time. *Development and Psychopathology*, 19, 367–383.

DeBellis, M. D., Baum, A. S., Birmaher, B., Keshavan, M. S., Ecard, C. H., A., Boring, A. M., Jenkins, F. J. & Ryan, N. D. (1999a). Developmental traumatology: Part 1. Biological stress systems. *Biological Psychiatry*, 9, 1259–1270.

DeBellis, M. D., Keshavan, M. S., Clark, D. B., Casey, B. J., Giedd, J. B., Boring, A. M., Frustaci, K. & Ryan, N. D. (1999b). Developmental traumatology: Part 2. Brain development. *Biological Psychiatry*, 45, 1271–1284.

Dozier, M., Peloso, E., Lindhiem, O., Gordon, M. K., Manni, M., Sepulveda, S., Ackerman, J., Bernier, A. & Levine, S. (2006). Preliminary evidence from a randomized clinical trial: Intervention effects on foster children's behavioral and biological regulation. *Journal of Social Issues*, 62, 767–785.

Egger, H. & Angold, A. (2004). Stressful life events and PTSD in preschool children. Paper presented at the Annual Meeting of the American

Academy of Child and Adolescent Psychiatry, Washington, DC.

Evans, G. W. (2004). The environment of childhood poverty. *American Psychologist, 59,* 77–92.

Evans, S. E., Davies, C., & DiLillo, D. (2008). Exposure to domestic violence: A meta-analysis of child and adolescent outcomes. *Aggression and Violent Behavior, 13,* 131–140.

Fantuzzo, J. W., Brouch, R., Beriama, A., & Atkins, M. (1997). Domestic violence and children: Prevalence and risk in five major U. S. cities. *Journal of the American Academy of Child and Adolescent Psychiatry, 36,* 116–122.

Felitti, V. J., Anda, R. F., Nordenberg, D., Williamson, D. F., Spitz, A. M., Edwards, V., Koss, M. P., & Marks, J. S. (1998). Relationship of childhood abuse and household dysfunction to many of the leading causes of death in adults: The adverse childhood experiences (ACE) study. *American Journal of Preventive Medicine, 14,* 245–258.

Finkelhor, D. (2008). *Childhood victimization: Violence, crime, and abuse in the lives of young people.* New York: Oxford University Press.

Fox, N. A., & Leavitt, L. A. (1995) The Violence Exposure Scale for Children-VEX. College Park, Md: Department of Human Development, University of Maryland.

Fraiberg, S., Adelson, E., & Shapiro, V. (1975). Ghosts in the nursery: Psychoanalytic approach to problems of impaired infant-mother relationships. *Journal of the American Academy of Child and Adolescent Psychiatry, 14,* 387–421.

Ghosh Ippen, C., Ford, J., Racusin, R., Acker, M., Bosquet, M., Rogers, K., Ellis, C., Schiffman, J., Ribbe, D., Cone, P., Lukovitz, M., Edwards, J., the Child Trauma Research Project of the Early Trauma Treatment Network, & the National Center for PTSD Dartmouth Child Trauma Research Group. (2002). *Traumatic Events Screening Inventory – Parent Report Revised.* San Francisco: University of California, San Francisco Early Trauma Treatment Network.

Gordis, E. G., Margolin, G., John, R. S. (1997). Marital aggression, observed parental hostility, and child behavior during dryadic family interaction. *Journal of Family Psychology, 11,* 76–89.

Grossman, D. C. (2000). The history of injury control and the epidemiology of child and adolescent injuries. In R. E. Behrman (Ed.), *The Future of Children: Unintentional Injuries of Childhood,* 10(1), 4–22. Los Altos, CA: David and Lucille Packard Foundation.

Grych, J. H., Fincham, F. D., Jouriles, E. N., & McDonald, R. (2000). Interparental conflict and child adjustment: Testing the mediational role of appraisals in the cognitive-contextual framework. *Child Development, 71,* 1648–1661.

Gunnar, M. R. (1992). Reactivity of the hypothalamic-pituitary-adrenocortical system to stressors in normal infants and children. *Pediatrics, 90,* 491–497.

Gunnar, M. (2005). Attachment and stress in early development: Does attachment add to the potency of social regulators of infant stress? In C. S. Carter, L. Ahnert, K. E. Grossman, S. B. Hrdy, M. E. Lamb, S. W. Porges, & N. Sacher (Eds.), *Attachment and bonding: A new synthesis,* pp. 245–255. Cambridge, MA: MIT Press.

Gunnar, M., & Donzella, B. (2002). Social regulation of the cortisol levels in early human development. *Psychoneuroendocrinology, 27,* 199–220.

Gunnar, M., & Quevedo, K. (2007). The neurobiology of stress and development. *Annual Review of Psychology, 58,* 145–173.

Gunnar, M. R., & Vazquez, D. M. (2001). Low cortisol and a flattening of expected daytime rhythm: Potential indices of risk in human development. *Development and Psychopathology, 13,* 515–538.

Harris, W. W., Lieberman, A. F., & Marans, S. (2007) In the best interests of society. *Journal of Child Psychology and Psychiatry, 48*(3/4), 392–411.

Harris, W. W., Putnam, F., & Fairbank, J. A. (2006). Mobilizing trauma resources for children. In A. F. Lieberman & R. DeMartino (Eds.), *Interventions for children exposed to violence,* 311–340. Johnson & Johnson Pediatric Round Table.

Holden, G. W., & Ritchie, K. L. (1991). Linking extreme marital discord, child rearing, and child behavior problems: Evidence from battered women. *Child Development, 62,* 311–327.

Jacobson, L., & Sopolsky, R. M. (1991). The role of the hippocampus in feedback regulation of the hypothalamic-pituitary-adrenocortical axis. *Endocrine Research, 12,* 118–134.

Janoff-Bulmann, R. (1992). *Shattered assumptions: Towards a new psychology of trauma.* New York: Free Press.

Jarvis, K. L., Gordon, E. E., Novaco, R. W. (2005) Psychological distress of children and mothers in domestic violence emergency shelters. *Journal of Family Violence, 20,* 389–402.

Johnson, V. K., & Lieberman, A. F. (2007). Variations in behavior problems of preschoolers exposed to domestic violence: The role of mothers' attunement to children's emotional experiences. *Journal of Family Violence*, 22, 297–308.

Katz, L. F., & Gottman, J. M. (1995). Vagal tone protects children from marital conflict. *Development and Psychopathology*, 7, 83–92.

Katz, L. F., Hessler, D. M., & Annest, A. (2007) Domestic violence, emotional competence, and child adjustment. *Social Development*, 16, 513–538.

Kitzmann, K. M., Gaylord, N. K., Holt, A. R., & Kenny, E. D. (2003). Child witnesses to domestic violence: A meta-analytic review. *Journal of Consulting and Clinical Psychology*, 71, 339–352.

Laor, N., Wolmer, L., & Cohen, D. J. (2001). Mothers' functioning and children's symptoms 5 years after a SCUD missile attack. *American Journal of Psychiatry*, 158, 1020–1026.

Leary, A., & Katz L. F. (2004). Coparenting, family-level processes, and peer outcomes: The moderating role of vagal tone. *Development and Psychopathology*, 16, 593–608.

LeDoux, J. (1995). Setting "stress" into motion: Brain mechanisms of stimulus evaluation. In M. J. Friedman, D. S. Charney, & A. Y. Deutch (Eds.), *Neurobiological and clinical consequences of stress: From normal adaptation to post-traumatic stress disorder*, pp. 125–134. New York: Lippincott-Raven Publishers.

LeDoux, J. (1996). *The emotional brain: The mysterious underpinnings of emotional life*. New York: Simon & Schuster.

LeDoux, J. (1998). Fear and the brain: Where have we been, and where are we going? *Biological Psychiatry*, 44, 1229–1238.

Levendosky, A. A., & Graham-Bermann, S. A. (1998). The moderating effects of parenting stress on children's adjustment in woman-abusing families. *Journal of Interpersonal Violence*, 13, 383–397.

Lewis, M. L., & Ghosh Ippen, C. (2004). Rainbows of tears, souls full of hope: Cultural issues related to young children and trauma. In J. D. Osofsky (ed.), *Young children and trauma: Intervention and treatment*, pp. 11–46. New York: Guilford.

Lewis, T., Armini, F., & Lannon, R. (2001). *A general theory of love*. New York: Vintage.

Lieberman, A. F. (1997). Toddlers' internalization of maternal attributions as a factor in the quality of attachment. In L. Atkinson &

K. L. Zuker (Eds.), *Attachment and psychopathology*, pp. 277–291. New York: Guilford Press.

Lieberman, A. F., Ghosh Ippen, C., & Van Horn, P. (2006). Child-parent psychotherapy: Six month follow-up of a randomized control trial. *Journal of the American Academy of Child and Adolescent Psychiatry*, 45, 913–918.

Lieberman, A. F., & Van Horn, P. (2008). *Psychotherapy with infants and young children: Repairing the effects of stress and trauma on early attachment*. New York: Guilford Press.

Lieberman, A. F., Van Horn, P., & Ghosh Ippen, C. Toward evidence-based treatment: Child-parent psychotherapy with preschoolers exposed to marital violence. *Journal of the American Academy of Child and Adolescent Psychiatry*, 44, 1241–1248.

Lieberman, A. F., Van Horn, P., & Ozer, E. J. (2005). Preschooler witnesses of marital violence: Predictors and mediators of child behavior problems. *Development and Psychopathology*, 17, 385–396.

Linares, L. O., Heeren, T., Bronfman, E., Zuckerman, B., Augustyn, M., & Tronick, E. (2001). A mediational model for the impact of exposure to community violence on early behavior problems. *Child Development*, 72, 639–652.

Lipschitz, D. S., Rasmusson, A. M., & Southwick, S. M. (1998). Childhood posttraumatic stress disorder: A review of neurobiologic sequelae. *Psychiatric Annals*, 28, 452–457.

Lynch, M. (2006) Children exposed to community violence. In M. M. Feerick & G. B. Silverman (Eds.), *Children exposed to violence*, pp. 9–52. Baltimore: Paul H. Brookes Publishing Co.

Lynch, M., & Cicchetti, D. (1998). An ecological-transactional analysis of children and context: The longitudinal interplay among child maltreatment, community violence, and children's symptomatology. *Development and Psychopathology*, 10, 235–257.

Margolin G., Gordis, E. B., & Oliver, P. H. (2004). Links between marital and parent-child interactions: Moderating role of husband-to-wife aggression. *Development and Psychopathology*, 16, 753–771.

Margolin G., & John R. S. (1997). Children's exposure to marital aggression: Direct and mediated effects. In G. K. Kantor & J. L. Jasinski (eds.), Out of the darkness: Perspectives on family violence, pp. 90–104. Thousand Oaks CA: Sage.

Margolin G., John R. S., Ghosh, C. &, Gordis, E. (1997). Family interaction process: An essential tool for exploring abusive relations. In D. D. Cahn & S. A. Lloyd (eds.), Family Abuse: A Communication Perspective, pp. 37–58. Thousand Oaks, CA: Sage.

McDonald, R., Jouriles, E., Ramisetty-Mikler, S., Caetano, R., & Green, C. (2006). Estimating the number of American children living in partner-violent families. Journal of Family Psychology, 20, 137–142.

McEwen, B. (1999). Development of the cerebral cortex: XIII. Stress and brain development II. Journal of the American Academy of Child and Adolescent Psychiatry, 38, 101–103.

McHale, J. P. (2007). Charting the bumpy road of coparenthood: Understanding the challenges of family life. Washington, DC: Zero to Three Press.

Mitchell, K. J., & Finkelhor, D. (2001). Risk of crime victimization among youth exposed to domestic violence. Journal of Interpersonal Violence, 16, 944–964.

National Research Council and Institute of Medicine (2000). From neurons to neighborhoods: The science of early childhood development. Committee on Integrating the Science of Early Childhood Development. In J. P. Shonkoff & D. A. Phillips (Eds.), Board on Children, Youth, and Families, Commission on Behavioral and Social Sciences and Education. Washington, DC: National Academy Press.

Noll, J. G., Trickett, P. K., Harris, W. W., & Putnam, F. W. (2008). The cumulative burden borne by offspring whose mothers were sexually abused as children. Journal of Interpersonal Violence OnlineFirst, doi:10.1177/0886260608317194.

Pollak, S. D., Cicchetti, D., Klorman, R., & Brumaghim, J. T. (1997). Cognitive brain event-related potentials and emotion processing in maltreated children. Child Development, 68, 773 – 787.

Porges, S. W. (1995). Orienting in a defensive world: Mammalian modifications of our evolutionary heritage: A polyvagal theory. Psychophysiology, 32, 301–318.

Proctor, L. J. (2006). Children growing up in a violent community: The role of the family. Aggression and Violent Behavior, 11, 558–576.

Pruett, K. D. (2000). Fatherneed: Why father care is as essential as mother care for your child. New York: Free Press.

Pynoos, R. S. (1997). The transgenerational repercussions of traumatic expectations. John F. Kennedy Lecture, Southern Florida Psychiatric Society, Miami, Florida, February, 1997.

Pynoos, R. S., Steinberg, A. M., & Piacentini, J. C. (1999) A developmental psychopathology model of childhood traumatic stress and intersections with anxiety disorders. Biological Psychiatry, 46, 1542–1554.

Radtke, K. M., Ruf, M., Gunter, H. M., Dohrmann, K., Schauer, M., Meyer, A., & Elbert, T. (2011). Transgenerational impact of intimate partner violence on methylation in the promoter of the glucocorticoid receptor. Translational Psychiatry, 1, e.

Richters, J. E., & Martinez, P. E. (1993). The NIMH Community Violence Project: Children as victims of and witnesses to violence. In D. Reiss, J. E. Richters, M. Radke-Yarrow, & D. Scharf (Eds.), Children and violence, pp. 7–21. New York: Guilford Press.

Rutter, M. (2000). Resilience reconsidered: Conceptual considerations, empirical findings, and policy implications. In J. P. Shonkoff & S. J. Meisels (eds.), Handbook of early childhood intervention, pp. 651–682. New York: Cambridge University Press.

Schwartz, D., & Proctor, L. (2000). Community violence exposure and children's social adjustment in the school peer group: The mediating roles of emotion regulation and social cognition. Journal of Consulting & Clinical Psychology, 68, 670–683.

Shahinfar, A. (1997). Preschool children's exposure to community violence: Prevalence, correlates, and moderating factors. Unpublished doctoral dissertation. College Park, MD: University of Maryland. Ann Arbor, MI: University Microfilms International, No. 9836528.

Shalev, A. Y., Peri, T., Canetti, L., & Schreiber, S. (1996). Predictors of PTSD in injured trauma survivors: A prospective study. American Journal of Psychiatry, 153, 219 – 225.

Sharfstein, S. (2006). New task force will address early childhood violence. Psychiatric News, 41, 3.

Skopp N. A., McDonald, R., Manke, B. (2005). Siblings in domestically violent families: Experience of interparent conflict and adjustment problems. Journal of Family Psychology, 19, 324–333.

Southwick, S. M., Yehuda, R., & Morgan, C. A. (1995). Clinical studies of neurotransmitter alterations in post-traumatic stress disorder. In M. J. Friedman, D. S. Charney, & A. Y. Deutch (Eds.), Neurobiological and clinical consequences of stress: From normal adaptation to post-traumatic stress disorder, pp. 335–350. New York: Lippincott-Raven Publishers.

Spaccarelli, S. (1995). Measuring abuse stress and negative cognitive appraisals in child sexual abuse: Validity data on two new scales. *Journal of Abnormal Child Psychology*, 23, 703–727.

Stern, D. N. (1985). *The interpersonal world of the infant*. New York: Basic Books.

Stern, D. N. (1995). *The motherhood constellation: A unified view of parent-infant psychotherapy*. New York: Basic Books.

Strathearn, L. (2007). Exploring the neurobiology of attachment. In L. Mayes, P. Fonagy, & M. Target (Eds.), *Developmental science and psychoanalysis: Integration and innovation*, pp. 117–130. London: Karnac Books.

Tamminen, T. (2006). How does culture promote the early development of identity? *Infant Mental Health Journal: Special Issue: Culture*, 27, 603–605.

Taylor, L., Zuckerman, B., Harik, V., & Groves, B. M. (1994). Witnessing violence by young children and their mothers. *Developmental and Behavioral Pediatrics*, 15, 120–123.

Toth, S. L., Maughan, A., Manly, J. T., Spagnola, M. & Cicchetti, D. (2002). The relative efficacy of two interventions in altering maltreated preschool children's representational models: Implications for attachment theory. *Development and psychopathology*, 14(4), 877–908.

Tronick, E. (2007). *The neurobehavioral and social-emotional development of infants and children*. New York: W. W. Norton & Company, Inc.

U.S. Department of Health and Human Services administration on Children, Youth, & Families. (2005). *Child maltreatment*, 2003. Washington, DC: U.S. Government Printing Office.

Van Horn, P., & Lieberman, A. F. (2011). Psychological impact and treatment of children exposed to domestic violence. In C. Jenny (ed.), *Child abuse and neglect: Diagnosis, treatment, and evidence*, pp. 501–515. Philadelphia: Elsevier.

Weinfield, N. S., Sroufe, L. A., & Egeland, B. (2000). Attachment from infancy to early adulthood in a high-risk sample: Continuity, discontinuity, and their correlates. *Child Development*, 71, 695–702.

White, B. P., Gunnar, M. R., Larson, M. C., Donzella, B., & Barr, R. G. (2000). Behavioral and physiological responsivity, and patterns of sleep and daily salivary cortisol in infants with and without colic. *Child Development*, 71, 862–877.

Winnicott, D. W. (1952/1958). Anxiety associated with insecurity. In *Through paediatrics to psycho-analysis*, pp. 97–100. London: Hogarth Press.

Winnicott, D. W. (1969/1989). The mother-infant experience of mutuality. In C. Winnicott, R. Shepherd, & M. Davis (Eds.), *Psycho-analytic explorations*, pp. 251–260. Cambridge, MA: Harvard University Press.

Wolfe, D. A., Crooks, C. V., Lee, V., McIntyre-Smith, A., & Jaffe, P. G. (2003). The effects of children's exposure to domestic violence: A meta-analysis and critique. *Clinical Child and Family Psychology Review*, 6, 171–187.

Yehuda, R., Giller, E. L., Levengood, R. A., Southwick, S. M., & Siever, L. J. (1995). Hypothalamic-pituitary-adrenal functioning in post-traumatic stress disorder: Expanding the concept of the stress response spectrum. In M. J. Friedman, D. S. Charney, & A. Y. Deutch (Eds.), *Neurobiological and clinical consequences of stress: From normal adaptation to post-traumatic stress disorder*, pp. 351–366. New York: Lippincott-Raven Publishers.

Yehuda, R., Giller, E. L., Southwick, S. M., Lowy, M. T., & Mason, J. W. (1991). Hypothalamic – pituitary – adrenal dysfunction in post-traumatic stress disorder. *Biological Psychiatry*, 30, 1031 – 1047.

Zeanah, C. H., & Scheeringa, M. S. (1997). *The experience and effects of violence in infancy*. In J. Osofsky (Ed.), *Children in a violent society*, pp. 97–123. New York, The Guilford Press.

CHAPTER 23

Child Maltreatment

A Pathogenic Relational Environment across Development

Julia Kim-Cohen, Sarah Rabbitt, Jessica S. Henry and Andrea L. Gold

The interplay between person and surround is total and complete, operating on every level. Environment and individual are mutually creating in an ongoing way.

(Sroufe, Egeland, Carlson, & Collins, 2005)

Child maltreatment is defined as an act or failure to act that presents an imminent risk of, or results in, serious harm to minors. The term, maltreatment, encompasses four primary types: neglect, physical abuse, sexual abuse, and emotional abuse that often co-occur (Manly et al., 2001). In addition to this basic definition, maltreatment experiences can also include more common occurrences such as sibling violence, exposure to violence between adults in the family, and severe corporal punishment. Aside from defining acts that constitute neglectful and abusive parenting, we view a maltreating *environment* as a dynamic condition characterizing the family environment over time rather than as an event or a set of isolated events. In line

with Cicchetti and Toth (2005), we conceptualize maltreatment as a "pathogenic relational environment" in which a child is at risk of harm due to a caregiver's failure to provide basic needs for safety, protection, and nurturance. We review the literature as it relates to the antecedents, predictors, and possible causes of child maltreatment and place our emphasis on continuities and discontinuities of abusive and neglectful environments as the parents and children age and develop within contexts that change (or do not change) along with them. Along with abuse, violence, and neglect, children may at times also experience warmth and positive attention from maltreating parents, but the central issue remains parents' abuse of power and control, or inability to act appropriately and control his or her impulses toward the child that lead to harm. Accordingly, we view such pathogenic and often inconsistent characteristics of a parent-child relationship to be at the core of an environment in which children are abused and neglected.

Although maltreatment may be perpetrated by strangers or individuals outside the immediate family, we will limit our discussion to parental maltreatment of children for two reasons. First, maltreatment that occurs within the backdrop of an ongoing relationship with parents is likely to have the greatest psychological significance and impact on the child's development. Second, parents are most frequently identified as the perpetrators of child maltreatment (U.S. Department of Health and Human Services, 2007). In many instances, physical abuse results when parents' efforts to discipline a child by using physical force lead to child harm (Gil, 1973; Kadushin & Martin, 1981). It has been argued that corporal punishment and physical abuse are not distinct, but are two points along a continuum in the cycle of violence (Gershoff, 2002). Thus, although we are primarily concerned with neglectful and abusive environments between parents and children, relevant findings having to do with corporal punishment of children will be incorporated where appropriate.

We will begin by summarizing rates of maltreatment and discussing key theoretical models on the etiology of maltreatment. We then propose a model by which parent and child development may interact over time to increase risk for a maltreating environment. We then review the literature that examines perpetrators' ages when they are most likely to commit abuse and neglect, and some of the reasons why developmental periods in parents' lives and their risk for psychopathology might be associated with risk for maltreatment. Finally, we will cover possible ways in which a maltreating environment is influenced by child characteristics over development, with a focus on child antisocial behavior.

Incidence of Child Abuse and Neglect

Although specific estimates of the incidence of child maltreatment vary depending upon the sampling methods and operational definitions of abuse and neglect, it is clear that large numbers of children are maltreated each year. The most recent national estimates come from the U.S. Department of Health and Human Services, which relies upon data from child protection agencies. In 2007, an alarming 3.5 million children in the U. S. were investigated for maltreatment by child welfare agencies and an estimated 794,000 cases were substantiated (U.S. Department of Health and Human Services, 2007). The majority of these children experienced neglect (59.0 percent); however, an additional 10.8 percent were physically abused, 7.6 percent were sexually abused, and 4.2 percent were emotionally or psychological abused or neglected. These rates present the extent to which each maltreatment type occurs. Somewhat older data available from the most recent National Incidence Study suggest rates of maltreatment as high as 2.3 percent to 4.2 percent each year (Sedlak & Broadhurst, 1996).

Research suggests that the continuity of maltreatment is high. In a sample of disadvantaged families, Pianta, Egeland, and Erickson (1989) found that the recurrence rate of maltreatment was 85 percent from age 1 to age 2 years, and 71 percent from age 1 to age 6 years. When discontinuity in maltreatment occurred in this sample, it appeared to be largely explained by the fact that children had moved into the care of other family members or had been adopted. Consequently, the estimates of recurrence, although high, actually could have been an underestimate. In a more recent, state-wide sample, the rate of re-referral to child welfare agencies was 40 percent within a 4-year period (Connell et al., 2007). Also, a nationally representative survey of youth victimization found that 36 percent of children maltreated in one year were maltreated again the following year (Finkelhor et al., 2007). However, other data show rates of recurrence to be lower, in the range of 15 percent to 20 percent over a 1-year period (Fluke et al., 1999). Taken together, these statistics indicate that maltreatment affects large numbers of children and that a significant proportion of maltreated children may be at risk of re-victimization.

Models for Understanding the Etiology of Child Maltreatment

A maltreating environment is a complex system that is multiply determined. Two complementary theoretical models have contributed substantially to the field's understanding of the causes of maltreatment: Belsky's (1980; 1993) social-contextual process model and Cicchetti and colleagues' ecological-transactional model (Cicchetti & Rizely, 1981; Cicchetti & Lynch, 1993; Cicchetti & Toth, 2005). After briefly describing each model, our goal is to propose an integration and extension of these etiological models by exploring ways in which the predictors of maltreatment change across the individual development of parents and children.

According to Belsky (1980; 1993), parental functioning – and malfunctioning in the case of maltreatment – emerges from the confluence of three broad categories of contributors to a relational environment. First, a parent's contributions to maltreatment risk consist of all of the dimensions that make her who she is beginning from the moment her child is conceived.[1] Her own childhood experiences of having been parented, her cognitive, emotional and social capacities, her personality, and history of psychopathology all shape her ability to function as a parent. Second, the child's characteristics play a role in the quality of the relational environment. At the outset, we must be clear that children alone do not cause their own maltreatment. As Belsky (1980) noted, "characteristics of the child make sense as elicitors for maltreatment only when considered vis-à-vis the caregiver's attributes" (p. 324). We recognize that children are not merely passive recipients of the world around them. Instead, they can influence the ways in which they are treated by others in their environment, including their caregivers. Third, contextual sources of stress and support influence the type and degree of demands that are made upon the parenting system. Belsky (1993) specifies that the qualities of the marital/romantic partnership, social network functioning, and

occupational experiences influence a parent's general well-being, which determines her ability to respond appropriately and adequately to her child. In addition, demographic variables such as single parenthood, parental age, a large family size, and low family income have been consistently linked to risk for child maltreatment (Cicchetti & Toth, 2005). Belsky (1980; 1993) underscores the fact that the parenting outcome is likely to result not from just one factor or from factors within just one broad category of determinants. Instead, the type and quality of parenting depend upon the dynamic interplay among all of the aforementioned factors.

In a similar but somewhat different fashion, Cicchetti and colleagues (Cicchetti & Rizely, 1981; Cicchetti & Lynch, 1993; Cicchetti & Toth, 2005) have conceptualized the risk for maltreatment as emerging from a balance of *potentiating or risk factors* that increase the likelihood of maltreatment and *compensatory or protective factors* that decrease the likelihood of maltreatment. Parental, child, and contextual characteristics, as discussed in Belsky's (1980; 1993) model, can be the source of both potentiating and compensatory factors that cut across multiple levels of analysis ranging from the biological (e.g., child's physical health problems or difficult temperament), historical (e.g., parents' history of having been maltreated as a child), psychological (e.g., parental personality or psychopathology), sociocultural (e.g., cultural attitudes toward childrearing practices), and situational (e.g., poverty, poor occupational opportunities). Moreover, potentiating and compensatory factors vary across a temporal dimension, in which some factors are thought to be stable and enduring over time and others are more transient and temporally limited. Cicchetti and Rizely's (1981) original formulation specified that the entire balance of factors that impinge upon risk for maltreatment and their transaction must be examined *over time*.

These two explanatory models of maltreatment risk have several overlapping principles. For instance, both models view

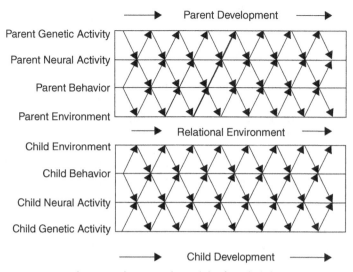

Figure 23.1. The metatheoretical model of probabilistic epigenesis views individual development as emerging from interactive influences over four levels of analysis: genetic activity, neural activity, behavior, and the environment (i.e., physical, social, and cultural). This modified model illustrates how the relational environment develops as child development and parent development each progress over time in interaction with multiple, bidirectional influences. (Adapted from Gottlieb 1998, 2007.)

parenting to be determined by the relative balance of risk and protective factors experienced by a given family. Both recognize multiple pathways by which individual (parent or child characteristics), historical (parent development), and social factors and processes combine to shape parental functioning. Both models view maltreatment as resulting from a dynamic, interactive process between parenting stresses, sometimes having to do directly with the child, and supports that bolster a parent's ability to cope positively. However, although both models imply that a maltreating environment develops over time, neither model speaks directly to the process by which this development may occur.

In conceptualizing the development of a maltreating environment, we apply the metatheoretical model of probabilistic epigenesis formulated by Gottlieb (1998; 2007). According to probabilistic epigenesis, individual development results from the completely bidirectional influences occurring within and between four broad levels

of analysis over time: genetic activity, neural activity, behavior, and the environment (Figure 23.1). This model argues against a common and prevailing notion that development originates in DNA and emerges deterministically and unidirectionally. Instead, it posits that development is an interactive process by which genes can influence brain development, behavior, and environmental characteristics, but at any point, genetic activity may also be influenced by neural activity, behavior, and the environment. Although Gottlieb's model is concerned primarily with the development of the individual, we extend its application toward understanding the development of the relational environment. For example, this model may be used to illustrate a family context in which multiple individuals, including caregivers, the target child, and siblings, are each undergoing their own developmental changes as a result of the dynamic interaction of their own genetic and neural makeup and behaviors over time. As parents and children mature, the contributions they bring to the family environment change according to the developmental issues that are salient to each individual. Conversely, the evolving family environment – whether typical or maltreating – influences how parents' and children's own ontogeny unfolds. In other words, the person and environment mutually influence one another over time, as Sroufe and colleagues (2005) have emphasized.

Parent and Child Development in Interaction

Despite interest in the possible role that parent age and child age might play in influencing rates and risk for maltreatment, as well as the wide acknowledgement that parenting tasks differ for children of different developmental periods, we know of no studies that have specifically documented how abusive and neglectful behavior changes according to the interplay between parent and child development. The few studies that have examined developmental and age effects on modifying parenting behavior tend to vary parent age while all children in the study are the same in age or developmental period, and to focus on parenting within the normal range (e.g., Bornstein et al., 2006; Bornstein & Putnick, 2007; Paikoff & Brooks-Gunn, 1991). Empirical studies have tended not to analyze how parent and child development dynamically and mutually influence the emerging relational environment and influence risk for maltreatment, perhaps because of the greater complexity such a model would involve.

Conceptually, it is logical to consider both parent and child development together because both change and mature over time. In Figure 23.2, we have illustrated how child developmental stages come together with parent developmental stages depending upon the age at which parents give birth. Parents were classified into three groups. First, adult parents who delay childbearing until they have reached adulthood experience, as adults, the varying demands and challenges presented by their children across all developmental periods from infancy

to adolescence. In the United States, the median maternal age at first birth, which has increased steadily in the past three decades, is approximately 25 years (Mathews & Hamilton, 2009). Although adults themselves may experience their own developmental changes, their psychological development is a relatively more stable and constant backdrop in which the more dramatic developmental changes in their growing children can unfold. Second, young adult parents are those who have children during the "emerging adulthood" years between ages 18–25. In the past, childbearing at this age period was more typical than in contemporary Western societies where there has been a trend toward postponing marriage and parenthood (Arnett, 2000). Instead of starting families, emerging adults tend to be more focused on self-development and exploration of many possible life paths. When parenthood is initiated during this stage, young adult parents are faced with children in the infancy to school-age periods before many of the parents mature into adulthood and establish relatively more stable lives. Third, for parents who have children during their adolescent years, their children are infants and preschoolers before the parents age-out of their own teen development. When these parents move into their young adult period (a time of self-focus and self-exploration, as mentioned earlier), their children are correspondingly moving through their school-age and adolescent development. This point, albeit a somewhat obvious one, illustrates how developmental stages of parents and children come together and change together over time to potentiate or protect against risk for abuse and neglect. For instance, parenting an aggressive child can be challenging to even mature, experienced caregivers; however, high rates of aggressive behavior that are common in very young children (Tremblay et al., 2004) may bestow exceptional parenting difficulties upon parents who are coping with the developmental demands of their own adolescence or emerging adulthood.

Finally, it is important to keep in mind that as parents grow older, they are likely

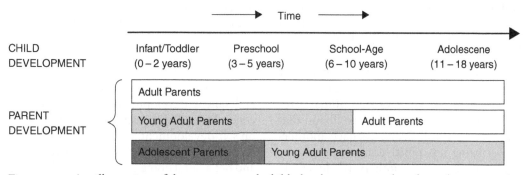

Figure 23.2. An illustration of how parent and child development overlap depending upon the developmental period during which parents first take on the parenting role.

to have more children, which raises two implications for the development of a maltreating environment. First, a larger number of children in the family is associated with a greater risk of maltreatment (Chaffin, Kelleher, & Hollenberg, 1996; Kotch et al., 1995). Second, with more than one child, parents must face not only an increased quantity of parenting demands, but must also simultaneously negotiate demands from children in different developmental stages (e.g., infancy and toddlerhood). Most parents in this situation cope well and derive much enjoyment and satisfaction from caring for their children, but in situations of low support and increased parenting stress because of multiple children in the home, the risk of maltreatment can increase.

Parent Development and Risk for Child Maltreatment

Parents are the most common perpetrators of maltreatment. In 2007, nearly 74 percent of identified perpetrators were parents of the victims (U.S. Department of Health and Human Services, 2007). Approximately 38.7 percent of child victims were maltreated by their mothers, 17.9 percent were maltreated by their fathers, and 16.8 percent were maltreated by both parents. In this section, we discuss how parental development and psychopathology over the life span may influence the likelihood of a maltreating environment.

Is Young Parental Age Associated with Increased Risk for Child Maltreatment?

In 2002 in the United States, approximately 425,000 babies were born to mothers between the ages of 15 and 19 years (Ventura, Abma, Mosher, & Henshaw, 2006), one of the highest rates of all developed nations. Although not all studies agree (e.g., Kinard, 2003), most of the available evidence suggests that young parental age is associated with an elevated risk for suboptimal parenting and child maltreatment. For instance, Canadian data have shown that as parental age increases, the risk for child neglect significantly decreases (Wekerle et al., 2007). Additionally, several researchers have shown that both younger age at first birth (Bolton et al., 1980; Connelly & Straus, 1992; George & Lee, 1997; Moffitt & The E-Risk Study Team, 2002) and younger age at the time of abuse (Benedict et al., 1985; Sidebotham & Golding, 2001) are reliably associated with higher rates of abuse and neglect. In the Environmental Risk (E-Risk) Longitudinal Twin Study (Moffitt & The E-Risk Study Team, 2002), parenting quality was compared between young mothers who were 20 years old or younger when they gave birth to their first child versus older mothers who delayed childbearing beyond age 20. At the time of the study, young mothers were, on average, 30 years old, and were significantly younger than the older mothers who were, on average, 36 years old. Despite the fact that the young mothers were well into their adulthood at the time of the study, the children of young mothers were at more than double the risk of being maltreated and placed in foster care (Moffitt & The E-Risk Study Team, 2002).

In addition to risk for maltreatment, per se, young parents are relatively more likely to engage in the kinds of suboptimal caregiving that may increase the likelihood that maltreatment will occur. Teenage mothers report being less positive about pregnancy than nonadolescent mothers (Culp et al., 1988) and rate themselves as being less satisfied with their parental roles than older parents (Ragozin et al., 1982). Young, first-time mothers also display less positive affect when interacting with their 4-month-old infants (Ragozin et al., 1982) and, by the time children are 14 months old, young mothers are observed to be less supportive, more detached, and more hostile in parent-child interactions (Berlin et al., 2002). In a sample of parents who ranged in age from 15–27 years at their child's birth, younger parents engaged in relatively more harsh and inconsistent parenting, even after psychiatric history and family-of-origin characteristics had been controlled (Jaffee et al., 2006). Younger parents are also more likely to use corporal punishment (Straus & Moynihan, 1994; Wolfner & Gelles, 1993), and to use it more frequently than older parents (Culp et al., 1999).

The association between teen parenthood and suboptimal parenting likely arises for at least two reasons. First, given the challenges that typically characterize adolescence, it should not be surprising that being a parent during this developmental period is generally associated with an increased risk for suboptimal parenting. Although approximately 80 percent of teenagers are thought to weather the "storm and stress" of adolescent development adequately with few or no major problems (Arnett, 1999), adolescence is a time when youths are at a substantially increased risk for morbidity and mortality because reckless, high-risk, and sensation-seeking behaviors that intensify emotional arousal are relatively more common (Dahl, 2004; Steinberg, 2007). Adolescence has been defined as "that awkward period between

sexual maturation and the attainment of adult roles and responsibilities" (Dahl, 2004, p. 9). Thus, adolescents who are faced with parenting responsibilities in contemporary Western societies are developmentally out-of-sync with the typical role expectations and salient developmental tasks of adolescence. Instead of focusing personal resources on self-development and enhancing competencies in academic or occupational, social, and behavioral domains (Masten et al., 1999), teenage parents must tend to the sometimes unpredictable needs and demands of their young offspring, which for many adolescent parents can be an overwhelming task that leads to frustration. Moreover, adolescent parenthood can curtail educational attainment and future occupational prospects, which set in motion a trajectory toward lasting adversity associated with socioeconomic disadvantage (Moffitt & The E-Risk Study Team, 2002).

Second, as indicated by the data demonstrating links between parental age at first birth and risk for maltreatment, factors that help explain why some teenage girls become pregnant may also explain why they have parenting difficulties. Teenage parenthood is associated with individual characteristics, such as impulsivity and poor planning ability, as well as greater socioeconomic disadvantage and family-of-origin adversities. Teenage mothers, relative to older parents, have fewer educational opportunities, poorer academic records, higher rates of unemployment and poverty, and less social support (Furstenberg et al., 1989) – factors that are known to increase the risk of maltreatment. The risk of teen parenting is associated with a history of sexual abuse, and personality disturbances or psychopathology, which can have enduring effects on functioning beyond the adolescent years (Roberts et al., 2004). Despite increased risk for maltreatment among children of young mothers, it is also imperative to note that most young parents do not maltreat their children (Sidebotham & Golding, 2001).

Parenting difficulties are not necessarily restricted to the adolescent period of the parents' life span. Although older mothers are generally considered to be at an advantage because of both greater maturity and better resources (e.g., education, income), it is also plausible that women bearing children later in life face challenges, such as health problems, that would interfere with optimal parenting (e.g., Mirowsky, 2002). In fact, recent studies indicate that some parenting behaviors improve throughout early adulthood (e.g., knowledge about parenting, parental satisfaction, limit setting, sensitivity) but then plateau around the age of 30 (Bornstein & Putnick, 2007). However, the effectiveness of some parenting behaviors demonstrates an inverted U-shaped curve with age. Specifically, in one study, the provision of a stimulating environment for infants was better for mothers in the middle of the age continuum, but significantly lower among both younger and older mothers (Bornstein et al., 2006).

How Does the Development of Parental Psychopathology Influence Risk for Maltreatment?

As parents grow older, their risk for abusing or neglecting their children may change in relation to their relative risks for developing various forms of psychopathology. Initially, when the phenomenon of child abuse came to public attention in the mid-20th century, it was believed that only mentally ill parents could be capable of causing serious physical harm to their children (Kempe & Kempe, 1978). The research evidence, however, revealed that parental psychopathology was involved in no more than 10 percent of physical abuse cases (Kempe & Kempe, 1978). Still, psychopathology, especially major depression, antisocial behavior, and substance abuse, in parents is associated with a significantly elevated risk for child neglect and abuse (Chaffin et al., 1996; Kim-Cohen et al., 2006).

A fairly large number of parents meet criteria for a psychiatric illness. Large-scale epidemiological studies indicate that almost half of the population will meet criteria for a psychiatric diagnosis over the course of their lifetime (Kessler et al., 2005).

Furthermore, many of these disorders onset by adolescence and the majority emerge before early adulthood (Kim-Cohen et al., 2003). Integrating these findings with the data on parental age, it is clear that by the time that most people become parents in their 20s, the individuals who are going to meet criteria for psychopathology already show psychiatric symptoms.

Parental psychopathology can compromise the quality of parenting in a number of ways, depending on several factors including the specific disorder, environmental supports and stressors, and the developmental stage of the child. For example, mothers meeting criteria for major depressive disorder (MDD) may, as a result of their low mood, lack of interest in activities, sadness, fatigue, or other symptoms, provide less social stimulation and expose their toddlers to fewer social situations. This may translate to a lack of interpersonal skills and social competence in the child's early school years (Zahn-Waxler et al., 2002). However, given the large number of people affected by mental illness, it is clear that most parental psychopathology is not associated with child abuse and neglect. Thus, the goal of this discussion is to focus on the particular circumstances in which poor parenting and maltreatment co-occur with parental psychopathology.

MAJOR DEPRESSION

There are two epidemiological patterns regarding major depressive disorder that have implications for understanding parental psychopathology and the development of a suboptimal parenting environment. First, females are twice as likely as males to meet diagnostic criteria for MDD (Hankin et al., 1998; Nolen-Hoeksema, 2002). Second, the rates of MDD in females rise dramatically in adolescence and remain elevated throughout the child-bearing years (Hankin et al., 1998). Some estimates show that up to a third of all women in their 20s and 30s meet diagnostic criteria for major depression (Kendler et al., 2003) and the presence of maternal depression has been shown to impair a parent's ability to adequately and appropriately care for her children. Depressed mothers have been shown to express more hostile, critical, and rejecting attitudes toward their children (e.g., Goodman & Gotlib, 1999; Goodman & Gotlib, 2002; Johnson et al., 2001; Radke-Yarrow, 1998). Even when an episode of major depression remits, a lifetime history of depression in mothers is associated with impaired parenting (Stein et al., 1991). Most depressed mothers do not maltreat their children. However, children of depressed mothers may be at elevated risk of exposure to a maltreating environment as a function of their mothers' depression (Kim-Cohen et al., 2006a).

ANTISOCIAL BEHAVIOR

Research on the development of antisocial behavior indicates that nearly all females who engage in antisocial behavior onset in adolescence and tend to have a variety of negative adult outcomes (Moffitt et al., 2001), which has implications for their functioning once they become parents. An adolescent history of conduct disorder is associated with greater socioeconomic disadvantage and more domestic violence compared with those with no psychiatric history or parents with a history of anxiety or depression (Jaffee et al., 2006). One study of a community sample of mothers and fathers found that parental personality disorders, including antisocial personality disorder (ASPD), were the most prevalent form of psychopathology in families where parents engaged in high numbers of maladaptive child rearing practices (Johnson et al., 2006). Antisocial women might be more likely to partner and mate with antisocial men, a phenomenon known as assortative mating (Krueger et al., 1998). In this way, children of antisocial parents may receive a "double dose" of the negative caregiving environment associated with ASPD as they are more likely to have both parents with disordered personalities (Kim-Cohen et al., 2006a).

Indeed, this is a valid concern given that several studies document poorer parenting in antisocial adults. In a study of children at 13 and 24 months of age, antisocial mothers were observed to be less understanding of toddler behavior than other mothers (Bosquet & Egeland, 2000). They also used more coercive parenting and shamed their children more frequently. Even mothers with subclinical antisocial characteristics (1 or more antisocial characteristic) have been shown to be less warm in parent-child interactions and more likely to maltreat their children compared with mothers without antisocial characteristics (Kim-Cohen et al., 2006a).

As discussed earlier, both parental depression and a history of antisocial behavior have independently been linked with a greater likelihood of child abuse and neglect, but in mothers, it appears to be the combination of the two that is associated with the highest risk for child maltreatment (Kim-Cohen, 2006; Kim-Cohen et al., 2006a). In a large cohort of British families, Kim-Cohen and colleagues (2006a) found that whereas the rate of probable or definite child maltreatment was 10 percent in "control" mothers with no depression and antisocial history, the rates were 19.4 percent and 16.2 percent in depressed-only or antisocial-only mothers, respectively. Strikingly, in the subset of mothers with both depression and a lifetime history of one or more symptoms of ASPD, the rate of probable or definite maltreatment was nearly 34 percent.

SUBSTANCE ABUSE

Substance use disorders typically onset between the ages of 18 and 27 years, with a median age of onset at 20 years (Kessler et al., 2005), which overlaps with prime childbearing years (Mathews & Hamilton, 2009). When substance use problems onset early in life, they are associated with greater severity. For instance, individuals who start drinking before the age of 15 are four times more likely to meet criteria for alcohol dependence than people who have their first drink at age 20 years or older (Grant & Dawson, 1997). For drug use disorders, early onset before age 18 years is associated with a significantly higher risk for comorbid personality disorders (Franken & Hendriks, 2000).

Substance abuse negatively affects parenting capacity through a number of different pathways, both direct and indirect. The effects of substances such as alcohol, marijuana, heroin and anxiolytics can lead to depressed mood, withdrawal, and memory impairment. Stimulants and amphetamines can cause poor affect regulation, impulse control problems, and irritability (Mayes & Truman, 2002). In both cases, parents may neglect major responsibilities, including child care, because of drug effects and the amount of time and effort involved in securing it. Particularly with illegal substances, addicted parents are more likely to be arrested and, consequently, separated from their children for prolonged periods (Haugaard & Hazan, 2003). Further complicating the situation is the frequent co-occurrence of substance use disorders with other psychiatric diagnoses and personality disorders (Hans et al., 1999; Regier et al., 1990). Substance abusing parents may represent a particularly psychologically impaired group, which may further compromise their parenting.

Substance abusing parents often hold misinformed or inappropriate attitudes about their children and may engage in a number of negative parenting behaviors. In terms of knowledge about parenting, mothers with substance use problems overestimate their children's abilities and show a lack of understanding of child development (Seagull et al., 1996). With regard to specific behavior, drug-abusing mothers engage in less positive behavior during mother-child interactions (Bernstein et al., 1986) and are observed as less enthusiastic and joyful when directly interacting with their infants (Burns et al., 1997). Furthermore, mothers with current or past substance use problems are more likely to engage in punitive behavior with their children (Miller et al., 1999). Studies also indicate that mothers with drug and alcohol problems engage in extreme criticism and yelling (Tucker, 1979).

In terms of maltreatment specifically, substance-abusing mothers are more likely to engage in physical abuse and neglect than mothers who do not have problems with drug and alcohol abuse. In a large, Canadian epidemiological sample, substance abuse by the caregiver was the single, strongest predictor of child maltreatment substantiation (Wekerle et al., 2007). As many as 22.5 percent of children living with alcoholic and opiate-addicted parents experience physical or sexual abuse and 41 percent experience neglect (Black & Mayer, 1980). Additionally, even greater risk for both physical abuse and neglect is seen in households in which both parents have a substance problem (Dube et al., 2001). It remains possible that substance-abusing parents increase the maltreatment risk by exposing their children to not only one, but two parents with compromised parenting abilities.

Child Development and Risk for Child Maltreatment

Although children by themselves cannot cause their own maltreatment to occur, they can contribute to the balance of potentiating and compensatory factors that influence maltreatment risk in the context of a relational environment that develops with their primary caregivers. For instance, low birth weight, poor health, and other developmental problems in infancy are associated with an elevated risk for maltreatment (Sidebotham et al., 2003). As both Cicchetti and colleagues (Cicchetti & Rizely, 1981; Cicchetti & Lynch, 1993; Cicchetti & Toth, 2005) and Belsky (1980) have pointed out, children's characteristics interact with parental and contextual variables to influence the degree to which abuse or neglect is likely to occur. This is logical given that maltreatment occurs as an "interactional" process between children and parents both embedded within a context. In this section, we review the literature on child effects on risk for maltreatment and suboptimal parenting, with an emphasis on how potentiating and protective effects may change along with the developmental trends in child antisocial behavior. But first, we begin by describing rates of maltreatment and harsh parenting by child age.

What Is the Incidence of Maltreatment by Child Age?

The evidence regarding child age and risk for various forms of maltreatment is somewhat inconsistent. According to national estimates of indicated maltreatment cases, rates of child abuse and neglect are generally highest for the youngest children and are inversely correlated with child age. This is due, in large part, to the fact that neglect is the most common form of maltreatment and occurs most frequently among infants and young children (U.S. Department of Health and Human Services, 2007). Except for sexual abuse, children ages 0–3 represented the largest age group experiencing victimization in 2007 compared to children ages 4–7, 8–11, 12–15, and 16–17 years. In the youngest age group, children under 1 year were at greatest risk of experiencing neglect and physical abuse (U.S. Department of Health and Human Services, 2007). However, an older national survey of family violence found that children ages 3–6 years were at greatest risk of physical violence, followed by children ages 7–12 years (Wolfner & Gelles, 1993). In a large, Canadian sample, older children were at increased risk for physical and sexual abuse substantiation (Wekerle et al., 2007). Other studies have reported no association between child age and risk for child maltreatment (Ammerman & Patz, 1996; Connelly & Straus, 1992).

Few studies have reported associations between child age and risk for maltreatment recurrence. Based on the available data, young children seem to be at relatively greater risk of experiencing a recurrence of maltreatment or suspected maltreatment. For instance, in one study, infants were at significantly elevated risk for a re-referral to authorities compared to children between the ages of 6–17 years (Connell et al., 2007). Older children may be less likely than younger children to experience maltreatment recurrence, in part, because they have relatively less time before gaining independence from their maltreating families (Connell et al., 2007; Fluke et al., 1999).

Child age is also associated with risk for corporal punishment, which elevates the risk that physical abuse might occur. Rates of corporal punishment are most common among preschool-aged children and decline with age as children grow older until rates drop off steeply in adolescence (for a review, see Gershoff, 2002). In a nationally representative telephone survey of 1,000 U.S. parents, Jackson and colleagues (1999) found that parents of younger children reported using more physical discipline, whereas parents of older children reported using more nonphysical discipline but also more verbal abuse, such as swearing. In line with this observation, a national survey conducted by the Gallup Organization found that younger children were not only more likely than older children to be physically punished, but they were also punished more frequently (Dietz, 2000).

In general, it appears that the youngest children are at highest risk of experiencing neglect, whereas physical abuse becomes a greater risk for children in their preschool and school-age years. Based on the evidence demonstrating that risk for maltreatment is not evenly distributed across children of all ages, it is likely that various changes across children's development may influence the likelihood that parents might maltreat them.

What Are Possible Reasons Why Child Age May Be Associated with Risk for Maltreatment?

There are several possible explanations behind age trends associated with child victimization. First, as noted earlier, physical force tends to be used more often against younger vs. older children (Jackson et al., 1999; Gershoff, 2002). Second, younger children spend more time with their caregivers than do older children who have entered school and spend more time with peers and in extracurricular activities. Third, younger children are physically more vulnerable than older children and are therefore, more prone to injury, which increases the likelihood that attention will be drawn to the child and a case will be officially substantiated. In addition to these possibilities, we briefly focus our review on a specific domain of child development that may influence how a physically maltreating environment can change over time: children's antisocial behavior.

Developmental Trends in Antisocial Behavior

In a longitudinal Canadian study, Tremblay and colleagues (2004) found that the earliest displays of physical aggression occur in the first year of life, although at relatively low rates. Through the toddler years, physically aggressive behaviors, including hitting, kicking, and biting, increase and reach their peak frequency in children between 24 and 42 months of age. Close to 50 percent of boys and 40 percent of girls engaged in physical aggression in the toddler period (Tremblay et al., 2004). These rates decline over childhood but two important points deserve consideration. First, aggressive behaviors remain elevated until children reach school age, with as many as 30 percent of children engaging in aggressive behavior at 5 years of age (Tremblay et al., 2004). Second, continuities in these negative behaviors are frequent. That is, the children who engage in aggressive behavior as toddlers are likely to engage in aggressive behavior over time (e.g., Keenan & Shaw, 1994).

Longitudinal epidemiological research has identified adolescence as another developmental period during which antisocial behaviors are especially salient. In adolescence, there is a dramatic increase in rates of delinquency and aggressive behaviors associated with a "maturity gap" when teenagers grow tired of their dependent status, demonstrate a greater sense of autonomy from their parents, and wish to try on adult roles and responsibilities before they have legal sanction to do so (Moffitt, 1993; Moffitt, 2003). The increase in antisocial behaviors during adolescence is thought to be a common occurrence, but it can nonetheless introduce new challenges for parents. Although many parents are able to weather these challenges

successfully, some parents may respond to their adolescents' defiant, rule-breaking behavior by utilizing harsh, negative control strategies that, in some instances, can cross the boundary into physically and emotionally abusive behavior.

Does Youth Antisocial Behavior Influence Risk for Physical Maltreatment?

Although parenting research has traditionally focused on the effects that parents have on children's developmental outcomes, research in the past several decades has demonstrated that children can affect the ways in which their parents treat them (Anderson et al., 1986; Bell, 1968; Kandel & Wu, 1995; O'Connor, 2002). In relation to antisocial behavior, researchers have identified coercive processes by which parents and children dynamically influence each other's behavior in a mutual, reciprocal fashion (Reid et al., 2002). Some of the strongest evidence for this comes from adoption studies that are able to control for a potential genetic confound presented by the fact that biological family members share both genes and an environment. In one study by Ge and colleagues (1996), adolescent adoptees who were presumed to be at risk for antisocial behavior on the basis of biological parent psychopathology were more likely than adoptees with no inherited risk for antisocial behavior to elicit harsh, negative parenting from their adoptive mothers. In another study by O'Connor and colleagues (1998), adopted children who had an inherited risk for externalizing problems elicited efforts to control behavior using hostility, guilt, and withdrawal from their adoptive parents. These examples, along with other research that finds heritable influences for both children's antisocial behavior (Arseneault et al., 2003; Rhee & Waldman, 2002) and for various measures of parenting (O'Connor, 2002; Reiss et al., 2000) have lead to speculation regarding whether children's genetically influenced traits might evoke maltreatment from parents.

To date, we are aware of only two studies that have directly addressed this proposition, both using data from the E-Risk Longitudinal Twin Study. First, Jaffee and colleagues (2004) found that whereas corporal punishment by parents showed some evidence of child genetic influences, physical maltreatment showed no significant genetic influences. Although they found that the covariation between children's antisocial behavior and corporal punishment was accounted for in large part by shared genetic influences, which suggests a genetically mediated child effect, this explanation did not apply to physical maltreatment. Instead, the reasons why some children are maltreated while others are not appear to be explained primarily by factors that differ between families, such as parental characteristics or contextual variables. As discussed earlier, the use of corporal punishment is linked to an increased risk for abuse. In Jaffee and colleagues' (2004) study, having been corporally punished was associated with a 2.5-fold increased risk for also having been physically maltreated. Thus, it is possible that if there are child effects on risk for maltreatment, it perhaps operates indirectly via children's behavior problems that may increase parents' use of physical discipline.

In another study, Kim-Cohen and colleagues (2006b) tested for a possible evocative gene-environment correlation having to do with a gene that encodes monoamine oxidase A (MAOA), an enzyme that selectively metabolizes serotonin, dopamine, and norepinephrine. The MAOA gene is of special interest because it has been shown to moderate the association between physical maltreatment experience and risk for antisocial behavior (Caspi et al., 2002; Foley et al., 2004; Taylor & Kim-Cohen, 2007). However, variants in the MAOA gene did not significantly predict differences in lifetime rates of physical maltreatment in 7-year-old boys (Kim-Cohen et al., 2006b), indicating that a specific gene associated with risk for antisocial behavior does not also elicit physical maltreatment from parents. Thus, the little evidence available to date rules-out the possibility that physical maltreatment is driven by children's genes or genetically influenced behavior problems. Further research is needed to replicate the findings from these two studies in older samples, with both sexes, with other candidate genes, and with regard to other types of maltreatment.

Conclusion

The notion of maltreatment as a relational environment is not new, and neither is the view that it is dynamic and subject to change over time (Belsky, 1993; Cicchetti & Toth, 2005). However, few studies have been conducted that empirically model the contributions of both parental and child development to a maltreating environment. Instead, most studies have focused on the age of the parent or the age of the child in association with maltreatment risk, yet there are limitations to focusing only on chronological age. As Rutter (1989) has aptly pointed out, age as a variable provides the most meaningful information when broken down into its components, such as cognitive level, type of life experiences, or number of life experiences. Along these lines, parental age can also be quantified in terms of maturity (Belsky & Vondra, 1989), both psychological and cognitive. In this sense, the key factor is the emotional, social, and cognitive maturation of the parent, rather than his or her chronological age. Understanding these developmental processes may advance meaningful explanations of how parent and child development relate to parenting outcomes in general, and to the development of a maltreating environment, in particular.

Notes

1   Although parent characteristics refer to both mothers and fathers, we use the feminine pronoun here because mothers typically spend more time than fathers caring for children.

References

Ammerman, R.T. & Patz, R. J. (1996). Determinants of child abuse potential: Contribution of parent and child factors. *Journal of Clinical Child Psychology*, 25, 300–307.

Anderson, K. E., Lytton, H., & Romney, D. M. (1986). Mothers' interactions with normal and conduct-disordered boys: Who affects whom? *Developmental Psychology*, 604–609.

Arnett, J. J. (1999). Adolescent storm and stress, reconsidered. *American Psychologist*, 54, 317–326.

Arnett, J. J. (2000). Emerging adulthood: A theory of development from the late teens through the twenties. *American Psychologist*, 55, 469–480.

Arseneault, L., Moffitt, T. E., Caspi, A., Taylor, A., Rijsdijk, F. V., Jaffee, S. R. et al. (2003). Strong genetic effects on cross-situational antisocial behaviour among 5-year-old children according to mothers, teachers, examiner-observers, and twins' self-reports. *Journal of Child Psychology and Psychiatry*, 832–848.

Bell, R. (1968). A reinterpretation of the direction of effects in studies of socialization. *Psychological Review*, 75, 81–95.

Belsky, J. (1980). Child maltreatment: An ecological integration. *American Psychologist*, 35, 320–335.

Belsky, J. (1993). Etiology of child maltreatment: A developmental ecological analysis. *Psychological Bulletin*, 114, 413–434.

Belsky, J. & Vondra, J. (1989). Lessons from child abuse: The determinants of parenting. In D. Cicchetti & V. Carlson (Eds.), *Child maltreatment: Theory and research on the causes and consequences of child abuse and neglect*, pp. 153–202. New York: Cambridge University Press.

Benedict, M. I., White, R. B., & Cornely, D. A. (1985). Maternal perinatal risk factors and child abuse. *Child Abuse & Neglect*, 9, 217–224.

Berlin, L. J., Brady-Smith, C., & Brooks-Gunn, J. (2002). Links between childbearing age and observed maternal behaviors with 14-month-olds in early Head Start research and evaluation program. *Infant Mental Health Journal*, 23, 104–129.

Bernstein, V. J., Jeruchimovicz, J. R., & Marcus, J. (1986). Mother-infant interaction in multiproblem families: Finding those at risk. *Journal of the American Academy of Child & Adolescent Psychiatry*, 25, 631–640.

Black, R. & Mayer, J. (1980). Parents with special problems: Alcoholism and opiate addiction. *Child Abuse & Neglect*, 4, 45–54.

Bolton, F. G., Laner, R. H., & Kane, S. P. (1980). Child maltreatment risk among adolescent mothers: A study of reported cases. *American Journal of Orthopsychiatry*, 60, 489–504.

Bornstein, M. H. & Putnick, D. L. (2007). Chronological age, cognitions, and practices in European American mothers: A multivariate study of parenting. *Developmental Psychology*, 43, 850–864.

Bornstein, M. H., Putnick, D. L., Suwalsky, J. T. D., & Gini, M. (2006). Maternal chronological age, prenatal and perinatal history, social support, and parenting of infants. *Child Development*, 77, 875–892.

Bosquet, M. & Egeland, B. (2000). Predicting parenting behaviors from Antisocial Practices content scale scores of the MMPI-2 administered during pregnancy. *Journal of Personality Disorders*, 74, 146–162.

Burns, K. A., Chetnik, L., Burns, W. J., & Clark, R. (1997). The early relationship of drug abusing mothers and their infants: an assessment at eight to twelve months of age. *Journal of Clinical Psychology*, 3, 279–287.

Caspi, A., McClay, J., Moffitt, T. E., Mill, J., Martin, J., Craig, I. W. et al. (2002). Role of genotype in the cycle of violence in maltreated children. *Science*, 297, 851–854.

Chaffin, M., Kelleher, K., & Hollenberg, J. (1996). Onset of physical abuse and neglect: Psychiatric, substance abuse, and social risk factors from prospective community data. *Child Abuse & Neglect*, 20, 191–203.

Cicchetti, D. & Lynch, M. (1993). Toward an ecological/transactional model of community violence and child maltreatment: Consequences for children's development. *Psychiatry*, 56, 96–118.

Cicchetti, D. & Rizely, R. (1981). Developmental perspectives on the etiology, intergenerational transmission, and sequelae of child maltreatment. *New Directions of Child Development*, 11, 31–55.

Cicchetti, D. & Toth, S. L. (2005). Child maltreatment. *Annual Review of Clinical Psychology*.

Connell, C. M., Bergeron, N., Katz, K. H., Saunders, L., & Tebes, J. K. (2007). Re-referral to child protective services: The influence of child, family, and case characteristics on risk status. *Child Abuse & Neglect*, 31, 573–588.

Connelly, C. D. & Straus, M. A. (1992). Mother's age and risk for physical abuse. *Child Abuse & Neglect*, 16, 709–718.

Culp, R. E., Appelbaum, M. I., Osofsky, J. D., & Levy, J. A. (1988). Adolescent and older mothers: Comparison between prenatal maternal variables and newborn interaction measures. *Infant Behavior and Mental Health*, 11, 353–362.

Culp, R. E., Culp, A. M., Dengler, B., & Maisano, P. C. (1999). First-time young mothers living in rural communities use corporal punishment with their toddlers. *Journal of Community Psychology*, 27, 503–509.

Dahl, R. E. (2004). Adolescent brain development: A period of vulnerabilities and opportunities. *Annals of the ew York Academy of Sciences*, 1021, 1–22.

Dietz, T. L. (2000). Disciplining children: Characteristics associated with the use of corporal punishment. *Child Abuse & Neglect*, 24, 1529–1542.

Dube, S. R., Anda, R. F., Felitti, V. J., Croft, J. B., Edwards, V. J., & Giles, W. H. (2001). Growing up with parental alcohol abuse: exposure to childhood abuse, neglect, and household dysfunction. *Child Abuse & Neglect*, 25, 1627–1640.

Finkelhor, D., Ormrod, R. K., & Turner, H. A. (2007). Re-victimization patterns in a national longitudinal sample of children and youth. *Child Abuse & Neglect*, 31, 479–502.

Fluke, J. D., Yuan, Y. Y., & Edwards, M. (1999). Recurrence of maltreatment: an application of the National Child Abuse and Neglect Data System (NCANDS). *Child Abuse & Neglect*, 23, 633–650.

Foley, D., Eaves, L., Wormley, B., Silberg, J. L., Maes, H., Kuhn, J., Riley, B. (2004). Childhood adversity, monoamine oxidase A genotype, and risk for conduct disorder. *Archives of General Psychiatry*, 61, 738–744.

Franken, I. H. A., & Hendriks, V. M. (2000). Early-onset of illicit substance use is associated with greater axis-II comorbidity, not with axis-I comorbidity. *Drug and Alcohol Dependence*, 59, 305–308.

Furstenberg, F. F., Brooks-Gunn, J., & Chase-Lansdale, L. (1989). Teenaged pregnancy and childbearing. *American Psychologist*, 44, 313–320.

Ge, X., Conger, R. D., Cadoret, R. J., Neiderhiser, J. M., Yates, W., Troughton, E. et al. (1996). The developmental interface between nature and nurture: A mutual influence model of child antisocial behavior and parent behaviors. *Developmental Psychology*, 32, 574–589.

Gershoff, E. T. (2002). Corporal punishment by parents and associated child behaviors and experiences: A meta-analytic and theoretical review. *Psychological Bulletin*, 128, 539–579.

Gil, D. (1973). *Violence against children*. Cambridge, MA: Harvard University Press.

George, R. M. & Lee, B. J. (1997). Abuse and neglect in young children. In R. A. Maynard (Ed.), *Kids having kids*, pp. 205–230. Washington DC: Urban Institute Press.

Goodman, S. H. & Gotlib, I. H. (1999). Risk for psychopathology in the children of depressed mothers: A developmental model for understanding mechanisms of transmission. *Psychological Review*, 106, 458–490.

Goodman, S. H. & Gotlib, I. H. (2002). *Children of depressed parents*. Washington, DC: American Psychological Association.

Gottlieb, G. (1998). Normally occurring environmental and behavioral influences on gene activity: From central dogma to probabilistic epigenesis. *Psychological Review*, 105, 792–802.

Gottlieb, G. (2007). Probabilistic epigenesis. *Developmental Science*, 10, 1–11.

Grant, B. F. & Dawson, D. A. (1997). Age at onset of alcohol use and its association with DSM-IV alcohol abuse and dependence: Results from the National Longitudinal Alcohol Epidemiologic Survey. *Journal of Substance Abuse*, 9, 103–110.

Hankin, B. L., Abramson, L. Y., Moffitt, T. E., Silva, P., McGee, R., & Angell, K. E. (1998). Development of depression from preadolescence to young adulthood: Emerging gender differences in a 10-year longitudinal study. *Journal of Abnormal Psychology*, 107, 128–140.

Hans, S. L., Bernstein, V. J., & Henson, L. G. (1999). The role of psychopathology in the parenting of drug dependent women. *Development & Psychopathology*, 11, 957–977.

Haugaard, J. J. & Hazan, C. (2003). Adoption as a natural experiment. *Development & Psychopathology*, 15, 909–926.

Jackson, S., Thompson, R. A., Christiansen, E. H., Colman, R. A., Wyatt, J., Buckendahl, C. W. et al. (1999). Predicting abuse-prone parental attitudes and discipline practices in a nationally representative sample. *Child Abuse & Neglect*, 23, 15–29.

Jaffee, S. R., Belsky, J., Harrington, H., Caspi, A., & Moffitt, T. E. (2006). When parents have a history of conduct disorder: How is the caregiving environment affected? *Journal of Abnormal Psychology*, 115, 309–319.

Jaffee, S. R., Caspi, A., Moffitt, T. E., Polo-Tomas, M., Price, T. S., & Taylor, A. (2004). The limits of child effects: Evidence for genetically mediated child effects on corporal punishment but not on physical maltreatment. *Developmental Psychology, 40*, 1047–1058.

Jaffee, S. R., Moffitt, T. E., Caspi, A., & Taylor, A. (2003). Life with (or without) father: The benefits of living with two biological parents depend on the father's antisocial behavior. *Child Development, 74*, 109–126.

Johnson, J. G., Cohen, P., Kasen, S., Ehrensaft, M. K., & Crawford, T. N. (2006). Associations of Parental Personality disorders and Axis I Disorders with childrearing behavior. *Psychiatry, 69*, 336–350.

Johnson, J. G., Cohen, P., Kasen, S., Smailes, E., & Brook, J. S. (2001). Association of maladaptive parental behavior with psychiatric disorder among parents and their offspring. *Archives of General Psychiatry, 58*, 453–460.

Kadushin, A. & Martin, J. A. (1981). *Child abuse: An interactional event.* New York: Columbia University Press.

Kandel, D. B. & Wu, P. (1995). Disentangling mother-child effects in the development of antisocial behavior. In J. McCord (Ed.), *Coercion and punishment in long-term perspectives*, pp. 106–123. Cambridge: Cambridge University Press.

Keenan, K. & Shaw, D. S. (1994). The development of aggression in toddlers: A study of low-income families. *Journal of Abnormal Child Psychology, 22*, 53–77.

Kempe, R. & Kempe, C. H. (1978). *Child abuse.* London: Fontana Open Books.

Kendler, K. S., Prescott, C. A., Myers, J., & Neale, M. C. (2003). The structure of genetic and environmental risk factors for common psychiatric and substance use disorders in men and women. *Archives of General Psychiatry, 60*, 929–937.

Kessler, R. C., Berglund, P., Demler, O., Jin, R., Merikangas, K. R., & Walters, E. E. (2005). Lifetime prevalence and age-of-onset distributions of DSM-IV Disorders in the National Comorbidity Survey Replication. *Archives of General Psychiatry, 62*, 593–602.

Kim-Cohen, J. (2006). Maternal depression and children's antisocial behaviour: More than just genetics. *ACAMH Occasional Papers, 25*, 39–49.

Kim-Cohen, J., Caspi, A., Moffitt, T. E., Harrington, H. L., Milne, B. J., & Poulton, R. (2003). Prior juvenile diagnoses in adults with mental disorder: Developmental follow-back of a prospective-longitudinal cohort. *Archives of General Psychiatry, 60*, 709–717.

Kim-Cohen, J., Caspi, A., Rutter, M., Polo Tomas, M., & Moffitt, T. E. (2006a). The caregiving environments provided to children by depressed mothers with or without an antisocial history. *American Journal of Psychiatry, 163*, 1009–1018.

Kim-Cohen, J., Caspi, A., Taylor, A., Williams, B., Newcombe, R., Craig, I. W. et al. (2006b). MAOA, maltreatment, and gene-environment interaction predicting children's mental health: new evidence and a meta-analysis. *Molecular Psychiatry, 11*, 903–913.

Kinard, E. M. (2003). Adolescent childbearers in later life: Maltreatment of their school-age children. *Journal of Family Issues, 24*, 687–710.

Kotch, J. B., Browne, D. C., Ringwalt, C. L., Stewart, P. W., Ruina, E., Holt, K. et al. (1995). Risk of child abuse or neglect in a cohort of low-income children. *Child Abuse & Neglect, 19*, 1115–1130.

Krueger, R. F., Moffitt, T. E., Caspi, A., Bleske, A., & Silva, P. (1998). Assortative mating for antisocial behavior: Developmental and methodological implications. *Behavior Genetics, 28*, 173–186.

Manly, J. T., Kim, J. E., Rogosch, F. A., & Cicchetti, D. (2001). Dimensions of child maltreatment and children's adjustment: contributions of developmental timing and subtype. *Development & Psychopathology, 13*, 759–782.

Masten, A., Hubbard, J. J., Gest, S. D., Tellegen, A., Garmezy, N., & Ramirez, M. (1999). Competence in the context of adversity: Pathways to resilience and maladaptation from childhood to late adolescence. *Development & Psychopathology, 11*, 143–169.

Mathews, T. J. & Hamilton, B. E. (2009). Delayed childbearing: More women are having their first child later in life. NCHS data brief, no 21. Hyattsville, MD: National Center for Health Statistics.

Mayes, L. C. & Truman, S. D. (2002). Substance abuse and parenting. In M. Bornstein (Ed.), *Handbook of parenting: Vol. 4. Social Conditions and applied parenting*, pp. 328–360. Mahwah, NJ: Lawrence Erlbaum Associates.

Miller, B. A., Smyth, N. J., & Mudar, P. J. (1999). Mothers' alcohol and other drug problems and their punitiveness toward their children. *Journal of Studies on Alcohol, 60*, 632–642.

Mirowsky, J. (2002). Parenthood and health: The pivotal and optimal age at first birth. *Social Forces, 81*, 315–349.

Moffitt, T. E. (1993). Adolescence-limited and life-course-persistent antisocial behavior: A developmental taxonomy. *Psychological Review, 100*, 674–701.

Moffitt, T. E. (2003). Life-course-persistent and adolescence-limited antisocial behavior: A 10-year research review and research agenda. In B. B. Lahey, T. E. Moffitt, & A. Caspi (Eds.), *Causes of Conduct Disorder and Juvenile Delinquency*, pp. 49–75. New York: Guilford Press.

Moffitt, T. E., Caspi, A., Rutter, M., & Silva, P. (2001). *Sex differences in antisocial behaviour.* Cambridge: Cambridge University Press.

Moffitt, T. E. & The E-Risk Study Team (2002). Teen-aged mothers in contemporary Britain. *Journal of Child Psychology and Psychiatry, 43*, 727–742.

Nolen-Hoeksema, S. (2002). Gender differences in depression. In I. H. Gotlib & C. L. Hammen (Eds.), *Handbook of Depression*, pp. 492–509. New York: Guilford Press.

O'Connor, T. G. (2002). Annotation. The "effects" of parenting reconsidered: Findings, challenges, and applications. *Journal of Child Psychology & Psychiatry, 43*, 555–572.

O'Connor, T. G., Deater-Deckard, K., Fulker, D., Rutter, M., & Plomin, R. (1998). Genotype-environment correlations in late childhood and early adolescence: Antisocial behavioral problems and coercive parenting. *Developmental Psychology, 34*, 970–981.

Paikoff, R. L. & Brooks-Gunn, J. (1991). Do parent-child relationships change during puberty? *Psychological Bulletin, 110*, 47–66.

Pianta, R., Eglena, B., & Erickson, M. F. (1989). The antecedents of maltreatment: Results of the mother-child interaction research project. In D. Cicchetti & V. Carlson (Eds.), *Child maltreatment: Theory and research on the causes and consequences of child abuse and neglect*, pp. 203–253. New York: Cambridge University Press.

Radke-Yarrow, M. (1998). *Children of Depressed Mothers*. Cambridge: Cambridge University Press.

Ragozin, A. S., Basham, R. B., Crnic, K. A., Greenberg, M. T., & Robinson, N. M. (1982). Effects of maternal age on parenting role. *Developmental Psychology, 18*, 627–634.

Regier, D. A., Farmer, M. E., Rae, B. Z., Locke, S. J., Keith, S. J., Judd, L. L. et al. (1990). Comorbidity of mental disorders with alcohol and other drug abuse: Results from the Epidemiologic Catchment Area (ECA) Study. *Journal of the American Medical Association, 264*.

Reid, J. B., Patterson, G. R., & Snyder, J. (2002). *Antisocial behavior in children and adolescents.*

Washington, DC: American Psychological Association.

Reiss, D., Neiderhiser, J. M., Hetherington, E. M., & Plomin, R. (2000). *The relationship code: Deciphering genetic and social influences on adolescent development.* Cambridge, MA: Harvard University Publishers.

Rhee, S. H. & Waldman, I. D. (2002). Genetic and environmental influences on antisocial behavior: A meta-analysis of twin and adoption studies. *Psychological Bulletin, 128*, 490–529.

Roberts, R., O'Connor, T., Dunn, J., & Golding, J. (2004). The effects of child sexual abuse in later family life: Mental health, parenting and adjustment of offspring. *Child Abuse & Neglect, 28*, 525–545.

Rutter, M. (1989). Age as an ambiguous variable in developmental research: Some epidemiological considerations from developmental research. *International Journal of Behavioral Development, 12*, 1–34.

Seagull, F. N., Mowery, J. L., Simpson, P. M., Robinson, T. R., Martier, S. S., Sokol, R. J. et al. (1996). Maternal assessment of infant development: associations with alcohol and drug use in pregnancy. *Child Pedriatrics, 35*, 628.

Sedlak, A. J. & Broadhurst, D. D. (1996). *The third National Incidence Study of child abuse and neglect.* Washington, DC: U.S. Department of Health and Human Services, Administration for Children, Youth, and Families.

Sidebotham, P. & Golding, J. (2001). Child maltreatment in the "Children of the Nineties": A longitudinal study of parental risk factors. *Child Abuse & Neglect, 25*, 1177–1200.

Sidebotham, P., Heron, J., & The ALSPAC Study Team (2003). Child maltreatment in the "children of the nineties:" The role of the child. *Child Abuse & Neglect, 27*, 337–352.

Sroufe, A. L., Egeland, B., Carlson, E. A., & Collins, W. A. (2005). *The development of the person: The Minnesota Study of risk and adaptation from birth to adulthood.* New York: Guilford Press.

Stein, A., Gath, D. H., Bucher, J., Bond, A., Day, A., & Cooper, P. J. (1991). The relationship between post-natal depression and mother-child interaction. *British Journal of Psychiatry, 158*, 46–52.

Steinberg, L. (2007). Risk taking in adolescence: New perspectives from brain and behavioral science. *Current Directions in Psychological Science, 16*, 55–59.

Straus, M. A. & Moynihan, M. M. (1994). Who spanks the most? In M. A. Straus (Ed.),

Beating the devil out of them: Corporal punishment in American families, pp. 49–63. New York: Lexington Books.

Taylor, A. & Kim-Cohen, J. (2007). Meta-analysis of gene-environment interactions in developmental psychopathology. *Development & Psychopathology, 19,* 1029–1037.

Tremblay, R. E., Nagin, D. S., Seguin, J. R., Zoccolillo, M., Zelazo, P. D., Boivin, M. et al. (2004). Physical aggression during early childhood: Trajectories and predictors. *Pediatrics, 114,* e43–e50.

Tucker, M. B. (1979). A descriptive and comparative analysis of the social support structure of heroin addicted women. In *Addicted women: Family dynamics, self-perceptions, and support systems*, pp. 37–79. Washington, DC: NIDA, Supt of Docs, U. S. Government Printing Office.

U.S. Department of Health and Human Services (2007). *Child maltreatment 2007.* Washington, DC: U.S. Department of Health and Human Services, Administration on Children, Youth and Families.

Ventura, S. J., Abma J. C., Mosher, W. D., & Henshaw, S. K. (2006). Recent trends in teenage pregnancy in the United States, 1990–2002. Health E-stats. Hyattsville, MD: National Center for Health Statistics.

Wekerle, C., Wall, A. M., Leung, E., & Trocme, N. (2007). Cumulative stress and substantiated maltreatment: The importance of caregiver vulnerability and adult partner violence. *Child Abuse & Neglect, 31,* 427–443.

Wolfner, G. D. & Gelles, R. J. (1993). A profile of violence toward children: A national study. *Child Abuse & Neglect, 17,* 197–212.

Zahn-Waxler, C., Duggal, S., & Gruber, R. (2002). Parental Psychopathology. In M. Bornstein (Ed.), *Handbook of parenting:* Vol. 4. *Social conditions and applied parenting*, pp. 295–328. Mahwah, NJ: Lawrence Erlbaum Associates.

CHAPTER 24

The Cultural Organization of Children's Environments

Sara Harkness and Charles M. Super

It's 7:30 AM, and Jane, a 3-year-old girl whose family lives in a pleasant Boston suburb, gets up to have breakfast with her mother and baby brother. Daddy has already left for work, but her mother, a part-time social worker, has planned a special day to make the most of her time with the children. After breakfast, they pile into the car and drive into town, where, after dropping off the little brother at his babysitter's, they meet another mother and her 3-year-old daughter at a theater to watch a performance of *Pinocchio*. After the show, the two mothers and daughters go to McDonald's for lunch. Jane and her mother stop at Sears department store to do some shopping and then pick up her little brother on their way home. Jane plays by herself in the back yard while her mother does housework. Then it is time for all three to leave for Jane's swimming class at the town pool (the little brother gets to go along for the trip). After going home at the end of the afternoon, Jane watches *Sesame Street* on TV, and then eats supper in her parents' bedroom while watching her mother fold laundry. Daddy gets home at 7:30, just in time

to read Jane a story and tuck her into bed at 8:15.

On the other side of the Atlantic, in the Dutch town of Bloemenheim, another 3-year-old girl has gotten up. Marja's day begins with a shower with Daddy at 7:00, followed by family breakfast with her mother, father, 7-year-old sister, and 5-year-old brother. By 8:15, Marja's sister has left for school. It's just a 5-minute bike ride away and usually their mother rides with both children on their own bikes while Marja sits in her toddler seat on the back, but today Mother will take the car as Marja's brother is staying home with a cold. When they get back home, Marja plays in the living room counting pennies in her piggy bank, then goes out to ride her bike in the child-safe neighborhood streets. At the end of the morning, it is time to go back to school to pick up Marja's sister, along with a younger neighbor child who will spend the afternoon at their home. They all have lunch together, then at 1:00 Mother takes Marja's sister back to school and Marja to the "Children's Playroom," where children her age go for a couple of hours twice a week in order to get used to being in a group outside home, prior to entering school the following year. Mother goes back at 3:00 to pick Marja up, then stops by school to pick up her sister, and they head home for a snack – the usual tea with milk and a cookie. By 4:00, Marja is outside riding her bike with other children in the neighborhood. At 5:30, Daddy arrives home on his bike from his job as a chemist at a nearby paint factory, and the children play together in the living room while their parents prepare dinner. At 6:00, the family sits down to eat together, then Daddy gets Marja ready for bed. By 6:50, after a story, Marja is tucked into bed and off to sleep.

Heading east and south almost to the equator, it is just about as far again from Bloemenheim to the community of Kokwet, located in the western highlands of Kenya, home of 3-year-old Chepkemoi and her family. Chepkemoi's day starts at 7:00 AM as she and three older siblings get up and wash their arms and legs in a bucket of water outside their sleeping hut, while their mother makes tea over the cooking fire inside. Baby sister lies nearby safely on a blanket spread on the ground to keep her from getting dirty, and the children keep a watchful eye on her as they bathe. The whole family including Chepkemoi's father gathers for breakfast at 8:00 (Father sits off to the side as he is not supposed to eat "with" the children). By 9:00, Mother is sweeping out the dirt floor of the hut with a bunch of loosely tied twigs, while Chepkemoi entertains herself by trying to jump over a stick. Mid-morning finds Chepkemoi at the edge of a maize field near the house, where she plays with a girl friend while their mothers weed between the rows of maize, swinging hoes over their heads as they bend to their task. Chepkemoi and her friend play at making a pot from the dirt for some time, then Chepkemoi takes care of her baby sister while their mothers continue weeding. Back at the hut, lunch for all the children is a simple bowl of maize porridge left over from yesterday, accompanied by sour milk from a gourd. Then it's back to the field again, running around with other children and helping to look for wild leafy vegetables that grow between the rows of

maize; Mother and many other women continue cultivating the rows of maize. By 3:00 in the afternoon, Chepkemoi is back running around the family hut with a friend while her father and another man sit nearby chatting together and Mother grinds maize on a stone for the family dinner. Chepkemoi joins her father, mother and older siblings as they drive the family's cattle to where they rest at night; then the whole family has dinner together outside their hut, including the wild vegetables that Chepkemoi helped to pick that afternoon (Father sits apart as usual). Darkness falls and by 8:00 Chepkemoi and her older siblings are asleep together, nestled in a light blanked on a raised sleeping place sculpted from the packed dirt floor of the hut. Later, their mother and baby sister will come in to sleep nearby, while their father will go to his own hut on the other side of the compound for the night.

These stories of a day in the life of three young girls, based on logs of actual days kept by their mothers in the first two cases and by "spot observations" over the course of 2 weeks in the last, are rich with information about the cultural organization of the girls' environments – in Weisner's phrase, the "cultural place" where each girl lives (Weisner, 1996). In this chapter, we offer an overview of theories and methods related to understanding the culturally structured environment of the child, with particular attention to integrative approaches. Recent decades have witnessed a rapid growth of interest within the psychological sciences in studying children's development in cultural context, and several distinctively different approaches are now represented in the research literature. Over the same period, anthropological concepts of culture have continued to evolve in response to challenges and new knowledge both within and outside the discipline. Following the famous dictum attributed to Kurt Lewin, "There is nothing so useful as a good theory," we first turn our attention to how culture has been conceptualized in these two disciplines; for how one thinks about culture determines how one studies and understands the child in cultural context.

Conceptualizations of Culture in Anthropology

The concept of culture has been a continuing focus of discussion within the field of anthropology since its earliest days. This follows in part from the distinctive focus of ethnographic fieldwork on particular kinds of communities. Anthropologist Robert Levy provided a classic definition of culture as he described research in such places: "Other less glamorous kinds of academics could study other kinds of ordering – generations, social classes, mobile people, or large, complex and heterogeneous urban conglomerations. But ethnographers were the proper students of those small, bounded, and coherent communities, whose order seemed to come from the deep-rooted art work that they and their ancestors had created and maintained – namely a local 'culture'" (Levy, 2005, p. 436).

The "small, bounded, and coherent communities" that ethnographers studied during the peak years of this enterprise were typically remote, non-Western communities that were relatively unconnected to the rest of the world. In this context, anthropologists, usually working alone, produced ethnographic accounts of the places they studied based on a general agreed-upon outline of topics to be covered (such as kinship), but away from the eyes of other observers who might have seen things differently. Their methods were primarily participant observation and informant interviews, often with only a small number of individuals who essentially became the ethnographer's guides to the local community. It was customary for the anthropologist to stay in the field site for a year or two, but with a myriad of topics to cover, it is not surprising that classical ethnographies tended toward general statements, often without reference to the source or type of information on which they were based. This included general characterizations of parenting and child development, as in Radcliffe-Brown's (1932/1964) study of the Andaman Islanders, based on field work carried out from 1906 to 1908:

We may turn now to the duties to one another of parents and children. During their infancy the children are in the care of the mother. Children are, however, such favourites with the Andamanese that a child is played with and petted and nursed not only by his own father and mother but by everyone in the village. A woman with an unweaned child will often give suck to the children of other women. Babies are not weaned till they are three or four years old. (p. 76)

In these classic studies, descriptions of informal customary practices were often interwoven with detailed documentation of more formal practices such as birth rituals, naming ceremonies, or rites of passage. Nevertheless, the importance of documenting the apparently "trivial incidents" of everyday life – especially for children and families – was recognized by these early ethnographers, as illustrated by Firth's (1936/1967) discussion of kinship among the Tikopia, residents of a remote Pacific island whom he studied in the 1920s:

In ethnographic lists of the "functions of kin" the reciprocal relations between parents and children are usually most ill-defined. They are more difficult to classify and enumerate than are the periodic devoirs to be rendered by kin outside this circle. Here, above all, the investigator's personal observation of behaviour must supplement and give perspective to the statements received from his informants, since from them it is impossible to obtain any adequate explicit formulation of the actual conditions. For accuracy of presentation, it is necessary to give actual examples of what seem to be trivial incidents, but which in reality form the substance of the kinship pattern. (p. 125)

In other words, the ethnographer in this tradition must be not only the documenter of what he or she learned about the culture from local informants, but also the interpreter of observed behavior. The basis for certainty in one's interpretations rested on the ethnographer's intensive involvement with a community over an extended period.

The anthropological study of childhood gained new importance in the "culture and personality" school of thought that reached its zenith in the 1950s and 1960s. A primary concern of this approach was to understand the actual processes through which culture is transmitted from one generation to the next, especially as it might operate through the formation of personality. Anthropologists turned to Freudian theory, to learning theory, and to cognitive approaches in their attempts to relate culturally structured childhood experiences to the "personality" of adult members of the culture, as expressed through customs, behaviors or belief systems. Although some systematic cross-cultural research was carried out in this tradition (LeVine, 2007), studies in culture and personality more typically focused on a single field site (see Jahoda, 1993). These studies, no matter how richly documented or theoretically persuasive, shared the disadvantage that causal relations that seemed reasonable in the context of one culture might not hold up in others. Furthermore, as more field studies made clear, there are many different kinds of personalities in any given cultural community.

In response to the evident methodological weakness of the culture and personality school, anthropologists John and Beatrice Whiting and their colleagues undertook a new kind of research in which methods from psychology were combined with traditional ethnographic methods in order to carry out systematic comparative studies of children and their families across cultures (Harkness & Super, 2001; Whiting, 1994; Worthman, 2010). Although their original paradigm was oriented primarily to understanding cultural beliefs and customs of the adult community, the Whitings' comparative field studies focused increasingly on parenting and the development of social behavior in childhood.

The Whitings' research was innovative in their choice of research sites, which differed considerably from the traditional "bounded communities" of classic ethnographic studies. The inclusion of an American middle-class community in their Six Culture Study (Whiting & Whiting, 1975), in particular, raised a new issue for cross-cultural research on children – namely, the question of "representativeness." The societies traditionally studied by anthropologists had been either too small or too unknown to provoke this question; in conventional psychology, the question also tended not to arise because of the assumption that one could study "the child" apart from the child's developmental context. For the Whitings, however, the issue of generalizability was one to be left for others to sort out, as their own interest lay in understanding the interactions among sociocultural organization, parenting practices, and child behavior and development in any given cultural place. The general conclusions to be drawn from this work had to do with different kinds of behavior in different kinds of societies, rather than establishing exactly what the geographic boundaries of any particular cultural pattern might be.

In historical parallel with the Whitings' research program, the "cognitive revolution" that swept linguistics and psychology also provoked a change of focus within anthropology from externally observable behavior to the internal workings of the mind (D'Andrade, 1984). Culture now came to be conceptualized as internalized ideas, values and motivations – in Quinn and Holland's (Quinn & Holland, 1987, p. 4) words, "what [people] must know in order to act as they do, make the things they make, and interpret their experience in the distinctive way they do." Correspondingly, Quinn and Holland (1987, p. 4) proposed the concept of "cultural models" as "presupposed, taken-for-granted models of the world that are widely shared (although not necessarily to the exclusion of other, alternative models) by the members of a society and that play an enormous role in their understanding of that world and their behavior in it." Notably, the "new" cognitive perspective in anthropology pointed not only forward to the next generation of empirical research, but also backward to the more holistic ideas of culture that had characterized earlier formulations (Harkness, 1992).

Drawing from these varied yet mutually supportive historical resources, anthropologists who study child development across cultures today are in general agreement on eight features of culture:

1) Culture is shared among members of a community: in LeVine's words (1984, p. 68), "culture represents a consensus on a wide variety of meanings among members of an interacting community," which he compares to shared meanings of language within a speech community.

2) Culture organizes meanings and actions across widely diverse domains within a community. As LeVine states (1984, p. 72), "Nothing is more characteristic of contemporary anthropologists than the conviction that the customs they study are connected and comprehensible only as parts of a larger organization – of beliefs, norms, values, or social actions." John and Beatrice Whiting, similarly, wrote that cultural systems of beliefs, values, and behaviors are "not only… internally integrated, but each type of custom is systematically related to the others. [They] form in combination a blueprint for action that has been called the custom complex." (Whiting & Whiting, 1960, p. 921)

3) Cultural beliefs exist in a variety of forms, from those that are encoded in law or ceremony to those that are implicit, taken-for-granted ideas about the right and natural way to do something. This aspect of culture is particularly important for the study of children's culturally structured environments, because it is the combination of the normative and descriptive, "the fusion of what is and [what] ought to be in a single vision … [that] gives distinctive cultural ideologies their singular psychological power." (LeVine, 1984, p. 78)

4) All cultures are unique, but none are totally different from all others. Rather, cultural communities tend to share some characteristics with other communities, including geographic neighbors, due in part to common historical roots and the diffusion of ideas and technologies. Thus, for example, the sub-Saharan region of Africa is characterized by many similar customs and beliefs related to children, along with important intraregional differences. Similarities among cultures also are related to common ecological demands and subsistence systems: simple agricultural societies, for example, have been shown to socialize children more strongly toward obedience, in contrast to hunting-and-gathering societies that encourage autonomy in their children (Barry, Child, & Bacon, 1959).

5) Cultural constellations of beliefs and values are resilient in the face of historical and ecological change. For example, the Dutch custom of putting babies outside for naps, even in cold weather, was documented in the 1960s by Rebelsky (1967); in the 1990s, we found Dutch parents carrying out the same custom, with the same rationale (Super et al., 1996). Studies of immigrant families generally find strong continuity in beliefs and practices, in addition to a variety of accommodations to the new surrounding culture (Moscardino, Nwobu, & Axia, 2006; Raghavan, Harkness, & Super, 2010; Rice, 2000).

6) Culture exists both as external environment and something "inside the head" of members of a cultural community (Handwerker, 2002). This apparent paradox can be understood with reference to language and the speech community: in both cases, there is a constant process of communication and transaction between the individual participant and the social environment.

7) Culture is *not* a larger version of personality. Although members of a cultural community share a common set of (often implicit) rules about things such as the nature of the child, the proper way to interact with other family members, and perceptions of the self, every

cultural community necessarily includes a wide variety of individually differing people. Further, the organization of individual differences is one feature of cultures (Wallace, 1961).

8) Ethnographic research about any particular cultural group necessarily involves a more complex, up-close and multimethod involvement on the researcher's part than does social behavioral research in which the culture is not considered (Weisner, 1996).

Concepts of Culture in Psychology

The concept of culture is a relatively new focus of interest in psychology. In contrast to the core consensus among anthropologists about what culture is and how it can be studied, psychological theories about culture tend to involve more distinctive constructs that may not overlap in either history or measurement. Several approaches have been particularly influential.

Culture Is Part of the "macrosystem"

The impetus for much of environmentally oriented psychology, at least as it was initially defined in the field of child development (McCall, 1977), was to move developmental psychology out of the laboratory and into "the real world." This world, for the typical North American developmental researcher, consisted mainly of U.S. populations at a time when cultural plurality was only barely on the intellectual horizon. Bronfenbrenner's ecological model (Bronfenbrenner, 1979) was the hallmark of the age, as he argued that children from minority backgrounds were shaped by ecologies that differed from children in the mainstream of U.S. society. In his model, culture is represented as the macrosystem, "the consistency observed within a given culture or subculture in the form and content of its constituent micro-, meso-, and exo-systems, as well as any belief systems or ideology underlying such consistencies" (Bronfenbrenner, 1979, p. 158). In visual representations of this model, with the child in the center of concentric circles, culture is placed as an outermost ring, separated from the child by the other systems that the child experiences more directly.

Culture and the Individual Are Part of Each Other

In contrast to Bronfenbrenner's model, cultural psychologists claim that culture and the individual person cannot be separated, as they are both part of a larger whole. In this approach, development itself is redefined as a joint project, "stretching to accomplish something together during participation in activities" (Miller & Goodnow, 1995, p. 53), rather than as a process of individual growth. In the strongest version of this approach, the idea of the child as separable from the environment is rejected. As Rogoff, Baker-Sennett, Lacasa, and Goldsmith (1995, p. 53–54) state:

> Viewing development as participation challenges the idea of a boundary between internal and external phenomena (for example, between arithmetic knowledge and the availability of order forms listing pricing information) – a boundary that is derived from use of the isolated individual as the unit of analysis. A person is a part of an activity in which he or she participates, not separate from it. Our perspective discards the idea that the social world is external to the individual and that development consists of acquiring knowledge and skills. Rather, a person develops through participation in an activity, changing to be involved in the situation at hand in ways that contribute both to the ongoing event and to the person's preparation for other involvement in other, similar events.

Culture Is a Social Address

There is a long-standing tradition in the behavioral sciences of conceptualizing culture as a social address. This approach, common in cross-cultural psychology of the late 20th century, leaves aside the question of what culture is, and instead treats it in research as an independent variable – sometimes along with other variables such as age, gender, birth order, or socioeconomic status – in order to explain group differences in people's behavior or responses to standardized measures (Adler, 1967; Walker, Torrance, & Walker, 1971). In one variant of this approach, some such variables are held constant in order for "cultural" effects to be more evident (Bornstein et al., 1998). Research within this tradition is carried out much like other mainstream psychological research on group differences, except that the groups are located in different societies around the world.

Cultures Can Be Categorized as "individualistic" or "collectivistic"

The Individualism/Collectivism (I/C) construct has been widely used to explain a variety of differences in behavior and thinking across cultures (Triandis, 1993). Kağitçibaşi (1997) stated that it was cited in about one-third of recently published cross-cultural studies at that time, and the trend seems to have continued. The I/C construct has been used to contrast many cultural groups including east Asian and Western cultures, modern middle-class Western populations and traditional rural African villagers, and U.S. middle-class versus Latin American immigrant groups (Greenfield, Quiroz, & Raeff, 2000; Keller, 2007; Marcus & Kitayama, 1991). Cross-cultural comparisons using this framework often refer to "assumed" psychological differences (at least among adult members of the community) without actually documenting them. For psychologists, the I/C construct (and other similar unidimensional models such as "independence" versus "interdependence") may hold special appeal because they offer a simple, unifying framework for understanding the child's cultural environment. Patricia Greenfield, whose research among the people of Zinacantan, Mexico has spanned some forty years, describes the benefits of understanding her research community in the context of individualism and collectivism:

> When I first went to Zinacantan in 1969, I was prepared by experienced members of the Harvard Chiapas Project. They gave me much useful information concerning how to act in specific situations. However, I perceived this information as disconnected bits and pieces that I had to memorize individually. When I went back to Zinacantan in 1991, I had just organized a conference on cross-cultural roots of minority child development (Greenfield & Cocking, 1994). Its major themes were the constructs of individualism and collectivism (Triandis, 1993) and how immigrants generally brought collectivistic cultural backgrounds with them from their homelands when they came to the United States. I took this conceptual framework with me when I returned to Zinacantan in 1991 for the first time in 21 years. What I found was the following. If I thought of Zinacantec culture as highly collectivistic, the culture as a whole made sense for the first time. Not only that: I could finally figure out how to act in (and understand) new situations – because I had a general principle, collectivism, that could be applied in a multitude of specific situations. I had a deep principle that was generative both for understanding Zinacantec behavior and attitudes and for producing appropriate behavior while I was in the Zinacantec Maya hamlet of Nabenchauk. I was much more successful and confident in integrating into the Zinacantec milieu once I had learned this one very general principle. (Greenfield, 2000, p. 573)

A Culture Is a Unique Collection of Unrelated Beliefs, Practices, and Values

Greenfield's description earlier of her first knowledge about the culture of Zinacantan as "disconnected bit and pieces" is the "default model" of culture as it may be encountered by some. As Greenfield noted, from this perspective customs, beliefs, practices and the material products of a cultural group may be recognizable as coming from the same origin, but there is no sense that they are interconnected in any meaningful way. Although this model is not often discussed as such, it seems to represent the assumptions of many behavioral scientists who undertake cross-cultural research.

Psychological Theories of Culture in Anthropological Perspective

Although the psychological conceptualizations of culture described earlier have generated a great deal of interesting research, from an anthropological perspective each approach has its limitations as a framework for understanding the cultural structuring of children's environments. For example, Bronfenbrenner's definition of culture as the consistency in relationships among social institutions and belief systems is not incompatible with anthropological approaches, but its placement in the macrosystem, at the outermost layer of a nested set of environments, leaves it with no direct connection to the individual – a contradiction of the anthropological view that culture is pervasive in individual experience.

Cultural psychology's central assertion about the inseparability of the child and the context poses a difficult challenge for research on children, as it becomes impossible to generalize about either the child (apart from the environment), or the environment (apart from the child). Furthermore, one cannot maintain this central assumption and at the same time identify a culture or a body of knowledge shared among community members that the child has not yet learned. In contrast, there is a long tradition within anthropology of studying processes of interaction and mutual influence *between* individuals and their culturally constructed environments.

Cross-cultural research using the social address model of culture has contributed greatly to knowledge about beliefs, customs and practices of various cultural groups. This research is limited, however, by the "etic" approach (Berry, 1989) in which instruments developed in middle-class Western societies, based on corresponding cultural assumptions, are applied to other cultural contexts in which the variables in question may have different meanings. In addition, the growing compendium of information on other cultural groups is itself confusing in the absence of a larger organizing framework. The very

success of this approach in adding to pieces to the global knowledge base about children's behavior and development, in a sense, has become its greatest drawback.

The constructs of Individualism and Collectivism (and related categories) have contributed to the broader understanding of culture as more than a random collection of beliefs, behaviors, and artifacts. Although the apparent simplicity of the model seems parsimonious, however, it is also a profound limitation in that it bypasses actual measurement of the environment. Thus all cultures labeled "collectivist" are assumed to be essentially the same (Hermans & Kempen, 1998; Kağitçibaşi, 1997). Consequently, there is no way to investigate questions such as variability in the meaning of "independence" among globally "individualistic" cultures (Harkness, Super, & van Tijen, 2000; Kağitçibaşi, 2007). Thus when developmental outcomes belie the unidimensional assumption, as they often do, the researcher has little recourse but to redefine the original prototypes or search for other, noncultural sources of difference (Harkness, 2008).

Integrative Frameworks

Drawing from both anthropological and psychological conceptualizations of culture, several integrative frameworks have been constructed for the study of child development in cultural context. Despite their somewhat different purposes, these models share a number of common features, in part because their proponents share an interdisciplinary background that includes training in both individual development and psychological anthropology. The "ecocultural niche" proposed by Weisner, Gallimore, and their colleagues pays special attention to the process of family adaptations in constructing daily life, as this process is influenced, for example, by culturally constituted goals, beliefs, and scripts for conduct (Bernheimer, Gallimore, & Weisner, 1990; Gallimore & Goldenberg, 1993; Gallimore, Goldenberg, & Weisner, 1993; Weisner & Garnier, 1992;

Weisner, Matheson, & Bernheimer, 1996). The "developmental microniche" proposed by Worthman takes a similar approach but focuses primarily on relationships among biology, behavior, and culture in shaping human development (Worthman, 2010; Worthman, 1994, 1995; Worthman, Stallings, & Jenkins, 1993). The present authors have proposed a third framework, the "developmental niche," further elaborated in relation to parents' cultural belief systems or "parental ethnotheories." We now turn to this last approach as it contributes to understanding the child's culturally constructed environment.

The Developmental Niche

The developmental niche is a theoretical framework for the integration of concepts and findings from multiple disciplines concerned with the development of children in cultural context (Harkness & Super, 1992; Super & Harkness, 1986, 2002). Two overarching principles reflect its origins in cultural anthropology and developmental psychology: first, that a child's environment is organized in a nonarbitrary manner as part of a cultural system; and second, that the child's own disposition, including a particular constellation of attributes, temperament, skills, and potentials, affects the process of development.

The features of the developmental niche are illustrated by the "days in the life" of the 3-year-old girls in diverse cultural settings described earlier: Jane in a Boston suburb in the northeastern United States, Marja in a Dutch town, and Chepkemoi in a Kipsigis village of western Kenya (Figure 24.1).

In the most immediate sense, we can only describe the niches of these three girls in terms of the particularities of their own characteristics and environments. Nevertheless, the niche framework is equally useful in deriving a generalized description of recurring patterns characteristic of their particular cultural communities.

Surrounding the child are the three major subsystems of the developmental niche:

Physical and Social Settings

The physical and social settings in which the child lives provide a scaffold upon which daily life is constructed, including where, with whom, and in what activities the child is engaged. These settings are the most evident aspect of the developmental niche, as they can be observed by a visitor or participant in the child's daily routines. The diaries or spot observations from which our "days in the life" are drawn illustrate one way to document the child's physical and social settings, and they also provide a framework for comparing them across cultural groups. Systematic analysis of such data would show what is evident from first impressions: for example, Jane spends more of her day away from her house than do the other two girls, but she is actually outdoors far less. Each girl's social settings are also distinctive. Jane spends more time alone or in the company of only her mother at home. Chepkemoi spends virtually all of her waking day outside either playing or helping out with family chores, and Marja spends some time outside playing with friends in the neighborhood as well as playing with other peers at the Children's Playroom.

These and many other features of the child's physical and social settings have profound developmental implications (Super & Harkness, 2010). For example, the daily cycle of natural light and darkness – which is more salient in Chepkemoi's niche than in Jane's – influences neural and hormonal activities that in turn influence integration of the overt circadian rhythms of sleep, digestion, and other physiological functions (Richter et al., 2004; Super & Harkness, 2010). Within the social environment, spending time in the company of infants and being assigned responsibility for their care has been shown to promote prosocial behaviors (Ember, 1973; Whiting & Edwards, 1988).

Systematic, quantitative analysis of children's settings of daily life may also provide a different picture from what is gained through qualitative ethnographic methods. For example, in an early report on mother-child

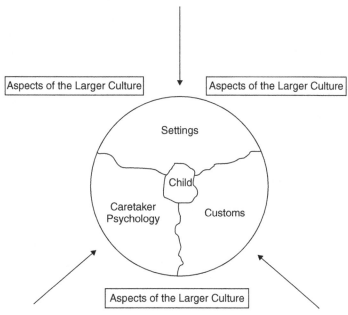

Figure 24.1. The developmental niche.

interaction in the Kipsigis community of Kokwet, we noted that, contrary to reports of maternal inattention to infants in sub-Saharan African villages, the mothers in Kokwet actually spent the same amount of time in face-to-face interaction with their infants as did middle-class American mothers in a U.S. study, but it was divided into shorter bouts. Furthermore, we found that the Kokwet babies received three times *more* face-to-face interaction than did the U.S. babies if one considered all interactive partners, not just the mother (Super & Harkness, 1974). This pattern has also been found in other African groups (Whaley, Sigman, Beckwith, Cohen, & Espinosa, 2002).

Customs and Practices of Care

The observation of settings can provide at least an initial guide to culturally regulated customs and practices of child care as they emerge from the ongoing flow of activities. Many such customs or practices are so commonly used by members of the community and so thoroughly integrated into the larger culture that individuals need not particularly rationalize them. To members of the culture, they seem obvious and natural solutions to everyday problems, developmental requirements, or social needs; their cultural nature becomes evident only when viewed from an outsider's perspective or when challenged in practice. For example, although it would seem self-evident to both Jane's and Marja's mothers that 3-year-olds are too young to be given real responsibilities such as caring for a younger sibling, to Chepkemoi's mother it was equally obvious that providing children with early experience in such activities was important for healthy development. In Kokwet (as in many African communities), helping with such tasks was considered so important for proper social and moral development that the last-born child, who never had as many opportunities for being responsible, was often perceived as selfish throughout life (see also Harkness, Super, Barry, Zeitlin, & Long, 2009).

Customs and practices of care, seen repeatedly in daily observations, signal particularly meaningful activities embedded in the settings of the child's life. As with settings, customs become most evident when viewed in cross-cultural perspective. Investigation of the meaning of such customs to parents, and eventually to children, links customs to the psychology of the caretakers, especially parental ethnotheories about children's development.

Psychology of the Caretakers

Aspects of the psychology of the caretakers can be inferred from observation of the child's settings of daily life and customs of care, but one needs to go further in exploring their meanings with the participants themselves. When talking with Jane's parents, for example, we might ask about the significance of the outing to a theater and then a restaurant. We would then learn (if we didn't already know as members of the same culture) that this activity is part of a class of activities that are marked as "special," and that are correspondingly seen as important for the child's cognitive development, relationship with the parent, and self-esteem. The theme of promoting children's cognitive development, in particular, is a striking element in current American parental ethnotheories. In our comparative studies of American and Dutch middle-class families, we found that the American parents tended to describe their children in terms of their intelligence (which they often found "amazing") much more than did the Dutch parents (Harkness et al., 2000). The American theme of cognitive qualities is present even in parents' talk about their young infants and it guides their ideas about good parenting practices (Harkness, Super et al., 2007).

In contrast, the Dutch parents who participated in our research tended to focus on other personal qualities such as sociability, temperament and especially self-regulation when they talked about their children. Regularity, a feature that we noted in Marja's day, was often invoked as a quality of the child – in particular children were described as "needing regularity" in order to maintain a calm but cheerful state (Super et al., 1996). Stimulation – a frequently cited theme among the American parents – was seen by these Dutch parents as something to avoid as it could easily disrupt the young child's healthy development.

Parental ethnotheories are often implicit, taken-for-granted ideas, and they have strong motivational properties; they are related to each other both across domains and in hierarchical fashion. Linking these ideas at all levels of specificity are cultural themes, which Quinn and Holland have called "general, all-purpose cultural models that are repeatedly incorporated into other cultural models developed for special purposes" (Quinn & Holland, 1987, p. 11). For example, the theme of "emotional closeness" has been identified in multiple contexts in research with Italian parents, including ideas about family life, parental support for children's success in school, and the child's most important developmental needs (Axia & Weisner, 2002; Harkness, Blom et al., 2007; Harkness, Super et al., 2007). Among Swedish parents, on the other hand, the concept of "rights" appears frequently in talk about family relationships, such as in the child's "right" to have access to physical closeness with parents at any time (Harkness et al., 2006; Welles-Nyström, 2005). It is important to note that the themes of "emotional closeness" and "rights" do not necessarily conflict with each other; rather, they seem to be concerned with different culturally shared yet largely unspoken premises.

Three Corollaries

The three subsystems of the developmental niche – settings, customs, and caretaker psychology – share the common function of mediating the child's developmental experience within the larger culture. Of particular significance for integrating research on these components are three corollaries:

1) The three components of the developmental niche operate together with powerful though incomplete coordination as a system. Thus, in an internally stable cultural environment, customs of care reflect parental ethnotheories about the child, as in the examples earlier, and they are further supported by the physical and social settings of daily life. In circumstances of rapid social

change, or immigration, however, the niche may become internally contradictory for a period as necessary changes in daily settings, for example, conflict with traditional customs and ethnotheories.

2) Each of the three subsystems of the niche is functionally embedded in other aspects of the human ecology in specific and unique ways; in other words, the three subsystems act as the primary channels through which the niche, as an open system, is influenced by outside forces. This corollary indicates that any one of the three components may be a primary route of influence. Economic or social change may lead to new settings for children, as it has for many sub-Saharan families now living in urban environments; the mothers' employment as street vendors may lead to inadequate care of infants who are left alone in the unsupervised care of siblings not yet old enough to manage this task independently. Likewise, historical change in what is recognized as "good parenting" – expressed in the public domain through the media as well as the advice of "experts" such as pediatricians or teachers – may directly affect parental ethnotheories, thereby activating change in customs and settings of care (Young, 1990). In the American context, for example, Lareau (2000) points out that the idea that parents should be responsible for their children's cognitive development is a relatively new phenomenon. Broad social shifts in values can also lay the groundwork for change, as seen in the successful introduction African-style baby carrying by a former Peace Corps volunteer (About. com, 2008) in the context of a general move toward interpersonal intimacy in the 1960s.

3) Each of the three subsystems of the niche is involved in a process of mutual adaptation with the individual child. Thus, the age, gender, temperament, interests and abilities of the individual child influence parents and others in the niche, modulating cultural

expectations and opportunities for the child at any given time. For example, a 6-year-old child in Kokwet who does not show qualities of being smart may be less likely to be asked to take a message to a neighbor or go to a local store to make a small purchase (Harkness et al., 2009). Interestingly, parents' perceptions of their child's individual qualities are formed at culturally recognized points in the child's development, making this timetable of expectations an aspect of parental ethnotheories in its own right. For example, mothers in Kokwet explained to us that all babies are alike, and individual differences can be seen only when the child becomes old enough to be given responsibilities (Super & Harkness, 1994). The American parents in our studies, in contrast, felt that they could judge their child's personality from the moment after birth (Harkness et al., 2009).

Cultural Themes

The developmental niche framework makes evident the kind of systematic regularity that culture provides – environmental organization that emphasizes repeatedly or with singular salience the culture's core "messages." It is through such cultural thematicity that the environment works its most profound influences on development. This quality of the developmental niche, which we have termed "contemporary redundancy," is important for the acquisition of skills and competencies as it offers multiple opportunities for learning the same thing, whether that "thing" is reading, sibling caretaking, or the communication of emotions (Super & Harkness, 1999). Similarly, the elaboration of themes over the course of developmental time reinforces lessons learned earlier and recasts them in a more adequate format for meeting the challenges of increasing maturity (Super & Harkness, 1999). In middle-class U.S. society, for example, the theme of "independence" is applied to the management of infant sleep, and later on to transitions to school, to parent-child relations during the teen-age years, and later still in advice to parents about "letting go" of their college-bound children (Harkness, Super, & Keefer, 1992). In these and other domains, children appear effortlessly to detect, abstract, and internalize culturally based rules of performance and systems of meaning. As an organizer of the environment, thus, culture assures that key meaning systems are elaborated in appropriate ways at different stages of development, and that the learning occurs across behavioral domains and various scales of time.

The Directive Force of Parental Ethnotheories

Although the developmental niche is conceptualized as a dynamic system in which the three subsystems influence each other, it is evident that parental ethnotheories play an important role in shaping customs and the organization of settings for children; or to put it in other terms, customs and settings can be seen as instantiations of parental ethnotheories. This is the case even though parents may provide practical rationales for their actions, with the obvious implication that their customs are simply what any reasonable person would do. As LeVine (1984, p. 79) commented, however, the "practicality" of certain customs may be predicated on other cultural assumptions about what is right and necessary:

> When Monica Wilson (1952) was told by a Nyakyusa informant that it was necessary to segregate adult generations into separate villages because otherwise the intergenerational avoidance taboos would cause inconvenience in daily life, the explanation was a rational one – but only if one assumes that the avoidance taboos represent a high priority for all concerned.

The directive force of parental ethnotheories is illustrated in a heuristic model (see Figure 24.2) in which general, often implicit ideas about the nature of the child, parenting and the family are conceptualized as a basic source of ideas about specific domains, such as infant sleep or social development. These in turn are closely tied to ideas about

appropriate practices, and further to imagined child or family outcomes. Ideas are translated into behavior as mediated by intervening factors such as child characteristics, situational variables, and competing cultural models and their related practices. The final results can be seen in actual parental practices or behaviors, and actual child and family outcomes.

Mapping out parental ethnotheories, practices and developmental outcomes within this model can be helpful for sorting out a variety of issues in the study of children's culturally organized environments. We offer three examples here: the problem of competing cultural models; the cultural organization of individual differences; and change and continuity of the developmental niche in the context of immigration.

Dealing with conflicting cultural models. Parental ethnotheories are not always evident in practice, in part because parents may be negotiating between the mandates of two or more conflicting cultural models. An example of this is discussed in Lareau's (2000) classic sociological study of families and schools in two communities. Fathers in the "working class" community were straightforward in expressing their view that involvement in their child's school was "her" job. Middle-class fathers, in contrast, thought that they *should* be more involved than they actually were. Further exploration of the topic in interviews with fathers suggested that all the fathers shared a more traditional American cultural model of gender roles, but the middle-class fathers were aware of a newer cultural model that dictated more equal sharing of childrearing roles and responsibilities. Even so, it seems evident that the traditional cultural model took precedence in the hierarchy of cultural models that these fathers carried around in their heads.

The cultural organization of individual differences. The developmental niche is responsive to individual differences in the child, including such aspects as temperament and intelligence (corollary 3). Nevertheless, the niche's response to such differences is predictably organized only within any given

Theoretical Model of Ethnotheories, Practice, and Outcomes

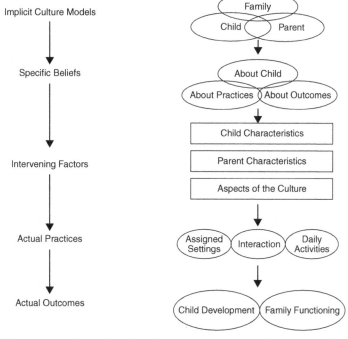

Figure 24.2. Parental ethnotheories, practices, and outcomes for children and families.

cultural place. Our research on cultural differences in what aspects of temperament are perceived by parents as "difficult" illustrates this point (Super et al., 2007). Parents of children aged 3 years, 4.5 years and 7–8 years in seven cultural communities filled out the Behavioral Style Questionnaire (McDevitt & Carey, 1978) to assess their children's temperaments in the framework of the nine-dimensional model developed by Thomas and Chess (1977). They also made a global rating of their child's overall "difficultness." Although parents in most of the cultural samples tended to associate difficultness with low adaptability and negative mood, there were important exceptions. The Italian parents, for example, did not associate negative mood with difficultness; on the other hand they did find being slow to warm up in new social situations to be a difficult aspect of young children's temperament. As they explained in interviews, the ability to move quickly and gracefully into new social situations was considered an important skill for

navigating various gatherings of family and friends from a young age.

Change and continuity in the developmental niche in the context of immigration. When families move from their culture of origin to a new environment, parents are confronted with the challenges of preserving the most meaningful aspects of their children's developmental niches while incorporating necessary changes. Research on Asian immigrant families in the United States suggests that parental ethnotheories travel relatively well, and that they are at least partially instantiated in parenting practices in the new environment. For example, Parmar, Harkness and Super (2004, 2008) found that Asian parents of preschoolers thought that they should be teachers rather than playmates to their young children, and that they actually did engage in more educational activities with their children than did a Euro-American comparison group. Likewise, Raghavan, Harkness and Super (2010) found that Asian Indian mothers focused more on qualities such as being hospitable and responsible when describing their daughters, in contrast to their Euro-American friends who described their daughters more in terms of independence and being athletic. Relatedly, the Indian immigrant daughters spent more time at home with their families and entertaining guests, whereas the Euro-American girls spent more time in sports. In contexts of increasing cultural diversity, a promising finding is that cultural beliefs and practices of the immigrant group may be incorporated into existing institutions such as day care for young children, as Huijbrechts and her colleagues found in a study of Moroccan, Turkish, Caribbean and native Dutch caregivers employed at child care centers in Amsterdam (Huijbrechts, Tavecchio, Leseman, & Hofenaar, 2009).

Revisiting Jane, Marja and Chepkemoi:

Understanding the Cultural Organization of Children's Environments

Imagine, for a moment, that Jane, Marja, and Chepkemoi can spend a day at each other's homes, where they are expected to fit in with the rest of their host family, doing the same things as their peer hostess. What would they find easy to understand and do, and where might they be challenged? What would they like, and what would they miss? Based on what we know about their developmental niches, we can make some educated guesses. On her visit with Marja in the Dutch town of Bloemenheim, Jane from the U. S. might be happy that she has other children to play with for most of the day, and she might be thrilled that she can go outside and play with other children on her own, without Mother there to supervise. Unfortunately, though, she has not learned how to ride a bicycle yet. Marja's bedtime story routine would be familiar to Jane, whose parents report having read to her "since before she was born." On the other hand, she might find Marja's bedtime very early! Marja, on the other hand, might find Jane's day in a suburban Boston town exciting but overstimulating, between the outing to see a play, lunch at a restaurant,

shopping, and a swimming lesson in the afternoon. Like all Dutch children, however, Marja has already taken swimming lessons and she knows how to swim quite well – an essential skill in their community that is crisscrossed with canals of all sizes. She might find it strange that Jane's father is away all day and that the family never seems to have a meal together, unlike home where much of her day is organized around family meals. Both girls would have a hard time understanding Chepkemoi's responsibilities in the village of Kokwet, Kenya, as they've never been asked to do any "chores" other than brush their teeth and pick up their toys (although by her mother's report, Marja loves helping with everything, even washing the windows). In fact, it probably wouldn't be wise for Chepkemoi's mother to leave the baby sister in the care of either Jane or Marja, even though she would be nearby to supervise. In short, the cultural competencies and expectations that these children have already learned during their first 3 years of life are strongly in evidence, illustrating both the plasticity of human development and the wealth of abilities that lie within each individual, waiting to be called forth by their environment.

As researchers, our challenges in studying other cultures are analogous to those that would confront Jane, Marja and Chepkemoi while visiting each other's communities. Like these little girls, we need ways to understand cultural differences that are fine-tuned enough to be able to identify specific cultural patterns, yet holistic enough to understand the internal organization of each environment. Like them, we need to be able to make predictions of behavior in situations other than the ones we have already seen – or as Greenfield put it, we need a theory that can correctly generate new behaviors in a given cultural setting. As researchers, we also need frameworks that are applicable beyond the level of a single culture, so that we will not have to start the entire process of ethnographic investigation from the beginning in each new site before undertaking research about children in their culturally organized environments. Likewise, when we encounter cultural diversity within the context of a single research site – an increasingly common phenomenon – we need to be alert to the possibility that "individual differences" among children and families, or even differences associated with social class – may actually be cultural differences that have their own rationale and their own expected developmental advantages from the perspective of their constituents. The usefulness of a good theory, to return to Lewin's phrase, is in large part a function of fit with the contexts of its application.

References

About.com. (2008). Ann Moore – Snugli, available online: http://inventors.about.com/library/inventors/bl_Ann_Moore.htm

Adler, L. L. (1967). A note on cross-cultural preferences: Fruit-tree preferences in children's drawings. *Journal of Psychology: Interdisciplinary and Applied*, 65(1), 15–22.

Axia, G., & Weisner, T. S. (2002). Infant stress reactivity and home cultural ecology of Italian infants and families. *Infant Behavior and Development*, 25(3), 255–268.

Barry, H., III, Child, I. L., & Bacon, M. K. (1959). Relations of child training to subsistence economy. *American Anthropologist*, 61, 51–63.

Bernheimer, L. P., Gallimore, R., & Weisner, T. S. (1990). Ecocultural theory as a context for the Individual Family Service Plan. *Journal of Early Intervention*, 14(3), 219–233.

Berry, J. W. (1989). Imposed etics – emics – derived etics: The operationalization of a compelling idea. *International Journal of Psychology*, 24, 721–735.

Bornstein, M. H., Haynes, O. M., Azuma, H., Galperín, C., Maital, S., Ogino, M. et al. (1998). A cross-national study of self-evaluations and attributions in parenting: Argentina, Belgium, France, Israel, Italy, Japan, and the United States. *Developmental Psychology*, 34(4), 662–676.

Bronfenbrenner, U. (1979). *The ecology of human development*. Cambridge, MA: Harvard University Press.

D'Andrade, R. G. (1984). Cultural meaning systems In R. A. Shweder & R. A. LeVine (Eds.), *Culture theory: Essays on mind, self, and emotion*, pp. 88–119. New York: Cambridge University Press.

Ember, C. R. (1973). Feminine task assignment and the social behavior of boys. *Ethos*, 1(4), 424–439.

Firth, R. W. (1936/1967). *Tikopia ritual and belief.* Boston: Beacon Press.

Gallimore, R., & Goldenberg, C. (1993). Activity settings of early literacy: Home and school factors in children's emergent literacy. In E. Forman, N. Minick & C. A. Stone (Eds.), *Contexts for learning: Sociocultural dynamics in children's development*, pp. 315–335. Oxford: Oxford University Press.

Gallimore, R., Goldenberg, C. N., & Weisner, T. S. (1993). The social construction and subjective reality of activity settings: Implications for community psychology. *American Journal of Community Psychology*, 21(4), 537–559.

Greenfield, P. M. (2000). What psychology can do for anthropology, or why anthropology took postmodernism on the chin. *American Anthropologist*, 102(3), 564–576.

Greenfield, P. M., & Cocking, R. R. (Eds.) (1994). *Cross-cultural roots of minority child development*. Hillsdale, NJ: Lawrence Erlbaum.

Greenfield, P. M., Quiroz, B., & Raeff, C. (2000). Cross-cultural conflict and harmony in the social construction of the child. In S. Harkness, C. Raeff & C. M. Super (Eds.), *Variability in the social construction of the child*, pp. 93–108. San Francisco: Jossey-Bass.

Handwerker, W. P. (2002). The construct validity of cultures: Cultural diversity, culture theory, and a method for ethnography. *American Anthropologist*, 104(1), 106–122.

Harkness, S. (2008). Human development in cultural context: One pathway or many? (Review of *Cultures of infancy* by Heidi Keller). *Human Development*, 51, 283–289.

Harkness, S., Blom, M. J. M., Oliva, A., Moscardino, U., Zylicz, P. O., Ríos Bermúdez, M. et al. (2007). Teachers' ethnotheories of the "ideal student" in five Western cultures. *Comparative Education*, 43(1), 113–135.

Harkness, S., Moscardino, U., Rios Bermudez, M., Zylicz, P. O., Welles-Nyström, B., Blom, M. J. M. et al. (2006). Mixed methods in international collaborative research: The experiences of the International Study of Parents, Children, and Schools. *Cross-Cultural Research*, 40(1), 65–82.

Harkness, S., & Super, C. M. (1992). The developmental niche: A theoretical framework for analyzing the household production of health. *Social Science and Medicine*, 38(2), 217–226.

Harkness, S., & Super, C. M. (2001). Culture and parenting. In M. H. Bornstein (Ed.), *Handbook of parenting* (2nd ed.). Hillsdale, NJ: Erlbaum.

Harkness, S., Super, C. M., Barry, O., Zeitlin, & M., Long, J. (2009). Assessing the environment of children's learning: The developmental niche in Africa. In E. Grigorenko (Ed.), *Multicultural psychoeducational assessment*, pp. 133–155. New York: Springer.

Harkness, S., Super, C. M., & Keefer, C. H. (1992). Learning to be an American parent: How cultural models gain directive force. In R. G. D'Andrade & C. Strauss (Eds.), *Human motives and cultural models*, pp. 163–178. New York: Cambridge University Press.

Harkness, S., Super, C. M., Moscardino, U., Rha, J.-H., Blom, M. J. M., Huitrón, B. et al. (2007). Cultural models and developmental agendas: Implications for arousal and self-regulation in early infancy. *Journal of Developmental Processes*, 1(2).

Harkness, S., Super, C. M., & van Tijen, N. (2000). Individualism and the "Western mind" reconsidered: American and Dutch parents' ethnotheories of children and family. In S. Harkness, C. Raeff & C. M. Super (Eds.), *Variability in the social construction of the child*, pp. 23–39, Vol. 87. New Directions for Child and Adolescent Development. San Francisco: Jossey-Bass.

Hermans, H. J. M., & Kempen, H. J. G. (1998). Moving cultures: The perilous problems of cultural dichotomies in a globalizing society. *American Psychologist*, 53(10), 1111–1120.

Huijbrechts, S. K., Tavecchio, L. W. C., Leseman, P. P. M., & Hofenaar, P. (2009). Childrearing in a group setting: Beliefs of Dutch, Caribbean-Dutch, and Mediterranean-Dutch caregivers in center-based care. *Journal of Cross-Cultural Psychology*, 40(5), 797–815.

Jahoda, G. (1993). *Crossroads between culture and mind: Continuities and change in theories of human nature*. Cambridge, MA: Harvard University Press.

Kağitçibaşi, Ç. (1997). Individualism and collectivism. In J. W. Berry, M. H. Segall & Ç. Kağitçibaşi (Eds.), *Handbook of cross-cultural psychology*: Vol. 3. *Social behavior and applications*, pp. 1–50. Boston: Allyn & Bacon.

Kağitçibaşi, Ç. (2007). *Family, self, and human development across cultures: Theory and Applications* (2nd Ed.). Mahwah, NJ: Erlbaum.

Keller, H. (2007). *Cultures of infancy*. Mahwah, NJ: Lawrence Erlbaum Associates Publishers.

Lareau, A. (2000). *Home advantage: Social class and parental intervention in elementary education*. Lanham, MD: Rowman & Littlefield.

LeVine, R. A. (1984). Properties of culture. In R. A. Shweder & R. L. LeVine (Eds.), *Culture theory: Essays on mind, self, and emotion*, pp. 67–87. New York: Cambridge University Press.

LeVine, R. A. (2007). Ethnographic studies of childhood: A historical overview. *American Anthropologist*, 109(2), 247–260.

Levy, R. (2005). Ethnography, comparison, and changing times. *Ethos*, 33(4), 435–458.

Marcus, R. M., & Kitayama, S. (1991). Culture and self: Implications for cognition, emotion, and motivation. *Psychological Review*, 98, 224–253.

McCall, R. B. (1977). Challenges to a science of developmental psychology. *Child Development*, 48, 333–344.

McDevitt, S. D., & Carey, W. B. (1978). The measurement of temperament in 3 to 7 year old children. *Journal of Child Psychology and Psychiatry*, 19(3), 245–253.

Miller, P. J., & Goodnow, J. J. (1995). Cultural practices: Toward an integration of culture and development. In J. J. Goodnow, P. J. Miller & F. Kessel (Eds.), *Cultural practices as contexts for development*, pp. 5–16, Vol. 67. New Directions for Child Development. San Francisco: Jossey-Bass.

Moscardino, U., Nwobu, O., & Axia, G. (2006). Cultural beliefs and practices related to infant health and development among Nigerian immigrant mothers in Italy. *Journal of Reproductive and Infant Psychology*, 24(3), 241–255.

Parmar, P., Harkness, S., & Super, C. M. (2004). Asian and Euro-American parents' ethnotheories of play and learning: effects on preschool children's home routines and school behavior. *International Journal of Behavioral Development*, 28(2), 97–104.

Parmar, P., Harkness, S., & Super, C. M. (2008). Teacher or playmate? Asian immigrant and Euro-American parents' participation in their young children's daily activities. *Social Behavior and Personality: An International Journal*, 36(2), 163–176.

Quinn, N., & Holland, D. (1987). Culture and cognition. In C. Holland & N. Quinn (Eds.), *Cultural models in language and thought*, pp. 3–42. Cambridge: Cambridge University Press.

Radcliffe-Brown, A. R. (1932/1964). *The Andaman Islanders*. New York: Free Press.

Raghavan, C., Harkness, S., & Super, C. M. (2010). Parental ethnotheories in the context of immigration: Asian Indian immigrant and Euro-American mothers and daughters in an American town. In C. P. Edwards & T. S. Weisner (guest Eds.), The contributions of Beatrice and John Whiting to the cross-cultural study of children and adolescents. *Journal of Cross Cultural Psychology*, 41(4), 617–632.

Rebelsky, F. G. (1967). Infancy in two cultures. *Nederlands Tijdschrift voor de Psychologie en Haar Grensgebeiden*, 22(6), 379–385.

Rice, P. L. (2000). Baby, souls, name and health: Traditional customs for a newborn infant among the Hmong in Melbourne. *Early Human Development*, 57(3), 189–203.

Richter, H. G., Torres-Farfán, C., Rojas-García, P. P., Campino, C., Torrealba, F., & Serón-Ferré, M. (2004). The circadian timing system: Making sense of day/night gene expression. *Biological Research*, 37(1), 11–28.

Rogoff, G., Baker-Sennett, J., Lacasa, P., & Goldsmith, D. (1995). Development through participation in sociocultural activity. In J. J. Goodnow, P. J. Miller & F. Kessel (Eds.), *Cultural practices as contexts for development*, pp. 45–66. Vol. 67. New Directions for Child Development. San Francisco: Jossey-Bass.

Super, C. M., Axia, G., Harkness, S., Welles-Nyström, B., Zylicz, P. O., Rios Bermudez, M. et al. (2007). Culture, temperament, and the "difficult child" in seven Western cultures. *European Journal of Developmental Science.*, 2(1–2), 136–157.

Super, C. M., & Harkness, S. (2002). Culture structures the environment for development. *Human Development*, 45(270–274).

Super, C. M., & Harkness, S. (1974). Patterns of personality in Africa: A note from the field. *Ethos*, 2(4), 377–386

Super, C. M., & Harkness, S. (1986). The developmental niche: A conceptualization at the interface of child and culture. *International Journal of Behavioral Development*, 9, 545–569.

Super, C. M., & Harkness, S. (1994). The cultural regulation of temperament-environment interactions. *Researching Early Childhood*, 2(1), 59–84.

Super, C. M., & Harkness, S. (1999). The environment as culture in developmental research. In T. Wachs & S. Friedman (Eds.), *Measurement of the environment in developmental research*, pp. 279–323. Washington, DC: American Psychological Association.

Super, C. M., & Harkness, S. (2010). Culture and infancy. In G. Bremner and T. D. Wachs (Eds.), *Blackwell handbook of infant development*, pp. 623–649, vol. 1. Oxford, UK: Blackwell.

Super, C. M., Harkness, S., van Tijen, N., van der Vlugt, E., Dykstra, J., & Fintelman, M. (1996). The three R's of Dutch child rearing and the socialization of infant arousal. In S. Harkness & C. M. Super (Eds.), *Parents' cultural belief systems: Their origins, expressions, and consequences*, pp. 447–466. New York: Guilford Press.

Thomas, A., & Chess, S. (1977). *Temperament and development*. New York: Brunner/Mazel.

Triandis, H. C. (1993). Collectivism and individualism as cultural syndromes. *Cross-Cultural Research: The Journal of Comparative Social Science*, 27(3), 155–180.

Walker, C., Torrance, E. P., & Walker, T. S. (1971). A cross-cultural study of the perception of situational causality. *Journal of Cross-Cultural Psychology*, 2(4), 401–404.

Wallace, A. F. C. (1961). *Culture and personality*. New York: Random House.

Weisner, T. S. (1996). Why ethnography should be the most important method in the study of human development. In A. Colby, R. Jessor & R. Shweder (Eds.), *Ethnography and human development: Context and meaning in social inquiry*, pp. 305–324. Chicago: University of Chicago Press.

Weisner, T. S., & Garnier, H. (1992). Nonconventional family life-styles and school achievement: A 12-year longitudinal study. *American Educational Research Journal*, 29(3), 605–632.

Weisner, T. S., Matheson, C. C., & Bernheimer, L. P. (1996). American cultural models of early influence and parent recognition of developmental delays: Is earlier always better than later? In S. Harkness & C. M. Super (Eds.), *Parents' cultural belief systems: Their origins, expressions, and consequences*, pp. 496–532. New York: Guillford.

Welles-Nyström, B. (2005). Co-sleeping as a window into Swedish culture: Considerations of gender and health care. *Scandinavian Journal of Caring Sciences*, 19(4), 354–360.

Whaley, S. E., Sigman, M., Beckwith, L., Cohen, S. E., & Espinosa, M. P. (2002). Infant-caregiver interaction in Kenya and the United States: The Importance of multiple caregivers and adequate comparison samples. *Journal of Cross-Cultural Psychology*, 33(3), 236–247.

Whiting, B. B., & Edwards, C. P. (1988). *Children of different worlds: the formation of social behavior.* Cambridge, MA: Harvard University Press.

Whiting, B. B., & Whiting, J. W. M. (1960). Contributions of anthropology to the methods of studying child rearing. In P. H. Mussen (Ed.), *Handbook of research methods in child development,* pp. 918–944. New York: Wiley.

Whiting, B. B., & Whiting, J. W. M. (1975). *The children of six cultures: A psychocultural analysis.* Cambridge, MA: Harvard University Press.

Whiting, J. W. M. (1994). Fifty years as a behavioral scientist: Autobiographical notes. In E. H. Chasdi (Ed.), *Culture and human development: The selected papers of John Whiting,* pp. 14–41. Cambridge: Cambridge University Press.

Wilson, M. H. (1952). *Good company: A study of the Nyakyusa age villages.* London: Oxford University Press.

Worthman, C. M. (1994). Developmental microniche: A concept for modeling relationships of biology, behavior, and culture in development. *American Journal of Physical Anthropology,* 18(Supplement), 210.

Worthman, C. M. (2010). The ecology of human development: Evolving models for cultural psychology. *Journal of Cross-Cultural Psychology,* 41(4), 546–562.

Worthman, C. M. (1995). Biocultural bases of human variation. *ISSBD Newsletter,* 27(1), 10–13.

Worthman, C. M., Stallings, J. F., & Jenkins, C. L. (1993). Developmental effects of sex-differentiated parental care among Hagahai foragers. *American Journal of Physical Anthropology* 16(Supplement), 212.

Young, K. T. (1990). American conceptions of infant development from 1955 to 1984: What the experts are telling parents. *Child Development,* 61, 17–28.

CHAPTER 25

Children and Electronic Media

Sandra L. Calvert

Children grow and develop in a media environment that is unprecedented in scope and influence. From birth throughout the adolescent years, youth living in the United States spend vast amounts of time in the presence of screen media. Media once were only observed or listened to by a mass audience (Calvert, 1999). Now youth interact with media, becoming the creators of content, not just the consumers of it (Pempek, Yermolayeva, & Calvert, 2009).

The creators of media have historically been large corporations with profit making as their goal. In the early 21st century, youth now join those corporations as they make their own media content, such as personal profiles on social networking websites like Facebook and videos viewed by others on youtube.com. The motives for these creations by youth are less about profit, and more about self-expression and communication with friends. New forums for interaction with others and new applications to distribute content online are also rapidly evolving, driven by advances in technology as well as by innovations by the young who live comfortably within the glow of the screen.

In this chapter, I explore the pervasive media environments that increasingly provide a context for development. I focus on media access, exposure, and effects on developmental outcomes. I end with a discussion of future research directions.

Children's Media Environments

Media is a cultural influence that crosses national borders. Most people with electricity own or have access to television sets, and those who live in developed countries typically have access to numerous media interfaces. Content often travels well, crossing the boundaries of time and space within a culture as well as being exported rather handily to other cultures. For instance, reruns of older television programs and films from other eras are easily accessed on U.S. television, providing quick availability to what life was like in decades past. Within or across cultures where there are numerous time zones and considerable ethnic diversity, media can provide a simultaneous viewing of the same content because of broadcast and cable television as well as through Internet access. Media content from countries like the United States, Canada, the United Kingdom, and Japan is often exported to other countries (Cahn, Kalagian & Lyon, 2008), making the world a much smaller place in the process. The Internet enables 24/7 access to virtually any content a user wants throughout the world, including television and film content as media options increasingly converge into a single screen interface.

The kinds of media available to children and youth are changing rapidly during the digital age. The point of entry for understanding the influence of this media environment on developmental outcomes is an assessment of the media available in children's homes.

Media Access and Penetration

Children who grow up in the United States live in an environment saturated with electronic media. In a nationally representative U.S. sample of 1,384 parents, Common Sense Media (2011) documented that 98 percent of 0-to-8 year-old children live in homes with at least one television set, 80 percent have a DVD player, 72 percent have a computer (68 percent with high speed Internet access), and 67 percent have a video game console. Forty-one percent of these parents own a smartphone, and 8% own tablets, such as an iPad (Common Sense Media, 2011).

Although numerous kinds of media are available to many young children when they are in their homes, socioeconomic and ethnic differences have been found in access to computers. Specifically, Calvert and colleagues (2005) found that well educated higher income families with 6 month to 6 year old children were more likely to own computers and to have Internet access from home than were families with lower incomes and lower educational levels. Hispanic families were least likely to own a computer, and Hispanic and African American families were less likely than Caucasian families to have Internet access at home. Consistent with these findings, 0-to-8-year-old children

who live in low-income households, who are Hispanic, or whose families are less well educated are less likely to have computers or high speed Internet access at home than are children whose families are wealthier, are Caucasian, or who are better educated (Common Sense Media, 2011).

Surveys conducted by the Kaiser Family Foundation for 8- to 18-year-olds yield similar findings for access to electronic media (Rideout, Foehr & Roberts, 2010). Ninety-nine percent of these youth live in homes with a television set (84 percent with cable or satellite options); 97% have a DVD or VCR player; 87% have a CD player; 94% have a radio; 93 percent have access to a computer (69 percent with Internet access, and 59 percent is high speed access); 87 percent have access to a videogame console; and 52 percent of homes have a digital video recorder, allowing viewers to easily shift viewing times. Most of these homes have multiple television sets, CD or tape players, and VCRs/DVD players. Two-thirds of all 8-to-18-year-old youth have a cell phone (Rideout et al., 2010).

Given the ubiquitous presence of so many electronic media in children's homes, it is not surprising that the household environments of 8- to 18-year-old U.S. youth were often oriented around media. The television set was usually on during meals for 64 percent of these households, 54 percent of these families had no rules about television viewing, and in 45 percent of these homes, the television set was turned on most of the time, even when no one was watching (Rideout et al., 2010). In short, television provides the backdrop in which many U.S. youth develop.

Media Exposure

For media to impact children and youth, exposure must occur. Media exposure is difficult to measure because of: 1) challenges in defining media exposure; and 2) measurement issues.

Defining media exposure. What does it mean to be exposed to media? In particular, the intense concentration of media available in children's homes and everyday environments means that some exposure is intentional whereas other exposure takes place simply because one happens to be in a place where a medium is on. Sometimes unintentional exposure is not perceived as important for developmental outcomes, but it is. Foreground content is often age-appropriate and potentially informative and meaningful to children whereas background content designed for adults can be a distractor from the important developmental tasks of childhood (D. R. Anderson & Pempek, 2005; Calvert, 2006). Background media exposure can create a world that is rarely quiet and typically noisy, which may disrupt internal regulation patterns, such as sleeping (Thompson & Christakis, 2005), concentrating (Christakis, Zimmerman, DiGiuseppe, & McCarty, 2004), and playing (Evans, Pempek, Kirkorian, Frankfield & D. R. Anderson, 2004).

Another key question is do we want to know how much or what kind of exposure is taking place (D. R. Anderson & Hansen, 2009; Calvert, 1999). *How much media content*, involving the quantity of media use, answers certain kinds of questions, such as the activities that media use displaces. For the American Academy of Pediatrics (1999), any exposure to media content before the age of 2 is thought to be detrimental to developmental outcomes, leading to inferior long-term cognitive performance because of a sensitive period in brain development during the infancy period. Valuable time spent with parents in activities, such as reading, may be displaced when parents place their very young children in front of a video screen while the parent does other activities. Longitudinal data specifically collected to answer this premise are sorely needed.

What kind of media content, which assesses the quality of the media environment, frames the second half of the question about media exposure. D. R. Anderson and Hanson (2009) use the analogy of a media diet to describe content influences. More specifically, exposure to certain kinds of programs, such as those involving educational and prosocial content, are linked to better short-term and long-term academic outcomes over time (D. R. Anderson et al., 2001; Wright et al, 2001). By contrast, exposure to violent or commercial content over time is linked to aggressive (C. Anderson, Gentile, & Buckley, 2007; Huessman, Moise-Titus, Podolski, & Eron, 2003) and overweight (McGinnis, Gootman & Craik, 2006) problems, respectively. The kind of media exposure is also captured by assessing foreground versus background media exposure (D. R. Anderson & Pempek, 2005; Calvert, 2006).

Measuring media exposure. Media exposure is assessed using several different approaches that are sometimes combined with one another to increase the reliability and the validity of the assessment. Six key methodological approaches assess media exposure (see D. R. Anderson & Hansen, 2009; Vandewater and Lee, 2009). One major method used is the *global time estimate*, in which parents or children (or both) estimate exposure to various media (e.g., How many hours did you play video games yesterday?). Kaiser Family Foundation Surveys, which are main sources of access and exposure data in the media literature area, rely on global estimates.

Diaries track both the amount and kind of media use that is occurring. *Time-use diaries*, in which parents of younger children or older children themselves write down all activities done in a set period, say 24 hours in length, is a highly reliable way to assess media exposure. However, this approach is very expensive and rarely used, with a few notable exceptions such as the Panel Study of Income Dynamics (PSID) that includes a subscale, the Child Development Supplement (CDS), that measures child media use patterns (Vandewater & Lee, 2009). *Media diaries*, a third approach to media use measurement, involve a variety of procedures. One approach is to provide participants with a booklet in which they check whether or not they use a particular medium in a specific time interval (e.g., 15 min), and they write in what they viewed or did (see, for example, D. R. Anderson, Field,

Collins, Lorch, & Nathan, 1986; Huston Wright, Rice, Kerkman & St. Peters, 1990).

In *experience sampling methods*, study participants are periodically contacted at random intervals and asked what they are doing at that exact moment in time as well as the quality of that experience. Users are often contacted via an electronic device, such as a pager (see Csikszentmihalyi & Kubey, 1981).

Direct observations can be made of children's media use patterns in the home, or by using video equipment to record exactly what children see on the screen at home using split screen technology (D. R. Anderson et al., 1986). While accurate, direct observations are far more expensive than other methods, such as surveys conducted with global estimates. Using video equipment to record viewing behavior, D. R. Anderson and colleagues (1986) documented that media diaries were a more accurate measure of the television set being turned on while viewers were present than were global estimates. Even so, global estimates and diaries were both positively correlated with the television set being on while a viewer was present in the room.

Finally, *electronic monitors*, such as the Nielsen People Meter, can track exactly who is viewing a specific television program, or *tracking software* can identify exactly where specific users have gone online (Vandewater & Lee, 2009). Electronic monitors are very expensive measurement techniques used by major corporations, such as the Nielsen Company who keeps their findings proprietary, opting to sell them for a profit. Tracking software on a computer, in which cookies lay a trail of a user's behavior, are accurate but raise privacy issues (Thornburgh & Lin, 2002).

Media exposure during the very early years. Nationally representative samples of media use patterns have been collected and examined by researchers primarily by using survey and diary methodologies to document children's media use patterns. The Zero to Six study documented children's early media use patterns using survey techniques in 2003 and 2006 and Common Sense Media documented similar media use patterns for children who were 0-to-8-years-old in 2011. The Child Development Supplement (CDS) of the Parent Study of Income Dynamics (PSID) is a longitudinal study in which time-use diaries track children's behaviors, including media use patterns. The PSID oversamples low-income ethnic minority groups, thereby illuminating similarities and differences in media use patterns between wealthier children who have more protective buffers and poorer children who may be more at risk for adverse developmental outcomes.

In the Zero to Six or Zero to Eight studies of very early media exposure of U.S. children (Common Sense Media, 2011; Rideout & Hamel, 2006; Rideout, Vandewater & Wartella, 2003), parents were asked questions about their youngster's media use patterns. For children who are younger than the age of 2, 66 percent have viewed television, and 52 percent have viewed a DVD (Common Sense Media,). On a typical day, 6-month to 2-year olds watch a television program or a DVD for an average of 61 min of daily screen exposure (Common Sense Media, 2011). Thirty percent of these children have a television set in their bedroom (Common Sense Media, 2011). This level of exposure contradicts the recommendation made by the American Academy of Pediatrics (1999) of limited or no screen exposure prior to age 2.

For 2- to 4-year-olds, screen media use averages 2 hours, 18 min daily which increases to 2 hours, 50 min of daily exposure for 5-to-8- year-old children (Common Sense Media, 2011). During this time frame, children increasingly use interactive media. Just over half of 2-to-4-year-old children have used a computer, which jumps to 90 percent for 5-to-8-year-old children. Similarly, mobile media use via a smart phone, video iPod, or Ipad jumps from 39 percent for 2-to-4-year-old children to 52 percent for 5-to-8-year-old children. An app gap has emerged as a new facet of the digital divide, with higher more so than lower income families exposing their children to content on these newer and mobile platforms. Twenty-three percent of 5-to-8-year-old children also multi-task, using more than one medium at a time, with television playing in the background for 21 percent of those children during some of the time that they are doing their homework (Common Sense Media, 2011). The latter pattern could disrupt concentration.

Parents generally perceived the kind of media content that children were exposed to favorably. Earlier studies by the Kaiser Family Foundation reported that 66 percent of parents reported that their children who were ages 0-to 6 imitated positive prosocial behaviors such as helping, while only 23 percent reported seeing their children imitate aggressive behaviors like hitting. Parents observed prosocial behavior the most when their children viewed children's educational programming. Parents reported that sons more so than daughters imitated aggressive behavior. Imitation increased at older ages with children who were a year old imitating less than those who were 2–3 years of age, and 4- to 6-year-olds imitating the most (Rideout & Hamel, 2006; Rideout, Vandewater & Wartella, 2003).

Parents also made discriminations across different kinds of media with computers holding a strong lead on perceptions of positive outcomes, television falling in the middle, and videogames going in a negative direction. Specifically, 69 percent of parents reported that computers mostly help their children versus only 8 percent who thought computers had a negative influence with 15 percent perceiving no influence. Thirty-eight percent of parents viewed television favorably for their children compared to 31 percent who viewed television as a negative influence, and 22 percent who saw no influence. Only 17 percent of parents viewed videogames favorably versus 49 percent who viewed videogames as a negative influence with 22 percent perceiving no influence (Rideout & Hamel, 2006). Although computers were perceived as the most favorable medium by parents, the television set was on approximately 6 hours a day in families' homes from the 2003 sample (Vandewater, Bickham, Lee, Cummings, Wartella, & Rideout, 2005).

The Kaiser Family Surveys on early media use were conducted in 2003 and in 2006.

Over that time frame, a significant decrease occurred in the number of households where the television set was on always or most of the time (37 percent in 2003 vs. 32 percent in 2005), as well as a significant decrease in television use during meals (35 percent in 2003 vs. 30 percent in 2005). Despite these declines, it is clear that media exposure is pervasive during the first six years of life. More recently, 39 percent of children under age 8 were found to live in heavy media use homes where the television set was on all or most of the time (Common Sense Media, 2011).

Media exposure from middle childhood through adolescence. The Kaiser Family Foundation and Panel Study of Income Dynamics data are also key sources of information about media exposure from middle childhood through the adolescent years. Survey data collected from 2,002 U.S. youth by the Kaiser Family Foundation in 2009 finds that media use for 8- to 18-year-olds is about 7.5 hours per day (Rideout et al., 2010). When overall media exposure, including multitasking is considered, that figure increases to 10 hours, 45 min per day. On a typical day, television viewing remains a dominant medium, commanding 4 hrs. 29 min. per day on average, followed by music at 2 hr, 31 min., computers at 1 hr., 29 min., videogames at 1 hour, 13 min., reading at 38 min, and movies at 25 min. per day. From 2004 to 2009, 8-to-18-year-old youths' ownership of mobile media increased dramatically with 66 percent owning a cell phone, 76 percent an iPod or MP3 player, and 29 percent a laptop in 2009 (Rideout et al., 2010). When using media, 7th to 12th graders report multitasking with another medium 58 percent of the time for at least one of the media (Rideout et al., 2010).

Using diary data from the Panel study of Income Dynamics, Bickham and colleagues (2003) found that African American children spent more time watching television and playing videogames than Caucasian or Hispanic children did. Caucasian children viewed more educational television programs than African American children, and Caucasian children also played more educational computer games than African

American or Hispanic children (Bickham, Vandewater, Huston, Lee, Gillman Caplovitz & Wright, 2003). The findings reinforce digital divide issues in relation to the quality of content. The implication is that Caucasian children are embedded in an educational media environment more so than children from African American and Hispanic households, a pattern which has implications for future academic and professional success.

Why Do Youth Use Media?

Uses and gratification theory (Rubin, 1994), grounded in the field of communications, provides an important framework for understanding media use patterns by children as well as by adolescents and adults. Uses involve the choices that children make to use different media. Gratification refers to the needs, such as companionship, that are filled by that use.

Using this framework, media are used for a variety of reasons including entertainment, communication, companionship, relieving boredom, and finding information. These choices are driven more by content area (e.g., news, entertainment) than by medium differences. For example, news content provided by online or televised news fills the same kind of need for information. However, how that information is understood does vary somewhat by medium. In particular, audiovisual images on television news come and go quickly whereas written online text can be read slowly or rapidly based on user skills (Calvert, 1999). Moreover, pictures and words together provide a different symbol system for processing information whereas only one symbol system is provided for processing written text alone (Calvert, 1999).

A companionship need that television and film content are particularly good at fulfilling is a parasocial relationship, in which a viewer acts as if they are in a relationship with an onscreen character (Hoffner, 2008). This kind of relationship is promoted in children's television programs by parasocial interactions in which the onscreen character looks directly at the audience through a camera lens and addresses the audience as if they are in an actual conversation. Fred Rogers pioneered this approach in *Mister Rogers' Neighborhood*. The technique of speaking directly to the audience is now a common technique in U.S. children's educational programs like *Blue's Clues* and *Dora the Explorer* where the characters look at children through the camera lens, talk to them, pause for a reply, and then act as if the child said something to them. Put another way, the feelings that children develop for media characters in these relationships become a tool to reach them and to deliver an educational message. The relationships that children form with characters have also been exploited to collect information from children for marketing purposes, as when Batman asked children to participate in an online "census" about their households for Gotham City (Montgomery & Pasnik, 1996).

Children and youth may also view television, films, and DVDs because they like to watch other people, becoming emotionally involved in the stories that are presented. Children's and youths' higher scores on fantasy empathy, which assesses how immersed one becomes in stories, predict emotional involvement with, and comprehension of, feature length DVDs (Calvert & Conger, 2007; Calvert, Strouse & Murray, 2006). Even adolescents on social networking websites like Facebook spend more time observing the content made by others, known as lurking, than in creating their own content (Pempek et al., 2009). For these reasons, observational media may never be fully replaced by interactive media in terms of children's and adolescents' time investment.

Effects of Media on Children's Developmental Outcomes

While overall exposure to content is important, the kind of content is a crucial organizer for understanding media effects (D. R. Anderson et al., 2001). Certain content can be constructive, leading to beneficial developmental outcomes, or content can be harmful, leading to negative developmental outcomes

Educational media. When the kind of media exposure is examined, a positive picture of media exposure emerges for certain content. Take, for example, the program *Sesame Street*, which was built from its inception on an educational curriculum. When *Sesame Street* was introduced, researchers were quick to assess the effects of home viewing on children's cognitive development. An initial evaluation conducted by Ball and Bogatz (1970) examined the effects of *Sesame Street* on 3- to 5-year-old children who were encouraged or not encouraged to view. The encouraged group received small toys and parents were given directions about how to use the program whereas the control group did not receive any toys or information. Because the program was so popular, however, most children watched the program. Thus, the, researchers created a strategy that divided children into quartiles based on the amount of home viewing. Boys and girls from different socioeconomic backgrounds who frequently viewed *Sesame Street* learned number and letter recognition, geometric forms, and classification and sorting information better than infrequent viewers did. For the children who entered school the next year, teachers rated the higher more so than the lower viewers of *Sesame Street* as having better attitudes about school and their peers.

In the second season of *Sesame Street*, Bogatz and Ball (1971) compared children who did and did not have access to *Sesame Street* by manipulating access to a cable that linked them to UHF stations where *Sesame Street* was then broadcast. The treatment group was given a cable, and the control group did not get a cable, thereby creating differences between the groups in who did and who did not view *Sesame Street*. Those who viewed *Sesame Street* were better than those who did not on a number of language and numerical skills, including Peabody Picture Vocabulary skills.

A subsequent study of *Sesame Street* conducted by Wright and colleagues focused solely on working-class or low-income disadvantaged children for a 3-year period. Two cohorts were compared: a 2-year-old group and a 4-year-old group. Naturalistic viewing patterns, as assessed by home diary measures, revealed that children from ages 2 to 4 viewed about two hours of educational television programs per week, most of which was *Sesame Street*. When the younger cohort was age 5, those who had been heavier viewers of *Sesame Street* performed better on Peabody Picture Vocabulary, math, and school readiness skills than the lighter viewers did. When the 5 year olds turned ages 6 and 7, those who had been heavier viewers of *Sesame Street* were better readers and better adjusted in school. Similarly, Rice and colleagues (1990) found that those who viewed *Sesame Street* more at age 3 had better vocabularies by age 5, but that *Sesame Street* was not as helpful for vocabulary acquisition for the cohort who began the study at age 5.

More than a decade after home viewing data were collected, the research teams headed by D. R. Anderson and by Huston and Wright joined forces to examine the long-term influences of educational television on children's outcomes, including academic success. These youth, who were now adolescents, were recontacted and asked various questions via a phone survey. Because of the time when the data were collected, most of the educational programming that children had viewed was *Sesame Street*. Early viewing of educational television programs was associated with long-term gains in the areas of science, math, and English grades in high school. Benefits of viewing educational television programs were stronger for boys than for girls. Frequent more so than infrequent viewers of educational television programs during childhood were also more creative, read more, and had more favorable attitudes about academic success when they were adolescents. Presumably, viewing educational programming early in life sets a trajectory associated with academic interests and gains over time. By contrast, girls who viewed heavy doses of action-oriented content, which tends to be associated with violent content, had lower academic achievement.

Other educational programs such as *Blue's Clues* yield beneficial outcomes for cognitive skills as well (D. R. Anderson, Bryant, Wilder, Crawley, Santomero, & Williams, 2000). In the diary data from the Panel Study of Income Dynamics, young children's use of educational television with a cognitive curriculum was related to better reading scores, a stabilizing factor for children who were growing up in stressful home environments (Vandewater & Bickham, 2004). Overall, then, television series with educational curricula yield beneficial educational outcomes.

Exposure to computers in the home environment is also associated with improved academic success by low-income children. For instance, Jackson and colleagues provided low-income 10- to 18-year-olds with computers and Internet access in their homes. Their Internet use was automatically and continuously recorded for a 16-month period. After 6 months, students who used the Internet more had higher reading comprehension scores than those who used the Internet less. After one year, students who used the Internet more frequently also had higher overall grade point averages than those who used the Internet less frequently. Grades in math were not affected. The authors suggest that time online was spent reading web pages and gathering information for class assignments, which, in turn, led to improved reading scores (Jackson, von Eye, Biocca, Barbatsis & Zhao, 2006).

While the quality of media content is associated with positive educational outcomes during childhood and adolescence (D. R. Anderson et al., 2001), growing up in the almost constant presence of television yields negative outcomes. Using data from the Kaiser Foundation *Zero to Six* study, analyses were conducted to examine the prevalence and developmental impact of "heavy-television" households on very young children. Thirty-five percent of the children lived in a home where the television is on "always" or "most of the time" (Vandewater et al, 2005). More than one third of children

who are between ages 0 and 6 had a television set in their bedroom (Rideout & Hamel, 2006). Regardless of their age, children from heavy-television households watched more television, read less, and spent less time doing homework than other children, particularly when they had a television set in their bedroom (Vandewater et al, 2005). Moreover, children exposed to constant television were less likely to be able to read than other children (Vandewater et al, 2005). These findings are supported by data from the Child Development Supplement in which television sets in the bedroom are associated with less home work activity, more television viewing, and less reading for older children and adolescents (Vandewater & Lee, 2007). Overall, the data link heavy television usage, particularly in children's bedrooms, to adverse cognitive outcomes.

Exposure to adult-directed television content, not child-directed content, appears to be a key reason for poor cognitive outcomes by young children. In one study (Barr, Lauricella, Zack & Calvert, 2010), 60 parents filled out 24-hour television diaries when their children were 1 and 4 years of age. At age 4, children completed a series of cognitive measures and their parents completed an assessment of their children's executive functioning skills. Results indicated that high levels of exposure to programs designed for adults during both infancy and at age 4, and high levels of household television usage during early childhood, was associated with poorer executive functioning skills at age 4. High exposure to television programs designed for adults during the early childhood years was also associated with poorer cognitive outcomes at age 4. In contrast, exposure to television programs designed for young children at either time point was not associated with any outcome measure at age 4.

Violent media. The effects of exposure to violent media on children's aggressive behavior has been a topic of hot debate for more than 50 years. In an early longitudinal study conducted by Eron (1963), children who were 8-years-old rated one another on how aggressive other children in their class acted.

Children's mothers were asked to identify which television programs their children viewed. Boys who viewed more aggressive television programs were more likely to be rated as aggressive by their peers. Ten years later, these children's aggressive behavior was tracked (Eron, Lefkowitz, Huesmann & Walder, 1972; Lefkowitz, Eron, Walder, & Huesmann, 1972). The boys whose mothers reported the heaviest viewing of violent programs at age 8 were the most aggressive youth at age 19. By contrast, being aggressive at age 8 did not predict viewing violent television programs at age 19. This research suggests that viewing violent content causes aggressive conduct. By age 30, the heavy early viewers of violence were more likely to have been convicted of violent crimes (Huessman & Miller, 1994). A follow-up study of more than 500 elementary-aged children revealed that boys and girls who reported more exposure to violent television were more aggressive when they were young adults 15 years later (Huessman, Moise-Titus, Podolski, & Eron, 2003). Similarly, a cross-cultural comparison of U.S. and Finnish boys and girls also found positive correlations between viewing television violence and peer nominations of aggressive behavior (Huesmann, Lagerspetz & Eron, 1984). D. R. Anderson and colleagues (2001) found that children who identified with media characters and who used aggressive media content in their play were more aggressive as adolescents. Intelligence also moderated aggressive influences in one study (Wiegerman, Kuttschreuter & Baarda, 1992), but not in another study (D. R. Anderson et al., 2001). Taken together, these studies implicate early exposure or investment with violent television content to long-term antisocial conduct by both boys and girls.

Negative effects of exposure to violent television are also found in field experiments. For example, Friedrich and Stein (1973) showed children aggressive cartoons, prosocial episodes from *Mister Rogers' Neighborhood,* or nature films. Exposure took place three times per week for a 1-month period in their preschools. Children's aggression at their preschool prior to exposure was compared to their aggression after exposure. Children who were initially more aggressive became even more aggressive after a steady diet of violent cartoons.

Violent videogame exposure over time has also been linked to children's aggressive conduct. In a study of third- and fifth-grade children, C. Anderson and colleagues (2007) found that those who reported playing more violent videogames were more aggressive five months later than those who did not play violent videogames. Increases occurred in both physical and verbal aggression. Meta-analyses that analyze bodies of experimental research also find that playing violent videogames increases children's aggressive behavior, their aggressive cognition, and lowers their prosocial behavior (C. Anderson, 2001).

Prosocial media. Media have the potential to enlighten and improve developmental outcomes by increasing prosocial behaviors like helping, sharing, and feeling empathy for others. Children who were exposed to *Mister Rogers' Neighborhood* in their preschools for a 1-month period, for example, increased in following rules, persisting at tasks, and in tolerating delays (Friedrich & Stein, 1973). Children who were from low-income backgrounds also became more nurturing, expressed their feelings more often, and cooperated better with others.

Teachers can use techniques in their classrooms to improve the effectiveness of exposure to prosocial television programs. For instance, Friedrich-Cofer and colleagues (1979) had Head Start teachers sing and engage in puppet play with children after the children viewed *Mister Rogers' Neighborhood.* Other groups of children viewed with materials in the classroom, with irrelevant materials in the classroom, or viewed neutral films with irrelevant materials in the classroom. Exposure and classroom activities took place over a 2-month period for 30 minutes each day. Prosocial interactions increased with peers the most when viewing the prosocial programs was accompanied by teacher-led rehearsal activities. Exposure to other prosocial programs, such as *Barney and Friends* and *Sesame Street,* yield similar beneficial prosocial outcomes when viewed in school settings with teacher-led discussions and materials that support the program message (Singer & Singer, 1998; Zielinska & Chambers, 1995).

Meta-analyses indicate that exposure to prosocial programs can improve altruism and other social behaviors, yielding moderate (Hearold, 1986) or weak-to-moderate effect sizes (Mares & Woodard, 2005). While Hearold (1986) found positive effects in both home and experimental studies, Mares and Woodard (2005) found stronger effects in experimental than in home situations.

Obesity. Obesity is a major epidemic in the United States as well as in many other areas of the world (Kaplan, Liverman, & Kraak, 2005). Energy balance is a key concept in obesity prevention and in weight control more generally. That is, to maintain a consistent weight, the amount of energy consumed must be balanced by the amount of calories burned through physical activity (Kaplan et al., 2005). Obesity may be caused by exposure to food commercials (an intake issue); or obesity can be caused by the sedentary patterns involved in most media experiences that may limit physical activity (an output issue); or both factors can contribute to obesity.

In an evaluation conducted by the Institute of Medicine and the Board on Children, Youth, and Families at the National Academies, the role that marketing plays in obesity and dietary patterns of children and youth was examined. After examining more than 100 studies, strong evidence was found that television advertising influences food and beverage preferences and purchase requests of children ages 2–11 years, strong evidence was found that television advertising influences the *short-term food consumption* of children ages 2–11 years, and strong evidence was found that diet-related health is associated with adiposity in children ages 2–11 years and teens ages 12–18 years though possible causal factors in that final link could not be ruled out definitively (for ethical reasons, experimental studies cannot be conducted that could make children obese, which are needed to establish that

final link causally) (McGinnis, Gootman & Kraak, 2006). Other data suggest that obesity is associated more with television advertising rather than the sedentary life styles that can come as a result of media exposure (Vandewater & Cummings, 2008).

Videogames have also been examined as a potential reason for overweight and obese youth. Using national diary data from the Panel Study of Income Dynamics, moderate video game play had a clearer negative impact on obesity than did heavy levels of television exposure (Vandewater, Shim & Caplovitz, 2004). However, videogames are increasingly being created as exergames that require gross motor movement for effective results. Youth who play Wii sports exergames, for instance, expend more calories than those who play a videogame (Graves, Stratton, Ridgers & Cable, 2007) or who work on a computer (Staiano & Calvert, 2011). Caloric expenditure is greatest when adolescents compete against a peer rather than solely against a machine (Staiano & Calvert, 2011). The pattern of results suggests complex and multifaceted reasons for obesity that are related to differential media use and exposure patterns.

Content analyses of the kinds of food products marketed on popular children's websites find the same high fat, low nutritional foods marketed online as those that are advertised on television (Alvy & Calvert, 2008). However, some of the same marketing techniques that lead to obesity could also be used to promote healthier eating habits. For example, a pacman advergame in which a child's character earned points for "eating" healthy snacks and beverages and lost points when their character "ate" unhealthy snacks led to healthier snack selections by low-income African American children than when a child's character was rewarded for eating the unhealthy snacks and punished for eating the healthy snacks (Pempek & Calvert, 2009).

Developmental considerations. What children bring to a media experience strongly influences what they take away. In the first two years of life, infants and toddlers demonstrate a video deficit in which they are able to imitate the behaviors demonstrated in a live presentation better than from a video demonstration of the same content. Repetition decreases the video deficit (Barr, Muentener, Gracia, Fujimoto, & Chávez, 2007) as does verbal labeling of the content (Barr & Wyss, 2008). Because very young children will watch the same video repeatedly, the video deficit may not be as big an issue in the home as it is when children are in experimental lab studies. Even so, the superiority of learning from live presentations by very young children should provide pause for those who market their video products as educational when they are directed at such a young audience. Motor skills that allow very young children to participate in computer activities are also poorly developed in toddlers. According to Kaiser Family survey data, children shift from using a computer from a parent's lap to autonomous computer use between ages 2½ to 3½ (Calvert et al., 2005). However, touchable tablet interfaces such as the iPad, which are easier for very young children to use than a mouse interface, could allow autonomous computer use at younger ages.

During the preschool through early childhood years, children experience considerable difficulty in comprehending plots, particularly those directed at an older audience (Calvert, Huston, Watkins & Wright, 1982). Mature plot comprehension requires children to separate the central plot relevant from the incidental irrelevant material, link those central events together in a temporal sequence, and draw inferences to connect that content together as well as infer how characters feel and what their motives are (Collins, Wellman, Keniston & Westby, 1978). Plot comprehension can be improved by live or onscreen adults who label content for children, repeated exposure to the content, and the judicious use of production features, such as pairing attention-getting auditory features with important central content (Calvert et al., 1982). Computer skills continue to be difficult for young children, with those who have better developed executive functioning skills demonstrating better skills at using a mouse (Lauricella, Barr & Calvert, 2009). Even so, Latina 4-year-old girls who interact with program content learn it better than those who view that content with an adult who does not describe or engage the child with the content in any way (Calvert, Strong, Jacobs, & Conger, 2007).

What youth do and say online reflects key developmental issues, such as identity development. Avatar construction of online characters in late childhood, for instance, remains an accurate reflection of biological sex (Calvert, Mahler, Zehnder, Jenkins & Lee, 2003; Calvert, Strouse, Strong, & Huffaker, & Lai, 2008), with girls and boys often struggling to find a common thread of interaction. For instance, whether children know each other or not, boys in multiuser domains (MUDs), which are online forums where children can interact with one another in settings like audiovisual animated backdrops, typically play by making up games or engaging in pretense whereas girls prefer to talk, reflecting traditional gender roles (Calvert et al, 2003; Calvert et al., 2008). Racial issues permeate online interactions. For instance, racist speech is present in online venues like chat rooms, even though the Internet *per se* offers the opportunity of a color-blind experience (Tynes, Reynolds, & Greenfield, 2004).

During adolescence, youth increasingly create rather than just consume media. For instance, youth create profiles on social networking websites such as myspace.com and facebook.com that reflect who they are, including their media preferences (Pempek et al., 2009). In their blogs, adolescents create and present intimate details of their lives, such as their sexual identity (Huffaker & Calvert, 2005). Coded language systems (e.g., the letter *u* represents the word *you*) are created that allow youth to discuss events in real time at about the speed of talking (Greenfield & Subramanyam, 2003).

Directions for Future Research

For an area that changes so rapidly, that is so pervasive, that covers so many different content areas, and that consumes so much of our children's time, it is striking that so much research fails to include measures of media influence on developmental outcomes. The Panel Study of Income Dynamics (PSID) and its associated Child Development Supplement (CDS), which tracks media use over time in relation to multiple developmental outcomes, is a notable exception. Inclusion of some of the questions from the PSID-CDS, such as those that address exposure to the newer media, would be highly useful for determining a range of developmental outcomes, including aggression, obesity, cognitive skills such as executive function skills, educational attainment, and prosocial behavior.

Although cross-sectional in nature, the media use survey conducted by the Kaiser Family Foundation provided a standard set of questions in which data were being systematically collected. Qualitative studies are also added to pursue some of the more interesting findings, such as why parents put television sets in very young children's bedrooms. Tracking multiple cohorts over time with this survey could be very fruitful. For instance, does having a television set in the bedroom create an environment where children go to sleep with a television set on? If so, how does this kind of experience set the stage not only for restful sleep, but also for academic performance and long-term self-regulation patterns over time.

Because multitasking is now the normal experience of middle childhood through the adolescent years (Rideout et al., 2005), it is important to update our knowledge about the reliability and validity of media exposure measures. This issue has not been tackled since the study conducted by Anderson and colleague in the early 1980s. Since then, a proliferation of media being used by children and youth simultaneously has complicated the task of reporting their own media use patterns. The use of newer technologies to quantify media exposure, such as time sampling measures in which children are called on cell phones and asked what they were just doing, could be highly informative. At a broader level, what does exposure mean if one is listening to music and writing a report on a computer while also replying to instance messages and visiting websites such as Facebook and youtube? Is there a primary task, a secondary task, and tertiary tasks, or all they all primary tasks that are rotated through very rapidly? How does such exposure influence basic cognitive processes such as attention and learning? Media interfaces are now mobile and touchable. How do these shifts in portability and mode of access (touching) influence media use patterns and the age at which children can readily use interactive media?

The United States recently transited to high definition digital television as the standard broadcast format, replacing the traditional analog format (Calvert, 2008). This shift allows youth a much more compelling media experience than that of generations past. How will the larger "television" sets and the surround sound home theaters that offer amazing visual and auditory clarity influence developmental outcomes?

Conclusion

Children's lives are embedded in an ever-changing media environment. Wherever they go, whatever they do, screen media are almost always with youth. Media content can delight, entertain, and educate our children. Or media content can lead to undesirable outcomes such as aggression and obesity. While the interfaces are rapidly changing, the developmental capabilities and needs of children are not. The challenge of the 21st century is for societies to accentuate the positive opportunities afforded by media while minimizing the negative ones. To do so, a clear understanding of how media effects take place in relation to multiple developmental outcomes, which is facilitated by reliable and valid measures of media exposure, is essential.

References

Alvy, E., & Calvert, S. L. (2008). Food marketing on popular children's websites: A content analysis. *Journal of the American Dietetic Association, 108,* 710–713.

American Academy of Pediatrics, Committee on Public Education. (1999). Media education. *Pediatrics, 104,* 341–342.

Anderson, C., & Bushman, B. (2001). Effects of violent videogames on aggressive behavior, aggressive cognition, aggressive affect, physiological arousal, and prosocial behavior: A meta-analytic review of the scientific literature. *Psychological Science, 12,* 353–359.

Anderson, D. R., Bryant, J., Wilder, A., Crawley, A., Santomero, A., & Williams, M. E. (2000). Researching *Blue's Clues*: Viewing behavior and impact. *Media Psychology, 2,* 179–194.

Anderson, C. A., Gentile, D. A., & Buckley, K. E. (2007). *Violent video game effects on children and adolescents: Theory, research, and public policy.* New York: Oxford University Press.

Anderson, D. R., & Hale, K. (2009). Children, media, and methodology. *American Behavioral Scientist, 52,* 1204–1219.

Anderson, D. R., Huston, A. C., Schmitt, K. L., Linebarger, D. L., & Wright, J. C. (2001). Early childhood television viewing and adolescent behavior: The recontact study. *Monographs of the Society for Research in Child Development, 66.*

Anderson, D. R., Lorch, E. P., Field, D. E., Collins, P. A., & Nathan, J. G. (1986). Television viewing at home: Age trends in visual attention and time with TV. *Child Development, 57,* 1024–1033.

Anderson, D. R., & Pempek, T. (2005). Television and very young children. *American Behavioral Scientist, 48,* 505–522.

Ball, S., & Bogatz, G. A. (1970). *The first year of Sesame Street: An evaluation.* Princeton, NJ: Educational Testing Service.

Barr, R., Lauricella, A., Zack, E. & Calvert, S. L. (2010). Infant and early childhood exposure to adult-directed and child-directed television programming: Relations with cognitive skills at age four. *Merrill Palmer Quarter, 56,* 21–48.

Barr, R., Muentener, P., Gracia, A., Fujimoto, M., & Chávez, V. (2007). The effect of repetition on imitation from television during infancy. *Developmental Psychology, 49,* 196–207.

Barr, R. & Wyss, N. (2008). Reenactment of televised content by 2-year-olds: Toddlers use language learned from television to solve a difficult imitation problem. *Infant Behavior and Development, 31,* 696–703.

Bogatz, G. A., & Ball, S. (1971). *The second year of Sesame Street: A continuing evaluation.* Princeton, NJ: Educational Testing Service.

Cahn, A., Kalagian, T. & Lyon, C. (2008). Business models for children's media. In S. L. Calvert & B. J. Wilson (Eds). *The handbook of children, media, and development.* Malden, MA: Wiley-Blackwell.

Calvert, S. L. (1999). *Children's journeys through the information age.* Boston: McGraw Hill.

Calvert, S. (2006). Media and early development. In K. McCartney & D. Phillips (Ed.), *Blackwell handbook of early childhood development,* pp. 508–530. Malden, MA: Blackwell Publishing.

Calvert, S. L. (2008). The Children's Television Act. In S. L. Calvert & B. J. Wilson (Eds). *The handbook of children, media, and development,* pp. 455–478. Malden, MA: Wiley-Blackwell.

Calvert, S. L., & Conger, E. A. (2007, March). Empathy for children's learning of DVD content. Paper presented at the Society for Research in Child Development, Boston, MA.

Calvert, S. L., Huston, A. C., Watkins, B. A., & Wright, J. C. (1982). The relation between selective attention to television forms and children's comprehension of content. *Child Development, 53,* 601–610.

Calvert, S. L., Mahler, B. A., Zehnder, S. M., Jenkins, A. & Lee, M (2003). Gender differences in preadolescent children's online interactions: Symbolic modes of self-presentation and self-expression. *Journal of Applied Developmental Psychology, 24,* 627–644.

Calvert, S. L., Rideout, V., Woolard, J., Barr, R., & Strouse, G. (2005). Age, ethnicity, and socioeconomic patterns in early computer use: A national survey. *American Behavioral Scientist, 48,* 590–607.

Calvert, S. L., Strong, B. L., Jacobs, E. L. & Conger, E. E. (2007). Interaction and participation for young Hispanic and Caucasian children's learning of media content. *Media Psychology, 9,* 431–445.

Calvert, S. L., Strouse, G. & Murray, K. (2006). The role of empathy in adolescents' role model selection and learning of DVD content. *Journal of Applied Developmental Psychology, 27,* 444–455.

Calvert, S. L., Strouse, G.A., Strong, B. & Huffaker, D. A. & Lai, S. (2008). Preadolescent boys' and girls' virtual MUD play. *Journal of Applied Developmental Psychology, 29,* 250–264.

Christakis, D. A., Zimmerman, F. J., DiGiuseppe, D. L., & McCarty, C. A. (2004). Early television exposure and subsequent attentional problems in children. *Pediatrics, 113,* 708–713.

Collins, W. A. Wellman, H., Keniston, A. & Westby, S. (1978). Age-related aspects of comprehension and inference from a televised dramatic narrative. *Child Development*, 49, 389–399.

Common Sense Media (Fall 2011). Zero to Eight: Children's Media Use in America. Available at http://www.commonsensemedia.org/research/zero-eight-childrens-media-use-america.

Csikszentmihalyi, M. & Kubey, R. (1981). Television and the rest of life: A systematic comparison of subjective experience. *Public Opinion Quarterly*, 45, 317–328.

Eron, L. (1963). Relationship of TV viewing habits and aggressive behavior in children. *Journal of Abnormal and Social Psychology*, 67, 193–196.

Eron, L. D., Lefkowitz, M. M., Huesmann, L. R., & Walder, L. O. (1972). Does television violence cause aggression? *American Psychologist*, 27, 253–263.

Evans, M. K., Pempek, T. A., Kirkorian, H. L., Frankenfield, A. E., & Anderson, D. R. (May 2004). *The impact of background television on complexity of play*. Presented at the biennial International Conference for Infant Studies, Chicago, IL.

Friedrich, L. K., & Stein, A. H. (1973). Aggressive and prosocial television programs and the natural behavior of preschool children. *Monographs of the Society for Research in Child Development*, 38(4), 1–63, Serial No. 151.

Friedrich-Cofer, L. K., Huston-Stein, A., Kipnis, D., Susman, E. & Clewit, A. (1979). Environmental enhancement of prosocial television content: Effect on interpersonal behavior, imaginative play, and self-regulation in a natural setting. *Developmental Psychology*, 15, 637–646.

Graves L., Stratton G., Ridgers N. D., Cable N. T. (2007). Comparison of energy expenditure in adolescents when playing new generation and sedentary computer games: a cross sectional study. *British Medical Journal*, 335, 1282–1284.

Greenfield, P. M. & Subramanyam, K. (2003). Online discourse in a teen chatroom: New codes and new modes of coherence in a visual medium. *Journal of Applied Developmental Psychology*, 24, 713–738.

Hearold, S. (1986). A synthesis of 1043 effects of television on social behavior. In G. Comstock (Ed.), *Public communication and behavior*, pp. 65–133, Vol. 1. New York: Academic Press.

Hoffner, C. (2008). Parasocial and online social relationships. In S. L. Calvert & B. J. Wilson (Eds). *The handbook of children, media, and development*. Malden, MA: Wiley-Blackwell.

Huesmann, L. R., & Eron, L. D. (Eds.) (1986). *Television and the aggressive child: A cross-national comparison*. Hillsdale, NJ: Erlbaum.

Huesmann, L. R., Lagerspetz, K. & Eron, L. (1984). Intervening variables in the TV-violence-aggression relation: Evidence from two countries. *Developmental Psychology*, 20, 746–755.

Huesmann, L. R. & Miller, L. (1994). Long-term effects of repeated exposure to media violence in childhood. In L. R. Huesmann (Ed)., *Aggressive behavior: Current perspectives*. New York: Plenum.

Huesmann, L. R., Moise-Titus, J., Podolski, C., & Eron, L. D. (2003). Longitudinal relations between children's exposure to TV violence and their aggressive and violent behavior in young adulthood: 1977–1992. *Developmental Psychology*, 39, 201–221.

Huffaker, D. A., & Calvert, S. L. (2005). Gender, identity, and language use in teenage blogs. *Journal of Computer-Mediated Communication*.

Huston, A. C., Wright, J. C., Rice, M. L., Kerkman, D., & St. Peters, M. (1990). Development of television viewing patterns in early-childhood – a longitudinal investigation. *Developmental Psychology*, 26(3), 409–420.

Jackson, L. A., von Ey, A., Biocca, F. A., Barbatsis, G., Zhao, Y., & Fitzgerald, H. E. (2006). Does home internet use influence the academic performance of low-income children? *Developmental Psychology*, 42, 429–435.

Kaplan, J. P., Liverman, C. T. & Kraak, V. I. (Eds.) and the Committee on Prevention of Obesity in Children and Youth (2005). *Preventing childhood obesity: Health in the balance*. Washington, DC: National Academies Press.

Lauricella, A., Barr, R. & Calvert, S. L. (2009). Emerging computer skills: Influences of young children's executive functioning abilities and parental scaffolding techniques, *Journal of Children and Media*, 3, 217–233.

Lefkowitz, M., Eron, L., Walder, L. & Huesmann, R. (1972). Television violence and child aggression: A follow-up study. In G. A. Comstock & E. A. Rubenstein (Eds.), *Television and social behavior, Vol, III*. Washington, DC: U.S. Government Printing Office.

Mares, M. L., & Woodard, E. (2005). Positive effects of television on children's social interactions: A meta-analysis. *Media Psychology*, 7, 301–322.

McGinnis J. M., Gootman J. A., Kraak V. I. (Eds.) and the Committee on Food Marketing and the Diets of Children and Youth, Food and

Nutrition Board, Board on Children, Youth, and Families, Institute of Medicine of the National Academies. (2006). *Food marketing to children and youth: Threat or opportunity?* Washington, DC: National Academies Press.

Montgomery, K., & Pasnik, S. (1996). Web of deception: Threats to children of online marketing. Washington, DC: Center for Media Education.

Pempek, T. A., & Calvert, S. L. (2009). Tipping the balance: Use of advergames to promote consumption of nutritious foods and beverages by low-income African American Children. *Archives of Pediatrics & Adolescent Medicine, 163*, 633–637.

Pempek, T. A., Yermolayeva, Y. & Calvert, S. L. (2009). College students social networking experiences on Facebook. *Journal of Applied Developmental Psychology, 30*, 227–238.

Rice, M. L., Huston, A. C., Truglio, R., & Wright, J. C. (1990). Words from *Sesame Street* – learning vocabulary while viewing. *Developmental Psychology, 26*, 421–428.

Rideout, V., Foehr, U.G. & Robert, D.E. (January 2010) *Generation M²: Media in the lives of 8- to 18-year-olds.* Menlo Park, CA: Kaiser Family Foundation.

Rideout, V., & Hamel, E. (2006). *The media family: Electronic media in the lives of infants, toddlers, preschoolers and their parents.* Menlo Park, CA: Kaiser Family Foundation.

Rideout, V., Roberts, D. F., & Foehr, U. G. (2005). *Generation M: Media in the lives of 8–18 year-olds. Executive Summary.* Menlo Park, CA: Kaiser Family Foundation.

Rideout, V., Vandewater, E., & Wartella, E. (2003). *Zero to six: Electronic media in the lives of infants, toddlers, and preschoolers.* Menlo Park, CA: Kaiser Family Foundation.

Rubin, A. (1994). Media uses and effects: A uses-and-gratification perspective. In J. Bryant & D. Zillmann (Eds.), *Media effects: Advances in theory and research.* Hillsdale, NJ: Erlbaum.

Singer, J. L., & Singer, D. G. (1998). Barney & Friends as entertainment and education. In J. K. Asamen & G. Berry (Eds.), *Research paradigms, television, and social behavior,* pp. 305–367. Thousand Oaks, CA: Sage.

Staiano, A. E., & Calvert, S. L. (2011). Wii tennis play for low-income African American adolescents' energy expenditure. *Cyberpsychology.* Available at http://cyberpsychology.eu/view.php?cisloclanku=2011060801&article=1.

Thompson, D. A., & Christakis, D. A. (2005). The association between television viewing and irregular sleep schedules among children less than 3 years of age. *Pediatrics, 116*, 851–856.

Thornburgh, D., & Lin, H. S. (Eds.) and the Committee to Study Tools and Strategies for Protecting Kids from Pornography and their Applicability to Other Internet Content (2002). *Youth, pornography, and the Internet.* Washington, DC: National Academy Press.

Tynes, B., Reynolds, L., & Greenfield, P. M. (2004). Adolescence, race and ethnicity on the Internet: A comparison of discourse in monitored and unmonitored chat rooms. *Journal of Applied Developmental Psychology, 25*, 667–684.

Vandewater, E., & Bickham, D. (2004). The impact of educational television on young children's reading in the context of family stress. *Journal of Applied Developmental Psychology, 25*, 717–728.

Vandewater, E., Bickham, D. S., & Lee, J. H. (2006). Time well spent? Relating television use to children's free-time activities. *Pediatrics, 117*, 181–191.

Vandewater, E. A., Bickham, D. S., Lee, J. H., Cummings, H. E., Wartella, E. A., & Rideout, V. J. (2005). When the television is always on: Heavy television exposure and young children's development. *American Behavioral Scientist, 48*, 562–577.

Vandewater, E., & Cummings, H. (2008). Media use and childhood obesity. In S. L. Calvert & B. J. Wilson (Eds). *The handbook of children, media, and development.* Malden, MA: Wiley-Blackwell.

Vandewater, E. A., & Lee, S. J. (2007, March). Can I have my own TV?: Relating bedroom television to adolescent activities and academic skills. Paper presented at the Society for Research in Child Development, Boston, MA.

Vandewater, E. A., & Lee, J. (2009). Measuring children's media use in the digital age. *American Behavioral Scientist, 52*, 1152–1176.

Vandewater, E. A., Park, S. E., Huang, X., & Wartella, E. A. (2005). "No – you can't watch that": Parental rules and young children's media use. *American Behavioral Scientist, 48*, 608–623.

Vandewater, E., Shim, M. & Caplovitz, A. (2004). Linking obesity and activity level with children's television and video game use. *Journal of Adolescence, 27*, 71–85.

Wiegerman, O., Kuttschreuter, M., & Baarda, B. (1992). A longitudinal study of the effects of television viewing on aggressive and prosocial behaviors. *British Journal of Social Psychology, 31*, 147–164.

Wright, J. C., Huston, A. C., Murphy, K. C., St Peters, M., Pinon, M., Scantlin, R. (2001). The relations of early television viewing to school readiness and vocabulary of children from low-income families: The early window project. *Child Development, 72*, 1347–1366.

Wright, J. C., Huston, S. C., Ross, R. P., Calvert, S. L., Rollandeli, D., Weeks, L. A. Raessi, P., & Potts, R. (1984). Pace and continuity of television programs: Effects on children's attention and comprehension. *Developmental Psychology, 20*, 653–666.

Zielinska, I. E., & Chambers, B. (1995). Using group viewing of television to teach preschool children social skills. *Journal of Educational Television, 21*, 85–95.

Part IV

MEASUREMENT

CHAPTER 26

Parenting Behavior as the Environment Where Children Grow

Ruth Feldman

Parenting behavior is not only the feature that defines the evolution of mammals and the component of parenting shared across mammalian species – it is the only aspect of the parenting phenomenon available to the infant. Following birth, both the parent's physiology and the parent's mindset are available to the infant only through the filter of the parent's relational behavior. As such, it can be argued that parenting *is* behavior – or repeatedly executed sets of specific behaviors of varying goals, rhythms, intensities, frequencies, and durations. Because of the critical importance of such behaviors for infant growth, survival, and well-being, the "parenting behavior" constellation consists of a highly conserved species-specific repertoire that may be more restricted and biologically based during the first postpartum period and gains richness, culture-specificity, flexibility, and individual variations as children grow. This early set of parenting behavior provides the foundation for the parent-infant bond, considered as the cornerstone of children's biological, cognitive, social, and emotional development (Feldman, 2007a; Leckman et al., 2004).

Ethological models, beginning with the seminal work of Lorenz (1950) and adapted to the study of human development by Bowlby (1969) and his followers, were the first to highlight the parent-infant bond as the central determinant of growth and maturation and advocated a behavioral, bottom-up approach to the study of bond formation. Bonding, according to these models, is expressed in a specific set of behaviors that emerge or intensify during periods of bond formation and such behaviors should be meticulously documented as a prerequisite for theory building. This behavior-focused perspective reorganized thinking in the field of infant development, especially with regards to the role of parenting behavior in the formulation of developmental theory. According to theoretical models derived from Ethology, observing the behaviors parents exhibit toward their young during the period of bond formation may provide the best entry point into the science of parenting and, consequently, into the study of human development.

Among the central questions in the conceptualization of parenting as an area of inquiry is: how are parenting behaviors "internalized" and become a part of the infant's mind, body, and behavior. Rutter and Sroufe (2000) argue that the central question for the study of social-emotional development in the next millennium should be: how do relational patterns experienced in infancy turn into the child's stable personality orientations across the lifespan. This question taps one of the central issues in development – the transformation from objective behavior into subjective mental content, from the interpersonal arena into the intrapsychic sphere, and from momentary parental behaviors to stable child competencies. Every theory of social-emotional growth, including attachment theory (Bowlby, 1969), psychoanalytic object-relations theory (Winnicott, 1956), and theories of socialization (Maccoby, 1992) and morality (Hoffman, 2000), is guided by the underlying assumption that the child's stable personality orientations – in terms of his sense of security in the world, the capacity for empathy, the development of emotion regulation, and the ability to accept societal rules and acquire a moral code – draw on the infant's earliest relationship with the parents. These repeated behavioral patterns and their long-term effects have been variously termed as "internal working model" (Bowlby, 1969), theorized as mental structures based on repeated experiences of maternal sensitivity across infancy, or "RIG – repeated interactions that have been generalized" (Stern, 1995), formulated as abstracted relational schemas that shape the child's emergent self. Psychoanalytic theories of human development have similarly proposed that development is based on the internalization of actual relationships experienced in infancy, beginning with Freud's (1916–1917) position on personality growth as emanating from a series of structural transformations in the infant's relationships with the mother, Kohut's (1971) emphasis on the role of repeatedly experienced maternal empathy for the consolidation of the self, Loewald's (1960) formulations on mother-infant ongoing attunement as the origins of the individual's internalizations,

and Winnicott's (1956) conceptualization of the "holding environment" as a framework of predictable maternal actions that provides the foundation for the child's creativity, authenticity, and the use of complex symbols throughout life.

The long-term effects of early parenting behavior on the development of personality echoes the dilemma that baffled philosophers since Plato – how do objective, quantifiable, and observable events turn into subjective experiences, the "stuff" of mind and personality, and what is the interface between the subjectively experienced inner world and external reality. Recent neurobiological models on self and consciousness have similarly grappled with the unexplainable gap between the third person objective assessment of consciousness – the specific brain structures, circuits, and neurons that support the conscious mind, and the first person phenomenological experience of subjectivity and individuality (Damasio, 2003; Edelman, 2004). The central hypothesis being proposed in this chapter is that parenting behavior, in particular the measurable "objective" experience coconstructed between parent and child during social interactions, variously termed as "reciprocity," "coregulation," "attunement," "mutual-influence," or "synchrony," provides a terminal station for the transformation of objective events into subjective experiences that support the formation of personality traits. This prototypical experience forms the interface where the parent's physiology, mental representations, affective state, and social networks are integrated into a specific parenting behavioral style; the infant's physiology, emerging mental world, and relational matrix is integrated into the child's behavioral style; and the behavioral patterns of the interacting partners shape each other in a reciprocal manner. Only through this interface of mutually influencing behaviors can the parent's physiology and representational world begin to have an impact on the child's mind and behavior and begin to provide the building blocks for the child's stable competencies, internal representations, well-being, and emotional growth. The

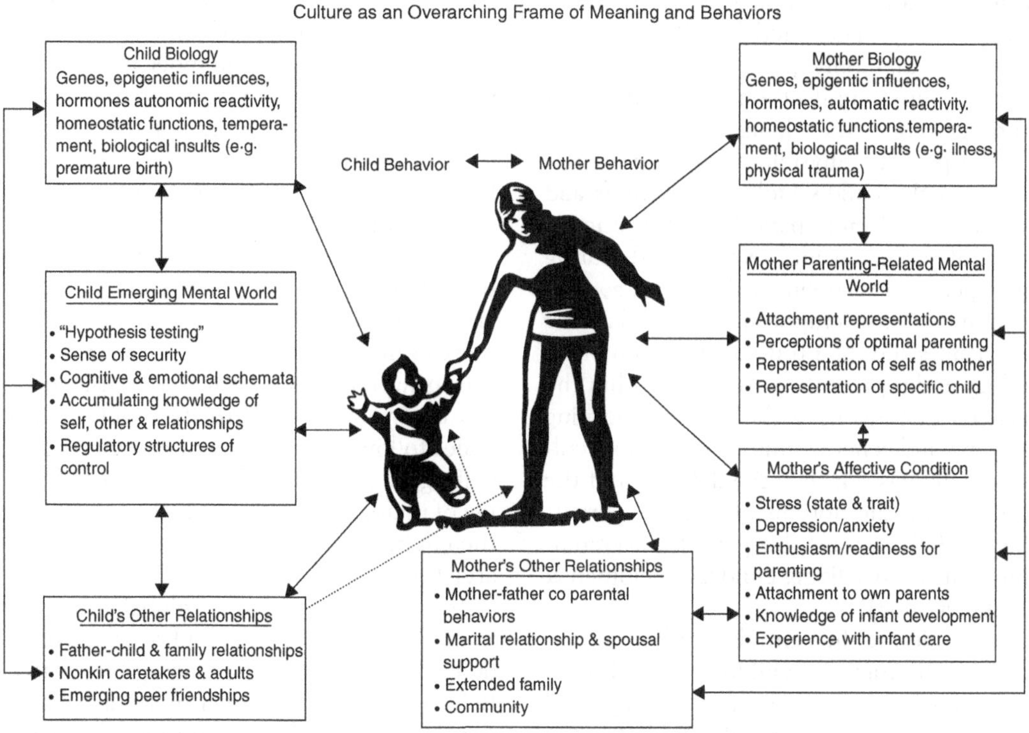

Culture as an Overarching Frame of Meaning and Behaviors

Figure 26.1. Parenting behavior as the interface of mutual influences between parent and child as reciprocally related to physiological, mental, affective, and contextual conditions.

proposed theoretical model is presented in Figure 26.1.

As seen in Figure 26.1, the central interface highlighted in the model is the mother-infant relational exchange. The term "mother" (rather than parent) is used to emphasize the associations of human parental behavior to its mammalian heritage and the absence of paternal care for 97 percent of species, but similar processes may be proposed for fathers (studies of both maternal and paternal behavior are detailed later). Maternal behavior is shaped by the mother's physiology, mental world, affective condition, and matrix of relationships and feeds back and reorganizes these components. In the same way, the infant's behavior is reciprocally connected to the child's biological dispositions, emerging mental structures, and other relationships. The only avenue by which maternal biology, affective state, and mental world can have a direct impact on the child's biological systems and internal representations is through

the central interface where the mother's behavior continuously remodels the infant's behavior and is reciprocally reorganized by it. The model contains one exception for a direct impact on the infant's behavior that is not by means of the mother-infant behavioral exchange – the mother-father coparental behavior, the father-child and family relational patterns, and the sibling relationship, all of which are behavioral components. According to theories of socialization (Asher & Gottman, 1981; Baumrind, 1973; Dunn, 1991; Hartup, 1989; Parke & Bhavnagri, 1989; Schneider, Attilit, Nadel, & Weissberg, 1989), children's social behavior is shaped by two contextual mechanisms: participation and observation. "Participation" refers to the shaping of social behavior through ongoing interactions in which the child is a participant and "observation" considers the direct impact of interparental or interfamily interaction patterns on child behavior in settings where the child is an observer of repeated interactions between significant others (Feldman, Masalha, & Derdikman-Eiron, 2010). The model still maintains, however, that only parental behavior can have a direct impact on infant behavior through repeated exchanges and the effects of the parent's physiology and representations on the child's biological systems and mental world must pass through the interface of actual events experienced during interpersonal relatedness (Feldman, 2007b). The model also emphasizes that relational exchanges and their mutual effects on physiology and representations occur within the general framework of the cultural meaning systems and general philosophies. These cultural schemas organize the definition of the self, dictate the notions of optimal parenting, and determine the parent's overarching goals in socializing children (Feldman & Masalha, 2007).

Considering the centrality of behavior in the development of children, it is thus of critical importance to form a language and develop systematic scientific tools for the observation of parenting behavior that would be valid across ages, cultures, and interacting adults; differentiate healthy from pathological development; and monitor the effects of intervention. For several decades, researchers have been searching for scientific ways to categorize parenting behavior, especially during the first year of life. The goal of these studies was to capture the parent's "sensitive," "responsive," and "mutually adaptive" style that is conducive for the infant's social-emotional growth and to define deviations from this optimal style in various forms of psychopathology. Studies have typically observed mother-infant free interactions (or less often father-infant interactions) at home or in a laboratory setting to assess the natural parental style that provides the "environment" for infant development. Two types of coding have been applied to address aspects of parenting behavior, microanalytic codes or global rating scales. Microanalytic coding includes a set of discrete behaviors, such as parent gaze at infant, "motherese" vocalizations, parental touch, or facial expressions, and the appearance of each behavior is marked for every small segment of time

and tallied across the entire interaction as frequencies (number of time a behavior occurred, for instance, number of time the parent touched the infant affectionately) or proportions (percentage of time out of the entire interaction this behavior was "on," for instance, proportion of time the parent expressed positive affect). Rating scales, on the other hand, were coded for the entire session on a Likert scale, often address more global aspects of the interaction, and may be more evaluative of the quality of the interaction, using constructs such as responsiveness, intrusiveness, or reciprocity. Such global scales follow the tradition of Ainsworth and colleagues (1978) and their use of global rating of maternal sensitivity, the key feature of the environment that promotes the infant's attachment security.

In this chapter, one global observational system of parent-child relationship is described in detail – the Coding Interactive Behavior – CIB (Feldman, 1998) as a window to the study of parenting behavior from infancy to adolescence. The CIB was developed more than a decade ago and has since been used in multiple studies of typically developing and high-risk samples ranging in age from newborns to adults and across a variety of cultures. In the following, the system is described, beginning with formulating the language for an observational system of parent-child interactions, continuing with the theoretical and methodological requirements of such a system, and concluding with the results of studies conducted with the system in different ages, pathological conditions, and cultural backgrounds. Associations between specific relational behaviors and specific components of the model – parent and child's physiology, representations, and social relationships – are presented to provide support for the proposed model. Longitudinal studies attesting to the stability of the parent and child's relational behavior and its prediction to stable components of the child's personality, adaptive behavior, and competence are presented using follow-up studies from infancy to adolescence. Results of these studies shed light on the development of parenting behavior as the environment where children grow and may begin to address the central question of social-emotional growth posed by Rutter and Sroufe (2000) – how do early relational patterns transform into stable personality orientations.

I. Formulating the Language for a Behavior Observation System

As a first step to formulating a system of behavior observation, one must define the main theoretically based constructs that are central to every human interaction. Such constructs provide the vectors against which the behaviors of specific social partners are evaluated and must tap the stable components of the individual and the dyadic interactive style. Relational constructs used should be broad enough to describe social interactions at every age, culture, and pathological condition yet specific enough as to not render the coding meaningless.

The CIB system is used to evaluate "free play" interactions between adults and children (or discussion sessions between adults and older children and adolescents or between romantic partners) and has been used for children from the newborn stage and up to adolescence, with a new version now available for interactions between romantic partners. The system contains 45 rating scales; 22 address the adult's behavior, 16 evaluate the child's behavior, five are dyadic codes, and two are overall codes, and codes are aggregated into several theoretically based constructs. Additional codes are available when the context is not that of free play, such as feeding, caregiving, cognitive problem-solving tasks, or book reading. A separate coding scheme is used when more than two people are interacting, typically a family, and this scheme evaluates the functioning of the family as a single unit. The CIB system uses global rating scales on a 5-point Likert scale and each code and the coding is not (apart from the newborn period) a time-sampling microlevel assessment of discrete behaviors. Yet, the system requires attention to various details, to multiple aspects of the

interaction, and to the specific behaviors of each partner as well as to the ongoing patterns of the relational unit.

The Architecture of Social Interactions

In the assessment of parenting behavior, the architecture of human relational behavior needs to be considered along three main lines: the level of observation, the target of observation, and the structure of observation, and each is discussed in turn.

a. *Level of observation.* The CIB system uses multiple discrete scales, which are first coded and then summarized into higher-order constructs. The system maintains both the discrete scales and the global constructs in order to enable different levels of observation that may be used to answer specific empirical questions and to assess how multiple aspects of behavior cohere into higher-order constructs under different conditions, such as age, culture, or pathology.

b. *Target of observation.* Most prior research on mother-infant interaction focused on the behavior of the mother, probably due to attachment theory's focus on maternal contributions to development. The CIB system considers behavior at both the level of individuals and the level of the interacting dyad or triad. The target of the analysis, therefore, first examines the separate behaviors of each individual (adult and child). Following, the target of the analysis shifts from the behaviors of each partner to the behaviors of the interacting dyad and the coding then addresses the organizational features of the dyadic system (Feldman, 2007c). In cases when interactions occur between more than two people – typically mother, father, and child or an entire family – the target of observation shifts again from individuals and dyads to the family system as a whole, consistent with perspectives on the development of family systems (Minuchin, 1985; Davies & Cicchetti, 2004). These shifting targets enable the researcher to consider the unique vectors that may be important for individuals during social action, for relational dyads during interpersonal exchanges, and for entire relational systems during interactions in order to capture the meaningful dimensions of social systems at each level of functioning.

c. *Structure of observation.* Every interaction consists of components that describe its "content" and components that describe its "form." Content refers to specific relational behaviors of each partner, for instance "parent positive affect," or "child vocalizations." These codes are based on discrete behaviors that always appear in a certain way, assess behaviors within a specific modality, and can be easily evaluated on the basis of the frequency and duration of their appearance. Codes related to form typically consider more subtle and fundamental aspects of the interaction, such as "parent intrusiveness," "child initiation," or "dyadic reciprocity." These codes may appear in various modalities, their level often depends on the response of the partner (e.g., certain maternal behaviors can be experienced as intrusive by some children but not by others), and their role is to describe the underlying organization of the interaction as it unfolds.

The CIB independent codes are aggregated into eight higher-order constructs. These constructs are based on theory and research in the field of early social development. The three adult constructs are sensitivity, intrusiveness, and limit-setting; the three child constructs are engagement-involvement, withdrawal, and compliance; and the two dyadic constructs are dyadic reciprocity and dyadic negative states. Additional codes and constructs are available for specific themes that appear in the child's play, for the level of the child's symbolic play, for feeding interactions, and for maternal and child negative affect and these constructs may be used in certain samples based on the research question. Each construct is built on a mixture of codes related

to "content" and codes related to "form." Similarly, each construct includes codes that are considered to be central for this construct at any age or culture and codes that may be part of the construct at some points in development but not in others or in some cultural settings but not in others. For instance, "parent acknowledgement" is a fundamental component of the "parent sensitivity" construct in any interaction at any age, whereas "parent affectionate touch" may be a more salient component of sensitivity in some cultures and the "parent imitation" code is a component of the sensitivity construct in the first months of life, but not thereafter.

Assessing Developmental Process

The social behavior of infants and young children changes dramatically during the first years of life: from the newborn's scant moments of attention, to the young infant's nonverbal involvement, to the preschooler's construction of complex play scenarios, to the older child and adolescent's complex verbal outputs. Parenting behavior, therefore, contains components that are meaningful across ages and codes that are specific to, or become salient at a certain time-window and serve a specific developmental goal during that period. For instance, during the 3- to 6-month stage, parents tend to move and manipulate the infant's arms and feet, rock the infant to and from a sitting position, or throw the baby in the air. These arousing forms of touch stimulate the child's physiological systems and create coherence between various nonverbal channels of communication, such as positive affect, vocalizations, gaze, and touch (Ferber, Feldman, & Makhul, 2008). During mother-child interactions in Western societies these patterns decrease significantly over the second six months of life, and in cases when physical manipulation is observed beyond the first year one should consider disturbances in the relationship. Yet, during father-child interactions, physical manipulation and "rough-and-tumble" play may be observed across the toddler and preschool years and even beyond, and the high father-child physical engagement is thought to promote the father-child bond (Lamb, 1977; Yogman, 1981). Similarly, in more traditional societies, father-child physical manipulation is the culturally accepted mode of relatedness, particularly with sons. For instance, father physical manipulation and "intrusive" behavior across the infant and toddler stages was found to predict *higher* child social competence at the childcare setting among Palestinian children, whereas similar intrusive patterns predicted *lower* social competence in Israeli toddlers (Feldman & Masalha, 2010), indicating that the growth-promoting components in one culture can be counterproductive in another.

Similar to differences related to cultural settings and interacting adults, there are parental behavior that may not be observed before a certain age. For instance, behaviors related to child compliance and parental limit setting, to joint attention, and to child on-task persistence are first observed toward the end of the first year and gain meaning as important vectors of the parent and child's social behavior only during the second year. Codes addressing the child's creative-symbolic play or competent use of the environment are likely to become meaningful aspect of the interaction during the second year of life, along with the maturation of symbols and the consolidation of intentional action (Bates, O'Connell, & Shore, 1987; Kagan, 1981; Messer, 1994). In this respect, the division of parenting behavior into codes that describe "content" and those that describe "form" may be useful. While the "content" of the interaction may change across development, in terms of the appearance or disappearance of specific behaviors along the maturation of cognitive, motor, and social skills, the organizational features of the interaction, the codes describing its "form," are likely to be meaningful across development, although levels of specific formal features may change with age. For instance, following the trajectory of the maternal sensitivity construct at six time points from birth to five years, it was found that sensitivity showed a curvilinear trajectory, with rapid increases during the first half-year, a decrease thereafter, and a plateau from two to five years of age (Feldman & Eidelman, 2009a).

In assessing parenting behavior as children's "environment," it may be useful to consider relational behaviors along five stages of social development from the newborn stage to adolescence, and examine the unique repertoire of parent and child's social behavior at each stage.

a. *The socially oriented newborn and the maternal postpartum repertoire.* The first post-partum month (or six weeks) is a unique period of "bio-behavioral transition" (Emde, Gaensbauer, & Harmon, 1976), when the newborn's homeostatic and self-regulatory functions and cycles of predictable caregiving start to consolidate (Sander, 1984). At this stage, infants are beginning to orient to the social world. Consistent with the work on maternal behavior in mammals (Meaney, 2001) and theoretical perspectives on bond formation (Leckman et al., 2005), parent-newborn observations should focus on the unfolding of the species-specific behaviors that support the parent-infant bond. At this stage, the CIB has a unique microlevel coding scheme that uses a time-sampling approach to assess parenting behaviors typical of the human mother in the postpartum period, including different forms of affectionate and functional touch, types of vocalizations, affective expressions, and gaze direction, as well as the infant state and gaze. Of the typical CIB rating scales, the only ones applicable for this age are maternal adaptation, maternal intrusiveness, maternal positive affect, and infant alertness. Feeding interactions begin to take shape as a central context for the emerging mother-infant bond and serve an important function for the development of the feeding relationship and the CIB system for newborn has a special version for feeding interactions that also consider the robustness of infant feeding and the nature of the mother's feeding behavior (Silberstein et al., 2009a).

b. *The relational infant.* Between the ages of three and twelve months, beginning with the emergence of face-to-face communication and up to the first signs of symbol use, infants are at the most social phase in life (Stern, 1985). Relational patterns in various modalities, such as gaze, affect, voice, touch, proximity position, body orientation, and arousal indicators, consolidate into configurations of dyad-specific behaviors, and parent and child begin to adapt to each other's pace and rhythms (Feldman, 2007a). Specific behaviors become markers of social interactions at this stage. Parents express positive affect and continuous gaze, emit "motherese" high-pitched vocalizations, acknowledge and elaborate the infant's signals in various interactive modalities, and engage in reciprocal ritualistic games. At the same time, parents develop a range of affective expressions, become resourceful in handling the child's changing mood and needs, and form a consistent style of relatedness. Infants show concrete social behaviors, such as gaze at the parent's face, social vocalizations, signs of positive affect, alertness and exuberance, and early forms of affectionate touch. During the second six months infants begin to initiate social interactions and the dyadic interacting style is marked by reciprocity, mutual adaptation, and a "dance-like" fluency and rhythm. These early face-to-face patterns are critical for the formation of the social brain circuitry (Johnson et al., 2005) and were found to predict a range of positive outcomes, including the development of self-regulation, symbolic skills, and empathy (Feldman, 2007a). Similarly, pathological conditions – whether stemming from the mother (e.g., postpartum depression), the infant (e.g., prematurity), or the context (e.g., poverty, war-related trauma) – are expressed in specific disruptions to the dyadic exchange at this stage.

c. *The just-verbal toddler.* With the development of symbol use and language (Nelson, 1985) and the child's emerging moral development at the second year (Kagan, 1984), parent-child interactions continue to show the positive indicators of social behavior observed in infancy, although face-to-face interactions are typically replaced by joint attention and manipulation of objects. These two emerging abilities – symbol formation and self-regulation – are expressed in new components of play. Toddlers begin to use elements of their environment for play, typically toys and objects, and the manner, complexity, and creativity of their use of the environment's offering is an important marker of their social and cognitive skills (Feldman, 2007d; Slade, 1987). At the same time, parents begin to socialize children to accepted social norms and interactions become more focused on the Dos and Don'ts of moral development (Emde, Biringen, Clyman, & Oppenheim, 1991). New parental behaviors related to limit setting and the child's willing compliance to the parental commands become markers of development in the social and moral domains. Other perspectives (Erikson, 1963; Patterson, Littman, & Bricker, 1967) highlight child autonomy as the central developmental milestone for the toddler stage and elements of the child's behavior, captured in codes such as "child initiation" and "child reliance on parent for help" mark the degree to which the child's social engagement is internally motivated and autonomous as opposed to being reliant and dependent. During the toddler stage, feeding interactions becomes an important context for the development of the parent-child relationship that may support or interfere with the child's emerging autonomy (Chatoor, 2000). Special feeding behaviors such as "negotiation during feeding" and "independent feeding" are important aspects of the feeding relationship and describe the development of autonomous feeding (Feldman, Keren, Gross-Rozval, & Tyano, 2004).

d. *The symbolic preschooler* From three to six years, play interactions develop markedly and the elements first noted at the toddler's play in their rudimentary form become more rich and complex, including creativity and symbolic expression, autonomy and initiation, compliance and self-regulation. In the preschool years, observational contexts other than free play may be used to index the parent-child relationship and its support of various developmental goals, such as a book-reading, a puppet show, or problem solving. With the development of the child's "internal state talk" (Bretherton & Beeghly, 1982) and theory-of-mind abilities, children become engaged in creating complex symbolic scenarios. In contrast to the toddler stage, when the coding focused on the complexity of the child's symbolic expression as a marker of development (Feldman, 2007d), in the play of preschoolers, coding the degree of complexity and creativity is complemented by a detailed assessment of the specific themes children enact during free play. Assessing these play themes may help shed light on the child's inner world of fantasy and guide diagnosis and treatment. In the preschool stage, the CIB has an additional appendix, which addresses typical themes that appear in the play of preschoolers, such as care and nurturance, construction and fixing, aggression, or adventure and travel. Play themes are coded for the frequency and intensity of their appearance and for whether they were initiated by the parent or child. Other behavioral elements that consolidate during the preschool years relate to the child's attention and affect. During this stage, play sessions become longer and enable the observer to focus on topics related to emotions and emotion regulation: Is the child able to maintain on-task persistence or does he/she gives in easily? Does the child's mood remain positive, negative, or alternates between energy and lethargy, engagement and disengagement?

Such observations may serve as early markers of later attention difficulties. Consistent with Erikson's (1963) view on the importance of initiation at the preschool years, the parent's handling of the child's independent action is an important parenting behavior that color the child's rearing environment at this stage, and codes such as "parent praising" and "parent criticizing" index the parent's appreciation or devaluation of the child's initiatives. Finally, as preschoolers begin to develop close peer friendships and to form independent relationships with parents and peers, it is important to differentiate the child's general affective expression during the observation from the affect directed to the parent. The distinction between codes such as "child positive affect," which assesses the child's global affect, and "child affection to parent" can serve as a specific marker of the attachment relationship at this stage

e. *The verbal-empathetic child.* During the school years, especially as children grow older, parent-child interactions no longer revolve around the parent and child's free play with toys. In studies of older children, two settings have been used for assessing the parent-child and whole-family interactions; a problem-solving or goal-directed activity (e.g., puzzle, joint drawing, art-work) and a joint discussion session on a preselected topic. For discussion sessions, dyads are either asked to choose a common conflict between them and try to reach a solution, or engage in a "positive" discussion and plan an enjoyable joint activity or remember a positive shared event. The coding of these discussions maintains the basic affective non-verbal codes ("content" codes) addressing the following specific social behaviors: Are partners comfortably gazing at each other or are they avoiding gaze? Is the overall affect warm and accepting? Is the vocal quality clear and warm? etc. Similarly, the original codes related to "form" are applicable in these contexts: Does parent acknowledge the child's viewpoint, position, plans, or memories? What is the level of child initiation of adaptable solution to conflicts? Can the dyadic atmosphere be described as reciprocal and fluent or as tense and constricted? Additional important codes created specifically for the conflict and positive discussions consider the parent's and child's capacity for empathetic resonance, which at this stage become central markers of the parenting environment. These makers of empathy, on the parts of both parent and child, chart the child's rearing environment as empathetic, involved, and facilitating of the child's individuality or as critical, harsh, or careless. During the discussion of conflicts it is important to evaluate the degree of perspective taking and empathic understanding: Is one partner "blaming" or "putting down" the other? Can parent and child see each other's point of view and show empathy to the needs of the other party despite inconvenience to the self? Is the style of discussion rational, practical, or emotional? At this age, children are expected to show empathy to the needs of others, including their parents. Data show that parents and school-age children typically discuss conflicts related to the child's responsibility for his/her room, clothes, pets, homework, or leisure rather than those being the responsibility of the parent and it would be expected of the child to show some acknowledgement of the parent's point of view. The degree of empathy the child expresses toward the parent's position becomes an important marker of the interaction and was found to predictor of the child's social and moral development in adolescence (Feldman, 2007e).

f. *The perspective-taking adolescent.* Two major developments occurring during adolescence are expressed in the types of social interactions adolescents create with their parents; the consolidation of and struggle for autonomy and identity formation, and the development of perspective taking, higher forms of empathy, and moral internalization. The conflict and positive discussions are used with adolescents as well. Additional codes at this stage include empathy and perspective taking, autonomy taking (child) and autonomy granting (parent), and child's manner of expressing his/her point of view. Dyadic codes address the dyad's assuming responsibility for raising appropriate solutions, the ability to flexibly move between the two positions and between present state, past experience, and future plans, and the dyadic readiness to tackle conflicts versus the tendency to gloss over conflicts or suppress them. Several studies of whole-families interactions with adolescents used goal-directed activities, such as build a kite from a kit, a problem-solving game, use a checkerboard for placing oneself in relation to other family members, and the family CIB codes consider the degree of family autonomy and intrusiveness, involvement, cooperation, activity level, didactiveness, creativity, and affective expression.

g. *The affectionate romantic partner.* In assessing the dialogue between romantic partners, three contexts are often used: conflict discussion, positive discussion, and support providing, a setting in which one partner discusses a difficult moment and the other is expected to provide support. Consistent with the central hypothesis guiding theories of adult attachment (e.g., Shaver & Mikulincer, 2002) – that the early parent-child relationship provides the internal working model upon which the individual's intimate relationships are founded – romantic relationships are coded along the same vectors as those of the parent-infant relationship. Nonverbal patterns related to specific modalities, including gaze, affect, and touch, as well as to the individual's general relational style, for instance, acknowledgement, appropriate range or affect, and consistency of style, take a new angle in contexts where interactions evolve between equals and not between parent and child. The degree of support provided by partners echo the "parent supportive presence" code of infancy, which is based on Winnicott's (1956) "holding environment," and the empathy and perspective taking assessment resemble the empathy required of adolescence in negotiating differences with their parents. Overall, the evaluation of romantic partners supports the attachment perspective (Bowlby, 1969) and indicates that the system's central constructs: sensitivity, intrusiveness, engagement, withdrawal, reciprocity, and tension are meaningful vectors against which social interactions between close partners can be assessed across the lifespan. Important to note in this context that all codes added across development as markers of the child's socio-cognitive maturation, do not take the place of the basic non-verbal elements observed in infancy: mutual gaze, positive and relaxed affective expression, warm vocal quality, proximity and body orientation, and fluent, natural fluctuations of arousal. These nonverbal patterns provide the "basso continuo" of interpersonal relationships learned in infancy upon which more complex social behaviors can be added as children grow and social interactions become more complex and multilayered (Feldman, 2007b).

Distinguishing Normative from Pathological Interactions

Behavior observations of the child's interactions with the primary caregiver are a central component of the diagnostic process in infancy and early childhood (Lieberman & Van Horn, 2008). During the first years of life, systematic observations of relational behavior may be the only tool available to the clinician for collecting direct information on the infant's emotional state that is not filtered by the mother's perspective. Observing the preverbal infant, therefore,

may be the only access into the infant's emerging "internal working model" and his or her hypotheses regarding the social world – whether it is secure, threatening, overstimulating, or uninvolved. At the toddler and preschool stages, direct observations may provide an important "port of entry" (Stern, 1995) into the child's emerging symbolic world, fantasy content, and increasingly complex relationships with the parents around issues of autonomy, compliance, self-regulation, and affect organization that are not available to the child's consciousness and cannot be reported by young children. Including systematic behavior observations into the clinical diagnosis of young children not only provides information that is otherwise unavailable, but can be used to guide the formulation of diagnostic classification systems and to differentiate transitory difficulties from stable pathological conditions that merit intervention (Feldman, 2008; Feldman & Keren, 2004).

In formulating the language for distinguishing normative from pathological interactions, an observation system must first determine the appropriate range of behaviors in normative processes across ages as a metric for evaluating deviation. Following, the system should chart specific profiles of the parent and child's relational behavior under specific risk conditions. Such relational profiles may be important not only for the diagnostic process, but can also serve as the basis for intervention and can be used to evaluate treatment outcomes. Furthermore, understanding the specific relational disruptions under each pathological condition may be an important step in theory building and can provide a deeper understanding of the various pathological conditions and their differential origins, lead to further conceptualizations in the field of developmental psychopathology, and advance progress in the study of developmental process as a whole.

Interactions between parents and children with a wide range of psychopathological conditions have been studied using the CIB system and conditions for which results are available are reported later. High risk conditions utilizing the CIB may be broadly divided into four groups; *(a) Conditions related to child biological risk* – includes cases in which the dyadic relatedness may be disrupted by the child's biologically based condition, such as prematurity, multiple birth (twins and triplets), intrauterine growth retardation, neurological conditions, physical disability (e.g., blindness, cerebral palsy), genetic syndromes (williams syndrome, velocardiofacial syndrome), mental retardation, and autism. *(b) Conditions related to child social-emotional risk* – children with a variety of psychiatric diagnoses but with no known physiological condition, including sleep and feeding disorders, affective disorders, regulatory disorders, PTSD, attachment disorders, and conduct disorders. *(c). Conditions related to maternal psychological risk* – includes cases in which mothers suffer a clinical or subclinical psychiatric condition, such as a major depressive disorder or high level of depressive symptoms, anxiety disorder or high level of anxious symptoms, PTSD, or personality disorders. *(d). Conditions of high contextual risk* – includes cases of high poverty and community violence, war-related trauma, maternal substance abuse, domestic violence, mothers in a sheltered settings, and incarcerated mothers. Because relationships function as systems, interactions are expected to be disturbed whether the risk is stemming from the parent, the child, or the context (Belsky, 1984; Sameroff, 1995). Furthermore, because of the systemic nature of development, the question of whether one can talk of the infant's own disorder apart from disordered early relationships and even from a disordered community is a matter of ongoing debate (Harris, Lieberman, & Marans, 2007).

In specifying the behavioral repertoire of each pathological condition, several points are of theoretical and clinical importance. First, research is still needed to determine whether each pathological condition exhibits a unique relational profile or whether conditions within each group (e.g., infant biological risk, maternal affective disorder, contextual risk) present a similar clinical picture. Second, possibly, for differential

diagnosis the use of individual codes (e.g., "acknowledgement") may be more informative than the higher-order constructs ("sensitivity"). Third, in some clinical conditions the relational profile points to *deficit* in the amounts and frequencies of positive parental behavior, for instance in cases of maternal postpartum depression; in others the relational profile is that of *negative parenting*, expressed in higher parental negative behavior (e.g., "criticizing," "parental hostility"), and in yet others the profile may be that of appropriate amounts of parental behavior that are not suited to the infant's signals, as observed, for instance, between parents and triplets. Assessing the specific disruptions to early relational behavior may therefore illuminate the nature of the condition and can serve to guide specific intervention. Finally, the developmental trajectories of parent and child's social behavior in each pathological condition should be assessed in the study of normative and disrupted relational processes. Whereas the deviations from normative social development decreases for some conditions, for instance among low-risk premature infants born to families of low social risk, the risk for other conditions may increase with age, for instance, the effects of maternal postpartum depression on the child's social engagement increased between two and five years (Feldman & Eidelman, 2009a). Because there is nearly no data on the development of relational patterns in different pathological conditions, assessing the trajectories of social behavior under various risk conditions requires much further research. Such data may be highly informative for a comprehensive understanding of the specific risk to infant development in conditions stemming from child biological conditions, parental psychopathology, or contextual risk.

Finally, another indicator for the disruptions to children's social-emotional development may be tapped by comparing the child's interaction with the mother to interactions with other adults. For instance, Field (1992) found that infants of depressed mothers interact in a "depressed" way even with nondepressed adults, indicating an internalization and generalization of a depressed mode of relatedness. Conversely, using the CIB system, it was found that when mothers are depressed and fathers are emotionally stable, infants of depressed mothers show more optimal interactive behaviors with their father (Feldman, 2007c). Comparing the two interactions in cases of maternal depression may describe the degree to which the relationship with the mother has been generalized to other social relationships (e.g., Stern's RIG) or whether other experiences available to the child enable the differentiation of depressed and nondepressed social partners. Among infants and young children with PTSD following exposure to war and violence, a greater difference between the interaction with mother and with a stranger was found as compared to controls. Infants with posttraumatic symptoms were significantly more frightened and withdrawn and showed lower engagement during play with a stranger compared to the mother, pointing to a basic mistrust of unknown adults that develops with repeated exposure to trauma (Feldman & Vengrober, 2011; Feldman, Vangrober, & Hallaq, 2007). On the other hand, children with Williams' syndrome displayed the opposite pattern. Whereas most children favor interactions with the mother and show more reciprocity and engagement with the attachment figure, these children prefer interactions with novel partners and show higher engagement, positive affect, attention, and vocalizations to the stranger. Thus, comparing interactions with mother and father or mother and stranger under various risk conditions may illuminate the nature of the child's attachment relationship and its exclusivity. Such analyses can trace the internalizations from the child's multiple social relationships and how these various internal models cohere to form the stable social "personality" or interactive style.

Evaluating Change Following Intervention

A behavior observation system that is directed toward the diagnosis of infant disorders must be sensitive to the effects of intervention. The central goal of intervention efforts in the early years – whether through various modes of parent-infant psychotherapy, psychoeducational programs, or home visitation, or by affording increased maternal-infant touch and contact – is to enhance the mother-infant bond. Such interventions all work on the assumption that a stronger bond and a greater parental investment would enhance the child's physiological, cognitive, social, emotional, and self-regulatory skills. Consistent with the theoretical model, the observation system should be able to detect changes in the mother's mental representations of parenting or physiological readiness for bonding by observing her concrete social behavior. In this respect, the system can help specify the effects of each intervention on specific pathological condition by using its own language. For instance, by using the distinctions between the level, target, and structure of observation, one can assess whether the intervention had an effect on specific relational codes or on the higher-order constructs (level of observation); whether the intervention had a greater impact on the behavior of mother, of child, or of the interacting dyad (target of observation); and whether the impact of the intervention was stronger on specific components of the dyadic exchange – the content – or on its formal features (structure of observation).

In addition to using the system to evaluate change in relational behavior following intervention, the system itself can be used in the *process* of intervention. Psychotherapeutic interventions for mothers and young infants are often directed to help mothers understand their infant's nonverbal communications and respond appropriately while at the same time understanding the emotional reasons for their interactive style and how it was shaped by their experiences as young children (Lieberman, Silverman, & Pawl, 2000). The codes of the CIB system can therefore be used to help mothers understand early interactions: What is considered "sensitive" parenting and how it is expressed by concrete maternal behavior?

What is intrusiveness and how she may be interfering with the child's flow of behavior? How can one reach reciprocity? At the same time, mothers can be introduced to children's social behavior; how does the child expresses engagement and withdrawal at each age, when is compliance appropriate and when it turn into reliance that interferes with the development of initiative and autonomy, and what are the specific ways infants signal overload (e.g., gaze aversion) or desire for more social stimulation (e.g., body orientation). Clinicians have often use video feedback to show mothers their videotaped interactions, pointing to moments of coordination and episodes of "miss," and attempting through these microlevel relational moments to enter into the mother's mental world and internalized behavioral style (Feldman & Keren, 2004). The language of the observation system, therefore, may provide a language for the therapeutic process, expanding the mother's ability to detect, respond, and monitor nonverbal social signals in herself and the child and understand their importance for the emerging relationship.

Psychometric Properties of the CIB System

Adequate psychometric properties are a basic requirement of any scientific tool. For a systematic collection of information, the observation system's psychometric properties must fulfill several conditions. In the following, these are detailed in relation to the CIB system.

(a) *Test-retest reliability.* In multiple samples of normative and high-risk populations and across ages, medium-to-high test-retest reliability is observed for the system's constructs. This is found for mother-child interactions in numerous contexts, such as play and feeding (Feldman, Keren et al., 2004; Keren & Feldman, 2002; Keren, Feldman, & Tyano, 2001; Silberstein et al., 2009b), or face-to-face and toy exploration (Feldman, Greenbaum, Mayes, & Erlich, 1997). Similarly test-retest reliability is found

between the child's interactions with different partners; between mothers and fathers in both infancy (Feldman, 2000; Feldman, Weller, Sirota, & Eidelman, 2003; Feldman, 2007c) and the preschool years (Geller, Diesendruck, & Feldman, 2007); between mothers, fathers, and caregivers (Feldman & Klein, 2003); and between mothers and strangers (Feldman, Vangrober, & Hallaq, 2007). In multiple longitudinal studies, coded independently by different observers, stability is found across time for the CIB constructs (Feldman, Eidelman, & Rotenberg, 2004; Feldman & Eidelman, 2005; 2006), with several studies showing stability across six time-points from birth to five years (Feldman & Eidelman, 2009a), and six time points from 3 months to 13 years (Feldman, 2010). Stability was also found for the CIB feeding codes from the newborn period to the end of the first year (Silberstein et al., 2009b). Similarly, stability was observed across cultures, following Israeli and Palestinian mothers, fathers, and infants from 5 months to 3 years (Feldman & Masalha, 2010). These studies demonstrate that the CIB constructs capture meaningful components of the individual's relational style, which are stable over lengthy periods of time as coded blindly by coders unfamiliar with the person's behavior at a previous time-point.

(b) *Construct validity.* The CIB constructs are theoretically based. Yet, in every sample studied so far, the same codes aggregated into the same higher-order constructs with adequate internal consistency. This was found across ages and in samples from different cultures. Each construct contains several codes that are considered the "core codes" and load on this construct in any observations and codes that may be more dependent on age and culture. For instance, affectionate touch is part of the "maternal sensitivity" construct in some cultures but not in others, whereas "mother acknowledgement of child's communication" is a core feature of the sensitivity construct at any age and an item-to-total analysis demonstrated that this code has the highest loading on the sensitivity construct in several samples. Finally, to validate the CIB constructs, we conducted a confirmatory factor analysis for 483 interactions. Results confirmed the four expected constructs; a positive and negative construct for the parent (sensitivity and intrusiveness) and a positive and negative construct for the child (social involvement and negative engagement), $X_2 = 56.12$, $p = .18$, goodness-of-fit-index (GFI) = .94, adjusted goodness-of-fit-index (AGFI) = .93, normed fit index (NFI) = .92, root mean square error of approximation (RMSEA) = .03.

(c) *Relations to other coding schemes.* An additional aspect of the "construct validity" of the system relates to its underlying theoretical definition. In several studies the CIB codes are made with other theoretically related coding schemes where both coding schemes were used for the same interactions by independent coders. Theoretically based associations were found between related constructs of the two systems. For instance, correlations were found between the CIB "reciprocity" construct and synchrony assessed by microanalytic coding (Moshe & Feldman, 2006; Harel, 2006), and between reciprocity and synchrony assessed with the "Monadic Phases" system (Tronick, Als, & Brazelton, 1980). Associations were also found between the CIB constructs and the Observing Mediational Interaction system (OMI, Klein, 1996), a coding scheme for parents' teaching behavior during interactions with toddlers (Klein & Feldman, 2007). Similarly, in comparing the Alarm Distress Baby Scale (Guedeney & Fermanian, 2001), a system that detects early signs of child withdrawal as a precursor to pediatric depression, correlations were found between withdrawal behavior assessed with the Alarm Distress Baby scale during a visit to the pediatrician and the CIB constructs of child involvement and withdrawal (Dollberg, Feldman, Keren, & Gudeney, 2006).

(d) *Predictive validity.* Finally, an important feature of an observation system that focuses on the first year of life is its ability to predict long-term outcomes in various developmental domains and the child's general well-being. Relational behaviors assessed with the CIB in the first year of life were found to predict IQ, behavior problems, symbolic complexity, self-regulation, social competence at a childcare setting, and empathy and peer friendship across childhood and up to adolescence (Feldman, 2007e; Feldman & Blatt, 1996; Feldman, Eidelman, & Rotenberg, 2004; Feldman & Eidelman, 2009a; Feldman & Masalha, 2010) as well as to differentiate between adjusted and less-adjusted adolescents at age thirteen (Feldman, 2010).

As seen, the CIB system demonstrates the psychometric requirements of an observation system and predicts to meaningful dimensions of child development. The multiple studies currently conducted using the CIB in the United States, France, Germany, United Kingdom, Belgium, Brazil, Italy, and Holland would provide further validation of the system across cultures and emerging data support its universal applicability. Cross-cultural studies would further specify the CIB and help tease apart the universal and stable components from the culture-specific application.

II. Findings: What Have We Learned from Observing Parent-Child Interactive Behavior

Studies have typically addressed the associations between observed relational behavior and components of the theoretical model – mother and child's physiology, mother's mental representations, child temperament, the child's mental world, mother and child's affective condition, and the relational matrix of the dyad. In the following, findings are presented for normative and pathological conditions and for intervention outcomes.

Normative Processes from Birth to Adolescence: Developmental Change, Correlates, and Prediction

Newborn stage. The infant's first social experience is marked by a unique repertoire of maternal behavior, including maternal gaze at the infant's face and body, "motherese" high-pitched vocalization, expression of positive affect, adaptation to infant cues, and affectionate touch – a behavior akin to the licking-and-grooming of mammals, and typical mothers naturally engage in such behaviors immediately after birth. This early encounters marks the infant's first experience in social contingencies. Infants engage in alert states for approximately 15 percent of the interaction and mothers were found to provide 65 percent of their behavior during these scant moments of alertness, establishing the infant's first experience of coordination between internal state and maternal behavior (Feldman & Eidelman, 2007). These maternal behavior serve an important function for infant growth, and the amount of maternal postpartum behavior has shown to predict infant-mother and infant-father synchrony at 3 months, neurobehavioral maturation at 6 months, cognitive and symbolic development at 1 year, and IQ and child social development at 5 years (Feldman & Eidelman, 2003, 2007, 2009; Feldman, Eidelman, & Rotenberg, 2004), highlighting the centrality of early maternal behavior for the infant's physical, emotional, and cognitive growth.

Maternal postpartum behavior is shaped by maternal and infant physiology. In a longitudinal study, mothers were followed at three time-points: first trimester of pregnancy, last trimester, and first postpartum month. Plasma oxytocin and cortisol were sampled at each time-point. Following birth, mothers were interviewed with regards to infant-related thoughts and worries and were observed interacting with their infants. Maternal oxytocin levels across this period were highly stable and levels at first

trimester predicted the amount of maternal postpartum behavior, particularly affectionate touch, and its coordination with infant state (Feldman, Zagoory-Sharon, Weller, & Levine, 2007), suggesting that affiliative hormones during pregnancy function to prime mothers to the initiation of bonding, similar to their role in other mammals (Insel & Young, 2001). A second study evaluating mothers' and fathers' oxytocin levels in the postpartum in relation to parenting behavior found that oxytocin correlated with the parent-specific repertoire: with affectionate touch, "motherese," and positive affect in mothers, and with stimulatory touch and object presentation in fathers (Gordon et al., 2010). Maternal behavior is shaped by the infant's physiological systems as well and was predicted by the newborn's cardiac vagal tone (Feldman & Eidelman, 2007), a measure of infant autonomic maturity that provides the foundation for social engagement (Porges, 2003). Maternal postpartum interactive behavior was also predicted by the mother's perception of labor pain – a psycho-physiological dimension of pain resilience. In particular, mothers with a tendency to "catastrophize" painful experiences reported labor as intensely painful and were less sensitive toward their infants at six weeks of age (Goldstein-Ferber & Feldman, 2005).

Infancy. Substantial changes occur across the first year of life in parents' and infants' interactive behavior. In comparison with the first months of face-to-face interactions, during the second six months of life, parents and infants begin to jointly attend and manipulate toys and, with the development of intersubjectivity (Trevarthen & Aitken, 1999), higher levels of reciprocity are observed and infants show higher involvement and initiation of joint activities. Between four and eight months infants' initiation show a marked increase and mothers' perception of infant intentionality grows accordingly. At eight months, mothers perceive their infants as intentional, goal-directed creatures who can selectively express emotions and purposefully attempt to achieve a goal (Feldman & Reznick, 1996).

Although individual stability is reported for maternal and infant behavior in all samples, interactive behaviors change in a dynamic fashion in relation to change in proximal and distal conditions. For instance, positive changes in interactive behavior between 3 and 9 months, that is, an increase in maternal sensitivity and infant social engagement and a decrease in maternal intrusiveness, were related to a decrease in maternal anxiety symptoms and an increase in father involvement, highlighting the ongoing dependence of interactive behavior on the constant fluctuations of individual and contextual determinants (Feldman et al., 1997). Similarly, the development of dyadic reciprocity across the first year was found to parallel the development of maternal touch patterns. Assessing infants at 3, 6, 9, and 12 months, affectionate touch decreased during the second six months while the level of dyadic reciprocity increased. The amount of early affectionate touch predicted the level of dyadic reciprocity in later infancy, pointing to the mother-infant loving physical contact as a foundation for the development of intersubjectivity (Goldstein-Ferber et al., 2008).

Father-infant patterns in the first year differ from the patterns observed between mothers and children mostly in factors related to "content" and less in factors related to "form." Overall, no differences were found in parent sensitivity or in infant social engagement between infant-mother and infant-father interactions at five months, although specific codes showed some differences. For instance, more physical manipulation, a quicker tempo of the interaction, and higher peaks of positive arousal were found for fathers, whereas more affectionate touch, longer episodes of social gaze, and more covocalization emerged for mothers (Feldman, 2003). Father involvement in childcare responsibilities, in terms of the amount and range of childcare activities the father undertakes (e.g., feeding, diapering, bathing, physician visits, taking for walks), predicted the degree of child social involvement during interactions with father, and both maternal and paternal sensitivity were related to the level of their marital satisfaction (Feldman, 2000), findings which support ecological models on the determinants of parenting (Belsky, 1984).

Toddler stage. Several studies examined typically developing children between 1 and 3 years, focusing on the emerging competencies of toddlers. Two-year olds were observed interacting with their mothers, fathers, and caregivers in order to assess individual stability in the child's social relatedness with the three meaningful adults and to examine the specific relational styles of each interaction. Overall, interactions between the three adults were individually stable, underscoring the child's contribution to the interaction even with non-kin adults. No differences were found in sensitivity among the three adults, but children showed the highest level of engagement with mother and the lowest with caregiver. Similarly, caregivers exhibited the highest level of limit setting in terms of a consistent style that maintained children on task. The parents' and caregivers' childrearing philosophies predicted the nature of their interaction as did the caregivers' style in interacting with the entire group of children (Feldman & Klein, 2003).

Another study with two-to-three year olds addressed the relations between the mother's mental representations and the mother and child's relational patterns. Mothers were interviewed with the Parenting Developmental Interview (PDI, Aber, Belsky, Slade, & Crnic, K., 1999), a narrative instrument that assesses the mother's state of mind with regards to attachment and her representations of self as a parent, the relationship with her own parents, and the representations of the specific child. Mothers whose representations were marked by more positive features, such as higher expression of joy, a more coherent narrative, less anger and guilt, and higher sense of parental competence, engaged in more positive interactions with their toddlers. These toddlers were also better able to regulate their emotions as observed in settings that required the regulation of frustration and joy (Dollberg, Feldman, & Keren, 2010; Feldman, Dollberg & Nadam, 2011).

Finally, a cross-cultural study of Israeli and Palestinian families, observed from 5 months to 3 years revealed that relational patterns in both infancy and the toddler stage were predictive of children's social competence, self-regulation, and aggressive behavior at the childcare setting. These findings indicate that relational behavior within the family context provide the foundation for the child's functioning within society at the stage when children make their first steps from the family microsystem into the larger social world (Feldman, Masalha, & Alony, 2006; Feldman & Masalha, 2010).

Preschool. The maturation of the child's theory of mind, complex symbolic play, and peer friendships requires support from the parent-child relationship. Assessing 3–4 year olds interacting with their mother, father, and the family, it was found that although the degree of sensitivity or the complexity of the child's symbolic play with mother and father were similar, children engaged in different play themes with each parent. Children expressed more "care" themes with mother, such as feeding, bathing, or dressing, and more "construction and fixing" and "travel" themes with father, and these parent-related themes were particularly notable in same-gender pairs: father-son and mother-daughter (Keren, Feldman, Namdari-Weinbaum, Spitzer, & Tyano, 2005). Similar to the findings that parent-infant synchrony is greater in gender-matched pairs (Feldman, 2003) and that the level of symbolic complexity is higher in gender-matched dyads (Feldman, 2007d), the symbolic content of children's play appears to be shaped not only by the parent's gender but also by the gender matching and mismatching status of the interacting dyad, with same-gender pairs possibly capitalizing on biologically based tendencies of both partners. Parent-child interactions were found to be predicted by child IQ and the quality of the marital relationships, pointing to the links between individual and contextual determinants and observed interactive behavior at the preschool stage.

In both infancy and the toddler stage, mother-child relationship is shaped by the mother's representations of both herself as a parent and the specific child. During the preschool years children's representations of their parents begin to have a more substantial contribution to the interaction. In a recent study of preschoolers, the child's internal representations of the parent were assessed among children aged 3.5 to 6.5 years. Children provided free narratives to ten TAT-like cards that depicted daily situations between parents and preschoolers. Several cards showed child with mother, others child with father, and yet others child with both parents (e.g., mother walking into a messy room and finds child sitting on floor and playing; mother, father, and child strolling pleasantly in the park). Children were then videotaped interacting separately with mother and father (Geller, Diesendruck, & Feldman, 2007). A developmental progression in children's social behavior was observed from 3 to 6 years, which differed for mother and father. Reciprocity and child engagement increased over time in both mother-child and father-child interactions, however, intrusiveness and withdrawal decreased with age only in mother-child interactions. These findings highlight the different developmental trajectories of children's relationship with each parent and point to the need to investigate interactions with each parent across childhood as contributors to the child's representational world. Children who perceived their parents as warmer, more nurturing, and less angry also engaged in more optimal interactions with these parents, in terms of higher reciprocity and social engagement, supporting the proposed links between the child's emerging mental representations of attachment relationships and actual behavioral patterns. The parent-specific patterns were associated with parent-specific representations, which point to the emerging specificity of the child's internal working models at both the behavioral and mental levels. Yet, the contribution of these specific behaviors and representations to long-term outcome requires much further research.

Adolescence. Several studies followed groups of healthy children from infancy to adolescence, periodically assessing parent-infant interactive patterns. In the first study, children were followed at six time-points from infancy to adolescence: at 3 and 9 months and at 2, 4, 6, and 13 years (Feldman, 2007e, 2010) and mother-child interactions were observed at each visit. Parent Sensitivity, Child Engagement, Parent Intrusiveness, and Dyadic Reciprocity were each found to follow a unique trajectory over time and often curvilinear trajectories were charted. Maternal sensitivity increased across the first year, then decreased and stayed at a medium level until adolescence, while reciprocity increased steadily until age 6 and decreased somewhat between childhood and adolescence. Relational patterns were individually stable from one observation to the next and the averaged level of maternal sensitivity and dyadic reciprocity across the entire period predicted children's depressive symptoms and behavior adaptation at 13 years (Feldman, 2010). In a second study, infants were observed at 5 months and 3 years with mothers, father, and the family and were then observed interacting with mother, father, the family triad, and their best friend at 13 years (Bamberger & Feldman, 2011). Results demonstrate stability in dyadic reciprocity across time – infancy to adolescence – as well as across partners: mother, father, and friend. Similar to the findings for newborns, the child's reciprocal relationship with friend was related to physiological support systems that enable social engagement and was predicted by cardiac vagal tone and the vagal brake. Reciprocity with mother and father across infancy predicted the child's ability to engage in a reciprocal, empathetic dialogue with a best friend in adolescence, indicating that the infant's first experiences with the attachment figures shapes the child's relationships with significant others at the point when peers take over the parents' position in being the adolescent's main target of closeness and intimacy. These longitudinal patterns from infancy to adolescence lend support the central hypothesis underlying theories of social-emotional growth: that early interactive patterns experienced

within attachment relationships shape the child's life-long patterns with close friends and intimate partners.

Family patterns. During the first months of life, family patterns consolidate and the family context begins to emerge as a unique interactive setting, particularly at the transition to parenthood when couples become families (Cowan & Cowan, 1992). At the transition to parenthood, parents who were better able to balance the conflicting demands of work and family following the mother's return to work from maternity leave engaged in more optimal family relational patterns, in terms of higher family cohesion and lower family rigidity (Feldman, Masalha, & Nadam, 2001). Family cohesion and rigidity are two higher-order constructs used by the CIB system to depict the family atmosphere. Cohesion describes the warm family, where individuals are autonomous and involved, play is creative, family members express positive affect, and the general atmosphere is that of collaboration and cooperation. Family rigidity indexes the "enmeshed" family, where members compete for attention, autonomy of each individual is discouraged, and the atmosphere is didactic and tense. These family patterns were found to be stable from infancy to the toddler stage and to predict children's social competence in the childcare setting (Feldman & Masalha, 2010). Family interactions, like dyadic relationships, appear to be characterized by distinct patterns that are stable across time and context. As family interactions provide the child's first experience in a "group" setting, these repeatedly experienced patterns are likely to be internalized and contribute to the child's working model of functioning in social groups.

In terms of symbolic content, assessment of 3-year olds playing with mother, father, and the family triad showed that the level of symbolic complexity and the richness of thematic content was significantly higher during parent-child interactions as compared to play (Keren et al., 2005). Possibly, navigating multiperson social systems, ability observed in infants already at the first months of life (Gordon & Feldman, 2008), requires significantly more effort from the child and may tax the resources available for complex symbolic expression. In general, family interactions provide an important context for the study of social development and should be evaluated from a cross-cultural perspective (Feldman, Masalha, & Alony, 2006) as families represent the smallest cultural "institution" that function to transmit cultural values, meaning systems, and relational behavior to the next generation. Family interactions also provide an important context to assess how the behaviors of individuals and the relationships between dyads within the family cohere into a higher-order process. Because of the role family interactions play in the development of children's well-being (Fincham, 1998), understanding the ways in which family-level processes support or undermine emotional growth may shed further light on the links between early social experiences and later social competencies.

Relational Patterns from Birth to Childhood: Developmental Psychopathology

Risk conditions to infant development have generally been divided along the lines of biological and social-emotional risks. In the following, findings are presented for the two types of risks and follow the developmental line of each from the newborn stage to later childhood.

BIOLOGICAL RISK
Prematurity. Premature birth is the most frequent biological risk condition in the industrial world, affecting 7–10 percent of births in Western societies. Technological advances enable smaller and smaller infants to survive each decade, yet much research has pointed to the high risk for cognitive and neurological disorders among these children and substantial difficulties to the development of early attachment. Several studies using the CIB focused on premature infants. In the neonatal period, mothers who were able to better resolve the trauma of premature birth, use the nursing staff for practical and emotional

assistance, deal with their anxiety and guilt, and feel more competent in the parental role upon discharge from the hospital also showed more positive maternal behavior, in terms of gaze, affect, adaptation, and affectionate touch, and their infants were more alert and less withdrawn (Keren, Feldman, Sirota, Eidelman, & Lester, 2003).

The effect of breastfeeding on the mother-preterm interaction and later development was examined in three groups of mothers of premature infants, according to the amount of breast-milk mothers expressed for the infant to feed (in a bottle): those who provided minimal (< 25 percent of infant nutrition), intermediate (25–75 percent), and substantial (> 75 percent) amounts of breast-milk. Mothers who provided substantial amounts of breast-milk reported less depressive symptoms and engaged in more maternal behavior, particularly affectionate touch. These findings are consistent with a neuroendocrinological model on the development of parenting behavior (Carter, 1998). Breastfeeding is likely to increase maternal oxytocin levels and its ensuing initiation of maternal behavior in typical mothers, however, the initiation of bonding is likely to be disrupted following premature birth which precludes full bodily contact and natural nursing (Feldman, Weller, Leckman, Kvint, & Eidelman, 1999). Since similar levels of oxytocin increase are reported for breast-pumping and natural breastfeeding (Zinaman, Hughes, Queenan, Labobok, & Albertson, 992), it is possible that breast-feeding among mothers of preterm infants helped to initiate the disrupted feedback loop of the oxytocin system. The degree of maternal behavior was found to predict the infant's neurological and cognitive development at six months and infants who were mainly breastfed showed better developmental outcome (Feldman & Eidelman, 2003).

Assessing feeding interactions between mothers and low-risk premature infants in the hospital using the CIB coding scheme for newborn feeding, mothers and infants who showed a faster and smoother transition from gavage to oral feeding engaged in more optimal feeding interactions. These infants showed a more robust sucking pattern during feeding and their mothers were less intrusive and more adaptive to the infant's feeding cues (Silberstein et al., 2009a). At one year of age, these infants were observed during feeding interactions at home, the home environment was assessed, and mothers were interviewed regarding their infants' feeding problems. Difficult feeders at one year, defined according to DC 0–3R criteria as infants showing minimal food consumption, no independent feeding, and engaging in constant struggle during feeding, showed lower reciprocity, engagement, and higher withdrawal and their mothers were less sensitive during feeding interactions at one year. Furthermore, the level of feeding difficulty at one year was predicted by feeding and nonfeeding interactions at the neonatal period, especially maternal affectionate touch during free interactions and maternal gaze aversion during feeding, highlighting the importance of early gaze and touch patterns for the development of the feeding relationship, particularly in the context of biological risk (Silberstein et al., 2009a).

Neonatal cardiac vagal tone and maternal postpartum behavior were examined in preterm and full-term infants as predictors of infant-mother and infant-father synchrony at 3 months. An interaction effect of premature birth and autonomic maturity was found and indicated that preterm infants with low vagal tone received the lowest amounts of maternal behavior in the postpartum and the least maternal affectionate touch at 3 months (Feldman & Eidelman, 2007). These findings are consistent with the "differential susceptibility to rearing conditions" hypothesis (Belsky, 1998). This hypothesis suggests that infants with higher disposition to disregulation require more attentive parenting yet such infants often receive lower amounts of parental behavior, placing them at even a greater developmental risk.

At three months, the mother's representations, measured with the Parenting Developmental Interview (PDI, Aber et al., 1999), relational behavior, and infant

performance on a visual novelty recognition task and an emotion regulation task were compared between preterm and full-term infants at 3 months of age (Harel et al., 2011). Results showed significant differences in the maternal narrative of attachment to her infant, suggesting fundamental difficulties in the mother's ability to bond with her premature infant. Mothers of premature infants had difficulty describing the infant in idealized terms, experienced guilt and a sense of incompetence as a mother, and often felt "disconnected" from the child. These representations were associated with the typical relational profile between mothers and premature infants – higher maternal intrusiveness, higher infant gaze aversion and withdrawal, lower dyadic reciprocity and adaptation, and higher dyadic tension and negative states. No differences emerged between groups on the visual recognition task but premature infants were less able to modulate their arousal during the emotion regulation task, and lower emotion regulation capacities were related to higher maternal intrusiveness.

Few studies examined interactions between premature infants and their mothers beyond infancy. In a study that followed mother-child relational patterns at six time-points from birth to five years, the trajectories of maternal sensitivity and child social engagement were examined among low-risk premature infants. Mother sensitivity increased from birth to six months, decreased from six to 12 months, and stayed stable from 12 months to five years. Child social engagement increased linearly from birth to five years, with higher increments during the first year and slower increases thereafter. Relational patterns were individually stable across the 5-year period and at all time-points between six months and five years, maternal sensitivity predicted both the child's concurrent IQ and the IQ score measured at the next time-point, highlighting the role of maternal sensitivity in the development of cognitive competencies among premature infants (Feldman & Eidelman, 2009a). However, because this study was conducted on a large cohort of preterm infants (N = 125) and no full-term controls, future research is needed to examine whether similar trajectories of social behavior is observed in full-term dyads.

Finally, in a follow-up of premature infants at 8 time-points from birth to ten years, a complex pattern of interaction emerged between mother-child relational patterns and the child's developmental competencies, particularly in the domains of physiological, emotional, and attentional regulation. Consistent with the transactional model of development (Sameroff, 1995), better emotion regulation capacities at one age predicted more reciprocal interactions at the next stage. Yet, the opposite pattern was also observed and more reciprocal interactions at one age predicted better regulatory capacities at the next step. These findings point to the complex mutual influences between relational patterns and the child's acquisition of regulatory skills and underscore the role of reciprocal exchanges for the aforementioned transformation from external interpersonal experiences to internal traits and phenomenological experiences of subjectivity.

Intrauterine Growth Retardation (IUGR). This condition implies that for some physiological reason the infant did not receive adequate nutrition or was not able to or achieve appropriate growth during pregnancy and was born weighing less than the 10th percentile of the growth curve for his/her gestational age. Studies have shown that IUGR infants are more irritable than those born with appropriate-for-gestation age birthweights, especially if the child is born both prematurely and with IUGR. Following a group of premature IUGR infants from birth to two years in comparison with both birthweight-matched and gestational-age-matched premature controls, it was found that IUGR infants displayed the highest levels of negative emotionality and their social signals were more unclear and inconsistent compared to both control groups. In parallel, mothers of IUGR infants showed the highest levels of intrusive behavior across infancy, marking especially high levels of intrusiveness and infant negative affect as

components of the relational profile of this risk group. Higher maternal intrusiveness, in turn, predicted lower cognitive abilities at 2 years (Feldman & Eidelman, 2006).

Multiple Birth – Triplets. Triplets are the fastest growing birth population in the Western world, yet very few studies examined the development of triplets across the first years of life. In a study following 23 sets of triplets matched to 23 sets of twins and 23 singleton infants from birth to five years. Relational patterns were examined at each time-point. Overall, triplets received lower levels of maternal sensitivity at 6, 12, and 24 months compared to singleton and twins, but differences at five years were no longer significant. Similarly, lower social engagement was found for triplets until 2 years (Feldman & Eidelman, 2005). The relational profile of parents and triplets during infancy was that of the parent providing adequate amounts of parenting behaviors (the "content" codes: gaze, positive affect, vocalizations), but these were not adapted to the child's pace and rhythms. These findings are interpreted in terms of evolutionary models on exclusive parenting as an essential component of the bonding process, which is disrupted when the parent needs to bond with three children simultaneously while being overwhelmed with their physical needs (Feldman & Eidelman, 2004). In 62 percent of the triplet sets there was one child who suffered IUGR in addition to being born as part of a triplet set and this child often received the lowest level of sensitive parenting as compared to the siblings. The IUGR child among the triplet set showed poorer cognitive and social-emotional development across childhood and received less sensitive and reciprocal parenting. The findings for triplets highlight the unique ecology of the triplet situation and the limited resources available to parents when faced with the task of raising three infants. As a result, the child who is more medically compromised paradoxically receives less sensitive care, which leads to irreversible negative outcomes, as suggested by the "differential susceptibility" model (Belsky, 1998). A follow up of these triplets at five years indicated that most triplets showed a developmental catch-up by five years and their cognitive, neuropsychological, and social-emotional development is similar to those of the matched singletons and twins, as is the level of social engagement during interactions. However, the IUGR child among the triplet set remains at a developmental risk and lower cognitive and social-emotional competencies as well as interactive engagement are observed for these children upon school entry (Feldman & Eidelman, 2009b), findings consistent with multirisk models of development.

Prenatal neurological risk. A study in Paris examined maternal representations and the emerging mother-infant relationship in cases when ultrasound examination discovers soft neurological signs in the infant during pregnancy (Viaux et al., 2012). Mothers were followed four times: at second trimester, third trimester, at birth, and at two months postpartum and were compared to controls. Maternal representations were evaluated at each point, infants were checked by pediatricians at birth, and mother-child interaction was observed at 2 months. Mothers of fetuses at neurological risk had narratives that were marked by more constriction, less development and flexibility of the representation, and less differentiation between self and fetus. Interactions between these mothers and their infants were characterized by lower maternal supportive presence, lower joint positive states, and higher joint negative states. Mothers also reported higher anxiety, which tended to increase over time. These findings emphasize the close links between maternal representations and dyadic behavior and highlight the pregnancy period as a critical time for the mother's mental preparation to motherhood and its disruption in cases of perinatal risk.

Genetic Disorders. A study of mother-child relationship in two groups of children with genetic disorders, Williams syndrome and velocardiofacial syndrome (VCF), in comparison with both age-matched and IQ-matched controls describes two distinct, highly stable relational profiles. Among the children with Williams' syndrome, children showed more relational behavior in terms of the content codes- gaze, affect, touch, vocalization – but were less able to manage a reciprocal dyadic exchange and little maturation was observed in social behavior from early childhood to adolescence. In contrast, children with VCF showed an "autistic-like" social behavior, marked by high social withdrawal, preoccupation with objects, no fluency or reciprocity, and little positive engagement or affection to mother. In both groups, children's social engagement and dyadic reciprocity were related to behavior adaptation and theory-of mind skills, pointing to the links between social behavior, social cognition, and psychological adjustment in cases of high risk (Burg-Malki, Feldman, Diesendruck, Geva, & Gothelf, 2010).

SOCIAL-EMOTIONAL RISK

Two classes of social-emotional risk conditions have been studied using the CIB: risk related to maternal affective condition and risk related to the child's social-emotional difficulties.

Maternal affective disorder. Maternal postpartum depression, affecting 12–15 percent of western women (Burt & Stein, 2002), is a disorder with long-term consequences to the mother-infant relationship and much research has addressed the effects of postpartum depressive symptoms on the mother-infant relationship, mostly during infancy. In several cohorts, associations were found between the mother's depressive symptoms and lower amounts of maternal affectionate touch, and the findings may be related to disruptions in the oxytocin bonding-related system (Feldman, Eidelman, Sirota, & Weller, 2002; Feldman, Keren et al., 2004; Feldman & Eidelman, 2003, 2007). Similarly, maternal postpartum depressive symptoms were related to lower sensitivity, reciprocity, and child engagement and to higher infant withdrawal in both infancy (Feldman, Masalha, & Nadam, 2001; Goldstein–Ferber & Feldman, 2005) and the toddler stage (Feldman, Keren et al., 2004; Dollberg et al., 2006). In the aforementioned study that followed low-risk premature infants from birth to five years (Feldman & Eidelman, 2009a), infants were divided into four groups on the basis of maternal postpartum depression (high, low) and infant autonomic maturity (high/low cardiac vagal tone) and the trajectories of cognitive development and child social engagement were charted for each group. Infants of postnatally depressed mothers, particularly those with lower cardiac vagal tone, showed the most delayed development in both domains. Interestingly, however, postpartum depression had the most notable effect on children's cognitive and social growth between 2 and 5 years, suggesting that depressed mothers may have a special difficulty in supporting the child's autonomy and emerging separateness and creativity that typically occur during this stage. A study in Germany using the CIB evaluated the relational patterns of 4-month old infants and their postnatally depressed mothers as compared to controls. Results showed that interactions between depressed mothers and their infants were characterized by lower infant social engagement, lower maternal sensitivity, and reduced dyadic reciprocity (Bartling et al., 2006).

Most studies of maternal postpartum depression examined women with high depressive symptoms and much less research assessed mothers diagnosed within a clinical depressive episode. A recent study (Feldman, Granat, Pariente, Kaneti, Kuint, & Gilboa-Schechtman, 2009) recruited a community cohort of 971 women who reported symptoms of depression and anxiety in the second post–birth day and 215 of those at the high and low end were reevaluated at 6 months. At 9 months women with a major depressive disorder ($N = 22$), anxiety disorders ($N = 19$) and matched controls ($N = 59$) were observed in mother-child interaction, in a fear paradigm, and cortisol was collected from mother and child. Infants of depressed mothers showed the poorest outcome on all measures: mothers displayed the lowest sensitivity and infants showed minimal social engagement at play. Infants of depressed mothers showed the highest level of negative affect and the lowest

amount of adaptive regulatory behavior during the emotion regulation paradigm. Finally, infants of depressed mothers had higher baseline cortisol levels and greater cortisol reactivity. Because regulatory capacities are built on the mother's "external regulatory" function in early infancy (Hofer, 1995; Field, 1994), the low capacities of infants of depressed mothers to self-regulate places these infants at a higher risk for regulatory difficulties across the lifespan. Moreover, the disruption to the physiological stress HPA system observed in infancy may point to a permanent damage to the stress response, as observed in animal research (Heim & Nemeroff, 2001).

Maternal anxiety disorder was expressed in a different relational profile, in which the tempo of the interaction was quick and jerky and the infant experienced over- rather than understimulation. The cycle between episodes of gaze synchrony, that is, between moments in which mother and child are looking at each other, was four time longer for depressed mothers and their infants as compared to controls but three time shorter for anxious mothers and their infants (Feldman, Granat, & Gilboa-Schechtman, 2005). The interactive style of anxious mothers was characterized by high intrusiveness and parent-led interactions. Although the amount of maternal behavior in the gaze, vocalization, and positive affect indicators was not lower than controls, these behaviors were not matched to the infant's signals and interactive moments when the infant averted gaze while the mother increased stimulation were often observed. Infants of anxious mothers were less able to regulate frustration, although no differences were found in the regulation of positive emotions.

Among the interesting question arising from the dichotomizing of risk conditions to those originating in the mother and those originating in the child is which risk is greater and carries a more negative impact on the development or early relationship. In a study using a matched-cohort design (Feldman, 2007c), six cohorts of 4-month old infants interacting with their mothers, father, and in a family triad were compared: a normative cohort, three cohorts of mother-related risk (anxious, depressed, and comorbid anxious and depressed), and two cohorts of infant-related risk (premature and IUGR infants). In all samples fathers were free of anxiety and depressive symptoms and in the infant-related conditions parents were nonsymptomatic. A linear decline pattern was found, with relationships most optimal in the healthy group, less in the mother-risk groups, and the least optimal in the infant-risk group. The relational components most sensitive to risk were parent intrusiveness and dyadic reciprocity, constructs that describe the systemic features of the dyadic relationship and the adaptation of parent and child to each other's rhythms. Family coherence and rigidity similarly showed a linear-decline pattern with most optimal patterns among control families, less among the mother-related risk groups, and lowest among the infant-risk groups. Dyadic and triadic relational patterns were interrelated with maternal and paternal reciprocity related to family cohesion and parental intrusiveness to family rigidity, confirming to the proposed coherence among the various subsystems in the family (Davies & Cicchetti, 2004).

Infant social-emotional risk. Research using the CIB among infants with social-emotional disorders has mainly observed young children referred to an infant mental health clinic who were diagnosed with a variety of psychiatric disorders of infancy. In comparison with nonreferred control families, relational patterns in the clinic-referred group were less optimal on all measures, including lower maternal sensitivity and limit-setting, higher maternal intrusiveness, lower child engagement and dyadic reciprocity, and higher child withdrawal (Keren, Feldman, & Tyano, 2001). The differences between the clinic and control groups increased during feeding interactions. The feeding situation, a setting that elicits more stress and calls for the fulfillment of a life-sustaining maternal function, elicited less adaptive behavior from the clinic children and their mothers and these patterns were related to less optimal home environment and to higher maternal psychopathology. Clinic-referred young children exhibited more withdrawal behavior during interactions, which were often directed toward the mother (Dollberg et al., 2006). Assessing maternal representations with the PDI, mothers of clinic-referred infants expressed less joy, more disregulated anger, and lower sense of competence in the parenting role, and these representations were associated with lower sensitivity and child engagement and higher maternal intrusiveness (Dollberg, Feldman, & Keren, 2010). In terms of the family relationships, using an extensive interview of the entire family based on the MacMaster model of family functioning (Epstein, Bishop, & Levine, 1978), clinic families showed lower overall family functioning, particularly in the domains of communication, affective expression, and role definition and these family patterns were related to higher maternal intrusiveness and lower sensitivity during mother-child interactions (Keren, Dollberg, Kosteff, Danino, & Feldman, 2010).

Apart from the overall understanding that social-emotional difficulties in infancy are linked with disrupted early relationships, an important next step is to describe the relational profile of each psychiatric disorder of infancy. Observing the interactions between mothers and infants with feeding disorders, infants with other Axis I disorders, and case-matched controls, the relational behavior most notable in the feeding disorder group was diminished maternal proximity and affectionate touch. Mothers of infants with feeding disorders tended to position the child out of arms' reach during mutual play, provided minimal amounts of affectionate or even instrumental touch, and the children showed signs of touch aversion (Feldman, Keren et al., 2004). The relations between touch, feeding, and growth has been demonstrated in premature infants and these findings show a similar problem in cases of feeding disorders, which can assist clinicians in both the diagnosis process and the direction of intervention.

Infant PTSD is another psychiatric disorder of infancy, which was studied using the CIB system (Feldman & Vengrober, 2011; Feldman, Vangrober, & Hallaq, 2007). Israeli and Palestinian infants aged 1.5 to 5 exposed to continuous war, terror, and violence were compared with controls. A most obvious difference between groups was that exposure to trauma markedly constricts the child's symbolic play, creativity, and thematic play content. The free play of PTSD infants was impoverished and often marked by a functional rather than symbolic use of play material. Mothers of infants exposed to terror were either withdrawn and aloof or highly anxious and overstimulating, and the dyadic atmosphere was tense and constricted. In assessing the differences between war-exposed children who developed PTSD as compared to children exposed to the same war-related stressors who did not developed psychopathology, it was found that children's physiological stress response in terms of cortisol and salivary alpha amylase were different in the two groups and more resilient children engaged in a more reciprocal interaction with their mothers (Feldman, Vengrober, Rothman-Eidelman, & Zagoory-Sharon, in press). In addition, lower symbolic competence during play and higher maternal and child anxiety were related to higher posttraumatic distress symptoms both concurrently and in a 1-year follow-up (Vengrober & Feldman, 2012). Finally, observing relational patterns in a large group of infants referred to a mental health clinic in Berlin (zero to five years) headed by Dr. Andreas Wiefel, the specific profiles of interactions are being studied among three diagnostic groups; infants with affective disorders, infants with regulatory disorders whose condition is initially biologically based, and infants with attachment disorders whose condition is initially relationship-based. Such research can begin to tease apart the separate contributions of biological and relational factors as they interact to shape specific relational profiles, can assist in providing more accurate differential diagnosis, and can serve in guiding intervention efforts.

Change in Relational Patterns Following Intervention

Studies using the CIB to assess change in relational patterns following intervention are generally divided to two types: change following touch-and-contact interventions for premature infants and change following various forms of psychotherapy.

Touch interventions for premature infants. In a large study of premature infants who received skin-to-skin intervention (Kangaroo Care), an intervention in which incubated newborns are placed naked on the mother's skin and thermoregulation is maintained by the mother's body heat, as compared to matched controls who received standard incubator care, interaction patterns of Kangaroo infants and controls were followed from birth to ten years. At each time-point interactions between mothers and infants in the Kangaroo group were more optimal. During the first year, Kangaroo mothers were more sensitive and less intrusive, infants were more engaged, and the dyadic atmosphere was more reciprocal. Such findings emerged for both mothers and fathers, although fathers did not participate in the kangaroo intervention, and the family patterns of the treated infants was more cohesive and less rigid (Feldman et al., 2002, 2003). Observations at 2, 5, and 10 years showed that kangaroo infants and their mothers engaged in more reciprocal interactions and children were more socially engaged. These findings highlight the central importance of the mother-infant bond during the initial period of bond formation for the long-term development of the mother-child relationship. During this critical period for bond formation maternal touch was precluded for the control infants but was provided for the kangaroo group. Similar to the function of "maternal proximity" during the immediate post–birth period in mammals (Hofer, 1995), mother-child physical closeness functions to establish the infant's physiological, attentional, and social regulatory abilities. Results of the longitudinal follow-up demonstrated that the improved early interactions predicted better regulatory capacities, which, in turn, helped preserve more positive inter-actions between mother and child across childhood (Feldman, 2004).

In addition to skin-to-skin contact mother-infant interactions were examined following massage therapy for premature infants, a regime of regular stroking of the infant's body which has shown to improve infant state and neurobehavioral maturation (Field, 1995). Three groups were tested in the hospital: infants receiving massage by moth-ers, infants receiving massage by nurses, and controls. At three months, infants receiv-ing massage in both groups showed higher alertness and involvement and mothers who provided massage themselves displayed higher sensitivity (Goldstein-Ferber et al., 2005). Results of the kangaroo and massage interventions may point to two mechanisms by which touch interventions improve dyadic relationships. First, touch interven-tions improve the infant's state and reduce the child's negative emotionality, and this, in turn, enables better child social engagement. Second, the close physical contact between mother and child increases maternal invest-ment, sense of competence, and familiar-ity with the infant's nonverbal signals and this leads to greater maternal sensitivity. As a result, the dyadic atmosphere becomes more reciprocal and less tense, mutually influencing child competencies and dyadic patterns.

Dyadic psychotherapy and psychosocial interventions. In a study assessing the out-comes of dyadic psychotherapy in the infant mental health clinic, mother-infant interac-tions were observed before treatment, fol-lowing a 6–8 months dyadic psychotherapy, and a year after the termination of treatment (Dollberg, Feldman, & Keren, 2006). At each time-point mothers were interviewed with the PDI (Aber et al., 1999) and mother-child interactions were observed. Results indi-cated that maternal sensitivity increased after treatment and slightly decreased a year later but was still significantly higher than its initial level, and similar findings emerged for the mother's joyful and coherent rep-resentations of herself in the parental role, indicating that a treatment which focuses

on the dyadic relationships improves both the mother's representations and relational behavior and that this change persists long after the treatment is terminated.

Several research programs have used the CIB to assess change following interventions. Paris, Weinberg, and Bolton (2008) evaluated a home-based intervention for postpartum depressed women in Boston. Results from the baseline assessment showed that mater-nal sensitivity during a structured interac-tion was negatively related to the mother's depression and maternal sensitivity during an unstructured interaction was associated with maternal suicidality. Infant involve-ment during the unstructured interaction was negatively related to maternal suicidal-ity. An intervention program for mothers who live in sheltered settings following acts of domestic violence is conducted in Jerusalem and at the Anna Freud Center in London. The London group is similarly conducting interventions with incarcer-ated mothers, using the CIB as a pre- and posttreatment evaluation tool. A French group is using the CIB for the evaluation of mother-infant psychotherapy, and a group in Dieseldorf, Germany is looking at the inter-actions of single mothers and their toddlers/preschoolers before and after a structured 20-session psycho-educational intervention. In all programs, change in individual scales is measured in addition to higher-order con-structs, in order to specify the components most amenable to the specific intervention in the population studied. At the same time, the coding scheme is used not only as a sci-entific tool but as a framework that provides the language for intervention, highlighting to the mother the content, form, and struc-ture of early social interactions.

Summary

Relationships are the context of infant growth. Parenting behavior is the force that underlies the development of relation-ships, carrying them from birth – when parents assume total control for the inter-action – to adolescence – when a more balanced exchange is called for. With each developmental progression, parents must modulate their parenting behavior, while keeping the same attuned, involved, and predictable style. Refining the language of behavior observation is required in order to anchor the study of human development in concrete measures of relationships, form theories based on a bottom-up methodologies, and expand the science of relationship in a rigorous, context-dependent, and comparative manner in order to provide a more detailed answer to the fundamental question of social emotional growth: how do early relationship shape the individual's body, mind, and personality.

References

Aber, L., Belsky, J., Slade, A., & Crnic, K. (1999). Stability and change in mothers' representations of their relationship with their toddlers. *Developmental Psychology*, 35, 1038–1047.

Ainsworth, M.D.S., Blehar, M.C., Waters, E., & Wall, S. (1978). *Patterns of attachment.* Hillsdale, NJ: Erlbaum.

Asher, S. R., & Gottman, J. M. (1981). *The development of children's friendships.* New York: Cambridge University Press.

Feldman, R., & Bamberger, E. (2011). Father-child reciprocity from infancy to adolescence shapes children's social and dialogical skills. Manuscript submitted for publication.

Bartling, K., Wiefel, A., Klapp, C., Jonkman, L., Lenz, K., & Lehmkuhl, U. (2006). Mother-child interaction and child's neuroendocrine stress regulation. Presented at the biennial meeting of the World Association for Infant Mental Health, Paris, France.

Bates, E., O'Connell, B., & Shore, C. (1987). Language and communication in infancy. In J. D. Osofsky (Ed.), *Handbook of infant development,* pp. 149–204 (2nd ed.). New York: Wiley.

Baumrind, D. (1973). The development of instrumental competence through socialization. In A. D. Pick (ed.), *Minnesota Symposia on Child Psychology,* pp. 3–46, Vol. 7. Minneapolis: University of Minnesota Press.

Belsky, J. (1984). The determinants of parenting: A process model. *Child Development,* 55, 83–96.

Belsky, J. (1998). Theory testing, effect-size evaluation, and differential susceptibility to rearing influence: The case of mothering and attachment. *Child Development,* 68, 598–600.

Bowlby, J. (1969). *Attachment and Loss,* Vol. 1. *Attachment.* New York: Basic.

Bretherton, I., & Beeghley, M. (1982). Talking about internal states: The acquisition of an explicit theory of mind. *Developmental Psychology,* 18, 906–921.

Burg-Malki, M., Feldman, R., Diesendruck, G., Geva, R., & Gothelf, D. (2010). Children with genetic disorders; Social cognition, social interaction, psychiatric evaluation, and daily skills. Paper submitted for publication.

Burt, V. K., & Stein, K. (2002). Epidemiology of depression throughout the female life-cycle. *Journal of Clinical Psychiatry,* 63 (Supplement 7), 9–15.

Carter, S. C. (1998). Neuroendocrine perspectives on social attachment and love. *Psychoneuroendocrinology,* 23, 779–818.

Chatoor, I. (2000). Feeding and eating disorders of infancy and early childhood. In H. I. Kaplan & B. J. Sadock (Eds.), *Comprehensive Textbook of Psychiatry,* pp 2704–2710, Vol. VII. Baltimore: Williams & Wilkins.

Cowan, P., & Cowan, C. (1992). *When partners become parents: The big life change for couples.* New York: Basic Books.

Damasio, A. R. (2003). *Looking for Spinoza: Joy, sorrow and the feeling brain.* New York: Harcourt.

Danino, K. (2007). Family functioning, maternal psychopathology, and mother-child relationship in clinic-referred and non-referred infants and toddlers. Master's Thesis. Department of Psychology, Bar-Ilan University.

Davies, P. T., & Cicchetti, D. (2004). Toward an integration of family systems and developmental psychopathology approaches. *Development and Psychopathology,* 16, 477–481.

Dollberg, D., Feldman, R., & Keren, M. (2006, July). Effects of dyadic psychotherapy on maternal representation and mother-infant relationship among infants referred to a community-based infant mental health center. Presented at the biennial meeting of the World Association for Infant Mental Health, Paris, France.

Dollberg, D., Feldman, R., & Keren, M. (2010). Maternal representations, child psychiatric status, and mother-child relationship in clinic-referred and non-referred infants. *European Journal of Child and Adolescent Psychiatry,* 19, 25–36.

Dollberg, D., Feldman, R., & Keren, M. (2008). Maternal representations, child psychiatric status, and mother-child relationship in clinic-referred and non-referred infants. Manuscript submitted for publication.

Dollberg, D., Feldman, R., Keren, M., & Gudeney, A. (2006). Sustained withdrawal behavior in clinic-referred and non-referred infants. *Infant Mental Health Journal*, 27, 292–309.

Dunn, J. (1991). Young children's understanding of other people: evidence from observations within the family. In D. Frye & C. Moore (eds.), *Children's theories of mind*, pp. 97–114. Hillsdale, NJ: LEA Inc.

Edelman, G. M. (2004). *Wider than the sky: The phenomenal gift of consciousness*. New Haven, CT: Yale University Press.

Emde, R. N., Biringen, Z., Clyman, R. B., & Oppenheim, D. (1991). The moral self of infancy: Affective core and procedural knowledge. *Developmental Review*, 11, 251–270.

Emde, R. N., Gaensbauer, T. J., & Harmon, R. J. (1976). Emotional expression in infancy: A biobehavioral study (Psychological issues Vol. 10, No. 37). New York: International Universities Press.

Epstein, N. B., Bishop, D. S., & Levine, S. (1978). The McMaster model of family functioning. *Journal of Marriage and Family Counseling*, 4, 19–31.

Erikson, E. E. (1963). *Childhood and society*. New York: Norton.

Feldman, R. (1998). *Coding Interactive Behavior (CIB) Manual*. Unpublished Manuscript. Bar-Ilan University.

Feldman, R. (2000). Parents' convergence on sharing and marital satisfaction, father involvement, and parent-child relationship at the transition to parenthood. *Infant Mental Health Journal*, 21, 176–191.

Feldman, R. (2003). Infant-mother and infant-father synchrony: The coregulation of positive arousal. *Infant Mental Health Journal*, 24, 1–23.

Feldman, R. (2004). Mother-infant skin-to-skin contact and the development of emotion regulation. In S. P. Shohov (Ed.), *Advances in psychology research*, pp. 113–131, Vol. 27. Hauppauge, NY; Nova Science.

Feldman, R. (2007a). Parent-infant synchrony and the construction of shared timing; Physiological precursors, developmental outcomes, and risk conditions. *Journal of Child Psychology and Psychiatry*, 48, 329–354.

Feldman, R. (2007b). Parent-infant synchrony: Biological foundations and developmental outcomes. *Current Directions in Psychological Science*, 16, 340–346.

Feldman, R. (2007c). Maternal versus child's risk and the development of parent-infant and family relationships in five high-risk populations. *Development & Psychopathology*, 19, 293–312.

Feldman, R. (2007d). On the origins of background emotions; From affect synchrony to symbolic expression. *Emotion*, 7, 601–611.

Feldman, R. (2007e). Mother-infant synchrony and the development of moral orientation in childhood and adolescence: Direct and indirect mechanisms of developmental continuity. *American Journal of Orthopsychiatry*, 77, 582–597.

Feldman, R. (2008). The intra-uterine environment, temperament, and development: including the biological foundations of individual differences in the study of psychopathology and wellness. *Journal of the American Academy of Child and Adolescent Psychiatry*, 47, 233–236.

Feldman, R. (2010). The relational basis of adolescent adjustment: Trajectories of mother-child interactive behaviors from infancy to adolescence shape adolescents' adaptation. *Attachment and Human Development*, 12, 173–192.

Feldman, R., & Blatt, S. J. (1996). Precursors of relatedness and self-definition in mother-infant interaction. In J. Masling & R. F. Bornstein (Eds.), *Psychoanalytic perspectives on developmental psychology*, pp. 1–42. Washington DC: American Psychological Association.

Feldman, R., Dollberg, D., & Nadam, R. (2011). The expression and regulation of anger in toddlers: Relations to maternal behavior and mental representations. *Infant Behavior and Development*, 34, 310–320.

Feldman, R., & Eidelman, A. I. (2003). Direct and indirect effects of maternal milk on the neurobehavioral and cognitive development of premature infants. *Developmental Psychobiology*, 43, 109–119.

Feldman, R., & Eidelman, A. I. (2004). Parent-infant synchrony and the social-emotional development of triplets. *Developmental Psychology*, 40, 1133–1147.

Feldman, R., & Eidelman, A. I. (2005). Does a triplet birth pose a special risk for infant development? Assessing cognitive development in relation to intrauterine growth and mother-infant interaction across the first two. *Pediatrics*, 115, 443–452.

Feldman, R., & Eidelman, A. I. (2006). Neonatal state organization, neuro- maturation, mother-infant relationship, and the cognitive

development of small-for-gestational-age premature infants. *Pediatrics*, 118, e869–e878.

Feldman, R. & Eidelman, A. I. (2007). Maternal
postpartum behavior and the emergence of
infant-mother and infant-father synchrony in
preterm and full-term infants: The role of neonatal vagal tone. *Developmental Psychobiology*,
49, 290–302.

Feldman, R., & Eidelman, A. I. (2009a). Biological
and environmental initial conditions shape
the trajectories cognitive and social-emotional
development across the first five years of life.
Developmental Science, 12, 194–200.

Feldman, R. & Eidelman, A. I. (2009b). Triplets
from birth to five years: The discordant infant
at birth remains at cognitive, social, and emotional risk. *Pediatrics*, 124, 316–323.

Feldman, R., Eidelman, A. I., & Rotenberg, N.
(2004). Parenting stress, infant emotion regulation, maternal sensitivity, and the cognitive
development of triplets: A model for parent
and child influences in a unique ecology. *Child
Development*, 75, 1774–1791.

Feldman, R., Eidelman, A. I., Sirota, L., & Weller,
A. (2002). Comparison of skin-to-skin (kangaroo) and traditional care: Parenting outcomes
and preterm infant development. *Pediatrics*,
110, 16–26.

Feldman, R., Granat, A., Gilboa-Schechtman, E.
(April 2005). Maternal anxiety and depression
and infant regulation of negative and positive emotions. Paper presented in the biennial
meeting of the Society for Research in Child
Development, Atlanta, GA.

Feldman, R., Granat, A., Pariente, C., Kaneti, H.,
Kuint, J. & Gilboa-Schechtman, E. (2009).
Maternal affective disorder across the postpartum year and infant social engagement,
fear regulation, and stress reactivity. *Journal of
the American Academy of Child and Adolescent
Psychiatry*, 48, 919–927.

Feldman, R., Greenbaum, C. W., Mayes, L. C.,&
Erlich, H. S. (1997). Change in mother-infant
interactive behavior: Relations to change in
the mother, the infant, and the social context.
Infant Behavior and Development, 20, 153–165.

Feldman, R., & Keren, M. (2004). Expanding the
scope of infant mental health assessment: A
community-based approach. In Del-Carmen-
Wiggins, R. & Carter, A. S. (Eds.), *Handbook
of infant mental health assessment*, pp. 443–465.
Cambridge: Oxford Press.

Feldman, R., Keren, M., Gross-Rozval, O., Tyano,
S. (2004). Mother and child's touch patterns in
infant feeding disorders; Relation to maternal,

child, and environmental factors. *Journal of
the American Academy of Child and Adolescent
Psychiatry*, 43, 1089–1097.

Feldman, R., & Klein, P. S. (2003). Toddlers' self-
regulated compliance with mother, caregiver,
and father: Implications for theories of socialization. *Developmental Psychology*, 39, 680–692.

Feldman, R., & Masalha, S. (2007). The role of
culture in moderating the links between early
ecological risk and young children's adaptation. *Development and Psychopathology*, 19,
1–21.

Feldman, R., & Masalha, S. (2010). Parent-child
and family antecedents of children's social
competence: Cultural specificity, universal process. *Developmental Psychology*, 46,
455–467.

Feldman, R., Masalha, S., & Alony, D. (2006).
Microregulatory patterns of family interactions: Cultural pathways to toddlers' self-
regulation. *Journal of Family Psychology*, 20,
614–623.

Feldman, R., Masalha, S. & Derdikman-Eiron,
R. (2010). Conflict resolution in the parent-
child, marital, and peer contexts and children's aggression in the peer-group: A cultural
perspective. *Developmental Psychology*, 46,
310–325.

Feldman, R., Masalha, S., & Nadam, R. (2001).
Cultural perspective on work and family:
Dual-earner Israeli-Jewish and Arab families
at the transition to parenthood. *Journal of
Family Psychology*, 15, 492–509.

Feldman, R., & Reznick, J. S. (1996). Maternal
perception of infant intentionality at 4 and 8
months. *Infant Behavior and Development*, 19,
485–498.

Feldman, R., & Vengrober, A. (2011). Post-
Traumatic Stress Disorder in infants and
young children exposed to war-related trauma.
*Journal of the American Academy of Child and
Adolescent Psychiatry*, 50, 645–658.

Feldman, R., Vengrober, A., & Hallaq, E. (August
2007). War and the young child; Mother-child
relationship, child symptoms, maternal well-
being, and mother and child's hormones in
infants and young children exposed to war,
terror, and violence. Paper presented at the
13th meeting of the European Society for
Child and Adolescent Psychiatry, Florence,
Italy.

Feldman, R., Vengrober, A., Eidelman-Rothman,
M., & Zagoory-Sharon, O. (in press). Stress
reactivity in war-exposed young children with
and without PTSD: Multi-level effects of

biology, parenting, and child emotionality and regulation. *Development and Psychopathology*

Feldman, R., Weller, A., Leckman, J. F., Kvint, J., & Eidelman, A. I. (1999). The nature of the mother's tie to her infant: Maternal bonding under conditions of proximity, separation, and potential loss. *Journal of Child Psychology and Psychiatry, 40*, 929–940.

Feldman, R., Weller, A., Sirota, L. & Eidelman, A. I. (2003). Testing a family intervention hypothesis: The Contribution of mother-infant skin-to-skin contact (Kangaroo Care) to family interaction and touch. *Journal of Family Psychology, 17*, 94–107.

Feldman, R., Weller, A., Zagoory-Sharon, O., & Levine, R. (2007). Evidence for a neuroendocrinological foundation of human affiliation; plasma oxytocin levels across pregnancy and the postpartum predict maternal-infant bonding. *Psychological Science, 19*, in press.

Ferber, S. G., & Feldman, R. & Makhoul, I. R. (2008). The development of maternal touch across the first year of life. *Early Human Development, 84*, 363–370.

Field, T. M. (1992). Infants of depressed mothers. *Development and Psychopathology, 4*, 49–66.

Field, T. M. (1994). The effects of mother's physical and emotional unavailability on emotion regulation. In N. A. Fox (Ed.), The development of emotion regulation: Biological and behavioral considerations. *Monographs of the Society for Research in Child Development, 59*(2–3), 208–227, Serial No. 240.

Field, T. M. (1995). Massage therapy for infants and children. *Journal of Behavioral and Developmental Pediatrics, 16*, 105–111.

Fincham, F. D. (1998). Child development and marital relations. *Child Development, 69*, 543–574.

Freud, S. (1916–1917). Introductory lectures on psycho-analysis. In *Standard Edition*, 16. London: Hogarth Press, 1955.

Geller, R., Diesendruck, G., & Feldman, R. (April 2007). Children's representations of their parents: Relationships with socio-cognitive capacities and parental interactive style. Poster presented in the biennial meeting of the Society for Research in Child Development, Boston.

Goldstein-Ferber, S. & Feldman, R. (2005). Delivery pain and the development of mother-infant interactions. *Infancy, 8*, 43–62.

Goldstein-Ferber, S., Feldman, R., Kohelet, D., Kuint, J., Dolberg, S., Arbel, E. & Weller, A. (2005). Massage therapy facilitates mother-infant interaction in premature infants. *Infant Behavior and Development, 28*, 74–81.

Gordon, I., & Feldman, R. (2008). Synchrony in the triad; A micro-level process model of coparenting and parent-child interactions. *Family Process, 47*, 465–479.

Gordon, I., Zagoory, O., Leckman, J. F., & Feldman, R. (2010). Oxytocin and the development of parenting in humans. *Biological Psychiatry, 68*, 377–382.

Guedeney, A., & Fermanian, J. (2001). A validity and reliability study of assessment and screening for sustained withdrawal reaction in infancy: The Alarm Distress Baby scale. *Infant Mental Health Journal, 22*, 559–575.

Johnson, M. H., Griffin, R., Csibra, G., Halit, H., Farroni, T., de Haan, M., Tucker, L. A., Baron-Cohen, S., & Richards, J. E. (2005). The emergence of the social brain network: Evidence from typical and atypical development. *Development and Psychopathology, 17*, 599–619.

Harel, H. (2006). Maternal representations, mother-infant interaction, and infant self-regulation in term and preterm infants. Ph.D. dissertation, Department of Psychology, Bar-Ilan University.

Harel, H., & Feldman, R. (April 2005). Maternal representations and mother-infant synchrony in full-term and preterm infants. Paper presented in the biennial meeting of the Society for Research in Child Development, Atlanta.

Harel, H., Gordon, I., Geva, R., & Feldman, R. (2011). Gaze behaviors of preterm and full-term infants in non-social and social contexts of increasing dynamics: Visual recognition, attention regulation, and gaze synchrony. *Infancy, 16*, 69–70

Hartup, W. W. (1989). Social relationships and their developmental significance. *American Psychologist, 44*, 120–126.

Harris, W. W., Lieberman, A. F., & Marans, S. (2007). In the best interests of society. *Journal of Child Psychology and Psychiatry, 48*, 392–411.

Heim, C., & Nemeroff, C. B. (2001). The role of childhood trauma in the neurobiology of mood and anxiety disorders: Preclinical and clinical studies. *Biological Psychiatry, 49*, 1023–1039.

Hofer, M. A. (1995). Hidden regulators: Implication for a new understanding of attachment, separation, and loss. In S. Goldberg, R. Muir & J. Kerr (eds.), *Attachment theory: Social, developmental, and clinical perspectives*, pp. 203–30. Hillsdale, NJ: Analytic Press.

Hoffman, M. L. (2000). *Empathy and moral development: Implications for caring and justice.* New York: Cambridge University Press.

Insel, T. R., & Young, L. J. (2001). The neurobiology of attachment. *Nature Reviews Neuroscience,* 2, 129–136.

Kagan, J. (1981). *The second year: The emergence of self awareness.* Cambridge, MA: Harvard University Press.

Kagan, J. (1984). *The nature of the child.* New York: Basic.

Keren, M., Dollberg, D., Kosteff, T., Danino, K., & Feldman, R. (2009). Family functioning and mother-child relational patterns in the context of infant psychiatric disorders. Manuscript submitted for publication.

Keren, M., Dollberg, D., Kosteff, T., Danino, K., & Feldman, R. (2010). Family functioning and mother-child relational patterns in the context of infant psychopathology. *Journal of Family Psychology,* 24, 597–604.

Keren, M., & Feldman, R. (2002). The role of feeding interaction assessment in the routine psychiatric evaluation of the infant. *Devenir,* 14, 5–16.

Keren, M., Feldman, R., Eidelman, A. I., Sirota, L., & Lester, B. (2003). Clinical interview for high-risk parents of premature infants (CLIP): Relations to mother-infant interaction. *Infant Mental Health Journal,* 24, 93–110.

Keren, M., Feldman, R., Namdari-Weinbaum, I., Spitzer S., & Tyano S. (2005). Symbolic play in toddlers: Relations with dyadic and triadic parent-child play interaction styles, child characteristics, and marital satisfaction. *Journal of Orthopsychiatry,* 75, 599–607.

Keren, M., Feldman, R., & Tyano, S. (2001). Emotional disturbances in infancy: Diagnostic classification and interactive patterns of infants referred to a community-based infant mental health clinic. *Journal of the American Academy of Child and Adolescent Psychiatry,* 40, 27–35.

Klein, P. S. (1996). *Early intervention: Cross-cultural experiences with a mediational approach.* New York: Gerland.

Klein, P. S., & Feldman, R. (2007). Mothers' and caregivers' interactive and teaching behavior with toddlers. *Early Child Development and Care,* 177, 383–402.

Kohut, H. (1971). *The analysis of the self.* New York: International Universities Press.

Lamb, M. E. (1977). Father-infant and mother-infant interaction in the first year of life. *Child Development,* 48, 167–181.

Leckman, J. F., Feldman, R., Swain, J. E., Eichler, V., Thompson, N., & Mayes, L. C. (2004). Primary parental preoccupation: Circuits, genes, and the crucial role of the environment. *Journal of Neural Transmission,* 11, 753–771.

Leckman, J. F. et al. (2005). Biobehavioral processes in attachment and bonding. In C. S. Carter & L. Ahnert (Eds.), *Attachment and Bonding: A New Synthesis.* Cambridge, MA: MIT Press.

Lieberman, A. F., Silverman, R., Pawl, J. H. (2000). Infant-parent psychotherapy. In C. H. Zeanah, Jr. (Ed.), *Handbook of infant mental health* (2nd ed.). New York: Guilford Press.

Lieberman, A. F., & Van Horn, P. (2008). *Psychotherapy for Infants and Young Children: Repairing the Effects of Stress and Trauma on Early Attachment.* New York: Guilford Publications, Inc.

Loewald, H. (1960). On the therapeutic action of psychoanalysis. *International Journal of Psychoanalysis,* 41, 16–33.

Lorenz, K. Z. (1950). The comparative method in studying innate behavior patterns. *Society for experimental biology: Physiological mechanisms in animal behavior* (Society's Symposium IV), pp. 221–268. Oxford, UK: Academic Press.

Maccoby, E. E. (1992). The role of parents in the socialization of children: An historical overview. *Developmental Psychology,* 28, 1006–1017.

Meaney, M. J. (2001). Maternal care, gene expression, and the transmission of individual differences in stress reactivity across generations. *Annual Review of Neuroscience,* 24, 1161–1192.

Messer, D. J. (1994). *The development of communication: From social interaction to language.* Chichester, UK: Wiley.

Minuchin, P. (1985). Families and individual development: Provocations from the field of family therapy. *Child Development,* 56, 289–302.

Moshe, M., & Feldman, R. (2006). Maternal and infant heart rhythms and mother-infant synchrony. A paper presented at the biennial conference of the World Association for Infant Mental Health. Paris, France.

Nelson, K. (1985). *Making sense: The acquisition of shared meaning.* New York: Academic Press.

Paris, R., Weinberg, M. K., & Bolton, R. (January 2008). *Postpartum depression and mother-infant interactions: Findings from a study of home-based interventions.* Boston: Society for Social Work Research.

Parke, R. D., & Bhavnagri, N. P. (1989). Parents as managers of children's peer relationships. In

D. Belle (ed.), *Children's social networks and social supports*, pp. 241–259. New York: Wiley.

Patterson, G. R., Littman, R. A., & Bricker, W. (1967). Assertive behavior in children; A step toward a theory of aggression. *Monographs for the Society of Research in Child Development*, 32, 1–43.

Porges, S. W. (2003). Social engagement and attachment; A polygenetic perspective. *Annals of the New York Academy of Sciences*, 1008, 31–47.

Rutter, M., & Sroufe, L. A. (2000). Developmental psychopathology: Concepts and challenges. *Development and Psychopathology*, 12, 265–296.

Sameroff, A. J. (1995). General systems theories and developmental psychopathology. In D. Cicchetti, D. J. Cohen, & F. D. Fincham (Eds.), (1998). *Child development and marital relations. Child Development*, 69, 543–574.

Sander, L. W. (1984). Polarity, paradox, and the organizing process in development. In J. D. call (Ed.), *Frontiers of infant psychiatry*, pp. 333–346. New York: Basic.

Schneider, B. H., Attili, G., Nadel, J., & Weissberg, R. P. (Eds.) (1989). *Social competence in developmental perspective*. Dordrecht: Kluwer.

Shaver, P., R., Mikulincer, M. (2002). Attachment-related psychodynamics. *Attachment & Human Development*, 4, 133–161.

Silberstein, D., Feldman, R., Gardner, J. M., Karmel, B. Z., Kuint, J., & Geva, R. (2009). The mother-infant feeding relationship across the first year and the development of feeding difficulties in low-risk premature infants. *Infancy*, 14, 1–25.

Silberstein, D., Geva, R., Feldman, R., Gardner, J. M., Karmel, B. Z., Rozen, C. & Kvint, J. (2009a). The transition to oral feeding in low-risk premature infants: Relations to neonatal neurobehavioral status and mother-infant feeding interaction. *Early Human Development*, 85, 157–162.

Slade, A. (1987). A longitudinal study of maternal involvement and symbolic play during the toddler period. *Child Development*, 21, 558–567.

Stern, D. N. (1985). *The interpersonal world of the infant*. New York: Basic.

Stern, D. N. (1995). *The Motherhood Constellation: A Unified View of Parent-Infant Psychotherapy*. New York: Basic Books.

Trevarthen, C., & Aitken (1999). Infant intersubjectivity; Research, theory, and clinical applications. *Journal of Child Psychology and Psychiatry*, 42, 3–48.

Tronick, E., Als, H., & Brazelton, T. B. (1980). Monadic phases: A structural descriptive analysis of infant–mother face–to–face interaction. *Merrill–Palmer Quarterly*, 26, 3–24.

Vengrober, A., & Feldman, R. (2012). Symbolic competence, play themes, and post-traumatic symptoms in war-exposed young children and their mothers. Manuscript submitted for publication

Viaux-Savelon, S., Dommergues, M., Rosenblum, O., Bodeau, N., Aidane, E., Phillippon, O., Mazet, P., Vibert-Guigue, C., Vauthier-Brouzes, D., Feldman, R., & Cohen, D. (2012). Prenatal ultrasound screening: False positive soft markers may alter maternal representations and mother-infant interactions. PLoSOne,2012;7(1):e30935

Winnicott, D. W. (1956). *Collected papers: Through pediatrics to psychoanalysis*. New York: Basic Books.

Yogman, M. W. (1981). Games fathers and mothers play with their infants. *Infant Mental Health Journal*, 2, 241–248.

Zinaman, M. J., Hughes, V., Queenan, J. T., Labobok, M. H., & Albertson, B. (1992). Acute prolactin and oxytocin responses and milk yields to infant suckling and artificial methods of expression in lactating women. *Pediatrics*, 89, 437–440.

CHAPTER 27

HOME Inventory

Robert H. Bradley

History and Purpose

The Home Observation or Measurement of the Environment (HOME) Inventory (Caldwell & Bradley, 2003) is one of the most widely used measures of the family environment in the world. HOME is designed to measure the quality and quantity of support, structure, and stimulation available to a child in the child's home setting. The focus is on the child as a recipient of inputs from objects, events, arrangements and transactions occurring in connection with life at home. The work of Bloom (1964) and Hunt (1961) provided a conceptual framework for constructing the original versions of the instrument in 1965. However, the principles used to guide selection of indicators to be included in the Inventory map closely on ecological-developmental theories such as those articulated by Bronfenbrenner (1995), Ford and Lerner (1992), and Wachs (2000). Accordingly, the measure is not limited to documenting just those circumstances and events that occur within the four walls of a child's residence but also includes the child's use of social networks and community resources outside the residence as they pertain to family life. This more capacious view of the home environment is consistent with the position of social anthropologists who contend that the social boundaries of household units often extend beyond the physical boundaries of their dwellings (Altman, 1977; Lawrence & Low, 1990).

There are 4 primary versions of HOME: (a) the Infant-Toddler version designed for children ages birth to 3, (b) the Early Childhood version designed for children ages 3 to 6, (c) the Middle Childhood version designed for children ages 6 to 10, and (d) the Early Adolescence version designed for children ages 10 to 15. The Infant-Toddler version (IT-HOME) was crafted and standardized in Syracuse, New York in the mid-1960s (Caldwell, Heider, & Kaplan, 1966) as was the original version of the Early Childhood version (EC-HOME) (NOTE: the scale was initially called the Preschool HOME). Both the IT-HOME and the EC-HOME were renormed in Little Rock, Arkansas in the early to mid-1970s, at which time the EC-HOME was restandardized to its current 55 items (Bradley & Caldwell,

1979). The Middle Childhood version (MC-HOME) was crafted and standardized in Little Rock in the mid-1980s (Bradley et al., 1988). The Early Adolescence version (EA-HOME) was crafted and standardized in Little Rock in the mid-1990s with support from colleagues in San Antonio, Los Angeles, and New York City (Bradley et al., 2000). In the mid-to-late 1980s specialized versions of the HOME were crafted and standardized in Arkansas to fit the needs of families having children with moderate to severe disabilities (Bradley et al., 1989). There are special forms for children with hearing impairments, visual impairments, motor impairments and severe cognitive impairments (Head, Bradley, & Rock, 1990; Holder-Brown et al., 1993; Rock et al., 1994). As part of the NICHD Study of Early Child Care, the IT-HOME and EC-HOME were modified for use in family child care arrangements with data gathered at all ten project sites around the United States (Bradley, Caldwell, & Corwyn, 2003).

Scale Characteristics

Content

HOME attempts to document the extent to which a child's environment contains experiences that promote the child's well-being and does not contain experiences that are inimical to well-being (e.g., parental warmth and responsiveness, the avoidance of restriction and harsh punishment, household order, appropriate discipline practices, family routines, appropriate rules and regulations, access to toys and materials for learning and recreation, access to enriching in-home and out-of-home experiences, provision of instruction, social stimulation and communication, connection to family and friendship networks, provision for safety). The items included in each version of HOME were guided by the research and theory available at the time the particular version was crafted, with a focus on age-appropriateness (i.e., the role of parenting for infants consists of providing almost everything directly to or for a child; but as

children grow older parenting increasingly involves the roles of arranger, broker, and mentor for experiences). Although HOME provides rather broad coverage of the things that might matter in terms of family promotion of well-being, it does not cover all domains of parenting/family life with equal depth (e.g., there is relatively scant coverage of most matters pertaining to safety and routines and even less about food provision). Moreover, as a measure of the family environment, HOME does not contain indicators of the quality of connected social environments such as child care, school, church or other social agencies.

The Infant-Toddler HOME is composed of 45 items clustered into 6 scales: (a) parental responsivity, (b) acceptance of child, (c) organization of the environment, (d) learning materials, (e) parental involvement, and (f) variety of experience. The Early Childhood HOME is composed of 55 items clustered into 8 scales: (a) learning materials, (b) language stimulation, (c) physical environment, (d) parental responsivity, (e) learning stimulation, (f) modeling of social maturity, (g) variety in experience, and (h) acceptance of child. The Middle Childhood HOME is composed of 59 items clustered into 8 scales: (a) parental responsivity, (b) physical environment, (c) learning materials, (d) active stimulation, (e) encouraging maturity, (f) emotional climate, (g) parental involvement, and (h) family participation. The Early Adolescence HOME is composed of 60 items clustered into 7 scales: (a) physical environment, (b) learning materials, (c) modeling, (d) instructional activities, (e) regulatory activities, (f) variety of experience, and (g) acceptance and responsivity. The specialized versions for families having children with disabilities are organized in the same manner as the original versions, except that they tend to contain a small number of additional indicators in particular scales and sometimes include minor adjustments in scoring procedures depending on the nature of the disability.

Cultural Issues. Although efforts have been made to include indicators in HOME that have wide applicability to children from different nationalities, ethnicities, and socioeconomic backgrounds, concerns have been raised about the applicability of particular items in particular groups. To a degree, the wide use of HOME throughout the world and in different subgroups within the United States offers a kind of imprimatur for the instrument writ large. By the same token, decisions have been made by many users to amend the scale so that it better fits local circumstances and practices. Modifications have taken many forms including dropping items, dropping scales, adding items and changing scoring criteria for items. In a few instances, researchers have constructed additional scales or created whole new measures that at least roughly parallel what HOME attempts to measures. Let me offer a few illustrations of the types of changes that have been made to address local concerns regarding the applicability of HOME.

Dropping individual items to suit local conditions has been fairly common. In St. Vincent, where there is not strong emphasis on independence and self-enhancement, the item "Parent spontaneously offers praise to child during visit" was not considered a very relevant indicator of parental responsiveness; therefore, it was dropped (Durbrow, Jones, Bozoky, Jimerson, & Adams, 1996). A similar judgment was made with respect to the Yoruba in Nigeria (Aina, Agiobu-Kemmer, Etta, Zeitlin, & Setiloane, 1993). Likewise, parents in Kilifi, Kenya do not tend to use terms of endearment for their children or encourage them to contribute to adult conversations, consistent with the cultural value that children should be deferent (Holding, 2003). In St. Vincent, decisions were made to drop "Child has access to musical instrument" because virtually no children did and "Family member has taken child on trip of over 50 miles in past year" because most families never leave the island. Dropping whole scales for conceptual or technical reasons has been relatively rare, but it has occurred. For example, Lamb and colleagues (1988) decided to use both IT-HOME and EC-HOME "as is" but eliminated half the EC-HOME scales

because of low reliability. In several studies done in North America and western Europe, the range of scores on some items was so minimal that items or scales were dropped for lack of variability – largely owing to high proportions of well-educated, well-resourced parents (Vedder et al., 1995). The opposite situation has emerged in a number of poor, developing countries. In communities or countries were families tend to have few material resources, decisions have often been made to adjust scoring criteria pertaining to books and other learning materials (Aina et al., 1993; Drotar et al., 1999; Grantham-McGregor et al., 1991; Lozoff et al., 1995; Richter & Grieve, 1991; & Zeitlin et al., 1995). Another common adjustment in more traditional societies pertains to items that concern discipline (spanking). In three different studies done in Africa, where spanking and other means of physical punishment are commonplace, decisions were made either to drop the spanking items on HOME or modify scoring criteria so that more spanking was allowed (Aina et al., 1993; Drotar et al., 1999; Holding, 2003) – similar adjustments were also made in Macedonia (personal communication). Likewise, Durbrow and colleagues (1996) modified items pertaining to parental loss of temper from the Middle Childhood Home in deference to cultural practice in the Caribbean. Although the most common responses (likely for practical reasons) for addressing concerns about HOME items has been to drop items or change scoring criteria, in a few instances researchers have added items or even whole scales so that the modified scale would more fully capture what the family environment affords by way of support for children's development (Hayes et al., 1991; Grantham-McGregor et al., 1982). Ertem and colleagues (1997) constructed a set of supplemental items to be used with the urban poor in the United States, items that give greater coverage to safety, routines, and food security. In Macedonia, where great emphasis is placed in the development of collaborative social skills, a new scale was developed just to measure family supports for this function.

Although the arguments made by researchers in the United States and elsewhere for changing HOME so that it more useful in particular eco-cultural niches seem generally sound, it is not known whether the various modifications made to the Inventory actually resulted in superior measurement. In two studies where culture-specific family environment measures were administered simultaneous to HOME (one in Japan, the second in Pakistan), the correlation between HOME and the culture-specific measure was greater than .80. In a third (this one in Brazil), findings with the culture-specific measure were quite similar to those using HOME (Anselmi, Piddinini, Bastos, & Lopes, 2004; Bastos, Almeida-Filho, & Pinho, 1998; Marturano, Ferriera, & Bacarji, 2004).

Short Forms. As part of the National Longitudinal Survey of Youth, abbreviated forms of the HOME were constructed (HOME-SF). These forms were modeled on the standard versions of IT-HOME, EC-HOME, and MC-HOME (those connected with NLSY constructed their own form for adolescents because there was no EA-HOME at the time the short forms were developed [http://www.nlsinfo.org/web-investigator/docs.php?mychrt=childya_03, accessed on November 1, 2007]). The primary difference in the short forms are that they contain only about half the number of items (hence there are no separate subscales), the information needed to score the items is a structured interview, and the items entail 4-point scales for scoring rather than the dichotomous scoring used in the standard HOME. However, the HOME-SF also uses 10 observational items from the original HOME that employ the standard dichotomous scoring.

Administration and Scoring

Administration. The HOME is administered as a semistructured interview and observation done at the target child's home place when both the child and the primary caregiver are present and awake (Caldwell & Bradley, 2003). Other members of the family may also be present but their presence

is not required. A minimum of 45 minutes is needed for the visit in order to allow sufficient time to make the required observations, but no more than 90 minutes are allowed. The home visit is designed to take place when there are no extraordinary constraints on parent or child behavior (in effect to allow for "natural" behavior to the greatest extent possible). The Manual recommends that exchanges between data gatherer and family be low-key, nonjudgmental, and non-threatening (i.e., conversational) so as to facilitate candid communication and natural behavior.

The method of interview with parent, child and anyone else present is semistructured. That is, the conversation is organized around broad probes concerning daily activities, child play, out-of-home excursions, family routines, child and parent interests, and the like. Caregivers are encouraged to express themselves in the normal ways, to continue household activities if needs be, and to allow the child freedom to play and communicate. The interviewer is urged to listen carefully and to encourage natural conversation about topics that arise, using follow-up questions so as to make certain that accurate information is obtained. Interviewers are trained to make family members feel comfortable and are cautioned against evaluative statements or leading questions.

Scoring. Each item is scored in binary (yes – no) fashion, with "yes" the desirable response in each case. Summary scores for component scales are derived by simply adding the number of "yes" scores for items in that scale. Likewise, the Total score is simply the total number of "yes" scores for all items.

Cut-points for scoring items generally are set at standards that discriminate between a "good enough" level of input and insufficient level of input rather than between adequate and optimal. Accordingly, there tends to be relatively high endorsement rates for most items. This leads to negative skews for most scale scores. Mean scores even for families in poor communities or poor countries tend to be above the mid-point.

Psychometric Properties

Reliability. The primary means of determining the consistency with which HOME measures the family environment is interrater reliability. Most reports on the measure indicate that there is about 90 percent agreement across raters who observe the same administration of the Inventory (Adams, Campbell, & Ramey, 1984; Bradley & Caldwell, 1979; Bradley et al., 1988, 1989, 2000; Caldwell, 1967; Coll, Vohr, Hoffman, & Oh, 1986; Gottfried & Gottfried, 1988; Johnson, 1979; Kurtz, Borkowski, & Deshmukh, 1988; Starr, 1982; Wilson & Matheny, 1983; Wulbert, Inglis, Kriegsman, & Mills, 1975). Recent data from the NICHD Study of Early Child Care and Youth Development also indicated interrater agreement to be > 90 percent. However, using raw percent agreement does not correct for base rate. Studies that have estimated interrater reliability using coefficients (intraclass, Pearson, Kappa) have generally found the reliability to be > .80 (Affleck, Allen, McGrade, & McQueeney, 1982; Belsky, Garduque, & Hrncir, 1984; Hollenbeck, 1978; Miller & Ottinger, 1983). Numerous researchers have also used coefficient alpha to estimate the reliability of HOME, with results generally showing rather high internal consistency for the total score (less so with some scale scores). However, this means of estimating of reliability is of dubious value as applied to HOME (Bradley, 2004).

Cause versus effect indicators. The distinction between cause (or formative) and effect (or reflective) indicators is becoming better understood throughout the social sciences (Bollen, 2002; Howell, Breivik, & Wilcox, 2007). Effect indicators arise from the phenomenon that is being measured; that is, they reflect the latent construct that is being measured and are inherently connected to it. By contrast, cause indicators do not emanate from the phenomenon being measured but rather have a functional relation to a separate phenomenon. The indicators contained in HOME were selected because of their presumed potential to affect children's behavior and development (i.e., they are cause indicators). The indicators contained in a particular scale may or may not emanate (reflect) the same latent construct, but that is immaterial to their inclusion in the scale. Consider just as an illustration four experiences that may help to foster language development (talking with momma, reading a book, going to a play at the community theater with dad, playing Scrabble with an older sibling). Each might be used as an indicator of "home environmental supports for language and literacy." However, what unites them is their presumed value for promoting language and literacy not their inherent relation to a single underlying phenomenon; that is, something that by its very nature gives rise to all four. The distinction between cause and effect indicators has rather broad implications in terms of using traditional approaches to constructing and evaluating measures. According to Bollen (2002, p. 617), "Factor analysis, reliability tests, and latent class analysis are examples of techniques that assume effect indicators." Even though factor analysis, coefficient alpha and item response theory have been used to help determine the usefulness of particular items and the organizational structure of HOME, their value to these purposes is questionable. There is no theoretical reason to assume any particular covariance structure for the indicators that make up HOME scales, nor is there any reason to assume that the structure should remain invariant across various socioeconomic or cultural groups. Indeed, according to Hui and Triandis (1985), it is likely that covariances among functionally similar indicators will vary across cultures. It can be interesting and useful to compare factor structures (or coefficient alphas) across groups, but finding a different structure does not mean that the set of indicators has greater validity or utility in one group versus another per se. The key, for measures like HOME (one composed of cause indicators), is whether the set of indicators predicts patterns of development in expected ways (Bradley, 2004).

The Context of Child Rearing

Access to Resources and HOME Scores

When families have access to resources, be they material, social, or political, it increases the likelihood children will be exposed to events, transactions, and conditions that increase the prospects of optimal development (Coleman, 1988). Not surprisingly, scores on the HOME are consistently associated with family income and wealth, level of parent education, age of mother at first birth, level of household crowding, access to social support, membership in a two-parent family, and related indicators of access to resources (Allen et al., 1984; Bradley & Caldwell, 1982; 1984; Bradley et al., 1988, 1989, 2000; Church & Katigbak, 1991; Coll et al., 1987; Field et al., 1990; Gottfried & Gottfried, 1984; Hollenbeck, 1978; Nihira et al., 1987; Pachter et al., 2006; Parks & Smeriglio, 1986; Ragozin et al., 1978). Although relations between HOME scores and various sociodemographic measures are sometimes only modest, as a study of working class mothers in Italy showed (Fein et al., 1993), evidence from throughout the world typically shows moderate to strong relations between HOME scores and access to resources (Aina et al., 1993, Blevins-Knabe & Austin, 2000; Broberg et al., 1997; Das & Padhee, 1993, Durbrow et al., 1996; Jacobson et al., 1995; Kurtz et al., 1988; Masud et al., 1994; Palacios et al., 1992; Palti et al., 1984; Perez & Moreno, 2004; Pinto, 2004; Richter & Grieve, 1991; Sahu & Devi, 1982; Tippie, 2003; Torralva & Cugnasco, 1996; Vedder, Eldering, & Bradley, 1995; Zeitlin et al., 1995). That said, there is at least some research suggesting that relations between available support and HOME scores may be complex. For example, among mothers with few obstetric complications Infant-Toddler HOME scores were unrelated to maternal resources or social support; but HOME scores for mothers with multiple obstetric complications were correlated strongly with availability of relatives, support from the baby's father, and support from friends (Wandersman & Unger, 1983). Pascoe and Earp (1984) found that HOME scores were related to social support but not life changes.

There are cultural differences in the patterns of relations observed, both with respect to overall strength and with respect to particular scales on HOME. These differences likely reflect the amount of variability in access to resources and the tightness of class structure within the society as well as particular cultural beliefs and practices – relations pertaining to material possessions being the most robust across samples, relations pertaining to discipline practices the least robust. Differences in parental beliefs about child rearing likely mediate some of the relations. For example, Palacios and colleagues (1992) found that parents with "modern" beliefs generally higher levels of education than parents with "traditional" beliefs (see also Zeitlin et al., 1995; Zevalkink & Riksen-Walraven, 2001).

In one of the most detailed investigations of relations between HOME scores and family demography, Bradley and colleagues (2001) compared high- and low-income families in three ethnic groups (European American, African American, Hispanic) on every indicator from the HOME-SF at every age from infancy through age 15. In this highly representative U.S. sample, of the 124 indicators examined, poor and nonpoor children were exposed to different levels of inputs on all but 15. Income differences emerged on the majority of indicators in all three ethnic groups. The mean effect size across all ethnic groups and all age periods was small ($h = .22$) but for about one-fourth of items the effect size was greater than .30. Ethnic group differences favoring whites and Asians also emerged on the majority of indicators but the mean effect size for ethnicity was < .20. That said, there were particular inputs where family income and ethnicity did not seem to matter (e.g., family visits relatives).

Parental History and Personality

Belsky (1984) identified parental history and personality as major determinants of the type of parenting children receive. Daggett et al. (2000) found that HOME scores were associated with parental life histories, particularly their perceptions of receiving harsh punishment. The findings by Palacios and colleagues (1992) regarding modernity beliefs testify to the connection between parenting attitudes and HOME scores for mothers in Spain. Studies also show that HOME scores are related to authoritarianism (Henderson, 1975), attitudes toward children and child rearing (Daggett et al., 2000; Greenberg & Crnic, 1988; Luster & Rhoades, 1989; Reis & Herz, 1987), knowledge of child development (Parks & Smeriglio, 1986; Reis et al., 1986), and depression (Allen et al., 1982; Pachter et al., 2006; Reis & Hertz, 1987). However, findings are not consistent across all studies or HOME scales; and neither does any particular personality characteristic tend to account for large amounts of variance. However, the relation between maternal intelligence and HOME tends to be at least moderately high in most populations (Bradley et al., 1994; Church & Katigbak, 1991; Longstreth et al., 1981; Plomin & Bergeman, 1991).

Just as HOME tends to show associations with various aspects of parental personality, so does it correlate with other types of parenting behavior. For example, breast feeding is associated with HOME scores as is smoking and the use of drugs and alcohol (LaVeck et al., 1984; Noll et al., 1989; Ragozin et al., 1978).

Relations with Other Measures of Parenting and Family Environment

For more than 30 years researchers have examined associations between HOME scores and other measures of parenting. One reason is to better understand the extent to which different parenting measures capture the same environmental supports for children's well-being in different social/cultural contexts; a second reason is to understand how family environment measures focused on different levels of analysis converge (Hui & Triandis, 1985). Ramey and Mills (1977) found that higher scores on the Infant-Toddler HOME were significantly correlated with observed maternal behavior in structured laboratory procedures among high-risk mothers. Mothers with high HOME scores interacted with the children more, talked to them more and watched TV less. Likewise, Barnard and Gortner (1977) observed that mothers with high HOME scores gave more positive and fewer negative messages to their infants during standardized teaching and feeding tasks. They also provided more useful assistance to children during the teaching task. Berlin et al. (1995) found that the warmth scale from EC-HOME was related to observed supportive presence and the learning stimulation was related to observed quality of assistance in both white and black families. More recently, Bradley and Corwyn (2005, 2007) found that scores on the Infant-Toddler, Early Childhood and Middle Childhood versions of HOME were moderately correlated with maternal sensitivity as measured using a structured laboratory procedure as part of the NICHD Study of Early Child Care and Youth Development. In fact, in several publications produced by the NICHD Early Child Care Research Network (Belsky et al., 2007), HOME has been combined with observed maternal sensitivity to construct an overall estimate of parenting quality. Zevalkink and Riksen-Walraven (1996) also found that HOME was moderately correlated with observed maternal sensitivity among Indonesian infants and preschoolers. Not surprisingly, Starr (1982) found that mothers identified by child protective service agencies as abusers had lower HOME scores of mothers with no record of abuse.

Several teams of researchers have observed moderate correlations between HOME scores and scores on another widely used measure of the family environment, the Family Environment Scale (Bradley et al., 1987; Gottfried & Gotfried, 1984, 1988; Mink & Nihira, 1987; Wandersman & Unger, 1987). As well, two groups of researchers have observed high correlations between HOME scores and measures of home quality developed for use in other countries (Japan: Anme & Takayama, 1989; Pakistan: Masud et al., 1994).

Child Well-Being

As stated earlier, HOME is designed to measure the quality and quantity of support, structure, and stimulation available to a child in the child's home setting. Consequently, hundreds of studies have examined relations between HOME scores and measures of child well-being.

Language, Cognitive Functioning and Achievement

Studies done throughout the world typically show low to moderate correlations (.20 – .60) between HOME scores and measures of children's language, cognitive functioning and achievement, beginning in the second year of life and extending through adolescence (Adams et al., 1984; Bakeman & Brown, 1980; Bee et al., 1982; Belsky et al., 1984, 2007; Bradley & Caldwell, 1976, 1979; 1984; Bradley et al., 1987, 1988, 1989; 2000; Character-Murchinson, 1988; Chua et al., 1989; Coll et al., 1987; Cravioto & DeLicardie, 1986; Elardo et al., 1975, 1977; Field et al., 1990; Gottfried & Gottfried, 1984; Jordan, 1978; Kurtz et al., 1988; McMichael et al., 1988; Mohite, 1987; Moore et al., 1989; Palti et al., 1984; Parks & Smeriglio, 1986; Pinto, 2004; Siegel, 1982; Stevenson & Lamb, 1979; Sahu & Devi, 1982; Wulbert et al., 1975). There is evidence that the kinds of processes measured by HOME help mediate the relation between family SES and children's competence (Bradley & Corwyn, 2003; Linver et al., 2002). However, the relation between HOME and children's competence is not simply a reflection of their joint relation to family SES (Mofese et al., 2003). Evidence supporting these associations emerged in a diversity of sociocultural groups, in children with various disabilities and biological problems, and with an array of different measures of competence (Kalmar, 1996). LaVeck et al. (1983) observed that children with minor anomalies who had low HOME scores often showed decreased activity level, motor skills, and language competence, but those with high HOME scores did not.

Part of the relation between HOME scores and measures of children's competence would seem to reflect parental teaching and exposure to quite specific skills (Jackson & Roberts, 2001). Part also reflects the development of proclivities, like academic achievement motivation and sustained attention, that help facilitate competence (Gottfried et al., 1998; NICHD Early Child Care Research Network, 2003).

Despite consistent findings that HOME scores are associated with cognitive functioning and achievement, research indicates that relations between HOME and children's cognitive and achievement outcomes are complex. Moreover, there is evidence that one cannot draw simple causal interpretations from the observed associations. For example, predictions are sometimes different depending on children's health status, culture and family demographics (Bradley et al., 1987, 1989, 2001; Church & Katigbak, 1991; Hadeed & Sylva, 1999; Hayes, 1980; Johnson et al., 1984; Lozoff et al., 1995; Richter Grieve, 1991; Wasserman et al., 1993; Wulbert et al., 1975). In poor communities, for instance, the dearth of material goods and opportunities for enrichment, together with poor nutrition, family instability and accumulated health problems, often resulted in lower correlations and changes made to HOME scales. In a sophisticated analysis using HOME-SF and the Peabody Individual Achievement Test data from the National Longitudinal Survey of Youth, Rowe et al. (1995) determined that there were strong genetic connections to the association. They also observed that linkages between home environmental processes and achievement were quite similar for European American, African American and Hispanic school children.

Social Development and Adaptive Behavior

Theoretically, aspects of parenting such as responsiveness and warmth should promote attachment security; and there is evidence of such a relation (Erickson et al,. 1985; Zevalkink et al., 2008). Bakeman and Brown

(1980) found that HOME Responsivity during the first year of life predicted the child's social involvement and participation; Bradley and Caldwell (1979) found that Early Childhood HOME scores were correlated with locus of control orientation in children ages 6 to 8; and Tedesco (1981) found that early HOME scores predicted classroom social competence. Even though responsiveness does not always the same characteristic form in all cultures, studies using HOME scales that capture warmth and responsiveness have shown associations with mental health problems in Brazil (Bastos et al., 1998), conduct problems in St. Vincent (Durbrow et al., 1996) and a composite measures of well-being among the Yoruba in Africa (Zeitlin et al., 1995). Mulhall et al. (1988) found that the total HOME score was related to behavioral disorders in preschool age Irish children as well. That said, when the acceptance and responsivity scale was combined with the regulatory activities scale to predict life satisfaction for adolescents from 5 cultural groups in the United States, it was often not a significant predictor. The physical environment scale actually performed better (Bradley & Corwyn, 2004); thus suggesting that different factors may have different implications for perceived well-being at different points in the life course.

Most studies of children social competence and adaptive behavior have observed complex relations between HOME, child characteristics and other measures of family context (Erickson et al., 1985; Linver et al., 2002; Mink & Nihira, 1987; Sroufe et al., 1990). For example, Carlson and Corcoran (2001) found that there was an interplay between family configuration and income in terms of the likelihood children would manifest behavior problems. Those relations were affected by maternal mental health and mediated by the quality of the home environment. Lamb et al. (1988) found that early development of a socially competent personality in Swedish children was a complex function of HOME scores, child temperament, and social support. Prodromidis et al. (1995) performed a follow-up analysis

and found relations between HOME scores and both aggression and compliance. Belsky's (2004) differential susceptibility hypothesis stipulates that children with difficult temperaments are more amenable to environmental influence. Bradley and Corwyn (2007) found further verification of this hypothesis using data from the NICHD Study of Early Child Care and Youth Development. Specifically, they observed that children with difficult temperaments were more likely to manifest externalizing behavior in first grade if their mothers were less sensitive and treated them more harshly (measured using HOME), whereas children with easy temperaments did not show such an effect. Likewise, children with difficult temperaments were more likely to show externalizing behavior if they had less opportunity for enriching activities (also measured using HOME) whereas children with easy temperaments show no such effect.

Not surprisingly, one of the most often studied relations is that between HOME scores and scores on the Child Behavior Checklist (Achenbach, 1991). Examples include a study done in low birth weight Dutch children (Weiglas-Kuperus et al., 1993) which found significant relations with the total problems score as well as with clinician ratings of behavior problems and a study done in Yugoslavia where HOME scores were related to CBCL scores (Wasserman et al., 1998). Gill and Kang (1995) found that the total HOME score was associated with externalizing behavior among preschool age children in India, albeit the patterns varied somewhat depending on whether the child lived in a rural or urban area. Likewise, Bradley (1994) and Bradley et al (2001) found that HOME was related to CBCL scores in European-American, African-American, and Mexican-American families from infancy through adolescence. In the former study, HOME was also related to measures of social competence as well. However, the correlations were stronger for European American children. Pachter et al. (2006) also found ethnic differences in patterns of relations. In one of the most ambitious studies, HOME (measured from age 2 through third grade) scores were related to patterns of aggression from infancy to middle childhood, controlling for a host of other child and environmental measures (NICHD Early Child Care Research Network, 2004).

In studies of conduct problems and externalizing behavior, scores on the HOME acceptance scale (with its focus on spanking) have been of particular interest. A study by Bradley et al. (2001) showed a relation to the acceptance scale, as did a study done in St. Vincent (Durbrow et al., 1996). Studies using data from the NICHD Study of Early Child Care and Youth Development suggest that relations between externalizing behavior and either the total HOME score or the acceptance scale are often mediated by meta-cognitive and self-regulatory behaviors (Bradley & Corwyn, 2005, 2007; NICHD Early Child Care Research Network, 2003). In Western societies, where there is emphasis on achievement and self-directedness, HOME items that tap stimulation and instruction also tend to be associated with reduced aggression and externalizing problems (Bradley et al., 2001; Bradley & Corwyn, 2005, 2007; Linver et al., 2002). Despite reasonably consistent findings pertaining to relations between HOME scales and measures of maladjustment, it's important not to interpret the findings as indicative of causal impacts. Plomin et al. (1985) found that HOME was not related to behavior problems among adopted children even though significant relations were observed in nonadopted children.

HOME scores obtained from infancy through adolescence have also shown relatively consistent relations with measures of classroom behavior such as task orientation, consideration and overall social skills from early childhood to adolescence (Belsky, 2007; Bradley et al., 1980, 1987, 2000; Gottfried & Gottfried, 1988; Laveck et al., 1983). These relations do not appear spurious in that they seem to hold despite controls on socioeconomic status; but the strength of association has varied somewhat depending on ethnicity and gender.

Health

Because HOME captures a diverse array of conditions and activities that are implicated in children's health and because it contains indicators that are correlated with other parenting practices and contextual conditions that are implicated in children's health, it is not surprising that some of the earliest studies using HOME involved children at risk for poor health (e.g., malnutrition, lead burden, failure-to-thrive). Neither is it surprising that HOME has been used as both an explanatory and a control variable in models aimed at explicating how environmental conditions affect the course of wellness in children throughout the world. For example, in the Australian Port Pirie study, HOME scores were related to postnatal blood lead levels (McMichael et al., 1992).

In their study of infants prenatally exposed to cocaine, Black et al. (1993) found that HOME was related to scores on the Brazleton Neonatal Behavior Assessment Scale. Nishimura (1992) also found that HOME scores were related to NBAS scores for Japanese children. In their study of fetal malnutrition in infants, Zeskind and Ramey (1978, 1981) found that a low ponderal index was associated with scores on the parental involvement scale from the Infant-Toddler HOME. HOME scores for children clinically malnourished were also lower than HOME scores for nonmalnourished children from similar socioeconomic backgrounds (Chase & Martin, 1970; Cravioto & DeLicardie, 1972, 1986). The academic stimulation scale from EC-HOME was correlated with the likelihood of having adequate intake of calories, protein, vitamin A, and iron among Javanese children between the ages of 25 and 73 months (Chomitz et al., 1992). Likewise, several studies have shown that children identified as nonorganic failure-to-thrive had lower scores on HOME scales such as responsivity, parental involvement, acceptance and learning materials than non-FTT children from similar SES backgrounds (Bradley et al., 1984; Kelleher et al. 1993; Pollitt et al., 1975). That said, studies also show that patterns of child growth tend not to have simple or inevitable relations with particular patterns of parenting or that one can easily forecast the specific health consequence for a given pattern of environmental conditions (Bradley et al., 1984; Drotar & Sturm, 1989; Grantham-McGregor et al., 1982). Studies of relations between HOME and children's growth provide evidence in support of general systems notions such as eqi-finality and multifinality; that is, several different patterns of environmental conditions may lead to the same health consequence and one pattern of environmental conditions may lead to several different developmental problems.

Although studies done world-wide demonstrate an association between the kinds of environmental indicators contained in HOME and a diverse array of child health measures, those relations have most often been observed for children at significant environmental risk. There is little to suggest that the same indicators are connected to common health conditions such as colds and flus in more general populations (NICHD Early Childhood Research Network, 2001, 2003).

CULTURAL ISSUES

Differences in cultural belief systems and socioeconomic circumstances appears to affect the extent to which parents display warmth and sensitivity to their children. Praising children and showing them affection in the presence of adults who are not family members is unlikely in some societies. That said, certain forms of physical affection are more common in some African societies than in most technologically developed societies, especially after early infancy. These variations notwithstanding, HOME scales that tap socioemotional support were related to measures of social and emotional development in most societies, albeit there relation to children's competence was less consistent. Scores on HOME scales that include indicators of physical punishment also varied greatly across societies, with spanking common in countries where respect for elders is considered important and there is little emphasis on developing

autonomy. Unlike the United States, where the use of spanking tends to coincide with parental demeaning of children, the two are not as consistently yoked in some collectivist societies where respect for adult authority is prized. Even so, low scores on the acceptance scale were associated with conduct problems even in some societies where respect for adults is highly valued and support for autonomy is low. Likewise, scores on the acceptance scale were correlated with child cognitive functioning in a number of non-Western societies. There is wide variation in the degree to which different societies emphasize the stimulation of young children and parental teaching of concepts related to schooling. In some parts of Africa and Asia, much greater attention is given to teaching practical skills and self-care. In some Latin American countries, it is partly a matter of timing, with parents waiting later to begin emphasizing certain types of learning. There is also wide variation in the likelihood children will have access to toys and materials for learning or enriching experiences within their communities. Even so, HOME scales such as learning materials, variety of stimulation, learning stimulation, parental involvement, enrichment, and family companionship tended to be associated with measures of language, cognitive functioning, and achievement in most groups. The correlations were sometimes lower in societies with very high poverty rates, where children were also more likely to have health problems and be exposed to adverse conditions.

Program Evaluation

Over the past 40 years the number of parent education programs has increased worldwide. The increase has been stimulated by concerns pertaining to school readiness, infant mental health, child safety, and the particular difficulties faced by children born with health problems. Because HOME taps a diverse array of parenting practices, household arrangements, and child-rearing conditions, it has been used either as an outcome measure in evaluations of parent education programs or as a mediator of early education program impacts on children where the program includes a parent component. One of the earliest efforts of this sort was a small study conducted in connection with the Parent-Child Center program in Washington (Hamilton, 1972). In this study of 16 parents, there was a 71 percent improvement on items tapping stimulation.

HOME has been used in several widely known programs aimed at improving the life prospects of children born in socioeconomically disadvantaged families, including the Parent-Child Development Center program (Johnson et al., 1984), Project CARE (Wasik et al., 1990), the Nurse Home Visitation program (Kitzman et al., 1997; Olds et al, 1985), and the Early Head Start National Evaluation study (Love et al., 2002). In each study, significant impacts on HOME scores were noted, sometimes on the total score and sometimes on scales such as acceptance, responsivity, learning materials, and learning stimulation. However, the national evaluation of the Comprehensive Child Development Program, which targeted low-income families beginning when children were age three, showed no impacts on HOME (St. Pierre & Layzer, 1999).

HOME was also used as an outcome measure in programs designed to assist parents of children born with medical problems, particularly those born prematurely and at low birth weight (Barnard & Bee, 1983; Barrera et al., 1986, 1990; Bradley et al., 1997; Ross, 1984). Although the services offered in these programs differed considerably, significant impacts (even lasting impacts) were observed in all studies. However, a study done in Australia found no evidence that positive impacts on parenting persisted 18 months after termination of the intervention (Fraser et al., 2000).

Bakermans-Kranenburg et al. (2005) published a meta-analysis of studies where HOME was used as an outcome. Their analysis included 56 studies involving 7,350 families. They found a combined effect size on the total HOME of $d = .20$, but the effects tended to be stronger for nonrandomized

than randomized designs. Interestingly, interventions of more modest duration had stronger average impacts than interventions with more than 16 sessions. Interventions started after children were six months old were also more effective than those started at birth. Home-based approaches produced more positive impacts on HOME than center-based approaches; and interventions that did not focus on improving children's cognitive development had stronger impacts than those that did focus on cognitive functioning directly. Programs also showed stronger impacts for adult than teenage parents and for middle class than low SES parents.

Most program evaluations involving use of HOME have been limited to program impacts on parenting. However, two studies have shown that impacts on parenting appear to mediate impacts on children's development (Bradley et al., 1994; Love et al., 2002). At present there are very few studies where HOME was used to examine the quality of the home environment as a mediator of program impacts on children's development. Therefore, it is not yet clear whether positive impacts on parenting generally lead to positive impacts on child adaptive functioning. Neither is it clear how often positive program impacts on children flow through parenting as contrasted to other mechanisms.

Final Comments on HOME

The HOME Inventory has been a durable and productive measure of the home environment for almost half a century. It clearly reflects the social and economic resources parents can bring to bear on child rearing; but it also reflects their personalities and other aspects of family context. The Inventory is a limited instrument. It more faithfully captures how certain groups provide the stimulation, support and structure needed for children to develop than how other groups do so. In addition, it does not capture all aspects of home life that are important for children. The indicators contained in HOME appear to be associated with a diverse array of developmental outcomes for many groups of children around the world, but less so developmental outcomes for children living in less economically and technologically developed non-Western societies. Although there are hundreds of studies using the HOME, much remains undetermined about its precise relation to aspects of culture, family life and child well-being, information that would inform the broader discourse on how environments are implicated in children's behavior and development. There would be advantages to restandardizing the HOME, based on newer research findings and the changing realities of 21st Century life.

Other Measures of the Home Environment

Although the HOME Inventory has enjoyed wide acceptance, there are numerous other measures that assess the quality of organization, stimulation, and support available to children at home. These include other measures developed in the United States and elsewhere designed to capture a diverse array of the actions, objects, events and conditions present in the home environment (Dave, 1963; Keeves, 1972; Marjoribanks, 1972). Most of the other broadly focused measures rely exclusively on interview with the parent, which makes them vulnerable to reporting biases. In addition, there are a number of measures that assess more narrowly targeted aspects of parenting and the home environment. Many provide greater depth of coverage to these narrower domains than does the HOME Inventory. For example, there are measures focused on food security (Cook & Frank, 2008), home dangers and safety (de Castro Ribas, Tymchuk, & Ribas, 2006), home literacy and media use (Farver, Xu, Eppe, & Lonigan, 2006; Griffin & Morrison, 1997; Marvin & Ogden, 2002), and family routines and rituals (Fiese & Klein, 1993). Although useful for those who wish to focus more narrowly on particular aspects of children's environments, most

of the measures have limited evidence for validity, have been used on relatively few groups, and are often targeted for use during a single developmental period. There are also measures of particular aspects of parenting practice: warmth and rejection (Dekovic et al., 2006), supervision and monitoring (Steinberg, Lamborn, Darling, Mounts, Dornbusch, 1994), control and autonomy (Calzada & Eyberg, 2002; Eccles, Buchanan, Midgley, Fuligni, & Flanagan, 1991). In some cases, these measures contain items the cover all the dimensions needed to classify parents as authoritative, authoritarian, or laissez faire in accordance with commonly used family style dimensions. For researchers and practitioners interested in particular aspects of parenting practices, such measures can be useful; but most are fully dependent on parent or child report, have limited evidence for validity in different cultural groups, and apply only to a narrow age span. Finally, some home environment measures use as an organizing principle family activities. Among these are very broadly focused measures such as might be used in ethnographic research (Weiser, Ryan, Reese, Kroesen, Bernheimer, & Gallimore, 2001) and some are narrowly focused on particular parent-child joint activities (Chandani, Prince, & Scott, 1997). Using activities as a framework can be revealing for certain scholarly and applied purposes; and it certain ways can be less culturally biased than is the case for other approaches used to document what children experience at home. However, these instruments vary as regards the method used for data collection (observation, parent report), the length of time needed to gather information, procedures for scoring, expertise required for data gathering, and applicability to children of different ages. Most of the measures also have limited evidence for validity. In overview, there are a variety of techniques available for documenting what children experience at home. Most are not as well established or as fully vetted as HOME; but, depending on the needs of the user, may function better to accomplish particular goals.

Dedication

This chapter is dedicated to Bettye Caldwell. Her early work set the tone for HOME and her ideas established a frame for the work done with it. Bettye would acknowledge the efforts of many colleagues who have contributed to its use and development – as do I – but it is she who gave HOME its direction.

References

Achenbach, T. M. (1991). *Manual for the Child Behavior Checklist 4–18 and 1991 profile*. Burlington: University of Vermont, Department of Psychiatry.

Adams, J. L., Campbell, F. A. & Ramey, C. T. (1984). Infants' home environments: A study of screening efficiency. *American Journal of Mental Deficiency, 89*, 133–139.

Affleck, G., Allen, D. A., McGrade, B. J., & McQueeney, M. (1982). Home environments for developmentally disabled infants as a function of parent and infant characteristics. *American Journal of Mental Deficiency, 86*, 445–452.

Aina, T. A., Agiobu-Kemmer, I., Etta, E. F., Zeitlin, M. F., & Setiloane, K. (1993). *Early child care and nutrition in Lagos State, Nigeria*. Medford, MA: Tufts University School of Nutrition & Policy for UNICEF.

Allen, D. A., Affleck, G., McGrade, B. J., & McQueeney, M. (1984). The effect of single parent status on mothers of their high-risk infants. *Infant Behavior and Development, 7*, 347–359.

Allen, D. A., McGrade, B. J., Affleck, G., & McQueeney, M. (1982). The predictive validity of neonatal intensive care nurses' judgments of parent-child relationships: A nine-month follow-up. *Journal of Pediatric Psychology, 7*, 125–134.

Altman, R. (1977). Privacy regulation: Culturally universal or culturally specific? *Journal of Social Issues, 33*, 66–84.

Anme, T., & Takayama, T. (1989). The study of evaluation of environmental stimulation for normal and handicapped children and health welfare system in Japan. Unpublished Manuscript. National Rehabilitation Center for the Disabled, Tokyo Japan.

Anselmi, L., Piccinini, C. A., Barros, F. C., & Lopes, R. S. (2004). Psychosocial determinants of behaviour problems in Brazilian preschool children. *Journal of Child Psychology and Psychiatry, 45*, 779–788.

Bakeman, R., & Brown, J. V. (1980). Early interaction: Consequences for social and mental development at three years. *Child Development, 51*, 4347–447.

Bakermans-Kranenburg, M. J., van Ijzendoorn, M. H., & Bradley, R. H. (2005). Those who have receive: The Matthew-effect in early childhood intervention. *Review of Educational Research, 75*, 1–26.

Barnard, K. E., & Bee, H. L. (1983). The impact of temporally patterned stimulation on the development of preschool infants. *Child Development, 54*, 1156–1167.

Barnard, K. E., & Gortner, S. R. (1977). *Child health assessment: 2-Results of the first twelve months of life*. U.S. Department of Health, Education, and Welfare, Public Health Services, Health Resources Administration, Bureau of Health Resources Development, Division of Nursing, DHEW pub. No. (HRA) 75–30. Bethesda, MD.

Barrera, M. E., Kitching, K. J., Cunningham, C. C., Doucet, D., & Rosenbaum, P. L. (1990). A 3-year early home intervention follow-up study with low birthweight infants and their parents. *Topics in Early Childhood Special Education 10*, 14–29.

Barrera, M. E., Rosenbaum, P. L., & Cunningham, C. E. (1986). Early home intervention with low-birthweight children and their parents. *Child Development, 57*, 20–33.

Bastos, A., Almeida-Filho, N., & Pinho, L. (1998). Experilncia inicialo, eventos de vida e ajustamento em adolescentes de um bairro popular de Salvador: Um de follow up. Unpublished manuscript.

Bee, H. L., Barnard, K. E., Eyres, S. J., Gray, C. A., Hammond, M. A., Spietz, A. L., Snyder, C., & Clark, B. (1982). Prediction of IQ and language skill from perinatal status, child performance, family characteristics, and mother-infant interaction. *ChildDevelopment, 53*, 1134–1156.

Belsky, J. (1984). The determinants of parenting: A process model. *Child Development, 55*, 83–96.

Belsky, J. (2004). Differential susceptibility to rearing influence: An evolutionary hypothesis and some evidence. In B. Ellis & D. Bjorklund (Eds.), *Origins of the social mind: Evolutionary psychology and child development*, pp. 139–163. New York: Guilford.

Belsky, J., Garduque, L., & Hrncir, E. (1984). Assessing performance, competence and executive capacity in infant play: Relations to home environment and security of attachment. *Developmental Psychology, 20*, 406–417.

Belsky, J., Vandell, D., Burchinal, M., Clarke-Stewart, A., McCartney, K., Owen, M. & the NICHD Early Child Care Research Network. (2007). Are there long term effects of early child care? *Child Development, 78*, 681–701.

Berlin, L. J., Brooks-Gunn, J., Spiker, D., Zaslow, M. (1995). Examining observational measures of emotional support and cognitive stimulation in Black and White mothers of preschoolers. *Journal of Family Issues, 16*, 664–686.

Black, M., Schuler, M., & Nair, P. (1993). Prenatal drug exposure: neurodevelopmental outcome and parenting environment. *Journal of Pediatric Psychology, 18*, 605–620.

Blevins-Knabe, B., & Austin, A. (April, 2000). The HOME: Working for cultural validity in rural Paraguay. Presented at the biennial meeting of the Society for Research in Child Development. Albuquerque, NM.

Bloom, B. S. (1964). Stability and change in human characteristics. New York: Wiley.

Bollen, K. (2002). Analysis of latent variables. *Annual Review of Psychology, 53*, 605–634.

Bradley, R. H. (1994). The HOME Inventory: Review and reflections. In H. Reese (Ed.), *Advances in child behavior and development*, pp. 241–288, Vol. 25. San Diego, CA: Academic Press.

Bradley, R. H. (2004). Chaos, culture, and covariance structures: A dynamic systems view of children's experiences at home. *Parenting: Science and Practice, 4*, 245–259.

Bradley, R. H., & Caldwell, B. M. (1976). The relationship of infants' home environment to mental test performance at fifty-four months: A follow-up study. *Child Development, 47*, 1172–1174.

Bradley, R. H., & Caldwell, B. M. (1979). Home environment and locus of control. *Journal of Clinical Child Psychology, 8*, 107–110.

Bradley, R. H., & Caldwell, B. M. (1979). Home observation for measurement of the environment: A revision of the preschool scale. *American Journal of Mental Deficiency, 84*, 235–244.

Bradley, R.H., & Caldwell, B.M. (1980). Home environment, cognitive competence and IQ

among males and females. *Child Development, 51*, 1140–1148.

Bradley, R. H., & Caldwell, B. M. (1982). The consistency of the home environment and its relation to child development. *International Journal of Behavioral Development, 5*, 445–465.

Bradley, R. H. & Caldwell, B. M. (1984). The HOME inventory and family demographics. *Developmental Psychology, 20*, 315–320.

Bradley, R. H., Caldwell, B. M., & Corwyn, R. F. (2003). The child care HOME Inventories: Assessing the quality of family child care homes. *Early Childhood Research Quarterly, 18*, 294–309.

Bradley, R. H., Caldwell, B. M., Rock, S. L., Barnard, K., Gray, C., Hammond, M., Mitchell, S., Siegel, L., Ramey, C., Gottfried, A., & Johnson, D. (1989). Home environment and cognitive development in the first 3 years of life: A collaborative study involving six sites and three ethnic groups in North America. *Developmental Psychology, 25*, 217–235.

Bradley, R. H., Caldwell, B. M., Rock, S. L., Casey, P. H., & Nelson, J. (1987). The early development of low-birthweight infants: Relationship to health, family status, family context, family processes, and parenting. *International Journal of Behavioral Development, 10*, 1–18.

Bradley, R. H., Caldwell, B. M., Rock, S. L., Hamrick, H. M., & Harris, P. (1988). Home Observation for Measurement of the Environment: Development of a HOME Inventory for use with families having children 6 to 10 years old. *Contemporary Educational Psychology, 13*, 58–71.

Bradley, R. H., Casey, P. H., & Caldwell, B. M. (1997). Quality of the home environment. In R. T. Gross, D. Spiker, & C. W. Haynes (Eds.), *Helping low birth-weight, premature infants: The infant health and development program*, pp. 242–256. Stanford, CA: Stanford University Press

Bradley, R. H., & Corwyn, R. F. (2003). Age and ethnic variations in family process mediators of SES. In M. H. Bornstein & R. H. Bradley (Eds.), *Socioeconomic status, parenting, and child development*, pp. 161–188. Mahwah, NJ: Erlbaum.

Bradley, R. H., & Corwyn, R. F. (2005). Productive activity and the prevention of behavior problems. *Developmental Psychology, 41*, 89–98.

Bradley, R. H., & Corwyn, R. F. (2004). Life satisfaction among European American, African American, Chinese American, Mexican American, and Dominican American adolescents. *International Journal of Behavioral Development*, 28, 385–400.

Bradley, R. H., & Corwyn, R. F. (2007). Externalizing problems in fifth grade: Relations with productive activity, maternal sensitivity, and harsh parenting from infancy through middle childhood. *Developmental Psychology*, 43, 1390–1401.

Bradley, R. H., & Corwyn, R. F. (2007). Infant temperament, parenting, and externalizing behavior in first grade: A test of the differential susceptibility hypothesis. *Journal of Child Psychology & Psychiatry*, 49, 124–131

Bradley, R. H., Corwyn, R. F., Caldwell, B. M., Whiteside-Mansell, L., Wasserman, G. A., & Mink, I. T. (2000). Measuring the home environments of children in early adolescence. *Journal of Research on Adolescence*, 10, 247–289.

Bradley, R. H., Corwyn, R. F., McAdoo, H. P., & Garcia Coll, C. (2001). The home environments of children in the United States: Part 1. Variations by age, ethnicity, and poverty status. *Child Development*, 72, 1844–1867.

Bradley, R. H., Rock, S. L., Caldwell, B. M., & Brisby, J. A. (1989). Uses of the HOME inventory for families with handicapped children. *American Journal of Mental Retardation*, 94, 313–330.

Bradley, R. H., Whiteside, L., Mundfrom, D. J., Casey, P. H., Caldwell, B. M., & Barrett, K. (1994). The impact of the Infant Health and Development Program on the home environments of low birthweight premature infants. *Journal of Educational Psychology*, 86, 531–541.

Broberg, A. G., Wessels, H., Lamb, M. E., & Hwang, C. P. (1997). Effects of day care on the development of cognitive abilities in 8-year-olds: A longitudinal study. *Developmental Psychology*, 33, 62–69.

Bronfenbrenner, U. (1995). The bioecological model from a life course perspective: Reflections from a participant observer. In P. Moen, G. H. Elder, & K. Luscher (Eds.), *Examining lives in context*, pp. 619–647. Washington, DC: American Psychological Association.

Caldwell, B. M. (1967). Descriptive evaluations of child development and developmental settings. *Pediatrics*, 40, 46–54.

Caldwell, B. M., & Bradley, R. H. (2003). *HOME Inventory administration manual*. Little Rock: University of Arkansas at Little Rock. http://www.ualr.edu/case.

Caldwell, B. M., Heider, J., & Kaplan, B. (August 1966). The Inventory of Home Stimulation. Paper presented at the annual meeting of the American Psychological Association.

Calzada, E. J., & Eyberg, S. M. (2002). Self-reported parenting practices in Dominican and Puerto Rican mothers of young children. *Journal of Clinical Child & Adolescent Psychology*, 31, 354–363.

Carlson, M. J., & Corcoran, M. E. (2001). Family structure and children's behavioral and cognitive outcomes. *Journal of Marriage and Family*, 63, 779–792.

Chandani, K., Prince, M. J., & Scott, S. (1999). Development and initial validation of the parent-child joint activity scale: A measure of joint engagement in activities between parent and preschool child. *International Journal of Methods in Psychiatric Research*, 8, 219–229.

Character-Murchinson, J. (1988). Family and environmental characteristics as they related to the language development of young hearing-impaired children. Unpublished masters's thesis, Utah State University, Logan.

Chase, H. P., & Martin, H. P. (1970). Undernutrition and child development. *New England Journal of Medicine*, 282, 933–939.

Chomitz, V. R., Zeitlin, M. F., Satoto, M., Peterson, K., Sockalingam, S., & Gershoff, S. (1992). Child care behaviors and environmental risk factors associated with short stature and low nutrient intake in Javanese preschool children. Report to UNICEF from the Tufts-UNICEF JNSP – Positive Deviance in Nutrition Research Project.

Chua, K. L., Kong, D. S., Wong, S. T., & Yoong, T. (1989). Quality of the home environment of toddlers: A validation study of the HOME Inventory. *Journal of the Singapore Paediatric Society*, 31, 38–45.

Church, A. T., & Katigbak, M. S. (1991). Home environment, nutritional status, and maternal intelligence as determinants of intellectual development in rural Phillipine preschool children. *Intelligence*, 15, 49–78.

Coleman, J. S. (1988). Social capital in the creation of human capital. *American Journal of Sociology*, 94(Suppl.), S95–S120.

Coll, C. G., Hoffman, J., & Oh, W. (1987). The social ecology and early parenting of Caucasian adolescent mothers. *Child Development*, 58, 955–963.

Coll, C. G., Vohr, O., Hoffman, J., & Oh, W. (1986). Maternal and environmental factors affecting developmental outcomes of infants of adolescent mothers. *Developmental & Behavioral Pediatrics*, 7, 230–236.

Cook, J. T., & Frank, D. A. (2008). Food security, poverty, and human development in the United States. *Annals of the New York Academy of Sciences*, 1136, 193–209.

Cravioto, J., & DeLicardie, E. R. (1986). Microenvironmental factors in severe protein-calorie malnutrition. In N. Scrimshaw & M. Behar (Eds.), *Nutrition and agricultural development*, pp. 25–36. New York: Plenum.

Cravioto, J., & DeLicardie, E. (1972). Environmental correlates of severe clinical malnutrition in survivors from kwashiorkor or marasmus. In *Nutrition, the nervous system, and behavior: Proceedings of the seminar on malnutrition in early life and subsequent mental development. Scientific Publication No. 251* (pp. 73– 94). Washington, DC: Pan American Health Organisation.

Daggett, J., O'Brien, M., Zanolli, K., Peyton, V. (2000). Parents' attitudes about children: Associations with parental life histories and child-rearing quality. *Journal of Family Psychology*, 14, 187–199.

Das, S., & Padhee, B. (1993). Level II abilities of socially disadvantaged children: Effects of home environment, caste and age. *Journal of Indian Psychology*, 11, 38–43.

Dave, R. (1963). The identification and measurement of environmental process variables that are related to educational achievement. Unpublished doctoral dissertation. University of Chicago.

De Castro Ribas, R., Tymchuk, A. J., & Ribas, A. (2006). Brazilian mothers's knowledge about home dangers and safety: An initial evaluation. *Social Science and Medicine*, 63, 1879–1888.

Dekovic, M., Have, M., Vollebergh, W., Pels T., Oosterwegel, A., Wissink, I., Winter, A., Verhulst, F., & Ormel, J. (2006). The cross-cultural equivalence of parental rearing measure: EMBU-C. *European Journal of Psychological Assessment*, 22, 85–91.

Drotar, D., Olness, K., Wiznitzer, M., Maruim, L., Guay, L., Hom, D., Svilar, G. Schatschneider, C., Fagan, J., Ndugwa, C., Mayengo, R. K. (1999). Neurodevelopmental outcomes of Ugandan infants with HIV infection: An application of growth curve analysis. *Health Psychology*, 18, 114–121.

Durbrow, E. H., Jones, E., Bozoky, I., Jimerson, S., & Adams, E. (July 1996). How well does the HOME Inventory predict Caribbean children's academic performance and behavior

problems? Paper presented at the biennial meeting of the International Society for the Study of Behavioral Development. Quebec City, Canada.

Eccles, J., Buchanan, C. M., Midgley, C., Fuligni, A. J., & Flanagan, C. (1991). Individuation reconsidered: Autonomy and control during early adolescence. *Journal of Social Issues*, 47, 53–68.

Elardo, R., Bradley, R. H., & Caldwell, B. M. (1975). The relation of infants' home environments to mental test performance from six to thirty-six months: A longitudinal analysis. *Child Development*, 46, 71–76.

Elardo, R., Bradley, R. H., & Caldwell, B. M. (1977). A longitudinal study of the relation of infants' home environments to language development at age three. *Child Development*, 48, 595–603.

Erickson, M. F., Sroufe, L. A., & Egeland, B. (1985). The relationship between quality of attachment and behavior problems in a high risk sample. *Monographs of the Society for Research in Child Development*, 50(1/2), 147–166.

Ertem, I. O., Forwyth, B. W. C., Avi-Singer, A. J., Damour, L. K. & Cicchetti, D. V. (1997). Development of a supplement to the HOME scale for children living in impoverished urban environments. *Journal of Developmental and Behavioral Pediatrics*, 18, 322–328.

Farver, J. M., Xu, Y., Eppe, S., & Lonigan, C. J. (2006). Home environment and young Latino children's school readiness. *Early Childhood Research Quarterly*, 21, 196–212.

Fein, G. G., Gariboldi, A., & Boni, R. (1993). Antecedents of maternal separation anxiety. *Merrill-Palmer Quarterly*, 39, 481–495.

Field, T. M., Widmayer, S. M., Adler, S., & DeCubas, M. (1990). Teenage parenting in different cultures, family constellations, and caregiving environments: Effects on infant development. *Infant Mental Health Journal*, 11, 158–174.

Fiese, B. H., & Kline, C. A. (1993). Development of the Family Ritual Questionnaire: Initial reliability and validation studies. *Journal of Family Psychology*, 6, 290–299.

Ford, D. H., & Lerner, R. M. (1992). *Developmental systems theory, an integrative approach*. Newbury Park, CA: Sage.

Fraser, J. A. Armstrong, K. L., Morris, J. P., & Dadds, M. R. (2000). Home visiting intervention for vulnerable families with newborns: Follow-up results of a randomized controlled trial. *Child Abuse and Neglect*, 24, 1399–1429.

Gill, R., Kang, T. (1995). Relationship of home environment with behavioral problems of pre-school children. *Indian Journal of Psychometry and Education, 26*, 77–82.

Gottfried, A. E., Fleming, J. S., Gottfried, A. W. (1998). Role of cognitively stimulating home environment in children's academic intrinsic motivation: A longitudinal study. *Child Development, 69*, 1448–1460.

Gottfried, A. E., & Gottfried, A. W. (1988). *Maternal employment and children's development: Longitudinal research.* New York: Plenum.

Gottfried, A. W., & Gottfried, A. E. (1984). Home environment and cognitive development in young children of middle-socioeconomic status families. In A. W. Gottfried & A. E. Gottfried (Eds.), *Home environment and early cognitive development*, pp. 329–242. Orlando, FL: Academic Press.

Grantham-McGregor, S. M. (1991). Nutritional supplementation, psychosocial stimulation, and mental development in stunted children: The Jamaican study. *Lancet, 338*, 1–5.

Grantham-McGregor, S. M., Powell, C., Stewart, M., & Schofield, W. N. (1982). Longitudinal study of growth and development of young Jamaican children recovering from severe protein-energy malnutrition. *Developmental Medicine and Child Neurology, 24*, 321–331.

Greenberg, M., & Crnic, K. (1988). Longitudinal predictors of developmental status and social interaction in premature and full-term infants at age two. *Child Development, 59*, 554–570.

Griffin, E. A., & Morrison, F. J. (1997). The unique contribution of home literacy environment to differences in early literacy skills. *Early Child Development and Care, 127–128*, 233–243.

Hadeed, J., & Sylva, K. (1999). Center care and education in Bahrain: Does it benefit children's development? *Early Child Development and Care, 136*, 45–55.

Hamilton, M. L. (1972). Evaluation of a parent and child center program. *Child Welfare, 51*, 248–258.

Hayes, J. S. (1980). Premature infant development: An investigation of the relationship of neonatal stimulation, birth condition, and home environment to development at age three years. *Pediatric Nursing, 6*(6), 33–36.

Hayes, J. S. (1996). Reliability and validity of the HOME preschool inventory in Jamaica. Unpublished manuscript.

Hayes, J., Lampart, R., Dreher, M., and Morgan, L. (1991). Five-year follow-up of rural Jamaican children whose mothers used marijuana during pregnancy. *West Indies Medical Journal, 40*, 120–123.

Head, D. N., Bradley, R. H., & Rock, S. L. (1990). Use of home environment measures with visually impaired children. *Journal of Visual Impairment and Blindness, 84*, 377–380.

Henderson, M. L. (1975). Home environment, maternal attitudes, marital adjustment, and SES: Their association with mental and motor development of two-year-old children. Unpublished Master's thesis. Kansas State University. Manhattan, KS.

Holder-Brown, L., Bradley, R. H., Whiteside, L., Brisby, J. A., & Parette, H. P. (1993). Using the HOME inventory with families of children with orthopedic disabilities. *Journal of Developmental and Physical Disabilities, 5*, 181–201.

Holding, P. (2003). Adaptation and use of the middle childhood HOME Inventory in Kilifi, Kenya. Unpublished manuscript.

Hollenbeck, A. R. (1978). Early infant home environments: Validation of the Home Observation for Measurement of the Environment inventory. *Developmental Psychology, 14*, 416–418.

Howell, R. D., Breivik, E., & Wilcox, J. B. (2007). Reconsidering formative measurement. *Psychological Methods, 12*, 205–218.

Hui, C. H., and Triandis, H. C. (1985). Measurement in cross-cultural psychology. *Journal of Cross-Cultural Psychology, 16*, 131–153.

Hunt, J. M. (1961). *Intelligence and experience.* New York: Ronald Press.

Jackson, S. C., Roberts, J. E. (2001). Complex syntax production of African American preschoolers. *Journal of Speech, Language & Hearing Research, 44*, 1083–1096.

Jacobson, J. L., Jacobson, S. W., Greenbaum, C., Schantz, S., Gornish, K., Ela, S., & Billings, R. L. (July 1995). Validity of the elementary version of HOME Inventory in two cultures. Presented at the biennial meeting of the International Society for the Study of Behavioral Development. Jyvaskyla, Finland.

Johnson, D. (July 1979). The influence of an intensive parent education program on behavioral continuity of mothers and children. Presented at the biennial meeting of the International Society for the Study of Behavioral Development. Lund, Sweden.

Johnson, D., Breckenridge, J. N., & McGowan, R. (1984). Home environment and early cognitive development in Mexican-American children. In A. Gottfried (Ed.), *Home environment and early cognitive development*, pp. 151–196. Orlando, FL: Academic Press.

Jordan, T. E. (1978). Influences on vocabulary attainment: A five-year prospective study. *Child Development, 49*, 1096–1106.

Kalmar, M. (1996). The Course of Intellectual Development in Preterm and Fullterm Children: An 8-year Longitudinal Study. *International Journal of Behavioral Development, 19*, 491–516.

Keeves, J. (1972). *Educational environment and student achievement*. Stockholm, Sweden: Malmquist & Wicksell.

Kelleher, K. J., Casey, P. H., Bradley, R. H., Pope, S. K., Whiteside, L., Barrett, K. W., Swanson, M. E. et al. (1993). Risk factors and outcomes for failure to thrive in low birth weight preterm infants. *Pediatrics, 91(5)*, 941–948.

Kitzman, H., Olds, D. L., Henderson, C. R., Hanks, C., Cole, R., Tatelbaum R., McConnochie, K M., Sidora, K., Luckey, D. W., Shaver, D., Engelhardt, K., James, D., & Barnard, K. (1997). Effect of prenatal and infancy home visitation by nurses on pregnancy outcomes, childhood injuries, and reported childbearing. *JAMA, 278*, 644–652.

Kurtz, B. C., Borkowski, J. G., & Deshmukh, K. (1988). Metamemory and learning in Maharashtrian children: Influences from home and school. *Journal of Genetic Psychology, 149*, 363–376.

Lamb, M. E., Hwang, C., Brookstein, F. L., Broberg, A., Hult, B., & Frodi, M. (1988). Determinants of social competence in Swedish preschoolers. *Developmental Psychology, 24*. 58–70.

LaVeck, B., Hammond, M. A., & LaVeck, G. D. (1984). Home environment and breast and bottle feeding. Unpublished manuscript. Seattle: Child Development and Mental Retardation Center, University of Washington.

LaVeck, B., Hammond, M. A., Telzrow, R., & LaVeck, G. D. (1983). Further observations on minor anomalies and behavior in different home environments. *Journal of Pediatric Psychology, 8*, 171–179.

Lawrence, D. L., & Low, S. M. (1990). The built environment in spatial form. *Annual Review of Anthropology, 19*, 453–505.

Linver M. R., Brooks-Gunn, J., Kohen, D. E. (2002) Family processes as pathways from income to young children's development. *Developmental Psychology, 38*, 719–734.

Longstreth, L., Davis, B., Carger, L., Flint, D., Owen, J., Rickert, M., & Taylor, E. (1981). Separation of home intellectual environment

and maternal IQ as determinants of child IQ. *Developmental Psychology, 17*, 532–541.

Love, J., Kisker, E., Ross, C., Schochet, P., Brooks-Gunn, J. et al. (2002). Making a difference in the lives of infants and toddlers and their families: The impacts of Early Head Start: Vol. 1. Final Technical Report. Washington, DC: U.S. Department of Health & Human Services, Administration on Children and Families, Office of Planning Research and Evaluation.

Lozoff, B., Park, A., Radan, A., & Wolf, A. (1995). Using the HOME Inventory with infants in Costa Rica. *International Journal of Behavioral Development, 18*, 277–295.

Luster, T. E., & Rhoades, K. (1989). The relation of child-rearing beliefs and the home environment in a sample of adolescent mothers. *Family Relations, 38*, 317–322.

Marjoribanks, K. (1972). Environment, social class, and mental abilities. *Journal of Educational Psychology, 43*, 103–109.

Marturano, E., Ferreira, M., & Bacarji, K. (2004). Development of an evaluation scale of family environment of children at risk for school failure. Unpublished manuscript: Sao Paolo, Brazil.

Marvin, C. A. & Ogden, N. J. (2002) A home literacy inventory: Assessing young children's contexts for emergent literacy. *Young Exceptional Children, 5*, 2–10.

Masud, S., Luster, T., & Youatt, J. (1994). Predictors of home environment and cognitive competence during early childhood in Pakistan. *Early Child Development and Care, 100*, 43–55.

McMichael, A. J. et al. (1992). Sociodemographic factors modifying the effect of environmental lead in neuropsychological development in early childhood. *Neurotoxicology and Teratology, 14*, 321–327.

McMichael, A. J., Baghurst, P. A., Wigg, N. R., Vinpani, G. V., Robertson, E. R., & Roberts, R. J. (1988). Port Pirie cohort study: Environmental exposure to lead and children's abilities at the age of four years. *New England Journal of Medicine, 319*, 468–475.

Miller, M. D., & Ottinger, D. R. (1983). Examination of the efficacy of a mother-completed questionnaire form of the Home Observation for Measurement of the Environment. Paper presented at the annual meeting of the Midwestern Psychological Association. Chicago.

Mink, I. T., & Nihira, K. (1987). Direction of effects: Family life styles and behavior of

TMR children. *American Journal of Mental Deficiency, 92*, 57–64.

Mohite, P. (July 1987). Mother-child interaction and its effect on child's learning. Paper presented at the Biennial Meeting of the International Society for the Study of Behavioral Development. Tokyo, Japan

Molfese, V. J., Modglin, A., & Molfese, D. L. (2003). The role of environment in the development of reading skills. *Journal of Learning Disabilities, 36*, 59–67.

Mulhall, D., Fitzgerald, M., & Kinsella, A. (1988). A study of the relationships between the home environment and psychiatric symptoms in children and parents. *Irish Journal of Psychiatry, 9*, 13–16.

NICHD Early Child Care Research Network1 (2001). Child care and common communicable illnesses. *Archives of Pediatrics and Adolescent Medicine, 155*, 481–488.

NICHD Early Child Care Research Network1 (2003). Child care and common communicable illnesses in children aged 37 to 54 months. *Archives of Pediatrics and Adolescent Medicine, 157*, 196–200.

NICHD Early Child Care Research Network1 (2003). Do children's attentional processes mediate the link between family predictors and school readiness? *Developmental Psychology, 39*, 451–469.

NICHD Early Child Care Research Network1 (2004). Trajectories of physical aggression from toddlerhood to middle childhood: Predictors, correlates, and outcomes. *Monographs of the Society for Research in Child Development, 69* (Whole No. 4).

Nihira, K., Tomiyasu, Y., & Oshio, C. (1987). Homes of TMR children: Comparison between American and Japanese families. *American Journal of Mental Deficiency, 91*, 486–495.

Nishimura, M., Imae, J., Tabuchi, N., Kanagawa, K., & Kawasaki, C. (October 1992). The relationships between child development and children's home environment at 1, 8, and 14 months of age in Japan. Presented at the First International Nursing Research Conference. Tokyo, Japan.

Noll, R. B., Zucker, R. A., Curtis, W. J., & Fitzgerald. H. E. (April 1989). Young male offspring of alcoholic fathers: Early developmental and cognitive findings. Presented at the biennial meeting of the Society for Research in Child Development. Kansas City, MO.

Olds, D. L., Henderson, C. R., Chamberlin, R. T., & Tatelbaum R. (1985). Preventing child abuse and neglect: A randomized trial of nurse home visitation. *Pediatrics, 77*, 16–28.

Pachter, L. M., Auinger, P., Palmer, R., & Weitzman, M. (2006). Do parenting and the home environment, maternal depression, neighborhood and chronic poverty affect child behavior problems differently in different racial-ethnic groups? *Pediatrics, 117*, 1329–1338.

Palacios, J., Gonzalez, M., & Moreno, C. (1992). Stimulating the child in the zone of proximal development: The role of parents' ideas. In I. Sigel, A. McGillicuddy-DeLisi, & J. Goodnow (Eds.), *Parental belief systems*, pp. 71–94. Hillsdale, NJ: Erlbaum.

Palti, H., Otrakkul, A., Belmaker, E., Tamair, D., & Tepper, D. (1984). Children's home environments: Comparison of a group exposed to stimulation intervention program with controls. *Early Child Development and Care, 13*, 193–212.

Parks, P. L., & Smeriglio, V. L. (1986). Relations among parenting knowledge, quality of stimulation in the home and infant development. *Family Relations, 35*, 411–416.

Pascoe, J. M. & Earp, J. A. (1984). The effect of mothers' social support and life changes on the stimulation of their children in the home. *American Journal of Public Health, 74*, 358–360.

Perez, P., & Moreno, C. (2004, September). Early childhood and middle childhood HOME inventories: A longitudinal study. Presented at Congreso Hispano-Portugues de Psicologia. Lisbon, Portugal.

Pinto, I. M. (September 2004). A escala HOME – Relacao com variavies do contexto ecologico das familias e com resultados nas criancas de idade pre-escolar. Presented at Congreso Hispano-Portugues de Psicologia. Lisbon, Portugal.

Plomin, R., & Bergeman, C. (1991). The nature of nurture: Genetic influence on "environmental" measures. *Behavior and Brain Sciences, 14*, 373–427.

Plomin, R., Loehlin, J. C., & DeFries, J. C. (1985). Genetic and environmental components of "environmental" influences. *Developmental Psychology, 21(3)*, 391–402.

Pollitt, E., Weisel Eichler, A., & Chan, C. K. (1975). Psychosocial development and behavior of mothers of failure-to-thrive children. *American Journal of Orthopsychiatry, 45*, 525–537.

Prodromidis, M., Lamb, M. E., Sternberg, K. J., Hwang, C. P., & Broberg, A. G. (1995). Aggression and noncompliance among Swedish children in centre-based care, family day care, and home care. *International Journal of Behavioral Development*, 18, 43–62.

Ragozin, A. S., Landesman-Dwyer, S., & Streissguth, A. P. (1978). The relationship between mothers' drinking habits and children's home environments. In F. Seixas (Ed.), *Currents in alcoholism: IV. Psychiatric, psychological, social and epidemiological studies*, pp. 39–49. New York: Grune & Stratton.

Ramey, C. AT., & Mills, P. Social and intellectual consequences of day care for high-risk infants. (1977). In R. Webb (Ed.), *Social development in childhood*, pp. 79–104. Baltimore, MD: Johns Hopkins Press.

Reis, J. S., & Herz, E. J. (1987). Correlates of adolescent parenting. *Adolescence*, 22, 599–609.

Reis, J. S., Barbera-Stein, L., & Bennett, S. (1986). Ecological determinants of parenting. *Family Relations*, 35, 547–554.

Richter, L. M., & Grieve, K. W. (1991). Home environment and cognitive development of black infants in impoverished South African families. *Infant Mental Health Journal*, 12, 88–102.

Rock, S. L., Head, D. N., Bradley, R. H., Whiteside, L., & Brisby, J. A. (1994). Use of the HOME inventory with families having children with disabilities. *Journal of Visual Impairment and Blindness*, 88, 140–151.

Ross, G. S. (1984). Home intervention for premature infants of low income families. *American Journal of Orthopsychiatry*, 54, 263–270.

Rowe, D. C., Vazsonyi, A. T., Flannery, D. (1995). Ethnic and racial similarity in developmental process: A study of academic achievement. *Psychological Science*, 6, 33–38.

Sahu, S., & Devi, B. (1982). Role of home environment in psycholinguistic abilities and intelligence of advantaged and disadvantaged preschool children. Unpublished manuscript (India).

Siegel, L. S. (1982). Reproductive, perinatal, and environmental factors as predictors of cognitive and language development in preterm and full term infants. *Child Development*, 53, 963–973.

Sroufe, L. A., Egeland, B., & Kreutzer, T. (1990). The fate of early experience following developmental change: Longitudinal approaches to individual adaptation in childhood. *Child Development*, 61, 1363–1373.

Starr, R. H. (1982). A research-based approach to the prediction of child abuse. In R. Starr (Ed.), *Child abuse prediction: Policy implications*, pp. 1–20. Cambridge, MA: Ballinger.

Steinberg, L., Lamborn, S. D., Darling, N., Mounts, N. S., & Dornbusch, S. M. (1994). Over-time changes in adjustment and competence among adolescents from authoritative, authoritarian, indulgent, and neglectful families. *Child Development*, 65, 754–770.

St. Pierre, R. G., & Layzer, J. I. (1999). Using home visits for multiple purposes: The Comprehensive Child Development Program. *The Future of Children*, 9, 134–151.

Tedesco, L. (1981). Early home experience, classroom social competence, and academic achievement. Unpublished doctoral dissertation. State University of New York, Buffalo.

Tippie, J. (April 2003). Psychometrics and cultural modifications of HOME in Chile. Paper presented at Assessing home environment for children from diverse backgrounds. Workshop: Center for human growth and development. University of Michigan.

Torralva, T., & Cugnasco, I. (1996) Estudios epidemiologicicos sobre desarrollo infantil. In A. O'Donnell & E. Carmuega (Eds.), *Hoy y manana, Salud y calidad de vida de la ninez Argentina*. Buenos Aires, Argentina: Centro de Estudios Sobre Nutricion Infantil.

Vedder, P., Eldering, L., & Bradley, R. H. (1995). The home environments of at risk children in the Netherlands. In J. J. Hox, B. F. van der Meulen, J. M. A. M. Janssens, J. J. F. ter Laak., & L. W. C. Tavecchio (Eds.), *Advances in family research*, pp. 69–76. Amsterdam: Thesis Publishers.

Wachs, T. D. (1989). The nature of the physical micro-environment: An expanded classification system. *Merrill-Palmer Quarterly*, 35, 399–419.

Wachs, T. D. (2000). *Necessary but not sufficient*. Washington, DC: American Psychological Association.

Wandersman, L. P., & Unger, D. G. (March 1983). Interaction of infant difficulty and social support in adolescent mothers. Paper presented at the biennial meeting of the Society for Research in Child Development. Detroit, MI.

Wasik, B. H., Ramey, C. T., Bryant, D. M., & Sparling, J. J. (1990). A longitudinal study of two early intervention strategies: Project CARE. *Child Development*, 61, 1682–1696.

Wasserman, G., Staghezza-Jaramillo B. Shrout, P., Popovac, D., Capuni-Paracka, S. Hadzialjevic, S., Lekic, V., Preteni-Redjepi, Elk Slavkovick, V., Musabegovic, A., Lolacono, N., & Graziano, J. (1998). The effect of lead exposure on preschool behavior problems. *American Journal of Public Health, 88*, 481–486.

Weiglas-Kuperus, N,. Koot, H. M., Baerts, W., Fetter, W. P., & Sauer, P. (1993). Behavior problems of very low-birthweight children. *Developmental Medicine and Child Neurology, 35*, 406–416

Weisner, T., Ryan, G., Reese, L., Kroesen, K., Bernheimer, L. et al. (2001). Behavior sampling and ethnography: Complementary methods for understanding home-school connections among Latino immigrant families. *Field Methods, 13*, 20–46.

Wilson, R. S., & Matheny, A. P. (1983). Mental development: Family environment and genetic influences. *Intelligence, 7*, 195–215.

Wulbert, M., Inglis, S., Kriegsmann, E., & Mills, B. (1975). Language delay and associated mother/child interactions. *Developmental Psychology, 2*, 61–70.

Zeitlin, M. F., Megawagni, R., Kramer, E. M., Coletta, N. D., Babatunde, E. D., & Carman, D. (1995). *Strengthening the family, Implications for international development.* Toyko: United Nations University Press.

Zeskind, P. S., & Ramey, C. T. (1978). Fetal malnutrition: An experimental study of its consequences on infant development in two caregiving environments. *Child Development, 49*, 1155–1162.

Zeskind, P. S., & Ramey, C. T. (1981). Preventing intellectual and interactional sequelae of fetal malnutrition: A longitudinal, transactional, and synergistic approach to development. *Child Development, 52*, 213–218.

Zevalkink, J., & Riksen-Walraven, J. (August 1996). Quality of maternal support and quality of children's home environments in two Indonesian communities. Paper presented at the biennial meeting of the International Society for the Study of Behavioral Development. Quebec City, Canada.

Zevalkink, J., & Riksen-Walraven, M.R. (2001). Parenting in Indonesia: Interand intracultural differences in mothers' interactions with their young children. *International Journal of Behavioral Development, 25*, 167–175.

Zevalkink, J., Riksen-Walraven, J. M., & Bradley, R.H. (2008). The quality of children's home environment an attachment security in Indonesia. *Journal of Genetic Psychology, 169*, 72–91.

CHAPTER 28

Measurement and Model Building in Studying the Influence of Socioeconomic Status on Child Development

Erika Hoff, Brett Laursen, and Kelly Bridges

The process of child development is shaped by experience, and children who live in different socioeconomic strata have different experiences. Thus, it should not be surprising that socioeconomic status (SES) is a pervasive predictor of child development. Children from higher SES families reliably fare better than children from lower SES families on a wide range of developmental outcomes from infancy to adulthood. Although some of the predictive power of SES may derive from its correlation with properties that are genetically transmitted from parents to their children (Rowe & Rodgers, 1997), a substantial literature argues that SES indexes properties of children's environments that affect development. Recent reviews of this substantial literature argue also that the processes by which SES exerts its well-attested effects are not adequately understood (Bradley & Corwyn, 2002; Bornstein & Bradley, 2003; Conger & Donnellan, 2007; National Research Council and Institute of Medicine, 2000).

Progress in understanding the mechanisms of SES influence requires measures that capture what about SES is relevant to children's experience and models that capture how SES exerts its influence. The questions of how to measure SES and to model its influence are the topics of this chapter. In the sections that follow, we lay out the issues involved and illustrate the approaches that have been taken with selected research examples.

Issues in Measuring Socioeconomic Status

Deciding how to measure SES requires deciding how to define SES. The traditional definition of SES is that it is an individual's or household's relative position in a social hierarchy based on access to, or control over, wealth, prestige, and power (Mueller & Parcel, 1981; Willms, 2003). A more recent conceptualization that has influenced work on child development comes from Coleman (1988), who identified financial capital, human capital, and social capital as the components of SES. Financial capital is the source of material resources – food, clothing, housing, and everything else that depends on money. Human capital is the source of nonmaterial resources such as knowledge and skills. Social capital is a less transparent concept; it is an individual's or household's connections to a larger social group, in the form of access to the expectations of that group, the norms of that group, and the channels of information that group provides (Coleman, 1988).

Measures of SES, both before and since Coleman's work, have typically included some index of household income, education level, and occupational prestige. Recent work guided by Coleman's theory is predicated on the argument that income indexes financial capital, education indexes human capital, and occupational status indexes social capital (Conger & Donnellan, 2007; Entwisle & Astone, 1994). Where poverty and its consequences are the focus of research, the predictors may also include other indicators such as measures of employment instability (Parke, Coltrane, Duffy et al., 2004) or material hardship (e.g., Gershoff, Aber, Raver, & Lennon, 2007).

In addition to selecting indicators, measuring SES requires also deciding whether to form a composite index from multiple indicators or to use the indicators separately and, for either the composite or multiple separate indicators, whether to treat them as continuous variables or as a basis for creating categories. The use of multiple separate indicators is consistent with the definition of SES as access to resources and with the view that indicators of access (albeit imperfect ones) can be directly measured (Entwisle & Antone, 1994). The use of a composite index is more consistent with the view that SES is greater than the sum of its parts and that the index serves as a proxy for an unmeasured underlying construct (Willms, 2003). The question of continuous or categorical treatment of SES arises for both individual and composite indices. With respect to individual indicators, the question is whether some junctures on the scale constitute category boundaries. For example, equal differences in years of education (as in the difference between leaving school one year before

high school graduation or finishing high school) may not map onto equal-size differences in human capital or the access to social capital that education affords. When the continuous or categorical variable question is asked with respect to combined indicators or a composite scale, the measurement question again meets the conceptual question of whether SES is truly a continuum in terms of the experiences it indexes, or whether different positions in the social hierarchy correspond to qualitatively different circumstances of living. The argument for categories is the argument that the combination of low levels of education, low income, and low occupational prestige (or, alternatively, limited access to multiple types of resources) creates an environment that is qualitatively different from the environment of a household in which the parents have high levels of education, income, and occupational prestige. This conceptualization tends to be associated with the use of the term *social class* more than with the term *socioeconomic status*. As the sociologist Melvin Kohn put it in his classic work on social class and parent-child relationships,

> *social class has proved to be so useful a concept because it refers to more than simply educational level, or occupation, or any of the large number of correlated variables. It is so useful because it captures the reality that the intricate interplay of all these variables creates different basic conditions of life at different levels of the social order.* (Kohn, 1963, p. 471)

It can also be argued that the underlying differences, while multiply determined, are nonetheless continuously distributed. If, however, continuous scales of measurement are used, then the question of whether SES is more than the sum of its parts cannot be adequately addressed. That is, so long as multiple indicators are combined in a regression analysis rather than used to create nonoverlapping groups, the variance accounted for by three linear predictors and their interactions will differ little from the variance accounted for by a composite of those indicators.

Approaches to Measuring Socioeconomic Status

The literature on the relation of SES to child development includes examples of each possible combination of the measurement decisions outlined earlier, but different approaches characterize the research of different periods and research with different goals.

Measuring SES Using a Composite Index

Much of the early literature makes use of a composite indicator (Hess, 1970; Hoff, Laursen, & Tardif, 2002) or, alternatively, a single indicator considered as a proxy for the correlated variables that define SES. The best known and most widely used composite measures of SES in the United States are the Hollingshead Four-Factor Index of Social Status and the Socioeconomic Index of Occupations (SEI) (Bornstein, Hahn, Suwalsky & Haynes, 2003). The Hollingshead is based on the education and occupation of each employed householder in the home; the SEI is a measure of occupational prestige that makes use of data on the educational requirements and income associated with occupations (see Bornstein et al. 2003, for a more complete discussion). Other composite indices that make use of these components and, sometimes, measures of wealth and educational and culturally related possessions, also exist (e.g., Willms, 1999, 2006).

Measuring SES Using Multiple Separate Indicators

The argument that SES is best understood as a composite variable has not won the day in studies of SES and child development. Ensminger and Fothergill (2003) found that the use of aggregate measures of SES was rare in studies of U.S. children and youth appearing in three major journals from 1991 to 2000. Current work frequently employs several separate indicators and makes use of more sophisticated statistical procedures than used in the early work to investigate the individual and combined predictive power of the indicators used. The dominant view in this recent work is that even when there is value to a composite index, separate effects of the constituent components of SES should also be examined (Bornstein & Bradley, 2003; Willms, 2003). Different components of SES have been argued to affect different outcomes (Duncan & Magnuson, 2003). Also, different components may affect the same outcome *via* different paths. For example, among 6- to 9-year-old sons of divorced mothers both maternal education and maternal occupation predicted children's school achievement, but the effect of education was mediated by the home skill-building activities mothers provided whereas the effect of occupation was not mediated by any measures of the home environment (DeGarmo, Forgatch, & Martinez, 1999).

Measuring SES Using a Single Scale

Often, however, SES has been measured using just one of the components of SES, and that component is typically maternal education. The same survey that found use of any composite index to be rare found that education (typically maternal education) alone was the most commonly used indicator of SES in recent child development research (Ensminger & Fothergill, 2003). One argument for this practice refers to ease of data collection and reliability of information. In particular, participants may be reluctant to provide income information, they may be less than entirely truthful when they do, and they may complain to the source providing participants thereby jeopardizing the whole research enterprise (Hoffman, 2003). Other arguments for using maternal education have to do with the instability of some components of SES. Whereas parental occupation and income may fluctuate widely over the course of an individual's childhood, parental education levels tend to be relatively stable (Duncan & Magnuson, 2003).

Empirical findings have also been the basis for arguments that maternal education is the best single indicator of SES in studies of child development (Bornstein et al., 2003; Hoffman, 2003). To illustrate, Bornstein et al. (2003) compared the predictive value of both composites, the Hollingshead and the SEI, with the predictive value of their components and found that maternal education was the most robust predictor of infant behavior at 5 months. DeGarmo et al. (1999) employed both the Hollingshead and measures of individual components of SES and found that maternal education was the strongest predictor of 8-year-old boys' school behavior and achievement.

The evidence that maternal education is the single best indicator of SES for predicting child outcomes is frequently interpreted as reflecting a process in which parenting behavior mediates the effect of SES on development and in which parenting behavior is more influenced by education than by income or occupation. For example, in the Canadian National Longitudinal Study of Children and Youth (NLSCY) data, maternal education was the best sociodemographic predictor of children's vocabulary because, Willms (1999) argued, maternal education is related to the nature of maternal speech, which affects children's vocabulary growth. Other findings support this proposed path of influence (Hoff, 2003a, 2003b, 2006). Similarly, Bornstein et al. (2003) found that the effect of maternal education on infant outcomes was related to several parenting behaviors, which mediated the effect of maternal education on child outcome, and Davis-Kean (2005) found that parents' education predicted parental expectations, which, *via* home activities, predicted 8- to 12-year-old children's academic knowledge.

Other outcomes at other ages are, however, predicted by parents' occupation or income. For example, parents' occupational status predicted their children's occupational attainment in adulthood in both Finnish and U.S. samples (Dubow, Huesmann, Boxer, Pulkkinen, & Kokko, 2006), and consistent poverty in childhood was found to predict aggression in 12-year-olds, holding maternal education constant (Tremblay, 1999). Such findings are consistent with arguments that depending on the outcome of interest, some components of SES are better

indicators of the real source of the effect of SES than others because different components of SES influence different aspects of children's experience and thus influence different developmental outcomes (Conger & Donnellan, 2007).

Measuring SES as a Categorical Variable

Studies in which SES is a categorical variable come in at least three varieties. In one, subjects are selected to span a range of levels of SES and then are grouped using natural or statistically identified junctures. For example, Dollaghan et al. (1999) found statistically significant linear trends for several measures of children's language across three levels of maternal education: less than high school graduate, high school graduate, and college graduate. Wadsworth and Achenbach (2005) found a significant effect of SES on childhood psychopathology, treating SES as 3-level categorical variable that was created by first using a continuous composite index of SES and then dividing their sample into low-, middle-, and high-SES groups.

In a second, conceptually similar approach, subjects are selected from discontinuous regions on the SES continuum, thus creating, by subject selection, discrete categories. The latter option is characteristic of small-scale studies in which the aim is to ask whether SES has an effect, without attempting to specify the function that relates SES to outcome across its range. This approach of selecting narrowly defined groups that represent nonadjacent positions on a continuum maximizes between group variance and minimizes within-group variance. For example, Hoff (2003b) identified SES-related differences in maternal speech and in child language development comparing households in which both parents had completed college and, if employed, worked in occupations that required a college education to households in which both parents had completed high school but had never attended any college and, if employed, worked in occupations consistent with that level of education. In this case, nonoverlapping and internally homogeneous groups in terms of parents' education and occupation were created.

In a third categorical approach, groups of interest are defined by the sociological landscape. In a great deal of research, the group of interest is those living in poverty. In much of the poverty research, income and other indices of poverty such as receiving government benefits are used to define a group, which is then compared to a group not living in poverty. Studies of the effects of poverty most frequently make use of large, longitudinal data bases (Ripke & Huston, 2006), but there are also examples of smaller-scale and more anthropological approaches to identifying groups. Heath (1983) found different styles of parent-child communication and different patterns of child language development in three distinct groups in the southeastern United States: a poor, African-American community; a nearby working-class white rural community; and the mainstream community that lived in town. Hart and Risley (1995) described language use and language development in three groups in the midwestern United States whom they labeled professional families, working-class families, and welfare families. The compelling findings in these latter studies are not in the form of regression coefficients for individual predictors but in the description of group differences. In both these studies, the groups that were compared no doubt differed on the standard measures of income, occupation, and education, but what is more salient in the results is the overwhelming picture of the qualitatively different environments in which children live. To echo Kohn (1963), the "basic conditions of life" are different for children living in a household supported by welfare payments, in which the adults are unemployed and have not graduated from high school, compared to children whose parents have professional degrees, occupations, and commensurate incomes.

In sum, the literature on the relation of SES to child development does not suggest a single best way to operationally define and measure SES. Rather, any measure that is selected entails a definition of SES; different measures entail different definitions.

In other words, the measurement question is not one that can be resolved in study design and then forgotten. Any findings with respect to the relation of SES to child development are actually findings of a relation of SES, defined and measured in a particular way, to the developmental outcome of interest.

Issues in Modeling the Influence of Socioeconomic Status

Describing how SES is related to child development requires not only operationalizing SES, but also making explicit and testable the hypothesized links between SES and child outcomes. Theories tend to be written in terms of the concepts and processes posited, using the vocabulary of ordinary language. Tests of hypotheses require, in contrast, models of the links among variables written in analytic terms. Although analytic models are inherent in theoretical models, achieving statistical formulation requires some translation from one vocabulary to another.

In the most frequently proposed and tested models, SES is a predictor variable. Conceptually, such models are social causation models; SES is posited as the cause of the child outcomes with which it is associated. Within this category of model, multiple types can be distinguished. The hypothesized causal path can be direct or mediated. In current work, models are more frequently models of mediated effects in which SES is linked to proximal variables such as parent behavior or household characteristics that, in turn, have consequences for children (e.g., Gershoff et al., 2007; Parke et al., 2004) (see Figure 28.1). Both direct and mediated effect models may posit linear or nonlinear relations between SES and child development. In linear models, incremental changes in SES are associated with incremental changes in child outcomes (see Figure 28.2). In nonlinear models, the posited effects of SES are not constant across its range. Often, the relation posited is one in which SES has linear (or even exponential)

Direct effects of family SES on child outcomes

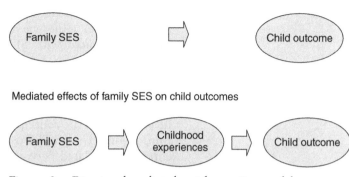

Mediated effects of family SES on child outcomes

Figure 28.1. Direct and mediated social causation models.

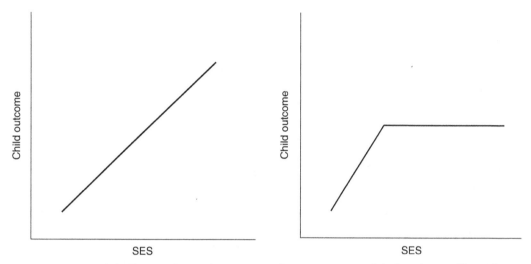

Figure 28.2. A model of linear effects of SES.

Figure 28.3. A model of nonlinear effects of SES.

effects below a certain threshold, but above that threshold, effects of SES are weak or nonexistent (see Figure 28.3).

The frequently cited family stress model is an example of such a model (Conger & Donnellan, 2007; Conger & Elder, 1994), although not all work in this vein labels itself as tests of a family stress model. What we propose here is that, labeling aside, all work that focuses on one part of the range of SES, usually on poverty, and ignores differences outside that range can be similarly described as testing a model of nonlinear or threshold effects (Laursen & Collins, 2009).

In another type of model, SES functions as a moderating variable. Such models typically

start from the premise that there are qualitative differences among SES groups. As a consequence, associations between predictor variables and outcome variables differ for those who occupy different social strata. SES may enhance risk, or it may buffer against adversity (see Figure 28.4). In some models, SES is not a predictor but an outcome or mediating variable. Again, within this category several models can be distinguished. In what are typically referred to as social selection models, the hypothesized direction of causation is from characteristics of individuals to SES – in which case SES in adulthood is the developmental outcome of interest. SES becomes a mediator

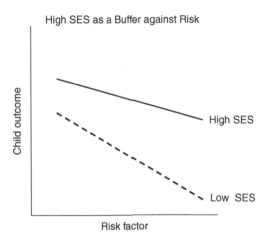

Figures 28.4. SES as a moderator variable.

when other behaviors or characteristics are the outcome of interest and the hypothesis under test is that one's SES in adulthood is an influence on behavior – separate from whatever caused that SES (see Figure 28.5). SES also functions as a mediator in models that posit that SES is part of a larger causal sequence in which characteristics of parents are responsible for family SES and family SES, in turn, shapes child outcomes (see Figure 28.6).

The final set of models is transactional, treating SES as both a predictor variable and a mediating variable. These are lifespan models and intergenerational transmission models in which there are bidirectional influences that unfold over time between characteristics of the child and characteristics and the environment that the child experiences. The SES of the household in which a child lives, via [CE: should "via" be in italics? See elsewhere as well]parent behavior, predicts child outcomes; these characteristics of the child in turn predict the child's SES as an adult, which then predicts behavioral outcomes in adulthood (see Figure 28.7). We will review each of these models in more detail in the section that follows, providing research examples of each.

All of the foregoing models involve SES as a real influence or meaningful outcome at some point in a causal sequence. In the social causation models, SES in childhood

causes, directly or indirectly, subsequent developmental outcomes. In models in which SES is a mediator, SES also causes adult outcomes, either via childhood experiences associated with SES or via influences of adult SES on behavior. In the social selection models the direction of causation is reversed; childhood characteristics and behaviors are the cause and SES in adulthood is the consequence. There is a third possibility, that SES is only a spurious correlate of related parent and child characteristics (which are themselves related to SES), and the real vehicle of transmission is genetic. Some research has begun to directly test this hypothesis, seeking to identify environmental effects that operate over and above genetically transmitted effects (see summaries in Caspi, 2002; Duncan & Magnuson, 2003).

Approaches to Modeling the Influence of Socioeconomic Status

SES as a Linear Predictor throughout Its Range

Continuous, linear models of the influence of SES posit that SES predicts child development across the entire range of socioeconomic strata and child outcomes. Put simply, the SES score of a child's family of origin should correspond with measures of social and cognitive functioning. Tests of models of direct effects of SES on child development may treat SES as a categorical variable and compare groups. This approach is characteristic of the many studies that use the social class terminology and compare development among children from lower class, working class, and middle class families (see Hess, 1970). The large body of research conducted in the 1960s on "the disadvantaged child" is also in this mold (Ginsburg, 1972; Williams, 1970). The findings from such work are typically in the form of a description of group differences. This approach is more characteristic of earlier work than of current work, it is more characteristic of work done outside the United States where

Direct effects of child characteristics on adult SES

SES as a mediator of effects of child characteristics on
adult behavioral outcomes

Figure 28.5. Direct and mediated social selection models.

Figure 28.6. A model of SES as a mediating variable.

Figure 28.7. A transactional model of the intergenerational influence
of SES.

notions of class do not elicit the same discomfort that they do in the United States (Hoff-Ginsberg & Tardif, 1995), and it is more characteristic of work done within the field of sociology than of work in developmental psychology (Argyle, 1994). In current work, even where groups are compared, the social class terminology has been supplanted and groups are referred to using vocabulary such as low, middle, or high SES (e.g., Hoff, 2003b; Wadsworth & Achenbach, 2006).

There are also tests of direct effects of SES in which SES is treated as a continuous variable. For example, Willms (1999) described the gradient or slope of association between SES and early vocabulary development in a large, nationwide sample of Canadian

preschool children (Willms, 1999). The findings from this sort of work are typically in the form of a function that maps SES to the associated outcome. In Willms (1999), the data indicated that 1 standard deviation increases in family SES are accompanied by one-third of a standard deviation increase in children's vocabulary scores.

Even where direct effects are tested and are of interest, current work almost always posits that SES exerts its influence indirectly. A central aim of much current research is to identify those indirect or mediated paths (Fernald & Marchman, 2011; Hoff, in press). Indirect or mediated effects can be tested within the approach that treats SES as a categorical variable. For example, Hoff (2003b) found that a sample of 2-year-old children of college-educated mothers used larger vocabularies in speaking than did the 2-year-old children of high school-educated mothers and that this association between SES and children's vocabulary size was fully mediated by differences between the two groups of mothers in properties of the speech they addressed to their children.

Indirect effects models are more often tested in large samples using structural equation modeling to determine whether intervening variables reduce or eliminate associations between SES and child outcomes. For example, results from a representative sample of U.S. grade school children indicated that associations between socioeconomic status and child behavior problems were partially mediated by a host of socialization variables including maternal warmth, values, and disciplinary practices (Dodge, Pettit, & Bates, 1994).

Both direct and mediated effects of SES may be moderated by other variables such that the magnitude or pattern of indirect associations from SES to child outcomes varies across categories of individuals. For example, country moderates the effect of SES on literacy: the socioeconomic gradients that relate SES to adolescents' literacy skills have different slopes in different countries (Willms, 1999). Age or developmental stage moderates the effect of SES on language development: there are SES-related differences in children's development of complex sentence structures but there are not SES-related differences in these same children's earlier development of simple sentence structure (Vasilyeva, Waterfall, & Huttenlocher, 2008). Ethnic group moderates the mediators of the effect of SES on literacy: associations between parent education and preadolescent school literacy were fully mediated by parental educational expectations among African Americans but only partially mediated among European Americans (Davis-Kean, 2005). Findings from the National Longitudinal Study of Youth also revealed ethnic group differences in patterns of mediation, specifically in links from SES, through home environment

measures, to school achievement and behavior problems (Bradley & Corwyn, 2003). In this case, home environment measures were more apt to emerge as mediators of effects of SES among European Americans than among African Americans and Hispanic Americans.

SES as a Predictor across a Partial Range (threshold Effects)

Truncated or discontinuous models of influence posit that SES predicts child development only within a restricted range. These models describe threshold effects. Within the literature there are different views regarding what determines the threshold below which differences have consequences for children. Some argue that associations between SES and child outcomes are limited to populations characterized by poverty and hardship. In this view, resource scarcity has a detrimental impact on child development, both directly and indirectly through its association with other proximal indicators (McLoyd, 1998). Others argue that resource scarcity, in and of itself, does not fully account for developmental difficulties, but rather the perception of need and the stress that accumulates with these perceptions. In this view, resource scarcity adversely influences child outcomes only when accompanied by perceptions of difficulty and hardship. Some analytic designs explicitly acknowledge the discontinuity assumption. Comparisons of families that lack resources and families that do not lack resources designate a threshold at which hardships are assumed to accrue and impact children. The threshold is typically defined in terms of a specific level of family income or a family-income-to-needs ratio, with children grouped according to whether and how often they have lived below this threshold. The National Institute of Child Health and Human Development (NICHD) Early Child Care Research Network (2005) adopted this approach to identify group differences in trajectories of child outcomes from age 2 to age 8. Children never living in poverty differed from children always living in poverty in terms of the intercept and sometimes also in terms of the slope of change in their cognitive skills and in their internalizing and externalizing behaviors; those experiencing poverty during some but not all of their lives typically had outcomes that fell in between these extremes. Despite the tremendous variability in affluence that exists above the poverty threshold, this approach makes no attempt to distinguish among nonpoverty groups. Thus, a discontinuous association is presumed such that family income predicts child outcomes only among the impoverished.

In some analytic models, the presumptions of nonlinearity can be difficult to discern. Tests of the family stress model, for example, typically make use of only a truncated range of responses on some of the predictor variables, that are, in principle continuous. For example, a model may include a measure of family income that represents the full spectrum of family finances, and a measure of negative financial events, which represents only the negative end – but not the positive end – of the potential range of financial changes. Mediator variables usually include family economic pressure, a parent-report measure describing financial hardships and unmet material needs, which also represents only the negative end of the potential range of perceived financial security. The finding that family income predicts perceptions of economic pressure, which, in turn, predicts parent mental health, parent marital quality, and parenting quality, which, in turn, predict child adjustment has been replicated in diverse samples (e.g., Conger, Wallace, Sun, Simons, McLoyd, & Brody, 2002; Solantaus, Leinonen, & Punamäki, 2004). Because the mediator variable is defined in terms of the presence of a specific condition or circumstance (e.g., financial cutbacks), the full model implies that family income has effects only when family income triggers perceptions of hardship. Thus, by virtue of the measures employed, these tests of the family stress model are tests of a threshold model of SES effects.

Threshold effects of SES are also sometimes moderated by other variables. Among children growing up during the depression of the 1930s, the effects of family economic hardship on long-term developmental outcomes varied according to the child's gender and the child's age when financial difficulties began (Elder, 1974). Boys who were older at the onset of the depression fared better than boys who were young, whereas the reverse was true for girls. Older boys were able to take on jobs outside the home to assist their families, reducing their exposure to family stress. Girls, in contrast, were forced to stay home, and older girls were less likely to be shielded from family difficulties than younger girls. One test of the family stress model indicates that adverse child outcomes are differentially linked to parent reactions to perceived economic pressures, depending on parent gender. In this study, child adjustment was linked to maternal, but not paternal, reports of depression and to paternal, but not maternal, reports of anxiety and social problems (Leinonen, Solantaus, & Punamäki, 2002). Ethnicity also may moderate parental reactions to perceived economic pressures. Hostile parenting has been found to be linked to child adjustment outcomes among European Americans, whereas marital problems were linked to child adjustment among Mexican Americans (Parke et al., 2004).

SES as a Moderator

SES functions as a moderator variable when the relations among other variables differ depending on SES. Models that incorporate SES as a moderator may use SES as a grouping variable or a measure of SES may be crossed with a predictor variable as an interaction term. One group of studies that includes SES as a potential moderator examines developmental risk and resilience. Considerable attention has focused on the possibility that lower levels of SES may increase detrimental outcomes (or inhibit positive outcomes) and that higher levels of SES may buffer against detrimental outcomes (or promote positive outcomes) (Masten & Coatsworth, 1998). These studies make explicit the notion that SES can function as both a developmental asset and a developmental liability.

SES also emerges as a robust moderator of development in studies not explicitly designed to focus on socioeconomic influences. For example, a study of the heritability of cognitive skills using a sample of siblings drawn from the National Longitudinal Study of Adolescent Health found the heritability of vocabulary was higher among adolescents with more educated parents and the heritability of vocabulary was lower among adolescents with less educated parents (Rowe, Jacobson, Van den Oord, 1999). A longitudinal study of Canadian youth indicated that parent education also moderates changes in young adult depressive symptoms (Galambos, Barker, & Krahn, 2006). Across young adulthood, depressive symptoms declined at a sharper rate among youth with highly educated parents than among youth with less educated parents. Finally, a large study of British youth indicated that parent occupation moderated changes in mental abilities scores during middle childhood (Feinstein & Bynner, 2004). Almost two-thirds of high SES children in the top quartile of cognitive performance at age 5 remained in the top quartile at age 10, compared with slightly more than one-quarter of low SES children; conversely, two-thirds of low SES children in the bottom quartile of cognitive performance at age 5 remained in the bottom quartile at age 10, compared with only one-third of high SES children. These studies provide converging evidence that trajectories of change in child outcomes vary as a function of SES.

The accumulating evidence for moderator effects of SES is an empirical argument for the position that different social classes constitute different environments such that the relations among other variables may be quite different in different socioeconomic groups (Hoffman, 2003). To capture the influence of such qualitative differences, scholars may need to reconsider variable-centered efforts to disaggregate sources of influence in favor of the person-centered practice of identifying clusters of individuals who share similar SES related traits (see Laursen & Hoff, 2006).

Identifying average relations between early and later cognitive performance may be neither scientifically interesting nor of practical use if the relations are different depending on SES. Similarly, distinguishing direct from indirect effects may be largely irrelevant if subgroups differ dramatically in terms of the constellation of SES-related components that predict child outcomes. Put another way, to capture how SES influences child development it may be necessary to identify the constellation of SES indicators that determine how other variables will operate. For example, parent education, neighborhood distress, and household chaos may be relevant only when more than one of these factors accompanies low income. Care must also be taken to ensure that SES is not used as a proxy for a correlated explanatory variable. For instance, data suggesting education and maternal employment are responsible for rates of mother-child conflict overlook the causal role played by single parenthood (Laursen, 1995, 2005a).

SES as an Outcome or Mediator

In the previously discussed models, SES was included as a predictor and the hypotheses under test have been some form of the hypothesis that SES exerts a causal influence on a developmental outcome of interest. SES can also be an outcome. The fact that an individual's SES is not perfectly predicted by his or her parents' SES means that other factors must come into play. Child traits unrelated to family SES may, for example, determine the child's ability to succeed in school and on the job, which, in turn, are responsible for later SES. The argument that individual characteristics cause SES was first developed to explain the fact that individuals with mental illness or very low intelligence tend to be socioeconomically disadvantaged as adults, regardless of the SES of their family of origin. This movement of such individuals down the SES scale was termed social drift (Dohrenwend & Dohrenwend, 1969). The hypothesis of social drift or social selection also applies to other individual characteristics such as temperament, personality, and intelligence that have sources other than SES but may contribute to the SES achieved in adulthood (Rowe & Rodgers, 1997).

In many models in which SES is posited to be the consequence of preceding individual characteristics, it is not just SES that is of interest as the outcome, but also the maladaptive behaviors associated with low SES. In this case SES functions as a mediator, linking the individual characteristics that caused SES to the behaviors that are caused by SES. For example, difficult, uncooperative children and those who lack intellectual capabilities may do poorly in school and fail to secure gainful employment, this may result in low SES, and that low SES in adulthood may increase stress and risks for maladaptive behaviors. Another model in which adult SES serves as a mediator is actually a social causation model in which the causal path has its origins in the SES experienced in childhood. For example, children who experience poverty, with its associated poor nutrition, chaotic living conditions, and deviant associates, are more likely than others to become low SES adults. Living in a low SES environment in adulthood may, in turn, be a cause of maladaptive behaviors.

Tests of models in which SES is the outcome or mediator ideally include measures for each individual of childhood characteristics, parent characteristics and family SES during childhood, SES as an adult, and outcomes as an adult. Long-term longitudinal studies are necessary to test such models. Caspi (2002) describes research strategies that can, in combination, untangle social selection from social causation effects. Three studies are mentioned here by way of example. Longitudinal studies in Finland and New Zealand indicate that ill-tempered, aggressive children tend to do poorly in school, which leads to dysfunctional, antisocial behavior and employment difficulties as an adult (Caspi, Elder, & Bem, 1987; Kokko & Pulkkinen, 2000). Both studies found that childhood behavior problems accounted for most of the variance in adulthood behavior problems, even after controlling for adult unemployment, suggesting that adult SES is, at best, only a partial mediator of longitudinal associations. Similar findings emerged from analyses of the National Longitudinal Surveys of Youth (McLeod & Kaiser, 2004). Childhood externalizing problems predicted the likelihood of high school completion and college enrollment, an association that was mediated by childhood experiences of academic failure but not by childhood socioeconomic disadvantage. The findings are consistent with social selection effects in which childhood characteristics – but not childhood SES – predict adult educational attainment. Taken together, the results of these and other studies suggest that SES may be as much a product as a cause of individual traits and behaviors.

An alternative to both social causation models and social selection models is that adult SES is merely a spurious covariate of associations between characteristics of the parent or child and the child's adult outcomes. In this view, attributes shared by parents and children determine later adult outcomes and also dictate adult SES. The latter argument is typically advanced in the context of a genetically informed model in which heritability is argued to account for most of the variance in adult outcomes and adult SES. To address this, it is necessary to assess the roles of both SES and genetics in a single sample. Caspi and colleagues (Caspi, Taylor, Moffitt, & Plomin, 2000) have done this, employing the twin design that is standard in research on heritability and including neighborhood SES as one environmental variable. They found a strong genetic influence on mental health, and they also found that growing up in deprived neighborhoods affects mental health, above and beyond the effect of genetic liability.

A Transactional Approach to Modeling the Influence of SES

It is well accepted that transactional influences operate between parents and children such that parents' behaviors shape children's behaviors, which, in turn, influence parent behaviors. Those who hold strong environmental or genetic positions might disagree, but it seems reasonable to us to assume that similar transactional process occur between SES and child development such that SES both shapes and is shaped by child outcomes. Thus, SES may function as predictor, mediator, and outcome in individual development over the lifespan. The best fitting models will capture this transactional nature of SES influences over time. Such analytic models will necessarily be quite complex, and testing such models will require longitudinal data from large samples. Concurrent assessments of both SES and individual developmental outcomes should be available during childhood and during adulthood. Data from and about multiple members of an individual's social network are needed (Laursen, 2005b). Three time points, at a minimum, are necessary to capture transactional processes. This is a tall order and few studies measure up completely.

We describe two studies that approach this ideal; each ends in young adulthood, when SES is fairly unstable, but they nevertheless demonstrate how SES may be both a cause and a consequence of individual traits and behaviors. In the first example, data from two studies of Iowa youth examined associations between family economic adversity during early adolescence, well-being during late adolescence, and individual economic adversity during young adulthood (Wickrama, Conger, & Abraham, 2005). Transactional patterns of influence were found such that greater economic adversity during adolescence predicted more problems during late adolescence, which, in turn, predicted economic difficulties during young adulthood. In the second example, two waves of data from the Dunedin Study examine associations between mental health data at ages 15 and 21, family SES at age 15, and individual educational attainment at age 21 (Miech, Caspi, Moffitt, Wright, & Silva, 1999). Controlling for concurrent associations at each time point, family SES during adolescence predicted subsequent young adult anxiety and antisocial behavior. Across this same period, conduct disorder and attention deficit disorder during adolescence predicted subsequent young adult educational

attainment. This latter study demonstrates social selection and social causation processes operating concurrently. Identifying transactional effects would require three or more time points. An example of a hypothesized transactional influence that could be tested against such longitudinal data is one in which the anxiety and antisocial behavior in young adulthood that was predicted by childhood SES in turn predicts (negatively) later occupational success, independent of the effects of educational achievement.

Even with long-term longitudinal data bases, there are limits to what variable-centered approaches can reveal about the multiple and complex transactional relations among SES and outcomes over time. Ultimately, apportioning variance among variables does little to inform us about individual developmental trajectories. Person-centered approaches are needed to demonstrate how changes in social class shape and are shaped by changes in other aspects of individual outcomes (Laursen & Hoff, 2006). Pattern-driven approaches pioneered by Elder (1974) and Block (1971) can be updated with new methods described by Nagin (2002) to model groups of individuals who share similar developmental and socioeconomic pathways. This is a strategy whose potential remains unfulfilled in this area of study. A growth mixture modeling approach could identify different lifespan trajectories of educational achievement or maladjustment, to identify those who share similar troubles. SES, or specific attributes of SES, could be similarly modeled, and SES group membership could be mapped onto adjustment trajectories.

Conclusion

This chapter has been an exercise in laying out the measures of socioeconomic status that have been employed and the causal models that have been tested in research on the relation of SES to child development. We reiterate some major points here:
The most frequent approach to studying the influence of SES on child development

in the current literature is to measure multiple components of family SES, typically parents' education, occupation, and income, and sometimes also indicators of poverty and to use variable-centered statistical techniques such as structural equation modeling to examine the unique and combined effects of these predictors on child outcomes. Also, most current work seeks to identify the mechanisms by which SES exerts its influence. Thus, most research on SES and child development includes an intermediate layer of variables, those hypothesized to carry the effects of SES. The findings yielded by this approach make it clear that the multiple facets of SES are associated with different proximal variables, with different functions relating these predictors to their associated mediating variables, and, in fact, with different developmental outcomes. The multiple potential indicators of SES are not interchangeable; there is no single best indicator; and the most appropriate indicator to use depends on the hypothesized outcome and path of influence.

Recent research has most frequently tested one of two models of the relation between SES and child outcome: a linear model in which increments in SES are associated with increments in child outcome throughout its range, or a threshold model in which increments, typically in income, are associated with increments in child outcome only below a certain threshold, typically poverty. Both approaches have revealed important effects on children, but, just as measures of SES are not equivalent, models of SES influences are not equivalent. For the purpose of interpretation, it should be remembered that effects of poverty are not effects of income throughout its range. For the purpose of research design, it should be remembered that like measurement decisions, data analytic decisions have inherent in them commitments to theories about how SES operates as an influence on child development.

The causal paths underlying the well-documented relations between SES and developmental outcomes are complex. The literature makes it clear that SES shapes parents' behavior and other aspects of children's environment, which, in turn, shape child outcomes. There is also evidence that SES can also function as a mediator of correlations between parent characteristics and child outcomes. Furthermore, there is evidence, when SES is studied as a developmental outcome, that individual characteristics of children lead some to be more successful and achieve higher socioeconomic status than others. And, it is clear that some of the correlations between parent SES and child outcome reflect genetic transmission of parent characteristics to their children. Large-scale longitudinal data bases, combined with sophisticated modeling techniques are beginning to untangle these intertwined and bidirectional influences. The use of sophisticated linear modeling techniques has substantially advanced scientific understanding of how SES exerts its influence on child development. With the increased use of this approach, however, the notion of social classes as qualitatively different groups and the corollary hypothesis that developmental processes may operate differently in these groups has largely been lost. The substantial evidence of moderator effects of SES suggests that this may be a mistake. There are person-centered data analytic techniques that might be applied to the question of whether there exist groups that differ in terms of the convergence of socioeconomic measures and patterns of relations among properties of children's experience and their development.

References

Argyle, M. (1994). *The psychology of social class.* London: Routledge.

Block, J. (1971). *Lives through time.* Berkeley, CA: Bancroft Books.

Bornstein, M. H., & Bradley, R. H. (Eds.) (2003). *Socioeconomic status, parenting, and child development.* Mahwah, NJ: Lawrence Erlbaum Associates.

Bornstein, M. H., Hahn, C., Suwalsky, J. T. D., & Haynes, O. M. (2003). Socioeconomic status, parenting, and child development: The Hollingshead Four-Factor Index of

Social Status and the Socioeconomic Index of Occupations. In M. H. Bornstein, & R. H. Bradley (Eds.), *Socioeconomic status, parenting, and child development*, pp. 29–82. Mahwah, NJ: Lawrence Erlbaum Associates.

Bradley, R. H., & Corwyn, R. F. (2003). Age and ethnic variations in family process mediators of SES. In M. H. Bornstein, & R. H. Bradley (Eds.), *Socioeconomic status, parenting, and child development*, pp. 161–188. Mahwah, NJ: Lawrence Erlbaum Associates.

Bradley, R. H., & Corwyn, R. F. (2002). Socioeconomic status and child development. *Annual Review of Psychology*, 53, 371–399.

Caspi, A. (2002). Social selection, social causation, and developmental pathways: Empirical strategies for better understanding how individuals and environments are linked across the life-course. In L. Pulkkinen, & A. Caspi (Eds.), *Paths to successful development: Personality in the life course*, pp. 281–301. Cambridge: Cambridge University Press.

Caspi, A., Elder, G. H., & Bem, D. J. (1987). Moving against the world: Life-course patterns of explosive children. *Developmental Psychology*, 23, 308–313.

Caspi, A., Taylor, A., Moffitt, T. E., & Plomin, R. (2000). Neighborhood deprivation affects children's mental health: Environmental risks identified in a genetic design. *Psychological Science*, 11, 338–342.

Coleman, J. S. (1988). Social capital in the creation of human capital. *American Journal of Sociology*, 94, S95-S120.

Conger, R. D., & Donnellan, M. B. (2007). An interactionist perspective on the socioeconomic context of human development. *Annual Review of Psychology*, 58, 177–199.

Conger, R. D., & Elder, G. H., Jr. (1994). *Families in troubled times: Adapting to change in rural America*. Hawthorne, NY: Aldine de Gruyter.

Conger, R. D., Wallace, L. E., Sun, Y., Simons, R. L., McLoyd, V. C., & Brody, G. H. (2002). Economic pressure in African American families: A replication and extension of the family stress model. *Developmental Psychology*, 38, 179–193.

Davis-Kean, P. E. (2005). The influence of parent education and family income on child achievement: The indirect role of parental expectations and the home environment. *Journal of Family Psychology*, 19, 294–304.

DeGarmo, D. S., Forgatch, M. S., & Martinez, Jr., C. R. (1999). Parenting of divorced mothers as a link between social status and boys'

academic outcomes: Unpacking the effects of socioeconomic status. *Child Development*, 70, 1231–1245.

Dodge, K. A., Pettit, G. S., & Bates, J. E. (1994). Socialization mediators of the relation between socioeconomic status and child conduct problems. *Child Development*, 65, 649–665.

Dohrenwend, B. P., & Dohrenwend, B. S. (1969). *Social status and psychological disorder: A causal inquiry*. New York: Wiley-Interscience A division of John Wiley & Sons.

Dollaghan, C. A., Campbell, T. F., Paradise, J. L., Feldman, H. M., Janosky, J. E., & Pitcairn, D. N. et al. (1999). Maternal education and measures of early speech and language. *Journal of Speech, Language, & Hearing Research*, 42, 1432–1443.

Dubow, E. F., Huesmann, L. R., Boxer, P., Pulkkinen, L., & Kokko, K. (2006). Middle childhood and adolescent contextual and personal predictors of adult educational and occupational outcomes: A mediational model in two countries. *Developmental Psychology*, 42, 937–949.

Duncan, G. J., & Magnuson, K. A. (2003). Off with Hollingshead: Socioeconomic resources, parenting, and child development. In M. H. Bornstein, & R. H. Bradley (Eds.), *Socioeconomic status, parenting, and child development*, pp. 83–106. Mahwah, NJ: Lawrence Erlbaum Associates.

Elder, G. H. (1974). *Children of the Great Depression: Social change in life experience*. Chicago: University of Chicago Press.

Ensminger, M. E., & Fothergill, K. E. (2003). A decade of measuring SES: What it tells us and where to go from here. In M. H. Bornstein, & R. H. Bradley (Eds.), *Socioeconomic status, parenting, and child development*, pp. 13–27. Mahwah, NJ: Lawrence Erlbaum Associates.

Entwisle, D. R., & Astone, N. M. (1994). Some practical guidelines for measuring youth's race/ethnicity and socioeconomic status. *Child Development*, 65, 1521–1540.

Feinstein, L., & Bynner, J. (2004). The importance of cognitive development in middle childhood for adulthood socioeconomic status, mental health, and problem behavior. *Child Development*, 75, 1329–1339.

Fernald, A. & Marchman, V. (2011). Causes and consequences of variability in early language learning. In I. Arnon & E. V. Clark (Eds.), *Experience, variation and generalization:*

Learning a first language, pp. 181–202. Philadelphia: John Benjamins Publishing Company.

Galambos, N. L., Barker, E. T., & Krahn, H. J. (2006). Depression, self-esteem, and anger in emerging adulthood: Seven-year trajectories. *Developmental Psychology, 42*, 350–365.

Gershoff, E. T., Aber, J. L., Raver, C. C., & Lennon, M. C. (2007). Income is not enough: Incorporating material hardship into models of income associations with parenting and child development. *Child Development, 78*, 70–90.

Ginsburg, H. (1972). *The myth of the deprived child: Poor children's intellect and education.* Englewood Cliffs, NJ: Prentice-Hall, Inc.

Hart, B., & Risley, T. R. (1995). *Meaningful differences in the everyday experience in young American children.* Baltimore: Paul H. Brookes Publishing Co.

Heath, S. B. (1983). *Ways with words: Language, life, and work in communities and classrooms.* London: Cambridge University Press.

Hess, R. D. (1970). Social class and ethnic influences upon socialization. In P. H. Mussen (Ed.), *Carmichael's manual of child psychology*, pp. 457–557 (3rd ed.). New York: John Wiley & Sons.

Hoff, E. (2003a). Causes and consequences of SES-related differences in parent-to-child speech. In M. H. Bornstein, & R. H. Bradley (Eds.), *Socioeconomic status, parenting, and child development*, pp. 147–160. Mahwah, NJ: Lawrence Erlbaum Associates.

Hoff, E. (2003b). The specificity of environmental influence: Socioeconomic status affects early vocabulary development via maternal speech. *Child Development, 74*, 1368–1378.

Hoff, E. (2006). How social contexts support and shape language development. *Developmental Review, 26*, 55–88.

Hoff, E. (in press). Interpreting the early language trajectories of children from low SES and language minority homes: Implications for closing achievement gaps. *Developmental Psychology.*

Hoff, E., Laursen, B., & Tardif, T. (2002). Socioeconomic status and parenting. In M. H. Bornstein (Ed.), *Handbook of parenting: Vol. 2. Biology and ecology of parenting*, pp. 231–252 (2nd ed.). Mahwah, NJ: Lawrence Erlbaum Associates.

Hoff-Ginsberg, E., & Tardif, T. (1995). Socioeconomic status and parenting. In M. H. Bornstein (Ed.), *Handbook of parenting: Vol. 2.*

Ecology and biology of parenting, pp. 161–188. Mahwah, NJ: Lawrence Erlbaum Associates.

Hoffman, L. W. (2003). Methodological issues in studies of SES, parenting, and child development. In M. H. Bornstein, & R. H. Bradley (Eds.), *Socioeconomic status, parenting, and child development*, pp. 125–143. Mahwah, NJ: Lawrence Erlbaum Associates.

Kohn, M. L. (1963). Social class and parent-child relationships: An interpretation. *American Journal of Sociology, 68*, 471–480.

Kokko, K., & Pulkkinen, L. (2000). Aggression in childhood and long-term unemployment in adulthood: A cycle of maladaptation and some protective factors. *Developmental Psychology, 36*, 463–472.

Laursen, B. (1995). Variations in adolescent conflict and social interaction associated with maternal employment and family structure. *International Journal of Behavioral Development, 18*, 151–164.

Laursen, B. (2005a). Conflict between mothers and adolescents in single-mother, blended, and two-biological-parent families. *Parenting: Science and Practice, 5*, 347–370.

Laursen, B. (2005b). Dyadic and group perspectives on close relationships. *International Journal of Behavioral Development, 29*, 97–100.

Laursen, B., & Collins, W. A. (2009). Parent-child relationships during adolescence. In R. M. Lerner & L. Steinberg (Eds.), *Handbook of adolescent psychology (3rd ed.): Vol. 2. Contextual influences on adolescent development*, pp. 3–42. New York: Wiley.

Laursen, B., & Hoff, E. (2006). Special issue: Person-centered and variable-centered approaches to longitudinal data. *Merrill-Palmer Quarterly, 52*, Whole volume no. 3.

Leinonen, J. A., Solantaus, T. S., & Punamäki, R. (2002). The specific mediating paths between economic hardship and the quality of parenting. *International Journal of Behavioral Development, 26*, 423–435.

Masten, A. S., & Coatsworth, J. D. (1998). The development of competence in favorable and unfavorable environments: Lessons from research on successful children. *American Psychologist, 53*, 205–220.

McLeod, J. D., & Kaiser, K. (2004). Childhood emotional and behavioral problems and educational attainment. *American Sociological Review, 69*, 636–658.

McLoyd, V. C. (1998). Socioeconomic disadvantage and child development. *American Psychologist, 53*, 185–204.

Miech, R. A., Caspi, A., Moffitt, T. E., Wright, B. R. E., & Silva, P. A. (1999). Low socioeconomic status and mental disorders: A longitudinal study of selection and causation during young adulthood. *American Journal of Sociology, 104,* 1096–1131.

Mueller, C. W., & Parcel, T. L. (1981). Measures of socioeconomic status: Alternatives and recommendations. *Child Development, 52,* 13–20.

Nagin, D. S. (2002). *Group-based modeling of development.* Cambridge, MA: Harvard University Press.

National Institute of Child Health and Human Development Early Child Care Research Network. (2005). Duration and developmental timing of poverty and children's cognitive and social development from birth through third grade. *Child Development, 76,* 795–810.

National Research Council and Institute of Medicine. (2000). From neurons to neighborhoods: The science of early childhood development. Committee on Integrating the Science of Early Childhood Development. In J. P. Shonkoff, & D. A. Phillips (Eds.), Board on Children, Youth, and Families, Commission on Behavioral and Social Sciences and Education. Washington, DC: National Academy Press.

Parke, R. D., Coltrane, S., Duffy, S., Buriel, R., Dennis, J., & Powers, J. et al. (2004). Economic stress, parenting, and child adjustment in Mexican American and European American families. *Child Development, 75,* 1632–1656.

Ripke, M. N. & Huston, A. C. (2006). Poverty: Consequences for children. In L. Balter, C. S. Tamis-LeMonda (Eds.), *Child psychology: A handbook of contemporary issues,* pp. 521–544 (2nd ed.). New York: Psychology Press.

Rowe, D. C., Jacobson, K. C., & Van den Oord, E. J. C. G. (1999). Genetic and environmental influences on vocabulary IQ: Parental education level as moderator. *Child Development, 70,* 1151–1162.

Rowe, D. C., & Rodgers, J. L. (1997). Poverty and behavior: Are environmental measures nature and nurture? *Developmental Review, 17,* 358–375.

Solantaus, T., Leinonen, J., & Punamäki, R. (2004). Children's mental health in times of economic recession: Replication and extension of the family economic stress model in Finland. *Developmental Psychology, 40,* 412–429.

Tremblay, R. E. (1999). When children's social development fails. In D. P. Keating, & C. Hertzman (Eds.), *Developmental health and the wealth of nations: Social, biological, and educational dynamics,* pp. 55–71. New York: Guilford Press.

Vasilyeva, M., Waterfall, H., & Huttenlocher, J. (2008). Emergence of syntax: Commonalities and differences across children. *Developmental Science, 11,* 84–97.

Wadsworth, M. E., & Achenbach, T. M. (2005). Explaining the link between low socioeconomic status and psychopathology: Testing two mechanisms of the social causation hypothesis. *Journal of Consulting and Clinical Psychology, 73,* 1146–1153.

Wickrama, K. A. S., Conger, R. D., & Abraham, W. T. (2005). Early adversity and later health: The intergenerational transmission of adversity through mental disorder and physical illness. *Journals of Gerontology: SERIES B, 60B,* 125–129.

Williams, F. (Ed.) (1970). *Language and poverty: Perspectives on a theme.* Chicago: Markham Publishing Company.

Willms, J. D. (1999). Quality and inequality in children's literacy: The effects of families, schools, and communities. In D. P. Keating, & C. Hertzman (Eds.), *Developmental health and the wealth of nations: Social, biological, and educational dynamics,* pp. 72–93. New York: Guilford Press.

Willms, J. D. (2003, February). Ten hypotheses about socioeconomic gradients and community differences in children's developmental outcomes. Applied Research Branch, Strategic Policy, Human Resources Development Canada, Final Report.

Willms, J. D. (2006). *Learning divides: Ten policy questions about the performance and equity of schools and schooling systems (No. 5).* Montreal: UNESCO Institute for Statistics.

CHAPTER 29

Assessment of Parental Psychopathology and Adaptive Functioning

Thomas M. Achenbach

Parents affect children's environments in many ways. (For brevity, I use "parents" to include birth, adoptive, step, and foster parents, as well as other adults who play parental roles; I use "children" to include infants and adolescents.) Parental competencies can contribute security, nurturance, encouragement, and healthy modeling for children's behavioral and emotional development. Conversely, parental problems can contribute insecurity, stress, discouragement, and unhealthy modeling.

Most parents have at least some competencies and some problems. The mix of competencies and problems manifested by particular parents may change as children develop. Equally important, parental characteristics that seem like competencies during one period of a child's development may seem like problems at later periods. For example, characteristics that make a parent exquisitely sensitive to the needs of a preverbal infant may be problematic in later periods when verbal communication of higher-level thoughts and emotions become important. Conversely, a highly intellectual parent may have little rapport with a preverbal infant but may contribute greatly to a child's later development.

Even within particular developmental periods, certain parental characteristics may be helpful in some contexts but less helpful in other contexts. For example, characteristics that contribute to close-knit family relationships might not help in meeting challenges outside the family, and vice versa. By the same token, characteristics that are highly valued by a parent's colleagues and bosses might alienate the parent's children. The important point is this: Parents, like all other humans, can be evaluated in terms of diverse characteristics that vary from one period of life to another and from one context to another within each period. To understand the possible effects of parental characteristics on children, it is necessary to take account of both quantitative and qualitative variations in these characteristics. It is also necessary to take account of how particular child characteristics interact with parental characteristics to produce particular outcomes. Moreover, accurate assessment of the characteristics of birth parents and their children is needed to understand genetic, as well as environmental, risk and protective factors.

This chapter focuses on assessment of parents in ways that mesh closely with assessment of children. Parallel assessments of parents and their children are needed for comprehensive evaluation of clinical cases where a child is the "identified patient," as well as cases where parental characteristics, such as psychopathology, addiction, or abusive behaviors, are identified as placing children at risk. If interventions are undertaken to prevent or ameliorate children's behavioral/emotional problems, it is usually as important to promote and assess changes in parents as in the children. By periodically readministering standardized assessment instruments, mental health workers can evaluate the progress and outcomes of interventions to help parents, as well as their children.

For research on the effects of different interventions, the same parallel parent and child assessment procedures should be used initially and then at subsequent points to compare the effects of each intervention on parents and their children. In addition to research on the effects of interventions, cross-sectional and longitudinal research on associations between parent and child characteristics, as well as tests of risk and protective factors for long-term outcomes, can greatly benefit from parallel assessment of parents and their children.

This chapter goes beyond traditional approaches that tend to view parental psychopathology mainly in terms of diagnoses. Although diagnoses provide one kind of lens through which to view parental functioning, I focus more on specific problems and adaptive characteristics that can be assessed through combinations of self-reports and other-reports, including reports by spouses, partners, children, and others who know the parents. Both the documentation provided by such reports and the processes involved in obtaining and comparing them can advance our understanding of the interplay between parent and child characteristics.

Specific topics addressed in this chapter include parental psychopathology and "biases" in parents' reports of their children's behavioral/emotional problems; the need for multi-informant assessment of children and parents; practical ways to use parallel assessment of children and parents; multicultural challenges; and research to advance our knowledge of the implications of parental psychopathology. As instructed by the editors of this volume, I provide my personal view of the issues, rather than an exhaustive review of the literature.

Assumptions That Parental Characteristics Cause Major Child Psychopathology

Numerous studies have found elevated levels of behavioral/emotional problems among children whose parents have psychiatric disorders such as depression, schizophrenia, antisocial personality, and substance abuse (e.g., Erlenmeyer-Kimling & Cornblatt, 1987; Jaffe, Moffit, Caspi, & Taylor, 2003; Mayes & Suchman, 2006; Zucker, 2006). Parental disorders might be associated with children's behavioral/emotional problems for reasons such as the following: (a) Children may inherit genetic vulnerabilities from disturbed parents; (b) disturbed parents' behavior toward their children may increase environmental risks; (c) disturbed parents may mate with partners who contribute to genetic and/or environmental risks; (d) disturbed parents' difficulties in holding jobs may create socioeconomic disadvantages for their children; (e) disturbed parents may be stigmatized in ways that cause children to be treated detrimentally; and (f) children's awareness of their parents' disturbance may adversely affect their self-concepts. Parental problems that do not meet diagnostic criteria for psychiatric disorders may also be associated with children's behavioral/emotional problems for similar reasons.

Until fairly recently, severe child psychopathology was blamed largely on parents.

A particularly egregious example was the pervasive assumption that conditions such as early infantile autism were caused by "refrigerator" parents who "wish that (their) child should not exist" (Bettelheim, 1967, p. 125) and "parents who inadvertently hated one another and used the child emotionally" (Wolman, 1970, p. vii). These assumptions stemmed partly from Kanner's (1943) description of parents of autistic children as being cold, although Kanner did not actually blame autism on the parents' behavior. Another example was the concept of the "schizophrenogenic mother" who was purportedly responsible for causing schizophrenia in her children.

Empirical research in recent years has debunked assumptions that autism and schizophrenia are caused by parents' attitudes, personality characteristics, or behavior. As the tendency to blame parents for these conditions has waned, diagnoses of autism and other pervasive developmental disorders, such as Asperger's disorder, have become far more common. Some have interpreted the increases in diagnoses of autistic disorders as indicating true increases in the prevalence of these disorders. However, there is considerable evidence that the increases in diagnoses reflect destigmatization of the diagnoses, more thorough case finding, and broadening of the phenotypic characteristics that evoke the diagnoses (Fombonne, 2005). It is also possible that mandates to provide intensive special educational services and evidence that such services can be beneficial have made diagnoses of pervasive developmental disorders more desirable than the diagnoses of mental retardation that such children often received in the past.

Parents' characteristics may indeed affect risks for psychopathology in their children. Yet, any such effects are likely to involve much more complex interactions between parent, child, and other variables than implied by earlier assumptions that parents' attitudes, personality characteristics, or behavior cause disorders such as autism and schizophrenia.

"Biases" in Parents' Reports of Child Psychopathology

For much of the 20th century, clinical assessment of children's behavioral/emotional problems depended heavily on impressions gleaned from unstandardized interviews with children and their parents in clinical settings. As an outgrowth of efforts to assess children's problems more systematically, standardized forms were developed to obtain parents' reports and ratings of their children's problems.

The "Depression-Distortion" Hypothesis

Studies of ratings by depressed mothers found that they tended to report more problems for their children than mothers who were not deemed to be depressed (e.g., Friedlander, Weiss, & Traylor, 1986; Griest, Forehand, Wells, & McMahon, 1980). These findings were interpreted to mean that depression caused mothers to exaggerate their children's problems (Breslau, Davis, & Prabucki, 1988; Panaccione & Wahler, 1986). The inferred tendency of depressed mothers' to distort their children's problems became known as the "depression-distortion hypothesis" (Richters & Pellegrini, 1989). However, studies that compared other sources of information about children's problems with reports by depressed versus nondepressed mothers revealed that the other sources, including direct observations, also indicated that children of depressed mothers had more problems than children of nondepressed mothers (Richters, 1992). Thus, rather than merely reflecting distortions by their mothers, elevated problem rates among children of depressed mothers were confirmed by other assessment procedures.

It is certainly possible that parents who are depressed or have other kinds of problems tend to report more problems for their children than other parents do. Yet, there are multiple reasons why children whose parents are depressed or have other problems may actually have elevated rates of problems. Examples of such reasons include: (a) the adverse effects of the parents' problems on the children's environment; (b) genetic vulnerabilities in children similar to those that make their parents vulnerable to particular problems; (c) tendencies for parents with problems to have partners who contribute genetic and/or environmental liabilities; and (d) reactions by both the parent and child to environmental stresses suffered by both of them, such as abuse by the other parent. Thus, findings that parents who have particular kinds of problems tend to report elevated rates of problems in their children may not necessarily reflect parental biases. Nevertheless, many factors, including parental psychopathology, may potentially influence particular informants' reports of children's problems, as well as the actual occurrence of problems during interactions with those informants.

Correlations between Reports by Different Informants

Meta-analyses have revealed low to moderate correlations between reports of children's problems by various combinations of informants (mothers vs. fathers vs. teachers vs. mental health workers vs. observers vs. children themselves) (Achenbach, McConaughy, & Howell, 1987). Although the meta-analyses were based on studies published before 1987, the findings of modest cross-informant correlations continue to be so consistent that they have been identified as being among "the most robust findings in child clinical research" (De Los Reyes & Kazdin, 2005, p. 483).

Because there is no single gold standard source of data about manifestations of children's problems in contexts such as home and school, each informant's report may be useful in its own right to document how that informant sees the child. Thus, although informant characteristics, such as depression, may be associated with what the informants report, attributing these associations merely to "bias" misses the following important point: There is no "unbiased" source to provide the gold standard truth that would enable us to detect "biases" in other sources.

Instead, for both clinical and research purposes, data from multiple sources are needed to distinguish between children's characteristics that are similarly reported by most informants versus those that are reported only by informants who see the child in a particular context (e.g., home or school) versus those that are reported by only a single informant.

Using Data from Multiple Informants

When certain potentially important characteristics are reported by only one out of several informants, this should prompt further investigation to answer questions such as the following: (a) Does the informant's report reflect behaviors by the child that are specific to the context in which that informant sees the child? (b) Does the informant's report reflect reactions by the child to that informant? (c) Does the informant's report reflect idiosyncrasies of the informant's judgments of the child that are not shared by other informants?

Most clinicians and researchers now understand the need for obtaining child assessment data from multiple sources. They also understand that agreement among different sources is usually modest. However, they may be less aware of how to use findings of specific agreements and disagreements among family members and between family members and nonfamily members, such as teachers. Documentation of specific agreements and disagreements can be extremely helpful in building therapeutic alliances and in motivating changes in the behavior of the relevant adults on behalf of a troubled child. For example, when a child's mother and father complete parallel standardized forms for assessing their child, the clinician can – with the parents' consent – elect to show both of them the results of their respective ratings. By displaying such ratings in terms of profiles of scales in relation to norms for parents' ratings, the clinician can highlight areas of agreement and disagreement between the parents' ratings. Concrete documentation of differences between their reports of their child's problems can facilitate parental insights into the differences in how they perceive and affect the child.

As an example, if one parent reports much more aggressive behavior than the other parent does, this might reflect the child's reactions to the first parent's more punitive and hostile behavior. On the other hand, if one parent reports many fewer problems than the other parent, this might reflect much less involvement with the child by the first parent than by the second parent. In either case, discussions with the parents may reveal reasons for their different reports about the child's functioning, reasons that can then become foci for interventions with the family. If the child and/or the child's teachers provide analogous reports of the child's functioning and if they consent, the clinician can also elect to show profiles scored from their reports to the parents. The child's self-reports and the teachers' reports can thus enlarge parents' perspectives on their child's functioning and on ways to improve it.

Clinical Applications of Parent Assessment

Helping parents understand variations in their child's functioning and in how the child is viewed can contribute immensely to helping the child. However, because parents' own views and behavior are often ingrained and multidetermined, improving their relationships with their child often requires them to enlarge their perspectives on their own functioning and their interactions with each other. The same approach to documenting multiple perspectives on the child's functioning can be applied to family-based assessment that includes the parents. Meta-analyses of agreement between adults' reports of their own problems and others' reports of the adults' problems have yielded cross-informant correlations as modest as the cross-informant correlations for reports of children's problems (Achenbach, Krukowski, Dumenci, & Ivanova, 2005). Consequently, many parents' self-reports

are apt to differ in important ways from their partners' reports about them.

Standardized forms are now widely used to obtain and compare informants' reports regarding children's functioning. Parents can complete analogous forms regarding their partner's and their own functioning. As an example, the Adult Behavior Checklist (ABCL; Achenbach, Newhouse, & Rescorla, 2007; Achenbach & Rescorla, 2003) has been developed as an adult analog of the Child Behavior Checklist (CBCL; Achenbach & Rescorla, 2000, 2001) for obtaining reports of children's problems and competencies from parent figures. The ABCL can be completed by a spouse, partner, sibling, adolescent/adult offspring, or anyone else who knows the adult well. The ABCL and CBCL are components of the Achenbach System of Empirically Based Assessment (ASEBA), which includes self- and other-report instruments for ages 1½ to 90+ years.

The ABCL assesses a very broad spectrum of behavioral, emotional, and social problems. Examples include *Argues a lot; Can't concentrate; Can't pay attention for long; Can't get mind off certain thoughts, obsessions (describe); Moods swing between elation and depression;* and *Unhappy, sad, or depressed.* The problem items are scored in terms of a variety of empirically derived syndrome constructs and broad-band groupings of syndromes designated as Internalizing and Externalizing. A Total Problems scale includes all the behavioral, emotional, and social problems rated on the ABCL. The ABCL is also scored on *DSM*-oriented scales, which consist of problem items identified by psychiatrists and psychologists from many cultures as being very consistent with diagnostic categories of the American Psychiatric Association's (1994) *Diagnostic and Statistical Manual,* 4th ed. *(DSM-IV).*

Answers to questions about tobacco use, drunkenness, and drug use are scored on substance use scales. Items tapping favorable characteristics are scored on scales for adaptive functioning and personal strengths. The adaptive functioning items pertain to areas such as relations with friends and spouse or partner (for those who have lived

Table 29.1: Scales of the Adult Behavior Checklist (ABCL) and Adult Self-Report (ASR)

Adaptive functioning	Empirically based syndromes	DSM-oriented	Substance use
Friends	Anxious/depressed (I)	Depressive problems	Tobacco
Spouse/partner	Withdrawn (I)	Anxiety problems	Alcohol
Family[a]	Somatic complaints (I)	Somatic problems	Drugs
Job[a]	Thought problems	Avoidant personality problems	Mean substance use
Education[a]	Attention problems	Attention deficit/ hyperactivity problems[b]	
Mean adaptive[a]	Aggressive behavior (E)	Antisocial personality problems	
Personal strengths	Rule-breaking behavior (E) Intrusive (E)		

[a] ASR only.

[b] The DSM-oriented Attention Deficit/Hyperactivity Problems scale includes subscales for Inattention and Hyperactivity-Impulsivity.

Note. A Critical Items scale comprises items identified by an international panel of psychiatrists and psychologists as being of particular clinical concern. A Total Problems scale comprises the sum of ratings on all problem items. I = syndromes that compose the Internalizing grouping; E = syndromes that compose the Externalizing grouping.

with a spouse/partner in the preceding 6 months). Examples of personal strengths items are *Works up to ability* and *Makes good decisions*.

The ABCL problem and personal strengths items are rated as 0 = *not true (as far as you know)*, 1 = *somewhat or sometimes true*, and 2 = *very true or often true*. These ratings are based on the preceding 6 months, although the rating period can be changed to suit the user's purposes. A Critical Items scale comprises problem items identified by an international panel of psychiatrists and psychologists as being of particular clinical concern. Examples of critical items include *Deliberately harms self or attempts suicide* and *Sees things that aren't there*. The adaptive functioning and substance use items have various response scales that are tailored to the content of the items. A parallel form, the Adult Self-Report (ASR; Achenbach & Rescorla, 2003; Achenbach et al., 2007), has first-person versions of the ABCL items, plus items that tap aspects of functioning not likely to be reportable by other people. Table 29.1 displays the names of the ASR and ABCL scales. Significant associations

with widely used methods for assessing adult psychopathology are reviewed later in the chapter.

Advantages of Including Parents in Family-Based Assessment

There are multiple advantages to having parents document their views of themselves and their partner or other adults relevant to a child's case on forms such as the ASR and ABCL. Adolescent and adult offspring can also complete the ABCL to describe their parents. Their ratings correlate with parents' self-ratings at about the same level as ABCL ratings by other informants (Achenbach, Newhouse, & Rescorla, 2004). Because parents can complete the forms independently in 15 to 20 minutes at home, on-line, or in a waiting room, no professional time is needed to ask about the diverse problems and adaptive characteristics assessed by the forms. Instead, the clinician can maximize the value of interview time by following up on the results of the assessment forms and by dealing with issues that need to be addressed in person. The ASR and ABCL are scored by hand or computer on profiles that display scores in relation to norms for the person's age and gender.

As illustrated in Figure 29.1 for a profile of syndromes scored from the ASR, the profile shows how an individual's scale scores compare with norms for the individual's age and gender. By looking at the profile in Figure 29.1, you can see broken lines that demarcate the borderline clinical range. Scores below the bottom broken line (at the 93rd percentile, equivalent to a T score of 65) are in the normal range. Scores above the top broken line (at the 97th percentile, equivalent to a T score of 69) are in the clinical range. And scores in the borderline clinical range (between the broken lines) are high enough to be of concern but are not as clearly deviant as those above the top broken line.

As Figure 29.1 shows, each syndrome's raw total score, T score, and percentile are displayed beneath the profile. The respondent's 0–1–2 ratings are also displayed for each item of each scale. (The wording of items in Figure 29.1 is abbreviated from the wording on the ASR.) A similar profile of syndrome scales is scored from the ABCL. Additional profiles display scores for the adaptive functioning, substance use, critical items, and *DSM*-oriented scales in relation to norms for each gender within particular age ranges.

Cross-Informant Comparisons of Parents

If each parent figure completes an ASR to describe themselves and an ABCL to describe the other parent figure or another adult relevant to the case, the clinician can visually compare the ASR and ABCL profiles for each individual. More systematic comparisons can be made by viewing bar graphs of all the ASR and ABCL scale scores, which the computer scoring program displays for the individual who is being assessed, as illustrated in Figure 29.2. This enables the clinician to quickly see the scales on which the ASR, ABCL, or neither form yield scores in the borderline or clinical range. If additional ABCLs are completed, as may be helpful in extended or blended families where more

than two adults are relevant to the case, their scale scores can also be displayed in the same bar graphs. To enable the clinician to systematically compare his or her own impression of each adult with reports by the adult and the collaterals, the clinician can also complete an ABCL whose scale scores are then displayed in the bar graphs. Additional profiles and cross-informant comparisons are produced for other ASR and ABCL scales, such as the *DSM*-oriented scales.

The computer software can display cross-informant comparisons of self-ratings and each other informant's ratings of each problem item for a particular adult. This enables the clinician to easily identify problems that are endorsed for that adult by all respondents, problems that are endorsed by only one respondent, and problems that are not endorsed by any respondents. The software can also display Q correlations between the problem item ratings obtained from each pair of respondents. (Q correlations measure the degree of agreement between many ratings obtained from two sources, such as ratings by the child's mother and father.) To help the clinician evaluate the degree of agreement indicated by the Q correlation between a particular ASR and ABCL, the software displays the 25th percentile, mean, and 75th percentile Q correlation obtained between ASRs and ABCLs in large reference samples of people. To translate the meaning of the Q correlations from a reference sample into words, the software prints *below average* if a Q correlation is below the 25th percentile, *average* if a Q correlation is between the 25th and 75th percentile, and *above average* if a Q correlation is above the 75th percentile of the reference sample correlations.

From the profiles and cross-informant bar graphs, the clinician can quickly identify areas in which the ASR and/or ABCLs indicate that a parent has enough problems to be in the borderline or clinical range. If more than one form indicates high levels of problems in similar areas, this would be especially good evidence that such problems may need clinical attention. Elevations on the *DSM*-oriented scales may suggest

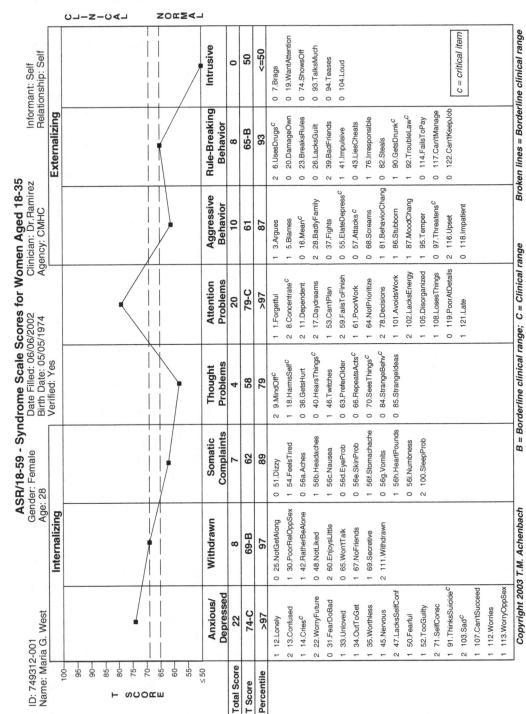

Figure 29.1. Profile of syndromes scored from the Adult Self-Report (ASR). (From Achenbach & Rescorla, 2003.)

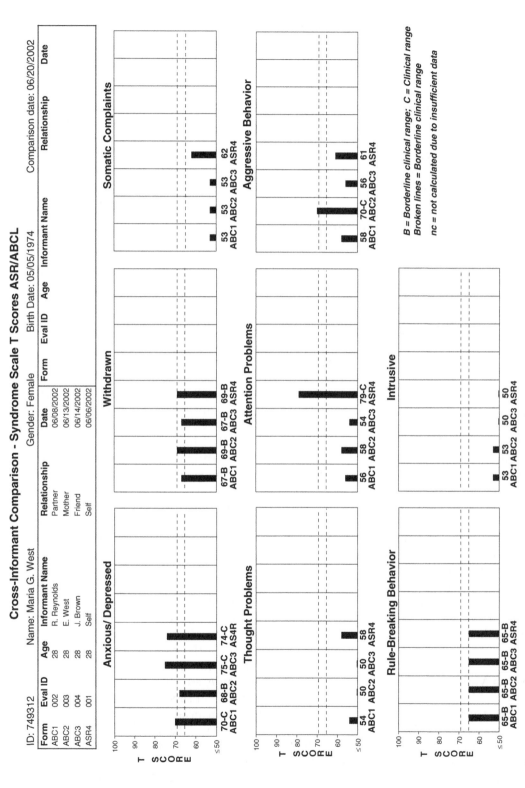

Figure 29.2. Comparisons of syndromes scored from the Adult Self-Report (ASR) and Adult Behavior Checklist (ABCL) completed for the same person by her partner, mother, and friend. (From Achenbach & Rescorla, 2003.)

particular diagnoses for the clinician to consider. Even if problem scales are not elevated, endorsement of critical items, such as those pertaining to suicidality, thought problems, and substance abuse, can alert the clinician to parents' needs for help. In any event, the ASR and ABCL findings can indicate whether parents' problems are of sufficient magnitude to warrant treatment in their own right, as well as indicating similarities and differences in how parents see each other and relations to the problems reported for their child.

Showing Cross-Informant Comparisons to Parents

If the clinician deems it appropriate, parents can be shown profiles and cross-informant bar graphs of scores obtained from parent, teacher, and self-ratings of the child who is the identified patient. Depending on the parents' reactions to seeing the similarities and differences between ratings of their child, the clinician may then elect to show them profiles and cross-informant bar graphs of their own ASR and ABCL scores. If they see that their problem scores are high and/or their adaptive functioning scores are low, this can help parents recognize needs for change in themselves. Important differences between ASR and ABCL scores can also become foci for dialogues between parents that may facilitate treatment of their child. The child and adult instruments can be periodically readministered to measure changes during and after treatment. If parents' problems cannot be ameliorated in the context of treatment for their child, the ASR and ABCL profiles can be used as a basis for referring them elsewhere for help.

Meeting Multicultural Challenges

Humans develop under amazingly diverse conditions. Their physical environments range from tropical jungles to arid deserts, mountains, densely packed cities, and arctic snow. Childrearing practices also contribute to major differences in environments for development, ranging from infant swaddling to laissez faire. Variations in attitudes, values, religion, education, rewards, punishments, opportunities, and role models associated with cultural differences may be more subtle but potentially just as influential.

In the 21st century, the need to take account of possible cultural variations in psychopathology is made especially urgent by cultural clashes, massive immigration, mixing of cultural groups, and economic globalization. Because most procedures for assessing child and parent psychopathology have been developed in a handful of societies, one multicultural challenge is to determine how such procedures work with people from other societies. Although cross-cultural research has a long history, it has tended to focus on differences between two or a few societies, each of which is assumed to be internally homogeneous and categorically distinct from the others (Hermans & Kemper, 1998, 1999).

From the traditional cross-cultural perspective, a difference between Society A and Society B implies that all members of Society A differ from all members of Society B. This neglects the fact that most human attributes vary widely within populations. Although a particular attribute may be distributed differently among members of Society A than Society B, this does not necessarily mean that all members of Society A differ from all or even most members of Society B on that attribute. Furthermore, if we compare only two or a few societies, we cannot know where differences between these societies stand in the bigger picture that would be provided by dozens of societies.

To take a concrete example, if the mean height of people in Society A is found to be greater than the mean height in Society B, we should not conclude that all members of Society A are taller than all members of Society B. Nor should we conclude that the difference in mean heights between Societies A and B is much larger (or smaller) than differences that would be found among dozens of societies. Although the mean height in Society A may be greater than in Society B, the mean height in both A and B may be much greater (or less) than the mean height in dozens of other societies.

A Multicultural Perspective

A multicultural perspective takes account of the fact that most human characteristics vary widely within the population of each society as well as within particular cultural groups who reside in a particular society. Consequently, to conceptualize both the similarities and differences between people from different societies and cultural groups, it is helpful to think of their attributes as forming multiple continua. For attributes such as height, it is obvious that the same standardized procedures can be used to measure people in different populations. Although more complicated than measurement of height, standardized procedures can also be used to assess psychopathology among the members of different populations. However, because assessment of psychopathology depends on people's reports of behavioral, emotional, and social problems, it must deal with greater challenges of translation, meaning, sampling, and respondent characteristics than assessment of physical attributes such as height. Nevertheless, multicultural understanding of psychopathology can be advanced via standardized assessment and comparison of people from many societies and cultural groups.

Research studies have compared the results of standardized procedures for obtaining parent, teacher, and self-reports of children in many societies (Achenbach & Rescorla, 2007b). For example, large samples of parents from 31 very diverse societies have been asked to complete the CBCL for their 6- to 18-year-old children. The societies were located in eastern, northern, southern, and western Europe, the Middle East, Africa, Asia, and the Caribbean, plus Australia and the United States (Rescorla et al., 2007). In all samples, confirmatory factor analyses (CFA) have supported the syndromal patterns of problems identified in U.S. samples (Ivanova et al., 2007). High correlations between the mean scores on each problem item across the different societies indicate

that particular items tend to receive similarly high, medium, or low scores in the different societies. Comparisons of mean scale scores have shown that mean scores for most societies cluster fairly closely around the "omnicultural mean" (the mean of scores from all the societies; Rescorla et al., 2007). However, small groups of societies were found to have mean scale scores that were more than 1 standard deviation below or more than 1 standard deviation above the omnicultural mean.

The multicultural support for a common set of syndromes and the availability of parent, teacher, and self-reports of children's problems in population samples from many societies create opportunities for multicultural clinical and research applications. To apply the multicultural data to clinical assessment, a computer scoring program is available that enables users to display scales scored from parent, teacher, and self-reports in relation to norms for societies where problem scores are relatively low, medium, or high (Achenbach & Rescorla, 2007a). Scale scores for children indigenous to societies where parents report relatively few problems can thus be displayed on profiles and on cross-informant bar graphs in relation to norms for societies where problem scores are relatively low. Similarly, scale scores for children indigenous to societies where problem scores are medium or high can be displayed in relation to norms appropriate for those societies. An analogous computer-scoring program is available for displaying scores from parent, preschool teacher, and daycare provider reports in relation to norms for many societies for ages 1½ through 5 years (Achenbach & Rescorla, 2010). A planned program for displaying ASR and ABCL scale scores in relation to multicultural norms will make it similarly possible to evaluate adult problems in relation to culturally appropriate norms.

Assessing Immigrant Children and Parents

In today's world, the millions of immigrants pose challenges for the mental health, educational, welfare, medical, and forensic systems of host societies. Because immigrant children and their parents often come from environments very different from those of the host society, assessment procedures need to take account of possible differences between norms for problems in the host society versus the immigrant's home society. Because parent figures are usually essential sources of information, it is especially important to take account of possible differences between norms for parent-reported problems in the host society versus the home society. Translations of structured forms such as the CBCL into many languages enable practitioners to obtain standardized reports of children's problems from parents who have not mastered the language of the host society. For parents who cannot complete forms independently, the CBCL can be administered orally by lay interviewers with no specialized training.

To determine whether a child's problem scores are clinically elevated according to norms appropriate for either the host society or the home society, the clinician can have the CBCL scale scores displayed in relation to norms for the host society and then the home society. If the scale scores are not clinically elevated according to either set of norms or are clinically elevated according to both sets of norms, the clinician can draw similar conclusions on the basis of both sets of norms. However, it would still be important to compare the parents' reports with reports by teachers and the child. Scores from the teacher and self-reports can also be displayed in relation to norms for societies where teacher and self-reports yield relatively low, medium, or high scores.

When different sets of norms relevant to a particular child yield different results, the clinician may need to tailor interventions for different contexts. For example, if parents' ratings of their child's problems are clinically elevated according to norms appropriate for the home society but the child's problem scores are not clinically elevated according to norms for parent, teacher, and/or self-reports for the host society, the clinician may need to help the parents understand differences between their views of their child's problems and people's views of children in the host society. Conversely, if the child's problem scores are clinically elevated according to norms for parent, teacher, and/or self-reports in the host society but not according to norms for the home society, the clinician may need to work with the family to reduce problems that conflict with the host society's standards. The ASR and ABCL can also be used for assessing immigrant parents and building therapeutic alliances to help children. The growing numbers of translations and multicultural studies of the ASR and ABCL are extending their applicability to more and more immigrant groups (e.g., Van Oort, Joung, van der Ende, Mackenbach, Verhulst, & Crijnen, 2006).

Research Applications of Parent Assessment

Research is needed on how to optimize use of parent assessment to advance understanding and treatment of children's problems. Although there is abundant research on adult psychopathology, there is far less research on how to mesh assessment of parents with assessment and treatment of their children. The ASR and ABCL provide examples of how parallel assessment procedures for parents and children can help users document similarities and differences between particular family members' self-perceptions and between their perceptions of each other.

Studies have shown significant associations of ASEBA adult scales with psychiatric diagnoses made from standardized diagnostic interviews. For example, Internalizing scores were significantly elevated in self- and other-ratings of adults who had been diagnosed with *DSM* major depression in Diagnostic Interview Schedule interviews administered three years earlier (Giaconia, Reinherz, Paradis, Hauf, & Stashwick, 2001). High scores on the ASEBA adult scales have also been found to predict *DSM* diagnoses made with the Composite International Diagnostic Interview (CIDI) six years later (Hofstra, van der Ende, & Verhulst, 2002).

Table 29.2: New Directions for Research on Assessment of Parent Psychopathology

1. Comparing parent and child psychopathology on parallel measures
2. Genetic and environmental influences on relations between parent and child psychopathology
3. Testing predictions of child psychopathology from measures of parent psychopathology
4. Effects of parent psychopathology on child treatment
5. Outcomes of parent psychopathology in relation to child treatment

ASEBA adult scales are significantly associated with other widely used methods for assessing adult psychopathology. Examples include: The Beck Anxiety Inventory, the Beck Depression Inventory, and the Relationship Scales Questionnaire (Laumann-Billings & Emery, 2000); several scales of the Minnesota Multiphasic Personality Inventory (MMPI) in a Turkish sample (Erol & Savasir, 2003); symptoms of Posttraumatic Stress Disorder (Muller, Lemieux, & Sicoli, 2001); and all scales of the Symptom Checklist-90 (SCL-90; Achenbach & Rescorla, 2003). Other studies have shown significant associations with preadult variables assessed years earlier, including histories of abuse (Silverman, Reinherz, & Giaconia, 1996); child and adolescent CBCL and YSR scores from as much as 10.5 years earlier in Dutch and American samples (Achenbach, Howell, McConaughy, & Stanger, 1995; Hofstra, van der Ende, & Verhulst, 2001; Stanger, MacDonald, McConaughy, & Achenbach, 1996; Heijmens Visser, van der Ende, Koot, & Verhulst, 2000); and receipt of counseling 15 years earlier and Child Depression Inventory scores 10 years earlier in a Finnish sample (Aronen & Arajarvi, 2000; Aronen & Soininen, 2000).

Instruments such as the ASR and ABCL that can be independently completed by parents can thus assess the kinds of adult psychopathology that are tapped by the Beck inventories, the MMPI, the SCL-90, and diagnostic interviews. Of particular importance for understanding children's problems, scores on the adult instruments are also significantly associated with a variety of scores obtained earlier on the childhood counterparts of the ASR and ABCL, as well as with childhood experiences such as abuse and counseling. The proliferation of translations and the growing multicultural data base for the ASR and ABCL support multicultural applications like those that are already widespread for the CBCL and related instruments (Achenbach & Rescorla, 2007b).

New Directions for Research on Assessment of Parent Psychopathology

Research on assessment of parental psychopathology is advancing, but much remains to be done. This section outlines some especially promising directions for such research, as summarized in Table 29.2. The emphasis is on empirically based assessment, also known as "evidence based assessment" (EBA). In keeping with the advance of the empirically based (or "evidence based") treatment (EBT) paradigm (Weisz, 2004), EBA is needed to ensure that decisions about diagnoses, treatment, and outcomes are firmly grounded in empirical data obtained with standardized procedures that are reliable, valid, generalizable, and informative about the relevant variables (Achenbach, 2005; Kazdin, 2005; Mash & Hunsley, 2005). EBA can contribute both to assessment of variables already recognized as important and to the identification of new variables and aggregations of variables whose value can then be tested.

Comparing Parent and Child Psychopathology

When a child is the identified patient, it can be very helpful to compare problems reported on parallel instruments for the child with problems reported for the child's parents. To determine whether particular kinds of parent problems tend to accompany particular kinds of child problems, research is needed on large samples of parents and children who are assessed with parallel instruments. It is desirable to include nonclinical samples of parents and children who are representative of general populations, in addition to clinical samples. Nonclinical samples are important for testing whether associations between parent and child problems are similar or different in nonclinical versus clinical samples. Representative general population samples typically include a wide range of problem levels, from low levels to levels that may approximate levels found in clinical samples. Consequently, general population samples afford opportunities for determining whether associations between child and parent problems are different when the children and/or their parents have low levels versus high levels of problems. For example, strong associations may be found between child and parent aggressive behavior when problem scores are high but not when problem scores are low. If this is the case, further analyses can be done to identify threshold areas on the continuum of child and parent aggressive behavior scores where the associations between them become informative.

Research on relations between child and parent problems should not be confined to associations between similar kinds of problems, such as aggressive behavior. Instead, tests of associations between parent and child problems should include multiple kinds of problems, such as those scored on the different scales listed in Table 29.1. By analyzing multiple kinds of problems, researchers can determine which parental problems are associated with similar versus different kinds of child problems. It may thus be found, for example, that parents who score high on the DSM-oriented Depressive Problems scale have children who score high on the DSM-oriented Oppositional Defiant Problems scale. Such a finding can be just as useful in prevention and intervention efforts as a finding of significant associations between the same kinds of parent and child problems. Findings of associations between parent and child problems can illuminate possible etiological pathways as well

as assisting clinicians in planning interventions with particular families.

Testing Genetic and Environmental Influences on Relations between Parent and Child Psychopathology

For etiological research on genetic and environmental factors in child psychopathology, standardized assessment of adult psychopathology can provide quantitative parameters for etiological models. Such models would typically be tested in longitudinal studies that assess the subsequent course of child psychopathology. The etiological models would include parents' scores on scales such as those in Table 29.1, but can also include other variables, such as genetic loadings for those scores, and possible environmental factors in children's development, such as abuse, physical traumas, and other stressful experiences. The child outcome variables can include scores on scales like the adult scales in Table 29.1, but can also include specific types of problems, such as suicidal behavior and substance abuse. Equally important, the outcome variables can include signs of disturbance such as expulsion from school and referral for mental health services.

Testing Predictions of Child Psychopathology from Measures of Parent Psychopathology

Somewhat analogous to the etiological research outlined in the preceding section is research designed to test parental psychopathology and adaptive functioning as predictors of child psychopathology, its course, and its outcome. Like etiological research, tests of prediction require longitudinal data spanning from assessment of candidate parent predictors at early points in children's development to assessment of outcome variables at later points in the children's development. To control for preexisting associations between parent and child characteristics, it is also desirable to assess the child characteristics concurrently with the initial assessment of parent characteristics. The parent characteristics can then be tested as predictors of continuity and changes in the child characteristics from the initial to subsequent assessments. As with tests of etiological models, tests of predictive models should include a variety of candidate predictors, such as the various scales listed in Table 29.1, plus other potential risk and protective factors, such as family constellation, socioeconomic status, and stressful experiences.

Testing Effects of Parental Psychopathology on Child Treatment

Previous sections have addressed the importance of assessing parental psychopathology and adaptive functioning in the course of assessing a child who is the identified patient. Whereas clinicians should consider parental characteristics when planning interventions for individual cases, an important research question concerns whether and how parental psychopathology and adaptive functioning affect the outcomes of different kinds of treatment. A key tenet of EBT is that it be subjected to controlled clinical trials for comparison with the efficacy of no treatment and/or other treatments. Children are typically recruited for controlled clinical trials according to preselected diagnostic categories and/or definitions of problems. It is increasingly recognized that EBA is needed to select children for controlled clinical trials (Mash & Hunsley, 2005). Research is also needed to advance understanding of the possible effects of parental characteristics on different kinds of treatments for different kinds of childhood problems. It may be difficult to add parental characteristics to other criteria needed for assigning children to conditions in controlled clinical trials. However, an initial start can be made by assessing parents with instruments such as the ASR and ABCL. Scale scores on these instruments can then be tested as covariates in analyses of the outcomes of different kinds of treatments for different kinds of child psychopathology. If parent scale scores are found to covary significantly with pre- to posttreatment changes in the children, subsequent studies can include scores on

these scales as criteria for assigning children to treatment conditions.

As an example, if high parental scores on the ASR and/or ABCL Attention Problems scale are associated with poor outcomes for treatment of children with ADHD, subsequent studies can use randomized blocks designs to insure similar distributions of parental Attention Problems scores in the different treatment conditions. If high parental Attention Problems scores are consistently associated with poor outcomes for children receiving different treatments, this would argue for adding treatment of parents who have high Attention Problems scores to treatment of children with ADHD. On the other hand, if certain child treatments are not adversely affected by parents with high Attention Problems scores, then these treatments of the children may be preferred over treatments that are adversely affected by parents with high Attention Problems scores.

Testing Outcomes of Parental Psychopathology in Relation to Child Treatment

Just as parental psychopathology and its treatment may affect children's problems, so, too, treatment of children's problems may affect parents' functioning. There are multiple reasons for assessing parental psychopathology and adaptive functioning before starting treatment for children. When this is done, it can provide baseline measures against which subsequent measures of parents' functioning can be compared. For example, if ASRs and ABCLs are completed prior to the onset of treatment of children in controlled clinical trials, readministration of the ASR and ABCL at the termination of treatment and at follow-up can be used to test changes in parents' functioning. Comparisons of parents' pretreatment versus posttreatment scores can also be used to evaluate changes in relation to the different treatment conditions. Because many treatments for children require active participation by parents as well as changes in parents' behavior, studies of this type can be used to determine whether child treatments improve parents' functioning and whether improvements in parents' functioning are associated with improvements in child functioning. As an example, Bögels and Siqueland (2006) used the ASR to assess changes in problems reported by Dutch parents who participated in family cognitive behavioral therapy targeted on their children's anxiety disorders. At follow-up assessments, significant improvements were found in ASR Externalizing scores for mothers and in Internalizing scores for both parents. CBCLs completed by both parents also showed significant improvements in the children's Internalizing and Externalizing scores. Adults' scores on these instruments have also been found to improve significantly following psychodynamically oriented psychotherapy for the adults themselves (Baruch & Faron, 2002).

Summary and Conclusions

Parents affect children in many ways. Most parents have at least some competencies and some problems. The mix of parental problems and competencies may change as children develop and may interact differently with different child characteristics. Until well into the 20th century, it was widely assumed that parents' characteristics caused their children to have disorders such as autism and schizophrenia. It was also assumed that parental characteristics such as depression caused parents to distort their reports of their children's problems. Although parents' behaviors and the genes they transmit can certainly affect their children's problems, relations between parent and child characteristics are apt to be far more complex and interactive than implied by assumptions that parents are unilateral causal agents.

It is now recognized that comprehensive assessment of children's problems requires data from multiple sources, that agreement among the sources is usually modest, and that there is no single gold standard of truth regarding children's problems. Instead,

informants differ in their knowledge of a child's functioning, their memories of it, and their candor in reporting it.

Although the need for standardized multisource assessment of children's functioning is now widely recognized, the need for standardized multisource assessment of parents is less widely recognized. When a child is the identified patient, comprehensive family-based assessment should include standardized, normed assessment of parents in ways that parallel assessment of the child. Considering the modest agreement between adults' self-reports of their own problems and reports by collaterals, it is especially helpful to have each parent provide self-ratings and ratings of their partner and/or other adults who are relevant to the child's case.

To meet the multicultural challenges of assessing parents and children, it is essential to recognize that important human attributes are broadly distributed within populations, such as societies and cultural groups residing within particular societies, as well as within cultural groups who reside in multiple societies. Quantitative assessment of problems and competencies in representative population samples can be used to document the distributions of these attributes within societies and cultural groups. Quantitative assessment also makes it possible to evaluate individuals' scores in relation to appropriate norms.

Research is needed on how to optimize assessment of parents in order to advance understanding and treatment of children's problems. Examples of new directions for such research include family-based assessment; comparisons of parent and child psychopathology; tests of genetic and environmental relations between parent and child psychopathology; tests of predictions of child psychopathology from measures of parental psychopathology; tests of effects of parental psychopathology on child treatment; and tests of outcomes of parental psychopathology in relation to child treatment. The availability of parallel standardized, quantified, self-report and collateral-report instruments for assessment of parent and child psychopathology offers opportunities to advance research in these directions.

References

Achenbach, T. M. (2005). Advancing assessment of children and adolescents: Commentary on evidence-based assessment of child and adolescent disorders. *Journal of Clinical Child and Adolescent Psychology*, 34, 541–547.

Achenbach, T. M., Howell, C. T., McConaughy, S. H., & Stanger, C. (1995). Six-year predictors of problems in a national sample: III. Transitions to young adult syndromes. *Journal of the American Academy of Child and Adolescent Psychiatry*, 34, 658–669.

Achenbach, T. M., Krukowski, R. A., Dumenci, L., & Ivanova, M. Y. (2005). Assessment of adult psychopathology: Meta-analyses and implications of cross-informant correlations. *Psychological Bulletin*, 131, 361–382.

Achenbach, T. M., McConaughy, S. H., & Howell, C. T. (1987). Child/adolescent behavioral and emotional problems: Implications of cross-informant correlations for situational specificity. *Psychological Bulletin*, 101, 213–232.

Achenbach, T. M., Newhouse, P. A., & Rescorla, L. A. (2004). *Manual for the ASEBA older adult forms & profiles*. Burlington: University of Vermont, Research Center for Children, Youth, and Families.

Achenbach, T. M., Newhouse, P. A., & Rescorla, L. A. (2007). *Guide for ASEBA Instruments for Adults/18–59 and Older Adults/60–90+* (2nd ed.). Burlington: University of Vermont, Research Center for Children, Youth, and Families.

Achenbach, T. M., & Rescorla, L. A. (2000). *Manual for the ASEBA Preschool Forms & Profiles*. Burlington: University of Vermont, Research Center for Children, Youth, and Families.

Achenbach, T. M., & Rescorla, L. A. (2001). *Manual for the ASEBA School-Age Forms & Profiles*. Burlington: University of Vermont, Research Center for Children, Youth, and Families.

Achenbach, T. M., & Rescorla, L. A. (2003). *Manual for the ASEBA Adult Forms & Profiles*. Burlington: University of Vermont, Research Center for Children, Youth, and Families.

Achenbach, T. M., & Rescorla, L. A. (2007a). *Multicultural supplement to the Manual for the ASEBA School-Age Forms & Profiles*. Burlington: University of Vermont Research Center for Children, Youth, and Families.

Achenbach, T. M., & Rescorla, L. A. (2007b). *Multicultural understanding of child and adolescent psychopathology: Implications for mental health assessment*. New York: Guilford Press.

Achenbach, T. M., & Rescorla, L. A. (2010). *Multicultural supplement to the Manual for the ASEBA Preschool Forms & Profiles*. Burlington: University of Vermont Research Center for Children, Youth, and Families.

American Psychiatric Association. (1994). *Diagnostic and statistical manual of mental disorders* (4th ed.). Washington, DC: Author.

Aronen, E. T., & Arajarvi, T. (2000). Effects of early intervention on psychiatric symptoms of young adults in low-risk and high-risk families. *American Journal of Orthopsychiatry*, 70, 223–232.

Aronen, E. T., & Soininen, M. (2000). Childhood depressive symptoms predict psychiatric problems in young adults. *Canadian Journal of Psychiatry*, 45, 465–470.

Baruch, G., & Fearon P. (2002). The evaluation of mental health outcome at a community-based psychodynamic psychotherapy service for young people: A 12-month follow-up based on self-report data. *Psychology and Psychotherapy: Theory, Research and Practice*, 75, 261–278.

Bettelheim, B. (1967). *The empty fortress*. New York: Free Press.

Bögels, S. M., & Siqueland, L. (2006). Family cognitive behavioral therapy for children and adolescents with clinical anxiety disorders. *Journal of the American Academy of Child and Adolescent Psychiatry*, 45, 134–141.

Breslau, N., Davis, G., & Prabucki, K. (1988). Depressed mothers as informants in family history research – are they accurate? *Psychiatry Research* 24, 345–359.

De Los Reyes, A., & Kazdin, A. E. (2005). Informant discrepancies in the assessment of childhood psychopathology: A critical review, theoretical framework, and recommendations for further study. *Psychological Bulletin*, 131, 483–509.

Erlenmeyer-Kimling, L., & Cornblatt, B. (1987). High risk research in schizophrenia: A summary of what has been learned. *Journal of Psychiatric Research*, 14, 401–411.

Erol, N., & Savasir, I. Data from Turkish translations of the MMPI and the Young Adult Self-Report. Reported in T. M. Achenbach, & L. A. Rescorla. (2003). *Manual for the ASEBA Adult Forms & Profiles*, pp. 122–124.

Burlington: University of Vermont, Research Center for Children, Youth, & Families.

Fombonne, E. (2005). Epidemiology of autistic disorder and other pervasive developmental disorders. *Journal of Clinical Psychiatry, 66* (Supplement 10), 3–8.

Friedlander, S., Weiss, D. S., & Traylor, J. (1986). Assessing the influence of maternal depression on the validity of the Child Behavior Checklist. *Journal of Abnormal Child Psychology, 14,* 123–133.

Giaconia, R. M., Reinherz, H. Z., Paradis, A. D., Hauf, A. M. C., & Stashwick, C. K. (2001). Major depression and drug disorders in adolescence: General and specific impairments in early adulthood. *Journal of the American Academy of Child and Adolescent Psychiatry, 40,* 1426–1433.

Griest, D. L., Forehand, R., Wells, K. C., & McMahon, R. J. (1980). An examination of differences between nonclinic and behavior problem clinic-referred children and their mothers. *Journal of Abnormal Psychology, 89,* 497–500.

Heijmens Visser, J., van der Ende, J., Koot, H. M., & Verhulst, F. C. (2000). Predictors of psychopathology in young adults referred to mental health services in childhood or adolescence. *British Journal of Psychiatry, 177,* 59–65.

Hermans, H. J. M., & Kempen, H. J. G. (1998). Moving cultures: The perilous problems of cultural dichotomies in a globalizing society. *American Psychologist, 53,* 1111–1120.

Hermans, H. J. M., & Kempen, H. J. G. (1999). Categorical thinking is the target. *American Psychologist, 54,* 840–841.

Hofstra, M. B., van der Ende, J., & Verhulst, F. C. (2001). Adolescents' self-reported problems as predictors of psychopathology in adulthood: 10-year follow-up study. *British Journal of Psychiatry, 179,* 203–209.

Hofstra, M. B., van der Ende, J., & Verhulst, F. C. (2002). Child and adolescent problems predict DSM-IV disorders in adulthood: A 14-year follow-up of a Dutch epidemiological sample. *Journal of the American Academy of Child and Adolescent Psychiatry, 41,* 182–189.

Ivanova, M. Y., Achenbach, T. M., Dumenci, L., Rescorla, L. A., Almqvist, F., Weintraub., S. et al. (2007). Testing the 8-syndrome structure of the Child Behavior Checklist in 30 societies. *Journal of Clinical Child and Adolescent Psychology, 36,* 405–417.

Jaffe, S. R., Moffitt, T. E., Caspi, A., & Taylor, A. (2003). Life with (or without) father: The benefits of living with two biological parents depend on the father's antisocial behavior. *Child Development, 74,* 109–126.

Kanner, L. (1943). Autistic disturbances of affective contact. *Nervous Child, 2,* 217–250.

Kazdin, A. E. (2005). Evidence-based assessment for children and adolescents: Issues in measurement development and clinical application. *Journal of Clinical Child and Adolescent Psychology, 34,* 548–558.

Laumann-Billings, L., & Emery, R. E. (2000). Distress among young adults from divorced families. *Journal of Family Psychology, 14,* 671–687.

Mash, E. J., & Hunsley, J. (2005). Evidence-based assessment of child and adolescent disorders: Issues and challenges. *Journal of Clinical Child and Adolescent Psychology, 34,* 362–379.

Mayes, L. C., & Suchman, N. E. (2006). Developmental pathways to substance abuse. In D. Cicchetti & D. J. Cohen (Eds.), *Developmental psychopathology:* Vol. 3. *Risk, disorder, and adaptation,* pp. 599–619 (2nd ed.). New York: Wiley.

Muller, R. T., Lemieux, K. E., & Sicoli, L. A. (2001). Attachment and psychopathology among formerly maltreated adults. *Journal of Family Violence, 16,* 151–169.

Panaccione, V. F., & Wahler, R. G. (1986). Child behavior, maternal depression, and social coercion as factors in the quality of child care. *Journal of Abnormal Child Psychology, 14,* 263–278.

Rescorla, L. A., Achenbach, T. M., Ivanova, M. Y., Dumenci, L., Almqvist, F., Bilenberg, N. et al. (2007). Behavioral and emotional problems reported by parents of children ages 6 to 16 in 31 societies. *Journal of Emotional and Behavioral Disorders, 15,* 130–142.

Richters, J. E. (1992). Depressed mothers as informants about their children: A critical review of the evidence for distortion. *Psychological Bulletin, 112,* 485–499.

Richters, J. E., & Pellegrini, D. (1989). Depressed mothers' judgments about their children: An examination of the depression-distortion hypothesis. *Child Development, 60,* 1068–1075.

Silverman, A. B., Reinherz, H. Z., & Giaconia, R. M. (1996). The long-term sequelae of child and adolescent abuse: A longitudinal community study. *Child Abuse & Neglect, 20,* 709–723.

Stanger, C., MacDonald, V., McConaughy, S. H., & Achenbach, T. M. (1996). Predictors of cross-informant syndromes among children and youths referred for mental health services. *Journal of Abnormal Child Psychology*, 24, 597–614.

Van Oort, F. V. A., Joung, I. M. A., van der Ende, J., Mackenbach, J. P., Verhulst, F. C., & Crijnen, A. A. M. (2006). Internalising and externalising behaviours in young adults: Dutch natives and Turkish migrants in the Netherlands. *Ethnicity and Health*, 11, 133–151.

Weisz, J. R. (2004). *Psychotherapy for children and adolescents: Evidence-based treatments and case examples*. Cambridge: Cambridge University Press.

Wolman, B. B. (1970). *Children without childhood*. New York: Grune & Stratton.

Zucker, R. A. (2006). Alcohol use and the alcohol use disorders: A developmental-biopsychosocial systems formulation covering the life course. In D. Cicchetti & D. J. Cohen (Eds.), *Developmental psychopathology*: Vol. 3. *Risk, disorder, and adaptation*, pp. 620–656 (2nd ed.). New York: Wiley.

CHAPTER 30

Assessment of Social Support, Social Network, and Social Capital

Brenda K. Bryant

Introduction

The concepts of social support, social networks, and social capital are complex and assessed to answer a variety of questions. Consequently, there is no one "correct" or "best" method of assessing social support, social network, or social capital. No one measure can be sufficient for every research endeavor. To guide the process by which individual researchers thoughtfully decide how they will assess social support, social networks, and/or social capital, this chapter presents a variety of perspectives for the researcher to consider prior to making choices as to what aspects of social support, social network and/or social capital they want to measure. Finally, social support, social networks, and social capital are dynamic concepts. Needs change with development and circumstance; Social networks change as interactions and changes in the lives of those in one's networks brings about changes (Cummings & Higgins, 2005); and social capital changes as relationships increase in depth or becomes more superficial. The dynamics of these social support

concepts is accepted but needs considerable longitudinal study to further our understanding of this aspect of social support, social networks, and social capital.

Multidimensional Nature of Social Support, Social Network, and Social Capital

How we can assess social support, social networks, and social capital is multidimensional. Table 30.1 summarizes the forms of support reviewed in this chapter.

Major dimensions in this regard include **structure, support provider characteristics** (gender, generation, and kind of relatedness), **function (e.g., activities; content), quantity** (e.g., size of network; frequency of support received), **quality** (e.g., the degree to which a person perceives the positive and/or negative valence of particular support types or providers), **accessibility, frequency, direct versus indirect** support, **formal** (e.g., membership in formal organization) **versus informal** sources of support, and **context** in which support is sought or provided, including the

Table 30.1: Specific Forms of Support

1. *Educational*

Information, transmission of knowledge (Grootaert et al., 2004; Reid et al., 1989; Malecki & Demaray, 2002; Davidson &Demaray, 2007; Feiring et al., 1987)

Ideas (Grootaert et al., 2004)

Advice (Feiring, et al., 1987; Lee, 1979; Taylor et al., 1993; Wolchik et al., 1984)

Guidance/counseling (Weiss, 1974; Barrera & Ainlay, 1983; Taylor et al., 1993; Feiring et al., 1987)

Feedback (Barrera & Ainlay, 1983)

Directive guidance/cognitive guidance (Barrera & Ainlay, 1983; Barrera, 1981; Hirsch & Reischl, 1985; Wolchik et al., 1987; Zelkowitz, 1984)

Appraisal (i.e., someone to talk to about one's problems)/problem solving (Cohen & Hoberman, 1983; Malecki & Davidson, 2002; Davidson & Demaray, 2007)

2. *Emotional*

Emotional/support/understanding; expression of concern and empathy (Fekete, 2006; Grootaert et al., 2004; Wolchik et al., 1984; Malecki & Demaray, 2002; Davidson & Demaray, 2007; Franks et al., 2006; Reid et al., 1989)

Listen (Barrera et al., 1981; Dakof & Taylor, 1990, Rook et al., 1990; Vinokur & Vinokur-Kaplan, 1990)

Caring (King et al., 2006)

Intimate talks (Bryant, 1985; Reid et al., 1989; Saunders, 1977; Cohen & Hoberman, 1983; Barrera & Ainlay, 1983; Furman & Buhrmester, 1985)

Appraisal may sometimes be emotional support as well as educational noted earlier

Provision of affection, nurturance (Zelkowitz, 1984; Saunders, 1977; Weiss, 1974; Furman & Buhrmester, 1985)

Agree (Barrera et al., 1981; Dakof & Taylor, 1990, Rook et al., 1990; Vinokur & Vinokur-Kaplan, 1990)

Positive feedback/agreement; self-esteem (Barrera & Ainlay, 1983; Cohen & Hoberman, 1983; Wolchik et al., 1984; Barrera, 1981; Hirsch & Reischl, 1985; Wolchik et al., 1987; Zelkowitz, 1984)

Provide emotional security/attachment (Weiss, 1974)

Encourage (Barrera, Sandler, & Ramsay, 1981; Dakof & Taylor, 1990; Rook et al., 1990; Vinokur & Vinokur-Kaplan,1990)

Reliable alliance/can count on (Weiss, 1974; Bryant & Donnellan, 2007; Furman & Buhrmester, 1985)

Nurturance/opportunity for(Weiss, 1974; Zelkowitz, 1984)

Nondirective support (Barrera & Ainlay, 1983)

3. *Inspirational*

Parental aspirations and expectations (Bryant et al., 2006)

Provision of good feelings of importance and pride (Bryant & Donnellan, 2007)

Provision of admiration (Bryant & Donnellan, 2007)

Improves self-esteem/status (Bryant & Donnellan, 2007; Cohen & Hoberman, 1983)

Reassurance of worth (acknowledge; value) (Weiss, 1974; Cohen & Hoberman, 1983; Furman & Buhrmester, 1985)

4. *Companionship*

Enjoyment/entertainment (Taylor et al., 1993)

Recreation/play (Zelkowitz, 1984; Wolchik et al., 1984; Barrera, 1981; Hirsch & Reischl, 1985; Zelkowitz, 1984)

Casual conversation (Bryant, 1985)

Belonging; social integration (Weiss, 1974; Barrera & Ainlay, 1983; Cohen & Hoberman, 1983)

Social cohesion/inclusion (Grootaert et al., 2004)

Read books (Zelkowitz, 1984)

Positive social interaction (Barrera & Ainlay, 1983)

Companionship (Reid et al., 1989; Furman & Buhrmester, 1985)

5. *Tangible*

Provision of access to services (health care, irrigation of fields; childcare; household upkeep help (Lee, 1979)

(continued)

Table 30.1 *continued*

Provision of goods and services (Feiring et al., 1987; Wolchik et al., 1984)

Improves income (Feiring et al., 1987; Lee, 1979)

Material aid (Barrera & Ainlay, 1983, Cohen & Hoberman, 1983)

Behavioral assistance (Barrera & Ainlay, 1983; Barrera et al., 1981; Dakof & Taylor, 1990, Rook et al., 1990; Vinokur & Vinokur-Kaplan, 1990; Barrera & Ainlay, 1983; Hirsch & Reischl, 1985; Wolchik et al., 1987; Zelkowitz, 1984)

Maintenance such as meal preparation, supervision, putting child to bed (Zelkowitz, 1984)

Instrumental (e.g., Reid et al., 1989; Furman & Buhrmester, 1985; Franks et al., 2006)**

6. *Structural*

One vs. two-parent family (Earls & Carlson, 2001; Sandler, 1980)

With older siblings or not (Sandler, 1980)

Ethnic congruence with community or not (Sandler, 1980)

Generation status (Bryant, 1985)

Formal vs. informal vs. Family (Cauce, 1982)

Pet vs. Human (Bryant, 1985)

Environmental climate (Moos, 2008; Trickett & Moos, 1973; Moos & Moos, 1978)

Spiritual vs. human (Genia, 1997)

---

* In some instances, researchers lump what I have separated in this table (e.g., Feiring et al., 1987 considered guidance to be advice and information).

** Instrumental was used by some researchers to subsume many forms of support, and this is not reflected in this table.

nature of stress or needs being studied in relation to social support, social network, and social capital. There is evidence that individuals prefer to solve their own problems without use of formal sources of support (e.g., professional support) (Cutrona & Cole, 2000). So the study of social support in daily life as well as crises that pull professional help is important. The nature of the measurements also varies. Dimensions to consider for choosing a measurement instrument include **objective** versus **subjective** evaluations of these matters; **qualitative** versus **quantitative**, and **observation** versus **self- or other-report**. Some of these dimensions require additional consideration.

Concept of Support

Social support at its most fundamental is one or more individuals providing for another's well-being. There is a wide range of functions or activities that can aid another's well-being. How researchers formulate such functions and provisions of support vary by the goal(s) of support being considered, the degree of specificity we study,

and the accessibility of receiving the support. Sometimes the support is direct and other times the support is viewed as indirect. Direct support is studied when the target of the support is provided directly to the person (e.g., infant), and, in this instance, support is indirect when we study support received by someone such as the mother whom we think will subsequently (i.e., indirectly) provide better support to the infant. Direct or indirect, social support has been characterized by function (e.g., Feiring & Lewis, 1989; Lewis & Feiring, 1979) or provisions provided in relationships (Cutrona, 1986).

Studies vary considerably in what functions or provisions of support are considered. Again, Table 30.1 identifies the range of formulations defining support that has been studied. One common framework used to develop several measures was based on Weiss' (1974) formulation of the 6 basic provisions offered in relationships. The six provisions are: (1) Attachment (emotional closeness and security); (2) social integration (i.e., belonging to a group of people who share interests or recreation activities);

(3) Reassurance of worth (i.e., acknowledgement and valuing of one's skills and strengths); (4) Reliable alliance (i.e., confident that one can count on others to address needs); (5) Guidance (i.e., advice and information); and (6) Opportunity for nurturance (i.e., sense of responsibility for the well-being of another). Factor analysis has provided some validity to this formulation (Russell & Cutrona, 1984, 1985).

Barrera and Ainlay (1983) presented a conceptual formulation of six categories of support, which included material aid, behavioral assistance, intimate interaction, guidance, feedback, and positive feedback, but then empirically generated only four unique factors of support, which he labeled as directive guidance, nondirective support, positive social interaction, and tangible assistance. Cohen & Hoberman (1983) used four aspects of perceived availability of support: tangible (material aid), appraisal (someone to talk to about one's problems), self-esteem (positive evaluation of oneself by others, and belonging (availability of people to do things with) support. Cohen and Hoberman report that perceived availability of esteem and appraisal support are the most effective in protecting people against the negative effects of stress. Whether or not one is studying support under particular stress conditions may influence what aspects of support a researcher will use.

Some selection of possible support provisions is studied in any one study. Barrera, Sandler, and Ramsay (1981), Dakof and Taylor (1990), Rook Thuras, and Lewis (1990), and Vinokur and Vinokur-Kaplan (1990) considered four types of support: listened, assisted, agreed with decisions, and encouraged. Zelkowitz (1984) considered: maintenance, nurturance, and recreation as the support variables of interest.

Others make broad dichotomies of types of support such as emotional support vs. instrumental support (Franks, Stephens, Rook, Frankin, Keteyian, & Artinan, 2006; Reid, Landesman, Treder, & Jaccard, 1989). Yet another type of support is called structural support, and this refers to a status where expectations are that one's status

automatically gets one support. For example, each available parent in a household is expected to provide support to children (e.g., 2-parent homes vs. 1-parent homes) or, marriage provides support from a spouse (e.g., married vs. single). These kinds of dichotomies may be useful to identify risk conditions from assumed low level of support provided children or mothers; it is not useful in examining the nature of support that is effective for specific goals or the actual of processes of support in development.

Thus far, I have described content of support. Another way to assess level of support is to obtain subjective evaluations as to satisfaction with the support received (cf., Sandler & Barrera, 1984). This approach uses a phenomenological approach and focuses on HOW support is received. Researchers are not limited to one type of definition of support, and, in fact, some researchers such as Sandler and Barrera (1984) advocate a multimethod approach for assessing support, using structural support, perceptions of being supported, frequency of support, and content of support.

Concept of Social Network

Social network is a summary term for the relationships which an individual has with others such as relatives, friends, neighbors, and coworkers (Unger & Powell, 1980) and beyond, including the relatives, friends, classmates and/or neighbors of those in one's immediate social network and so on, much like a genealogical tree forms branches and connections. Historically, with respect to child development, we began by looking at mothers to the exclusion of others. This restricted view has greatly expanded. We added fathers, siblings, neighbors, peers, teachers, among others to our view of influencing development, and, in doing this, we began looking at the social support figures, the social network, of children themselves and of those who buttress child development (Cochran & Brassard, 1979; Lewis, 1982; Lewis & Feiring, 1978;1979). When there is no detail regarding the kinds of support that people in the network provide, this is an identification of social connection with others in the environments, and this condition has been called "social embeddedness," (Wolchik, Beals, & Sandler, 1989). When networks are identified as people who will provide support, they reflect particular sorts of social embeddedness. At times, research participants focus on one type of social support such as "emotional support" (Belle & Longfellow, 1983; Bryant, 1985).

Bryant (1985) asked, for example, "To whom would you go if you were sad and needed someone to talk to?" Belle and Longfellow (1983) used Saunder's (1977) Nurturance scale to operationalize social support as confiding in others. This scale, then, is a measure of social embeddedness for one type of supportive transactions, confiding about either positive and/or negative events. Others include, not just one, but rather multiple forms of support such as cognitive guidance, tangible assistance, positive feedback and recreation (Barrera, 1981; Hirsch & Reischl, 1985; Wolchik, Sandler & Braver, 1987; Zelkowitz, 1984).

Early on, Lewis and Feiring (1978, 1979) proposed a model for studying children's social networks that included identifying individuals (i.e., social objects) and the functions (i.e., activities) that these individuals provided that were designed to promote the child's well-being. While social support could occur within the context of a dyad, this view of social network raised awareness that people provide care within a larger context of their social network. How one assesses social networks for a particular study will depend, in part, on what aspect of development is under consideration because different individuals may play a role in certain aspects of development but not in others and because the functions or activities required for particular activities will drive the actual assessment of social networks in a given study.

Once we identify possible support providers, we find that some individuals provide several different forms of support and others provide just one form. Multiplexity is the term that addresses the degree to which individuals in the network provide multiple

forms of support by combining a consideration of source (i.e., individual) of support in relation to each function of support considered (Wolchik et al., 1984). Multiplexity is an index of a more supportive relationship between network member and child (Zelkowitz, 1989). Zelkowitz further reports that both children and mothers were clearly able to distinguish between uniplex and multiplex relationship. In addition, Wolchik et al. (1984) provide evidence for further relevance of the concept of multiplexity when they found that having multiplex relationships were related to greater satisfaction with both support received and with the supporters.

Overinvolvement in a stressed individual's life can interfere with constructive provision of support (Cutrona & Cole, 2000). For example, sometimes the support provider begins to think that they are responsible to assure that a patient adheres exactly to all medical regimens (Coyne, Wortman, & Lehman, 1988). Because of this perception of responsibility, the support provider can become highly critical and demanding and the patient or young person may sabotage treatment as a means of asserting independence (Cutrona & Cole, 2000). Thus, when studying the process of support providing and receiving, assessment of provider overinvolvement, or critical and demanding nature support is relevant to consider.

Other characteristics are used to describe social networks. Networks of support vary according to the extent or expression of conflict among network members (Wolchik et al, 1984). Thus, some networks are characterized by a number of supporters who are also sources of interpersonal conflict (Barrera, 1981). Undermining behavior is one form of conflict. Social support providers may also engage in socially undermining behavior (Vinokur & Vinokur-Kaplan, 1990). These researchers operationally define social undermining by the support provider as "acting in an unpleasant or angry manner," "making life difficult for the support seeker," "making one feel unwanted," "getting on one's nerves," and/or "criticizing the one being supported," even when providers are coupling this with some form of support. Because asking for support might activate conflict, this factor of network conflict is relevant to assess when the process related to support asking is under study.

Concept of Social Capital

The concept of *social capital* considers the relations among people, institutions, and organizations of the community outside the immediate family structure (Parke, 2004). It is, at its core, a relationship construct. This includes support from whom, frequency of the support, on what terms is support given, and how one joins or becomes a member of a group that will provide support.

The concept of "social capital" has become a heuristic in visioning social support as well from this broader perspective (cf. Coleman, 1988), coming from sociology and embraced by child development researchers (e.g., Bryant, Zvonkovic, & Reynolds, 2006; Parke, 2004), adding political scientists, economists and community advocates to those interested in studying social networks (Grootaert, Narayan, Jones, & Woolcock, 2004). Social capital is defined by function within social structures between two or more individuals. The functions include providing obligations, expectations, trustworthiness, information channels, and norms and effective sanctions (Coleman, 1988). Social capital often parlays into access to or development of financial capital (i.e., wealth, income, what money can buy) and human capital (i.e., skills and capabilities) (Coleman, 1988; Bryant et al., 2006). The social capital of a family can include parents' and children's social capital in social structures both within the family (i.e., nuclear and extended) and outside the family (e.g., parental friends and work associates) that bear on opportunities for enhancing the development of children (Bryant et al., 2006). Social capital in relation to child development commonly includes "presence of two parents in a child's home, extended family support, maternal support, number of children in the family, neighborhood support, and church attendance" (Earls & Carlson, 2001). This notion of social capital coordinates with the view that family context operates in a complex arena of daily life. While the family is still central to child development, this increasingly appreciated social capital perspective also acknowledges that individuals function within a broad context of support, both direct and indirect social support.

Social capital often refers to the resources (e.g., information, ideas, emotional support) that individuals are able to procure by virtue of their relationships with other people (Grootaert et al., 2004). These resources are capital and they are social because they are only accessible through these relationships. Grootaert and colleagues further define the individuals who provide resources as the social network, and its structure is characterized by who interacts with whom, how frequently, and on what terms, all of which have influence on the flow of resources through the network.

Political scientists focus on organizations, which "contain" people to define social capital (Grootaert et al., 2004). In this case, social capital refers to the nature and extent of one's involvement in various formal and informal organizations (e.g., political party) or defined groups of people (e.g., neighbors). As Grootaert and colleagues explain, this view of social capital characterizes how a given community's members interact.

The concept and assessment of social capital has also been used and made by community planners, social policy makers, and world institutions such as the World Bank (Grootaert et al., 2004). The unit of analysis varies primarily by discipline. The unit of analysis varies from a focus on the individual (e.g., child development; Bryant, 1985; Feiring, Taska, & Lewis, 1998) to a focus on the community (Grootaert et al., 2004).

Competing Developmental Requirements Impacts Assessment of Support

Other dimensions of support recognize dual requirements of development and functioning with others. "Support in relation to autonomy" as well as "support in relation to control" are two important conceptual considerations for the study and assessment of support.

"Support and Autonomy"

I conceptualize support as including both experiences of relatedness to others and the experience of autonomy from others. Social support calls attention for the need and value of others to development (Bryant, 1985). Issues of relatedness are of central importance to developmental psychologists because the very survival of a human organism requires human bonding and attachment formation with at least one nurturing other. The need for and extent of relatedness to others varies with developmental stages or issues. Equally important for growth and development is the competing developmental requirement of separateness from others and development of autonomous functioning, initially a matter of adequate integration of basic vegetative functions (Murphy, 1974).

Issues of both autonomy from and relatedness to others operate in intimate relationships. Proshansky, Ittelson, & Rivlin (1972) conceptualized intimacy as one of four basic states of privacy, and intimacy as protected communication serves a critical function of autonomy (Westin, 1967). Intimacy in social relationships can reflect the need for sharing with someone while withholding, or, more benignly, remaining autonomous from others. Blythe (1982) found that, of all the people identified by a sample of seventh graders as important in their lives, only 27 percent of the important people offered intimate encounters (i.e., encounters in which these youth reported sharing their feelings a lot). Intimate relations are not characteristic of all important support figures, but intimate relations can be considered as expressions of issues involving both relatedness and autonomy and, as such, will be differentiated from nonintimate relatedness to others. Being mindful of the dual need for relatedness and autonomy can influence how we assess support figures. Bryant (1985) differentiated intimate from

nonintimate sources of support with differentiation of this matter reflected in differentiated findings pertaining to social support and psychological well-being.

"Support and Control"

Similar in importance of the dichotomy of support and autonomy is the dichotomy of support and control. Control and support are interrelated but distinct (Fekete, Stephens, Druley, & Greene, 2006). According to these researchers, support reduces stress and control gets someone to do something. In this study, control was assessed by a measure developed by Lewis and Rook (1999). Fekete et al., as did Lewis and Rook, distinguished between positive control, motivating (e.g., complimenting and motivating), and negative control, pressuring (e.g., criticizing and nagging). They distinguish positive support, emotional understanding (showing affection, pointing out patients strengths) from problematic support, dismissing (e.g., changing the topic, telling patients not to worry). Problematic support minimizes or undermines the recipient's emotional needs (Stephens & Clark, 1997). The link between control and support is that effectiveness of control depends on the quality of support that has been experienced in the relationship (Fekete et al., 2006). The concept of social capital encompasses both support and control. Complimenting someone (i.e., supporting self-esteem) may help build trust and work to establish the need to be reciprocally supportive in future interchanges. Developing trust and support includes being open to some control; This is at the crux of social capital in relation to child development. Nonetheless, control and support may both be independently assessed to further this developmental consideration.

Context Impacts Assessment of Support

Accessibility and Frequency

Accessibility of support can include physical availability, approachability, communication skills (Bryant et al., 2006) and trust (Grootaert, 2004). Such factors of accessibility affect how others are able to serve as resources of support (Bryant et al., 2006). Accessibility can also include frequency of access or actual use, mode of accessibility such as phone or in-person, and perceived satisfaction and expectations met or unmet pertaining to support received. More recently, the Internet can enlarge someone's social network, sometimes simply a virtual network and at other times, a path to enlarging one's social network in public life.

Value of the Subjective Perspective

While we might objectively define support, we must realize that given support is not always perceived by the receiver as helpful. Belle (1982) and Coletta and Gregg (1981) have demonstrated that the degree of satisfaction with support is an important dimension for understanding the role of social support in affecting mother's behavior. While most researchers ask support network questions as though membership in one's support network is stable, Wahler (1980) combined an evaluation of valence of interpersonal interactions on a daily basis and linked this daily variation to the quality of their maternal behavior. The perception of quality of social contacts was linked to more positive parenting behavior and, consistent with this, to children being more positive with their mothers. And, importantly, the quality of social contacts and the quality of parenting can vary daily.

There is evidence that cognitions of the one needing support influences how they perceive support (Cutrona & Cole, 2000). Cutrona and Cole (2000) argue that early family experiences bias the evaluation of support provided. Two such sources of bias have to do with mistrusting others as sources of support and the tendency to view oneself as unworthy of support. Measures of trust and self-concept in this regard is relevant when considering an assessment of social support, social networks, and social capital.

While social support can have a positive impact, there are often costs associated with maintaining membership in a social network (Belle, 1983). When individuals have excessive demands made on them by their network members, this can strain a mutually supportive relationship to the point of dissolution of the relationship (Tietjen, 1980). Heavy involvement in a social network that is otherwise benign can produce costs (i.e., negative consequences) when membership in the network creates an overload of responsibility and heightened psychological distress (Belle, 1983). Among low-income mothers, large networks have been shown to provide stress and support in almost equal quantities, so that there was no advantage to having a large social network (Belle, 1983). Demands of network members can be more draining than rewarding.

Conflict in relationships with network members has been linked to maladaptive coping (Cutrona & Cole, 2000). Stressed individuals may avoid support or a potential support provider may withhold support because of the conflictual nature of the relationship, or the conditions of reciprocity may be greater than normal when support comes from someone with whom there is ongoing conflict.

Stress often derives from interaction with persons in one's social network (Belle, 1983). When someone is a source of support, negative interchanges with this person is more distressing and linked to magnified harmful psychological effects (Major, Zubek, Cooper, Cozzarelli, & Richards, 1997). Thus, receiving support can jeopardize one's ability to have disagreements without negative fallout in the relationship.

Not all members of a stressed individual's social network are necessarily positive influences on the struggling individual (Cutrona & Cole, 2000). This is particularly true with fellow drug users when one is trying to end an addiction. Visits from critical or controlling relatives can also be costly (Belle, 1983)

Subjective assessment of support received is one dimension. In addition, the perceived cost of support is another. Assessment of support, ideally, accounts for both of these matters.

Relationship Context

We need to consider the relationship context in which support is given and received. Different support providers appear in differing relationship contexts. Relative power of those receiving and providing support is relevant as is the importance of the relationship in which support is sought or provided (Furman & Buhrmester, 1985). Relationship types such as parent-child, friendship, and sibling relationship each have a number of core features. Support from parents typically occurs within the context of attachment, secure base, and a sense of security. At times, there is also a constructive relationship between support and control (i.e., discipline) and, as such, is a base from which socialization occurs. Support from siblings comes from a relationship context whose core aspects are conflict and caregiving (Bryant, 1982). Support from friends typically comes from a context of reciprocity, although the nature of reciprocity can vary (e.g., sharing secrets; playmates on a team). Clearly, what relationships we study will influence how we choose to assess social support and social networks. Design of studies of support would benefit from a consideration of the unique characteristics of the relationship context factors.

In research that focuses on a limited set of social support figures, assessing the nature of attachment, conflict and caregiving, and reciprocity might usefully be included. Considering the nature of the relationship in which support is sought and received warrants further attention.

Kin outside the immediate family are more likely to provide assistance in major crises whereas friends are more likely to give help for day-to-day problems (Croog, Lipson, & Levile, 1972; Lee, 1979; Troll & Bengston, 1979). Kin/non-kin status is frequently a dimension measured when studying social support.

Provider Intended Support vs. Recipient Perceived Support

Support is often motivated by benevolence, but this intended support is not always perceived as helpful by the recipient (Coyne, Ellard, & Smith, 1990). Assessing provider intention and recipient perception allows for clearer valuation of social support. To address this issue of ambiguity, Bryant and Crockenberg (1980) distinguished maternal "help asked for" versus maternal "help not asked for." In this study mothers were helping two daughters. Researchers could not with certainty know from observing whether the support was perceived as wanted or not (i.e., intrusive or controlling versus welcomed support). By noting whether the "help" was asked for or not, they reduced lumping unwanted and wanted help, and the results indicate that it was a useful dichotomy because "help asked for," but not "help not asked for," was linked to infrequent antisocial and frequent prosocial behavior between the siblings. In contrast, maternal support not asked for was unrelated to prosocial behavior between her children. Considering whether or not the support given was wanted and optimally matched to the need of the stressed individual are both relevant to consider in an assessment of support provision and their relation to development.

The same actions can be perceived as helpful from some "helpers" and not others (Dakof & Taylor, 1990). For example, intimate others (i.e., close relatives and friends) providing esteem and emotional support are viewed as the most helpful, whereas tangible aid and informational support from relatives and close friends is less valued. The intended help from people with the same health problem and from doctors were most appreciated when they provided information as compared to when they offered esteem/emotional support. Source of support by provider's role in relation to the support receiver is relevant to assess in most situations.

When adults are able to solve their own problems, high levels of advice are not viewed favorably, but when the stressed person is not able to solve (i.e., control) the stressful situation, high levels of advice from a family member (i.e., spouse) led to high satisfaction (Cutrona & Suhr, 1992). This is assuming that the stressed person believes the helper has some expertise. This study of adults also indicates that high levels of emotional support (e.g., caring, empathy, sympathy) was viewed favorably by the stressed individual in both stressful situations that were and were not controllable. Cutrona and Suhr found that, even though active problem solving is needed to resolve the stress, emotionally soothing interactions may help the stressed person calm themselves and tackle the problem with a calmer frame of mind. These findings may be equally true for children and adolescents *vis a vis* their parents. Assessing the child's self-evaluation of their ability to solve a problem under study, the perception of level of expertise perceived by the child needing to problem solve and the soothing nature of interactions are worthy of assessment. The assessment of perceived expertise may be particularly relevant when studying adolescent development, especially when considering both adult and peer support because adolescents may consider their peers as more knowledgeable than their parents or other adults "who do not understand what it is like to be a teenager in today's world."

Timing of the provision of support is yet another relevant support factor to consider because stressed individuals are more likely to receive support to change during a crisis, more so than after the crisis has been either positively or negatively resolved (Cutrona & Cole, 2000). Timing of support is rarely studied, but the field would benefit from considering this aspect of support provisions.

Approaches to Measuring

The approach to measuring social support and social networks can be quantitative and qualitative. Appendix A provides a summary of the specifics of measures reviewed later. Interviewing has been the most common form of assessment of social support and social networks, but observation has also been a useful tool for measurement. Interviews can be self-report or other report and can be given in oral form or in paper-and-pencil format. While qualitative research is designed to formulate central factors or processes previously unexplored, quantitative studies offer a priori design measures. Given the variety of contexts and domains of study noted earlier, there is no one best method. In this section, I will discuss several measures to highlight how methods of assessing vary. How we conceptualize our research goals is another way of differentiating context. Four major contexts in which researchers have studied social support, networks of support, and social capital include: a. support in relation to child development; b. support in relation to achieving health; c. support in relation to adapting to specific stresses; and d. social capital available and used in communities.

Both qualitative and quantitative approaches to assessment have been used. Most commonly, for both of these approaches, self- and other-report have predominated. Parent or teacher report often supplements a child's report. Fortunately, some have used the more objective approach of observation. All approaches have enhanced our study of social support.

Focus Group Method: Example Studying Support for Chronic Illness

This assessment approach is a qualitative method designed to determine what constitutes specific actions of support from family and friends for self-management by adults with a chronic health problem (arthritis, diabetes, and/or heart disease) (Gallant, Spitze, & Prohaska, 2007). The methodology provides a model for the use of focus groups with other age groups. It may not be an appropriate method for use with the very young.

In the Gallant et al. (2007) study, thirteen focus groups, segregated by gender and race, were conducted. Relevant questions of assessing their social support network and how the support network functioned included: (1) Does anyone help you to take care of yourself? Who? Do they live with your, or nearby? (2) In what ways do members of your family (or friends) make it easier for you to take care of your chronic illness? (3) Are there things that family members do or say that get in the way of managing your chronic illness or make it harder for you? (4) Do your friends do anything that gets in the way of managing your chronic illness or make it harder for you? (5) Do you know other people (e.g., friends, siblings) who have the same chronic illness? Who are they? Do they offer you advice or any special kind of support? Each focus group included four to nine participants. There were four groups of white women, five groups with black women, three groups with white men, and one group with black men. The number of women groups met the standard "rule of thumb" criterion or four to six groups before saturation for a group such as white women (Morgan, 1996).

The Social Provisions Model: Foundation for Several Quantitative Measures of Support

The most comprehensive set of quantitative measures of support is based on a Social Provisions model in accord with Weiss' (1974) conceptualization of the functions of relationships. Weiss formulates that relationships have the potential of providing the following important six basic provisions: (1) Attachment (emotional closeness and security); (2) social integration (i.e., belonging to a group of people who share interests or recreation activities); (3) Reassurance of worth (i.e., acknowledgement and valuing of one's skills and strengths); (4) Reliable alliance (i.e., confident that one can count on others to address needs); (5) Guidance (i.e., advice and information); and (6) Opportunity for nurturance (i.e., sense of responsibility for the well-being of another). One of the derivative measures is a structured self-report measure called the Social Provisions Scale (Cutrona & Russell, 1987). A second form uses a diary format that requires monitoring actual incidents of social interaction that includes checklists and ratings of the actual interactions. This is called the Social Contact Record (Cutrona, 1986). The next three measures employ observation, using

Weiss' six provisions of support as the basis for coding of behavior (Cutrona, Shaffer, Wesner, and Gardner, 2007). One of these observational measures is the Social Support Elicitation Behavior Code (Cutrona, Suhr, & MacFarlane, 1990; Jensen, 2001), a second is the Social Support Behavior Code (Suhr, Cutrona, Krebs, & Jensen, 2004), and the third is a rating scale administered after a videotaped interaction (Cutrona, 2007). The social provisions model forms a conceptual and measurable foundation for studying support in relation to adaptation to stress.

The Social Provisions Scale

This is a self-report measure of perceived social support based on Weiss' (1974) characterization of the six functions of social relationships (Cutrona & Russell, 1987). This scale consists of 22 items comprising six subscales; items are rated on a 4-point response scale (1= strongly disagree to 4 = strongly agree). The measure was designed for administering to adults, but I see no reason why this could not be used or adapted for children and youth. Factor analysis has confirmed a six-factor structure that corresponds to the six social provisions (Russell & Cutrona, 1984, 1985). Green, Furrer, and McAllister (2007) used the Social Provisions Scale (SPS) and found the subscales were significantly correlated with each other [$r(129) = .32 - .78$], and so they used a total scale score in their study, and the Cronbach alpha for all 22 items was .89. The alpha coefficients for the individual subscales ranged from .64 to .76. Several studies further support the validity of the Social Provisions Scale. Among first-year college students, the six social provisions together accounted for 66 percent of the variance in scores on the UCLA Loneliness Scale (Cutrona, 1982). Similar validity studies, using both cross-sectional and longitudinal designs, have replicated the negative association between the having social provisions and problem emotional states across diverse populations, including postpartum mothers (Cutrona, 1984), public school teachers (Russell, Altmaier, & Van Velzen, 1987), and nurses (Russell & Cutrona, 1984). Response bias caused by mood, personality (e.g., self-esteem; neuroticism), and social desirability was found not to be a problem as discriminant validity was documented in a study with a college student sample (Russell & Cutrona, 1985).

SOCIAL PROVISIONS SCALE – PARENT VERSION (SPS-P)

There is also a parent version of the Social Provisions Scale (Cutrona, 1989; Cutrona & Russell, 1987; Cutrona, Cole, Colangelo, Assouline, & Russell, 1994). Two items, one that describes the presence and one that delineates the absence of the provision in the young person's relationship with their parents assess each of the 6 provisions of support. This format was intended to minimize the effects of acquiescence. There are a total of 12 items. The reliability for the scale ranges from .81 to .91 across a range of samples (Cutrona, 1989; Cutrona & Russell, 1987; Cutrona et al., 1994). In Cutrona et al (1994), the internal consistency of the 2-item subscales ranged from .47 (opportunity to provide nurturance) to .72 (attachment). Validity evidence of the SPS among both adult and adolescent populations has been reported (Cutrona, 1989; Cutrona & Russell, 1987).

Cutrona (1989) also used this measure with pregnant adolescent females. A sources specific adaptation was also included. This adaptation evaluated the extent to which each of the six provision of social support was currently available from each of three sources: parents, friends, and male partner. Internal consistency for these scales were .69, 63, and .78, respectively. Correlations with the source specific subscales correlated .44(df = 109, $p<.001$) for the parent support, .56 ($p< .001$) for friend support, and .31 ($p< .001$), and .31 ($p< .001$) for male-partner support. One gains a more refined picture of social support when using the source specific format.

THE SOCIAL CONTACT RECORD

Using the same conceptual framework of Weiss's (1974) provisions of support, this is a paper-and-pencil task in which respondents are to note the duration of each interaction over a series of days and to complete a series of checklists in which they indicate the number and relationship to themselves of the individuals with whom they interacted and the occurrence of help-oriented exchanges (e.g., provided information) and non-help-oriented activities (e.g., engaged in a recreational activity together). Help oriented activities were: emotional sustenance (e.g., express concern), self-esteem bolstering (e.g., give compliment), information/feedback (e.g., give advice), and tangible assistance ("did something to help solve a problem"). In addition, the participants rated each interaction on pleasantness, helpfulness, and the degree to which the interaction changed their mood.

THE SOCIAL SUPPORT ELICITATION BEHAVIOR CODE

The Social Support Elicitation Behavior Code (ssebc: Cutrona, Suhr, & Macfarlane, 1990; Jensen, 2001)measure is used to code behavior of the support seeker during a 10-minute videotaped interaction task. It was developed for use with marital partners but is generic to others in interaction as well. Two of the subscales, "Requests Information" and "Describes Emotions" were used by Cutrona et al. (2007) and, based on two coders of 25 percent of the videotapes, obtained interrater reliability using kappa coefficients of .98 and .68 respectively. Validity of this measure is reported in Jensen (2001).

THE SOCIAL SUPPORT BEHAVIOR CODE

The social support behavior code (SSBC) (Suhr, Cutrona, Krebs, & Jensen, 2004) assesses the frequency of 26 specific behaviors that were initially collapsed into 4 subscales: Information Support (e.g., information, advice, or suggestions about how to handle the problem), Esteem Support (bolstering the other's sense of competence or self-worth), and Caring Support (expressions of affection or concern). The Esteem Support and Caring Support subscales were highly correlated ($r = .70$) in a study by Cutrona et al. (2007) and so they were collapsed into one subscale named "Emotional Support." Interrater reliability as indexed by kappa coefficients was excellent (.92) for Informational Support and .88 for Emotional Support. A fourth subscale is the Negative Behavior subscale (e.g., criticizing; sarcasm) and had a kappa coefficient of .70. The validity for this measure is reported in Krebs, 2000).

Partner Sensitive Responsiveness Measure

This measure was designed to be administered after the 10-minute interaction and consists of 5 items measuring partner sensitivity (Cutrona et al., 2007). Items tapped components of interactions that lead to intimacy according to Reis and Shaver (1988): validation, understanding, and caring. A sample item is: "My _____(spouse) made me feel comfortable about myself and my feelings." Reliability of a sample of young married couples was .87. Validity of the measure has been attributed to a significant correlation with observer-rated listener responsiveness (Krebs, 2000). Because sensitive responsiveness is at the core of the development of a secure attachment, this measure may usefully be adapted to child and adolescent parent-child relationships.

Network of Relationship Inventory

This inventory was designed for use with children in the fifth and sixth grades and made use of Weiss' (1974) provisions of relationships as well (Furman & Buhrmester, 1985). Nine relationships involving the child respondent, if available in the child's life, were assessed separately: mother, father, grandparent, older and younger brother, older and younger sister, best friend, and teacher. A 5-point Likert scale with a low of 1 (little or non) to a high of 5 (the most) was used to quantify the various forms of support in relation to provider. The kinds of support that are assessed includes: affection, intimacy, reliable alliance, enhancement of worth, companionship, and instrumental help. Satisfaction of support, conflict in relationship being assessed, relative power

in the relationship being assessed were also systematically considered. The relationship, and importance of each specific support were also assessed. Internal consistency based on Cronbach alphas averaged .80. Only "companionship with teacher" where alpha was .47 and "conflict with grandparents" with alpha only .57 were low on internal consistency. Beginning validity has been established because children reported seeking different kinds of support from different individuals, and this is consistent with what one would expect from Weiss' (1974) theory of relationships. In addition, results were basically replicated in a sample of Costa Rican children in the same grades as those in the original network inventory, and this indicates the robustness of the components of support measured.

The Integrated Questionnaire Measurement of Social Capital (SC-IQ)

This measure can be administered in paper-and-pencil form or in an interview format (Grootaert et al. 2004). Grootaert et al. present both a long and short version of this measure. The short version consists of 27 questions while the long version contains 95 questions. Six dimensions of social capital are assessed: (1) groups and networks; (2) trust and solidarity; (3) collective action and cooperation; (4) information and communication; (5) social cohesion and inclusion; (6) empowerment and political action. The assessment is done at the household level and, as such, assesses the social capital of families (or other compositions of households). This measure may be particularly useful when designing community based social support interventions for enhanced development of children and parents.

Groups and networks questions consider the nature and extent of all household member's participation in various kinds of social organizations and informal groups, the range of contributions that household members give and receive from organizations, the diversity of each group's membership, how its leadership is selected, and how one's involvement has changed over time. Included, among others, are work related groups, cultural groups, religious groups, financial groups, ethnic-based community groups, sports groups, youth groups, health groups, education groups.

Trust and solidarity is determined by questions pertaining to trust towards neighbors, key service providers, and strangers, and how these perceptions have changed over time. Collective action and cooperation pertains to whether and how household members have worked with others in the their community on joint projects and/ or in response to a crisis.

Grootaert and colleagues report that all questions are drawn from prior survey work on social capital and each item has demonstrated reliability, validity and usefulness. Although an external panel of experts critiqued the questionnaire, it is unfortunate that actual research references pertaining to measurement characteristics are not provided for the researcher to review in detail.

Collective action and cooperation questions determine whether and how household members have worked with others in their community on joint projects and/or response to a crisis. Also considered is the consequence of violating community expectations regarding participation.

Information and communication questions determines the most common ways and means by which households receive information (e.g., radio) regarding economic conditions and public services, and the extent of their access to communications infrastructure.

Social cohesion and inclusion refers to identifying if there is diversity and the degree to which this diversity creates conflicts in the community, the mechanisms by which the conflicts are managed, and which groups are excluded from key public services. Everyday social interactions are also included.

Empowerment and political action questions explore household members' sense of happiness, personal efficacy, and capacity to influence both local events and broader political outcomes.

The Arizona Social Support Inventory

This is a structured interview that represents a multimethod approach. It frames questions according to experiences respondents have had during the past month (Wolchik, Sandler, & Braver, 1984; Barrera, 1980). What results is a structure of ties to others, perceptions of being supported, frequency of support, and content of support. In addition to network size, six kinds of support are considered: (1) talk about private feelings, (2) material aid, (3) advice and information; (4) positive feedback; (5) physical assistance; and (6) social participation. Barrera obtained test-retest reliability of .88 for this inventory. In addition, respondents are asked to identify people in their lives whom they can expect to make them angry and upset. In this way, scores are made to reflect conflicted and nonconflicted support networks. The test-retest reliability was .59 for conflicted networks and .87 for nonconflicted networks. This notion of conflicted networks may be particularly relevant in clinical situations.

Wolchik, Sandler, and Braver (1984) and, later, Kaufman (1991) have made adaptations of this measure to use with children. These two adaptations will be described later, each with its own emphases relevant to their programs of research

The Children's Inventory of Social Support

In the process of Wolchik studying children of divorce, this scale was adapted from the Arizona Social Support Inventory (Wolchik, Sandler, &: Braver, 1984; Barrera, 1980) and so, similarly construes social support as a multidimensional construct. Support network characteristics (e.g., relatives/nonrelatives), specific kinds of support received, and satisfaction with supporters. The five kinds of support were: (1)recreation/play; (2) advice/ information; (3) Goods/services; (4) emotional; and (5) positive feedback. Scores result for network size, number of supporters within each support function (e.g., the number of family members who provided positive feedback); multiplexity (the total number of relationships that provided more than one support function); satisfaction of each support provider; and conflicted network size (i.e., this network both provides support AND makes the one receiving the support feel "angry, bad, or upset").

The internal consistency of total number of support functions among groups of support providers (e.g., family adults, nonfamily adults, family children, and nonfamily children) ranged from .79–.90 and test-retest reliability ranged from .52–.85. Test-retest reliability was lowest with respect to adults and highest for nonfamily children. Satisfaction with support had internal consistency scores of .52 for family and .71 for nonfamily. Test-retest was highest for satisfaction with family and lowest for nonfamily support providers.

The Arizona Social Support Inventory as Adapted by Kaufman (1991) for Use with Children

Kaufman (1991) has been studying social support as one of several moderators of the relationship between childhood maltreatment and depression among school aged children (ages 8–12). Like Wolchik et al. (1984), Kaufman (1991) adapted the language and focus of Barrera's (1980) Arizona Social Support Inventory as follows: Children were asked to name: (a) people they talk to about very personal things, (b) those people they count on to buy the things they need, (c) people they share good news with, (d) the adults and children they get together with to have fun, (e) those they go to if they need advice, and (f) the people who make them angry or upset. To increase children's comprehension, a visual (pictorial) aid in the form of a graduated heart was used to clarify a 5-point Likert scale. Children were asked to rate how much they feel each source of support person previously named cares about them, and how much they care about each support person. Five scores were then derived from the ASSIS interview: (1) Total Support, the total number of people listed in the positive support categories, weighted by the number of times each source of support was listed; (2) Negative Relationships, the number of people listed in the antagonistic relationship category; (3) Conflictual Relationships, the number of people listed in both the antagonistic relationship category and one of the positive support categories; (4) Perceived Affection from Supporters, the average of the ratings of how much the children felt each support provider cared for them; and (5) Reported Affection for Supporters, the average of the ratings of how much the children stated they cared about each person who provided social support.

Two ways of assessing the reliability of this adaptation have been reported (Kaufman, 1991). Split-half reliability for the total support score was computed based on the first two and last three positive support categories, resulting in a coefficient of .72 ($p < .01$). Correlations computed separately for the older and younger children were not significantly different (Fisher's $p < .05$). Unfortunately, not all scores used in the analyses (Kaufman, 1991; Kaufman et al., 2006) had any reliability data. There is a need to attend to reliability in future use of this measure with school-aged children because the work with this measure appears promising and useful in looking at the relationship between child abuse and genotype in relation to risk for depression in children. Social support appears influential in interacting with genetic and environmental forces to reduce the risk of psychopathology (Kaufman, 1991; Kaufman et al., 2006).

"My Family and Friends"

This is an interview procedure designed to measure the perception of a child or young adolescent regarding their existing social supports (Reid et al., 1989). The first part of the interview consists of identifying those individuals and their role within the child's support network. Following this, a card is made for each member of the network (e.g., mother, father, friend, teacher). The child then enters into five different sets of dialogue in situations involving emotional support (e.g., When you want to talk about your feelings to whom do you go?). At the end of each dialogue task, there is a ranking task that requires the child to rank individuals within their network in an order indicative of how often they approach each particular person for emotional support (most often to least often). There were four major domains of support considered: emotional support, information support, instrumental support, and companionship. Respondents also rated support providers by indicating their level of satisfaction with the support they receive from each person. These ratings involved a barometer scale for children to indicate their degree of satisfaction with the support they receive from each person. Scores were derived separately for mother, father, sibling(s), friends, other relatives and teachers. Overall, this interview takes approximately 30 minutes to administer (Reid et al., 1989).

Test-retest reliability among children varies. Overall, the median test-retest reliability is .68 for rankings and .69 for ratings. Eighty-six percent of the "unreliable" children were from families that home visitors had described as experiencing stress or upheaval such as bitter divorce and separation problems, parental depression and marital dissatisfaction, and parent-child conflict or estrangement (Reid et al., 1989).

The Network Interview

This interview was designed for use with mothers of young infants (Feiring, Fox, Jaskir, & Lewis, 1987). It focuses on those kinds of stresses and the concomitant support that mothers of young infants experience. It assesses the nature of mothers' social networks and the type of support they had received in the past 3 months. Within each of four categories of support (goods, services, money, and advice), a mother is asked to name any person, their relationships to her (e.g., relative, friend), and what was given. Goods included such things as clothing, furniture, and baby supplies. Services included baby-sitting, household chores. Advice included parenting information, and emotional support. Financial support was

how much money was provided. The categories in this study are more specific than those used in Weiss' (1974) categorization, with guidance and reliable alliance the only provisions relevant to Weiss' categories that were included. It is instructive to consider both general provisions and more specific provisions for particular circumstances.

Social Network Matrix

What people constitute the social network and what they do within the social network (i.e., their social functions) can be conceptualized as the social network matrix (Lewis & Feiring, 1979; Feiring & Lewis, 1989). The members of the social network are listed along the vertical and the social functions are listed on the horizontal axis. Within the matrix, each person by support function can be assigned a frequency score. This matrix is flexible in that there is no exhaustive list of functions of support, and it accommodates and recognizes that the salience of certain support functions will change depending on the age or developmental phase of the children being studied. By examining the matrix, researchers can determine which social network members are present, what functions are being satisfied, and which support functions are fulfilled by which social network members (Feiring & Lewis, 1989). A broadening of the size of network over time can be an index of developing autonomy whereas consistency in network membership in multiple functions (Feiring & Lewis, 1989) can be an index of a sense of belonging and security.

The Neighborhood Walk

This is an interview for use with children in middle childhood and calls for children to report on their social networks and to some extent their emotional support figures within the network (Bryant, 1985). The Neighborhood Walk assesses all the places where the child acts and reacts to a notable degree. Of primary interest is whether or not children find support in each of these places. The interview appraises how children differ in their access to and interaction with (a) intrapersonal sources of support (hobbies, fantasies, skill development), (b) others as resources (persons in various generations; pets), and (c) environmental sources of support in their communities (i.e., places to join others and places to get off to by self). Thus, both formal and informal sources of support are assessed. The interview includes identifying individuals with whom they casual kinds of interactions (i.e., knows and interacts with) and with whom they have intimate kinds of interactions (i.e., talks about stressful experiences). Grandparent, parent, peer, and "pet" generation scores are possible. This interview of a child's neighborhood sources of support is a psychological rather than sociological description of the child's neighborhood.

The test-retest reliability for The Neighborhood Walk has been reported >.85. While this interview was developed to be administered during a walk around the child's neighborhood so that visual and kinesthetic cues might enhance reliability, there has been no study of whether the walking is necessary to have good reliability. Validity of the measure comes from the documented links between support and psychological function, although it should be noted that these findings were typically moderated by family size, developmental level, and sex of child.

The Child and Adolescent Social Support Scale

This self-report measure is used to assess perceived frequency and importance of social support from five key sources (parents, teachers, classmates, close friends, school) with respect to four types of support (emotional, appraisal, instrumental, and informational types) (Malecki & Demaray, 2002; Davidson & Demaray, 2007). A 6-point Likert scale is used to quantify frequency of support and a 3-point Likert scale is used to rate importance receiving the support. Internal consistency for subscales and total score for frequency scores have all been >.90. Test-retest correlations

are modest, ranging from .60 to .76 on the subscales and .70 on the total score. Convergent validity was supported by a correlation of .70 between scores on the child and adolescent social support scale (CASS) and Harter's (1985) social support scale for children.

The Adult Kinship Relations Measure

This is a measure using adolescents as reporter of adult kinship support (Taylor, Casten, & Flickinger, 1993). Special attention to kinship support is justified by the finding that kin support is more effective than that provided by nonkin (Dakof & Taylor, 1990). Regardless of relative merit, child and adult adjustment benefit from an available kinship network (Dressler, 1985; Kellam, Adams, Brown, & Ensminger, 1982). Taylor's et al. (1993) kinship relations measure consists of two parts: First, respondents are asked to name "people like your grandparents, your aunts or uncles or other adult relative." Second, the measure has questions about the frequency of contact with adult kin, the number of adult kin living within an hour of the adolescents' residence; and the degree of endorsement (4 point rating) of 13 items examining social support. Advice and counseling, socialization and entertainment, and problem solving were the forms of support included in this measure. Using the Cronbach alpha, internal reliability was calculated for adolescent respondents, and the internal consistency was .72. The questions pertaining to social support were of two types: (1) the adolescent's personal satisfaction with the support of their adult kin and (2) the adolescent's knowledge of explicit behavior of kin in offering help and the actions of their family in seeking help. Previous work had indicated that adolescent report and parent report of kinship social support was high ($r = .85$). With respect to validity, the findings of Taylor et al (1993) were comparable to those of Taylor and Roberts (1995) using parental reports to assess kinship support and authoritative parenting. Specifically, adult kinship social support was positively correlated with adolescent adjustment and authoritative parenting (Taylor et al., 1993).

Youth-Nominated Support Team

This is an interview or paper-and-pencil measure (King, Kramer, Preuss, Kerr, Weisse, and Venkataraman, 2006). The support team was specifically designed to supplement the customary care given to adolescents who had recently been hospitalized because of acute suicidal thoughts and behavior. The adolescents identified people in their lives whom they thought provided support to them. They were encouraged to consider caring persons from all domains of their lives, including school, neighborhood/community, and family. They were also told that (a) a total of four support persons would actually participate in the intervention, (b) only a subset of nominated persons would likely be available, and (c) informed consent by the appropriate person would be needed for each nominated person. No reliability information is available. The Youth-Nominated Support Team was readily endorsed by the administrative staff (i.e., experienced mental health professionals) at the hospital sites involved. The proportion of nominated individuals who participated was relatively high. This endorsement by experts provides face validity to the selection process. Unfortunately, it is not clear what "relatively high" means. Although the measurement qualities of reliability or validity of the identified support network was absent or weak, this treatment approach is innovative.

Social Climate Scales

Just as people can be supportive to an individual's well-being, so can environments such as a family environment, group environment, work environment, a community environment, and a classroom environment. Moos (2008) has developed a series of measures to do just that. A support subscale is part of the Community Environment Scale. The Family Environment Scale has subscales of "cohesion" and "conflict" among other scales. In the Group Environment Scale,

subscales of cohesion and leadership support are of interest when studying support. In the Work Environment Scale, coworker cohesion, supervisor support, and autonomy are all relevant to the study of social support. Each of the scales are paper-and-pencil in format. Beyond the scope of this chapter is a delineation of each of these scales, but they have developed and been tested with large sample sizes.

As an example, take the support subscale of the Classroom Environment Scale (Trickett and Moos, 1973; Moos & Moos, 1978). This measure was designed and tested on adolescents in 38 junior high and high school classrooms (Trickett & Moos, 1973). This measure is a 90-item (10 items per dimension) perceived environment scale that assesses nine dimension (e.g., teacher support). Each of the subscales significantly discriminates among the 38 classrooms in the standardization sample (Trickett & Moos, 1973). The internal consistency of the subscales and the overall profile stability are high. All items produced very low correlations ($r = .2$ or less) with the Marlowe-Crowne Social Desirability Scale. The support subscale measures the extent to which the teacher expresses a personal interest in the students. Internal consistency correlations (Cronbach alpha) ranged from .67 – .86 with the support subscale having an internal consistency of .84 (Trickett & Moos, 1973). Validity comes from the finding that classes with high absenteeism rates were in classrooms in which students perceptions were that teacher support was low (Moos & Moos, 1978).

NEGOPY Social Network Computer Program

Social networks have been a challenge to measure (Richards & Rice, 1981). Of interest has been friendship groups, both loose groupings and tight cliques. Friendship groups are groups of adolescents (or others) who are connected by reciprocal friendship choices. NEGOPY is a network analysis computer program used to describe pair-wise linkage between people to define friendship groups and cliques. A friendship choice between individuals is a link.

Social network data sets managed by NEGOPY are based on adolescents (or others) writing down the name of their best friend and then their other friends (typically prescribed to be in school or other specified setting). This forms the basis for the reciprocated friendship choices which NEGOPY uses to identify friendship groups and cliques.

NEGOPY assigns individuals to groups on the basis of the following criteria: (a) Each group member must have at least two links within a group. (b) The individual must have most (50 percent or more) of their links into the group, and (c) the group must stay intact even when 15 percent of the links are removed. NEGOPY groups have been verified by sociograms (Urberg, Degirmencioglu, & Pilgrim, 1997).

Developmental Adaptations for Assessing

Social Support and Social Networks

Social support has relevance across the lifespan and across cultures; it is a basic human need. Adaptations in measuring social support or networks have been made to accommodate linguistic differences across samples, the amount of time available to assess, variations in the local culture and sensitivities and variations in age and developmental status of respondent. In particular, the type of response format may need to be adapted. For example, Zelkowitz (1984) found that a preschool child could draw a distinction between people who "never" did something vs. people who did it "a lot," "sometimes," and "a little bit," but they could not reliability distinguish between "a lot" vs. sometimes vs. "a little bit." The use of frequency rating scales with preschoolers seems questionable. This reduced range of answers is also probably the foundation for why the reliability of children's interview data is typically lower than mothers.' The importance of pilot work of one's chosen wording for an assessment of social support and

social networks is invaluable in determining the unanticipated reactions/responses of respondents under study. As Grootaert et al. (2004) note, this also reminds us of the importance of training interviewers with care.

Often one chooses a measure with fewer distinctions required for the young and the elderly. For example, rather than use a 4-point scale, Aquino, Russell, Cutrona, & Altmaier (1996), in a study of the elderly, used a reduced "yes" – "no" format for the Social Provision Scale of Cutrona and Russell (1987). The reliability was affected by the simplification of the response format. Instead of an internal consistency of .92 found previously with the full response format (Cutrona, Russell, & Rose, 1986), the internal consistency was .71 for the simplified format (Aquino et al., 1996).

Because preschool children's ability to generate reliable data, mother report of the child's network has been considered. Mothers and children show good agreement about the number of friends from preschool to early school age (Feiring & Lewis, 1989; Zelkowitz, 1989; Feiring & Lewis, 1991a), but by middle childhood, mothers' reports underestimate the number of friends in the child's network (Feiring & Lewis, 1989; Feiring & Lewis, 1991b; Garbarino, Burston, Raber, Russell, & Crouter, 1978).

The categorization of social support and social network data is wide ranging. It may be a simple dichotomy according to size of network, such as "broad based" versus "limited" network. It may categorize social support by generation (e.g., Bryant, 1985; Feiring & Lewis, 1991a). The categorization might focus on the relevant aspects of a child's network of support for particular situations of needs for support. For example, who is available for support in low or ordinary daily kinds of stress conditions, typically of short duration (Bryant, 1985) versus who is available to support in high stress situations such as divorce (Wolchik, Sandler, & Ramsey, 1984) and recovering from an illness (Croog et al., 1972; Lee, 1979; Troll & Bengston, 1979). The kinds of high stress conditions may vary as well and the relevant social network (people with resources; support functions needed) may change accordingly.

Working cross-culturally with different languages can also be a challenge. For example, the French have more distinctions among "friends" than do Americans. While Americans use this one word to encompass all kinds of relations (friends from school, casual friends at work), the French emphatically distinguish between "pals/classmates," colleagues, and very emotionally close friends, having specific words to make these distinctions, and they find the distinctions rather important in everyday conversation. A team of researchers struggled to translate the terms "get along," "togetherness" and "fairness" in Nigeria (Grootaert et al., 2004). A translation back and forth by "blind" translators can be helpful in negotiating these matters, but there are times when no translation is available, and, therefore, irrelevant for a particular culture. It certainly complicates measurement issues in cross-cultural research. Distinctions among types of support or support providers appear to be quite important. There is evidence that a global approach to assessing social support may obscure important differences in the relationships between measures of social support and indices of well-being, especially among different ethnic, age, and gender groups (Cauce, 1982).

Personality may affect how people respond to questionnaires (Cutrona, 1989). In particular, various response styles can lead to an artifactual product of the measurement method. Examples of problematic response styles are: self-desirability, acquiescence, extreme response tendency, and deviant response tendency (Nunnally, 1987). Other personality factors such as self-esteem, need affiliation, extraversion, and locus of control (Sarason, Levine, Basham, & Sarason, 1983; Cutrona, 1989) may influence how an individual responds to questions. Individuals who are depressed tend to evaluate themselves and others more negatively than when they are not depressed (Alloy & Abramson, 1988; Beck, 1967). These factors warrant consideration when designing studies. When intrusive factors such as those described earlier cannot be accommodated, such factors may be used as covariates to help us understand the findings of a given study of social support, social networks, and/or social capital.

Summary

Methodological problems pertaining to assessment have historically suffered because of a lack of distinguishing between social network from social support and social support from support satisfaction. Social capital expands the notion of social network and social support. Social networks refer to individuals characterized by number, age, gender, and type of relationship (e.g., family members, friends, professionals). Social networks assess the range of social relationships available to an individual, but it does not refer to the depth or quality of these relationships. Social support refers to the giving or exchanging of something intended to help another, often called functions of support. This can be objectively coded by an observer or by the person who provided the support or it can by coded by the recipient of support. These variations may not be synonymous, and so the researcher needs to be clear as to who codes the social support. In addition to kinds (functions) of support, accessibility and frequency of such support can be measured. Also central to understanding development with respect to social network, social support, and social capital is the satisfaction of support, referring to the valence (positive or negative) of how support is experienced by the recipient of support.

Social support is always provided within a context of competing developmental requirements and various contexts in which the support is offered and received. Concepts of accessibility and frequency, subjective and objective perspective, relationship context, and support provider in relation to support receiver experience all add to the multidimensional nature of social support, network, and capital. A range of both quantitative and qualitative measures of social network, social support, and social capital are available. In addition, objective and subjective assessments as well as self- and other report approaches to measurement are choices. Special considerations are warranted when we consider the constraints of child cognitive capacities and the meaning given to social events across cultures. Furthermore, assessing social networks, social support, and social capital as it occurs in daily life appears critical both because people prefer it, but it also appears to be most effective (Werner & Smith, 1982). Measuring both benefits and costs attached to various forms of support will provide a more complete understanding of why support is offered and/or received and used. There is no "best" form of social support. Support goals, support provisions, and support costs can usefully be mapped in the study of the consequences of support given and received.

Acknowledgments

Funding for this chapter has come from USDA, Agriculture Experiment Station funds.

References

Alloy, L. B., & Abramson, L. Y. (1988).Depressive realism: Four theoretical perspectives. In L. B. Alloy (Ed.),*Cognitive processes in depression*, pp. 223–265. New York: Guilford Press.

Aquino, J. A., Russell, D. W., Cutrona, C. E., & Altmaier, E. M. (1996). Employment status, social support, and life satisfaction among the elderly. *Journal of Consulting Psychology*, 43, 480–489.

Barrera, J., Jr., Sandler, I. N., & Ramsay, T. B. (1981). Preliminary development of a scale of social support: Studies in college students. *American Journal of Community Psychology*, 9, 435–447.

Barrera, M (1980) A method for the assessment of social support networks in community survey research. Connections 3:8–13 as cited by Kaufman (1991) Depressive disorders in maltreated children. *Journal of the American Academy of child and Adolescent Psychiatry*, 30, 257–265.

Barrera, M. (1981). Social support in the adjustment of pregnant adolescents: Assessment issues. In B. H. Gottlieb (Ed.), *Social networks of social support*, pp. 69–96. Beverly Hills, CA: Sage Publications.

Barrera, M., & Ainlay, S. L. (1983). The structure of social support: A conceptual and empirical analysis. *Journal of Community Psychology*, 11, 133–143.

Beck, A. T. (1967). *Depression: Clinical, experimental, and theoretical aspects*. New York: Harper and Row.

Belle, D. (1982). Social ties and social support. In D. Belle (Ed.), *Lives in stress: Women and depression*, pp.89–103. Beverly Hills, CA: Sage.

Belle, D. (1983). The impact of poverty on social networks and supports. *Marriage and Family Review*, 5, 89–103.

Belle, D., & Longfellow, C. (April 1983). Emotional support and children's well-being: An exploratory study of children's confidants. Paper presented at the biennial meeting of the Society for Research in Child Development, Detroit.

Blythe, D. (1982). Mapping the social world of adolescents: Issues, techniques, and problems. In F. Serafica (Ed.), *Social cognition, context, and social behavior: A developmental perspective*. New York: Guilford Press.

Bryant, B. K. (1982). Sibling relationships in middle childhood. In M. Lamb & B. Sutton-Smith (Eds.), *Sibling relationships: Their nature and significance across the lifespan*. Hillsdale, NJ: Lawrence Erlbaum Associates, Inc.

Bryant, B. K. (1985). The neighborhood walk: Sources of support in middle childhood: With commentary by Ross D. Parke. *Monographs of the Society for Research in Child Development*, 50(3), Serial No. 210.

Bryant, B. K., & Crockenberg, S. (1980).Correlates and dimensions of prosocial behavior: A study of female siblings with their mothers. *Child Development*, 51, 529–544.

Bryant, B. K., & Donnellan, B. (2007). The relation between socio-economic status concerns and angry peer conflict resolution is moderated by pet provisions of support. *Anthrozoos*, 20, 213–223.

Bryant, B. K., Zvonkovic, A. M., & Reynolds, P. (2006). Parenting in relation to child and adolescent vocational development. *Journal of Vocational Behavior*, 69, 149–175.

Cauce, A. (1982). Social support in high-risk adolescents: Structural components and adaptive impact. *American Journal of Community Psychology*, 10, 417–428.

Cochran, M., & Brassard, J. (1979). Child development and personal social networks. *Child Development*, 50, 601–616.

Cohen, S., & Hoberman, H. (1983). Positive events and social support as buffers of life change stress. *Journal of Applied Social Psychology*, 13, 99–125.

Coleman, J. S. (1988). Social capital in the creation of human capital. *American Journal of Sociology*, 94, 95–120.

Coletta, N. D., & Gregg, C. H. (1981). Adolescent mothers vulnerability to stress. *Journal of Nervous and Mental Disease*, 169, 50–54.

Coyne, J. C., Ellard, J. H., & Smith, D. A. F. (1990). Social support, interdependence and the dilemmas of helping. In B. R. Sarason, I. G., Sarason, and G. R. Pierce (Eds.), *Social support: An interactional view*, pp. 129–149. New York: Wiley.

Coyne, J. C., Wortman, C. B., & Lehman, D. R. (1988). The other side of support. In *Marshalling social support: Formats, processes, and effects*, pp. 305–330. Newbury Park, CA: Sage.

Croog, S. Lipson, A., & Levile, S. (1972). Help patterns in severe illness: The role of kin network, nonfamily resources and institutions. *Journal of Marriage and the Family*, 34, 32–41.

Cummings, J. N., & Higgins, M. C. (2006). Relational instability at the network core: Support dynamics in developmental networks. *Social Networks*, 28, 38–55.

Cutrona, C. E. (1982). Transition to college: Loneliness and the process of social adjustment. In L. A. Peplau & D. Perlman (Eds.), *Loneliness: A sourcebook of current research, theory, and therapy*, pp. 291–309. New York: Wiley Interscience.

Cutrona, C. E. (1984). Social support in the transition to parenthood. *Journal of Abnormal Psychology*, 93, 378–390.

Cutrona, C. E. (1986). Behavioral manifestations of social support: A microanalytic investigation. *Journal of Personality and Social Psychology*, 51, 201–208.

Cutrona, C. E. (1989). Ratings of social support by adolescents and adult informants: Degree of correspondence and prediction of depressive symptoms. *Journal of Personality and Social Psychology*, 57, 723–730.

Cutrona, C. E., & Cole, V. (2000). Optimizing support in the natural network. In S. Cohen, L. G. Underwood, B. H. Gottlieb (Eds.), *Social support measurement and intervention: A guide for health and social scientists*, pp. 278–308. New York: Oxford University Press.

Cutrona, C. E., & Cole, V., Colangelo, N., Assouline, S. G., & Russell, D. W. (1994). *Journal of Personality and Social Psychology*, 66, 369–378.

Cutrona, C. E., Russell, D. W. (1987). The provisions of social relationships and adaptation to stress. *Advances in personal relationships*, pp. 37–67, Vol. 1. Greenwich, CT: JAI Press.

Cutrona, C. E., Shaffer, P. A., Wesner, K. A., & Gardner, K. A. (2007). Optimally matching support and perceived spousal sensitivity. *Journal of Family Psychology*, 21, 754–758.

Cutrona, C. E., & Suhr, J. A. (1992) Controllability of stressful events and satisfaction with spouse support behaviors. *Communication Research*, 19, 154–174.

Cutrona, C. E., Suhr, J. A., & MacFarlane, R. (1990). Interpersonal transactions and the psychological sense of support. In S. Duck & R. C. Silver (Eds.), *Personal relationships and social support*, pp. 30–45. Newbury Park, CA: Sage.

Cutrona, C. E., & Troutman, B. R. (1986). Social support, infant temperament, and parenting self-efficacy: A mediational model of postpartum depression. *Child Development*, 57, 1507–1518.

Dakof, G. A., & Taylor, S. E. (1990). Perceptions of social support: What is helpful from whom. *Journal of Personality and Social Psychology*, 58, 80–89.

Davidson, l. M., & Demaray, M. K. (2007). Social support as a moderator between victimization and internalizing-externalizing distress from bullying. *School Psychology Review*, 36, 383–405.

Dressler, W. W. (1985). Extended family relationships, social support and mental health in a southern black community. *Journal of Health and Social Behavior*, 26, 39–49.

Earls, F., & Carlson, M. (2001). The social ecology of child health and well-being. *Annual Review of Public Health*, 22, 143–166.

Feiring, C., Fox, N. Jaskir, J., & Lewis, M. (1987). The relation between social support, infant risk assessment, and mother-infant interaction. *Developmental Psychology*, 23, 400–405.

Feiring, C., & Lewis, M. (1989). The social networks of girls and boys from early through middle childhood. In D. Belle (Ed.), *Children's social networks and social supports*, pp. 119–150. New York: John Wiley & Sons.

Feiring, C., & Lewis, M. (1991a). The transition from middle childhood to early adolescence: Sex differences in the social network and perceived self-competence. *Sex roles*, 24, 489–509.

Feiring, C., & Lewis, M. (1991b). The development of social networks from early to middle childhood: Gender differences and the relation to school competence. *Sex Roles, 25*(3–4), 237–253.

Feiring, C., Taska, L. S., Lewis, M. (1998). Social support and children's and adolescents' adaptation to sexual abuse. *Journal of Interpersonal Violence, 13*(2), 240–260.

Fekete, E., M. Stephens, M. A. P. Druley, J. A., & Greene, K. A. (2006). Effects of spousal control and support on older adults' recovery from knee surgery. *Journal of Family Psychology, 20,* 302–310.

Franks, M. M., Stephens, M. A. P., Rook, K. S., Frankin, B. A., Keteyian, S. J., & Artinan, N. T. (2006). Spouses' provision of health-related support and control to patients participating in cardiac rehabilitation, *Journal of Family Psychology, 20,* 311–318.

Furman, W., & Buhrmester, D. (1985). Children's perceptions of the personal relationships in their social networks. *Developmental Psychology, 20,* 277–290.

Furman, W., & Buhrmester, D. (1992). Age and sex differences in perceptions of networks of personal relationships, *Developmental Psychology, 21,* 103–115.

Gallant, M. P., Spitze, G. D., & Prohaska T. R. (2007). Help or hindrance? How family and friends influence chronic illness self-management among older adults. *Research in Aging, 29,* 375–409.

Garbarino, Burston, Raber, Russell, & Crouter (1978). The social maps of children approaching adolescence: Studying the ecology of youth development. *Journal of Youth and Adolescence 7,* 417–428

Genia, V. (1997). Spiritual Experience Index: Revision and reformulation. *Review of Religious Research, 38,* 344–361.

Green, B. L., Furrer, C., & McAllister, C. (2007). How do relationships support parenting? Effects of attachment style and social support on parenting behavior in an at-risk population. *American Journal of Community Psychology, 40,* 96–108.

Grootaert, C., Narayan, D., Jones, V. N., & Woolcock, M. (2004). *Measuring social capital: An integrated questionnaire.* Washington, DC: World Bank.

Harter, S. (1985). Manual for the Social Support Scale for Children. Denver: University of Denver. Cited in Davidson, L. M. & Demaray, M. K. (2007). Social Support as a moderator

between victimization and internalizing-externalizing distress from bullying. *School Psychology Review, 36,* 383–405.

Hirsch, B. J., & Reischl, T. M. (1985). Social networks and developmental psychopathology: A comparison of adolescent children of depressed, arthritic or normal parents. *Journal of Abnormal Psychology, 94,* 272–281.

Jensen, S. L. (2001). Development of a scale to code the elicitation of social support. Unpublished doctoral dissertation, Iowa State University, Ames, Iowa, Cited by Cutrona, C. E., Shaffer, P. A., Wesner, K. A., & Gardner, K. A. (2007). Optimally matching support and perceived spousal sensitivity. *Journal of Family Psychology, 21,* 754–758.

Kaufman, J. (1991). Depressive disorders in maltreated children. *Journal of the American Academy of Child and Adolescent Psychiatry, 30,* 257–265.

Kaufman, J., Yang, B. Douuglas-Palumberi, H., Crouse-Artus, M., Lipschitz, D., Krystal, J. H., & Gelenter, J. (2006). Genetic and environmental predictors of early alcohol use. *Biological Psychiatry, 59,* 673–680.

Kellam, S. G., Adams, R. G., Brown, C. H., & Ensminger, M. A. (1982). The long-term evolution of the family structure of teenage and older mothers. *Journal of Marriage and the Family, 46,* 539–554.

King, C. A., Kramer, A., Preuss, L., Kerr, D. C. R., Weisse, L., & Venkataraman, S. (2006). Youth-Nominated Support Team for suicidal adolescents (Version 1): A randomized controlled trial. *Journal of Consulting and Clinical Psychology, 74*(1), 199–206.

Krebs, K. K. (2000). Comparison of macro and micro observational methods for measuring marital social support. Unpublished doctoral dissertation. Iowa State University: Ames, Iowa. Cited by Cutrona, C. E., Shaffer, P. A., Wesner, K. A., & Gardner, K. A. (2007). Optimally matching support and perceived spousal sensitivity. *Journal of Family Psychology, 21,* 754–758.

Lee, G. R. (1979). Effects of social networks on the family. In W. R. Burr, A., Hill, F. I. Nye, & L. L. Reiss (Eds.), *Contemporary theories about the family,* pp. 27–66, Vol. 1. New York: Free Press.

Lewis, M (1982). The social network systems model: Toward a theory of social development. In T. Field (Ed.), *Review in human development.* New York: John Wiley.

Lewis, M., & Feiring, C. (1978). The child's social world. In R. M. Lerner and G. B. Spanier

(Eds.), *Child influences on marital and family interaction: A life-span perspective.* New York: Plenum.

Lewis, M., & Feiring, C. (1979). The child's social network: Social object, social functions, and their relationships. In M. Lewis and L. A. Rosenblum (Ed.), *The child and its family*, pp. 21–48. New York: Plenum.

Lewis, M. A., & Rook, K. S. (1999). Social control in personal relationships: Impact on health behaviors and psychological distress. *Health Psychology, 18,* 63–71.

Major, B., Zubek, J. M., Cooper, M. L., Zubek, C., Cooper, M. L., Cozzarelli, C., & Richards, C. (1997). Mixed messages: Implications of social conflict and social support within close relationships for adjustment to a stressful life even. *Journal of Social and Personality Psychology, 72,* 1349–1363.

Malecki, C. K., & Demaray, M. K. (2002). Measuring perceived social support: Development of the child and adolescent social support scale (CASS). *Psychology in the Schools, 39,* 1–18.

Moos, Rudolph (2008). Social Climate Scales. http://www.mindgarden.com/products/scsug.htm (Accessed September 24, 2008).

Moos, R., & Moos, B. (1978). Classroom social climate and student absences and grades. *Journal of Educational Psychology, 70,* 263–269.

Morgan, D. (1996). Focus groups. *Annual Review of Sociology. 22,* 129–52.

Murphy, L. (1974). Coping, vulnerability, and resilience in childhood. In G. V. Coelho, D. A. Hamburg, & J. E. Adams (Eds.), *Coping and adaptation*, pp. 69–100. New York: Basic Books.

Nunnally, J. C. (1978). *Psychometric theory* (2nd ed). New York: McGraw-Hill.

Parke, R. D. (2004). Development in the family. *Annual Review of Psychology, 55,* 365–99.

Proshansky, H. M., Ittelson, W. H., & Rivlin, L. G. (1972). Freedom of choice and behavior in a physical setting. In J. F. Wohlwill & D. H. Carson (Eds.), *Environment and the social sciences: Perspectives and applications.* Washington, DC: American Psychological Association.

Reid, M., Landesman, S., Treder, R., & Jaccard, J. (1989). "My family and friends": Six- to twelve-year-old children's perceptions of social support. *Child Development, 60,* 896–910.

Reis, H. T., & Shaver, P. (1988). Intimacy as an interpersonal process. In S. W. Duck (Ed.), *Handbook of personal relationships*, pp. 367–389. Chichester, UK: Wiley.

Richards, W. D., & Rice, R. E. (1981). The NEGOPY network analysis program. *Social Networks, 3,* 215–223.

Rook, K. S., Thuras, P. D., & Lewis, M. A. (1990). Social control, health risk taking, and psychological distress among the elderly, *Psychology and Aging, 5,* 327–334.

Russell, D. W., Altmaier, E., & Van Velzen, D. (1987). Job related stress, social support, and burnout among classroom teachers. *Journal of Applied Psychology, 72,* 269–274.

Russell, D. W., & Cutrona, C. E. (August 1984). The provisions of social relationships and adaptation to stress. Paper presented at the annual meeting of the American Psychological Association, Toronto; cited in Aquino, J. A., Russell, D. W., Cutrona, C. E., & Altmaier, E. M. (1996). Employment status, social support, and life satisfaction among the elderly. *Journal of Consulting Psychology, 43,* 480–489.

Russell, D. W., & Cutrona, C. E. (1985). The Social Provisions Scale: A qualitative measure of facets of social support. Unpublished manuscript. Cited by Cummins, R. C. (1988). Perceptions of social support, receipt of supportive behaviors, and locus of control as moderators of the effects of chronic stress. *American Journal of Community Psychology, 16,* 685–700.

Sandler, I. N. (1980). Social support resources, stress and maladjustment of poor children. *American Journal of Community Psychology, 8,* 41–52.)

Sandler, I. N., & Barrera, M. (1984). Toward a multimethod approach to assessing the effects of social support. *American Journal of Community Psychology, 12,* 37–52.

Sarason, I. G. Levine, H. M., Basham, R. B., & Sarason, B. R. (1983). Assessing social support: The social supportquestionnaire. *Journal of Personality and Social Psychology, 44,* 127–139.

Saunders, E. B. (1977). The Nurturance Scale. Unpublished report, Stress and Families Project, Harvard University. Cited by Wolchik, S. A., Beals, J., & Sandler, I. N. Mapping children's support networks: Conceptual and methodological Issues. In D. Belle (Ed.) (1989). *Children's social networks and social supports*, pp. 191–220. New York: John Wiley & Sons.

Stephens, M. A. P., & Clark, S. L. (1997). Reciprocity in the expression of emotional support among later-life couples coping with stroke. In B. Gottlieb (Ed.), *Coping with chronic stress*, pp. 221–242. The Plenum series on stress and coping. New York: Plenum Press.

Suhr, J. A., Cutrona, C. E., Krebs, K. K., & Jensen, S. L. (2004). The Social Support Behavior Code. In P. K Kerig & D. Baucom (Eds.), Couple observational coding systems, pp. 311–318. Mahwah, NJ: Erlbaum.

Taylor, R. D., Casten, R., & Flickinger, S. M. (1993). Influence of kinship social support on the parenting experiences and psychosocial adjustment of African-American adolescents. *Developmental Psychology, 29*, 382–388.

Taylor, R. D., & Roberts (1995) Kinship support and adolescent well-being in economically disadvantaged African-American families. *Child Development, 66*, 1585–1597.

Taylor, S. E., Welch, W. T., Kim, H. S., & Sherman, D. K. (2007). Cultural differences in the impact of social support on psychological and biological stress responses. *Psychological Science, 18*, 831–837.

Tietjen, A. M. (1980). Integrating formal and informal support systems: The Swedish experience. In J. Garbarino, S. H. Stocking, and associates, *Protecting children from abuse and neglect: Developing and maintaining effective support systems for families*. San Francisco: Jossey-Bass.

Trickett, E. J., & Moos, R. H. (1973). Social environment of junior high and high school classrooms, *Journal of Educational Psychology, 65*, 93–103.

Trickett, T. L., & Bengston, V. (1979). Generations in the family. In W. R. Burr, R. Hill, F. I. Nye, & I. L. Reiss (Eds.), *Contemporary theories about the family*: Vol. 1. *Research-based theories*, pp. 127–161. New York: Free Press.

Unger, D. G., & Powell, D. R. (1980). Supporting families under stress: The role of social networks. *Family Relations, 29*, 566–574.

Urberg, K. A., Degirmencioglu, S. M., & Pilgrim C. (1997). *Developmental Psychology, 33*, 834–844.

Vinokur, A., & Vinokur-Kaplan, D. (1990). "In sickness and in health:" Patterns of support and undermining in older married couples. *Journal of Aging and Health, 2*, 215–241.

Wahler, R. (1980). The insular mother: Her problems in parent-child treatment. *Journal of Applied Behavior Analysis, 13*, 207–219.

Weiss, R. (1974). The provisions of social relationships. In Z. Rubin (Ed.), *Doing unto others*, pp. 17–26. Englewood Cliffs, NJ: Prentice-Hall.

Werner, E. E. (1982). *Vulnerable but invincible: A longitudinal study of resilient children and youth*. New York: McGraw-Hill.

Westin, A. F. (1967). *Privacy and freedom*. New York: Atheneum.

Wolchik, S. A., Beals, J., & Sandler, I. N. (1989). Mapping children's support networks: Conceptual and methodological Issues. In D. Belle (Ed.), *Children's social networks and social supports*, pp. 191–220. New York: John Wiley & Sons.

Wolchik, S. A., Sandler, I. N., & Braver, S. (August 1984). The social support networks of children of divorce. Poster presented at the annual meeting of the American Psychological Association, Toronto.

Wolchik, S. A., Sandler, I. N., & Braver, S. L. (1987). Social support: Its assessment and relations to children's adjustment. In N. Eisenberg (Ed.), *Contemporary topics in developmental psychology*, pp. 319–349. New York: Wiley.

Zelkowitz, P. (1984). Comparing maternal and child reports of children's social networks. Poster presented at the annual meeting of the American Psychological Association, Toronto.

Zelkowitz, P. (1989). Parents and children as informants concerning children's social networks. In D. Belle (Ed.), *Children's social networks and social supports*, pp. 221–237. Oxford, UK: John Wiley & Sons.

Appendix A: Summary of Support Measures

Reference	Measure	Informant	Length	What Measured
Gallant, Spitze, & Prohaska (2007)	**Focus Group Method**	Variable – all but the very young; need metacognitive ability; responses to questions that vary with the study	Variable	Variable – can be individualized
Cutrona & Russell (1987)	**Social Provisions Scale: Paper-and-Pencil**	Self-report	22 items 6 subscales	Six kinds of social provisions
Cutrona (1989); Cutrona & Russell (1987); Cutrona et al. (1994)	**Social Provisions Scale – Parent Version**	Parent	12 items	Presence and absence of six provisions in the parent-child relationship
Cutrona (1986)	**Social Contact Record**	Self-report; diary method; note interactions	Variable; not predetermined	Number of interactions; relationship to self; help- vs. no-help-oriented support; rated pleasantness and change of mood in interaction
Cutrona, Suhr, & MacFarlane (1990); Jensen (2001)	**Social Support Elicitation Behavior Code**	Objective, trained observer	10-minute interaction task	Codes the support seeker behavior: "Requests information" and "describes emotions" subscales
Suhr, Cutrona, Krebs, & Jensen (2004); Krebs (2000)	**Social Support Behavior Code**	Objective, trained observer	Length of Interaction task	26 specific behaviors, collapsed into 4 subscales: Information support; Esteem support; Caring support; Negative behavior (Note: Esteem support + Caring support = Emotional Support)
Cutrona et al. (2007); Krebs (2000)	**Partner Sensitive Responsivity Scale**	Self-report of individual participants in earlier 10-minute interaction	5-item questionnaire after 10-minute interaction	After interaction, 5 items rated: Components of interactions that lead to intimacy: validation, understanding, and caring
Furman & Buhrmester (1985)	**Network of Relationships Inventory**	Children (originally for 5th and 6th graders); self-report; paper-and-pencil	108 questions; 5-point Likert scale	Assessed separately, nine relationships on 6 provisions of support (affection, intimacy, reliable alliance, enhancement of worth, companionship, and instrumental help) and importance of each specific kind of support for each of the nine relationships assessed

(continued)

Appendix A *continued*

Reference	Measure	Informant	Length	What Measured
Grootaert et al. (2004)	**Integrated Question-naire Mea-sure of Social Capital**	Self-report for family; paper-and-pencil or interview format	Short form = 26 items Long form = 95 items	Assesses social capital of fami-lies; six dimensions of social capital assessed: groups and networks, trust and solidarity, collective action and cooper-ation, information and com-munication, social cohesion and inclusion, empowerment and political action
Barrera (1980; 1981; Bar-rera & Ain-lay, 1983)	**Arizona Social Support Inventory**	Self-report; adult structured inter-view referring to past month experiences	Length of interview depends on size of interview-ee's social network	Identifies significant ties to others with respect to six kinds of support (talk about private feelings; material aid; advice and informa-tion; positive feedback; physical assistance; social participation; conflicted and nonconflicted support net-works; perceptions of being supported, frequency of support; content of support; network size)
Wolchik, Sandler, & Braver (1984)	**Children's Inventory of Social Support**	Self-report; struc-tured interview with ranking ratings using a barometer scale to indicate level of support figures	Approxi-mately 30 minutes	Characterizes number of sup-porters within each func-tion of support, network size, multiplexity of each relationship (i.e., number of relationships that provided more than one support function, satisfaction of each support provider, con-flicted network size, emo-tional support, information support, instrumental sup-port, and companionship)
Kaufman (1991)	**Arizona Social Support Inventory adapted for school-aged children**	Self-report; struc-tured interview; Adaptation of Barrera (1980) with language and focus com-fortable for school-aged children	Length of interview depends on size of interview-ee's social network	Five scores then derived from the ASSIS inter-view: (1) Total Support, (2) Negative Relationships, (3) Conflictual Relationships, (4) Perceived Affection from Supporters, and (5) Reported Affection for Supporters
Reid et al. (1989)	**"My Family and Friends"**	Structured inter-view, self-report, open-ended plus ranking and ratings (using a barometer scale)	About 20 minutes	Four major domains of sup-port considered: emotional support, information sup-port, instrumental sup-port, and companionship; scoring derived separately for mother, father, sibling(s), friends, other relatives, and teachers

Reference	Measure	Informant	Length	What Measured
Feiring et al. (1987)	**Network Interview**	For use with mothers of young children; structured interview; focuses on experiences of the past 3 months	Varies according to size of support network	Focuses on kinds of stresses and concomitant support that mothers of young infants experience; four categories of support: goods, services, money, and advice
Feiring & Lewis (1989)	**Social Support Matrix**	Provides a template that individual researchers can use and tailor to their interests (e.g., support needed varies with age of one's child); adult report	Length varies according to social functions researcher is studying and the size of social network of interviewee	Results with list of social network members available, what functions being satisfied, and which support functions are fulfilled by which social network members; over time, can measure the changes in size of network and consistency over time in network membership in multiple functions; index of sense of belonging and security
Bryant (1985)	**Neighborhood Walk**	Structured interview; child self-report	Variable, but generally about 45 minutes	Appraises how children differ in their access to and interaction with intrapersonal sources of support (e.g., hobbies), others as resources (e.g., person in various generations), and environmental sources of support (e.g., places to join others and places to go to be alone; formal and informal sources of support; casual and intimate kinds of interactions
Malecki & Demaray (2002); Davidson & Demaray (2007)	**Child and Adolescent Social Support Scale**	Self-report; paper-and-pencil	60 questions; 6-point Likert scale and 3-point Likert scale	Five key sources of support considered (i.e., parents, teachers, classmates, close friends, school); 4 types of support (i.e., emotional, appraisal, instrumental, and informational); quantifies frequency of support and importance of support
Taylor, Casten,& Flickinger (1993)	**Adult Kinship Relations Measure**	Adolescent reports adult kinship support; structured interview	Identify adult kin; then 13 questions using 4-point rating scale	Two parts to interview: (1) grandparent, aunts, or other adult relative are names; (2) questions about frequency of contact with adult kin the number of adult kin, frequency of contact with adult kin, number of adult kin living within hour of adolescent's home; degree

(continued)

Appendix A *continued*

Reference	Measure	Informant	Length	What Measured
				of endorsement of social support received; forms of support studied were (a) advice and counseling, (b) socialization and entertainment, (c) problem solving
King, Kramer, Preuss, Kerr, Weisse, & Venkatkaraman (2006)	**Youth Nominated Support Team**	Adolescent receives either open-ended interview or paper-and-pencil format	Variable according to who they thought provided support in daily life contexts;	Interview yielded a list of support persons, four of whom were invited to participate in therapeutic intervention
Moos (2008)	**Social Climate Scales**	Self-report from individuals in a given context and then aggregate analyses by context		**Community Environment Scale** with support subscale; **Family Environment Scale** with cohesion and conflict subscales; **Group Environment Scale** with cohesion and leadership support subscales;
e.g., Trickett & Moos (1973); Moos & Moos (1978)		Individual report; paper-and-pencil; junior and senior high school students	90 items	**Work Environment Scale** with coworker cohesion, supervisor support, and autonomy subscales
				Classroom Environment Scale with support subscale

CHAPTER 31

Stress Reactivity in Child Development Research

Indices, Correlates, and Future Directions

Jelena Obradović and W. Thomas Boyce

A handbook on strategies for measuring salient dimensions of developmental environments would be decidedly incomplete without a consideration of childhood stress and children's biobehavioral responses to the challenges and misfortunes occurring within social environments. North American children and those of other industrialized nations are no strangers to stress and adversity, and children and youth in developing countries contend with a vast range of added threats to health, well-being and survival, beyond the normative challenges and stressors of a child's everyday life. Even a brief consideration of such challenges is sufficient to remind us that, while childhood remains a time of innocence and protection, it is also, for many children, a time of deep exigency and disappointing realities. More than 13 million children in the United States – more than one in six – live in conditions of poverty (Children's Defense Fund, 2008), and more than 12 million live in homes where reliable access to food is limited or uncertain (Cook & Frank, 2008). Beyond such fundamental threats to survival and development, more than 900,000

U.S. children are abused or neglected each year, and more than 500,000 are placed in foster care (Children's Defense Fund, 2008). Approximately one in eleven infants have mothers with major depression during the infant's first year of life, and among disadvantaged populations, as many as 50 percent of mothers with young children are clinically depressed (Center on the Developing Child at Harvard University, 2009). Approximately half of North American children see their parents' marriages end in divorce, an event that results in 30–40 percent of parents developing significant depressive symptoms and creates substantive psychological hardships and mental health problems among affected children, as well (U.S. Surgeon General's Office, 1999).

At the more global level (UNICEF, 2009), one billion children worldwide live on less than $2 per day, and more children are living in poverty today than were 10 years ago. As many as a million children are forced or lured into prostitution each year. More than 500 million children live in contexts of family, community or national violence, and an estimated 300,000 children under 18 have fought in war and other armed conflicts (Lustig et al., 2004). Approximately half of the world's 20 million refugees are children, and more than 121 million children are not attending school, of which 60 percent are girls. Taken together, these markers of stress, adversity and missed opportunity indicate that large numbers of children in today's world, endure early lives replete with poverty, unmet needs, parental dysfunction, and exposures to discord and violence.

Against this backdrop of troubled childhoods and early adversities, researchers have emphasized the importance of studying the stressors inherent within developmental contexts and addressing children's responses to such stressors across multiple levels of analysis, from the cell to the society (Keating & Hertzman, 1999). Stress reactivity has emerged as an important area of research, as it allows us to examine how early environmental experiences "get under the skin" and shape future development (Hertzman, 1999). Recent studies made possible by advances in the assessment of neurobiological responses to diverse challenges and stressors have revealed associations between various indices of stress reactivity and adaptive functioning. However, more research is needed to better understand how stress reactivity interacts with environmental factors to influence positive and negative domains of adaptation across various developmental periods. In reviewing the current state of literature and suggesting new avenues of stress reactivity research, we hope to stimulate a new generation of studies that examines the role that stress reactivity plays in children's development in more nuanced and dynamic ways.

This chapter is organized in two sections. In the first section, we describe the indices of stress response most frequently examined in children, and we review known developmental correlates of these stress reactivity measures as well as important methodological considerations. In the second section, we examine existing research pitfalls, identify new work occupying the advancing "edge" of this field, and suggest potential future directions.

Indices of Stress Response and Their Developmental Correlates

There are numerous ways of assessing children's biological responses to stress, as there are many, complex neurobiological systems involved. We focus our review on the noninvasive and relatively inexpensive indices of stress response that are most commonly used in developmental and epidemiological field research. While we highlight general methodological considerations associated with each approach, comprehensive guidelines for individual measures are beyond the scope of the chapter. We urge researchers interested in applying these indices to see the references provided for a more detailed description of methods and instrumentation.

Autonomic Nervous System

Environmental threats to an individual's well-being trigger a highly integrated cascade of biological responses within brain circuitry and peripheral neuroendocrine pathways. The initial set of stress responses, known collectively as the "fight-or-flight" response, activates the autonomic nervous system (ANS). The ANS initiates a series of quick biobehavioral changes, increasing heart rate, diverting blood flow from the skin and stomach to the muscles and brain, stimulating production of glucose, dilating pupils, raising cardiac output, and launching a variety of other preparatory physiologic processes. The ANS consists of two branches: the sympathetic nervous system (SNS), which initiates physiological arousal, and the parasympathetic nervous system (PNS), which modulates SNS input to the heart and other target organs, regulating recovery and restoring autonomic homeostasis. For a more detailed description of ANS responses to stress, the reader should consult the work of Cacioppo, Berntson, and Porges (e.g., Berntson, Cacioppo, & Quigley, 1994; Berntson, Quigley, & Lozano, 2007; Cacioppo et al., 1998; Porges, 2007).

Two general approaches have been employed in measuring ANS reactivity in response to challenging or stressful tasks. The first approach uses a change score (Δ), created by subtracting a basal ANS value from the ANS value during the challenge task, or a standardized residual score, created by regressing ANS values during the challenge task on basal ANS values. The second, more novel approach uses multiple measures of ANS reactivity during the challenge task to derive a more dynamic measure of stress reactivity, which can also reveal how effectively the child regulates the initial stress response.

Basal ANS activity levels are generally measured while children are relaxed and resting. Because young children often find it difficult to be physically still, researchers sometimes utilize the reading of a calming story as a means of inducing a state of quiet restfulness. However, recently, some researchers have emphasized the importance of isolating psychological responses to the experimental stressor and controlling for peripheral triggers of cardiovascular activation, such as muscle movement (Bush, Alkon, Obradović, Stamperdahl, & Boyce, 2011; Kamarck & Lovallo, 2003). As both SNS and PNS can be activated by simple psychomotor activities, such as speaking, focused attending, and nonchallenging social engagement (Porges et al., 2007; Tomaka, Blascovich & Swart, 1994), researchers have begun to assess baseline ANS activity levels during specific control tasks that are designed to parallel the motor and engagement demands of the challenge task without the challenge or stressful component (e.g., Obradović, Bush, Stamperdahl, Adler, & Boyce, 2010).

A majority of studies examine ANS reactivity to a particular task, such as watching an emotion-inducing video or completing a cognitive task. However, other studies employ a series of tasks that assess reactivity across different types of stimuli. For example, Boyce and colleagues have designed a stress reactivity protocol that includes social, cognitive, sensory, and emotional tasks designed to approximate normative challenges that children may encounter in their everyday environment. Stress responses are then averaged across multiple tasks to produce an overall index of ANS reactivity (Alkon et al., 2003; Boyce et al., 2001; Obradović et al., 2010).

Sympathetic Nervous System

Skin Conductance Level. Skin conductance level (SCL), also known as electrodermal activity or galvanic skin response, is an index of electrical skin conductance, often expressed in microSiemens (μS). Skin conductance varies with the levels of sweat in sweat gland ducts, which when elevated cause skin to be less resistant and more conductive (Dawson, Schell, & Filion, 2007). Since postganglionic sympathetic neurons form cholinergic synapses with eccrine sweat glands, the levels of sweat in sweat ducts across various glands can be used to measure peripheral SNS activity (Dawson et al., 2007). SCL has been found to vary with demographic variables, such as age, gender, and ethnicity, as well as with the nature of stimuli, the season, the time of the day, and the type of measurement (Boucsein, 1992; Venables & Mitchell, 1996). Washing hands decreases skin conductance, so participants should wash their hands prior to SCL measurement in order to standardize the time since the last hand-washing. Abrasive soaps and alcohol should be avoided, as they further alter conductive skin properties (Venables & Christie, 1980). Changes from baseline SCL in response to stressful or challenging tasks indicate SCL reactivity, which is a measure of sympathetic response to such tasks. Changes in SCL can be assessed in response to both discrete and continuous stimuli, beginning 1 to 3 seconds after the stimuli presentation (Dawson et al., 2007). Both baseline SCL and SCL reactivity to a cognitive challenge have demonstrated moderate, 2-year stability across childhood (El-Sheikh, 2007).

Some researchers have argued that the electrodermal response reflects individual differences in the behavioral inhibition system (BIS) and passive avoidance tendencies, as SCL increases under the threat of punishment, but is unaffected by reward

(Beauchaine, 2001; Fowles, Kochanska, & Murray, 2000; Shannon, Beauchaine, Brenner, Neuhaus, Gatzke- Kopp, 2007). Accordingly, SCL can be conceptualized as a biological marker of state and trait anxiety. Indeed, high SCL reactivity in response to stressful or challenging laboratory tasks has been linked to higher levels of internalizing problems in children, such as behavioral inhibition (Scarpa, Raine, Venables, & Mednick, 1997), anxiety (Weems, Zakem, Costa, Cannon, & Watts, 2005), and fearfulness (Fowles et al., 2000).

In contrast, children and adolescents prone to externalizing behavioral problems tend to show diminished SCL reactivity (Crowell et al., 2006; Gatzke-Kopp et al., 2002). A recent meta-analysis confirms that both low basal SCL and low SCL reactivity to negatively charged stimuli are related to conduct problems in children (Lorber, 2004). In addition, reduced baseline SCL and SCL reactivity have been observed in preschoolers and adolescents with attention-deficit/hyperactivity disorder (Beauchaine, Katkin, Strassberg, & Snarr, 2001; Crowell et al., 2006), suggesting that attenuated SCL may also mark impulsivity and disinhibition. Given the opposite relations between SCL reactivity and internalizing and externalizing behavior problems, it is important that researchers take into account comorbid symptoms when studying SCL as a biological marker of developmental psychopathology. For example, Crowell and colleagues (2005) found no differences in SCL between parasuicidal adolescent girls and age-matched controls. However, the study also found that parasuicidal girls showed higher levels of both internalizing and externalizing symptoms, and some girls reported violent self-injurious behavior, which may have confounded results.

Although low SCL and low SCL reactivity have been robustly linked to psychopathy in adults, Lorber (2004) found this relation to be less clear in children and adolescents. However, a recent study by Fung and colleagues (2005) revealed a similar pattern of low SCL reactivity in adolescent boys with psychopathic tendencies.

As a majority of the studies examining SCL correlates of externalizing symptoms have been conducted with older boys, it remains to be determined whether underarousal of the SNS as indexed by low SCL presents a risk factor for antisocial and callous-unemotional behavior in girls and younger children. Furthermore, a recent study examining SCL reactivity in response to losing a game as a result of peer cheating further illustrates the complexity of the association between SCL reactivity and categories of aggressive behavior (Hubbard et al., 2002). A higher trajectory of SCL reactivity across the entire game was associated with reactive aggression but not with proactive aggression. Children high in reactive aggression showed the lowest levels of SCL at the beginning of the game but had the steepest increase in SCL during the game, underscoring the importance of obtaining multiple measures of reactivity and capturing variability in individuals' response trajectories.

A few studies have demonstrated that the relation between SCL reactivity and adjustment may vary across different levels of adversity exposure. Children who demonstrate higher levels of SCL reactivity to emotional or cognitive stressors tend to be more susceptible to various adverse experiences in their lives. For example, children who exhibited high SCL reactivity had higher levels of behavioral, social, and cognitive problems than their low reactive peers, but only in contexts of high family adversity, such as paternal depression and marital conflict (Cummings, El-Sheikh, Kouros, & Keller, 2007; El-Sheikh, Keller, & Erath, 2007). However, the underlying processes also seem to vary by gender.

Pre-ejection Period. Cardiac pre-ejection period (PEP) is the period of isovolumetric contraction, indexed by the time in millisecond (ms) from left ventricular depolarization to the opening of the aortic valve and the discharge of blood from the left ventricle. PEP is thus measured as the interval between the Q-wave on the electrocardiogram (ECG) (i.e., the onset of electromechanical systole) and the B-point on an impedence cardiographic (ICG) signal (i.e., the opening of the aortic valve and the passage of blood from the left ventricular outflow tract). PEP is the only noninvasive cardiac measure of pure SNS activation that has been validated via pharmacological blockade in adults (Berntson, Cacioppo, & Quigley, 1994). Shorter PEP intervals indicate higher sympathetic activation and are correlated with faster heart rate and increased cardiac output.

Individual differences in PEP across various tasks are stable, as indexed by high intertask PEP correlations in children and adolescence (McGrath & O'Brien, 2001; Quigley & Stifter, 2006). Furthermore, PEP reactivity shows longitudinal stability over short and long periods in both children and adolescents (Matthews, Salomon, Kenyon, & Allen, 2002; McGrath & O'Brien, 2001). Children have been shown to have shorter baseline PEPs than adolescents, commensurate with the higher heart rates found at younger ages (Alkon et al., 2003; Allen & Matthews, 1997; Matthews et al., 2002); however, adolescents show greater decreases in PEP in response to a cognitive task (Allen & Matthews, 1997). Although gender differences have not been found consistently in younger children (Alkon et al., 2003), adolescent girls were found to have shorter baseline PEP values and higher PEP reactivity (Matthews et al., 2002; Allen & Matthews, 1997).

Beauchaine and colleagues have proposed that, as a cardiac index of SNS activity, PEP reflects individual differences in the behavioral activation system (BAS) and reward sensitivity, because behavioral approach tendencies require SNS-regulated increases in both cardiac and energy outputs (Beauchaine, 2001; Brenner, Beauchaine, & Sylvers, 2005; Crowell et al., 2005). Indeed, decreases in PEP in response to reward have been observed in normative groups of children and adolescents; however, children with clinical levels of externalizing symptoms showed both a longer baseline PEP and lower PEP reactivity in response to reward, indicating hyporesponsivity of the SNS and reward insensitivity (Beauchaine, Gatzke-Kopp, & Mead, 2007; Crowell et al., 2006).

Similar findings have been seen in community samples of children with high levels of externalizing symptoms, who exhibit lower PEP reactivity in response to a series of challenges than children who have low levels of behavioral symptoms (Boyce et al., 2001).

It is important to note that PEP reactivity can be difficult to elicit in young children (Alkon et al., 2003; Buss, Goldsmith & Davidson, 2005; Quigley & Stifter, 2006). For example, in a study of three samples of children aged 3–8 years, Alkon and colleagues (2003) utilized a protocol that included cognitive, social, sensory, and emotional tasks and found no significant changes in PEP in two samples and anomalously lower sympathetic activation in a third sample. However, children showed changes in heart rate and parasympathetic activity in response to the various challenges, suggesting that the tasks were appropriately designed to elicit stress reactivity. Quigley and Stiffer (2006) suggest several possible reasons for the absence of PEP reactivity in young children. Young children (1) may be incapable of producing a phasic sympathetic cardiac response, (2) may have no physiological need for sympathetic reactivity, given that they show good parasympathetic regulation, or (3) may have sufficiently low basal PEPs to preclude any additional shortening. Future research is needed to examine these hypotheses.

Salivary Alpha-Amylase. Salivary alpha-amylase (sAA), expressed in units per milliliter (U/ml), is an enzyme produced by salivary glands in the mouth that can serve as an index of SNS activity. Although blood levels of epinephrine (EP) and norepinephrine (NE) index SNS activity, the salivary levels of these hormones do not reflect SNS activity. However, under conditions of physical and psychological stress, an increase in plasma levels of NE in response to SNS activation has been linked to elevated sAA levels in adults (Nater et al., 2006). Salivary glands and surrounding tissues contain adrenergic receptors, and in response to NE secretion from sympathetic nerves, the glands increase the ratio of sAA-to-fluid in saliva (Granger et al., 2007). Further, sAA reactivity to stressors has been linked to other cardiovascular measures of stress reactivity (El-Sheikh, Erath, Buckhalt, Granger, & Mize, 2008; Nater et al., 2006; Stroud, Handwerger, Kivlighan, Granger, & Niaura, 2005). As the primary functions of sAA are to aid digestion and to reduce levels of oral bacteria, both diet and oral health may affect basal levels of sAA (Granger, Kivlighan, El-Sheikh, Gordis, & Stroud, 2007).

In recent years, Granger and colleagues have advocated for inclusion of sAA in developmental research as an index of children's SNS response to stress (Granger et al., 2006, 2007). The levels of sAA in children seem to be robust, unaffected by collection, storage, and handling procedures, and tend to be stable across multiple same-day assessments (Granger et al., 2006). Studies of oral biology indicate that sAA is absent in newborns, emerges toward the end of the first year, when children are introduced to solid foods, and reaches adult levels in 5 to 6-year-olds (Granger et al., 2006). In children and adolescents, sAA basal levels and sAA reactivity have been positively correlated with pubertal status and age (El-Sheikh, Mize, & Granger, 2005; Susman, Granger, Dockray, Heaton, & Dorn, 2006; Stroud et al., 2005). It is important to note that, unlike PEP and SCL, sAA reactivity in response to a social stressor peaks 5–10 minutes after the stressor onset (Gordis, Granger, Susman, & Trickett, 2006). Thus, researchers need to collect multiple samples of sAA to accurately assess SNS reactivity. For a more detailed discussion of measurement issues, see Granger et al. (2007).

A few studies have linked sAA reactivity to indices of adaptive functioning. In middle childhood, high sAA reactivity to emotional and cognitive stressors was associated with poor health, social problems, externalizing, and academic problems (El-Sheikh et al., 2005). In adolescents, higher sAA reactivity in response to social and cognitive stressors was associated with feelings of fearfulness (Stroud et al., 2005). In contrast, low sAA reactivity to a modified TSST was related to adolescents' self-report of oppositional defiant disorder and conduct disorder symptoms in boys (Susman et al., 2006). Although sAA

is emerging as a viable index of SNS stress reactivity, more research is needed to establish its validity, reliability and stability in children and to examine the effects of gender or ethnicity.

Summary. Investigators seeking to measure SNS responses to standardized challenges in studies of child development currently have three options from which to choose, with different profiles of methodological strengths and weaknesses. SCL offers an accurate, simple, and established index of sympathetic arousal using electrodes and equipment for detecting, amplifying, and recording the skin conductance signal. SCL also has the advantages of being relatively inexpensive to measure, being harmless to child participants, and requiring only the use of palmar electrodes. Downsides of SCL include its relatively long response latency (about 1–3 seconds) and its linkages to a variety of psychological processes, including arousal, attention, and affective responses. PEP is more difficult to measure, involving impedance cardiography, the use of spot or band electrodes on the neck and thorax, and the processing of data with relatively sophisticated signal analysis software. On the other hand, impedance cardiography is now quite feasible using out-of-the-box instrumentation that is easy to use and requires only moderate expertise in the acquisition and analysis of physiological signals. Finally, sAA, the most recent addition to the array of available SNS markers, is a simple and promising measure, involving the collection of saliva, and the laboratory processing of samples using a quantitative enzyme kinetic method. An emerging literature on sAA in psychophysiological research will eventually provide investigators with useful information on its reliability and validity in studies of child development.

Parasympathetic Nervous System

Respiratory Sinus Arrhythmia. Respiratory sinus arrhythmia (RSA) is a measure of PNS stress response and refers to high frequency heart rate variation controlled by efferent fibers of the vagus (tenth cranial) nerve during the respiratory cycle. RSA is estimated as the natural logarithm of heart period variance within the high frequency range corresponding to respiration (Bar-Haim, Marshall, & Fox, 2000). Vagal regulation, in the form of increases and decreases in RSA, has been regarded as a measure of children's capacity to control responses to positive and negative environmental demands (Beauchaine, 2001; Beauchaine et al., 2007; Porges, 2003, 2007). In situations of rest and calm, efferent projections of the vagal nerve presynaptically suppress sympathetic tone to the heart, producing the baseline heart rate, whereas in stressful or challenging situations, the vagal nerve withdraws its suppression, allowing SNS to generate a faster heart rate, as indexed by a decrease in RSA (Porges, 2003; 2007).

Baseline RSA values increase over time and reach adult levels around age 5 years, which may reflect the development of regulatory capacities during early childhood (Beauchaine, 2001). Similarly, short- and long-term stability of baseline RSA increases from infancy to adulthood (Alkon et al., 2003; Matthews, Salomon, Brady, & Allen, 2003). These developmental changes in basal RSA may account for the shifting relations between RSA and adaptation from infancy to early childhood. For example, high levels of basal RSA in infancy have been linked to temperamental difficulty and emotional negativity (Porges, Doussard-Roosevelt, & Maiti, 1994; Stifter & Fox, 1990), whereas high levels of basal RSA later in childhood have been associated with positive outcomes, such as social competence, empathy, and emotion regulation (Beauchaine, 2001; Blair & Peters, 2003; Fabes, Eisenberg, & Eisenbud, 1993). Researchers have argued that low basal RSA may reflect emotional lability and dysregulation, as it has been linked to behavior problems in both at-risk, community, and clinical samples across childhood and adolescence (Beauchaine, 2001; Beauchaine et al. 2007; Pine et al., 1998). However, recent studies of community, nonclinical samples have found a positive relation, or no significant relation, between resting RSA and

externalizing symptoms (Calkins, Graziano, & Keane, 2007; Dietrich et al., 2007).

Further, researchers have examined changes in RSA in response to stressful laboratory challenges. High reactivity, as indexed by decreases in RSA from basal levels (i.e., greater vagal withdrawal), has been associated with more sustained attention, better emotion regulation, and increased engagement during challenge tasks (Calkins, 1997; Suess, Porges, & Plude, 1994). Additionally, Santucci et al. (2008) reported that lower vagal recovery following an emotional challenge was associated with poor emotion regulation strategies in response to frustration.

RSA reactivity is less stable longitudinally, but tends to show stability across different tasks (Calkins & Keane, 2004; Doussard-Roosevelt, Montgomery, & Porges, 2003). In children and adolescents, RSA reactivity has been found to predict basal RSA levels three years later, over and above the continuity of basal RSA (Salomon, 2005). Further, children who demonstrated stable high RSA reactivity in response to challenges at ages 2 and 4.5 years were described as less negatively reactive, more socially competent, and better behaved than children who demonstrated stable low RSA reactivity or children whose RSA reactivity level increased (Calkins & Keane, 2004).

In community samples of kindergarten children, higher RSA reactivity to various challenge tasks has been linked to positive indices of adaptation, such as high levels of sociability, attention, and work abilities (Blair & Peters, 2003; Doussard-Roosevelt et al., 2003), as well as to high levels of internalizing symptoms (Boyce et al., 2001). Some of the inconsistencies across studies may be explained by the nature of the sample and the nature of their symptoms. For example, low RSA reactivity has been associated with externalizing symptoms in normative samples of young children (Boyce et al., 2001; Calkins et al., 2007), whereas high RSA reactivity has been observed in children with clinical levels of behavior problems (Beauchaine et al., 2007; Crowell et al., 2005). In addition, children at risk for comorbid internalizing and externalizing behavior problems show high RSA reactivity (Boyce et al., 2001; Calkins et al., 2007; Calkins & Dedmon, 2000; Crowell et al., 2005; Kibler, Prosser, & Ma, 2004).

Several studies have revealed that relations between RSA and adjustment may vary across different levels of adversity exposure. Studies of community samples have shown that high basal RSA levels and high RSA reactivity in response to emotion-evoking stimuli buffered children from the effects of marital conflict on behavior problems, academic achievement, and health problems (El-Sheikh & Whitson, 2006; Katz, 2007; Katz & Gottman, 1997). Only children with low baseline RSA and low RSA reactivity were at risk for maladaptation in the context of high marital conflict. However, these findings varied across gender, type of marital conflict (e.g., verbal, physical), and children's outcomes. Similarly, high RSA reactivity to interpersonal stressors emerged as a protective factor against the effects of hostile-withdrawn parenting (Leary & Katz, 2004). In contrast, in a clinical sample, parental psychopathology had a negative effect on children's emotional and behavioral problems only in children with high baseline RSA (Shannon et al., 2007).

In summary, investigators testing hypotheses linking PNS reactivity measures to developmental outcomes have only one choice of measure: the magnitude of RSA or vagal regulation. Although RSA is a singular index of parasympathetic activation or withdrawal, there are a variety of both hardware and software solutions for operationalizing this measure. Each of these requires the acquisition of ECG signal, using several thoracic and extremity electrodes, and spectral analyses of high frequency, respiration-related variation in heart rate.

Integrative ANS Measures

Heart Rate. There are two indices of how fast the heart is beating: (1) heart period (HP), which measures the time in milliseconds (msec) between two beats as indexed by the adjacent R-waves on an electrocardiogram,

and (2) heart rate (HR), which measures the number of beats per minute (bpm). Although the two measures are directly related, as one can be derived from the other, research shows that the change in ANS input affects HR and HP differently (Berntson, Cacioppo, & Quigley, 1995). The effect of ANS change on HP is linear and independent of basal HP levels, whereas the effect of the same ANS change on HR varies depending on basal HR levels.

Regulation of HR, referred to as cardiac chronotropic control, is influenced by both SNS and PNS. The effect of PNS on HR is more direct, larger, and faster than that of SNS and tends to be more pronounced during basal conditions (Berntson et al., 2007). However, the interaction of SNS and PNS has also been found to influence HR (Berntson et al., 1995). HR responses to stimuli may thus reflect an increase in sympathetic input, parasympathetic withdrawal, or a combination of both, rendering HR and HP measures useful only to broadly assess whether and how psychophysiology relates to behavioral outcomes.

Baseline HR is a moderately stable measure across childhood (Marshall & Stevenson-Hinde, 1998). Low baseline HR is a well-established correlate of aggression, conduct problems, and antisocial behavior in both children and adolescents, according to numerous studies and two recent meta-analyses (Dietrich et al., 2007; Lorber, 2004; Ortiz & Raine, 2004; Williams, Lochman, Phillips, & Barry, 2003). The strength of the association does not vary across many covariates, including age and gender (Ortiz & Raine, 2004). However, a few studies found no significant relations among baseline HR and indices of behavior problems in young children (Calkins & Dedmon, 2000; Calkins & Keane, 2004), and others report positive associations between baseline HR and aggression (Schneider, Nicolotti, & Delamater, 2002). The inconsistency of these findings may be due in part to comorbidity of externalizing and internalizing symptoms, as high resting HR has been generally associated with internalizing symptoms (Dietrich et al., 2007; Scarpa et al., 1997).

As with basal HR, concurrent and longitudinal associations between HR reactivity and internalizing symptoms have generally been positive (Marshall & Stevenson-Hinde, 1998; Weems et al., 2005). However, studies of HR reactivity reveal a complex association with externalizing behavioral problems. In toddlers, HR reactivity was found to relate to concurrent negative affect, and changes in HR reactivity tracked changes in negative affect (Buss et al., 2005). In children, high HR reactivity to stressful and challenging tasks was associated with aggression and conduct problems (Lorber, 2004), whereas low HR reactivity was associated with more antisocial behaviors (Ortiz & Raine, 2004). The link between HR reactivity and externalizing behavior problems also seems to vary by type of aggression. Lower HR reactivity to losing a game as a result of peer cheating was associated with higher reactive aggression, but not with proactive aggression (Hubbard et al., 2002). There is a need for more systematic examination of HR reactivity in children prone to reactive, proactive, relational, and physical aggression.

Furthermore, Lorber (2004) found that the association between HR reactivity and externalizing symptoms varied with the nature of stimuli used to elicit changes in HR, with positive associations emerging in the context of negative stimuli and negative associations emerging in the context of non-negative stimuli. For example, high HR reactivity to provocative and conflict-inducing stimuli was associated with reports of higher levels of aggression (Van Goozen et al., 1998), whereas high HR reactivity to cognitive challenges was linked to lower levels of aggression and misconduct (Kibler et al., 2004; Schneider et al., 2002). However, it is important that researchers go beyond simple linear tests of associations between psychophysiology and behavior, as Williams et al. (2003) have shown that relations between HR reactivity and aggression may be curvilinear.

Blood Pressure. Blood pressure (BP) is the force exerted by circulating blood against the wall of arteries and veins, is expressed in millimeters of mercury (mmHg), and is one of the cardinal "vital signs." Like HR, BP is affected by both PNS and SNS activity. There are several different measures of BP. Systolic blood pressure (SBP) is a measure of highest arterial pressure during systole, that is, ventricular contraction, whereas diastolic blood pressure (DBP) is a measure of lowest arterial pressure during diastole, or ventricular relaxation and filling. Mean arterial pressure (MAP) is an average pressure during one cardiac cycle and is calculated by summing one-third of the SBP value and two-thirds of the DBP value, since diastole lasts twice as long as systole.

The measure of BP is influenced by various factors outside of researchers' control, such as the diameter and type of blood vessel, structural resistance inside vessels, and the viscosity of blood. However, researchers can control for confounding factors such as recent diet, caffeine/nicotine intake, and physical activity. In addition, it is important to standardize the location of measurement and the participant's position and to use the appropriate size and placement of measuring cuff, preferably at the height of the heart in order to lessen the confounding effect of hydrostatic pressure (Berntson, Quigley, & Lozano, 2007). For an overview of measurement issues and approaches see Berntson et al. (2007).

There is significant stability in baseline and reactivity measures of BP in children and adolescents over a multiyear period, with BP reactivity predicting longitudinal change in resting BP (Matthews et al., 2003; Matthews et al., 2002). However, BP reactivity shows higher reliability within the same task than across different types of challenges (Kelsey, Ornduff, & Alpert, 2007). Different measures of BP have been shown to vary with gender, age, and ethnicity with males, African Americans, and older individuals exhibiting higher levels of BP (Murphy, Alpert, & Walker, 1992; Wang et al., 2006).

Studies examining linkages between BP reactivity and socioemotional and cognitive development are relatively scarce. Associations between BP reactivity and indices of hostility and aggression are well-established in the adult literature; however, the relation of BP and externalizing behavior problems in children is less clear. While a few studies indicate significant associations between high BP reactivity and externalizing in boys (Dobkin, Treiber, & Tremblay, 2000), others have found no significant differences in SBP and DBP in boys with and without externalizing symptoms (Van Goozen et al., 1998). Moreover, a recent meta-analysis concluded that these effects were weak and not significant (Kibler et al., 2004). Evidence is emerging that associations with BP reactivity may be more complex and may be moderated by other risk factors and individual characteristics. For example, Schneider and colleagues (2002) found that basal and reactivity SBP and DBP levels had no direct relation to aggression, but among children with a parental history of hypertension, aggressive children showed higher baseline SBP and DBP than nonaggressive children. Murray-Close and Crick (2007) showed that SBP reactivity in response to a recollection of relational stressors was positively related to teacher reports of relational aggression in girls, but not in boys.

Several studies indicate that exposures to stress and adversity are associated with increased basal and reactivity BP levels in children and adolescents (Brady & Matthews, 2006; Evans & English, 2002; Wilson, Kliewer, Plybon, & Sica, 2000). Brady and Matthews (2006) reported that having a high number of chronic, negative life events was linked to high ambulatory SBP and DBP in boys and SBP in girls, controlling for confounds and demographic variables. Moreover, various processes have been found to mediate or moderate relations between adversity and BP. Using structural equation modeling, Gump, Matthews, and Räikkönen (1999) found that hostility mediated the effects of both neighborhood and family socioeconomic status on BP in African American children and adolescents, with higher levels of hostility predicting higher BP reactivity to cognitive and physical challenges. In contrast, only lower family socioeconomic status directly predicted higher BP reactivity in white children and adolescents. Hostile interpretations of ambiguous stimuli were also found to partially mediate concurrent and longitudinal associations between low socioeconomic status and increased BP reactivity in both children and adolescents (Chen, Langer, Raphaelson, & Matthews, 2004).

Increased BP is a well-established risk factor for cardiovascular illness in adults (Jones & Jose, 2005). Boyce and colleagues (1995) examined whether MAP reactivity to various laboratory challenges was a risk factor for short-term physical health problems in children. Interactions between MAP reactivity and exposures to environmental stressors predicted the incidence of respiratory illnesses, such that highly reactive children had the highest incidence of illnesses in the context of high stress and the lowest incidence of illnesses in the context of low stress.

Summary. Researchers seeking broader measures of ANS responses to environmental stimuli may turn to assessments of HR or BP, which offer an integrative, summative index of overall autonomic reactivity, with both sympathetic and parasympathetic components. Both are easily measured using relatively inexpensive automatic instrumentation readily available from medical supply companies.

Hypothalamic-Pituitary-Adrenocortical Axis

In addition to ANS response, the human body reacts to stressful or challenging experiences by activating the hypothalamic-pituitary-adrenocortical (HPA) axis and the resultant production of glucocorticoids (GCs). GCs bind to two types of receptors – mineralocorticoid receptors (MRs) and glucocorticoid receptors (GRs). MRs are responsible for the daily adaptive functions of the HPA axis, facilitating glucose transport and utilization, stimulating appetite and feeding, and enabling memory formation and learning. As GCs show greater affinity for MRs than for GRs, most MRs are occupied at basal levels of HPA activation. During stress, the additional GCs bind to available GRs, whose function is to reverse the effects of the MRs and prepare the organism for more chronic exposures to stress. GRs also activate a negative feedback loop, which leads to lower production of GCs and restoration of homeostasis. For a more detailed description of the HPA response to stress, see Gunnar and Vazquez (2006) and Sapolsky, Romero, and Munck (2000).

Cortisol. Cortisol is the human GC hormone secreted by the adrenal glands and passively diffused into saliva. Cortisol levels can be measured in blood, urine, and saliva, but most recent studies of cortisol in children measure salivary levels, as this is the simplest and least invasive procedure. Salivary cortisol reflects the levels of unbound and biologically active cortisol circulating in the blood and can thus be used as an index of HPA activation. Salivary cortisol is most frequently expressed in nanomoles per liter (nmol/L) or micrograms per deciliter (μg/dl), with 1 nmol/L equaling 27.58 μg/dl. Cortisol levels follow a daily rhythm, starting with a peak 30–40 minutes after waking, known as the cortisol awakening response (CAR), and gradually decreasing throughout the day, until levels reach their lowest values in the middle of the night, several hours after sleep onset. Thus, it is important to measure cortisol levels at the same time after waking in all participants, or to control for time of collection in order to avoid measurement artifacts associated with circadian rhythm. Measurement of the CAR is especially sensitive to the precise time of collection (Kudielka, Broderick, & Kirschbaum, 2003). In addition to this daily fluctuation, several other confounds may have direct effects on cortisol levels in saliva, including recent or concurrent food intake, physically or psychologically stressful events, illnesses, and certain medications. Recent studies have shown that certain medications can influence cortisol levels, and researchers advocate monitoring the effects of medications containing exogenous GCs (Masharani et al., 2005) or medications prescribed to control children's behavior (Hibel, Granger, Cicchetti, & Rogosch, 2007).

There are numerous ways of examining HPA stress responses, depending on the number and timing of cortisol samples. Repeated measures are very important in assessing daily cortisol fluctuation. Researchers interested in cortisol reactivity can collect two measurement points to determine change in cortisol secretion over a certain period using difference or residual scores. With two or more measurement points, studies have examined the so-called "area under the curve," which can be calculated in relation to the ground if examining daily cortisol secretion (i.e., the full amount of expressed cortisol) or in relation to the baseline if examining cortisol output post stressor onset (i.e., subtracting individual baseline cortisol levels) (Pruessner, Kirschbaum, Meinlschmid, & Hellhammer, 2003). Cortisol trajectory patterns can also be examined using two or more measurement points. In addition, researchers have compared children who show a significant increase in response to an event (i.e., responder group) with children who do not show a significant increase in cortisol levels. In addition to examining daily patterns of cortisol across different contexts (e.g., home, school, foster care), populations (e.g., maltreated children, orphans), and time (e.g., pre- and postadoption), studies have examined cortisol reactivity to particular cognitive and emotional challenges. However, unlike ANS stress responses, the cortisol response to stressful and challenging tasks cannot be measured concurrently, as cortisol levels in saliva reach their peak approximately 15 to 20 minutes following stressor onset (Dickerson & Kemeny, 2004). Ramsay and Lewis (2003) found considerable variability in the timing of the cortisol peak in infants, which was unrelated to the slope of cortisol dampening response post peak. Thus, they argue that a single post-stressor measure of cortisol is not adequate to capture variability in cortisol reactivity. Moreover, some children show the highest cortisol elevation immediately prior to a stressor in anticipation of a negative experience (Kestler & Lewis, 2009).

Cortisol levels show relative short-term stability (Klimes-Dougan, Hastings, Granger, Usher, & Zahn-Waxler, 2001; Schiefelbein &

Susman, 2006). However, variability in cortisol levels is due largely to state-like, situational factors, rather than stable, trait-like factors (Shirtcliff, Granger, Booth, & Johnson, 2005). Consequently, cortisol collection should be replicated across multiple days to ensure a more reliable measure. Cortisol levels and reactivity have also been found to vary with age, gender, and ethnicity (DeSantis et al., 2007; Gunnar, Wewerka, Frenn, Long, & Griggs, 2009; Klimes-Dougan et al., 2001), but more studies are needed to further examine these individual differences in children.

Elevated cortisol levels have been associated with concurrent or incident internalizing behavior problems and social wariness, especially in girls (Gunnar et al., 2009, Schiefelbein & Susman, 2006; Smider et al., 2002). Comparison studies of children and adolescents with and without depressive symptoms show that high symptom levels and persistence of symptoms were associated with higher cortisol levels in the morning (Halligan, Herbert, Goodyer, & Murray, 2007) and in the evening (Goodyer, Park, & Herbert, 2001). A recent study indicates that feelings of sadness and loneliness have been associated with the higher CAR the following day (Adam, Hawkley, Kudielka, & Cacioppo, 2006).

In most studies, low cortisol levels have been linked to concurrent and longitudinal externalizing behavior problems, especially aggression, in both community and clinical samples (Oosterlaan, Geurts, Knol, & Sergeant, 2005; Shirtcliff et al., 2005; Van Goozen et al., 1998); however, there are a few exceptions (Klimes-Dougan et al., 2001). Given the opposite relation of cortisol with internalizing and externalizing symptoms, children with comorbid symptoms should be examined separately, as they may show very different patterns of HPA activity (McBurnett et al., 1991). For example, in community samples of kindergarten children, cortisol was positively related to the combined severity of externalizing and internalizing symptoms (Essex, Klein, Cho, & Kalin, 2002).

Cortisol elevation in response to normative stressful events, such as starting a new school year or attending a daycare, has been associated with negative affectivity, impulsivity, poor effortful control, and peer rejection (Dettling, Parker, Lane, Sebanc, & Gunnar, 2000; Gunnar, Sebanc, Tout, Donzella, & Van Dulmen, 2003). However, these associations with stress-related cortisol levels may vary across context and time. For example, Dettling et al. (2000) reported that elevation in cortisol was found in preschoolers attending low-quality daycare centers, but not in those attending high-quality care settings. Moreover, elevated cortisol during the first weeks of school, when children forge new peer groups and connections, may be an adaptive response, as it has been linked to higher social competence. On the other hand, elevated cortisol later in the school year, when peer groups have been fully formed, may indicate maladaptation, as it has been linked to solitary and negative behaviors (Gunnar, Tout, de Haan, Pierce, & Stansbury, 1997). Researchers interested in studying cortisol levels in the school context should be aware that the season of the year and the day of the week may influence daily cortisol levels assessed in the classroom (Bukowski & Lopez, 2008).

The correlates of cortisol reactivity to specific laboratory tasks can change with the nature of these tasks. High cortisol reactivity to a conflict-oriented parent-child interaction has been associated with higher concurrent and longitudinal social withdrawal, social problems, and anxiety (Granger, Weisz, & Kauneckis, 1994). In response tasks designed to elicit provocation and frustration, children with comorbid internalizing and externalizing symptoms exhibited higher cortisol reactivity than children with no behavior problems, while children with only externalizing symptoms exhibited lower cortisol reactivity (Snoek, Van Goozen, Matthys, Buitelaar, & Van Engeland, 2004; Van Goozen et al., 1998). However, moderately elevated cortisol in response to cognitively challenging, attention demanding tasks has been found to be adaptive. Children who showed higher average cortisol levels or elevated cortisol during testing performed better on various executive functioning tasks and demonstrated stronger self-regulatory capacities in the classroom (Blair, Granger, & Razza, 2005; Davis, Bruce, & Gunnar, 2002). Moreover, children who retained an ADHD diagnosis over a 2-year period showed lower cortisol reactivity after completing a battery of achievement and attention tasks than children who no longer had ADHD (King, Barkley, & Barrett, 1998).

HPA activity has been examined in various populations of at-risk children, including children raised in orphanages, living in poverty, or with a history of abuse and neglect. A study of children living in low-income, urban areas of Mexico found that living with depressed mothers was associated with lower baseline cortisol and lower cortisol reactivity in response to cognitive testing (Fernald, Burke, & Gunnar, 2008). Not unexpectedly, extreme levels of adversity have also been found to alter the daily pattern of cortisol secretion. For example, blunted early morning cortisol and flattened diurnal rhythms have been detected in children raised in Romanian and Russian orphanages (Carlson & Earls, 1997; Gunnar & Vazquez, 2001) and in children living in foster homes in the United States (Dozier et al., 2006). However, recent intervention programs show promise in normalizing HPA activity in foster children (Dozier, Peloso, Lewis, Laurenceau, & Levine, 2008; Fisher, Stoolmiller, Gunnar, & Burraston, 2007).

Exposure to risk and adversity has also been associated with elevated cortisol expression (Evans & English, 2002; Evans & Kim, 2007; Lupien, King, Meaney, & McEwen, 2001). In general, maltreated children show elevated basal cortisol levels across the day when compared to nonmaltreated children (Cicchetti & Rogosch, 2001). However, cortisol levels in maltreated children vary with the nature of symptoms that the children exhibit. Elevated cortisol levels have been found most consistently in maltreated children with internalizing symptoms (Cicchetti & Rogosch, 2001, Gunnar & Vazquez, 2006). In contrast, the difference in cortisol levels found between maltreated children with externalizing symptoms and nonmaltreated children has been less consistent, possibly because of the countered effects of maltreatment and externalizing on the HPA axis (Tarullo & Gunnar, 2006). Studies of cortisol in disadvantaged children need to take various factors known to affect the HPA axis into account, including history of abuse and neglect, the nature of symptoms, and recent adversity.

In summary, assessments of GC reactivity and basal activation of the HPA were rendered simple and accessible by the advent of ELISA assays of salivary cortisol. The reviewed work of Gunnar and others has provided the field with a body of careful, systematic observations of how such measures can inform and illuminate the science of child development.

Promising Future Directions

Longitudinal design. The paucity of studies examining relations between stress reactivity and adaptive functioning over time is striking. Future studies should address this gap in the literature. As stress reactivity is a dynamic process, evolving with neurobiological maturation and environmental exposures, it is important to examine whether and how associations between stress reactivity and adaptive functioning change across different developmental periods within the same individuals (Kraemer, Yesavage, Taylor, & Kupfer, 2000). Future research will need to employ more advanced, longitudinal analytical procedures when examining the role of stress reactivity in development. To date, most studies of stress reactivity have relied on simple bivariate correlations, analyses of variance, and regression analyses. Many new statistical approaches would yield more sophisticated understandings of these associations. A complete review of these techniques is beyond the scope of this chapter, but we mention a few here.

Structural equation modeling allows researchers to construct latent measures of stress reactivity and to examine separately the variability in stress response that is common across different tasks or stable across different days (Shirtcliff et al., 2005). It can also be used to examine bi-directional effects between stress reactivity and adaptation across multiple time points and controlling for the continuity and within-time covariation of stress reactivity and adaptation. Such a model would provide a rigorous test of whether stress reactivity shapes adaptation over time and/or vice versa. *Growth curve modeling* can be used to examine whether trajectories of stress response show linear or nonlinear change during a task, across a day, or over a longer period. These techniques also allow researchers to identify various static and dynamic covariates of stress response trajectories. For example, Shirtcliff and Essex (2008) used growth curves to examine whether interindividual variability in basal cortisol levels and diurnal trajectories predict adolescent mental health during fifth and seventh grade. Growth curves would also be appropriate when examining whether other indices of development, such as pubertal onset and pace, track changes in stress reactivity over time. *Group-based trajectory modeling* is an exploratory analytic procedure that can be employed to identify groups of children who have similar stress reactivity trajectories and examine antecedents and correlates of each group. For example, Gunnar and colleagues used this technique to identify groups of children who show unique diurnal patterns of cortisol secretion (Van Ryzin, Chatham, Kryzer, Kertes, & Gunnar, 2009).

Multidimensionality of adaptive functioning. Studies to date have focused primarily on linking stress reactivity to indices of psychopathology, particularly externalizing and internalizing symptoms. Although many studies converge in their findings, a significant number of inconsistencies exist. Future studies should employ a more nuanced investigation of different types of behavior problems. Given that physical and relational aggression, as well as proactive and reactive aggression, show different developmental antecedents and correlates, it is likely that children prone to these behavioral difficulties also exhibit different stress reactivity patterns. Researchers should also take into account comorbidity of symptoms, as many

studies indicate that children who suffer from both internalizing and externalizing symptoms differ significantly from children that show only one type of behavior problem (Boyce et al., 2001; Calkins et al., 2007; Essex et al., 2002). Most importantly, researchers should examine how stress reactivity relates to positive indices of functioning, such as the developmentally salient domains of competence. Studies of RSA and cortisol reactivity levels have shown that stress reactivity is significantly associated with indices of executive functioning, academic achievement, peer competence, and prosocial behaviors (Blair et al., 2005; Blair & Peters, 2003; Davis et al., 2002; Doussard-Roosevelt et al., 2003; Gunnar et al., 1997; Katz & Gottman, 1997). These findings need to be replicated and extended to other indices of stress reactivity in both clinical and community samples across different developmental periods in order to gain a more comprehensive understanding of the role that stress reactivity plays in positive adaptation.

Effect modification and moderators of reactivity-outcome associations. Various factors and processes modify the associations among stress reactivity and indices of health and adaptive functioning. First, a more systematic examination of individual differences, including age, gender, ethnicity, puberty status, and temperament, is needed. Second, studies should strive to examine how processes salient to children's development, such as nurturing interpersonal relations with parents, peers, and teachers influence children's reactivity to stress. For example, recent studies have shown that the quality of the parent-child relationship moderated the effect of temperament on SCL reactivity to fear-inducing films, such that fearful children with low quality parenting showed high reactivity, while fearful children with high quality parenting showed low reactivity (Gilissen, Koolstra, Van IJzendoorn, Bakermans-Kranenburg, & Van der Veer, 2007). Third, processes linking stress reactivity to adaptation should be examined across various populations of children and various contextual experiences. Children who have experienced extreme stress and adversity, such as deprivation, neglect, and abuse, have been found to exhibit different cortisol patterns than children faced with more normative daily stressors and challenges (Carlson & Earls, 1997; Dozier et al., 2006; Gunnar & Vazquez, 2001). For example, maltreatment status was found to moderate the link between physical aggression and diurnal cortisol pattern, such that physically aggressive children who were maltreated showed a flatter decline in cortisol levels across the day than children who were not maltreated (Murray-Close, Han, Cicchetti, Crick, & Rogosch, 2008).

Biological sensitivity to context. Traditionally, high stress reactivity has been seen as a risk factor for or marker of maladaptation. However, Boyce and colleagues (Boyce & Ellis, 2005; Ellis, Essex, & Boyce 2005) have challenged this notion, suggesting that high stress reactivity is not simply a unitary, pathogenic response to adversity, but rather a reflection of high biological sensitivity to both positive and negative contexts. As such, high biological sensitivity may be maladaptive in the context of adversity, but adaptive or even salubrious in contexts of support and protection. Thus, it becomes crucial to address social context when examining associations between stress reactivity and adaptation. A growing number of studies, examining indices of RSA, SCL, and cortisol reactivity in the contexts of various types of adversities (e.g., marital conflict, parental psychopathology, financial stress), support the notion that associations between stress reactivity and adaptation vary across different levels of adversity exposure (Boyce et al., 1995; Cummings et al., 2007; El-Sheikh et al., 2007; El-Sheikh & Whitson, 2006; Leary & Katz, 2004; Obradović et al., 2010; Shannon et al., 2007).

This theory of biological sensitivity to context is consistent with research on behavioral reactivity indicating that children with high levels of negative affectivity are particularly susceptible to both negative and positive experiences (Belsky, Bakermans-Kranenburg, & Van IJzendoorn, 2007; Klein Velderman, Bakermans-Kranenburg, Juffer, & Van IJzendoorn, 2006) and also

parallels recent research showing that genetic polymorphisms can moderate the effects of adversity on adaptive functioning (Bakermans-Kranenburg & Van IJzendoorn, 2007; Caspi et al., 2002; Taylor et al., 2006). Future studies are needed to determine whether these behavioral, physiological, and genetic markers of susceptibility to contextual factors constitute the same phenomena expressed at different levels of assessment or represent different types of susceptibility that may have cumulative or multiplicative effects on development (Obradović & Boyce, 2009).

Following this theory of biological sensitivity to context, Boyce and colleagues (Boyce & Ellis, 2005) have proposed that the quality of early experience may shape stress reactivity through conditional adaptations to developmental contexts. Children raised in stimulating and nurturing environments may develop high biological sensitivity in order to take advantage of positive influences. Children growing up in harsh and threatening environments may also develop biological sensitivity in order to maintain high levels of vigilance necessary for survival. In contrast, children raised in environments between these two extremes may conform to profiles of lower context sensitivity, as their social setting is neither highly nurturant nor highly threatening. Thus, the relation between early experience and stress reactivity has been hypothesized to be curvilinear and U-shaped; high reactivity phenotypes should be most prevalent in the contexts of low and high adversity exposure. However, only longitudinal studies of the interplay between environmental effects and stress reactivity starting with prenatal development and within broadly variable social contexts can provide credible empirical evidence for this hypothesis. It would also be important to examine whether stress reactivity phenotypes change with intervention efforts designed to improve caregiving and behaviors of children exposed to early adversity. Studies of foster care children living in the United States, for example, provide early evidence that psychosocial interventions may indeed modify children's cortisol diurnal rhythms (Dozier et al., 2008; Fisher et al., 2007).

The nature of stressors and challenges. Most extant studies of stress reactivity either employ a single challenge task or average the stress response across various tasks. Findings across different studies seem to show that the nature of the challenge task may influence the relation between reactivity and adaptation; however, researchers rarely examine whether reactivity to cognitive, social, or emotional tasks relate differently to developmental outcomes within the same study. Chen, Matthews, Salomon, and Ewart (2002) reported different correlates of cardiovascular reactivity to social and nonsocial stressors. Obradović, Bush and Boyce (2011) reported that the interaction between stress reactivity and marital conflict significantly predicted children's externalizing symptoms, but the direction of the effect varied with the nature of the challenge task. In contrast, two recent studies found that the interaction effects of adversity and SCL reactivity on children's internalizing and externalizing symptoms were mostly consistent across cognitive and emotional tasks, although some differences did emerge (Cummings et al., 2007; El-Sheikh et al., 2007). Future studies should examine whether stress reactivity that varies across different tasks indicates homologous or unique risks for maladaptation and disorders. Finally, at-risk children may be more reactive to certain types of stressors that are more salient in their lives. For example, bullied children may more reactive to stressors that simulate peer provocation, whereas maltreated children may be more reactive to fear-inducing stimuli. New studies should test these hypotheses, as the findings would advance our understanding of the processes linking adversity, stress reactivity, and adaptation.

Stress reactivity profiles: SNS and PNS. Studies of ANS stress response frequently employ different indices of SNS and PNS activity. Although researchers report correlations between different measures, they rarely examine SNS and PNS activity concurrently within the same person. Some studies show orthogonality between concurrent measures of SNS and PNS activity, as indexed by the lack of correlation between RSA and PEP measures (Alkon et al., 2003; Buss et al., 2005). Nonetheless, the two systems respond to stress in a highly integrated manner that may vary across different groups of children. For example, using PEP and RSA measures as indices of SNS and PNS activity, Alkon et al. (2003) examined four different autonomic response profiles: (1) *coactivation*, as indexed by concurrent SNS and PNS activation; (2) *coinhibition*, as indexed by SNS and PNS withdrawal; (3) *reciprocal parasympathetic activation*, as indexed by SNS withdrawal and PNS activation; and (4) *reciprocal sympathetic activation*, as indexed by SNS activation and PNS withdrawal. The prevalence of the reciprocal sympathetic activation profile declined with age, whereas coinhibition and reciprocal parasympathetic activation profiles increased with age, suggesting that with maturation, children show less arousal and better regulation. Moreover, Salomon, Matthews, and Allen (2000) found that percentages of children who demonstrated the four reactivity profiles varied across different tasks. The reciprocal sympathetic profile was the most common profile across all tasks, followed by a coactivation profile for cognitive and coinhibition profile for social and sensory tasks.

Boyce and colleagues (2001) examined how different autonomic stress reactivity profiles – as indexed by RSA, PEP, HR, and MAP reactivity to social, cognitive, sensory, and emotional challenges – relate to presyndromal behavior problems. Stress reactivity profiles differentiated four groups of children who showed high internalizing symptoms, high externalizing symptoms, high comorbid internalizing and externalizing symptoms, or low symptoms. In comparison with the low symptom group, internalizers were characterized by heightened reactivity as indexed by parasympathetic withdrawal, externalizers showed diminished reactivity via maintenance of the parasympathetic tone and low sympathetic arousal, and children with comorbid symptoms exhibited only low sympathetic arousal. Future studies should continue this line of work by examining associations between ANS stress reactivity profiles and positive and negative indices of socioemotional, cognitive, and physical development across time. In addition to using person-focused approaches to examine the interplay between two systems, researchers should also employ variable-focused analyses by testing interactions between SNS and PNS measures.

Stress reactivity profiles: ANS and HPA axis. A few studies have examined associations between indices of both ANS and HPA stress reactivity; however, the findings are inconsistent and vary with age and different measures of PNS and SNS activity. In newborns, concurrent basal and reactive levels of RSA and cortisol were unrelated, but higher levels of basal RSA were associated with higher cortisol reactivity to a physical stressor (Gunnar, Porter, Wolf, Rigatuso, & Larson, 1995). In kindergarten children, higher RSA reactivity to an emotionally negative task was related to a larger increase in cortisol responses across the testing session (Doussard-Roosevelt et al., 2003). Other studies have found no relations between RSA and cortisol (Donzella, Gunnar, Krueger, & Alwin, 2000). Similarly, covariation between BP and cortisol reactivity has been found in some studies (Evans & Kim, 2007) but not others (Van Goozen et al., 1998). Initial work found no relations between sAA and cortisol levels in infancy, early and middle childhood, and adolescence (El-Sheikh et al., 2005; Stroud et al., 2005); however, a few recent papers report significant covariation between sAA and cortisol reactivity to stressful tasks (El-Sheikh et al., 2008; Gordis et al., 2006). Another recent study sheds some light on the potential source of these discrepancies. Lewis, Ramsay and Sullivan (2006) reported that autonomic reactivity was uniquely associated with experiences of anger, whereas cortisol reactivity was uniquely associated with sadness.

Bauer, Quas, and Boyce (2002) emphasized the importance of examining interaction effects between indices of ANS and HPA activity in relation to behavior problems. They have proposed two different stress response models that may be associated with higher risk for behavior problems. The *additive model* suggests that the two systems independently augment each other, so that children who show either concurrently low or high activation of both the ANS and HPA axis may be at highest risk for maladaptation. In contrast, an *interactive model* would assert, as advanced by Sapolsky, Romero and Munck (2000), that glucocorticoids act both to augment and suppress sympathetically mediated changes in physiological functions and that optimal, self-limited stress responses require a coordinated *symmetry of activation* between the ANS and SNS. Under this assumption, the highest adaptive risks would therefore be borne by children showing unbalanced, asymmetrical arousal in the autonomic and sympathetic nervous systems. Gordis and colleagues (2006) tested these alternate models by examining sAA and cortisol reactivity to social and cognitive stressors. They found that low cortisol reactivity was related to higher levels of externalizing symptoms only in adolescents who also demonstrated low sAA reactivity. Similarly, El-Sheikh et al. (2008) examined the interactive effects of sAA, SCL, and cortisol reactivity for behavior problems in a community sample of 8 to 9-year-olds. The interaction between sAA and cortisol predicted both internalizing and externalizing symptom, whereas the interaction between SCL and cortisol predicted only internalizing problems. Children who exhibited high levels of both SNS and HPA reactivity were at highest risk for behavior problems, whereas the lowest levels of symptoms were found in children with asymmetrical SNS and HPA levels. The two studies provide initial evidence for the additive model, although results from Gordis et al. (2006) indicate that underarousal presents the highest risk for maladaptation, whereas those from El-Sheikh et al. (2008) indicate that overarousal presents the highest risk. Discrepancies in findings highlight the importance of further examining these models across different stressors, developmental periods, and in relation to multiple indices of adaptation.

Allostatic load. The burden of childhood adversities is associated not only contemporaneously with an increased risk for mental and physical disorders in early life, but with longer-term disease risks extending into adult life. The Adverse Childhood Experiences Study, for example, demonstrated that adults reporting more traumatic events in childhood have substantially greater risks for an extensive array of health impairments including coronary artery disease, chronic pulmonary disease, cancer, alcoholism, depression, and drug abuse (Edwards, Holden, Felitti, & Anda, 2003; Felitti et al., 1998), as well as life-threatening psychiatric disorders (Felitti et al., 1998), comorbid mental health problems (Anda et al., 2006), and cardiovascular risk factors, such as obesity, physical inactivity, and smoking (Dong et al., 2004). Other longitudinal studies have found similar linkages between childhood stressful life events and adult disease (Caspi, Harrington, Moffitt, Milne, & Poulton, 2006; Rutter, Kim-Cohen, & Maughan, 2006). Cumulative-exposure accounts of chronic disease risks in adult life are consistent with research addressing the breakdown of physiological steady state under conditions of stress and chronic challenge – a phenomenon referred to as "allostatic load" (McEwen, 1998). Under such circumstances, activation of the stress reactivity systems detailed earlier results in the expression of a repertoire of responses involving the secretion of stress hormones, increases in heart rate and blood pressure, protective mobilization of nutrients, redirection of blood perfusion to the brain, and the induction of vigilance and fear (McEwen, 2000). These neurobiological responses are, as noted earlier, essential and generally protective, but when activated persistently under circumstances of chronic or overwhelming adversity, can become pathogenic (Boyce & Ellis, 2005; Gunnar & Vazquez, 2006). Recent research documenting patterns of allostatic load that parallel racial disparities in health suggests, for example, that chronic physiological stress plays a key

role in the premature and disproportionate illness experienced by African-Americans and other groups who experience discrimination (Geronimus, Hicken, Keene, & Bound, 2006). More studies of the short- and long-term effects of "allostatic load" on cognitive and socioemotional development in childhood are needed.

Beyond Physiological Measures – Examining Circuits, Receptors and Epigenetic Changes. Ultimately, reactivity to stress is subserved by a set of neurobiological processes that can be described, understood, and measured at multiple levels of abstraction. The blood pressure and HR reactivity assessments that characterized early studies of stress reactivity are integrative measures of autonomic arousal, which can now be decomposed into their sympathetic and parasympathetic components using cardiac impedance and spectral analyses of HR variability, i.e., PEP and RSA, respectively. Further, as noted earlier, salivary cortisol provides an accessible, accurate index of HPA activation. Increasingly, however, measures of PEP, RSA and salivary cortisol are giving way to more direct evaluations of downstream effects on target end-organs, such as the immune system, and upstream molecular differences in glucocorticoid and neurotransmitter receptor densities and structures, central neural circuitry, allelic variations in neuroregulatory genes, and epigenetic markings that bear, at an even deeper level, on the observed individual differences in children's responsivity to stressors. Thus, the work of Sheridan and colleagues in studies of animal models (e.g., Avitsur, Hunzeker, & Sheridan, 2006) and Cohen, Manuck, and colleagues in experimental studies of human subjects (e.g., Marsland, Bachen, Cohen, Rabin, & Manuck, 2002) has shown how individual differences in the intensity and character of immune reactivity to stressors calibrates host susceptibility to viral and other infectious agents. In studies pursuing the neurobiological substrates of stress reactivity, Derijk and colleagues have demonstrated associations among polymorphisms in the genes coding for the mineralocorticoid (MR) and glucocorticoid receptors (GR), stress responsiveness, and vulnerability to major depression (Derijk, Van Leeuwen, Klok, & Zitman, 2008). Other work by Gianaros et al. (2008) has revealed that individuals with exaggerated blood pressure responses to stressors also show heightened activation of the amygdala and greater functional connectivity between the amygdala and the perigenual anterior cingulate cortex, a circuit implicated in the extinction of negative affect. Moreover, Pezawas et al. (2005) have found that individuals carrying a short allele of the serotonin transporter gene showed higher levels of temperamental anxiety and a relative uncoupling of the amygdala-perigenual cingulate circuit during perceptual processing of fearful stimuli.

Finally, the modification of stress-responsive gene expression by epigenetic modifications of chromatin structure, DNA methylation, and histone acetylation will likely figure largely into the unfolding molecular story of the genesis of individual differences in stress reactivity. Experience- and exposure-related alterations in the chromatin packaging of DNA can calibrate the transcription of genes involved, either peripherally or centrally, in the development and regulation of stress reactivity. Rokutan and colleagues (2005), for example, studied 1,467 genes in peripheral blood leukocytes before and after a 6-hour examination in a sample of Japanese doctoral students. Their comparisons yielded 49 up-regulated genes and 21 down-regulated, most of which coded for cytokines, cytokine receptors, growth- or apoptosis-related molecules, and heat shock proteins. These findings suggest that stressful events can trigger acute responses in leukocytes that are mediated by changes in gene expression. McGowan, Meaney, and Szyf (2008) have summarized evidence that naturally occurring variation in both maternal behavior and diet in rats can effect changes in offspring stress reactivity through glucocorticoid receptor gene expression. These regulatory influences are associated with altered histone acetylation, DNA methylation, and NGFI-A transcription factor binding. Further, in a study of human infants, Oberlander and colleagues (2008) have presented data indicating that fetal exposure to third trimester maternal depression is related to increased methylation of the GR gene (NR3C1) at an NGFI-A binding site and exaggerated salivary cortisol responses to a stressor at three months of age. Taken together, these human and animal studies offer promising, new insights into the epigenetic processes by which early environmental exposures and the expression of stress-responsive genes shape and tune the individual's physiological responsivity to challenge.

Conclusion

This chapter has aspired to present a theoretical and practical overview of the measurement of stress reactivity by describing the basic neurobiological processes involved in the stress response, by enumerating currently accessible measures of reactivity and their varied strengths, shortcomings, and relations to developmental endpoints, and by envisioning the scientific frontier of this field in the emerging epigenetic and neurobiological accounts of the origins of reactive phenotypes. An international human epigenome project – in planning by the Alliance for the Human Epigenome and Disease (American Association for Cancer Research Human Epigenome Task Force & European Union, 2008) – will produce, as just one outcome of its work, new knowledge of the ontogeny of individual differences in stress reactivity and the linkages of such differences to complex, multifactorial human disorders. What began, decades ago, as a fledgling scientific enterprise attempting to account for varying individual risks for the development of hypertension has become a complex, multidisciplinary field yielding new understanding of how humans adaptively respond to environmental threats and challenges and how the magnitude and character of such responses are shaped by early life experiences.

Acknowledgments

Preparation of this chapter was supported in part by a Killam Postdoctoral Research Fellowship from the University of British Columbia to Dr. Obradović. Dr. Obradović is the Great-West Life Junior Fellow in the Canadian Institute for Advanced Research's Experience-based Brain and Biological Development Program and Junior Fellow Academy. Dr. Boyce is a Fellow of the Canadian Institute for Advanced Research and holds the Sunny Hill Health Centre/BC Leadership Chair in Child Development at the University of British Columbia.

References

Adam, E. K., Hawkley, L. C., Kudielka, B. M., & Cacioppo, J. T. (2006). Day-to-day dynamics of experience – cortisol associations in a population-based sample of older adults. *Proceedings of the National Academy of Sciences*, 103, 17058–17063.

Alkon, A., Goldstein, L. H., Smider, N., Essex, M. J., Kupfer, D. J., & Boyce, W. T. (2003). Developmental and contextual influences on autonomic reactivity in young children. *Developmental Psychobiology*, 42, 64–78.

Allen, M. T., & Matthews, K. A. (1997). Hemodynamic responses to laboratory stressors in children and adolescents: The influences of age, race, and gender. *Psychophysiology*, 34, 329–339.

American Association for Cancer Research Human Epigenome Task Force, E. U., N. o. E., Scientific Advisory Board. (2008). Moving AHEAD with an international human epigenome project. *Nature*, 454(7205), 711–715.

Anda, R. F., Felitti, V. J., Bremner, J. D., Walker, J. D., Whitfield, C., Perry, B. D. et al. (2006). The enduring effects of abuse and related adverse experiences in childhood: A convergence of evidence from neurobiology and epidemiology. *European Archives of Psychiatry and Clinical Neuroscience*, 256, 174–186.

Avitsur, R., Hunzeker, J., & Sheridan, J. F. (2006). Role of early stress in the individual differences in host response to viral infection. *Brain Behavior and Immunity*, 20, 339–348.

Bakermans-Kranenburg, M. J., & Van IJzendoorn, M. H. (2007). Genetic vulnerability or differential susceptibility in child development: The case of attachment. *Journal of Child Psychology & Psychiatry*, 48, 1160–1173.

Bar-Haim, Y., Marshall, P. J., & Fox, N. A. (2000). Developmental changes in heart period and high-frequency heart period variability from 4 months to 4 years of age. *Developmental Psychobiology*, 37, 44–56.

Bauer, A., Quas, J. A., & Boyce, W. T. (2002). Associations between physiological reactivity and children's behavior: Advantages of a multisystem approach. *Journal of Developmental and Behavioral Pediatrics*, 23, 102.

Beauchaine, T. (2001). Vagal tone, development, and Gray's motivational theory: Toward an integrated model of autonomic nervous system functioning in psychopathology. *Development and Psychopathology*, 13, 183–214.

Beauchaine, T. P., Gatzke-Kopp, L., & Mead, H. K. (2007). Polyvagal theory and developmental psychopathology: Emotion dysregulation and conduct problems from preschool to adolescence. *Biological Psychology*, 74, 174–184.

Beauchaine, T. P., Katkin, E. S., Strassberg, Z., & Snarr, J. (2001). Disinhibitory psychopathology in male adolescents: Discriminating conduct disorder from attention-deficit/hyperactivity disorder through concurrent assessment of multiple autonomic states. *Journal of Abnormal Psychology*, 110, 610–624.

Belsky, J., Bakermans-Kranenburg, M. J., & Van IJzendoorn, M. H. (2007). For better and for worse: Differential susceptibility to environmental influences. *Current Directions in Psychological Science*, 16, 300–304.

Berntson, G. G., Cacioppo, J. T., & Quigley, K. S. (1994). Autonomic cardiac control: I. Estimation and validation from pharmacological blockades. *Psychophysiology*, 31, 572–585.

Berntson, G. G., Cacioppo, J. T., & Quigley, K. S. (1995). The metrics of cardiac chronotropism: Biometric perspectives. *Psychophysiology*, 32, 162–171.

Berntson, G. G., Quigley, K. S., & Lozano, D. (2007). Cardiovascular psychophysiology. In *Handbook of Psychophysiology*, pp. 182–210 (3rd ed.). Cambridge: Cambridge University Press.

Blair, C., Granger, D., & Razza, R. P. (2005). Cortisol reactivity is positively related to executive function in preschool children attending head start. *Child Development*, 76, 554–567.

Blair, C., & Peters, R. (2003). Physiological and neurocognitive correlates of adaptive behavior in preschool among children in head start. *Developmental Neuropsychology*, 24(1), 479–497.

Boucsein, W. (1992). *Electrodermal Activity*. New York: Plenum Press.

Boyce, W. T., Chesney, M., Alkon-Leonard, A., Tschann, J., Adams, S., Chesterman, B. et al. (1995). Psychobiologic reactivity to stress and childhood respiratory illnesses: Results of two prospective studies. *Psychosomatic Medicine*, 57, 411–422.

Boyce, W. T., & Ellis, B. J. (2005). Biological sensitivity to context: An evolutionary-developmental theory of the origins and functions of stress reactivity. *Development and Psychopathology*, 17, 271–301.

Boyce, W. T., Quas, J., Alkon, A., Smider, N., Essex, M., & Kupfer, D. J. (2001). Autonomic reactivity and psychopathology in middle childhood. *British Journal of Psychiatry*, 179, 144–150.

Brady, S. S., & Matthews, K. A. (2006). Chronic stress influences ambulatory blood pressure in adolescents. *Annals of Behavioral Medicine*, 31, 80–88.

Brenner, S. L., Beauchaine, T. P., & Sylvers, P. D. (2005). A comparison of psychophysiological and self report measures of BAS and BIS activation. *Psychophysiology*, 42, 108–115.

Bukowski, W. M., & Lopez, L. M. (2008, March). Using multilevel modeling to study within- and between persons variation in cortisol during early adolescence. Paper presented at the biannual meeting of Society of Research on Adolescence. Chicago.

Bush, N. R., Alkon, A., Obradović, J., Stamperdahl, J., & Boyce, W. T. (2011). Differentiating challenge reactivity from psychomotor activity in studies of children's psychophysiology: Considerations for theory and measurement. *Journal of Experimental Child Psychology*, 110, 62–79.

Buss, K. A., Goldsmith, H. H., & Davidson, R. J. (2005). Cardiac reactivity is associated with changes in negative emotion in 24-month-olds. *Developmental Psychobiology*, 46, 118–132.

Cacioppo, J. T., Berntson, G. G., Malarkey, W. B., Kiecolt-Glaser, J. K., Sheridan, J. F., Poehlmann, K. M. et al. (1998). Autonomic, neuroendocrine, and immune responses to psychological stress: The reactivity hypothesis. *Annals of the New York Academy of Sciences*, 840, 664–673.

Calkins, S. D. (1997). Cardiac vagal tone indices of temperamental reactivity and behavioral regulation in young children. *Developmental Psychobiology*, 31, 125–135.

Calkins, S. D., & Dedmon, S. E. (2000). Physiological and behavioral regulation in two-year-old children with aggressive/destructive behavior problems. *Journal of Abnormal Child Psychology*, 28, 103–118.

Calkins, S. D., Graziano, P. A., & Keane, S. P. (2007). Cardiac vagal regulation differentiates among children at risk for behavior problems. *Biological Psychology*, 74, 144–153.

Calkins, S. D., & Keane, S. P. (2004). Cardiac vagal regulation across the preschool period: Stability, continuity, and implications for childhood adjustment. *Developmental Psychobiology*, 45, 101–112.

Carlson, M., & Earls, F. (1997). Psychological and neuroendocrinological sequelae of early social deprivation in institutionalized children in Romania. *Annals of the New York Academy of Sciences*, 807, 419–428.

Caspi, A., Harrington, H., Moffitt, T. E., Milne, B. J., & Poulton, R. (2006). Socially isolated children 20 years later: Risk of cardiovascular disease. *Archives of Pediatrics and Adolescent Medicine*, 160, 805–811.

Caspi, A., McClay, J., Moffitt, T., Mill, J., Martin, J., Craig, I. et al. (2002). Role of genotype in the cycle of violence in maltreated children. *Science*, 297, 851–854.

Chen, E., Langer, D. A., Raphaelson, Y. E., & Matthews, K. A. (2004). Socioeconomic status and health in adolescents: The role of stress interpretations. *Child Development*, 75, 1039–1052.

Chen, E., Matthews, K. A., Salomon, K., & Ewart, C. K. (2002). Cardiovascular reactivity during social and nonsocial stressors: Do children's personal goals and expressive skills matter? *Health Psychology*, 21, 16–24.

Children's Defense Fund. (2008). *The state of America's children 2008*. Washington, DC: Children's Defense Fund.

Cicchetti, D., & Rogosch, F. A. (2001). The impact of child maltreatment and psychopathology on neuroendocrine functioning. *Development and Psychopathology*, 13, 783–804.

Cook J. T., & Frank D. A. (2008). Food security, poverty, and human development in the United States. *Annals of the New York Academy of Sciences*, 1136, 193–209.

Crowell, S. E., Beauchaine, T. P., Gatzke-Kopp, L., Sylvers, P., Mead, H., & Chipman-Chacon, J. (2006). Autonomic correlates of attention-deficit/hyperactivity disorder and oppositional defiant disorder in preschool children. *Journal of Abnormal Psychology*, 115, 174–178.

Crowell, S. E., Beauchaine, T. P., McCauley, E., Smith, C. J., Stevens, A. L., & Sylvers, P. (2005). Psychological, autonomic, and serotonergic correlates of parasuicide among adolescent girls. *Development and Psychopathology, 17,* 1105–1127.

Cummings, M. E., El-Sheikh, M., Kouros, C. D., & Keller, P. S. (2007). Children's skin conductance reactivity as a mechanism of risk in the context of parental depressive symptoms. *Journal of Child Psychology and Psychiatry, 48,* 436–445.

Davis, E. P., Bruce, J., & Gunnar, M. R. (2002). The anterior attention network: Associations with temperament and neuroendocrine activity in 6-year-old children. *Developmental Psychobiology, 40,* 43–56.

Dawson, M. E., Schell, A. M., & Filion, D. L. (2007). The electrodermal system. In *Handbook of Psychophysiology,* pp. 159–180 (3rd ed.). Cambridge.

Derijk, R. H., Van Leeuwen, N., Klok, M. D., & Zitman, F. G. (2008). Corticosteroid receptor-gene variants: Modulators of the stress-response and implications for mental health. *European Journal of Pharmacology, 585*(2–3), 492–501.

DeSantis, A. S., Adam, E. K., Doane, L. D., Mineka, S., Zinbarg, R. E., & Craske, M. G. (2007). Racial/ethnic differences in cortisol diurnal rhythms in a community sample of adolescents. *Journal of Adolescent Health, 41,* 3–13.

Dettling, A. C., Parker, S. W., Lane, S., Sebanc, A., & Gunnar, M. R. (2000). Quality of care and temperament determine changes in cortisol concentrations over the day for young children in childcare. *Psychoneuroendocrinology, 25,* 819–836.

Dickerson, S. S., & Kemeny, M. E. (2004). Acute stressors and cortisol responses: a theoretical integration and synthesis of laboratory research. *Psychological Bulletin, 130,* 355–391.

Dietrich, A., Riese, H., Sondeijker, F. E. P. L., Graces-Lord, K., Van Roon, A. M., Ormel, J. et al. (2007). Externalizing and internalizing problems in relation to autonomic function: A population-based study in preadolescents. *Journal of American Academy of Child and Adolescent Psychiatry, 46,* 378–386.

Dobkin, P. L., Treiber, F. A., & Tremblay, R. E. (2000). Cardiovascular reactivity in adolescent boys of low socioeconomic status previously characterized as anxious, disruptive, anxious-disruptive or normal during childhood. *Psychotherapy and Psychosomatics, 69,* 50–56.

Dong, M., Giles, W. H., Felitti, V. J., Dube, S. R., Williams, J. E., Chapman, D. P. et al. (2004). Insights into causal pathways for ischemic heart disease: Adverse childhood experiences study. *Circulation, 110,* 1761–1766.

Donzella, B., Gunnar, M., R., Krueger, W. K., & Alwin, J. (2000). Cortisol and vagal tone responses to competitive challenges in preschoolers: Associations with temperament. *Developmental Psychobiology, 37,* 209–220.

Doussard-Roosevelt, J. A., Montgomery, L. A., & Porges, S. W. (2003). Short-term stability of physiological measures in kindergarten children: Respiratory sinus arrhythmia, heart period, and cortisol. *Developmental Psychobiology, 43,* 230–242.

Dozier, M., Manni, M., Gordon, M. K., Peloso, E., Gunnar, M. R., Stovall-McClough, K. C. et al. (2006). Foster children's diurnal production of cortisol: An exploratory study. *Child Maltreatment, 11,* 189–197.

Dozier, M., Peloso, E., Lewis, E., Laurenceau, J.-P., & Levine, S. (2008). Effects of an attachment-based intervention on the cortisol production of infants and toddlers in foster care. *Development and Psychopathology, 20,* 845–859.

Edwards, V. J., Holden, G. W., Felitti, V. J., & Anda, R. F. (2003). Relationship between multiple forms of childhood maltreatment and adult mental health in community respondents: Results from the adverse childhood experiences study. *American Journal of Psychiatry, 160,* 1453–1460.

Ellis, B. J., Essex, M. J., & Boyce, W. T. (2005). Biological sensitivity to context: II. Empirical explorations of an evolutionary-developmental theory. *Development and Psychopathology, 17,* 303–328.

El-Sheikh, M. (2007). Children's skin conductance level and reactivity: Are these measures stable over time and across tasks. *Developmental Psychobiology, 49,* 180–186.

El-Sheikh, M., Erath, S. A., Buckhalt, J. A., Granger, D. A., & Mize, J. (2008). Cortisol and children's adjustment: The moderating role of sympathetic nervous system activity. *Journal of Abnormal Child Psychology, 36,* 601–611.

El-Sheikh, M., Keller, P. S., & Erath, S. A. (2007). Marital conflict and risk for child maladjustment over time: Skin conductance level reactivity as a vulnerability factor. *Journal of Abnormal Child Psychology, 35,* 715–727.

El-Sheikh, M., Mize, J., & Granger, D. A. (March 2005). Endocrine and parasympathetic responses to stress predict child adjustment, physical health, and cognitive functioning.

Paper presented at the biennial meeting of Society for Research in Child Development. Atlanta.

El-Sheikh, M., & Whitson, S. A. (2006). Longitudinal relations between marital conflict and child adjustment: Vagal regulation as a protection factor. *Journal of Family Psychology*, 20, 30–39.

Essex, M. J., Klein, M. H., Cho, E., & Kalin, N. H. (2002). Maternal stress beginning in infancy may sensitize children to later stress exposure: Effects on cortisol and behavior. *Biological Psychiatry*, 52, 776–784.

Evans, G. W., & English, K. (2002). The environment of poverty: Multiple stressor exposure, psychophysiological stress, and socioemotional adjustment. *Child Development*, 73, 1238–1248.

Evans, G. W., & Kim, P. (2007). Childhood poverty and health: Cumulative risk exposure and stress dysregulation. *Psychological Science*, 18, 953–956.

Fabes, R. A., Eisenberg, N., & Eisenbud, L. (1993). Behavioral and physiological correlates of children's reactions to others in distress. *Developmental Psychology*, 29, 655–663.

Felitti, V. J., Anda, R. F., Nordenberg, D., Williamson, D. F., Spitz, A. M., Edwards, V. et al. (1998). Relationship of childhood abuse and household dysfunction to many of the leading causes of death in adults. The Adverse Childhood Experiences (ACE) Study. *American Journal of Preventive Medicine*, 14, 245–258.

Fernald, L. C. H., Burke, H. M., & Gunnar, M. R. (2008). Salivary cortisol levels in children of low-income women with high depressive symptomatology. *Development and Psychopathology*, 20, 423–436.

Fisher, P. A., Stoolmiller, M., Gunnar, M. R., & Burraston, B. O. (2007). Effects of a therapeutic intervention for foster preschoolers on diurnal cortisol activity. *Psychoneuroendocrinology*, 32, 892–905.

Fowles, D., Kochanska, G., & Murray, K. (2000). Electrodermal activity and temperament in preschool children. *Psychophysiology*, 37, 777–787.

Fung, M. T., Raine, A., Loeber, R., Lynam, D. R., Steinhauer, S. R., Venables, P. H. et al. (2005). Reduced electrodermal activity in psychopathy-prone adolescents. *Journal of Abnormal Psychology*, 114, 187–196.

Gatzke-Kopp, L., Raine, A., Loeber, R., Stouthamer-Loeber, M., & Steinhauer, S. R.

(2002). Serious delinquent behavior, sensation seeking, and electrodermal arousal. *Journal of Abnormal Child Psychology*, 30, 477–486.

Geronimus, A. T., Hicken, M., Keene, D., & Bound, J. (2006). "Weathering" and age patterns of allostatic load scores among blacks and whites in the United States. *American Journal of Public Health*, 96, 826–833.

Gianaros, P. J., Sheu, L. K., Matthews, K. A., Jennings, J. R., Manuck, S. B., & Hariri, A. R. (2008). Individual differences in stressor-evoked blood pressure reactivity vary with activation, volume, and functional connectivity of the amygdala. *Journal of Neuroscience*, 28, 990–999.

Gilissen, R., Koolstra, C., M., Van IJzendoorn, M. H., Bakermans-Kranenburg, M. J., & Van der Veer, R. (2007). Physiological reactions of preschoolers to fear-inducing film clips: Effects of temperamental fearfulness and quality of the parent-child relationship. *Developmental Psychobiology*, 49, 187–195.

Goodyer, I. M., Park, R. J., & Herbert, J. (2001). Psychosocial and endocrine features of chronic first-episode major depression in 8–16 year olds. *Biological Psychiatry*, 50, 351–357.

Gordis, E. B., Granger, D. A., Susman, E. J., & Trickett, P. K. (2006). Asymmetry between salivary cortisol and a-amylase reactivity to stress: Relation to aggressive behavior in adolescents. *Psychoneuroendocrinology*, 31, 976–987.

Granger, D. A., Kivlighan, K. T., Blair, C., El-Sheikh, M., Mize, J., Lisonbee, J. A. et al. (2006). Integrating the measurement of salivary alpha-amylase into studies of child health, development, and social relationships. *Journal of Social and Personal Relationships*, 23, 267.

Granger, D. A., Kivlighan, K. T., El-Sheikh, M., Gordis, E. B., & Stroud, L. R. (2007). Recent developments and applications. *Annals of the New York Academy of Sciences*, 1098, 122–144.

Granger, D. A., Weisz, J. R., & Kauneckis, D. (1994). Neuroendocrine reactivity, internalizing behavior problems, and control-related cognitions in clinic-referred children and adolescents. *Journal of Abnormal Psychology*, 103, 267–276.

Gump, B. B., Matthews, K. A., & Räikkönen, K. (1999). Modeling relationships among socioeconomic status, hostility, cardiovascular reactivity, and left ventricular mass in African American and White children. *Health Psychology*, 18, 140–150.

Gunnar, M. R., Porter, F. L., Wolf, C. M., Rigatuso, J., & Larson, M. C. (1995). Neonatal stress reactivity: Predictions to later emotional temperament. *Child Development, 66,* 1–13.

Gunnar, M. R., Sebanc, A. M., Tout, K., Donzella, B., & Van Dulmen, M. M. (2003). Peer rejection, temperament, and cortisol activity in preschoolers. *Developmental Psychobiology, 43,* 346–358.

Gunnar, M. R., Tout, K., de Haan, M., Pierce, S., & Stansbury, K. (1997). Temperament, social competence, and adrenocortical activity in preschoolers. *Developmental Psychobiology, 31,* 65–85.

Gunnar, M. R., & Vazquez, D. M. (2001). Low cortisol and a flattening of expected daytime rhythm: Potential indices of risk in human development. *Development and Psychopathology, 13,* 515–538.

Gunnar, M. R., & Vazquez, D. M. (2006). Stress neurobiology and developmental psychopathology. In D. Cicchetti & D. J. Cohen (Eds.), *Development and Psychopathology,* pp. 533–577 (2nd ed.)

Gunnar, M. R., Wewerka, S. S., Frenn, K., Long, J. D., & Griggs, C. (2009). Developmental changes in HPA activity over the transition to adolescence: Normative changes and associations with puberty. *Development and Psychopathology, 21,* 69–85.

Halligan, S. L., Herbert, J., Goodyer, I., & Murray, L. (2007). Disturbances in morning cortisol secretion in association with maternal postnatal depression predict subsequent depressive symptomatology in adolescents. *Biological Psychiatry, 62,* 40–46.

Hertzman, C. (1999). The biological embedding of early experience and its effects on health in adulthood. *Annals of the New York Academy of Sciences, 896,* 85–95.

Hibel, L. C., Granger, D. A., Cicchetti, D., & Rogosch, F. (2007). Salivary biomarker levels and diurnal variation: Associations with medications prescribed to control children's problem behavior. *Child Development, 78,* 927–937.

Hubbard, J. A., Smithmyer, C. M., Ramsden, S. R., Parker, E. H., Flanagan, K. D., Dearing, K. F. et al. (2002). Observational, physiological, and self-report measures of children's anger: Relations to reactive versus proactive aggression. *Child Development, 73,* 1101–1118.

Jones, J. E., & Jose, P. A. (2005). Hypertension in young children and neonates. *Current Hypertension Reports, 7,* 454–460.

Kamarck, T. W., & Lovallo, W. R. (2003). Cardiovascular reactivity to psychological challenge: Conceptual and measurement considerations. *Psychosomatic Medicine, 65,* 9–21.

Katz, L. F. (2007). Domestic violence and vagal reactivity to peer provocation. *Biological Psychology, 74,* 154–164.

Katz, L. F., & Gottman, J. M. (1997). Buffering children from marital conflict and dissolution. *Journal of Clinical Child Psychology, 26,* 157–171.

Keating, D. P., & Hertzman, C. (1999). *Developmental Health and the Wealth of Nations: Social, Biological, and Educational Dynamics.* New York: Guilford Press.

Kelsey, R. M., Ornduff, S. R., & Alpert, B. S. (2007). Reliability of cardiovascular reactivity to stress: Internal consistency. *Psychophysiology, 44,* 216–225.

Kestler, L. P., & Lewis, M. (2009). Cortisol response to inoculation in 4-year-old children. *Psychoneuroendocrinology, 34,* 743–751.

Kibler, J. L., Prosser, V. L., & Ma, M. (2004). Cardiovascular correlates of misconduct in children and adolescents. *Journal of Psychophysiology, 18,* 184–189.

King, J. A., Barkley, R. A., & Barrett, S. (1998). Attention-deficit hyperactivity disorder and the stress response. *Biological Psychiatry, 44,* 72–74.

Klein Velderman, M., Bakermans-Kranenburg, M. J., Juffer, F., & Van IJzendoorn, M. H. (2006). Effects of attachment-based interventions on maternal sensitivity and infant attachment: Differential susceptibility of highly reactive infants. *Journal of Family Psychology, 20,* 266–274.

Klimes-Dougan, B., Hastings, P. D., Granger, D. A., Usher, B. A., & Zahn-Waxler, C. (2001). Adrenocortical activity in at-risk and normally developing adolescents: Individual differences in salivary cortisol basal levels, diurnal variation, and responses to social challenges. *Development and Psychopathology, 13,* 695–719.

Kraemer H. C., Yesavage J. A., Taylor J. L., & Kupfer D. (2000). How can we learn about developmental processes from cross-sectional studies, or can we? *American Journal of Psychiatry, 157,* 163–171.

Kudielka, B. M., Broderick, J. E., & Kirschbaum, C. (2003). Compliance with saliva sampling protocols: Electronic monitoring reveals invalid cortisol daytime profiles in noncompliant subjects. *Psychosomatic Medicine, 65,* 313–319.

Leary, A., & Katz, L. F. (2004). Coparenting, family-level processes, and peer outcomes: The moderating role of vagal tone. *Development and Psychopathology, 16*, 593–608.

Lewis, M., Ramsay, D. S., & Sullivan, M. W. (2006). The relations of ANS and HPA activation to infant anger and sadness response to goal blockage. *Developmental Psychobiology, 48*, 397–405.

Lorber, M. F. (2004). Psychophysiology of aggression, psychopathy, and conduct problems: A meta-analysis. *Psychological Bulletin, 130*, 531–552.

Lupien, S. J., King, S., Meaney, M. J., & McEwen, B. S. (2001). Can poverty get under your skin? Basal cortisol levels and cognitive function in children from low and high socioeconomic status. *Development and Psychopathology, 13*, 653–676.

Lustig, S. L., Kia-Keating, M., Knight, W. G., Geltman, P., Ellis, H., Kinzie, J. D. et al. (2004). Review of child and adolescent refugee mental health. *Journal of American Academy of Child & Adolescent Psychiatry, 43*, 24–36.

Marshall, P. J., & Stevenson-Hinde, J. (1998). Behavioral inhibition, heart period, and respiratory sinus arrhythmia in young children. *Developmental Psychobiology, 33*, 283–292.

Marsland, A. L., Bachen, E. A., Cohen, S., Rabin, B., & Manuck, S. B. (2002). Stress, immune reactivity and susceptibility to infectious disease. *Physiology and Behavior, 77*(4–5), 711–716.

Masharani, U., Shiboski, S., Eisner, M. D., Katz, P. P., Janson, S. L., Granger, D. A. et al. (2005). Impact of exogenous glucocorticoid use on salivary cortisol measurements among adults with asthma and rhinitis. *Psychoneuroendocrinology, 30*, 744–752.

Matthews, K. A., Salomon, K., Brady, S. S., & Allen, M. T. (2003). Cardiovascular reactivity to stress predicts future blood pressure in adolescence. *Journal of American Heart Association, 65*, 410–415.

Matthews, K. A., Salomon, K., Kenyon, K., & Allen, M. T. (2002). Stability of children's and adolescents' hemodynamic responses to psychological challenge: A three-year longitudinal study of a multiethnic cohort of boys and girls. *Psychophysiology, 39*, 826–834.

McBurnett, K. M., Lahey, B. B., Frick, P. J., Risch, C., Loeber, R., Hart, E. L. et al. (1991). Anxiety, inhibition, and conduct disorder in children: II. Relation to salivary cortisol. *Journal of the American Academy of Child and Adolescent Psychiatry, 30*, 192–196.

McEwen, B. S. (1998). Protective and damaging effects of stress mediators. *New England Journal of Medicine, 338*, 171–179.

McEwen, B. S. (2000). The neurobiology of stress: From serendipity to clinical relevance. *Brain Research, 886*(1–2), 172–189.

McGowan, P. O., Meaney, M. J., & Szyf, M. (2008). Diet and the epigenetic (re)programming of phenotypic differences in behavior. *Brain Research, 1237*, 12–24.

McGrath, J. J., & O'Brien, W. H. (2001). Pediatric impedance cardiography: Temporal stability and intertask consistency. *Psychophysiology, 38*, 479–484.

Murphy, J. K., Alpert, B. S., & Walker, S. S. (1992). Ethnicity, pressor reactivity, and children's blood pressure. Five years of observations. *Journal of American Heart Association, 20*, 327–332.

Murray-Close, D., & Crick, N. R. (2007). Gender differences in the association between cardiovascular reactivity and aggressive conduct. *International Journal of Psychophysiology, 65*, 103–113.

Murray-Close, D., Han, G., Cicchetti, D., Crick, N. R., & Rogosch, F. (2008). Neuroendocrine regulation and physical and relational aggression: The moderating roles of child maltreatment and gender. *Developmental Psychology, 44*, 1160–1176.

Nater, U. M., La Marca, R., Florin, L., Moses, A., Langhans, W., Koller, M. M. et al. (2006). Stress-induced changes in human salivary alpha-amylase activity – associations with adrenergic activity. *Psychoneuroendocrinology, 31*, 49–58.

Center on the Developing Child at Harvard University. (2009). Maternal Depression Can Undermine the Development of Young Children: Working Paper No. 8. Available online: http://www.developingchild.harvard.edu.

Oberlander, T. F., Weinberg, J., Papsdorf, M., Grunau, R., Misri, S., & Devlin, A. M. (2008). Prenatal exposure to maternal depression, neonatal methylation of human glucocorticoid receptor gene (NR3C1) and infant cortisol stress response. *Epigenetics, 3*, 97–106.

Obradović, J., Bush, N. R., & Boyce, W. T. (2011). The interactive effect of marital conflict and stress reactivity on externalizing and internalizing symptoms: The role of laboratory stressors. *Development and Psychopathology, 23*, 101–114.

Obradović, J. & Boyce, W. T. (2009). Individual differences in behavioral, physiological, and genetic sensitivities to contexts: Implications for development and adaptation. *Developmental Neuroscience, 31,* 300–308.

Obradović, J., Bush, N. R., Stamperdahl, J., Adler, N. A., & Boyce, W. T. (2010). Biological sensitivity to context: The interactive effects of stress reactivity and family adversity on socio-emotional behavior and school readiness. *Child Development, 81,* 270–289.

Oosterlaan, J., Geurts, H., M., Knol, D., L., & Sergeant, J., A. (2005). Low basal salivary cortisol is associated with teacher-reported symptoms of conduct disorder. *Psychiatry Research, 134,* 1–10.

Ortiz, J., & Raine, A. (2004). Heart rate level and antisocial behavior in children and adolescents: A meta-analysis. *Journal of the American Academy of Child and Adolescent Psychiatry, 43,* 154.

Pezawas, L., Meyer-Lindenberg, A., Drabant, E. M., Verchinski, B. A., Munoz, K. E., Kolachana, B. S. et al. (2005). 5-HTTLPR polymorphism impacts human cingulate-amygdala interactions: A genetic susceptibility mechanism for depression. *Nature Neuroscience, 8,* 828–834.

Pine, D. S., Wasserman, G. A., Miller, L., Coplan, J. D., Bagiella, E., Kovelenku, P. et al. (1998). Heart period variability and psychopathology in urban boys at risk for delinquency. *Psychophysiology, 35,* 521–529.

Porges, S. W. (2003). The polyvagal theory: Phylogenetic contributions to social behavior. *Physiology and Behavior, 79,* 503–513.

Porges, S. W. (2007). The polyvagal perspective. *Biological Psychology, 74,* 116–143.

Porges, S. W., Doussard-Roosevelt, J. A., & Maiti, A. K. (1994). Vagal tone and the physiological regulation of emotion. *Monographs of the Society for Research in Child Development, 59*(2–3), Serial No. 240.

Porges, S. W., Heilman, K. J., Bazhenova, O. V., Bal, E., Doussard-Roosevelt, J. A., & Koledin, M. (2007). Does motor activity during psychophysiological paradigms confound the quantification and interpretation of heart rate and heart rate variability measures in young children? *Developmental Psychobiology, 49,* 485–494.

Pruessner J. C., Kirschbaum C., Meinlschmid G., & Hellhammer, D. H. (2003). Two formulas for computation of the area under the curve represent measures of total hormone concentration versus time-dependent change. *Psychoneuroendocrinology, 28,* 916–931.

Quigley, K. S., & Stifter, C. A. (2006). A comparative validation of sympathetic reactivity in children and adults. *Psychophysiology, 43,* 357–365.

Ramsay, D., & Lewis, M. (2003). Reactivity and regulation in cortisol and behavioral responses to stress. *Child Development, 74,* 456–464.

Rokutan, K., Morita, K., Masuda, K., Tominaga, K., Shikishima, M., Teshima-Kondo, S. et al. (2005). Gene expression profiling in peripheral blood leukocytes as a new approach for assessment of human stress response. *Journal of Medical Investigation, 52,* 137–144.

Rutter, M., Kim-Cohen, J., & Maughan, B. (2006). Continuities and discontinuities in psychopathology between childhood and adult life. *Journal of Child Psychology and Psychiatry, 47,* 276–295.

Salomon, K. (2005). Respiratory sinus arrhythmia during stress predicts resting respiratory sinus arrhythmia 3 years later in a pediatric sample. *Health Psychology, 24,* 68–76.

Salomon, K., Matthews, K. A., & Allen, M. T. (2000). Patterns of sympathetic and parasympathetic reactivity in a sample of children and adolescents. *Psychophysiology, 37,* 842–849.

Santucci, A. K., Silk, J., S., Shaw, D. S., Gentzler, A., Fox, N., A., & Kovacs, M. (2008). Vagal tone and temperament as predictors of emotion regulation strategies in young children. *Developmental Psychobiology, 50,* 205–216.

Sapolsky, R. M., Romero, L. M., & Munck, A. U. (2000). How do glucocorticoids influence stress responses? Integrating permissive, suppressive, stimulatory, and preparative actions. *Endocrine Reviews, 21,* 55–89.

Scarpa, A., Raine, A., Venables, P. H., & Mednick, S. A. (1997). Heart rate and skin conductance in behaviorally inhibited Mauritian children. *Journal of Abnormal Psychology, 106,* 182–190.

Schiefelbein, V. L., & Susman, E. J. (2006). Cortisol levels and longitudinal cortisol change as predictors of anxiety in adolescents. *Journal of Early Adolescence, 26,* 397.

Schneider, K. M., Nicolotti, L., & Delamater, A. (2002). Aggression and cardiovascular response in children. *Journal of Pediatric Psychology, 27,* 565–573.

Shannon, K. E., Beauchaine, T. P., Brenner, S. L., Neuhaus, E., & Gatzke-Kopp, L. (2007). Familial and temperamental predictors of resilience in children at risk for conduct disorder and depression. *Development and Psychopathology, 19,* 701–727.

Shirtcliff, E. A., & Essex, M. (2008). Concurrent and longitudinal associations of basal and diurnal cortisol with mental health symptoms in early adolescence. *Development and Psychopathology, 50,* 690–703.

Shirtcliff, E. A., Granger, D. A., Booth, A., & Johnson, D. (2005). Low salivary cortisol levels and externalizing behavior problems in youth. *Development and Psychopathology, 17,* 167–184.

Smider, N. A., Essex, M. J., Kalin, N. H., Buss, K. A., Klein, M. H., Davidson, R. J. et al. (2002). Salivary cortisol as a predictor of socioemotional adjustment during kindergarten: A prospective study. *Child Development, 73,* 75–92.

Snoek, H., Van Goozen, S. H. M., Matthys, W., Buitelaar, J., & Van Engeland, H. (2004). Stress responsivity in children with externalizing behavior disorders. *Development and Psychopathology, 16,* 389–406.

Stifter, C. A., & Fox, N. A. (1990). Infant reactivity: Physiological correlates of newborn and 5-month temperament. *Developmental Psychology, 26,* 582–588.

Stroud, L. R., Handwerger, K. L., Kivlighan, K. T., Granger, D. A., & Niaura, R. (2005, March). Alpha amylase stress-reactivity in youth: Age differences and relation to cortisol, cardiovascular, and affective responses. Paper presented at the biennial meeting of Society for Research in Child Development. Atlanta, GA.

Suess, P. E., Porges, S. W., & Plude, D. J. (1994). Cardiac vagal tone and sustained attention in school-age children. *Psychophysiology, 31,* 17–22.

Susman, E. J., Granger, D. A., Dockray, S., Heaton, J., & Dorn, L. D. (March 2006). Alpha-amylase, timing of puberty and disruptive behavior in young adolescents: A test of the attenuation hypothesis. Paper presented at the biennial meeting of the Society for Research on Adolescence. San Francisco.

Tarullo, A. R., & Gunnar, M. R. (2006). Child maltreatment and the developing HPA axis. *Hormones and Behavior, 50,* 632–639.

Taylor, S. E., Way, B. M., Welch, W. T., Hilmert, C. J., Lehman, B. J., & Eisenberger, N. I. (2006). Early family environment, current adversity, the serotonin transporter polymorphism, and depressive symptomatology. *Biological Psychiatry, 60,* 671–676.

Tomaka, J., Blascovich, J., & Swart, L. (1994). Effects of vocalization on cardiovascular and electrodermal responses during mental arithmetic. *International Journal of Psychophysiology, 18,* 23–33.

UNICEF (2009). *The state of the world's children 2009: Childhood under threat* (No. 9280635328). New York: UNICEF.

U. S. Surgeon General's Office (1999). *Mental health: A report of the surgeon general* (No. ISBN 0–16–050300–0). Rockville, MD: Department of Health and Human Services.

Van Goozen, S. H. M., Matthys, W., Cohen-Kettenis, P. T., Gispen-de Wied, C., Wiegant, V. M., & Van Engeland, H. (1998). Salivary cortisol and cardiovascular activity during stress in oppositional-defiant disorder boys and normal controls. *Biological Psychiatry, 43,* 531–539.

Van Ryzin, M. J., Chatham, M., Kryzer, E., Kertes, D. A. & Gunnar, M. R. (2009). Identifying atypical cortisol patterns in young children: The benefits of group-based trajectory modeling. *Psychoneuroendocrinology, 34,* 50–61.

Venables, P. H., & Christie, M. (1980). Electrodermal activity. In L. Martin & P. H. Venables (Eds.), *Techniques in Psychophysiology,* pp. 3–67. New York: Wiley.

Venables, P. H., & Mitchell, D. A. (1996). The effects of age, sex and time of testing on skin conductance activity. *Biological Psychology, 43,* 87–101.

Wang, X., Poole, J. C., Treiber, F. A., Harshfield, G. A., Hanevolt, C. D., & Snieder, H. (2006). Ethnic and gender differences in ambulatory blood pressure trajectories: Results from a 15-year longitudinal study in youth and young adults. *Journal of American Heart Association, 114,* 2780–2787.

Weems, C. F., Zakem, A. H., Costa, N. M., Cannon, M. F., & Watts, S. E. (2005). Physiological response and childhood anxiety: Association with symptoms of anxiety disorders and cognitive bias. *Journal of Clinical Child and Adolescent Psychology, 34,* 712–723.

Williams, S. C., Lochman, J. E., Phillips, N. C., & Barry, T. D. (2003). Aggressive and nonaggressive boys' physiological and cognitive processes in response to peer provocations. *Journal of Clinical Child and Adolescent Psychology, 32,* 568–576.

Wilson, D. K., Kliewer, W., Plybon, L., & Sica, D. A. (2000). Socioeconomic status and blood pressure reactivity in healthy black adolescents. *Hypertension, 35,* 496–500.

CHAPTER 32

Mixed Model Analyses for Repeated-Measures Data

Peter J. Molfese, Yaacov Petscher,
and David L. Molfese

Purpose

This chapter gives a brief introduction to mixed models analyses in the context of repeated-measures data analyses. While the details of mixed models can be complex, this chapter introduces the basic theory as well as the application of that theory using modern day statistical software. Theory will take the form of descriptive text and equations, while application will be presented as SAS syntax with corresponding output using two examples. In order to best utilize the contents of this chapter, the reader should be familiar with multiple regression analysis. A reader wishing to brush up on multiple regression is directed to Pedhazur (1997). Additionally, we will devote the majority of this chapter to examples and refer the interested reader to additional materials.

While many of the chapters in this book have used a variety of analyses approaches to answer substantive questions, mixed model analyses offer both a fresh look at traditional problems as well as introduce ways to examine new types of questions in data. Often when exploring the impacts of environment

on development, researchers are interested in two sets of questions (1) change over time, for instance, do individuals get better at a task over time; and (2) what accounts for those changes, for instance, does poverty impact (or account for) differences in ability at a particular time point, or even change over time. It is primarily this second set of questions that a special type of mixed models called Hierarchical Linear Models are well known for. This chapter seeks to introduce these concepts to the reader.

Introduction

A cursory glance of the published manuscripts in journals of education and psychology over the past ten years shows a dramatic increase in the number of authors analyzing data collected over several time points. With the multitude of statistical techniques available to researchers today, deciding how to analyze data with repeated-measures could be more difficult than the actual analysis. Beyond attempting to answer substantive research questions, the choice of analytic procedure is influenced by the number of measurements or time points in a dataset, the number of variables under study, how the research questions are framed, and often times, the researchers' knowledge of both statistics and statistical software.

Analytic approaches are influenced by the structure of the data. Specifically, whether data fit a hierarchy, such as children nested within classrooms and schools, or repeated-measures nested within an individual. Analyses of these research designs are require mixed models that are referred to by a number of names, including multilevel modeling, mixed effects model analysis, random coefficient models, and growth curve modeling. For simplicity, we will simply refer to these models as mixed models.

Repeated-Measures Analysis

Repeated-measures data can take multiple forms. Two of the more common types of repeated-measures data are (1) repeated-measures within a participant at a single time point (e.g., a measure of reading and a measure of language); and (2) repeated-measures within a participant across time in a longitudinal design (e.g., measures of reading in the fall and spring of the school year). As this chapter will demonstrate, analysis approaches to repeated-measures data have changes to allow new types of repeated-measures data as well as new research questions to be addressed.

One way of analyzing repeated-measures data is to use a simple difference score (also known as change or gain score), which represents a minimally sufficient procedure to repeated measures analysis. The creation and test of the simple difference score has received much attention in the literature describing how to analyze repeated measures data (e.g., Cronbach & Furby, 1970; Rogosa, 1995; Rogosa, Brandt, & Zimowski, 1982, Rogosa & Willett, 1985, Zumbo, 1999), and was one of the earliest methods used to analyze data measured over multiple time points (Lord, 1956, 1963). An analysis of difference scores is appealing because such results provide information on the gain

raw score values observed in individuals in the same metric. Simple difference scores, and variations of the difference score (e.g., covariance adjusted scores) are frequently reported in the literature, yet despite the prevalence of these scores, Rogosa et al. (1982) have cautioned researchers that – "Two waves of data are better than one, but maybe not much better" (p. 744). Indicating that even more waves of data may be necessary for sufficient analysis of repeated-measures data. Though factually correct, this declaration is often difficult to heed. Many researchers find it difficult to collect multiple waves of data with limited resources and funding. Moreover, even when longitudinal data are collected, many researchers still opt to use the first and last assessment to estimate overall change. This result is often unsatisfactory, as change scores continue to paraphrase the information available by giving similar values to individuals changing from a score of 50 to 60 as an individual changing from a score of 90 to 100.

While analysis of change scores, including pre/post scores, is straightforward and fits in the context of analyses such as dependent t-tests and the Analysis of Covariance (ANCOVA), increasing the numbers of data points introduces the need for more sophisticated analysis techniques (Maxwell, 1998). The most common of these other techniques are (1) the repeated-measures ANOVA and (2) mixed models. A special subset of mixed models, called growth curve models, are advocated by Rogosa (1995) as they can be used to make up for the shortcomings of change scores in order to improve the validity of straight-line growth as well as to improve the precision (or specificity) of the change parameters. Similarly, Maxwell (1998) demonstrated that in the context of randomized experiments, repeated measures growth models could be used to reduce the number of participants in designs while still maintaining high levels of precision and power.

We do not wish to imply that t-tests, ANCOVA, and repeated-measures ANOVAs are outdated. Indeed, these methods are well suited to analyze many types

(a)

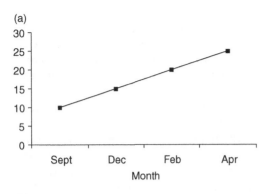

(b)

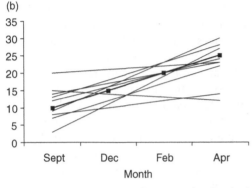

Figure 32.1. Comparison of mean and individual growth curves.

of data; mixed models simply offer an alternative that in many cases can be both more flexible and in some cases more appropriate to analyzing data. Additionally, mixed models facilitate greater flexibility in interpretations of the results, particularly when data are nested. Mixed models often include both fixed effects (means) and random effects (variance of individuals around the means), which aids in examining differences in how students, classes, or schools grow on a dependent variable, such a student achievement in reading. In a traditional fixed effects model, the mean scores of each time point may be plotted to visually understand the nature of the average trend over time. By including random effects, the types of visual trends that can be plotted will change. For example, rather than static fit lines that only indicate the general trend obtained from the mean scores, random effects lend themselves to more dynamic individual growth curves that vary in slopes. Figure 32.1 shows the differences in types of plots that

can be generated between the two models. The plot for a sample fixed effects model (a), while useful for displaying the average amount of growth, says little about how individual differences change across time of measurement. Conversely, a plot for a random effects model (b) can demonstrate not just the mean growth across all participants in the sample, but each individual's growth trajectory. In this case we can observe that some students grew faster than the average slope, some grew more slowly, and some decreased in their amount of change over the year. This simple example can be extended to instances where data are nested in order to understand how higher level clustering (e.g., classes, schools, districts) differ in the amount of change.

Benefits of Mixed Models

There are many advantages to using the mixed model family of analyses over more traditional methods. We focus on three specific benefits to the use of mixed models: (1) the ability to correctly handle nested data; (2) the ability to include participants with missing data; and (3) the ability to specify and model multiple random effects for analyses. The first major advantage that separates traditional methods from the Mixed Models family of analyses is the ability to analyze nested data. The assumption of independent observations is central to most classical statistical techniques; however, data are not always independent. A sample of students, for example, can be viewed as being nested within a particular classroom, whereby the education and experience of a teacher impacts all students in the classroom (Brown, Molfese, & Molfese, 2008). In this example, scores obtained from individual students are not assumed to be independent from one another. In cases of repeated-measures over time on the same participant, observations are nested within a participant, and one would predict that performance at one point in time would be related to performance at future observations – again the scores are not independent. The nesting of data points introduces

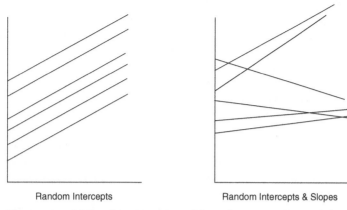

Random Intercepts　　　　　　　Random Intercepts & Slopes

Figure 32.2. (a) Random intercepts; (b) random intercepts and slopes.

dependence or correlation between two data points. If dependence is ignored, it can lead to incorrect standard errors and significance tests (Goldstein, 1995). Mixed model analysis offers the ability to model (or specify) the pattern of correlations that are present in the data.

The second advantage of using mixed models is the inclusion of participants with missing data. Using traditional methods, if a participant is missing a single measurement, the participant's data are excluded from further analyses. Missing data is a particularly difficult problem in longitudinal research, including data collection techniques where partial data loss also is common. By using Maximum Likelihood Estimation (instead of Ordinary Least Squared), Mixed Models are able to use all available data from participants, even those with missing data points. In addition to handling of missing data better, mixed models can also allow for participants in a longitudinal design to be tested at different intervals of time, a distinct advantage in testing for changes over time (Hox, 2002). In addition to Maximum Likelihood, other estimators (such as restricted maximum likelihood, and Generalized Least Squares) are available; see Littell et al. (2006).

The final advantage to the use of mixed models is the ability to specify more than one random effect. This is another benefit to using Maximum Likelihood Estimation (ML), because ML is iterative, mixed

models can specify effects as fixed or random at the beginning of the estimation process, instead of at the end, which is typical of ANOVA with random effects (Maxwell & Delaney, 2004). This applies to many cases of mixed model analyzes, such as allowing for random intercept and random slope models. Examples of the use of these two models are depicted in Figure 32.2, showing that unlike traditional regression analyses where all participants are assumed to have the same regression line with the same intercept and slope, and all deviations from the fixed intercept and slope are caused by error, mixed models allows each participant (or cluster) to have a unique intercept or unique slope and then identify sources that account for variability of the intercept and slope (Raudenbush & Bryk, 2001). Mixed models also allow the user to structure the covariance of the random effects. This allows further structuring of the relationships between and within groups; the interested reader is directed to Littell et al. (2006).

To illustrate these advantages and introduce the reader to practical applications of mixed modes, we now present two examples. The first example uses repeated-measures within a participant at a single time point. This type of model is a Multivariate Multilevel model (Goldstein, 1995; Hox, 2002) and is also known as a Mixed Model Analysis of Repeated-Measures data (Littell, Milliken, Stroup, Wolfinger, & Schabenberger,

2006). This example serves to demonstrate that this particular type of mixed model can substitute for traditional MANOVA, particularly when there are missing data (Hox, 2002). Our second example uses repeated-measures for an individual across multiple time points, and is often referred to as a multilevel growth model (Raudenbush & Bryk, 2001). We consider the multilevel application of repeated measures as an extension of the more well known repeated measures ANOVA. The illustration used in this chapter will demonstrate the flexibility in modeling and the unique type of data achieved when treating time as a random effect.

The user interested in replicating these analyses should be aware that data analyzed with PROC GLM (the SAS procedure used here for traditional repeated-measures ANOVA) is presented in multivariate format, where each individual has one and only one row (or case). Data analyzed using PROC MIXED (the SAS procedure used to analyzed mixed models) is in the univariate format, where each time point for an individual is a row (or case). Examples are shown later.

Example 1: Repeated-Measures within Participant

Our first example investigates a problem in molecular neuroscience (Molfese, Sweatt, & Lubin, Accepted) looking at the impacts of different types of fear conditioning on histone protein tail methylation in a study of rodent memory. For the purposes of this chapter, a subset ($n = 55$ rats) of the total data was used, involving just three conditions and only investigating one of the time points. The three conditions included: (1) a control group of rats ($n = 25$) that was handled every day, but never received any foot shocks; (2) a contextual fear conditioning group of rats ($n = 16$) that received foot shocks shortly after being introduced to a novel environment; (3) a latent inhibition group of rats ($n = 14$) that were exposed to the novel environment for two hours, after which they received a foot shock.

After receiving foot shocks, animals were sacrificed and the hippocampus was removed and split into three distinct areas: CA1, CA3, and the Dentate Gyrus (DG). At different points in the extraction and measurement of the histone proteins, data points were lost because of damaged tissue or poor signal-to-noise, which resulted in unequal sample size numbers. To alleviate some of the missing data, data from the two hemispheres were averaged together, since hemisphere differences were not suspected. The substantive questions for these analyses are whether the three groups differ from each other and how those differences involve the three brain structures measured. The design has one between-group factor Condition (Control, Context + Shock, Latent Inhibition), as well as a within-subjects factor Brain Region (CA1, CA3, and DG). Code for running these analyses using both PROC MIXED and PROC GLM is presented in Table 32.1. The corresponding SAS output for PROC MIXED is presented on the next page.

The PROC MIXED syntax follows the same format as other SAS code. The first line identifies the procedure to run and the data set to use. The addition of "method=REML" tells SAS to use the default Reduced Maximum Likelihood, which has the advantages of being less biased for smaller samples as well as giving the same estimates as ANOVA in balanced designs (Hox, 2002). The second line identifies the categorical or class variables COND (short for condition) and REGION (short for brain region or CA1, DG, CA3). The third line specifies the model, the dependent variable, or the measurement of the protein (COL1), as it is generically named. The independent (or predictor) variables are on the right side of the equal sign (condition, region and the interaction of the two). There is also a "/noint" to specify that there is no intercept in this model, as there is no case when all predictor variables will be 0 and interpretation of the intercept is not possible. The REPEATED statement is the same, except that MIXED needs to know the second-level indicator in which measurements are

Table 32.1: Example of Univariate and Multivariate Data Sets

Multivariate Format	Univariate Format
Subject ID, IQ1, IQ2, IQ3	Subject ID, Time Point, IQ
Tim, 100, 101, 103	Tim, 1, 100
Beth, 102, 108, 105	Tim, 2, 101
	Tim, 3, 103
	Beth, 1, 102
	Beth, 2, 108
	Beth, 3, 105

nested (SUBJECT=ID), so our ID variable has unique identifiers that are represented on multiple lines. It is also important to specify the structure of the covariance matrix using (TYPE=UN), here we specify that the covariance matrix is unstructured (Figure 32.3a) and that we would like SAS to estimate each variance and covariance from the data with no restrictions on the values. Other covariance structures exist (VC = Variance Components, CS = Compound Symmetry; Figures 32.4b and 32.4a), and can be found in the PROC MIXED chapter of the SAS/STAT User's Guide (SAS Institute Inc.). One advantage to using an unstructured covariance matrix is that it does not assume a compound symmetry (a type of sphericity) structure to the data.

Model Information

Data Set	WORK.P2
Dependent Variable	COL1
Covariance Structure	Unstructured
Subject Effect	SUBJ
Estimation Method	REML
Residual Variance Method	None
Fixed Effects SE Method	Model-Based
Degrees of Freedom Method	Between-Within

Class Level Information

Class	Levels	Values
COND	3	1 2 3
REGION	3	1 2 3

Dimensions

Covariance Parameters	6
Columns in X	16
Columns in Z	0
Subjects	55
Max Obs Per Subject	3

Number of Observations

Number of Observations Read	165
Number of Observations Used	99
Number of Observations Not Used	66

Iteration History

Iteration	Evaluations	-2 Res Log Like	Criterion
0	1	1002.14162844	
1	2	994.91095496	0.00289138
2	1	993.39653694	0.00120225
3	1	992.76310404	0.00046713
4	1	992.52656354	0.00010989
5	1	992.47398156	0.00000958
6	1	992.46977340	0.00000010
7	1	992.46973245	0.00000000

Convergence criteria met.

Covariance Parameter Estimates

Cov Parm	Subject	Estimate
UN(1,1)	SUBJ	3145.72
UN(2,1)	SUBJ	80.6906
UN(2,2)	SUBJ	4180.34
UN(3,1)	SUBJ	−2924.14
UN(3,2)	SUBJ	−426.64
UN(3,3)	SUBJ	3988.50

Fit Statistics

−2 Res Log Likelihood	992.5
AIC (smaller is better)	1004.5
AICC (smaller is better)	1005.5
BIC (smaller is better)	1016.5

Null Model Likelihood Ratio Test

DF	Chi-Square	Pr > ChiSq
5	9.67	0.0851

Type 3 Tests of Fixed Effects

Effect	Num DF	Den DF	F Value	Pr > F
COND	2	51	10.67	0.0001
REGION	2	51	0.94	0.3964
COND* REGION	4	51	6.99	0.0001

The SAS output is shown earlier, the "Model Information" provides the basic elements of our analysis: here we see that the covariance structure (unstructured) and the estimation method (REML) match our code. Table 32.2 shows our class variables and the levels (3 conditions, 3 regions). The dimensions table refers to the matrices that SAS generates internally to represent the data. The X matrix refers to the dummy variables SAS creates to represent the 15 levels of the predictor variables (3 levels of Region, 3 levels of Condition, and 9 levels of Interaction). SAS would normally create 16 columns, with one representing the intercept, but we have removed this using our code. Because there are no random effects in this model, there are no columns in the Z matrix.

The first table in the SAS output also tells us that the analysis had 55 subjects, matching our data and a maximum of 3 observations per subject. SAS also gives information on the number of observations used, which identifies that some participants had missing data, but the available data from all participants was still included in the model. The next two tables of the SAS output show model fit calculations as well as our residual covariance structure, which was estimated from the data. For more information on these tables as well as the model fit indices and chi-square, see Littell et al. (2006). Finally, the last table presents the fixed effects results for this model. As shown in earlier, there is a significant main effect for condition, as well as a significant Condition X Region interaction $F(4, 51) = 6.99$, $p = 0.0001$. Post hoc tests of this interaction identified that this effect was driven by Condition differences between control animals and Context+Shock animals in CA1 as well as differences between Context+Shock and latent inhibition animals

in CA1. Differences were also found between all three groups for region CA3, with only one difference in region DG between control animals and the latent group.

These results can be interpreted as showing that histone protein tail methylation is altered by contextual fear conditioning and by latent inhibition. The effect of pairing Context with Shock was only observed in area CA1 of the hippocampus. A 2-hour preexposure to the context, however (latent inhibition), did not alter histone tail methylation in area CA1, but these proteins were modified in DG and CA3. That one form of behavioral conditioning appears to induce changes in one region of hippocampus while a different learning paradigm alters other hippocampus subregions supports the hypothesis that spatial encoding of distinct memories occur at the molecular level.

In a second analysis (not shown), animals were sacrificed after a delay of 48 hours following initial conditioning without being reexposed to the conditioning environment. The results of these analyses were interpreted a showing that the effects of both Context+Shock and latent inhibition are no longer observed in any region of hippocampus. However, if the memory was extinguished through daily reexposures to the conditioning environment without foot shock over those same 48 hours, an elevation in histone methylation is again observed in area CA1 and also in area CA3. These finding were interpreted as showing that extinction of the fear memory may employ some of the same molecular mechanisms as initial encoding of the memory, but new circuitry may also be recruited.

Compared to a standard MANOVA (PROC GLM), using a mixed-model approach to this data analysis has two immediate advantages for this dataset. First, PROC MIXED allows for the use of all available data, while MANOVA (PROC GLM) requires complete data for each participant. The same analyses conducted in PROC GLM identified a condition effect $F(2, 17) = 7.21$, $p = 0.0054$, but no condition*region interaction. The condition effects were driven entirely by differences in CA3, which identified differences between

Table 32.2: Code for PROC MIXED and PROC GLM

PROC MIXED	PROC GLM
PROC MIXED DATA = P1 method=reml; CLASS COND REGION; MODEL COL1 = COND REGION COND*REGION / noint; REPEATED REGION / SUBJECT=SUBJ TYPE=UN; RUN;	PROC GLM DATA = P1_MV; CLASS COND; MODEL P1CA1 P1DG P1CA3 = COND; REPEATED REGION 3; RUN;

the control animals and the context animals, as well as differences between the context animals and the latent inhibition animals. In the case of these data, the MIXED analyses were able to use all 55 subjects (with varying degrees of missing data), compared to PROC GLM that utilized only the 19 subjects with complete data. Thus, using PROC MIXED may allow for a better representation of data when there is missing data.

The second major advantage to using PROC MIXED is the ability to model the within-subject residuals. The more traditional approach using PROC GLM makes the assumption that the data has a compound-symmetric structure to it (see Figure 32.4a where all variances are equal, and all covariances are equal). While there are corrections for violations of this assumption (e.g., Greenhouse Geisser), PROC MIXED allows for the modeling of these covariances to reduce the residual. PROC MIXED also allows the estimation of a full covariance matrix using the "unstructured" setting on the repeated line (Figure 32.3a). This is shown in the SAS output labeled "Covariance Parameter Estimates."

Example 2: Longitudinal Data

Longitudinal data structures refer to instances where data at more than one time-point are collected on a sample. How the data are analyzed becomes important as the choice of analysis is dependent on particular assumptions that the researcher is making about the data. Generally speaking, longitudinal data analyses may be decomposed into two types of models, namely fixed effects and random effects models. Fixed effects models describe

applications where all of the variables in the study have a set number of levels specified in the design of the study, and the generalizations from the analysis are specific to the levels of the variables in the study. A random effects model for a study is where the levels of the variables are randomly selected from a population of possible levels, as might be the case if an existing large data set is available and only specific variables are selected for analyses. In this case, the generalizations from this type of model can be extended to all possible levels of the variable, not solely the ones tested in the experiment. More conceptually, the primary difference between a fixed and random effects model is how the variability between individuals in a sample is treated; whereby the fixed effect model constrains the variability and random effects allow it to be freely estimated.

Fixed effects models are often attractive as they allow researchers to eliminate potential bias by controlling for the stable characteristics of the sample (Allison, 2005). Additionally, they are less restrictive in assumptions and are more likely to characterize data in pragmatic ways compared to random effects models. Despite these advantages, applying a fixed effects model to longitudinal data has several drawbacks. Using fixed effects will often increase the sampling variability compared to other models because of the way that the fixed models treats the variance that occurs between individuals. When individuals are measured on successive occasions, the scores on the assessment will vary both across individuals within one time-point and within a particular individual across multiple time-points. Fixed effects models ignore the variation that occurs between individuals, and instead

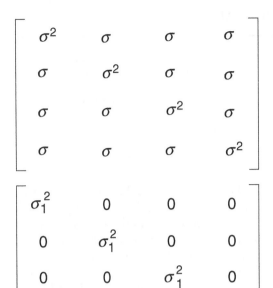

Figure 32.3. (a) Compound symmetric covariance structure; (b) variance components covariance structure.

centers on how each individuals change over time. Although these models produce estimates that are not affected by unmeasured individual attributes, ignoring variance that truly exists has implications for model results. It is well known that in longitudinal models, most of the variance can

be estimated between individuals rather than within individuals. Ignoring this variance component, therefore, is not only methodologically incorrect, but statistically will result in inflated standard errors which affect decisions about whether or not the null hypothesis should be rejected.

By using PROC GLM and PROC MIXED we can demonstrate the differences that will be observed when using fixed or random effects models. Data from this example are from 3,034 students who were assessed on their oral reading fluency (ORF) ability four times during the schools year. The fixed effect model can be represented with.

$$ORF_{it} = \beta_0 + X_{it}(TIME) + r_{it}, \qquad \text{Eq. 1}$$

In Table 32.3, ORF_{it} is a student's ORF score for student i at time t; X_{it} is the predictor of ORF, in this instance TIME, and r_{it} is the error term. This model can be estimated with PROC GLM (Table 32.3):

where the *class* command is used to handle the month of assessment because it takes on multiple values for each wave of assessment. The *model* command allows for the specification of the fixed effects model, in this case that we wish to predict our outcome ORF with our independent variable TIME. The results from the fixed effect model are shown below.

Source	DF	Sum of Squares	Mean Square	F Value	Pr > F
Model	3	2460438.659	820146.220	1877.49	<.0001
Error	11927	5210086.201	436.831		
Corrected Total	11930	7670524.860			

Source	DF	Type III SS	Mean Square	F Value	Pr > F
TIME	3	2460438.659	820146.220	1877.49	<.0001

Parameter	Estimate	Standard Error	t Value	Pr > |t|
Intercept	48.82360699	0.37950774	128.65	<.0001
TIME 1	−37.29204779	0.54135425	−68.89	<.0001
TIME 2	−30.71444849	0.54005011	−56.87	<.0001
TIME 3	−16.32294210	0.53781900	−30.35	<.0001
TIME 4	0.00000000	.	.	.

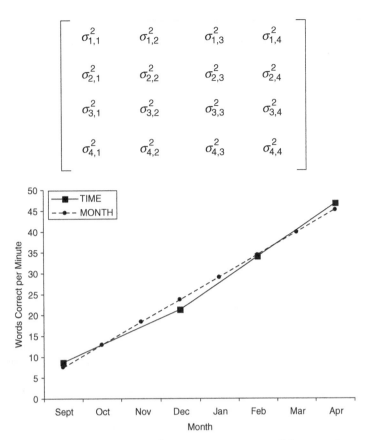

$$
\begin{bmatrix}
\sigma_{1,1}^2 & \sigma_{1,2}^2 & \sigma_{1,3}^2 & \sigma_{1,4}^2 \\
\sigma_{2,1}^2 & \sigma_{2,2}^2 & \sigma_{2,3}^2 & \sigma_{2,4}^2 \\
\sigma_{3,1}^2 & \sigma_{3,2}^2 & \sigma_{3,3}^2 & \sigma_{3,4}^2 \\
\sigma_{4,1}^2 & \sigma_{4,2}^2 & \sigma_{4,3}^2 & \sigma_{4,4}^2
\end{bmatrix}
$$

Figure 32.4 (a) Unstructured covariance structure; (b) comparison of slopes from models..

Table 32.3: PROC GLM Code

```
proc glm data=rsn;
class time;
model ORF = time /solution;
run;
quit;
```

As shown, the main effect of TIME is statistically significant with scores on ORF increasing over time. The intercept value in this model (48.82) represents the mean ORF score at the fourth time point and because values for times 1–4 are additive to the intercept we can calculate that mean ORF score for time 1 = 11.53 (48.82 − 37.29 = 11.53), time 2 ORF = 18.11 (48.82 − 30.71 = 18.11), and time 3 ORF = 32.50 (48.82 − 16.32 = 32.50).

If instead of a fixed effects model, we chose run in a random effects framework, our initial equation would change from Eq X.1 to

$$ORF_{it} = \beta_0 + X_{it}(TIME) + u_t + r_{it} \qquad \text{Eq 2}$$

where u_t is a parameter that describes the random effect for the mean ORF score, and can be estimated using PROC MIXED with (Table 32.4)

The difference in syntax here highlights the estimation differences in the fixed and random models. Inclusion of the *random* statement in PROC MIXED specifies that we want to estimate the amount of variance that occurs in the intercept. Results from the random effects model are shown below.

Covariance Parameter Estimates

Cov Parm	Subject	Estimate	Standard Error	Z Value	Pr > Z
Intercept	STUDENT_ID	329.04	9.1937	35.79	<.0001
Residual		109.41	1.6411	66.67	<.0001

Solution for Fixed Effects

Effect	TIME	Estimate	Standard Error	DF	t Value	Pr > |t|
Intercept		48.8225	0.3802	3033	128.42	<.0001
TIME	1	−37.4353	0.2719	8894	−137.67	<.0001
TIME	2	−30.8832	0.2711	8894	−113.94	<.0001
TIME	3	−16.3459	0.2695	8894	−60.65	<.0001
TIME	4	0	.	.	.	.

The primary differences between the output from PROC GLM and PROC MIXED are not only the addition of the estimate of variance of ORF between-students but also in the magnitude of the standard errors. While the mean values for each time point are nearly identical, the standard errors for the GLM model twice as large as in the MIXED model. Because the random effects model does not control for the differences that are observed between individuals, it improves on an ordinary least squares approach by accounting for the within-person correlation that occurs with repeated measures data. Allison (2005) noted that the decision to use the fixed effect model is based on weighing the trade-off between increased sampling variability with reduced bias; however this recommendation appears to oversimplify the choice of models. Rather than subjectively weigh the decision to use fixed or random effects models, it is more important to use empirical data to guides the decision of which type of model to utilize to answer specific research questions.

Model Building and Evaluation

A common question that arises when beginning to use mixed models for repeated measures across time is how to correctly specify the parameters and how estimates from the model should be used to evaluate aspects of model estimation. Often times, researchers fail to comprehensively describe the process by which they obtained a final prediction model, to what extent the variances can be partitioned across different levels of nesting, and how much of the variance the different predictors will explain. While these processes are fairly straightforward, there is a great deal of latitude in the model building process that the researcher should be aware of, thus, it is important that the research questions and theory guide the decision-making.

The first step when building the multi-level model is testing a completely unconditional model. An unconditional model includes no predictors, unlike a conditional model, which calculates the mean scores for the dependent variable as *conditional* based on performance on an independent variable. This analysis seeks to test if there is any variability in scores for the dependent variable, and is typically represented by a general form of Eq. 3.

$$Y_{it} = \beta_0 + u_r + r_{it}$$

where Y_{it} is the outcome score for student i at time-point t, β_0 is the mean score

Table 32.4: PROC MIXED code

```
proc mixed data=rsn covtest;
class student_id time;
model ORF = time /solution ddfm=bw;
random intercept /subject=student_id;
run;.
```

across all students i, and time-points t, u_t is the random effect that describes the amount of variability around the mean scores, and r_{it} is the error.

Once this model is tested, the researcher should check for two important pieces of information before moving forward. First, it is important to determine if there is a statistically significant fixed effect, or mean score. If there is no statistically significant coefficient for β_0, then there is no merit in further modeling as the score does not meaningfully differ from zero. From example 2, this information can be found in the SAS output section entitled *Solutions for Fixed Effects*. If there is a statistically significant fixed effect, the researcher should examine the random effect (found in the section entitled *Covariance Parameter Estimates*) and whether or not there is a significant result. A nonsignificant random effect would indicate that modeling should stop as there is no variability in scores, however, a p-value < .05 for the random term would suggest that individuals vary on their scores. Because no time covariates are included in this model, the random effect does not indicate that there is significant growth, but merely that some students meaningfully differ in their scores. At this point, the model should be developed further by adding a covariate that describes the nature of time, such as

$$Y_{it} = \beta_0 + X_{it}(TIME) + u_r + r_{it} \qquad \text{Eq. 4}$$

where TIME is centered at the first time point of assessment over three time points. As before, the fixed and random effects should be examined for significance.

Additionally, with the inclusion of time as a fixed effect in the model, an associated random effect may be considered. If there is significant variation in both students' mean scores *and* growth, then an intraclass correlation coefficient can be used to answer the question, "Of the total amount of variability in scores, how much of the variance is due to differences in the intercept and how much is due to differences in growth?" This is calculated by dividing the variance for the parameter of interest by the total variance (see Hox, 2002).

Examining where the variance in the sample exists and what accounts for this variance is what drives research questions as well as helps in model building. For example, should more variability exist in slopes than in intercepts, it's possible that the researcher is more interested in using predictors to explain that variance than in the intercept. If there is not a statistically significant random effect for the intercept and/or slope in the conditional model, then the model can be adjusted by removing the parameter from the random statement in SAS. As a rule of thumb, when building the mixed model for repeated measures in SAS, the following should be tested to help arrive at the most parsimonious model: 1) fixed intercept and no slope; 2) random intercept with no slope; 3) random intercept and fixed slope; and 4) random intercept and random slope. Each model allows for testing incremental changes to best describe performance on the intercept and slope.

Centering

In many longitudinal studies, subjects are not simultaneously tested on the same day. Rather, researchers will assess students across multiple days, weeks, or even a month, and then consider all scores within a time period to be collapsed within a "testing window." This is useful so that inferences can be made about expected student performance on a measure at a given point during the year. For example, during the national *Reading First* initiative as part of the No Child Left Behind Act, students in a number of states were assessed on basic literacy skills once in the fall, twice during the winter, and once during the spring of the school year. Rather than prescribe a simultaneous, standardized administration day; schools were given the flexibility to manage testing windows. The initial assessment in the fall did not need to occur on August 15th; instead the students were allowed to be assessed during a 30–45 day window. It could be argued that a student's score tested on day 1 is very different from a student tested on day 30 or day 45. Moreover, when looking at coding decisions for all instructional windows, multiple conclusions could be reached on how to treat time: one could code the actual day and treat time more flexibly (0–364); a more restrictive method would account only for the month of testing (0–11); and the most restrictive case would code time for the assessment window (0–3). In these examples, zero is included as the first number to serve as the comparison assessment to which all other time points are compared to in the model. In the example where students are administered on a measure of

oral reading fluency four times a year, time is typically treated as a categorical variable corresponding to the number of assessments (e.g., 1, 2, 3, and 4). Students were assessed during the months of September, December, February, and April. Although coding of time as 1–4 provides meaningful information (amount of change between time points), such coding restricts the general findings because there are not equal intervals between each time point. That is, more time elapsed between the September and December assessments (3 months) than the December-February or February-April assessments (2 months). By treating time more flexibly and recoding time to indicate the month of assessment, rather than the wave number gives the researcher greater specificity in interpretation of the growth parameter estimates.

Consider an example where time is structured sequentially as times points 1–4 and assumes equal interval spacing between assessments. Initially, these values must be recoded to center the score at a particular assessment point so that the intercept is interpretable. For the following results, the data were centered at the first time point, thus the data were recoded from 1, 2, 3, and 4 to 0, 1, 2, and 3:

Covariance Parameter Estimates

Cov Parm	Subject	Estimate	Standard Error	Z Value	Pr Z
UN(1,1)	STUDENT_ID	167.90	5.3187	31.57	<.0001
UN(2,1)	STUDENT_ID	26.3900	1.8953	13.92	<.0001
UN(2,2)	STUDENT_ID	40.7579	1.3312	30.62	<.0001
Residual		50.5165	0.9306	54.28	<.0001

Solution for Fixed Effects

Effect	Estimate	Standard Error	DF	t Value	Pr > |t|
Intercept	8.6445	0.2606	3033	33.17	<.0001
time2	12.6919	0.1300	8896	97.62	<.0001

The results shown earlier demonstrate that, on average, students mean ORF score at the fall time point was 8.63 words correct per minute, and that they grew an average 12.70 words correct per minute per *time period*. Alternatively, when time is recoded to reflect the month of the year students were assessed, the time variable takes on values of 0, 3, 5, and 7 to reflect the distance, in months, between assessments. The results from this model are shown below.

in the estimated ORF score. This can be attributed to the unequal spacing of time when treating growth categorically, and as a greater amount of time elapses between the first two assessments than other intervals, the amount of growth that occurs between those assessments is deflated.

This change in how growth is characterized not only has implications for the fixed effects, but also for the random effect of the slope. In the first model, the amount of variance in ORF growth was 40.75, which indicated that

Covariance Parameter Estimates

Cov Parm	Subject	Estimate	Standard Error	Z Value	Pr Z
UN(1,1)	STUDENT_ID	138.86	5.2360	26.52	<.0001
UN(2,1)	STUDENT_ID	13.9710	0.8052	17.35	<.0001
UN(2,2)	STUDENT_ID	6.3240	0.2427	26.06	<.0001
Residual		74.9807	1.3796	54.35	<.0001

Solution for Fixed Effects

Effect	Estimate	Standard Error	DF	t Value	Pr > |t|
Intercept	7.6106	0.2570	3033	29.61	<.0001
MONTH	5.3568	0.05513	8896	97.17	<.0001

These results initially appear to be quite different from the first model in that the mean ORF score for fall performance has decreased from 8.63 to 7.61. More striking is that the growth has changed from 12.70 to 5.35. It is important to note; however, that the metric of the first model describes growth in terms of increased fluency per time period, while the second model changes this terminology to be increased fluency per *month*. One way to examine how different these estimates are from each other is to plot the mean performance and compare the average growth trajectories. Figure 32.3b shows what the mean growth would look like when time is coded sequentially (TIME) compared to when it is treated more flexibly (MONTH). When plotted, the average slopes across the year are very close, yet in December there is a noticeable difference

approximately 15 percent of the variance in ORF scores was attributable to differences in slope. Conversely, slope differences in the second model only accounted for 3 percent of the overall variance. Depending on the nature of the research questions, very different conclusions would be drawn from these models, with different approaches taken using predictors to explain the variance. The selection of the model should be based on theory and research questions, but this illustration highlights the importance of model selection and the care that one should take in applying mixed models.

Software

As mixed models become more common in research, the types software capable of

Table 32.5: List of Statistical Programs That Handle Mixed Models

Name	Specialization	Platform	Web Site
HLM	MultiLevel Models	Windows	http://www.ssicentral.com/hlm/index.html
MLwiN	Multilevel Models	Windows	http://www.cmm.bristol.ac.uk/MLwiN/index.shtml
MPlus	Structural Equations Modeling	Windows	http://www.statmodel.com/
R	General Statistics and Data Management	Macintosh, Linux, Windows	http://www.r-project.org/
SAS	General Statistics and Data Management Program	Linux, Windows	http://www.sas.com/
SPSS	General Statistics and Data Management Program	Macintosh, Linux, Windows	http://www.spss.com/
Stata	General Statistics and Data Management Program	Macintosh, Linux, Windows	http://www.stata.com/

performing the analyses have become more numerous. This section identifies some of the common software applications for performing mixed model analyses, ranging from specialized programs (e.g., HLM, MLWin),to general statistics programs (e.g., R, SAS, SPSS, Stata) and the addition of Structural Equation Modeling software (e.g., MPlus).

Specialized software programs handle a specific task, in this case fitting mixed or multilevel models. The advantage to these programs is that they are often very easy to understand within the context of their specialized analyses. The advantage to using more generalized software, however, is that this software may be more readily available to researchers and allow all of the data management and analysis to take place within the same program, perhaps reducing some confusion. A list of programs, the platform (Operating System) they run on, and type (general vs. specialized) are shown in Table 32.5.

While we have demonstrated the use of SAS for fitting mixed models here in this chapter, the authors still use HLM, Mplus, SuperMix and R for particular problem sets. The decision to present this chapter in SAS was a combination of familiarity and popularity. Researchers approaching these types of questions from a Structural Equations framework should see Mehta and West (2000).

Conclusion

This chapter has briefly covered both some of the theory behind mixed model analyses as well as two brief examples of data analyses using mixed models. In both of these examples, the substantive questions were change over. However, the first example focused more on condition differences in a way similar to MANOVA, while the second example focused on growth over time and accounting for that growth using predictors, which is more analogous to regression. We present some references to further readings that we have found useful for further understanding and applying these techniques. These are separated out by topic area below:

- Introduction and Background
  - Maxwelland Delaney (2003)
  - Raudenbush and Bryk (2001)
  - Hox (2002)
- Applications to Repeated-Measures Data
  - Littell et al. (2006)
  - Singer & Willett (2003)
  - Maxwell & Delaney (2003)
- SAS Specific Code and Examples
  - Littell et al. (2006)
  - Singer (1998)

References

Allison, P.D. (2005). Fixed effects regression methods for longitudinal data using SAS. Cary, NC: SAS Institute.

Brown, E. T., Molfese, V., & Molfese, P. (2008). Preschool student learning in literacy and mathematics: impact of teacher experience, qualifications, and beliefs on an at-risk sample. *Journal of Education for Students Placed at Risk*, 13, 106–126.

Cronbach, L., & Furby, L. (1970). How should we measure change – or should we? *Psychological Bulletin*, 74, 68–80.

Goldstein, H. (1995). Multilevel Statistical Models, 2nd ed. New York: Halstead Press.

Hox, J. (2002). Multilevel analysis: techniques and applications. Mahwah, NJ: Lawrence Earlbaum Associates, Inc.

Littell, R. C., Milliken, G. A., Stroup, W. W., Wolfinger, R. D., Schabenberger, O. (2006). *SAS for Mixed Models*. Cary, NC: SAS Institute, Inc.

Lord, F. M. (1956). The measurement of growth. *Educational and Psychological Measurement*, 16, 421–437.

Lord, F. M. (1963). Elementary models for measuring change. In C. W. Harris (Ed.), *Problems in measuring change*. Madison: University of Wisconsin Press.

Maxwell, S. E. (1998). Longitudinal designs in randomized group comparison: When will intermediate observations increase statistical power? *Psychological Methods*, 3, 275–290.

Maxwell, S. E., & Delaney, H. D. (2004). *Designing experiments and analyzing data: A model comparison perspective* (2nd ed.). Mahwah, NJ: Lawrence Erlbaum.

McCulloch, C. E., & Searle, S. R. (2001). *Generalized, linear, and mixed models*. New York: Wiley.

Mehta, P. D., & West, S. G. (2000). Putting the individual back into individual growth curves. *Psychological Methods*, 5(1), 23–43.

Molfese, D. L., Sweatt, J. D., & Lubin, F. D. (In press). Histone methylation as an epigenetic marker of memory extinction. *Neurobiology of Learning and Memory*.

Pedhazur, E. J. (1997). *Multiple Regression In Behavioral Research* (3rd ed.). Orlando, FL: Harcourt Brace College Publishers.

Raudenbush, S. W., & Bryk, A. S. (2001). *Hierarchical Linear Models: Applications and Data Analysis Methods* (2nd ed.). Thousand Oaks, CA: Sage Publications, Inc.

Rogosa, D. R. (1995). Myths and methods: Myths about longitudinal research plus supplemental questions. In J. M. Gottman (Ed.), *The analysis of change*, pp. 4–66. Mahwah, NJ: Lawrence Erlbaum Associates.

Rogosa, D. R., Brandt, D., & Zimowski, M. (1982). A growth curve approach to the measurement of change. *Psychological Bulletin*, 92, 726–748.

Rogosa, D. R., & Willett, J. B. (1985). Understanding correlates of change by modeling individuals differences in growth. *Psychometrika*, 50, 203–228.

SAS Institute Inc. (2008). SAS/STAT® 9.2 User's Guide. Cary, NC: SAS Institute Inc.

Singer, J. D. (1998). Using SAS PROC MIXED to fit multilevel models, hierarchical models, and individual growth models. *Journal of Educational and Behavioral Statistics*, 24(4), 323–355.

Singer, J. D., & Willett, J. B. (2003). *Applied longitudinal data analysis: modeling change and event occurrence*. New York: Oxford University Press.

Zumbo, B. D. (1999). The simple difference score as an inherently poor measure of change: Some reality, much mythology. In Bruce Thompson (Ed.), *Advances in Social Science Methodology*, pp. 269–304. Greenwich, CT: JAI Press.

Index

CPSIA information can be obtained at www.ICGtesting.com
Printed in the USA
BVOW10s1859090915

417304BV00004B/31/P